Voting Rights and
Election Law

Voting Rights and Election Law

Cases, Explanatory Notes, and Problems

THIRD EDITION

Michael R. Dimino
PROFESSOR OF LAW
WIDENER UNIVERSITY COMMONWEALTH LAW SCHOOL

Bradley A. Smith
JOSIAH H. BLACKMORE II/SHIRLEY M. NAULT PROFESSOR OF LAW
CAPITAL UNIVERSITY LAW SCHOOL

Michael E. Solimine
DONALD P. KLEKAMP PROFESSOR OF LAW
UNIVERSITY OF CINCINNATI COLLEGE OF LAW

CAROLINA ACADEMIC PRESS
Durham, North Carolina

ISBN 978-1-5310-1906-8
eISBN 978-1-5310-1907-5
LCCN 2020942179

Carolina Academic Press
700 Kent Street
Durham, North Carolina 27701
Telephone (919) 489-7486
Fax (919) 493-5668
E-mail: cap@cap-press.com
www.cap-press.com

Printed in the United States of America

To Jennifer, for loving me . . . and tolerating election law;
and
To Justice Scalia, for his civic courage, "without which democracy is doomed."*
M.R.D.

To Henry, Sophia, Edward, Robert, Grace, Peter, & Eva, that they
may inherit a prosperous, free, and democratic republic.
B.A.S.

To Pat, Jane, and Jimmy.
M.E.S.

---

* *Doe v. Reed*, 561 U.S. 186, 228 (2010) (Scalia, J., concurring in the judgment).

Contents

Table of Cases

Table of Scholarly Authorities

C

Preface

The law of politics is one of the most exciting, consequential, and fun subjects in the law-school curriculum. Disputes about political power involve much more than a single controversy; rather, they set the rules for the resolution of future disputes and go a long way toward determining who will resolve those disputes and how those disputes will be resolved. But courts don't (or aren't supposed to) make up these rules themselves; it is the political process itself that sets its own rules. Evaluating the judicial role in overseeing those rules and the process that creates them is a constant theme throughout this text. We hope the subject fascinates you as it fascinates us.

The third edition is the product of a comprehensive review and streamlining of the second. This edition is shorter than the previous one, owing to the deletion of several principal cases and close editing of the ones that remain. Our overall philosophy in editing this book has remained true to our original impetus for writing it: We wanted to present the subject in a thorough but understandable way that approaches election law primarily as *law* rather than as an exercise in political theory. That is, we have written this book not primarily for political-science students but for law students, whether or not they intend to practice in the field. This book, therefore, combines an emphasis on doctrine with Notes and Questions that encourage students to think about the proper role for the courts in policing politics.

In accordance with these goals, we have presented narrative introductions and Notes that clearly set forth and explain the law, while generally editing cases to allow the students to appreciate judicial reasoning by reading the courts' own words. On occasion, however, we have summarized courts' language to save space. We have also provided several Problems to test students' understanding of the material and to provide opportunities to apply the law to real-life scenarios. We believe that the final product presents the law in a form that is both teachable and sophisticated.

There have been several additional changes in this edition besides its more efficient presentation of the subject. We have, of course, updated the text to account for developments in election law and voting rights over the last five years. Users of the second edition will note the reorganization of several parts of the book. Material on congressional power to enact the original Voting Rights Act of 1965 has been moved from Chapter 1 to Chapter 3, where it joins our (slimmed-down) coverage of preclearance. The second edition's coverage of the political-question doctrine in

Chapter 2 and the one-person, one-vote doctrine in Chapter 3 have been combined in a new Chapter 2 on "Redistricting and One Person, One Vote." That change has permitted us to address partisan gerrymandering (a political-question topic) after the one-person, one-vote cases that are central to the partisan-gerrymandering debate.

Our coverage of third parties and ballot access has been split from the rest of the former Chapter 6 on political parties' rights, and it now joins the term-limits material in the former Chapter 7 to form a new Chapter 6 that gives comprehensive coverage to states' power to design, and to control access to, the ballot. We have also moved the material on anonymous speech out of the former Chapter 8, and we have moved the material on campaign-finance disclosure rules out of the former Chapter 9. Both of those sections now combine to form a new Chapter 9 that comprehensively considers the tradeoffs between disclosure and anonymity.

Finally, we have also thoroughly redesigned the coverage of election administration. Whereas the second edition treated polling-place restrictions and vote-counting rules in separate chapters, Chapter 10 of this edition covers all manner of election-day rules. In practice, disputes over the casting and counting of ballots overlap because often whether a vote should be counted depends on the manner in which it was cast. Therefore, vote-casting and vote-counting disputes are often analytically similar and it makes sense to consider them in a single chapter. This new structure also allows us to devote attention to the electoral college and to other federal rules that affect the casting and counting of votes, even as elections are administered by state and local officials.

Readers should be aware of certain conventions we have used in editing cases. Footnotes, citations, and section headings have been deleted without indication. Our deletions of text are marked by asterisks ("* * *"). Ellipses (". . .") appear in the material we are quoting. Our insertions of text are indicated by brackets ("[]"). Footnotes appearing in the cases have retained their original numbers; our footnotes are indicated by letters. Paragraph breaks have occasionally been altered. We use braces ("{}") to indicate that text has been moved.

There are many persons with whom we have shared portions of this book, and whose suggestions have improved the final product. Among those persons, Heather Gerken, Allison Hayward, and Gene Mazo deserve special mention. We wish to express our thanks to the students who have taken our classes and seminars in election law; this new edition has benefited from their input. We are also indebted to others whose scholarship has created a field of election law, and whose work has enriched our understanding of the subject: Rick Hasen, Sam Issacharoff, Pam Karlan, Dan Lowenstein, Rick Pildes, and Dan Tokaji. In addition, we have benefited from several on-line resources, including Hasen's Election Law Blog and listserv, as well as Election Law @ Moritz and Ballot Access News.

We are thankful for the administrative support of Connie Miller, as well as the research assistance of Lisa Bemboom, Kaleigh Boyer, Bill Cash, Alexander

Czebiniak, Gregory Darr, Jacob Dean, Keely Espinar, Megan Harmon, Carol Herdman, Joe Holaska, Aaron Kaufer, Jessica Lehman, Lauren Linsenbach, Cecille Lucero, Clarke Madden, Julie Olivas, Evelyn Stoner, Justin Swartz, Jesse Unruh, and Shawn-Ryan White.

Dimino wishes to extend additional thanks to Professors Smith and Solimine. They have been delightful co-authors, and it has been a great pleasure to work with both. Their expertise, good humor, and cooperative attitudes have been essential in the more than two years it took to write the first edition and the ten years since its publication. Without their agreement to become part of this book it never would have been written, and without their insights it would not be as good as it is.

This is the first edition published by Carolina Academic Press. We would like to thank all the friendly and professional staff at CAP, particularly Linda Lacy and Susan Trimble, who have welcomed us with great patience and kindness.

Please contact us with ideas for improving the book in the next edition.

Michael R. Dimino
mrdimino@widener.edu

Bradley A. Smith
bsmith@law.capital.edu

Michael E. Solimine
michael.solimine@uc.edu

Voting Rights and
Election Law

Chapter 1

Voting Qualifications

A. Introduction

The law governing the political process involves conflicts among some of the values most important to a free society and an organized system of democratic self-governance. Liberty, speech, equality, and democracy collide when courts are called upon to police the methods by which the citizenry can influence government. Indeed, election law is so interesting and important not just because the questions presented are difficult and the facts are often dramatic, but because the stakes are so high. Rules affecting the distribution of political power favor certain interests at the expense of others,[a] affecting policy many years into the future. Accordingly, "it is as important to regulate in a republic, in what manner, by whom, to whom, and concerning what suffrages are to be given, as it is in a monarchy to know who is the prince, and after what manner he ought to govern." 2 Charles de Secondat, Baron de Montesquieu, The Spirit of the Laws ch. 2, at 9 (Thomas Nugent trans. 1949) (1748); *see also* The Federalist No. 52, at 354 (James Madison) (Jacob E. Cooke ed. 1961) ("The definition of the right of suffrage is very justly regarded as a fundamental article of republican government.").

The "right to vote" itself does not appear explicitly in the Constitution. Despite the fact that the Constitution establishes a representative democracy for the nation as a whole, and despite the fact that Article IV, § 4 requires Congress to guarantee the states "a Republican Form of Government," the Constitution "does not confer the right of suffrage upon any one." *Minor v. Happersett*, 88 U.S. (21 Wall.) 162, 178 (1875). "Although the Constitution was promulgated in the name of 'We, the people of the United States,' the individual states retained the power to define just who 'the people' were." Alexander Keyssar, The Right to Vote: The Contested History of Democracy in the United States 20 (rev. ed. 2009).

The Constitution leaves questions about the scope of the franchise to states in the first instance,[b] subject to the prerogative of Congress under Article I, § 4 to "make

---

a. All such decisions have the effect of favoring certain interests, whether or not the decisions are made with that purpose in mind. But in practice, of course, electoral rules are often constructed so as to achieve certain practical consequences—a practice political scientist William Riker labeled "heresthetics." William H. Riker, The Art of Political Manipulation ix (1986).

b. *See* The Federalist No. 52, at 326 (James Madison) (Clinton Rossiter ed., 1961) ("To have reduced the different qualifications [for voting in elections for members of the House of Representatives] in the different States to one uniform rule would probably have been as dissatisfactory

3

or alter * * * Regulations" concerning the "Times, Places, and Manner of holding Elections for Senators and Representatives," and subject to the further limitation that persons able to vote for the most numerous branch of the state legislature must be able to vote for senators and representatives. Article I, § 2, cl. 1 (representatives); Amendment XVII (senators).

Since the Constitution's ratification, several Amendments have broadened the scope of the franchise, but not by granting an affirmative right to vote. Instead, the Constitution continues to leave such questions to the states, but prohibits states from denying voting rights based on particular criteria: religion (Amendment I); "race, color, or previous condition of servitude" (Amendment XV; *see, e.g., Ex Parte Yarbrough*, 110 U.S. 651 (1884)); sex (Amendment XIX, *overturning Minor v. Happersett, supra*); failure to pay a poll tax (Amendment XXIV (which is applicable according to its terms only in federal elections)); and age for citizens eighteen or older (Amendment XXVI).

All these anti-discrimination provisions, however, fail to establish a right to vote that would bar states from limiting the franchise on the basis of any number of other characteristics, or even eliminating some elections entirely.[c] For example, there is nothing in the constitutional provisions cited above that would prohibit the use of literacy tests, poll taxes in state elections, or property qualifications. One would be mistaken, however, to conclude that states are entirely free to enact such measures. This Chapter will explore the ways in which statutes and court decisions have limited the ability of states to control access to the voting booth.

---

to some of the States as it would have been difficult to the convention. The provision made by the convention appears, therefore, to be the best that lay within their option. It must be satisfactory to every State, because it is conformable to the standard already established, or which may be established, by the State itself. It will be safe to the United States, because, being fixed by the State constitutions, it is not alterable by the State governments, and it cannot be feared that the people of the States will alter this part of their constitutions in such a manner as to abridge the rights secured to them by the federal Constitution.").

c. *See San Antonio Independent School District v. Rodriguez*, 411 U.S. 1, 35 n.78 (1973) ("[T]he right to vote, *per se*, is not a constitutionally protected right * * *."); *Rodriguez v. Popular Democratic Party*, 457 U.S. 1 (1982) (upholding a law giving political parties the power to fill vacancies in the Puerto Rican legislature); *Valenti v. Rockefeller*, 393 U.S. 405 (1969) (*per curiam*), *summarily aff'g* 292 F. Supp. 851 (W.D.N.Y. 1968) (upholding a law giving the governor power to fill vacancies in the U.S. Senate); *Fortson v. Morris*, 385 U.S. 231 (1966) (upholding a provision of the Georgia Constitution authorizing the state legislature to choose the governor from among the two candidates receiving the greatest number of popular votes if no candidate received a majority). *See generally* Richard H. Pildes, *The Future of Voting Rights Policy: From Anti-Discrimination to the Right to Vote*, 49 How. L.J. 741 (2006); Jamin Raskin, *A Right-to-Vote Amendment for the U.S. Constitution: Confronting America's Structural Democracy Deficit*, 3 ELECTION L.J. 559 (2004); Richard Briffault, *The Contested Right to Vote*, 100 MICH. L. REV. 1506 (2002) (book review).

One of the foundational cases establishing a constitutional right to vote[d] was the criminal case of *United States v. Classic*, 313 U.S. 299 (1941). The defendants were Louisiana election commissioners who committed election fraud in counting and certifying the votes in a Democratic primary election to nominate a candidate for Congress. They were indicted for violating two federal statutes that made it a crime to violate others' constitutional rights. The government argued that the defendants violated the statutes by depriving voters of their right to vote for members of Congress. Accordingly, it was necessary for the Court to determine whether the Federal Constitution protected the right to a fair count of one's vote in a primary election for the House of Representatives.

The Court concluded that it did, despite the fact that the Constitution did not explicitly guarantee any individual the right to vote in a general election, let alone in a primary. The Court reasoned that Article I, § 2 was designed "to secure to the people the right to choose representatives * * * by some form of election." 313 U.S. at 318. And because the primary occupied an important position in the electoral mechanism that culminated in the general election, the right to vote in the primary was included within Article I, § 2 as well: "Where the state law has made the primary an integral part of the procedure of choice [of representatives in Congress], or where in fact the primary effectively controls the choice, the right of the elector to have his ballot counted at the primary is likewise included in the right protected by Article I, § 2." 313 U.S. at 318. With *Classic* having tethered voting rights to the Constitution, the stage was set for the Court to reshape American election law by defining those rights.

Understanding court decisions expounding the rights to vote and to participate in politics requires a familiarity with basic constitutional doctrine. The remainder of this section is presented as a refresher for students who need to be reminded of some concepts of constitutional law, and as a primer for students who have not yet studied equal protection and fundamental rights.[e]

Challenges to the constitutionality of restrictions on the right to vote may be based on either the Due Process Clauses of the Fifth and Fourteenth Amendments or the Equal Protection Clause of the Fourteenth Amendment. The Due Process Clause of the Fifth Amendment is applicable to the federal government, while the

---

d. Or "manufactur[ing it] out of whole cloth." Nathaniel Persily, *Forty Years in the Political Thicket: Judicial Review of the Redistricting Process Since* Reynolds v. Sims, *in* Party Lines: Competition, Partisanship, and Congressional Redistricting 67, 71 (Thomas E. Mann & Bruce E. Cain eds., 2005).

e. Students who need a more thorough treatment of these issues should consult one of the excellent secondary sources on constitutional law, including John B. Attanasio & Joel K. Goldstein, Understanding Constitutional Law (4th ed. 2012); Erwin Chemerinsky, Constitutional Law: Principles and Policies (6th ed. 2019); Daniel Farber & Neil S. Siegel, United States Constitutional Law (2019); John E. Nowak & Ronald D. Rotunda, Principles of Constitutional Law (3d ed. 2007)).

Due Process Clause of the Fourteenth Amendment is applicable to the states. There is only one Equal Protection Clause—applicable by its terms to the states—but the Supreme Court has long interpreted the Fifth Amendment Due Process Clause as binding the federal government to the same principles of equality that are contained in the Equal Protection Clause. *See Adarand Constructors, Inc. v. Peña*, 515 U.S. 200, 235–37 (1995); *Bolling v. Sharpe*, 347 U.S. 497 (1954).

Actions of private parties—as opposed to actions of government—do not violate any of those Clauses. Indeed, with the important exception of the Thirteenth Amendment, which prohibits slavery by both private individuals and the government, the entire Constitution restricts the power of government only. This "state-action" doctrine means that whether a constitutional violation occurs depends not only on what conduct occurs, but on *who* performs the conduct. For example, acts of violence designed to intimidate voters do not violate the Constitution if committed by private individuals, even though the acts may have the effect of preventing groups of people from exercising their constitutional rights. *See United States v. Cruikshank*, 92 U.S. 542, 554 (1875). Government may not avoid constitutional limits, however, by delegating all its power to seemingly private parties. Individuals who exercise "public functions" will be deemed to be state actors, even if they appear to be free from governmental control. The Supreme Court has held that conducting elections is one such public function, and has extended this reasoning to apply constitutional restrictions to political parties in nominating candidates. *See, e.g., Ray v. Blair*, 343 U.S. 214, 225–27 (1952); *Smith v. Allwright*, 321 U.S. 649 (1944) [p. 418]. We will consider state action more closely in Chapter 5, § B, when we confront the "White Primary Cases."

Most challenges to government action, under either the Due Process Clauses or the Equal Protection Clause, proceed under the "rational-basis test." Under that test, government action will be upheld unless the challenger proves that the action is not rationally related to a legitimate government interest. The rational-basis test is extraordinarily deferential to government, almost invariably resulting in the challenged law being upheld. It is possible to find some legitimate interest that is advanced by just about any statute, and there is no requirement that the state's actual purpose be to advance that interest, as long as a rational legislator *might* have thought the statute would do so. *See, e.g., Williamson v. Lee Optical*, 348 U.S. 483 (1955); *Railway Express Agency, Inc. v. New York*, 336 U.S. 106 (1949).

"Strict scrutiny" occupies the opposite side of the spectrum from the rational-basis test. Strict scrutiny requires the government to prove that its regulation is narrowly tailored to advance a compelling interest. Narrow tailoring means that the regulation must not harm the plaintiff any more than necessary to accomplish its goal. This test is extraordinarily difficult to satisfy, both because few tasks performed by government are truly "compelling" and because virtually all government regulation achieves its goals imperfectly. Speed limits, for example, serve a compelling interest (traffic safety), but they would fail strict scrutiny because they are not narrowly tailored. They unnecessarily slow some safe drivers and fail to catch some drivers who are "unsafe at any speed." But the administrative costs of enforcing more narrowly tailored regulations are often prohibitive and it is often difficult to write narrowly tailored regulations without providing excessive discretion to law enforcement.

Historically, review under strict scrutiny has been "'strict' in theory but fatal in fact," meaning that a law evaluated under that test was almost certain to be unconstitutional, while the rational-basis test has operated as a rubber stamp, validating all manner of government restrictions. Gerald Gunther, *The Supreme Court, 1971 Term — Foreword: In Search of Evolving Doctrine on a Changing Court: A Model for a Newer Equal Protection*, 86 HARV. L. REV. 1, 8 (1972). There are, however, a few counter-examples, where the Court has applied strict scrutiny and upheld a law, or struck down a law while applying only rational-basis scrutiny. *See McConnell v. Federal Election Commission*, 540 U.S. 93, 203–09 (2003) [p. 829]; *Grutter v. Bollinger*, 539 U.S. 306 (2003); *Burson v. Freeman*, 504 U.S. 191 (1992) [p. 1024] (plurality opinion); *Lawrence v. Texas*, 539 U.S. 558 (2003); *City of Cleburn v. Cleburn Living Center*, 473 U.S. 432 (1985).

Although the Due Process Clauses speak only of providing appropriate procedures before government deprives a person of life, liberty, or property, the Court has read the clauses to provide *substantive* protection as well, meaning that certain "fundamental" liberties may not be abridged by government regardless of the procedures afforded. Exactly which rights are "fundamental," however, has always been a matter of considerable debate. The Court has reasoned that most rights contained in the first eight Amendments, such as the right to criminal juries, the freedoms of speech and religious exercise, and the freedom from unreasonable searches and seizures, are so important and historically recognized as to be fundamental. Accordingly, the Court has "incorporated" them through the Due Process Clause of the Fourteenth Amendment and applied them to the states, even though those rights were originally guaranteed as against only the federal government. *See Barron v. Mayor and City Council of Baltimore*, 32 U.S. (7 Pet.) 243 (1833). Not all fundamental rights, however, are listed in the Bill of Rights. The Court has also declared certain unenumerated rights to be fundamental, including the right to privacy, the right to direct the upbringing of one's children, the right to marry, and — most relevant here — the right to vote.

Once a right is determined to be fundamental, neither the state nor the federal government may infringe that right unless doing so is necessary to accomplish a compelling state interest, *i.e.*, unless the government satisfies strict scrutiny. If a claimed right is not fundamental, states may infringe it unless the law fails the rational-basis test.

Governments obviously infringe rights when they prohibit persons from exercising them, but restrictions short of complete bans may constitute infringements as well. *See generally* CHEMERINSKY, *supra* note e, at 860–61 (from which the material in this paragraph is drawn); Michael C. Dorf, *Incidental Burdens on Fundamental Rights*, 109 HARV. L. REV. 1175 (1996); Kathleen Sullivan, *Unconstitutional Conditions*, 102 HARV. L. REV. 1413 (1989). Thus, for example, the Supreme Court held that imposing a filing fee on indigent persons wishing to obtain a divorce was an unconstitutional infringement on the fundamental right to marry people other then their current spouses. *Boddie v. Connecticut*, 401 U.S. 371 (1971). Similarly, the right to marry was infringed by a state law prohibiting individuals from obtaining marriage licenses if they were behind in child-support payments. *Zablocki v. Redhail*, 434 U.S. 374 (1978). On the other hand, the Court did not apply strict scrutiny in upholding a law providing that disabled children would lose government benefits when they married. *Califano v. Jobst*, 434 U.S. 47 (1977). The standard applied by the Court to determine if a fundamental right has been infringed is to gauge the "directness and substantiality of the interference." *Redhail*, 434 U.S. at 387 n.12.

In cases involving alleged infringements on the right to vote, strict scrutiny will obtain where the challenged law places a "severe" restriction on the right. Laws imposing lesser burdens are subject to a balancing test that considers the extent of the laws' interference with fundamental rights, the state interests served by the laws, and the relationship between the laws and the state interests they serve. *See Crawford v. Marion County Election Board*, 553 U.S. 181, 190 n.8 (2008) [p. 999] (opinion of Stevens, J.). Such laws will be upheld if they are "reasonable" and "nondiscriminatory." *Clingman v. Beaver*, 544 U.S. 581, 586–87 (2005) [p. 460]; *Timmons v. Twin Cities Area New Party*, 520 U.S. 351, 358 (1997) [p. 526]; *Burdick v. Takushi*, 504 U.S. 428 (1992) [p. 990]; *Anderson v. Celebrezze*, 460 U.S. 780 (1983) [p. 517].

In contrast to a due-process claim, in which the challenger argues that the government may not interfere with his or her individual rights regardless of the government's actions toward anyone else, an equal-protection claim argues that the statute in question unjustifiably treats the challenger worse than it treats others. For example, a statute that limits the right to vote to people who own land may be challenged under the Equal Protection Clause by a landless would-be voter. When a law treats different groups of people unequally, the courts must assess whether such different treatment is constitutional; they do so by applying the rational-basis and strict-scrutiny tests discussed above.

Differential treatment on the ground of race or ethnicity triggers strict scrutiny, regardless of whether it is designed to benefit or burden minorities. *See, e.g., Rice v. Cayetano*, 528 U.S. 495 (2000) (invalidating a statute that limited the right to vote to persons with ancestors living in Hawaii in 1778); *City of Richmond v. J.A. Croson Co.*, 488 U.S. 469 (1989) (invalidating a set-aside program designed to assist minorities in the awarding of public contracts); *Davis v. Guam*, 932 F.3d 822 (9th Cir. 2019) (striking down a law restricting voting to "native inhabitants of Guam" as imposing a racial classification); *Davis v. Commonwealth Election Commission*, 844 F.3d 1087 (9th Cir. 2016) (striking down a provision of the Northern Mariana Constitution restricting voting to individuals of "Northern Marianas descent"). Whenever the law on its face makes a racial classification—providing one rule for a certain race and a different rule for another race—strict scrutiny is triggered and the classification will be sustained only if it is narrowly tailored to a compelling interest.

Laws may discriminate against a "suspect class," however, without expressly classifying people based on their membership in that class. For example, the Supreme Court held that a state statute establishing a literacy test for voting, but which grandfathered all lineal descendants of persons entitled to vote in 1865 or earlier, created a racial classification in violation of the Fifteenth Amendment. *Guinn v. United States*, 238 U.S. 347 (1915). *See also Rice, supra*, 528 U.S. at 514–17 (treating the Hawaii statute's use of ancestry as a proxy for race); *Gomillion v. Lightfoot*, 364 U.S. 339, 341 (1960) [p. 279] (striking down a law re-drawing city boundaries in a manner that would have excluded "all save only four or five of its 400 Negro voters while not removing a single white voter or resident"); *Davis, supra*, 844 F.3d at 1093 (treating the Northern Mariana ancestry-based voting restriction as race-based because "the stated intent of the provision is to make ethnic distinctions").

But not every law that has the effect of treating racial or ethnic groups differently is "discrimination on the ground of race or ethnicity." Rather, laws having different effects on different racial groups—but which do not make an express distinction between racial or ethnic groups—are subject to strict scrutiny only if they were enacted for the purpose of treating one racial group better than another. *See, e.g., Washington v. Davis*, 426 U.S. 229 (1976); *Jefferson v. Hackney*, 406 U.S. 535 (1972).

Discrimination on the ground of sex triggers intermediate scrutiny, which requires that the law be "substantially tailored to an important government interest." *Craig v. Boren*, 429 U.S. 190, 197 (1976). As with race discrimination, sex discrimination triggers heightened scrutiny when laws explicitly classify on the basis of sex or where a facially neutral classification is adopted for a discriminatory purpose and produces disparate effects between the sexes. *See Personnel Administrator v. Feeney*, 442 U.S. 256 (1979). If a facially sex-neutral law has both a disparate effect on the sexes and a discriminatory purpose, intermediate scrutiny applies; if either or both is absent, then courts evaluate the constitutionality of the classification by applying the rational-basis test.

Discrimination on the ground of citizenship triggers only rational-basis scrutiny if the discriminatory law is federal, but strict scrutiny if the discrimination is contained in state law. *Compare Nyquist v. Mauclet*, 432 U.S. 1 (1977), *with Mathews v. Diaz*, 426 U.S. 67 (1976). The difference is due to Congress's "broad power over immigration and naturalization." *Mauclet*, 432 U.S. at 7 n.8. *See also* JOHN E. NOWAK & RONALD D. ROTUNDA, PRINCIPLES OF CONSTITUTIONAL LAW § 14.11 at 442 (3d ed. 2007) (citing "[t]he federal interest in international affairs, as well as the federal power over immigration and naturalization").

Discrimination on other grounds, such as education, wealth, disability, and hair color, ordinarily triggers rational-basis scrutiny. Occasionally, however, the Court will strike down distinctions even on grounds such as these, where the unequal treatment is motivated by "irrational prejudice" rather than a "legitimate government interest." *See, e.g., Cleburne Living Center, supra.*

Voting rights present important questions under both equal protection and due process because, while few rights are as fundamental to a self-governing people as the right to vote, and while we are suspicious of measures to limit the voting power of certain groups, it may be equally fundamental to preserve the ability of states and communities to set standards for who will determine the future policies of those areas. *See City of Rome v. United States*, 446 U.S. 156, 201 (1980) (Powell, J., dissenting) (noting that the Voting Rights Act imposes costs on "local control of the means of self-government, one of the central values of our polity"). As you read the remainder of this Chapter, as well as the rest of the book, ask yourself whether the court decisions balancing these interests are—or can be—neutral choices of constitutional principle, or whether the judges and Justices are giving effect to their political philosophies.

B. Defining the Community and Excluding Outsiders

1. The Illiterate

Beginning with Connecticut in 1855, many states adopted literacy tests as qualifications for voting, some of which remained in effect until outlawed by the Voting Rights Act (first in 1965 in "covered jurisdictions" mainly in the South, and then, in 1970, nationwide). There were three stated justifications for the tests: First, "illiterate men lacked the intelligence or knowledge necessary to be wise or even adequate voters." Second, "English-language literacy was essential for the foreign-born to become properly acquainted with American values and institutions." Third, "tying voting to literacy would encourage assimilation and education, which would benefit American society as well as immigrants themselves." Alexander Keyssar, The Right to Vote: The Contested History of Democracy in the United States 116 (rev. ed. 2009). Unstated, but powerful, was the further justification that literacy tests would reduce the voting power of immigrants and illiterate native-born Americans (who were almost exclusively Southern blacks). The effect was significant: "[A] minimum of several hundred thousand voters—and likely more than a million—were barred by these tests, *outside* of the South." *Id.* at 118 (emphasis added). The following case upheld the North Carolina literacy test against a constitutional challenge.

Lassiter v. Northampton County Board of Elections

Supreme Court of the United States

360 U.S. 45, 79 S. Ct. 985, 3 L. Ed. 2d 1072 (1959)

Mr. Justice Douglas delivered the opinion of the Court [in which Mr. Chief Justice Warren, Mr. Justice Black, Mr. Justice Frankfurter, Mr. Justice Clark, Mr. Justice Harlan, Mr. Justice Brennan, Mr. Justice Whittaker, and Mr. Justice Stewart join].

* * * Appellant, a Negro citizen of North Carolina, * * * applied for registration as a voter. Her registration was denied by the registrar because she refused to submit to a literacy test as required by [a] North Carolina statute.[1] * * *

* * * [W]hile the right of suffrage is established and guaranteed by the Constitution it is subject to the imposition of state standards which are not discriminatory and which do not contravene any restriction that Congress, acting pursuant to its constitutional powers, has imposed. While §2 of the Fourteenth Amendment, which provides for apportionment of Representatives among the States according to their respective numbers counting the whole number of persons in each State (except Indians not taxed), speaks of "the right to vote," the right protected "refers to the right to vote as established by the laws and constitution of the state." *McPherson v. Blacker*, 146 U.S. 1, 39 [(1892)] [p. 1065].

We do not suggest that any standards which a State desires to adopt may be required of voters. But there is wide scope for exercise of its jurisdiction. Residence requirements, age, [and] previous criminal record are obvious examples indicating factors which a State may take into consideration in determining the qualifications of voters. The ability to read and write likewise has some relation to standards designed to promote intelligent use of the ballot. Literacy and illiteracy are neutral on race, creed, color, and sex, as reports around the world show. Literacy and intelligence are obviously not synonymous. Illiterate people may be intelligent voters. Yet in our society where newspapers, periodicals, books, and other printed matter canvass and debate campaign issues, a State might conclude that only those who are literate should exercise the franchise.[7] * * * We do not sit in judgment on the wisdom of that policy. We cannot say, however, that it is not an allowable one measured by constitutional standards.

Of course a literacy test, fair on its face, may be employed to perpetuate that discrimination which the Fifteenth Amendment was designed to uproot. No such influence is charged here. * * * The present requirement, applicable to members of

---

1. This Act, passed in 1957, provides * * * as follows: "Every person presenting himself for registration shall be able to read and write any section of the Constitution of North Carolina in the English language." * * *

7. Nineteen States, including North Carolina, have some sort of literacy requirement as a prerequisite to eligibility for voting. * * *

all races, is that the prospective voter "be able to read and write any section of the Constitution of North Carolina in the English language." That seems to us to be one fair way of determining whether a person is literate, not a calculated scheme to lay springes for the citizen. Certainly we cannot condemn it on its face as a device unrelated to the desire of North Carolina to raise the standards for people of all races who cast the ballot.

Affirmed.

Notes and Questions

1. Until they were banned by the Voting Rights Act, literacy tests of various strengths were imposed by states. Some tests, like those of North Carolina at issue in *Lassiter*, and of New York, reprinted on pages 233–34 n.3, *infra*, were relatively mild. Others, however, required greater language ability and a greater knowledge of civics. Alabama, for example, employed a test that asked applicants to write certain sections of the Constitution dictated to them by registration officials, and in addition required them to answer a group of four questions "without assistance." There were twelve different groupings of four questions each, and the groups would be rotated to make it more difficult to predict the questions that would be asked of any particular applicant. Here are the questions in the rotation, taken from the appendix to *United States v. Parker*, 236 F. Supp. 511, 519–29 (M.D. Ala. 1964):

What city is the capital of the United States?

How many states are there in the United States?

How many senators from each state are in the United States Senate?

The president of the United States is elected for a term of how many years?

What city is the capital of Alabama?

How old must a person be in order to be eligible to vote in Alabama?

What is the lawmaking body of the United States called?

The Constitution of the United States provides that Congress shall make no law respecting an establishment of religion, or prohibiting the free exercise thereof. (True or false)

In what town or city is the court-house located in this county?

How many stars are there in the United States Flag?

What is the lawmaking body of Alabama called?

Those who shall be convicted of any crime punishable by imprisonment in the state penitentiary shall be disqualified from voting in Alabama. (True or false)

What is the chief executive of the United States called?

Name the two major political parties in the United States.

Who coins money, the state or the United States?

If the president dies, who takes his place?

What is the chief executive of Alabama called?

Are post offices operated by the state or federal government?

What is the name of the president of the United States?

To what national lawmaking body does each state send senators and representatives?

What is the name of the governor of Alabama?

Of what political party is the president of the United States a member?

Name one of the United States senators from Alabama.

When residents of a city elect their officials, the voting is called a municipal election. (True or false)

2. It is important to keep in mind that while literacy tests were used as one of several techniques to prevent disfavored groups (mainly blacks in the South and immigrants in the North) from voting, there was no allegation by Lassiter that North Carolina's literacy test was being applied discriminatorily. Indeed, Lassiter refused to submit to the test at all. As a result, the Court's holding was necessarily limited. It rejected Lassiter's facial challenge to the literacy test, but did not uphold the constitutionality of all literacy tests.

Three types of literacy tests would fail a constitutional challenge even under the standard applied in *Lassiter*. First, a test applied differently to applicants of different races (or other suspect classes) would violate the Equal Protection Clause, just as a neutrally written statute requiring a permit to operate a business would violate the Constitution if minorities' permit applications were uniformly denied. *See Yick Wo v. Hopkins*, 118 U.S. 356 (1886). For example, in *United States v. Louisiana*, 225 F. Supp. 353, 383–84 (E.D. La. 1963), *aff'd*, 380 U.S. 145 (1965), the district court pointed to "unmistakable evidence" that white applicants had been given the answers to a literacy test (and one white applicant even signed the answer sheet by mistake), while black applicants received no such assistance.

In *Louisiana*, voting registrars discriminated against blacks both in the choice of constitutional provisions they were to interpret and in the grading of responses:

[F]requently the choice of difficult sections has made it impossible for many Negro applicants to pass. White applicants were more often given easy sections, many of which could be answered by short, stock phrases such as "freedom of speech," "freedom of religion," "States' rights," and so on. Negro applicants, on the other hand, were given parts of the Louisiana Constitution [that were much harder to interpret]. * * *

As in the selection process, gross abuses of discretion appear in the evaluation of the interpretations. One rejected Negro applicant stated that the registrar "said what I was saying was right, but it wasn't like she wanted me to say it." * * *

Registrars were easily satisfied with answers from white voters. In one instance "FRDUM FOOF SPETGH" was an acceptable response to the request to interpret [the portion] of the Louisiana Constitution [protecting the freedom of speech].

On the other hand, the record shows that Negroes whose application forms and answers indicate that they are highly qualified by literacy standards and have a high degree of intelligence have been turned down although they had given a reasonable interpretation of fairly technical clauses of the constitution.

Id. See also BRIAN K. LANDSBERG, FREE AT LAST TO VOTE: THE ALABAMA ORIGINS OF THE 1965 VOTING RIGHTS ACT 43–44, 121–22 (2007). As Landsberg summarized some of the discrimination,

Was a white applicant illiterate? A registrar would fill out the applicant's form. Did the white applicant know no one to serve as a supporting witness? A registrar would find a witness. But for African Americans, registration was a privilege, to be earned only by meeting some undefined and flexible standard, depending on the registrars' and potential witnesses' exercise of a sort of lesè-majesté.

LANDSBERG, *supra*, at 68.

Second, a literacy test could violate the Constitution if its terms left too much discretion in the officials administering the test. Thus, a test that required an applicant not only to "read and write" a provision of the state constitution, but to "understand and explain" it was held unconstitutional in *Davis v. Schnell*, 81 F. Supp. 872 (S.D. Ala.), *aff'd*, 336 U.S. 933 (1949). *See also United States v. Louisiana*, 225 F. Supp. at 384 (striking down Louisiana's test, which required potential voters to "interpret" part of the Louisiana Constitution and left "unlimited discretion" in the registrars). Are *Davis* and *Louisiana* consistent with the reasoning of *Lassiter*? *See Williams v. Mississippi*, 170 U.S. 213, 225 (1898) ("The[] [provisions of Mississippi law requiring voters to "read" or "understand" a provision of the Constitution] do not on their face discriminate between the races, and it has not been shown that their actual administration was evil; only that evil was possible under them."); *id.* at 222–23. Was the Alabama test reprinted above invalid under *Davis* and *Louisiana*?

Third, even neutrally *applied* literacy tests may have been established for the purpose of disqualifying disproportionate numbers of ethnic or racial minorities. Contrary to the Court's remark that "[l]iteracy and illiteracy are neutral on race, creed, color, and sex, as reports around the world show," there was a clear racial disparity in literacy. According to the National Center for Education Statistics (which relies on census data), the overall rate of illiteracy in the United States in 1959, the year *Lassiter* was decided, was 2.2%. (North Carolina's was higher: 4%.) The rate of white illiteracy in the United States was lower—1.6%, but the rate of minority illiteracy was 7.5%. *See* National Center for Education Statistics, National Assessment of Adult Literacy, *at* https://nces.ed.gov/naal/lit_history.asp. A state wishing to disenfranchise blacks could, therefore, have adopted a facially neutral literacy test, confident that the result of the test would be to disqualify far more blacks than whites. But of course, the same disparity would be produced if the state was not trying to discriminate by race and was instead simply trying to ensure that the ballot would be used "intelligent[ly]."

Literacy tests having *both* the purpose and effect of discriminating on the ground of race or ethnicity would be examined under strict scrutiny and invalidated. The South, in particular, saw disproportionate effects from several types of voting restrictions that combined "to disfranchise nearly all blacks and many poor whites." Keyssar, *supra*, at 182. The situation was both predictable and intended: "[A]s Senator Theodore Bilbo observed in 1946, in Mississippi 'a man to register must be able to read and explain . . . a Constitution that damn few white men and no n****rs at all can explain.'" *Id*. We will again confront the issue of discriminatorily motivated voting restrictions when we examine *Hunter v. Underwood*, 471 U.S. 222 (1985) [p. 41], later in this Chapter.

3. Even with the qualifications noted above, literacy tests enabled a great deal of discrimination in practice. Should the Court have prevented the potentially discriminatory use of literacy tests by striking down even those literacy tests that were applied without regard to race (or where discrimination was not proven)?

4. For what reasons other than discriminatory ones would a state adopt a literacy test? In other words, why does the Court say that literacy tests "ha[ve] some relation to standards designed to promote intelligent use of the ballot"? Could a state constitutionally require that voters attain a certain level of education, perhaps the successful completion of high school? Could a state accord different weight to people's votes depending on the levels of education the voters received? *See* John Stuart Mill, *Considerations on Representative Government, in* On Liberty and Other Essays 334–37 (John Gray ed., Oxford University Press 1991).

5. Could a state constitutionally employ a literacy test that would exclude all blind persons (or all persons blind at the time of their attempted registration) from the franchise? Would it make a difference if part of the reason for the literacy test were to limit the political influence of the disabled?

6. Shortly after 1959, when *Lassiter* was decided, the Court assumed a much greater role in addressing the constitutionality of distributions of political power than it had previously exercised. *Colegrove v. Green*, 328 U.S. 549 (1946) [p. 90], had applied the political-question doctrine to hold that federal courts lacked jurisdiction to adjudicate constitutional challenges to malapportioned districts. *Baker v.*

Carr, 369 U.S. 186 (1962) [p. 97], overruled *Colegrove* and concluded that courts could decide reapportionment challenges under the Equal Protection Clause, but did not decide that unequally populated districts actually violated that Clause.

That conclusion would come two years later in *Reynolds v. Sims*, 377 U.S. 533 (1964) [p. 122]. *Reynolds* established the "one-person, one-vote" requirement in holding that each house of a state legislature must be elected from districts "substantially equal" in population. *See also Lucas v. Forty-Fourth General Assembly of Colorado*, 377 U.S. 713 (1964) (requiring both state house and senate districts to be apportioned by population); *Wesberry v. Sanders*, 376 U.S. 1 (1964) [p. 116] (applying the one-person, one-vote requirement to elections for the United States House of Representatives). Both the jurisdictional question and the merits of the one-person, one-vote doctrine are covered in depth in Chapter 2.

In another important election-law development, 1964 saw the ratification of the Twenty-Fourth Amendment, which prohibited poll taxes in federal elections. Further, the Civil Rights Act of 1964 and the Voting Rights Act of 1965 radically altered the degree of federal intervention in areas that theretofore had been left to the states. We will consider the Voting Rights Act extensively in later Chapters.

Thus, by 1966, the law of elections had significantly changed from the way it was in 1959. Both the Court and Congress had committed themselves to greater involvement in protecting voting rights.[f] Of comparable importance, there had been significant changes in the Court's membership. In 1962, Eisenhower-appointee Charles Whittaker retired because of a mental disability and Roosevelt-appointee Felix Frankfurter retired because of the effect of two strokes. Frankfurter had written the plurality opinion in *Colegrove* and had been a vociferous critic of judicial involvement in the districting process. (Indeed, some, including apparently Frankfurter himself, have attributed the cause of the strokes to *Baker*. *See More Perfect: The Political Thicket*, WNYC Studios (June 10, 2016), https://www.wnycstudios.org/podcasts/radiolabmoreperfect/episodes/the-political-thicket (37:35).) His departure left Justice Harlan as the only member of the Court who would reliably encourage the Court to exercise judicial restraint in reviewing election cases. President Kennedy appointed Byron White and Arthur Goldberg to succeed Whittaker and Frankfurter, and when Goldberg resigned his seat to serve as Ambassador to the United Nations, President Johnson appointed Abe Fortas to take his place.

---

f. In the early part of the twentieth century, the Court was reticent about enforcing voting rights against uncooperative states. In *Giles v. Harris*, 189 U.S. 475 (1903), for example, the Court refused to intervene to correct the allegedly unconstitutional voting registration system of Alabama, which required voters to pass tests but exempted those voters registered before the new requirements went into effect. The Court held that it could not decide the case, in part because it would be powerless to effect the equality to which the plaintiff was entitled: "Unless we are prepared to supervise the voting in that State by officers of the court, it seems to us that all that the plaintiff could get from equity would be an empty form." *Id*. at 488. The plaintiff's only recourse, according to the Court, was with Congress and the state itself. *See id*.

2. The Poor

Harper v. Virginia State Board of Elections

Supreme Court of the United States

383 U.S. 663, 86 S. Ct. 1079, 16 L. Ed. 2d 169 (1966)

MR. JUSTICE DOUGLAS delivered the opinion of the Court [in which MR. CHIEF JUSTICE WARREN, MR. JUSTICE CLARK, MR. JUSTICE BRENNAN, MR. JUSTICE WHITE, and MR. JUSTICE FORTAS join].

These are suits by Virginia residents to have declared unconstitutional Virginia's poll tax.[1] * * *

While the right to vote in federal elections is conferred by Art. I, § 2, of the Constitution (*United States* v. *Classic*, 313 U.S. 299, 314–15 [(1941)]), the right to vote in state elections is nowhere expressly mentioned. It is argued that the right to vote in state elections is implicit, particularly by reason of the First Amendment and that it may not constitutionally be conditioned upon the payment of a tax or fee.[2] We do not stop to canvass the relation between voting and political expression. For it is enough to say that once the franchise is granted to the electorate, lines may not be drawn which are inconsistent with the Equal Protection Clause of the Fourteenth Amendment. That is to say, the right of suffrage "is subject to the imposition of state standards which are not discriminatory and which do not contravene any restriction that Congress, acting pursuant to its constitutional powers, has imposed." *Lassiter* v. *Northampton County Board of Elections*, 360 U.S. 45, 51 [(1959)] [p. 11]. We were speaking there of a state literacy test which we sustained, warning that the result would be different if a literacy test, fair on its face, were used to discriminate against a class. *Id.* at 53. But the *Lassiter* case does not govern the result here, because, unlike a poll tax, the "ability to read and write * * * has some relation to standards designed to promote intelligent use of the ballot." *Id.* at 51.

We conclude that a State violates the Equal Protection Clause of the Fourteenth Amendment whenever it makes the affluence of the voter or payment of any fee an electoral standard. Voter qualifications have no relation to wealth nor to paying or

---

1. Section 173 of Virginia's Constitution directs the General Assembly to levy an annual poll tax not exceeding $1.50 [approximately $12.50 in today's dollars — Eds.] on every resident of the State 21 years of age and over (with exceptions not relevant here). * * * Section 18 of the Constitution includes payment of poll taxes as a precondition for voting. Section 20 provides that a person must "personally" pay all state poll taxes for the three years preceding the year in which he applies for registration. By § 21 the poll tax must be paid at least six months prior to the election in which the voter seeks to vote. * * *

2. * * * "If the State of Texas placed a tax on the right to speak at the rate of one dollar and seventy-five cents per year, no court would hesitate to strike it down as a blatant infringement of the freedom of speech. Yet the poll tax as enforced in Texas is a tax on the equally important right to vote." *United States* v. *Texas*, 252 F. Supp. 234, 254 ([W.D. Tex.] 1966).

not paying this or any other tax.[4] Our cases demonstrate that the Equal Protection Clause of the Fourteenth Amendment restrains the States from fixing voter qualifications which invidiously discriminate. Thus without questioning the power of a State to impose reasonable residence restrictions on the availability of the ballot, we held in *Carrington* v. *Rash*, 380 U.S. 89 [(1965)] [p. 71], that a State may not deny the opportunity to vote to a bona fide resident merely because he is a member of the armed services. * * * Previously we had said that neither homesite nor occupation "affords a permissible basis for distinguishing between qualified voters within the State." *Gray* v. *Sanders*, 372 U.S. 368, 380 [(1963)] [p. 111]. We think the same must be true of requirements of wealth or affluence or payment of a fee.

Long ago in *Yick Wo* v. *Hopkins*, 118 U.S. 356, 370 [(1886)], the Court referred to "the political franchise of voting" as a "fundamental political right, because preservative of all rights." Recently in *Reynolds* v. *Sims*, 377 U.S. 533, 561–562 (1964) [p. 122], we said, "Undoubtedly, the right of suffrage is a fundamental matter in a free and democratic society. Especially since the right to exercise the franchise in a free and unimpaired manner is preservative of other basic civil and political rights, any alleged infringement of the right of citizens to vote must be carefully and meticulously scrutinized." * * *

We say the same whether the citizen, otherwise qualified to vote, has $1.50 in his pocket or nothing at all, pays the fee or fails to pay it. The principle that denies the State the right to dilute a citizen's vote on account of his economic status or other such factors by analogy bars a system which excludes those unable to pay a fee to vote or who fail to pay.

It is argued that a State may exact fees from citizens for many different kinds of licenses; that if it can demand from all an equal fee for a driver's license, it can demand from all an equal poll tax for voting. But we must remember that the interest of the State, when it comes to voting, is limited to the power to fix qualifications. Wealth, like race, creed, or color, is not germane to one's ability to participate intelligently in the electoral process. Lines drawn on the basis of wealth or property, like those of race, are traditionally disfavored. *See Edwards* v. *California*, 314 U.S. 160, 184–185 [(1941)] (Jackson, J., concurring); *Griffin* v. *Illinois*, 351 U.S. 12 [(1956)]; *Douglas* v. *California*, 372 U.S. 353 [(1963)].[g] To introduce wealth or payment of a fee as a measure of a voter's qualifications is to introduce a capricious or irrelevant factor. The degree of the discrimination is irrelevant. In this context—that is, as a

---

4. Only a handful of States today condition the franchise on the payment of a poll tax. Alabama and Texas each impose a poll tax of $1.50. Mississippi has a poll tax of $2. Vermont has recently eliminated the requirement that poll taxes be paid in order to vote.

g. *Edwards* struck down, on Commerce Clause grounds, a California law prohibiting the importation of "indigent person[s]" into the state. Justice Jackson's concurrence argued that one's indigency should be "constitutionally an irrelevance, like race, creed, or color." *Griffin* required states to provide an indigent criminal defendant a transcript free of charge to enable him to file an appeal. *Douglas* required states to provide counsel for a criminal defendant during an initial appeal, where state law provided the defendant such an appeal as of right. —Eds.

condition of obtaining a ballot—the requirement of fee paying causes an "invidious" discrimination that runs afoul of the Equal Protection Clause. * * *

* * * In determining what lines are unconstitutionally discriminatory, we have never been confined to historic notions of equality, any more than we have restricted due process to a fixed catalogue of what was at a given time deemed to be the limits of fundamental rights. Notions of what constitutes equal treatment for purposes of the Equal Protection Clause *do* change. * * *

* * * [W]e held [in *Reynolds* v. *Sims, supra,*] that "the opportunity for equal participation by all voters in the election of state legislators" is required. We decline to qualify that principle by sustaining this poll tax. Our conclusion, like that in *Reynolds* v. *Sims,* is founded not on what we think governmental policy should be, but on what the Equal Protection Clause requires.

We have long been mindful that where fundamental rights and liberties are asserted under the Equal Protection Clause, classifications which might invade or restrain them must be closely scrutinized and carefully confined.

Those principles apply here. For to repeat, wealth or fee paying has, in our view, no relation to voting qualifications; the right to vote is too precious, too fundamental to be so burdened or conditioned.

Reversed.

Mr. Justice Black, dissenting.

In *Breedlove* v. *Suttles,* 302 U.S. 277 [(1937)], * * * we unanimously upheld the right of the State of Georgia to make payment of its state poll tax a prerequisite to voting in state elections. We rejected at that time contentions that the state law violated the Equal Protection Clause of the Fourteenth Amendment because it put an unequal burden on different groups of people according to their age, sex, and ability to pay. * * *

* * * Later, * * * *Butler* v. *Thompson,* 341 U.S. 937 [(1951)], uph[eld], over the dissent of Mr. Justice Douglas, the Virginia state poll tax law challenged here against the same equal protection challenges. * * * I would adhere to the holding of those cases. * * *

It should be pointed out at once that the Court's decision is to no extent based on a finding that the Virginia law as written or as applied is being used as a device or mechanism to deny Negro citizens of Virginia the right to vote on account of their color. * * * What the Court does hold is that the Equal Protection Clause necessarily bars all States from making payment of a state tax, any tax, a prerequisite to voting.

I think the interpretation that this Court gave the Equal Protection Clause in *Breedlove* was correct. The mere fact that a law results in treating some groups differently from others does not, of course, automatically amount to a violation of the Equal Protection Clause. To bar a State from drawing any distinctions in the application of its laws would practically paralyze the regulatory power of legislative bodies. * * * Voting laws are no exception to this principle. All voting laws treat some persons differently from others in some respects. Some bar a person from voting who is under 21 years of age; others bar those under 18. Some bar convicted felons or the insane, and some have attached a freehold or other property qualification for voting. * * *

* * * State poll tax legislation can "reasonably," "rationally" and without an "invidious" or evil purpose to injure anyone be found to rest on a number of state policies including (1) the State's desire to collect its revenue, and (2) its belief that voters who pay a poll tax will be interested in furthering the State's welfare when they vote. Certainly it is rational to believe that people may be more likely to pay taxes if payment is a prerequisite to voting. And if history can be a factor in determining the "rationality" of discrimination in a state law * * *, then whatever may be our personal opinion, history is on the side of "rationality" of the State's poll tax policy. Property qualifications existed in the Colonies and were continued by many States after the Constitution was adopted. Although I join the Court in disliking the policy of the poll tax, this is not in my judgment a justifiable reason for holding this poll tax law unconstitutional. Such a holding on my part would, in my judgment, be an exercise of power which the Constitution does not confer upon me.[4] * * *

The Court's justification for consulting its own notions rather than following the original meaning of the Constitution, as I would, apparently is based on the belief of the majority of the Court that for this Court to be bound by the original meaning of the Constitution is an intolerable and debilitating evil; that our Constitution should not be "shackled to the political theory of a particular era," and that to save the country from the original Constitution the Court must have constant power to renew it and keep it abreast of this Court's more enlightening theories of what is best for our society. It seems to me that this is an attack not only on the great value of our Constitution itself but also on the concept of a written constitution which is to survive through the years as originally written unless changed through the amendment process which the Framers wisely provided. Moreover, when a "political theory" embodied in our Constitution becomes outdated, it seems to me that a majority of the nine members of this Court are not only without constitutional

---

4. The opinion of the Court, in footnote two, quotes language from a federal district court's opinion which implies that since a tax on speech would not be constitutionally allowed a tax which is a prerequisite to voting likewise cannot be allowed. But a tax or any other regulation which burdens and actually abridges the right to speak would, in my judgment, be a flagrant violation of the First Amendment's prohibition against abridgments of the freedom of speech which prohibition is made applicable to the States by the Fourteenth Amendment. There is no comparable specific constitutional provision absolutely barring the States from abridging the right to vote. Consequently States have from the beginning and do now qualify the right to vote because of age, prior felony convictions, illiteracy, and various other reasons. Of course the First and Fourteenth Amendments forbid any State from abridging a person's right to speak because he is under 21 years of age, has been convicted of a felony, or is illiterate.

power but are far less qualified to choose a new constitutional political theory than the people of this country proceeding in the manner provided by Article V. * * *

The people have not found it impossible to amend their Constitution to meet new conditions. The Equal Protection Clause itself is the product of the people's desire to use their constitutional power to amend the Constitution to meet new problems. Moreover, the people, in § 5 of the Fourteenth Amendment, designated the governmental tribunal they wanted to provide additional rules to enforce the guarantees of that Amendment. The branch of Government they chose was not the Judicial Branch but the Legislative. I have no doubt at all that Congress has the power under § 5 to pass legislation to abolish the poll tax in order to protect the citizens of this country if it believes that the poll tax is being used as a device to deny voters equal protection of the laws. But this legislative power which was granted to Congress by § 5 of the Fourteenth Amendment is limited to Congress. * * *

MR. JUSTICE HARLAN, whom MR. JUSTICE STEWART joins, dissenting.

The final demise of state poll taxes, already totally proscribed by the Twenty-Fourth Amendment with respect to federal elections and abolished by the States themselves in all but four States with respect to state elections, is perhaps in itself not of great moment. But the fact that the *coup de grace* has been administered by this Court instead of being left to the affected States or to the federal political process should be a matter of continuing concern to all interested in maintaining the proper role of this tribunal under our scheme of government. * * *

* * * In substance the Court's analysis of the equal protection issue goes no further than to say that the electoral franchise is "precious" and "fundamental," and to conclude that "[t]o introduce wealth or payment of a fee as a measure of a voter's qualifications is to introduce a capricious or irrelevant factor." These are of course captivating phrases, but they are wholly inadequate to satisfy the standard governing adjudication of the equal protection issue: Is there a rational basis for Virginia's poll tax as a voting qualification? I think the answer to that question is undoubtedly "yes."[5] * * *

[I]t is only by fiat that it can be said, especially in the context of American history, that there can be no rational debate as to [property qualifications'] advisability. Most of the early Colonies had them; many of the States have had them during much of their histories; and, whether one agrees or not, arguments have been and still can be made in favor of them. For example, it is certainly a rational argument that payment of some minimal poll tax promotes civic responsibility, weeding out

---

5. I have no doubt that poll taxes that deny the right to vote on the basis of race or color violate the Fifteenth Amendment and can be struck down by this Court. * * * The Virginia poll tax is on its face applicable to all citizens, and there was no allegation that it was discriminatorily enforced. The District Court explicitly found "no racial discrimination * * * in its application as a condition to voting." * * *

those who do not care enough about public affairs to pay $1.50 or thereabouts a year for the exercise of the franchise. It is also arguable, indeed it was probably accepted as sound political theory by a large percentage of Americans through most of our history, that people with some property have a deeper stake in community affairs, and are consequently more responsible, more educated, more knowledgeable, more worthy of confidence, than those without means, and that the community and Nation would be better managed if the franchise were restricted to such citizens. Nondiscriminatory and fairly applied literacy tests, upheld by this Court in *Lassiter* v. *Northampton County Board of Elections*, find justification on very similar grounds.

These viewpoints, to be sure, ring hollow on most contemporary ears. Their lack of acceptance today is evidenced by the fact that nearly all of the States, left to their own devices, have eliminated property or poll-tax qualifications; by the cognate fact that Congress and three-quarters of the States quickly ratified the Twenty-Fourth Amendment; and by the fact that rules such as the "pauper exclusion" in Virginia law have never been enforced.

Property and poll-tax qualifications, very simply, are not in accord with current egalitarian notions of how a modern democracy should be organized. It is of course entirely fitting that legislatures should modify the law to reflect such changes in popular attitudes. However, it is all wrong, in my view, for the Court to adopt the political doctrines popularly accepted at a particular moment of our history and to declare all others to be irrational and invidious, barring them from the range of choice by reasonably minded people acting through the political process. It was not too long ago that Mr. Justice Holmes felt impelled to remind the Court that the Due Process Clause of the Fourteenth Amendment does not enact the *laissez-faire* theory of society, *Lochner* v. *New York*, 198 U.S. 45, 75–76 [(1905)]. The times have changed, and perhaps it is appropriate to observe that neither does the Equal Protection Clause of that Amendment rigidly impose upon America an ideology of unrestrained egalitarianism.

I would affirm the decision of the District Court.

Notes and Questions

1. *Harper* was one of a series of cases from the 1950s and 1960s calling into question the constitutionality of government distinctions based on wealth. By 1966, the Court had required states to provide counsel to criminal defendants on trial for felonies (*Gideon* v. *Wainwright*, 372 U.S. 335 (1963) (later extended to any crime punished by imprisonment, *Argersinger* v. *Hamlin*, 407 U.S. 25 (1972))) and during an appeal as of right, *i.e.*, which the appellate court must hear (*Douglas* v. *California*, 372 U.S. 353 (1963)). Further, the Court held that states must provide a transcript free of charge for an indigent defendant who needs the transcript to file an appeal (*Griffin* v. *Illinois*, 351 U.S. 12 (1956)), and, most famously, that accused persons subject to custodial interrogation had a right to counsel at state expense (*Miranda* v.

Arizona, 384 U.S. 436, 479 (1966). For similar holdings into the early 1970s, see also *Boddie v. Connecticut*, 401 U.S. 371 (1971) (invalidating a filing fee for divorce cases, as applied to persons unable to pay the fee); *Goldberg v. Kelly*, 397 U.S. 254 (1970) (holding that welfare recipients possessed a property right in anticipated government benefits, such that the benefits could not be terminated without a hearing); *Shapiro v. Thompson*, 394 U.S. 618 (1969) (invalidating laws that imposed a one-year residency requirement on the receipt of welfare benefits).

Note that the Court often used the Equal Protection Clause to prevent states from discriminating against certain classes of people, particularly with regard to important aspects of personal liberty. Even where the Court was unwilling to strike down a law under the Due Process Clause, it was sometimes willing to apply strict scrutiny under the Equal Protection Clause, resulting in the invalidation of laws that in practice allowed only some people to exercise those important rights. *See Skinner v. Oklahoma ex rel. Williamson*, 316 U.S. 535 (1942) (per Douglas, J.) (using the Equal Protection Clause to strike down a law providing for the sterilization of some (but not all) habitual criminals).

Soon after the appointment of Chief Justice Burger to replace Chief Justice Warren, the Court's jurisprudence began to shift away from a concern about the unequal distribution of property. The Court held that wealth was not a suspect classification and, applying the rational-basis test, upheld laws that limited a family's welfare benefits regardless of the number of children in the family (*Dandridge v. Williams*, 397 U.S. 471 (1970)); that funded local public schools by property taxes so that children in poorer school districts attended schools less well funded than schools in wealthier areas (*San Antonio Independent School District v. Rodriguez*, 411 U.S. 1 (1973)); and that paid childbirth expenses for indigent women but did not pay for abortions (*Maher v. Roe*, 432 U.S. 464 (1977)).

The Court has not overruled the cases striking down wealth classifications, though. Instead, the Court has applied strict scrutiny only to those classifications that discriminate on the basis of wealth *as to the exercise of a fundamental right.* Voting is considered a fundamental right, so *Harper* continues to be good law. Similarly, because running for office is a fundamental right, states may not impose filing fees on candidates who are unable to afford them. *Lubin v. Panish*, 415 U.S. 709 (1974).

2. *Harper* claimed that "[l]ines drawn on the basis of wealth or property, like those of race, are traditionally disfavored." Was the Court correct to treat the Virginia statute as such a "line," or was the $1.50 requirement a nondiscriminatory one, applicable to all voters regardless of their assets?

3. Would the tax in *Harper* be constitutional if the poor—*i.e.*, those unable to pay the tax—were given an exemption?

4. *Problem.* Suppose that instead of requiring all voters to pay a tax, Virginia had required potential voters either to pay the $1.50 poll tax or to watch a thirty-minute

candidate debate or panel discussion of the issues involved in the election. The purpose of both would be to ensure that voters considered the election sufficiently important to justify the expenditure of time or money, and also to increase the likelihood that voters would be knowledgeable about the relevant issues. Would such a requirement be constitutional? If not, is there a constitutional problem with requiring voters to register prior to election day, on the belief that only people sufficiently motivated to register should be permitted to vote? *Cf. Harmon v. Forssenius*, 380 U.S. 528 (1965) (holding unconstitutional a Virginia law requiring voters in federal elections either to pay a poll tax or file a certificate of residency six months before the election).

5. The Court's discovery of a "tradition" against "[l]ines drawn on the basis of wealth or property" is curious given Anglo-American law's centuries-long explicit wealth discrimination. *See generally* CHILTON WILLIAMSON, AMERICAN SUFFRAGE: FROM PROPERTY TO DEMOCRACY, 1760–1860 (1960). "By the middle of the eighteenth century, all the American colonies save one had adopted property qualifications for the suffrage." Robert J. Steinfeld, *Property and Suffrage in the Early American Republic*, 41 STAN. L. REV. 335, 336 (1989). For a helpful catalogue of suffrage qualifications in the early years of the United States, see ALEXANDER KEYSSAR, THE RIGHT TO VOTE: THE CONTESTED HISTORY OF DEMOCRACY IN THE UNITED STATES 306–33 (rev. ed. 2009); *see also Wesberry v. Sanders*, 376 U.S. 1, 25 n.7 (1964) [p. 116] (Harlan, J., dissenting). Even as property and taxpaying requirements were being eliminated in the nineteenth century, they were often replaced by "pauper exclusions" (to which Justice Harlan referred in his *Harper* dissent) that barred persons on public assistance from voting. *See* KEYSSAR, *supra*, at 49–50, 321–23. By 1900, fourteen states had pauper exclusions. *See* Steinfeld, *supra*, at 335.

Professor Steinfeld has noted that the debate over property qualifications and pauper exclusions presented a conflict between the traditional idea that only property ownership gave a voter true independence—a "will of his own"—and the notion that all men were "by nature equally free and independent." *Id.* at 338. As Blackstone stated the traditional view,

> If it were probable that every man would give his vote freely and without influence of any kind, then, upon the true theory and genuine principles of liberty, every member of the community, however poor, should have a vote in electing those delegates, to whose charge is committed the disposal of his property, his liberty, and his life. But, since that can hardly be expected in persons of indigent fortunes, or such as are under the immediate dominion of others, all popular states have been obliged to establish certain qualifications; whereby some, who are expected to have no will of their own, are excluded from voting, in order to set other individuals, whose wills may be supposed independent, more thoroughly upon a level with each other.

1 WILLIAM BLACKSTONE, COMMENTARIES ON THE LAWS OF ENGLAND *171 (1765). Professor Steinfeld has further stated that "[i]n the decades after the [American] Revolution, hardly anyone disputed the proposition that property ownership was necessary for personal independence." Steinfeld, *supra*, at 342. Was *Harper* right to regard such a view as "irrational"? Or is wealth in reality more than a "capricious or irrelevant factor" in determining one's qualifications to vote? In particular, is wealth less related to one's ability to cast a vote intelligently and virtuously than is one's ability to pass a literacy test, as in *Lassiter*?

6. According to Professor Keyssar, the concern with the non-propertied class's lack of "independence" "coexisted with an altogether contradictory argument, often expressed by the same people: the poor, or the propertyless, should not vote because they would threaten the interests of property—that is, they would have too much will of their own." KEYSSAR, *supra*, at 9. Professor Keyssar went on to suggest that the Blackstonian invocation of concerns about independence "mask[ed]" the true class-based reasons for property qualifications, and "provid[ed] an ostensibly egalitarian defense of an overtly anti-egalitarian policy." *Id.*

7. On the propriety of property qualifications, consider the thoughts of Benjamin Franklin:

> Today a man owns a jackass worth fifty dollars and he is entitled to vote; but before the next election the jackass dies. The man in the mean time has become more experienced, his knowledge of the principles of government, and his acquaintance with mankind, are more extensive, and he is therefore better qualified to make a proper selection of rulers—but the jackass is dead and the man cannot vote. Now gentlemen, pray inform me, in whom is the right of suffrage? In the man or in the jackass?

4 BENJAMIN FRANKLIN, THE CASKET, OR FLOWERS OF LITERATURE, WIT AND SENTIMENT 181 (1828).

8. *Problem.* A state statute limits participation in city bond elections to those residents who have taxable property listed with the city tax assessor. Both real and personal property qualify, and listing any property, no matter how little the value, satisfies the statute. (Another statute requires city residents to list all their taxable property with the assessor yearly. There is no penalty for failing to do so, however.) The objective is to have such elections decided by the people who will have to pay the cost of any debt incurred by the city. Is the limitation constitutional? *See Hill v. Stone*, 421 U.S. 289 (1975).

9. Is there any constitutional difference between requiring people to pay a fee in order to vote and requiring people to pay a fee for *failing* to vote? Is there a fundamental right *not* to vote? *See* Glenn Blain, *New Yorkers Who Don't Vote Would Pay $10 Fine Under Assemblywoman's Bill*, N.Y. DAILY NEWS (Mar. 17, 2017), *at* http://www.nydailynews.com/news/politics/new-yorkers-don-vote-pay-10-proposed-bill-article-1.3001499?cid=bitly.

3. The Law-Breaking

Richardson v. Ramirez

Supreme Court of the United States
418 U.S. 24, 94 S. Ct. 2655, 41 L. Ed. 2d 551 (1974)

MR. JUSTICE REHNQUIST delivered the opinion of the Court [in which MR. CHIEF JUSTICE BURGER, MR. JUSTICE STEWART, MR. JUSTICE WHITE, MR. JUSTICE BLACKMUN, and MR. JUSTICE POWELL join].

The three individual respondents in this case were convicted of felonies and have completed the service of their respective sentences and paroles. * * * They claimed, on behalf of themselves and others similarly situated, that application to them of the provisions of the California Constitution and implementing statutes which disenfranchised persons convicted of an "infamous crime" denied them the right to equal protection of the laws under the Federal Constitution. The Supreme Court of California [agreed]. * * *

Article XX, §11, of the California Constitution has provided since its adoption in 1879 that "[l]aws shall be made" to exclude from voting persons convicted of bribery, perjury, forgery, malfeasance in office, "or other high crimes." At the time respondents were refused registration, former Art. II, §1, of the California Constitution provided in part that "no alien ineligible to citizenship, no idiot, no insane person, no person convicted of any infamous crime, no person hereafter convicted of the embezzlement or misappropriation of public money, and no person who shall not be able to read the Constitution in the English language and write his or her name, shall ever exercise the privileges of an elector in this State." Sections 310 and 321 of the California Elections Code provide that an affidavit of registration shall show whether the affiant has been convicted of "a felony which disqualifies [him] from voting." * * *

Each of the individual respondents was convicted of one or more felonies, and served some time in jail or prison followed by a successfully terminated parole. * * * All three respondents were refused registration because of their felony convictions.[9] * * *

Unlike most claims under the Equal Protection Clause, for the decision of which we have only the language of the Clause itself as it is embodied in the Fourteenth Amendment, respondents' claim implicates not merely the language of the Equal

---

9. Respondent Ramirez was convicted in Texas of the felony of "robbery by assault" in 1952. He served three months in jail and successfully terminated his parole in 1962. * * * Respondent Lee was convicted of the felony of heroin possession in California in 1955, served two years in prison, and successfully terminated his parole in 1959. * * * Respondent Gill was convicted in 1952 and 1967 of second-degree burglary in California, and in 1957 of forgery. He served some time in prison on each conviction, followed by a successful parole. * * *

Protection Clause of § 1 of the Fourteenth Amendment, but also the provisions of the less familiar § 2 of the Amendment:

> "Representatives shall be apportioned among the several States according to their respective numbers, counting the whole number of persons in each State, excluding Indians not taxed. But when the right to vote at any election for the choice of electors for President and Vice President of the United States, Representatives in Congress, the Executive and Judicial officers of a State, or the members of the Legislature thereof, is denied to any of the male inhabitants of such State, being twenty-one years of age, and citizens of the United States, or in any way abridged, *except for participation in rebellion, or other crime*, the basis of representation therein shall be reduced in the proportion which the number of such male citizens shall bear to the whole number of male citizens twenty-one years of age in such State." (Emphasis supplied.)

Petitioner contends that the italicized language of § 2 expressly exempts from the sanction of that section disenfranchisement grounded on prior conviction of a felony. She goes on to argue that those who framed and adopted the Fourteenth Amendment could not have intended to prohibit outright in § 1 of that Amendment that which was expressly exempted from the lesser sanction of reduced representation imposed by § 2 of the Amendment. This argument seems to us a persuasive one unless it can be shown that the language of § 2, "except for participation in rebellion, or other crime," was intended to have a different meaning than would appear from its face.

The problem of interpreting the "intention" of a constitutional provision is, as countless cases of this Court recognize, a difficult one. Not only are there deliberations of congressional committees and floor debates in the House and Senate, but an amendment must thereafter be ratified by the necessary number of States. The legislative history bearing on the meaning of the relevant language of § 2 is scant indeed; the framers of the Amendment were primarily concerned with the effect of reduced representation upon the States, rather than with the two forms of disenfranchisement which were exempted from that consequence by the language with which we are concerned here. Nonetheless, what legislative history there is indicates that this language was intended by Congress to mean what it says.

Throughout the floor debates in both the House and the Senate, in which numerous changes of language in § 2 were proposed, the language "except for participation in rebellion, or other crime" was never altered. The language of § 2 attracted a good deal of interest during the debates, but most of the discussion was devoted to its foreseeable consequences in both the Northern and Southern States, and to arguments as to its necessity or wisdom. What little comment there was on the phrase in question here supports a plain reading of it. * * *

Further light is shed on the understanding of those who framed and ratified the Fourteenth Amendment, and thus on the meaning of § 2, by the fact that at the time of the adoption of the Amendment, 29 States had provisions in their constitutions which prohibited, or authorized the legislature to prohibit, exercise of the franchise by persons convicted of felonies or infamous crimes.

More impressive than the mere existence of the state constitutional provisions disenfranchising felons at the time of the adoption of the Fourteenth Amendment is the congressional treatment of States readmitted to the Union following the Civil War. For every State thus readmitted, affirmative congressional action in the form of an enabling act was taken, and as a part of the readmission process the State seeking readmission was required to submit for the approval of the Congress its proposed state constitution. * * * The Act admitting Arkansas, the first State to be so admitted, attached a condition to its admission. That Act provided:

> "* * * [t]hat the constitution of Arkansas shall never be so amended or changed as to deprive any citizen or class of citizens of the United States of the right to vote who are entitled to vote by the constitution herein recognized, except as a punishment for such crimes as are now felonies at common law, whereof they shall have been duly convicted, under laws equally applicable to all the inhabitants of said State * * *."

* * * The same "fundamental condition" as was imposed by the act readmitting Arkansas was also, with only slight variations in language, imposed by the Act readmitting North Carolina, South Carolina, Louisiana, Georgia, Alabama, and Florida, enacted three days later. That condition was again imposed by the Acts readmitting Virginia, Mississippi, Texas, and Georgia early in 1870. * * *

Despite this settled historical and judicial understanding of the Fourteenth Amendment's effect on state laws disenfranchising convicted felons, respondents argue that our recent decisions invalidating other state-imposed restrictions on the franchise as violative of the Equal Protection Clause require us to invalidate the disenfranchisement of felons as well. * * *

As we have seen, however, the exclusion of felons from the vote has an affirmative sanction in § 2 of the Fourteenth Amendment, a sanction which was not present in the case of the other restrictions on the franchise which were invalidated in the cases on which respondents rely. We hold that the understanding of those who adopted the Fourteenth Amendment, as reflected in the express language of § 2 and in the historical and judicial interpretation of the Amendment's applicability to state laws disenfranchising felons, is of controlling significance in distinguishing such laws from those other state limitations on the franchise which have been held invalid under the Equal Protection Clause by this Court. We * * * may rest on the demonstrably sound proposition that § 1, in dealing with voting rights as it does, could not have been meant to bar outright a form of disenfranchisement which was expressly exempted from the less drastic sanction of reduced representation which § 2 imposed for other forms of disenfranchisement. * * *

We therefore hold that the Supreme Court of California erred in concluding that California may no longer, consistent with the Equal Protection Clause of the

Fourteenth Amendment, exclude from the franchise convicted felons who have completed their sentences and paroles. * * * Accordingly, we reverse and remand for further proceedings not inconsistent with this opinion.

It is so ordered.

Mr. Justice Marshall, with whom Mr. Justice Brennan joins, dissenting.

The Court today holds that a State may strip ex-felons who have fully paid their debt to society of their fundamental right to vote without running afoul of the Fourteenth Amendment. This result is, in my view, based on an unsound historical analysis which already has been rejected by this Court. * * *

* * * The Court construes § 2 of the Fourteenth Amendment as an express authorization for the States to disenfranchise former felons. Section 2 does except disenfranchisement for "participation in rebellion, or other crime" from the operation of its penalty provision. As the Court notes, however, there is little independent legislative history as to the crucial words "or other crime"; the proposed § 2 went to a joint committee containing only the phrase "participation in rebellion" and emerged with "or other crime" inexplicably tacked on. * * *

The historical purpose for § 2 itself is, however, relatively clear and, in my view, dispositive of this case. The Republicans who controlled the 39th Congress were concerned that the additional congressional representation of the Southern States which would result from the abolition of slavery might weaken their own political dominance. There were two alternatives available — either to limit southern representation, which was unacceptable on a long-term basis, or to insure that southern Negroes, sympathetic to the Republican cause, would be enfranchised; but an explicit grant of suffrage to Negroes was thought politically unpalatable at the time. Section 2 of the Fourteenth Amendment was the resultant compromise. It put Southern States to a choice — enfranchise Negro voters or lose congressional representation. * * *

It is clear that § 2 was not intended and should not be construed to be a limitation on the other sections of the Fourteenth Amendment. Section 2 provides a special remedy — reduced representation — to cure a particular form of electoral abuse — the disenfranchisement of Negroes. There is no indication that the framers of the provisions intended that special penalty to be the exclusive remedy for all forms of electoral discrimination. This Court has repeatedly rejected that rationale. *See Reynolds* v. *Sims*, 377 U.S. 533 (1964) [p. 122]; *Carrington* v. *Rash*, 380 U.S. 89 (1965) [p. 71]. Rather, a discrimination to which the penalty provision of § 2 is inapplicable must still be judged against the Equal Protection Clause of § 1 to determine whether judicial or congressional remedies should be invoked. * * *

The Court's references to congressional enactments contemporaneous to the adoption of the Fourteenth Amendment * * * are inapposite. They do not explain the purpose for the adoption of § 2 of the Fourteenth Amendment. They merely indicate that disenfranchisement for participation in crime was not uncommon in the States at the time of the adoption of the Amendment. Hence, not surprisingly, that form of disenfranchisement was excepted from the application of the special penalty provision of § 2. But because Congress chose to exempt one form of electoral discrimination from the reduction-of-representation remedy provided by § 2 does not necessarily imply congressional approval of this disenfranchisement.[24] By providing a special remedy for disenfranchisement of a particular class of voters in § 2, Congress did not approve all election discriminations to which the § 2 remedy was inapplicable, and such discriminations thus are not forever immunized from evolving standards of equal protection scrutiny. There is no basis for concluding that Congress intended by § 2 to freeze the meaning of other clauses of the Fourteenth Amendment to the conception of voting rights prevalent at the time of the adoption of the Amendment. * * *

In my view, the disenfranchisement of ex-felons must be measured against the requirements of the Equal Protection Clause of § 1 of the Fourteenth Amendment. That analysis properly begins with the observation that because the right to vote "is of the essence of a democratic society, and any restrictions on that right strike at the heart of representative government," *Reynolds* v. *Sims*, 377 U.S., at 555, voting is a "fundamental" right. * * *

To determine that the compelling-state-interest test applies to the challenged classification is, however, to settle only a threshold question. * * * I think it clear that the State has not met its burden of justifying the blanket disenfranchisement of former felons presented by this case. There is certainly no basis for asserting that ex-felons have any less interest in the democratic process than any other citizen. Like everyone else, their daily lives are deeply affected and changed by the decisions of government. * * *

[One] asserted purpose [of disenfranchising ex-felons] is to keep former felons from voting because their likely voting pattern might be subversive of the interests of an orderly society. Support for the argument that electors can be kept from the ballot box for fear they might vote to repeal or emasculate provisions of the criminal code, is drawn primarily from this Court's decisions in *Murphy* v. *Ramsey*, 114 U.S. 15 (1885), and *Davis* v. *Beason*, 133 U.S. 333 (1890). In *Murphy*, the Court upheld the disenfranchisement of anyone who had ever entered into a bigamous or polygamous marriage and in *Davis*, the Court sanctioned, as a condition to the exercise of franchise, the requirement of an oath that the elector did not "teach,

---

24. To say that § 2 of the Fourteenth Amendment is a direct limitation on the protection afforded voting rights by § 1 leads to absurd results. If one accepts the premise that § 2 authorizes disenfranchisement for any crime, the challenged California provision could * * * require disenfranchisement for seduction under promise of marriage, or conspiracy to operate a motor vehicle without a muffler. Disenfranchisement extends to convictions for vagrancy in Alabama or breaking a water pipe in North Dakota, to note but two examples. Even a jaywalking or traffic conviction could conceivably lead to disenfranchisement, since § 2 does not differentiate between felonies and misdemeanors.

advise, counsel, or encourage any person to commit the crime of bigamy or polyg-amy." The Court's intent was clear—"to withdraw all political influence from those who are practically hostile to" the goals of certain criminal laws. *Murphy*, 114 U.S. at 45; *Davis*, 133 U.S., at 334.

To the extent *Murphy* and *Davis* approve the doctrine that citizens can be barred from the ballot box because they would vote to change the existing criminal law, those decisions are surely of minimal continuing precedential value. We have since explicitly held that such "differences of opinion cannot justify for excluding [any] group from . . . 'the franchise,'" *Cipriano* v. *City of Houma*, 395 U.S. 701, 705–706 (1969). * * *

Although, in the last century, this Court may have justified the exclusion of vot-ers from the electoral process for fear that they would vote to change laws con-sidered important by a temporal majority, I have little doubt that we would not countenance such a purpose today. The process of democracy is one of change. Our laws are not frozen into immutable form, they are constantly in the process of revi-sion in response to the needs of a changing society. The public interest, as conceived by a majority of the voting public, is constantly undergoing reexamination. This Court's holding in *Davis* and *Murphy*, that a State may disenfranchise a class of voters to "withdraw all political influence from those who are practically hostile" to the existing order, strikes at the very heart of the democratic process. A tem-poral majority could use such a power to preserve inviolate its view of the social order simply by disenfranchising those with different views. Voters who opposed the repeal of prohibition could have disenfranchised those who advocated repeal "to prevent persons from being enabled by their votes to defeat the criminal laws of the country." Today, presumably those who support the legalization of marihuana could be barred from the ballot box for much the same reason. The ballot is the democratic system's coin of the realm. To condition its exercise on support of the established order is to debase that currency beyond recognition. Rather than resur-rect *Davis* and *Murphy*, I would expressly disavow any continued adherence to the dangerous notions therein expressed. * * *

I think it clear that measured against the standards of this Court's modern equal protection jurisprudence, the blanket disenfranchisement of ex-felons cannot stand.

I respectfully dissent.

Mr. Justice Douglas * * * dissents from a reversal of the judgment below as he cannot say that it does not rest on an independent state ground.

Notes and Questions

1. According to Professor Gabriel Chin, the Fifteenth Amendment's self-enforcing prohibition on racial discrimination in voting was inconsistent with (and pro-voked by the failure of) the more limited remedy specified in § 2 of the Fourteenth Amendment. As a result, the Fifteenth Amendment should be understood to have

repealed § 2 of the Fourteenth Amendment, on which the Court relied in *Ramirez*. *See* Gabriel J. Chin, *Reconstruction, Felon Disenfranchisement, and the Right to Vote: Did the Fifteenth Amendment Repeal Section 2 of the Fourteenth Amendment?*, 92 GEO. L.J. 259 (2004). If the Supreme Court reconsiders the constitutionality of felon disenfranchisement without relying on § 2, as Chin proposes, might felon disenfranchisement still be constitutional?

2. In the years since *Ramirez*, several states have liberalized their laws and permitted (ex-)felons to vote. Maine and Vermont even permit felons to vote during their periods of incarceration. In 2007, Florida and Maryland changed their laws to permit most released felons to regain their voting rights. In 2014, Virginia made two changes that make it easier for felons to become re-eligible to vote. Violent felons in that state used to have to wait five years before they could petition to be eligible to vote, but that period has been reduced to three years. And drug offenses have been reclassified as non-violent, so Virginia's drug felons can now petition for a restoration of their voting rights as soon as they complete their prison time and pay court costs. *See* Larry O'Dell, *Va. Gov. Changes Policy on Felons' Voting Rights*, WASH. TIMES (Apr. 18, 2014), *at* http://www.washingtontimes.com/news/2014/apr/18/mcauliffe-alters-felons-voting-rights-procedures/.

Since 2017, Wyoming has re-enfranchised first-time nonviolent felons upon their release from prison. In New York, a 2018 executive order established a new policy to make parolees eligible for re-enfranchisement, following a review of their records by the governor's office. In 2019, Colorado automatically re-enfranchised parolees. A 2019 Nevada law automatically re-enfranchised all offenders once released from prison. Also in 2019, a Louisiana law took effect that automatically restored voting rights to felons five years after their release from prison. (Delaware removed a similar five-year waiting period for most offenders in 2013.) And in 2020, a New Jersey law took effect that re-enfranchised offenders on probation or parole.

Some states, however, are moving in the opposite direction and making it more difficult for felons to vote. Massachusetts and Utah disenfranchised currently incarcerated felons in 2000 and 1998. South Dakota has joined this counter-trend, extending its voting ban, which had prohibited imprisoned felons and parolees from voting, to probationers as well. Further, in 2011, both Florida (which, as noted above, had loosened its laws in 2007) and Iowa tightened their laws concerning the restoration of felons' voting rights. Whereas each had previously automatically restored the franchise to felons who had fulfilled all the requirements of their sentences, the 2011 amendments required felons to petition individually for the reestablishment of their voting rights. As discussed below in Note 11, Florida has changed its laws yet again. In 2018, Florida's voters amended the state constitution to restore voting rights to most felons automatically upon completion of all the "terms of sentence."

Eleven states (Alabama, Arizona, Delaware, Florida, Iowa, Maryland, Mississippi, Missouri, Kentucky, Tennessee, and Wyoming) impose some form of voting restriction on at least some felons even after they are no longer in prison, on parole, or on probation, though these states vary in the particulars of their schemes. One important difference is between the states that automatically restore felons' rights after some period and those that require felons to petition for the restoration of rights. There are other important differences as well. Arizona, for example, permanently disenfranchises persons who have committed two felonies. Iowa disenfranchises people who have committed "infamous" crimes, but it is not clear which crimes qualify. *See Chiodo v. Section 43.24 Panel*, 846 N.W.2d 845 (Iowa 2014). As an indication of how confusing the law can be in this area, consider the breakdown of the Iowa Supreme Court justices in *Chiodo*: The plurality opinion for three of the seven justices would have held that the term "infamous" crimes includes no misdemeanors (such as a second offense for operating a vehicle while impaired, the aggravated misdemeanor that was at issue in that case) and it includes only those felonies that suggest that the felons would "tend to undermine the process of democratic governance through elections." Two other justices believed that "infamous" crimes should mean all felonies and no misdemeanors. Another justice believed that the term included all felonies and some misdemeanors as well. And the seventh justice was recused.

Between those states permanently disenfranchising all felons and those for which criminal conviction does not affect voting rights at all, are the states that have adopted some temporary exclusion of felons. Such measures include suspension of voting rights while the offender is in prison, while the offender is in prison or on parole, and while the offender is in prison, on parole, or on probation. Nebraska restores voting rights two years after felons' release from prison, parole, or probation. California bans felons from voting while imprisoned in the state prison or on parole, but permits people to vote while serving a sentence in a county jail. For summaries of states' laws, see Sentencing Project, *Felony Disenfranchisement,* at http://www.sentencingproject.org/issues/felony-disenfranchisement; Brennan Center for Justice, *Disenfranchisement Laws,* at https://www.brennancenter.org/issues/ensure-every-american-can-vote/voting-rights-restoration/disenfranchisement-laws.

In addition to laws that have actually been enacted, there is a bewildering variety of laws that are being considered by lawmakers in the several states. Consider this summary from 2012:

> South Dakota lawmakers have sent the governor a bill to block voting by felons on probation or parole. However, legislators in New Jersey and New York are considering bills that would do the opposite by letting parolees and probationers vote. Legislation pending in Tennessee would stop requiring that convicts pay their restitution, court costs and child support before they can vote again. But Washington state legislators are considering a bill that would add the same repayment obligations that Tennessee may end. Some felons could vote absentee from their prison cells under bills introduced in Hawaii and Tennessee. A South Carolina bill would block registered

sex offenders from voting at all. Lawmakers in New Jersey, New York and Pennsylvania could require state officials to help offenders register to vote as they complete their incarceration, probation or parole.

Don Thompson, *Group Sues California, Wants Criminals to Be Able to Vote*, THE REPORTER (Vacaville, Cal.) (Mar. 8, 2012), *at* http://www.sentencingproject.org /template/page.cfm?id=133.

Felon-disenfranchisement laws continue to be the subject of much reform. Delaware, which had amended its Constitution in 2013 to eliminate the five-year waiting period for the restoration of voting rights, further liberalized its laws in 2016. Under the previous law, felons had to serve their prison sentences and satisfy all financial obligations before being eligible to have their voting rights restored. Now, although they must still complete their prison sentences, a failure to satisfy the financial obligations will not render them ineligible to vote. *See Governor Signs Legislation Expanding Access to the Ballot Box, Builds on Record of Criminal Justice Reform*, NEWS.DELAWARE.GOV (July 13, 2016), *at* http://news.delaware.gov/2016 /07/13/governor-signs-legislation-expanding-access-to-the-ballot-box-builds-on -record-of-criminal-justice-reform/.

Virginia's Democratic governor attempted to use his clemency power to restore the voting rights of 200,000 felons who were no longer in prison, on parole, or on probation (although the governor's executive order also included, apparently by mistake, several felons who were still in prison and 132 sex offenders under supervision). By a 4-3 vote, the Virginia Supreme Court invalidated the governor's order, holding that the governor could not grant voting rights to 200,000 felons in a single order. *Howell v. McAuliffe*, 788 S.E.2d 706 (Va. 2016). In response, the governor vowed to sign individual clemency orders for each of the felons, and on August 13, 2016, the governor announced that he had restored the voting rights of 13,000 felons "after reviewing their cases individually." Margaret Chadbourn, *Va. Gov. Terry McAuliffe Restores Voting Rights of Felons*, ABC NEWS (Aug. 22, 2016), *at* http:// abcnews.go.com/Politics/va-gov-terry-mcauliffe-restores-voting-rights-felons/story ?id=41572956.

Of course, each side accused the other of partisanship. The governor characterized opposition to his executive order as "a disgrace" and "overtly political," while Republicans accused the governor of attempting to increase the number of Democratic voters in an attempt to improve Hillary Clinton's chances of winning the state's presidential electors in the 2016 election. *See* Fenit Nirappil & Jenna Portnoy, *Va. High Court Invalidates McAuliffe's Order Restoring Felon Voting Rights*, WASH. POST (July 22, 2016), *available at* https://www.washingtonpost.com/local/virginia -politics/virginia-court-invalidates-gov-terry-mcauliffes-order-restoring-felon -voting-rights/2016/07/22/3e1d45f6-5058-11e6-a7d8-13d06b37f256_story.html. In 2019, Kentucky's governor similarly restored the voting rights of 140,000 non-violent felons.

3. If Florida had permitted felons to vote in 2000, the result of the presidential election likely would have been different. Because felons are more likely than the general population to be poor, to be of a minority race, and to have relatively low levels of education—all of which are indications of Democratic sympathies—most analysts believe they would have preferred the Democrat Gore to the Republican Bush, and the differential would have been sufficient to overcome Bush's minuscule margin of victory.[h] If this analysis is accurate, does it indicate that the election of President Bush was illegitimate because it was predicated on the exclusion of potential voters, or that a Gore presidency predicated on the votes of convicted felons would have been the illegitimate outcome? In this light, consider that then-Democratic presidential candidate Barack Obama's campaign received briefings and advice concerning the registration of felons whose voting rights had recently been restored. The Obama campaign, however, was "reluctant to acknowledge any concerted effort" because of the potential negative reaction at being identified as the candidate of choice for felons. Solomon Moore, *States Restore Voting Rights for Ex-Convicts, but Issue Remains Politically Sensitive*, N.Y. Times Sept. 14, 2008, at A22. *See also* Traci Burch, *Did Disenfranchisement Laws Help Elect President Bush?: New Evidence on the Turnout Rates and Candidate Preferences of Florida's Ex-Felons*, 34 Political Behavior 1 (2012); Traci Burch, *Turnout and Party Registration Among Criminal Offenders in the 2008 General Election*, 45 Law and Society Rev. 699 (2011); Alan Gerber et al., *Can Incarcerated Felons Be (Re)integrated into the Political System? Results from a Field Experiment* (working paper 2013), available at http://onlinelibrary.wiley.com/doi/10.1111/ajps.12166/abstract; Vesla Weaver & Amy E. Lerman, *Political Consequences of the Carceral State*, 104 Am. Pol. Sci. Rev. 817 (2010).

After assuming office, the Obama administration continued its support for restoring felons' voting rights. In 2014, Attorney General Holder "call[ed] upon state leaders and other elected officials across the country to pass clear and consistent reforms to restore the voting rights of all who have served their terms in prison or jail, completed their parole or probation, and paid their fines." Nicole Flatow, *U.S. Attorney General: Time to Restore Voting Rights of Every Person Who Has Completed Their [sic] Criminal Sentence*, Think Progress (Feb. 11, 2014) *at* http://thinkprogress.org/justice/2014/02/11/3277531/attorney-general-time-restore -voting-rights-person-completed-criminal-sentence/.

4. Justice Marshall argued that the Constitution did not permit states to limit felons' voting rights by pointing to the bad effects that would flow from having

---

h. *See* Jeff Manza & Christopher Uggen, Locked Out: Felon Disenfranchisement and American Democracy 191–93 (2006) (arguing that the 2000 election would have turned out differently had Florida not disenfranchised felons who completed their sentences, and further citing the 1960 and 1976 elections as ones that would have resulted in victories for the Republican candidates if those years had seen felon-disenfranchisement rates comparable to those in effect today). *But see id.* at 144–51 (arguing that disenfranchised felons' policy preferences are similar to those of people who are permitted to vote).

politicians appeal to the felon constituency. For a contrary view, consider *Green v. Board of Elections*, 380 F.2d 445, 451–52 (2d Cir. 1967) (Friendly, J.):

> The early exclusion of felons from the franchise by many states could well have rested on Locke's concept, so influential at the time, that by entering into society every man "authorizes the society, or which is all one, the legislature thereof, to make laws for him as the public good of the society shall require, to the execution whereof his own assistance (as to his own decrees) is due." [John Locke, *An Essay Concerning the True Original, Extent and End of Civil Government* 89 (1689).] A man who breaks the laws he has authorized his agent to make for his own governance could fairly have been thought to have abandoned the right to participate in further administering the compact. On a less theoretical plane, it can scarcely be deemed unreasonable for a state to decide that perpetrators of serious crimes shall not take part in electing the legislators who make the laws, the executives who enforce these, the prosecutors who must try them for further violations, or the judges who are to consider their cases. This is especially so when account is taken of the heavy incidence of recidivism and the prevalence of organized crime. A contention that the equal protection clause requires New York to allow convicted mafiosi to vote for district attorneys or judges would not only be without merit but as obviously so as anything can be.

Is there a difference between (a) allowing Mafiosi to vote for district attorneys, (b) allowing welfare recipients to vote for officials who will determine how much public assistance will be distributed, and (c) allowing billionaires to vote for officials who will determine the amount of the capital-gains tax?

   5. The original justification for felon disenfranchisement—which dates from Ancient Greece and which came to the United States through Britain during the colonial period, *see* Alec C. Ewald, *"Civil Death": The Ideological Paradox of Criminal Disenfranchisement Law in the United States*, 2002 Wis. L. Rev. 1045, 1059–61 (2002)—was not a fear that felons would vote for politicians who were soft on crime, but rather was the attitude that an infamous criminal was an outsider to the community, ineligible for all of the civil benefits that accompanied membership, including legal protection of his property.[i] Somewhat similarly, today we might defend felon disenfranchisement by arguing that people who have shown an unwillingness to abide by society's most important commands should not have a role in making the rules others are bound to follow. *See* Roger Clegg et al., *The Case Against*

---

   i. *See* Howard Itzkowitz & Lauren Oldak, *Restoring the Ex-Offender's Right to Vote: Background and Developments*, 11 Am. Crim. L. Rev. 695 (1973). *See also* Gabriel J. Chin, *Felon Disenfranchisement and Democracy in the Late Jim Crow Era*, 5 Ohio St. J. Crim. L. 329, 337 (2007) (book review) ("When men wore powdered wigs and knee breeches, felon disenfranchisement was entirely consistent with an elite franchise, restricted as well by race, sex and wealth. Now, however, voting is thought of as a 'right' enjoyed by all adults.").

Felon Voting, 2 U. St. Thomas J.L. & Pub. Pol'y 1 (2008). Is there anything unconstitutional about excluding felons from the political community and labeling them as outsiders?

6. Is it better for disenfranchisement of felons to take effect automatically upon conviction, or would it be better to incorporate disenfranchisement into the sentencing process, leaving it to the sentencing judge to determine whether disenfranchisement is appropriate, considering "the type of crime committed, the impact of that crime on the victim, and the individual's prior criminal record"? Susan E. Marquardt, Comment, *Deprivation of a Felon's Right to Vote: Constitutional Concerns, Policy Issues and Suggested Reform for Felony Disenfranchisement Law*, 82 U. Det. Mercy L. Rev. 279, 297 (2005). Disenfranchisement might be particularly appropriate for election-related crimes or other crimes indicating a lack of trustworthiness. *See id.* at 297–98. Would it be constitutional for an executive-branch agency to decide whether to restore voting rights? *See Hand v. Scott*, 285 F. Supp. 3d 1289 (N.D. Fla.) (striking down Florida's procedure for restoring felons' voting rights, which provided "unfettered discretion" to the state's Executive Clemency Board), *stay granted*, 888 F.3d 1206 (11th Cir. 2018) (concluding that the government was likely to succeed on the merits), *vacated as moot sub nom. Hand v. DeSantis*, 946 F.3d 1272 (11th Cir. 2020).

7. Are there any limits on the crimes for which a state may disenfranchise convicts? May a state strip jaywalkers of their voting rights? Drunk drivers? *See* footnote 24 of Justice Marshall's *Ramirez* dissent.

8. Section 2 of the Voting Rights Act, 52 U.S.C. § 10301, as amended in 1982, 96 Stat. 134, prohibits voting qualifications that "result[] in" certain citizens "hav[ing] less opportunity than other members of the electorate to participate in the political process and to elect representatives of their choice." Section 2 comprises an important part of election law and will be covered extensively in Chapter 4. For present purposes, consider whether § 2 outlaws felon-disenfranchisement laws that disenfranchise a disproportionate number of minorities. If § 2 does ban felon-disenfranchisement, does § 2 exceed Congress's power under the Fourteenth and Fifteenth Amendments? The First, Second, Sixth, and Eleventh Circuits have concluded that § 2 should be read not to outlaw felon-disenfranchisement, because a contrary holding would raise serious constitutional questions. *See Simmons v. Galvin*, 575 F.3d 24 (1st Cir. 2009); *Hayden v. Pataki*, 449 F.3d 305 (2d Cir. 2006) (*en banc*); *Johnson v. Governor*, 405 F.3d 1214 (11th Cir. 2005) (*en banc*); *Wesley v. Collins*, 791 F.2d 1255 (6th Cir. 1986). *See also Baker v. Pataki*, 85 F.3d 919 (2d Cir. 1996) (*en banc*) (dividing 5-5 on the question whether the VRA reaches felon-disenfranchisement). The Ninth Circuit initially concluded that Washington State's felon-disenfranchisement law violated VRA § 2, *Farrakhan v. Gregoire*, 590 F.3d 989, *vacated*, 603 F.3d 1072 (9th Cir. 2010). After taking the case *en banc*, however, the court held that § 2 would not be violated absent a showing of intentional discrimination. *Farrakhan v. Gregoire*, 623 F.3d 990, 993–94 (9th Cir. 2010) (*en banc*).

9. Some members of Congress have proposed legislation that would require states to re-enfranchise convicted felons. Most proposals have received support overwhelmingly from Democrats, but in 2014 Republican Rand Paul introduced a bill that would require states to restore the voting rights of "non-violent" felons (a category that would be clarified by the attorney general) one year after their release from prison or probation. Other proposals favored by supporters of expanded voting rights for criminals do not carve out violent felons and do not have the one-year delay. *See* Burgess Everett, *Rand Paul Seeks to Expand Voting Rights to Some Ex-Cons*, POLITICO (June 22, 2014), *at* http://www.politico.com/story/2014/06/rand-paul-voting-rights-ex-felons-108156.html. Would such measures be constitutional ways of enforcing the Fourteenth Amendment?

10. *Problem*. New Vermont not only prohibits incarcerated felons from voting, but excludes from the franchise anyone who is confined, whether awaiting trial or as the result of a misdemeanor or felony conviction. Is the exclusion unconstitutional as to either pretrial detainees or convicted misdemeanants? *Cf. O'Brien v. Skinner*, 414 U.S. 524 (1974) (holding unconstitutional under the Equal Protection Clause a state law permitting pre-trial detainees to vote by absentee ballot if confined outside their home counties, but not permitting pre-trial detainees to vote if confined within their home counties).

Problem. Ohio permits all registered voters to vote by absentee ballot as long as they request an absentee ballot by noon, three days before election day. That deadline does not apply, however, for one class of voters: those who are hospitalized (or whose minor children are hospitalized) because of an unforeseeable accident or medical emergency that occurs after the deadline has passed. Those voters have until 3:00 p.m. on election day to request an absentee ballot. Tommy is a registered voter who plans to vote in-person on election day. At 7:00 p.m. on the Saturday before election day (after the noon deadline), Tommy is arrested. He is subsequently arraigned and jailed, and it is clear that he will not be released until after election day. He asks jail officials to permit him to vote, but they refuse. Does the refusal to permit Tommy to vote violate his constitutional right to vote? Does it violate equal protection to permit unexpectedly hospitalized voters to request a ballot until 3:00 p.m. on election day while holding unexpectedly jailed voters to the earlier deadline? *See Mays v. LaRose*, 951 F.3d 775 (6th Cir. 2020).

11. *Problem*. West Dakota allows felons to vote upon completion of all requirements of their sentences, including the payment of court costs, fees, and victim restitution. Is such a law constitutional under *Ramirez*, or does it violate the Equal Protection Clause under *Harper* to deny the right to vote to a felon who would be permitted to vote except for his inability (or unwillingness) to satisfy financial obligations? *See Madison v. State*, 163 P.3d 757 (Wash. 2007); *Johnson v. Bredesen*, 624 F.3d 742 (6th Cir. 2010); *Harvey v. Brewer*, 605 F.3d 1067 (9th Cir. 2010).

Florida has been involved in a similar controversy. In November 2018, voters passed Amendment 4, which provided that felons would have their voting rights "restored upon completion of all terms of sentence including parole or probation."

The following summer, the state's Republican-controlled legislature passed, and the Republican governor signed, a law providing that the "terms of sentence" include fines and court costs, so that a felon who had been released from prison but who was unable or unwilling to pay fines or court costs would not have his voting rights restored. The law was immediately challenged and preliminarily enjoined, *Jones v. DeSantis*, 410 F. Supp. 3d 1284 (N.D. Fla. 2019), *aff'd*, 950 F.3d 795 (11th Cir. 2020). The district court later issued a permanent injunction, *Jones v. DeSantis*, __ F. Supp. 3d __, 2020 WL 2618062 (N.D. Fla. 2020), but the Eleventh Circuit granted initial hearing *en banc* and stayed the judgment pending appeal. *McCoy v. Governor of Florida*, 2020 WL 4012843 (11th Cir. 2020) (*en banc*). Over the dissent of Justice Sotomayor, joined by Justices Ginsburg and Kagan, the Supreme Court declined to vacate the stay. *Raysor v. DeSantis*, 591 U.S. __, 140 S. Ct. __, 2020 WL 4006868 (2020). The *en banc* Eleventh Circuit then, in a 6-4 decision, reversed the district court and vacated the injunction. *Jones v. Governor of Florida*, __ F.3d __, 2020 WL 5493770 (11th Cir. 2020) (*en banc*).

12. The Court's opinions in *Ramirez*, *Lassiter*, and *Harper* (as well as the *Harper* dissents) stressed that the regulations at issue in those cases were not put in place for the *purpose* of discriminating against disfavored racial groups, even though the regulations may have had the *effect* of disenfranchising proportionately more racial minorities than whites. But consider the situation where a plaintiff alleges that a restriction on voting *was* enacted for a discriminatory purpose. How is a court supposed to determine whether in fact the discriminatory purpose was present? And why should purpose matter at all?

In *Fletcher v. Peck*, 10 U.S. (6 Cranch) 87, 130 (1810), the Supreme Court confronted the question whether Georgia could rescind a land deal that had been entered into because the legislature had been bribed. Writing for the Court, Chief Justice Marshall discussed the problems with considering legislative purpose, and "doubted how far the validity of a law depends upon the motives of its framers":

> If the principle be conceded, that an act of the supreme sovereign power may be declared null by a court, in consequence of the means which procured it, still would there be much difficulty in saying to what extent those means must be applied to produce this effect. Must the vitiating cause operate on a majority, or on what number of its members? Would the act be null, whatever might be the wish of the nation, or would its obligation or nullity depend upon the public sentiment?

Similarly, in *Palmer v. Thompson*, 403 U.S. 217, 225 (1971), the Court refused to consider evidence of legislative purpose when the Jackson, Mississippi, city council closed all the public swimming pools after being faced with a judgment declaring segregation of the pools unconstitutional. As the Court stated,

> It is difficult or impossible for any court to determine the "sole" or "dominant" motivation behind the choices of a group of legislators. Furthermore, * * * [i]f the law is struck down [because of the bad motives of its

supporters], * * * it would presumably be valid as soon as the legislature or relevant governing body repassed it for different reasons.

Even if it is agreed that legislative purpose is relevant, determining the legislature's purpose is difficult, and therefore conclusions about legislative purpose can be the subject of dispute. To nobody's surprise, legislators often say things that aren't exactly true. Relying on legislators' explanations for their votes, therefore, might allow legislators to conceal improper, or unconstitutional, motives. *See generally* McNollgast, *Positive Canons: The Role of Legislative Bargains in Statutory Interpretation*, 80 GEO. L.J. 705 (1992).

Further, legislators, like everyone else, take actions for several different reasons. If a legislator votes in favor of a bill partly out of racial prejudice, partly because doing so will get him votes, partly because doing so will get him more campaign contributions, and partly because he thinks the bill actually represents good policy, is his vote the product of a "discriminatory purpose"? Are courts supposed to assess whether he would have voted for the bill if he were not prejudiced? How might a court undertake such an inquiry?

The inquiry is still more complicated, as *Fletcher* recognized, when one attempts to assess the purposes of multiple legislators. Whose purpose matters if 40% of the legislature voted in favor of a statute for legitimate reasons, 15% voted in favor of the statute for unconstitutional reasons, and 45% voted against the statute? Should the views of legislative sponsors or committee chairs be given extra weight? *See* WILLIAM N. ESKRIDGE, JR., ET AL., LEGISLATION AND STATUTORY INTERPRETATION 221–30 (2d ed. 2006); CALEB NELSON, STATUTORY INTERPRETATION 341–62 (2011); Frank H. Easterbrook, *Statutes' Domains*, 50 U. CHI. L. REV. 533 (1983); McNollgast, *supra*; Kenneth A. Shepsle, *Congress Is a "They," Not an "It"*, 12 INT'L REV. L. & ECON. 239 (1992). *Cf. Edwards v. Aguillard*, 482 U.S. 578, 636–38 (1987) (Scalia, J., dissenting) (discussing the same difficulty in determining under the Establishment Clause whether a law was passed because of a secular legislative purpose).

Despite the difficulty of articulating both why and how a court would look to legislative purpose in assessing constitutionality, it is settled that legislative purpose *does* matter in some instances. When a facially neutral statute produces a discriminatory effect against a "suspect class," courts will apply strict scrutiny to that statute if, but only if, the statute was enacted because of a discriminatory purpose. *See Hunter v. Underwood*, 471 U.S. 222 (1985), below; *see also Rogers v. Lodge*, 458 U.S. 613 (1982) (declaring an at-large voting system unconstitutional because it had been maintained for a discriminatory purpose). If the statute was enacted for a different, legitimate purpose, rational-basis scrutiny applies. *See Village of Arlington Heights v. Metropolitan Housing Development Corp.*, 429 U.S. 252 (1977); *Washington v. Davis*, 426 U.S. 229 (1976). *See also Yick Wo v. Hopkins*, 118 U.S. 356 (1886). The Court, in *Arlington Heights*, specified that once the legislature's improper purpose is proven, the defendant bears "the burden of establishing that the same decision would have resulted even had the impermissible purpose not been considered." If the defendant meets that standard, then "the injury complained of [cannot be attributed] to improper consideration of a discriminatory purpose." 429 U.S. at 270.

Lastly, the Court has confronted the ambiguity of the term "purpose" in the context of legislative indifference to the disparate effects caused by statutes. Statutes may be enacted or maintained not out of hostility toward a disaffected group, but simply because the decision-maker does not care that the group is being harmed. Such a case was presented in *Personnel Administrator v. Feeney,* 442 U.S. 256 (1979), which involved a challenge to a veterans' preference for civil-service positions. The challengers argued that the preference advanced the job prospects of men much more than it advanced the prospects of women because the class of veterans was overwhelmingly male. The Court held, however, that rational-basis scrutiny was appropriate unless the challenged action was taken "at least in part 'because of,' not merely 'in spite of,' its adverse effects upon an identifiable group." *Id.* at 279. As a result, it did not matter whether the legislature would have reacted differently if men had been disadvantaged by the preference to the extent that women were.

Hunter v. Underwood

Supreme Court of the United States
471 U.S. 222, 105 S. Ct. 1916, 85 L. Ed. 2d 222 (1985)

Justice Rehnquist delivered the opinion of the Court [in which Chief Justice Burger, Justice Brennan, Justice White, Justice Marshall, Justice Blackmun, Justice Stevens, and Justice O'Connor join].

We are required in this case to decide the constitutionality of Art. VIII, § 182, of the Alabama Constitution of 1901, which provides for the disenfranchisement of persons convicted of, among other offenses, "any crime . . . involving moral turpitude." Appellees Carmen Edwards, a black, and Victor Underwood, a white, have been blocked from the voter rolls pursuant to § 182 by the Boards of Registrars for Montgomery and Jefferson Counties, respectively, because they each have been convicted of presenting a worthless check. * * *

The predecessor to § 182 was Art. VIII, § 3, of the Alabama Constitution of 1875, which denied persons "convicted of treason, embezzlement of public funds, malfeasance in office, larceny, bribery, or other crime punishable by imprisonment in the penitentiary" the right to register, vote or hold public office. These offenses were largely, if not entirely, felonies. The drafters of § 182, which was adopted by the 1901 convention, expanded the list of enumerated crimes substantially to include the following:

> "treason, murder, arson, embezzlement, malfeasance in office, larceny, receiving stolen property, obtaining property or money under false pretenses, perjury, subornation of perjury, robbery, assault with intent to rob, burglary, forgery, bribery, assault and battery on the wife, bigamy, living in adultery, sodomy, incest, rape, miscegenation, [and] crime against nature."

The drafters retained the general felony provision—"any crime punishable by imprisonment in the penitentiary"—but also added a new catchall provision covering "any . . . crime involving moral turpitude." This latter phrase is not defined, but it was subsequently interpreted by the Alabama Supreme Court to mean an act that is "immoral in itself, regardless of the fact whether it is punishable by law * * *."

The enumerated crimes contain within them many misdemeanors. If a specific crime does not fall within one of the enumerated offenses, the Alabama Boards of Registrars consult Alabama case law or, in absence of a court precedent, opinions of the Alabama Attorney General to determine whether it is covered by § 182. Various minor nonfelony offenses such as presenting a worthless check and petty larceny fall within the sweep of § 182, while more serious nonfelony offenses such as second-degree manslaughter, assault on a police officer, mailing pornography, and aiding the escape of a misdemeanant do not because they are neither enumerated in § 182 nor considered crimes involving moral turpitude. It is alleged, and the Court of Appeals found, that the crimes selected for inclusion in § 182 were believed by the delegates to be more frequently committed by blacks.

Section 182 on its face is racially neutral, applying equally to anyone convicted of one of the enumerated crimes or a crime falling within one of the catchall provisions. Appellee Edwards nonetheless claims that the provision has had a racially discriminatory impact. [T]he Court of Appeals implicitly found the evidence of discriminatory impact indisputable:

> "The registrars' expert estimated that by January 1903 section 182 had disfranchised approximately ten times as many blacks as whites. This disparate effect persists today. In Jefferson and Montgomery Counties blacks are by even the most modest estimates at least 1.7 times as likely as whites to suffer disfranchisement under section 182 for the commission of nonprison offenses."

So far as we can tell the impact of the provision has not been contested, and we can find no evidence in the record below or in the briefs and oral argument in this Court that would undermine this finding by the Court of Appeals.

Presented with a neutral state law that produces disproportionate effects along racial lines, the Court of Appeals was correct in applying the approach of *Arlington Heights* [v. *Metropolitan Housing Development Corp.*, 429 U.S. 252, 264–65 (1977)] to determine whether the law violates the Equal Protection Clause of the Fourteenth Amendment:

> "[O]fficial action will not be held unconstitutional solely because it results in a racially disproportionate impact. . . . Proof of racially discriminatory intent or purpose is required to show a violation of the Equal Protection Clause."

See Washington v. *Davis*, 426 U.S. 229, 239 (1976). Once racial discrimination is shown to have been a "substantial" or "motivating" factor behind enactment of the law, the burden shifts to the law's defenders to demonstrate that the law would have been enacted without this factor.

Proving the motivation behind official action is often a problematic undertaking. * * * With respect to Congress, the Court said in *United States* v. *O'Brien*, 391 U.S. 367, 383–384 (1968):

> "Inquiries into congressional motives or purposes are a hazardous matter. When the issue is simply the interpretation of legislation, the Court will look to statements by legislators for guidance as to the purpose of the legislature, because the benefit to sound decision-making in this circumstance is thought sufficient to risk the possibility of misreading Congress' purpose. It is entirely a different matter when we are asked to void a statute that is, under well-settled criteria, constitutional on its face, on the basis of what fewer than a handful of Congressmen said about it. What motivates one legislator to make a speech about a statute is not necessarily what motivates scores of others to enact it, and the stakes are sufficiently high for us to eschew guesswork."

But the sort of difficulties of which the Court spoke in *O'Brien* do not obtain in this case. Although understandably no "eyewitnesses" to the 1901 proceedings testified, testimony and opinions of historians were offered and received without objection. These showed that the Alabama Constitutional Convention of 1901 was part of a movement that swept the post-Reconstruction South to disenfranchise blacks. The delegates to the all-white convention were not secretive about their purpose. John B. Knox, president of the convention, stated in his opening address: "And what is it that we want to do? Why it is within the limits imposed by the Federal Constitution, to establish white supremacy in this State."

Indeed, neither the District Court nor appellants seriously dispute the claim that this zeal for white supremacy ran rampant at the convention.

* * * Having reviewed this evidence, we are persuaded that * * * § 182 was enacted with the intent of disenfranchising blacks. * * * At oral argument in this Court appellants' counsel essentially conceded this point, stating: "I would be very blind and naive [to] try to come up and stand before this Court and say that race was not a factor in the enactment of Section 182; that race did not play a part in the decisions of those people who were at the constitutional convention of 1901 and I won't do that."

In their brief to this Court, appellants maintain on the basis of their expert's testimony that the real purpose behind § 182 was to disenfranchise poor whites as well as blacks. * * * Even were we to accept this explanation as correct, it hardly saves § 182 from invalidity. The explanation concedes both that discrimination against blacks, as well as against poor whites, was a motivating factor for the provision and that § 182 certainly would not have been adopted by the convention or ratified by the electorate in the absence of the racially discriminatory motivation.

[A]ppellants make the further argument that the existence of a permissible motive for § 182, namely, the disenfranchisement of poor whites, trumps any proof of a parallel impermissible motive. Whether or not intentional disenfranchisement of poor whites would qualify as a "permissible motive," * * * an additional purpose to discriminate against poor whites would not render nugatory the purpose to discriminate against all blacks, and it is beyond peradventure that the latter was a "but-for" motivation for the enactment of § 182. * * *

At oral argument in this Court, the appellants' counsel suggested that, regardless of the original purpose of § 182, events occurring in the succeeding 80 years had legitimated the provision. Some of the more blatantly discriminatory selections, such as assault and battery on the wife and miscegenation, have been struck down by the courts, and appellants contend that the remaining crimes — felonies and moral turpitude misdemeanors — are acceptable bases for denying the franchise. Without deciding whether § 182 would be valid if enacted today without any impermissible motivation, we simply observe that its original enactment was motivated by a desire to discriminate against blacks on account of race and the section continues to this day to have that effect. As such, it violates equal protection under *Arlington Heights.*

* * * The single remaining question is whether § 182 is excepted from the operation of the Equal Protection Clause of § 1 of the Fourteenth Amendment by the "other crime" provision of § 2 of that Amendment. Without again considering the implicit authorization of § 2 to deny the vote to citizens "for participation in rebellion, or other crime," *see Richardson* v. *Ramirez,* 418 U.S. 24 (1974) [p. 26], we are confident that § 2 was not designed to permit the purposeful racial discrimination attending the enactment and operation of § 182 which otherwise violates § 1 of the Fourteenth Amendment. Nothing in our opinion in *Richardson* v. *Ramirez* suggests the contrary.

The judgment of the Court of Appeals is

Affirmed.

JUSTICE POWELL took no part in the consideration or decision of this case.

Notes and Questions

1. Despite the Court's reliance on legislative history to understand the purpose behind the voting exclusion, the expert testimony in *Underwood* disclosed that the legislative history may not have completely and accurately reflected the motivations of the individuals who voted for the provision:

> A. * * * Repeatedly through the debates, the delegates say that they are interested in disfranchising blacks and not interested in disfranchising whites. And in fact, they go out of their way to make that point. . . . But the point that I am trying to make is that this is really speaking to the galleries, that it is attempting to say to the white electorate that must ratify this constitution

what it is necessary for that white electorate to be convinced of in order to get them to vote for it, and not merely echoing what a great many delegates say. . . . [I]n general, the delegates aggressively say that they are not interested in disfranchising any whites. I think falsely, but that's what they say.

Q. So they were simply trying to overplay the extent to which they wanted to disenfranchise blacks, but that they did desire to disenfranchise practically all of the blacks?

A. Oh, absolutely, certainly.

Does this exchange indicate that legislative history is not to be trusted as a way of understanding legislative purpose, or, instead, that legislative history can be a powerful tool for understanding legislative purpose if placed in proper context?

2. The opinion of the Court concluded "that § 182 certainly would not have been adopted by the convention *or ratified by the electorate* in the absence of the racially discriminatory motivation." 471 U.S. at 231 (emphasis added). Does the Court mean to imply that *voters*, acting out of racial prejudice, could render unconstitutional a facially neutral law? What if the provision were enacted as part of an initiative? Conversely, could a pure motive on the part of "the electorate" save a referendum that was presented to the voters by a biased legislature?

3. If, one year after *Underwood* was decided, Alabama were to enact a law identical to the provision struck down in that case, would it violate the Equal Protection Clause? Would such a law be distinguishable from the one in *Richardson v. Ramirez*? *See Johnson v. Governor*, 405 F.3d 1214, 1223–24 (11th Cir. 2005) (holding that the 1968 re-enactment of Florida's 1868 disenfranchisement law "eliminated any taint from the allegedly discriminatory 1868 provision, particularly in light of the passage of time and the fact that, at the time of the 1968 enactment, no one had ever alleged that the 1868 provision was motivated by racial animus"); *Cotton v. Fordice*, 157 F.3d 388 (5th Cir. 1988) (holding that Mississippi's 1950 and 1968 revisions of a discriminatory 1890 disenfranchisement law, removing burglary and adding murder and rape as disenfranchising crimes, rendered the law constitutional). *Cf. McCreary County v. ACLU*, 545 U.S. 844, 870–74 (2005) (holding in an Establishment Clause case that previous religious displays could demonstrate the purpose behind a later display that included the Ten Commandments, but that "we do not decide that the Counties' past actions forever taint any effort on their part to" display the Ten Commandments as part of an educational message about the foundations of American law).

4. If the hypothetical law discussed in Note 3 would be constitutional, was there any justification for the Court to strike down the actual provision? In other words, should a discriminatory purpose for a law passed generations ago nullify modern attempts to enforce it for legitimate reasons?

5. If a felon-disenfranchisement provision were enacted for the sole purpose, and had the effect, of stripping the vote from poor persons of all races, would it be constitutional?

6. Although the expansion of the franchise has proceeded unevenly, American democracy has seen several barriers to political participation fall, often through or enabled by the Supreme Court's interpretations of the Constitution. As this section has discussed, these barriers include qualifications based on property ownership, wealth, payment of taxes, literacy, race, sex, and age (at least for those who have reached age eighteen), and the barrier to political participation by convicted felons has shown some signs of weakening despite *Ramirez's* holding that it is constitutional. Does this history convince you that John Adams was correct in predicting that "[o]nce it was acknowledged that people had a *right* to vote, it would be difficult to deny the right to anyone: there would 'be no end of it' * * *"? ALEXANDER KEYSSAR, THE RIGHT TO VOTE: THE CONTESTED HISTORY OF DEMOCRACY IN THE UNITED STATES 11 (rev. ed. 2009). Alexis de Tocqueville made a similar prediction in his classic *Democracy in America*:

> When a nation begins to modify the elective qualification, it may easily be foreseen that, sooner or later, that qualification will be entirely abolished. There is no more invariable rule in the history of society: the further electoral rights are extended, the greater is the need of extending them; for after each concession the strength of the democracy increases, and its demands increase with its strength. The ambition of those who are below the appointed rate is irritated in exact proportion to the great number of those who are above it. The exception at last becomes the rule; concession follows concession, and no stop can be made short of universal suffrage.

ALEXIS DE TOCQUEVILLE, DEMOCRACY IN AMERICA 57 (Richard D. Heffner trans., Mentor 1956) (1835).

4. The Disinterested

Kramer v. Union Free School District No. 15

Supreme Court of the United States
395 U.S. 621, 89 S. Ct. 1886, 23 L. Ed. 2d 583 (1969)

MR. CHIEF JUSTICE WARREN delivered the opinion of the Court [in which MR. JUSTICE DOUGLAS, MR. JUSTICE BRENNAN, MR. JUSTICE WHITE, and MR. JUSTICE MARSHALL join].[j]

In this case we are called on to determine whether § 2012 of the New York Education Law is constitutional. The legislation provides that in certain New York school districts residents who are otherwise eligible to vote in state and federal elections may vote in the school district election only if they (1) own (or lease) taxable real property within the district, or (2) are parents (or have custody of) children enrolled in the local public schools. Appellant, a bachelor who neither owns nor

---

j. Justice Abe Fortas resigned one month before this decision was released; only eight Justices participated in it. —Eds.

leases taxable real property, filed suit in federal court claiming that § 2012 denied him equal protection of the laws in violation of the Fourteenth Amendment. * * * Finding that § 2012 does violate the Equal Protection Clause of the Fourteenth Amendment, we reverse. * * *

Appellant is a 31-year-old college-educated stockbroker who lives in his parents' home in the Union Free School District No. 15, a district to which § 2012 applies. He is a citizen of the United States and has voted in federal and state elections since 1959. However, since he has no children and neither owns nor leases taxable real property, appellant's attempts to register for and vote in the local school district elections have been unsuccessful. After the school district rejected his 1965 application, appellant instituted the present class action challenging the constitutionality of the voter eligibility requirements. * * *

At the outset, it is important to note what is not at issue in this case. The requirements of § 2012 that school district voters must (1) be citizens of the United States, (2) be bona fide residents of the school district, and (3) be at least 21 years of age are not challenged. Appellant agrees that the States have the power to impose reasonable citizenship, age, and residency requirements on the availability of the ballot. The sole issue in this case is whether the additional requirements of § 2012 — requirements which prohibit some district residents who are otherwise qualified by age and citizenship from participating in district meetings and school board elections — violate the Fourteenth Amendment's command that no State shall deny persons equal protection of the laws.

"In determining whether or not a state law violates the Equal Protection Clause, we must consider the facts and circumstances behind the law, the interests which the State claims to be protecting, and the interests of those who are disadvantaged by the classification." And, in this case, we must give the statute a close and exacting examination. "[S]ince the right to exercise the franchise in a free and unimpaired manner is preservative of other basic civil and political rights, any alleged infringement of the right of citizens to vote must be carefully and meticulously scrutinized." *Reynolds* v. *Sims*, 377 U.S. 533, 562 (1964) [p. 122]. This careful examination is necessary because statutes distributing the franchise constitute the foundation of our representative society. Any unjustified discrimination in determining who may participate in political affairs or in the selection of public officials undermines the legitimacy of representative government.

Thus, state apportionment statutes, which may dilute the effectiveness of some citizens' votes, receive close scrutiny from this Court. No less rigid an examination is applicable to statutes denying the franchise to citizens who are otherwise qualified by residence and age. Statutes granting the franchise to residents on a selective basis always pose the danger of denying some citizens any effective voice in the governmental affairs which substantially affect their lives. Therefore, if a challenged state statute grants the right to vote to some bona fide residents of requisite age and citizenship and denies the franchise to others, the Court must determine whether the exclusions are necessary to promote a compelling state interest.

And, for these reasons, the deference usually given to the judgment of legislators does not extend to decisions concerning which resident citizens may participate in the election of legislators and other public officials. Those decisions must be carefully scrutinized by the Court to determine whether each resident citizen has, as far as is possible, an equal voice in the selections. Accordingly, when we are reviewing statutes which deny some residents the right to vote, the general presumption of constitutionality afforded state statutes and the traditional approval given state classifications if the Court can conceive of a "rational basis" for the distinctions made are not applicable. The presumption of constitutionality and the approval given "rational" classifications in other types of enactments are based on an assumption that the institutions of state government are structured so as to represent fairly all the people. However, when the challenge to the statute is in effect a challenge of this basic assumption, the assumption can no longer serve as the basis for presuming constitutionality. And, the assumption is no less under attack because the legislature which decides who may participate at the various levels of political choice is fairly elected. Legislation which delegates decision making to bodies elected by only a portion of those eligible to vote for the legislature can cause unfair representation. Such legislation can exclude a minority of voters from any voice in the decisions just as effectively as if the decisions were made by legislators the minority had no voice in selecting. [10]

The need for exacting judicial scrutiny of statutes distributing the franchise is undiminished simply because, under a different statutory scheme, the offices subject to election might have been filled through appointment. [11] States do have latitude in determining whether certain public officials shall be selected by election or chosen by appointment and whether various questions shall be submitted to the voters. * * * However, "once the franchise is granted to the electorate, lines may not be drawn which are inconsistent with the Equal Protection Clause of the Fourteenth Amendment." *Harper* v. *Virginia Bd. of Elections*, 383 U.S. 663, 665 (1966) [p. 17]. * * *

Appellant asserts that excluding him from participation in the district elections denies him equal protection of the laws. He contends that he and others of his class are substantially interested in and significantly affected by the school meeting decisions. All members of the community have an interest in the quality and structure of public education, appellant says, and he urges that "the decisions taken by local boards * * * may have grave consequences to the entire population." Appellant also argues that the level of property taxation affects him, even though he does not

---

10. Thus, statutes structuring local government units receive no less exacting an examination merely because the state legislature is fairly elected. See *Avery* v. *Midland County*, 390 U.S. 474, 481, n.6 (1968).

11. Similarly, no less a showing of a compelling justification for disenfranchising residents is required merely because the questions scheduled for the election need not have been submitted to the voters.

own property, as property tax levels affect the price of goods and services in the community.

We turn therefore to question whether the exclusion is necessary to promote a compelling state interest. First appellees argue that the State has a legitimate interest in limiting the franchise in school district elections to "members of the community of interest"—those "primarily interested in such elections." Second, appellees urge that the State may reasonably and permissibly conclude that "property taxpayers" (including lessees of taxable property who share the tax burden through rent payments) and parents of the children enrolled in the district's schools are those "primarily interested" in school affairs.

We do not understand appellees to argue that the State is attempting to limit the franchise to those "subjectively concerned" about school matters. Rather, they appear to argue that the State's legitimate interest is in restricting a voice in school matters to those "directly affected" by such decisions. The State apparently reasons that since the schools are financed in part by local property taxes, persons whose out-of-pocket expenses are "directly" affected by property tax changes should be allowed to vote. Similarly, parents of children in school are thought to have a "direct" stake in school affairs and are given a vote.

Appellees argue that it is necessary to limit the franchise to those "primarily interested" in school affairs because "the ever increasing complexity of the many interacting phases of the school system and structure make it extremely difficult for the electorate fully to understand the whys and wherefores of the detailed operations of the school system." Appellees say that many communications of school boards and school administrations are sent home to the parents through the district pupils and are "not broadcast to the general public"; thus, nonparents will be less informed than parents. Further, appellees argue, those who are assessed for local property taxes (either directly or indirectly through rent) will have enough of an interest "through the burden on their pocketbooks, to acquire such information as they may need."

We need express no opinion as to whether the State in some circumstances might limit the exercise of the franchise to those "primarily interested" or "primarily affected." * * * For, assuming, *arguendo*, that New York legitimately might limit the franchise in these school district elections to those "primarily interested in school affairs," close scrutiny of the § 2012 classifications demonstrates that they do not accomplish this purpose with sufficient precision to justify denying appellant the franchise.

Whether classifications allegedly limiting the franchise to those resident citizens "primarily interested" deny those excluded equal protection of the laws depends, *inter alia*, on whether all those excluded are in fact substantially less interested or affected than those the statute includes. In other words, the classifications must be tailored so that the exclusion of appellant and members of his class is necessary to achieve the articulated state goal.[14] Section 2012 does not meet the exacting standard of precision we require of statutes which selectively distribute the franchise. The classifications in § 2012 permit inclusion of many persons who have, at best, a remote and indirect interest in school affairs and, on the other hand, exclude others who have a distinct and direct interest in the school meeting decisions.[15]

Nor do appellees offer any justification for the exclusion of seemingly interested and informed residents—other than to argue that the § 2012 classifications include those "whom the State could understandably deem to be the most intimately interested in actions taken by the school board," and urge that "the task of * * * balancing the interest of the community in the maintenance of orderly school district elections against the interest of any individual in voting in such elections should clearly remain with the Legislature." But the issue is not whether the legislative judgments are rational. A more exacting standard obtains. The issue is whether the § 2012 requirements do in fact sufficiently further a compelling state interest to justify denying the franchise to appellant and members of his class. The requirements of § 2012 are not sufficiently tailored to limiting the franchise to those "primarily interested" in school affairs to justify the denial of the franchise to appellant and members of his class.

The judgment of the United States District Court for the Eastern District of New York is therefore reversed. The case is remanded for further proceedings consistent with this opinion.

It is so ordered.

Mr. Justice Stewart, with whom Mr. Justice Black and Mr. Justice Harlan join, dissenting. * * *

Although at times variously phrased, the traditional test of a statute's validity under the Equal Protection Clause is a familiar one: a legislative classification is invalid only "if it rest[s] on grounds wholly irrelevant to achievement of the regulation's objectives." It was under just such a test that the literacy requirement involved in *Lassiter* [v. *Northampton County Board of Elections*, 360 U.S. 45 (1959)] [p. 11] was upheld. The premise of our decision in that case was that a State may constitutionally impose upon its citizens voting requirements reasonably "designed to promote intelligent use of the ballot." A similar premise underlies the proposition, consistently endorsed by this Court, that a State may exclude nonresidents from participation in

---

14. Of course, if the exclusions are necessary to promote the articulated state interest, we must then determine whether the interest promoted by limiting the franchise constitutes a compelling state interest. We do not reach that issue in this case.

15. For example, appellant resides with his parents in the school district, pays state and federal taxes and is interested in and affected by school board decisions; however, he has no vote. On the other hand, an uninterested unemployed young man who pays no state or federal taxes, but who rents an apartment in the district, can participate in the election.

its elections. Such residence requirements, designed to help ensure that voters have a substantial stake in the outcome of elections and an opportunity to become familiar with the candidates and issues voted upon, are entirely permissible exercises of state authority. Indeed, the appellant explicitly concedes, as he must, the validity of voting requirements relating to residence, literacy, and age. Yet he argues—and the Court accepts the argument—that the voting qualifications involved here somehow have a different constitutional status. I am unable to see the distinction.

Clearly a State may reasonably assume that its residents have a greater stake in the outcome of elections held within its boundaries than do other persons. Likewise, it is entirely rational for a state legislature to suppose that residents, being generally better informed regarding state affairs than are nonresidents, will be more likely than nonresidents to vote responsibly. And the same may be said of legislative assumptions regarding the electoral competence of adults and literate persons on the one hand, and of minors and illiterates on the other. It is clear, of course, that lines thus drawn cannot infallibly perform their intended legislative function. Just as "[i]lliterate people may be intelligent voters," [*Lassiter*, 360 U.S. at 52], nonresidents or minors might also in some instances be interested, informed, and intelligent participants in the electoral process. Persons who commute across a state line to work may well have a great stake in the affairs of the State in which they are employed; some college students under 21 may be both better informed and more passionately interested in political affairs than many adults. But such discrepancies are the inevitable concomitant of the line drawing that is essential to law making. So long as the classification is rationally related to a permissible legislative end, therefore—as are residence, literacy, and age requirements imposed with respect to voting—there is no denial of equal protection.

Thus judged, the statutory classification involved here seems to me clearly to be valid. New York has made the judgment that local educational policy is best left to those persons who have certain direct and definable interests in that policy: those who are either immediately involved as parents of school children or who, as owners or lessees of taxable property are burdened with the local cost of funding school district operations. True, persons outside those classes may be genuinely interested in the conduct of a school district's business—just as commuters from New Jersey may be genuinely interested in the outcome of a New York City election. But unless this Court is to claim a monopoly of wisdom regarding the sound operation of school systems in the 50 States, I see no way to justify the conclusion that the legislative classification involved here is not rationally related to a legitimate legislative purpose. * * *

With good reason, the Court does not really argue the contrary. Instead, it strikes down New York's statute by asserting that the traditional equal protection standard is inapt in this case, and that a considerably stricter standard—under which classifications relating to "the franchise" are to be subjected to "exacting judicial scrutiny"—should be applied. But the asserted justification for applying such a standard cannot withstand analysis.

The Court is quite explicit in explaining why it believes this statute should be given "close scrutiny":

> "The presumption of constitutionality and the approval given 'rational' classifications in other types of enactments are based on an assumption that the institutions of state government are structured so as to represent fairly all the people. However, when the challenge to the statute is in effect a challenge of this basic assumption, the assumption can no longer serve as the basis for presuming constitutionality."

I am at a loss to understand how such reasoning is at all relevant to the present case. The voting qualifications at issue have been promulgated, not by Union Free School District No. 15, but by the New York State Legislature, and the appellant is of course fully able to participate in the election of representatives in that body. There is simply no claim whatever here that the state government is not "structured so as to represent fairly all the people," including the appellant. * * *

In any event, it seems to me that under any equal protection standard, short of a doctrinaire insistence that universal suffrage is somehow mandated by the Constitution, the appellant's claim must be rejected. First of all, it must be emphasized—despite the Court's undifferentiated references to what it terms "the franchise"— that we are dealing here, not with a general election, but with a limited, special-purpose election.[9] The appellant is eligible to vote in all state, local, and federal elections in which general governmental policy is determined. He is fully able, therefore, to participate not only in the processes by which the requirements for school district voting may be changed, but also in those by which the levels of state and federal financial assistance to the District are determined. He clearly is not locked into any self-perpetuating status of exclusion from the electoral process.

Secondly, the * * * appellant's status is merely that of a citizen who says he is interested in the affairs of his local public schools. If the Constitution requires that he must be given a decision-making role in the governance of those affairs, then it seems to me that any individual who seeks such a role must be given it. * * *

---

9. Special-purpose governmental authorities such as water, lighting, and sewer districts exist in various sections of the country, and participation in such districts is undoubtedly limited in many instances to those who partake of the agency's services and are assessed for its expenses. The constitutional validity of such a policy is, it seems to me, unquestionable. And while it is true, as the appellant argues, that a school system has a more pervasive influence in the community than do most other such special-purpose authorities, I cannot agree that that difference in degree presents anything approaching a distinction of constitutional dimension.

Notes and Questions

1. Note the slippery way in which Chief Justice Warren used the term "interested." New York sought to bar from voting people who lacked an "interest" in the outcome of school board elections, *i.e.*, those people who would not be "directly affected" thereby. In holding that the voting restriction was not narrowly tailored to accomplish that purpose, however, the Court (in footnote 15) pointed out that Kramer was "interested in and affected by school board decisions." The Court thus appeared to use "interest" in the sense of "subjectively concerned"—precisely the sense in which the state was *not* using the term. *See* WEBSTER'S NEW UNIVERSAL UNABRIDGED DICTIONARY 993 (2003) (defining "interested" to mean both "having the attention or curiosity engaged" and "influenced by personal or selfish motives").[k]

2. In what way was Kramer "affected by school board decisions"? Why should he have any say in the making of school policy? For information on Kramer and the background of the case, see Eugene D. Mazo, *The Right to Vote in Local Elections: The Story of* Kramer v. Union Free School District No. 15, *in* ELECTION LAW STORIES 87 (Joshua A. Douglas & Eugene D. Mazo eds., 2016).

3. Dissenting from the three-judge district-court decision that was reversed by the opinion you have just read, Judge Weinstein pointed to other types of individuals who were denied the ability to vote under § 2012:

1. young adults such as plaintiff residing in family homes;

2. boarders and lodgers;

3. elder citizens and others living in the homes of their children or other relatives;

4. spouses of persons renting homes;

5. parents not owning or renting homes whose children attend private or parochial schools;

6. parents, not owning or renting homes, whose children attend special public schools outside the district;

7. parents, not owning or renting homes, whose children are too young or too old to attend public schools; and

---

k. Similarly, "uninterested" and (especially) "disinterested" are ambiguous. They may refer to lack of bias or to indifference. "DISINTERESTED and UNINTERESTED share a confused and confusing history. DISINTERESTED was originally used to mean 'not interested, indifferent'; UNINTERESTED in its earliest use meant 'impartial.' By various developmental twists, DISINTERESTED is now used in both senses. UNINTERESTED is used mainly in the sense 'not interested, indifferent.' It is occasionally used to mean 'not having a personal or property interest.' Many object to the use of DISINTERESTED to mean 'not interested, indifferent.' They insist that DISINTERESTED can mean only 'impartial': *A disinterested observer is the best judge of behavior.* However, both senses are well established in all varieties of English, and the sense intended is almost always clear from the context." WEBSTER'S NEW UNIVERSAL UNABRIDGED DICTIONARY 566 (2003). *Almost* always.

8. clergy, military, and others living on tax exempt property.

Kramer v. Union Free School District No. 15, 282 F. Supp. 70, 75 (E.D.N.Y. 1968) (Weinstein, J., dissenting), *rev'd*, 395 U.S. 621 (1969). Should states be able to exclude any of these groups from voting? All of them? Does *Kramer* permit the exclusion of any of these groups?

4. Suppose New York had prohibited persons convicted of certain lewd acts involving minors from voting. Would such an exclusion be narrowly tailored to a compelling interest? What if the exclusion extended to all sex-related crimes? Failure to pay child support?

5. Was the more important narrow-tailoring problem not that too few people (such as Kramer) were permitted to vote, but rather that *too many* people were permitted to vote? Could New York have complied with the Equal Protection Clause by excluding persons such as the Court's hypothetical "uninterested unemployed young man who pays no state or federal taxes, but who rents an apartment in the district"?

6. If the "uninterested"—those who are subjectively unconcerned—are unlikely to vote when given the opportunity, why should the Equal Protection Clause be violated if a state permits them to vote? In other words, should New York be able to defend its decision to allow all leaseholders to vote by saying, "We want decisions in school-board elections to be made by interested voters, but there is no harm in allowing an 'uninterested unemployed young man' to vote because he won't show up at the polls anyway"? In answering, be conscious of the ambiguity of the term "interested," as discussed in Note 1.

7. Imagine that you are counsel to the New York Legislature, and are charged with drafting a replacement for § 2012. Can you construct voter qualifications that would limit the franchise to "interested" persons and pass the Court's narrow-tailoring analysis?

8. *Problem.* Analyze the constitutionality of the restrictions on the franchise in these hypothetical school districts' elections:

    A. Chester A. Arthur School District permits all district residents who have reached age eighteen to vote. The statute is challenged by Alice, a seventeen-year-old, honor-roll high-school student, who alleges that excluding her from voting because of age violates the Equal Protection Clause.

    B. James Buchanan School District permits all district residents who have reached age eighteen to vote, except that it prohibits current students in the district from voting. The rationale is that current students are too likely to vote out of short-term self-interest, and not to support policies that are designed to provide long-lasting educational benefits. Bianca, an eighteen-year-old high-school senior, challenges the restriction.

    C. Grover Cleveland School District permits all district residents who have reached age eighteen to vote and, in addition, permits students currently enrolled at Calvin Coolidge High School, the only public high school in the district, to vote regardless of age. The scheme is challenged by Carter, a resident of the district and a sixteen-year-old junior at the Chesterfield Academy, a private high school located within the district.

9. *Problem.* Dissatisfied with the performance of the city's public schools, the mayor of Los Angeles proposes that control of the schools be shifted from the Los Angeles Unified School District to a nonprofit organization. To be adopted in any individual school, the proposal must receive a majority vote of all teachers at that school and a majority of the votes cast by parents of students at the school. No one besides teachers and parents is permitted to vote. Further, parents' votes are not distributed on a one-parent, one-vote basis; rather, votes are accorded to parents based on the number of *children* they have in the school. *See* Howard Blume & Duke Helfand, *An Odd Civics Lesson for 7 L.A. Schools*, L.A. Times, Dec. 12, 2007, at 1. The nonprofit will seek to implement reforms that are "locally driven; increase autonomy and school site decision making; increase accountability; leverage city resources; and invest private and philanthropic resources." Each school will develop its own plan for achieving those goals, but the exact character of the reforms is vague. How would you defend the voting system against constitutional attack?

10. *Problem.* After *Kramer*, do states have any ability to restrict the franchise as a way of "promot[ing] intelligent use of the ballot," in *Lassiter*'s words? Could a state, for example, exclude from voting any person who is suffering from mental incapacity? If so, how should a state delimit the exclusion so as to satisfy *Kramer*'s demand that such a law be narrowly tailored? *See Doe v. Rowe*, 156 F. Supp. 2d 35 (D. Me. 2001) (striking down a voting exclusion applicable to persons with "mental illness" because the term did not include other mental incapacities that were just as severe); *Minnesota Voters Alliance v. Ritchie*, 890 F. Supp. 2d 1106 (D. Minn. 2012) (upholding Minnesota's constitutional provision prohibiting voting by "a person under guardianship, or a person who is insane or not mentally competent," but interpreting it to apply only to people judicially determined to be incapable of voting); *In re Guardianship of Erickson*, 2012 Minn. Dist. LEXIS 193 (Minn. Dist. Ct. 2012) (striking down the same provision insofar as it categorically barred from voting all persons under guardianship); Elizabeth R. Schiltz, *The Ties That Bind Idiots and Infamous Criminals: Disenfranchisement of Persons with Cognitive Impairments*, 13 U. St. Thomas L.J. 100 (2016); Hillary May, Note, *The Last Frontier of Disenfranchisement: A Fundamental Right for Individuals with Cognitive Disabilities*, 59 Wm. & Mary L. Rev. 693 (2017).

11. Remember that narrow tailoring is only part of the strict-scrutiny analysis. If strict scrutiny is applied to a classification, the classification is unconstitutional unless narrowly tailored *to a compelling government interest*. In *Kramer*, the Court struck down § 2012 because it was not sufficiently tailored to the government's cited interest in limiting the franchise to "interested" persons. Accordingly, the Court did not need to reach the question whether the interest was compelling. If § 2012 had been narrowly tailored, by permitting all persons—but only those

persons—"interested" in school policy to vote, could the classification have survived the compelling-interest prong?

In this regard, consider Rex E. Lee, *Mr. Herbert Spencer and the Bachelor Stockbroker:* Kramer v. Union Free School District No. 15, 15 ARIZ. L. REV. 457, 464–65 (1973):

> Clearly, there is no compelling reason why the State of New York should not allow Kramer and all other resident bachelors of voting age to vote in the school board elections for Union Free School District No. 15. For that matter, neither is there any compelling reason for denying the franchise to intelligent and well-informed 17 year olds, convicted felons, non-residents or non-citizens. * * * Indeed, there is no governmental regulation as to which some person cannot make a case for the proposition that it affects him unfairly vis-à-vis someone else. * * *

> The net result [of requiring a compelling reason to deny an individual a right], nominally, is total and absolute equality where judicially declared "fundamental" interests are involved. Ironically, however, since application of the test will almost certainly result in constitutional invalidity, the real consequence of the Court's new equal protection test is a shift away from questions concerning equality and a new concentration on what is "fundamental."

12. Before the Twenty-Sixth Amendment prohibited states and the national government from denying the right to vote to anyone eighteen or older on account of age, Congress attempted to accomplish the same result by statute. The 1970 amendments to the Voting Rights Act, 84 Stat. 314, purported to lower the voting age across the nation to eighteen. In *Oregon v. Mitchell*, 400 U.S. 112 (1970), the Supreme Court considered the constitutionality of that provision. Four Justices (Douglas, Brennan, White, and Marshall) thought the provision constitutional as a means of enforcing the Equal Protection Clause. Four Justices (Burger, Harlan, Stewart, and Blackmun) thought that Congress had no authority to alter the voting age. As Justice Harlan reasoned, "the suggestion that members of the age group between 18 and 21 are threatened with unconstitutional discrimination * * * is little short of fanciful. [A]ll the evidence indicates that Congress—led on by recent decisions of this Court—thought simply that 18-year-olds were fairly entitled to vote and that Congress could give it to them by legislation." *Id.* at 212–13 (Harlan, J., concurring in part and dissenting in part).

The controlling opinion of Justice Black held that Congress could lower the voting age in federal elections, but not in state ones. Justice Black reasoned that Congress's power to "make or alter" the "Manner" of congressional elections gave it the power to lower the qualifications for voters in such elections, and "[i]t cannot be seriously contended that Congress has less power over the conduct of presidential elections than it has over congressional elections." *Id.* at 124 (opinion of Black, J.). As to state elections, however, Justice Black held that the Constitution preserved the autonomous authority of states to set voting qualifications. Can the combination of these two halves of Justice Black's reasoning be squared with Art. I, §2 of the Constitution and the Seventeenth Amendment, which provide that voters in congressional elections "shall have the Qualifications requisite for Electors of the most numerous Branch of the State Legislature"?

The Supreme Court appears to have rejected Justice Black's reasoning. In *Arizona v. Inter Tribal Council of Arizona, Inc.*, 570 U.S. 1 (2013), the Court held that Arizona's requirement that persons registering to vote present proof of citizenship was preempted by a federal requirement in the National Voter Registration Act that states "accept and use" a federal form which demanded no proof of citizenship. 52 U.S.C. §20505(a)(1). Arizona had insisted that if the federal form prevented it from requiring such proof, it would be an unconstitutional interference with the state power to determine voter qualifications. The Court suggested that Arizona may well have been correct (*see* 570 U.S. at 17 ("Arizona is correct that it would raise serious constitutional doubts if a federal statute precluded a State from obtaining the information necessary to enforce its voter qualifications.")), but that there was a way to avoid the conflict: Arizona could demand that the Election Assistance Commission amend the form to add a state-specific instruction telling Arizona registrants to present proof of citizenship.

For present purposes, the key question is the extent of Congress's power to regulate the registration process as part of its authority under the Elections Clause, U.S. Const. art. I, §4, cl. 1, to "make or alter" regulations concerning the "Times, Places and Manner of holding Elections for Senators and Representatives." *Inter Tribal Council* provided a bright-line rule: "[T]he Elections Clause empowers Congress to regulate *how* federal elections are held, but not *who* may vote in them." 570 U.S. at 16.

This rule, although consistent with the Clause itself, is inconsistent with the outcome in *Oregon v. Mitchell. Inter Tribal Council* quoted approvingly from the dissent in *Mitchell*, which argued that "[i]t is difficult to see how words could be clearer in stating what Congress can control and what it cannot control. Surely nothing in these provisions lends itself to the view that voting qualifications in federal elections are to be set by Congress." 570 U.S. at 16 (quoting *Mitchell*, 400 U.S. at 210 (Harlan, J., concurring in part and dissenting in part)). Although Justice Black's opinion in *Mitchell* did conclude that Congress could invoke the Elections Clause to require states to permit 18 year-olds to vote, *Inter Tribal Court* brushed it aside: "That result, which lacked a majority rationale, is of minimal precedential value here." *Inter Tribal Council*, 570 U.S. at 16 n.8.

In *Kobach v. United States Election Assistance Commission*, 6 F. Supp. 3d 1252 (D. Kan. 2014), the district court followed the Supreme Court's suggestion and held that the EAC was required to include a proof-of-citizenship requirement among the state-specific instructions for Kansas and Arizona on the NVRA form. The Tenth Circuit reversed, however, holding that the EAC was "not compulsorily mandated to approve state-requested changes to the Federal Form." 772 F.3d 1183 (10th Cir. 2014).

13. States' processes for selecting judges can give disproportionate influence to lawyers. Under the method of selection known as the "Missouri Plan" or "merit selection," commissions are used to screen potential judicial nominees. Details differ across states, but the commission commonly selects a certain number of candidates, and the governor must choose from among the candidates approved by the commission. The commission, therefore, has considerable power in the selection process.

The membership of the commissions is determined by a variety of methods in the states using forms of the Missouri Plan, but lawyers—and in particular the organized bar—are sometimes given disproportionate influence in the selection of commissioners. *See* Stephen J. Ware, *The Missouri Plan in National Perspective*, 74 Mo. L. Rev. 751 (2009). Some states' commissions, for example, have a certain number of members chosen by the organized bar; in Kansas, a majority of the nine-member commission is elected by the bar.[1]

Does such a system violate the Equal Protection Clause, as interpreted in *Kramer*? Would it matter if a state used its commission to choose candidates to run in judicial *elections* rather than to be appointed by the governor? *See* Nelson Lund, *May Lawyers Be Given the Power to Elect Those Who Choose Our Judges? "Merit Selection" and Constitutional Law*, 34 Harv. J.L. & Pub. Pol'y 1043 (2011). *Cf. Hellebust v. Brownback*, 42 F.3d 1331 (10th Cir. 1994) (striking down Kansas's procedure for selecting members of the state's Board of Agriculture because the procedure empowered delegates from private agricultural associations to select members of the board).

14. Did it violate the Equal Protection Clause for states to restrict voting to twenty-one-year-olds, as forty-six of the states did at the time suit was filed in *Oregon v. Mitchell*? (Only two states, Georgia and Kentucky, permitted eighteen-year-olds to vote; Hawaii and Alaska set the voting age above eighteen but below twenty-one.) If not, how can Congress be held to be "enforc[ing]" the Equal Protection Clause by requiring states to grant the vote to eighteen-year-olds? *Compare Katzenbach v. Morgan*, 384 U.S. 641 (1966) [p. 227].

Did the Voting Rights Act itself violate the Constitution by setting the voting age at eighteen, rather than seventeen or a lower age? *See Oregon v. Mitchell*, 400 U.S. at 142 (Douglas, J., concurring in the judgment in part and dissenting in part) ("It is said, why draw the line at 18? Why not 17? Congress can draw lines and I see no reason why it cannot conclude that 18-year-olds have that degree of maturity which entitles them to the franchise.").

---

1. The power granted to the bar may result in candidates approved by the commissions who are more ideologically attuned to the interests of the organized bar than would be the case if the bar lacked such influence. *See* Brian T. Fitzpatrick, *The Politics of Merit Selection*, 74 Mo. L. Rev. 675 (2009).

15. With the ratification of the Twenty-Sixth Amendment, states and the federal government are prohibited from denying or abridging the voting rights of any U.S. citizen eighteen years or older on account of age. May a state make special accommodation for the elderly without violating the Amendment? Texas permits no-excuse voting by mail for voters age sixty-five and older. Does that policy violate the rights of voters younger than 65, by abridging their right to vote on account of age? *See Texas Democratic Party v. Abbott*, 961 F.3d 389, 406–08 (5th Cir.), *motion to vacate stay denied*, 140 S. Ct. 2015 (2020).

16. In footnote 9 of his *Kramer* dissent, Justice Stewart argued that the school district should have been treated as a special-purpose district, exempt from the constitutional requirements applicable to governments exercising more general authority. The Court later reaffirmed *Kramer*'s implicit conclusion that school districts' "powers are general enough and have sufficient impact throughout the district" to trigger the fundamental constitutional right to vote and the one-person, one-vote rule. *Hadley v. Junior College District*, 397 U.S. 50, 54 (1970).

Nevertheless, there are some special-purpose districts for which those constitutional requirements do not apply. One such district was at issue in *Salyer Land Co. v. Tulare Lake Basin Water Storage District*, 410 U.S. 719 (1973). The special district in that case had limited powers, all focused on "the acquisition, storage, and distribution of water for farming." Accordingly, its activities disproportionately affected landowners. Further, all costs of the district's projects and charges for its services were assessed in proportion to the benefits received. Because the impact of the district was felt based on the amount of land owned rather than on an equal basis across the population, the Court, applying rational-basis scrutiny, held that it was constitutional to restrict the vote in district elections to landowners and to weigh votes according to the amount of land owned.

In *Ball v. James*, 451 U.S. 355 (1981), the Court, 5-4, applied *Salyer* to the Salt River Project, a district that stored and delivered water to almost half the population of Arizona, including much of Phoenix. The operating costs of the Project were raised through the sale of electric power, not by assessments according to land value, as was the case in *Salyer*. Bonds issued by the Project were, however, secured by landowners' property. The Court upheld the method of selecting Project's directors, which was to apportion voting power by acreage owned, and to exclude non-landowners from the directorial elections entirely.

> The [Salt River] District * * * cannot impose ad valorem property taxes or sales taxes. It cannot enact any laws governing the conduct of citizens, nor does it administer such normal functions of government as the maintenance of streets, the operation of schools, or sanitation, health, or welfare services.
>
> * * * The District * * * do[es] not own, sell, or buy water, nor do[es it] control the use of any water [it] ha[s] delivered. * * * [A]ll water delivered

by the Salt River District, like the water delivered by the Tulare Lake Basin Water Storage District, is distributed according to land ownership[.] * * *

[N]either the existence nor size of the District's power business affects the legality of its property-based voting scheme. [T]he provision of electricity is not a traditional element of governmental sovereignty, and so is not in itself the sort of general or important governmental function that would make the government provider subject to [one person, one vote].

[N]o matter how great the number of nonvoting residents buying electricity from the District, the relationship between them and the District's power operations is essentially that between consumers and a business enterprise from which they buy. * * *

* * * [The District bears a disproportionate relationship] to the specific class of people whom the system makes eligible to vote. The voting landowners are the only residents of the District whose lands are subject to liens to secure District bonds. Only these landowners are subject to the acreage-based taxing power of the District, and voting landowners are the only residents who have ever committed capital to the District through stock assessments * * *. The *Salyer* opinion did not say that the selected class of voters for a special public entity must be the only parties at all affected by the operations of the entity, or that their entire economic well-being must depend on that entity. Rather, the question was whether the effect of the entity's operations on them was disproportionately greater than the effect on those seeking the vote.

Id. at 366–71. The Court applied rational basis and upheld the voting scheme.

17. According to the U.S. Census Bureau, there are 38,542 special-purpose districts in the United States. *See* U.S. Census Bureau, America Counts Staff, *From Municipalities to Special Districts, Official Count of Every Type of Local Government in 2017 Census of Governments* 3 (2019), *available at* https://www.census.gov/content/dam/Census/library/visualizations/2019/econ/from_municipalities_to_special_districts_america_counts_october_2019.pdf. That number represents an increase of approximately 50% over the number of special-purpose districts in existence in 1972, and well over twice the number of districts in 1952. The districts fulfill myriad functions, including providing services relating to education, social services, transportation, environment and housing, and utilities. The largest category of single-function districts is fire districts, of which there are 5,975, but there are far more districts with functions relating to the environment and housing or community development.

18. Recall that in *Kramer*, the Court was careful to note that the case did not present a challenge to the residency requirement for voting, and indeed residency requirements have been uniformly upheld. But was Kramer any more "affected" by the decisions of the school board because he *resided* in the district? One might

question whether Kramer's interest was any more significant than, for example, that of a resident of a neighboring district who employed graduates of the school district in which he wished to vote. Should states be required to permit such non-residents to vote in school-district elections?

Or must states *prohibit* non-residents from voting, on the ground that if non-residents vote, they dilute the voting strength of residents? *Compare May v. Town of Mountain Village*, 132 F.3d 576 (10th Cir. 1997) (permitting voting by non-residents), *with Board of County Commissioners of Shelby County v. Burson*, 121 F.3d 244 (6th Cir. 1997) (striking down a scheme permitting Memphis city residents to vote for officials of both the Memphis City School District and the Shelby County School District, which was comprised of the areas of the county not including the city).

Should the Constitution recognize a difference between "dual residents," who maintain bona fide residences in multiple locales, and nonresident property owners? *See* Ashira Pelman Ostrow, Note, *Dual Resident Voting: Traditional Disenfranchisement and Prospects for Change*, 102 COLUM. L. REV. 1954 (2002). Professor Gerald Frug has argued that extending the franchise to people who work, but do not live, in a locality could foster a sense of "regional citizenship." Gerald E. Frug, *Beyond Regional Government*, 115 HARV. L. REV. 1763, 1828–30 (2002). Should such a concept play a role in expounding the constitutional right to vote?

The next principal case forces us to examine the often-overlooked assumption that voting rights should be tied to residence.

Holt Civic Club v. City of Tuscaloosa

Supreme Court of the United States
439 U.S. 60, 99 S. Ct. 383, 58 L. Ed. 2d 292 (1978)

MR. JUSTICE REHNQUIST delivered the opinion of the Court [in which MR. CHIEF JUSTICE BURGER, MR. JUSTICE STEWART, MR. JUSTICE BLACKMUN, MR. JUSTICE POWELL, and MR. JUSTICE STEVENS join].

Holt is a small, largely rural, unincorporated community located on the northeastern outskirts of Tuscaloosa, the fifth largest city in Alabama. Because the community is within the three-mile police jurisdiction circumscribing Tuscaloosa's corporate limits, its residents are subject to the city's "police [and] sanitary regulations." Holt residents are also subject to the criminal jurisdiction of the city's court, and to the city's power to license businesses, trades, and professions. Tuscaloosa, however, may collect from businesses in the police jurisdiction only one-half of the license fee chargeable to similar businesses conducted within the corporate limits. * * *

In 1973 appellants, an unincorporated civic association and seven individual residents of Holt, brought this statewide class action * * * challenging the constitutionality of these Alabama statutes. They claimed that the city's extraterritorial exercise of police powers over Holt residents, without a concomitant extension of the franchise on an equal footing with those residing within the corporate limits, denies residents of the police jurisdiction rights secured by the Due Process and Equal Protection Clauses of the Fourteenth Amendment. * * *

[The Court summarized *Kramer* v. *Union Free School Dist.*, 395 U.S. 621 (1969) [p. 46], and *Cipriano* v. *City of Houma*, 395 U.S. 701 (1969), which held that states may not limit the franchise to property taxpayers in elections to approve the issuance of revenue bonds.] Appellants also place heavy reliance on *Evans* v. *Cornman*, 398 U.S. 419 (1970). In *Evans* the Permanent Board of Registry of Montgomery County, Md., ruled that persons living on the grounds of the National Institutes of Health (NIH), a federal enclave located within the geographical boundaries of the State, did not meet the residency requirement of the Maryland Constitution. Accordingly, NIH residents were denied the right to vote in Maryland elections. This Court rejected the notion that persons living on NIH grounds were not residents of Maryland: "Appellees clearly live within the geographical boundaries of the State of Maryland, and they are treated as state residents in the census and in determining congressional apportionment. * * *"

Thus, because inhabitants of the NIH enclave were residents of Maryland and were "just as interested in and connected with electoral decisions as they were prior to 1953 when the area came under federal jurisdiction and as their neighbors who live off the enclave," the State could not deny them the equal right to vote in Maryland elections.[7]

From these and our other voting qualifications cases a common characteristic emerges: The challenged statute in each case denied the franchise to individuals who were physically resident within the geographic boundaries of the governmental entity concerned. No decision of this Court has extended the "one man, one vote" principle to individuals residing beyond the geographic confines of the governmental entity concerned, be it the State or its political subdivisions. On the contrary, our cases have uniformly recognized that a government unit may legitimately restrict the right to participate in its political processes to those who reside within its borders. * * *

Appellants' argument that extraterritorial extension of municipal powers requires concomitant extraterritorial extension of the franchise proves too much. The imaginary line defining a city's corporate limits cannot corral the influence of municipal actions. A city's decisions inescapably affect individuals living immediately outside its borders. The granting of building permits for high rise apartments, industrial plants, and the like on the city's fringe unavoidably contributes to

---

7. In this case residents of the police jurisdiction are excluded only from participation in municipal elections since they reside outside of Tuscaloosa's corporate limits. * * * Treatment of the plaintiffs in *Evans* as nonresidents of Maryland had repercussions not merely with respect to their right to vote in city elections, but with respect to their right to vote in national, state, school board, and referendum elections.

problems of traffic congestion, school districting, and law enforcement immediately outside the city. A rate change in the city's sales or ad valorem tax could well have a significant impact on retailers and property values in areas bordering the city. The condemnation of real property on the city's edge for construction of a municipal garbage dump or waste treatment plant would have obvious implications for neighboring nonresidents. Indeed, the indirect extraterritorial effects of many purely internal municipal actions could conceivably have a heavier impact on surrounding environs than the direct regulation contemplated by Alabama's police jurisdiction statutes. Yet no one would suggest that nonresidents likely to be affected by this sort of municipal action have a constitutional right to participate in the political processes bringing it about. * * *

The extraterritorial exercise of municipal powers is a governmental technique neither recent in origin nor unique to the State of Alabama. In this country 35 States authorize their municipal subdivisions to exercise governmental powers beyond their corporate limits. Although the extraterritorial municipal powers granted by these States vary widely, several States grant their cities more extensive or intrusive powers over bordering areas than those granted under the Alabama statutes.[8]

In support of their equal protection claim, appellants suggest a number of "constitutionally preferable" governmental alternatives to Alabama's system of municipal police jurisdictions. For example, exclusive management of the police jurisdiction by county officials, appellants maintain, would be more "practical." From a political science standpoint, appellants' suggestions may be sound, but this Court does not sit to determine whether Alabama has chosen the soundest or most practical form of internal government possible. Authority to make those judgments resides in the state legislature, and Alabama citizens are free to urge their proposals to that body. Our inquiry is limited to the question whether "any state of facts reasonably may be conceived to justify" Alabama's system of police jurisdictions, and in this case it takes but momentary reflection to arrive at an affirmative answer.

The Alabama Legislature could have decided that municipal corporations should have some measure of control over activities carried on just beyond their "city limit" signs, particularly since today's police jurisdiction may be tomorrow's annexation to the city proper. Nor need the city's interests have been the only concern of the legislature when it enacted the police jurisdiction statutes. Urbanization of any area brings with it a number of individuals who long both for the quiet of suburban or

---

8. * * * We do not have before us, of course, a situation in which a city has annexed outlying territory in all but name, and is exercising precisely the same governmental powers over residents of surrounding unincorporated territory as it does over those residing within its corporate limits. * * * While the burden was on appellants to establish a difference in treatment violative of the Equal Protection Clause, we are bound to observe that among the powers *not* [exercised by the city outside its borders] are the vital and traditional authorities of cities and towns to levy ad valorem taxes, invoke the power of eminent domain, and zone property for various types of uses.

country living and for the career opportunities offered by the city's working environment. Unincorporated communities like Holt dot the rim of most major population centers in Alabama and elsewhere, and state legislatures have a legitimate interest in seeing that this substantial segment of the population does not go without basic municipal services such as police, fire, and health protection. Established cities are experienced in the delivery of such services, and the incremental cost of extending the city's responsibility in these areas to surrounding environs may be substantially less than the expense of establishing wholly new service organizations in each community.

Nor was it unreasonable for the Alabama Legislature to require police jurisdiction residents to contribute through license fees to the expense of services provided them by the city. The statutory limitation on license fees to half the amount exacted within the city assures that police jurisdiction residents will not be victimized by the city government. * * *

* * * Alabama's police jurisdiction statute, enacted in 1907, was a rational legislative response to the problems faced by the State's burgeoning cities. Alabama is apparently content with the results of its experiment, and nothing in the Equal Protection Clause of the Fourteenth Amendment requires that it try something new. * * *

Affirmed.

Mr. Justice Stevens, concurring.

* * * While I join the opinion of the Court, I write separately to emphasize that this holding does not make all exercises of extraterritorial authority by a municipality immune from attack under the Equal Protection Clause of the Fourteenth Amendment.

* * * Certainly there is nothing in the Federal Constitution to prevent a suburb from contracting with a nearby city to provide municipal services for its residents, even though those residents have no voice in the election of the city's officials or in the formulation of the city's rules. That is essentially what Alabama has accomplished here, through the elected representatives of all its citizens in the state legislature.[1] * * *

* * * The statutory scheme created by the Alabama Legislature is not unconstitutional by its terms, but it may well be, as the opinion of the Court recognizes, *ante,* n.8, that that scheme or another much like it might sometimes operate to deny the franchise to individuals who share the interests of their voting neighbors. * * *

---

1. I recognize that there is a difference between a suburb's decision to contract with a nearby city and a decision by the state legislature requiring all suburbs to do so. In some situations that difference might justify a holding that a particular extraterritorial delegation of power is unconstitutional. It does not, however, justify the view that all such delegations are invalid.

Mr. Justice Brennan, with whom Mr. Justice White and Mr. Justice Marshall join, dissenting. * * *

[Residency requirements "preserve the basic conception of a political community" and for that reason are exempt from strict scrutiny, provided they are "appropriately defined" to serve that purpose.] At the heart of our basic conception of a "political community," however, is the notion of a reciprocal relationship between the process of government and those who subject themselves to that process by choosing to live within the area of its authoritative application. Statutes such as those challenged in this case, which fracture this relationship by severing the connection between the process of government and those who are governed in the places of their residency, thus undermine the very purposes which have led this Court in the past to approve the application of bona fide residency requirements.

There is no question but that the residents of Tuscaloosa's police jurisdiction are governed by the city. * * * The Court seems to imply, however, that residents of the police jurisdiction are not governed enough to be included within the political community of Tuscaloosa, since they are not subject to Tuscaloosa's powers of eminent domain, zoning, or ad valorem taxation. But this position is sharply contrary to our previous holdings.

The residents of Tuscaloosa's police jurisdiction are vastly more affected by Tuscaloosa's decisionmaking processes than were the plaintiffs in either *Kramer* or *Cipriano* affected by the decisionmaking processes from which they had been unconstitutionally excluded. * * * A municipality, for example, may use its police powers to regulate, or even to ban, common professions and businesses. * * * The Court today does not explain why being subjected to the authority to exercise such extensive power does not suffice to bring the residents of Tuscaloosa's police jurisdiction within the political community of the city. Nor does the Court in fact provide any standards for determining when those subjected to extraterritorial municipal legislation will have been "governed enough" to trigger the protections of the Equal Protection Clause. * * *

The criterion of geographical residency is thus entirely arbitrary when applied to this case. It fails to explain why, consistently with the Equal Protection Clause, the "government unit" which may exclude from the franchise those who reside outside of its geographical boundaries should be composed of the city of Tuscaloosa rather than of the city together with its police jurisdiction. It irrationally distinguishes between two classes of citizens, each with equal claim to residency (insofar as that can be determined by domicile or intention or other similar criteria), and each governed by the city of Tuscaloosa in the place of their residency.

The Court argues, however, that if the franchise were extended to residents of the city's police jurisdiction, the franchise must similarly be extended to all those indirectly affected by the city's actions. This is a simple non sequitur. There is a crystal-clear distinction between those who reside in Tuscaloosa's police jurisdiction, and who are therefore subject to that city's police and sanitary ordinances, licensing fees, and the jurisdiction of its municipal court, and those who reside in neither the city nor its police jurisdiction, and who are thus merely affected by the indirect impact of the city's decisions. This distinction * * * is consistent with, if not mandated by, the very conception of a political community underlying constitutional recognition of bona fide residency requirements.

Appellants' equal protection claim can be simply expressed: The State cannot extend the franchise to some citizens who are governed by municipal government in the places of their residency, and withhold the franchise from others similarly situated, unless this distinction is necessary to promote a compelling state interest. No such interest has been articulated in this case. Neither Tuscaloosa's interest in regulating "activities carried on just beyond [its] 'city limit' signs," nor Alabama's interest in providing municipal services to the unincorporated communities surrounding its cities are in any way inconsistent with the extension of the franchise to residents of Tuscaloosa's police jurisdiction. Although a great many States may presently authorize the exercise of extraterritorial lawmaking powers by a municipality, and although the Alabama statutes involved in this case may be of venerable age, neither of these factors * * * can serve to justify practices otherwise impermissible under the Equal Protection Clause of the Fourteenth Amendment. * * *

Notes and Questions

1. Was Justice Brennan correct that there was a "crystal-clear" distinction between the residents of the police jurisdiction and outsiders? Or was the Court correct that the very principle Justice Brennan used to extend the franchise to residents of the police jurisdiction argued for extending it infinitely further?

2. Professor James Gardner has argued that the Court's opinion in *Holt*

> entirely missed the point of the plaintiffs' claim. The plaintiffs were not trying to minimize the fact that they lived in a different community—that was precisely their point. The problem, in their view, was that they were governed by a political community different from the one to which they belonged. * * * While the Court was correct that the actions of one jurisdiction inevitably have some kind of "spillover" effect on neighboring jurisdictions, there is a significant difference between living *with* neighbors and living *under* those neighbors—the difference between comity under independent self-government and outright political subjection.

James A. Gardner, *Liberty, Community and the Constitutional Structure of Political Influence: A Reconsideration of the Right to Vote*, 145 U. Pa. L. Rev. 893, 910–11 (1997). Do you agree?

3. If some line must be drawn based on residence, was Alabama's choice rational? Would it pass strict scrutiny? What is the justification for tying voting rights to geography in the first place? Not everyone agrees that residence should be so important:

The Miami Herald won a Pulitzer Prize for an investigation proving that many of the ballots cast in the [1997] Miami city election were cast by people who did not, if you wanted to get picky about it, reside in Miami. The *Herald* contacted some of these people, who gave some truly wonderful, even heartwarming, explanations, including these, which I am not making up: * * *

A man who had moved to Hialeah, but continued to vote in Miami: "I've always felt more in tune with things in Miami than anywhere else. Look, I'm an American citizen and I feel you don't violate the law when you vote. It's my right as an American citizen."

Damn right! This is *America*, where a person has the fundamental right to vote in the municipality of his choosing, regardless of where he lives!

DAVE BARRY, DAVE BARRY HITS BELOW THE BELTWAY 145–46 (2001).

4. Can *Holt* be squared with *Kramer*? As Professor Gardner noted, "[c]ompared to the plaintiffs in *Holt*, the plaintiff in *Kramer* had a far less plausible claim that his inability to vote impaired in any significant way his ability to protect his rights and liberties from government infringement." Gardner, *supra*, at 911–12. Perhaps, though, Kramer was harmed by "the *fact* of his exclusion, not the *result* of it," in that the exclusion from voting itself signaled that Kramer—despite residing within the school district—was "not a member of the community." *Id.* at 912.

5. *Problem. Holt* gave controlling significance to the geographical limits of municipalities, and treated only residents as possessing a fundamental right to vote in municipal elections. How far should this principle extend? A South Dakota statute provides:

Every municipality shall have power to exercise jurisdiction for all authorized purposes over all territory within the corporate limits * * *, and in and over all places, except within the corporate limits of another municipality, within one mile of the corporate limits * * *, for the purpose of promoting the health, safety, morals, and general welfare of the community, and of enforcing its ordinances and resolutions relating thereto.

S.D. CODIFIED LAWS § 9-29-1. May South Dakota refuse to allow residents within one mile of municipalities to vote in municipal elections? Consider footnote 8 in *Holt*. *See Little Thunder v. South Dakota*, 518 F.2d 1253 (8th Cir. 1975) (holding unconstitutional a similar South Dakota law providing that "[t]he county commissioners of any organized county to which any unorganized county is attached shall have all of the jurisdiction, rights, powers, duties, and liabilities for the administration of the affairs of the unorganized county or counties which may be attached to said organized county as they may have in the organized county, excepting in cases where it is otherwise expressly provided by law.").

6. *Problem.* How are voting rights to be determined in instances where the whole point of voting is to establish municipal lines? Suppose a county is served by two

school districts. Residents seek to form a third district out of land formerly controlled by each of the two existing districts. If the question of the creation of the third district is put to the voters in a ballot measure, is it constitutional to limit the franchise to residents of the area that would be within the new district? *See City of Herriman v. Bell*, 590 F.3d 1176 (10th Cir. 2010).

7. *Problem.* Counties in Ohio contain townships, which themselves may contain municipal corporations, such as villages. Freeholders in townships containing municipal corporations may petition for the creation of a new township, excluding the municipal corporation. If a majority of freehold electors in the township, but outside the municipal corporation, so petitions, the Board of County Commissioners shall establish the new township. Thus, the group permitted to petition for the creation of the new township is limited to (1) freeholders (2) who own land in the township but outside the municipal corporation. Does this scheme violate the Equal Protection Clause by discriminating against either non-freehold residents or residents of the municipal corporation who are also residents of the existing township? As to each of the two limitations, should a court apply strict or rational-basis scrutiny? *See Board of Lucas County Commissioners v. Waterville Township Board of Trustees*, 870 N.E.2d 791 (Ohio Ct. App. 2007).

8. States may prohibit resident aliens — even permanent-resident aliens — from "basic governmental processes," such as voting, regardless of the aliens' interest in the outcome. As the Supreme Court has explained, "Self-government, whether direct or through representatives, begins by defining the scope of the community of the governed and thus of the governors as well: Aliens are by definition those outside of this community." *Cabell v. Chavez-Salido*, 454 U.S. 432, 439–40 (1982). *See Sugarman v. Dougall*, 413 U.S. 634, 649 (1975) ("[I]mplicit in many of this Court's voting rights decisions is the notion that citizenship is a permissible criterion for limiting such rights."); *Skafte v. Rorex*, 553 P.2d 830 (Colo. 1976). Of what relevance is § 2 of the Fourteenth Amendment, which reduces the representation of states that deny the vote to "any of the male inhabitants of such state, being twenty-one years of age, *and citizens of the United States* * * * except for participation in rebellion or other crime" (emphasis added)? *Cf. Richardson v. Ramirez*, 418 U.S. 24, 43 (1974) [p. 26] (upholding the disenfranchisement of felons); *Minor v. Happersett*, 88 U.S. (21 Wall.) 162, 174–75 (1875) (upholding the disenfranchisement of women).

9. The United States Constitution, though leaving the question of voter qualifications largely to the states, does restrict the voter pool in a significant respect: Only "the People of the several States" may select representatives and senators,[m] and only the states (and the District of Columbia, by virtue of the Twenty-Third Amendment)

---

m. *See Alexander v. Mineta*, 531 U.S. 940 (2000), *summarily aff'g Adams v. Clinton*, 90 F. Supp. 2d 35 (D.D.C. 2000) (holding that District of Columbia residents possess no constitutional right to elect congressional representatives). Territories and the District of Columbia do select *non-voting* delegates to Congress, however.

have the privilege of appointing members of the electoral college. Accordingly, residents of U.S. territories, though they may be U.S. citizens, are not entitled to vote in presidential elections, or to select voting members of Congress. "That the franchise for choosing electors is confined to 'states' cannot be 'unconstitutional' because it is what the Constitution itself provides. Hence it does no good to stress how important is 'the right to vote' for President." *Igartúa-de la Rosa v. United States*, 417 F.3d 145, 148 (1st Cir. 2005).[n]

Might one argue that the Fifth Amendment, with its Due Process Clause and "equal protection component," superseded the original Constitution's restriction of the vote to state residents? Such an argument would presumably require the national government to provide the vote to "all persons" in territories, rather than to U.S. citizens alone, because the Fifth Amendment does not limit its protections to citizens. By the same reasoning, however, the Seventeenth Amendment's provision for the direct election of U.S. senators from "each State" would appear to trump any equal-protection norm contained in the Fifth Amendment as to the composition of the Senate.

10. Is it constitutional for Congress to grant voting rights to *former* residents of states, who have taken up residence in a foreign country? *See* Uniformed and Overseas Citizens Absentee Voting Act, 52 U.S.C. § 20310(5)(c) (requiring states to count the absentee votes of "person[s] who reside[] outside the United States and (but for such residence) would be qualified to vote in the last place in which the person[s] [were] domiciled before leaving the United States").

5. The Newly Resident

Pope v. Williams

Supreme Court of the United States
193 U.S. 621, 24 S. Ct. 573, 48 L. Ed. 817 (1904)

Statement by MR. JUSTICE PECKHAM: * * *

Plaintiff in error on September 29, 1903, presented his application to the board of registry of election district No. 7, Montgomery county, Maryland, * * * to be registered and entered as a qualified voter on the registry of voters of that election district, which application the board refused and declined to comply with, for the

---

n. *See also Attorney General of Territory of Guam v. United States*, 738 F.2d 1017 (9th Cir. 1984); Jamin B. Raskin, *Is This America? The District of Columbia and the Right to Vote*, 34 HARV. C.R.-C.L. L. REV. 39 (1999); Amber L. Cottle, Comment, *Silent Citizens: United States Territorial Residents and the Right to Vote in Presidential Elections*, 1995 U. CHI. LEGAL F. 315 (1995). For a similarly frivolous argument concerning *candidates* rather than voters, see *Lindsay v. Bowen*, 750 F.3d 1061 (9th Cir. 2014) (rejecting the argument of a twenty-seven year-old who claimed a constitutional right to be placed on the presidential ballot despite the Constitution's command that "[n]o Person * * * [shall] be eligible to [the presidency] who shall not have attained to the Age of thirty five Years, and been fourteen Years a Resident within the United States"). U.S. CONST. art II, § 1, cl. 5.

sole reason that he had not [registered with the clerk of the county's circuit court, as required by state law].{†} [Pope subsequently] alleged that he had, on June 7, 1902, with his wife and child, removed from the city of Washington, District of Columbia, into Montgomery county, in the state of Maryland, "having then had, and ever since and now having, the intention of making the state of Maryland the permanent domicil of himself and his family, and of becoming a citizen of said state[.]" * * *

[Pope argued that the statute violated the Constitution for three reasons: First, Pope alleged that the statute violated § 1 of the Fourteenth Amendment by failing to treat new residents as citizens of the state until the residents complied with the law. Second, he claimed that the statute violated the Equal Protection Clause. Third, he argued that the statute unreasonably burdened the ability to travel and migrate interstate.] * * *

MR. JUSTICE PECKHAM, after making the above statement of facts, delivered the opinion of the court [in which MR. CHIEF JUSTICE FULLER, MR. JUSTICE HARLAN, MR. JUSTICE BREWER, MR. JUSTICE BROWN, MR. JUSTICE WHITE, MR. JUSTICE McKENNA, MR. JUSTICE HOLMES, and MR. JUSTICE DAY join]: * * *

* * * The simple matter to be herein determined is whether, with reference to the exercise of the privilege of voting in Maryland, the legislature of that state had the legal right to provide that a person coming into the state to reside should make the declaration of intent a year before he should have the right to be registered as a voter of the state.

The privilege to vote in any state is not given by the Federal Constitution, or by any of its amendments. It is not a privilege springing from citizenship of the United States. It may not be refused on account of race, color, or previous condition of servitude, but it does not follow from mere citizenship of the United States. In other words, the privilege to vote in a state is within the jurisdiction of the state itself, to be exercised as the state may direct, and upon such terms as to it may seem proper, provided, of course, no discrimination is made between individuals, in violation of the Federal Constitution. The state might provide that persons of foreign birth could vote without being naturalized, and * * * such persons were allowed to vote in several of the states upon having declared their intentions to become citizens of the United States. Some states permit women to vote; others refuse them that privilege. A state, so far as the Federal Constitution is concerned, might provide by its

---

† * * * "All persons who * * * shall remove into any county of this state or into the city of Baltimore from any other state, district, or territory, shall indicate their intent to become citizens and residents of this state by registering their names in a suitable record book, to be procured and kept for the purpose by the clerk of the circuit court for the several counties * * *; such record to contain their names, residence, age, and occupation * * *. And no person coming into this state from any other state, district, or territory shall be entitled to registration as a legal voter of this state until one year after his intent to become such legal voter shall be thus evidenced by such entry in such record book[.] * * *"

own constitution and laws that none but native-born citizens should be permitted to vote, as the Federal Constitution does not confer the right of suffrage upon any one, and the conditions under which that right is to be exercised are matters for the states alone to prescribe, subject to the conditions of the Federal Constitution, already stated; although it may be observed that the right to vote for a member of Congress is not derived exclusively from the state law. *See* Fed. Const. art. 1, § 2. But the elector must be one entitled to vote under the state statute. In this case no question arises as to the right to vote for electors of President and Vice President, and no decision is made thereon. The question whether the conditions prescribed by the state might be regarded by others as reasonable or unreasonable is not a Federal one. We do not wish to be understood, however, as intimating that the condition in this statute is unreasonable or in any way improper.

We are unable to see any violation of the Federal Constitution in the provision of the state statute for the declaration of the intent of a person coming into the state before he can claim the right to be registered as a voter. The statute * * * is neither an unlawful discrimination against any one in the situation of the plaintiff in error nor does it deny to him the equal protection of the laws, nor is it repugnant to any fundamental or inalienable rights of citizens of the United States, nor a violation of any implied guaranties of the Federal Constitution. The right of a state to legislate upon the subject of the elective franchise as to it may seem good, subject to the conditions already stated, being, as we believe, unassailable, we think it plain that the statute in question violates no right protected by the Federal Constitution. * * *

[T]he judgment of the Court of Appeals of Maryland is, therefore,

Affirmed.

Carrington v. Rash

Supreme Court of the United States
380 U.S. 89, 85 S. Ct. 775, 13 L. Ed. 2d 675 (1965)

Mr. Justice Stewart delivered the opinion of the Court [in which Mr. Justice Black, Mr. Justice Douglas, Mr. Justice Clark, Mr. Justice Brennan, Mr. Justice White, and Mr. Justice Goldberg join].

A provision of the Texas Constitution prohibits "[a]ny member of the Armed Forces of the United States" who moves his home to Texas during the course of his military duty from ever voting in any election in that State "so long as he or she is a member of the Armed Forces." The question presented is whether this provision * * * deprives the petitioner of a right secured by the Equal Protection Clause of the Fourteenth Amendment. * * *

The petitioner, a sergeant in the United States Army, entered the service from Alabama in 1946 at the age of 18. The State concedes that he has been domiciled in Texas since 1962, and that he intends to make his home there permanently. He has purchased a house in El Paso where he lives with his wife and two children. He is also the proprietor of a small business there. The petitioner's post of military duty is not in Texas, but at White Sands, New Mexico. He regularly commutes from his home in El Paso to his Army job at White Sands. He pays property taxes in Texas and has his automobile registered there. But for his uniform, the State concedes that the petitioner would be eligible to vote in El Paso County, Texas.

Texas has unquestioned power to impose reasonable residence restrictions on the availability of the ballot. There can be no doubt either of the historic function of the States to establish, on a nondiscriminatory basis, and in accordance with the Constitution, other qualifications for the exercise of the franchise. * * *

This Texas constitutional provision, however, is unique.[3] Texas has said that no serviceman may ever acquire a voting residence in the State so long as he remains in service. It is true that the State has treated all members of the military with an equal hand. * * * But the fact that a State is dealing with a distinct class and treats the members of that class equally does not end the judicial inquiry. * * *

It is argued that this absolute denial of the vote to servicemen like the petitioner fulfills two purposes. First, the State says it has a legitimate interest in immunizing its elections from the concentrated balloting of military personnel, whose collective voice may overwhelm a small local civilian community. Secondly, the State says it has a valid interest in protecting the franchise from infiltration by transients, and it can reasonably assume that those servicemen who fall within the constitutional exclusion will be within the State for only a short period of time.

The theory underlying the State's first contention is that the Texas constitutional provision is necessary to prevent the danger of a "takeover" of the civilian community resulting from concentrated voting by large numbers of military personnel in bases placed near Texas towns and cities. A base commander, Texas suggests, who opposes local police administration or teaching policies in local schools, might influence his men to vote in conformity with his predilections. Local bond issues may fail, and property taxes stagnate at low levels because military personnel are unwilling to invest in the future of the area. We stress—and this a theme to be reiterated—that Texas has the right to require that all military personnel enrolled to vote be bona fide residents of the community. But if they are in fact residents, with the intention of making Texas their home indefinitely, they, as all other qualified residents, have a right to an equal opportunity for political representation. "Fencing out" from the franchise a sector of the population because of the way they may vote is constitutionally impermissible. "[T]he exercise of rights so vital to the maintenance of democratic institutions" cannot constitutionally be obliterated because of a fear of the political views of a particular group of bona fide residents. Yet, that is what Texas claims to have done here.

---

3. While many States have rules which prescribe special tests for qualifying military personnel for the vote, none goes so far as completely to foreclose from the franchise all servicemen who were nonresidents before induction.

The State's second argument is that its voting ban is justified because of the transient nature of service in the Armed Forces. * * * The Texas Constitution provides that a United States citizen can become a qualified elector if he has "resided in this State one (1) year next preceding an election and the last six (6) months within the district or county in which such person offers to vote." It is the integrity of this qualification of residence which Texas contends is protected by the voting ban on members of the Armed Forces.

But only where military personnel are involved has Texas been unwilling to develop more precise tests to determine the bona fides of an individual claiming to have actually made his home in the State long enough to vote. The State's law reports disclose that there have been many cases where the local election officials have determined the issue of bona fide residence. * * * By statute, Texas deals with particular categories of citizens who, like soldiers, present specialized problems in determining residence. Students at colleges and universities in Texas, patients in hospitals and other institutions within the State, and civilian employees of the United States Government may be as transient as military personnel. But all of them are given at least an opportunity to show the election officials that they are bona fide residents. * * *

We deal here with matters close to the core of our constitutional system. * * * States may not casually deprive a class of individuals of the vote because of some remote administrative benefit to the State. By forbidding a soldier ever to controvert the presumption of non-residence, the Texas Constitution imposes an invidious discrimination in violation of the Fourteenth Amendment. * * *

Reversed.

The Chief Justice [Warren] took no part in the consideration or decision of this case.

Mr. Justice Harlan, dissenting. * * *

I deplore the added impetus which this decision gives to the current tendency of judging constitutional questions on the basis of abstract "justice" unleashed from the limiting principles that go with our constitutional system. Constitutionally principled adjudication, high in the process of which is due recognition of the just demands of federalism, leaves ample room for the protection of individual rights. A constitutional democracy which in order to cope with seeming needs of the moment is willing to temporize with its basic distribution and limitation of governmental powers will sooner or later find itself in trouble. * * *

* * * The question here is simply whether the differentiation in voting eligibility requirements which Texas has made is founded on a rational classification. In judging this question I think that the dictates of history, even though the Court has seen fit to disregard them for the purpose of determining whether it should get into

the matter at all, should cause the Court to take a hard look before striking down a traditional state policy in this area as rationally indefensible.

Essentially the Texas statute establishes a rule that servicemen from other States stationed at Texas bases are to be treated as transients for voting purposes. No one disputes that in the vast majority of cases Texas' view of things accords with fact. Although it is doubtless true that this rule may operate in some instances contrary to the actual facts, I do not think that the Federal Constitution prevents the State from ignoring that possibility in the overall picture. In my opinion Texas could rationally conclude that such instances would likely be too minimal to justify the administrative expenditure involved in coping with the "special problems" entailed in winnowing out the bona fide permanent residents from among the transient servicemen living off base and sending their children to local schools.

Beyond this, I think a legitimate distinction may be drawn between those who come voluntarily into Texas in connection with private occupations and those ordered into Texas by military authority. Residences established by the latter are subject to the doubt, not present to the same degree with the former, that when the military compulsion ends, so also may the desire to remain in Texas.

And finally, I think that Texas, given the traditional American notion that control of the military should always be kept in civilian hands * * *, could rationally decide to protect state and local politics against the influences of military voting strength by, in effect, postponing the privilege of voting otherwise attaching to a service-acquired domicile until the serviceman becomes a civilian and by limiting Texas servicemen to voting in the counties of their original domicile. Such a policy on Texas' part may seem to many unduly provincial in light of modern conditions, but it cannot, in my view, be said to be unconstitutional. * * *

Dunn v. Blumstein

Supreme Court of the United States
405 U.S. 330, 92 S. Ct. 995, 31 L. Ed. 2d 274 (1972)

MR. JUSTICE MARSHALL delivered the opinion of the Court [in which MR. JUSTICE DOUGLAS, MR. JUSTICE BRENNAN, MR. JUSTICE STEWART, and MR. JUSTICE WHITE join].

* * * [Appellee James] Blumstein moved to Tennessee on June 12, 1970, to begin employment as an assistant professor of law at Vanderbilt University in Nashville. With an eye toward voting in the upcoming August and November elections, he attempted to register to vote on July 1, 1970. The county registrar refused to register him, on the ground that Tennessee law authorizes the registration of only those persons who, at the time of the next election, will have been residents of the State for a year and residents of the county for three months. * * *

I

* * * Appellee does not challenge Tennessee's power to restrict the vote to bona fide Tennessee residents. Nor has Tennessee ever disputed that appellee was a bona fide resident of the State and county when he attempted to register. But Tennessee insists that, in addition to *being* a resident, a would-be voter must *have been* a resident for a year in the State and three months in the county. It is this additional *durational* residence requirement that appellee challenges.

Durational residence laws penalize those persons who have traveled from one place to another to establish a new residence during the qualifying period. Such laws divide residents into two classes, old residents and new residents, and discriminate against the latter to the extent of totally denying them the opportunity to vote. The constitutional question presented is whether the Equal Protection Clause of the Fourteenth Amendment permits a State to discriminate in this way among its citizens.

* * * In considering laws challenged under the Equal Protection Clause, this Court has evolved more than one test, depending upon the interest affected or the classification involved. First, then, we must determine what standard of review is appropriate. In the present case, whether we look to the benefit withheld by the classification (the opportunity to vote) or the basis for the classification (recent interstate travel) we conclude that * * * durational residence laws must be measured by a strict equal protection test: they are unconstitutional unless the State can demonstrate that such laws are "*necessary* to promote a *compelling* governmental interest." * * *

It is not sufficient for the State to show that durational residence requirements further a very substantial state interest. In pursuing that important interest, the State cannot choose means that unnecessarily burden or restrict constitutionally protected activity. Statutes affecting constitutional rights must be drawn with "precision," and must be "tailored" to serve their legitimate objectives. And if there are other, reasonable ways to achieve those goals with a lesser burden on constitutionally protected activity, a State may not choose the way of greater interference. If it acts at all, it must choose "less drastic means."

II

We turn, then, to the question of whether the State has shown that durational residence requirements are needed to further a sufficiently substantial state interest. We emphasize again the difference between bona fide residence requirements and durational residence requirements. We have in the past noted approvingly that the States have the power to require that voters be bona fide residents of the relevant political subdivision.[7] An appropriately defined and uniformly applied

---

7. Appellants * * * rely on *Pope v. Williams*, 193 U.S. 621 (1904) [p. 69]. Carefully read, that case simply *holds* that federal constitutional rights are not violated by a state provision requiring

requirement of bona fide residence may be necessary to preserve the basic conception of a political community, and therefore could withstand close constitutional scrutiny. But *durational* residence requirements, representing a separate voting qualification imposed on bona fide residents, must be separately tested by the stringent standard. * * *

Tennessee tenders "two basic purposes" served by its durational residence requirements:

> "(1) INSURE PURITY OF BALLOT BOX—Protection against fraud through colonization and inability to identify persons offering to vote, and
>
> "(2) KNOWLEDGEABLE VOTER—Afford some surety that the voter has, in fact, become a member of the community and that as such, he has a common interest in all matters pertaining to its government and is, therefore, more likely to exercise his right more intelligently."

We consider each in turn.

A

Preservation of the "purity of the ballot box" is a formidable-sounding state interest. The impurities feared, variously called "dual voting" and "colonization," all involve voting by nonresidents, either singly or in groups. The main concern is that nonresidents will temporarily invade the State or county, falsely swear that they are residents to become eligible to vote, and, by voting, allow a candidate to win by fraud. Surely the prevention of such fraud is a legitimate and compelling government goal. But it is impossible to view durational residence requirements as necessary to achieve that state interest. * * *

Durational residence laws may once have been necessary to prevent a fraudulent evasion of state voter standards, but today in Tennessee, as in most other States, this purpose is served by a system of voter registration. Given this system, the record is totally devoid of any evidence that durational residence requirements are in fact necessary to identify bona fide residents. The qualifications of the would-be voter in Tennessee are determined when he registers to vote, which he may do until 30 days before the election. His qualifications—including bona fide residence—are established then by oath. There is no indication in the record that Tennessee routinely goes behind the would-be voter's oath to determine his qualifications. Since false swearing is no obstacle to one intent on fraud, the existence of burdensome voting qualifications like durational residence requirements cannot prevent corrupt nonresidents from fraudulently registering and voting. As long as the State relies on the oath-swearing system to establish qualifications, a durational residence requirement

---

a person who enters the State to make a "declaration of his intention to become a citizen before he can have the right to be registered as a voter and to vote in the state." In other words, the case simply stands for the proposition that a State may require voters to be bona fide residents. To the extent that dicta in that opinion are inconsistent with the test we apply or the result we reach today, those dicta are rejected.

adds nothing to a simple residence requirement in the effort to stop fraud. The non-resident intent on committing election fraud will as quickly and effectively swear that he has been a resident for the requisite period of time as he would swear that he was simply a resident. Indeed, the durational residence requirement becomes an effective voting obstacle only to residents who tell the truth and have no fraudulent purposes.

Moreover, to the extent that the State makes an enforcement effort after the oath is sworn, it is not clear what role the durational residence requirement could play in protecting against fraud. * * * As long as the State permits registration up to 30 days before an election, a lengthy durational residence requirement does not increase the amount of time the State has in which to carry out an investigation into the sworn claim by the would-be voter that he is in fact a resident.

* * * Fixing a constitutionally acceptable period is surely a matter of degree. It is sufficient to note here that 30 days appears to be an ample period of time for the State to complete whatever administrative tasks are necessary to prevent fraud — and a year, or three months, too much. This was the judgment of Congress in the context of presidential elections.° And, on the basis of the statutory scheme before us, it is almost surely the judgment of the Tennessee lawmakers as well. * * *

---

o. In 1970, Congress amended the Voting Rights Act to prohibit durational-residency require-ments for presidential elections. *See* 52 U.S.C. § 10502(c). Further, the amendment required states to accept registrants until thirty days prior to an election. *See* 52 U.S.C. § 10502(d). Congress declared that durational-residency requirements, as applied to presidential elections, "den[y] or abridge[] the inherent constitutional right of citizens to vote for their President and Vice President," "den[y] or abridge[] the inherent constitutional right of citizens to enjoy their free movement across State lines," violate the Privileges and Immunities Clause of Article IV, have "the effect" of denying rights protected by the Fourteenth Amendment, and "do[] not bear a reasonable relationship to any compelling State interest in the conduct of presidential elections." 52 U.S.C. § 10502(a).

Congress also stated that a durational-residency requirement in presidential elections "in some instances has the impermissible purpose or effect of denying citizens the right to vote for such offi-cers because of the way they may vote." 52 U.S.C. § 10502(a)(4). It may appear odd to say that a law or policy may create an "effect . . . *because of* the way [new residents] may vote" (emphasis added) without having the "purpose" of so doing. *See Texas Dep't of Housing & Community Affairs v. Inclu-sive Communities Project*, 135 S. Ct. 2507, 2536 (2015) (Alito, J., dissenting) ("In ordinary English usage, when a person [acts] 'because of' some factor, that factor must be a reason for the act."). The Supreme Court, however, has interpreted similar language in other antidiscrimination laws not to require a discriminatory purpose. *See id*. at 2523 (opinion of the Court) (interpreting §§ 804(a) and 805(a) of the Fair Housing Act, 42 U.S.C. §§ 3604(a), 3605(a), which outlaw housing discrimina-tion "because of race [and other prohibited characteristics]" to prohibit the use of factors that have a discriminatory impact on racial minorities unless necessary to achieve a valid interest); *Smith v. City of Jackson, Mississippi*, 544 U.S. 228 (2005) (plurality opinion) (interpreting § 4(a)(2) of the Age Discrimination in Employment Act, 29 U.S.C. § 623(a)(2), which prohibits discrimination "because of [an employee's] age," to impose liability on employers for policies that produce a dis-parate impact on older workers, even in the absence of a discriminatory purpose); *Griggs v. Duke Power Co.*, 401 U.S. 424 (1971) (interpreting § 703(a)(2) of Title VII of the Civil Rights Act of 1964, 42 U.S.C. § 2000e2(a), which prohibits discrimination "because of [an employee's] race, color, reli-gion, sex, or national origin," to impose liability on employers for policies that produce disparate impacts on racial minorities). —Eds.

B * * *

[The State argues that in pursuing its goal of having "knowledgeable voters,"] it may require a period of residence sufficiently lengthy to impress upon its voters the local viewpoint. This is precisely the sort of argument this Court has repeatedly rejected. In *Carrington* v. *Rash*, for example, the State argued that military men newly moved into Texas might not have local interests sufficiently in mind, and therefore could be excluded from voting in state elections. This Court replied:

> "But if they are in fact residents, . . . they, as all other qualified residents, have a right to an equal opportunity for political representation. . . . 'Fencing out' from the franchise a sector of the population because of the way they may vote is constitutionally imper missible." 380 U.S. [89], 94 [(1965)] [p. 71].

Similarly here, Tennessee's hopes for voters with a "common interest in all matters pertaining to [the community's] government" is impermissible.[27] To paraphrase what we said elsewhere, "All too often, lack of a ['common interest'] might mean no more than a different interest." "[D]ifferences of opinion" may not be the basis for excluding any group or person from the franchise. "[T]he fact that newly arrived [Tennesseeans] may have a more national outlook than longtime residents, or even may retain a viewpoint characteristic of the region from which they have come, is a constitutionally impermissible reason for depriving them of their chance to influence the electoral vote of their new home State."

Finally, * * * Tennessee argues that people who have been in the State less than a year and the county less than three months are likely to be unaware of the issues involved in the congressional, state, and local elections, and therefore can be barred from the franchise. We note that the criterion of "intelligent" voting is an elusive one, and susceptible of abuse. But without deciding as a general matter the extent to which a State can bar less knowledgeable or intelligent citizens from the franchise, we conclude that durational residence requirements cannot be justified on this basis. * * *

[T]he durational residence requirements in this case founder because of their crudeness as a device for achieving the articulated state goal of assuring the knowledgeable exercise of the franchise. The classifications created by durational residence requirements obviously permit any longtime resident to vote regardless of his knowledge of the issues—and obviously many longtime residents do not have any. On the other hand, the classifications bar from the franchise many other, admittedly new, residents who have become at least minimally, and often fully, informed

---

27. It has been noted elsewhere, and with specific reference to Tennessee law, that "[t]he historical purpose of [durational] residency requirements seems to have been to deny the vote to undesirables, immigrants and outsiders with different ideas." We do not rely on this alleged original purpose of durational residence requirements in striking them down today.

about the issues. Indeed, recent migrants who take the time to register and vote shortly after moving are likely to be those citizens, such as appellee, who make it a point to be informed and knowledgeable about the issues. Given modern communications, and given the clear indication that campaign spending and voter education occur largely during the month before an election, the State cannot seriously maintain that it is "necessary" to reside for a year in the State and three months in the county in order to be knowledgeable about congressional, state, or even purely local elections. * * *

It is pertinent to note that Tennessee has never made an attempt to further its alleged interest in an informed electorate in a universally applicable way. Knowledge or competence has never been a criterion for participation in Tennessee's electoral process for longtime residents. * * * If the State seeks to assure intelligent use of the ballot, it may not try to serve this interest only with respect to new arrivals.

It may well be true that new residents as a group know less about state and local issues than older residents; and it is surely true that durational residence requirements will exclude some people from voting who are totally uninformed about election matters. But as devices to limit the franchise to knowledgeable residents, the conclusive presumptions of durational residence requirements are much too crude. They exclude too many people who should not, and need not, be excluded. * * * We are aware that classifications are always imprecise. By requiring classifications to be tailored to their purpose, we do not secretly require the impossible. Here, there is simply too attenuated a relationship between the state interest in an informed electorate and the fixed requirement that voters must have been residents in the State for a year and the county for three months. Given the exacting standard of precision we require of statutes affecting constitutional rights, we cannot say that durational residence requirements are necessary to further a compelling state interest. * * *

Affirmed.

MR. JUSTICE POWELL and MR. JUSTICE REHNQUIST took no part in the consideration or decision of this case.

MR. JUSTICE BLACKMUN, concurring in the result.

I cannot so blithely explain *Pope* v. *Williams* away, as does the Court, by asserting that if that opinion is "[c]arefully read," one sees that the case was concerned simply with a requirement that the new arrival declare his intention. The requirement was that he make the declaration *a year* before he registered to vote; time as well as intent was involved. For me, therefore, the Court today really overrules the holding in *Pope* v. *Williams* and does not restrict itself, as footnote 7 says, to rejecting what it says are mere dicta. * * *

The Tennessee plan, based both in statute and in the State's constitution, is not ideal. I am content that the one-year and three-month requirements be struck down for want of something more closely related to the State's interest. It is, of course, a matter of line drawing, as the Court concedes. But if 30 days pass constitutional muster, what of 35 or 45 or 75? The resolution of these longer measures, less than those today struck down, the Court leaves, I suspect, to the future.

Mr. Chief Justice Burger, dissenting.

The holding of the Court in *Pope* v. *Williams* is as valid today as it was at the turn of the century. It is no more a denial of equal protection for a State to require newcomers to be exposed to state and local problems for a reasonable period such as one year before voting, than it is to require children to wait 18 years before voting. In both cases some informed and responsible persons are denied the vote, while others less informed and less responsible are permitted to vote. Some lines must be drawn. To challenge such lines by the "compelling state interest" standard is to condemn them all. So far as I am aware, no state law has ever satisfied this seemingly insurmountable standard, and I doubt one ever will, for it demands nothing less than perfection.

The existence of a constitutional "right to travel" does not persuade me to the contrary. If the imposition of a durational residency requirement for voting abridges the right to travel, surely the imposition of an age qualification penalizes the young for being young, a status I assume the Constitution also protects.

Notes and Questions

1. Recall the discussion, earlier in this Chapter, of felon disenfranchisement. Is there a constitutionally significant difference between the attempt to exclude outside influences in *Carrington* and *Blumstein*, on the one hand, and the attempt to limit the political influence of criminals, on the other?

2. *Carrington* and *Blumstein* establish that states must allow bona-fide residents to vote, and cannot conclusively presume that certain categories of persons lack an intent to remain in the state permanently. Nevertheless, many college students and persons serving in the military intend to move elsewhere upon graduation or termination of their military service. How may a state identify which individuals within those classes intend to establish permanent residency? In *Symm v. United States*, 439 U.S. 1105 (1979), the Court summarily affirmed a lower-court judgment that held unconstitutional Waller County, Texas's, use of a residency questionnaire. The County, which is the home of Prairie View A&M University, a predominantly black institution, distributed the questionnaire to persons registering to vote. The questionnaire asked whether the applicant was a college student. Those applicants answering in the affirmative were then asked follow-up questions:

[W]here do you attend school? How long have you been a student at such school? Where do you live while in college? How long have you lived in Texas? In Waller County? Do you intend to reside in Waller County indefinitely? How long have you considered yourself to be a bona fide resident of Waller County? What do you plan to do when you finish your college education? Do you have a job or position in Waller County? Own any home or other property in Waller County? Have an automobile registered in Waller County? Have a telephone listing in Waller County? Belong to a Church, Club or some Waller County Organization other than college related? If so, please name them[.] Where do you live when the college is not in session? What address is listed as your home address with the college? Give any other information which might be helpful:

United States v. Texas, 445 F. Supp. 1245, 1262 (S.D. Tex. 1978), *summarily aff'd*, 439 U.S. 1105 (1978). The official in charge of voter registration testified that he did not rely on any of these factors alone, but considered them together to determine residency. *Id.* at 1251. He further testified that "generally students are not regarded by him as residents unless they do something to qualify as permanent residents, such as marrying and living with their spouse or obtaining a promise of a job in Waller County when they complete school." *Id.* In what way(s) did Waller County's registration procedures violate the Constitution?

3. Generally speaking, people are able to vote in the place where they are domiciled, even if the state law governing eligibility speaks in terms of "residence." *See Wit v. Berman*, 306 F.3d 1256, 1261 (2d Cir. 2002); Annotation, *Residence of Students for Voting Purposes*, 44 A.L.R.3d 797 § 2, at 801 (1972). College students, however, typically do not intend to reside permanently in the place where they attend school, so they are not domiciliaries of their college towns, even if they are residents there. Should college students be able to vote where they temporarily live, even if they do not intend to stay after graduation? *See Hershkoff v. Board of Registrars of Voters of Worcester*, 321 N.E.2d 656 (Mass. 1974) (permitting students to establish a domicile in the place where they attend school). *See generally* John B. Graebe, *A Federal Baseline for the Right to Vote*, 112 Colum. L. Rev. Sidebar 62 (2012); Richard G. Niemi et al., *Where Can College Students Vote: A Legal and Empirical Perspective*, 8 Election L.J. 327 (2009).

Recently there has been controversy in New Hampshire about that state's attempt to delineate the residency requirements for voting. As a result of a 2015 ruling, college students and other non-permanent residents could be considered domiciliaries and thus qualified to vote, but might not be "residents" obligated to comply with other laws, such as ones requiring residents to register motor vehicles in the state and to obtain a state driver's license. *See Guare v. State*, 117 A.3d 731 (N.H. 2015). (Strangely, New Hampshire law provided that residents had to establish both domicile and an intent to remain "for the indefinite future." Domiciliaries, on the other hand, merely needed to show "a physical presence and . . . an intent to maintain a single continuous presence for domestic, social, and civil purposes relevant to participating in democratic self-government.") In response to the *Guare* decision, New Hampshire passed a law that re-defined "residence" by deleting "for the indefinite future," and thus making the definition of "residence" "effectively the same" as that of "domicile." *In re: Request of the Governor and Council*, 191 A.3d 1245, 1254 (N.H. 2018). Under the new law, anyone who has sufficient connection with the state to qualify that person to vote must also comply with the other obligations of state residency. The state supreme court upheld the constitutionality of the 2018 law by a 3-2 vote. *See In re: Request of the Governor and Council, supra.*

May a person establish a domicile in a place where he resides *involuntarily*, as by imprisonment or institutionalization? *See Dane v. Board of Registrars of Voters of Concord*, 371 N.E.2d 1358 (Mass. 1977) (permitting prisoners to establish a domicile in the place of incarceration, but establishing a rebuttable presumption that prisoners retain their former domiciles).

4. *Problem.* You are counsel to the city council in Sleepyville, a quiet city with a population that is mostly elderly. The state has decided to create a large new state university, and locate it in Sleepyville. The residents are concerned that if resident university students vote in local elections, their strength will overcome the votes of the long-term residents, with the result that zoning regulations will be relaxed to permit more bars, nightclubs, tattoo parlors, and the like. City ordinances establish the qualifications for voting in city elections. What can you do to minimize the likelihood that the university students will elect councilors with views in line with those of the students? Keep in mind that intentional discrimination against young voters may violate the Twenty-Sixth Amendment. *See League of Women Voters v. Detzner*, 314 F. Supp. 3d 1205 (N.D. Fla. 2018) (enjoining a ban on early voting at college or university campuses).

5. *Carrington* and *Blumstein* may lead one to believe that all but the most minimal registration requirements for voting will be subjected to strict scrutiny and invalidated. Not so. *Rosario v. Rockefeller*, 410 U.S. 752 (1973), upheld a requirement that persons wishing to vote in a primary election join the party before the preceding general election, *i.e.*, eight to eleven months before the primary election. The requirement was not designed to further the government's interest in guarding against voter registration fraud or ensuring that bureaucrats had sufficient time to compile the list of registered voters; rather, the purpose was to prevent "party raiding"—the practice of joining a party with which one disagrees, for the purpose of altering the results of its primary.

Congress has required states to accept voter registrations until thirty days before an election. 52 U.S.C. § 10502(d). As far as the Constitution is concerned, however, thirty days is not a magic number. *Marston v. Lewis*, 410 U.S. 679 (1973), decided two days before *Rosario* and one year after *Blumstein* (but with the participation of Justices Powell and Rehnquist), upheld Arizona's fifty-day durational-residency requirement, despite *Blumstein*'s dictum that thirty days would be sufficient time to manage the voter rolls. Arizona's situation was unusual, however: It relied on a system of volunteer deputy registrars whose mistakes needed to be corrected by professional staff. Given the practical difficulties that Arizona would have in processing all registrations within thirty days, the Court, 6-3, held that the fifty-day requirement was "necessary to permit preparation of accurate voter lists." *Id.* at 681. In dissent, Justice Marshall protested that Arizona's inability to process registrations within thirty days could be solved if the state hired more registrars and trained them properly. *Id.* at 682–83 (Marshall, J., dissenting).

In the modern Internet age, it is difficult to believe that any state would have an adequate excuse to close registrations more than thirty days before an election. More than twenty states permit same-day voter registration (that is, a voter can register and cast a ballot on the same day). The other states require voters to register between eight and thirty days before the election. *See* National Conference of State Legislatures, *Same Day Voter Registration*, *at* https://www.ncsl.org/research/elections-and -campaigns/same-day-registration.aspx. Despite technological advancements, it remains true that states may require registration up to thirty days in advance of the election. *See Luft v. Evers*, 963 F.3d 665, 675–76 (7th Cir. 2020) (upholding Wisconsin's twenty-eight-day rule).

6. Note that the materials in this portion of the Chapter involve durational-residency requirements for *voting*. The history of such requirements is detailed in Eugene D. Mazo, *Residency and Democracy: Durational Residency Requirements from the Framers to the Present*, 43 Fla. St. U. L. Rev. 611 (2016). Durational-residency requirements for *candidacy* for state office are subject to much less stringent constitutional review.[p] (Durational-residency requirements for federal office are unconstitutional because they add to the Constitution's exclusive list of qualifications for the

---

p. *See Sununu v. Stark*, 420 U.S. 958 (1975), *summarily aff'g* 383 F. Supp. 1287 (D.N.H. 1974) (upholding a seven-year durational-residency requirement for state senators); *Chimento v. Stark*, 414 U.S. 802 (1973), *summarily aff'g* 353 F. Supp. 1211 (D.N.H.) (upholding a seven-year durational-residency requirement for governor); *City of Akron v. Bell*, 660 F.2d 166 (6th Cir. 1981) (upholding a one-year durational-residency requirement for ward councilors); *Mobley v. Armstrong*, 978 S.W.2d 307 (Ky. 1998) (upholding a two-year durational-residency requirement for district judges); *Rivera v. Erie County Board of Elections*, 560 N.Y.S.2d 536 (App. Div. 1990) (upholding a one-year durational-residency requirement for members of the common council); *State ex rel. Brown v. Board of Elections*, 545 N.E.2d 1256 (Ohio 1989) (upholding two-year durational-residency requirement for city councilors); *White v. Manchin*, 318 S.E.2d 470 (W. Va. 1984) (upholding one-year durational-residency requirement for state senators). *But see Matthews v. City of Atlantic City*, 417 A.2d 1011 (N.J. 1980) (striking down a two-year durational-residency requirement for city commissioners in some New Jersey municipalities). *See also Schiavone v. Destefano*, 852 A.2d 862 (Conn. Super. Ct. 2001) (holding that a five-year residency requirement for mayor complied with the United States Constitution, but violated the Connecticut Constitution's Equal Protection Clause). *Compare Castner v. Homer*, 598 P.2d 953 (Alaska 1979) (upholding a durational-residency requirement of one year for city councilors), *with Peloza v. Freas*, 871 P.2d 687 (Alaska 1994) (striking down, under the state constitution, a different city's three-year durational-residency requirement for city councilors).

House and Senate, which require only habitation in the state at the time of election. *See* U.S. Const. art. I, §2, cl. 2; art. I, §3, cl. 3. *See also, e.g., Schaefer v. Townsend,* 215 F.3d 1031 (9th Cir. 2000); *cf. U.S. Term Limits, Inc. v. Thornton,* 514 U.S. 779 (1995) [p. 538].)

7. After studying this Chapter, do you agree with Professor Gardner's assessment "that the right to vote has become so indeterminate that every observer may see in it whatever he or she wishes"? James A. Gardner, *Liberty, Community and the Constitutional Structure of Political Influence: A Reconsideration of the Right to Vote,* 145 U. Pa. L. Rev. 893, 896 (1997).

Chapter 2

Redistricting and One Person, One Vote

A. Introduction

Under certain circumstances, federal and state courts will refuse to reach the merits of cases properly before them, on the basis that the case presents a "political question" more properly resolved by the other branches of government. Because the topics covered in this Casebook all involve "political" issues to varying degrees, the political-question doctrine has the potential, depending how broadly and rigorously it is applied, to prevent many election-law disputes from being resolved by the courts. Whether this result is good or bad depends on what one thinks about the appropriateness of courts deciding election issues.

The political-question doctrine in the federal courts has a venerable, if confusing and controversial, history. The doctrine can be traced back to no less than *Marbury v. Madison*, 5 U.S. (1 Cranch) 137, 170 (1803), in which Chief Justice John Marshall spoke of certain powers of the President lying in his sole discretion, beyond the control of courts. Challenges to the President's exercise of such discretionary authority presented "[q]uestions, in their nature political," unfit for judicial resolution. As the Court explained:

> Where the head of a department acts in a case, in which executive discretion is to be exercised; in which he is the mere organ of executive will; * * * any application to a court to control, in any respect, his conduct, would be rejected without hesitation.

> But where he is directed by law to do a certain act affecting the absolute rights of individuals, in the performance of which he is not placed under the particular direction of the President, and the performance of which, the President cannot lawfully forbid, and therefore is never presumed to have forbidden * * *, it is not perceived on what ground the courts of the country are further excused from the duty of giving judgment, that right be done to an injured individual, than if the same services were to be performed by a person not the head of a department.

Id. at 170–71.

The Supreme Court has since considered whether the political-question doctrine applies to issues beyond the unique facts presented in *Marbury*. Some of these cases involved various aspects of election law. Although the Court held that some such claims were justiciable, *see, e.g., Nixon v. Herndon*, 273 U.S. 536, 540 (1927) (holding racial discrimination in the Texas Democratic primary unconstitutional, and remarking that to invoke the political-question doctrine because the political process was at issue was "little more than a play upon words"), the Court has always been troubled that cases challenging the distribution of political power do not lend themselves to judicial resolution. The Court's doubts, as expressed in *Colegrove v. Green*, 328 U.S. 549 (1946) [p. 90] (plurality opinion), were overcome in *Baker v. Carr*, 369 U.S. 186 (1962) [p. 97], when the Court held that it had jurisdiction to resolve an equal-protection challenge to districts that varied wildly in population. Ever since, the Court has exercised jurisdiction in cases challenging malapportioned districts. *Baker* has become the Court's seminal case on the political-question doctrine because of its canonical distillation of the situations, discussed below, where the doctrine applies.

The doctrine has generated a large amount of scholarly commentary. Some writers defend it, arguing that federal judges should be able to exercise prudential judgment to avoid the merits of particularly difficult or contentious issues, which are better resolved by the other, more democratically accountable branches of government. *E.g.,* Alexander Bickel, The Least Dangerous Branch (1962). In contrast, other writers argue that the doctrine is an inappropriate and unprincipled exercise of authority by judges. On this account, the courts have a duty to reach the merits of cases properly before them, particularly when constitutional rights are involved, and the doctrine itself is based on "political" considerations that judges should not take into account. *E.g.,* Martin H. Redish, *Judicial Review and the Political Question*, 79 Nw. U. L. Rev. 1031 (1985). For a sample of the large scholarly literature, see Rachel E. Barkow, *More Supreme than Court? The Fall of the Political Question Doctrine*, 102 Colum. L. Rev. 237 (2002); Jesse Choper, *The Political Question Doctrine: Suggested Criteria*, 54 Duke L.J. 1457 (2005); Richard F. Fallon, Jr., *Judicially Manageable Standards and Constitutional Meaning*, 119 Harv. L. Rev. 1275 (2006). As you read the cases in the remainder of this Chapter, consider whether election cases are more or less likely to raise "political" questions than are cases in other fields, such as separation-of-powers conflicts between Congress and the President.

The political-question doctrine has also been applied by state courts considering legal challenges to the actions of other branches of the state government. To the extent they apply the doctrine, some states borrow the criteria developed in federal courts. But on the whole, the doctrine has been applied less robustly by many state courts, in part because state constitutions are typically much longer and more detailed than the Federal Constitution, and seem to call for more judicial interpretation and application of those provisions. Since most state judges are subject to periodic elections to attain or retain office, some have argued that the doctrine is less appropriate at the state level than at the federal level. *Compare* Helen Hershkoff, *State Courts and the "Passive Virtues": Rethinking the Judicial Function*, 114 Harv. L. Rev. 1833 (2001) (advancing such an argument), *with* Christine M. Durham, *The*

Judicial Branch in State Government: Parables of Law, Politics, and Power, 76 N.Y.U. L. Rev. 1601 (2001) (expressing skepticism of an activist role by state judiciaries). *See generally* Nat Stern, *Don't Answer That: Revisiting the Political Question Doctrine in State Courts*, 21 U. Pa. J. Const. L. 153 (2018).

Once *Baker v. Carr* held that districting challenges under the Equal Protection Clause could be adjudicated according to judicially manageable standards, the Court was forced to reach the merits of such challenges and to determine what constraints, if any, the Constitution placed on electoral districting. It took little time for the Court to provide an answer: *Reynolds v. Sims*, 377 U.S. 533 (1964) [p. 122], established the famous one-person, one-vote rule. Under that rule, both houses of state legislatures must be apportioned on a population basis, and all the districts of each house must be "as nearly of equal population as is practicable." *Id*. at 577. Although we are all familiar with the phrase "one person, one vote," states do not technically have an obligation to give all votes the same weight, in the sense of requiring that there be the same number of votes—or even voters—in each district. Rather, the Court has held that the Constitution is satisfied so long as districts have the same total population, even if the number of eligible or registered voters differs from district to district. *See Evenwel v. Abbott*, 578 U.S. __, 136 S. Ct. 1120 (2016) [p. 145].

Before the Court considered the mandate of the Equal Protection Clause in state-legislative districts in *Sims*, the Court was faced with two challenges to voting schemes in other contexts. In *Gray v. Sanders*, 372 U.S. 368 (1963) [p. 111], the Court held unconstitutional Georgia's scheme for selecting United States senators and statewide officers. Georgia had used a unit system that operated much like the federal electoral college. Because the electoral power of each county was not based solely on population, the system did not give each voter equal influence in the election. The Court held the unit system unconstitutional, reasoning that the state could not treat its voters unequally by effectively weighting votes from less populous counties more heavily than the votes from other counties.

Wesberry v. Sanders, 376 U.S. 1 (1964) [p. 116], considered a constitutional challenge to population differentials in congressional districts. Rather than relying on the Equal Protection Clause, however, *Wesberry* held that Article I, § 2's requirement that members of the House of Representatives be elected "by the People of the several States" "means that as nearly as is practicable one man's vote in a congressional election is to be worth as much as another's." *Id*. at 7–8.

Article I, § 2 obviously had no applicability to state-legislative districts, so *Reynolds v. Sims* rested the one-person, one-vote rule for those districts on the Equal Protection Clause. Under *Sims*, districts were to be "substantially equal" in population. 377 U.S. at 568. Immediately after *Sims*, however, it was (and to some extent it still remains) unclear what level of population inequality would qualify as "substantial," and what reasons a state could offer to justify population differentials. According to *Sims*,

> So long as the divergences from a strict population standard are based on legitimate considerations incident to the effectuation of a rational state

policy, some deviations from the equal-population principle are constitutionally permissible with respect to the apportionment of seats in either or both of the two houses of a bicameral state legislature. But neither history alone, nor economic or other sorts of group interests, are permissible factors in attempting to justify disparities from population-based representation.

Id. at 579–80 (footnote omitted). *Sims* suggested that one justification in particular—allowing political subdivisions to have representation by drawing district lines along municipal boundaries—might permit states to enjoy "[s]omewhat more flexibility . . . with respect to state legislative apportionment than in congressional districting." *Id.* at 578.

As in *Gray v. Sanders*, *Sims* rejected a districting plan resembling the system established in the Constitution for the national government. *Gray* rejected a system resembling the Constitution's allocation of votes in selecting the President; *Sims* rejected a system resembling the Constitution's creation of different constituencies for the two houses of Congress. The United States Senate, of course, is not based on population, as each state is allocated two senators. *See* U.S. Const. art. I, § 3, cl. 1. *Sims* held that Alabama could not similarly allocate one state senator to each county. In the Court's view, the United States Senate was a necessary compromise among formerly independent states, while Alabama's counties were merely convenient administrative units and did not need independent representation in the state legislature. *See Sims*, 377 U.S. at 571–77.

Mahan v. Howell, 410 U.S. 315 (1973) [p. 163], took up *Sims*'s suggestion that states may justify population disparities by citing a desire to allow political subdivisions some representation in state legislatures. *Howell* upheld Virginia's districting plan even though the districts varied in population by as much as 16.4%, reasoning that such a disparity was necessary for Virginia to allow its counties some influence in the state-legislative debates, especially regarding local legislation directed to particular political subdivisions.

By contrast, the Court has required states to justify even the smallest disparities in population between congressional districts. In *Kirkpatrick v. Preisler*, 394 U.S. 526 (1969) [p. 154], and *Karcher v. Daggett*, 462 U.S. 725 (1983), the Court struck down congressional districting plans where the population of the largest districts exceeded the population of the smallest by approximately 6% and 1%, respectively, but where the states failed to explain the need for even those differentials.

Similarly minuscule differences in state-legislative districts would not even make out a *prima facie* case of an equal-protection violation and, as a result, the state need not justify such population disparities. *See Gaffney v. Cummings*, 412 U.S. 735 (1973) [p. 168]. A small difference in the populations of state-legislative districts does not completely insulate them from challenge, however; as *Cox v. Larios*, 542 U.S. 947 (2004) [p. 175], shows, small disparities created to effectuate a partisan gerrymander will cause a plan to be struck down.

The nagging concerns about the judiciary's capacity to resolve districting cases were never completely resolved, however. While the Court came to accept its ability to decide apportionment on the basis of the easy-to-apply one-person, one-vote standard, it never settled on a judicially manageable standard for deciding cases alleging partisan gerrymandering—the practice of manipulating district lines to produce politically advantageous results even while adhering to one person, one vote. After decades of uncertainty, the Supreme Court finally concluded in *Rucho v. Common Cause*, 588 U.S. __, 139 S. Ct. 2484 (2019) [p. 180], that it lacked jurisdiction to adjudicate such claims.

The Court's attitude toward redistricting, then, has continued to center around the ideas about politics and judicial power that the Justices debated at the very outset of the "reapportionment revolution." That debate is enormously consequential in terms of politics, constitutional rights, and the proper role of the judiciary.

B. The Political Thicket

Article IV, §4 of the U.S. Constitution states that "[t]he United States shall guarantee to every State in this Union a Republican Form of Government." Beginning with the canonical decision in *Luther v. Borden*, 48 U.S. (7 How.) 1 (1849), the Supreme Court has held that federal courts cannot hear legal challenges to state governmental structures or processes on the ground that they violate the Guarantee Clause. *Luther* involved a series of changes to the state constitution of Rhode Island, which resulted in controversy and confusion about the proper governmental authority in that state. The case came before the Court due to a challenge to a search undertaken by a sheriff of the Rhode Island government. The challenger argued that the search was unlawful, since it was undertaken on behalf of a government that was not in a republican form. The Court held that the challenge was non-justiciable, since it was up to Congress to enforce the Guarantee Clause. *See id.* at 42. Among other things, the Court observed that there were no clear standards to determine whether a state's government was sufficiently republican to satisfy the Constitution. *See id.* at 45–46.

The Court subsequently held in *Pacific States Telephone & Telegraph Co. v. Oregon*, 223 U.S. 118 (1912), that challenges under the Guarantee Clause to the exercise of direct democracy would fail on political-question grounds. That case involved a challenge to Oregon's adoption of the initiative and referendum, a common reform during the Progressive Era, respectively permitting voters to enact laws (or amendments to state constitutions) by placing them on the ballot, or to review laws passed by the state legislature. These provisions, the argument ran, took power away from state legislatures and thus made Oregon's form of government democratic, rather than republican. Citing *Luther*, the Court dismissed the case for want of jurisdiction as a nonjusticiable political question. The challenge to a statute passed by initiative was of a "political nature," since it concerned the "framework and political character of the government." The Guarantee Clause, the Court held, reserved those issues for review by Congress. *Luther* and *Pacific States* did not, however, completely resolve the issue of judicial enforcement of the Clause, as the following cases indicate.

Colegrove v. Green

Supreme Court of the United States
328 U.S. 549, 66 S. Ct. 1198, 90 L. Ed. 1432 (1946)

Mr. Justice Frankfurter announced the judgment of the Court and an opinion in which Mr. Justice Reed and Mr. Justice Burton concur.

* * * [Appellants] are three qualified voters in Illinois districts which have much larger populations than other Illinois Congressional districts. They brought this suit against the Governor, the Secretary of State, and the Auditor of the State of Illinois, as members *ex officio* of the Illinois Primary Certifying Board, to restrain them, in effect, from taking proceedings for an election in November 1946, under the provisions of Illinois law governing Congressional districts. * * *

We are of opinion that the petitioners ask of this Court what is beyond its competence to grant. This is one of those demands on judicial power which cannot be met by verbal fencing about "jurisdiction." It must be resolved by considerations on the basis of which this Court, from time to time, has refused to intervene in controversies. It has refused to do so because due regard for the effective working of our Government revealed this issue to be of a peculiarly political nature and therefore not meet for judicial determination.

This is not an action to recover for damage because of the discriminatory exclusion of a plaintiff from rights enjoyed by other citizens. The basis for the suit is not a private wrong, but a wrong suffered by Illinois as a polity. Compare *Nixon v. Herndon*, 273 U.S. 536 [(1927)] and *Lane v. Wilson*, 307 U.S. 268 [(1939)], with *Giles v. Harris*, 189 U.S. 475 [(1903)]. In effect this is an appeal to the federal courts to reconstruct the electoral process of Illinois in order that it may be adequately represented in the councils of the Nation. Because the Illinois legislature has failed to revise its Congressional Representative districts in order to reflect great changes, during more than a generation, in the distribution of its population, we are asked to do this, as it were, for Illinois.

Of course no court can affirmatively re-map the Illinois districts so as to bring them more in conformity with the standards of fairness for a representative system. At best we could only declare the existing electoral system invalid. * * * Nothing is clearer than that this controversy concerns matters that bring courts into immediate and active relations with party contests. From the determination of such issues this Court has traditionally held aloof. It is hostile to a democratic system to involve the judiciary in the politics of the people. And it is not less pernicious if such judicial intervention in an essentially political contest be dressed up in the abstract phrases of the law.

The petitioners urge with great zeal that the conditions of which they complain are grave evils and offend public morality. The Constitution of the United States gives ample power to provide against these evils. But due regard for the Constitution as a viable system precludes judicial correction. Authority for dealing with such problems resides elsewhere. Article I, § 4 of the Constitution provides that "The Times, Places and Manner of holding Elections for . . . Representatives, shall be prescribed in each State by the Legislature thereof; but the Congress may at any time by Law make or alter such Regulations, . . ." The short of it is that the Constitution has conferred upon Congress exclusive authority to secure fair representation by the States in the popular House and left to that House determination whether States have fulfilled their responsibility. If Congress failed in exercising its powers, whereby standards of fairness are offended, the remedy ultimately lies with the people. Whether Congress faithfully discharges its duty or not, the subject has been committed to the exclusive control of Congress. An aspect of government from which the judiciary, in view of what is involved, has been excluded by the clear intention of the Constitution cannot be entered by the federal courts because Congress may have been in default in exacting from States obedience to its mandate.

The one stark fact that emerges from a study of the history of Congressional apportionment is its embroilment in politics, in the sense of party contests and party interests. The Constitution enjoins upon Congress the duty of apportioning Representatives "among the several States . . . according to their respective Numbers." Article I, § 2. Yet, Congress has at times been heedless of this command and not apportioned according to the requirements of the Census. It never occurred to anyone that this Court could issue mandamus to compel Congress to perform its mandatory duty to apportion. * * * Until 1842 there was the greatest diversity among the States in the manner of choosing Representatives because Congress had made no requirement for districting. 5 Stat. 491. Congress then provided for the election of Representatives by districts. Strangely enough the power to do so was seriously questioned; it was still doubted by a Committee of Congress as late as 1901. In 1850 Congress dropped the requirement. 9 Stat. 428, 432–33. The Reapportionment Act of 1862 required that the districts be of contiguous territory. 12 Stat. 572. In 1872 Congress added the requirement of substantial equality of inhabitants. 17 Stat. 28. This was reinforced in 1911. 37 Stat. 13, 14. But the 1929 Act * * * dropped these requirements. 46 Stat. 21. Throughout our history, whatever may have been the controlling Apportionment Act, the most glaring disparities have prevailed as to the contours and the population of districts. * * *

To sustain this action would cut very deep into the very being of Congress. Courts ought not to enter this political thicket. The remedy for unfairness in districting is to secure State legislatures that will apportion properly, or to invoke the ample powers of Congress. The Constitution has many commands that are not enforceable by courts because they clearly fall outside the conditions and purposes that circumscribe judicial action. Thus, "on Demand of the executive Authority," Art. IV, § 2, of a State it is the duty of a sister State to deliver up a fugitive from justice. But the fulfillment of this duty cannot be judicially enforced. *Kentucky* v. *Dennison*, [65 U.S.] 24 How. 66 [(1860)]. The duty to see to it that the laws are faithfully executed cannot be brought under legal compulsion. *Mississippi* v. *Johnson*, [71 U.S.] 4 Wall. 475 [(1866)]. Violation of the great guaranty of a republican form of government in States cannot be challenged in the courts. *Pacific States Telephone Co.* v. *Oregon*, 223 U.S. 118 [(1912)]. The Constitution has left the performance of many duties in our governmental scheme to depend on the fidelity of the executive and legislative action and, ultimately, on the vigilance of the people in exercising their political rights.

Dismissal of the complaint is affirmed.

Mr. Justice Jackson took no part in the consideration or decision of this case.

Mr. Justice Rutledge. * * *

[T]his complaint should be dismissed for [want of equity]. Assuming that the controversy is justiciable, I think the cause is of so delicate a character * * * that the jurisdiction should be exercised only in the most compelling circumstances. * * *

If the constitutional provisions on which appellants rely give them the substantive rights they urge, other provisions qualify those rights in important ways by vesting large measures of control in the political subdivisions of the Government and the state. There is not, and could not be except abstractly, a right of absolute equality in voting. At best there could be only a rough approximation. And there is obviously considerable latitude for the bodies vested with those powers to exercise their judgment concerning how best to attain this, in full consistency with the Constitution.

The right here is not absolute. And the cure sought may be worse than the disease.

I think, therefore, the case is one in which the Court may properly, and should, decline to exercise its jurisdiction. Accordingly, the judgment should be affirmed and I join in that disposition of the cause.

Mr. Justice Black, dissenting. * * *

It is difficult for me to see why the 1901 State Apportionment Act does not deny petitioners equal protection of the laws. The failure of the Legislature to reapportion the congressional election districts for forty years, despite census figures indicating great changes in the distribution of the population, has resulted in election districts the populations of which range from 112,000 to 900,000. One of the petitioners lives in a district of more than 900,000 people. His vote is consequently much less effective than that of each of the citizens living in the district of 112,000. And such a gross inequality in the voting power of citizens irrefutably demonstrates a complete lack of effort to make an equitable apportionment. The 1901 State Apportionment Act if applied to the next election would thus result in a wholly indefensible discrimination against petitioners and all other voters in heavily populated districts. The equal protection clause of the Fourteenth Amendment forbids such discrimination. It does not permit the states to pick out certain qualified citizens or groups of citizens and deny them the right to vote at all. See *Nixon* v. *Herndon*, 273 U.S. [at] 541; *Nixon* v. *Condon*, 286 U.S. 73 [(1932)]. No one would deny that the equal protection clause would also prohibit a law that would expressly give certain citizens a half-vote and others a full vote. The probable effect of the 1901 State Apportionment Act in the coming election will be that certain citizens, and among them the appellants, will in some instances have votes only one-ninth as effective in choosing representatives to Congress as the votes of other citizens. Such discriminatory legislation seems to me exactly the kind that the equal protection clause was intended to prohibit.

The 1901 State Apportionment Act in reducing the effectiveness of appellants' votes abridges their privilege as citizens to vote for Congressmen and violates Article I of the Constitution. Article I provides that Congressmen "shall be . . . chosen . . . by the People of the several States." It thus gives those qualified a right to vote and a right to have their vote counted. *Ex parte Yarbrough*, 110 U.S. 651 [(1884)]; *United States* v. *Mosley*, 238 U.S. 383 [(1915)]. This Court in order to prevent "an interference with the effective choice of the voters" has held that this right extends to primaries. *United States* v. *Classic*, 313 U.S. 299, 314 [(1941)]. While the Constitution contains no express provision requiring that Congressional election districts established by the States must contain approximately equal populations, the constitutionally guaranteed right to vote and the right to have one's vote counted clearly imply the policy that state election systems, no matter what their form, should be designed to give approximately equal weight to each vote cast. To some extent this implication of Article I is expressly stated by § 2 of the Fourteenth Amendment which provides that "Representatives shall be apportioned among the several States according to their respective numbers . . ." The purpose of this requirement is obvious: It is to make the votes of the citizens of the several States equally effective in the selection of members of Congress. It was intended to make illegal a nation-wide "rotten borough" system as between the States. The policy behind it is broader than that. It prohibits as well Congressional "rotten boroughs" within the States, such as the ones here involved. The policy is that which is laid down by all the Constitutional provisions regulating the election of members of the House of Representatives, including Article I which guarantees the right to vote and to have that vote effectively counted: All groups, classes, and individuals shall to the extent that it is practically feasible be given equal representation in the House of Representatives, which, in conjunction with the Senate, writes the laws affecting the life, liberty, and property of all the people. * * *

Had Illinois passed an Act requiring that all of its twenty-six Congressmen be elected by the citizens of one county, it would clearly have amounted to a denial to the citizens of the other counties of their Constitutionally guaranteed right to vote. And I cannot imagine that an Act that would have apportioned twenty-five

Congressmen to the State's smallest county and one Congressman to all the others, would have been sustained by any Court. Such an Act would clearly have violated the constitutional policy of equal representation. The 1901 Apportionment Act here involved violates that policy in the same way. The policy with respect to federal elections laid down by the Constitution, while it does not mean that the courts can or should prescribe the precise methods to be followed by state legislatures and the invalidation of all Acts that do not embody those precise methods, does mean that state legislatures must make real efforts to bring about approximately equal representation of citizens in Congress. Here the legislature of Illinois has not done so. Whether that was due to negligence or was a wilful effort to deprive some citizens of an effective vote, the admitted result is that the Constitutional policy of equality of representation has been defeated. Under these circumstances it is the Court's duty to invalidate the state law.

It is contended, however, that a court of equity does not have the power, or even if it has the power, that it should not exercise it in this case. To do so, it is argued, would mean that the Court is entering the area of "political questions." I cannot agree with that argument. * * *

It is true that voting is a part of elections and that elections are "political." But as this Court said in *Nixon* v. *Herndon, supra,* it is a mere "play on words" to refer to a controversy such as this as "political" in the sense that courts have nothing to do with protecting and vindicating the right of a voter to cast an effective ballot. * * *

MR. JUSTICE DOUGLAS and MR. JUSTICE MURPHY join in this dissent.

Notes and Questions

1. Does (or should) *Luther v. Borden* stand for the proposition that *all* Guarantee Clause claims are non-justiciable in federal court? If so, why weren't *Pacific States* and *Colegrove* disposed of in short opinions citing *Luther*? Are *Pacific States* and *Colegrove* more difficult to resolve than *Luther*? Is it relevant to the more recent cases if and how Congress (and perhaps other political actors) might consider and resolve issues related to Guarantee Clause claims?

2. While most cases seem to read *Luther* and *Pacific States* for the proposition that all legal challenges on Guarantee Clause grounds are non-justiciable, that has not prevented commentators from arguing that some forms of direct democracy can violate the Clause. *See, e.g.,* Fred O. Smith, *Due Process, Republicanism, and Direct Democracy,* 89 N.Y.U. L. Rev. 582 (2014) (arguing that the initiative process can violate the Clause if it deprives individuals of liberty or property); Jacob M. Heller, Note, *Death by a Thousand Cuts: The Guarantee Clause Regulation of State Constitutions,* 62 Stan. L. Rev. 1711 (2010) (arguing that frequent use of initiative in California arguably to micromanage legislative functions violates the Clause). *Compare* Robert G. Natelson, *A Republic, Not a Democracy? Initiative, Referendum, and the*

Constitution's Guarantee Clause, 80 Tex. L. Rev. 807 (2002) (originalist defense of direct democracy).

3. Justice Frankfurter's opinion for a plurality in *Colegrove* is a classic exposition of the limits of federal judicial power. Did he adequately respond to the argument in Justice Black's dissent that the plaintiffs' equal-protection claims were being ignored? Conversely, did Justice Black fully appreciate the apparent dangers of courts entering the "political thicket," as described by Justice Frankfurter?

4. One central argument of those who would permit courts to take jurisdiction of election controversies is that judicial action is necessary to avoid a "political lockup." That is, without court orders forcing reapportionment, legislatures would not change the districts because, after all, those legislators were elected from the existing districts. *See* John Hart Ely, Democracy and Distrust: A Theory of Judicial Review 103 (1980); Samuel Issacharoff & Richard H. Pildes, *Politics as Markets: Partisan Lockups of the Democratic Process*, 50 Stan. L. Rev. 643 (1998). Should that rationale apply to challenges to congressional districts, which are initially drawn by states but which can be changed by Congress?

5. In 1947, immediately after *Colegrove*, the governor of Illinois recommended a reapportionment. The state legislature not only reapportioned the electoral districts in that year, but did so again in 1951. Should that information be relevant to us in interpreting the political-question doctrine?

6. What are the limits of the principle behind *Colegrove*? If a state drew districts for the purpose of reducing the political influence of a particular group, would a challenge to that action be justiciable? Would it make a difference if the gerrymandering were for the purpose of reducing (or increasing) the power of a racial group, a political party, or voters who live in a certain part of the state? In *Gomillion v. Lightfoot*, 364 U.S. 339 (1960), considered in more detail in Chapter 4 at page 279, the Supreme Court considered the constitutionality of a law redrawing the boundary of Tuskegee, Alabama, from a square into an "uncouth twenty-eight-sided figure." *Id.* at 340. The new boundary "remove[d] from the city all save four or five of its 400 Negro voters while not removing a single white voter or resident." *Id.* at 341.

In opinion by Justice Frankfurter, the author of *Colegrove v. Green*, the Supreme Court held the law to be in violation of the Fifteenth Amendment. In addressing the state's argument that the case presented a political question under *Colegrove*, the Court responded as follows:

> * * * The appellants in *Colegrove* complained only of a dilution of the strength of their votes as a result of legislative inaction over a course of many years. The petitioners here complain that affirmative legislative action deprives them of their votes and the consequent advantages that the ballot affords. When a legislature thus singles out a readily isolated segment of a racial minority for special discriminatory treatment, it violates

the Fifteenth Amendment. In no case involving unequal weight in voting distribution that has come before the Court did the decision sanction a differentiation on racial lines whereby approval was given to unequivocal withdrawal of the vote solely from colored citizens. Apart from all else, these considerations lift this controversy out of the so-called "political" arena and into the conventional sphere of constitutional litigation.

In sum, as Mr. Justice Holmes remarked, when dealing with a related situation, in *Nixon* v. *Herndon*, 273 U.S. 536, 540 [(1927)], "Of course the petition concerns political action," but "The objection that the subject-matter of the suit is political is little more than a play upon words." A statute which is alleged to have worked unconstitutional deprivations of petitioners' rights is not immune to attack simply because the mechanism employed by the legislature is a redefinition of municipal boundaries. According to the allegations here made, the Alabama Legislature has not merely redrawn the Tuskegee city limits with incidental inconvenience to the petitioners; it is more accurate to say that it has deprived the petitioners of the municipal franchise and consequent rights and to that end it has incidentally changed the city's boundaries. While in form this is merely an act redefining metes and bounds, if the allegations are established, the inescapable human effect of this essay in geometry and geography is to despoil colored citizens, and only colored citizens, of their theretofore enjoyed voting rights. That was no *Colegrove* v. *Green*.

When a State exercises power wholly within the domain of state interest, it is insulated from federal judicial review. But such insulation is not carried over when state power is used as an instrument for circumventing a federally protected right. * * *

Id. at 346–47. Are you convinced by the Court's attempt to distinguish *Colegrove*?

Justice Whittaker, concurring in the judgment in *Gomillion*, argued that the redrawing of Tuskegee's boundaries violated the Fourteenth Amendment, rather than the Fifteenth. In addition to other arguments, he contended that a decision grounded in the Fourteenth Amendment "clearly would not involve * * * the *Colegrove* problem." *Id.* at 349 (Whittaker, J., concurring). Do you agree? Consider your answer as you read ahead.

As we have seen, litigants and judges engaged in various efforts—some successful, some not—to circumvent the limits of *Luther* and other Guarantee Clause cases through explicit reliance on other constitutional provisions, particularly the Equal Protection Clause of the Fourteenth Amendment. But the jurisprudential shift to the Equal Protection Clause raised complications of its own, and did not automatically dispose of concerns raised by the political-question doctrine, as the following cases show.

Baker v. Carr

Supreme Court of the United States
369 U.S. 186, 82 S. Ct. 691, 7 L. Ed. 2d 663 (1962)

Mr. Justice Brennan delivered the opinion of the Court [in which Mr. Chief Justice Warren, Mr. Justice Black, Mr. Justice Douglas, Mr. Justice Clark, and Mr. Justice Stewart join]. * * *

[Plaintiffs, Tennessee voters, brought suit alleging that the apportionment of state-legislative districts debased their votes in violation of the Equal Protection Clause.]

The General Assembly of Tennessee consists of the Senate with 33 members and the House of Representatives with 99 members. * * * [The Tennessee Constitution requires redistricting every ten years according to] the total number of qualified voters resident in the respective counties, subject to only minor qualifications. Decennial reapportionment in compliance with the constitutional scheme was effected by the General Assembly each decade from 1871 to 1901. * * * In the more than 60 years since [passage of the 1901 Apportionment Act, however], all proposals in both Houses of the General Assembly for reapportionment have failed to pass.

Between 1901 and 1961, Tennessee has experienced substantial growth and redistribution of her population. In 1901 the population was 2,020,616, of whom 487,380 were eligible to vote. The 1960 Federal Census reports the State's population at 3,567,089, of whom 2,092,891 are eligible to vote. The relative standings of the counties in terms of qualified voters have changed significantly. It is primarily the continued application of the 1901 Apportionment Act to this shifted and enlarged voting population which gives rise to the present controversy.

Indeed, the complaint alleges that the 1901 statute, even as of the time of its passage, "made no apportionment of Representatives and Senators in accordance with the constitutional formula . . . , but instead arbitrarily and capriciously apportioned representatives in the Senate and House without reference . . . to any logical or reasonable formula whatever." It is further alleged that "because of the population changes since 1900, and the failure of the Legislature to reapportion itself since 1901," the 1901 statute became "unconstitutional and obsolete." Appellants also argue that, because of the composition of the legislature effected by the 1901 Apportionment Act, redress in the form of a state constitutional amendment to change the entire mechanism for reapportioning, or any other change short of that, is difficult or impossible.[14] The complaint concludes that "these plaintiffs and others

---

14. The appellants claim that no General Assembly constituted according to the 1901 Act will submit reapportionment proposals either to the people or to a Constitutional Convention. There is no provision for popular initiative in Tennessee. Amendments proposed in the Senate or House must first be approved by a majority of all members of each House and again by two-thirds of the members in the General Assembly next chosen. The proposals are then submitted to the people at the next general election in which a Governor is to be chosen. Alternatively, the

similarly situated, are denied the equal protection of the laws accorded them by the Fourteenth Amendment to the Constitution of the United States by virtue of the debasement of their votes." They seek a declaration that the 1901 statute is unconstitutional and an injunction restraining the appellees from acting to conduct any further elections under it. They also pray that unless and until the General Assembly enacts a valid reapportionment, the District Court should either decree a reapportionment by mathematical application of the Tennessee constitutional formulae to the most recent Federal Census figures, or direct the appellees to conduct legislative elections, primary and general, at large. * * *

In holding that the subject matter of this suit was not justiciable, the District Court relied on *Colegrove* v. *Green*, [328 U.S. 549 (1946)] [p. 90], and subsequent *per curiam* cases. * * * We hold that the claim pleaded here neither rests upon nor implicates the Guaranty Clause and that its justiciability is therefore not foreclosed by our decisions of cases involving that clause. * * * [Our review of "political question" cases reveals that] it is the relationship between the judiciary and the coordinate branches of the Federal Government, and not the federal judiciary's relationship to the States, which gives rise to the "political question."

We have said that "In determining whether a question falls within [the political question] category, the appropriateness under our system of government of attributing finality to the action of the political departments and also the lack of satisfactory criteria for a judicial determination are dominant considerations." *Coleman* v. *Miller*, 307 U.S. 433, 454–455 [(1939)]. The nonjusticiability of a political question is primarily a function of the separation of powers. Much confusion results from the capacity of the "political question" label to obscure the need for case-by-case inquiry. Deciding whether a matter has in any measure been committed by the Constitution to another branch of government, or whether the action of that branch exceeds whatever authority has been committed, is itself a delicate exercise in constitutional interpretation, and is a responsibility of this Court as ultimate interpreter of the Constitution. * * *

It is apparent that several formulations which vary slightly according to the settings in which the questions arise may describe a political question, although each has one or more elements which identify it as essentially a function of the separation of powers. Prominent on the surface of any case held to involve a political question is found a textually demonstrable constitutional commitment of the issue to a coordinate political department; or a lack of judicially discoverable and manageable standards for resolving it; or the impossibility of deciding without an initial policy

---

legislature may submit to the people at any general election the question of calling a convention to consider specified proposals. Such as are adopted at a convention do not, however, become effective unless approved by a majority of the qualified voters voting separately on each proposed change or amendment at an election fixed by the convention. Conventions shall not be held oftener than once in six years. [Legislation in 1951 and 1957] provided that delegates to the 1953 and 1959 conventions were to be chosen from the counties and floterial districts just as are members of the State House of Representatives. * * *

determination of a kind clearly for nonjudicial discretion; or the impossibility of a court's undertaking independent resolution without expressing lack of the respect due coordinate branches of government; or an unusual need for unquestioning adherence to a political decision already made; or the potentiality of embarrassment from multifarious pronouncements by various departments on one question.

Unless one of these formulations is inextricable from the case at bar, there should be no dismissal for non-justiciability on the ground of a political question's presence. The doctrine of which we treat is one of "political questions," not one of "political cases." The courts cannot reject as "no law suit" a bona fide controversy as to whether some action denominated "political" exceeds constitutional authority. The cases we have reviewed show the necessity for discriminating inquiry into the precise facts and posture of the particular case, and the impossibility of resolution by any semantic cataloguing.

But it is argued that this case shares the characteristics of decisions that constitute a category not yet considered, cases concerning the Constitution's guaranty, in Art. IV, § 4, of a republican form of government. A conclusion as to whether the case at bar does present a political question cannot be confidently reached until we have considered those cases with special care. We shall discover that Guaranty Clause claims involve those elements which define a "political question," and for that reason and no other, they are nonjusticiable. In particular, we shall discover that the nonjusticiability of such claims has nothing to do with their touching upon matters of state governmental organization. * * *

* * * The question here is the consistency of state action with the Federal Constitution. We have no question decided, or to be decided, by a political branch of government coequal with this Court. Nor do we risk embarrassment of our government abroad, or grave disturbance at home if we take issue with Tennessee as to the constitutionality of her action here challenged. Nor need the appellants, in order to succeed in this action, ask the Court to enter upon policy determinations for which judicially manageable standards are lacking. Judicial standards under the Equal Protection Clause are well developed and familiar, and it has been open to courts since the enactment of the Fourteenth Amendment to determine, if on the particular facts they must, that a discrimination reflects *no* policy, but simply arbitrary and capricious action.

This case does, in one sense, involve the allocation of political power within a State, and the appellants might conceivably have added a claim under the Guaranty Clause. Of course, as we have seen, any reliance on that clause would be futile. But because any reliance on the Guaranty Clause could not have succeeded it does not follow that appellants may not be heard on the equal protection claim which in fact they tender. True, it must be clear that the Fourteenth Amendment claim is not so enmeshed with those political question elements which render Guaranty Clause claims nonjusticiable as actually to present a political question itself. But we have found that not to be the case here. * * *

We conclude then that the nonjusticiability of claims resting on the Guaranty Clause which arises from their embodiment of questions that were thought "political," can have no bearing upon the justiciability of the equal protection claim presented in this case. Finally, we emphasize that it is the involvement in Guaranty Clause claims of the elements thought to define "political questions," and no other feature, which could render them nonjusticiable. Specifically, we have said that such claims are not held nonjusticiable because they touch matters of state governmental organization. * * *

When challenges to state action respecting matters of "the administration of the affairs of the State and the officers through whom they are conducted" have rested on claims of constitutional deprivation which are amenable to judicial correction, this Court has acted upon its view of the merits of the claim. For example, * * * only last Term, in *Gomillion* v. *Lightfoot*, 364 U.S. 339 [(1960)] [p. 279], we applied the Fifteenth Amendment to strike down a redrafting of municipal boundaries which effected a discriminatory impairment of voting rights, in the face of what a majority of the Court of Appeals thought to be a sweeping commitment to state legislatures of the power to draw and redraw such boundaries. * * *

We conclude that the complaint's allegations of a denial of equal protection present a justiciable constitutional cause of action upon which appellants are entitled to a trial and a decision. The right asserted is within the reach of judicial protection under the Fourteenth Amendment.

The judgment of the District Court is reversed and the cause is remanded for further proceedings consistent with this opinion.

Reversed and remanded.

Mr. Justice Whittaker did not participate in the decision of this case.

Mr. Justice Douglas, concurring.

While I join the opinion of the Court and, like the Court, do not reach the merits, a word of explanation is necessary.[1] I put to one side the problems of "political" questions involving the distribution of power between this Court, the Congress, and the Chief Executive. We have here a phase of the recurring problem of the relation of the federal courts to state agencies. More particularly, the question is the extent to which a State may weight one person's vote more heavily than it does another's. * * *

With the exception of *Colegrove* v. *Green*; *MacDougall* v. *Green*, 335 U.S. 281 [(1948)]; *South* v. *Peters*, 339 U.S. 276 [(1950)], and the decisions they spawned, the

---

1. I feel strongly that many of the cases cited by the Court and involving so-called "political" questions were wrongly decided. In joining the opinion, I do not approve those decisions but only construe the Court's opinion in this case as stating an accurate historical account of what the prior cases have held.

Court has never thought that protection of voting rights was beyond judicial cognizance. Today's treatment of those cases removes the only impediment to judicial cognizance of the claims stated in the present complaint.

The justiciability of the present claims being established, any relief accorded can be fashioned in the light of well-known principles of equity.

Mr. Justice Clark, concurring.

* * * I believe it can be shown that this case is distinguishable from earlier cases dealing with the distribution of political power by a State, that a patent violation of the Equal Protection Clause of the United States Constitution has been shown, and that an appropriate remedy may be formulated. * * *

The controlling facts cannot be disputed. It appears from the record that 37% of the voters of Tennessee elect 20 of the 33 Senators while 40% of the voters elect 60 of the 99 members of the House. But this might not on its face be an "invidious discrimination," *Williamson* v. *Lee Optical of Oklahoma*, 348 U.S. 483, 489 (1955), for a "statutory discrimination will not be set aside if any state of facts reasonably may be conceived to justify it."

* * * The frequency and magnitude of the inequalities in the present districting [however] admit of no policy whatever. * * * [The] apportionment picture in Tennessee is a topsy-turvical of gigantic proportions. This is not to say that some of the disparity cannot be explained, but when the entire table is examined—comparing the voting strength of counties of like population as well as contrasting that of the smaller with the larger counties—it leaves but one conclusion, namely that Tennessee's apportionment is a crazy quilt without rational basis. * * *

The truth is that—although this case has been here for two years and has had over six hours' argument (three times the ordinary case) and has been most carefully considered over and over again by us in Conference and individually—no one, not even the State nor the dissenters, has come up with any rational basis for Tennessee's apportionment statute.

No one * * * contends that mathematical equality among voters is required by the Equal Protection Clause. But certainly there must be some rational design to a State's districting. The discrimination here does not fit any pattern—as I have said, it is but a crazy quilt. My Brother Harlan contends that other proposed apportionment plans contain disparities. Instead of chasing those rabbits he should first pause long enough to meet appellants' proof of discrimination by showing that in fact the present plan follows a rational policy. Not being able to do this, he merely counters with such generalities as "classic legislative judgment," no "significant discrepancy," and "de minimis departures." I submit that even a casual glance at the present apportionment picture shows these conclusions to be entirely fanciful. If present representation has a policy at all, it is to maintain the *status quo* of invidious discrimination at any cost. * * *

Although I find the Tennessee apportionment statute offends the Equal Protection Clause, I would not consider intervention by this Court into so delicate a field if there were any other relief available to the people of Tennessee. But the majority of the people of Tennessee have no "practical opportunities for exerting their political weight at the polls" to correct the existing "invidious discrimination." Tennessee has no initiative and referendum. I have searched diligently for other "practical opportunities" present under the law. I find none other than through the federal courts. The majority of the voters have been caught up in a legislative strait jacket. Tennessee has an "informed, civically militant electorate" and "an aroused popular conscience," but it does not sear "the conscience of the people's representatives." This is because the legislative policy has riveted the present seats in the Assembly to their respective constituencies, and by the votes of their incumbents a reapportionment of any kind is prevented. The people have been rebuffed at the hands of the Assembly; they have tried the constitutional convention route, but since the call must originate in the Assembly it, too, has been fruitless. They have tried Tennessee courts with the same result,[9] and Governors have fought the tide only to flounder. It is said that there is recourse in Congress and perhaps that may be, but from a practical standpoint this is without substance. To date Congress has never undertaken such a task in any State. We therefore must conclude that the people of Tennessee are stymied and without judicial intervention will be saddled with the present discrimination in the affairs of their state government. * * *

MR. JUSTICE STEWART, concurring.

The separate writings of my dissenting and concurring Brothers stray so far from the subject of today's decision as to convey, I think, a distressingly inaccurate impression of what the Court decides. For that reason, I think it appropriate, in joining the opinion of the Court, to emphasize in a few words what the opinion does and does not say. * * *

The complaint in this case asserts that Tennessee's system of apportionment is utterly arbitrary—without any possible justification in rationality. The District Court did not reach the merits of that claim, and this Court quite properly expresses no view on the subject. Contrary to the suggestion of my Brother HARLAN, the Court does not say or imply that "state legislatures must be so structured as to reflect with approximate equality the voice of every voter." The Court does not say or imply that there is anything in the Federal Constitution "to prevent a State, acting not irrationally, from choosing any electoral legislative structure it thinks best suited to the interests, temper, and customs of its people." And contrary to the suggestion of my Brother DOUGLAS, the Court most assuredly does not decide the

---

9. It is interesting to note that state judges often rest their decisions on the ground that this Court has precluded adjudication of the federal claim.

question, "may a State weight the vote of one county or one district more heavily than it weights the vote in another?" * * *

Mr. Justice Frankfurter, whom Mr. Justice Harlan joins, dissenting.

The Court today reverses a uniform course of decision established by a dozen cases, including one by which the very claim now sustained was unanimously rejected only five years ago. The impressive body of rulings thus cast aside reflected the equally uniform course of our political history regarding the relationship between population and legislative representation—a wholly different matter from denial of the franchise to individuals because of race, color, religion or sex. Such a massive repudiation of the experience of our whole past in asserting destructively novel judicial power demands a detailed analysis of the role of this Court in our constitutional scheme. Disregard of inherent limits in the effective exercise of the Court's "judicial Power" not only presages the futility of judicial intervention in the essentially political conflict of forces by which the relation between population and representation has time out of mind been and now is determined. It may well impair the Court's position as the ultimate organ of "the supreme Law of the Land" in that vast range of legal problems, often strongly entangled in popular feeling, on which this Court must pronounce. The Court's authority—possessed of neither the purse nor the sword—ultimately rests on sustained public confidence in its moral sanction. Such feeling must be nourished by the Court's complete detachment, in fact and in appearance, from political entanglements and by abstention from injecting itself into the clash of political forces in political settlements.

A hypothetical claim resting on abstract assumptions is now for the first time made the basis for affording illusory relief for a particular evil even though it foreshadows deeper and more pervasive difficulties in consequence. The claim is hypothetical and the assumptions are abstract because the Court does not vouchsafe the lower courts—state and federal—guidelines for formulating specific, definite, wholly unprecedented remedies for the inevitable litigations that today's umbrageous disposition is bound to stimulate in connection with politically motivated reapportionments in so many States. In such a setting, to promulgate jurisdiction in the abstract is meaningless. It is as devoid of reality as "a brooding omnipresence in the sky," for it conveys no intimation what relief, if any, a District Court is capable of affording that would not invite legislatures to play ducks and drakes with the judiciary. For this Court to direct the District Court to enforce a claim to which the Court has over the years consistently found itself required to deny legal enforcement and at the same time to find it necessary to withhold any guidance to the lower court how to enforce this turnabout, new legal claim, manifests an odd—indeed an esoteric—conception of judicial propriety. * * * Even assuming the indispensable intellectual disinterestedness on the part of judges in such matters, they do not have accepted legal standards or criteria or even reliable analogies to draw upon for making judicial judgments. To charge courts with the task of accommodating the incommensurable factors of policy that underlie these mathematical puzzles is to attribute, however flatteringly, omnicompetence to judges. * * *

* * * [T]here is not under our Constitution a judicial remedy for every political mischief, for every undesirable exercise of legislative power. The Framers carefully and with deliberate forethought refused so to enthrone the judiciary. In this situation, as in others of like nature, appeal for relief does not belong here. Appeal must be to an informed, civically militant electorate. In a democratic society like ours, relief must come through an aroused popular conscience that sears the conscience of the people's representatives. In any event there is nothing judicially more unseemly nor more self-defeating than for this Court to make *in terrorem* pronouncements, to indulge in merely empty rhetoric, sounding a word of promise to the ear, sure to be disappointing to the hope. * * *

The *Colegrove* doctrine, in the form in which repeated decisions have settled it, was not an innovation. It represents long judicial thought and experience. From its earliest opinions this Court has consistently recognized a class of controversies which do not lend themselves to judicial standards and judicial remedies. To classify the various instances as "political questions" is rather a form of stating this conclusion than revealing of analysis.[10] * * *

The Court has been particularly unwilling to intervene in matters concerning the structure and organization of the political institutions of the States. The abstention from judicial entry into such areas has been greater even than that which marks the Court's ordinary approach to issues of state power challenged under broad federal guarantees. * * *

The cases involving Negro disfranchisement are no exception to the principle of avoiding federal judicial intervention into matters of state government in the absence of an explicit and clear constitutional imperative. For here the controlling command of Supreme Law is plain and unequivocal. An end of discrimination against the Negro was the compelling motive of the Civil War Amendments. The Fifteenth expresses this in terms, and it is no less true of the Equal Protection Clause of the Fourteenth. * * *

The influence of these converging considerations—the caution not to undertake decision where standards meet for judicial judgment are lacking, the reluctance to interfere with matters of state government in the absence of an unquestionable and effectively enforceable mandate, the unwillingness to make courts arbiters of the broad issues of political organization historically committed to other institutions and for whose adjustment the judicial process is ill-adapted—has been decisive of the settled line of cases, reaching back more than a century, which holds that Art. IV, §4, of the Constitution, guaranteeing to the States "a Republican Form of Government," is not enforceable through the courts. * * * The subject was fully considered in *Pacific States Telephone & Telegraph Co. v. Oregon*, 223 U.S. 118 [(1912)], in

---

10. See Bickel, *Foreword: The Passive Virtues*, 75 Harv. L. Rev. 40, 45 *et seq.* (1961).

which the Court dismissed for want of jurisdiction a writ of error attacking a state license tax statute enacted by the initiative, on the claim that this mode of legislation was inconsistent with a Republican Form of Government and violated the Equal Protection Clause and other federal guarantees. * * *

The present case involves all of the elements that have made the Guarantee Clause cases non-justiciable. It is, in effect, a Guarantee Clause claim masquerading under a different label. But it cannot make the case more fit for judicial action that appellants invoke the Fourteenth Amendment rather than Art. IV, §4, where, in fact, the gist of their complaint is the same—unless it can be found that the Fourteenth Amendment speaks with greater particularity to their situation. * * * But where judicial competence is wanting, it cannot be created by invoking one clause of the Constitution rather than another. When what was essentially a Guarantee Clause claim was sought to be laid, as well, under the Equal Protection Clause in *Pacific States Telephone & Telegraph Co.* v. *Oregon*, the Court had no difficulty in "dispelling any mere confusion resulting from forms of expression, and considering the substance of things." * * *

What, then, is this question of legislative apportionment? Appellants invoke the right to vote and to have their votes counted. But they are permitted to vote and their votes are counted. They go to the polls, they cast their ballots, they send their representatives to the state councils. Their complaint is simply that the representatives are not sufficiently numerous or powerful—in short, that Tennessee has adopted a basis of representation with which they are dissatisfied. Talk of "debasement" or "dilution" is circular talk. One cannot speak of "debasement" or "dilution" of the value of a vote until there is first defined a standard of reference as to what a vote should be worth. What is actually asked of the Court in this case is to choose among competing bases of representation—ultimately, really, among competing theories of political philosophy—in order to establish an appropriate frame of government for the State of Tennessee and thereby for all the States of the Union.

In such a matter, abstract analogies which ignore the facts of history deal in unrealities; they betray reason. This is not a case in which a State has, through a device however oblique and sophisticated, denied Negroes or Jews or redheaded persons a vote, or given them only a third or a sixth of a vote. That was *Gomillion* v. *Lightfoot*. What Tennessee illustrates is an old and still widespread method of representation—representation by local geographical division, only in part respective of population—in preference to others, others, forsooth, more appealing. Appellants contest this choice and seek to make this Court the arbiter of the disagreement. They would make the Equal Protection Clause the charter of adjudication, asserting that the equality which it guarantees comports, if not the assurance of equal weight to every voter's vote, at least the basic conception that representation ought to be proportionate to population, a standard by reference to which the reasonableness of apportionment plans may be judged.

To find such a political conception legally enforceable in the broad and unspecific guarantee of equal protection is to rewrite the Constitution. See *Luther* v. *Borden*. Certainly, "equal protection" is no more secure a foundation for judicial judgment of the permissibility of varying forms of representative government than is "Republican Form." Indeed since "equal protection of the laws" can only mean an equality of persons standing in the same relation to whatever governmental action is challenged, the determination whether treatment is equal presupposes a determination concerning the nature of the relationship. This, with respect to apportionment, means an inquiry into the theoretic base of representation in an acceptably republican state. For a court could not determine the equal-protection issue without in fact first determining the Republican-Form issue, simply because what is reasonable for equal-protection purposes will depend upon what frame of government, basically, is allowed. To divorce "equal protection" from "Republican Form" is to talk about half a question.

The notion that representation proportioned to the geographic spread of population is so universally accepted as a necessary element of equality between man and man that it must be taken to be the standard of a political equality preserved by the Fourteenth Amendment—that it is, in appellants' words "the basic principle of representative government"—is, to put it bluntly, not true. However desirable and however desired by some among the great political thinkers and framers of our government, it has never been generally practiced, today or in the past. It was not the English system, it was not the colonial system, it was not the system chosen for the national government by the Constitution, it was not the system exclusively or even predominantly practiced by the States at the time of adoption of the Fourteenth Amendment, it is not predominantly practiced by the States today. Unless judges, the judges of this Court, are to make their private views of political wisdom the measure of the Constitution—views which in all honesty cannot but give the appearance, if not reflect the reality, of involvement with the business of partisan politics so inescapably a part of apportionment controversies—the Fourteenth Amendment, "itself a historical product," provides no guide for judicial oversight of the representation problem. * * *

[MR. JUSTICE FRANKFURTER followed with a detailed historical review of legislative apportionment in Great Britain, in the 13 Colonies, and in the States demonstrating, as he saw it, the many different approaches to the issue.]

* * * Detailed recent studies are available to describe the present-day constitutional and statutory status of apportionment in the fifty States. They demonstrate a decided twentieth-century trend away from population as the exclusive base of representation. Today, only a dozen state constitutions provide for periodic legislative reapportionment of both houses by a substantially unqualified application of the population standard, and only about a dozen more prescribe such reapportionment for even a single chamber. * * * More than twenty States now guarantee each county at least one seat in one of their houses regardless of population, and in nine others county or town units are given equal representation in one legislative

branch, whatever the number of each unit's inhabitants. Of course, numerically considered, "These provisions invariably result in over-representation of the least populated areas. . . ." And in an effort to curb and political dominance of metropolitan regions, at least ten States now limit the maximum entitlement of any single county (or, in some cases, city) in one legislative house—another source of substantial numerical disproportion. * * *

Manifestly, the Equal Protection Clause supplies no clearer guide for judicial examination of apportionment methods than would the Guarantee Clause itself. Apportionment, by its character, is a subject of extraordinary complexity, involving—even after the fundamental theoretical issues concerning what is to be represented in a representative legislature have been fought out or compromised—considerations of geography, demography, electoral convenience, economic and social cohesions or divergencies among particular local groups, communications, the practical effects of political institutions like the lobby and the city machine, ancient traditions and ties of settled usage, respect for proven incumbents of long experience and senior status, mathematical mechanics, censuses compiling relevant data, and a host of others. Legislative responses throughout the country to the reapportionment demands of the 1960 Census have glaringly confirmed that these are not factors that lend themselves to evaluations of a nature that are the staple of judicial determinations or for which judges are equipped to adjudicate by legal training or experience or native wit. And this is the more so true because in every strand of this complicated, intricate web of values meet the contending forces of partisan politics. The practical significance of apportionment is that the next election results may differ because of it. Apportionment battles are overwhelmingly party or intraparty contests. It will add a virulent source of friction and tension in federal-state relations to embroil the federal judiciary in them. * * *

Dissenting opinion of MR. JUSTICE HARLAN, whom MR. JUSTICE FRANKFURTER joins. * * *

The Court has said time and again that the Equal Protection Clause does not demand of state enactments either mathematical identity or rigid equality. * * * It is not inequality alone that calls for a holding of unconstitutionality; only if the inequality is based on an impermissible standard may this Court condemn it.

What then is the basis for the claim made in this case that the distribution of state senators and representatives is the product of capriciousness or of some constitutionally prohibited policy? It is not that Tennessee has arranged its electoral districts with a deliberate purpose to dilute the voting strength of one race, cf. *Gomillion* v. *Lightfoot*, or that some religious group is intentionally underrepresented. Nor is it a charge that the legislature has indulged in sheer caprice by allotting representatives to each county on the basis of a throw of the dice, or of some other determinant bearing no rational relation to the question of apportionment. Rather, the claim is that the State Legislature has unreasonably retained substantially the same allocation of senators and representatives as was established by statute in 1901, refusing to recognize the great shift in the population balance between urban and rural communities that has occurred in the meantime. * * *

A Federal District Court is asked to say that the passage of time has rendered the 1901 apportionment obsolete to the point where its continuance becomes vulnerable under the Fourteenth Amendment. But is not this matter one that involves a classic legislative judgment? Surely it lies within the province of a state legislature to conclude that an existing allocation of senators and representatives constitutes a desirable balance of geographical and demographical representation, or that in the interest of stability of government it would be best to defer for some further time the redistribution of seats in the state legislature.

Indeed, I would hardly think it unconstitutional if a state legislature's expressed reason for establishing or maintaining an electoral imbalance between its rural and urban population were to protect the State's agricultural interests from the sheer weight of numbers of those residing in its cities. A State may, after all, take account of the interests of its rural population in the distribution of tax burdens, and recognition of the special problems of agricultural interests has repeatedly been reflected in federal legislation. Does the Fourteenth Amendment impose a stricter limitation upon a State's apportionment of political representatives to its central government? I think not. These are matters of local policy, on the wisdom of which the federal judiciary is neither permitted nor qualified to sit in judgment.

The suggestion of my Brother FRANKFURTER that courts lack standards by which to decide such cases as this, is relevant not only to the question of "justiciability," but also, and perhaps more fundamentally, to the determination whether any cognizable constitutional claim has been asserted in this case. Courts are unable to decide when it is that an apportionment originally valid becomes void because the factors entering into such a decision are basically matters appropriate only for legislative judgment. And so long as there exists a possible rational legislative policy for retaining an existing apportionment, such a legislative decision cannot be said to breach the bulwark against arbitrariness and caprice that the Fourteenth Amendment affords. * * *

In conclusion, it is appropriate to say that one need not agree, as a citizen, with what Tennessee has done or failed to do, in order to deprecate, as a judge, what the majority is doing today. Those observers of the Court who see it primarily as the last refuge for the correction of all inequality or injustice, no matter what its nature or source, will no doubt applaud this decision and its break with the past. Those who consider that continuing national respect for the Court's authority depends in large measure upon its wise exercise of self-restraint and discipline in constitutional adjudication, will view the decision with deep concern.

I would affirm.

Notes and Questions

1. *Baker* concluded that the equal-protection challenge to Tennessee's electoral districts was justiciable even though a Guarantee Clause challenge would have presented a political question under *Colegrove*. That is, Baker distinguished—and did not overrule—*Colegrove*. Was the Court's distinction convincing?

2. The Court concluded that "the nonjusticiability of a political question is primarily a function of the separation of powers." That is, the political-question doctrine prevents the courts from usurping the powers that are properly exercised by the "political" branches of government. *Baker* involved a challenge to state-legislative districts, so the case did not risk a conflict with the authority of Congress or the President. Sometimes, however, the political-question doctrine limits the judiciary's ability to decide certain issues even when such a limit would do nothing to protect the powers of the other branches of the national government. For example, a case might require "an initial policy determination of a kind clearly for nonjudicial discretion." Alternatively, the standards for deciding a case might not be "judicially discoverable and manageable." This last concern was a principal reason that Guarantee Clause claims were held not to be justiciable—courts would have no manageable standard for assessing the limits of "Republican" government.

3. *Baker* argued that, by contrast, the standards for deciding equal-protection cases were "well developed and familiar." The Court had, of course, decided several cases (most prominently *Brown v. Board of Education*, 347 U.S. 483 (1954)) challenging official action under the Equal Protection Clause. None of those cases, however, established a standard for determining the constitutionality of districting plans; the one-person, one-vote doctrine, which we will study in the next section, was not established until later. Accordingly, *Baker* suggested that an equal-protection violation would occur if a districting plan "reflect[ed] *no* policy, but simply arbitrary and capricious action." Is that standard judicially manageable in the context of a challenge to a districting plan? To take Justice Harlan's example, would it be arbitrary or capricious to construct districts "to protect the State's agricultural interests from the sheer weight of numbers of those residing in its cities"?

4. If the Tennessee apportionment was constitutional in 1901 when it was first made, and became unconstitutional sometime over the next sixty years due to the migration of the state's population, when precisely did the apportionment become unconstitutional? Was it unconstitutionally arbitrary for the state simply to leave the 1901 apportionment in place if legislators could not agree on a replacement?

5. Should it matter that if courts were powerless to intervene in reapportionment cases, the plaintiffs would likely be without any remedy at all? The legislators who were elected under the 1901 districting plan obviously had little incentive to change it, and therefore many observers have been dissatisfied with the dissenters' insistence that the only recourse in reapportionment cases should lie with the people's representatives. To turn Justice Frankfurter's words against him, we might argue that suggesting that reapportionment remedies could come from legislatures would

be "to indulge in merely empty rhetoric, sounding a word of promise to the ear, sure to be disappointing to the hope." Still, should we insist that the courts be available to correct every defect in the political process? What would be wrong in concluding that courts are powerless to redraw electoral districts, even if that meant that nobody else would do so either? Sometimes limits on courts' jurisdiction result in legal claims going unaddressed. *See, e.g., United States v. Richardson*, 418 U.S. 166 (1974) (refusing to hear a claim under the Statement of Account Clause, art. I, § 9, cl. 7); *Schlesinger v. Reservists Committee to Stop the War*, 418 U.S. 208 (1974) (refusing to hear a claim under the Incompatibility Clause, art. I, § 6); *Marbury v. Madison*, 5 U.S. (1 Cranch) 137 (1803) (refusing to order the government to grant a wrongfully withheld judicial commission). As you will see, the same question returned to the Court when the issue was not whether there were judicially manageable standards for deciding how many people should be in districts, but whether there were judicially manageable standards for determining whether a districting plan unconstitutionally favored the interests of one political party. *See Rucho v. Common Cause*, 588 U.S. __, 139 S. Ct. 2484 (2019) [p. 180].

6. It is difficult to appreciate how controversial *Baker v. Carr* was at the time it was decided, or how significant it has been for the subsequent development of the law. The Court's deliberations were so contentious that they forced two Justices to leave the Supreme Court. Justice Charles Whittaker could not handle the pressure of deciding the Court's momentous cases, and *Baker* was the case that pushed him over the edge. Having served on the Court for only five years, he had a mental breakdown and left the Court, effective a week after *Baker*. He participated in the deliberations about the case, but could not make up his mind and did not cast a vote when the case was finally handed down. Justice Felix Frankfurter did participate in the decision, but was so affected by the Court's activism that he had a massive stroke two weeks after the case and was found by his secretary, sprawled on the floor of his office. He left the Court that summer because of his medical condition and died two and one-half years later. *See More Perfect: The Political Thicket*, WNYC Studios (June 10, 2016), https://www.wnycstudios.org/podcasts/radiolabmoreperfect/episodes/the-political-thicket.

7. By accepting that federal courts would have jurisdiction to determine the constitutionality of laws allocating political power, *Baker* began the "reapportionment revolution." In a sense, therefore, the entire discipline of election law stems from *Baker*. *Baker*, then, deserves some of the credit—or blame—for decisions involving not just districting but the regulation of politics more generally, from campaign finance, *see Buckley v. Valeo*, 424 U.S. 1 (1976) [p. 728] (*per curiam*), to ballot access, *see Anderson v. Celebrezze*, 460 U.S. 780 (1983) [p. 517], and to vote counting, *see Bush v. Gore*, 531 U.S. 98 (2000) [p. 1085]. As you read the remainder of this Casebook and as you study the remainder of the course, consider whether Justice Frankfurter and Justice Harlan were prophetic in their warnings about courts entering the "political thicket."

C. The Constitutional Basis for One Person, One Vote

Before 1963, the Constitution placed virtually no judicially enforceable constraints on the ability of states to allocate political power to different interests through legislative apportionment. *Gomillion v. Lightfoot*, 364 U.S. 339 (1960) [p. 279], ensured that states could not use the districting process to shut out racial minorities, but the "reapportionment revolution" begun with *Baker v. Carr*, 369 U.S. 186 (1962) [p. 97], and continued most prominently in *Reynolds v. Sims*, 377 U.S. 533 (1964) [p. 122], involved the federal judiciary in districting disputes to an extent unimaginable a short time earlier. This section traces the Court's discovery of the one-person, one-vote standard in both the Equal Protection Clause and the constitutional requirement that members of the Federal House of Representatives be elected "by the People of the several States." U.S. CONST. art. I, § 2, cl. 1.

Gray v. Sanders

Supreme Court of the United States

372 U.S. 368, 83 S. Ct. 801, 9 L. Ed. 2d 821 (1963)

MR. JUSTICE DOUGLAS delivered the opinion of the Court [in which MR. CHIEF JUSTICE WARREN, MR. JUSTICE BLACK, MR. JUSTICE CLARK, MR. JUSTICE BRENNAN, MR. JUSTICE STEWART, MR. JUSTICE WHITE, and MR. JUSTICE GOLDBERG join].

This suit was instituted by appellee, who is qualified to vote in primary and general elections in Fulton County, Georgia, to restrain appellants from using Georgia's county unit system as a basis for counting votes in a Democratic primary for the nomination of a United States Senator and statewide officers, and for declaratory relief. * * * Appellee alleges that the use of the county unit system in counting, tabulating, consolidating, and certifying votes cast in primary elections for statewide offices violates the Equal Protection Clause and the Due Process Clause of the Fourteenth Amendment and the Seventeenth Amendment. * * *

[Under the county unit system, candidates compete for the votes of each county, rather than for the votes of individuals. The winner is the candidate who wins the most unit (county) votes—not the one who wins the most individual votes. The candidate receiving the most votes in any particular county receives all the unit votes of that county, regardless of the closeness of the election in that county. Unit votes were apportioned in part by counties' populations, but with a significant weighting in favor of less-populous counties.]

This case * * * does not involve a question of the degree to which the Equal Protection Clause of the Fourteenth Amendment limits the authority of a State Legislature in designing the geographical districts from which representatives are chosen either for the State Legislature or for the Federal House of Representatives. * * * Nor does it present the question, inherent in the bicameral form of our

Federal Government, whether a State may have one house chosen without regard to population. * * *

* * * The inclusion of the electoral college in the Constitution, as the result of specific historical concerns, validated the collegiate principle despite its inherent numerical inequality, but implied nothing about the use of an analogous system by a State in a statewide election.{8} No such specific accommodation of the latter was ever undertaken, and therefore no validation of its numerical inequality ensued. Nor does the question here have anything to do with the composition of the state or federal legislature. And we intimate no opinion on the constitutional phases of that problem beyond what we said in *Baker* v. *Carr*, [369 U.S. 186 (1962)] [p. 97]. The present case is only a voting case. Georgia gives every qualified voter one vote in a statewide election; but in counting those votes she employs the county unit system which in end result weights the rural vote more heavily than the urban vote and weights some small rural counties heavier than other larger rural counties. * * *

The Fifteenth Amendment prohibits a State from denying or abridging a Negro's right to vote. The Nineteenth Amendment does the same for women. If a State in a statewide election weighted the male vote more heavily than the female vote or the white vote more heavily than the Negro vote, none could successfully contend that that discrimination was allowable. How then can one person be given twice or 10 times the voting power of another person in a statewide election merely because he lives in a rural area or because he lives in the smallest rural county? Once the geographical unit for which a representative is to be chosen is designated, all who participate in the election are to have an equal vote—whatever their race, whatever their sex, whatever their occupation, whatever their income, and wherever their home may be in that geographical unit. This is required by the Equal Protection Clause of the Fourteenth Amendment. The concept of "we the people" under the Constitution visualizes no preferred class of voters but equality among those who meet the basic qualifications. * * *

The only weighting of votes sanctioned by the Constitution concerns matters of representation, such as the allocation of Senators irrespective of population and the use of the electoral college in the choice of a President. Yet when Senators are chosen, the Seventeenth Amendment states the choice must be made "by the people." Minors, felons, and other classes may be excluded. See *Lassiter* v. *Northampton County Election Board*, 360 U.S. [45,] 51 [(1959)] [p. 11]. But once the class of voters is chosen and their qualifications specified, we see no constitutional way by which

---

8. The electoral college was designed by men who did not want the election of the President to be left to the people. * * * Passage of the Fifteenth, Seventeenth, and Nineteenth Amendments shows that this conception of political equality belongs to a bygone day, and should not be considered in determining what the Equal Protection Clause of the Fourteenth Amendment requires in statewide elections.

equality of voting power may be evaded.{[12]} * * * The conception of political equality from the Declaration of Independence, to Lincoln's Gettysburg Address, to the Fifteenth, Seventeenth, and Nineteenth Amendments can mean only one thing—one person, one vote. * * *

[*Vacated and remanded.*]

Mr. Justice Stewart, whom Mr. Justice Clark joins, concurring.

In joining the opinion and judgment of the Court, I emphasize what—but for my Brother Harlan's dissent—I should have thought would be apparent to all who read the Court's opinion. This case does not involve the validity of a State's apportionment of geographic constituencies from which representatives to the State's legislative assembly are chosen, nor any of the problems under the Equal Protection Clause which such litigation would present. * * * This case, on the contrary, involves statewide elections of a United States Senator and of state executive and judicial officers responsible to a statewide constituency. Within a given constituency, there can be room for but a single constitutional rule—one voter, one vote.

Mr. Justice Harlan, dissenting. * * *

The Court's holding surely flies in the face of history. For, as impressively shown by the opinion of Frankfurter, J., in *Baker* v. *Carr*, "one person, one vote" has never been the universally accepted political philosophy in England, the American Colonies, or in the United States. The significance of this historical fact seems indeed to be recognized by the Court, for it implies that its newfound formula might not obtain in a case involving the apportionment of seats in the "State Legislature or for the Federal House of Representatives."

But * * * any such distinction finds persuasive refutation in the Federal Electoral College whereby the President of the United States is chosen on principles wholly opposed to those now held constitutionally required in the electoral process for statewide office. One need not close his eyes to the circumstance that the Electoral College was born in compromise, nor take sides in the various attempts that have been made to change the system, in order to agree with the court below that it "could hardly be said that such a system used in a state among its counties, assuming rationality and absence of arbitrariness in end result, could be termed invidious." * * *

* * * In my dissent in *Baker* v. *Carr*, I expressed the view that a State might rationally conclude that its general welfare was best served by apportioning more seats in the legislature to agricultural communities than to urban centers, lest the legitimate

---

12. The county unit system * * * would allow the candidate winning the popular vote in the county to have the entire unit vote of that county. Hence the weighting of votes would continue, even if unit votes were allocated strictly in proportion to population. Thus if a candidate won 6,000 of 10,000 votes in a particular county, he would get the entire unit vote, the 4,000 other votes for a different candidate being worth nothing and being counted only for the purpose of being discarded.

interests of the former be submerged in the stronger electoral voice of the latter. In my opinion, recognition of the same factor cannot be deemed irrational in the present situation[.] * * *

Notes and Questions

1. The Court's footnote 8 argued that the Fifteenth, Seventeenth, and Nineteenth Amendments should have relevance to the interpretation of the *Fourteenth* Amendment. Certainly, constitutional amendments can change the meaning of earlier-enacted portions of the Constitution; for example, the Twenty-First Amendment repealed the Eighteenth, and the Eleventh Amendment altered the prior understanding of the limits of the judicial power established in Article III. Indeed, changing the meaning of the existing Constitution is the entire point of proposing and ratifying an Amendment. But the Court's argument here was different. The Court was stating that the democratic ideals in the background of the Fifteenth, Seventeenth, and Nineteenth Amendments changed the meaning of the Fourteenth Amendment, *without there being any clear conflict.* Is it proper for the Court to use later amendments in this way?

2. If one accepts the Court's methodological approach and the substantive conclusion in *Gray*, is the Electoral College itself—or states' practice of awarding delegates on a winner-take-all basis—unconstitutional? *See Lyman v. Baker*, 954 F.3d 351 (1st Cir. 2020); *New v. Pelosi*, 374 Fed. Appx. 158 (2d Cir. 2010); *New v. Ashcroft*, 293 F. Supp. 2d 256 (E.D.N.Y. 2003); *Williams v. Virginia State Board of Elections*, 288 F. Supp. 622 (E.D. Va. 1968), *aff'd* 393 U.S. 320 (1969). The Fifth Amendment contains an equal protection "component," *see Adarand Constructors, Inc. v. Peña*, 515 U.S. 200, 212–18 (1995); *Bolling v. Sharpe*, 347 U.S. 497, 499–500 (1954); why should that Amendment not be reinterpreted in light of the Fifteenth, Seventeenth, and Nineteenth Amendments?

3. *Problem.* Maine and Nebraska allocate their presidential electors in part by congressional district, and have done so since 1972 and 1996, respectively. Those states award two electors to the statewide plurality winner, and one elector for each congressional district won. (Maine has two congressional districts, and Nebraska has three.) Does such a system contravene *Gray*, especially footnote 12, even though the districts contain the same number of people? Does the answer to the constitutional question depend on the size of the state's congressional delegation?

4. The Court is surely correct that states may not give disproportionate weight to the votes of whites or males. Is there a reason for a different rule to obtain when the votes of rural-area residents are favored?

5. *Problem. Gray* held that "[o]nce the geographical unit for which a representative is to be chosen is designated, all who participate in the election are to have an equal vote." It is clear that states have some flexibility in designating the "geographical unit." For example, as we will explore in considerable detail in Chapter 4, states may provide that certain representatives be chosen at large in multimember

districts. That is, voters in a single electoral district may elect multiple representatives. Alternatively, representatives may be chosen individually from smaller districts, which in local races, are often called "wards." States may also choose to have at-large elections, but to impose residency requirements so that the legislative body contains members residing in each of the wards.

The six members of Tucson, Arizona's city council are nominated in primary elections conducted in individual wards. Only residents of those wards are permitted to vote in the primaries. Once nominated, however, the two candidates run against each other in a general election in which all residents in the city are permitted to vote. The winner then receives a place on the city council, where he represents the entire city—not merely the ward that nominated him. The residents of each ward, however, could be expected to have a disproportionate influence on their home councilman, however, as those ward residents would determine whether he would be re-nominated. (The effect might be especially pronounced in one-party jurisdictions, where the primary election effectively controls the ultimate outcome.) See *Public Integrity Alliance v. City of Tucson*, 805 F.3d 876 (2015), *vacated and reh'g en banc granted*, 820 F.3d 1075, *rev'd*, 836 F.3d 1019 (9th Cir. 2016) (*en banc*).

Does such a system violate the Constitution? A panel of the Ninth Circuit initially held the system unconstitutional, but the *en banc* court upheld it. In the view of the panel, "every otherwise eligible voter who will be a constituent of the winner of the general election must have an equal opportunity to participate in each election cycle through which that candidate is selected." 805 F.3d at 881. Tucson's system, in the view of the panel majority, "gives some of a representative's constituents—those in his home ward—a vote of disproportionate weight. That is the very result the Supreme Court's one person, one vote jurisprudence is meant to foreclose." *Id.*

On the other hand, each voter in the city is able to vote in the general election and in his ward's primary, so perhaps Tucson's system does not feature the kind of discrimination that caused the Supreme Court to strike down Georgia's system in *Gray*. The *en banc* court held that Tucson's system was "a careful, longstanding choice . . . as to how best to achieve a city council with members who represent Tucson as a whole but reflect and understand all of the city's wards." 836 F.3d at 1020.

Is it proper to view the "geographical unit" as the entire city, so that members of the ward appear to have more influence and power than voters elsewhere in the city? Alternatively, is the "geographical unit" better thought to be different for the primaries and the general election, such that the "geographical unit" for the primaries would be each ward (within which each voter in the primary election is treated equally) and the "geographical unit" for the general election would be the whole city (within which each voter in the general election is treated equally)?

6. Did *Gray* effectively foreordain the extension of one-person, one-vote to congressional and state-legislative races, or were Justices Stewart and Clark correct that the issues were distinguishable?

Wesberry v. Sanders

Supreme Court of the United States
376 U.S. 1, 84 S. Ct. 526, 11 L. Ed. 2d 481 (1964)

MR. JUSTICE BLACK delivered the opinion of the Court [in which MR. CHIEF JUS-
TICE WARREN, MR. JUSTICE DOUGLAS, MR. JUSTICE BRENNAN, MR. JUSTICE WHITE,
and MR. JUSTICE GOLDBERG join].

Appellants are citizens and qualified voters of Fulton County, Georgia, and as
such are entitled to vote in congressional elections in Georgia's Fifth Congressional District. That district, one of ten created by a 1931 Georgia statute, * * * has a
population according to the 1960 census of 823,680. The average population of the
ten districts is 394,312, less than half that of the Fifth. * * * Since there is only one
Congressman for each district, this inequality of population means that the Fifth
District's Congressman has to represent from two to three times as many people as
do Congressmen from some of the other Georgia districts. * * *

We hold that, construed in its historical context, the command of Art. I, § 2, that
Representatives be chosen "by the People of the several States" means that as nearly
as is practicable one man's vote in a congressional election is to be worth as much as
another's.[10] * * * It would be extraordinary to suggest that * * * the votes of inhabitants of some parts of a State * * * could be weighted at two or three times the value of
the votes of people living in more populous parts of the State * * *. We do not believe
that the Framers of the Constitution intended to permit the same vote-diluting discrimination to be accomplished through the device of districts containing widely
varied numbers of inhabitants. To say that a vote is worth more in one district than
in another would not only run counter to our fundamental ideas of democratic government, it would cast aside the principle of a House of Representatives elected "by
the People," a principle tenaciously fought for and established at the Constitutional
Convention. The history of the Constitution, particularly that part of it relating to
the adoption of Art. I, § 2, reveals that those who framed the Constitution meant
that, no matter what the mechanics of an election, whether statewide or by districts, it was population which was to be the basis of the House of Representatives.
* * *It would defeat the principle solemnly embodied in the Great Compromise—
equal representation in the House for equal numbers of people—for us to hold that,
within the States, legislatures may draw the lines of congressional districts in such
a way as to give some voters a greater voice in choosing a Congressman than others.
The House of Representatives, the Convention agreed, was to represent the people
as individuals, and on a basis of complete equality for each voter. The delegates
were quite aware of what [James] Madison called the "vicious representation" in
Great Britain whereby "rotten boroughs" with few inhabitants were represented in

---

10. We do not reach the arguments that the Georgia statute violates the Due Process, Equal Protection and Privileges and [sic] Immunities Clauses of the Fourteenth Amendment.

Parliament on or almost on a par with cities of greater population. * * * The delegates referred to rotten borough apportionments in some of the state legislatures as the kind of objectionable governmental action that the Constitution should not tolerate in the election of congressional representatives.

Madison in *The Federalist* described the system of division of States into congressional districts, the method which he and others assumed States probably would adopt: "The city of Philadelphia is supposed to contain between fifty and sixty thousand souls. It will therefore form nearly two districts for the choice of Fœderal Representatives." "[N]umbers," he said, * * * "are the only proper scale of representation." In the state conventions, speakers urging ratification of the Constitution emphasized the theme of equal representation in the House which had permeated the debates in Philadelphia. Charles Cotesworth Pinckney told the South Carolina Convention, "the House of Representatives will be elected immediately by the people, and represent them and their personal rights individually. . . ." Speakers at the ratifying conventions emphasized that the House of Representatives was meant to be free of the malapportionment then existing in some of the State legislatures * * * and argued that the power given Congress in Art. I, § 4,[43] was meant to be used to vindicate the people's right to equality of representation in the House. * * *

It is in the light of such history that we must construe Art. I, § 2, of the Constitution, which, carrying out the ideas of Madison and those of like views, provides that Representatives shall be chosen "by the People of the several States" and shall be "apportioned among the several States . . . according to their respective Numbers." It is not surprising that our Court has held that this Article gives persons qualified to vote a constitutional right to vote and to have their votes counted. *United States* v. *Mosley*, 238 U.S. 383 [(1915)]; *Ex parte Yarbrough*, 110 U.S. 651 [(1884)]. Not only can this right to vote not be denied outright, it cannot, consistently with Article I, be destroyed by alteration of ballots, see *United States* v. *Classic*, 313 U.S. 299 [(1941)], or diluted by stuffing of the ballot box, see *United States* v. *Saylor*, 322 U.S. 385 [(1944)]. No right is more precious in a free country than that of having a voice in the election of those who make the laws under which, as good citizens, we must live. Other rights, even the most basic, are illusory if the right to vote is undermined. * * *

While it may not be possible to draw congressional districts with mathematical precision, that is no excuse for ignoring our Constitution's plain objective of making equal representation for equal numbers of people the fundamental goal for the House of Representatives. That is the high standard of justice and common sense which the Founders set for us.

Reversed and remanded.

---

43. "The Times, Places and Manner of holding Elections for Senators and Representatives, shall be prescribed in each State by the Legislature thereof; but the Congress may at any time by Law make or alter such Regulations, except as to the Places of chusing Senators. . . ."

Mr. Justice Clark, concurring in part and dissenting in part.

* * * [I]n my view, Brother Harlan has clearly demonstrated that both the historical background and language preclude a finding that Art. I, § 2, lays down the *ipse dixit* "one person, one vote" in congressional elections.

On the other hand, I agree with the majority that congressional districting is subject to judicial scrutiny. * * * I therefore cannot agree with Brother Harlan that the supervisory power granted to Congress under Art. I, § 4, is the exclusive remedy.

I would examine the Georgia congressional districts against the requirements of the Equal Protection Clause of the Fourteenth Amendment. * * * The trial court, however, did not pass upon the merits of the case * * *. In my view we should therefore vacate this judgment and remand the case for a hearing on the merits. * * *

Mr. Justice Harlan, dissenting.

I had not expected to witness the day when the Supreme Court of the United States would render a decision which casts grave doubt on the constitutionality of the composition of the House of Representatives. * * *

Disclaiming all reliance on other provisions of the Constitution, in particular those of the Fourteenth Amendment on which the appellants relied below and in this Court, the Court holds that the provision in Art, I, § 2, for election of Representatives "by the People" means that congressional districts are to be "as nearly as is practicable" equal in population.{[4]} Stripped of rhetoric and a "historical context" which bears little resemblance to the evidence found in the pages of history, the Court's opinion supports its holding only with the bland assertion that "the principle of a House of Representatives elected 'by the People'" would be "cast aside" if "a vote is worth more in one district than in another," *i.e.*, if congressional districts within a State, each electing a single Representative, are not equal in population. The fact is, however, that Georgia's 10 Representatives are elected "by the People" of Georgia, just as Representatives from other States are elected "by the People of the several States." This is all that the Constitution requires.

Although the Court finds necessity for its artificial construction of Article I in the undoubted importance of the right to vote, that right is not involved in this case.

---

4. The Court's "as nearly as is practicable" formula sweeps a host of questions under the rug. How great a difference between the populations of various districts within a State is tolerable? Is the standard an absolute or relative one, and if the latter to what is the difference in population to be related? Does the number of districts within the State have any relevance? Is the number of voters or the number of inhabitants controlling? Is the relevant statistic the greatest disparity between any two districts in the State or the average departure from the average population per district, or a little of both? May the State consider factors such as area or natural boundaries (rivers, mountain ranges) which are plainly relevant to the practicability of effective representation? There is an obvious lack of criteria for answering questions such as these, which points up the impropriety of the Court's whole-hearted but heavy-footed entrance into the political arena.

All of the appellants do vote. The Court's talk about "debasement" and "dilution" of the vote is a model of circular reasoning, in which the premises of the argument feed on the conclusion. Moreover, by focusing exclusively on numbers in disregard of the area and shape of a congressional district as well as party affiliations within the district, the Court deals in abstractions which will be recognized even by the politically unsophisticated to have little relevance to the realities of political life.

In any event, the very sentence of Art. I, § 2, on which the Court exclusively relies confers the right to vote for Representatives only on those whom *the State* has found qualified to vote for members of "the most numerous Branch of the State Legislature." So far as Article I is concerned, it is within the State's power to confer that right only on persons of wealth or of a particular sex or, if the State chose, living in specified areas of the State. Were Georgia to find the residents of the Fifth District unqualified to vote for Representatives to the State House of Representatives, they could not vote for Representatives to Congress, according to the express words of Art. I, § 2. Other provisions of the Constitution would, of course, be relevant, *but, so far as Art. I, § 2, is concerned*, the disqualification would be within Georgia's power. How can it be, then, that this very same sentence prevents Georgia from apportioning its Representatives as it chooses? The truth is that it does not.

[Under Art. I, § 2,] Representatives were to be apportioned among the States on the basis of free population plus three-fifths of the slave population. Since no slave voted, the inclusion of three-fifths of their number in the basis of apportionment gave the favored States representation far in excess of their voting population. If, then, slaves were intended to be without representation, Article I did exactly what the Court now says it prohibited: it "weighted" the vote of voters in the slave States. * * *

There is a further basis for demonstrating the hollowness of the Court's assertion that Article I requires "one man's vote in a congressional election . . . to be worth as much as another's." Nothing that the Court does today will disturb the fact that although in 1960 the population of an average congressional district was 410,481, the States of Alaska, Nevada, and Wyoming each have a Representative in Congress, although their respective populations are 226,167, 285,278, and 330,066. In entire disregard of population, Art. I, § 2, guarantees each of these States and every other State "at Least one Representative." It is whimsical to assert in the face of this guarantee that an absolute principle of "equal representation in the House for equal numbers of people" is "solemnly embodied" in Article I. All that there is is a provision which bases representation in the House, generally but not entirely, on the population of the States. The provision for representation of *each State* in the House of Representatives is not a mere exception to the principle framed by the majority; it shows that no such principle is to be found.

Finally in this array of hurdles to its decision which the Court surmounts only by knocking them down is § 4 of Art. I which states simply:

"The Times, Places and *Manner* of holding Elections for Senators and Representatives, shall be prescribed in each State by the Legislature thereof;

but the Congress may at any time by Law make or alter such Regulations, except as to the Places of chusing Senators." (Emphasis added.)

* * * It cannot be supposed that delegates to the Convention would have labored to establish a principle of equal representation only to bury it, one would have thought beyond discovery, in § 2, and omit all mention of it from § 4, which deals explicitly with the conduct of elections. Section 4 states without qualification that the state legislatures shall prescribe regulations for the conduct of elections for Representatives and, equally without qualification, that Congress may make or alter such regulations. There is nothing to indicate any limitation whatsoever on this grant of plenary initial and supervisory power. * * *

There is dubious propriety in turning to the "historical context" of constitutional provisions which speak so consistently and plainly. But, as one might expect when the Constitution itself is free from ambiguity, the surrounding history makes what is already clear even clearer.

* * * [T]he statements [at the Constitutional Convention] approving population-based representation were focused on the problem of how representation should be apportioned among the States in the House of Representatives. The Great Compromise concerned representation *of the States* in the Congress. In all of the discussion surrounding the basis of representation of the House and all of the discussion whether Representatives should be elected by the legislatures or the people of the States, there is nothing which suggests even remotely that the delegates had in mind the problem of districting within a State. * * *

[T]he language of Art. I, §§ 2 and 4, the surrounding text, and the relevant history are all in strong and consistent direct contradiction of the Court's holding. The constitutional scheme vests in the States plenary power to regulate the conduct of elections for Representatives, and, in order to protect the Federal Government, provides for congressional supervision of the States' exercise of their power. Within this scheme, the appellants do not have the right which they assert, in the absence of provision for equal districts by the Georgia Legislature or the Congress. The constitutional right which the Court creates is manufactured out of whole cloth. * * *

Congress exercised its power to regulate elections for the House of Representatives for the first time in 1842, when it provided that Representatives from States "entitled to more than one Representative" should be elected by districts of contiguous territory, "no one district electing more than one Representative." The requirement was later dropped, and reinstated. In 1872, Congress required that Representatives "be elected by districts composed of contiguous territory, and containing as nearly as practicable an equal number of inhabitants, . . . no one district electing more than one Representative." This provision for equal districts which the Court exactly duplicates in effect, was carried forward in each subsequent apportionment statute through 1911. There was no reapportionment following the 1920 census. The provision for equally populated districts was dropped in 1929, and has not been revived[.] * * *

Although there is little discussion of the reasons for omitting the requirement of equally populated districts, the fact that such a provision was included in the bill as it was presented to the House, and was deleted by the House after debate and notice of intention to do so, leaves no doubt that the omission was deliberate. [See *Wood v. Broom*, 287 U.S. 1, 7 (1932).] * * * Bills which would have imposed on the States a requirement of equally or nearly equally populated districts were regularly intro duced in the House. None of them became law. * * *

Today's decision has portents for our society and the Court itself which should be recognized. This is not a case in which the Court vindicates the kind of individual rights that are assured by the Due Process Clause of the Fourteenth Amendment, whose "vague contours" of course leave much room for constitutional develop- ments necessitated by changing conditions in a dynamic society. Nor is this a case in which an emergent set of facts requires the Court to frame new principles to protect recognized constitutional rights. The claim for judicial relief in this case strikes at one of the fundamental doctrines of our system of government, the sepa- ration of powers. In upholding that claim, the Court attempts to effect reforms in a field which the Constitution, as plainly as can be, has committed exclusively to the political process.

This Court, no less than all other branches of the Government, is bound by the Constitution. The Constitution does not confer on the Court blanket authority to step into every situation where the political branch may be thought to have fallen short. The stability of this institution ultimately depends not only upon its being alert to keep the other branches of government within constitutional bounds but equally upon recognition of the limitations on the Court's own functions in the constitutional system.

What is done today saps the political process. The promise of judicial interven- tion in matters of this sort cannot but encourage popular inertia in efforts for politi- cal reform through the political process, with the inevitable result that the process is itself weakened. By yielding to the demand for a judicial remedy in this instance, the Court in my view does a disservice both to itself and to the broader values of our system of government.

Believing that the complaint fails to disclose a constitutional claim, I would affirm the judgment below dismissing the complaint.

MR. JUSTICE STEWART.

I think it is established that "this Court has power to afford relief in a case of this type as against the objection that the issues are not justiciable," and I cannot subscribe to any possible implication to the contrary which may lurk in MR. JUS- TICE HARLAN's dissenting opinion. With this single qualification I join the dissent because I think MR. JUSTICE HARLAN has unanswerably demonstrated that Art. I,

§ 2, of the Constitution gives no mandate to this Court or to any court to ordain that congressional districts within each State must be equal in population.

Notes and Questions

1. What did Justice Harlan mean when he charged the majority with "circular reasoning" in its "talk about 'debasement' and 'dilution' of the vote"? *See also Baker v. Carr*, 369 U.S. 186, 300 (1962) (Frankfurter, J., dissenting) ("Talk of 'debasement' or 'dilution' is circular talk. One cannot speak of 'debasement' or 'dilution' of the value of a vote until there is first defined a standard of reference as to what a vote should be worth.").

2. What does "as nearly as is practicable" mean? At the very end of its opinion, the Court stated that precise equality "may not be possible." Should the standard require equality unless it is "[im]possible"? If a more lenient standard is to be applied, what might be sufficient reasons for deviating from precise mathematical equality?

3. Note Justice Harlan's attempt to distinguish the question in this case from issues involving the Due Process Clause. Was he convincing in arguing that the Due Process Clause, but not Article I, §§ 2 and 4, calls for "constitutional developments necessitated by changing conditions in a dynamic society"? (Three years earlier, in *Poe v. Ullman*, 367 U.S. 497 (1961) (dissenting opinion), Justice Harlan had famously called for an active judicial role in protecting the privacy of marital relationships through the Due Process Clause.) Should the Court's interpretation of the Equal Protection Clause take on a similarly dynamic character? *Wesberry v. Sanders* found it unnecessary to address the Equal Protection Clause, but that Clause was at the heart of the next case.

Reynolds v. Sims

Supreme Court of the United States
377 U.S. 533, 84 S. Ct. 1362, 12 L. Ed. 2d 506 (1964)

MR. CHIEF JUSTICE WARREN delivered the opinion of the Court [in which MR. JUSTICE BLACK, MR. JUSTICE DOUGLAS, MR. JUSTICE BRENNAN, MR. JUSTICE WHITE, and MR. JUSTICE GOLDBERG join]. * * *

[Voters in Jefferson County, Alabama, challenged the apportionment of the State's legislature, which consisted of a 35-member Senate and a 106-member House of Representatives, as violating the Equal Protection Clause. Alabama's 1901 Constitution required the State to reapportion districts following each decennial census, but this had not been done. In the years since 1900, Alabama's proportion of city residents had greatly increased, causing the districts' population-variance ratios to be as high as 41-to-1 in the Senate and 16-to-1 in the House. The 1901 Constitution also required each county to have at least one representative and provided that no county could be divided between two Senate districts.

[During this litigation, the Alabama legislature passed a proposed constitutional amendment, which was to be submitted to the voters and would have created a 67-member Senate with 1 senator from each county, and would have given each county one representative in the 106-member House, with the remaining 39 representatives distributed according to population. The District Court held both the existing system and the proposed amendment unconstitutional.]

* * * The right to vote freely for the candidate of one's choice is of the essence of a democratic society, and any restrictions on that right strike at the heart of representative government. And the right of suffrage can be denied by a debasement or dilution of the weight of a citizen's vote just as effectively as by wholly prohibiting the free exercise of the franchise. * * *

Gray [v. *Sanders*, 372 U.S. 368 (1963)] [p. 111] and *Wesberry* [v. *Sanders*, 376 U.S. 1 (1964)] [p. 116] are of course not dispositive of or directly controlling on our decision in these cases involving state legislative apportionment controversies. * * * But neither are they wholly inapposite. *Gray*, though not determinative here since involving the weighting of votes in statewide elections, established the basic principle of equality among voters within a State, and held that voters cannot be classified, constitutionally, on the basis of where they live, at least with respect to voting in statewide elections. And our decision in *Wesberry* * * * clearly established that the fundamental principle of representative government in this country is one of equal representation for equal numbers of people, without regard to race, sex, economic status, or place of residence within a State. Our problem, then, is to ascertain, in the instant cases, whether there are any constitutionally cognizable principles which would justify departures from the basic standard of equality among voters in the apportionment of seats in state legislatures.

A predominant consideration in determining whether a State's legislative apportionment scheme constitutes an invidious discrimination violative of rights asserted under the Equal Protection Clause is that the rights allegedly impaired are individual and personal in nature. * * * While the result of a court decision in a state legislative apportionment controversy may be to require the restructuring of the geographical distribution of seats in a state legislature, the judicial focus must be concentrated upon ascertaining whether there has been any discrimination against certain of the State's citizens which constitutes an impermissible impairment of their constitutionally protected right to vote. Like *Skinner* v. *Oklahoma*, 316 U.S. 535 [(1942)], such a case "'touches a sensitive and important area of human rights,' and 'involves one of the basic civil rights of man,'" presenting questions of alleged "invidious discriminations . . . against groups or types of individuals in violation of the constitutional guaranty of just and equal laws." Undoubtedly, the right of suffrage is a fundamental matter in a free and democratic society. Especially since the right to exercise the franchise in a free and unimpaired manner is preservative of other basic civil and political rights, any alleged infringement of the right of citizens to vote must be carefully and meticulously scrutinized. Almost a century ago, in *Yick Wo* v. *Hopkins*, 118 U.S.

356 [(1886)], the Court referred to "the political franchise of voting" as "a funda-mental political right, because preservative of all rights."

Legislators represent people, not trees or acres. Legislators are elected by voters, not farms or cities or economic interests. As long as ours is a representative form of government, and our legislatures are those instruments of government elected directly by and directly representative of the people, the right to elect legislators in a free and unimpaired fashion is a bedrock of our political system. It could hardly be gainsaid that a constitutional claim had been asserted by an allegation that certain otherwise qualified voters had been entirely prohibited from voting for members of their state legislature. And, if a State should provide that the votes of citizens in one part of the State should be given two times, or five times, or 10 times the weight of votes of citizens in another part of the State, it could hardly be contended that the right to vote of those residing in the disfavored areas had not been effectively diluted. * * * And it is inconceivable that a state law to the effect that, in counting votes for legislators, the votes of citizens in one part of the State would be multiplied by two, five, or 10, while the votes of persons in another area would be counted only at face value, could be constitutionally sustainable. Of course, the effect of state legislative districting schemes which give the same number of representatives to unequal numbers of constituents is identical. * * * Weighting the votes of citizens differently, by any method or means, merely because of where they happen to reside, hardly seems justifiable. * * *

[R]epresentative government is in essence self-government through the medium of elected representatives of the people, and each and every citizen has an inalienable right to full and effective participation in the political processes of his State's legislative bodies. Most citizens can achieve this participation only as qualified voters through the election of legislators to represent them. Full and effective participation by all citizens in state government requires, therefore, that each citizen have an equally effective voice in the election of members of his state legislature. Modern and viable state government needs, and the Constitution demands, no less.

Logically, in a society ostensibly grounded on representative government, it would seem reasonable that a majority of the people of a State could elect a majority of that State's legislators. To conclude differently, and to sanction minority control of state legislative bodies, would appear to deny majority rights in a way that far surpasses any possible denial of minority rights that might otherwise be thought to result. Since legislatures are responsible for enacting laws by which all citizens are to be governed, they should be bodies which are collectively responsive to the popular will. And the concept of equal protection has been traditionally viewed as requiring the uniform treatment of persons standing in the same relation to the governmental action questioned or challenged. With respect to the allocation of legislative representation, all voters, as citizens of a State, stand in the same relation regardless of where they live. Any suggested criteria for the differentiation of citizens are insufficient to justify any discrimination, as to the weight of their votes, unless relevant to the permissible purposes of legislative apportionment. Since the achieving of fair and effective representation for all citizens is concededly the basic aim of legislative apportionment, we conclude that the Equal Protection Clause guarantees the opportunity for equal participation by all voters in the election of state legislators. Diluting the weight of votes because of place of residence impairs basic constitutional rights under the Fourteenth Amendment just as much as invidious discriminations based upon factors such as race or economic status. Our constitutional system amply provides for the protection of minorities by means other than giving them majority control of state legislatures. And the democratic ideals of equality and majority rule, which have served this Nation so well in the past, are hardly of any less significance for the present and the future.

We are told that the matter of apportioning representation in a state legislature is a complex and many-faceted one. We are advised that States can rationally consider factors other than population in apportioning legislative representation. We are admonished not to restrict the power of the States to impose differing views as to political philosophy on their citizens. We are cautioned about the dangers of entering into political thickets and mathematical quagmires. Our answer is this: a denial of constitutionally protected rights demands judicial protection; our oath and our office require no less of us. * * * To the extent that a citizen's right to vote is debased, he is that much less a citizen. The fact that an individual lives here or there is not a legitimate reason for overweighting or diluting the efficacy of his vote. The complexions of societies and civilizations change, often with amazing rapidity. A nation once primarily rural in character becomes predominantly urban. Representation schemes once fair and equitable become archaic and outdated. But the basic principle of representative government remains, and must remain, unchanged—the weight of a citizen's vote cannot be made to depend on where he lives. Population is, of necessity, the starting point for consideration and the controlling criterion for judgment in legislative apportionment controversies. A citizen, a qualified voter, is no more nor no less so because he lives in the city or on the farm. This is the clear and strong command of our Constitution's Equal Protection Clause. This is an essential part of the concept of a government of laws and not men. This is at the heart of Lincoln's vision of "government of the people, by the people, [and] for the people." The Equal Protection Clause demands no less than substantially equal state legislative representation for all citizens, of all places as well as of all races.

We hold that, as a basic constitutional standard, the Equal Protection Clause requires that the seats in both houses of a bicameral state legislature must be apportioned on a population basis. Simply stated, an individual's right to vote for state legislators is unconstitutionally impaired when its weight is in a substantial fashion diluted when compared with votes of citizens living in other parts of the State. * * *

Since neither of the houses of the Alabama Legislature * * * was apportioned on a population basis, we would be justified in proceeding no further. However, * * * the so-called 67-Senator Amendment, at least superficially resembles the scheme of legislative representation followed in the Federal Congress. Under this plan, each of

Alabama's 67 counties is allotted one senator, and no counties are given more than one Senate seat. Arguably, this is analogous to the allocation of two Senate seats, in the Federal Congress, to each of the 50 States, regardless of population. Seats in the Alabama House, under the proposed constitutional amendment, are distributed by giving each of the 67 counties at least one, with the remaining 39 seats being allotted among the more populous counties on a population basis. This scheme, at least at first glance, appears to resemble that prescribed for the Federal House of Representatives, where the 435 seats are distributed among the States on a population basis, although each State, regardless of its population, is given at least one Congressman. Thus, although there are substantial differences in underlying rationale and result, the 67-Senator Amendment, as proposed by the Alabama Legislature, at least arguably presents for consideration a scheme analogous to that used for apportioning seats in Congress.

* * * We * * * find the federal analogy inapposite and irrelevant to state legislative districting schemes. * * *

The system of representation in the two Houses of the Federal Congress is one ingrained in our Constitution, as part of the law of the land. It is one conceived out of compromise and concession indispensable to the establishment of our federal republic. Arising from unique historical circumstances, it is based on the consideration that in establishing our type of federalism a group of formerly independent States bound themselves together under one national government. Admittedly, the original 13 States surrendered some of their sovereignty in agreeing to join together "to form a more perfect Union." But at the heart of our constitutional system remains the concept of separate and distinct governmental entities which have delegated some, but not all, of their formerly held powers to the single national government. The fact that almost three-fourths of our present States were never in fact independently sovereign does not detract from our view that the so-called federal analogy is inapplicable as a sustaining precedent for state legislative apportionments. The developing history and growth of our republic cannot cloud the fact that, at the time of the inception of the system of representation in the Federal Congress, a compromise between the larger and smaller States on this matter averted a deadlock in the Constitutional Convention which had threatened to abort the birth of our Nation. * * *

Political subdivisions of States—counties, cities, or whatever—never were and never have been considered as sovereign entities. Rather, they have been traditionally regarded as subordinate governmental instrumentalities created by the State to assist in the carrying out of state governmental functions. * * * The relationship of the States to the Federal Government could hardly be less analogous.

Thus, we conclude that the plan contained in the 67-Senator Amendment for apportioning seats in the Alabama Legislature cannot be sustained by recourse to the so-called federal analogy. Nor can any other inequitable state legislative apportionment scheme be justified on such an asserted basis. This does not necessarily mean that such a plan is irrational or involves something other than a "republican form of government." We conclude simply that such a plan is impermissible for the States under the Equal Protection Clause, since perforce resulting, in virtually every case, in submergence of the equal-population principle in at least one house of a state legislature.

Since we find the so-called federal analogy inapposite to a consideration of the constitutional validity of state legislative apportionment schemes, we necessarily hold that the Equal Protection Clause requires both houses of a state legislature to be apportioned on a population basis. The right of a citizen to equal representation and to have his vote weighted equally with those of all other citizens in the election of members of one house of a bicameral state legislature would amount to little if States could effectively submerge the equal-population principle in the apportionment of seats in the other house. If such a scheme were permissible, an individual citizen's ability to exercise an effective voice in the only instrument of state government directly representative of the people might be almost as effectively thwarted as if neither house were apportioned on a population basis. Deadlock between the two bodies might result in compromise and concession on some issues. But in all too many cases the more probable result would be frustration of the majority will through minority veto in the house not apportioned on a population basis, stemming directly from the failure to accord adequate overall legislative representation to all of the State's citizens on a nondiscriminatory basis. In summary, we can perceive no constitutional difference, with respect to the geographical distribution of state legislative representation, between the two houses of a bicameral state legislature.

We do not believe that the concept of bicameralism is rendered anachronistic and meaningless when the predominant basis of representation in the two state legislative bodies is required to be the same — population. A prime reason for bicameralism, modernly considered, is to insure mature and deliberate consideration of, and to prevent precipitate action on, proposed legislative measures. Simply because the controlling criterion for apportioning representation is required to be the same in both houses does not mean that there will be no differences in the composition and complexion of the two bodies. Different constituencies can be represented in the two houses. One body could be composed of single-member districts while the other could have at least some multimember districts. The length of terms of the legislators in the separate bodies could differ. The numerical size of the two bodies could be made to differ, even significantly, and the geographical size of districts from which legislators are elected could also be made to differ. And apportionment in one house could be arranged so as to balance off minor inequities in the representation of certain areas in the other house. In summary, these and other factors could be, and are presently in many States, utilized to engender differing complexions and collective attitudes in the two bodies of a state legislature, although both are apportioned substantially on a population basis.

By holding that as a federal constitutional requisite both houses of a state legislature must be apportioned on a population basis, we mean that the Equal Protection Clause requires that a State make an honest and good faith effort to construct districts, in both houses of its legislature, as nearly of equal population as is practicable. We realize that it is a practical impossibility to arrange legislative districts so that each one has an identical number of residents, or citizens, or voters. Mathematical exactness or precision is hardly a workable constitutional requirement.

In *Wesberry* v. *Sanders, supra,* the Court stated that congressional representation must be based on population as nearly as is practicable. In implementing the basic constitutional principle of representative government as enunciated by the Court in *Wesberry*—equality of population among districts—some distinctions may well be made between congressional and state legislative representation. Since, almost invariably, there is a significantly larger number of seats in state legislative bodies to be distributed within a State than congressional seats, it may be feasible to use political subdivision lines to a greater extent in establishing state legislative districts than in congressional districting while still affording adequate representation to all parts of the State. To do so would be constitutionally valid, so long as the resulting apportionment was one based substantially on population and the equal-population principle was not diluted in any significant way. Somewhat more flexibility may therefore be constitutionally permissible with respect to state legislative apportionment than in congressional districting. Lower courts can and assuredly will work out more concrete and specific standards for evaluating state legislative apportionment schemes in the context of actual litigation. For the present, we deem it expedient not to attempt to spell out any precise constitutional tests. What is marginally permissible in one State may be unsatisfactory in another, depending on the particular circumstances of the case. Developing a body of doctrine on a case-by-case basis appears to us to provide the most satisfactory means of arriving at detailed constitutional requirements in the area of state legislative apportionment. Thus, we proceed to state here only a few rather general considerations which appear to us to be relevant.

A State may legitimately desire to maintain the integrity of various political subdivisions, insofar as possible, and provide for compact districts of contiguous territory in designing a legislative apportionment scheme. Valid considerations may underlie such aims. Indiscriminate districting, without any regard for political subdivision or natural or historical boundary lines, may be little more than an open invitation to partisan gerrymandering. Single-member districts may be the rule in one State, while another State might desire to achieve some flexibility by creating multimember or floterial districts.[a] Whatever the means of accomplishment, the overriding objective must be substantial equality of population among the various

---

a. A floterial district combines multiple single-member districts, where the conglomeration would be entitled to more representation than the total number of representatives allocated to each smaller district individually. For example, if the ideal district has 100,000 people, a state might create a floterial district out of four districts with populations of 125,000. Each of the four districts

districts, so that the vote of any citizen is approximately equal in weight to that of any other citizen in the State.

History indicates, however, that many States have deviated, to a greater or lesser degree, from the equal-population principle in the apportionment of seats in at least one house of their legislatures. So long as the divergences from a strict population standard are based on legitimate considerations incident to the effectuation of a rational state policy, some deviations from the equal-population principle are constitutionally permissible with respect to the apportionment of seats in either or both of the two houses of a bicameral state legislature. But neither history alone, nor economic or other sorts of group interests, are permissible factors in attempting to justify disparities from population-based representation. Citizens, not history or economic interests, cast votes. Considerations of area alone provide an insufficient justification for deviations from the equal-population principle. Again, people, not land or trees or pastures, vote. Modern developments and improvements in transportation and communications make rather hollow, in the mid-1960's, most claims that deviations from population-based representation can validly be based solely on geographical considerations. Arguments for allowing such deviations in order to insure effective representation for sparsely settled areas and to prevent legislative districts from becoming so large that the availability of access of citizens to their representatives is impaired are today, for the most part, unconvincing.

A consideration that appears to be of more substance in justifying some deviations from population-based representation in state legislatures is that of insuring some voice to political subdivisions, as political subdivisions. Several factors make more than insubstantial claims that a State can rationally consider according political subdivisions some independent representation in at least one body of the state legislature, as long as the basic standard of equality of population among districts is maintained. Local governmental entities are frequently charged with various responsibilities incident to the operation of state government. In many States much of the legislature's activity involves the enactment of so-called local legislation, directed only to the concerns of particular political subdivisions. And a State may legitimately desire to construct districts along political subdivision lines to deter the possibilities of gerrymandering. However, permitting deviations from population-based representation does not mean that each local governmental unit or political subdivision can be given separate representation, regardless of population. Carried too far, a scheme of giving at least one seat in one house to each political subdivision (for example, to each county) could easily result, in many States, in a total subversion of the equal-population principle in that legislative body. This would be especially true in a State where the number of counties is large and many of them are sparsely populated, and the number of seats in the legislative body being apportioned does not significantly exceed the number of counties. Such a result, we conclude, would be constitutionally impermissible. And careful judicial scrutiny

---

would be entitled to its one representative, and there would be an additional "floater" elected by the entire floterial district. —Eds.

must of course be given, in evaluating state apportionment schemes, to the character as well as the degree of deviations from a strict population basis. But if, even as a result of a clearly rational state policy of according some legislative representation to political subdivisions, population is submerged as the controlling consideration in the apportionment of seats in the particular legislative body, then the right of all of the State's citizens to cast an effective and adequately weighted vote would be unconstitutionally impaired.

One of the arguments frequently offered as a basis for upholding a State's legislative apportionment arrangement, despite substantial disparities from a population basis in either or both houses, is grounded on congressional approval, incident to admitting States into the Union, of state apportionment plans containing deviations from the equal-population principle. * * * Nevertheless, * * * Congress presumably does not assume, in admitting States into the Union, to pass on all constitutional questions relating to the character of state governmental organization. In any event, congressional approval, however well-considered, could hardly validate an unconstitutional state legislative apportionment. Congress simply lacks the constitutional power to insulate States from attack with respect to alleged deprivations of individual constitutional rights.

That the Equal Protection Clause requires that both houses of a state legislature be apportioned on a population basis does not mean that States cannot adopt some reasonable plan for periodic revision of their apportionment schemes. Decennial reapportionment appears to be a rational approach to readjustment of legislative representation in order to take into account population shifts and growth. * * * Limitations on the frequency of reapportionment are justified by the need for stability and continuity in the organization of the legislative system, although undoubtedly reapportioning no more frequently than every 10 years leads to some imbalance in the population of districts toward the end of the decennial period and also to the development of resistance to change on the part of some incumbent legislators. In substance, we do not regard the Equal Protection Clause as requiring daily, monthly, annual or biennial reapportionment, so long as a State has a reasonably conceived plan for periodic readjustment of legislative representation. While we do not intend to indicate that decennial reapportionment is a constitutional requisite, compliance with such an approach would clearly meet the minimal requirements for maintaining a reasonably current scheme of legislative representation. And we do not mean to intimate that more frequent reapportionment would not be constitutionally permissible or practicably desirable. But if reapportionment were accomplished with less frequency, it would assuredly be constitutionally suspect. * * *

   * * * [W]e affirm the judgment below and remand the case for further proceedings consistent with the views stated in this opinion.

It is so ordered.

Mr. Justice Clark, concurring in the affirmance. * * *

It seems to me that all that the Court need say in this case is that each plan considered by the trial court is "a crazy quilt," clearly revealing invidious discrimination in each house of the Legislature and therefore violative of the Equal Protection Clause. See my concurring opinion in *Baker* v. *Carr,* 369 U.S. 186, 253–258 (1962) [p. 97].

I, therefore, do not reach the question of the so-called "federal analogy." But in my view, if one house of the State Legislature meets the population standard, representation in the other house might include some departure from it so as to take into account, on a rational basis, other factors in order to afford some representation to the various elements of the State.

Mr. Justice Stewart.

All of the parties have agreed * * * that legislative inaction for some 60 years in the face of growth and shifts in population has converted Alabama's legislative apportionment plan enacted in 1901 into one completely lacking in rationality. Accordingly, for the reasons stated in my dissenting opinion in *Lucas* v. *Forty-Fourth General Assembly of Colorado,* [377 U.S. 713 (1964) (discussed in the Notes following this case)], I would affirm the judgment of the District Court holding that this apportionment violated the Equal Protection Clause. * * *

Mr. Justice Harlan, dissenting. * * *

* * * Stripped of aphorisms, the Court's argument boils down to the assertion that appellees' right to vote has been invidiously "debased" or "diluted" by systems of apportionment which entitle them to vote for fewer legislators than other voters, an assertion which is tied to the Equal Protection Clause only by the constitutionally frail tautology that "equal" means "equal." * * *

The Court relies exclusively on that portion of § 1 of the Fourteenth Amendment which provides that no State shall "deny to any person within its jurisdiction the equal protection of the laws," and disregards entirely the significance of § 2, which reads:

> "Representatives shall be apportioned among the several States according to their respective numbers, counting the whole number of persons in each State, excluding Indians not taxed. *But when the right to vote at any election for* the choice of electors for President and Vice President of the United States, Representatives in Congress, *the Executive and Judicial officers of a State, or the members of the Legislature thereof, is denied* to any of the male inhabitants of such State, being twenty-one years of age, and citizens of the United States, *or in any way abridged,* except for participation in rebellion, or other crime, the basis of representation therein shall be reduced in the proportion which the number of such male citizens shall bear to the whole

number of male citizens twenty-one years of age in such State." (Emphasis added.)

* * * Whatever one might take to be the application to these cases of the Equal Protection Clause if it stood alone, I am unable to understand the Court's utter disregard of the second section which expressly recognizes the States' power to deny "or in any way" abridge the right of their inhabitants to vote for "the members of the [State] Legislature," and its express provision of a remedy for such denial or abridgment. * * * If indeed the words of the Fourteenth Amendment speak for themselves, as the majority's disregard of history seems to imply, they speak as clearly as may be against the construction which the majority puts on them. But we are not limited to the language of the Amendment itself.

The history of the adoption of the Fourteenth Amendment provides conclusive evidence that neither those who proposed nor those who ratified the Amendment believed that the Equal Protection Clause limited the power of the States to apportion their legislatures as they saw fit. Moreover, the history demonstrates that the intention to leave this power undisturbed was deliberate and was widely believed to be essential to the adoption of the Amendment. [MR. JUSTICE HARLAN discussed the legislative history surrounding the proposal of the Fourteenth Amendment, arguing that § 2 was seen as a politically acceptable alternative to requiring States to grant equal voting rights.]

* * * Of the 23 loyal States which ratified the Amendment before 1870, five had constitutional provisions for apportionment of at least one house of their respective legislatures which wholly disregarded the spread of population. Ten more had constitutional provisions which gave primary emphasis to population, but which applied also other principles, such as partial ratios and recognition of political subdivisions, which were intended to favor sparsely settled areas. Can it be seriously contended that the legislatures of these States, almost two-thirds of those concerned, would have ratified an amendment which might render their own States' constitutions unconstitutional? * * *

Each of the 10 "reconstructed" States was required to ratify the Fourteenth Amendment before it was readmitted to the Union. The Constitution of each was scrutinized in Congress. * * * The Constitutions of six of the 10 States contained provisions departing substantially from the method of apportionment now held to be required by the Amendment. * * *

It is incredible that Congress would have exacted ratification of the Fourteenth Amendment as the price of readmission, would have studied the State Constitutions for compliance with the Amendment, and would then have disregarded violations of it.

The facts recited above show beyond any possible doubt:

(1) that Congress, with full awareness of and attention to the possibility that the States would not afford full equality in voting rights to all their

citizens, nevertheless deliberately chose not to interfere with the States' plenary power in this regard when it proposed the Fourteenth Amendment;

(2) that Congress did not include in the Fourteenth Amendment restrictions on the States' power to control voting rights because it believed that if such restrictions were included, the Amendment would not be adopted; and

(3) that at least a substantial majority, if not all, of the States which ratified the Fourteenth Amendment did not consider that in so doing, they were accepting limitations on their freedom, never before questioned, to regulate voting rights as they chose. * * *

The years following 1868, far from indicating a developing awareness of the applicability of the Fourteenth Amendment to problems of apportionment, demonstrate precisely the reverse: that the States retained and exercised the power independently to apportion their legislatures. [MR. JUSTICE HARLAN noted the subordination of population equality in the constitutions of Alabama, Florida, Georgia, Louisiana, Mississippi, Missouri, Montana, New Hampshire, New York, North Carolina, Oklahoma, Pennsylvania, South Carolina, Utah, and Wyoming.]

Since the Court now invalidates the legislative apportionments in six States, and has so far upheld the apportionment in none, it is scarcely necessary to comment on the situation in the States today, which is, of course, as fully contrary to the Court's decision as is the record of every prior period in this Nation's history. As of 1961, the Constitutions of all but 11 States, roughly 20% of the total, recognized bases of apportionment other than geographic spread of population, and to some extent favored sparsely populated areas by a variety of devices[.] * * *

In this summary of what the majority ignores, note should be taken of the Fifteenth and Nineteenth Amendments. The former prohibited the States from denying or abridging the right to vote "on account of race, color, or previous condition of servitude." The latter, certified as part of the Constitution in 1920, added sex to the prohibited classifications. * * * If constitutional amendment was the only means by which all men and, later, women, could be guaranteed the right to vote at all, even for federal officers, how can it be that the far less obvious right to a particular kind of apportionment of state legislatures * * * can be conferred by judicial construction of the Fourteenth Amendment? * * *

It should by now be obvious that these cases do not mark the end of reapportionment problems in the courts. Predictions once made that the courts would never have to face the problem of actually working out an apportionment have proved false. This Court, however, continues to avoid the consequences of its decisions, simply assuring us that the lower courts "can and . . . will work out more concrete and specific standards." Deeming it "expedient" not to spell out "precise constitutional tests," the Court contents itself with stating "only a few rather general considerations."

Generalities cannot obscure the cold truth that cases of this type are not amenable to the development of judicial standards. No set of standards can guide a court which has to decide how many legislative districts a State shall have, or what the shape of the districts shall be, or where to draw a particular district line. No judicially manageable standard can determine whether a State should have single-member districts or multimember districts or some combination of both. No such standard can control the balance between keeping up with population shifts and having stable districts. In all these respects, the courts will be called upon to make particular decisions with respect to which a principle of equally populated districts will be of no assistance whatsoever. Quite obviously, there are limitless possibilities for districting consistent with such a principle. Nor can these problems be avoided by judicial reliance on legislative judgments so far as possible. Reshaping or combining one or two districts, or modifying just a few district lines, is no less a matter of choosing among many possible solutions, with varying political consequences, than reapportionment broadside. * * *

Although the Court—necessarily, as I believe—provides only generalities in elaboration of its main thesis, its opinion nevertheless fully demonstrates how far removed these problems are from fields of judicial competence. Recognizing that "indiscriminate districting" is an invitation to "partisan gerrymandering," the Court nevertheless excludes virtually every basis for the formation of electoral districts other than "indiscriminate districting." In one or another of today's opinions, the Court declares it unconstitutional for a State to give effective consideration to any of the following in establishing legislative districts:

(1) history;

(2) "economic or other sorts of group interests";

(3) area;

(4) geographical considerations;

(5) a desire "to insure effective representation for sparsely settled areas";

(6) "availability of access of citizens to their representatives";

(7) theories of bicameralism (except those approved by the Court);

(8) occupation;

(9) "an attempt to balance urban and rural power."

(10) the preference of a majority of voters in the State.

So far as presently appears, the *only* factor which a State may consider, apart from numbers, is political subdivisions. But even "a clearly rational state policy" recognizing this factor is unconstitutional if "population is submerged as the controlling consideration."

I know of no principle of logic or practical or theoretical politics, still less any constitutional principle, which establishes all or any of these exclusions. Certain it is that the Court's opinion does not establish them. So far as the Court says anything at all on this score, it says only that "legislators represent people, not trees or acres"; that "citizens, not history or economic interests, cast votes"; that "people, not land or trees or pastures, vote." All this may be conceded. But it is surely equally obvious, and, in the context of elections, more meaningful, to note that people are not ciphers and that legislators can represent their electors only by speaking for their interests—economic, social, political—many of which do reflect the place where the electors live. The Court does not establish, or indeed even attempt to make a case for the proposition that conflicting interests within a State can only be adjusted by disregarding them when voters are grouped for purposes of representation. * * *

Notes and Questions

1. Few Americans today have any recollection or knowledge of the extent of malapportionment in American legislatures at the time that the Court began to decide reapportionment cases under the Equal Protection Clause. No state even came close to using equally populated districts, and the differences, in all regions of the country, were sometimes stunning. In Connecticut, state house districts ranged in population from a low of 192 to a high of 81,096. In Florida, they ranged from 2868 to 311,682. Minnesota state senate districts ran the gamut from 4896 to 359,982; Nevada's from 568 to 127,016. One state house district in Vermont had a population of just 24, while the most populous district in the state represented 35,531 people. *See* STEPHEN ANSOLABEHERE & JAMES M. SNYDER, JR., THE END OF INEQUALITY: ONE PERSON, ONE VOTE, AND THE TRANSFORMATION OF AMERICAN POLITICS 26–27, Table 2.1 (2008). Do such numbers emphasize the need for the Court to act, or do they indicate that the Constitution was understood not to require equally populated districts?

2. Is there an inconsistency between the Court's rejection of the "federal analogy" and its concession that some population disparity is acceptable to "insur[e] some voice to political subdivisions, as political subdivisions"?[b] Why should that interest trump absolute population equality? What "voice" do political subdivisions need if they are only "subordinate governmental instrumentalities created by the State to assist in the carrying out of state governmental functions"? Reconsider these questions after reading *Mahan v. Howell*, 410 U.S. 315 (1973) [p. 163], and *Gaffney v. Cummings*, 412 U.S. 735 (1973) [p. 168], later in this Chapter.

Considering the matter from another perspective, why should population equality trump other goals states might try to achieve through their representational structures? Why can states not seek to apportion legislatures to balance the political power of economic, social, or political groups?

---

b. *See also Board of Estimate v. Morris*, 489 U.S. 688, 702–03 & 703 n.10 (1989) (holding unconstitutional New York City's method of selecting the Board, under which each borough president received a seat regardless of the borough's population, and rejecting the proposition that "exigencies of history or convenience" could justify such a departure from the one-person, one-vote rule).

3. In *Baker*, the plaintiffs and Solicitor General Archibald Cox argued that states should and would have great leeway in devising new districts. Cox specifically argued that equal population in both houses of a state legislature was not constitutionally mandated. Rather, the state merely needed to provide a rational basis for deviating from strict population equality. "States," said Cox, "would have great freedom to apportion, according to their own theories." A reasoned approach to redistricting, though it might not create equally populated districts, would presumably be constitutional. Tennessee's approach, he argued, was neither reasoned nor reasonable. Transcript of Oral Argument at 36, *Baker v. Carr*, 369 U.S. 186 (1962) (No. 6).

If this approach seems appealing, put yourself in the position of a state legislator trying to draw districts. What would be allowed? Consider that within six months of *Baker*, legal challenges to districting plans had been filed in thirty-one states. Of the first fifteen cases decided, eleven plans were struck down and just four were upheld, but those numbers don't begin to account for the wide range of theories and differing reasons given by the courts. *See* Guy Uriel-Charles & Luis Fuentes Rohwer, *Reynold Revisited*, *in* ELECTION LAW STORIES 21, 26–27 (Joshua A. Douglas & Eugene D. Mazo eds., 2016).

Justices Clark and Stewart in *Sims* seemed to apply a similar approach to the one suggested by Solicitor General Cox in *Baker*. Those two Justices voted to strike down Alabama's districting because they viewed it as irrational. They understood the "well developed and familiar" standards of equal protection to embody the traditional rational-basis test applied to adjudicate equal-protection challenges to laws *not* implicating fundamental rights. (The Court rejected the rational-basis test in *Sims* by analogizing the right to an equally weighted vote to the fundamental right to procreate, at issue in *Skinner v. Oklahoma*, 316 U.S. 535 (1942), abridgments of which trigger strict scrutiny.) In *Lucas v. Forty-Fourth General Assembly of Colorado*, 377 U.S. 713 (1964), decided the same day as *Reynolds v. Sims*, Justice Stewart further explained how he would apply the rational-basis test to legislative apportionment.

Lucas involved a challenge to the apportionment of Colorado's state legislature, and the companion case of *WMCA, Inc. v. Lomenzo*, 377 U.S. 633 (1964), involved a challenge to the apportionment of New York's. The Court struck down each, but Justices Stewart and Clark dissented, finding the plans "rational":

> Representative government is a process of accommodating group interests through democratic institutional arrangements. Its function is to channel the numerous opinions, interests, and abilities of the people of a State into the making of the State's public policy. Appropriate legislative apportionment, therefore, should ideally be designed to ensure effective representation in the State's legislature[.] * * *

> [A] system of legislative apportionment which might be best for South Dakota, might be unwise for Hawaii with its many islands, or Michigan with its Northern Peninsula. * * * Montana with its vast distances is not

Rhode Island with its heavy concentrations of people. [There are also] great variations among the several States in their historic manner of distributing legislative power [including powers of initiative and referendum, Governors' Councils, gubernatorial veto powers, and home-rule provisions for cities]. The Court today declines to give any recognition to these considerations and countless others, tangible and intangible, in holding unconstitutional the particular systems of legislative apportionment which these States have chosen. Instead, the Court says that the requirements of the Equal Protection Clause can be met in any State only by the uncritical, simplistic, and heavy-handed application of sixth-grade arithmetic.

But legislators do not represent faceless numbers. They represent people, or, more accurately, a majority of the voters in their districts — people with identifiable needs and interests which require legislative representation, and which can often be related to the geographical areas in which these people live. * * *

The fact is, of course, that population factors must often to some degree be subordinated in devising a legislative apportionment plan which is to achieve the important goal of ensuring a fair, effective, and balanced representation of the regional, social, and economic interests within a State. And the further fact is that throughout our history the apportionments of State Legislatures have reflected the strongly felt American tradition that the public interest is composed of many diverse interests, and that in the long run it can better be expressed by a medley of component voices than by the majority's monolithic command. What constitutes a rational plan reasonably designed to achieve this objective will vary from State to State, since each State is unique, in terms of topography, geography, demography, history, heterogeneity and concentration of population, variety of social and economic interests, and in the operation and interrelation of its political institutions. But so long as a State's apportionment plan reasonably achieves, in the light of the State's own characteristics, effective and balanced representation of all substantial interests, without sacrificing the principle of effective majority rule, that plan cannot be considered irrational. * * *

* * * I think that the Equal Protection Clause demands but two basic attributes of any plan of state legislative apportionment. First, it demands that, in the light of the state's own characteristics and needs, the plan must be a rational one. Secondly, it demands that the plan must be such as not to permit the systematic frustration of the will of a majority of the electorate of the State. I think it is apparent that any plan of legislative apportionment which could be shown to reflect no policy, but simply arbitrary and capricious action or inaction, and that any plan which could be shown systematically to prevent ultimate effective majority rule, would be invalid under accepted Equal Protection Clause standards. But, beyond this, I think there is nothing in the Federal Constitution to prevent a State from choosing any

electoral legislative structure it thinks best suited to the interests, temper, and customs of its people.

Lucas, 377 U.S. at 749–51, 753–54 (Stewart, J., joined by Clark, J., dissenting). Colorado's plan, Justice Stewart contended, was a rational means of representing the interests of the vastly different geographical areas of the state, while New York's was a rational way of ensuring that the population of New York City did not overwhelm the interests of the rest of the state. *See id*. at 754–65. *See also Wesberry v. Sanders*, 376 U.S. 1, 21 n.4 (1964) [p. 116] (Harlan, J., dissenting) (arguing that states should be able to take into account "the practicability of effective representation" in drawing district lines that conform to "natural boundaries (rivers, mountain ranges)"). The Court, however, held that neither concern was an adequate excuse for not apportioning districts on a population basis, partially because of "[m]odern developments and improvements in transportation and communications," which minimized the effect of those natural boundaries.

Is Justice Stewart's rationality standard capable of consistent application? Is ensuring that the population of New York City does not overwhelm the rest of the state just a nicer way of characterizing "the systematic frustration of the will of a majority of the electorate"?

4. Part of the attraction of the Court's one-person, one-vote rule is the capacity of other systems to "lock-up" the political process by permitting those with political power to determine the appropriate "balance" of political power for the future. *See generally* Richard L. Hasen, *The "Political Market" Metaphor and Election Law: A Comment on Issacharoff and Pildes*, 50 STANFORD L. REV. 719 (1998); Samuel Issacharoff & Richard H. Pildes, *Politics as Markets: Partisan Lockups of the Democratic Process*, 50 STANFORD L. REV. 643 (1998); Michael J. Klarman, *Majoritarian Judicial Review: The Entrenchment Problem*, 85 GEO. L.J. 491 (1997). Voters in cities, for example, may have no effective way of altering a representational structure giving rural interests disproportionate representation, if those rural interests will control any consideration of reapportionment. But what if a state's apportionment was a deliberate choice by the people, rather than a self-interested power-grab?

In *Lucas, supra*, Colorado's federal model of representation was passed by referendum. It received two-thirds of the statewide vote and majorities in every county, including those counties "underrepresented" by the plan. Nevertheless, the Court was not impressed. In a 6-3 decision, the Court, with Chief Justice Warren authoring the opinion, applied *Sims* to hold the plan invalid:

> An individual's constitutionally protected right to cast an equally weighted vote cannot be denied even by a vote of a majority of a State's electorate, if the apportionment scheme adopted by the voters fails to measure up to the requirements of the Equal Protection Clause. Manifestly, the fact that an apportionment plan is adopted in a popular referendum is insufficient to sustain its constitutionality[.] * * * A citizen's constitutional rights can hardly be infringed simply because a majority of the people choose that it

be. We hold that the fact that a challenged legislative apportionment plan was approved by the electorate is without federal constitutional significance, if the scheme adopted fails to satisfy the basic requirements of the Equal Protection Clause, as delineated in our opinion in *Reynolds* v. *Sims*.

377 U.S. at 736–37. Can a group of people democratically vote to "underrepresent" themselves vis-à-vis other parts of the state?

5. What is the significance of Chief Justice Warren's insistence that the right to an equally weighted vote is an "individual," "personal" right? Does such a conclusion make sense? *See* Samuel Issacharoff, *Groups and the Right to Vote*, 44 EMORY L.J. 869 (1995). *Cf.* Heather K. Gerken, *Understanding the Right to an Undiluted Vote*, 114 HARV. L. REV. 1663, 1681–89 (2001).

6. Should the Court have rested its holding on the Guarantee Clause rather than the Equal Protection Clause? *See* Michael W. McConnell, *The Redistricting Cases: Original Mistakes and Current Consequences*, 24 HARV. J.L. & PUB. POL'Y 103 (2000).

7. *Problem.* The districts used to select Louisiana's seven supreme-court justices had not been reapportioned between 1921 and 1972, and as a result ranged in population from 369,485 to 682,072. Does the difference between the duties of judges and members of the "political" branches justify excusing judicial elections from the one-person, one-vote rule? *See Wells v. Edwards*, 347 F. Supp. 453 (M.D. La. 1972), *aff'd*, 409 U.S. 1095 (*per curiam*) (holding judicial elections immune from one person, one vote, because the doctrine is in place only "to preserve a truly representative form of government"). *But cf. Chisom v. Roemer*, 501 U.S. 380 (1991) (interpreting the Voting Rights Act, which requires states to provide members of racial groups an equal opportunity to elect "representatives" of their choice, to reach claims of minority vote dilution in judicial elections).

8. In distributing legislative seats, some states count prison populations as part of the districts in which the prisons are located, even though the prisoners are not permitted to vote. (This practice is sometimes derisively called "prison gerrymandering.") The effect is to give greater voting power to the others living in those districts, including prison guards' families, whose interests may not coincide with those of the inmates. By the same token, the areas in which the inmates used to live are not granted the influence they would possess if the prisoners were counted as residing in the last place they lived before imprisonment. Does this practice violate one person, one vote? Does it matter that minority races are disproportionately represented in prison populations and that prisons are often located in rural, mainly white, areas? *See* Dale Ho, *Captive Constituents: Prison-Based Gerrymandering and the Current Redistricting Cycle*, 22 STAN. L. & POL'Y REV. 355 (2011). Several states have recently reformed their laws to provide that prisoners should be counted as residing at their last pre-prison address. *See* Prison Policy Initiative, *Prison Gerrymandering Project*, *at* https://www.prisonersofthecensus.org.

In *Fletcher v. Lamone*, 567 U.S. 930 (2012), *summarily aff'g* 831 F. Supp. 2d 887 (D. Md. 2011) (three-judge court), Maryland adopted a redistricting plan that counted prisoners as residing at their last addresses before incarceration. The plan was challenged as diluting minority communities' voting strength (even though Maryland's intent was to augment it). The district court turned away the challenge, holding that Maryland could constitutionally treat inmates as residing at their pre-prison addresses even if it did not accord similar treatment to members of the military and students (who, as the court pointed out, presented different situations from prisoners in that they could vote during their service and schooling). The Supreme Court unanimously summarily affirmed.

9. So far, we have encountered several ways states may use electoral systems to allocate political power. For example, states may exclude groups of people from voting or draw district lines to affect the amount of political influence certain voters can exercise. Electoral systems can allocate power in other ways, too. Super-majority requirements (such as a requirement that tax increases receive the affirmative vote of 60% or two-thirds of the voters before they can become law) prevent simple majorities from exercising political power, and allow a minority to maintain the status quo.[c] Accordingly, such requirements can be viewed as undermining the principle of majority rule underlying the one-person, one-vote standard. *See Reynolds v. Sims*, 377 U.S. 533, 565 (1964) [p. 122] ("Logically, in a society ostensibly grounded on representative government, it would seem reasonable that a majority of the people of a State could elect a majority of that State's legislators."); *id.* at 576 (condemning "frustration of the majority will through minority veto" if one house of a state legislature were permitted to be apportioned on a basis other than population). *See also Whitcomb v. Chavis*, 403 U.S. 124, 166 (1971) [p. 282] (opinion of Harlan, J.) (suggesting that the one-person, one-vote "cases can best be understood * * * as reflections of deep *personal* commitments by some members of the Court to the principles of pure majoritarian democracy").

Nevertheless, the Supreme Court has not been as hostile to super-majority requirements as it has been to rules that use more overt ways of weighting some votes more heavily than others. In *Gordon v. Lance*, 403 U.S. 1 (1971), the Court upheld a West Virginia law prohibiting localities from taking out bonds or raising taxes without a referendum in which at least 60% of the voters approved of the measure. The Court stressed that the law did not discriminate against any "independently identifiable group or category that favors bonded indebtedness over other forms of financing," and therefore, the law did not discriminate against any "sector

---

c. The Constitution itself, of course, employs this technique repeatedly. *See* U.S. Const. art. I, §5, cl. 2 (requiring a two-thirds vote of the Senate to convict an impeached official); *id.* (requiring a two-thirds vote of either the House or the Senate to expel a member); *id.* art. I, §7, cls. 2, 3 (requiring a two-thirds vote of each House to override a presidential veto); *id.* art. II, §2, cl. 2 (requiring a two-thirds vote of the Senate to ratify a treaty); *id.* art. V (establishing super-majority requirements for amending the Constitution); *id.* art. VII (requiring nine states to ratify the Constitution before the document would take effect). Additionally, the bicameralism requirements and even the substantive limits on legislation contained in such provisions as the Bill of Rights can be seen as supermajority requirements. *See generally* The Federalist No. 51 (James Madison); John O. McGinnis & Michael B. Rappaport, *Our Supermajoritarian Constitution*, 80 Tex. L. Rev. 703 (2002).

of the population" "because of the way they will vote." *Id*. at 5. The Court held that so long as super-majority requirements avoided "discrimination against any identifiable class," they were constitutional. *Id*. at 7. Is *Lance* consistent with *Reynolds v. Sims*? *See Whitcomb v. Chavis*, 403 U.S. 124, 170 (1971) (separate opinion of Harlan, J.) [p. 282] (arguing that *Lance* represented a retreat from the majoritarianism exhibited in the one-person, one-vote cases, and hoping that "the day will come when the Court will frankly recognize the error of its ways in ever having undertaken to restructure state electoral processes."). Is there any constitutional limit to states' ability to insulate policy decisions from majority control? If a state prohibited amendments to its constitution, would it comport with the Equal Protection Clause?

Was the Court correct that the law in *Lance* did not discriminate against any "identifiable class"? Don't tax and bond measures impose benefits and costs on identifiable portions of the public? Would it be constitutional for a minority of wealthy voters to block the majority from raising taxes? *See Brenner v. School District of Kansas City, Missouri*, 403 U.S. 913 (1971), *summarily aff'g* 315 F. Supp. 627 (W.D. Mo. 1970); *Santa Clara County Local Transportation Authority v. Guardino*, 902 P.2d 225 (Cal. 1995). (Note that *Gordon* itself involved a super-majority requirement applicable both to bond indebtedness and taxation.) Should it change the result if a super-majority was required to enact only a certain kind of bond, for example, bonds to finance road construction or schools, or bonds with interest rates exceeding a certain percentage? Would the answer depend on which kinds of bond were subject to the requirement? *See In re Contest of a Certain Special Election*, 659 P.2d 1294 (Ariz. Ct. App. 1982).

10. In the same way that super-majority requirements can amount to a minority veto of the desired policies of a majority, requirements that support for a measure come from geographically disparate areas can also limit the power of majorities. The Court has sent mixed signals regarding the constitutionality of such geographical-distribution requirements. Illinois law, for example, required independent candidates petitioning to be on the presidential ballot to collect 25,000 signatures, with at least 200 signatures from each of at least 50 counties. The Court initially upheld the law. *MacDougall v. Green*, 335 U.S. 281 (1948). In *Moore v. Ogilvie*, 394 U.S. 814 (1969), however, the Court overruled *MacDougall*, concluding that the law "discriminate[d] against the residents of the populous counties of the State in favor of rural sections." *Id*. at 819.

Yet in *Town of Lockport v. Citizens for Community Action at the Local Level, Inc.*, 430 U.S. 259 (1977), the Court upheld a New York law permitting a new county charter to go into effect only if it was approved in a referendum by both a majority of the county's city residents and the county's non-city residents. The Court concluded that the dual-majority requirement was constitutional because city residents and non-city residents would be differently affected by the charter, given that the charter would affect the distribution of governmental authority between the county and the localities. "The real and long-term impact of a restructuring of local government is felt quite differently by the different county constituent units that in a sense compete to provide similar governmental services." *Id.* at 272. Is *Citizens for Community Action* consistent with *Moore v. Ogilvie*? Is it consistent with *Reynolds v. Sims* to structure the political process to allow for the representation of different interests? *Compare Citizens for Community Action* with Justice Stewart's dissenting opinion in *Lucas v. Forty-Fourth General Assembly of Colorado*, 377 U.S. 713 (1964), discussed and quoted at pages 136–38, *supra*.

Problem. For initiatives to appear on the ballot in Idaho, supporters must collect the signatures of six percent of the state's qualified voters, including six percent of the qualified voters in each of at least half of the state's forty-four counties. Are those requirements distinguishable from those in *Moore*? *See Idaho Coalition United for Bears v. Cenarrusa*, 342 F.3d 1073 (9th Cir. 2003). *See also Gallivan v. Walker*, 54 P.3d 1069 (Utah 2002).

11. *Which* populations must be equalized across state-legislative districts? Must a state equalize districts' total populations, or may a state equalize other populations, such as registered voters, eligible voters, voting-age population, or something else? May a districting plan that equalizes total population nonetheless violate the Constitution because of differences in the numbers of voting-eligible citizens?

The answer depends on which equality principle one gleans from *Reynolds v. Sims*:

> While apportionment by population and apportionment by number of eligible electors normally yield precisely the same result, they are based on radically different premises and serve materially different purposes. Apportionment by raw population embodies the principle of equal representation; it assures that all persons living within a district—whether eligible to vote or not—have roughly equal representation in the governing body. A principle of equal representation serves important purposes. It assures that constituents have more or less equal access to their elected officials, by assuring that no official has a disproportionately large number of constituents to satisfy. Also, assuming that elected officials are able to obtain benefits for their districts in proportion to their share of the total membership of the governing body, it assures that constituents are not afforded unequal government services depending on the size of the population in their districts.
>
> Apportionment by proportion of eligible voters serves the principle of electoral equality. This principle recognizes that electors—persons eligible to vote—are the ones who hold the ultimate political power in our democracy. * * * Apportionment by proportion of eligible voters assures that, regardless of the size of the whole body of constituents, political power, as defined by the number of those eligible to vote, is equalized as between districts holding the same number of representatives. It also assures that those eligible to vote do not suffer dilution of that important right by having their vote given less weight than that of electors in another location.

Garza v. County of Los Angeles, 918 F.2d 763, 781–82 (9th Cir. 1990) (Kozinski, J., concurring and dissenting in part). See also Ronald Keith Gaddie et al., *Seats, Votes, Citizens, and the One Person, One Vote Problem*, 23 STAN. L. & POL'Y REV. 431 (2012).

Does it matter that the Fourteenth Amendment requires congressional districts to be apportioned among the states based on total population? *See* U.S. CONST. amend. XIV, § 2 ("Representatives shall be apportioned among the several States according to their respective numbers, counting the whole number of persons in each State, excluding Indians not taxed."). Might the Constitution require equality of different populations in congressional districts and state-legislative ones?

Surprisingly, although in several cases the Court appeared to assume the permissibility (if not the necessity) of using total population as the basis for representation, the Court directly addressed the issue only once before 2016. In *Burns v. Richardson*, 384 U.S. 73 (1966), a case decided at the beginning of the reapportionment revolution, the Supreme Court upheld the constitutionality of a Hawaii state-legislative districting plan that was based on the number of registered voters, rather than the number of citizens or total persons. Because many military personnel and tourists temporarily residing on the island of Oahu were counted in the census as part of Hawaii's total population but could not vote, the choice of relevant population affected the distribution of legislative seats. The Court held that the use of registered voters was permissible, but only because such use "produced a distribution of legislators not substantially different from that which would have resulted from the use of a permissible population basis" such as citizen population. *Id.* at 93. As the Court explained,

> [T]he Equal Protection Clause does not require the States to use total population figures derived from the federal census as the standard by which [] substantial population equivalency is to be measured. Although total population figures were in fact the basis of comparison in [*Reynolds v. Sims*] and most of the other[] [cases] decided that day, our discussion carefully left open the question what population was being referred to. At several points, we discussed substantial equivalence in terms of voter population or citizen population, making no distinction between the acceptability of such a test and a test based on total population.[20] Indeed, in *WMCA, Inc. v. Lomenzo*, 377 U.S. 633 [(1964)], decided the same day, we treated an apportionment based upon United States citizen population as presenting problems no different from apportionments using a total population

---

20. Thus we spoke of "[t]he right of a citizen to equal representation and to have his vote weighted equally with those of all other citizens. . . ." *Reynolds v. Sims*, 377 U.S., at 576. We also said: "[I]t is a practical impossibility to arrange legislative districts so that each one has an identical number of residents, or citizens, or voters." *Id.*, at 577. "[T]he overriding objective must be substantial equality of population among the various districts, so that the vote of any citizen is approximately equal in weight to that of any other citizen in the State." *Id.*, at 579.

measure. Neither in *Reynolds* v. *Sims* nor in any other decision has this Court suggested that the States are required to include aliens, transients, short-term or temporary residents, or persons denied the vote for conviction of crime, in the apportionment base by which their legislators are distributed and against which compliance with the Equal Protection Clause is to be measured. The decision to include or exclude any such group involves choices about the nature of representation with which we have been shown no constitutionally founded reason to interfere. Unless a choice is one the Constitution forbids, cf., *e.g.*, *Carrington* v. *Rash*, 380 U.S. 89 [(1965)] [p. 71], the resulting apportionment base offends no constitutional bar, and compliance with the rule established in *Reynolds* v. *Sims* is to be measured thereby.

Use of a registered voter or actual voter basis presents an additional problem. Such a basis depends not only upon criteria such as govern state citizenship, but also upon the extent of political activity of those eligible to register and vote. Each is thus susceptible to improper influences by which those in political power might be able to perpetuate underrepresentation of groups constitutionally entitled to participate in the electoral process, or perpetuate a "ghost of prior malapportionment." Moreover, "fluctuations in the number of registered voters in a given election may be sudden and substantial, caused by such fortuitous factors as a peculiarly controversial election issue, a particularly popular candidate, or even weather conditions." Such effects must be particularly a matter of concern where, as in the case of Hawaii apportionment, registration figures derived from a single election are made controlling for as long as 10 years. In view of these considerations, we hold that the present apportionment satisfies the Equal Protection Clause only because on this record it was found to have produced a distribution of legislators not substantially different from that which would have resulted from the use of a permissible population basis.

384 U.S. at 91–93. Justice Harlan disagreed with the Court's limitation on states' ability to base apportionment calculations on the number of registered voters, arguing that *Reynolds v. Sims* required only that states use a rational system for ensuring that legislatures represent "'people,' not other interests." *Id*. at 99 (Harlan, J., concurring in the result).

In 2016, the issue of the appropriate population basis returned to the Court in the following case, *Evenwel v. Abbott*. Whereas *Burns* involved a plaintiff's allegation that the state violated the Constitution by using a population basis other than total population, *Evenwel* involved an allegation that the state violated the Constitution by equalizing total population rather than citizen-voting-age population.

Evenwel v. Abbott

Supreme Court of the United States
578 U.S. __, 136 S. Ct. 1120, 194 L. Ed. 2d 291 (2016)

JUSTICE GINSBURG delivered the opinion of the Court [in which CHIEF JUSTICE ROBERTS, JUSTICE KENNEDY, JUSTICE BREYER, JUSTICE SOTOMAYOR, and JUSTICE KAGAN join].[d]

Texas, like all other States, draws its legislative districts on the basis of total population. Plaintiffs-appellants are Texas voters; they challenge this uniform method of districting on the ground that it produces unequal districts when measured by voter-eligible population. Voter-eligible population, not total population, they urge, must be used to ensure that their votes will not be devalued in relation to citizens' votes in other districts. We hold, based on constitutional history, this Court's decisions, and longstanding practice, that a State may draw its legislative districts based on total population. * * *

* * * After the 2010 census, Texas redrew its State Senate districts using a total-population baseline. [The plan that was ultimately adopted had a] maximum total-population deviation [of] 8.04%, safely within the presumptively permissible 10% range [discussed in the next section—Eds.]. But measured by a voter-population baseline—eligible voters or registered voters—the map's maximum population deviation exceeds 40%. * * *

The parties and the United States advance different positions in this case. [A]ppellants insist that the Equal Protection Clause requires jurisdictions to draw state and local legislative districts with equal voter-eligible populations, thus protecting "voter equality," *i.e.*, "the right of eligible voters to an equal vote."[7] To comply with their proposed rule, appellants suggest, jurisdictions should design districts based on citizen-voting-age-population (CVAP) data from the Census Bureau's American Community Survey (ACS), an annual statistical sample of the U.S. population. * * *

[W]e reject appellants' attempt to locate a voter-equality mandate in the Equal Protection Clause. As history, precedent, and practice demonstrate, it is plainly permissible for jurisdictions to measure equalization by the total population of state and local legislative districts.

We begin with constitutional history. At the time of the founding, the Framers confronted a question analogous to the one at issue here: On what basis should congressional districts be allocated to States? The Framers' solution, now known as the Great Compromise, was to provide each State the same number of seats in the Senate, and to allocate House seats based on States' total populations. * * * In other

---

d. Justice Scalia died before the decision in this case, so only eight Justices participated. —Eds.

7. In the District Court, appellants suggested that districting bodies could also comply with the one-person, one-vote rule by equalizing the registered-voter populations of districts, but appellants have not repeated that argument before this Court.

words, the basis of *representation* in the House was to include all inhabitants—although slaves were counted as only three-fifths of a person—even though States remained free to deny many of those inhabitants the right to participate in the selection of their representatives.[8] Endorsing apportionment based on total population, Alexander Hamilton declared: "There can be no truer principle than this—that every individual of the community at large has an equal right to the protection of government."

When debating what is now the Fourteenth Amendment, Congress reconsidered the proper basis for apportioning House seats. Concerned that Southern States would not willingly enfranchise freed slaves, and aware that "a slave's freedom could swell his state's population for purposes of representation in the House by one person, rather than only three-fifths," the Framers of the Fourteenth Amendment considered at length the possibility of allocating House seats to States on the basis of voter population.

* * * Supporters of apportionment based on voter population employed the same voter-equality reasoning that appellants now echo. See, *e.g.*, [Cong. Globe, 39th Cong., 1st Sess., 380 (1866)] (remarks of Rep. Orth) ("[T]he true principle of representation in Congress is that voters alone should form the basis, and that each voter should have equal political weight in our Government. . . ."); *id.*, at 404 (remarks of Rep. Lawrence) (use of total population "disregards the fundamental idea of all just representation, that every voter should be equal in political power all over the Union").

Voter-based apportionment proponents encountered fierce resistance from proponents of total-population apportionment. Much of the opposition was grounded in the principle of representational equality. "As an abstract proposition," argued Representative James G. Blaine, a leading critic of allocating House seats based on voter population, "no one will deny that population is the true basis of representation; for women, children, and other non-voting classes may have as vital an interest in the legislation of the country as those who actually deposit the ballot." *Id.*, at 141. See also *id.*, at 358 (remarks of Rep. Conkling) (arguing that use of a voter-population basis "would shut out four fifths of the citizens of the country—women and children, who are citizens, who are taxed, and who are, and always have been, represented"); *id.*, at 434 (remarks of Rep. Ward) ("[W]hat becomes of that large class of non-voting tax-payers that are found in every section? Are they in no matter to be represented? They certainly should be enumerated in making up the whole number of those entitled to a representative.").

---

8. * * * Restrictions on the franchise left large groups of citizens, including women and many males who did not own land, unable to cast ballots, yet the Framers understood that these citizens were nonetheless entitled to representation in government.

The product of these debates was §2 of the Fourteenth Amendment, which retained total population as the congressional apportionment base. * * *

Appellants ask us to find in the Fourteenth Amendment's Equal Protection Clause a rule inconsistent with this [theory of population-based representation]. But, as the Court recognized in *Wesberry* [v. *Sanders*, 376 U.S. 1 (1964)] [p. 116], this theory underlies not just the method of allocating House seats to States; it applies as well to the method of apportioning legislative seats within States. * * * "While it may not be possible to draw congressional districts with mathematical precision," the Court acknowledged, "that is no excuse for ignoring our Constitution's plain objective of making equal representation for *equal numbers of people* the fundamental goal for the House of Representatives." *Id.*, at 18 (emphasis added). It cannot be that the Fourteenth Amendment calls for the apportionment of congressional districts based on total population, but simultaneously prohibits States from apportioning their own legislative districts on the same basis. * * *

Consistent with constitutional history, this Court's past decisions reinforce the conclusion that States and localities may comply with the one-person, one-vote principle by designing districts with equal total populations. Quoting language from those decisions that, in appellants' view, supports the principle of equal voting power—and emphasizing the phrase "one-person, one-vote"—appellants contend that the Court had in mind, and constantly meant, that States should equalize the voter-eligible population of districts. See *Reynolds*, 377 U.S., at 568 ("[A]n individual's right to vote for State legislators is unconstitutionally impaired when its weight is in a substantial fashion diluted when compared with votes of citizens living on other parts of the State."); *Gray*, 372 U.S., at 379–380 ("The concept of 'we the people' under the Constitution visualizes no preferred class of voters but equality among those who meet the basic qualifications."). Appellants, however, extract far too much from selectively chosen language and the "one-person, one-vote" slogan.

For every sentence appellants quote from the Court's opinions, one could respond with a line casting the one-person, one-vote guarantee in terms of equality of representation, not voter equality. In *Reynolds*, for instance, the Court described "the fundamental principle of representative government in this country" as "one of equal representation for equal numbers of people." 377 U.S., at 560–561. And the Court has suggested, repeatedly, that districting based on total population serves *both* the State's interest in preventing vote dilution *and* its interest in ensuring equality of representation. See *Board of Estimate of City of New York v. Morris*, 489 U.S. 688, 693–694 (1989) ("If districts of widely unequal population elect an equal number of representatives, the voting power of each citizen in the larger constituencies is debased and the citizens in those districts have a smaller share of representation than do those in the smaller districts."). See also *Kirkpatrick* [v. *Preisler*], 394 U.S. [526], 531 [(1969)] [p. 154] (recognizing in a congressional-districting case that "[e]qual representation for equal numbers of people is a principle designed to prevent debasement of voting power and diminution of access to elected representatives").[12]

Moreover, from *Reynolds* on, the Court has consistently looked to total-population figures when evaluating whether districting maps violate the Equal Protection Clause by deviating impermissibly from perfect population equality. Appellants point to no instance in which the Court has determined the permissibility of deviation based on eligible- or registered-voter data. It would hardly make sense for the Court to have mandated voter equality *sub silentio* and then used a total-population baseline to evaluate compliance with that rule. More likely, we think, the Court has always assumed the permissibility of drawing districts to equalize total population. * * *

What constitutional history and our prior decisions strongly suggest, settled practice confirms. Adopting voter-eligible apportionment as constitutional command would upset a well-functioning approach to districting that all 50 States and countless local jurisdictions have followed for decades, even centuries. Appellants have shown no reason for the Court to disturb this longstanding use of total population. As the Framers of the Constitution and the Fourteenth Amendment comprehended, representatives serve all residents, not just those eligible or registered to vote. Nonvoters have an important stake in many policy debates—children, their parents, even their grandparents, for example, have a stake in a strong public-education system—and in receiving constituent services, such as help navigating public-benefits bureaucracies. By ensuring that each representative is subject to requests and suggestions from the same number of constituents, total-population apportionment promotes equitable and effective representation.[14]

In sum, the rule appellants urge has no mooring in the Equal Protection Clause. The Texas Senate map, we therefore conclude, complies with the requirements of the one-person, one-vote principle.[15] Because history, precedent, and practice suffice to reveal the infirmity of appellants' claims, we need not and do not resolve whether, as Texas now argues, States may draw districts to equalize voter-eligible population rather than total population. * * *

---

12. Appellants also observe that standing in one-person, one-vote cases has rested on plaintiffs' status as voters whose votes were diluted. But the Court has not considered the standing of nonvoters to challenge a map malapportioned on a total-population basis. This issue, moreover, is unlikely ever to arise given the ease of finding voters willing to serve as plaintiffs in malapportionment cases.

14. Appellants point out that constituents have no constitutional right to equal access to their elected representatives. But a State certainly has an interest in taking reasonable, nondiscriminatory steps to facilitate access for all its residents.

15. Insofar as appellants suggest that Texas could have roughly equalized both total population and eligible-voter population, this Court has never required jurisdictions to use multiple population baselines. In any event, appellants have never presented a map that manages to equalize both measures, perhaps because such a map does not exist, or because such a map would necessarily ignore other traditional redistricting principles, including maintaining communities of interest and respecting municipal boundaries.

JUSTICE THOMAS, concurring in the judgment.

* * * I agree with the majority that our precedents do not require a State to equal-ize the total number of voters in each district. States may opt to equalize total popu-lation. I therefore concur in the majority's judgment that appellants' challenge fails.

I write separately because this Court has never provided a sound basis for the one-person, one-vote principle. For 50 years, the Court has struggled to define what right that principle protects. * * *

This inconsistency (if not opacity) is not merely a consequence of the Court's equivocal statements on one person, one vote. The problem is more fundamental. There is simply no way to make a principled choice between interpreting one person, one vote as protecting eligible voters or as protecting total inhabitants within a State. That is because, though those theories are noble, the Constitution does not make either of them the exclusive means of apportionment for state and local representa-tives. In guaranteeing to the States a "Republican Form of Government," Art. IV, § 4, the Constitution did not resolve whether the ultimate basis of representation is the right of citizens to cast an equal ballot or the right of all inhabitants to have equal representation. The Constitution instead reserves these matters to the people. The majority's attempt today to divine a single "theory of the Constitution"—appor-tionment based on representation—rests on a flawed reading of history and wrongly picks one side of a debate that the Framers did not resolve in the Constitution. * * *

The Court's attempt to impose its political theory upon the States has produced a morass of problems. These problems are antithetical to the values that the Fram-ers embraced in the Constitution. These problems confirm that the Court has been wrong to entangle itself with the political process.

First, in embracing one person, one vote, the Court has arrogated to the Judi-ciary important value judgments that the Constitution reserves to the people. * * * [T]o control factions that would legislate against the common good, individual voting strength must sometimes yield to countermajoritarian checks. And this principle has no less force within States than it has for the federal system. Instead of large States versus small States, those interests may pit urban areas versus rural, manufacturing versus agriculture, or those with property versus those without. There is no single method of reconciling these competing interests. And it is not the role of this Court to calibrate democracy in the vain search for an optimum solution. * * *

Second, the Court's efforts to monitor the political process have failed to provide any consistent guidance for the States. Even if it were justifiable for this Court to enforce some principle of majority rule, it has been unable to do so in a principled manner. Our precedents do not address the myriad other ways that minorities (or fleeting majorities) entrench themselves in the political system. States can place pol-icy choices in their constitutions or have supermajoritarian voting rules in a legisla-tive assembly. In theory, of course, it does not seem to make a difference if a state legislature is unresponsive to the majority of residents because the state assembly requires a 60% vote to pass a bill or because 40% of the population elects 51% of the representatives.

So far as the Constitution is concerned, there is no single "correct" way to design a republican government. Any republic will have to reconcile giving power to the people with diminishing the influence of special interests. The wisdom of the Framers was that they recognized this dilemma and left it to the people to resolve. In trying to impose its own theory of democracy, the Court is hopelessly adrift amid political theory and interest-group politics with no guiding legal principles. * * *

I agree with the majority's ultimate disposition of this case. As far as the original understanding of the Constitution is concerned, a State has wide latitude in selecting its population base for apportionment. It can use total population, eligible voters, or any other nondiscriminatory voter base. And States with a bicameral legislature can have some mixture of these theories, such as one population base for its lower house and another for its upper chamber.

Our precedents do not compel a contrary conclusion. Appellants are correct that this Court's precedents have primarily based its one-person, one-vote jurisprudence on the theory that eligible voters have a right against vote dilution. But this Court's jurisprudence has vacillated too much for me to conclude that the Court's precedents preclude States from allocating districts based on total population instead. Under these circumstances, the choice is best left for the people of the States to decide for themselves how they should apportion their legislature. * * *

JUSTICE ALITO, with whom JUSTICE THOMAS joins * * *, concurring in the judgment. * * *

Both practical considerations and precedent support the conclusion that the use of total population is consistent with the one-person, one-vote rule. The decennial census required by the Constitution tallies total population. These statistics are more reliable and less subject to manipulation and dispute than statistics concerning eligible voters. Since *Reynolds*, States have almost uniformly used total population in attempting to create legislative districts that are equal in size. And with one notable exception, *Burns v. Richardson*, 384 U.S. 73 (1966), this Court's post-*Reynolds* cases have likewise looked to total population. Moreover, much of the time, creating districts that are equal in total population also results in the creation of districts that are at least roughly equal in eligible voters. I therefore agree that States are permitted to use total population in redistricting plans. * * *

The Court does not purport to decide whether a State may base a districting plan on something other than total population, but the Court, picking up a key component of the Solicitor General's argument, suggests that the use of total population is supported by the Constitution's formula for allocating seats in the House of Representatives among the States. * * * [But] reliance on the Constitution's allocation of congressional representation is profoundly ahistorical. When the formula for allocating House seats was first devised in 1787 and reconsidered at the time of the adoption of the Fourteenth Amendment in 1868, the overwhelming concern was far removed from any abstract theory about the nature of representation. Instead, the dominant consideration was the distribution of political power among the States. * * *

After the Civil War, when the Fourteenth Amendment was being drafted, the question of the apportionment formula arose again. Thaddeus Stevens, a leader of the so-called radical Republicans, unsuccessfully proposed that apportionment be based on eligible voters, rather than total population. The opinion of the Court suggests that the rejection of Stevens' proposal signified the adoption of the theory that representatives are properly understood to represent all of the residents of their districts, whether or not they are eligible to vote. As was the case in 1787, however, it was power politics, not democratic theory, that carried the day.

In making his proposal, Stevens candidly explained that the proposal's primary aim was to perpetuate the dominance of the Republican Party and the Northern States. As Stevens spelled out, if House seats were based on total population, the power of the former slave States would be magnified. Prior to the Civil War, a slave had counted for only three-fifths of a person for purposes of the apportionment of House seats. As a result of the Emancipation Proclamation and the Thirteenth Amendment, the former slaves would now be fully counted even if they were not permitted to vote. By Stevens' calculation, this would give the South 13 additional votes in both the House and the electoral college. [JUSTICE ALITO discussed additional evidence from the legislative history of the Fourteenth Amendment to demonstrate that Members of Congress who focused on equalizing numbers of voters were concerned about giving the South additional representation (because of the freed slaves) at the expense of the States that had been loyal to the Union.] * * *

The bottom line is that in the leadup to the Fourteenth Amendment, claims about representational equality were invoked, if at all, only in service of the *real* goal: preventing southern States from acquiring too much power in the National Government.

After much debate, Congress eventually settled on the compromise that now appears in § 2 of the Fourteenth Amendment. Under that provision, House seats are apportioned based on total population, but if a State wrongfully denies the right to vote to a certain percentage of its population, its representation is supposed to be reduced proportionally. Enforcement of this remedy, however, is dependent on action by Congress, and — regrettably — the remedy was never used during the long period when voting rights were widely abridged.

In light of the history of Article I, § 2, of the original Constitution and § 2 of the Fourteenth Amendment, it is clear that the apportionment of seats in the House of Representatives was based in substantial part on the distribution of political power among the States and not merely on some theory regarding the proper nature of representation. It is impossible to draw any clear constitutional command from this complex history.

For these reasons, I would hold only that Texas permissibly used total population in drawing the challenged legislative districts. I therefore concur in the judgment of the Court.

Notes and Questions

1. *Evenwel* held that the Constitution did not compel states to equalize the number of voters (or vote-eligible citizens) when drawing state-legislative districts. The Court reached this conclusion on the basis of "constitutional history, this Court's decisions, and longstanding practice." Should each of those factors be relevant? How important is each of those factors relative to the others? Why do you suppose the Court did not list "constitutional text" as one of its reasons for reaching the result that it did?

2. It may be an easy matter to conclude, as *Evenwel* did, that there is no constitutional *obligation* to draw districts using voter-based apportionment. That is, the Constitution *permits* a state to base its apportionment on total population, *if the state chooses to do so.* But may a state choose to reject total-population apportionment in favor of equalizing citizen-voting-age population? In other words, *Evenwel* held that states *may* base their state-legislative-district apportionments on total population. Should a future case hold that states *must* base their state-legislative-district apportionments on total population? What did each of the opinions in *Evenwel* say (or imply) about that question?

3. *Problem.* Disney County, Florida, is the home of Castro State Penitentiary. The penitentiary houses thousands of inmates from all over the state, with the vast majority coming from outside Disney County. When it re-draws its districts for county commissioners and school board members, the County constructs districts that are equal in population. All of the inmates of the penitentiary, who cannot vote, are counted as residing in the district encompassing the penitentiary. One effect of the districting scheme is to increase the voting power of the other residents of the district, because although their district contains the same number of people as all the other districts, it contains far fewer eligible voters. Is the districting plan vulnerable to a one-person, one-vote challenge? Are prison inmates different from children or aliens, who cannot vote but who are nonetheless "represented" by their legislators? *See Davidson v. City of Cranston*, 837 F.3d 135 (1st Cir. 2016) (holding a similar districting plan constitutional, and reasoning that under *Evenwel*, "the decision whether to include * * * prisoners in Cranston's apportionment is one for the political process"), *rev'g* 188 F. Supp. 3d 146, 149–51 (D.R.I. 2016) (finding an equal-protection violation, and distinguishing *Evenwel* on the basis that the prison inmates "don't have a stake in the Cranston public school system and they are not receiving constituent services, such as help with public-benefits bureaucracies. They are not making requests of and suggestions to Cranston elected officials (or if they

are, they are receiving no response), nor are they receiving 'the protection of government,' at least not from Cranston elected officials."). *See also Calvin v. Jefferson County Board of Commissioners*, 172 F. Supp. 3d 1292 (N.D. Fla. 2016) (finding an equal-protection violation, although the case was decided pre-*Evenwel*). For further discussion of the treatment of prisoners for population purposes, see Amee Frodle, Note, *Where Does a Prisoner Live? Furthering the Goals of Representational and Voter Equality Through Counting Prisoners*, 107 GEO. L.J. 175 (2018) (arguing that prisoners should be counted at their homes, in part because most cannot vote while imprisoned).

4. Do you agree with Justice Thomas that the Court was wrong to enter the political thicket? If so, should the cases of the reapportionment revolution be reconsidered, or should *stare decisis* insulate those decisions from challenge?

5. In *Department of Commerce v. New York*, 588 U.S. __, 139 S. Ct. 2551 (2019), the Supreme Court addressed the highly charged issue of whether the Trump Administration could add a question about citizenship to the 2020 census forms. The census had asked the question at various times, most recently in 1950. The Secretary of Commerce wanted to add the question to the census ostensibly because the information was necessary for the Department of Justice to enforce the Voting Rights Act. Critics argued that the real reason was that undocumented immigrants were less likely to participate in the census if they knew they would need to answer the question, which in turn would mean there would be fewer (usually Democratic) congressional districts with those persons in the population. Adding the citizenship question would also provide states with data needed to draw districts based on the number of citizens rather than total population, which would reduce the political power of geographic areas with large numbers of immigrants (whether entitled to be present in the United States or not) and, correspondingly, increase representation of other areas. The Secretary was sued by the State of New York and other plaintiffs, who argued that his decision violated the Enumeration Clause, the Census Act, and the Administrative Procedure Act (APA).

In a lead opinion authored by Chief Justice Roberts, and joined by shifting numbers of the other Justices on various issues, the Court rejected the challenges based on the Enumeration Clause and the Census Act, held that the government had not complied with the APA, and remanded for further proceedings. Regarding the Census Act, the Court held that the Secretary had ample authority to make the change as a matter of policy. Nevertheless, the Court held that the Secretary's decision violated the APA because the voting-rights-enforcement rationale was pretextual and contrived. Evidence before the district court showed that the Secretary had been planning to add the question since the early days of the Administration, and only later settled on the VRA enforcement rationale.

Justice Thomas, joined by Justices Gorsuch and Kavanaugh, concurred in the holdings on the Enumeration Clause and the Census Act, but dissented on the APA holding, on the basis that there was no evidence that the Secretary's decision was contrived. Justice Breyer, joined by Justices Ginsburg, Sotomayor, and Kagan, dissented in part on the basis that the Secretary's decision was "arbitrary and capricious" under the Census Act and the APA. Justice Breyer argued that the Secretary failed to give appropriate deference to the findings of the Census Bureau that citizenship data could be gleaned from other sources. Justice Alito dissented in part on the basis that the Secretary's decision was not reviewable under the APA.

The majority of the Court remanded for further proceedings at the administrative level, leaving it unclear if the question might be able to be added if the Secretary were able to offer a more convincing rationale. The Trump Administration, after sending conflicting signals, eventually decided to abandon any attempt to add the question to the 2020 census.

D. How Equal Is Equal Enough?: One Person, One Vote (More or Less)

It is one thing to establish a constitutional standard of "substantially equal" district populations and to apply it where the population disparities are as broad as they were in *Baker v. Carr* and *Reynolds v. Sims*. It is quite another to apply that standard where the disparities are much narrower. Is the constitutional guarantee of equality offended if districts differ in their populations by as little as 1%?

As the following cases demonstrate, the Court has held congressional districts to a strict requirement of population equality, but has been more lenient with respect to state-legislative districts. In the latter context, the Court has permitted states to draw districts that correspond to boundaries of political subdivisions, even if doing so causes slight population variances across districts.

Kirkpatrick v. Preisler[e]

Supreme Court of the United States
394 U.S. 526, 89 S. Ct. 1225, 22 L. Ed. 2d 519 (1969)

MR. JUSTICE BRENNAN delivered the opinion of the Court [in which MR. CHIEF JUSTICE WARREN, MR. JUSTICE BLACK, MR. JUSTICE DOUGLAS, and MR. JUSTICE MARSHALL join].

In *Wesberry v. Sanders*, 376 U.S. 1 (1964) [p. 116], we held that "* * * Art. I, §2, of the Constitution requires that "as nearly as is practicable one man's vote in a

---

e. This case was argued with, and decided the same day as, *Wells v. Rockefeller*, 394 U.S. 542 (1969). *Wells* held unconstitutional New York's congressional districting plan, which divided the state into seven regions, and divided each of the regions into congressional districts. Although each district within a given region had the same population, the regions themselves varied in population. As a result, the population of the districts statewide varied by as much as 13%. The Court struck down the plan as indistinguishable from the plan in *Kirkpatrick v. Preisler*. The dissents of Justice Harlan and Justice White, reprinted here, appear in the U.S. Reports as part of *Wells*, though they apply to both cases. — Eds.

congressional election is to be worth as much as another's." *Id.*, at 7–8. We are required in these cases to elucidate the "as nearly as practicable" standard.

The Missouri congressional redistricting statute challenged in these cases [was enacted in 1967. At that time, the best population data available were the 1960 United States census figures, according to which] absolute population equality among Missouri's 10 congressional districts would mean a population of 431,981 in each district. The districts created by the 1967 Act, however, varied from this ideal within a range of 12,260 below it to 13,542 above it. The difference between the least and most populous districts was thus 25,802. In percentage terms, the most populous district was 3.13% above the mathematical ideal, and the least populous was 2.84% below. * * *

We reject Missouri's argument that there is a fixed numerical or percentage population variance small enough to be considered *de minimis* and to satisfy without question the "as nearly as practicable" standard. The whole thrust of the "as nearly as practicable" approach is inconsistent with adoption of fixed numerical standards which excuse population variances without regard to the circumstances of each particular case. The extent to which equality may practicably be achieved may differ from State to State and from district to district. Since "equal representation for equal numbers of people [is] the fundamental goal for the House of Representatives," *Wesberry* v. *Sanders, supra,* at 18, the "as nearly as practicable" standard requires that the State make a good-faith effort to achieve precise mathematical equality. See *Reynolds* v. *Sims,* 377 U.S. 533, 577 (1964) [p. 122]. Unless population variances among congressional districts are shown to have resulted despite such effort, the State must justify each variance, no matter how small.

There are other reasons for rejecting the *de minimis* approach. We can see no nonarbitrary way to pick a cutoff point at which population variances suddenly become *de minimis.* Moreover, to consider a certain range of variances *de minimis* would encourage legislators to strive for the range rather than for equality as nearly as practicable. * * *

Equal representation for equal numbers of people is a principle designed to prevent debasement of voting power and diminution of access to elected representatives. Toleration of even small deviations detracts from these purposes. Therefore, the command of Art. I, §2, that States create congressional districts which provide equal representation for equal numbers of people permits only the limited population variances which are unavoidable despite a good-faith effort to achieve absolute equality, or for which justification is shown.

Clearly, the population variances among the Missouri congressional districts were not unavoidable. Indeed, it is not seriously contended that the Missouri Legislature came as close to equality as it might have come. * * * Legislative proponents of the 1967 Act frankly conceded at the District Court hearing that resort to the simple device of transferring entire political subdivisions of known population between contiguous districts would have produced districts much closer to numerical equality. The District Court found, moreover, that the Missouri Legislature relied on inaccurate data in constructing the districts, and that it rejected without consideration a plan which would have markedly reduced population variances among the districts. Finally, it is simply inconceivable that population disparities of the magnitude found in the Missouri plan were unavoidable. * * *

We therefore turn to the question whether the record establishes any legally acceptable justification for the population variances. It was the burden of the State "to present . . . acceptable reasons for the variations among the populations of the various . . . districts. . . ." *Swann* v. *Adams*, [385 U.S. 440,] 443–444 [(1967)]. * * *

Missouri contends that variances were necessary to avoid fragmenting areas with distinct economic and social interests and thereby diluting the effective representation of those interests in Congress. But to accept population variances, large or small, in order to create districts with specific interest orientations is antithetical to the basic premise of the constitutional command to provide equal representation for equal numbers of people. "[N]either history alone, nor economic or other sorts of group interests, are permissible factors in attempting to justify disparities from population-based representation. Citizens, not history or economic interests, cast votes." *Reynolds* v. *Sims, supra*, at 579–580.

We also reject Missouri's argument that "[t]he reasonableness of the population differences in the congressional districts under review must . . . be viewed in the context of legislative interplay. The legislative leaders all testified that the act in question was in their opinion a reasonable legislative compromise. * * *" We agree with the District Court that "the rule is one of 'practicability' rather than political 'practicality.'" Problems created by partisan politics cannot justify an apportionment which does not otherwise pass constitutional muster.

Similarly, we do not find legally acceptable the argument that variances are justified if they necessarily result from a State's attempt to avoid fragmenting political subdivisions by drawing congressional district lines along existing county, municipal, or other political subdivision boundaries. The State's interest in constructing congressional districts in this manner, it is suggested, is to minimize the opportunities for partisan gerrymandering. But an argument that deviations from equality are justified in order to inhibit legislators from engaging in partisan gerrymandering[4] is no more than a variant of the argument, already rejected, that considerations of practical politics can justify population disparities.

Missouri further contends that certain population variances resulted from the legislature's taking account of the fact that the percentage of eligible voters among the total population differed significantly from district to district—some districts contained disproportionately large numbers of military personnel stationed at bases

---

4. It is dubious in any event that the temptation to gerrymander would be much inhibited, since the legislature would still be free to choose which of several subdivisions, all with their own political complexion, to include in a particular congressional district. Besides, opportunities for gerrymandering are greatest when there is freedom to construct unequally populated districts. * * *

maintained by the Armed Forces and students in attendance at universities or colleges. There may be a question whether distribution of congressional seats except according to total population can ever be permissible under Art. I, § 2.[f] But assuming without deciding that apportionment may be based on eligible voter population rather than total population, the Missouri plan is still unacceptable. Missouri made no attempt to ascertain the number of eligible voters in each district and to apportion accordingly. At best it made haphazard adjustments to a scheme based on total population[.] * * *

Missouri also argues that population disparities between some of its congressional districts result from the legislature's attempt to take into account projected population shifts. We recognize that a congressional districting plan will usually be in effect for at least 10 years and five congressional elections. Situations may arise where substantial population shifts over such a period can be anticipated. Where these shifts can be predicted with a high degree of accuracy, States that are redistricting may properly consider them. By this we mean to open no avenue for subterfuge. Findings as to population trends must be thoroughly documented and applied throughout the State in a systematic, not an *ad hoc*, manner. Missouri's attempted justification * * * falls far short of this standard. * * *

Finally, Missouri claims that some of the deviations from equality were a consequence of the legislature's attempt to ensure that each congressional district would be geographically compact. However, in *Reynolds* v. *Sims, supra,* at 580, we said, "Modern developments and improvements in transportation and communications make rather hollow, in the mid-1960's, most claims that deviations from population-based representation can validly be based solely on geographical considerations. Arguments for allowing such deviations in order to insure effective representation for sparsely settled areas and to prevent legislative districts from becoming so large that the availability of access of citizens to their representatives is impaired are today, for the most part, unconvincing." In any event, Missouri's claim of compactness is based solely upon the unaesthetic appearance of the map of congressional boundaries that would result from an attempt to effect some of the changes in district lines which, according to the lower court, would achieve greater equality. A State's preference for pleasingly shaped districts can hardly justify population variances.

Affirmed.

Mr. Justice Fortas, concurring [in the judgment]. * * *

In *Wesberry* v. *Sanders,* this Court recognized that "it may not be possible to draw congressional districts with mathematical precision," and it held that the

---

f. Recall that *Burns v. Richardson,* 384 U.S. 73 (1966), discussed at pages 143–44, which upheld an apportionment based on numbers of registered voters, concerned an equal-protection challenge to state-legislative districts, not congressional districts. —Eds.

Constitution requires that they be drawn so that, "as nearly as is practicable," each representative should cast a vote on behalf of the same number of people.

The Court now not only interprets "as nearly as practicable" to mean that the State is required to "make a good-faith effort to achieve precise mathematical equality," but it also requires that any remaining population disparities "no matter how small," be justified. It then proceeds to reject, *seriatim*, every type of justification that has been — possibly, every one that could be — advanced.

I agree that the state legislatures should be required to make "a good-faith effort to achieve" a result that allocates the population or the residents of the State in roughly equal numbers to each district, based upon some orderly and objective method. In my view, the State could properly arrive at figures for current population by taking the latest census returns and making modifications to allow for population movements since the last census (which the Court seems to find acceptable). It could also, in my opinion, discount the census figures to take account of the presence of significant transient or nonresident population in particular areas (an adjustment as to which the Court indicates doubt). If the State should proceed on some appropriate population basis such as I have suggested, producing approximately equal districts, trial courts, in my judgment, would be justified in declining to disapprove the result merely because of small disparities, in the absence of evidence of gerrymandering—the deliberate and arbitrary distortion of district boundaries and populations for partisan or personal political purposes.

In considering whether the State has "approximated" an equal division and allocation of the population, I sympathize with the majority's view that a *de minimis* rule of allowable disparities tends to demean in theory and in practice the constitutional objective because it suggests that it is not necessary even to aim at equality. On the other hand, to reject *de minimis* as a statement of the limits on the rule of equality should not lead us to toss aside the wise recognition of the inscrutability of fact and the imperfection of man which is implicit in the *Wesberry* standard: "as nearly as practicable." This phrase does not refer merely to arithmetical possibilities. Arithmetically, it is possible to achieve division of a State into districts of precisely equal size, as measured by the decennial census or any other population base. To carry out this theoretical possibility, however, a legislature might have to ignore the boundaries of common sense, running the congressional district line down the middle of the corridor of an apartment house or even dividing the residents of a single-family house between two districts. The majority opinion does not suggest so extreme a practical application of its teaching, and I mention it only because the example may dramatize the fallacy of inflexible insistence upon mathematical exactness, with no tolerance for reality.

Whatever might be the merits of insistence on absolute equality if it could be attained, the majority's pursuit of precision is a search for a will-o'-the-wisp. The fact is that any solution to the apportionment and districting problem is at best an approximation because it is based upon figures which are always to some degree obsolete. No purpose is served by an insistence on precision which is unattainable because of the inherent imprecisions in the population data on which districting must be based. * * *

Nothing that I have said should be taken as indicating that I do not believe that the *Wesberry* standard requires a high degree of correspondence between the demonstrated population or residence figures and the district divisions. Nor would I fix, at least at this relatively early stage of the reapportionment effort, a percentage figure for permissible variation.

In the present cases, however, I agree that the judgment of the District Court should be affirmed. The history of this reapportionment and of the legislature's failure to comply with the plain and patient directions of the three-judge District Court and the failure of the legislature to use either accurate 1960 census figures or other systematically obtained figures for all the districts—these factors strongly support the District Court's refusal to accept the Missouri plan. * * *

MR. JUSTICE HARLAN, with whom MR. JUSTICE STEWART joins, dissenting.

Whatever room remained under this Court's prior decisions for the free play of the political process in matters of reapportionment is now all but eliminated by today's Draconian judgments. Marching to the nonexistent "command of Art. I, §2" of the Constitution, the Court now transforms a political slogan into a constitutional absolute. Straight indeed is the path of the righteous legislator. Slide rule in hand, he must avoid all thought of county lines, local traditions, politics, history, and economics, so as to achieve the magic formula: one man, one vote.

As my Brothers WHITE and FORTAS demonstrate, insistence on mathematical perfection does not make sense even on its own terms. Census figures themselves are inexact; our mobile population rapidly renders them obsolete; large groups of ineligible voters are unevenly distributed throughout the State. Nevertheless, the Court refuses to permit any room for legislative common sense to compensate for Census Bureau inadequacies. If no "scientific" data are available to justify a divergence from census figures, the Court holds that nothing can be done—"we mean to open no avenue for subterfuge."

This all-pervasive distrust of the legislative process is completely alien to established notions of judicial review. Nor does it have precedent in the prior reapportionment decisions themselves. * * * Even more important, the Court's exclusive concentration upon arithmetic blinds it to the realities of the political process. The fact of the matter is that the rule of absolute equality is perfectly compatible with "gerrymandering" of the worst sort. A computer may grind out district lines which can totally frustrate the popular will on an overwhelming number of critical issues. The legislature must do more than satisfy one man, one vote; it must create a structure which will in fact as well as theory be responsive to the sentiments of the community. * * *

* * * Of course, all districting decisions inevitably involve choices between different interest groups. But as *Reynolds* recognized, legislatures prefer to follow traditional county and regional lines so that the demands of blatant partisanship will be tempered by the constraints of history and tradition. If the Court believes it has struck a blow today for fully responsive representative democracy, it is sorely mistaken. Even more than in the past, district lines are likely to be drawn to maximize the political advantage of the party temporarily dominant in public affairs.

We do not deal here with the hopelessly malapportioned legislature unwilling to set its own house in order. Rather, the question before us is whether the Constitution requires that mathematics be a substitute for common sense in the art of statecraft. * * * I dissent. * * *

MR. JUSTICE WHITE, dissenting. * * *

* * * I would not quibble with the legislative judgment [concerning apportionment] if variations between districts were acceptably small. And I would be willing to establish a population variation figure which if not exceeded would normally not call for judicial intervention. As a rule of thumb, a variation between the largest and the smallest district of no more than 10% to 15% would satisfy me, absent quite unusual circumstances not present in any of these cases. At the very least, at this trivial level, I would be willing to view state explanations of the variance with a more tolerant eye.

This would be far more reasonable than the Court's demand for an absolute but illusory equality or for an apportionment plan which approaches this goal so nearly that no other plan can be suggested which would come nearer. As MR. JUSTICE FORTAS demonstrates, the 1960 census figures were far from accurate when they were compiled by professional enumerators and statisticians bent on precision, in 1960. Massive growth and shifts in population since 1960 made the 1960 figures even more inaccurate by 1967. That is why a new census is taken every 10 years. When the Court finds a 3% variation from substantially inexact figures constitutionally impermissible it is losing perspective and sticking at a trifle. * * *

Today's decisions on the one hand require precise adherence to admittedly inexact census figures, and on the other downgrade a restraint on a far greater potential threat to equality of representation, the gerrymander. Legislatures intent on minimizing the representation of selected political or racial groups are invited to ignore political boundaries and compact districts so long as they adhere to population equality among districts using standards which we know and they know are sometimes quite incorrect. I see little merit in such a confusion of priorities.

Moreover, today's decisions will lead to an unnecessary intrusion of the judiciary into legislative business. It would be one thing if absolute equality were possible. But, admittedly, it is not. The Court may be groping for a clean-cut, *per se* rule which will minimize confrontations between courts and legislatures while also satisfying the Fourteenth Amendment. If so, the Court is wide of the mark. Today's results simply shift the area of dispute a few percentage points down the scale; the courts will now be engaged in quibbling disputes over such questions as whether a plan with a 1% variation is "better" than one with a larger variation, say 1.1% or even 2%. If county and municipal boundaries are to be ignored, a computer can produce countless plans for absolute population equality, one differing very little from another, but each having its own very different political ramifications. * * * Not only will the Court's new rule necessarily precipitate a new round of congressional and legislative districting, but also I fear that in the long run the courts, rather than the legislatures or nonpartisan commissions, will be making most of the districting decisions in the several States. Since even at best, with compact and equal districts, the final boundary lines unavoidably have significant political repercussions, the courts should not draw district lines themselves unnecessarily. I therefore dissent.

Notes and Questions

1. *Kirkpatrick v. Preisler* was reaffirmed and extended in *Karcher v. Daggett*, 462 U.S. 725 (1983). In that case, New Jersey's congressional districts varied in population by an average of 726 people (0.1384%), and the largest district exceeded the smallest by 3,674 people (0.6984% of the average district). Nevertheless, there were other proposed districting plans available with even smaller population differences.

The government argued that where the population difference between districts is less than the error rate of the census, the population difference should be constitutionally irrelevant. The Court rejected the argument, pointing out that

> the census data provide the only reliable—albeit less than perfect—indication of the districts' "real" relative population levels. Even if one cannot say with certainty that one district is larger than another merely because it has a higher census count, one *can* say with certainty that the district with a larger census count is more likely to be larger than the other district than it is to be smaller or the same size.

Id. at 738. Note, however, that in *Gaffney v. Cummings*, 412 U.S. 735 (1973) [p. 168], which appears as a principal case later in this Chapter, the Court did refer to the error rate of the census in holding that states need not justify minimal population differences between *state-legislative* districts. Not coincidentally, Justice White was among the dissenters in *Kirkpatrick* and *Daggett*, and authored the opinion of the Court in *Gaffney*.

2. Is it reasonable to force states to justify population deviations of less than one percent? Is there *any* threshold under which states should not have to defend population differences between districts? Is one's right to an equally weighted vote or "fair and effective representation" abridged in any meaningful way if one's district is over-populated by a handful of people? *See generally* Heather K. Gerken, *The Costs and Causes of Minimalism in Voting Cases:* Baker v. Carr *and Its Progeny*, 80 N.C. L. Rev. 1411, 1437–41 (2002).

3. *Kirkpatrick* required states to bear the burden of proof when justifying population disparities between districts. In *Daggett*, 462 U.S. at 730–31, the Court elaborated:

> [T]wo basic questions shape litigation apportioning congressional districts. First, the court must consider whether the population differences among districts could have been reduced or eliminated altogether by a good-faith effort to draw districts of equal population. Parties challenging apportionment legislation must bear the burden of proof on this issue, and if they fail to show that the differences could have been avoided the apportionment scheme must be upheld. If, however, the plaintiffs can establish that the population differences were not the result of a good-faith effort to achieve equality, the State must bear the burden of proving that each significant variance between districts was necessary to achieve some legitimate goal.

In *Tennant v. Jefferson County Commission*, 567 U.S. 758 (2012) (*per curiam*), the Supreme Court applied *Daggett* to uphold a West Virginia districting plan with a population variance of 0.79%. Alternative plans with smaller variations were considered, but none was effective at achieving three of the state's objectives: keeping counties intact, keeping incumbents in different districts, and limiting population shifts from the previous districts. The Court approved each of those objectives as "valid" and "neutral," and applied a balancing test to hold that they sufficed to justify the 0.79% population variance: "[G]iven the small 'size of the deviations,' as balanced against 'the importance of the State's interests, the consistency with which the plan as a whole reflects those interests,' and the lack of available 'alternatives that might substantially vindicate those interests yet approximate population equality more closely,' [the plan] is justified by the State's legitimate objectives." *Id.* at 765 (quoting *Daggett*, 462 U.S. at 741).

4. What is the effect of the one-person, one-vote requirement on partisan gerrymandering? Defenders of one-person, one-vote, such as Justice Brennan, argue that an equal-population principle places limits on the ability of states to draw district lines for partisan purposes, and that at the very least the principle does no harm. *See Daggett*, 462 U.S. at 734 n.6. Without such a mandate, states would have one more tool available to effectuate a gerrymander. Critics respond that in the absence of a strict one-person, one-vote requirement states would face pressures to draw district lines that track political subdivisions and other established communities. While legally there might be no obligation to do so, legislators would be expected to draw lines in that fashion and gerrymanders would therefore attract considerable public attention. If, however, political subdivisions must be cut to equalize district populations, then a strict interpretation of one person, one vote, the argument goes, gives legislators cover to draw district lines for partisan purposes. You have seen this debate in *Reynolds* and *Kirkpatrick*; it continued in *Daggett*, with Justice Stevens, in concurrence, and Justices White and Powell, in dissent, particularly criticizing partisan gerrymanders as undercutting the right to an effective vote. *See id.* at 752–65 (Stevens, J., concurring); 775–78 (White, J., dissenting); 786–90 (Powell, J., dissenting).

Mahan v. Howell

Supreme Court of the United States
410 U.S. 315, 93 S. Ct. 979, 35 L. Ed. 2d 320 (1973)

MR. JUSTICE REHNQUIST delivered the opinion of the Court [in which MR. CHIEF JUSTICE BURGER, MR. JUSTICE STEWART, MR. JUSTICE WHITE, and MR. JUSTICE BLACKMUN join]. * * *

[The issue in this case is the constitutionality of the Virginia General Assembly's 1971 apportionment for the election of its House of Delegates. The apportionment] provided for a combination of 52 single-member, multimember, and floater delegate districts from which 100 delegates would be elected. As found by the lower court, the ideal district in Virginia consisted of 46,485 persons per delegate, and the maximum percentage variation from that ideal under the Act was 16.4% — the 12th district being overrepresented by 6.8% and the 16th district being underrepresented by 9.6%. The population ratio between these two districts was 1.18 to 1. The average percentage variance under the plan was 3.89%, and the minimum population percentage necessary to elect a majority of the House was 49.29%. Of the 52 districts, 35 were within 4% of perfection and nine exceeded a 6% variance from the ideal. With one exception, the delegate districts followed political jurisdictional lines of the counties and cities. That exception, Fairfax County, was allotted 10 delegates but was divided into two five-member districts.

Relying on *Kirkpatrick v. Preisler*, 394 U.S. 526 (1969) [p. 154], *Wells v. Rockefeller*, 394 U.S. 542 (1969), and *Reynolds v. Sims*, 377 U.S. 533 (1964) [p. 122], the District Court concluded that the 16.4% variation was sufficient to condemn the House statute under the "one person, one vote" doctrine. While it noted that the variances were traceable to the desire of the General Assembly to maintain the integrity of traditional county and city boundaries, and that it was impossible to draft district lines to overcome unconstitutional disparities and still maintain such integrity, it held that the State proved no governmental necessity for strictly adhering to political subdivision lines. Accordingly, it undertook its own redistricting and devised a plan having a percentage variation of slightly over 10% from the ideal district[.] * * *This Court first recognized that the Equal Protection Clause requires both houses of a bicameral state legislature to be apportioned substantially on a population basis in *Reynolds v. Sims*. In so doing, it suggested that in the implementation of the basic constitutional principle — equality of population among the districts — more flexibility was constitutionally permissible with respect to state legislative reapportionment than in congressional redistricting. 377 U.S., at 578. Consideration was given to the fact that, almost invariably, there is a significantly larger number of seats in state legislative bodies to be distributed within a State than congressional seats, and that therefore it may be feasible for a State to use political subdivision lines to a greater extent in establishing state legislative districts than congressional districts while still affording adequate statewide representation. *Ibid.* Another possible justification for deviation from population-based representation in state legislatures was stated to be:

> "[T]hat of insuring some voice to political subdivisions, as political sub-divisions. Several factors make more than insubstantial claims that a State can rationally consider according political subdivisions some independent representation in at least one body of the state legislature, as long as the basic standard of equality of population among districts is maintained. Local governmental entities are frequently charged with various responsibilities incident to the operation of state government. In many States much of the legislature's activity involves the enactment of so-called local legislation, directed only to the concerns of particular political subdivisions. And a State may legitimately desire to construct districts along political subdivision lines to deter the possibilities of gerrymandering." *Id.*, at 580–581. * * *

We conclude, therefore, that the constitutionality of Virginia's legislative redistricting plan was not to be judged by the more stringent standards that *Kirkpatrick* and *Wells* make applicable to congressional reapportionment, but instead by the equal protection test enunciated in *Reynolds* v. *Sims.* We reaffirm its holding that "the Equal Protection Clause requires that a State make an honest and good faith effort to construct districts, in both houses of its legislature, as nearly of equal population as is practicable." 377 U.S., at 577. We likewise reaffirm its conclusion that "[s]o long as the divergences from a strict population standard are based on legitimate considerations incident to the effectuation of a rational state policy, some deviations from the equal-population principle are constitutionally permissible with respect to the apportionment of seats in either or both of the two houses of a bicameral state legislature." *Id.*, at 579. * * *

* * * The inquiry then becomes whether it can reasonably be said that the state policy urged by Virginia to justify the divergences in the legislative reapportionment plan of the House is, indeed, furthered by the plan adopted by the legislature, and whether, if so justified, the divergences are also within tolerable limits. For a State's policy urged in justification of disparity in district population, however rational, cannot constitutionally be permitted to emasculate the goal of substantial equality.

There was uncontradicted evidence offered in the District Court to the effect that the legislature's plan, subject to minor qualifications, "produces the minimum deviation above and below the norm, keeping intact political boundaries." That court itself recognized that equality was impossible if political boundaries were to be kept intact in the process of districting. But it went on to hold that since the State "proved no governmental necessity for strictly adhering to political subdivision lines," the legislative plan was constitutionally invalid. As we noted above, however, the proper equal protection test is not framed in terms of "governmental necessity," but instead in terms of a claim that a State may "rationally consider." *Reynolds* v. *Sims, supra,* at 580–581. * * *

We hold that the legislature's plan for apportionment of the House of Delegates may reasonably be said to advance the rational state policy of respecting the boundaries of political subdivisions. The remaining inquiry is whether the population disparities among the districts that have resulted from the pursuit of this plan exceed constitutional limits. We conclude that they do not. * * *

Neither courts nor legislatures are furnished any specialized calipers that enable them to extract from the general language of the Equal Protection Clause of the Fourteenth Amendment the mathematical formula that establishes what range of percentage deviations is permissible, and what is not. The 16-odd percent maximum deviation that the District Court found to exist in the legislative plan for the reapportionment of the House is substantially less than the percentage deviations that have been found invalid in the previous decisions of this Court [including *Reynolds v. Sims*, in which the largest district had a population more than forty times greater than that of the smallest]. While this percentage may well approach tolerable limits, we do not believe it exceeds them. Virginia has not sacrificed substantial equality to justifiable deviations.

The policy of maintaining the integrity of political subdivision lines in the process of reapportioning a state legislature, the policy consistently advanced by Virginia as a justification for disparities in population among districts that elect members to the House of Delegates, is a rational one. It can reasonably be said, upon examination of the legislative plan, that it does in fact advance that policy. The population disparities that are permitted thereunder result in a maximum percentage deviation that we hold to be within tolerable constitutional limits. We, therefore, hold the General Assembly's plan for the reapportionment of the House of Delegates constitutional and reverse the District Court's conclusion to the contrary. * * *

[R]eversed in [relevant] part.

MR. JUSTICE POWELL took no part in the consideration or decision of th[is] cas[e].

MR. JUSTICE BRENNAN, with whom MR. JUSTICE DOUGLAS and MR. JUSTICE MARSHALL join, * * * dissenting[.] * * *

* * * In my view, the problem in the case before us is in no sense one of first impression, but is squarely controlled by our prior decisions[, whose] * * * holdings * * * can be restated in two unequivocal propositions. First, the paramount goal of reapportionment must be the drawing of district lines so as to achieve precise equality in the population of each district. * * * The Constitution does not permit a State to relegate considerations of equality to secondary status and reserve as the primary goal of apportionment the service of some other state interest.

Second, it is open to the State, in the event that it should fail to achieve the goal of population equality, to attempt to justify its failure by demonstrating that precise equality could not be achieved without jeopardizing some critical governmental interest. The Equal Protection Clause does not exalt the principle of equal representation to the point of nullifying every competing interest of the State. But we have held firmly to the view that variations in weight accorded each vote can be approved only where the State meets its burden of presenting cogent reasons in explanation of the variations, and even then only where the variations are small.

The validity of these propositions and their applicability to the case before us are not at all diminished by the fact that *Kirkpatrick* v. *Preisler* and *Wells* v. *Rockefeller*—two of the many cases in which the propositions were refined and applied—concerned the division of States into federal congressional districts rather than legislative reapportionment. Prior to today's decision, we have never held that different constitutional *standards* are applicable to the two situations. True, there are significant differences between congressional districting and legislative apportionment, and we have repeatedly recognized those differences. In *Reynolds* v. *Sims*, for example, we termed "more than insubstantial" the argument that "a State can rationally consider according political subdivisions some independent representation in at least one body of the state legislature, as long as the basic standard of equality of population among districts is maintained." But the recognition of these differences is hardly tantamount to the establishment of two distinct controlling standards. What our decisions have made clear is that certain state interests that are pertinent to legislative reapportionment can have no possible relevance to congressional districting. Thus, the need to preserve the integrity of political subdivisions as political subdivisions may, in some instances, justify small variations in the population of districts from which state legislators are elected. But that interest can hardly be asserted in justification of malapportioned congressional districts. While the State may have a broader range of interests to which it can point in attempting to justify a failure to achieve precise equality in the context of legislative apportionment, it by no means follows that the State is subject to a lighter burden of proof or that the controlling constitutional standard is in any sense distinguishable. * * * On the contrary, the "as nearly as practicable" standard with which we were concerned [in *Kirkpatrick*] is identical to the standard that *Reynolds* v. *Sims* specifically made applicable to controversies over state legislative apportionment.

* * * The Court assumes that county representation is an important goal of Virginia's reapportionment plan, and appellants suggest that the plan can be justified, at least in part, by the effort "to give an independent voice to the cities and counties [the legislature] daily governs." * * * That argument assumes that some significant number of issues will have an impact squarely on [a single c]ounty, while having no impact, or a differing impact, on the surrounding areas. For on issues affecting the entire region or the Commonwealth as a whole—presumably the vast majority of issues—the critical concern is not that each vote in [a c]ounty be cast in a single district, but that each vote cast be precisely equal in weight to votes in every other part of the Commonwealth. And the argument also assumes that the issues affecting only one county are of predominant concern to the voters. Under a representative form of government, the voters participate indirectly through the

election of delegates. It should be obvious that as a voter's concern with regional or statewide issues increases relative to his interest in county issues, the significance of voting outside the county will correspondingly diminish.

But even if a substantial number of issues do have an impact primarily on a single county, and even if those issues are of deep concern to the voters, it still does not follow that the legislature's apportionment plan is a rational attempt to serve an important state interest. The plan would by no means provide, even in the legislature's own terms, effective representation for each county [because small counties are combined to form individual House districts]. * * *

In short, the best that can be said of appellants' efforts to secure county representation is that the plan can be effective only with respect to some unspecified but in all likelihood small number of issues that affect a single county and that are overwhelmingly important to the voters of that county; and even then it provides effective representation only where the affected county represents a large enough percentage of the voters in the district to have a significant impact on the election of the delegate. * * *

On this record—without any showing of the specific need for county representation or a showing of how such representation can be meaningfully provided to small counties whose votes would be submerged in a multi-county district—I see no basis whatsoever for upholding the Assembly's 1971 plan and the resulting substantial variations in district population. Accordingly, I would affirm the judgment of the District Court holding the plan invalid under the Equal Protection Clause of the Fourteenth Amendment.

Notes and Questions

1. What was the Court's rationale for subjecting state-legislative apportionment to a more lenient standard than the one applicable to congressional districting? Is the distinction convincing?

2. Did the Court or Justice Brennan have the better argument based on precedent?

3. If *Howell's* standard of rationality were applied to *Reynolds v. Sims*, would that case have been decided differently? How can one tell when a given apportionment system is "irrational"?

4. Why did the Court say that the Virginia plan "may well approach tolerable limits"? What are those limits?

5. Practically speaking, would the dissent's application of the one-person, one-vote standard ever permit a state to deviate from precise mathematical equality?

6. *Problem.* Wyoming's Constitution has provided since statehood in 1890 that each county shall be entitled to at least one member of the state Senate and one member of the state House of Representatives. The 1981 statute apportioning the legislature established a 64-member House. Dividing Wyoming's population by 64

yielded an ideal district size of 7,337 persons. Wyoming's smallest county, Niobrara County, however, had only 2,924 persons. Giving Niobrara County its own representative, therefore, yielded a total deviation of 89% of the ideal district. If each of the other districts was made equal in population, would the district for Niobrara County render the entire plan unconstitutional? *See Brown v. Thomson*, 462 U.S. 835 (1983); *see also Abate v. Mundt*, 403 U.S. 182 (1971).

7. Should states be permitted to vary from one person, one vote to keep *neighborhoods* together? Suppose that within the relatively well-to-do Town of Amherst, there is a neighborhood comprised of low-income housing, known derisively as Looney Acres. In drawing district lines for the town board or county legislature, may the government defend its overpopulation of the Looney Acres district on the ground that it wishes to preserve the representation of neighborhoods? What if the Looney Acres district were *under*-populated so as to increase the power of the low-income community?

Gaffney v. Cummings

Supreme Court of the United States
412 U.S. 735, 93 S. Ct. 2321, 37 L. Ed. 2d 298 (1973)

MR. JUSTICE WHITE delivered the opinion of the Court [in which MR. CHIEF JUSTICE BURGER, MR. JUSTICE STEWART, MR. JUSTICE BLACKMUN, MR. JUSTICE POWELL, and MR. JUSTICE REHNQUIST join].

The questions in this case are whether the population variations among the election districts provided by a reapportionment plan for the Connecticut General Assembly, proposed in 1971, made out a prima facie case of invidious discrimination under the Equal Protection Clause and whether an otherwise acceptable reapportionment plan is constitutionally vulnerable where its purpose is to provide districts that would achieve "political fairness" between the political parties.

I

[After the 1970 census, the Connecticut General Assembly and an eight-member bipartisan commission were unable to agree on a reapportionment plan, so a three-member Apportionment Board was appointed and eventually adopted a plan by a 2-1 vote.] According to the 1970 census data before the Board, the population of Connecticut is 3,032,217. The Board's reapportionment plan provides for a Senate consisting of 36 senators elected from single-member districts. The ideal senatorial district, in terms of population, would thus contain 84,228 people. The districts actually created deviate, on the average, by 0.45% from this ideal, the median deviation being 0.47%. The largest and smallest senatorial districts deviate by +0.88% and -0.93%, respectively, making the total maximum deviation 1.81%.

The reapportionment plan proposed a House of 151 single-member districts. The population of the ideal assembly district would be 20,081. The average deviation from perfect equality for all the plan's assembly districts is 1.9%, the median deviation, 1.8%. The maximum deviation from the ideal is +3.93% and -3.9%. The maximum deviation between any two districts thus totals 7.83%.

* * * [T]o reach what it thought to be substantial population equality, the Board cut the boundary lines of 47 of the State's 169 towns. The Board also consciously and overtly adopted and followed a policy of "political fairness," which aimed at a rough scheme of proportional representation of the two major political parties. Senate and House districts were structured so that the composition of both Houses would reflect "as closely as possible . . . the actual [statewide] plurality of vote on the House or Senate lines in a given election." Rather than focusing on party membership in the respective districts, the Board took into account the party voting results in the preceding three statewide elections, and, on that basis, created what was thought to be a proportionate number of Republican and Democratic legislative seats.

In November 1971, * * * an action was brought in federal district court seeking declaratory and injunctive relief against implementation of the plan. * * * [T]he District Court * * * invalidat[ed] the Board plan and permanently enjoin[ed] its use in future elections. * * *

II

We think that appellees' showing of numerical deviations from population equality among the Senate and House districts in this case failed to make out a prima facie violation of the Equal Protection Clause of the Fourteenth Amendment, whether those deviations are considered alone or in combination with the additional fact that another plan could be conceived with lower deviations among the State's legislative districts. Put another way, the allegations and proof of population deviations among the districts fail in size and quality to amount to an invidious discrimination under the Fourteenth Amendment which would entitle appellees to relief, absent some countervailing showing by the State. * * *

We doubt that *Reynolds* [v. *Sims*, 377 U.S. 533 (1964)] [p. 122], would mandate any other result, if for no other reason than that the basic statistical materials which legislatures and courts usually have to work with are the results of the United States census taken at 10-year intervals and published as soon as possible after the beginning of each decade. [I]t makes little sense to conclude from relatively minor "census population" variations among legislative districts that any person's vote is being substantially diluted. The "population" of a legislative district is just not that knowable to be used for such refined judgments.

What is more, it must be recognized that total population, even if absolutely accurate as to each district when counted, is nevertheless not a talismanic measure of the weight of a person's vote under a later adopted reapportionment plan. The United States census is more of an event than a process. It measures population at only a single instant in time. District populations are constantly changing, often at different rates in either direction, up or down. Substantial differentials in population growth rates are striking and well-known phenomena. So, too, if it is the weight of a person's vote that matters, total population — even if stable and accurately taken — may not actually reflect that body of voters whose votes must be counted and weighed for the purposes of reapportionment, because "census persons" are not voters. [See *Burns v. Richardson*, 384 U.S. 73, 91–92 (1966).] The proportion of the census population too young to vote or disqualified by alienage or nonresidence varies substantially among the States and among localities within the States. The six congressional districts in Connecticut, for example, vary from one another by as much as 4% in their age-eligible voters, with the first district having 68% of its census population at voting age while the sixth district has 64% at 18 years or older. Other States have congressional districts that vary from one another by as much as 29% and as little as 1% with respect to their age-eligible voters. And these figures tell us nothing of the other ineligibles making up the substantially equal census populations among election districts: aliens, nonresident military personnel, nonresident students, for example. Nor do these figures tell anything at all about the proportion of all those otherwise eligible individuals whose vote cannot be counted or weighed because they either failed to register or failed to vote.

Reynolds v. *Sims*, of course, dealt with more than the statistical niceties involved in equalizing individual voting strength. It * * * recognized that "the achieving of fair and effective representation for all citizens is . . . the basic aim of legislative apportionment," [377 U.S.,] at 565–566, and it was for that reason that the decision insisted on substantial equality of populations among districts.

This is a vital and worthy goal, but surely its attainment does not in any commonsense way depend upon eliminating the insignificant population variations involved in this case. Fair and effective representation may be destroyed by gross population variations among districts, but it is apparent that such representation does not depend solely on mathematical equality among district populations. * * *

Nor is the goal of fair and effective representation furthered by making the standards of reapportionment so difficult to satisfy that the reapportionment task is recurringly removed from legislative hands and performed by federal courts which themselves must make the political decisions necessary to formulate a plan or accept those made by reapportionment plaintiffs who may have wholly different goals from those embodied in the official plan. * * * We doubt that the Fourteenth Amendment requires repeated displacement of otherwise appropriate state decisionmaking in the name of essentially minor deviations from perfect census-population equality that no one, with confidence, can say will deprive any person of fair and effective representation in his state legislature.

That the Court was not deterred by the hazards of the political thicket when it undertook to adjudicate the reapportionment cases does not mean that it should become bogged down in a vast, intractable apportionment slough, particularly when there is little, if anything, to be accomplished by doing so. * * *

* * * We have repeatedly recognized that state reapportionment is the task of local legislatures or of those organs of state government selected to perform it. Their work should not be invalidated under the Equal Protection Clause when only minor population variations among districts are proved. Here, the proof at trial demonstrated that the House districts under the State Apportionment Board's plan varied in population from one another by a maximum of only about 8% and that the average deviation from the ideal House district was only about 2%. The Senate districts had even less variations. On such a showing, we are quite sure that a prima facie case of invidious discrimination under the Fourteenth Amendment was not made out.

III

State legislative districts may be equal or substantially equal in population and still be vulnerable under the Fourteenth Amendment. A districting statute otherwise acceptable, may be invalid because it fences out a racial group so as to deprive them of their pre-existing municipal vote. *Gomillion* v. *Lightfoot*, 364 U.S. 339 (1960) [p. 279]. * * * We must, therefore, respond to appellees' claims in this case that even if acceptable populationwise, the Apportionment Board's plan was invidiously discriminatory because a "political fairness principle" was followed in making up the districts in both the House and Senate.

The record abounds with evidence, and it is frankly admitted by those who prepared the plan, that virtually every Senate and House district line was drawn with the conscious intent to create a districting plan that would achieve a rough approximation of the statewide political strengths of the Democratic and Republican Parties, the only two parties in the State large enough to elect legislators from discernible geographic areas. Appellant insists that the spirit of "political fairness" underlying this plan is not only permissible, but a desirable consideration in laying out districts that otherwise satisfy the population standard of the reapportionment cases. Appellees, on the other hand, label the plan as nothing less than a gigantic political gerrymander, invidiously discriminatory under the Fourteenth Amendment.[18]

We are quite unconvinced that the reapportionment plan offered by the three-member Board violated the Fourteenth Amendment because it attempted to reflect the relative strength of the parties in locating and defining election districts. It would be idle, we think, to contend that any political consideration taken into account in fashioning a reapportionment plan is sufficient to invalidate it. * * * The very essence of districting is to produce a different—a more "politically fair"— result than would be reached with elections at large, in which the winning party would take 100% of the legislative seats. Politics and political considerations are

---

18. Appellees also maintain that the shapes of the districts would not have been so "indecent" had the Board not attempted to "wiggle and joggle" boundary lines to ferret out pockets of each party's strength. That may well be true * * *. But compactness or attractiveness has never been held to constitute an independent federal constitutional requirement for state legislative districts.

inseparable from districting and apportionment. The political profile of a State, its party registration, and voting records are available precinct by precinct, ward by ward. These subdivisions may not be identical with census tracts, but, when over-laid on a census map, it requires no special genius to recognize the political conse-quences of drawing a district line along one street rather than another. It is not only obvious, but absolutely unavoidable, that the location and shape of districts may well determine the political complexion of the area. District lines are rarely neutral phenomena. They can well determine what district will be predominantly Demo-cratic or predominantly Republican, or make a close race likely. Redistricting may pit incumbents against one another or make very difficult the election of the most experienced legislator. The reality is that districting inevitably has and is intended to have substantial political consequences.

It may be suggested that those who redistrict and reapportion should work with census, not political, data and achieve population equality without regard for politi-cal impact. But this politically mindless approach may produce, whether intended or not, the most grossly gerrymandered results; and, in any event, it is most unlikely that the political impact of such a plan would remain undiscovered by the time it was proposed or adopted, in which event the results would be both known and, if not changed, intended.

It is much more plausible to assume that those who redistrict and reapportion work with both political and census data. Within the limits of the population equality standards of the Equal Protection Clause, they seek, through compromise or otherwise, to achieve the political or other ends of the State, its constituents, and its officeholders. * * * Even more plainly, judicial interest should be at its lowest ebb when a State purports fairly to allocate political power to the parties in accordance with their voting strength and, within quite tolerable limits, succeeds in doing so. There is no doubt that there may be other reapportionment plans for Connecticut that would have different political consequences and that would also be consti-tutional. Perhaps any of appellees' plans would have fallen into this category, as would the court's, had it propounded one. But neither we nor the district courts have a constitutional warrant to invalidate a state plan, otherwise within tolerable population limits, because it undertakes, not to minimize or eliminate the politi-cal strength of any group or party, but to recognize it and, through districting, provide a rough sort of proportional representation in the legislative halls of the State.

Reversed.

MR. JUSTICE BRENNAN, with whom MR. JUSTICE DOUGLAS and MR. JUSTICE MARSHALL join, dissenting[.] * * *

Although not purporting to quarrel with the principle that precise mathematical equality is the constitutionally mandated goal of reapportionment, the Court today establishes a wide margin of tolerable error, and thereby undermines the effort to effectuate the principle. * * *

[I]t is important to understand that the demand for precise mathematical equality rests neither on a scholastic obsession with abstract numbers nor a rigid insensitivity to the political realities of the reapportionment process. Our paramount concern has remained an individual and personal right — the right to an equal vote. * * * We have demanded equality in district population precisely to insure that the weight of a person's vote will not depend on the district in which he lives. The conclusion that a State may, without any articulated justification, deliberately weight some persons' votes more heavily than others, seems to me fundamentally at odds with the purpose and rationale of our reapportionment decisions. * * *

Notes and Questions

1. In *Gaffney* and other cases, the Court established that 10% was the figure that divided "minor deviations" from more significant ones, for which the state needed to provide a justification. *See Evenwel v. Abbott*, 578 U.S. __, 136 S. Ct. 1120, 1124 (2016) [p. 145] ("Where the maximum population deviation between the largest and smallest district is less than 10%, the Court has held, a state or local legislative map presumptively complies with the one-person, one-vote rule."); *Brown v. Thomson*, 462 U.S. 835, 842 (1983) ("Our decisions have established, as a general matter, that an apportionment plan with a maximum population deviation under 10% falls within this category of minor deviations."). *See also Evenwel*, 136 S. Ct. at 1124 n.2 ("Maximum population deviation is the sum of the percentage deviations from perfect population equality of the most- and least-populated districts.") (citing *Chapman v. Meier*, 420 U.S. 1, 22 (1975)). *White v. Regester*, 412 U.S. 755 (1973) [p. 288], which was decided the same day as *Gaffney*, held that a Texas redistricting plan having a maximum deviation of 9.9% came within the *Gaffney* safe harbor. *Id.* at 764. In *Abate v. Mundt*, 403 U.S. 182 (1971), however, the Court held that a plan with a maximum deviation of 11.9% required a justification. Is there anything in the Constitution that can reasonably be interpreted as establishing a 10% safe harbor? If not, do you find acceptable the approach under *Kirkpatrick v. Preisler*, 394 U.S. 526 (1969) [p. 154], and *Karcher v. Daggett*, 462 U.S. 725 (1983), according to which virtually no population deviations are constitutional? Is there a third possibility?

2. In distinguishing *Kirkpatrick* and holding that a 16.4% population difference between state-legislative (but not congressional) districts could be justified, *Mahan v. Howell* reasoned that state legislatures are large enough to have representatives who can serve the interests of identifiable political subdivisions, and that state legislatures enact local legislation for which it would be useful to have legislators who can represent municipalities. Thus, keeping municipalities intact may be a sufficient reason to create state-legislative districts that differ slightly in population, even if the same justification would be insufficient to defend population disparities in congressional districts.

Was there a comparable reason for *Gaffney* to distinguish *Kirkpatrick* on the question whether it is necessary to provide a justification at all for population differences of less than 10%? Why would the Constitution require states to justify small deviations in the population of congressional districts, but not to justify similar deviations in state-legislative districts?

3. The one-person, one-vote rule applies to districts for the election of representatives to local governments as well as to Congress and state legislatures. *See Avery v. Midland County*, 390 U.S. 474 (1968). *Abate v. Mundt, supra*, elaborated on the permissible deviations from mathematical equality for local-government districts:

> [V]iable local governments may need considerable flexibility in municipal arrangements if they are to meet changing societal needs, and * * * a desire to preserve the integrity of political subdivisions may justify an apportionment plan which departs from numerical equality. These observations, along with the facts that local legislative bodies frequently have fewer representatives than do their state and national counterparts and that some local legislative districts may have a much smaller population than do congressional and state legislative districts, lend support to the argument that slightly greater percentage deviations may be tolerable for local government apportionment schemes.

Is this explanation consistent with the Court's explanation of its different tolerances for population variation in congressional and state-legislative districts? How much variation would qualify as a "slightly greater percentage deviation[]"? Nineteen percent? *See Blackmoon v. Charles Mix County*, 386 F. Supp. 2d 1108 (D.S.D. 2005).

4. In *Gaffney*, the Court permitted Connecticut to impose slight population variations across districts in an effort to achieve "political fairness," by which the state meant a more nearly proportional distribution of legislative seats between the major parties. Is it constitutional for a state to achieve the same goal in a more overt way by forbidding any party from holding more than a certain number of seats? In two cases in the 1970s, the Supreme Court summarily affirmed lower-court judgments upholding the constitutionality of such laws. *See Hechinger v. Martin*, 411 F. Supp. 650 (D.D.C. 1976) (three-judge court) (upholding a law guaranteeing at least some representation on the D.C. Council to political minorities), *summarily aff'd*, 429 U.S. 1030 (1977); *LoFrisco v. Schaffer*, 341 F. Supp. 743 (D. Conn.) (similarly upholding a law guaranteeing representation for political minorities by limiting the number of candidates a party may nominate), *summarily aff'd*, 409 U.S. 972 (1972). Are such laws inconsistent with the majoritarianism that the Court constitutionalized in *Reynolds v. Sims*?

Cox v. Larios

Supreme Court of the United States
542 U.S. 947, 124 S. Ct. 2806, 159 L. Ed. 2d 831 (2004)

Affirmed on appeal from D.C. N.D. Ga. Reported below: 300 F. Supp. 2d 1320.

JUSTICE STEVENS, with whom JUSTICE BREYER joins, concurring.

Today we affirm the District Court's judgment that Georgia's legislative reapportionment plans for the State House of Representatives and Senate violate the one-person, one-vote principle of the Equal Protection Clause. [The maximum population variance was 9.8%.] The District Court's findings disclose two reasons for the unconstitutional population deviations in the state legislative reapportionment plans. The first was "a deliberate and systematic policy of favoring rural and inner-city interests at the expense of suburban areas north, east, and west of Atlanta." The second was "an intentional effort to allow incumbent Democrats to maintain or increase their delegation, primarily by systematically underpopulating the districts held by incumbent Democrats, by overpopulating those of Republicans, and by deliberately pairing numerous Republican incumbents against one another." * * * The District Court correctly held that the drafters' desire to give an electoral advantage to certain regions of the State and to certain incumbents (but not incumbents as such) did not justify the conceded deviations from the principle of one person, one vote.

In challenging the District Court's judgment, appellant invites us to weaken the one-person, one-vote standard by creating a safe harbor for population deviations of less than 10 percent, within which districting decisions could be made for any reason whatsoever. The Court properly rejects that invitation. After our recent decision in *Vieth* v. *Jubelirer*, 541 U.S. 267 (2004), the equal-population principle remains the only clear limitation on improper districting practices, and we must be careful not to dilute its strength. * * *

Drawing district lines that have no neutral justification in order to place two incumbents of the opposite party in the same district is probative of the same impermissible intent as the "uncouth twenty-eight-sided figure" that defined the boundary of Tuskegee, Alabama, in *Gomillion* v. *Lightfoot*, 364 U.S. 339, 340 (1960) [p. 279], or the "dragon descending on Philadelphia from the west" that defined Pennsylvania's District 6 in *Vieth*, 541 U.S., at 340 (STEVENS, J., dissenting). The record in this case, like the allegations in *Gomillion* and in *Vieth*, reinforce my conclusion that "the unavailability of judicially manageable standards" cannot justify a refusal "to condemn even the most blatant violations of a state legislature's fundamental duty to govern impartially." *Vieth*, 541 U.S., at 341. I remain convinced that in time the present "failure of judicial will" will be replaced by stern condemnation of partisan gerrymandering that does not even pretend to be justified by neutral principles.

JUSTICE SCALIA, dissenting.

When reviewing States' redistricting of their own legislative boundaries, we have been appropriately deferential. See *Mahan* v. *Howell*, 410 U.S. 315, 327 (1973) [p. 163]. A series of our cases established the principle that "minor deviations" among districts—deviations of less than 10%—are "insufficient to make out a prima facie case of invidious discrimination under the Fourteenth Amendment so as to require justification by the State." *Brown* v. *Thomson*, 462 U.S. 835, 842 (1983) (quoting *Gaffney* v. *Cummings*, 412 U.S. 735, 745 (1973) [p. 168]); see also *Voinovich* v. *Quilter*, 507 U.S. 146, 160–162 (1993). This case presents a question that *Brown*, *Gaffney*, and *Voinovich* did not squarely confront—whether a districting plan that *satisfies* this 10% criterion may nevertheless be invalidated on the basis of circumstantial evidence of partisan political motivation.

The state officials who drafted Georgia's redistricting plan believed the answer to that question was "no," reading our cases to establish a 10% "safe harbor" with which they meticulously complied. The court below disagreed. No party here contends that, beyond grand generalities in cases such as *Reynolds* v. *Sims*, 377 U.S. 533, 577 (1964) [p. 122], this Court has addressed the question. The opinion below is consistent with others to have addressed the issue; there is no obvious conflict among the lower courts. This is not a petition for certiorari, however, but an appeal, and we should not summarily affirm unless it is clear that the disposition of this case is correct.

In my view, that is not clear. A substantial case can be made that Georgia's redistricting plan *did* comply with the Constitution. Appellees do not contend that the population deviations—all less than 5% from the mean—were based on race or some other suspect classification. They claim only impermissible *political* bias— that state legislators tried to improve the electoral chances of Democrats over Republicans by underpopulating inner-city and rural districts and by selectively protecting incumbents, while ignoring "traditional" redistricting criteria. The District Court agreed.

The problem with this analysis is that it assumes "politics as usual" is not *itself* a "traditional" redistricting criterion. In the recent decision in *Vieth* v. *Jubelirer*, all but one of the Justices agreed that it *is* a traditional criterion, and a constitutional one, so long as it does not go too far. It is not obvious to me that a legislature goes too far when it stays within the 10% disparity in population our cases allow. To say that it does is to invite allegations of political motivation whenever there is population disparity, and thus to destroy the 10% safe harbor our cases provide. Ferreting out political motives in minute population deviations seems to me more likely to encourage politically motivated litigation than to vindicate political rights.

I would set the case for argument.

Notes and Questions

1. In reconciling *Larios* with *Rucho v. Common Cause*, 588 U.S. ___, 139 S. Ct. 2484 (2019) [p. 180], (and with *Vieth v. Jubelirer*, which was decided two months before *Larios*), remember that *Larios* involved not just a partisan gerrymander, but a partisan gerrymander that achieved its results in part through deviations from one person, one vote. *Larios* thus stands for the proposition (questioned by Justice Scalia in dissent) that deviations from population equality—even where those deviations are less than the 10% "safe harbor"—are unconstitutional if they are justified only by a desire to produce a partisan advantage.

2. Does this case spell the end of the "safe harbor"? *See In re Municipal Reapportionment of Township of Haverford*, 873 A.2d 821, 834–36 (Pa. Commw. Ct. 2005). Under *Brown* and *Gaffney*, deviations of less than 10% were "insufficient to make out a prima facie case of invidious discrimination," and therefore required no justification from the state. *Larios* held that Georgia's justification for its less-than-10% deviations was insufficient, but such a conclusion is logically possible only if the state is obligated to provide some justification in the first place.

Consider one court's attempt to explain the proper approach to follow after *Cox v. Larios*:

> The formulaic [ten-percent] threshold is not an absolute determinant. Rather, it effectively allocates the burden of proof. Population deviation less than ten percent, for example, is not *per se* nondiscriminatory and is not an absolute bar to a claim of vote dilution. At the same time, a deviation in population equality greater than ten percent establishes a *prima facie* case of discrimination and shifts the evidentiary burden to the state, requiring justification for the deviation. With a deviation less than ten percent, a plaintiff must prove that the redistricting process was tainted by arbitrariness or discrimination. That is, a deviation less than ten percent is not a safe harbor, barring any claim of discrimination[.] * * * [M]inor deviations do not amount to a *prima facie* case of discrimination under the Fourteenth Amendment, but they do not foreclose the possibility of success altogether; there may be other evidence.

Moore v. Itawamba County, 431 F.3d 257, 259–60 (5th Cir. 2005) (*per curiam*) (footnotes omitted). *Cf. Batson v. Kentucky*, 476 U.S. 79 (1986) (establishing a similar burden-shifting framework for addressing claims of racial discrimination in the use of peremptory challenges for jurors). If *Moore* is correct, why aren't challenges such as *Larios* barred by *Rucho*? That is, once it is established that the population variance does not create a prima facie case of discrimination, the plaintiff is left to make essentially the same claim that *Rucho* refused to adjudicate.

How much "other evidence" of "arbitrariness or discrimination" should plaintiffs have to present to succeed in a challenge to a plan with a total deviation of less than 10%? The easier it is to make such a claim, the less significance there will be to the 10% threshold. Justice Scalia seemed to imply that after *Larios*, it will be too easy for plaintiffs in "politically motivated litigation" to make allegations of improper motivation in districting. Was he correct?

3. In *Harris v. Arizona Independent Redistricting Commission*, 578 U.S. __, 136 S. Ct. 1301 (2016), the Supreme Court clarified the standard that plaintiffs must meet when challenging population variances of less than 10% in state-legislative districts. According to *Harris*, "those attacking a state-approved plan must show that it is more probable than not that a deviation of less than 10% reflects the predominance of illegitimate reapportionment factors"—presumably including partisanship. *Id.* at 1307; *see also id.* at 1309. The Court noted its expectation that, "[g]iven the inherent difficulty of measuring and comparing factors that may legitimately account for small deviations from strict mathematical equality," such challenges would "only rarely" succeed. *Id.* at 1307. And so, even though partisanship played "some role" in the adoption of the districting plan at issue in *Harris*, the principal motivation appeared to be compliance with the Voting Rights Act, and so the Court unanimously upheld the districting plan. *Id.* at 1306 (quoting the opinion below, 993 F. Supp. 2d 1042, 1046 (D. Ariz. 2014)).

4. If Georgia's plan had been designed to help all incumbent legislators, instead of just Democrats, should the result have been different? More broadly, what "reapportionment factors" should be considered "illegitimate"? Was Justice Stevens correct in *Larios* to draw a parallel between partisan gerrymandering and the racial gerrymandering declared unconstitutional in *Gomillion v. Lightfoot*?

5. Challenges to the apportionment of congressional districts or statewide legislative districts are heard in federal court not by a single district judge, as is the usual practice, but by a court of three judges, at least one of whom must be a circuit judge. *See* 28 U.S.C. § 2284(b)(1). Appeals from such courts proceed directly to the Supreme Court, and the Court must decide those appeals; they are not subject to the *certiorari* process that permits the Court to determine most of its own docket. *See* 28 U.S.C. § 1253. Thus, as Justice Scalia noted, the Court did not have the ability to deny *certiorari* in *Larios* and leave the issues presented for another day. *See generally* Michael E. Solimine, *The Three-Judge District Court in Voting Rights Litigation*, 30 U. MICH. J.L. REF. 79 (1996).

Not every case subject to the Supreme Court's "mandatory" jurisdiction is given full consideration, however. Sometimes, as in *Larios*, the Court decides such appeals summarily, without oral argument. It takes six Justices to invoke the summary process. Despite the cursory treatment the Court gives to such cases, however, they are entitled to precedential weight and must be treated as binding by lower courts. *See Hicks v. Miranda*, 422 U.S. 332 (1975).[g] The Supreme Court itself,

---

g. Nevertheless, "[s]ummary actions * * * should not be understood as breaking new ground but as applying principles established by prior decisions to the particular facts involved." *Mandel v.*

however, will give summary dispositions less precedential weight than it gives to decisions reached after full consideration. *See, e.g., Edelman v. Jordan*, 415 U.S. 651, 671 (1974). *See generally* Stephen M. Shapiro et al., Supreme Court Practice § 4.28 (11th ed. 2019); Michael E. Solimine, *Institutional Process, Agenda Setting, and the Development of Election Law on the Supreme Court*, 68 Ohio St. L.J. 767, 792–93 (2007).

E. Partisan Gerrymandering

The Supreme Court's insistence on districts with equal populations forced districters to draw district lines that deviated from reasonably objective divisions between communities. After the "reapportionment revolution," district lines routinely crossed municipal and geographic boundaries, such as rivers and major roads, that tended to create defined communities. Once there was no longer an expectation that districts would conform to such boundaries, there was little to stop politicians from drawing districts to accomplish political or personal goals, such as the election of candidates belonging to a favored party or the reelection of a particular politician.[h]

Districting had been used for a long time to accomplish those goals—the term "gerrymander" dates from Massachusetts Governor Elbridge Gerry's creation of a salamander-shaped district in 1812—but the Court's decisions hastened the demise of some norms that had kept gerrymandering in check. The development of increasingly powerful computer technology at the end of the twentieth century helped make gerrymandering more precise and easier, so that by the 1980s, many observers complained that districting had become more of a partisan game than a genuine attempt to represent the people in various communities within a jurisdiction. The Supreme Court was asked again to enter the political thicket to limit politicians' ability to manipulate district lines for partisan ends.

The constitutionality of partisan gerrymandering involved many of the same concerns about political fairness and judicial competence that lay behind the Court's earlier one-person, one-vote decisions. On the one hand, trusting districting to politicians would leave the fox guarding the henhouse. It could even be thought to undermine the one-person, one-vote principle, as districts could be drawn to advantage certain political interests that might not represent the views of

---

Bradley, 432 U.S. 173, 176 (1977).

h. You may recall that Justice Harlan warned about this very possibility. *See Reynolds v. Sims*, 377 U.S. 533, 622 (1964) [p. 122] (Harlan, J., dissenting) ("Recognizing that 'indiscriminate districting' is an invitation to 'partisan gerrymandering,' *ante* pp. 578–579, the Court nevertheless excludes virtually every basis for the formation of electoral districts other than 'indiscriminate districting.'").

the people. Certain voters could be denied fair representation—the value of their votes could be diluted—because of their political views, and the government itself would be stacking the deck to produce a pre-determined electoral outcome. On the other hand, judicial involvement would presuppose that there was a judicially manageable standard for determining what the views of the people were and what electoral results would be fair. And unlike the one-person, one-vote doctrine, where there was a ready mathematical formula for assessing compliance, it would be very difficult—perhaps impossible—for the judiciary to determine whether districting decisions had been made with too much concern for politics.

When partisan gerrymandering reached the Supreme Court, the Court's decisions were equivocal, even Delphic. In *Davis v. Bandemer*, 478 U.S. 109 (1986), the Court (6-3) held that partisan-gerrymandering claims did implicate constitutional rights under the Equal Protection Clause, *see id.* at 118–27, but the Court could not agree on a standard by which to evaluate those claims. Justice White, in an opinion joined by Justices Brennan, Marshall, and Blackmun, argued that partisan gerrymandering was unconstitutional when a group had been denied the ability to influence the political process as a whole—an inquiry that involved, but was not limited to, an analysis of election results. *See id.* at 132–33 (plurality opinion). Justices Powell and Stevens would have asked, instead, "whether the boundaries of the voting districts have been distorted deliberately and arbitrarily to achieve illegitimate ends." *Id.* at 165 (Powell, J., concurring in part and dissenting in part).

Partisan gerrymandering was back at the Court in 2004 with *Vieth v. Jubelirer*, 541 U.S. 267 (2004). Again, the Court was split. A plurality of four Justices, in an opinion by Justice Scalia, concluded that there were no judicially manageable standards for adjudicating partisan-gerrymandering claims, and so such claims presented political questions and were non-justiciable. *See id.* at 305 (plurality opinion). The fifth Justice, Justice Kennedy, agreed to dismiss the case because no judicially manageable standards had yet been developed, but he suggested that partisan-gerrymandering claims might be justiciable if judicially manageable standards were to be developed in the future. *See id.* at 309–10, 311–12 (Kennedy, J., concurring in the judgment).

With the issue still unresolved fifteen years later, the Court tried yet again.

Rucho v. Common Cause

Supreme Court of the United States
588 U.S. __, 139 S. Ct. 2484, 204 L. Ed. 2d 931 (2019)

CHIEF JUSTICE ROBERTS delivered the opinion of the Court [in which JUSTICE THOMAS, JUSTICE ALITO, JUSTICE GORSUCH, and JUSTICE KAVANAUGH join]. * * *

These cases require us to consider once again whether claims of excessive partisanship in districting are "justiciable"—that is, properly suited for resolution by the federal courts. This Court has not previously struck down a districting plan as an unconstitutional partisan gerrymander, and has struggled without success over the past several decades to discern judicially manageable standards for deciding such claims. The districting plans at issue here are highly partisan, by any measure. The question is whether the courts below appropriately exercised judicial power when they found them unconstitutional as well.

I

The first case [*Rucho* v. *Common Cause*] involves a challenge to the congressional redistricting plan enacted by the Republican-controlled North Carolina General Assembly in 2016. The Republican legislators leading the redistricting effort instructed their mapmaker to use political data to draw a map that would produce a congressional delegation of ten Republicans and three Democrats. * * * One Democratic state senator objected that entrenching the 10–3 advantage for Republicans was not "fair, reasonable, [or] balanced" because, as recently as 2012, "Democratic congressional candidates had received more votes on a statewide basis than Republican candidates." The General Assembly was not swayed by that objection and approved the 2016 Plan by a party-line vote. * * *

The plaintiffs challenged the 2016 Plan on multiple constitutional grounds. First, they alleged that the Plan violated the Equal Protection Clause of the Fourteenth Amendment by intentionally diluting the electoral strength of Democratic voters. Second, they claimed that the Plan violated their First Amendment rights by retaliating against supporters of Democratic candidates on the basis of their political beliefs. Third, they asserted that the Plan usurped the right of "the People" to elect their preferred candidates for Congress, in violation of the requirement in Article I, §2, of the Constitution that Members of the House of Representatives be chosen "by the People of the several States." Finally, they alleged that the Plan violated the Elections Clause by exceeding the State's delegated authority to prescribe the "Times, Places and Manner of holding Elections" for Members of Congress.

After a four-day trial, the three-judge District Court unanimously concluded that the 2016 Plan violated the Equal Protection Clause and Article I of the Constitution. The court further held, with Judge Osteen dissenting, that the Plan violated the First Amendment. * * *

The second case before us is *Lamone* v. *Benisek*. In 2011, the Maryland Legislature—dominated by Democrats—undertook to redraw the lines of that State's eight congressional districts. The Governor at the time, Democrat Martin O'Malley, led the process. * * * The Governor later testified that his aim was to "use the redistricting process to change the overall composition of Maryland's congressional delegation to 7 Democrats and 1 Republican by flipping" one district. * * * Overall, the Plan reduced the number of registered Republicans in the Sixth District by about 66,000 and increased the number of registered Democrats by about 24,000. The map was adopted by a party-line vote. It was used in the 2012 election and succeeded in flipping the Sixth District. A Democrat has held the seat ever since.

In November 2013, three Maryland voters filed this lawsuit. They alleged that the 2011 Plan violated the First Amendment, the Elections Clause, and Article I, § 2, of the Constitution. [T]he District Court entered summary judgment for the plaintiffs. * * *

II * * *

Partisan gerrymandering is nothing new. Nor is frustration with it. The practice was known in the Colonies prior to Independence, and the Framers were familiar with it at the time of the drafting and ratification of the Constitution. During the very first congressional elections, George Washington and his Federalist allies accused Patrick Henry of trying to gerrymander Virginia's districts against their candidates—in particular James Madison, who ultimately prevailed over fellow future President James Monroe.

In 1812, Governor of Massachusetts and future Vice President Elbridge Gerry notoriously approved congressional districts that the legislature had drawn to aid the Democratic-Republican Party. The moniker "gerrymander" was born when an outraged Federalist newspaper observed that one of the misshapen districts resembled a salamander. E. Griffith, The Rise and Development of the Gerrymander 17–19 (1907). "By 1840, the gerrymander was a recognized force in party politics and was generally attempted in all legislation enacted for the formation of election districts. It was generally conceded that each party would attempt to gain power which was not proportionate to its numerical strength." *Id.*, at 123.

The Framers addressed the election of Representatives to Congress in the Elections Clause. Art. I, § 4, cl. 1. That provision assigns to state legislatures the power to prescribe the "Times, Places and Manner of holding Elections" for Members of Congress, while giving Congress the power to "make or alter" any such regulations. * * *

Congress has regularly exercised its Elections Clause power, including to address partisan gerrymandering. The Apportionment Act of 1842, which required single-member districts for the first time, specified that those districts be "composed of contiguous territory," Act of June 25, 1842, ch. 47, 5 Stat. 491, in "an attempt to forbid the practice of the gerrymander," Griffith, *supra*, at 12. Later statutes added requirements of compactness and equality of population. Act of Jan. 16, 1901, ch. 93, § 3, 31 Stat. 733; Act of Feb. 2, 1872, ch. 11, § 2, 17 Stat. 28. (Only the single member district requirement remains in place today. 2 U.S.C. § 2c.) * * *

Appellants suggest that, through the Elections Clause, the Framers set aside electoral issues such as the one before us as questions that only Congress can resolve. We do not agree. In two areas—one-person, one-vote and racial gerrymandering—our cases have held that there is a role for the courts with respect to at least some issues that could arise from a State's drawing of congressional districts. See *Wesberry* v. *Sanders*, 376 U.S. 1 (1964) [p. 116]; *Shaw* v. *Reno*, 509 U.S. 630 (1993) (*Shaw I*) [p. 362]. * * *

Partisan gerrymandering claims have proved far more difficult to adjudicate [than are cases in those two areas]. The basic reason is that, while it is illegal for a jurisdiction to depart from the one-person, one-vote rule, or to engage in racial discrimination in districting, "a jurisdiction may engage in constitutional political gerrymandering." *Hunt* v. *Cromartie*, 526 U.S. 541, 551 (1999); *Miller* v. *Johnson*, 515 U.S. 900, 916 (1995) [p. 376]; *Shaw I*, 509 U.S., at 646). See also *Gaffney* v. *Cummings*, 412 U.S. 735, 753 (1973) [p. 168] (recognizing that "[p]olitics and political considerations are inseparable from districting and apportionment").

To hold that legislators cannot take partisan interests into account when drawing district lines would essentially countermand the Framers' decision to entrust districting to political entities. The "central problem" is not determining whether a jurisdiction has engaged in partisan gerrymandering. It is "determining when political gerrymandering has gone too far." *Vieth* [v. *Jubelirer*], 541 U.S. [267], 296 [(2004)] (plurality opinion). See *League of United Latin American Citizens* v. *Perry*, 548 U.S. 399, 420 (2006) (*LULAC*) [p. 395] (opinion of Kennedy, J.) (difficulty is "providing a standard for deciding how much partisan dominance is too much"). * * *

III

A

In considering whether partisan gerrymandering claims are justiciable, we are mindful of Justice Kennedy's counsel in *Vieth*: Any standard for resolving such claims must be grounded in a "limited and precise rationale" and be "clear, manageable, and politically neutral." 541 U.S., at 306–308 (opinion concurring in judgment). * * * An expansive standard requiring "the correction of all election district lines drawn for partisan reasons would commit federal and state courts to unprecedented intervention in the American political process," *Vieth*, 541 U.S., at 306 (opinion of Kennedy, J.).

As noted, the question is one of degree: How to "provid[e] a standard for deciding how much partisan dominance is too much." And it is vital in such circumstances that the Court act only in accord with especially clear standards: "With uncertain limits, intervening courts—even when proceeding with best intentions—would risk assuming political, not legal, responsibility for a process that often produces ill will and distrust." *Vieth*, 541 U.S., at 307 (opinion of Kennedy, J.). If federal courts are to "inject [themselves] into the most heated partisan issues" by adjudicating partisan gerrymandering claims, [*Davis* v.] *Bandemer*, 478 U.S. [109], 145 [(1986)] (opinion of O'Connor, J.), they must be armed with a standard that can reliably differentiate unconstitutional from "constitutional political gerrymandering." *Cromartie*, 526 U.S., at 551.

B

Partisan gerrymandering claims rest on an instinct that groups with a certain level of political support should enjoy a commensurate level of political power and influence. Explicitly or implicitly, a districting map is alleged to be unconstitutional because it makes it too difficult for one party to translate statewide support into seats in the legislature. But such a claim is based on a "norm that does not exist" in our electoral system—"statewide elections for representatives along party lines." *Bandemer*, 478 U.S., at 159 (opinion of O'Connor, J.).

Partisan gerrymandering claims invariably sound in a desire for proportional representation. As Justice O'Connor put it, such claims are based on "a conviction that the greater the departure from proportionality, the more suspect an apportionment plan becomes." *Ibid.* "Our cases, however, clearly foreclose any claim that the Constitution requires proportional representation or that legislatures in reapportioning must draw district lines to come as near as possible to allocating seats to the contending parties in proportion to what their anticipated statewide vote will be." *Id.*, at 130 (plurality opinion).

The Founders certainly did not think proportional representation was required. For more than 50 years after ratification of the Constitution, many States elected their congressional representatives through at-large or "general ticket" elections. Such States typically sent single-party delegations to Congress. That meant that a party could garner nearly half of the vote statewide and wind up without any seats in the congressional delegation. * * *

Unable to claim that the Constitution requires proportional representation outright, plaintiffs inevitably ask the courts to make their own political judgment about how much representation particular political parties *deserve*—based on the votes of their supporters—and to rearrange the challenged districts to achieve that end. But federal courts are not equipped to apportion political power as a matter of fairness, nor is there any basis for concluding that they were authorized to do so. As Justice Scalia put it for the plurality in *Vieth*:

> "'Fairness' does not seem to us a judicially manageable standard. . . . Some criterion more solid and more demonstrably met than that seems to us necessary to enable the state legislatures to discern the limits of their districting discretion, to meaningfully constrain the discretion of the courts, and to win public acceptance for the courts' intrusion into a process that is the very foundation of democratic decisionmaking." 541 U.S., at 291.

The initial difficulty in settling on a "clear, manageable and politically neutral" test for fairness is that it is not even clear what fairness looks like in this context. There is a large measure of "unfairness" in any winner-take-all system. Fairness may mean a greater number of competitive districts. Such a claim seeks to undo packing and cracking so that supporters of the disadvantaged party have a better shot at electing their preferred candidates. But making as many districts as possible more competitive could be a recipe for disaster for the disadvantaged party. As Justice White has pointed out, "[i]f all or most of the districts are competitive . . . even a narrow statewide preference for either party would produce an overwhelming majority for the winning party in the state legislature." *Bandemer*, 478 U.S., at 130 (plurality opinion).

On the other hand, perhaps the ultimate objective of a "fairer" share of seats in the congressional delegation is most readily achieved by yielding to the gravitational pull of proportionality and engaging in cracking and packing, to ensure each party its "appropriate" share of "safe" seats. Such an approach, however, comes at the expense of competitive districts and of individuals in districts allocated to the opposing party.

Or perhaps fairness should be measured by adherence to "traditional" districting criteria, such as maintaining political subdivisions, keeping communities of interest together, and protecting incumbents. But protecting incumbents, for example, enshrines a particular partisan distribution. And the "natural political geography" of a State—such as the fact that urban electoral districts are often dominated by one political party—can itself lead to inherently packed districts. As Justice Kennedy has explained, traditional criteria such as compactness and contiguity "cannot promise political neutrality when used as the basis for relief. Instead, it seems, a decision under these standards would unavoidably have significant political effect, whether intended or not." *Vieth*, 541 U.S., at 308–309 (opinion concurring in judgment).

Deciding among just these different visions of fairness (you can imagine many others) poses basic questions that are political, not legal. There are no legal standards discernible in the Constitution for making such judgments, let alone limited and precise standards that are clear, manageable, and politically neutral. Any judicial decision on what is "fair" in this context would be an "unmoored determination" of the sort characteristic of a political question beyond the competence of the federal courts.

And it is only after determining how to define fairness that you can even begin to answer the determinative question: "How much is too much?" At what point does permissible partisanship become unconstitutional? If compliance with traditional districting criteria is the fairness touchstone, for example, how much deviation from those criteria is constitutionally acceptable and how should mapdrawers prioritize competing criteria? Should a court "reverse gerrymander" other parts of a State to counteract "natural" gerrymandering caused, for example, by the urban concentration of one party? If a districting plan protected half of the incumbents but redistricted the rest into head to head races, would that be constitutional? A court would have to rank the relative importance of those traditional criteria and weigh how much deviation from each to allow.

If a court instead focused on the respective number of seats in the legislature, it would have to decide the ideal number of seats for each party and determine at what point deviation from that balance went too far. If a 5–3 allocation corresponds most closely to statewide vote totals, is a 6–2 allocation permissible, given that legislatures have the authority to engage in a certain degree of partisan gerrymandering? Which seats should be packed and which cracked? Or if the goal is as many competitive districts as possible, how close does the split need to be for the district to be considered competitive? Presumably not all districts could qualify, so how to choose? Even assuming the court knew which version of fairness to be looking for, there are no discernible and manageable standards for deciding whether there has been a violation. The questions are "unguided and ill suited to the development of judicial standards," *Vieth*, 541 U.S., at 296 (plurality opinion), and "results from one gerrymandering case to the next would likely be disparate and inconsistent," *id.*, at 308 (opinion of Kennedy, J.).

Appellees contend that if we can adjudicate one-person, one-vote claims, we can also assess partisan gerrymandering claims. But the one-person, one-vote rule is relatively easy to administer as a matter of math. The same cannot be said of partisan gerrymandering claims, because the Constitution supplies no objective measure for assessing whether a districting map treats a political party fairly. It hardly follows from the principle that each person must have an equal say in the election of representatives that a person is entitled to have his political party achieve representation in some way commensurate to its share of statewide support.

More fundamentally, "vote dilution" in the one-person, one-vote cases refers to the idea that each vote must carry equal weight. In other words, each representative must be accountable to (approximately) the same number of constituents. That requirement does not extend to political parties. It does not mean that each party must be influential in proportion to its number of supporters. * * *

Nor do our racial gerrymandering cases provide an appropriate standard for assessing partisan gerrymandering. "[N]othing in our case law compels the conclusion that racial and political gerrymanders are subject to precisely the same constitutional scrutiny. In fact, our country's long and persistent history of racial discrimination in voting—as well as our Fourteenth Amendment jurisprudence, which always has reserved the strictest scrutiny for discrimination on the basis of race—would seem to compel the opposite conclusion." *Shaw I*, 509 U.S., at 650. Unlike partisan gerrymandering claims, a racial gerrymandering claim does not ask for a fair share of political power and influence, with all the justiciability conundrums that entails. It asks instead for the elimination of a racial classification. A partisan gerrymandering claim cannot ask for the elimination of partisanship.

IV

Appellees and the dissent propose a number of "tests" for evaluating partisan gerrymandering claims, but none meets the need for a limited and precise standard that is judicially discernible and manageable. And none provides a solid grounding for judges to take the extraordinary step of reallocating power and influence between political parties.

A

The *Common Cause* District Court * * * first required the plaintiffs to prove "that a legislative mapdrawer's predominant purpose in drawing the lines of a particular district was to 'subordinate adherents of one political party and entrench a rival party in power.'" The District Court next required a showing "that the dilution of the votes of supporters of a disfavored party in a particular district—by virtue of cracking or packing—is likely to persist in subsequent elections such that an elected representative from the favored party in the district will not feel a need to be responsive to constituents who support the disfavored party." Finally, after a prima facie showing of partisan vote dilution, the District Court shifted the burden to the defendants to prove that the discriminatory effects are "attributable to a legitimate state interest or other neutral explanation."

The District Court's "predominant intent" prong is borrowed from the racial gerrymandering context. In racial gerrymandering cases, we rely on a "predominant intent" inquiry to determine whether race was, in fact, the reason particular district boundaries were drawn the way they were. If district lines were drawn for the purpose of separating racial groups, then they are subject to strict scrutiny because "race-based decisionmaking is inherently suspect." *Miller*, 515 U.S., at 915. But determining that lines were drawn on the basis of partisanship does not indicate that the districting was improper. A permissible intent—securing partisan advantage—does not become constitutionally impermissible, like racial discrimination, when that permissible intent "predominates."

The District Court tried to limit the reach of its test by requiring plaintiffs to show, in addition to predominant partisan intent, that vote dilution "is likely to persist" to such a degree that the elected representative will feel free to ignore the concerns of the supporters of the minority party. But "[t]o allow district courts to strike down apportionment plans on the basis of their prognostications as to the outcome of future elections . . . invites 'findings' on matters as to which neither judges nor anyone else can have any confidence." *Bandemer*, 478 U.S., at 160 (opinion of O'Connor, J.). And the test adopted by the *Common Cause* court requires a far more nuanced prediction than simply who would prevail in future political contests. Judges must forecast with unspecified certainty whether a prospective winner will have a margin of victory sufficient to permit him to ignore the supporters of his defeated opponent (whoever that may turn out to be). Judges not only have to pick the winner—they have to beat the point spread. * * *

Even the most sophisticated districting maps cannot reliably account for some of the reasons voters prefer one candidate over another, or why their preferences may change. Voters elect individual candidates in individual districts, and their selections depend on the issues that matter to them, the quality of the candidates, the tone of the candidates' campaigns, the performance of an incumbent, national events or local issues that drive voter turnout, and other considerations. Many voters split their tickets. Others never register with a political party, and vote for candidates from both major parties at different points during their lifetimes. For all of those reasons, asking judges to predict how a particular districting map will perform in future elections risks basing constitutional holdings on unstable ground outside judicial expertise.

It is hard to see what the District Court's third prong—providing the defendant an opportunity to show that the discriminatory effects were due to a "legitimate redistricting objective"—adds to the inquiry. The first prong already requires the plaintiff to prove that partisan advantage predominates. Asking whether a legitimate purpose other than partisanship was the motivation for a particular districting map just restates the question.

B

The District Courts also found partisan gerrymandering claims justiciable under the First Amendment, coalescing around a basic three-part test: proof of intent to burden individuals based on their voting history or party affiliation; an actual burden on political speech or associational rights; and a causal link between the invidious intent and actual burden. Both District Courts concluded that the districting plans at issue violated the plaintiffs' First Amendment right to association. * * *

The plaintiffs' argument is that partisanship in districting should be regarded as simple discrimination against supporters of the opposing party on the basis of political viewpoint. Under that theory, any level of partisanship in districting would constitute an infringement of their First Amendment rights. But as the Court has explained, "[i]t would be idle . . . to contend that any political consideration taken into account in fashioning a reapportionment plan is sufficient to invalidate it." *Gaffney*, 412 U.S., at 752. The First Amendment test simply describes the act of districting for partisan advantage. It provides no standard for determining when partisan activity goes too far.

As for actual burden, * * * this too is not a serious standard for separating constitutional from unconstitutional partisan gerrymandering. The District Courts relied on testimony about difficulty drumming up volunteers and enthusiasm. How much of a decline in voter engagement is enough to constitute a First Amendment burden? How many door knocks must go unanswered? How many petitions unsigned? How many calls for volunteers unheeded? * * *

These cases involve blatant examples of partisanship driving districting decisions. But the First Amendment analysis below offers no "clear" and "manageable" way of distinguishing permissible from impermissible partisan motivation. * * * The decisions below prove the prediction of the *Vieth* plurality that "a First Amendment claim, if it were sustained, would render unlawful *all* consideration of political affiliation in districting," contrary to our established precedent.

C

The dissent proposes using a State's own districting criteria as a neutral baseline from which to measure how extreme a partisan gerrymander is. * * *

As an initial matter, it does not make sense to use criteria that will vary from State to State and year to year as the baseline for determining whether a gerrymander violates the Federal Constitution. The degree of partisan advantage that the Constitution tolerates should not turn on criteria offered by the gerrymanderers themselves. It is easy to imagine how different criteria could move the median map toward different partisan distributions. As a result, the same map could be constitutional or not depending solely on what the mapmakers said they set out to do. That possibility illustrates that the dissent's proposed constitutional test is indeterminate and arbitrary.

Even if we were to accept the dissent's proposed baseline, it would return us to "the original unanswerable question (How much political motivation and effect is too much?)." Would twenty percent away from the median map be okay? Forty percent? Sixty percent? Why or why not? * * * The dissent's answer says it all: "This much is too much." That is not even trying to articulate a standard or rule. * * *

D

The North Carolina District Court further concluded that the 2016 Plan violated the Elections Clause and Article I, § 2. We are unconvinced by that novel approach.

Article I, § 2, provides that "[t]he House of Representatives shall be composed of Members chosen every second Year by the People of the several States." The Elections Clause provides that "[t]he Times, Places and Manner of holding Elections for Senators and Representatives, shall be prescribed in each State by the Legislature thereof; but the Congress may at any time by Law make or alter such Regulations, except as to the Places of chusing Senators." Art. I, § 4, cl. 1.

* * * [T]he plurality in *Vieth* concluded—without objection from any other Justice—that neither § 2 nor § 4 of Article I "provides a judicially enforceable limit on the political considerations that the States and Congress may take into account when districting." 541 U.S., at 305. The District Court nevertheless asserted that partisan gerrymanders violate "the core principle of [our] republican government" preserved in Art. I, § 2, "namely, that the voters should choose their representatives, not the other way around." That seems like an objection more properly grounded in the Guarantee Clause of Article IV, § 4, which "guarantee[s] to every State in [the] Union a Republican Form of Government." This Court has several times concluded, however, that the Guarantee Clause does not provide the basis for a justiciable claim. See, *e.g., Pacific States Telephone & Telegraph Co. v. Oregon*, 223 U.S. 118 (1912).

V

Excessive partisanship in districting leads to results that reasonably seem unjust. But the fact that such gerrymandering is "incompatible with democratic principles," *Arizona State Legislature* [v. *Arizona Independent Redistricting Comm'n*], 576 U.S. [787], 791 [(2015)] [p. 200], does not mean that the solution lies with the federal judiciary. We conclude that partisan gerrymandering claims present political questions beyond the reach of the federal courts. Federal judges have no license to reallocate political power between the two major political parties, with no plausible grant of authority in the Constitution, and no legal standards to limit and direct their decisions. "[J]udicial action must be governed by *standard*, by *rule*," and must be "principled, rational, and based upon reasoned distinctions" found in the Constitution or laws. *Vieth*, 541 U.S., at 278, 279 (plurality opinion). Judicial review of partisan gerrymandering does not meet those basic requirements.

Today the dissent essentially embraces the argument that the Court unanimously rejected in *Gill* [v. *Whitford,* 585 U.S. __, 138 S. Ct. 1916 (2018)]: "this Court *can* address the problem of partisan gerrymandering because it *must.*" 585 U.S., at __, 138 S. Ct. at 1929. That is not the test of our authority under the Constitution; that document instead "confines the federal courts to a properly judicial role." * * *

Our conclusion does not condone excessive partisan gerrymandering. Nor does our conclusion condemn complaints about districting to echo into a void. The States, for example, are actively addressing the issue on a number of fronts. In 2015, the Supreme Court of Florida struck down that State's congressional districting plan as a violation of the Fair Districts Amendment to the Florida Constitution. *League of Women Voters of Florida v. Detzner,* 172 So. 3d 363 ([Fla.] 2015). The dissent wonders why we can't do the same. The answer is that there is no "Fair Districts Amendment" to the Federal Constitution. Provisions in state statutes and state constitutions can provide standards and guidance for state courts to apply. (We do not understand how the dissent can maintain that a provision saying that no districting plan "shall be drawn with the intent to favor or disfavor a political party" provides little guidance on the question.) Indeed, numerous other States are restricting partisan considerations in districting through legislation. One way they are doing so is by placing power to draw electoral districts in the hands of independent commissions. For example, in November 2018, voters in Colorado and Michigan approved constitutional amendments creating multimember commissions that will be responsible in whole or in part for creating and approving district maps for congressional and state legislative districts. Missouri is trying a different tack. Voters there overwhelmingly approved the creation of a new position — state demographer — to draw state legislative district lines.

Other States have mandated at least some of the traditional districting criteria for their mapmakers. Some have outright prohibited partisan favoritism in redistricting. See Fla. Const., Art. III, § 20(a) ("No apportionment plan or individual district shall be drawn with the intent to favor or disfavor a political party or an incumbent."); Mo. Const., Art. III, § 3 ("Districts shall be designed in a manner that achieves both partisan fairness and, secondarily, competitiveness. 'Partisan fairness' means that parties shall be able to translate their popular support into legislative representation with approximately equal efficiency."); Iowa Code § 42.4(5) (2016) ("No district shall be drawn for the purpose of favoring a political party, incumbent legislator or member of Congress, or other person or group."); Del. Code Ann., Tit. xxix, § 804 (2017) (providing that in determining district boundaries for the state legislature, no district shall "be created so as to unduly favor any person or political party").

As noted, the Framers gave Congress the power to do something about partisan gerrymandering in the Elections Clause. The first bill introduced in the 116th Congress would require States to create 15-member independent commissions to draw congressional districts and would establish certain redistricting criteria, including protection for communities of interest, and ban partisan gerrymandering. H. R. 1, 116th Cong., 1st Sess., §§ 2401, 2411 (2019).

Dozens of other bills have been introduced to limit reliance on political considerations in redistricting. In 2010, H. R. 6250 would have required States to follow standards of compactness, contiguity, and respect for political subdivisions in redistricting. It also would have prohibited the establishment of congressional districts "with the major purpose of diluting the voting strength of any person, or group, including any political party," except when necessary to comply with the Voting Rights Act of 1965.

Another example is the Fairness and Independence in Redistricting Act, which was introduced in 2005 and has been reintroduced in every Congress since. That bill would require every State to establish an independent commission to adopt redistricting plans. The bill also set forth criteria for the independent commissions to use, such as compactness, contiguity, and population equality. It would prohibit consideration of voting history, political party affiliation, or incumbent Representative's residence.

We express no view on any of these pending proposals. We simply note that the avenue for reform established by the Framers, and used by Congress in the past, remains open.

* * *

No one can accuse this Court of having a crabbed view of the reach of its competence. But we have no commission to allocate political power and influence in the absence of a constitutional directive or legal standards to guide us in the exercise of such authority. * * *

The judgments [below] are vacated, and the cases are remanded with instructions to dismiss for lack of jurisdiction.

It is so ordered.

Justice Kagan, with whom Justice Ginsburg, Justice Breyer, and Justice Sotomayor join, dissenting. * * *

* * * The partisan gerrymanders in these cases deprived citizens of the most fundamental of their constitutional rights: the rights to participate equally in the political process, to join with others to advance political beliefs, and to choose their political representatives. In so doing, the partisan gerrymanders here debased and dishonored our democracy, turning upside-down the core American idea that all governmental power derives from the people. These gerrymanders enabled politicians to entrench themselves in office as against voters' preferences. They promoted partisanship above respect for the popular will. They encouraged a politics of polarization and dysfunction. If left unchecked, gerrymanders like the ones here may irreparably damage our system of government.

And checking them is *not* beyond the courts. The majority's abdication comes just when courts across the country, including those below, have coalesced around manageable judicial standards to resolve partisan gerrymandering claims. Those standards satisfy the majority's own benchmarks. They do not require—indeed, they do not permit—courts to rely on their own ideas of electoral fairness, whether proportional representation or any other. And they limit courts to correcting only egregious gerrymanders, so judges do not become omnipresent players in the political process. But yes, the standards used here do allow—as well they should—judicial intervention in the worst-of-the-worst cases of democratic subversion, causing blatant constitutional harms. In other words, they allow courts to undo partisan gerrymanders of the kind we face today from North Carolina and Maryland. In giving such gerrymanders a pass from judicial review, the majority goes tragically wrong. * * *

Partisan gerrymandering of the kind before us not only subverts democracy (as if that weren't bad enough). It violates individuals' constitutional rights as well. That statement is not the lonesome cry of a dissenting Justice. This Court has recognized extreme partisan gerrymandering as such a violation for many years.

Partisan gerrymandering operates through vote dilution—the devaluation of one citizen's vote as compared to others. A mapmaker draws district lines to "pack" and "crack" voters likely to support the disfavored party. He packs supermajorities of those voters into a relatively few districts, in numbers far greater than needed for their preferred candidates to prevail. Then he cracks the rest across many more districts, spreading them so thin that their candidates will not be able to win. Whether the person is packed or cracked, his vote carries less weight—has less consequence—than it would under a neutrally drawn (non-partisan) map. In short, the mapmaker has made some votes count for less, because they are likely to go for the other party.

That practice implicates the Fourteenth Amendment's Equal Protection Clause. The Fourteenth Amendment, we long ago recognized, "guarantees the opportunity for equal participation by all voters in the election" of legislators. *Reynolds* v. *Sims*, 377 U.S. 533, 566 (1964) [p. 122]. And that opportunity "can be denied by a debasement or dilution of the weight of a citizen's vote just as effectively as by wholly prohibiting the free exercise of the franchise." *Id.*, at 555. Based on that principle, this Court in its one-person-one-vote decisions prohibited creating districts with significantly different populations. A State could not, we explained, thus "dilut[e] the weight of votes because of place of residence." *Id.*, at 566. The constitutional injury in a partisan gerrymandering case is much the same, except that the dilution is based on party affiliation. In such a case, too, the districters have set out to reduce the weight of certain citizens' votes, and thereby deprive them of their capacity to "full[y] and effective[ly] participat[e] in the political process[]." *Id.*, at 565. * * *

And partisan gerrymandering implicates the First Amendment too. That Amendment gives its greatest protection to political beliefs, speech, and association. Yet partisan gerrymanders subject certain voters to "disfavored treatment"—again, counting their votes for less—precisely because of "their voting history [and] their expression of political views." *Vieth*, 541 U.S., at 314 (opinion of Kennedy, J.). And added to that strictly personal harm is an associational one. Representative democracy is "unimaginable without the ability of citizens to band together in [support of] candidates who espouse their political views." *California Democratic Party* v. *Jones*, 530 U.S. 567, 574 (2000) [p. 449]. By diluting the votes of certain citizens, the State frustrates their efforts to translate those affiliations into political effectiveness. In both those ways, partisan gerrymanders of the kind we confront here undermine the protections of "democracy embodied in the First Amendment." * * *

Though different Justices have described the constitutional harm in diverse ways, nearly all have agreed on this much: Extreme partisan gerrymandering (as happened in North Carolina and Maryland) violates the Constitution. [T]he majority never disagrees; it appears to accept the "principle that each person must have an equal say in the election of representatives." * * *

So the only way to understand the majority's opinion is as follows: In the face of grievous harm to democratic governance and flagrant infringements on individuals' rights—in the face of escalating partisan manipulation whose compatibility with this Nation's values and law no one defends—the majority declines to provide any remedy. For the first time in this Nation's history, the majority declares that it can do nothing about an acknowledged constitutional violation because it has searched high and low and cannot find a workable legal standard to apply. * * *

* * * Over the past several years, federal courts across the country—including, but not exclusively, in the decisions below—have largely converged on a standard for adjudicating partisan gerrymandering claims (striking down both Democratic and Republican districting plans in the process). See also *Ohio A. Philip Randolph Inst.* [v. *Householder*], 373 F. Supp. 3d 978 [(SD Ohio 2019)]; *League of Women Voters of Michigan* v. *Benson*, 373 F. Supp. 3d 867 (ED Mich. 2019). And that standard does what the majority says is impossible. The standard does not use any judge-made conception of electoral fairness—either proportional representation or any other; instead, it takes as its baseline a State's *own* criteria of fairness, apart from partisan gain. And by requiring plaintiffs to make difficult showings relating to both purpose and effects, the standard invalidates the most extreme, but only the most extreme, partisan gerrymanders. * * *

Start with the standard the lower courts used. * * * [B]oth courts (like others around the country) used basically the same three-part test to decide whether the plaintiffs had made out a vote dilution claim. As many legal standards do, that test has three parts: (1) intent; (2) effects; and (3) causation. First, the plaintiffs challenging a districting plan must prove that state officials' "predominant purpose" in drawing a district's lines was to "entrench [their party] in power" by diluting the votes of citizens favoring its rival. Second, the plaintiffs must establish that the lines drawn in fact have the intended effect by "substantially" diluting their votes. And third, if the plaintiffs make those showings, the State must come up with a legitimate, non-partisan justification to save its map. If you are a lawyer, you know that this test looks utterly ordinary. It is the sort of thing courts work with every day.

Turn now to the test's application. First, did the North Carolina and Maryland districters have the predominant purpose of entrenching their own party in power? Here, the two District Courts catalogued the overwhelming direct evidence that they did. * * *

The majority's response to the District Courts' purpose analysis is discomfiting. The majority does not contest the lower courts' findings; how could it? Instead, the majority says that state officials' intent to entrench their party in power is perfectly "permissible," even when it is the predominant factor in drawing district lines. But that is wrong. True enough, that the intent to inject "political considerations" into districting may not raise any constitutional concerns. In *Gaffney* v. *Cummings*, for example, we thought it non-problematic when state officials used political data to ensure rough proportional representation between the two parties. And true enough that even the naked purpose to gain partisan advantage may not rise to the level of constitutional notice when it is not the driving force in mapmaking or when the intended gain is slight. But when political actors have a specific and predominant intent to entrench themselves in power by manipulating district lines, that goes too far. * * * It cannot be permissible and thus irrelevant, as the majority claims, that state officials have as their purpose the kind of grotesquely gerrymandered map that, according to all this Court has ever said, violates the Constitution.

On to the second step of the analysis, where the plaintiffs must prove that the districting plan substantially dilutes their votes. * * * Consider the sort of evidence used in North Carolina first. There, the plaintiffs demonstrated the districting plan's effects mostly by relying on what might be called the "extreme outlier approach." (Here's a spoiler: the State's plan was one.) The approach—which also has recently been used in Michigan and Ohio litigation—begins by using advanced computing technology to randomly generate a large collection of districting plans that incorporate the State's physical and political geography and meet its declared districting criteria, *except for* partisan gain. For each of those maps, the method then uses actual precinct-level votes from past elections to determine a partisan outcome (*i.e.*, the number of Democratic and Republican seats that map produces). Suppose we now have 1,000 maps, each with a partisan outcome attached to it. We can line up those maps on a continuum—the most favorable to Republicans on one end, the most favorable to Democrats on the other. We can then find the median outcome—that is, the outcome smack dab in the center—in a world with no partisan manipulation. And we can see where the State's actual plan falls on the spectrum—at or near the median or way out on one of the tails? The further out on the tail, the more extreme the partisan distortion and the more significant the vote dilution.

Using that approach, the North Carolina plaintiffs offered a boatload of alternative districting plans—all showing that the State's map was an out-out-out-outlier. One expert produced 3,000 maps, adhering in the way described above to the districting criteria that the North Carolina redistricting committee had used, other than partisan advantage. * * * The results were, shall we say, striking. Every single one of the 3,000 maps would have produced at least one more Democratic House Member than the State's actual map, and 77% would have elected three or four more. A second expert obtained essentially the same results with maps conforming to more generic districting criteria (*e.g.*, compactness and contiguity of districts). Over 99% of that expert's 24,518 simulations would have led to the election of at least one more Democrat, and over 70% would have led to two or three more. Based on those and other findings, the District Court determined that the North Carolina plan substantially dilutes the plaintiffs' votes.

Because the Maryland gerrymander involved just one district, the evidence in that case was far simpler—but no less powerful for that. * * * In the old Sixth, 47% of registered voters were Republicans and only 36% Democrats. But in the new Sixth, 44% of registered voters were Democrats and only 33% Republicans. That reversal of the district's partisan composition translated into four consecutive Democratic victories, including in a wave election year for Republicans (2014). In what was once a party stronghold, Republicans now have little or no chance to elect their preferred candidate. The District Court thus found that the gerrymandered Maryland map substantially dilutes Republicans' votes. * * *

By substantially diluting the votes of citizens favoring their rivals, the politicians of one party had succeeded in entrenching themselves in office. They had beat democracy.

The majority's broadest claim, as I've noted, is that this is a price we must pay because judicial oversight of partisan gerrymandering cannot be "politically neutral" or "manageable." * * * Consider neutrality first. Contrary to the majority's suggestion, the District Courts did not have to—and in fact did not—choose among competing visions of electoral fairness. That is because they did not try to compare the State's actual map to an "ideally fair" one (whether based on proportional representation or some other criterion). Instead, they looked at the difference between what the State did and what the State would have done if politicians hadn't been intent on partisan gain. Or put differently, the comparator (or baseline or touchstone) is the result not of a judge's philosophizing but of the State's own characteristics and judgments. * * * Under their approach, in other words, the State selected its own fairness baseline in the form of its other districting criteria. All the courts did was determine how far the State had gone off that track because of its politicians' effort to entrench themselves in office.

* * * So in North Carolina, for example, all the [randomly generated comparator] maps adhered to the traditional criteria of contiguity and compactness. But the comparator maps in another State would have incorporated different objectives— say, the emphasis Arizona places on competitive districts or the requirement Iowa imposes that counties remain whole. The point is that the assemblage of maps, reflecting the characteristics and judgments of the State itself, creates a neutral baseline from which to assess whether partisanship has run amok. Extreme outlier as to what? As to the other maps the State could have produced given its unique political geography and its chosen districting criteria. *Not* as to the maps a judge, with his own view of electoral fairness, could have dreamed up.

The Maryland court lacked North Carolina's fancy evidence, but analyzed the gerrymander's effects in much the same way—not as against an ideal goal, but as against an *ex ante* baseline. * * * The court did not strike down the new Sixth District because a judicial ideal of proportional representation commanded another Republican seat. It invalidated that district because the quest for partisan gain made the State override *its own* political geography and districting criteria. So much, then, for the impossibility of neutrality.

The majority's sole response misses the point. According to the majority, "it does not make sense to use" a State's own (non-partisan) districting criteria as the baseline from which to measure partisan gerrymandering because those criteria "will vary from State to State and year to year." But that is a virtue, not a vice—a feature, not a bug. Using the criteria the State itself has chosen at the relevant time prevents any judicial predilections from affecting the analysis—exactly what the majority claims it wants. At the same time, using those criteria enables a court to measure just what it should: the extent to which the pursuit of partisan advantage—by these legislators at this moment—has distorted the State's districting decisions. * * *

The majority's "how much is too much" critique fares no better than its neutrality argument. How about the following for a first-cut answer: This much is too much. By any measure, a map that produces a greater partisan skew than any of 3,000 randomly generated maps (all with the State's political geography and districting criteria built in) reflects "too much" partisanship. Think about what I just said: The absolute worst of 3,001 possible maps. The *only one* that could produce a 10–3 partisan split even as Republicans got a bare majority of the statewide vote. And again: How much is too much? This much is too much: A map that without any evident non-partisan districting reason (to the contrary) shifted the composition of a district from 47% Republicans and 36% Democrats to 33% Republicans and 42% Democrats. A map that in 2011 was responsible for the largest partisan swing of a congressional district in the country. Even the majority acknowledges that "[t]hese cases involve blatant examples of partisanship driving districting decisions." If the majority had done nothing else, it could have set the line here. How much is too much? At the least, any gerrymanders as bad as these.

And if the majority thought that approach too case-specific, it could have used the lower courts' general standard—focusing on "predominant" purpose and "substantial" effects—without fear of indeterminacy. I do not take even the majority to claim that courts are incapable of investigating whether legislators mainly intended to seek partisan advantage. That is for good reason. Although purpose inquiries carry certain hazards (which courts must attend to), they are a common form of analysis in constitutional cases. Those inquiries would be no harder here than in other contexts.

Nor is there any reason to doubt, as the majority does, the competence of courts to determine whether a district map "substantially" dilutes the votes of a rival party's supporters from the everything-but-partisanship baseline described above.

(Most of the majority's difficulties here really come from its idea that ideal visions set the baseline. But that is double-counting—and, as already shown, wrong to boot.) * * * [C]ontrary to the majority's suggestion, courts all the time make judgments about the substantiality of harm without reducing them to particular percentages. If courts are no longer competent to do so, they will have to relinquish, well, substantial portions of their docket.

And the combined inquiry used in these cases set the bar high, so that courts could intervene in the worst partisan gerrymanders, but no others. Or to say the same thing, so that courts could intervene in the kind of extreme gerrymanders that nearly every Justice for decades has thought to violate the Constitution. * * *

The majority, in the end, fails to understand both the plaintiffs' claims and the decisions below. Everything in today's opinion assumes that these cases grew out of a "desire for proportional representation" or, more generally phrased, a "fair share of political power." And everything in it assumes that the courts below had to (and did) decide what that fair share would be. But that is not so. The plaintiffs objected to one specific practice—the extreme manipulation of district lines for partisan gain. Elimination of that practice could have led to proportional representation. Or it could have led to nothing close. What was left after the practice's removal could have been fair, or could have been unfair, by any number of measures. That was not the crux of this suit. The plaintiffs asked only that the courts bar politicians from entrenching themselves in power by diluting the votes of their rivals' supporters. And the courts, using neutral and manageable—and eminently legal—standards, provided that (and only that) relief. This Court should have cheered, not overturned, that restoration of the people's power to vote. * * *

* * * With respect but deep sadness, I dissent.

Notes and Questions

1. Are partisan-gerrymandering claims non-justiciable because there are no judicially manageable standards for adjudicating them, or because the Constitution simply contains no right to be free from excessive partisanship in districting? *See* Michael R. Dimino, *You've Got (Political) Questions? We've Got No Answers*, 71 MERCER L. REV. 719 (2020). *Cf. Baker v. Carr*, 369 U.S. 186, 337 (1962) (Harlan, J., dissenting) ("The suggestion of my Brother FRANKFURTER that courts lack standards by which to decide [reapportionment cases] is relevant not only to the question of 'justiciability,' but also, and perhaps more fundamentally, to the determination whether any cognizable constitutional claim has been asserted in this case."). Both rationales might be described as holding that partisan-gerrymandering claims are "political questions," but they are significantly different. In the former, partisan gerrymandering violates the Constitution, but the violation cannot be remedied by the federal courts. In the latter, there is no constitutional violation at all. *See generally* Jonathan R. Siegel, *Political Questions and Political Remedies, in* THE POLITICAL QUESTION DOCTRINE AND THE SUPREME COURT OF THE UNITED STATES 243 (Nada

Mourtada-Sabbah & Bruce E. Cain eds., 2007); Louis Henkin, *Is There a Political Question Doctrine?*, 85 YALE L.J. 597 (1976). In thinking about your response, consider what the majority's response was to the dissent's claim that the lower courts' standards *were* judicially manageable.

2. If partisan gerrymandering does amount to a substantive violation of the Constitution, should litigants be able to receive a remedy from *state* courts that do not face the same case-or-controversy limitations that federal courts are bound to obey? *Compare* Tara Leigh Grove, *The Lost History of the Political Question Doctrine*, 90 N.Y.U. L. REV. 1908 (2015), *and* John Harrison, *The Political Question Doctrines*, 67 AM. U. L. REV. 457 (2017) (no), *with* Michael Solimine, *State Courts as Forums for Partisan Gerrymandering Claims after* Common Cause v. Rucho, June 30, 2019, *at* https://electionlawblog.org/?p=105902 (yes). For further discussions of remedies in state courts under state law, post-*Rucho*, see Samuel S.-H. Wang, Richard F. Ober, Jr. & Ben Williams, *Laboratories of Democracy Reform: State Constitutions and Partisan Gerrymanders*, 22 U. PA. J. CONST. L. 203 (2019).

3. How could the Court conclude that federal courts are powerless to determine whether partisan considerations "predominate" in districting, when, in evaluating racial-gerrymandering claims under *Miller v. Johnson*, 515 U.S. 900, 916 (1995) [p. 376], courts must determine whether considerations of race predominate in districting? Did the Court conclude that there was no judicially manageable standard for assessing whether partisanship predominated, or was the majority's objection something different?

4. The Court asserted that "securing partisan advantage" was a "permissible intent." Do you agree? If not, why should such an intent be impermissible? If you do agree that securing partisan advantage should be a permissible intent, what is the legitimate purpose served by such an intent?

5. The Court noted that the Article I objection to partisan gerrymandering closely resembled (if it did not wholly duplicate) a claim under the Guarantee Clause. Couldn't it be said that the equal-protection claim in *Baker v. Carr* closely resembled, if it did not wholly duplicate, the Guarantee Clause claim in *Colegrove v. Green*? *See Baker v. Carr*, 369 U.S. 186, 297 (1962) (Frankfurter, J., dissenting) ("The present case involves all of the elements that have made the Guarantee Clause cases nonjusticiable. It is, in effect, a Guarantee Clause claim masquerading under a different label.").

6. Could there be a judicially manageable standard tied to the "efficiency gap" — a measure of how well each party can translate votes into legislative seats under a given districting plan? *See* Nicholas O. Stephanopoulos & Eric M. McGhee, *Partisan Gerrymandering and the Efficiency Gap*, 82 U. CHI. L. REV. 831 (2015); Eric M. McGhee, *Measuring Partisan Bias in Single-Member District Electoral Systems*, 39 LEG. STUDIES Q. 55 (2014). The "efficiency gap" tallies the number of "wasted" votes for each party by counting the votes for losing candidates and the extra votes for

winning candidates—the number of votes in excess of the minimum necessary for that candidate to prevail—and yields a quantifiable measure of a gerrymander's effectiveness. (Is it appropriate to characterize such votes as "wasted"?) Under this measure, the party with the fewest wasted votes has most efficiently translated its votes into seats, and has benefited most from the districting plan. Could there be a judicially manageable standard in insisting that the efficiency gap not exceed a certain number?

7. In response to the Court's persistent demand for a standard to determine "how much [partisan gerrymandering] is too much," the dissent said, "This much is too much." Is that any more determinate than "I know it when I see it," Justice Stewart's infamous "test" for obscenity? *Jacobellis v. Ohio*, 378 U.S. 184, 197 (1964) (Stewart, J., concurring). Did Justice Kagan's dissent in effect concede that there is no standard for deciding how much is too much?

8. The dissent stressed that not all uses of partisan considerations in districting should be unconstitutional; only the most extreme partisan gerrymanders should be struck down. Do you believe that the dissent's standard, if it had been adopted by the Court, would have been so limited? Recall that when *Baker v. Carr* held that federal courts had the power to hear reapportionment cases under the Equal Protection Clause, Justices Clark and Stewart wrote concurring opinions arguing that only extreme, irrational malapportionments would be held to violate the Constitution. As we have seen, that is not how the doctrine evolved.

9. Should the public look to courts to save them from partisan gerrymandering, or would it be better to focus attention on Congress? The Constitution's Elections Clause grants Congress the authority to ban or limit partisan gerrymandering, although Congress has not enacted any limitation on states' ability to use districting for partisan advantage. *See* U.S. Const. art. I, § 4, cl. 1 ("The Times, Places and Manner of holding Elections for Senators and Representatives, shall be prescribed in each State by the Legislature thereof; but the Congress may at any time by Law make or alter such Regulations * * *."). For an argument that partisan-gerrymandering claims should be presented to Congress, rather than the courts, see Troy McCurry, *Leeway to Judicial Usurpation: Ignoring the Default of the Elections Clause in The Texas Redistricting Cases*, 25 Quinnipiac L. Rev. 631 (2006).

10. In *Rucho*, the majority opinion by Chief Justice Roberts suggested that states could limit the effect of politics in redistricting by trusting the task to independent commissions rather than legislatures. But could such commissions constitutionally draw districts for congressional elections? In the following case, the Arizona Legislature argued that the Elections Clause meant that only the state legislature itself could draw lines for congressional districts. The Court rejected the challenge in a 5-4 decision, with the majority holding that the Clause did not prevent a state from creating redistricting commissions by popular initiative, as occurred in Arizona. The dissenters, led by the Chief Justice, agreed with the Arizona Legislature's literal interpretation of the Clause.

Arizona State Legislature v. Arizona Independent Redistricting Commission

Supreme Court of the United States
576 U.S. 787, 135 S. Ct. 2652, 192 L. Ed. 2d 704 (2015)

JUSTICE GINSBURG delivered the opinion of the Court [in which JUSTICE KENNEDY, JUSTICE BREYER, JUSTICE SOTOMAYOR, and JUSTICE KAGAN join]. * * *

In 2000, Arizona voters adopted an initiative, Proposition 106, aimed at "ending the practice of gerrymandering and improving voter and candidate participation in elections." Proposition 106 amended Arizona's Constitution to remove redistricting authority from the Arizona Legislature and vest that authority in an independent commission, the Arizona Independent Redistricting Commission (AIRC or Commission). After the 2010 census, as after the 2000 census, the AIRC adopted redistricting maps for congressional as well as state legislative districts.

The Arizona Legislature challenged the map the Commission adopted in January 2012 for congressional districts [on the ground] that the Commission and its map violated the "Elections Clause" of the U.S. Constitution. That Clause, critical to the resolution of this case, provides:

> "The Times, Places and Manner of holding Elections for Senators and Representatives, shall be prescribed in each State by the Legislature thereof; but the Congress may at any time by Law make or alter such Regulations. . . ." Art. I, §4, cl. 1. * * *

I * * *

* * * The AIRC convenes after each census, establishes final district boundaries, and certifies the new districts to the Arizona Secretary of State. The legislature may submit nonbinding recommendations to the AIRC, and is required to make necessary appropriations for its operation. The highest ranking officer and minority leader of each chamber of the legislature each select one member of the AIRC from a list compiled by Arizona's Commission on Appellate Court Appointments. The four appointed members of the AIRC then choose, from the same list, the fifth member, who chairs the Commission. A Commission's tenure is confined to one redistricting cycle; each member's time in office "expire[s] upon the appointment of the first member of the next redistricting commission."

Holders of, or candidates for, public office may not serve on the AIRC, except candidates for or members of a school board. No more than two members of the Commission may be members of the same political party, and the presiding fifth member cannot be registered with any party already represented on the Commission. Subject to the concurrence of two-thirds of the Arizona Senate, AIRC members may be removed by the Arizona Governor for gross misconduct, substantial neglect of duty, or inability to discharge the duties of office.

Several other States, as a means to curtail partisan gerrymandering, have also provided for the participation of commissions in redistricting. Some States, in common with Arizona, have given nonpartisan or bipartisan commissions binding authority over redistricting.[6] The California Redistricting Commission, established by popular initiative, develops redistricting plans which become effective if approved by public referendum.[7] Still other States have given commissions an auxiliary role, advising the legislatures on redistricting,[8] or serving as a "backup" in the event the State's representative body fails to complete redistricting.[9] Studies report that nonpartisan and bipartisan commissions generally draw their maps in a timely fashion and create districts both more competitive and more likely to survive legal challenge. See Miller & Grofman, *Redistricting Commissions in the Western United States*, 3 U.C. Irvine L. Rev. 637, 661, 663–664, 666 (2013).

On January 17, 2012, the AIRC approved final congressional and state legislative maps based on the 2010 census. Less than four months later, on June 6, 2012, the Arizona Legislature filed suit in the United States District Court for the District of Arizona, [seeking] both a declaration that Proposition 106 and congressional maps adopted by the AIRC are unconstitutional, and, as affirmative relief, an injunction against use of AIRC maps for any congressional election after the 2012 general election.

* * * [D]ividing two to one, the District Court granted the AIRC's motion to dismiss the complaint for failure to state a claim. Decisions of this Court, the majority concluded, "demonstrate that the word 'Legislature' in the Elections Clause refers to the legislative process used in [a] state, determined by that state's own constitution and laws." As the "lawmaking power" in Arizona "plainly includes the power to enact laws through initiative," the District Court held, the "Elections Clause permits [Arizona's] establishment and use" of the Commission. * * * We * * * now affirm.

II * * *

[The Court held that the Arizona Legislature had standing to bring the challenge.]

III * * *

Before focusing directly on the * * * constitutional prescriptions in point, we summarize this Court's precedent relating to appropriate state decisionmakers for redistricting purposes. Three decisions compose the relevant case law: *Ohio ex rel. Davis* v. *Hildebrant*, 241 U.S. 565 (1916); *Hawke* v. *Smith (No. 1)*, 253 U.S. 221 (1920); and *Smiley* v. *Holm*, 285 U.S. 355 (1932).

Davis v. *Hildebrant* involved an amendment to the Constitution of Ohio vesting in the people the right, exercisable by referendum, to approve or disapprove by popular vote any law enacted by the State's legislature. A 1915 Act redistricting the State for the purpose of congressional elections had been submitted to a popular vote, resulting in disapproval of the legislature's measure. State election officials

---

6. See Haw. Const., Art. IV, § 2, and Haw. Rev. Stat. §§ 25–1 to 25–9; Idaho Const., Art. III, § 2; Mont. Const., Art. V, § 14; N.J. Const., Art. II, § 2; Wash. Const., Art. II, § 43.

7. See Cal. Const., Art. XXI, § 2; Cal. Govt. Code Ann. §§ 8251–8253.6.

8. See Iowa Code §§ 42.1–42.6; Ohio Rev. Code Ann. § 103.51; Me. Const., Art. IV, pt. 3, § 1–A.

9. See Conn. Const., Art. III, § 6; Ind. Code § 3–3–2–2.

asked the State's Supreme Court to declare the referendum void. That court rejected the request, holding that the referendum authorized by Ohio's Constitution, "was a part of the legislative power of the State[.]" * * * In upholding the state court's decision, we recognized that the referendum was "part of the legislative power" in Ohio, [241 U.S., at 567], legitimately exercised by the people to disapprove the legislation creating congressional districts. For redistricting purposes, *Hildebrant* thus established, "the Legislature" did not mean the representative body alone. Rather, the word encompassed a veto power lodged in the people.

Hawke v. *Smith* involved the Eighteenth Amendment to the Federal Constitution. Ohio's Legislature had ratified the Amendment, and a referendum on that ratification was at issue. Reversing the Ohio Supreme Court's decision upholding the referendum, we held that "ratification by a State of a constitutional amendment is not an act of legislation within the proper sense of the word." 253 U.S., at 229. * * * The Court contrasted the ratifying function, exercisable exclusively by a State's legislature, with "the ordinary business of legislation." *Id.*, at 229. *Davis* v. *Hildebrant*, the Court explained, involved the enactment of legislation, *i.e.*, a redistricting plan, and properly held that "the referendum [was] part of the legislative authority of the State for [that] purpose." 253 U.S., at 230.

Smiley v. *Holm* raised the question whether legislation purporting to redistrict Minnesota for congressional elections was subject to the Governor's veto. * * * We * * * held, for the purpose at hand, Minnesota's legislative authority includes not just the two houses of the legislature; it includes, in addition, a make-or-break role for the Governor. In holding that the Governor's veto counted, we distinguished instances in which the Constitution calls upon state legislatures to exercise a function other than lawmaking. State legislatures, we pointed out, performed an "electoral" function "in the choice of United States Senators under Article I, section 3, prior to the adoption of the Seventeenth Amendment," a "ratifying" function for "proposed amendments to the Constitution under Article V," as explained in *Hawke* v. *Smith*, and a "consenting" function "in relation to the acquisition of lands by the United States under Article I, section 8, paragraph 17." 285 U.S., at 365–366.

In contrast to those other functions, we observed, redistricting "involves lawmaking in its essential features and most important aspect." *Id.*, at 366. * * * And the Elections Clause, we explained, respected the State's choice to include the Governor in that [legislative] process, although the Governor could play no part when the Constitution assigned to "the Legislature" a ratifying, electoral, or consenting function. Nothing in the Elections Clause, we said, "attempt[ed] to endow the legislature of the State with power to enact laws in any manner other than that in which the constitution of the State ha[d] provided that laws shall be enacted." *Id.*, at 368.

THE CHIEF JUSTICE, in dissent, features, indeed trumpets repeatedly, the pre-Seventeenth Amendment regime in which Senators were "chosen [in each State] by the Legislature thereof." Art. I, § 3. If we are right, he asks, why did popular election proponents resort to the amending process instead of simply interpreting "the Legislature" to mean "the people"? *Smiley*, as just indicated, answers that question.

Article I, § 3, gave state legislatures "a function different from that of lawgiver," 85 U.S., at 365; it made each of them "an electoral body" charged to perform that function to the exclusion of other participants, *ibid.* So too, of the ratifying function. As we explained in *Hawke*, "the power to legislate in the enactment of the laws of a State is derived from the people of the State." 253 U.S., at 230. Ratification, however, "has its source in the Federal Constitution" and is not "an act of legislation within the proper sense of the word." *Id.*, at 229–230.

Constantly resisted by THE CHIEF JUSTICE, but well understood in opinions that speak for the Court: "[T]he meaning of the word 'legislature,' used several times in the Federal Constitution, differs according to the connection in which it is employed, depend[ent] upon the character of the function which that body in each instance is called upon to exercise." *Atlantic Cleaners & Dyers, Inc.* v. *United States,* 286 U.S. 427, 434 (1932) (citing *Smiley*). Thus "the Legislature" comprises the referendum and the Governor's veto in the context of regulating congressional elections. *Hildebrant*; *Smiley.* In the context of ratifying constitutional amendments, in contrast, "the Legislature" has a different identity, one that excludes the referendum and the Governor's veto. *Hawke.*[17]

In sum, our precedent teaches that redistricting is a legislative function, to be performed in accordance with the State's prescriptions for lawmaking, which may include the referendum and the Governor's veto. The exercise of the initiative, we acknowledge, was not at issue in our prior decisions. But as developed below, we see no constitutional barrier to a State's empowerment of its people by embracing that form of lawmaking. * * *

In accord with the District Court, we hold that the Elections Clause permits the people of Arizona to provide for redistricting by independent commission. To restate the key question in this case, the issue centrally debated by the parties: Absent congressional authorization, does the Elections Clause preclude the people of Arizona from creating a commission operating independently of the state legislature to establish congressional districts? The history and purpose of the Clause weigh heavily against such preclusion, as does the animating principle of our Constitution that the people themselves are the originating source of all the powers of government.

We note, preliminarily, that dictionaries, even those in circulation during the founding era, capaciously define the word "legislature." Samuel Johnson defined

---

17. The * * * constitutional provisions in which the word "legislature" appears * * * [are] illustrative of the variety of functions state legislatures can be called upon to exercise. For example, Art. I, § 2, cl. 1, superseded by the Seventeenth Amendment, assigned an "electoral" function. See *Smiley,* 285 U.S., at 365. Article I, § 3, cl. 2, assigns an "appointive" function. Article I, § 8, cl. 17, assigns a "consenting" function, see *Smiley,* 285 U.S., at 366, as does Art. IV, § 3, cl. 1. "[R]atifying" functions are assigned in Art. V, Amdt. 18, § 3, Amdt. 20, § 6, and Amdt. 22, § 2. See *Hawke,* 253 U.S., at 229. But Art. I, § 4, cl. 1, unquestionably calls for the exercise of lawmaking authority. That authority can be carried out by a representative body, but if a State so chooses, legislative authority can also be lodged in the people themselves.

"legislature" simply as "[t]he power that makes laws." 2 A Dictionary of the English Language (1st ed. 1755); *ibid.* (6th ed. 1785); *ibid.* (10th ed. 1792); *ibid.* (12th ed. 1802). Thomas Sheridan's dictionary defined "legislature" exactly as Dr. Johnson did: "The power that makes laws." 2 A Complete Dictionary of the English Language (4th ed. 1797). Noah Webster defined the term precisely that way as well. Compendious Dictionary of the English Language 174 (1806). And Nathan Bailey similarly defined "legislature" as "the Authority of making Laws, or Power which makes them." An Universal Etymological English Dictionary (20th ed. 1763).[23]

As to the "power that makes laws" in Arizona, initiatives adopted by the voters legislate for the State just as measures passed by the representative body do. As well in Arizona, the people may delegate their legislative authority over redistricting to an independent commission just as the representative body may choose to do. * * *

The Arizona Legislature maintains that, by specifying "the Legislature thereof," the Elections Clause renders the State's representative body the sole "component of state government authorized to prescribe . . . regulations . . . for congressional redistricting." THE CHIEF JUSTICE, in dissent, agrees. But it is characteristic of our federal system that States retain autonomy to establish their own governmental processes. "Through the structure of its government, and the character of those who exercise government authority, a State defines itself as a sovereign." *Gregory* v. *Ashcroft*, 501 U.S. 452, 460 (1991). Arizona engaged in definition of that kind when its people placed both the initiative power and the AIRC's redistricting authority in the portion of the Arizona Constitution delineating the State's legislative authority.

This Court has "long recognized the role of the States as laboratories for devising solutions to difficult legal problems." *Oregon* v. *Ice*, 555 U.S. 160, 171 (2009); see *United States* v. *Lopez*, 514 U.S. 549, 581 (1995) (KENNEDY, J., concurring) ("[T]he States may perform their role as laboratories for experimentation to devise various solutions where the best solution is far from clear."); *New State Ice Co.* v. *Liebmann*, 285 U.S. 262, 311 (1932) (Brandeis, J., dissenting) ("It is one of the happy incidents of the federal system that a single courageous State may, if its citizens choose, serve as a laboratory; and try novel social and economic experiments without risk to the rest of the country."). Deference to state lawmaking "allows local policies 'more sensitive to the diverse needs of a heterogeneous society,' permits 'innovation and experimentation,' enables greater citizen 'involvement in democratic processes,' and makes government 'more responsive by putting the States in competition for a mobile citizenry.'" *Bond* v. *United States*, 564 U.S. 211, 221, 131 S. Ct. 2355, 2364 (2011) (quoting *Gregory*, 501 U.S., at 458).

---

23. Illustrative of an embracive comprehension of the word "legislature," Charles Pinckney explained at South Carolina's ratifying convention that America is "[a] republic, where the people at large, either collectively or by representation, form the legislature." 4 Debates on the Federal Constitution 328 (J. Elliot 2d ed. 1863). Participants in the debates over the Elections Clause used the word "legislature" interchangeably with "state" and "state government."

We resist reading the Elections Clause to single out federal elections as the one area in which States may not use citizen initiatives as an alternative legislative process. Nothing in that Clause instructs, nor has this Court ever held, that a state legislature may prescribe regulations on the time, place, and manner of holding federal elections in defiance of provisions of the State's constitution. * * *

The Framers may not have imagined the modern initiative process in which the people of a State exercise legislative power coextensive with the authority of an institutional legislature. But the invention of the initiative was in full harmony with the Constitution's conception of the people as the font of governmental power. * * * As this Court stated, quoting Hamilton: "[T]he true principle of a republic is, that the people should choose whom they please to govern them." *Powell* v. *McCormack*, 395 U.S. 486, 540–541 (1969). In this light, it would be perverse to interpret the term "Legislature" in the Elections Clause so as to exclude lawmaking by the people, particularly where such lawmaking is intended to check legislators' ability to choose the district lines they run in, thereby advancing the prospect that Members of Congress will in fact be "chosen . . . by the People of the several States," Art. I, § 2. * * *

Independent redistricting commissions, it is true, "have not eliminated the inevitable partisan suspicions associated with political line-drawing." But "they have succeeded to a great degree [in limiting the conflict of interest implicit in legislative control over redistricting]." They thus impede legislators from choosing their voters instead of facilitating the voters' choice of their representatives.

Banning lawmaking by initiative to direct a State's method of apportioning congressional districts would do more than stymie attempts to curb partisan gerrymandering, by which the majority in the legislature draws district lines to their party's advantage. It would also cast doubt on numerous other election laws adopted by the initiative method of legislating.

The people, in several States, functioning as the lawmaking body for the purpose at hand, have used the initiative to install a host of regulations governing the "Times, Places and Manner" of holding federal elections. Art. I, § 4. For example, the people of California provided for permanent voter registration, specifying that "no amendment by the Legislature shall provide for a general biennial or other periodic reregistration of voters." Cal. Elec. Code Ann. § 2123 (West 2003). The people of Ohio banned ballots providing for straight-ticket voting along party lines. Ohio Const., Art. V, § 2a. The people of Oregon shortened the deadline for voter registration to 20 days prior to an election. Ore. Const., Art. II, § 2. None of those measures permit [*sic*] the state legislatures to override the people's prescriptions. The Arizona Legislature's theory—that the lead role in regulating federal elections cannot be wrested from "the Legislature," and vested in commissions initiated by the people—would endanger all of them.

The list of endangered state elections laws, were we to sustain the position of the Arizona Legislature, would not stop with popular initiatives. Almost all state constitutions were adopted by conventions and ratified by voters at the ballot box, without involvement or approval by "the Legislature." Core aspects of the electoral process regulated by state constitutions include voting by "ballot" or "secret ballot," voter registration, absentee voting, vote counting, and victory thresholds. Again, the States' legislatures had no hand in making these laws and may not alter or amend them.

The importance of direct democracy as a means to control election regulations extends beyond the particular statutes and constitutional provisions installed by the people rather than the States' legislatures. The very prospect of lawmaking by the people may influence the legislature when it considers (or fails to consider) election-related measures. Turning the coin, the legislature's responsiveness to the people its members represent is hardly heightened when the representative body can be confident that what it does will not be overturned or modified by the voters themselves.

* * *

* * * Both parts of the Elections Clause are in line with the fundamental premise that all political power flows from the people. So comprehended, the Clause doubly empowers the people. They may control the State's lawmaking processes in the first instance, as Arizona voters have done, and they may seek Congress' correction of regulations prescribed by state legislatures. * * *

For the reasons stated, the judgment of the United States District Court for the District of Arizona is

Affirmed.

CHIEF JUSTICE ROBERTS, with whom JUSTICE SCALIA, JUSTICE THOMAS, and JUSTICE ALITO join, dissenting. * * *

* * * Nowhere does the majority explain how a constitutional provision that vests redistricting authority in "the Legislature" permits a State to wholly exclude "the Legislature" from redistricting. Arizona's Commission might be a noble endeavor — although it does not seem so "independent" in practice — but the "fact that a given law or procedure is efficient, convenient, and useful . . . will not save it if it is contrary to the Constitution." *INS* v. *Chadha*, 462 U.S. 919, 944 (1983). No matter how concerned we may be about partisanship in redistricting, this Court has no power to gerrymander the Constitution. I respectfully dissent.

I

* * * The Elections Clause both imposes a duty on States and assigns that duty to a particular state actor: In the absence of a valid congressional directive to the contrary, States must draw district lines for their federal representatives. And that duty "shall" be carried out "in each State by the Legislature thereof."

In Arizona, however, redistricting is not carried out by the legislature. Instead, as the result of a ballot initiative, an unelected body called the Independent Redistricting Commission draws the lines. The key question in the case is whether the Commission can conduct congressional districting consistent with the directive that such authority be exercised "by the Legislature."

The majority concedes that the unelected Commission is not "the Legislature" of Arizona. The Court contends instead that the people of Arizona as a whole constitute "the Legislature" for purposes of the Elections Clause, and that they may delegate the congressional districting authority conferred by that Clause to the Commission. The majority provides no support for the delegation part of its theory, and I am not sure whether the majority's analysis is correct on that issue. But even giving the Court the benefit of the doubt in that regard, the Commission is still unconstitutional. Both the Constitution and our cases make clear that "the Legislature" in the Elections Clause is the representative body which makes the laws of the people.

A * * *

* * * The Court seems to conclude, based largely on its understanding of the "history and purpose" of the Elections Clause, that "the Legislature" encompasses any entity in a State that exercises legislative power. That circular definition lacks any basis in the text of the Constitution or any other relevant legal source.

The majority's textual analysis consists, in its entirety, of one paragraph citing founding era dictionaries. The majority points to various dictionaries that follow Samuel Johnson's definition of "legislature" as the "power that makes laws." The notion that this definition corresponds to the entire population of a State is strained to begin with, and largely discredited by the majority's own admission that "[d]irect lawmaking by the people was virtually unknown when the Constitution of 1787 was drafted." Moreover, Dr. Johnson's first example of the usage of "legislature" is this: "Without the concurrent consent of all three parts of the legislature, no law is or can be made." 2 A Dictionary of the English Language (1st ed. 1755) (emphasis deleted). Johnson borrowed that sentence from Matthew Hale, who defined the "Three Parts of the Legislature" of England as the King and the two houses of Parliament. History of the Common Law of England 2 (1713). (The contrary notion that the people as a whole make the laws would have cost you your head in England in 1713.) Thus, even under the majority's preferred definition, "the Legislature" referred to an institutional body of representatives, not the people at large.

Any ambiguity about the meaning of "the Legislature" is removed by other founding era sources. "[E]very state constitution from the Founding Era that used the term legislature defined it as a distinct multimember entity comprised of representatives." Morley, *The Intratextual Independent "Legislature" and the Elections Clause*, 109 Nw. U. L. Rev. Online 131, 147, and n. 101 (2015) (citing eleven State Constitutions). The Federalist Papers are replete with references to "legislatures" that can only be understood as referring to representative institutions. *E.g.*, The Federalist No. 27, pp. 174–175 (C. Rossiter ed. 1961) (A. Hamilton) (describing "the State legislatures" as "select bodies of men"); *id.*, No. 60, at 368 (contrasting "the State legislatures" with "the people"). Noah Webster's heralded American Dictionary of the English Language defines "legislature" as "[t]he body of men in a state or kingdom, invested with power to make and repeal laws." 2 An American Dictionary of the English Language (1828). It continues, "The legislatures of most of the states in America . . . consist of two houses or branches." *Ibid.* (emphasis deleted).

I could go on, but the Court has said this before. As we put it nearly a century ago, "Legislature" was "not a term of uncertain meaning when incorporated into the Constitution." *Hawke*, 253 U.S., at 227. "What it meant when adopted it still means for the purpose of interpretation." *Ibid.* "A Legislature" is "the representative body which ma[kes] the laws of the people." *Ibid.*; see *Smiley*, 285 U.S., at 365 (relying on this definition).

B

The unambiguous meaning of "the Legislature" in the Elections Clause as a representative body is confirmed by other provisions of the Constitution that use the same term in the same way. When seeking to discern the meaning of a word in the Constitution, there is no better dictionary than the rest of the Constitution itself. * * *

The Constitution includes seventeen provisions referring to a State's "Legislature." Every one of those references is consistent with the understanding of a legislature as a representative body. More importantly, many of them are only consistent with an institutional legislature—and flatly incompatible with the majority's reading of "the Legislature" to refer to the people as a whole.

Start with the Constitution's first use of the term: "The House of Representatives shall be composed of Members chosen every second Year by the People of the several States, and the Electors in each State shall have the Qualifications requisite for Electors of the most numerous Branch of the State Legislature." Art. I, § 2, cl. 1. This reference to a "Branch of the State Legislature" can only be referring to an institutional body, and the explicit juxtaposition of "the State Legislature" with "the People of the several States" forecloses the majority's proposed reading.

The next Section of Article I describes how to fill vacancies in the United States Senate: "if Vacancies happen by Resignation, or otherwise, during the Recess of the Legislature of any State, the Executive thereof may make temporary Appointments until the next Meeting of the Legislature, which shall then fill such Vacancies." § 3, cl. 2. The references to "the Recess of the Legislature of any State" and "the next Meeting of the Legislature" are only consistent with an institutional legislature, and make no sense under the majority's reading. The people as a whole (schoolchildren and a few unnamed others excepted) do not take a "Recess."

The list goes on. Article IV provides that the "United States shall guarantee to every State in this Union a Republican Form of Government, and shall protect each of them against Invasion; and on Application of the Legislature, or of the Executive (when the Legislature cannot be convened), against domestic Violence." § 4. * * *

Article VI provides that the "Senators and Representatives before mentioned, and the Members of the several State Legislatures, and all executive and judicial Officers, both of the United States and of the several States, shall be bound by Oath or Affirmation, to support this Constitution." Cl. 3. Unless the majority is prepared to make all the people of every State swear an "Oath or Affirmation, to support this Constitution," this provision can only refer to the "several State Legislatures" in their institutional capacity.

Each of these provisions offers strong structural indications about what "the Legislature" must mean. But the most powerful evidence of all comes from the Seventeenth Amendment. Under the original Constitution, Senators were "chosen by the Legislature" of each State, Art. I, § 3, cl. 1, while Members of the House of Representatives were chosen "by the People," Art. I, § 2, cl. 1. * * *

Before long, reformers * * * launched a protracted campaign to amend the Constitution. * * * At no point in this process did anyone suggest that a constitutional amendment was unnecessary because "Legislature" could simply be interpreted to mean "people." * * * Yet that is precisely what the majority does to the Elections Clause today * * *. The majority's revision renders the Seventeenth Amendment an 86-year waste of time, and singles out the Elections Clause as the only one of the Constitution's seventeen provisions referring to "the Legislature" that departs from the ordinary meaning of the term. * * *

* * * The majority observes that "the Legislature" of a State may perform different functions under different provisions of the Constitution. * * * The majority, however, leaps from the premise that "the Legislature" performs different *functions* under different provisions to the conclusion that "the Legislature" assumes different *identities* under different provisions.

As a matter of ordinary language and common sense, however, a difference in function does not imply a difference in meaning. A car, for example, generally serves a transportation function. But it can also fulfill a storage function. At a tailgate party or a drive-in movie, it may play an entertainment function. In the absence of vacancies at the roadside motel, it could provide a lodging function. To a neighbor with a dead battery, it offers an electricity generation function. And yet, a person describing a "car" engaged in any of these varied functions would undoubtedly be referring to the same thing.

The Constitution itself confirms this point. [The Constitution assigns a variety of functions to the House, the Senate, the President, and the courts, but n]either the majority nor the Commission points to a single instance in which the identity of these actors changes as they exercise different functions.

The majority attempts to draw support from precedent, but our cases only further undermine its position. In *Hawke*, this Court considered the meaning of "the

Legislatur[e]" in Article V, which outlines the process for ratifying constitutional amendments. The Court concluded that "Legislature" meant "the representative body which ma[kes] the laws of the people." 253 U.S., at 227. * * * The Court concluded that "Legislature" refers to a representative body, whatever its function. As the Court put it, "There can be no question that the framers of the Constitution clearly understood and carefully used the terms in which that instrument referred to the action of the legislatures of the States. When they intended that direct action by the people should be had they were no less accurate in the use of apt phraseology to carry out such purpose." [*Id.*, at 228.]

Smiley, the leading precedent on the meaning of "the Legislature" in the Elections Clause, reaffirmed the definition announced in *Hawke*[:] "* * * As this Court said in *Hawke* . . . the term was not one 'of uncertain meaning when incorporated into the Constitution. What it meant when adopted it still means for purposes of interpretation. A Legislature was then the representative body which made the laws of the people.'" 285 U.S., at 365 (quoting *Hawke*, 253 U.S., at 227). * * *

C

The history of the Elections Clause further supports the conclusion that "the Legislature" is a representative body. The first known draft of the Clause to appear at the Constitutional Convention provided that "Each state shall prescribe the time and manner of holding elections." 1 Debates on the Federal Constitution 146 (J. Elliot ed. 1836). After revision by the Committee of Detail, the Clause included the important limitation at issue here: "The times and places, and the manner, of holding the elections of the members of each house, shall be prescribed *by the legislature of each state*; but their provisions concerning them may, at any time, be altered *by the legislature of the United States.*" *Id.*, at 225 (emphasis added). The insertion of "the legislature" indicates that the Framers thought carefully about which entity within the State was to perform congressional districting. And the parallel between "the legislature of each state" and "the legislature of the United States" further suggests that they meant "the legislature" as a representative body. * * *

The majority contends that its counterintuitive reading of "the Legislature" is necessary to advance the "animating principle" of popular sovereignty. But the ratification of the Constitution was the ultimate act of popular sovereignty, and the people who ratified the Elections Clause did so knowing that it assigned authority to "the Legislature" as a representative body. The Elections Clause was not, as the majority suggests, an all-purpose "safeguard against manipulation of electoral rules by politicians." Like most provisions of the Constitution, the Elections Clause reflected a compromise—a pragmatic recognition that the grand project of forging a Union required everyone to accept some things they did not like. See The Federalist No. 59, at 364 (describing the power allocated to state legislatures as "an evil which could not have been avoided"). This Court has no power to upset such a compromise simply because we now think that it should have been struck differently. As we explained almost a century ago, "[t]he framers of the Constitution might have adopted a different method," but it "is not the function of courts . . . to alter the method which the Constitution has fixed." *Hawke*, 253 U.S., at 227.

D

In addition to text, structure, and history, several precedents interpreting the Elections Clause further reinforce that "the Legislature" refers to a representative body.

The first precedent comes not from this Court, but from Congress. Acting under its authority to serve as "the Judge of the Elections, Returns and Qualifications of its own Members," Art. I, § 5, cl. 1, the House of Representatives in 1866 confronted a dispute about who should be seated as the Congressman from the Fifth District of Michigan. At a popular convention, Michigan voters had amended the State Constitution to require votes to be cast within a resident's township or ward. The Michigan Legislature, however, passed a law permitting soldiers to vote in alternative locations. If only the local votes counted, one candidate (Baldwin) would win; if the outside votes were included, the other candidate (Trowbridge) would be entitled to the seat.

The House Elections Committee explained that the Elections Clause conferred power on "the Legislature" of Michigan to prescribe election regulations. "But," the Committee asked, "what is meant by 'the legislature?' Does it mean the legislative power of the State, which would include a convention authorized to prescribe fundamental law; or does it mean the legislature *eo nomine*, as known in the political history of the country?" The Committee decided, and the full House agreed, that "the Legislature" in the Elections Clause was the "legislature *eo nominee*"—the legislature *by that name*, a representative body. That conclusion followed both from the known meaning of "the Legislature" at the time of the framing and the many other uses of the word in the Constitution that would not be compatible with a popular convention. Thus, "[w]here there is a conflict of authority between the constitution and legislature of a State in regard to fixing place of elections, the power of the legislature is paramount." * * *

The next relevant precedent is this Court's decision in *McPherson* v. *Blacker*, 146 U.S. 1 (1892) [p. 1065]. That case involved a constitutional provision with considerable similarity to the Elections Clause, the Presidential Electors Clause of Article II: "Each State shall appoint, in such Manner *as the Legislature thereof* may direct, a Number of Electors. . . ." § 1, cl. 2 (emphasis added). The question was whether the state legislature, as a body of representatives, could divide authority to appoint electors across each of the State's congressional districts. The Court upheld the law and emphasized that the plain text of the Presidential Electors Clause vests the power to determine the manner of appointment in "the Legislature" of the State. That power, the Court explained, "*can neither be taken away nor abdicated.*" 146 U.S., at 35 (emphasis added).

Against that backdrop, the Court decided two cases regarding the meaning of "the Legislature" in the Elections Clause. In *Ohio ex rel. Davis* v. *Hildebrant*, 241 U.S. 565 (1916), the Ohio Legislature passed a congressional redistricting law. Under the Ohio Constitution, voters held a referendum on the law and rejected it. A supporter of the law sued on behalf of the State, contending that the referendum "was not and could not be a part of the legislative authority of the State and therefore could have no influence on . . . the law creating congressional districts" under the Elections Clause. *Id.*, at 567.

This Court rejected the challenger's constitutional argument as a nonjusticiable claim that the referendum "causes a State . . . to be not republican" in violation of the Guarantee Clause of the Constitution. *Id.*, at 569 (citing Art. IV, § 4). * * * *Hildebrant* in no way suggested that the state legislature could be displaced from the redistricting process, and *Hildebrant* certainly did not hold—as the majority today contends—that "the word ['Legislature' in the Elections Clause] encompassed a veto power lodged in the people." *Hildebrant* simply approved a State's decision to employ a referendum *in addition to* redistricting by the Legislature. The result of the decision was to send *the Ohio Legislature* back to the drawing board to do the redistricting.

In *Smiley*, the Minnesota Legislature passed a law adopting new congressional districts, and the Governor exercised his veto power under the State Constitution. * * * The Court [held] that the Elections Clause did not prevent a State from applying the usual rules of its legislative process—including a gubernatorial veto—to election regulations prescribed by the legislature. 285 U.S., at 373. As in *Hildebrant*, the legislature was not displaced, nor was it redefined; it just had to start on a new redistricting plan.

* * * There is a critical difference between allowing a State to *supplement* the legislature's role in the legislative process and permitting the State to *supplant* the legislature altogether. Nothing in *Hildebrant*, *Smiley*, or any other precedent supports the majority's conclusion that imposing some constraints on the legislature justifies deposing it entirely.

The constitutional text, structure, history, and precedent establish a straightforward rule: Under the Elections Clause, "the Legislature" is a representative body that, when it prescribes election regulations, may be required to do so within the ordinary lawmaking process, but may not be cut out of that process. Put simply, the state legislature need not be exclusive in congressional districting, but neither may it be excluded.

The majority's contrary understanding requires it to accept a definition of "the Legislature" that contradicts the term's plain meaning, creates discord with the Seventeenth Amendment and the Constitution's many other uses of the term, makes nonsense of the drafting and ratification of the Elections Clause, and breaks with the relevant precedents. In short, the effect of the majority's decision is to erase the words "by the Legislature thereof" from the Elections Clause. That is a judicial error of the most basic order. * * *

The Court also overstates the effects of enforcing the plain meaning of the Constitution in this case. There is no dispute that Arizona may continue to use its Commission to draw lines for state legislative elections. The representatives chosen in those elections will then be responsible for congressional redistricting as members of the state legislature, so the work of the Commission will continue to influence Arizona's federal representation.

Moreover, reading the Elections Clause to require the involvement of the legislature will not affect most other redistricting commissions. As the majority notes, many States have commissions that play an "auxiliary role" in congressional redistricting. But in these States, unlike in Arizona, the legislature retains primary authority over congressional redistricting.

The majority also points to a scattered array of election-related laws and constitutional provisions enacted via popular lawmaking that it claims would be "endangered" by interpreting the Elections Clause to mean what it says. Reviewing the constitutionality of these far-flung provisions is well outside the scope of this case. Suffice it to say that none of them purports to do what the Arizona Constitution does here: set up an unelected, unaccountable institution that permanently and totally displaces the legislature from the redistricting process. "[T]his wolf comes as a wolf." *Morrison* v. *Olson*, 487 U.S. 654, 699 (1988) (SCALIA, J., dissenting).

Absent from the majority's portrayal of the high motives that inspired the Arizona Commission is any discussion of how it has actually functioned. The facts described in a recent opinion by a three-judge District Court detail the partisanship that has affected the Commission on issues ranging from staffing decisions to drawing the district lines. See *Harris* v. *Arizona Independent Redistricting Comm'n*, 993 F. Supp. 2d 1042 ([D.] Ariz. 2014). The *per curiam* opinion explained that "partisanship played some role in the design of the map," that "some of the commissioners were motivated in part in some of the linedrawing decisions by a desire to improve Democratic prospects in the affected districts," and that the Commission retained a mapping consultant that "had worked for Democratic, independent, and nonpartisan campaigns, but no Republican campaigns." *Id.*, at 1046, 1047, 1053. * * *

Judge Silver's separate opinion noted that "the very structure of Arizona's reformed redistricting process reflects that partisanship still plays a prominent role." 993 F. Supp. 2d, at 1083. Judge Wake's separate opinion described the Commission's "systematic overpopulation of Republican plurality districts and underpopulation of Democratic plurality districts" as "old-fashioned partisan malapportionment." *Id.*, at 1091, 1108. * * *

The District Court concluded by a two-to-one margin that this partisanship did not rise to the level of a constitutional violation.[i] * * * But a finding that the partisanship in the redistricting plan did not violate the Constitution hardly proves that

---

i. The Court subsequently affirmed the district court's conclusion that "the population deviations were primarily a result of good-faith efforts to comply with the Voting Rights Act . . . even though partisanship played some role," finding that conclusion to be "well supported in the record." *Harris v. Arizona Independent Redistricting Commission*, 578 U.S. __, __, 136 S. Ct. 1301, 1309 (2016). "[A]s a result, appellants have not shown that it is more probable than not that illegitimate considerations were the predominant motivation behind the plan's deviations from mathematically the Commission is operating free of partisan influence—and certainly not that it complies with the Elections Clause.

* * *

The people of Arizona have concerns about the process of congressional redistricting in their State. For better or worse, the Elections Clause of the Constitution does not allow them to address those concerns by displacing their legislature. But it does allow them to seek relief from Congress, which can make or alter the regulations prescribed by the legislature. And the Constitution gives them another means of change. They can follow the lead of the reformers who won passage of the Seventeenth Amendment. Indeed, several constitutional amendments over the past century have involved modifications of the electoral process. Amdts. 19, 22, 24, 26. Unfortunately, today's decision will only discourage this democratic method of change. Why go through the hassle of writing a new provision into the Constitution when it is so much easier to write an old one out?

I respectfully dissent.

Justice Scalia, with whom Justice Thomas joins, dissenting.

I do not believe that the question the Court answers is properly before us. Disputes between governmental branches or departments regarding the allocation of political power do not in my view constitute "cases" or "controversies" committed to our resolution by Art. III, § 2, of the Constitution. * * *

Normally, having arrived at that conclusion, I would express no opinion on the merits unless my vote was necessary to enable the Court to produce a judgment. In the present case, however, the majority's resolution of the merits question ("legislature" means "the people") is so outrageously wrong, so utterly devoid of textual or historic support, so flatly in contradiction of prior Supreme Court cases, so obviously the willful product of hostility to districting by state legislatures, that I cannot avoid adding my vote to the devastating dissent of The Chief Justice.

Justice Thomas, with whom Justice Scalia joins, dissenting. * * *

The ballot initiative in this case * * * was unusually democracy-reducing. It did not ask the people to approve a particular redistricting plan through direct democracy, but instead to take districting away from the people's representatives and give it to an unelected committee, thereby reducing democratic control over the process in the future. The Court's characterization of this as direct democracy at its best is rather like praising a plebiscite in a "banana republic" that installs a strongman as

---

equal district populations—deviations that were under 10%. Consequently, they have failed to show that the Commission's plan violates the Equal Protection Clause * * *." *Id.* —Eds.

President for Life. And wrapping the analysis in a cloak of federalism does little to conceal the flaws in the Court's reasoning.

I would dispense with the faux federalism and would instead treat the States in an evenhanded manner. That means applying the Constitution as written. Although the straightforward text of Article I, § 4, prohibits redistricting by an unelected, independent commission, Article III limits our power to deciding cases or controversies. Because I agree with JUSTICE SCALIA that the Arizona Legislature lacks Article III standing to assert an institutional injury against another entity of state government, I would dismiss its suit. I respectfully dissent.

Notes and Questions

1. Was *Arizona Independent Redistricting Commission* distinguishable from *Smiley*? That is, if it was constitutional for the governor of a state to veto a redistricting bill and thereby deny effect to the will of the state legislature, must it also be constitutional for the people of a state to strip the redistricting power from the state legislature entirely? For further discussion of non-partisan or bipartisan redistricting commissions, see Bruce E. Cain, *Redistricting Commissions: A Better Political Buffer?*, 121 YALE L.J. 1808 (2012).

2. Does *Arizona State Legislature* mean that a state constitution can place substantive constraints on congressional districting, such as forbidding considerations of partisanship or incumbency protection? Presumably yes. The whole point of independent redistricting commissions is to free the districting process from the legislature's control. If *Arizona State Legislature* was willing to approve independent districting commissions, it is hard to believe that the Court would forbid other means of limiting the effects of partisanship in districting. *See League of Women Voters v. Commonwealth*, 178 A.3d 282 (Pa.) (holding that political gerrymandering of congressional districts violated the Pennsylvania Constitution, and further holding that the state constitution's restrictions on the state legislature's prerogative to draw district lines did not violate the Elections Clause), *cert. denied* 139 S. Ct. 445 (2018). Yet does such a conclusion create problems under *U.S. Term Limits v. Thornton*, 514 U.S. 779 (1995) [p. 538]? In *Term Limits*, the Court held that states could not impose additional qualifications on candidates for Congress beyond the qualifications that were listed in Article I, § 2, cl. 2 and Article I, § 3, cl. 3 of the Constitution. If a state were to impose substantive constraints on congressional districting, would it be committing the same kind of violation by adding a restriction on the choice of members of Congress beyond the limitations set forth in the Constitution?

3. If states are permitted to vest the congressional-redistricting power in an independent commission despite the Constitution's reference to the "Legislature," may a state similarly strip its legislature of the power to determine the "Manner" of selecting presidential electors? U.S. CONST. art. II, § 1, cl. 2 ("Each State shall Appoint, in such Manner as the Legislature thereof may direct, a Number of Electors * * *."). *See McPherson v. Blacker*, 146 U.S. 1, 35 (1892) [p. 1065] (stating that this power

"can neither be taken away nor abdicated"). *See also Bush v. Gore*, 531 U.S. 98, 111–22 (2000) (Rehnquist, C.J., concurring) (arguing that the Florida Supreme Court unconstitutionally interfered with the Florida Legislature's authority to determine the method of selecting electors); *Bush v. Palm Beach County Canvassing Board*, 531 U.S. 70 (2000) (vacating a decision of the Florida Supreme Court because of uncertainty whether the Florida Constitution limited the state legislature's authority to choose presidential electors); *Coleman v. Miller*, 307 U.S. 433, 446–47 (1939) (dividing equally on whether the Court had jurisdiction to determine if a state legislature's authority to ratify U.S. constitutional amendments, U.S. Const. art. V, was violated when the lieutenant governor broke a tie in favor of ratification).

4. In *Rucho v. Common Cause*, 588 U.S. __, 139 S. Ct. 2484 (2019) [p. 180], the majority opinion by the Chief Justice, who dissented in *Arizona State Legislature*, cited the *Arizona* decision seemingly as good law, and also cited various states' redistricting commissions as examples of how redistricting reform could take place at that level. After *Rucho*, is there any doubt that *Arizona* is good law?

Chapter 3

Congressional Power and the Voting Rights Act

A. Introduction

This Chapter examines congressional power, paying particular attention to the "preclearance" requirement of the Voting Rights Act of 1965 (VRA). Several post-Civil-War Amendments, including the Thirteenth, Fourteenth, Fifteenth, Nineteenth, and Twenty-Sixth, not only prohibit certain governmental actions, but also give Congress the power to "enforce" the Amendments' substantive provisions "by appropriate legislation." The scope of Congress's authority under these "Enforcement Clauses," however, is controversial. Congress can certainly provide mechanisms for investigating and punishing constitutional violations. *See, e.g.*, 42 U.S.C. § 1983 (providing a private right of action against state actors who cause "the deprivation of any rights, privileges, or immunities secured by the Constitution and laws"); 28 U.S.C. § 1343(a)(3) (granting original jurisdiction in the district courts for actions to redress constitutional violations). It is clear, therefore, that Congress has the power to prevent and punish "first-generation" barriers to voting, such as discrimination in voting registration, the casting of votes, or vote-counting.

What is unclear, however, is the extent to which Congress may use the Enforcement Clauses to punish conduct that is not itself a constitutional violation. Because states can dilute minorities' voting power without denying them the ability to cast valid votes, some have argued that Congress needs the ability to address "second-generation" barriers—which address voting *strength* rather than access to the ballot—in order to make the right to vote effective. Others respond that Congress's enforcement power should be limited to protecting the rights that are guaranteed by the substantive portions of the Amendments. Because the Constitution protects against discrimination in voting but does not guarantee electoral results, some have been wary of allowing Congress to "enforce" those Amendments by banning state laws that do not violate the Constitution. To understand those modern controversies, it is necessary to understand the history surrounding the Voting Rights Act.

The VRA did much to combat the country's disgraceful history of race discrimination in voting, and, by almost any standard, the VRA was one of the most successful legislative acts of the twentieth century. Its impact was forceful and immediate; its "historic accomplishments * * * undeniable." *Northwest Austin*

Municipal Utility District Number One v. Holder, 557 U.S. 193, 201 (2009). "In Mississippi, black registration went from less than 10 percent in 1964 to almost 60 percent in 1968; in Alabama, the figure rose from 24 percent to 57 percent. In the [South] as a whole, roughly a million new voters were registered within a few years after the bill became law, bringing African-American registration to a record 62 percent." ALEXANDER KEYSSAR, THE RIGHT TO VOTE: THE CONTESTED HISTORY OF DEMOCRACY IN THE UNITED STATES 212 (rev. ed. 2009). By 1967, a majority of African Americans were registered to vote in 9 of the 13 Southern states. The number of elected African-American state legislators in the former Confederacy rose from just three in 1965 to 176 by 1985. Bernard Grofman & Lisa Handley, *The Impact of the Voting Rights Act on Black Representation in Southern State Legislatures*, 16 LEGIS. STUD. Q. 111, 113 (1991). Today, voter registration and turnout for blacks and whites are at virtual parity, with blacks registering and voting at slightly higher numbers than whites in some of the Southern states. *See* H.R. Rep. No. 109–478, at 12–18 (2006).

Key portions of the Act included §§ 6-8, which provided for federal examiners to help register minority voters and to police election administration, and § 4(a), which immediately suspended literacy tests in certain Southern states. (The provisions for federal examiners were repealed in the 2006 renewal of the Act, under a broad consensus that the provision had served its purpose and was no longer necessary; the ban on literacy tests was extended nationwide in 1970 and made permanent in the 1975 renewal of the Act.) Another key portion was § 2, which prohibits discrimination in voting practices and procedures, and which is covered extensively in Chapter 4. But the most innovative part of the VRA was § 5, the "preclearance" provision.

Until the passage of the VRA, Southern state officials bent on denying blacks political power could exact enormous costs on opposition forces simply by requiring plaintiffs to litigate. A plaintiff wishing to put a stop to unconstitutionally discriminatory limits on the right to vote, for example, would have to spend resources pursuing a court case. Even if the plaintiff were successful in court, however, the state could simply replace the challenged law with another discriminatory one, and by staying one step ahead of plaintiffs, the state could significantly delay compliance.

Congress sought to correct this situation by "shift[ing] the advantage of time and inertia from the perpetrators of the evil to its victims." *South Carolina v. Katzenbach*, 383 U.S. 301, 328 (1966) [p. 220]. Instead of placing the burden on plaintiffs to demonstrate the unconstitutionality of election laws, § 5 of the VRA imposed upon certain governments the obligation to prove the laws' legality *before* those laws could go into effect. Under the preclearance provision, a state or political subdivision wishing to change its election laws was required to submit its proposed change to the Attorney General of the United States or obtain a declaratory judgment from the United States District Court for the District of Columbia. Under either route, preclearance would be granted and the proposed change would be permitted to take effect only if the change had neither the purpose nor the effect of "denying or abridging the right to vote on account of race or color." 52 U.S.C. § 10304. (The Act was since extended to cover laws denying or abridging language minorities' right to vote. *See* 52 U.S.C. § 10303(f)(2).) Thus, even a nondiscriminatory change in election law—one that would be consistent with the Fourteenth and Fifteenth Amendments—could not be enforced until the federal government gave permission. *South Carolina v. Katzenbach* upheld the preclearance procedure against a states'-rights challenge, but did not fully resolve the scope of congressional authority under the Enforcement Clauses.

May Congress, for example, "enforce" the right to vote by prohibiting literacy tests, even though the tests themselves do not violate the Constitution?[a] In *Katzenbach v. Morgan*, 384 U.S. 641, 650–51 (1966) [p. 227], the Court upheld the Voting Rights Act's literacy-test ban. In doing so, it interpreted the enforcement authority as granting Congress the power to pass legislation that, in the judgment of Congress, furthered the goals of the Amendments. *Cf. McCulloch v. Maryland*, 17 U.S. (4 Wheat.) 316, 421 (1819) (granting Congress similar authority under the Necessary and Proper Clause, Art. 1, § 8, cl. 18). Such an interpretation gave Congress broad discretion to determine for itself what the limits of its authority were, but the Supreme Court cut back on that discretion in *City of Boerne v. Flores*, 521 U.S. 507 (1997). Concerned that *Morgan*'s interpretation could undermine the Constitution's plan for limiting the federal government's powers, *Flores* held that Congress's authority under the Enforcement Clauses extended only to those statutes "congruent" with and "proportional" to the *courts'* understanding of the substantive meaning of the Amendments. *Id*. at 534–35.

The preclearance provision did not apply to the entire country. Its scope was restricted to "covered jurisdictions," which were identified in § 4(b) of the VRA, 52 U.S.C. § 10303(b), as those states or political subdivisions that used "tests or devices" in determining voter eligibility and in which fewer than 50% of the voting-age residents were registered or voted in the presidential elections of 1964, 1968, or 1972. The Act further defined a "test or device" as "any requirement that a person as a prerequisite for voting or registration for voting (1) demonstrate the ability to read, write, understand, or interpret any matter, (2) demonstrate any educational achievement or his knowledge of any particular subject, (3) possess good moral character, or (4) prove his qualifications by the voucher of registered voters or members of any other class." 52 U.S.C. § 10303(c).

Section 4(b)'s coverage formula was upheld in *South Carolina v. Katzenbach*, but was struck down nearly fifty years later in *Shelby County, Alabama v. Holder*, 570 U.S. 529 (2013) [p. 244]. Congress had not updated the formula in decades, so the 2006 re-authorization of the VRA (which allowed the VRA to continue in effect until 2031) still based coverage decisions on data from the presidential elections of

---

a. Recall that in *Lassiter v. Northampton County Board of Elections*, 360 U.S. 45 (1959) [p. 11], the Court upheld a fairly administered literacy test against a claim that it violated the Equal Protection Clause. The Supreme Court has never overruled *Lassiter*.

1964, 1968, and 1972. The Supreme Court held that the outdated coverage formula was not a rational way of identifying jurisdictions that would be required to obtain preclearance, and the Court therefore struck down the law as an unconstitutional method of enforcing the Fifteenth Amendment. Proposals have been introduced in Congress to update the coverage formula, but none has been enacted.

The preclearance provision was limited not only in its geographic scope, but also in that it did not apply to all changes to laws that might conceivably affect voting power. Rather, the preclearance obligation extended only to "voting qualification[s] or prerequisite[s] to voting, or standard[s], practice[s], or procedure[s] with respect to voting." 52 U.S.C. § 10304. Although the Supreme Court recognized that this phrase implied that some laws need not be precleared, the Court gave it a broad interpretation, extending its coverage to such matters as the hours and locations of polling places, the drawing of district lines, whether certain government offices should be elective, and limitations on ballot access. *See Allen v. State Board of Elections*, 393 U.S. 544 (1969) [p. 252].

As the Supreme Court interpreted § 5, preclearance guarded against "retrogression"—laws that reduce the political power of minority groups as compared to the power they held before the proposed change. *See Beer v. United States*, 425 U.S. 130 (1976). Preclearance did not demand that states improve the lot of minorities, that minorities be given any particular share in political power, or even that states end discriminatory practices. Existing discrimination in voting practices and procedures was prohibited by § 2 of the VRA, which applied nationwide, and which is discussed in the next Chapter. Section 5 merely required that any changes to election laws in certain covered jurisdictions not make the situation *worse*. If, however, the *purpose* of a proposed change (as distinguished from its effect) was to discriminate against minorities, preclearance was to be denied. *See* 52 U.S.C. § 10304(c).

B. Preclearance and Prophalaxis

South Carolina v. Katzenbach

Supreme Court of the United States
383 U.S. 301, 86 S. Ct. 803, 15 L. Ed. 2d 769 (1966)

Mr. Chief Justice Warren delivered the opinion of the Court [in which Mr. Justice Douglas, Mr. Justice Clark, Mr. Justice Harlan, Mr. Justice Brennan, Mr. Justice Stewart, Mr. Justice White, and Mr. Justice Fortas join].

* * * South Carolina * * * seek[s] a declaration that selected provisions of the Voting Rights Act of 1965 violate the Federal Constitution, and ask[s] for an injunction against enforcement of these provisions by the Attorney General. * * * We hold that the sections of the Act which are properly before us are an appropriate means for carrying out Congress' constitutional responsibilities and are consonant with all other provisions of the Constitution. * * *

II.

The Voting Rights Act of 1965 reflects Congress' firm intention to rid the country of racial discrimination in voting. The heart of the Act is a complex scheme of stringent remedies aimed at areas where voting discrimination has been most flagrant. Section 4(a)–(d) lays down a formula defining the States and political subdivisions to which these new remedies apply. The first of the remedies, contained in §4(a), is the suspension of literacy tests and similar voting qualifications for a period of five years from the last occurrence of substantial voting discrimination. Section 5 prescribes a second remedy, the suspension of all new voting regulations pending review by federal authorities to determine whether their use would perpetuate voting discrimination. The third remedy, covered in §§6(b), 7, 9, and 13(a), is the assignment of federal examiners on certification by the Attorney General to list qualified applicants who are thereafter entitled to vote in all elections. * * *

Coverage formula.

The remedial sections of the Act assailed by South Carolina automatically apply to any State, or to any separate political subdivision such as a county or parish, for which two findings have been made: (1) the Attorney General has determined that on November 1, 1964, it maintained a "test or device," and (2) the Director of the Census has determined that less than 50% of its voting-age residents were registered on November 1, 1964, or voted in the presidential election of November 1964. These findings are not reviewable in any court and are final upon publication in the Federal Register. §4(b). As used throughout the Act, the phrase "test or device" means any requirement that a registrant or voter must "(1) demonstrate the ability to read, write, understand, or interpret any matter, (2) demonstrate any educational achievement or his knowledge of any particular subject, (3) possess good moral character, or (4) prove his qualifications by the voucher of registered voters or members of any other class." §4(c).

Statutory coverage of a State or political subdivision under §4(b) is terminated if the area obtains a declaratory judgment from the District Court for the District of Columbia, determining that tests and devices have not been used during the preceding five years to abridge the franchise on racial grounds. * * *

South Carolina was brought within the coverage formula of the Act on August 7, 1965, pursuant to appropriate administrative determinations which have not been challenged in this proceeding. On the same day, coverage was also extended to Alabama, Alaska, Georgia, Louisiana, Mississippi, Virginia, 26 counties in North Carolina, and one county in Arizona. Two more counties in Arizona, one county in Hawaii, and one county in Idaho were added to the list on November 19, 1965. * * *

Suspension of tests.

In a State or political subdivision covered by §4(b) of the Act, no person may be denied the right to vote in any election because of his failure to comply with a "test or device." §4(a).

On account of this provision, South Carolina is temporarily barred from enforcing the portion of its voting laws which requires every applicant for registration to show that he: "Can both read and write any section of [the State] Constitution submitted to [him] by the registration officer or can show that he owns, and has paid all taxes collectible during the previous year on, property in this State assessed at three hundred dollars or more." * * * Similar tests and devices have been temporarily suspended in the other sections of the country listed above.

Review of new rules.

In a State or political subdivision covered by § 4(b) of the Act, no person may be denied the right to vote in any election because of his failure to comply with a voting qualification or procedure different from those in force on November 1, 1964. This suspension of new rules is terminated, however, under either of the following circumstances: (1) if the area has submitted the rules to the Attorney General, and he has not interposed an objection within 60 days, or (2) if the area has obtained a declaratory judgment from the District Court for the District of Columbia, determining that the rules will not abridge the franchise on racial grounds. * * * § 5.

South Carolina altered its voting laws in 1965 to extend the closing hour at polling places from 6 p.m. to 7 p.m. The State has not sought judicial review of this change in the District Court for the District of Columbia, nor has it submitted the new rule to the Attorney General for this scrutiny, although at our hearing the Attorney General announced that he does not challenge the amendment. * * *

Federal examiners.

In any political subdivision covered by § 4(b) of the Act, the Civil Service Commission shall appoint voting examiners whenever the Attorney General certifies either of the following facts: (1) that he has received meritorious written complaints from at least 20 residents alleging that they have been disenfranchised under color of law because of their race, or (2) that the appointment of examiners is otherwise necessary to effectuate the guarantees of the Fifteenth Amendment. In making the latter determination, the Attorney General must consider, among other factors, whether the registration ratio of non-whites to whites seems reasonably attributable to racial discrimination, or whether there is substantial evidence of good-faith efforts to comply with the Fifteenth Amendment. § 6(b). These certifications are not reviewable in any court and are effective upon publication in the Federal Register. § 4(b).

The examiners who have been appointed are to test the voting qualifications of applicants * * *. §§ 7(a) and 9(b). Any person who meets the voting requirements of state law, insofar as these have not been suspended by the Act, must promptly be placed on a list of eligible voters. * * *

III.

These provisions of the Voting Rights Act of 1965 are challenged on the fundamental ground that they exceed the powers of Congress and encroach on an area reserved to the States by the Constitution. * * * The ground rules for resolving this question are clear. * * * As against the reserved powers of the States, Congress may use any rational means to effectuate the constitutional prohibition of racial discrimination in voting. We turn now to a more detailed description of the standards which govern our review of the Act.

Section 1 of the Fifteenth Amendment declares that "[t]he right of citizens of the United States to vote shall not be denied or abridged by the United States or by any State on account of race, color, or previous condition of servitude." * * * South Carolina contends that [although the Amendment gives the *courts* authority to strike down statutes and procedures,] to allow an exercise of this authority by Congress would be to rob the courts of their rightful constitutional role. On the contrary, § 2 of the Fifteenth Amendment expressly declares that "Congress shall have power to enforce this article by appropriate legislation." By adding this authorization, the Framers indicated that Congress was to be chiefly responsible for implementing the rights created in § 1. "It is the power of Congress which has been enlarged. Congress is authorized to *enforce* the prohibitions by appropriate legislation. Some legislation is contemplated to make the [Civil War] amendments fully effective." *Ex parte Virginia*, 100 U.S. 339, 345 [(1880)]. Accordingly, in addition to the courts, Congress has full remedial powers to effectuate the constitutional prohibition against racial discrimination in voting. * * *

The basic test to be applied in a case involving § 2 of the Fifteenth Amendment is the same as in all cases concerning the express powers of Congress with relation to the reserved powers of the States. Chief Justice Marshall laid down the classic formulation, 50 years before the Fifteenth Amendment was ratified: "Let the end be legitimate, let it be within the scope of the constitution, and all means which are appropriate, which are plainly adapted to that end, which are not prohibited, but consist with the letter and spirit of the constitution, are constitutional." *McCulloch v. Maryland*, [17 U.S.] 4 Wheat. 316, 421 [(1819)].

The Court has subsequently echoed his language in describing each of the Civil War Amendments: "Whatever legislation is appropriate, that is, adapted to carry out the objects the amendments have in view, whatever tends to enforce submission to the prohibitions they contain, and to secure to all persons the enjoyment of perfect equality of civil rights and the equal protection of the laws against State denial or invasion, if not prohibited, is brought within the domain of congressional power." *Ex parte Virginia*, 100 U.S., at 345–346.[b] * * *

We therefore reject South Carolina's argument that Congress may appropriately do no more than to forbid violations of the Fifteenth Amendment in general terms—that the task of fashioning specific remedies or of applying them to particular localities must necessarily be left entirely to the courts.

---

b. *Ex parte Virginia* upheld an act of Congress that made it a crime to disqualify jurors "on account of race, color, or previous condition of servitude." —Eds.

Congress is not circumscribed by any such artificial rules under § 2 of the Fifteenth Amendment. * * *

IV.

Congress exercised its authority under the Fifteenth Amendment in an inventive manner when it enacted the Voting Rights Act of 1965. First: The measure prescribes remedies for voting discrimination which go into effect without any need for prior adjudication. This was clearly a legitimate response to the problem, for which there is ample precedent under other constitutional provisions [citing Commerce Clause cases]. Congress had found that case-by-case litigation was inadequate to combat widespread and persistent discrimination in voting, because of the inordinate amount of time and energy required to overcome the obstructionist tactics invariably encountered in these lawsuits. After enduring nearly a century of systematic resistance to the Fifteenth Amendment, Congress might well decide to shift the advantage of time and inertia from the perpetrators of the evil to its victims. The question remains, of course, whether the specific remedies prescribed in the Act were an appropriate means of combatting the evil, and to this question we shall presently address ourselves.

Second: The Act intentionally confines these remedies to a small number of States and political subdivisions which in most instances were familiar to Congress by name. This, too, was a permissible method of dealing with the problem. Congress had learned that substantial voting discrimination presently occurs in certain sections of the country, and it knew no way of accurately forecasting whether the evil might spread elsewhere in the future. In acceptable legislative fashion, Congress chose to limit its attention to the geographic areas where immediate action seemed necessary. * * *

Coverage formula.

We now consider the related question of whether the specific States and political subdivisions within § 4(b) of the Act were an appropriate target for the new remedies. South Carolina contends that the coverage formula is awkwardly designed in a number of respects and that it disregards various local conditions which have nothing to do with racial discrimination. These arguments, however, are largely beside the point. Congress began work with reliable evidence of actual voting discrimination in a great majority of the States and political subdivisions affected by the new remedies of the Act. The formula eventually evolved to describe these areas was relevant to the problem of voting discrimination, and Congress was therefore entitled to infer a significant danger of the evil in the few remaining States and political subdivisions covered by § 4(b) of the Act. No more was required to justify the application to these areas of Congress' express powers under the Fifteenth Amendment. * * *

* * * Tests and devices are relevant to voting discrimination because of their long history as a tool for perpetrating the evil; a low voting rate is pertinent for the obvious reason that widespread disenfranchisement must inevitably affect the number

of actual voters. Accordingly, the coverage formula is rational in both practice and theory. It was therefore permissible to impose the new remedies on the few remaining States and political subdivisions covered by the formula, at least in the absence of proof that they have been free of substantial voting discrimination in recent years. * * *

It is irrelevant that the coverage formula excludes certain localities which do not employ voting tests and devices but for which there is evidence of voting discrimination by other means. Congress had learned that widespread and persistent discrimination in voting during recent years has typically entailed the misuse of tests and devices, and this was the evil for which the new remedies were specifically designed. At the same time, * * * Congress strengthened existing remedies for voting discrimination in other areas of the country. Legislation need not deal with all phases of a problem in the same way, so long as the distinctions drawn have some basis in practical experience. See *Williamson* v. *Lee Optical Co.*, 348 U.S. 483, 488–489 [(1955)]; *Railway Express Agency* v. *New York*, 336 U.S. 106 [(1949)]. There are no States or political subdivisions exempted from coverage under §4(b) in which the record reveals recent racial discrimination involving tests and devices. This fact confirms the rationality of the formula. * * *

Suspension of tests.

We now arrive at consideration of the specific remedies prescribed by the Act for areas included within the coverage formula. South Carolina assails the temporary suspension of existing voting qualifications, reciting the rule laid down by *Lassiter* v. *Northampton County Bd. of Elections*, 360 U.S. 45 [(1959)] [p. 11], that literacy tests and related devices are not in themselves contrary to the Fifteenth Amendment. In that very case, however, the Court went on to say, "Of course a literacy test, fair on its face, may be employed to perpetuate that discrimination which the Fifteenth Amendment was designed to uproot." *Id.*, at 53. The record shows that in most of the States covered by the Act, including South Carolina, various tests and devices have been instituted with the purpose of disenfranchising Negroes, have been framed in such a way as to facilitate this aim, and have been administered in a discriminatory fashion for many years. Under these circumstances, the Fifteenth Amendment has clearly been violated. See *Louisiana* v. *United States*, 380 U.S. 145 [(1965)]; *Alabama* v. *United States*, 371 U.S. 37 [(1962)]; *Schnell* v. *Davis*, 336 U.S. 933 [(1949)].

The Act suspends literacy tests and similar devices for a period of five years from the last occurrence of substantial voting discrimination. This was a legitimate response to the problem, for which there is ample precedent in Fifteenth Amendment cases. Underlying the response was the feeling that States and political subdivisions which had been allowing white illiterates to vote for years could not sincerely complain about "dilution" of their electorates through the registration of Negro illiterates. Congress knew that continuance of the tests and devices in use at the present time, no matter how fairly administered in the future, would freeze the effect of past discrimination in favor of unqualified white registrants. Congress permissibly rejected the alternative of requiring a complete re-registration of all voters, believing that this would be too harsh on many whites who had enjoyed the franchise for their entire adult lives.

Review of new rules.

The Act suspends new voting regulations pending scrutiny by federal authorities to determine whether their use would violate the Fifteenth Amendment. This may have been an uncommon exercise of congressional power, as South Carolina contends, but the Court has recognized that exceptional conditions can justify legislative measures not otherwise appropriate. Congress knew that some of the States covered by § 4(b) of the Act had resorted to the extraordinary stratagem of contriving new rules of various kinds for the sole purpose of perpetuating voting discrimination in the face of adverse federal court decrees. Congress had reason to suppose that these States might try similar maneuvers in the future in order to evade the remedies for voting discrimination contained in the Act itself. Under the compulsion of these unique circumstances, Congress responded in a permissibly decisive manner. * * *

Federal examiners.

The Act authorizes the appointment of federal examiners to list qualified applicants who are thereafter entitled to vote, subject to an expeditious challenge procedure. This was clearly an appropriate response to the problem, closely related to remedies authorized in prior cases. In many of the political subdivisions covered by § 4(b) of the Act, voting officials have persistently employed a variety of procedural tactics to deny Negroes the franchise, often in direct defiance or evasion of federal court decrees. Congress realized that merely to suspend voting rules which have been misused or are subject to misuse might leave this localized evil undisturbed. * * *

After enduring nearly a century of widespread resistance to the Fifteenth Amendment, Congress has marshalled an array of potent weapons against the evil, with authority in the Attorney General to employ them effectively. * * * We here hold that the portions of the Voting Rights Act properly before us are a valid means for carrying out the commands of the Fifteenth Amendment. * * *

The bill of complaint is

Dismissed.

Mr. Justice Black, concurring and dissenting.

I agree with substantially all of the Court's opinion sustaining the power of Congress under § 2 of the Fifteenth Amendment to suspend state literacy tests and similar voting qualifications and to authorize the Attorney General to secure the appointment of federal examiners to register qualified voters in various sections of the country. * * * I also agree with the judgment of the Court upholding § 4(b) of the Act which sets out a formula for determining when and where the major remedial sections of the Act take effect. I reach this conclusion, however, for a somewhat different reason than that stated by the Court, which is that "the coverage formula is rational in both practice and theory." I do not base my conclusion on the fact that the formula is rational, for it is enough for me that Congress by creating this formula has merely exercised its hitherto unquestioned and undisputed power to decide when, where, and upon what conditions its laws shall go into effect. * * *

Though, as I have said, I agree with most of the Court's conclusions, I dissent from its holding that every part of § 5 of the Act is constitutional. * * * Section 5, by providing that some of the States cannot pass state laws or adopt state constitutional amendments without first being compelled to beg federal authorities to approve their policies, so distorts our constitutional structure of government as to render any distinction drawn in the Constitution between state and federal power almost meaningless. One of the most basic premises upon which our structure of government was founded was that the Federal Government was to have certain specific and limited powers and no others, and all other power was to be reserved either "to the States respectively, or to the people." Certainly if all the provisions of our Constitution which limit the power of the Federal Government and reserve other power to the States are to mean anything, they mean at least that the States have power to pass laws and amend their constitutions without first sending their officials hundreds of miles away to beg federal authorities to approve them. Moreover, it seems to me that § 5 which gives federal officials power to veto state laws they do not like is in direct conflict with the clear command of our Constitution that "The United States shall guarantee to every State in this Union a Republican Form of Government." I cannot help but believe that the inevitable effect of any such law which forces any one of the States to entreat federal authorities in far-away places for approval of local laws before they can become effective is to create the impression that the State or States treated in this way are little more than conquered provinces. And if one law concerning voting can make the States plead for this approval by a distant federal court or the United States Attorney General, other laws on different subjects can force the States to seek the advance approval not only of the Attorney General but of the President himself or any other chosen members of his staff. It is inconceivable to me that such a radical degradation of state power was intended in any of the provisions of our Constitution or its Amendments.

Katzenbach v. Morgan

Supreme Court of the United States
384 U.S. 641, 86 S. Ct. 1717, 16 L. Ed. 2d 828 (1966)

MR. JUSTICE BRENNAN delivered the opinion of the Court [in which MR. CHIEF JUSTICE WARREN, MR. JUSTICE BLACK, MR. JUSTICE CLARK, MR. JUSTICE WHITE, and MR. JUSTICE FORTAS join, and in which MR. JUSTICE DOUGLAS joins in part].

These cases concern the constitutionality of § 4(e) of the Voting Rights Act of 1965. That law, in the respects pertinent in these cases, provides that no person who has successfully completed the sixth primary grade in a public school in, or a private school accredited by, the Commonwealth of Puerto Rico in which the language of instruction was other than English shall be denied the right to vote in any election because of his inability to read or write English. * * *[3] * * * We hold that * * * § 4(e) is a proper exercise of the powers granted to Congress by § 5 of the Fourteenth Amendment[5] and that by force of the Supremacy Clause, the New York English literacy requirement cannot be enforced to the extent that it is inconsistent with § 4(e). * * *

The Attorney General of the State of New York argues that an exercise of congressional power under § 5 of the Fourteenth Amendment that prohibits the enforcement of a state law can only be sustained if the judicial branch determines that the state law is prohibited by the provisions of the Amendment that Congress sought to enforce. More specifically, he urges that § 4(e) cannot be sustained as appropriate legislation to enforce the Equal Protection Clause unless the judiciary decides — even with the guidance of a congressional judgment — that the application of the English literacy requirement prohibited by § 4(e) is forbidden by the Equal Protection Clause itself. We disagree. Neither the language nor history of § 5 supports such a construction. * * * A construction of § 5 that would require a judicial determination that the enforcement of the state law precluded by Congress violated the Amendment, as a condition of sustaining the congressional enactment, would depreciate both congressional resourcefulness and congressional responsibility for implementing the Amendment. It would confine the legislative power in this context to the insignificant role of abrogating only those state laws that the judicial branch was prepared to adjudge unconstitutional, or of merely informing the judgment of the judiciary by particularizing the "majestic generalities" of § 1 of the Amendment.

Thus our task in this case is not to determine whether the New York English literacy requirement as applied to deny the right to vote to a person who successfully completed the sixth grade in a Puerto Rican school violates the Equal Protection Clause. Accordingly, our decision in *Lassiter* v. *Northampton Election Bd.*, 360 U.S. 45 (1959) [p. 11], sustaining the North Carolina English literacy requirement as not in all circumstances prohibited by the first sections of the Fourteenth and Fifteenth Amendments, is inapposite. *Lassiter* did not present the question before

---

3. [A]side from the schools in the Commonwealth of Puerto Rico, there are no public or parochial schools in the territorial limits of the United States in which the predominant language of instruction is other than English and which would have generally been attended by persons who are otherwise qualified to vote save for their lack of literacy in English.

5. "Section 5. The Congress shall have power to enforce, by appropriate legislation, the provisions of this article."

It is therefore unnecessary for us to consider whether § 4(e) could be sustained as an exercise of power under the Territorial Clause, Art. IV, § 3 * * *. Nor need we consider whether § 4(e) could be sustained insofar as it relates to the election of federal officers as an exercise of congressional power under Art. I, § 4; nor whether § 4(e) could be sustained, insofar as it relates to the election of state officers, as an exercise of congressional power to enforce the clause guaranteeing to each State a republican form of government, Art. IV, § 4; Art. I, § 8, cl. 18.

us here: Without regard to whether the judiciary would find that the Equal Protection Clause itself nullifies New York's English literacy requirement as so applied, could Congress prohibit the enforcement of the state law by legislating under §5 of the Fourteenth Amendment? In answering this question, our task is limited to determining whether such legislation is, as required by §5, appropriate legislation to enforce the Equal Protection Clause.

By including §5 the draftsmen sought to grant to Congress, by a specific provision applicable to the Fourteenth Amendment, the same broad powers expressed in the Necessary and Proper Clause.[9] The classic formulation of the reach of those powers was established by Chief Justice Marshall in *McCulloch v. Maryland*, 17 U.S. (4 Wheat.) 316, 421 (1819): "Let the end be legitimate, let it be within the scope of the constitution, and all means which are appropriate, which are plainly adapted to that end, which are not prohibited, but consist with the letter and spirit of the constitution, are constitutional." *Ex parte Virginia*, 100 U.S. (10 Otto) 339, 345–346 (1880), decided 12 years after the adoption of the Fourteenth Amendment, held that congressional power under §5 had this same broad scope:

> "Whatever legislation is appropriate, that is, adapted to carry out the objects the amendments have in view, whatever tends to enforce submission to the prohibitions they contain, and to secure to all persons the enjoyment of perfect equality of civil rights and the equal protection of the laws against State denial or invasion, if not prohibited, is brought within the domain of congressional power."

Section 2 of the Fifteenth Amendment grants Congress a similar power to enforce by "appropriate legislation" the provisions of that amendment; and we recently held in *South Carolina v. Katzenbach*, 383 U.S. 301, 326 (1966) [p. 220], that "[t]he basic test to be applied in a case involving §2 of the Fifteenth Amendment is the same as in all cases concerning the express powers of Congress with relation to the reserved powers of the States." That test was identified as the one formulated in *McCulloch v. Maryland*. Thus the *McCulloch v. Maryland* standard is the measure of what constitutes "appropriate legislation" under §5 of the Fourteenth Amendment. Correctly viewed, §5 is a positive grant of legislative power authorizing Congress to exercise its discretion in determining whether and what legislation is needed to secure the guarantees of the Fourteenth Amendment.

We therefore proceed to the consideration whether §4(e) is "appropriate legislation" to enforce the Equal Protection Clause, that is, under the *McCulloch v. Maryland* standard, whether §4(e) may be regarded as an enactment to enforce the Equal

---

9. In fact, earlier drafts of the proposed Amendment employed the "necessary and proper" terminology to describe the scope of congressional power under the Amendment. The substitution of the "appropriate legislation" formula was never thought to have the effect of diminishing the scope of this congressional power.

Protection Clause, whether it is "plainly adapted to that end" and whether it is not prohibited by but is consistent with "the letter and spirit of the constitution."[10]

There can be no doubt that § 4(e) may be regarded as an enactment to enforce the Equal Protection Clause. Congress explicitly declared that it enacted § 4(e) "to secure the rights under the fourteenth amendment of persons educated in American-flag schools in which the predominant classroom language was other than English." The persons referred to include those who have migrated from the Commonwealth of Puerto Rico to New York and who have been denied the right to vote because of their inability to read and write English, and the Fourteenth Amendment rights referred to include those emanating from the Equal Protection Clause. More specifically, § 4(e) may be viewed as a measure to secure for the Puerto Rican community residing in New York nondiscriminatory treatment by government — both in the imposition of voting qualifications and the provision or administration of governmental services, such as public schools, public housing and law enforcement.

Section 4(e) may be readily seen as "plainly adapted" to furthering these aims of the Equal Protection Clause. The practical effect of § 4(e) is to prohibit New York from denying the right to vote to large segments of its Puerto Rican community. Congress has thus prohibited the State from denying to that community the right that is "preservative of all rights." *Yick Wo* v. *Hopkins*, 118 U.S. 356, 370 (1886). This enhanced political power will be helpful in gaining nondiscriminatory treatment in public services for the entire Puerto Rican community. Section 4(e) thereby enables the Puerto Rican minority better to obtain "perfect equality of civil rights and the equal protection of the laws." It was well within congressional authority to say that this need of the Puerto Rican minority for the vote warranted federal intrusion upon any state interests served by the English literacy requirement. It was for Congress, as the branch that made this judgment, to assess and weigh the various conflicting considerations — the risk or pervasiveness of the discrimination in governmental services, the effectiveness of eliminating the state restriction on the right to vote as a means of dealing with the evil, the adequacy or availability of alternative remedies, and the nature and significance of the state interests that would be affected by the nullification of the English literacy requirement as applied to residents who have successfully completed the sixth grade in a Puerto Rican school. It is not for us to review the congressional resolution of these factors. It is enough that we be able to perceive a basis upon which the Congress might resolve the conflict as it did. There plainly was such a basis to support § 4(e) in the application in question in this case.

---

10. Contrary to the suggestion of the dissent, § 5 does not grant Congress power to exercise discretion in the other direction and to enact "statutes so as in effect to dilute equal protection and due process decisions of this Court." We emphasize that Congress' power under § 5 is limited to adopting measures to enforce the guarantees of the Amendment; § 5 grants Congress no power to restrict, abrogate, or dilute these guarantees. Thus, for example, an enactment authorizing the States to establish racially segregated systems of education would not be — as required by § 5 — a measure "to enforce" the Equal Protection Clause since that clause of its own force prohibits such state laws.

Any contrary conclusion would require us to be blind to the realities familiar to the legislators.

The result is no different if we confine our inquiry to the question whether § 4(e) was merely legislation aimed at the elimination of an invidious discrimination in establishing voter qualifications. We are told that New York's English literacy requirement originated in the desire to provide an incentive for non-English speaking immigrants to learn the English language and in order to assure the intelligent exercise of the franchise. Yet Congress might well have questioned, in light of the many exemptions provided,[13] and some evidence suggesting that prejudice played a prominent role in the enactment of the requirement,[14] whether these were actually the interests being served. Congress might have also questioned whether denial of a right deemed so precious and fundamental in our society was a necessary or appropriate means of encouraging persons to learn English, or of furthering the goal of an intelligent exercise of the franchise. Finally, Congress might well have concluded that as a means of furthering the intelligent exercise of the franchise, an ability to read or understand Spanish is as effective as ability to read English for those to whom Spanish-language newspapers and Spanish-language radio and television programs are available to inform them of election issues and governmental affairs. Since Congress undertook to legislate so as to preclude the enforcement of the state law, and did so in the context of a general appraisal of literacy requirements for voting, to which it brought a specially informed legislative competence, it was Congress' prerogative to weigh these competing considerations. Here again, it is enough that we perceive a basis upon which Congress might predicate a judgment that the application of New York's English literacy requirement to deny the right to vote to a person with a sixth grade education in Puerto Rican schools in which the language of instruction was other than English constituted an invidious discrimination in violation of the Equal Protection Clause.

There remains the question whether the congressional remedies adopted in § 4(e) constitute means which are not prohibited by, but are consistent "with the letter and spirit of the constitution." The only respect in which appellees contend that § 4(e) fails in this regard is that the section itself works an invidious discrimination in violation of the Fifth Amendment by prohibiting the enforcement of the English literacy requirement only for those educated in American-flag schools (schools located

---

13. The principal exemption complained of is that for persons who had been eligible to vote before January 1, 1922.

14. This evidence consists in part of statements made in the Constitutional Convention first considering the English literacy requirement, such as the following made by the sponsor of the measure: "More precious even than the forms of government are the mental qualities of our race. While those stand unimpaired, all safe. They are exposed to a single danger, and that is that by constantly changing our voting citizenship through the wholesale, but valuable and necessary infusion of Southern and Eastern European races * * *. The danger has begun. * * * We should check it." * * * This evidence was reinforced by an understanding of the cultural milieu at the time of proposal and enactment, spanning a period from 1915 to 1921 — not one of the enlightened eras of our history.

within United States jurisdiction) in which the language of instruction was other than English, and not for those educated in schools beyond the territorial limits of the United States in which the language of instruction was also other than English. This is not a complaint that Congress, in enacting §4(e), has unconstitutionally denied or diluted anyone's right to vote but rather that Congress violated the Constitution by not extending the relief effected in §4(e) to those educated in non-American-flag schools. We need not pause to determine whether appellees have a sufficient personal interest to have §4(e) invalidated on this ground, since the argument, in our view, falls on the merits.

* * * In deciding [whether Congress may limit §4(e)'s protection to persons educated in American-flag schools], the principle that calls for the closest scrutiny of distinctions in laws denying fundamental rights is inapplicable; for the distinction challenged by appellees is presented only as a limitation on a reform measure aimed at eliminating an existing barrier to the exercise of the franchise. Rather, in deciding the constitutional propriety of the limitations in such a reform measure we are guided by the familiar principles that a "statute is not invalid under the Constitution because it might have gone farther than it did," that a legislature need not "strike at all evils at the same time," and that "reform may take one step at a time, addressing itself to the phase of the problem which seems most acute to the legislative mind," *Williamson* v. *Lee Optical Co.*, 348 U.S. 483, 489 (1955).

Guided by these principles, we are satisfied that appellees' challenge to this limitation in §4(e) is without merit. In the context of the case before us, the congressional choice to limit the relief effected in §4(e) may, for example, reflect Congress' greater familiarity with the quality of instruction in American-flag schools, a recognition of the unique historic relationship between the Congress and the Commonwealth of Puerto Rico, an awareness of the Federal Government's acceptance of the desirability of the use of Spanish as the language of instruction in Commonwealth schools, and the fact that Congress has fostered policies encouraging migration from the Commonwealth to the States. We have no occasion to determine in this case whether such factors would justify a similar distinction embodied in a voting-qualification law that denied the franchise to persons educated in non-American-flag schools. We hold only that the limitation on relief effected in §4(e) does not constitute a forbidden discrimination since these factors might well have been the basis for the decision of Congress to go "no farther than it did."

We therefore conclude that §4(e), in the application challenged in this case, is appropriate legislation to enforce the Equal Protection Clause and that the judgment of the District Court must be and hereby is reversed.

Reversed.

Mr. Justice Douglas joins the Court's opinion except for the discussion of the question whether the congressional remedies adopted in §4(e) constitute means which are not prohibited by, but are consistent with "the letter and spirit of the constitution." On that question, he reserves judgment until such time as it is presented by a member of the class against which that particular discrimination is directed.

Mr. Justice Harlan, whom Mr. Justice Stewart joins, dissenting.

Worthy as its purposes may be thought by many, I do not see how § 4(e) of the Voting Rights Act of 1965 can be sustained except at the sacrifice of fundamentals in the American constitutional system—the separation between the legislative and judicial function and the boundaries between federal and state political authority. * * *

When recognized state violations of federal constitutional standards have occurred, Congress is of course empowered by § 5 to take appropriate remedial measures to redress and prevent the wrongs. But it is a judicial question whether the condition with which Congress has thus sought to deal is in truth an infringement of the Constitution, something that is the necessary prerequisite to bringing the § 5 power into play at all. * * *

* * * The question here is not whether the statute is appropriate remedial legislation to cure an established violation of a constitutional command, but whether there has in fact been an infringement of that constitutional command, that is, whether a particular state practice or, as here, a statute is so arbitrary or irrational as to offend the command of the Equal Protection Clause of the Fourteenth Amendment. That question is one for the judicial branch ultimately to determine. Were the rule otherwise, Congress would be able to qualify this Court's constitutional decisions under the Fourteenth and Fifteenth Amendments, let alone those under other provisions of the Constitution, by resorting to congressional power under the Necessary and Proper Clause. In view of this Court's holding in *Lassiter* that an English literacy test is a permissible exercise of state supervision over its franchise,{[3]} I do not

---

3. * * * The 1943 test, submitted by the Attorney General of New York as representative, is reproduced below: * * *

Read this and then write the answers to the questions[.]

Read it as many times as you need to[.]

The legislative branch of the National Government is called the Congress of the United States. Congress makes the laws of the Nation. Congress is composed of two houses. The upper house is called the Senate and its members are called Senators. There are 96 Senators in the upper house, two from each State. Each United States Senator is elected for a term of six years. The lower house of Congress is known as the House of Representatives. The number of Representatives from each state is determined by the population of that state. At present there are 435 members of the House of Representatives. Each Representative is elected for a term of two years. Congress meets in the Capital at Washington.

The answers to the following questions are to be taken from the above paragraph[.]

1 How many houses are there in Congress?

2 What does Congress do?

3 What is the lower house of Congress called?

4 How many members are there in the lower house?

think it is open to Congress to limit the effect of that decision as it has undertaken to do by § 4(e). In effect the Court reads § 5 of the Fourteenth Amendment as giving Congress the power to define the substantive scope of the Amendment. If that indeed be the true reach of § 5, then I do not see why Congress should not be able as well to exercise its § 5 "discretion" by enacting statutes so as in effect to dilute equal protection and due process decisions of this Court. In all such cases there is room for reasonable men to differ as to whether or not a denial of equal protection or due process has occurred, and the final decision is one of judgment. Until today this judgment has always been one for the judiciary to resolve.

I do not mean to suggest in what has been said that a legislative judgment of the type incorporated in § 4(e) is without any force whatsoever. Decisions on questions of equal protection and due process are based not on abstract logic, but on empirical foundations. To the extent "legislative facts" are relevant to a judicial determination, Congress is well equipped to investigate them, and such determinations are of course entitled to due respect. * * *

But no such factual data provide a legislative record supporting § 4(e) by way of showing that Spanish-speaking citizens are fully as capable of making informed decisions in a New York election as are English-speaking citizens. Nor was there any showing whatever to support the Court's alternative argument that § 4(e) should be viewed as but a remedial measure designed to cure or assure against unconstitutional discrimination of other varieties, *e.g.*, in "public schools, public housing and law enforcement," to which Puerto Rican minorities might be subject in such communities as New York. * * *

Thus, we have here not a matter of giving deference to a congressional estimate, based on its determination of legislative facts, bearing upon the validity *vel non* of a statute, but rather what can at most be called a legislative announcement that Congress believes a state law to entail an unconstitutional deprivation of equal protection. Although this kind of declaration is of course entitled to the most respectful consideration, coming as it does from a concurrent branch and one that is knowledgeable in matters of popular political participation, I do not believe it lessens our responsibility to decide the fundamental issue of whether in fact the state enactment violates federal constitutional rights. * * * At least in the area of primary state concern a state statute that passes constitutional muster under the judicial standard of rationality should not be permitted to be set at naught by a mere contrary congressional pronouncement unsupported by a legislative record justifying that conclusion. * * *

---

5 How long is the term of office of a United States Senator?

6 How many Senators are there from each state?

7 For how long a period are members of the House of Representatives elected?

8 In what city does Congress meet?

Notes and Questions

1. The Court in *Morgan* proclaimed *Lassiter* "inapposite" because the question in *Morgan* was not whether New York's literacy test was constitutional, but instead whether Congress's ban on literacy tests was constitutional. The answer to that question depended on the extent of Congress's power to "enforce" the provisions of the Civil War Amendments. *Lassiter* and *Morgan* can coexist only if Congress has the power under the Enforcement Clauses to prohibit, by statute, at least *some* conduct that does not itself violate the Constitution. *Morgan* did not, however, settle the question of what limits, if any, the Constitution places on the enforcement power.

2. *Katzenbach v. Morgan* can be read narrowly or broadly. The narrow reading focuses on the Court's discussion of the discrimination against minorities — "both in the imposition of voting qualifications and the provision or administration of governmental services, such as public schools, public housing and law enforcement" — that elimination of the literacy test could rectify. Under this narrow theory of *Morgan*, Congress is permitted to "enforce" the Civil War Amendments by adopting remedial measures when Congress has made a rational judgment that actual violations of the Amendments are occurring but would be difficult to prove.

By contrast, the broad reading of *Morgan* permits Congress to expand the substance of the Amendment. This reading focuses on *Morgan*'s language providing Congress discretion to take actions "'plainly adapted' to furthering the[] aims of the Equal Protection Clause," leaving it to Congress to determine whether national legislation is appropriate.

3. The Supreme Court has since rejected the broad theory of *Morgan*. In *City of Boerne v. Flores*, 521 U.S. 507 (1997), the Court explained that while Congress possesses broad discretion to determine the appropriate way to enforce the protections of the Amendments, such "remedial" power does not include the ability to redefine what the Amendments mean:

> * * * The design of the [Fourteenth] Amendment and the text of § 5 are inconsistent with the suggestion that Congress has the power to decree the substance of the Fourteenth Amendment's restrictions on the States. * * * Congress does not enforce a constitutional right by changing what the right is. It has been given the power "to enforce," not the power to determine what constitutes a constitutional violation. Were it not so, what Congress would be enforcing would no longer be, in any meaningful sense, the "provisions of [the Fourteenth Amendment]."

While the line between measures that remedy or prevent unconstitutional actions and measures that make a substantive change in the governing law is not easy to discern, and Congress must have wide latitude in determining where it lies, the distinction exists and must be observed. There must be a congruence and proportionality between the injury to be prevented or remedied and the means adopted to that end. Lacking such a connection, legislation may become substantive in operation and effect.

History and our case law support drawing the distinction, one apparent from the text of the Amendment.

Id. at 519–20. *Flores* interpreted *Morgan* as approving Congress's "reasonable attempt to combat" "unconstitutional discrimination by New York," rather than granting Congress the power to "interpret the Constitution." *Id.* at 528.

4. Recall that in *Morgan* the Court relied in part on an early draft of the Fourteenth Amendment for the proposition that Congress's enforcement power was to be coextensive with its power under the Necessary and Proper Clause to "carr[y] into Execution" the other powers of the national government. *See* footnote 9. *Flores* countered *Morgan*'s view of history, contending that the replacement of the language of the draft with the narrower "enforce" language established that Congress's power was to be more limited:

> In February [1866], Republican Representative John Bingham of Ohio reported the following draft Amendment to the House of Representatives on behalf of the Joint Committee:
>
> "The Congress shall have power to make all laws which shall be necessary and proper to secure to the citizens of each State all privileges and immunities of citizens in the several States, and to all persons in the several States equal protection in the rights of life, liberty, and property." Cong. Globe, 39th Cong., 1st Sess., 1034 (1866).
>
> The proposal encountered immediate opposition, which continued through three days of debate. Members of Congress from across the political spectrum criticized the Amendment, and the criticisms had a common theme: The proposed Amendment gave Congress too much legislative power at the expense of the existing constitutional structure. Democrats and conservative Republicans argued that the proposed Amendment would give Congress a power to intrude into traditional areas of state responsibility, a power inconsistent with the federal design central to the Constitution. * * *
>
> As a result of these objections having been expressed from so many different quarters, the House voted to table the proposal until April. The congressional action was seen as marking the defeat of the proposal. * * * The Amendment in its early form was not again considered. Instead, the Joint Committee began drafting a new article of Amendment[.] * * *
>
> Under the revised Amendment, Congress' power was no longer plenary but remedial. * * * The revised Amendment proposal did not raise the concerns expressed earlier regarding broad congressional power to prescribe uniform national laws with respect to life, liberty, and property. [T]he new measure passed both Houses and was ratified in July 1868 as the Fourteenth Amendment.

Flores, 521 U.S. at 520–23.

5. As a result of *Flores*, the test when considering the constitutionality of an act of Congress ostensibly enacted to enforce the Civil War Amendments is whether the statute is "congruent" with and "proportional" to violations of constitutional rights, *as those rights are interpreted by the judiciary. See* 521 U.S. at 534–35. Thus, the prevailing test is not, as *Morgan* suggested, whether Congress could rationally have found that the statute advances the purpose of the Amendments, nor is the test whether the activity punished by the congressional statute itself violates the Constitution. Rather, after *Flores*, the Court will permit Congress to enact statutes that are somewhat over-inclusive relative to the constitutional violations they are designed to remedy, as long as the statutes are not *too* over-inclusive.

Such over-inclusive statutes are referred to as "prophylactic remedies" because they interpose a statutory prohibition against conduct that approaches (but does not violate) the prohibition established by the Constitution, so as to ensure that the Constitution itself will not be violated. To give a practical example, a total nationwide ban on literacy tests (at issue in *Oregon v. Mitchell*, which is discussed in Note 6, *infra*) helps ensure that literacy tests will not be used to discriminate against potential voters on racial grounds. After all, if there can be no literacy tests, there certainly can be no discriminatory ones. Nevertheless, the effect of a nationwide ban is to prohibit the use of some literacy tests that could be administered constitutionally under *Lassiter*. Might *Flores*, as well as *Morgan*, give too much power to Congress by enabling the creation of these prophylactic remedies? Consider *Tennessee v. Lane*, 541 U.S. 509, 556, 558–60 (2004) (Scalia, J., dissenting):

> I joined the Court's opinion in *Boerne* with some misgiving. I have generally rejected tests based on such malleable standards as "proportionality," because they have a way of turning into vehicles for the implementation of individual judges' policy preferences. * * * I would replace "congruence and proportionality" with another test—one that provides a clear, enforceable limitation supported by the text of § 5. Section 5 grants Congress the power "to *enforce*, by appropriate legislation," the other provisions of the Fourteenth Amendment. *Morgan* notwithstanding, one does not, within any normal meaning of the term, "enforce" a prohibition by issuing a still broader prohibition directed to the same end. One does not, for example, "enforce" a 55-mile-per-hour speed limit by imposing a 45-mile-per-hour speed limit—even though that is indeed directed to the same end of automotive safety and will undoubtedly result in many fewer violations of the 55-mile-per-hour limit. * * * That is simply not what the power to enforce means—or ever meant. The 1860 edition of Noah Webster's American Dictionary of the English Language, current when the Fourteenth Amendment was adopted, defined "enforce" as: "To put in execution; to cause to take effect; as, to *enforce* the laws." Nothing in § 5 allows Congress to go *beyond* the provisions of the Fourteenth Amendment to proscribe, prevent, or "remedy" conduct that does not *itself* violate any provision of the

Fourteenth Amendment. So-called "prophylactic legislation" is reinforcement rather than enforcement.

> *Morgan* asserted that this commonsense interpretation "would confine the legislative power . . . to the insignificant role of abrogating only those state laws that the judicial branch was prepared to adjudge unconstitutional, or of merely informing the judgment of the judiciary by particularizing the 'majestic generalities' of § 1 of the Amendment." That is not so. * * * Section 5 authorizes Congress to create a cause of action through which the citizen may vindicate his Fourteenth Amendment rights. * * * Section 5 would also authorize measures that do not restrict the States' substantive scope of action but impose requirements directly related to the *facilitation* of "enforcement" — for example, reporting requirements that would enable violations of the Fourteenth Amendment to be identified. But what § 5 does *not* authorize is so-called "prophylactic" measures, prohibiting primary conduct that is itself not forbidden by the Fourteenth Amendment.

See also The Civil Rights Cases, 109 U.S. 3, 11, 13 (1883) ("[T]he last section of the amendment invests congress with power to enforce it by appropriate legislation. To enforce what? To enforce the prohibition. * * * [Congressional legislation under § 5] should be adapted to the mischief and wrong which the amendment was intended to provide against; and that is, state laws or state action of some kind adverse to the rights of the citizen secured by the amendment.").

6. As originally enacted, § 4(a) of the Voting Rights Act of 1965 temporarily suspended literacy tests in southern states. The literacy-test ban was expanded in 1970 to apply nationwide. In *Oregon v. Mitchell*, 400 U.S. 112 (1970), the Court upheld the nationwide ban despite Arizona's complaint that it had not discriminated on the ground of race and therefore should not be forced to suffer a remedy for such discrimination. As Justices Brennan, White, and Marshall explained,

> Arizona argues that it is and has been providing education of equal quality for all its citizens; that its literacy test is both fair and fairly administered; and that there is no evidence in the legislative record upon which Congress could have relied to reach a contrary conclusion. It urges that to the extent that any citizens of Arizona have been denied the right to vote because of illiteracy resulting from discriminatory government practices, the unlawful discrimination has been by governments other than the State of Arizona or its political subdivisions. Arizona, it suggests, should not have its laws overridden to cure discrimination on the part of governmental bodies elsewhere in the country.

Id. at 233 (Brennan, White, and Marshall, JJ., concurring in the judgment in part and dissenting in part). Every Justice rejected Arizona's argument, though in several different opinions. Justices Brennan, White, and Marshall pointed to the unequal educational opportunities provided to different racial groups,[c] in Arizona and elsewhere, as well as the racially disparate impact of the literacy test. *See id.* at 234–35. Chief Justice Burger and Justices Black, Stewart, and Blackmun noted that discrimination in education affected more states than simply the ones where the discrimination was practiced. Further, race discrimination was a problem faced by the entire country, though in different particulars, and therefore those Justices found no problem with Congress's nationwide ban. *See id.* at 133–34 (opinion of Black, J.); 283–84 (Stewart, J., joined by Burger, C.J., and Blackmun, J., concurring in part and dissenting in part). Justice Douglas thought it sufficient to note that Congress was aware that literacy tests had been used to discriminate against minorities. *See id.* at 147 (Douglas, J., concurring in the judgment in part and dissenting in part). Finally, Justice Harlan thought "the issue [wa]s not free from difficulty," but believed the nationwide ban was constitutional because "Congress could have determined that racial prejudice is prevalent throughout the Nation, and that literacy tests unduly lend themselves to discriminatory application, either conscious or unconscious." *Id.* at 216 (Harlan, J., concurring in part and dissenting in part).

7. Justice Harlan concurred in the Court's opinion in *South Carolina v. Katzenbach*, dissented in *Katzenbach v. Morgan*, and concurred in that part of *Oregon v. Mitchell* that upheld the nationwide literacy-test ban. Can his positions be reconciled?

8. The literacy-test ban was made permanent in 1975. *See* 52 U.S.C. § 10303(e)(2), 89 Stat. 400 (1975). Can Congress constitutionally ban literacy tests across the country *today*? Is there any point at which the federal literacy-test ban will become unconstitutional? *Cf. Shelby County, Alabama v. Holder*, 570 U.S. 529, 535, 547–50 (2013) [p. 244] (looking to "current conditions" and relying on improvements in the protection of voting rights since 1965 to strike down the Voting Rights Act's preclearance formula).

De jure school segregation has been outlawed for more than half a century, but many school districts with large concentrations of minorities are poorly funded relative to wealthier, suburban, and largely white districts. Such disparities in funding, *per se*, do not violate the Constitution. *See San Antonio Independent School District v. Rodriguez*, 411 U.S. 1 (1973). May Congress nevertheless point to the funding

---

c. On the importance of disparities in educational opportunities in establishing a basis for banning literacy tests, see *Gaston County, North Carolina v. United States*, 395 U.S. 285 (1969). The Voting Rights Act of 1965 had permitted states to reinstate literacy tests upon proving that they had not used such tests with the purpose or effect of racially discriminating for the preceding five years. The County claimed that its test was neutrally applied, but the Court found that insufficient. The County's literacy test carried a discriminatory effect, according to the Court, because minorities of voting age had been educated in inferior schools, relative to the schools reserved for whites. *See id.* at 291. The result was that the County had made it more difficult for minorities to pass a literacy test, and for that reason the County was not permitted to use one.

disparity between largely white and largely minority schools in prohibiting states from enacting literacy tests?

9. In *City of Mobile v. Bolden*, 446 U.S. 55 (1980) [p. 302], a plurality of the Court held that facially neutral election laws trigger strict scrutiny under the Fifteenth Amendment only if they have both a discriminatory purpose and a disparate effect based on race or some other suspect classification. The VRA, however, requires the Attorney General to deny preclearance to a proposed change in election law whenever it would have *either* a discriminatory purpose *or* a discriminatory effect. *South Carolina v. Katzenbach* had reasoned that the preclearance requirement was "appropriate" legislation to enforce the Fifteenth Amendment because it placed the burden on the state to prove its compliance with the Constitution rather than on individuals to demonstrate the unconstitutionality of a challenged law. But what if the state proves that it did *not* have a discriminatory purpose? If discriminatory effect alone is enough under the VRA to defeat preclearance, does the VRA "appropriate[ly]" "enforce" a constitutional provision that requires both discriminatory purpose and effect? The Supreme Court confronted that issue in *City of Rome v. United States*, 446 U.S. 156 (1980), decided the same day as *Bolden*. In upholding the VRA's preclearance requirement as applied to changes in voting practices that had only a discriminatory effect, the Court reasoned as follows:

> The Court's treatment in *South Carolina* v. *Katzenbach* of the Act's ban on literacy tests demonstrates that, under the Fifteenth Amendment, Congress may prohibit voting practices that have only a discriminatory effect. The Court had earlier held in *Lassiter* v. *Northampton County Board of Elections*, 360 U.S. 45 (1959) [p. 11], that the use of a literacy test that was fair on its face and was not employed in a discriminatory fashion did not violate § 1 of the Fifteenth Amendment. In upholding the Act's *per se* ban on such tests in *South Carolina* v. *Katzenbach*, the Court found no reason to overrule *Lassiter*. Instead, the Court recognized that the prohibition was an appropriate method of enforcing the Fifteenth Amendment because for many years most of the covered jurisdictions had imposed such tests to effect voting discrimination and the continued use of even nondiscriminatory, fairly administered literacy tests would "freeze the effect" of past discrimination by allowing white illiterates to remain on the voting rolls while excluding illiterate Negroes. This holding makes clear that Congress may, under the authority of § 2 of the Fifteenth Amendment, prohibit state action that, though in itself not violative of § 1, perpetuates the effects of past discrimination. [The Court also discussed *Katzenbach* v. *Morgan* and *Oregon* v. *Mitchell*, concluding that they "recognize Congress' broad power to enforce the Civil War Amendments."] * * *

It is clear, then, that under § 2 of the Fifteenth Amendment Congress may prohibit practices that in and of themselves do not violate § 1 of the Amendment, so long as the prohibitions attacking racial discrimination in voting are "appropriate," as that term is defined in *McCulloch* v. *Maryland* and *Ex parte Virginia*. In the present case, we hold that the Act's ban on electoral changes that are discriminatory in effect is an appropriate method of promoting the purposes of the Fifteenth Amendment, even if it is assumed that § 1 of the Amendment prohibits only intentional discrimination in voting. Congress could rationally have concluded that, because electoral changes by jurisdictions with a demonstrable history of intentional racial discrimination in voting create the risk of purposeful discrimination, it was proper to prohibit changes that have a discriminatory impact. We find no reason, then, to disturb Congress' considered judgment that banning electoral changes that have a discriminatory impact is an effective method of preventing States from "'[undoing] or [defeating] the rights recently won' by Negroes."

446 U.S. at 175–78.

Then-Justice Rehnquist was not persuaded:

Neither reason nor precedent supports the conclusion that here it is "appropriate" for Congress to attempt to prevent purposeful discrimination by prohibiting conduct which a locality proves is *not* purposeful discrimination.

Congress had before it evidence that various governments were enacting electoral changes and annexing territory to prevent the participation of blacks in local government by measures other than outright denial of the franchise. Congress could of course remedy and prevent such purposeful discrimination on the part of local governments. And given the difficulties of proving that an electoral change or annexation has been undertaken for the purpose of discriminating against blacks, Congress could properly conclude that as a remedial matter it was necessary to place the burden of proving lack of discriminatory purpose on the localities. But all of this does not support the conclusion that Congress is acting remedially when it continues the presumption of purposeful discrimination even after the locality has disproved that presumption. Absent other circumstances, it would be a topsy-turvy judicial system which held that electoral changes which have been affirmatively proved to be permissible under the Constitution nonetheless violate the Constitution.

446 U.S. at 214–15 (Rehnquist, J., dissenting). Do you agree with then-Justice Rehnquist that *City of Rome* is incompatible with the remedial theory of Congress's § 5 powers? If so, did *Flores* overrule *City of Rome*?

Several states—including some formerly covered jurisdictions—have recently passed laws requiring voters to show identification (often photo identification) at the polls. Critics charge that the laws disproportionately burden the elderly, the poor, and racial minorities. Nevertheless, the Supreme Court upheld one such law against a facial challenge. *See Crawford v. Marion County Election Bd.*, 553 U.S. 181 (2008) [p. 999]. The Obama Justice Department, after denying preclearance to some such laws, argued that photo-ID requirements produce a discriminatory effect because minorities are less likely than whites to possess IDs and to have access to cars— making it more difficult for them to obtain an ID, especially in counties not served by public transportation. Should such facts, if true, lead to a denial of preclearance? *See* Daniel P. Tokaji, *If It's Broke, Fix It: Improving Voting Rights Act Preclearance*, 49 How. L.J. 785 (2006). If so, does that affect the question of § 5's constitutionality?

10. Section 4(e) provided special rights to persons educated in Puerto Rican schools that were not afforded to persons who learned Spanish in foreign countries. Should that favoritism for "American-flag" schools violate equal protection? What is the Court's response? What is the Court's reason for applying rational-basis scrutiny?

11. Section 4(e) forbade states from enforcing English-literacy tests only against "person[s] who ha[d] successfully completed the sixth primary grade." Is it constitutional for Congress to limit the VRA's coverage in that manner? Recall Note 4 following *Lassiter*, on page 15, which asked whether it would be constitutional for a state to restrict the franchise to persons attaining a certain level of education.

12. The Court decided the constitutionality of the preference for "American-flag" schools despite the fact that no party to the case was discriminated against because of the preference. Such an approach would not be followed today (unless the merits claim were "frivolous" or "insubstantial"). *Steel Co. v. Citizens for a Better Environment*, 523 U.S. 83, 89 (1998). Standing is considered a threshold question, and the power of the federal courts to reach the merits comes into being only upon the existence of an actual controversy. *See id.* at 101 ("Hypothetical jurisdiction produces nothing more than a hypothetical judgment—which comes to the same thing as an advisory opinion . . ."). *See also* Scott C. Idleman, *The Demise of Hypothetical Jurisdiction in the Federal Courts*, 52 VAND. L. REV. 235, 280–85 (1999).

13. The plaintiffs-appellees in *Katzenbach v. Morgan* were New York voters who claimed that the Voting Rights Act diluted their votes by permitting persons to vote who were ineligible to vote under New York law. Did the plaintiffs have standing? *Cf. United States v. Hays*, 515 U.S. 737 (1995); *Baker v. Carr*, 369 U.S. 186, 204–08 (1962); *United States v. Saylor*, 322 U.S. 385 (1944); Pamela S. Karlan, *Politics by Other Means*, 85 VA. L. REV. 1697, 1719 (1999).

14. The Court was careful to note that Congress possesses no "power to exercise discretion in the other direction and to enact" measures that *limit* constitutional rights as pronounced by the Court. *See* footnote 10. This conclusion has become known (redundantly) as the "one-way ratchet" theory because it permits Congress to expand upon, but not to contract, constitutional rights as interpreted by the courts. Is the Court correct that any enactment limiting the courts' reading of constitutional rights would be unconstitutional because it would not be "enforc[ing]" the Constitution, or is Justice Harlan correct that the theory underlying the majority

opinion permits Congress to alter the meaning of the Constitution in any direction it chooses?

15. The constitutionality of preclearance and the coverage formula would return to the Court more than 40 years later, after Congress in 2006 reauthorized the VRA for another 25 years but continued to use the same coverage formula that had been in place since 1975. Under that formula, a jurisdiction would be subject to preclearance if it had used voting tests and it had less than 50% voter registration or turnout in 1964, 1968, or 1972.

In *Northwest Austin Municipal Utility District No. One v. Holder*, 557 U.S. 193 (2009), the utility district, located in Texas, complained that Congress could not constitutionally require preclearance on the basis of an outdated coverage formula that rendered the state a covered jurisdiction. The Court dodged the constitutional issue, instead holding that the district was eligible to bail out of §5's preclearance obligations if it could show that it met the requirements of 52 U.S.C. §10303(a)(1): that within the preceding ten years it had not used a voting test, had not been denied preclearance, and had not been found guilty of other voting rights violations.

Even though the case thus turned on the statutory bailout question, the Court warned that Congress may have exceeded its constitutional power in passing the 2006 reauthorization:

> * * * Things have changed in the South. Voter turnout and registration rates now approach parity. Blatantly discriminatory evasions of federal decrees are rare. And minority candidates hold office at unprecedented levels.
>
> These improvements are no doubt due in significant part to the Voting Rights Act itself, and stand as a monument to its success. Past success alone, however, is not adequate justification to retain the preclearance requirements. It may be that these improvements are insufficient and that conditions continue to warrant preclearance under the Act. But the Act imposes current burdens and must be justified by current needs.
>
> The Act also differentiates between the States, despite our historic tradition that all the States enjoy "equal sovereignty." Distinctions can be justified in some cases. * * * But a departure from the fundamental principle of equal sovereignty requires a showing that a statute's disparate geographic coverage is sufficiently related to the problem that it targets.

557 U.S. at 202–03. In 2013, the Court faced another constitutional challenge to preclearance, this time by an Alabama county that was ineligible for bailout because it had been denied preclearance within the prior ten years. The Court, therefore, was presented with the constitutional question that it had avoided in *Northwest Austin*.

Shelby County, Alabama v. Holder

Supreme Court of the United States
570 U.S. 529, 133 S. Ct. 2612 (2013)

CHIEF JUSTICE ROBERTS delivered the opinion of the Court [in which JUSTICE SCALIA, JUSTICE KENNEDY, JUSTICE THOMAS, and JUSTICE ALITO join].

The Voting Rights Act of 1965 employed extraordinary measures to address an extraordinary problem. Section 5 of the Act required States to obtain federal permission before enacting any law relating to voting—a drastic departure from basic principles of federalism. And §4 of the Act applied that requirement only to some States—an equally dramatic departure from the principle that all States enjoy equal sovereignty. This was strong medicine, but Congress determined it was needed to address entrenched racial discrimination in voting * * *. Reflecting the unprecedented nature of these measures, they were scheduled to expire after five years.

Nearly 50 years later, they are still in effect; indeed, they have been made more stringent, and are now scheduled to last until 2031. There is no denying, however, that the conditions that originally justified these measures no longer characterize voting in the covered jurisdictions. By 2009, "the racial gap in voter registration and turnout [was] lower in the States originally covered by §5 than it [was] nationwide." *Northwest Austin Municipal Util. Dist. No. One* v. *Holder*, 557 U.S. 193, 203–04 (2009). Since that time, Census Bureau data indicate that African-American voter turnout has come to exceed white voter turnout in five of the six States originally covered by §5, with a gap in the sixth State of less than one half of one percent.

At the same time, voting discrimination still exists; no one doubts that. The question is whether the Act's extraordinary measures, including its disparate treatment of the States, continue to satisfy constitutional requirements. As we put it a short time ago, "the Act imposes current burdens and must be justified by current needs." *Northwest Austin*, 557 U.S., at 203. * * *

In 1965, the States could be divided into two groups: those with a recent history of voting tests and low voter registration and turnout, and those without those characteristics. Congress based its coverage formula on that distinction. Today the Nation is no longer divided along those lines, yet the Voting Rights Act continues to treat it as if it were.

The Government's defense of the formula is limited. First, the Government contends that the formula is "reverse-engineered": Congress identified the jurisdictions to be covered and *then* came up with criteria to describe them. Under that reasoning, there need not be any logical relationship between the criteria in the formula and the reason for coverage; all that is necessary is that the formula happen to capture the jurisdictions Congress wanted to single out.

The Government suggests that [*South Carolina* v.] *Katzenbach* [383 U.S. 301 (1966)] [p. 220] sanctioned such an approach, but the analysis in *Katzenbach* was quite different. *Katzenbach* reasoned that the coverage formula was rational because the "formula . . . was relevant to the problem": "Tests and devices are relevant to voting discrimination because of their long history as a tool for perpetrating the evil; a low voting rate is pertinent for the obvious reason that widespread disenfranchisement must inevitably affect the number of actual voters." 383 U.S., at 329, 330.

Here, by contrast, the Government's reverse-engineering argument does not even attempt to demonstrate the continued relevance of the formula to the problem it targets. And in the context of a decision as significant as this one—subjecting a disfavored subset of States to "extraordinary legislation otherwise unfamiliar to our federal system," *Northwest Austin*, [557 U.S.,] at 211—that failure to establish even relevance is fatal.

The Government falls back to the argument that because the formula was relevant in 1965, its continued use is permissible so long as any discrimination remains in the States Congress identified back then—regardless of how that discrimination compares to discrimination in States unburdened by coverage. This argument does not look to "current political conditions," *Northwest Austin*, *supra*, at 203, but instead relies on a comparison between the States in 1965. That comparison reflected the different histories of the North and South. It was in the South that slavery was upheld by law until uprooted by the Civil War, that the reign of Jim Crow denied African-Americans the most basic freedoms, and that state and local governments worked tirelessly to disenfranchise citizens on the basis of race. The Court invoked that history—rightly so—in sustaining the disparate coverage of the Voting Rights Act in 1966.

But history did not end in 1965. By the time the Act was reauthorized in 2006, * * * largely because of the Voting Rights Act, voting tests were abolished, disparities in voter registration and turnout due to race were erased, and African-Americans attained political office in record numbers. And yet the coverage formula that Congress reauthorized in 2006 ignores these developments, keeping the focus on decades-old data relevant to decades-old problems, rather than current data reflecting current needs. * * *

* * * The dissent [in attempting to justify the disparate coverage under § 4] relies on "second-generation barriers," which are not impediments to the casting of ballots, but rather electoral arrangements that affect the weight of minority votes. That does not cure the problem. Viewing the preclearance requirements as targeting such efforts simply highlights the irrationality of continued reliance on the § 4 coverage formula, which is based on voting tests and access to the ballot, not vote dilution. We cannot pretend that we are reviewing an updated statute, or try our hand at updating the statute ourselves, based on the new record compiled by Congress. Contrary to the dissent's contention, we are not ignoring the record; we are simply recognizing that it played no role in shaping the statutory formula before us today. * * *

There is no valid reason to insulate the coverage formula from review merely because it was previously enacted 40 years ago. If Congress had started from scratch in 2006, it plainly could not have enacted the present coverage formula. It would have been irrational for Congress to distinguish between States in such a fundamental way based on 40-year-old data, when today's statistics tell an entirely different story. And it would have been irrational to base coverage on the use of voting tests 40 years ago, when such tests have been illegal since that time. But that is exactly what Congress has done. * * *

Our decision in no way affects the permanent, nationwide ban on racial discrimination in voting found in § 2. We issue no holding on § 5 itself, only on the coverage formula. Congress may draft another formula based on current conditions. Such a formula is an initial prerequisite to a determination that exceptional conditions still exist justifying such an "extraordinary departure from the traditional course of relations between the States and the Federal Government." Our country has changed, and while any racial discrimination in voting is too much, Congress must ensure that the legislation it passes to remedy that problem speaks to current conditions.

The judgment of the Court of Appeals is reversed.

It is so ordered.

JUSTICE THOMAS, concurring.

I join the Court's opinion in full but write separately to explain that I would find § 5 of the Voting Rights Act unconstitutional as well. * * *

While the Court claims to "issue no holding on § 5 itself," its own opinion compellingly demonstrates that Congress has failed to justify "current burdens" with a record demonstrating "current needs." By leaving the inevitable conclusion unstated, the Court needlessly prolongs the demise of that provision. For the reasons stated in the Court's opinion, I would find § 5 unconstitutional.

JUSTICE GINSBURG, with whom JUSTICE BREYER, JUSTICE SOTOMAYOR, and JUSTICE KAGAN join, dissenting.

In the Court's view, the very success of § 5 of the Voting Rights Act demands its dormancy. Congress was of another mind. Recognizing that large progress has been made, Congress determined, based on a voluminous record, that the scourge of discrimination was not yet extirpated. The question this case presents is who decides whether, as currently operative, § 5 remains justifiable, this Court, or a Congress charged with the obligation to enforce the post-Civil War Amendments "by appropriate legislation." With overwhelming support in both Houses, Congress concluded that, for two prime reasons, § 5 should continue in force, unabated. First, continuance would facilitate completion of the impressive gains thus far made; and second, continuance would guard against backsliding. Those assessments were well within Congress' province to make and should elicit this Court's unstinting approbation. * * *

I begin with the evidence on which Congress based its decision to continue the preclearance remedy. The surest way to evaluate whether that remedy remains in order is to see if preclearance is still effectively preventing discriminatory changes to voting laws. On that score, the record before Congress was huge. In fact, Congress found there were *more* DOJ objections between 1982 and 2004 (626) than there were between 1965 and the 1982 reauthorization (490).

All told, between 1982 and 2006, DOJ objections blocked over 700 voting changes based on a determination that the changes were discriminatory. Congress found that the majority of DOJ objections included findings of discriminatory intent and that the changes blocked by preclearance were "calculated decisions to keep minority voters from fully participating in the political process." On top of that, over the same time period the DOJ and private plaintiffs succeeded in more than 100 actions to enforce the § 5 preclearance requirements.

In addition to blocking proposed voting changes through preclearance, DOJ may request more information from a jurisdiction proposing a change. In turn, the jurisdiction may modify or withdraw the proposed change. The number of such modifications or withdrawals provides an indication of how many discriminatory proposals are deterred without need for formal objection. Congress received evidence that more than 800 proposed changes were altered or withdrawn since the last reauthorization in 1982. Congress also received empirical studies finding that DOJ's requests for more information had a significant effect on the degree to which covered jurisdictions "compl[ied] with their obligatio[n]" to protect minority voting rights.

Congress also received evidence that litigation under § 2 of the VRA was an inadequate substitute for preclearance in the covered jurisdictions. Litigation occurs only after the fact, when the illegal voting scheme has already been put in place and individuals have been elected pursuant to it, thereby gaining the advantages of incumbency. An illegal scheme might be in place for several election cycles before a § 2 plaintiff can gather sufficient evidence to challenge it. And litigation places a heavy financial burden on minority voters. Congress also received evidence that preclearance lessened the litigation burden on covered jurisdictions themselves, because the preclearance process is far less costly than defending against a § 2 claim, and clearance by DOJ substantially reduces the likelihood that a § 2 claim will be mounted. * * *

I turn next to the evidence on which Congress based its decision to reauthorize the coverage formula in § 4(b). Because Congress did not alter the coverage formula, the same jurisdictions previously subject to preclearance continue to be covered by this remedy. The evidence just described, of preclearance's continuing efficacy in blocking constitutional violations in the covered jurisdictions, itself grounded Congress' conclusion that the remedy should be retained for those jurisdictions. * * *

{But, the Court insists, the coverage formula is no good; it is based on "decades-old data and eradicated practices." Even if the legislative record shows, as engaging with it would reveal, that the formula accurately identifies the jurisdictions with the worst conditions of voting discrimination, that is of no moment, as the Court sees it. Congress, the Court decrees, must "star[t] from scratch." I do not see why that should be so. * * *

{* * * By [2006], the formula had been in effect for many years, and *all* of the jurisdictions covered by it were "familiar to Congress by name." [*Katzenbach*, 383 U.S.], at 328. The question before Congress: Was there still a sufficient basis to support continued application of the preclearance remedy in each of those already-identified places? There was at that point no chance that the formula might inadvertently sweep in new areas that were not the subject of congressional findings. And Congress could determine from the record whether the jurisdictions captured by the coverage formula still belonged under the preclearance regime. If they did, there was no need to alter the formula. * * *}

[E]ven after 40 years and thousands of discriminatory changes blocked by preclearance, conditions in the covered jurisdictions demonstrated that the formula was still justified by "current needs." *Northwest Austin*, 557 U.S., at 203. * * * Although covered jurisdictions account for less than 25 percent of the country's population, * * * they accounted for 56 percent of successful § 2 litigation since 1982. Controlling for population, there were nearly *four* times as many successful § 2 cases in covered jurisdictions as there were in noncovered jurisdictions. [F]urther[,] § 2 lawsuits are more likely to succeed when they are filed in covered jurisdictions than in noncovered jurisdictions. From these findings—ignored by the Court—Congress reasonably concluded that the coverage formula continues to identify the jurisdictions of greatest concern. * * *

Notes and Questions

1. The Court's holding striking down the coverage formula was grounded in "the principle that all States enjoy equal sovereignty"—a principle the Court deemed "highly pertinent in assessing * * * disparate treatment of States" by Congress. Using that principle, the Court held that the coverage formula could not stand unless the formula was at least a rational way of identifying states where voting discrimination was the most problematic. Is it appropriate to presume the unconstitutionality of laws that treat states differently? The dissent countered that it is common to treat states differently, and that the equal-sovereignty presumption should apply only in the context in which it was first developed—the entry of new states into the Union.

2. The United States argued that the coverage formula resulted in identifying states with voting discrimination. The Court, however, held that the formula must do more than result in outcomes that make some sense; rather, the formula itself must be "relevan[t] * * * to the problem it targets." That is, even if the covered jurisdictions happen to be the ones where voting discrimination is most prevalent currently, the voting data from 1964, 1968, and 1972 do not have anything to do with that fact.

Why should this make any difference? If a state has a voting-discrimination problem, why does it matter if Congress identified that state based on its history, the number of letters in the state's name, or the flip of a coin? Alternatively, would the constitutionality of §5 be affected if Congress had specified the covered jurisdictions by name rather than relying on the coverage formula in §4(b)? In other words, should it matter that the coverage formula relies on old data if those data still identify jurisdictions for which discrimination continues to be a problem?

3. Is it appropriate for a court to defer to Congress's judgment that the reason there have been few recent instances of overt discrimination in covered jurisdictions is that §5 has deterred potential violators? The Court rejected the deterrence argument, because it would render §5 "effectively immune from scrutiny; no matter how 'clean' the record of covered jurisdictions, the argument could always be made that it was deterrence that accounted for the good behavior." 570 U.S. at 550. The dissent argued that Congress's conclusions should be evaluated deferentially under the rational-basis test. Which side has the better of the argument? Would accepting deterrence allow Congress to escape limits on its power, or (as the dissent charged) would failing to accept a deterrence argument be "like throwing away your umbrella in a rainstorm because you are not getting wet"? *Id.* at 590 (Ginsburg, J., dissenting).

4. More generally (and to change metaphors), should Congress be able to assume that where there is smoke there is fire? That is, if Congress cannot point to many constitutional violations (because, for example, there is no showing of the jurisdiction's discriminatory intent), should it nonetheless be able to act on its belief that preclearance is necessary to prevent constitutional violations?

5. As mentioned above in Note 3, the dissent argued that the 2006 reauthorization should have been evaluated under the rational-basis test. The majority was not so clear about whether the rationality standard or the congruence-and-proportionality standard from *City of Boerne v. Flores* was more appropriate. In *Northwest Austin*, the Court acknowledged the two conflicting lines of precedent, but concluded that it was unnecessary to decide which standard applied. *Northwest Austin Municipal Utility Dist. No. 1 v. Holder*, 557 U.S. 193, 204 (2009). Likewise, the majority in *Shelby County* concluded that the 2006 reauthorization was irrational, and therefore unconstitutional regardless of whether rational basis or congruence and proportionality applied. *Shelby County, Alabama v. Holder*, 570 U.S. 529, 554, 556 (2013).

6. Perhaps the most striking aspect of *Shelby County* is the Court's refusal to engage in the debate about whether Congress had sufficient proof of voting discrimination in the covered jurisdictions. Whereas the dissent at some length discussed Congress's evidence about "second-generation" barriers, DOJ objections, requests for more information, §2 suits, and the like, the majority brushed off all those statistics by claiming that they do not relate to the coverage formula that Congress used in §4. Was the Court correct to treat those data as beside the point? If

Congress did update § 4 to rely on current conditions, and if it used § 2 suits as an indication of those current needs, would Congress be acting constitutionally or would Congress be exceeding its power because § 2 violations need not include discriminatory intent—a requirement for a violation of the Fourteenth and Fifteenth Amendments, which Congress would be attempting to enforce?

7. What effect did preclearance have on the representatives elected from districts that were subject to § 5? A recent article found that representatives from such districts were more likely to be supportive of civil-rights legislation than were other representatives, especially if the precleared districts were competitive or had an exceptionally high proportion of black constituents. *See* Sophie Schuit & Jon C. Rogowski, *Race, Representation, and the Voting Rights Act*, 61 AM. J. POL. SCI. 513 (2017).

8. With the demise of the coverage formula in § 4 of the VRA, the bail-in provisions of § 3 have assumed greater prominence. According to § 3, "[i]f in any proceeding instituted by the Attorney General or an aggrieved person under any statute to enforce the voting guarantees of the Fourteenth or Fifteenth Amendment in any State or political subdivision the court finds that violations of the Fourteenth or Fifteenth Amendment justifying equitable relief have occurred within the territory of such State or political subdivision, the court, in addition to such relief as it may grant, shall retain jurisdiction for such period as it may deem appropriate and during such period" preclearance shall be required. 52 U.S.C. § 10302(c). *See generally* Travis Crum, Note, *The Voting Rights Act's Secret Weapon: Pocket Trigger Litigation and Dynamic Preclearance*, 119 YALE L.J. 1992 (2010).

Thus, § 3 permits a jurisdiction-by-jurisdiction identification of the places where preclearance is required, rather than the wholesale approach of § 4, which involved application of the formula struck down in *Shelby County*. Further, the decision whether to require preclearance under § 3 belongs with the courts. So far, most jurisdictions to have been bailed-in accepted that status through a consent decree. *But see Jeffers v. Clinton*, 740 F. Supp. 585 (E.D. Ark. 1990).

Note that the bail-in procedure requires a finding of a constitutional violation—not simply a violation of the prophylactic guarantees of § 2, which protect minorities from laws that result in an abridgement of their ability to elect their candidates of choice. This standard makes it difficult for "aggrieved person[s]" to win a bail-in suit and requires the court to find intentional discrimination. But while it may be difficult to force a state or political subdivision to be bailed-in, it is not impossible.

Texas is the battleground for bail-in under VRA Section 3. In several different post-*Shelby County* cases, courts have found that Texas or its political subdivisions intentionally discriminated against minorities. *See Perez v. Abbott*, 274 F. Supp. 3d 624 (W.D. Tex. 2017) (three-judge court) (2-1) (finding intentional discrimination in the drawing of congressional districts); *Veasey v. Abbott*, 265 F. Supp. 3d 384 (S.D. Tex. 2017) (finding discriminatory intent in passage of voter-ID law), *rev'd*, 888 F.3d 792 (5th Cir. 2018) (holding that discriminatory intent behind a repealed voter-ID law did not justify enjoining the law that replaced it). And in one case, a federal district court took the next step and bailed-in the city of Pasadena, Texas, after finding intentional discrimination against Latinos in the City's creation of an at-large district. Having found that the City had thus violated the Constitution, the court invoked VRA § 3 to bail-in the City, making it subject to preclearance for the next six years. *See Patino v. City of Pasadena, Texas*, 230 F. Supp. 3d 667 (S.D. Tex. 2017), *stay denied*, 677 Fed. Appx. 950 (5th Cir. 2017).

9. In response to *Shelby County*, some members of Congress have introduced bills that would amend the VRA's coverage formula and effect other changes. The current bill is referred to as the Voting Rights Advancement Act of 2019. H.R. 4, 116th Cong. The new coverage formula is based on a rolling 25-year calendar. States would be covered if (1) 15 federal voting-rights violations—constitutional or statutory—occurred in that state within the preceding 25 years, or (2) 10 violations occurred in the state, any one of which was committed by the state itself, instead of being committed only by political subdivisions. Political subdivisions would be covered if they committed three federal violations in the same 25-year period. "Violations" would include not only final judgments finding a constitutional or VRA violation, but also denials of preclearance (either by the Attorney General or the court), settlements, and consent decrees resulting in the "alteration or abandonment of a voting practice" that was challenged as discriminating on the ground of race, color, or membership in a language minority group.

This rolling 25-year calendar was designed to address *Shelby County*'s insistence that Congress must be able to point to current evidence—and not just voting data from the 1964, 1968, and 1972 elections—to justify overriding the equal sovereignty of states. The updated coverage formula might not solve the VRA's constitutional problems, however. In the first place, as stated above, preclearance under the amendment would be triggered by violations of federal statutory law, such as § 2 of the VRA—not merely violations of the Federal Constitution. Because those statutes sometimes prohibit laws that have a discriminatory effect and not just those laws that are motivated by a discriminatory purpose, states might be covered under the proposed VRA amendment without having committed constitutional violations. Similarly, the amendments would expand the bail-in provisions of § 3 to permit jurisdictions to be covered on the basis of statutory violations not necessarily indicative of discriminatory purpose. The Bill passed the House of Representatives in late 2019, but has not passed the Senate.

10. Covered jurisdictions under the 1965 VRA had the option of seeking preclearance from the attorney general or the U.S. District Court for the District of Columbia—not one of the district courts sitting in the covered jurisdiction itself. "The common assumption at the time was that if Section 5 provided for local venue, its application would be placed at risk by hostile or unsympathetic federal district judges." Michael E. Solimine, *Rethinking District of Columbia Venue in Voting Rights Preclearance Actions*, 103 Geo. L.J. Online 29, 35 (2014). If preclearance is reinstituted, should declaratory-judgment actions for preclearance continue to be venued exclusively in the D.C. District? One of us has argued that they should not. *See id.*

11. If Congress were to pass an updated coverage formula, the Supreme Court would have to consider not only the constitutionality of that new formula, but of § 5 itself—a question that the Court avoided in both *Northwest Austin* and *Shelby County*. Has preclearance itself become an inappropriate way of enforcing the Fourteenth and Fifteenth Amendments? Suppose Congress abandoned the idea of requiring preclearance of only certain jurisdictions. Would Congress have the power to apply the preclearance requirement throughout the entire country?

C. Standards, Practices, and Procedures with Respect to Voting

The preclearance procedure applied to only a subset of laws passed or administered by covered jurisdictions. Specifically, preclearance was required whenever a covered jurisdiction "enact[ed] or s[ought] to administer any voting qualification or prerequisite to voting, or standard, practice, or procedure with respect to voting." 52 U.S.C. § 10304. There was little controversy as to the meaning of "voting qualification or prerequisite to voting," but the remaining statutory language was the subject of important litigation.

Disputes concerning the meaning of "standard, practice, or procedure with respect to voting" confronted two competing concerns. On the one hand, all manner of state and local laws can diminish the significance of the right to vote without directly stopping any person from casting a ballot. Consequently, the purposes of the Voting Rights Act would be undermined by an interpretation that permitted states to avoid its strictures through clever devices that formally did not involve voting. On the other hand, however, Congress did not intend to require *every* state and local law to be precleared. Requiring preclearance for changes "with respect to voting," in other words, implied the existence of laws not respecting voting, which would not be subject to preclearance. Exactly which laws fell within that category, however, has long been the subject of dispute, as the following case attests.

Allen v. State Board of Elections

Supreme Court of the United States
393 U.S. 544, 89 S. Ct. 817, 22 L. Ed. 2d 1 (1969)

Mr. Chief Justice Warren delivered the opinion of the Court [in which Mr. Justice Brennan, Mr. Justice Stewart, Mr. Justice White, and Mr. Justice Fortas join, and in which Mr. Justice Douglas and Mr. Justice Marshall join in relevant part]. * * *

In these four cases, the States have passed new laws or issued new regulations. The central issue is whether these provisions fall within the prohibition of § 5 that prevents the enforcement of "any voting qualification or prerequisite to voting, or standard, practice, or procedure with respect to voting" unless the State first complies with one of the section's [preclearance] procedures.

No. 25, *Fairley v. Patterson*, involves a 1966 amendment to § 2870 of the Mississippi Code of 1942. The amendment provides that the board of supervisors of each county may adopt an order providing that board members be elected at large by all qualified electors of the county. * * *

No. 26, *Bunton v. Patterson*, concerns a 1966 amendment to § 6271-08 of the Mississippi Code. The amendment provides that in 11 specified counties, the county superintendent of education shall be appointed by the board of education. Before the enactment of this amendment, all these counties had the option of electing or appointing the superintendent. * * *

No. 36, *Whitley v. Williams*, involves a 1966 amendment to § 3260 of the Mississippi Code, which changed the requirements for independent candidates running in general elections. The amendment makes four revisions: (1) it establishes a new rule that no person who has voted in a primary election may thereafter be placed on the ballot as an independent candidate in the general election; (2) the time for filing a petition as an independent candidate is changed to 60 days before the primary election from the previous 40 days before the general election; (3) the number of signatures of qualified electors needed for the independent qualifying petition is increased substantially; and (4) a new provision is added that each qualified elector who signs the independent qualifying petition must personally sign the petition and must include his polling precinct and county. * * *

In all three of these cases, the three-judge District Court ruled that the amendments to the Mississippi Code did not come within the purview of and are not covered by § 5, and dismissed the complaints. Appellants brought direct appeals to this Court. * * *

No. 3, *Allen v. State Board of Elections*, concerns a bulletin issued by the Virginia Board of Elections to all election judges. The bulletin was an attempt to modify the provisions of § 24-252 of the Code of Virginia of 1950 which provides, *inter alia*, that "any voter [may] place on the official ballot the name of any person *in his own handwriting*. . . ." The Virginia Code further provides that voters with a physical incapacity may be assisted in preparing their ballots. * * * However, no statutory provision is made for assistance to those who wish to write in a name, but who are unable to do so because of illiteracy. When Virginia was brought under the coverage of the Voting Rights Act of 1965, Virginia election officials apparently thought that the provision in § 24-252, requiring a voter to cast a write-in vote in the voter's own handwriting was incompatible with the provisions of § 4(a) of the Act suspending the enforcement of any test or device as a prerequisite to voting. Therefore, the Board of Elections issued a bulletin to all election judges, instructing that the election judge could aid any qualified voter in the preparation of his ballot, if the voter so requests and if the voter is unable to mark his ballot due to illiteracy.

Appellants are functionally illiterate registered voters from the Fourth Congressional District of Virginia. They * * * clai[m] that [in requiring the voter's choice to be in his or her own handwriting] § 24-252 and the modifying bulletin violate the

Equal Protection Clause of the Fourteenth Amendment and the Voting Rights Act of 1965. [They wanted to "write-in" the name of their preferred candidate by attaching a sticker to the ballot. They objected to being forced to rely on the assistance of the election judge, thus potentially compromising anonymity, when a disabled voter could be assisted by "a person of [the voter's] choice."] A three-judge court was convened and the complaint dismissed. * * *

These suits were instituted by private citizens; an initial question is whether private litigants may invoke the jurisdiction of the district courts to obtain the relief requested in these suits. * * *

The Voting Rights Act does not explicitly grant or deny private parties authorization to seek a declaratory judgment that a State has failed to comply with the provisions of the Act. However, § 5 does provide that "no person shall be denied the right to vote for failure to comply with [a new state enactment covered by, but not approved under, § 5]." Analysis of this language in light of the major purpose of the Act indicates that appellants may seek a declaratory judgment that a new state enactment is governed by § 5. Further, after proving that the State has failed to submit the covered enactment for § 5 approval, the private party has standing to obtain an injunction against further enforcement, pending the State's submission of the legislation pursuant to § 5.

The Act was drafted to make the guarantees of the Fifteenth Amendment finally a reality for all citizens. Congress realized that existing remedies were inadequate to accomplish this purpose and drafted an unusual, and in some aspects a severe, procedure for insuring that States would not discriminate on the basis of race in the enforcement of their voting laws.

The achievement of the Act's laudable goal could be severely hampered, however, if each citizen were required to depend solely on litigation instituted at the discretion of the Attorney General. For example, the provisions of the Act extend to States and the *subdivisions thereof.* The Attorney General has a limited staff and often might be unable to uncover quickly new regulations and enactments passed at the varying levels of state government. It is consistent with the broad purpose of the Act to allow the individual citizen standing to insure that his city or county government complies with the § 5 approval requirements. * * *

* * * The guarantee of § 5 that no person shall be denied the right to vote for failure to comply with an unapproved new enactment subject to § 5, might well prove an empty promise unless the private citizen were allowed to seek judicial enforcement of the prohibition. * * *

Finding that these cases are properly before us, we turn to a consideration of whether these state enactments are subject to the approval requirements of § 5. These requirements apply to "any voting qualification or prerequisite to voting, or standard, practice, or procedure with respect to voting. . . ." 42 U.S.C. § 1973c [now 52 U.S.C. § 10304—Eds.]. The Act further provides that the term "voting" "shall include all action necessary to make a vote effective in any primary, special, or general election, including, but not limited to, registration, listing . . . or other action required by law prerequisite to voting, casting a ballot, and having such ballot counted properly and included in the appropriate totals of votes cast with respect to candidates for public or party office and propositions for which votes are received in an election." [52 U.S.C. § 10310(c)(1)]. Appellees in the Mississippi cases maintain that § 5 covers only those state enactments which prescribe who may register to vote. While accepting that the Act is broad enough to insure that the votes of all citizens should be cast, appellees urge that § 5 does not cover state rules relating to the qualification of candidates or to state decisions as to which offices shall be elective.

Appellees rely on the legislative history of the Act to support their view, citing the testimony of former Assistant Attorney General Burke Marshall before a subcommittee of the House Committee on the Judiciary:

> "Mr. CORMAN. We have not talked at all about whether we have to be concerned with not only who can vote, but who can run for public office and that has been an issue in some areas in the South in 1964. Have you given any consideration to whether or not this bill ought to address itself to the qualifications for running for public office as well as the problem of registration?

> "Mr. MARSHALL. The problem that the bill was aimed at was the problem of registration, Congressman. If there is a problem of another sort, I would like to see it corrected, but that is not what we were trying to deal with in the bill."

Appellees in No. 25 also argue that § 5 was not intended to apply to a change from district to at-large voting, because application of § 5 would cause a conflict in the administration of reapportionment legislation. They contend that under such a broad reading of § 5, enforcement of a reapportionment plan could be enjoined for failure to meet the § 5 approval requirements, even though the plan had been approved by a federal court. Appellees urge that Congress could not have intended to force the States to submit a reapportionment plan to two different courts.[29]

We must reject the narrow construction that appellees would give to § 5. The Voting Rights Act was aimed at the subtle, as well as the obvious, state regulations which have the effect of denying citizens their right to vote because of their race. * * * We are convinced that in passing the Voting Rights Act, Congress intended that state enactments such as those involved in the instant cases be subject to the § 5 approval requirements.

---

29. Appellees in No. 3 also argue that § 5 does not apply to the regulation in their case, because that regulation was issued in an attempt to comply with the provisions of the Voting Rights Act. They argue that if § 5 applies to the Virginia regulation, covered States would be prohibited from quickly complying with the Act. We cannot accept this argument, however. A State is not exempted from the coverage of § 5 merely because its legislation is passed in an attempt to comply with the provisions of the Act. To hold otherwise would mean that legislation, allegedly passed to meet the requirements of the Act, would be exempted from § 5 coverage — even though it would have the effect of racial discrimination. It is precisely this situation Congress sought to avoid in passing § 5.

The legislative history on the whole supports the view that Congress intended to reach any state enactment which altered the election law of a covered State in even a minor way. For example, § 2 of the Act, as originally drafted, included a prohibition against any "qualification or procedure." During the Senate hearings on the bill, Senator Fong expressed concern that the word "procedure" was not broad enough to cover various practices that might effectively be employed to deny citizens their right to vote. In response, the Attorney General said he had no objection to expanding the language of the section, as the word "procedure" "was intended to be all-inclusive of any kind of practice." Indicative of an intention to give the Act the broadest possible scope, Congress expanded the language in the final version of § 2 to include any "voting qualifications or prerequisite to voting, or standard, practice, or procedure." [52 U.S.C. § 10301]. Similarly, in the House hearings, it was emphasized that § 5 was to have a broad scope[.] * * *

Also, the remarks of both opponents and proponents during the debate over passage of the Act demonstrate the Congress was well aware of another admonition of the Attorney General. He had stated in the House hearings that two or three types of changes in state election law (such as changing from paper ballots to voting machines) could be specifically excluded from § 5 without undermining the purpose of the section. He emphasized, however, that there were "precious few" changes that could be excluded "because there are an awful lot of things that could be started for purposes of evading the 15th amendment if there is the desire to do so." It is significant that Congress chose not to include even these minor exceptions in § 5, thus indicating an intention that all changes, no matter how small, be subjected to § 5 scrutiny.

In light of the mass of legislative history to the contrary, especially the Attorney General's clear indication that the section was to have a broad scope and Congress' refusal to engraft even minor exceptions, the single remark of Assistant Attorney General Burke Marshall cannot be given determinative weight. Indeed, in any case where the legislative hearings and debate are so voluminous, no single statement or excerpt of testimony can be conclusive. * * *

The weight of the legislative history and an analysis of the basic purposes of the Act indicate that the enactment in each of these cases constitutes a "voting qualification or prerequisite to voting, or standard, practice, or procedure with respect to voting" within the meaning of § 5.

No. 25 involves a change from district to at-large voting for county supervisors. The right to vote can be affected by a dilution of voting power as well as by an absolute prohibition on casting a ballot. See *Reynolds* v. *Sims*, 377 U.S. 533, 555 (1964) [p. 122]. Voters who are members of a racial minority might well be in the majority in one district, but in a decided minority in the county as a whole. This type of change could therefore nullify their ability to elect the candidate of their choice just as would prohibiting some of them from voting.

In No. 26 an important county officer in certain counties was made appointive instead of elective. The power of a citizen's vote is affected by this amendment; after the change, he is prohibited from electing an officer formerly subject to the approval of the voters. Such a change could be made either with or without a discriminatory purpose or effect; however, the purpose of § 5 was to submit such changes to scrutiny.

The changes in No. 36 appear aimed at increasing the difficulty for an independent candidate to gain a position on the general election ballot. These changes might also undermine the effectiveness of voters who wish to elect independent candidates. One change involved in No. 36 deserves special note. The amendment provides that no person who has voted in a primary election may thereafter be placed on the ballot as an independent candidate in the general election. This is a "procedure with respect to voting" with substantial impact. One must forego his right to vote in his party primary if he thinks he might later wish to become an independent candidate.

The bulletin in No. 3 outlines new procedures for casting write-in votes. As in all these cases, we do not consider whether this change has a discriminatory purpose or effect. It is clear, however, that the new procedure with respect to voting is different from the procedure in effect when the State became subject to the Act; therefore, the enactment must meet the approval requirements of § 5 in order to be enforceable. * * *

In No. 3 the judgment of the District Court is vacated; in Nos. 25, 26, and 36 the judgments of the District Court are reversed. All four cases are remanded to the District Courts with instructions to issue injunctions restraining the further enforcement of the enactments until such time as the States adequately demonstrate compliance with § 5.

It is so ordered.

Mr. Justice Harlan, concurring in part and dissenting in part. * * *[1]

* * * It is best to begin by delineating the precise area of difference between the position the majority adopts and the one which I consider represents the better view of the statute. We are in agreement that in requiring federal review of changes in any "standard, practice, or procedure with respect to voting," Congress intended to include all state laws that changed the process by which voters were registered and had their ballots counted. The Court, however, goes further to hold that a State covered by the Act must submit for federal approval all those laws that could arguably have an impact on Negro voting power, even though the manner in which the election is conducted remains unchanged. I believe that this reading of the statute

---

1. I concur in the Court's disposition of the complex jurisdictional issues these cases present. * * *

should be rejected on several grounds. It ignores the place of § 5 in the larger structure of the Act; it is untrue to the statute's language; and it is unsupported by the legislative history.

First, and most important, the Court's construction ignores the structure of the complex regulatory scheme created by the Voting Rights Act. The Court's opinion assumes that § 5 may be considered apart from the rest of the Act. In fact, however, the provision is clearly designed to march in lock-step with § 4—the two sections cannot be understood apart from one another. Section 4 is one of the Act's central provisions, suspending the operation of all literacy tests and similar "devices" for at least five years in States whose low voter turnout indicated that these "tests" and "devices" had been used to exclude Negroes from the suffrage in the past. Section 5, moreover, reveals that it was not designed to implement new substantive policies but that it was structured to assure the effectiveness of the dramatic step that Congress had taken in § 4. The federal approval procedure found in § 5 only applies to those States whose literacy tests or similar "devices" have been suspended by § 4. As soon as a State regains the right to apply a literacy test or similar "device" under § 4, it also escapes the commands of § 5.

The statutory scheme contains even more striking characteristics which indicate that § 5's federal review procedure is ancillary to § 4's substantive commands. A State may escape § 5, *even though it has consistently violated this provision*, so long as it has complied with § 4, and has suspended the operation of literacy tests and other "devices" for five years. On the other hand, no matter how faithfully a State complies with § 5, it remains subject to its commands so long as it has not consistently obeyed § 4.

As soon as it is recognized that § 5 was designed solely to implement the policies of § 4, it becomes apparent that the Court's decision today permits the tail to wag the dog. * * * The fourth section of the Act had the profoundly important purpose of permitting the Negro people to gain access to the voting booths of the South once and for all. But the action taken by Congress in § 4 proceeded on the premise that once Negroes had gained free access to the ballot box, state governments would then be suitably responsive to their voice, and federal intervention would not be justified. * * *

The Court's construction of § 5 is even more surprising in light of the Act's regional application. For the statute, as the Court now construes it, deals with a problem that is national in scope. I find it especially difficult to believe that Congress would single out a handful of States as requiring stricter federal supervision concerning their treatment of a problem that may well be just as serious in parts of the North as it is in the South.[4]

---

4. Indeed, I would have very substantial constitutional difficulties with the statute if I were to accept such a construction.

The difficulties with the Court's construction increase even further when the language of the statute is considered closely.{[7]} When standing alone, the statutory formula requiring federal approval for changes in any "standard, practice, or procedure with respect to voting" can be read to support either the broad construction adopted by the majority or the one which I have advanced. But the critical formula does not stand alone. Immediately following the statute's description of the federal approval procedure, § 5 proceeds to describe the type of relief an aggrieved voter may obtain if a State enforces a new statute without obtaining the consent of the appropriate federal authorities: "no person shall be denied the right to vote *for failure to comply* with such qualification, prerequisite, standard, practice, or procedure." (Emphasis supplied.) This remedy serves to delimit the meaning of the formula in question. Congress was clearly concerned with changes in procedure with which voters could *comply*. But a law, like that in *Fairley* v. *Patterson*, No. 25, which permits all members of the County Board of Supervisors to run in the entire county and not in smaller districts, does not require a voter *to comply* with anything at all, and so does not come within the scope of the language used by Congress. * * *

The majority is left, then, relying on its understanding of the legislative history. With all deference, I find that the history the Court has garnered undermines its case, insofar as it is entitled to any weight at all. I refer not only to the unequivocal statement of Assistant Attorney General Burke Marshall, which the Court concedes to be diametrically opposed to the construction it adopts. For the lengthy testimony of Attorney General Katzenbach, upon which the Court seems to rely, actually provides little more support for its position. Mr. Katzenbach, unlike his principal assistant, was never directly confronted with the question raised here, and we are left to guess as to his views. If guesses are to be made, however, surely it is important to note that though the Attorney General used many examples to illustrate the operation of § 5, each of them concerned statutes that had an immediate impact on voter qualifications or which altered the manner in which the election

---

7. The Court seeks to strengthen its case by looking to the language of one of the definitional sections of the Act. Section 14(c)(1) defines the term "vote" or "voting" to "include all action necessary to make a vote *effective* in any primary, special, or general election, *including, but not limited to*, registration, listing pursuant to this Act, or other action required by law prerequisite to voting, casting a ballot, and having such ballot counted properly and included in the appropriate totals of votes cast with respect to candidates for public or party office and propositions for which votes are received in an election." (Emphasis supplied.) All of the aspects of voting that are enumerated in this definition concern the procedures by which voters are processed. When the statute cautions that its enumeration of stages in the election process is not exclusive, it merely indicates that the change of any other procedure that prevents the voter from having his ballot finally counted is also included within the range of the Act's concern. Surely the Court is entirely ignoring the textual context when it seeks to read the italicized phrases as embracing all electoral laws that affect the amount of political power Negroes will derive from the exercise of the franchise, even when the way in which voters are processed remains unchanged.

was conducted.[8] One would imagine that if the Attorney General believed that § 5 had the remarkable sweep the majority has now given it, one of his hypotheticals would have betrayed that fact.

Section 5, then, should properly be read to require federal approval only of those state laws that change either voter qualifications or the manner in which elections are conducted.

[Applying this standard, MR. JUSTICE HARLAN concluded that preclearance was required in all of the cases under review except *Fairley* v. *Patterson*, No. 25, which involved a statute "giv[ing] each county the right to elect its Board of Supervisors on an at-large basis." In his view, the nomination process for independents was the "functional equivalent of the political primary," which was explicitly covered by the Act; making a formerly elective office appointive took away the right to vote for that office; and Virginia's regulations concerning illiterates' write-in votes "quite obviously altered the manner in which an election is conducted."]

[MR. JUSTICE MARSHALL, joined by MR. JUSTICE DOUGLAS, concurred in most of the Court's opinion, but dissented as to an omitted portion giving only prospective relief in the Mississippi cases.]

MR. JUSTICE BLACK, dissenting.

Assuming the validity of the Voting Rights Act of 1965, as the Court does, I would agree with its careful interpretation of the Act, and would further agree with its holding as to jurisdiction and with its disposition of the four cases now before us. But I am still of the opinion that for reasons stated in my separate opinion in *South Carolina* v. *Katzenbach*, 383 U.S. 301, 355–362 (1966) [p. 220], a part of § 5 violates the United States Constitution. Section 5 * * * is reminiscent of old Reconstruction days * * *. The Southern States were at that time deprived of their right to pass laws on the premise that they were not then a part of the Union and therefore could be treated with all the harshness meted out to conquered provinces. The constitutionality of that doctrine was certainly not clear at that time. And whether the doctrine was constitutional or not, I had thought that the whole Nation had long since repented of the application of this "conquered province" concept, even as to the time immediately following the bitter Civil War. I doubt that any of the 13 Colonies would have agreed to our Constitution if they had dreamed that the time might come when they would have to go to a United States Attorney General or a District of Columbia court with hat in hand begging for permission to change their laws. Still less would any of these Colonies have been willing to agree to a Constitution that gave the Federal Government power to force one Colony to go

---

8. The examples given by the Attorney General concerned changes in a State's voting age, residence, or property requirements; changes in the frequency that registrars' offices are open; and changes from paper ballots to machines or vice versa.

through such an onerous procedure while all the other former Colonies, now supposedly its sister States, were allowed to retain their full sovereignty. * * *

I would hold § 5 of the 1965 Voting Rights Act unconstitutional insofar as it commands certain selected States to leave their laws in any field unchanged until they get the consent of federal agencies to pass new ones.

Notes and Questions

1. In what way can the regulations at issue in this case be characterized as "standard[s], practice[s], or procedure[s] with respect to voting"?

2. It is important to understand that the issue in this case was only whether the regulations needed to go through the preclearance process. Changes in voting procedures in "covered jurisdictions" had to be submitted for preclearance even if those regulations were not themselves discriminatory; indeed, the purpose of the preclearance process was to evaluate whether they were discriminatory before they took effect. Thus, in holding that preclearance was necessary for each of the regulations, the Court did *not* conclude that the regulations violated either the VRA or the Constitution.

3. You know from reading Chapter 2 that states must redraw districts at least every ten years to account for population shifts reported in the census. *Allen*, however, held that changes to voting procedures—including redrawn districts—could not go into effect until they obtained preclearance. As a result, covered jurisdictions found themselves between a rock and a hard place, being constitutionally compelled to redraw districts but being unable to make such changes effective until the preclearance process was complete.

Perry v. Perez, 565 U.S. 388 (2012), presented such a dilemma. As a result of the 2010 census, Texas (a covered jurisdiction) received four additional congressional districts and was required to draw new district lines before the 2012 elections. The state passed a plan and submitted it to the D.C. District Court for preclearance, but there the process stalled. Not only was no timely decision on preclearance forthcoming, but the plan was challenged in a separate suit as violating the Constitution and § 2 of the Voting Rights Act for allegedly diluting the strength of minorities' votes. That suit likewise would not be resolved in time to make whatever adjustments would be required before the 2012 elections.

In reviewing the case, a nearly unanimous Supreme Court reaffirmed what it had earlier written in *Connor v. Finch*, 431 U.S. 407 (1977)—that where a state's existing districts have been rendered unconstitutional by a subsequent census, a federal district court must itself draw interim districts if the political process is unable to yield new districts on its own. Very well. But what standards should the district court use in crafting an interim plan? In particular, what consideration should be given to the plan that has been passed but that is awaiting preclearance?

The Court responded that even though such a plan may not have legal effect itself, it is an "important starting point" for the district court to use in devising an interim plan. "It provides important guidance that helps ensure that the district court appropriately confines itself to drawing interim maps that comply with the Constitution and the Voting Rights Act, without displacing legitimate state policy judgments with the court's own preferences." *Perez*, 565 U.S. at 394.

Recall, however, that the state's new plan not only had not yet received preclearance; it had also been challenged as violating § 2 and the Equal Protection Clause. If the district court simply adopted the state's plan, it could be giving effect to an illegal or unconstitutional plan. If, on the other hand, the district court shied away from the state's plan, it would be preventing a state's policies from having effect simply because of an *allegation* of illegality—an action that would have federalism costs and would encourage the filing of meritless allegations in the future. Further, if the district court were to decide for itself whether the state's plan should be precleared, it would be usurping the role assigned by the VRA to the D.C. District Court and the Attorney General.

The Supreme Court's answer was that the district court should peek at the merits of the preclearance issue and any other challenges to the new districts, but should back away from actually deciding their legality. In the Court's words, "Where a State's plan faces challenges under the Constitution or § 2 of the Voting Rights Act, a district court should still be guided by that plan, except to the extent those legal challenges are shown to have a likelihood of success on the merits." *Id.* at 942. Similarly, with regard to the preclearance issue, the state's plan should provide guidance to the district court except to the extent it contains elements "that stand a reasonable probability of failing to gain § 5 preclearance. And by 'reasonable probability' this Court means in this context that the § 5 challenge is not insubstantial." *Id.*

Eight members of the Court joined the *per curiam* opinion; Justice Thomas concurred in the judgment, arguing that § 5 was unconstitutional.

4. Should the choice between at-large and district-based voting structures be a decision subject to preclearance? If so, how should the attorney general or the D.C. District Court decide if such a choice is discriminatory? In an omitted portion of his opinion in *Allen*, Justice Harlan posited that "courts cannot intelligently compare" the benefits of an at-large system with those of one based on single-member districts: "Under one system, Negroes have *some* influence in the election of *all* officers; under the other, minority groups have *more* influence in the selection of *fewer* officers." 393 U.S. at 586 (Harlan, J., concurring in part and dissenting in part). Accordingly, he argued, the Supreme Court should have been reluctant to read the VRA as forcing courts to make such choices, as the D.C. District Court must do in deciding whether to grant preclearance to plans that switch from single-member to multi-member districts, or vice-versa.

5. Are the relative benefits of at-large and single-member-district systems any harder to discern than are the relative benefits of elective and appointive offices? Recall that Justice Harlan was willing to require changes of the latter type to be precleared.

6. *Problem.* Would the following actions require preclearance if passed in a covered jurisdiction?

A. A board of education passes a rule requiring its employees to take unpaid leaves of absence while they campaign for office. Would it matter in terms of the need for preclearance if the rule were passed one month after an employee — the first black person from the county to run for elective office in recent memory — declared his candidacy? What if the rule requires employees to take leaves of absence whenever they would be absent from their duties, rather than singling out absenteeism caused by an employee's campaign? *See Dougherty County Board of Education v. White,* 439 U.S. 32 (1978).

B. A county commission is restructured from a four-member body (with all four members being white) to a six-member body (including one black member). After the new commissioners take office, the commission reorganizes its members' responsibilities, reserving authority over the county's roads to the holdover white commissioners. What if a different county commission transfers authority over road construction from itself to a county engineer appointed by the commission? *See Presley v. Etowah County Commission,* 502 U.S. 491 (1992).

C. A county commission passes a resolution changing the commissioners' control over funds. Before the resolution, the county was divided into districts, with each commissioner having full control over the expenditure of money within his own district. Afterwards, the distribution of all money was to be controlled by the entire commission, meaning that expenditures would have to be approved by a majority of the commission and minority members could be outvoted. *See id.*

7. The cases we have encountered thus far in this section have involved the question whether certain types of laws required preclearance. They therefore focused on *what* the new law was. Later cases had to confront the *who* question. Specifically, covered jurisdictions must preclear voting changes that they "enact or seek to administer," but not every voting law *administered* by a covered jurisdiction is *enacted* by that jurisdiction. In *Lopez v. Monterey County,* 525 U.S. 266 (1999), the Supreme Court considered whether the County (a covered jurisdiction) was required to preclear changes when those changes were imposed by the law of California (not a covered jurisdiction). The Court concluded that preclearance was required, even if the County did not exercise any discretion in implementing the state law. The Court relied on "the face of the [Voting Rights] Act itself" in holding that preclearance was required whenever a covered jurisdiction "enacts *or* seeks to administer" a voting change, whether or not that jurisdiction exercises discretion. *See id.* at 278.

8. But what if the covered jurisdiction "seeks to administer" a change that is required not by state law, but by a federal court? Again, the answer is complicated. Where the federal court is entirely responsible for the content of the change, the

Court has created an exemption to the preclearance requirement. Because it would raise grave separation-of-powers concerns to require a federal court's decision to be precleared by the Attorney General or the D.C. District Court, *cf. Hayburn's Case*, 2 U.S. (2 Dall.) 409 (1792), the Court concluded that the federal court's plan need not be precleared. *See Connor v. Johnson*, 402 U.S. 690 (1971) (*per curiam*). *See also Lopez*, 525 U.S. at 286, 287 (describing *Connor* as exempting from preclearance those plans "crafted wholly by a federal district court in the first instance," and "wholly court-developed"). Where, however, the federal court orders a change that had been submitted to it by the covered jurisdiction, preclearance is necessary. *See McDaniel v. Sanchez*, 452 U.S. 130 (1981). Further, because *Connor's* separation-of-powers concerns are absent when a voting change is ordered by a *state* court, such changes must be precleared. *See Branch v. Smith*, 538 U.S. 254, 262 (2003) (noting the lack of dispute on the point).

9. *Allen* apparently settled the question whether private parties may sue to enforce VRA §5. *Reaves v. Department of Justice*, 355 F. Supp. 2d 510, 515–16 (D.D.C. 2005) (three-judge court) (*per curiam*) (rejecting South Carolina's claim of immunity to a suit by private parties to enforce §5). The Supreme Court has never decided whether private parties may sue to enforce §2, however. Because of concerns about sovereign immunity, the Constitution ordinarily prohibits private parties from suing states without the states' consent. *See, e.g., Seminole Tribe of Florida v. Florida*, 517 U.S. 44 (1996). Congress may abrogate states' sovereign immunity when it is enforcing the Civil War Amendments, *see Fitzpatrick v. Bitzer*, 427 U.S. 445 (1976), but Congress must use statutory language that is both express and "unmistakably clear" for such an abrogation to be effective. *Atascadero State Hospital v. Scanlon*, 473 U.S. 234, 242 (1985). Section 3 of the VRA refers to suits initiated by "the Attorney General or an aggrieved person." 52 U.S.C. § 10302. Nowhere, however, is there an explicit abrogation of the states' sovereign immunity. Nevertheless, the courts that have considered the question have held that §2 does abrogate states' sovereign immunity in suits by private parties. *See Alabama State Conference of the NAACP v. Alabama*, 949 F.3d 647 (11th Cir. 2020); *OCA-Greater Houston v. Texas*, 867 F.3d 604, 614 (5th Cir. 2017); *Mixon v. Ohio*, 193 F.3d 389, 398–99 (6th Cir. 1999); *Georgia State Conference of the NAACP v. Georgia*, 269 F. Supp. 3d 1266, 1274–75 (N.D. Ga. 2017) (three-judge court).

D. Retrogression

Once it has been determined that a particular proposed change is "with respect to voting" and therefore requires preclearance, it becomes necessary to examine the standards by which the Attorney General or the D.C. District Court will decide to grant or deny preclearance. The VRA provides that preclearance should be granted only if the proposed change "does not have the purpose and will not have the effect of denying or abridging the right to vote on account of race or color." 52 U.S.C. § 10304. But what does it mean to "deny[]" or "abridg[e]" the right to vote? Specifically, what is the baseline against which to compare the proposed change? Should preclearance be denied only if the change makes the existing situation worse, *i.e.*, abridges voting power relative to the status quo? Or should preclearance be denied to any plan that fails to give racial groups the voting power to which they are enti tled, even if the proposed change modestly improves the existing situation?

In *Beer v. United States*, 425 U.S. 130 (1976), the Court interpreted "abridg[e]" to mean a reduction in voting power as compared to the status quo. Thus, a proposed change that had the effect of improving the political power of a racial group could not be said to have abridged it, even if neither the proposed plan nor the existing one gave the group the representation to which it was entitled. As the Court later explained, "The term 'abridge' * * *—whose core meaning is 'shorten'—necessarily entails a comparison. * * * In § 5 preclearance proceedings—which uniquely deal only and specifically with *changes* in voting procedures—the baseline is the status quo that is proposed to be changed." *Reno v. Bossier Parish School Board*, 528 U.S. 320, 333–34 (2000). Further, the Court provided a policy-based justification for its "retrogressive" interpretation: "To deny preclearance to a plan that is *not* retrogressive—*no matter how unconstitutional it may be*—would risk leaving in effect a status quo that is even worse." *Id.* at 336.

Bossier Parish extended *Beer* to hold that the "purpose" to discriminate proscribed by § 5 was a retrogressive purpose. Thus, after *Bossier Parish*, preclearance was to be denied only if a proposed change actually reduced a racial minority's voting power relative to the status quo, or was intended to do so.

In 2006, Congress amended § 5 to overturn the *Bossier Parish* holding, but it left the *Beer* holding intact. Title 52 U.S.C. § 10304(c) now provides that "purpose" in the preclearance provisions "shall include any discriminatory purpose." Thus, the VRA now provides that preclearance should be denied when a covered jurisdiction acts with a "discriminatory," albeit nonretrogressive, purpose, or with a retrogressive effect. Thus, the "effect" inquiry uses the existing law as the baseline of comparison, while the "purpose" inquiry uses a hypothetical nondiscriminatory regime as its baseline. Does the new provision render the preclearance requirement unconstitutional? *See* Abigail Thernstrom, Voting Rights—and Wrongs: The Elusive Quest for Racially Fair Elections 176–78 (2009); Nathaniel Persily, *The Promise and Pitfalls of the New Voting Rights Act*, 117 Yale L.J. 174, 217 n.165 (2007).

Retrogression is not always as simple as comparing the numbers of majority-minority districts in the challenged plan and the benchmark plan. The next case looks at Georgia's creation of "influence" districts and examines how they affect the retrogression analysis.

Georgia v. Ashcroft

Supreme Court of the United States
539 U.S. 461, 123 S. Ct. 2498, 156 L. Ed. 2d 428 (2003)

JUSTICE O'CONNOR delivered the opinion of the Court [in which CHIEF JUSTICE REHNQUIST, JUSTICE SCALIA, JUSTICE KENNEDY, and JUSTICE THOMAS join].

In this case, we decide whether Georgia's [2001] State Senate redistricting plan should have been precleared under § 5 of the Voting Rights Act of 1965, 42 U.S.C. § 1973c [now 52 U.S.C. § 10304 — Eds.]. * * *

All parties here concede that the 1997 plan is the benchmark plan for this litigation because it was in effect at the time of the 2001 redistricting effort. The 1997 plan drew 56 districts, 11 of them with a total black population of over 50%, and 10 of them with a black voting age population of over 50%. The 2000 census revealed that these numbers had increased so that 13 districts had a black population of at least 50%, with the black voting age population exceeding 50% in 12 of those districts.

After the 2000 census, the Georgia General Assembly began the process of redistricting the Senate once again. No party contests that a substantial majority of black voters in Georgia vote Democratic, or that all elected black representatives in the General Assembly are Democrats. The goal of the Democratic leadership — black and white — was to maintain the number of majority-minority districts and also increase the number of Democratic Senate seats. * * * Part of the Democrats' strategy was not only to maintain the number of majority-minority districts, but to increase the number of so-called "influence" districts, where black voters would be able to exert a significant — if not decisive — force in the election process. * * *

The plan as designed by the Senate "unpacked" the most heavily concentrated majority-minority districts in the benchmark plan, and created a number of new influence districts. The new plan drew 13 districts with a majority-black voting age population, 13 additional districts with a black voting age population of between 30% and 50%, and 4 other districts with a black voting age population of between 25% and 30%. According to the 2000 census, as compared to the benchmark plan, the new plan reduced by five the number of districts with a black voting age population in excess of 60%. Yet it increased the number of majority-black voting age population districts by one, and it increased the number of districts with a black voting age population of between 25% and 50% by four. As compared to the benchmark plan enacted in 1997, the difference is even larger. Under the old census figures, Georgia had 10 Senate districts with a majority-black voting age population, and 8 Senate districts with a black voting age population of between 30% and 50%. The new plan thus increased the number of districts with a majority black voting age population by three, and increased the number of districts with a black voting age population of between 30% and 50% by another five.

The Senate adopted its new districting plan on August 10, 2001, by a vote of 29 to 26. Ten of the eleven black Senators voted for the plan. The Georgia House of

Representatives passed the Senate plan by a vote of 101 to 71. Thirty-three of the thirty-four black Representatives voted for the plan. No Republican in either the House or the Senate voted for the plan, making the votes of the black legislators necessary for passage. The Governor signed the Senate plan into law on August 24, 2001, and Georgia subsequently sought to obtain preclearance [from the D.C. District Court]. * * * A three-judge panel of the District Court held that Georgia's State Senate apportionment violated § 5, and was therefore not entitled to preclearance. * * *

After the District Court refused to preclear the plan, Georgia enacted another plan, largely similar to the one at issue here, except that it added black voters to Districts 2, 12, and 26. The District Court precleared this plan. No party has contested the propriety of the District Court's preclearance of the Senate plan as amended. Georgia asserts that it will use the plan as originally enacted if it receives preclearance.

We noted probable jurisdiction to consider whether the District Court should have precleared the plan as originally enacted by Georgia in 2001, and now vacate the judgment below. * * *

Georgia argues that * * * its State Senate plan should be precleared because it does not lead to "a retrogression in the position of racial minorities with respect to their effective exercise of the electoral franchise." *Beer* v. *United States*, [425 U.S. 130,] 141 [(1976)].

While we have never determined the meaning of "effective exercise of the electoral franchise," this case requires us to do so in some detail. First, the United States and the District Court correctly acknowledge that in examining whether the new plan is retrogressive, the inquiry must encompass the entire statewide plan as a whole. Thus, while the diminution of a minority group's effective exercise of the electoral franchise in one or two districts may be sufficient to show a violation of § 5, it is only sufficient if the covered jurisdiction cannot show that the gains in the plan as a whole offset the loss in a particular district.

Second, any assessment of the retrogression of a minority group's effective exercise of the electoral franchise depends on an examination of all the relevant circumstances, such as the ability of minority voters to elect their candidate of choice, the extent of the minority group's opportunity to participate in the political process, and the feasibility of creating a nonretrogressive plan. See, *e.g.*, *Johnson* v. *De Grandy*, 512 U.S. 997, 1011–1012, 1020–1021 (1994) [p. 334]; *Thornburg* v. *Gingles*, [478 U.S. 30,] 97–100 [(1986)] [p. 316] (O'CONNOR, J., concurring in judgment). "No single statistic provides courts with a shortcut to determine whether" a voting change retrogresses from the benchmark. *De Grandy, supra,* at 1020–1021.

In assessing the totality of the circumstances, a court should not focus solely on the comparative ability of a minority group to elect a candidate of its choice. While this factor is an important one in the § 5 retrogression inquiry, it cannot be dispositive or exclusive. The standard in § 5 is simple—whether the new plan "would lead to a retrogression in the position of racial minorities with respect to their effective exercise of the electoral franchise." *Beer,* 425 U.S., at 141.

The ability of minority voters to elect a candidate of their choice is important but often complex in practice to determine. In order to maximize the electoral success of a minority group, a State may choose to create a certain number of "safe" districts, in which it is highly likely that minority voters will be able to elect the candidate of their choice. Alternatively, a State may choose to create a greater number of districts in which it is likely—although perhaps not quite as likely as under the benchmark plan—that minority voters will be able to elect candidates of their choice.

Section 5 does not dictate that a State must pick one of these methods of redistricting over another. Either option "will present the minority group with its own array of electoral risks and benefits," and presents "hard choices about what would truly 'maximize' minority electoral success." On one hand, a smaller number of safe majority-minority districts may virtually guarantee the election of a minority group's preferred candidate in those districts. Yet even if this concentration of minority voters in a few districts does not constitute the unlawful packing of minority voters, such a plan risks isolating minority voters from the rest of the state, and risks narrowing political influence to only a fraction of political districts. And while such districts may result in more "descriptive representation" because the representatives of choice are more likely to mirror the race of the majority of voters in that district, the representation may be limited to fewer areas.

On the other hand, spreading out minority voters over a greater number of districts creates more districts in which minority voters may have the opportunity to elect a candidate of their choice. Such a strategy has the potential to increase "substantive representation" in more districts, by creating coalitions of voters who together will help to achieve the electoral aspirations of the minority group. It also, however, creates the risk that the minority group's preferred candidate may lose. * * * Section 5 gives States the flexibility to choose one theory of effective representation over the other.

In addition to the comparative ability of a minority group to elect a candidate of its choice, the other highly relevant factor in a retrogression inquiry is the extent to which a new plan changes the minority group's opportunity to participate in the political process. "The power to influence the political process is not limited to winning elections." *Thornburg* v. *Gingles, supra,* at 99 (O'CONNOR, J., concurring in judgment) (quoting *Davis* v. *Bandemer,* 478 U.S. 109, 132 (1986)); see also *White* v. *Regester,* 412 U.S. 755, 766–767 (1973) [p. 288]; *Whitcomb* v. *Chavis,* 403 U.S. 124, 149–160 (1971) [p. 282]; *Johnson* v. *De Grandy,* 512 U.S., at 1011–1012.

Thus, a court must examine whether a new plan adds or subtracts "influence districts"—where minority voters may not be able to elect a candidate of choice but can play a substantial, if not decisive, role in the electoral process. In assessing the comparative weight of these influence districts, it is important to consider "the likelihood that candidates elected without decisive minority support would be willing to take the minority's interests into account." *Id.*, at 100 (O'CONNOR, J., concurring in judgment). * * *

Section 5 leaves room for States to use * * * influence and coalitional districts. Indeed, the State's choice ultimately may rest on a political choice of whether substantive or descriptive representation is preferable. The State may choose, consistent with §5, that it is better to risk having fewer minority representatives in order to achieve greater overall representation of a minority group by increasing the number of representatives sympathetic to the interests of minority voters. See [*id.*], at 87–89, 99.

In addition to influence districts, one other method of assessing the minority group's opportunity to participate in the political process is to examine the comparative position of legislative leadership, influence, and power for representatives of the benchmark majority-minority districts. * * * Indeed, in a representative democracy, the very purpose of voting is to delegate to chosen representatives the power to make and pass laws. The ability to exert more control over that process is at the core of exercising political power. A lawmaker with more legislative influence has more potential to set the agenda, to participate in closed-door meetings, to negotiate from a stronger position, and to shake hands on a deal. Maintaining or increasing legislative positions of power for minority voters' representatives of choice, while not dispositive by itself, can show the lack of retrogressive effect under §5.

And it is also significant, though not dispositive, whether the representatives elected from the very districts created and protected by the Voting Rights Act support the new districting plan. * * * The representatives of districts created to ensure continued minority participation in the political process have some knowledge about how "voters will probably act" and whether the proposed change will decrease minority voters' effective exercise of the electoral franchise. * * *

Given the evidence submitted in this case, we find that Georgia likely met its burden of showing nonretrogression. * * * Section 5 gives States the flexibility to implement the type of plan that Georgia has submitted for preclearance—a plan that increases the number of districts with a majority-black voting age population, even if it means that in some of those districts, minority voters will face a somewhat reduced opportunity to elect a candidate of their choice. * * *

The purpose of the Voting Rights Act is to prevent discrimination in the exercise of the electoral franchise and to foster our transformation to a society that is no longer fixated on race. * * * While courts and the Department of Justice should be vigilant in ensuring that States neither reduce the effective exercise of the electoral franchise nor discriminate against minority voters, the Voting Rights Act, as properly interpreted, should encourage the transition to a society where race no longer matters: a society where integration and color-blindness are not just qualities to be proud of, but are simple facts of life.

The District Court is in a better position to reweigh all the facts in the record in the first instance in light of our explication of retrogression. The judgment of the District Court for the District of Columbia, accordingly, is vacated, and the case is remanded for further proceedings consistent with this opinion.

It is so ordered.

JUSTICE KENNEDY, concurring.

As is evident from the Court's accurate description of the facts in this case, race was a predominant factor in drawing the lines of Georgia's State Senate redistricting map. If the Court's statement of facts had been written as the preface to consideration of a challenge brought under the Equal Protection Clause or under § 2 of the Voting Rights Act of 1965, a reader of the opinion would have had sound reason to conclude that the challenge would succeed. Race cannot be the predominant factor in redistricting under our decision in *Miller* v. *Johnson*, 515 U.S. 900 (1995) [p. 376]. Yet considerations of race that would doom a redistricting plan under the Fourteenth Amendment or § 2 seem to be what save it under § 5.

I agree that our decisions controlling the § 5 analysis require the Court's ruling here. The discord and inconsistency between §§ 2 and 5 should be noted, however; and in a case where that issue is raised, it should be confronted. There is a fundamental flaw, I should think, in any scheme in which the Department of Justice is permitted or directed to encourage or ratify a course of unconstitutional conduct in order to find compliance with a statutory directive. This serious issue has not been raised here, and, as already observed, the Court is accurate both in its summary of the facts and its application of the controlling precedents. With these observations, I join the opinion of the Court.

JUSTICE THOMAS, concurring.

I continue to adhere to the views expressed in my opinion in *Holder* v. *Hall*, 512 U.S. 874, 891 (1994) [p. 343] (opinion concurring in judgment). I join the Court's opinion because it is fully consistent with our § 5 precedents.

JUSTICE SOUTER, with whom JUSTICE STEVENS, JUSTICE GINSBURG, and JUSTICE BREYER join, dissenting.

I agree with the Court that reducing the number of majority-minority districts within a State would not necessarily amount to retrogression barring preclearance under § 5 of the Voting Rights Act of 1965. The prudential objective of § 5 is hardly betrayed if a State can show that a new districting plan shifts from supermajority districts, in which minorities can elect their candidates of choice by their own voting power, to coalition districts, in which minorities are in fact shown to have a similar opportunity when joined by predictably supportive nonminority voters.

Before a State shifts from majority-minority to coalition districts, however, the State bears the burden of proving that nonminority voters will reliably vote along with the minority. It must show not merely that minority voters in new districts may have some influence, but that minority voters will have effective influence translatable into probable election results comparable to what they enjoyed under the existing district scheme. And to demonstrate this, a State must do more than produce reports of minority voting age percentages; it must show that the probable voting behavior of nonminority voters will make coalitions with minorities a real prospect. If the State's evidence fails to convince a factfinder that high racial polarization in voting is unlikely, or that high white crossover voting is likely, or that other political and demographic facts point to probable minority effectiveness, a reduction in supermajority districts must be treated as potentially and fatally retrogressive, the burden of persuasion always being on the State. * * *

The Court * * * alternatively suggest[s] that a potentially retrogressive redistricting plan could satisfy § 5 if a sufficient number of so-called "influence districts," in addition to "coalition districts" were created, or if the new plan provided minority groups with an opportunity to elect a particularly powerful candidate. On either alternative, the § 5 requirement that voting changes be nonretrogressive is substantially diminished and left practically unadministrable. * * *

The history of § 5 demonstrates that it addresses changes in state law intended to perpetuate the exclusion of minority voters from the exercise of political power. * * * In addressing the burden to show no retrogression, therefore, "influence" must mean an opportunity to exercise power effectively.

The Court, however, says that influence may be adequate to avoid retrogression from majority-minority districts when it consists not of decisive minority voting power but of sentiment on the part of politicians: influence may be sufficient when it reflects a willingness on the part of politicians to consider the interests of minority voters, even when they do not need the minority votes to be elected. The Court holds, in other words, that there would be no retrogression when the power of a voting majority of minority voters is eliminated, so long as elected politicians can be expected to give some consideration to minority interests.

The power to elect a candidate of choice has been forgotten; voting power has been forgotten. It is very hard to see anything left of the standard of nonretrogression * * *.

Indeed, to see the trouble ahead, one need only ask how on the Court's new understanding, state legislators or federal preclearance reviewers under § 5 are supposed to identify or measure the degree of influence necessary to avoid the retrogression the Court nominally retains as the § 5 touchstone. Is the test purely *ad hominem*, looking merely to the apparent sentiments of incumbents who might run in the new districts? Would it be enough for a State to show that an incumbent had previously promised to consider minority interests before voting on legislative measures? Whatever one looks to, however, how does one put a value on influence that falls short of decisive influence through coalition? Nondecisive influence is worth less than majority-minority control, but how much less? Would two influence districts offset the loss of one majority-minority district? Would it take three? Or four? The Court gives no guidance for measuring influence that falls short of the voting strength of a coalition member, let alone a majority of minority voters. Nor do I see how the Court could possibly give any such guidance. The Court's "influence" is simply not functional in the political and judicial worlds.

Identical problems of comparability and administrability count at least as much against the Court's further gloss on nonretrogression, in its novel holding that a State may trade off minority voters' ability to elect a candidate of their choice against their ability to exert some undefined degree of influence over a candidate likely to occupy a position of official legislative power. The Court implies that one majority-minority district in which minority voters could elect a legislative leader could replace a larger number of majority-minority districts with ordinary candidates, without retrogression of overall minority voting strength. Under this approach to § 5, a State may value minority votes in a district in which a potential committee chairman might be elected differently from minority votes in a district with ordinary candidates.

It is impossible to believe that Congress could ever have imagined § 5 preclearance actually turning on any such distinctions. In any event, if the Court is going to allow a State to weigh minority votes by the ambitiousness of candidates the votes might be cast for, it is hard to see any stopping point. I suppose the Court would not go so far as to give extra points to an incumbent with the charisma to attract a legislative following, but would it value all committee chairmen equally? (The committee chairmen certainly would not.) And what about a legislator with a network of influence that has made him a proven dealmaker? Thus, again, the problem of measurement: is a shift from 10 majority-minority districts to 8 offset by a good chance that one of the 8 may elect a new Speaker of the House? * * *One is left to ask who will suffer most from the Court's new and unquantifiable standard. If it should turn out that an actual, serious burden of persuasion remains on the States, States that rely on the new theory of influence should be guaranteed losers: nonretrogression cannot be demonstrated by districts with minority influence too amorphous for objective comparison. But that outcome is unlikely, and if in subsequent cases the Court allows the State's burden to be satisfied on the pretense that unquantifiable influence can be equated with majority-minority power, § 5 will simply drop out as a safeguard against the "unremitting and ingenious defiance of the Constitution" that required the procedure of preclearance in the first place.

Notes and Questions

1. In applying *Georgia v. Ashcroft*, how is one to know when a decrease in majority-minority districts has been offset by other increases in the political power of a minority group? *Cf. Whitcomb v. Chavis*, 403 U.S. 124, 170 (1971) [p. 282] (opinion of Harlan, J.) ("If there are less appropriate subjects for federal judicial inquiry [than the relative influence of legislators], they do not come readily to mind.").

2. Did the 2001 plan improve black voting strength over that experienced under the 1997 plan? Is that a different question from asking whether the 2001 plan improved *Democratic* voting strength?

3. Should this case have come out differently if the black legislative delegation were more evenly split on the wisdom of the 2001 plan?

4. The 2006 amendments to the Voting Rights Act added a new provision, now codified at 52 U.S.C. § 10304(b), which provides, "Any voting qualification or pre-requisite to voting, or standard, practice, or procedure with respect to voting that has the purpose of or will have the effect of diminishing the ability of any citizens of the United States on account of race or color, or [status as a language minority], to elect their preferred candidates of choice denies or abridges the right to vote within the meaning of" the statute, and should therefore result in a denial of preclear-ance. To what extent does the amendment overrule *Georgia v. Ashcroft*? *See* Abigail Thernstrom, Voting Rights — and Wrongs: The Elusive Quest for Racially Fair Elections 178–82 (2009); Nathaniel Persily, *The Promise and Pitfalls of the New Voting Rights Act*, 117 Yale L.J. 174, 216–51 (2007). Is it fair to characterize the amendment as placing covered jurisdictions in a "straitjacket" by requiring them to perform "a dual obligation: creating both majority-minority districts and main-taining those in which minority representation is increased by the potential for cre-ating political coalitions in which black or Hispanic voters are a political force"? Thernstrom, *supra*, at 179.

5. Under the 2006 amendments, how is one to determine whether a change in an election law would have the effect of "diminishing [minorities' ability] to elect their preferred candidates of choice"? *Alabama Legislative Black Caucus v. Alabama*, 575 U.S. 254 (2015), involved a redistricting plan put in place by the Alabama leg-islature. In an attempt to gain preclearance, the state attempted to ensure that the new plan not only preserved the number of majority-minority districts, but also minorities' voting strength within each majority-minority district. For example, if a district under the previous plan was 70% minority, the line-drawers attempted to ensure that the district would continue to be 70% minority. Otherwise, Alabama feared, the new plan would diminish minorities' voting strength. After all, as we have learned, because not all eligible voters turn out, and because of crossover votes, a slim population majority in a district hardly ensures that a group will be able to elect its candidates of choice. Thus, a reduction of minority population from 70% to, say, 55% in a district could diminish the minority's ability to elect its candidates of choice, even if the number of majority-minority districts remained constant.

The Supreme Court held that §5 of the VRA was not so constraining. In the Court's view, the question of the diminishment of minority voting strength required a more "complex" analysis than simply a comparison of the percentage of minori-ties in a district before and after the district lines were redrawn. *Id.* at 278. Rather, it required courts to "take account of all significant circumstances" bearing on minor-ities' voting power. *Id.* Thus, while reducing the percentage of minorities in a district *might* decrease that group's ability to elect its preferred candidates, it might not.

In dissent, Justice Thomas criticized the Court's vague standard as "requir[ing] States to analyze race even *more* exhaustively, not less, by accounting for black voter registration and turnout statistics." *Id.* at 305 (Thomas, J., dissenting). Was Justice

Thomas correct that "States covered by § 5 have been whipsawed, first required to create 'safe' majority-black districts, then told not to 'diminis[h]' the ability to elect, and now told they have been too rigid in preventing and 'diminishing' of the ability to elect"? *Id.*

6. *Problem.* West Carolina, a covered jurisdiction, submits to the Attorney General a proposed change to its election laws that would keep the polls open an additional hour from 6:00 p.m. until 7:00 p.m. The purpose is to reduce lines at the polls and to make voting more convenient. Because a greater proportion of whites than blacks have jobs ending between 5:00 and 7:00, however, the effect of the change would be to dilute black voting strength by permitting a higher percentage of whites to vote than would be the case if polls closed at 6:00. Should the Attorney General grant preclearance?

7. In protesting the Court's entry into the "political thicket," Justices Frankfurter and Harlan argued that there can be no judicially manageable standards for the allocation of political power. In particular, Justice Harlan's dissent in *Reynolds v. Sims*, 377 U.S. 533 (1964) [p. 122], which we encountered in Chapter 2, noted that

> cases of this type are not amenable to the development of judicial standards. No set of standards can guide a court which has to decide how many legislative districts a State shall have, or what the shape of the districts shall be, or where to draw a particular district line. No judicially manageable standard can determine whether a State should have single member districts or multi-member districts or some combination of both.

Id. at 621 (Harlan, J., dissenting). And in *Baker v. Carr*, 369 U.S. 186 (1962) [p. 97], which also appears in Chapter 2, Justice Frankfurter argued that the Equal Protection Clause provided no judicially manageable standards against which to evaluate the constitutionality of apportionment decisions:

> Appellants invoke the right to vote and to have their votes counted. But they are permitted to vote, and their votes are counted. They go to the polls, they cast their ballots, they send their representatives to the state councils. Their complaint is simply that the representatives are not sufficiently numerous or powerful—in short, that Tennessee has adopted a basis of representation with which they are dissatisfied. Talk of "debasement" or "dilution" is circular talk. One cannot speak of "debasement" or "dilution" of the value of a vote until there is first defined a standard of reference as to what a vote should be worth. What is actually asked of the Court in this case is to choose among competing bases of representation—ultimately, really, among competing theories of political philosophy—in order to establish an appropriate frame of government for the State of Tennessee, and thereby for all the States of the Union.

Id. at 299–300 (Frankfurter, J., dissenting). Does the Court's difficulty in formulating a test for retrogression under § 5 prove that Justices Frankfurter and Harlan were correct?

Chapter 4

Race-Conscious Districting

A. Introduction

Preventing and remedying racial discrimination were the principal objectives of both the Voting Rights Act and the Civil War Amendments. As with race-conscious decisions concerning employment and school admissions, however, the use of race in electoral districting is controversial. Some argue that states (in drawing district lines) and Congress (in passing the VRA) should be able to protect minorities' interests by ensuring that they have an opportunity to influence the political process, even if such efforts involve the explicit consideration of race. Others, however, note that the use of race by government is constitutionally suspect, and argue that the goal of a color-blind society is unlikely to be achieved if we promote racial and ethnic separatism by drawing district lines according to race and ethnicity.

In the next section of this Chapter, we examine the degree to which the Equal Protection Clause prevents states from minimizing the electoral influence of minorities. The one-person, one-vote doctrine and the constitutional protection of the right to vote ensure that members of minority groups have some access to the ballot. But the right to vote does little by itself to ensure effective political power. Districts can be drawn to absorb minority voices within larger communities, resulting in those voices going unheard. Yet individual voters do not have a right to be in a district of their choice or to have their favored candidates elected. Accordingly, while it can be intuitively obvious that drawing district lines to exclude minorities should be unconstitutional, *see Gomillion v. Lightfoot*, 364 U.S. 339 (1960) [p. 279], it is not as obvious why any individual excluded from a particular district has been deprived of either his right to vote or the equal protection of the laws.

Constitutional challenges to the distribution of political power beg an important question: How much political power *should* any group possess? The Court has been consistent in holding that nothing in the Constitution entitles groups to representation proportional to their share of the population. Short of that standard, however, it is difficult or impossible to agree on another way to determine whether a given policy denies a group the power it is due. The Court has addressed this problem by holding that minorities may not prevail on a claim of vote dilution simply by showing a lack of success at the polls. Rather, a successful plaintiff must demonstrate that access to the broader political process has been hindered, or that minorities' electoral prospects have been minimized over a series of electoral cycles. Racial discrimination or burdensome registration requirements, for example, may comprise part of a state scheme that unconstitutionally dilutes minorities' political influence beyond merely producing disproportionate results in a given election.

Even those election laws that dilute minorities' political influence in election after election may not be unconstitutional. In fact, they may not even trigger strict scrutiny. Rather, as a plurality of the Court held in *City of Mobile v. Bolden*, 446 U.S. 55 (1980) [p. 302], the Fifteenth Amendment requires plaintiffs to prove both a disparate *effect* on minorities' political power and a discriminatory *purpose* on the part of the state.

Congress's reaction to *Bolden* forms the basis for § C of this Chapter. There we confront the 1982 amendments to § 2 of the Voting Rights Act. Those amendments replaced statutory language modeled on the Fifteenth Amendment (and therefore, *Bolden* held, required proof of both discriminatory purpose and effect) with a strictly effects-based test. The amended § 2 declared unlawful a state's voting practice or procedure "which results in a denial or abridgement of the right of any citizen of the United States to vote on account of race or color" or status as a member of a language minority. 52 U.S.C. § 10301(a). The statute further directed courts to find violations where, "based on the totality of circumstances, it is shown that the political processes leading to nomination or election in the State or political subdivision are not equally open to participation by members of a class of citizens protected by subsection (a) in that its members have less opportunity than other members of the electorate to participate in the political process and to elect representatives of their choice." 52 U.S.C. § 10301(b).

In *Thornburg v. Gingles*, 478 U.S. 30 (1986) [p. 316], the Court determined that plaintiffs in a § 2 suit must satisfy three "preconditions" before a court will proceed to the totality-of-the-circumstances test.

> First, the minority group must be able to demonstrate that it is sufficiently large and geographically compact to constitute a majority in a single-member district. * * * Second, the minority group must be able to show that it is politically cohesive. * * * Third, the minority must be able to demonstrate that the white majority votes sufficiently as a bloc to enable it * * * usually to defeat the minority's preferred candidate.

Id. at 50–51. The second and third requirements together are referred to as "racially polarized voting."

If a plaintiff can satisfy the three *Gingles* preconditions, the plaintiff still must demonstrate that, considering the totality of the circumstances, members of the plaintiff's minority group have an unequal opportunity "to participate in the political process and to elect representatives of their choice." 52 U.S.C. § 10301(b). In determining whether a minority group's opportunity is equal to that of other voters, courts will take into account whether the group controls a "roughly proportional" number of legislative seats compared to its population. *See Johnson v. De Grandy*, 512 U.S. 997, 1000 (1994) [p. 334].

Section D continues to examine VRA § 2, concentrating on the section's scope. Section 2, like § 5, applies to "standard[s], practice[s], and procedure[s]," and in general the meaning of the § 2 phrase tracks the meaning of the corollary provision in § 5, which was covered in Chapter 3. Because the purposes of §§ 2 and 5 are different, however (§ 5 protects against retrogression, while § 2 protects minorities from laws that diminish their voting power relative to the strength they "should" possess), occasionally controversies arise. For example, in *Chisom v. Roemer*, 501 U.S. 380 (1991), the Court held that § 2's protection of the equal opportunity to elect "representatives" extended to vote-dilution claims involving judicial elections. And in *Holder v. Hall*, 512 U.S. 874 (1994) [p. 343], the Court considered whether the size of a governmental body—concededly within the scope of § 5's preclearance requirement—could be the subject of a § 2 challenge. The Court held that it could not, although the five Justices agreeing on that conclusion were badly split as to rationale.

We return to the Equal Protection Clause in § E. There, we consider the Court's racial-gerrymandering decisions that limit the ability of states to draw district lines according to race, even as a way of protecting minorities' voting power. *Shaw v. Reno*, 509 U.S. 630 (1993) [p. 362], established a constitutional cause of action for a gerrymander that segregates voters by race, and *Miller v. Johnson*, 515 U.S. 900 (1995) [p. 376], clarified that the constitutional violation recognized by *Shaw* occurs when the state disregards traditional districting criteria, such as the districts' compactness, and predominantly focuses on race.

The VRA and *Shaw* placed districters between a rock and a hard place. VRA § 2 required states to consider race in creating majority-minority districts, while *Shaw* forbade states from excessively considering race in creating majority-minority districts. Section F considers that quandary. The Court has held, consistent with *Gingles*'s language, that § 2 provides no right for a minority group to control the election of a representative unless the minority group is numerous enough to comprise a majority in a single-member district. *See Bartlett v. Strickland*, 556 U.S. 1 (2009). However, states may decide for themselves to create "influence" or "coalition" districts, in which minorities exercise control or influence over the selection of representatives despite not having a majority of the district's population. In "influence" districts, minorities do not have the ability to elect their preferred candidates, but can influence the choice of candidates. In "coalition" districts, minorities do elect their candidates of choice, but with the assistance of majority "crossover" voters who vote for the minority's preferred candidate. The power minorities exercise in such districts may be relevant to determining whether a state has violated § 2 or § 5 in depriving minority voters of the political power to which they are entitled. *See Georgia v. Ashcroft*, 539 U.S. 461 (2003) [p. 266].

B. Constitutional Constraints on Minority Vote Dilution

We introduced the next case, *Gomillion v. Lightfoot*, in Chapter 2. There, we were primarily concerned with the question whether federal courts had jurisdiction to adjudicate the constitutionality of laws setting district and municipal boundaries. We return to *Gomillion* now and focus on the merits question: To what degree does the Constitution limit government's ability to draw electoral districts so as to minimize the political power of minorities? As you will see, *Gomillion's* rationale was difficult to determine, and after the decision it remained unclear exactly what showing would be necessary to prove that a districting scheme abridged the constitutional right to vote. The fundamental problem in articulating such a standard is the same problem we saw in Chapter 2, namely, that it is necessary to establish a baseline representing the political power that a group should enjoy before it is possible to determine whether a law "dilutes" that amount.

In a series of cases in the 1970s, the Court attempted to clarify the constitutional protection against vote dilution. The Court was unwilling to accept one potential baseline—that the Constitution entitles groups to legislative representation commensurate with their share of the population. In the Court's view, all political groups should bear the risks that come with politics—that the popularity of candidates and parties varies from year to year, for example, and accordingly no group should be guaranteed a proportional share of representation when such a guarantee would free those groups from fielding popular candidates and appealing to voters. The Court also did not want to limit its consideration of political influence to a group's ability to elect its favored candidates. Political power, said the Court, was more nuanced than simple vote totals. Accordingly, in *White v. Regester*, 412 U.S. 755, 766 (1973) [p. 288], the Court held that a vote-dilution claim could succeed only when the plaintiffs demonstrated that they "had less opportunity than did other residents in the district to participate in the political process and to elect legislators of their choice."

In *City of Mobile v. Bolden*, 446 U.S. 55 (1980) [p. 302], a plurality of the Court held that plaintiffs must show not only that the challenged law had the effect of disproportionately reducing the political power of the disfavored group, but also that the law was motivated by a discriminatory purpose. Congress reacted to *Bolden* by amending § 2 of the Voting Rights Act to forbid states from taking actions that had the effect of diluting the political power of minorities, regardless of the purpose behind those actions. That amendment is the subject of the next section.

Gomillion v. Lightfoot

Supreme Court of the United States
364 U.S. 339, 81 S. Ct. 125, 5 L. Ed. 2d 110 (1960)

MR. JUSTICE FRANKFURTER delivered the opinion of the Court [in which MR. CHIEF JUSTICE WARREN, MR. JUSTICE BLACK, MR. JUSTICE DOUGLAS, MR. JUSTICE CLARK, MR. JUSTICE HARLAN, MR. JUSTICE BRENNAN, and MR. JUSTICE STEWART join].

This litigation challenges the validity, under the United States Constitution, of Local Act No. 140, passed by the Legislature of Alabama in 1957, redefining the boundaries of the City of Tuskegee. * * * Petitioners' claim is that enforcement of the statute, which alters the shape of Tuskegee from a square to an uncouth twenty-eight-sided figure, will constitute a discrimination against them in violation of the Due Process and Equal Protection Clauses of the Fourteenth Amendment to the Constitution and will deny them the right to vote in defiance of the Fifteenth Amendment. * * *

* * * The complaint, charging that Act 140 is a device to disenfranchise Negro citizens, alleges the following facts: Prior to Act 140 the City of Tuskegee was square in shape; the Act transformed it into a strangely irregular twenty-eight-sided figure as indicated in the diagram appended to this opinion. The essential inevitable effect of this redefinition of Tuskegee's boundaries is to remove from the city all save four or five of its 400 Negro voters while not removing a single white voter or resident. The result of the Act is to deprive the Negro petitioners discriminatorily of the benefits of residence in Tuskegee, including, *inter alia*, the right to vote in municipal elections.

These allegations, if proven, would abundantly establish that Act 140 was not an ordinary geographic redistricting measure even within familiar abuses of gerrymandering. If these allegations upon a trial remained uncontradicted or unqualified, the conclusion would be irresistible, tantamount for all practical purposes to a mathematical demonstration, that the legislation is solely concerned with segregating white and colored voters by fencing Negro citizens out of town so as to deprive them of their pre-existing municipal vote.

It is difficult to appreciate what stands in the way of adjudging a statute having this inevitable effect invalid in light of the principles by which this Court must judge, and uniformly has judged, statutes that, howsoever speciously defined, obviously discriminate against colored citizens. "The [Fifteenth] Amendment nullifies sophisticated as well as simple-minded modes of discrimination." *Lane* v. *Wilson*, 307 U.S. 268, 275 [(1939)].

The complaint amply alleges a claim of racial discrimination. Against this claim the respondents have never suggested, either in their brief or in oral argument, any countervailing municipal function which Act 140 is designed to serve. The respondents invoke generalities expressing the State's unrestricted power—unlim-ited, that is, by the United States Constitution—to establish, destroy, or reorganize by contraction or expansion its political subdivisions, to wit, cities, counties, and other local units. We freely recognize the breadth and importance of this aspect of the State's political power. To exalt this power into an absolute is to misconceive the reach and rule of this Court's [prior] decisions[.] * * *

This line of authority conclusively shows that the Court has never acknowledged that the States have power to do as they will with municipal corporations regard-less of consequences. Legislative control of municipalities, no less than other state power, lies within the scope of relevant limitations imposed by the United States Constitution. * * * The opposite conclusion, urged upon us by respondents, would sanction the achievement by a State of any impairment of voting rights whatever so long as it was cloaked in the garb of the realignment of political subdivisions. "It is inconceivable that guaranties embedded in the Constitution of the United States may thus be manipulated out of existence." *Frost & Frost Trucking Co.* v. *Railroad Commission of California*, 271 U.S. 583, 594 [(1926)].

* * * The petitioners here complain that affirmative legislative action deprives them of their votes and the consequent advantages that the ballot affords. When a legislature thus singles out a readily isolated segment of a racial minority for special discriminatory treatment, it violates the Fifteenth Amendment. * * * A statute which is alleged to have worked unconstitutional deprivations of petition-ers' rights is not immune to attack simply because the mechanism employed by the legislature is a redefinition of municipal boundaries. According to the allega-tions here made, the Alabama Legislature has not merely redrawn the Tuskegee city limits with incidental inconvenience to the petitioners; it is more accurate to say that it has deprived the petitioners of the municipal franchise and consequent rights and to that end it has incidentally changed the city's boundaries. While in form this is merely an act redefining metes and bounds, if the allegations are established, the inescapable human effect of this essay in geometry and geogra-phy is to despoil colored citizens, and only colored citizens, of their theretofore enjoyed voting rights. * * *

When a State exercises power wholly within the domain of state interest, it is insulated from federal judicial review. But such insulation is not carried over when state power is used as an instrument for circumventing a federally protected right. * * *

For these reasons, the principal conclusions of the District Court and the Court of Appeals are clearly erroneous and the decision below must be

Reversed.

MR. JUSTICE DOUGLAS, while joining the opinion of the Court, adheres to the dissents in *Colegrove* v. *Green* and *South* v. *Peters*, 339 U.S. 276 [(1950)].

CHART SHOWING TUSKEGEE, ALABAMA, BEFORE AND AFTER ACT 140

(The entire area of the square comprised the City prior to
Act 140. The irregular black-bordered figure within the
square represents the post-enactment city.)

MR. JUSTICE WHITTAKER, concurring.

I concur in the Court's judgment, but not in the whole of its opinion. It seems to
me that the decision should be rested not on the Fifteenth Amendment, but rather
on the Equal Protection Clause of the Fourteenth Amendment to the Constitution.
I am doubtful that the averments of the complaint, taken for present purposes to be
true, show a purpose by Act No. 140 to abridge petitioners' "right . . . to vote," in the
Fifteenth Amendment sense. It seems to me that the "right . . . to vote" that is guaranteed by the Fifteenth Amendment is but the same right to vote as is enjoyed by
all others within the same election precinct, ward or other political division. And,
inasmuch as no one has the right to vote in a political division, or in a local election
concerning only an area in which he does not reside, it would seem to follow that
one's right to vote in Division A is not abridged by a redistricting that places his
residence in Division B if he there enjoys the same voting privileges as all others in
that Division, even though the redistricting was done by the State for the purpose of
placing a racial group of citizens in Division B rather than A.

But it does seem clear to me that accomplishment of a State's purpose—to use
the Court's phrase—of "fencing Negro citizens out of" Division A and into Division B is an unlawful segregation of races of citizens, in violation of the Equal

Protection Clause of the Fourteenth Amendment, *Brown* v. *Board of Education*, 347 U.S. 483 [(1954)]; *Cooper* v. *Aaron*, 358 U.S. 1 [(1959)]; and, as stated, I would think the decision should be rested on that ground * * *.

Notes and Questions

1. Under *Gomillion*, how can one determine whether someone's constitutional rights are violated by a boundary line that keeps him outside a district or a municipality? Was the "uncouth" shape of the post-Act-140 city relevant to the holding? Was Act 140 unconstitutional because of the Alabama legislature's purpose? What evidence was there of the legislature's purpose?

2. Justice Whittaker preferred to rest *Gomillion* on the Fourteenth Amendment rather than the Fifteenth. Was he right to do so? How were the plaintiffs denied the right to vote? How were they denied the equal protection of the laws?

Whitcomb v. Chavis

Supreme Court of the United States
403 U.S. 124, 91 S. Ct. 1858, 29 L. Ed. 2d 363 (1971)

Mr. Justice White delivered the opinion of the Court [in which Mr. Chief Justice Burger, Mr. Justice Black, Mr. Justice Stewart, and Mr. Justice Blackmun join.] * * *

Indiana has a bicameral general assembly consisting of a house of representatives of 100 members and a senate of 50 members. Eight of the 31 senatorial districts and 25 of the 39 house districts are multi-member districts, that is, districts that are represented by two or more legislators elected at large by the voters of the district. Under the statutes here challenged, Marion County is a multi-member district electing eight senators and 15 members of the house. * * *

{Plaintiffs level two quite distinct challenges to the Marion County district. The first charge is that any multi-member district bestows on its voters several unconstitutional advantages over voters in single-member districts or smaller multi-member districts. The other allegation is that the Marion County district, on the record of this case, illegally minimizes and cancels out the voting power of a cognizable racial minority in Marion County. The District Court sustained the latter claim and considered the former sufficiently persuasive to be a substantial factor in prescribing uniform, single-member districts as the basic scheme of the court's own plan.}

The question of the constitutional validity of multi-member districts has been pressed in this Court since the first of the modern reapportionment cases. * * * [S]uch a district is not *per se* illegal under the Equal Protection Clause. *Fortson* v. *Dorsey*, 379 U.S. 433 (1965); *Burns* v. *Richardson*, 384 U.S. 73 (1966); *Kilgarlin* v. *Hill*, 386 U.S. 120 (1967). That voters in multi-member districts vote for and are represented by more legislators than voters in single-member districts has so far not demonstrated an invidious discrimination against the latter. But we have deemed the validity of multi-member district systems justiciable, recognizing also that they may be subject to challenge where the circumstances of a particular case may "operate to minimize or cancel out the voting strength of racial or political elements of the voting population." *Fortson*, 379 U.S., at 439, and *Burns*, 384 U.S., at 88. Such a tendency, we have said, is enhanced when the district is large and elects a substantial proportion of the seats in either house of a bicameral legislature, if it is multi-member for both houses of the legislature or if it lacks provision for at-large candidates running from particular geographical subdistricts, as in *Fortson*. *Burns*, 384 U.S., at 88. But we have insisted that the challenger carry the burden of proving that multi-member districts unconstitutionally operate to dilute or cancel the voting strength of racial or political elements. We have not yet sustained such an attack. * * *

In asserting discrimination against voters outside Marion County, plaintiffs recognize that *Fortson*, *Burns*, and *Kilgarlin* proceeded on the assumption that the dilution of voting power suffered by a voter who is placed in a district 10 times the population of another is cured by allocating 10 legislators to the larger district instead of the one assigned to the smaller district. Plaintiffs challenge this assumption at both the voter and legislator level. They demonstrate mathematically that in theory voting power does not vary inversely with the size of the district and that to increase legislative seats in proportion to increased population gives undue voting power to the voter in the multimember district since he has more chances to determine election outcomes than does the voter in the single-member district. [The theory analyzes the chance of any particular voter in a district casting a tie-breaking or "critical" vote. Because voters in multi-member districts can determine the election of multiple representatives, their ability to cast a "critical" vote is enhanced.] This consequence obtains wholly aside from the quality or effectiveness of representation later furnished by the successful candidates. The District Court did not quarrel with plaintiffs' mathematics, nor do we. But like the District Court we note that the position remains a theoretical one and, as plaintiffs' witness conceded, knowingly avoids and does "not take into account any political or other factors which might affect the actual voting power of the residents, which might include party affiliation, race, previous voting characteristics or any other factors which go into the entire political voting situation." The real-life impact of multi-member districts on individual voting power has not been sufficiently demonstrated, at least on this record, to warrant departure from prior cases.

The District Court was more impressed with the other branch of the claim that multi-member districts inherently discriminate against other districts. This was the assertion that whatever the individual voting power of Marion County voters in choosing legislators may be, they nevertheless have more effective representation in the Indiana general assembly for two reasons. First, each voter is represented by more legislators and therefore, in theory at least, has more chances to influence critical legislative votes. Second, since multimember delegations are elected at large and represent the voters of the entire district, they tend to vote as a bloc, which is tantamount to the district having one representative with several votes. * * *

We are not ready, however, to agree that multi-member districts, wherever they exist, overrepresent their voters as compared with voters in single-member districts, even if the multi-member delegation tends to bloc voting. The theory that plural representation itself unduly enhances a district's power and the influence of its voters remains to be demonstrated in practice and in the day-to-day operation of the legislature. * * *

* * * Moreover, Marion County would have no less advantage, if advantage there is, if it elected from individual districts and the elected representatives demonstrated the same bloc-voting tendency, which may also develop among legislators representing singlemember districts widely scattered throughout the State. Of course it is advantageous to start with more than one vote for a bill. But nothing before us shows or suggests that any legislative skirmish affecting the State of Indiana or Marion County in particular would have come out differently had Marion County been subdistricted and its delegation elected from single-member districts.

Rather than squarely finding unacceptable discrimination against outstate voters in favor of Marion County voters, the trial court struck down Marion County's multi-member district because it found the scheme worked invidiously against a specific segment of the county's voters as compared with others. The court identified an area of the city as a ghetto, found it predominantly inhabited by poor Negroes with distinctive substantive-law interests and thought this group unconstitutionally underrepresented because the proportion of legislators with residences in the ghetto elected from 1960 to 1968 was less than the ghetto's proportion of the population, less than the proportion of legislators elected from Washington Township, a less populous district, and less than the ghetto would likely have elected had the county consisted of single-member districts. We find major deficiencies in this approach.

First, * * * there is no suggestion here that Marion County's multi-member district, or similar districts throughout the State, were conceived or operated as purposeful devices to further racial or economic discrimination. * * *

Nor does the fact that the number of ghetto residents who were legislators was not in proportion to ghetto population satisfactorily prove invidious discrimination absent evidence and findings that ghetto residents had less opportunity than did other Marion County residents to participate in the political processes and to elect legislators of their choice. We have discovered nothing in the record or in the court's findings indicating that poor Negroes were not allowed to register or vote, to choose the political party they desired to support, to participate in its affairs or to be equally represented on those occasions when legislative candidates were chosen. Nor did the evidence purport to show or the court find that inhabitants of the ghetto were regularly excluded from the slates of both major parties, thus denying them the chance of occupying legislative seats. It appears reasonably clear that the Republican Party won four of the five elections from 1960 to 1968, that Center Township ghetto voted heavily Democratic and that ghetto votes were critical to Democratic Party success. [Democrats appear to have slated candidates satisfactory to the ghetto throughout that period, but prevailed only in 1964.] * * * [I]t seems reasonable to infer that had the Democrats won all of the elections or even most of them, the ghetto would have had no justifiable complaints about representation. The fact is, however, that four of the five elections were won by Republicans, which was not the party of the ghetto and which would not always slate ghetto candidates—although in 1962 it nominated and elected one representative and in 1968 two representatives from that area. If this is the proper view of this case, the failure of the ghetto to have legislative seats in proportion to its population emerges more as a function of losing elections than of built-in bias against poor Negroes. The voting power of ghetto residents may have been "cancelled out" as the District Court held, but this seems a more euphemism for political defeat at the polls.

On the record before us plaintiffs' position comes to this: that although they have equal opportunity to participate in and influence the selection of candidates and legislators, and although the ghetto votes predominantly Democratic and that party slates candidates satisfactory to the ghetto, invidious discrimination nevertheless results when the ghetto, along with all other Democrats, suffers the disaster of losing too many elections. But typical American legislative elections are district-oriented, head-on races between candidates of two or more parties. As our system has it, one candidate wins, the others lose. Arguably the losing candidates' supporters are without representation since the men they voted for have been defeated; arguably they have been denied equal protection of the laws since they have no legislative voice of their own. This is true of both single-member *and* multi-member districts. But we have not yet deemed it a denial of equal protection to deny legislative seats to losing candidates, even in those so-called "safe" districts where the same party wins year after year.

* * * [T]he District Court thought the ghetto voters' claim to the partial allegiance of eight senators and 15 representatives was not equivalent to the undivided allegiance of one senator and two representatives; nor was the ghetto voters' chance of influencing the election of an entire slate as significant as the guarantee of one ghetto senator and two ghetto representatives. As the trial court saw it, ghetto voters could not be adequately and equally represented unless some of Marion County's general assembly seats were reserved for ghetto residents serving the interests of the ghetto majority. But are poor Negroes of the ghetto any more underrepresented than poor ghetto whites who also voted Democratic and lost, or any more discriminated against than other interest groups or voters in Marion County with allegiance to the Democratic Party, or, conversely, any less represented than Republican areas or voters in years of Republican defeat? We think not. The mere fact that one interest group or another concerned with the outcome of Marion County elections has found itself outvoted and without legislative seats of its own provides no basis for invoking constitutional remedies where, as here, there is no indication that this segment of the population is being denied access to the political system. * * *

The District Court's holding, although on the facts of this case limited to guaranteeing one racial group representation, is not easily contained. It is expressive of the more general proposition that any group with distinctive interests must be represented in legislative halls if it is numerous enough to command at least one scat and represents a majority living in an area sufficiently compact to constitute a single-member district. This approach would make it difficult to reject claims of Democrats, Republicans, or members of any political organization in Marion County who live in what would be safe districts in a single-member district system but who in one year or another, or year after year, are submerged in a one-sided multi-member district vote. There are also union oriented workers, the university community, religious or ethnic groups occupying identifiable areas of our hetero-geneous cities and urban areas. Indeed, it would be difficult for a great many, if not most, multi-member districts to survive analysis under the District Court's view unless combined with some voting arrangement such as proportional representa-tion or cumulative voting aimed at providing representation for minority parties or interests. At the very least, affirmance of the District Court would spawn endless litigation concerning the multi-member district systems now widely employed in this country.[37]

We are not insensitive to the objections long voiced to multi-member district plans. Although not as prevalent as they were in our early history, they have been with us since colonial times and were much in evidence both before and after the adoption of the Fourteenth Amendment.[39] Criticism is rooted in their winner-take-all aspects, their tendency to submerge minorities and to overrepresent the winning party as compared with the party's statewide electoral position, a general prefer-ence for legislatures reflecting community interests as closely as possible and disen-chantment with political parties and elections as devices to settle policy differences between contending interests. The chance of winning or significantly influencing intraparty fights and issue-oriented elections has seemed to some inadequate protec-tion to minorities, political, racial, or economic; rather, their voice, it is said, should also be heard in the legislative forum where public policy is finally fashioned. In our view, however, experience and insight have not yet demonstrated that multi-member districts are inherently invidious and violative of the Fourteenth Amendment. * * * Moreover, if the problems of multi-member districts are unbearable or even uncon-stitutional it is not at all clear that the remedy is a single-member district system with its lines carefully drawn to ensure representation to sizable racial, ethnic, economic, or religious groups and with its own capacity for overrepresenting and underrep-resenting parties and interests and even for permitting a minority of the voters to control the legislature and government of a State. The short of it is that we are unpre-pared to hold that district-based elections decided by plurality vote are unconstitu-tional in either single- or multi-member districts simply because the supporters of

---

37. As of November 1970, 46% of the upper houses and 62% of the lower houses in the States contained some multi-member districts. * * *

39. In colonial days, "[m]ultiple districts were the rule, single ones the exception," and "[f]or nearly a century and a half after the Declaration of Independence the American states elected by far the greater part of their lawmakers in multiple constituencies." * * *

losing candidates have no legislative seats assigned to them. As presently advised we hold that the District Court misconceived the Equal Protection Clause in applying it to invalidate the Marion County multi-member district. * * *

We therefore reverse the judgment of the District Court and remand the case to that court for further proceedings consistent with this opinion.

It is so ordered.

[Mr. Justice Stewart joins the portions of the Court's opinion reprinted here, but dissents from an omitted portion concerning one person, one vote.]

Separate opinion of Mr. Justice Harlan. * * *

[The Court neither suggests a manner of determining when voting power has been unconstitutionally distributed] nor considers the consequences of its inability to measure what it purports to be equalizing. Instead it becomes enmeshed in the haze of slogans and numerology which for 10 years has obscured its vision in this field, and finally remands the case "for further proceedings consistent with [its] opinion." This inexplicit mandate is at least subject to the interpretation that the court below is to inquire into such matters as "the actual influence of Marion County's delegation in the Indiana Legislature" and the possibility of "recurring poor performance by Marion County's delegation with respect to Center Township ghetto," with a view to determining whether "any legislative skirmish affecting the State of Indiana or Marion County in particular would have come out differently had Marion County been subdistricted and its delegation elected from single-member districts." If there are less appropriate subjects for federal judicial inquiry, they do not come readily to mind. The suggestion implicit in the Court's opinion that appellees may ultimately prevail if they can make their record in these and other like respects should be recognized for what it is: a manifestation of frustration by a Court that has become trapped in the "political thicket" and is looking for the way out.

* * * I hope the day will come when the Court will frankly recognize the error of its ways in ever having undertaken to restructure state electoral processes. * * *

Mr. Justice Douglas, with whom Mr. Justice Brennan and Mr. Justice Marshall concur, dissenting in part and concurring in the result in part. * * *

The problem of the gerrymander is how to defeat or circumvent the sentiments of the community. The problem of the law is how to prevent it. * * *

It is said that if we prevent racial gerrymandering today, we must prevent gerrymandering of any special interest group tomorrow, whether it be social, economic, or ideological. I do not agree. Our Constitution has a special thrust when it come to voting; the Fifteenth Amendment says the right of citizens to vote shall not be "abridged" on account of "race, color, or previous condition of servitude."

Our cases since *Baker* v. *Carr* have never intimated that "one man, one vote" meant "one white man, one vote." Since "race" may not be gerrymandered, I think the Court emphasizes the irrelevant when it says that the effect on "the actual voting power" of the blacks should first be known. They may be all Democratic or all Republican; but once their identity is purposely washed out of the system, the system, as I see it, has a constitutional defect. It is asking the impossible for us to demand that the blacks first show that the effect of the scheme was to discourage or prevent poor blacks from voting or joining such party as they chose. On this record, the voting rights of the blacks have been "abridged," as I read the Constitution. * * *

I would affirm the judgment.

Notes and Questions

1. Why did the Court disregard the mathematical analysis of voting power offered by the plaintiffs? Do you agree with Justice Harlan's criticism (in an omitted portion of his separate opinion) that "[t]he only relevant difference between the elementary arithmetic on which the Court relies [in the 'one man, one vote' cases] and the elementary probability theory on which [plaintiffs] rel[y] is that calculations in the latter field cannot be done on one's fingers"? 403 U.S. at 168 n.2 (opinion of Harlan, J.).

2. What rule results from this case? What must plaintiffs show to demonstrate that electoral districts—though complying with the one-person, one-vote mandate—nevertheless allocate political power unconstitutionally? The next case may provide some insight . . . or further confusion.

White v. Regester

Supreme Court of the United States
412 U.S. 755, 93 S. Ct. 2332, 37 L. Ed. 2d 314 (1973)

Mr. Justice White delivered the opinion of the Court [in which Mr. Chief Justice Burger, Mr. Justice Douglas, Mr. Justice Brennan, Mr. Justice Stewart, Mr. Justice Marshall, Mr. Justice Blackmun, Mr. Justice Powell, and Mr. Justice Rehnquist join]. * * *

* * * [The 150-member Texas House of Representatives is selected from] 79 single-member and 11 multimember districts. [Plaintiffs sued, alleging that the] multimember districts for Bexar County and Dallas County operated to dilute the voting strength of racial and ethnic minorities. [The District Court held the multimember districts unconstitutional and ordered that they be redrawn into single-member districts. We affirm.] * * *

* * * Plainly, under our cases, multimember districts are not *per se* unconstitutional, nor are they necessarily unconstitutional when used in combination with single-member districts in other parts of the State. *Whitcomb* v. *Chavis*, 403 U.S. 124 (1971) [p. 282]. But we have entertained claims that multimember districts are being used invidiously to cancel out or minimize the voting strength of racial groups. To

sustain such claims, it is not enough that the racial group allegedly discriminated against has not had legislative seats in proportion to its voting potential. The plaintiffs' burden is to produce evidence to support findings that the political processes leading to nomination and election were not equally open to participation by the group in question—that its members had less opportunity than did other residents in the district to participate in the political processes and to elect legislators of their choice. [*Id.*] at 149–150.

With due regard for these standards, the District Court first referred to the history of official racial discrimination in Texas, which at times touched the right of Negroes to register and vote and to participate in the democratic processes. It referred also to the Texas rule requiring a majority vote as a prerequisite to nomination in a primary election and to the so-called "place" rule limiting candidacy for legislative office from a multimember district to a specified "place" on the ticket, with the result being the election of representatives from the Dallas multimember district reduced to a head-to-head contest for each position. These characteristics of the Texas electoral system, neither in themselves improper nor invidious, enhanced the opportunity for racial discrimination, the District Court thought.[10] More fundamentally, it found that since Reconstruction days, there have been only two Negroes in the Dallas County delegation to the Texas House of Representatives and that these two were the only two Negroes ever slated by the Dallas Committee for Responsible Government (DCRG), a white-dominated organization that is in effective control of Democratic Party candidate slating in Dallas County. That organization, the District Court found, did not need the support of the Negro community to win elections in the county, and it did not therefore exhibit good-faith concern for the political and other needs and aspirations of the Negro community. The court found that as recently as 1970 the DCRG was relying upon "racial campaign tactics in white precincts to defeat candidates who had the overwhelming support of the black community." Based on the evidence before it, the District Court concluded that "the black community has been effectively excluded from participation in the Democratic primary selection process," and was therefore generally not permitted to enter into the political process in a reliable and meaningful manner. These findings and conclusions are sufficient to sustain the District Court's judgment with respect to the Dallas multimember district and, on this record, we have no reason to disturb them.

The same is true of the order requiring disestablishment of the multimember district in Bexar County. * * * Surveying the historic and present condition of the Bexar County Mexican-American community, which is concentrated for the most part on the west side of the city of San Antonio, the court observed, based upon prior cases and the record before it, that the Bexar community, along with other Mexican-Americans in Texas, had long "suffered from, and continues to suffer

---

10. There is no requirement that candidates reside in subdistricts of the multimember district. Thus, all candidates may be selected from outside the Negro residential area.

from, the results and effects of invidious discrimination and treatment in the fields of education, employment, economics, health, politics and others." The bulk of the Mexican-American community in Bexar County occupied the Barrio, an area consisting of about 28 contiguous census tracts in the city of San Antonio. Over 78% of Barrio residents were Mexican-Americans, making up 29% of the county's total population. The Barrio is an area of poor housing; its residents have low income and a high rate of unemployment. The typical Mexican-American suffers a cultural and language barrier that makes his participation in community processes extremely difficult, particularly, the court thought, with respect to the political life of Bexar County. "[A] cultural incompatibility . . . conjoined with the poll tax and the most restrictive voter registration procedures in the nation have operated to effectively deny Mexican-Americans access to the political processes in Texas even longer than the Blacks were formally denied access by the white primary." The residual impact of this history reflected itself in the fact that Mexican-American voting registration remained very poor in the county and that only five Mexican-Americans since 1880 have served in the Texas Legislature from Bexar County. Of these, only two were from the Barrio area. The District Court also concluded from the evidence that the Bexar County legislative delegation in the House was insufficiently responsive to Mexican-American interests.

Based on the totality of the circumstances, the District Court evolved its ultimate assessment of the multimember district, overlaid, as it was, on the cultural and economic realities of the Mexican-American community in Bexar County and its relationship with the rest of the county. Its judgment was that Bexar County Mexican-Americans "are effectively removed from the political processes of Bexar [County] in violation of all the *Whitcomb* standards, whatever their absolute numbers may total in that County." Single-member districts were thought required to remedy "the effects of past and present discrimination against Mexican-Americans," and to bring the community into the full stream of political life of the county and State by encouraging their further registration, voting, and other political activities.

The District Court apparently paid due heed to *Whitcomb* v. *Chavis*, did not hold that every racial or political group has a constitutional right to be represented in the state legislature, but did, from its own special vantage point, conclude that the multimember district, as designed and operated in Bexar County, invidiously excluded Mexican-Americans from effective participation in political life, specifically in the election of representatives to the Texas House of Representatives. On the record before us, we are not inclined to overturn these findings, representing as they do a blend of history and an intensely local appraisal of the design and impact of the Bexar County multimember district in the light of past and present reality, political and otherwise.

Affirmed in part, reversed in part, and remanded.

[MR. JUSTICE BRENNAN, with MR. JUSTICE DOUGLAS and MR. JUSTICE MAR-SHALL, joins the portion of the Court's opinion reprinted here, but dissents from the Court's acceptance, in this case and in *Gaffney* v. *Cummings*, 412 U.S. 735 (1973) [p. 168], of variations up to 9.9% in the populations of state-legislative districts.]

Notes and Questions

1. What accounted for the different results in this case and in *Whitcomb v. Chavis*?

2. By the time *Regester* was argued and decided, Justices Black and Harlan had left the Court and had been replaced by Justices Powell and Rehnquist. If Justice Harlan were still on the Court, what would his reaction have been to the *Regester* opinion? Imagine that you are his law clerk, and draft a separate opinion that would reflect his thoughts.

United Jewish Organizations, Inc. v. Carey

Supreme Court of the United States
430 U.S. 144, 97 S. Ct. 996, 51 L. Ed. 2d 229 (1977)

MR. JUSTICE WHITE announced the judgment of the Court and filed an opinion in which MR. JUSTICE STEVENS joined; Parts I, II, and III of which are joined by MR. JUSTICE BRENNAN and MR. JUSTICE BLACKMUN; and Parts I and IV of which are joined by MR. JUSTICE REHNQUIST.

* * * The question presented is whether, in the circumstances of this case, the use of racial criteria by the State of New York in its attempt to comply with § 5 of the Voting Rights Act and to secure the approval of the Attorney General violated the Fourteenth or Fifteenth Amendment.

I

Kings County [Brooklyn], N.Y., together with New York (Manhattan) and Bronx Counties, became subject to §§ 4 and 5 of the Act, by virtue of a determination by the Attorney General that a literacy test was used in these three counties as of November 1, 1968, and a determination by the Director of the Census that fewer than 50% of the voting-age residents of these three counties voted in the Presidential election of 1968. * * * On January 31, 1974, the provisions of the [1972] statute districting these counties for congressional, state senate, and state assembly seats were submitted to the Attorney General. * * * On April 1, 1974, the Attorney General concluded that, as to certain districts in Kings County covering the Bedford-Stuyvesant area of Brooklyn, the State had not met the burden placed on it by § 5 and the regulations thereunder to demonstrate that the redistricting had neither the purpose nor the effect of abridging [blacks' and Puerto Ricans'] right to vote by reason of race or color.{[5]}

---

5. * * * The NAACP [which submitted a memorandum to the Attorney General opposing the 1972 plan], the Attorney General, and the court below classified Puerto Ricans in New York together with blacks as a minority group entitled to the protections of the Voting Rights Act. * * *

Under § 5, the State could have challenged the Attorney General's objections to the redistricting plan by filing a declaratory judgment action in a three-judge court in the District of Columbia. Instead, the State sought to meet what it understood to be the Attorney General's objections and to secure his approval in order that the 1974 primary and general elections could go forward under the 1972 statute. A revised plan, submitted to the Attorney General on May 31, 1974, in its essentials did not change the number of districts with nonwhite majorities, but did change the size of the nonwhite majorities in most of those districts. * * * The report of the legislative committee on reapportionment stated that these changes were made "to overcome Justice Department objections" by creating more "substantial nonwhite majorities" in two assembly districts and two senate districts. [The Attorney General precleared the 1974 plan.]

One of the communities affected by these revisions in the Kings County reapportionment plan was the Williamsburgh area, where about 30,000 Hasidic Jews live. Under the 1972 plan, the Hasidic community was located entirely in one assembly district (61% nonwhite) and one senate district (37% nonwhite); in order to create substantial nonwhite majorities in these districts, the 1974 revisions split the Hasidic community between two senate and two assembly districts. A staff member of the legislative reapportionment committee testified that in the course of meetings and telephone conversations with Justice Department officials, he "got the feeling . . . that 65 percent would be probably an approved figure" for the nonwhite population in the assembly district in which the Hasidic community was located, a district approximately 61% nonwhite under the 1972 plan. To attain the 65% figure, a portion of the white population, including part of the Hasidic community, was reassigned to an adjoining district. * * *

Shortly after the State submitted this revised plan for Kings County to the Attorney General, petitioners sued on behalf of the Hasidic Jewish community of Williamsburgh, alleging that the 1974 plan "would dilute the value of each plaintiff's franchise by halving its effectiveness," solely for the purpose of achieving a racial quota and therefore in violation of the Fourteenth Amendment. Petitioners also alleged that they were assigned to electoral districts solely on the basis of race, and that this racial assignment diluted their voting power in violation of the Fifteenth Amendment. [The District Court dismissed the complaint, and the Court of Appeals affirmed.] * * *

II

Petitioners argue that the New York Legislature, although seeking to comply with the Voting Rights Act as construed by the Attorney General, has violated the Fourteenth and Fifteenth Amendments by deliberately revising its reapportionment plan along racial lines. * * * [But] neither the Fourteenth nor the Fifteenth Amendment mandates any *per se* rule against using racial factors in districting and apportionment. * * * [Further, t]he permissible use of racial criteria is not confined to eliminating the effects of past discriminatory districting or apportionment.[19]

Moreover, in the process of drawing black majority districts in order to comply with § 5, the State must [place a certain percentage of minorities in a district] as a necessary means to ensure the opportunity for the election of a black representative and to obtain approval of its reapportionment plan. [A] reapportionment cannot violate the Fourteenth or Fifteenth Amendment merely because a State uses specific numerical quotas in establishing a certain number of black majority districts. Our cases under § 5 [which permit the federal government to deny preclearance to "retrogressive" districting plans that reduce the number of districts controlled by minorities] stand for at least this much.

III

[W]e turn to the * * * question * * * whether the racial criteria New York used in this case—the revision of the 1972 plan to create 65% nonwhite majorities in two additional senate and two additional assembly districts—were constitutionally infirm. We hold they are not, on two separate grounds. * * *

The first ground is that petitioners have not shown, or offered to prove, that New York did more than the Attorney General was authorized to require it to do under the non-retrogression principle of *Beer* [*v. United States*, 425 U.S. 130 (1976)], a principle that, as we have already indicated, this Court has accepted as constitutionally valid. Under *Beer*, the acceptability of New York's 1972 reapportionment for purposes of § 5 depends on the change in nonwhite voting strength in comparison with the previous apportionment, which occurred in 1966. Yet there is no evidence in the record to show whether the 1972 plan increased or decreased the number of senate or assembly districts with substantial nonwhite majorities of 65%. For all that petitioners have alleged or proved, the 1974 revisions may have accomplished nothing more than the restoration of nonwhite voting strength to 1966 levels. To be successful in their constitutional challenge to the racial criteria used in New York's revised plan, petitioners must show at a minimum that minority voting strength was increased under the 1974 plan in comparison with the 1966 apportionment; otherwise the challenge amounts to a constitutional attack on compliance with the statutory rule of non-retrogression.

In the absence of any evidence regarding nonwhite voting strength under the 1966 apportionment, the creation of substantial nonwhite majorities in approximately 30% of the senate and assembly districts in Kings County was reasonably

---

19. Petitioners also insist that, because the Attorney General concluded not that the 1972 plan would have a discriminatory effect but only that the State had failed to demonstrate that the plan would not have such an effect, there was insufficient justification for racial redistricting. This argument overlooks the central role of the shift in burden of proof in the congressional effort to combat discriminatory voting laws. Our cases have upheld this shift. * * *

related to the constitutionally valid statutory mandate of maintaining nonwhite voting strength. The percentage of districts with nonwhite majorities was less than the percentage of nonwhites in the county as a whole (35%). The size of the nonwhite majorities in those districts reflected the need to take account of the substantial difference between the nonwhite percentage of the total population in a district and the nonwhite percentage of the voting-age population.[22] * * * We think it was reasonable for the Attorney General to conclude in this case that a *substantial* nonwhite population majority—in the vicinity of 65%—would be required to achieve a nonwhite majority of eligible voters.

Petitioners have not shown that New York did more than accede to a position taken by the Attorney General that was authorized by our constitutionally permissible construction of § 5. New York adopted the 1974 plan because it sought to comply with the Voting Rights Act. * * *

IV

[Additionally there is] a second, and independent, ground for sustaining the particulars of the 1974 plan for Kings County. Whether or not the plan was authorized by or was in compliance with § 5 of the Voting Rights Act, New York was free to do what it did as long as it did not violate the Constitution, particularly the Fourteenth and Fifteenth Amendments; and we are convinced that neither Amendment was infringed.

There is no doubt that in preparing the 1974 legislation the State deliberately used race in a purposeful manner. But its plan represented no racial slur or stigma with respect to whites or any other race, and we discern no discrimination violative of the Fourteenth Amendment nor any abridgment of the right to vote on account of race within the meaning of the Fifteenth Amendment.

It is true that New York deliberately increased the nonwhite majorities in certain districts in order to enhance the opportunity for election of nonwhite representatives from those districts. Nevertheless, there was no fencing out the white population from participation in the political processes of the county, and the plan did not minimize or unfairly cancel out white voting strength. Compare *White* v. *Regester*, 412 U.S. [755,] 765–767 [(1973)] [p. 288], and *Gomillion* v. *Lightfoot*, 364 U.S. 339 (1960) [p. 279], with *Gaffney* v. *Cummings*, 412 U.S. 735, 751–754 (1973) [p. 168]. Petitioners have not objected to the impact of the 1974 plan on the representation of white voters in the county or in the State as a whole. [T]he plan left white majorities in approximately 70% of the assembly and senate districts in Kings County, which had a countywide population that was 65% white. Thus, even if voting in the county occurred strictly according to race, whites would not be underrepresented relative to their share of the population.

---

22. The NAACP, intervenor in this action, submitted census data to the Attorney General showing that roughly 75% of all whites in Kings County but only about 55% of all nonwhites were eligible to vote. * * *

In individual districts where nonwhite majorities were increased to approximately 65%, it became more likely, given racial bloc voting, that black candidates would be elected instead of their white opponents, and it became less likely that white voters would be represented by a member of their own race; but as long as whites in Kings County, as a group, were provided with fair representation, we cannot conclude that there was a cognizable discrimination against whites or an abridgment of their right to vote on the grounds of race.[24] Furthermore, the individual voter in the district with a nonwhite majority has no constitutional complaint merely because his candidate has lost out at the polls and his district is represented by a person for whom he did not vote. Some candidate, along with his supporters, always loses. See *Whitcomb* v. *Chavis*, 403 U.S. [124,] 153–160 [(1971)] [p. 282].

Where it occurs, voting for or against a candidate because of his race is an unfortunate practice. But it is not rare; and in any district where it regularly happens, it is unlikely that any candidate will be elected who is a member of the race that is in the minority in that district. However disagreeable this result may be, there is no authority for the proposition that the candidates who are found racially unacceptable by the majority, and the minority voters supporting those candidates, have had their Fourteenth or Fifteenth Amendment rights infringed by this process. Their position is similar to that of the Democratic or Republican minority that is submerged year after year by the adherents to the majority party who tend to vote a straight party line.

It does not follow, however, that the State is powerless to minimize the consequences of racial discrimination by voters when it is regularly practiced at the polls. In *Gaffney* v. *Cummings*, the Court upheld a districting plan "drawn with the conscious intent to . . . achieve a rough approximation of the statewide political strengths of the Democratic and Republican Parties." 412 U.S., at 752. We there recognized that districting plans would be vulnerable under our cases if "*racial or political groups* have been fenced out of the political process and their voting strength invidiously minimized," *id.*, at 754 (emphasis added); but that was not the case there, and no such purpose or effect may be ascribed to New York's 1974 plan. Rather, that plan can be viewed as seeking to alleviate the consequences of racial voting at the polls and to achieve a fair allocation of political power between white and nonwhite voters in Kings County.

In this respect New York's revision of certain district lines is little different in kind from the decision by a State in which a racial minority is unable to elect

---

24. We also note that the white voter who as a result of the 1974 plan is in a district more likely to return a nonwhite representative will be represented, to the extent that voting continues to follow racial lines, by legislators elected from majority white districts. The effect of the reapportionment on whites in districts where nonwhite majorities have been increased is thus mitigated by the preservation of white majority districts in the rest of the county. Of course, if voting does not follow racial lines, the white voter has little reason to complain that the percentage of nonwhites in his district has been increased.

representatives from multimember districts to change to single-member districting for the purpose of increasing minority representation. This change might substantially increase minority representation at the expense of white voters, who previously elected all of the legislators but who with single-member districts could elect no more than their proportional share. If this intentional reduction of white voting power would be constitutionally permissible, as we think it would be, we think it also permissible for a State, employing sound districting principles such as compactness and population equality, to attempt to prevent racial minorities from being repeatedly outvoted by creating districts that will afford fair representation to the members of those racial groups who are sufficiently numerous and whose residential patterns afford the opportunity of creating districts in which they will be in the majority. * * *

The judgment is

Affirmed.

MR. JUSTICE MARSHALL took no part in the consideration or decision of this case.

MR. JUSTICE BRENNAN, concurring in part.

I join Parts I, II, and III of MR. JUSTICE WHITE's opinion. * * * Yet, because this case carries us further down the road of race-centered remedial devices than we have heretofore traveled—with the serious questions of fairness that attend such matters—I offer this further explanation of my position. * * *

If we were presented here with a classification of voters motivated by racial animus, or with a classification that effectively downgraded minority participation in the franchise, we promptly would characterize the resort to race as "suspect" and prohibit its use. Under such circumstances, the tainted apportionment process would not necessarily be saved by its proportional outcome, for the segregation of voters into "separate but equal" blocs still might well have the intent or effect of diluting the voting power of minority voters. It follows, therefore, that if the racial redistricting involved here, imposed with the avowed intention of clustering together 10 viable nonwhite majorities at the expense of preexisting white groupings, is not similarly to be prohibited, the distinctiveness that avoids this prohibition must arise from either or both of two considerations: the permissibility of affording preferential treatment to disadvantaged nonwhites generally, or the particularized application of the Voting Rights Act in this instance.

The first and broader of the two plausible distinctions rests upon the general propriety of so-called benign discrimination: The challenged race assignment may be permissible because it is cast in a remedial context with respect to a disadvantaged class rather than in a setting that aims to demean or insult any racial group. Even in the absence of the Voting Rights Act, this preferential policy plausibly could find expression in a state decision to overcome nonwhite disadvantages in voter registration or turnout through redefinition of electoral districts—perhaps, as here, through the application of a numerical rule—in order to achieve a proportional distribution of voting power. Such a decision, in my view, raises particularly sensitive issues of doctrine and policy. Unlike Part IV of Mr. Justice White's opinion,[1] I am wholly content to leave this thorny question until another day, for I am convinced that the existence of the Voting Rights Act makes such a decision unnecessary and alone suffices to support an affirmance of the judgment before us.

* * * As a focus for consideration of what * * * problems might or might not [arise from the use of race-conscious remedies], it is instructive to consider some of the objections frequently raised to the use of overt preferential race-assignment practices.

First, a purportedly preferential race assignment may in fact disguise a policy that perpetuates disadvantageous treatment of the plan's supposed beneficiaries. Accordingly, courts might face considerable difficulty in ascertaining whether a given race classification truly furthers benign rather than illicit objectives. An effort to achieve proportional representation, for example, might be aimed at aiding a group's participation in the political processes by guaranteeing safe political offices, or, on the other hand, might be a "contrivance to segregate" the group, thereby frustrating its potentially successful efforts at coalition building across racial lines. Indeed, even the present case is not entirely free of complaints that the remedial redistricting in Brooklyn is not truly benign. Puerto Rican groups, for example, who have been joined with black groups to establish the "nonwhite" category, protested to the Attorney General that their political strength under the 1974 reapportionment actually is weaker than under the invalidated 1972 districting. A black group similarly complained of the loss of a "safe" seat because of the inadequacy of the 65% target figure. These particular objections, as the Attorney General argued in his memorandum endorsing the 1974 reapportionment, may be ill-advised and unpersuasive. Nevertheless, they illustrate the risk that what is presented as an instance of benign race assignment in fact may prove to be otherwise. This concern, of course,

---

1. Part IV limits its endorsement of proportional distribution of voting power to instances where the voters are polarized along racial lines and where the State intends "no racial slur or stigma with respect to" any race. I agree that, without such qualifications, the position taken in Part IV plainly would be intolerable. Yet, even as so limited, problems remain that, in my view, merit further consideration. For example, questions concerning the polarization of voters and the motives of the state policymakers may place formidable factfinding responsibilities on the courts. Such responsibilities, I believe, are greatly lessened when the Voting Rights Act is involved. Furthermore, I am not at rest with the notion that a "cognizable discrimination" cannot be found so long as whites "as a group [are] provided with fair representation." While voting may differ from other activities or entitlements in that one group of voters often derives benefits indirectly from a legislator serving a different constituency—and to that extent I agree that the adverse effects of a racial division are "mitigated"—I am not satisfied that this vicarious benefit fully answers the Hasidim's complaint of injustice. Finally, I have serious doubts that the Court's acceptance of political-party apportionment in *Gaffney* v. *Cummings* necessarily applies to apportionment by race. Political affiliation is the keystone of the political trade. Race, ideally, is not.

does not undercut the theoretical legitimacy or usefulness of preferential policies. At the minimum, however, it does suggest the need for careful consideration of the operation of any racial device, even one cloaked in preferential garb. And if judicial detection of truly benign policies proves impossible or excessively crude, that alone might warrant invalidating any race-drawn line.

Second, even in the pursuit of remedial objectives, an explicit policy of assignment by race may serve to stimulate our society's latent race consciousness, suggesting the utility and propriety of basing decisions on a factor that ideally bears no relationship to an individual's worth or needs. Furthermore, even preferential treatment may act to stigmatize its recipient groups, for although intended to correct systemic or institutional inequities, such policy may imply to some the recipients' inferiority and especial need for protection. Again, these matters would not necessarily speak against the wisdom or permissibility of selective, benign racial classifications. But they demonstrate that the considerations that historically led us to treat race as a constitutionally "suspect" method of classifying individuals are not entirely vitiated in a preferential context.

Third, especially when interpreting the broad principles embraced by the Equal Protection Clause, we cannot well ignore the social reality that even a benign policy of assignment by race is viewed as unjust by many in our society, especially by those individuals who are adversely affected by a given classification. This impression of injustice may be heightened by the natural consequence of our governing processes that the most "discrete and insular" of whites often will be called upon to bear the immediate, direct costs of benign discrimination. Perhaps not surprisingly, there are indications that this case affords an example of just such decisionmaking in operation. For example, the respondent-intervenors take pains to emphasize that the mandated 65% rule could have been attained through redistricting strategies that did not slice the Hasidic community in half. State authorities, however, chose to localize the burdens of race reassignment upon the petitioners rather than to redistribute a more varied and diffused range of whites into predominantly non-white districts. I am in no position to determine the accuracy of this appraisal, but the impression of unfairness is magnified when a coherent group like the Hasidim disproportionately bears the adverse consequences of a race-assignment policy.

In my view, if and when a decisionmaker embarks on a policy of benign racial sorting, he must weigh the concerns that I have discussed against the need for effective social policies promoting racial justice in a society beset by deep-rooted racial inequities. But I believe that Congress here adequately struck that balance in enacting the carefully conceived remedial scheme embodied in the Voting Rights Act. However the Court ultimately decides the constitutional legitimacy of "reverse discrimination" pure and simple, I am convinced that the application of the Voting Rights Act substantially minimizes the objections to preferential treatment, and legitimates the use of even overt, numerical racial devices in electoral redistricting.

The participation of the Attorney General, for example, largely relieves the judiciary of the need to grapple with the difficulties of distinguishing benign from malign discrimination. * * * [The preclearance requirement], coupled with the fact-finding competence of the Justice Department, substantially reduces the likelihood that a complicated reapportionment plan that silently furthers malign racial policies would escape detection by appropriate officials. As a practical matter, therefore, I am prepared to accord considerable deference to the judgment of the Attorney General that a particular districting scheme complies with the remedial objectives furthered by the Voting Rights Act. * * *

This leaves, of course, the objection expressed by a variety of participants in this litigation: that this reapportionment worked the injustice of localizing the direct burdens of racial assignment upon a morally undifferentiated group of whites, and, indeed, a group that plausibly is peculiarly vulnerable to such injustice. This argument has both normative and emotional appeal, but for a variety of reasons I am convinced that the Voting Rights Act drains it of vitality.

First, it is important to recall that the Attorney General's oversight focuses upon jurisdictions whose prior practices exhibited the purpose or effect of infringing the right to vote on account of race, thereby triggering § 4 of the Act. This direct nexus to localities with a history of discriminatory practices or effects enhances the legitimacy of the Attorney General's remedial authority over individuals within those communities who benefited (as whites) from those earlier discriminatory voting patterns. Moreover, the obvious remedial nature of the Act and its enactment by an elected Congress that hardly can be viewed as dominated by nonwhite representatives belie the possibility that the decisionmaker intended a racial insult or injury to those whites who are adversely affected by the operation of the Act's provisions.[7] Finally, petitioners have not been deprived of their right to vote, a consideration that minimizes the detrimental impact of the remedial racial policies governing the § 5 reapportionment. True, petitioners are denied the opportunity to vote as a group in accordance with the earlier districting configuration, but they do not press any legal claim to a group voice as Hasidim. In terms of their voting interests, then, the burden that they claim to suffer must be attributable solely to their relegation to increased nonwhite-dominated districts. Yet, to the extent that white and nonwhite interests and sentiments are polarized in Brooklyn, the petitioners still are indirectly "protected" by the remaining white assembly and senate districts within the county, carefully preserved in accordance with the white proportion of the total county population. While these considerations obviously do not satisfy petitioners, I am persuaded that they reinforce the legitimacy of this remedy.

---

7. In this regard, it is important that * * * petitioners themselves do not protest that their treatment under the 1974 plan was motivated by anti-Semitism. Indeed, it is undeniable that the Hasidic community is contiguous to several nonwhite neighborhoods, and, therefore, understandably is a candidate for redistricting given the goal of creating 10 viable nonwhite voting majorities.

Since I find nothing in the first three parts of MR. JUSTICE WHITE's opinion that is inconsistent with the views expressed herein, I join those parts.

MR. JUSTICE STEWART, with whom MR. JUSTICE POWELL joins, concurring in the judgment. * * *

Under the Fourteenth Amendment the question is whether the reapportionment plan represents purposeful discrimination against white voters. *Washington v. Davis*, 426 U.S. 229 [(1976)]. Disproportionate impact may afford some evidence that an invidious purpose was present. *Arlington Heights* v. *Metropolitan Housing Dev. Corp.*, 429 U.S. 252, 266 [(1977)]. But the record here does not support a finding that the redistricting plan undervalued the political power of white voters relative to their numbers in Kings County. That the legislature was aware of race when it drew the district lines might also suggest a discriminatory purpose. Such awareness is not, however, the equivalent of discriminatory intent. The clear purpose with which the New York Legislature acted in response to the position of the United States Department of Justice under the Voting Rights Act forecloses any finding that it acted with the invidious purpose of discriminating against white voters.*

Having failed to show that the legislative reapportionment plan had either the purpose or the effect of discriminating against them on the basis of their race, the petitioners have offered no basis for affording them the constitutional relief they seek. Accordingly, I join the judgment of the Court.

MR. CHIEF JUSTICE BURGER, dissenting. * * *

* * * If *Gomillion* [v. *Lightfoot*, 364 U.S. 339 (1960)] [p. 279] teaches anything, I had thought it was that drawing of political boundary lines with the sole, explicit objective of reaching a predetermined racial result cannot ordinarily be squared with the Constitution. The record before us reveals and it is not disputed that this is precisely what took place here. In drawing up the 1974 reapportionment scheme, the New York Legislature did not consider racial composition as merely one of several political characteristics; on the contrary, race appears to have been the one and only criterion applied. * * *

Although reference to racial composition of a political unit may, under certain circumstances, serve as "a starting point in the process of shaping a remedy," rigid

---

* It is unnecessary to consider whether the position of the Department of Justice in this case was required or even authorized by the Voting Rights Act. It is enough to note that the Voting Rights Act and the procedures used to implement it are constitutionally valid, and that the procedures followed in this case were consistent with the Act. Congress has established an exclusive forum—the District Court for the District of Columbia—and provided exclusive standing in the State or political subdivision to raise the issue of substantive compliance with the Act. That procedure was not invoked by New York here, and the issue of statutory compliance is consequently not properly before us.

adherence to quotas, especially in a case like this, deprives citizens such as petitioners of the opportunity to have the legislature make a determination free from unnecessary bias for or against any racial, ethnic, or religious group. * * * While petitioners certainly have no constitutional right to remain unified within a single political district, they do have, in my view, the constitutional right not to be carved up so as to create a voting bloc composed of some other ethnic or racial group through the kind of racial gerrymandering the Court condemned in *Gomillion* v. *Lightfoot*. * * *

The result reached by the Court today in the name of the Voting Rights Act is ironic. The use of a mathematical formula tends to sustain the existence of ghettos by promoting the notion that political clout is to be gained or maintained by marshaling particular racial, ethnic, or religious groups in enclaves. It suggests to the voter that only a candidate of the same race, religion, or ethnic origin can properly represent that voter's interests, and that such candidate can be elected only from a district with a sufficient minority concentration. The device employed by the State of New York, and endorsed by the Court today, moves us one step farther away from a truly homogeneous society. * * *

Notes and Questions

1. How would you articulate the alleged "right" that formed the basis of the United Jewish Organizations' claim? Did the various opinions in *UJO* treat the right as one held by individuals or groups?

2. The plurality characterized its holdings in Parts III and IV as "independent." As such, in the view of some Justices at least, an unconstitutional race-conscious districting plan might be authorized by the VRA and thereby legitimized. Should Congress be able to authorize states to engage in otherwise-unconstitutional conduct?

3. The Court's usual practice is not to offer alternative holdings, especially in constitutional cases, because it prefers to decide questions of constitutional interpretation only when the proper case outcome depends on such a construction. Why might an exception have been made in this case?

4. Justice White and Justice Brennan suggested that the interests of the white residents of majority-minority districts may benefit from the support of white legislators from other districts—a concept that has come to be called "virtual representation." Do you think the Hasidim could be virtually represented by white legislators from other districts? Do you believe that a violation of one group's rights of political access can be mitigated by the representation of that group's interests within a legislative body as a whole? Reconsider this last question after you read *LULAC v. Perry*, 548 U.S. 399 (2006) [p. 395], later in this Chapter.

5. In Part II of its opinion, the plurality accepted as constitutional "specific numerical quotas" concerning the minimum number of minorities in majority-minority districts. Is such a permissive attitude toward racial quotas consistent with

modern equal-protection law? *Cf. Grutter v. Bollinger*, 539 U.S. 306 (2003); *Gratz v. Bollinger*, 539 U.S. 244 (2003).

6. In Part IV, the plurality held that states may use race-conscious means to provide minorities "fair representation," provided that they use "sound districting principles such as compactness and population equality." Even Chief Justice Burger, in dissent, accepted that states may take race into account in drawing district lines, although he believed the influence of race on the 1974 plan was constitutionally excessive. Do you agree that states may use race to some extent without violating the Constitution? How significant must racial considerations be before the constitutional threshold is crossed? Why might the constitutionality of a districting program turn on compactness? The Court, as we will see, has demonstrated a renewed interest in these questions with the line of cases beginning with *Shaw v. Reno*, 509 U.S. 630 (1993) [p. 362], which is discussed later in this Chapter.

7. Was it proper to evaluate the Hasidim as part of the white "majority" in permitting New York to sacrifice their interests to those of the Puerto Rican and black communities? *Cf. Regents of the University of California v. Bakke*, 438 U.S. 265, 295 (1978) (opinion of Powell, J.) ("[T]he white 'majority' itself is composed of various minority groups, most of which can lay claim to a history of prior discrimination at the hands of the State and private individuals."). Should the Court have treated the Hasidim themselves as a racial minority, permitting them to claim that the 1974 plan diluted their voting strength in violation of § 2 of the Voting Rights Act? How should the Constitution and the Voting Rights Act protect "minority" groups within the white "majority"?

8. Should Puerto Ricans and blacks have been considered together as a racial group of "nonwhites"? Are "Hispanics" a racial group? What about "nonwhite Hispanics"? Latinos? As each of these questions illustrates, *UJO* forces us to ask what race means, and why we view racial identity as so central to American politics. As you read the remainder of this Chapter (and the remainder of this book), consider how answers to those questions may have changed since the middle of the twentieth century.

City of Mobile v. Bolden

Supreme Court of the United States
446 U.S. 55, 100 S. Ct. 1490, 64 L. Ed. 2d 47 (1980)

MR. JUSTICE STEWART announced the judgment of the Court and delivered an opinion, in which THE CHIEF JUSTICE [BURGER], MR. JUSTICE POWELL, and MR. JUSTICE REHNQUIST joined.

The city of Mobile, Ala., has since 1911 been governed by a City Commission consisting of three members elected by the voters of the city at large. {The three Commissioners jointly exercise all legislative, executive and administrative power in the municipality. * * * As required by the state law enacted in 1911, each candidate for the Mobile City Commission runs for election in the city at large for a term of four years in one of three numbered posts, and may be elected only by a majority of the total vote. This is the same basic electoral system that is followed by literally thousands of municipalities and other local governmental units throughout the Nation.}

The appellees brought this suit in the Federal District Court for the Southern District of Alabama as a class action on behalf of all Negro citizens of Mobile. * * * The complaint alleged that the practice of electing the City Commissioners at large unfairly diluted the voting strength of Negroes in violation of § 2 of the Voting Rights Act of 1965, of the Fourteenth Amendment, and of the Fifteenth Amendment. Following a bench trial, the District Court found that the constitutional rights of the appellees had been violated, entered a judgment in their favor, and ordered that the City Commission be disestablished and replaced by a municipal government consisting of a Mayor and a City Council with members elected from single-member districts. The Court of Appeals affirmed[.] * * *

[Appellees' complaint contains not only constitutional claims, but also a] statutory claim — that the Mobile electoral system violates § 2 of the Voting Rights Act of 1965. Even a cursory examination of that claim, however, clearly discloses that it adds nothing to the appellees' complaint.

Section 2 of the Voting Rights Act provides:

"No voting qualification or prerequisite to voting, or standard, practice, or procedure shall be imposed or applied by any State or political subdivision to deny or abridge the right of any citizen of the United States to vote on account of race or color." 42 U.S.C. § 1973 [now 52 U.S.C. § 10301 — Eds.].

[I]t is apparent that the language of § 2 no more than elaborates upon that of the Fifteenth Amendment, and the sparse legislative history of § 2 makes clear that it was intended to have an effect no different from that of the Fifteenth Amendment itself.

Section 2 was an uncontroversial provision in proposed legislation whose other provisions engendered protracted dispute. The House Report on the bill simply recited that § 2 "grants . . . a right to be free from enactment or enforcement of voting qualifications . . . or practices which deny or abridge the right to vote on account of race or color." The view that this section simply restated the prohibitions already contained in the Fifteenth Amendment was expressed without contradiction during the Senate hearings. Senator Dirksen indicated at one point that all States, whether or not covered by the preclearance provisions of § 5 of the proposed legislation, were prohibited from discriminating against Negro voters by § 2, which he termed "almost a rephrasing of the 15th [A]mendment." Attorney General Katzenbach agreed.

In view of the section's language and its sparse but clear legislative history, it is evident that this statutory provision adds nothing to the appellees' Fifteenth Amendment claim. * * *

Our decisions * * * have made clear that action by a State that is racially neutral on its face violates the Fifteenth Amendment only if motivated by a discriminatory purpose. In *Guinn* v. *United States*, 238 U.S. 347 [(1915)], this Court struck down a "grandfather" clause in a state constitution exempting from the requirement that voters be literate any person or the descendants of any person who had been entitled to vote before January 1, 1866 * * *, because it was not "possible to discover any basis in reason for the standard thus fixed other than the purpose" to circumvent the Fifteenth Amendment. *Id.*, at 365.

The Court's more recent decisions confirm the principle that racially discriminatory motivation is a necessary ingredient of a Fifteenth Amendment violation. In *Gomillion* v. *Lightfoot*, 364 U.S. 339 [(1960)] [p. 279], the Court held that allegations of a racially motivated gerrymander of municipal boundaries stated a claim under the Fifteenth Amendment. The constitutional infirmity of the state law in that case, according to the allegations of the complaint, was that in drawing the municipal boundaries the legislature was "solely concerned with segregating white and colored voters by fencing Negro citizens out of town so as to deprive them of their pre-existing municipal vote." *Id.*, at 341. The Court made clear that in the absence of such an invidious purpose, a State is constitutionally free to redraw political boundaries in any manner it chooses. *Id.*, at 347.

In *Wright* v. *Rockefeller*, 376 U.S. 52 [(1964)], the Court upheld by like reasoning a state congressional reapportionment statute against claims that district lines had been racially gerrymandered, because the plaintiffs failed to prove that the legislature "was either motivated by racial considerations or in fact drew the districts on racial lines"; or that the statute "was the product of a state contrivance to segregate on the basis of race or place of origin." *Id.*, at 56, 58. See also *Lassiter* v. *Northampton Election Bd.*, 360 U.S. 45 [(1959)] [p. 11]; *Lane* v. *Wilson*, 307 U.S. 268, 275–277 [(1939)]. * * *

The answer to the appellees' argument is that, as the District Court expressly found, their freedom to vote has not been denied or abridged by anyone. The Fifteenth Amendment does not entail the right to have Negro candidates elected, and * * * prohibits only purposefully discriminatory denial or abridgment by government of the freedom to vote "on account of race, color, or previous condition of servitude." Having found that Negroes in Mobile "register and vote without hindrance," the District Court and Court of Appeals were in error in believing that the appellants invaded the protection of that Amendment in the present case. * * *

The Court of Appeals also agreed with the District Court that Mobile's at-large electoral system violates the Equal Protection Clause of the Fourteenth Amendment. There remains for consideration, therefore, the validity of its judgment on that score. * * *

Likewise, only if there is purposeful discrimination can there be a violation of the Equal Protection Clause of the Fourteenth Amendment. See *Washington* v. *Davis*, 426 U.S. 229 [(1976)]; *Arlington Heights* v. *Metropolitan Housing Dev. Corp.*, 429 U.S. 252 [(1977)]; *Personnel Administrator of Mass.* v. *Feeney*, 442 U.S. 256 [(1979)]. The Court explicitly indicated in *Washington* v. *Davis* that this principle applies to claims of racial discrimination affecting voting just as it does to other claims of racial discrimination. [See *Davis*, 426 U.S., at 240.] * * *

In only one case has the Court sustained a claim that multimember legislative districts unconstitutionally diluted the voting strength of a discrete group. That case was *White* v. *Regester* [412 U.S. 755 (1973)] [p. 288]. There the Court * * * held that the plaintiffs had been able to "produce evidence to support findings that the political processes leading to nomination and election were not equally open to participation by the group[s] in question." 412 U.S., at 766, 767. In so holding, the Court relied upon evidence in the record that included a long history of official discrimination against minorities as well as indifference to their needs and interests on the part of white elected officials. The Court also found in each county additional factors that restricted the access of minority groups to the political process. In one county, Negroes effectively were excluded from the process of slating candidates for the Democratic Party, while the plaintiffs in the other county were Mexican-Americans who "suffer[ed] a cultural and language barrier" that made "participation in community processes extremely difficult, particularly . . . with respect to the political life" of the county. *Id.* at 768.

White v. *Regester* is thus consistent with "the basic equal protection principle that the invidious quality of a law claimed to be racially discriminatory must ultimately be traced to a racially discriminatory purpose," *Washington* v. *Davis*, 426 U.S., at 240. * * * Of course, "[t]he impact of the official action — whether it 'bears more heavily on one race than another' — may provide an important starting point." *Arlington Heights*, *supra*, at 266. But where the character of a law is readily explainable on grounds apart from race, as would nearly always be true where, as here, an entire system of local governance is brought into question, disproportionate impact alone cannot be decisive, and courts must look to other evidence to support a finding of discriminatory purpose. See *ibid.*; *Washington* v. *Davis*, *supra*, at 242.

* * * [I]t is clear that the evidence in the present case fell far short of showing that the appellants "conceived or operated [a] purposeful devic[e] to further racial . . . discrimination." *Whitcomb* v. *Chavis*, 403 U.S. [124], 149 [(1971)] [p. 282]. * * *

* * * The theory of [Mr. Justice Marshall's] dissenting opinion * * * appears to be that every "political group," or at least every such group that is in the minority, has a federal constitutional right to elect candidates in proportion to its numbers.[22] * * *

---

22. The dissenting opinion seeks to disclaim this description of its theory by suggesting that a claim of vote dilution may require, in addition to proof of electoral defeat, some evidence of "historical and social factors" indicating that the group in question is without political influence. Putting to the side the evident fact that these gauzy sociological considerations have no constitutional basis, it remains far from certain that they could, in any principled manner, exclude the claims of any discrete political group that happens, for whatever reason, to elect fewer of its candidates than arithmetic indicates it might. Indeed, the putative limits are bound to prove illusory if the express

Whatever appeal the dissenting opinion's view may have as a matter of political theory, it is not the law. The Equal Protection Clause of the Fourteenth Amendment does not require proportional representation as an imperative of political organization. The entitlement that the dissenting opinion assumes to exist simply is not to be found in the Constitution of the United States. * * *

The dissenting opinion erroneously discovers the asserted entitlement to group representation within the "one person-one vote" principle of *Reynolds* v. *Sims* [377 U.S. 533 (1964)] [p. 122] and its progeny.[25] * * * There can be, of course, no claim that the "one person, one vote" principle has been violated in this case, because the city of Mobile is a unitary electoral district and the Commission elections are conducted at large. It is therefore obvious that nobody's vote has been "diluted" in the sense in which that word was used in the *Reynolds* case.

The dissenting opinion places an extraordinary interpretation on these decisions, an interpretation not justified by *Reynolds* v. *Sims* itself or by any other decision of this Court. It is, of course, true that the right of a person to vote on an equal basis with other voters draws much of its significance from the political associations that its exercise reflects, but it is an altogether different matter to conclude that political groups themselves have an independent constitutional claim to representation.[26] And the Court's decisions hold squarely that they do not. See *United Jewish Organizations* v. *Carey*, 430 U.S. 144, 166–167 [(1977)] [p. 291]; *id.*, at 179–180 (opinion concurring in judgment); *White* v. *Regester*, 412 U.S., at 765–766; *Whitcomb* v. *Chavis*, 403 U.S., at 149–150, 153–154, 156–157.

---

purpose informing their application would be, as the dissent assumes, to redress the "inequitable distribution of political influence."

25. The dissenting opinion also relies upon several decisions of this Court that have held constitutionally invalid various voter eligibility requirements * * *. But there is in this case no attack whatever upon any of the voter eligibility requirements in Mobile. * * * It is difficult to perceive any similarity between the excluded person's right to equal electoral participation in the cited cases, and the right asserted by the dissenting opinion in the present case, aside from the fact that they both in some way involve voting.

26. It is difficult to perceive how the implications of the dissenting opinion's theory of group representation could rationally be cabined. Indeed, certain preliminary practical questions immediately come to mind: Can only members of a minority of the voting population in a particular municipality be members of a "political group"? How large must a "group" be to be a "political group"? Can any "group" call itself a "political group"? If not, who is to say which "groups" are "political groups"? Can a qualified voter belong to more than one "political group"? Can there be more than one "political group" among white voters (*e.g.*, Irish-American, Italian-American, Polish-American, Jews, Catholics, Protestants)? Can there be more than one "political group" among nonwhite voters? Do the answers to any of these questions depend upon the particular demographic composition of a given city? Upon the total size of its voting population? Upon the size of its governing body? Upon its form of government? Upon its history? Its geographic location? The fact that even these preliminary questions may be largely unanswerable suggests some of the conceptual and practical fallacies in the constitutional theory espoused by the dissenting opinion, putting to one side the total absence of support for that theory in the Constitution itself.

The fact is that the Court has sternly set its face against the claim, however phrased, that the Constitution somehow guarantees proportional representation. * * *

The judgment is reversed, and the case is remanded to the Court of Appeals for further proceedings.

It is so ordered.

Mr. Justice Blackmun, concurring in the result.

Assuming that proof of intent is a prerequisite to appellees' prevailing on their constitutional claim of vote dilution, I am inclined to agree with Mr. Justice White that, in this case, "the findings of the District Court amply support an inference of purposeful discrimination." I concur in the Court's judgment of reversal, however, because I believe that the relief afforded appellees by the District Court was not commensurate with the sound exercise of judicial discretion. * * *

Contrary to the District Court, I do not believe that, in order to remedy the unconstitutional vote dilution it found, it was necessary to convert Mobile's city government to a mayor-council system. In my view, the District Court at least should have considered alternative remedial orders that would have maintained some of the basic elements of the commission system Mobile long ago had selected — joint exercise of legislative and executive power, and citywide representation. In the first place, I see no reason for the court to have separated legislative and executive power in the city of Mobile by creating the office of mayor. In the second place, the court could have, and in my view should have, considered expanding the size of the Mobile City Commission and providing for the election of at least some commissioners at large. Alternative plans might have retained at-large elections for all commissioners while imposing district residency requirements that would have insured the election of a commission that was a cross section of all of Mobile's neighborhoods, or a plurality-win system that would have provided the potential for the effective use of single-shot voting by black voters. In failing to consider such alternative plans, it appears to me that the District Court was perhaps overly concerned with the elimination of at-large elections *per se,* rather than with structuring an electoral system that provided an opportunity for black voters in Mobile to participate in the city's government on an equal footing with whites. * * *

Mr. Justice Stevens, concurring in the judgment. * * *

* * * In this case, if the commission form of government in Mobile were extraordinary, or if it were nothing more than a vestige of history, with no greater justification than the grotesque figure in *Gomillion*, it would surely violate the Constitution. That conclusion would follow simply from its adverse impact on black voters plus the absence of any legitimate justification for the system, without reference to the subjective intent of the political body that has refused to alter it.

Conversely, I am also persuaded that a political decision that affects group voting rights may be valid even if it can be proved that irrational or invidious factors have played some part in its enactment or retention. The standard for testing the acceptability of such a decision must take into account the fact that the responsibility for drawing political boundaries is generally committed to the legislative process and that the process inevitably involves a series of compromises among different group interests. If the process is to work it must reflect an awareness of group interests and it must tolerate some attempts to advantage or to disadvantage particular segments of the voting populace. * * * The standard cannot, therefore, be so strict that any evidence of a purpose to disadvantage a bloc of voters will justify a finding of "invidious discrimination"; otherwise, the facts of political life would deny legislatures the right to perform the districting function. Accordingly, a political decision that is supported by valid and articulable justifications cannot be invalid simply because some participants in the decisionmaking process were motivated by a purpose to disadvantage a minority group.

The decision to retain the commission form of government in Mobile, Ala., is such a decision. I am persuaded that some support for its retention comes, directly or indirectly, from members of the white majority who are motivated by a desire to make it more difficult for members of the black minority to serve in positions of responsibility in city government. I deplore that motivation and wish that neither it nor any other irrational prejudice played any part in our political processes. But I do not believe otherwise legitimate political choices can be invalidated simply because an irrational or invidious purpose played some part in the decisionmaking process. * * * A contrary view "would spawn endless litigation concerning the multi-member district systems now widely employed in this country," *id.*, at 157, and would entangle the judiciary in a voracious political thicket.

In sum, I believe we must accept the choice to retain Mobile's commission form of government as constitutionally permissible even though that choice may well be the product of mixed motivation, some of which is invidious. For these reasons I concur in the judgment of reversal.

Mr. Justice Brennan, dissenting.

I dissent because I agree with Mr. Justice Marshall that proof of discriminatory impact is sufficient * * *. I also dissent because, even accepting the plurality's premise that discriminatory purpose must be shown, I agree with Mr. Justice Marshall and Mr. Justice White that the appellees have clearly met that burden.

Mr. Justice White, dissenting.

* * * The Court's decision is flatly inconsistent with *White* v. *Regester* and it cannot be understood to flow from our recognition in *Washington* v. *Davis* that the Equal Protection Clause forbids only purposeful discrimination. Both the District

Court and the Court of Appeals properly found that an invidious discriminatory purpose could be inferred from the totality of facts in this case. The Court's cryptic rejection of their conclusions ignores the principles that an invidious discriminatory purpose can be inferred from objective factors of the kind relied on in *White* v. *Regester* and that the trial courts are in a special position to make such intensely local appraisals. * * *

In the instant case the District Court and the Court of Appeals faithfully applied the principles of *White* v. *Regester* in assessing whether the maintenance of a system of at-large elections for the selection of Mobile City Commissioners denied Mobile Negroes their Fourteenth and Fifteenth Amendment rights. Scrupulously adhering to our admonition that "[t]he plaintiffs' burden is to produce evidence to support findings that the political processes leading to nomination and election were not equally open to participation by the group in question," *id.*, at 766, the District Court conducted a detailed factual inquiry into the openness of the candidate selection process to blacks. The court noted that "Mobile blacks were subjected to massive official and private racial discrimination until the Voting Rights Act of 1965" and that "[t]he pervasive effects of past discrimination still substantially affec[t] black political participation." Although the District Court noted that "[s]ince the Voting Rights Act of 1965, blacks register and vote without hindrance," the court found that "local political processes are not equally open" to blacks. Despite the fact that Negroes constitute more than 35% of the population of Mobile, no Negro has ever been elected to the Mobile City Commission. The plaintiffs introduced extensive evidence of severe racial polarization in voting patterns during the 1960's and 1970's with "white voting for white and black for black if a white is opposed to a black," resulting in the defeat of the black candidate or, if two whites are running, the defeat of the white candidate most identified with blacks. * * * After single-member districts were created in Mobile County for state legislative elections, "three blacks of the present fourteen member Mobile County delegation have been elected." Based on th[is] evidence, the District Court found "that the structure of the at-large election of city commissioners combined with strong racial polarization of Mobile's electorate continues to effectively discourage qualified black citizens from seeking office or being elected thereby denying blacks equal access to the slating or candidate selection process."

The District Court also reviewed extensive evidence that the City Commissioners elected under the at-large system have not been responsive to the needs of the Negro community. The court found that city officials have been unresponsive to the interests of Mobile Negroes in municipal employment, appointments to boards and committees, and the provision of municipal services in part because of "the political fear of a white backlash vote when black citizens' needs are at stake." The court also found that there is no clear-cut state policy preference for at-large elections and that past discrimination affecting the ability of Negroes to register and to vote "has helped preclude the effective participation of blacks in the election system today." The adverse impact of the at-large election system on minorities was found to be enhanced by the large size of the citywide election district, the majority vote requirement, the provision that candidates run for positions by place or number, and the lack of any provision for at-large candidates to run from particular geographical subdistricts.

After concluding its extensive findings of fact, the District Court addressed the question of the effect of *Washington* v. *Davis* on the *White* v. *Regester* standards. The court concluded that the requirement that a facially neutral statute involve purposeful discrimination before a violation of the Equal Protection Clause can be established was not inconsistent with *White* v. *Regester* in light of the recognition in *Washington* v. *Davis* that the discriminatory purpose may often be inferred from the totality of the relevant facts, including the discriminatory impact of the statute. After noting that "whenever a redistricting bill of any type is proposed by a county delegation member, a major concern has centered around how many, if any, blacks would be elected," the District Court concluded that there was "a present purpose to dilute the black vote . . . resulting from intentional state legislative *inaction.*" Based on an "exhaustive analysis of the evidence in the record," the court held that "[t]he plaintiffs have met the burden cast in *White* and *Whitcomb*," and that "the multi-member at-large election of Mobile City Commissioners . . . results in an unconstitutional dilution of black voting strength." * * *

[T]he Court of Appeals reviewed the District Court's findings of fact, found them not to be clearly erroneous and held that they "compel the inference that [Mobile's at-large] system has been maintained with the purpose of diluting the black vote, thus supplying the element of intent necessary to establish a violation of the fourteenth amendment and the fifteenth amendment." The court observed that the District Court's "finding that the legislature was acutely conscious of the racial consequences of its districting policies," coupled with the attempt to assign different functions to each of the three City Commissioners "to lock in the at-large feature of the scheme," constituted "direct evidence of the intent behind the maintenance of the at-large plan." * * *

* * * Although the totality of the facts relied upon by the District Court to support its inference of purposeful discrimination is even more compelling than that present in *White* v. *Regester*, the plurality today rejects the inference of purposeful discrimination apparently because each of the factors relied upon by the courts below is alone insufficient to support the inference. The plurality states that the "fact [that Negro candidates have been defeated] alone does not work a constitutional deprivation," that evidence of the unresponsiveness of elected officials "is relevant only as the most tenuous and circumstantial evidence," that "the substantial history of official racial discrimination . . . [is] of limited help," and that the features of the electoral system that enhance the disadvantages faced by a voting minority "are far from proof that the at-large electoral scheme represents purposeful discrimination." By viewing each of the factors relied upon below in isolation, and ignoring the fact that racial bloc voting at the polls makes it impossible to elect

a black commissioner under the at-large system, the plurality rejects the "totality of the circumstances" approach we endorsed in *White* v. *Regester*, *Washington* v. *Davis*, and *Arlington Heights* v. *Metropolitan Housing Dev. Corp.*, and leaves the courts below adrift on uncharted seas with respect to how to proceed on remand.

Because I believe that the findings of the District Court amply support an inference of purposeful discrimination in violation of the Fourteenth and Fifteenth Amendments, I respectfully dissent.

Mr. Justice Marshall, dissenting. * * *

In my view, our vote dilution decisions require only a showing of discriminatory impact to justify the invalidation of a multimember districting scheme, and, because they are premised on the fundamental interest in voting protected by the Fourteenth Amendment, the discriminatory impact standard adopted by them is unaffected by *Washington* v. *Davis* and its progeny. Furthermore, an intent requirement is inconsistent with the protection against denial or abridgment of the vote on account of race embodied in the Fifteenth Amendment and in § 2 of the Voting Rights Act of 1965. * * *

The Court does not dispute the proposition that multimember districting can have the effect of submerging electoral minorities and over-representing electoral majorities.[3] * * * Although we have held that multimember districts are not unconstitutional *per se*, there is simply no basis for the plurality's conclusion that, under our prior cases, proof of discriminatory intent is a necessary condition for the invalidation of multimember districting.

In *Fortson* v. *Dorsey*, 379 U.S. 433 (1965), the first vote-dilution case to reach this Court, we stated explicitly that such a claim could rest on either discriminatory purpose or effect:

> "It might well be that, *designedly or otherwise*, a multimember constituency apportionment scheme, under the circumstances of a particular case, would *operate* to minimize or cancel out the voting strength of racial or political elements of the voting population." *Id.* at 439 (emphasis added).

---

3. * * * The electoral schemes in these cases involve majority-vote, numbered-post, and staggered-term requirements. These electoral rules exacerbate the vote-dilutive effects of multimember districting. A requirement that a candidate must win by a majority of the vote forces a minority candidate who wins a plurality of votes in the general election to engage in a runoff election with his nearest competitor. If the competitor is a member of the dominant political faction, the minority candidate stands little chance of winning in the second election. A requirement that each candidate must run for a particular "place" or "post" creates head-to-head contests that minority candidates cannot survive. When a number of positions on a governmental body are to be chosen in the same election, members of a minority will increase the likelihood of election of a favorite candidate by voting only for him. If the remainder of the electorate splits its votes among the other candidates, the minority's candidate might well be elected by the minority's "single-shot voting." If the terms of the officeholders are staggered, the opportunity for single-shot voting is decreased.

We reiterated these words in *Burns* v. *Richardson*, 384 U.S. 73 (1966), interpreted them as the correct test to apply to vote-dilution claims, and described the standard as one involving "invidious effect," *id.* at 88. * * * It could not be plainer that the Court in *Burns* considered discriminatory effect a sufficient condition for invalidating a multimember districting plan.

In *Whitcomb* v. *Chavis*, 403 U.S. 124 (1971) [p. 282], we again repeated and applied the *Fortson* standard, but determined that the Negro community's lack of success at the polls was the result of partisan politics, not racial vote dilution. The Court stressed that both the Democratic and Republican Parties had nominated Negroes, and several had been elected. Negro candidates lost only when their entire party slate went down to defeat. * * *

More recently, in *White* v. *Regester*, 412 U.S. 755 (1973) [p. 288], we invalidated the challenged multimember districting plans because their characteristics, when combined with historical and social factors, had the discriminatory effect of denying the plaintiff Negroes and Mexican-Americans equal access to the political process. * * *

It is apparent that a showing of discriminatory intent in the creation or maintenance of multimember districts is as unnecessary after *White* as it was under our earlier vote-dilution decisions. Under this line of cases, an electoral districting plan is invalid if it has the effect of affording an electoral minority "less opportunity than . . . other residents in the district to participate in the political processes and to elect legislators of their choice," *id.* at 766. It is also apparent that the Court in *White* considered equal access to the political process as meaning more than merely allowing the minority the opportunity to vote. *White* stands for the proposition that an electoral system may not relegate an electoral minority to political impotence by diminishing the importance of its vote. The plurality's approach requiring proof of discriminatory purpose in the present cases is, then, squarely contrary to *White* and its predecessors.

The plurality fails to apply the discriminatory-effect standard of *White* v. *Regester* because that approach conflicts with what the plurality takes to be an elementary principle of law. "[O]nly if there is purposeful discrimination," announces the plurality, "can there be a violation of the Equal Protection Clause of the Fourteenth Amendment." That proposition is plainly overbroad. It fails to distinguish between two distinct lines of equal protection decisions: those involving suspect classifications, and those involving fundamental rights. {Whatever may be the merits of applying motivational analysis to the allocation of constitutionally gratuitous benefits, that approach is completely misplaced where, as here, it is applied to the distribution of a constitutionally protected interest [such as the right to vote].} * * *

Reynolds v. *Sims* and its progeny focused solely on the discriminatory *effects* of malapportionment. They recognize that, when population figures for the representational districts of a legislature are not similar, the votes of citizens in larger districts do not carry as much weight in the legislature as do votes cast by citizens in smaller districts. The equal protection problem attacked by the "one person, one vote" principle is, then, one of vote dilution: under *Reynolds*, each citizen must have an "equally effective voice" in the election of representatives. In the present cases, the alleged vote dilution, though caused by the combined effects of the electoral structure and social and historical factors, rather than by unequal population distribution, is analytically the same concept: the unjustified abridgment of a fundamental right. It follows, then, that a showing of discriminatory intent is just as unnecessary under the vote-dilution approach adopted in *Fortson* v. *Dorsey*, and applied in *White* v. *Regester*, as it is under our reapportionment cases. * * *

The plurality's response is that my approach amounts to nothing less than a constitutional requirement of proportional representation for groups. That assertion amounts to nothing more than a red herring: I explicitly reject the notion that the Constitution contains any such requirement. The constitutional protection against vote dilution found in our prior cases does not extend to those situations in which a group has merely failed to elect representatives in proportion to its share of the population. To prove unconstitutional vote dilution, the group is also required to carry the far more onerous burden of demonstrating that it has been effectively fenced out of the political process. * * *

[I]t is beyond dispute that a standard based solely upon the motives of official decisionmakers creates significant problems of proof for plaintiffs and forces the inquiring court to undertake an unguided, tortuous look into the minds of officials in the hope of guessing why certain policies were adopted and others rejected. An approach based on motivation creates the risk that officials will be able to adopt policies that are the products of discriminatory intent so long as they sufficiently mask their motives through the use of subtlety and illusion. * * *

* * * If this Court refuses to honor our long-recognized principle that the Constitution "nullifies sophisticated as well as simple-minded modes of discrimination," it cannot expect the victims of discrimination to respect political channels of seeking redress. I dissent.

Notes and Questions

1. It is important to recognize that *Bolden* involved two separate holdings, both of which are significant. First, interpreting § 2 of the Voting Rights Act, the plurality held that the statutory language prohibited only the same "abridge[ments]" of the right to vote already prohibited by the Fifteenth Amendment. Thus, for the plaintiffs to succeed, they had to show that the City's districting violated their constitutional rights.

Second, interpreting the Fifteenth Amendment itself, the plurality held that the constitutional prohibition extended to vote dilution only where there was both the purpose and effect of diminishing the political power of minorities. Because, in the view of the plurality, the plaintiffs could not prove discriminatory intent, they could not succeed on either the constitutional claim or the statutory claim.

2. Justice Marshall, in dissent, pointed to *Reynolds v. Sims* and the Court's other one-person, one-vote cases in arguing that the Constitution provided a right against measures that diluted the voting strength of groups, regardless of the government's intent. Was the plurality right to dismiss those cases as inapposite?

3. Did *White v. Regester* require plaintiffs to prove discriminatory intent?

4. *Bolden*'s intent requirement for proving violations of the Fifteenth Amendment mirrors the intent requirement in Fourteenth Amendment jurisprudence. Plaintiffs must demonstrate that the challenged action was instituted or maintained "at least in part 'because of,' not merely 'in spite of,' its adverse effects upon an identifiable group." *Personnel Administrator v. Feeney*, 442 U.S. 256, 279 (1979). Is that definition of "purpose" appropriate, or should plaintiffs be able to succeed merely by proving that the government was indifferent to the effect of a law on the political power of minorities?

5. How should a court determine whether there is intentional vote dilution against a racial minority when a Republican legislature minimizes minorities' voting power not because of any racial animus but because of a desire to advance Republican prospects? In a word, it is "complicated." *Abbott v. Perez*, 585 U.S. __, __, 138 S. Ct. 2305, 2314 (2018). "[B]ecause a voter's race sometimes correlates closely with political party preference, *see Cooper* v. *Harris*, 581 U.S. __, __-__, 137 S. Ct. 1455, 1473–1474 (2017); *Easley* v. *Cromartie*, 532 U.S. 234, 243 (2001), it may be very difficult for a court to determine whether a districting decision was based on race or party preference." *Perez*, 138 S. Ct. at 2314. *Bolden* may suggest that a legislature's desire to advance one party's prospects would not be racially discriminatory even if a minority's voting power were minimized as the *means* of achieving the political goal. Some cases, however, suggest that intentionally minimizing the voting power of a racial minority may be discriminatory even if done for political reasons.

For a recent example, see *Michigan State A. Philip Randolph Institute v. Johnson*, 326 F. Supp. 3d 532, 569 (E.D. Mich.) (finding intentional discrimination against African Americans in Michigan's elimination of straight-ticket voting, even though there was no evidence of racial animus), *stayed as likely clearly erroneous*, 749 Fed. Appx. 342, 354 (6th Cir.), *motion to vacate stay denied*, 139 S. Ct. 50 (2018), *and vacated as moot*, 2019 WL 4145547 (6th Cir. 2019). *See also One Wisconsin Institute, Inc. v. Thomsen*, 198 F. Supp. 3d 896 (W.D. Wis. 2016) (finding intentional racial discrimination in a measure reducing absentee voting as a way of suppressing minority votes for Democratic candidates).

Of course, everybody realizes that most minority groups prefer Democrats to Republicans. Given that understanding, is there a meaningful difference between (1) a party-motivated Republican measure that minimizes Democratic votes (including minority votes); (2) a race-motivated Republican measure that minimizes (mostly Democratic) minority votes; and (3) a Republican measure that dilutes minority voting power not because of racial prejudice but as a way of minimizing the strength of an easily identifiable core group of Democratic voters? Would it be better to ask only whether the legislature is motivated by animus against a racial minority, as opposed to a desire to harm an opposition party even if there is an incidental effect on a racial minority?

6. Should the purpose requirement be satisfied by a showing that an at-large district was *maintained* (but not instituted) for a discriminatory purpose? *See Rogers v. Lodge*, 458 U.S. 613, 622, 626 (1982).

C. Section 2's Post-1982 Results Test

The plurality's constitutional holding in *City of Mobile v. Bolden* remains good law. Outright prohibitions on voting or registering violate the Fifteenth Amendment whether or not they were enacted for a discriminatory purpose. Measures that make a group's votes less *effective* than votes of other groups, however, are unconstitutional only if plaintiffs can show a discriminatory purpose in addition to the dilutive effect.

Bolden's statutory holding, on the other hand, had a very short life indeed. Congress reacted to *Bolden* by amending §2 in 1982. The amendment attempted to overrule *Bolden* by making clear that a §2 violation could be shown by pointing to a state "standard, practice, or procedure" that "*results* in a denial or abridgement" of citizens' votes on account of race, color, or membership in a language minority. 52 U.S.C. §10301, 96 Stat. 134 (1982) (emphasis added). Thus, *Bolden's* focus on discriminatory intent was replaced by amended §2's "results test." This amendment made clear that §2 was intended to have a broader scope than the Fifteenth Amendment, and accordingly most litigation under §2 focuses on the application of the results test.[a] *Thornburg v. Gingles*, which appears immediately below, was the Court's first attempt to interpret the language of amended §2. The three "preconditions" established by *Gingles* have proven central to later cases interpreting §2.

---

a. For an extensive and balanced discussion of the legislative history of the 1982 amendments, see Thomas M. Boyd & Stephen J. Markman, *The 1982 Amendments to the Voting Rights Act: A Legislative History*, 40 Wash. & Lee L. Rev. 1347 (1983).

Thornburg v. Gingles

Supreme Court of the United States

478 U.S. 30, 106 S. Ct. 2752, 92 L. Ed. 2d 25 (1986)

Justice Brennan announced the judgment of the Court and delivered the opinion of the Court with respect to Parts I, II, III-A, III-B, IV-A, and V [in which Justice White, Justice Marshall, Justice Blackmun, and Justice Stevens join], an opinion with respect to Part III-C, in which Justice Marshall, Justice Blackmun, and Justice Stevens join, and an opinion with respect to Part IV-B, in which Justice White joins. * * *

I

In April 1982, the North Carolina General Assembly enacted a legislative redistricting plan for the State's Senate and House of Representatives. Appellees, black citizens of North Carolina who are registered to vote, challenged seven districts, one single-member and six multimember districts, alleging that the redistricting scheme impaired black citizens' ability to elect representatives of their choice in violation of the Fourteenth and Fifteenth Amendments to the United States Constitution and of § 2 of the Voting Rights Act.

After appellees brought suit, but before trial, Congress amended § 2. The amendment was largely a response to this Court's plurality opinion in *Mobile* v. *Bolden*, 446 U.S. 55 (1980) [p. 302], which had declared that, in order to establish a violation either of § 2 or of the Fourteenth or Fifteenth Amendments, minority voters must prove that a contested electoral mechanism was intentionally adopted or maintained by state officials for a discriminatory purpose. Congress substantially revised § 2 to make clear that a violation could be proved by showing discriminatory effect alone and to establish as the relevant legal standard the "results test," applied by this Court in *White* v. *Regester*, 412 U.S. 755 (1973) [p. 288], and by other federal courts before *Bolden*. S. Rep. No. 97–417, p.28 (1982) (hereinafter S. Rep.).

Section 2, as amended, 96 Stat. 134, reads as follows:

> "(a) No voting qualification or prerequisite to voting or standard, practice, or procedure shall be imposed or applied by any State or political subdivision in a manner which results in a denial or abridgement of the right of any citizen of the United States to vote on account of race or color, or in contravention of the guarantees set forth in section 4(f)(2), as provided in subsection (b).

> "(b) A violation of subsection (a) is established if, based on the totality of circumstances, it is shown that the political processes leading to nomination or election in the State or political subdivision are not equally open to participation by members of a class of citizens protected by subsection (a) in that its members have less opportunity than other members of the electorate to participate in the political process and to elect representatives of their choice. The extent to which members of a protected class have been

elected to office in the State or political subdivision is one circumstance which may be considered: *Provided*, That nothing in this section establishes a right to have members of a protected class elected in numbers equal to their proportion in the population." Codified at 42 U.S.C. § 1973 [now 52 U.S.C. § 10301 — Eds.].

The Senate Judiciary Committee majority Report accompanying the bill that amended § 2 elaborates on the circumstances that might be probative of a § 2 violation, noting the following "typical factors":[4]

"1. the extent of any history of official discrimination in the state or political subdivision that touched the right of the members of the minority group to register, to vote, or otherwise to participate in the democratic process;

"2. the extent to which voting in the elections of the state or political subdivision is racially polarized;

"3. the extent to which the state or political subdivision has used unusually large election districts, majority vote requirements, anti-single shot provisions, or other voting practices or procedures that may enhance the opportunity for discrimination against the minority group;

"4. if there is a candidate slating process, whether the members of the minority group have been denied access to that process;

"5. the extent to which members of the minority group in the state or political subdivision bear the effects of discrimination in such areas as education, employment and health, which hinder their ability to participate effectively in the political process;

"6. whether political campaigns have been characterized by overt or subtle racial appeals;

"7. the extent to which members of the minority group have been elected to public office in the jurisdiction.

"Additional factors that in some cases have had probative value as part of plaintiffs' evidence to establish a violation are:

"whether there is a significant lack of responsiveness on the part of elected officials to the particularized needs of the members of the minority group.

"whether the policy underlying the state or political subdivision's use of such voting qualification, prerequisite to voting, or standard, practice or procedure is tenuous." S. Rep., at 28–29.

---

4. These factors were derived from the analytical framework of *White* v. *Regester*, as refined and developed by the lower courts, in particular by the Fifth Circuit in *Zimmer* v. *McKeithen*, 485 F.2d 1297 (1973) (en banc), aff'd *sub nom. East Carroll Parish School Board* v. *Marshall*, 424 U.S. 636 (1976) *(per curiam)*. S. Rep., at 28, n.113. [Accordingly, they have become known as the "*Zimmer* factors." — Eds.]

The District Court applied the "totality of the circumstances" test set forth in § 2(b) to appellees' statutory claim, and, relying principally on the factors outlined in the Senate Report, held that the redistricting scheme violated § 2 because it resulted in the dilution of black citizens' votes in all seven disputed districts. In light of this conclusion, the court did not reach appellees' constitutional claims. * * *

II * * *

Appellees contend that the legislative decision to employ multimember, rather than single-member, districts in the contested jurisdictions dilutes their votes by submerging them in a white majority, thus impairing their ability to elect representatives of their choice.[12]

The essence of a § 2 claim is that a certain electoral law, practice, or structure interacts with social and historical conditions to cause an inequality in the opportunities enjoyed by black and white voters to elect their preferred representatives. * * * The theoretical basis for this type of impairment is that where minority and majority voters consistently prefer different candidates, the majority, by virtue of its numerical superiority, will regularly defeat the choices of minority voters. Multimember districts and at-large election schemes, however, are not *per se* violative of minority voters' rights. S. Rep., at 16. Minority voters who contend that the multimember form of districting violates § 2 must prove that the use of a multimember electoral structure operates to minimize or cancel out their ability to elect their preferred candidates.

While many or all of the factors listed in the Senate Report may be relevant to a claim of vote dilution through submergence in multimember districts, unless there is a conjunction of the following circumstances, the use of multimember districts generally will not impede the ability of minority voters to elect representatives of their choice.[15] Stated succinctly, a bloc voting majority must *usually* be able to defeat

---

12. The claim we address in this opinion is one in which the plaintiffs alleged and attempted to prove that their ability *to elect* the representatives of their choice was impaired by the selection of a multimember electoral structure. We have no occasion to consider whether § 2 permits, and if it does, what standards should pertain to, a claim brought by a minority group, that is not sufficiently large and compact to constitute a majority in a single-member district, alleging that the use of a multimember district impairs its ability *to influence* elections.

We note also that we have no occasion to consider whether the standards we apply to respondents' claim that multimember districts operate to dilute the vote of geographically cohesive minority groups that are large enough to constitute majorities in single-member districts and that are contained within the boundaries of the challenged multimember districts, are fully pertinent to other sorts of vote dilution claims, such as a claim alleging that the splitting of a large and geographically cohesive minority between two or more multimember or single-member districts resulted in the dilution of the minority vote.

15. Under a "functional" view of the political process mandated by § 2, S. Rep., at 30, n.120, the most important Senate Report factors bearing on § 2 challenges to multimember districts are the "extent to which minority group members have been elected to public office in the jurisdiction" and the "extent to which voting in the elections of the state or political subdivision is racially polarized." If present, the other factors, such as the lingering effects of past discrimination, the use

candidates supported by a politically cohesive, geographically insular minority group. These circumstances are necessary preconditions for multimember districts to operate to impair minority voters' ability to elect representatives of their choice for the following reasons. First, the minority group must be able to demonstrate that it is sufficiently large and geographically compact to constitute a majority in a single-member district. If it is not, as would be the case in a substantially integrated district, the *multimember form* of the district cannot be responsible for minority voters' inability to elect its candidates.[17] Second, the minority group must be able to show that it is politically cohesive. If the minority group is not politically cohesive, it cannot be said that the selection of a multimember electoral structure thwarts distinctive minority group interests. Third, the minority must be able to demonstrate that the white majority votes sufficiently as a bloc to enable it—in the absence of special circumstances, such as the minority candidate running unopposed—usually to defeat the minority's preferred candidate. In establishing this last circumstance, the minority group demonstrates that submergence in a white multimember district impedes its ability to elect its chosen representatives.

Finally, we observe that the usual predictability of the majority's success distinguishes structural dilution from the mere loss of an occasional election.

III * * *

A * * *

* * * The District Court found that blacks and whites generally preferred different candidates and, on that basis, found voting in the districts to be racially correlated [to a statistically significant extent]. * * * [T]he court [further] found that

---

of appeals to racial bias in election campaigns, and the use of electoral devices which enhance the dilutive effects of multimember districts when substantial white bloc voting exists—for example antibullet voting laws and majority vote requirements, are supportive of, but *not essential to*, a minority voter's claim.

* * * It is obvious that unless minority group members experience substantial difficulty electing representatives of their choice, they cannot prove that a challenged electoral mechanism impairs their ability "to elect." And, where the contested electoral structure is a multimember district, * * * in the absence of significant white bloc voting it cannot be said that the ability of minority voters to elect their chosen representatives is inferior to that of white voters. Consequently, if difficulty in electing and white bloc voting are not proved, minority voters have not established that the multimember structure interferes with their ability to elect their preferred candidates. * * *

17. The reason that a minority group making such a challenge must show, as a threshold matter, that it is sufficiently large and geographically compact to constitute a majority in a single-member district is this: Unless minority voters possess the *potential* to elect representatives in the absence of the challenged structure or practice, they cannot claim to have been injured by that structure or practice. The single-member district is generally the appropriate standard against which to measure minority group potential to elect because it is the smallest political unit from which representatives are elected. Thus, if the minority group is spread evenly throughout a multimember district, or if, although geographically compact, the minority group is so small in relation to the surrounding white population that it could not constitute a majority in a single-member district, these minority voters cannot maintain that they would have been able to elect representatives of their choice in the absence of the multimember electoral structure.

in all but 2 of the 53 elections the degree of racial bloc voting was "so marked as to be substantively significant, in the sense that the results of the individual election would have been different depending upon whether it had been held among only the white voters or only the black voters."

The court also reported its findings * * * that a high percentage of black voters regularly supported black candidates and that most white voters were extremely reluctant to vote for black candidates. The court then considered the relevance to the existence of legally significant white bloc voting of the fact that black candidates have won some elections. It determined that in most instances, special circumstances, such as incumbency and lack of opposition, rather than a diminution in usually severe white bloc voting, accounted for these candidates' success. The court also suggested that black voters' reliance on bullet voting [in which voters can allocate multiple votes to a single candidate] was a significant factor in their successful efforts to elect candidates of their choice. Based on all of the evidence before it, the trial court concluded that each of the districts experienced racially polarized voting "in a persistent and severe degree."

B * * *

The Senate Report states that the "extent to which voting in the elections of the state or political subdivision is racially polarized" is relevant to a vote dilution claim. * * *

The purpose of inquiring into the existence of racially polarized voting is twofold: to ascertain whether minority group members constitute a politically cohesive unit and to determine whether whites vote sufficiently as a bloc usually to defeat the minority's preferred candidates. Thus, the question whether a given district experiences legally significant racially polarized voting requires discrete inquiries into minority and white voting practices. A showing that a significant number of minority group members usually vote for the same candidates is one way of proving the political cohesiveness necessary to a vote dilution claim and, consequently, establishes minority bloc voting within the context of § 2. And, in general, a white bloc vote that normally will defeat the combined strength of minority support plus white "crossover" votes rises to the level of legally significant white bloc voting. The amount of white bloc voting that can generally "minimize or cancel" black voters' ability to elect representatives of their choice, however, will vary from district to district according to a number of factors, including the nature of the allegedly dilutive electoral mechanism; the presence or absence of other potentially dilutive electoral devices, such as majority vote requirements, designated posts, and prohibitions against bullet voting; the percentage of registered voters in the district who are members of the minority group; the size of the district; and, in multimember districts, the number of seats open and the number of candidates in the field.

Because loss of political power through vote dilution is distinct from the mere inability to win a particular election, a pattern of racial bloc voting that extends over a period of time is more probative of a claim that a district experiences legally significant polarization than are the results of a single election. Also for this reason, in a district where elections are shown usually to be polarized, the fact that racially polarized voting is not present in one or a few individual elections does not necessarily negate the conclusion that the district experiences legally significant bloc voting. Furthermore, the success of a minority candidate in a particular election does not necessarily prove that the district did not experience polarized voting in that election; special circumstances, such as the absence of an opponent, incumbency, or the utilization of bullet voting, may explain minority electoral success in a polarized contest.

As must be apparent, the degree of racial bloc voting that is cognizable as an element of a § 2 vote dilution claim will vary according to a variety of factual circumstances. Consequently, there is no simple doctrinal test for the existence of legally significant racial bloc voting. However, the foregoing general principles should provide courts with substantial guidance in determining whether evidence that black and white voters generally prefer different candidates rises to the level of legal significance under § 2. * * *

C

North Carolina and the United States * * * argue that the term "racially polarized voting" must, as a matter of law, refer to voting patterns for which the *principal cause* is race. * * *

Whether appellants and the United States believe that it is the voter's race or the candidate's race that must be the primary determinant of the voter's choice is unclear[.] * * * In either case, we disagree: For purposes of § 2, the legal concept of racially polarized voting incorporates neither causation nor intent. It means simply that the race of voters correlates with the selection of a certain candidate or candidates; that is, it refers to the situation where different races (or minority language groups) vote in blocs for different candidates. * * *

The first reason we reject appellants' argument that racially polarized voting refers to voting patterns that are in some way *caused by race*, rather than to voting patterns that are merely *correlated with the race of the voter*, is that the reasons black and white voters vote differently have no relevance to the central inquiry of § 2. By contrast, the correlation between race of voter and the selection of certain candidates is crucial to that inquiry.

Both § 2 itself and the Senate Report make clear that the critical question in a § 2 claim is whether the use of a contested electoral practice or structure results in members of a protected group having less opportunity than other members of the electorate to participate in the political process and to elect representatives of their choice. As we explained, multimember districts may impair the ability of blacks to elect representatives of their choice where blacks vote sufficiently as a bloc as to be able to elect their preferred candidates in a black majority, single-member district and where a white majority votes sufficiently as a bloc usually to defeat the candidates chosen by blacks. It is the *difference* between the choices made by blacks and whites—not the reasons for that difference—that results in blacks having less opportunity than whites to elect their preferred representatives. Consequently, we conclude that under the "results test" of § 2, only the correlation between race of voter and selection of certain candidates, not the causes of the correlation, matters. * * *

[Additionally, reading "racially polarized voting" to refer only] to voting patterns that are *determined primarily by the voter's race*, rather than by the voter's other socioeconomic characteristics * * * ignores the fact that members of geographically insular racial and ethnic groups frequently share socioeconomic characteristics, such as income level, employment status, amount of education, housing and other living conditions, religion, language, and so forth. Where such characteristics are shared, race or ethnic group not only denotes color or place of origin, it also functions as a shorthand notation for common social and economic characteristics. Appellants' definition of racially polarized voting is even more pernicious where shared characteristics are causally related to race or ethnicity. The opportunity to achieve high employment status and income, for example, is often influenced by the presence or absence of racial or ethnic discrimination. A definition of racially polarized voting which holds that black bloc voting does not exist when black voters' choice of certain candidates is most strongly influenced by the fact that the voters have low incomes and menial jobs—when the reason most of those voters have menial jobs and low incomes is attributable to past or present racial discrimination—runs counter to the Senate Report's instruction to conduct a searching and practical evaluation of past and present reality, S. Rep., at 30, and interferes with the purpose of the Voting Rights Act to eliminate the negative effects of past discrimination on the electoral opportunities of minorities.

Furthermore, under appellants' theory of racially polarized voting, even uncontrovertible evidence that candidates strongly preferred by black voters are *always* defeated by a bloc voting white majority would be dismissed for failure to prove racial polarization whenever the black and white populations could be described in terms of other socioeconomic characteristics. * * *

North Carolina's and the United States' suggestion that racially polarized voting means that voters select or reject candidates *principally* on the basis of the *candidate's race* is also misplaced.

First, both the language of § 2 and a functional understanding of the phenomenon of vote dilution mandate the conclusion that the race of the candidate *per se* is irrelevant to racial bloc voting analysis. Section 2(b) states that a violation is established if it can be shown that members of a protected minority group "have less opportunity than other members of the electorate to . . . elect representatives *of their choice*." (Emphasis added.) Because both minority and majority voters often select members of their own race as their preferred representatives, it will frequently be the case that a black candidate is the choice of blacks, while a white candidate is the choice of whites. Indeed, the facts of this case illustrate that tendency—blacks preferred black candidates, whites preferred white candidates. Thus, as a matter of convenience, we and the District Court may refer to the preferred representative of black voters as the "black candidate" and to the preferred representative of white voters as the "white candidate." Nonetheless, the fact that race of voter and race of candidate is often correlated is not directly pertinent to a §2 inquiry. Under §2, it is the *status* of the candidate as the *chosen representative of a particular racial group*, not the race of the candidate, that is important. * * *

Second, appellants' suggestion that racially polarized voting refers to voting patterns where whites vote for white candidates because they prefer members of their own race or are hostile to blacks, as opposed to voting patterns where whites vote for white candidates because the white candidates spent more on their campaigns, utilized more media coverage, and thus enjoyed greater name recognition than the black candidates, fails for another, independent reason. This argument, like the argument that the race of the voter must be the primary determinant of the voter's ballot, is inconsistent with the purposes of §2 and would render meaningless the Senate Report factor that addresses the impact of low socioeconomic status on a minority group's level of political participation.

* * * If, because of inferior education and poor employment opportunities, blacks earn less than whites, they will not be able to provide the candidates of their choice with the same level of financial support that whites can provide theirs. Thus, electoral losses by candidates preferred by the black community may well be attributable in part to the fact that their white opponents outspent them. But, the fact is that, in this instance, the economic effects of prior discrimination have combined with the multimember electoral structure to afford blacks less opportunity than whites to participate in the political process and to elect representatives of their choice. It would be both anomalous and inconsistent with congressional intent to hold that, on the one hand, the effects of past discrimination which hinder blacks' ability to participate in the political process tend to prove a §2 violation, while holding on the other hand that, where these same effects of past discrimination deter whites from voting for blacks, blacks cannot make out a crucial element of a vote dilution claim.

Finally, we reject the suggestion that racially polarized voting refers only to white bloc voting which is caused by white voters' *racial hostility* toward black candidates. To accept this theory would frustrate the goals Congress sought to achieve by repudiating the intent test of *Mobile* v. *Bolden* and would prevent minority voters who have clearly been denied an opportunity to elect representatives of their choice from establishing a critical element of a vote dilution claim. * * *

The grave threat to racial progress and harmony which Congress perceived from requiring proof that racism caused the adoption or maintenance of a challenged electoral mechanism is present to a much greater degree in the proposed requirement that plaintiffs demonstrate that racial animosity determined white voting patterns. Under the old intent test, plaintiffs might succeed by proving only that a limited number of elected officials were racist; under the new intent test plaintiffs would be required to prove that most of the white community is racist in order to obtain judicial relief. It is difficult to imagine a more racially divisive requirement.

A second reason Congress rejected the old intent test was that in most cases it placed an "inordinately difficult burden" on § 2 plaintiffs. The new intent test would be equally, if not more, burdensome. In order to prove that a *specific factor*—racial hostility—*determined* white voters' ballots, it would be necessary to demonstrate that other potentially relevant *causal factors*, such as socioeconomic characteristics and candidate expenditures, do not correlate better than racial animosity with white voting behavior. * * *

[Finally, f]ocusing on the discriminatory intent of the voters, rather than the behavior of the voters, also asks the wrong question. All that matters under § 2 and under a functional theory of vote dilution is voter behavior, not its explanations. * * *

In sum, we would hold that the legal concept of racially polarized voting, as it relates to claims of vote dilution, refers only to the existence of a correlation between the race of voters and the selection of certain candidates. Plaintiffs need not prove causation or intent in order to prove a prima facie case of racial bloc voting and defendants may not rebut that case with evidence of causation or intent.

IV

A

North Carolina and the United States maintain that the District Court failed to accord the proper weight to the success of some black candidates in the challenged districts. Black residents of these districts, they point out, achieved improved representation in the 1982 General Assembly election. * * * Essentially, appellants and the United States contend that if a racial minority gains proportional or nearly proportional representation in a single election, that fact alone precludes, as a matter of law, finding a § 2 violation.

Section 2(b) provides that "[the] extent to which members of a protected class have been elected to office . . . is one circumstance which may be considered." The Senate Committee Report also identifies the extent to which minority candidates have succeeded as a pertinent factor. However, the Senate Report expressly states that "the election of a few minority candidates does not 'necessarily foreclose the possibility of dilution of the black vote[.]'" * * * The Senate Report also emphasizes that the question whether "the political processes are 'equally open' depends upon a searching practical evaluation of the 'past and present reality.'" *Id.*, at 30. Thus, the language of § 2 and its legislative history plainly demonstrate that proof that some minority candidates have been elected does not foreclose a § 2 claim. * * *

Nothing in the statute or its legislative history prohibited the court from viewing with some caution black candidates' success in the 1982 election, and from deciding on the basis of all the relevant circumstances to accord greater weight to blacks' relative lack of success over the course of several recent elections. Consequently, we hold that the District Court did not err, as a matter of law, in refusing to treat the fact that some black candidates have succeeded as dispositive of appellees' § 2 claim. Where multimember districting generally works to dilute the minority vote, it cannot be defended on the ground that it sporadically and serendipitously benefits minority voters.

B

The District Court did err, however, in ignoring the significance of the *sustained* success black voters have experienced in House District 23. In that district, the last six elections have resulted in proportional representation for black residents. This persistent proportional representation is inconsistent with appellees' allegation that the ability of black voters in District 23 to elect representatives of their choice is not equal to that enjoyed by the white majority.

In some situations, it may be possible for § 2 plaintiffs to demonstrate that such sustained success does not accurately reflect the minority group's ability to elect its preferred representatives,[38] but appellees have not done so here. Appellees presented evidence relating to black electoral success in the last three elections; they failed utterly, though, to offer any explanation for the success of black candidates in the previous three elections. Consequently, we believe that the District Court erred, as a matter of law, in ignoring the sustained success black voters have enjoyed in House District 23, and would reverse with respect to that District.

V * * *

The District Court in this case carefully considered the totality of the circumstances and found that in each district racially polarized voting; the legacy of official discrimination in voting matters, education, housing, employment, and health services; and the persistence of campaign appeals to racial prejudice acted in concert with the multimember districting scheme to impair the ability of geographically insular and politically cohesive groups of black voters to participate equally in the political process and to elect candidates of their choice. It found that the success a few black candidates have enjoyed in these districts is too recent, too limited, and, with regard to the 1982 elections, perhaps too aberrational, to disprove its conclusion. Excepting House District 23, with respect to which the District Court committed legal error, we affirm the District Court's judgment. We cannot say that the District Court, composed of local judges who are well acquainted with the political realities of the State, clearly erred in concluding that use of a multimember electoral structure has caused black voters in the districts other than House District 23 to have less opportunity than white voters to elect representatives of their choice.

The judgment of the District Court is

Affirmed in part and reversed in part.

---

38. We have no occasion in this case to decide what types of special circumstances could satisfactorily demonstrate that sustained success does not accurately reflect the minority's ability to elect its preferred representatives.

JUSTICE WHITE, concurring.

I join Parts I, II, III-A, III-B, IV-A, and V of the Court's opinion and agree with JUSTICE BRENNAN's opinion as to Part IV-B. I disagree with Part III-C of JUSTICE BRENNAN's opinion.

JUSTICE BRENNAN states in Part III-C that the crucial factor in identifying polarized voting is the race of the voter and that the race of the candidate is irrelevant. Under this test, there is polarized voting if the majority of white voters vote for different candidates than the majority of the blacks, regardless of the race of the candidates. I do not agree. Suppose an eight-member multimember district that is 60% white and 40% black, the blacks being geographically located so that two safe black single-member districts could be drawn. Suppose further that there are six white and two black Democrats running against six white and two black Republicans. Under JUSTICE BRENNAN's test, there would be polarized voting and a likely § 2 violation if all the Republicans, including the two blacks, are elected, and 80% of the blacks in the predominantly black areas vote Democratic. I take it that there would also be a violation in a single-member district that is 60% black, but enough of the blacks vote with the whites to elect a black candidate who is not the choice of the majority of black voters. This is interest-group politics rather than a rule hedging against racial discrimination. I doubt that this is what Congress had in mind in amending § 2 as it did, and it seems quite at odds with the discussion in *Whitcomb* v. *Chavis*, 403 U.S. 124, 149–160 (1971) [p. 282]. Furthermore, on the facts of this case, there is no need to draw the voter/candidate distinction. The District Court did not and reached the correct result except, in my view, with respect to District 23.

JUSTICE O'CONNOR, with whom THE CHIEF JUSTICE [BURGER], JUSTICE POWELL, and JUSTICE REHNQUIST join, concurring in the judgment. * * *

In construing this compromise legislation, we must make every effort to be faithful to the balance Congress struck. This is not an easy task. We know that Congress intended to allow vote dilution claims to be brought under § 2, but we also know that Congress did not intend to create a right to proportional representation for minority voters. There is an inherent tension between what Congress wished to do and what it wished to avoid, because any theory of vote dilution must necessarily rely to some extent on a measure of minority voting strength that makes some reference to the proportion between the minority group and the electorate at large. * * * Put simply, in order to decide whether an electoral system has made it harder for minority voters to elect the candidates they prefer, a court must have an idea in mind of how hard it "should" be for minority voters to elect their preferred candidates under an acceptable system. * * *

The Court's definition of the elements of a vote dilution claim is simple and invariable: a court should calculate minority voting strength by assuming that the minority group is concentrated in a single-member district in which it constitutes a voting majority. Where the minority group is not large enough, geographically concentrated enough, or politically cohesive enough for this to be possible, the minority group's claim fails. Where the minority group meets these requirements, the representatives that it could elect in the hypothetical district or districts in which it constitutes a majority will serve as the measure of its undiluted voting strength. Whatever plan the State actually adopts must be assessed in terms of the effect it has on this undiluted voting strength. * * *

* * * The Court requires the minority group that satisfies the threshold requirements of size and cohesiveness to prove that it will *usually* be unable to elect as many representatives of its choice under the challenged districting scheme as its undiluted voting strength would permit. This requirement, then, constitutes the true test of vote dilution. * * *

This measure of vote dilution, taken in conjunction with the Court's standard for measuring undiluted minority voting strength, creates what amounts to a right to *usual, roughly* proportional representation on the part of sizable, compact, cohesive minority groups. If, under a particular multimember or single-member district plan, qualified minority groups usually cannot elect the representatives they would be likely to elect under the most favorable single-member districting plan, then §2 is violated. Unless minority success under the challenged electoral system regularly approximates this rough version of proportional representation, that system dilutes minority voting strength and violates §2. * * *

To be sure, the Court also requires that plaintiffs prove that racial bloc voting by the white majority interacts with the challenged districting plan so as usually to defeat the minority's preferred candidate. In fact, however, this requirement adds little that is not already contained in the Court's requirements that the minority group be politically cohesive and that its preferred candidates usually lose. * * * If the minority can prove that it could constitute a majority in a single-member district, that it supported certain candidates, and that those candidates have not usually been elected, then a finding that there is "legally significant white bloc voting" will necessarily follow. Otherwise, by definition, those candidates would usually have won rather than lost.

As shaped by the Court today, then, the basic contours of a vote dilution claim require no reference to most of the "*Zimmer* factors" that were developed by the Fifth Circuit to implement *White*'s results test and which were highlighted in the Senate Report. If a minority group is politically and geographically cohesive and large enough to constitute a voting majority in one or more single-member districts, then unless white voters usually support the minority's preferred candidates in sufficient numbers to enable the minority group to elect as many of those candidates as it could elect in such hypothetical districts, it will routinely follow that a vote dilution claim can be made out, and the multimember district will be invalidated. * * *

In enacting §2, Congress codified the "results" test this Court had employed, as an interpretation of the Fourteenth Amendment, in *White* and *Whitcomb*. The factors developed by the Fifth Circuit and relied on by the Senate Report simply fill in the contours of the "results" test as described in those decisions, and do not purport to redefine or alter the ultimate showing of discriminatory effect required by *Whitcomb* and *White*. In my view, therefore, it is to *Whitcomb* and *White* that we should look in the first instance in determining how great an impairment of minority voting strength is required to establish vote dilution in violation of § 2. * * *

* * * The vote dilution analysis adopted by the Court today clearly bears little resemblance to the "results" test that emerged in *Whitcomb* and *White*. The Court's test for vote dilution, combined with its standard for evaluating "voting potential," means that any racial minority with distinctive interests must *usually* "be represented in legislative halls if it is numerous enough to command at least one seat and represents a minority living in an area sufficiently compact to constitute" a voting majority in "a single member district." *Whitcomb*, 403 U.S., at 156. Nothing in *Whitcomb*, *White*, or the language and legislative history of § 2 supports the Court's creation of this right to usual, roughly proportional representation on the part of every geographically compact, politically cohesive minority group that is large enough to form a majority in one or more single-member districts.

I would adhere to the approach outlined in *Whitcomb* and *White* and followed, with some elaboration, in *Zimmer* and other cases in the Courts of Appeals prior to *Bolden*. Under that approach, a court should consider all relevant factors bearing on whether the minority group has "less opportunity than other members of the electorate to participate in the political process *and* to elect representatives of their choice." [52 U.S.C. § 10301] (emphasis added). The court should not focus solely on the minority group's ability to elect representatives of its choice. Whatever measure of undiluted minority voting strength the court employs in connection with evaluating the presence or absence of minority electoral success, it should also bear in mind that "the power to influence the political process is not limited to winning elections." *Davis v. Bandemer*, [478 U.S. 109,] 132 [(1986)]. Of course, the relative lack of minority electoral success under a challenged plan, when compared with the success that would be predicted under the measure of undiluted minority voting strength the court is employing, can constitute powerful evidence of vote dilution. Moreover, the minority group may in fact lack access to or influence upon representatives it did not support as candidates. Nonetheless, a reviewing court should be required to find more than simply that the minority group does not usually attain an undiluted measure of electoral success. The court must find that even substantial minority success will be highly infrequent under the challenged plan before it may conclude, on this basis alone, that the plan operates "to cancel out or minimize the voting strength of [the] racial [group]." *White, supra*, at 765.

Only three Justices of the Court join Part III-C of JUSTICE BRENNAN's opinion, which addresses the validity of the statistical evidence on which the District Court relied in finding racially polarized voting in each of the challenged districts. Insofar as statistical evidence of divergent racial voting patterns is admitted solely to establish that the minority group is politically cohesive and to assess its prospects for electoral success, I agree that defendants cannot rebut this showing by offering evidence that the divergent racial voting patterns may be explained in part by causes other than race, such as an underlying divergence in the interests of minority and white voters. I do not agree, however, that such evidence can never affect the overall vote dilution inquiry. Evidence that a candidate preferred by the minority group in a particular election was rejected by white voters for reasons other than those which made that candidate the preferred choice of the minority group would seem clearly relevant in answering the question whether bloc voting by white voters will consistently defeat minority candidates. Such evidence would suggest that another candidate, equally preferred by the minority group, might be able to attract greater white support in future elections.

I believe Congress also intended that explanations of the reasons why white voters rejected minority candidates would be probative of the likelihood that candidates elected without decisive minority support would be willing to take the minority's interests into account. In a community that is polarized along racial lines, racial hostility may bar these and other indirect avenues of political influence to a much greater extent than in a community where racial animosity is absent although the interests of racial groups diverge. * * * Similarly, I agree with Justice White that Justice Brennan's conclusion that the race of the candidate is always irrelevant in identifying racially polarized voting conflicts with *Whitcomb* and is not necessary to the disposition of this case. * * *

* * * I agree with Justice Brennan that consistent and sustained success by candidates preferred by minority voters is presumptively inconsistent with the existence of a § 2 violation. Moreover, I agree that this case presents no occasion for determining what would constitute proof that such success did not accurately reflect the minority group's actual voting strength in a challenged district or districts. * * *

I do not propose that consistent and virtually proportional minority electoral success should always, as a matter of law, bar finding a § 2 violation. But, as a general rule, such success is entitled to great weight in evaluating whether a challenged electoral mechanism has, on the totality of the circumstances, operated to deny black voters an equal opportunity to participate in the political process and to elect representatives of their choice. With respect to House District 23, the District Court's failure to accord black electoral success such weight was clearly erroneous, and the District Court identified no reason for not giving this degree of success preclusive effect. Accordingly, I agree with Justice Brennan that appellees failed to establish a violation of § 2 in District 23. * * *

Compromise is essential to much if not most major federal legislation, and confidence that the federal courts will enforce such compromises is indispensable to their creation. I believe that the Court today strikes a different balance than Congress intended to when it codified the results test and disclaimed any right to proportional representation under § 2. For that reason, I join the Court's judgment but not its opinion.

JUSTICE STEVENS, with whom JUSTICE MARSHALL and JUSTICE BLACKMUN join, concurring in part and dissenting in part.

In my opinion, the findings of the District Court * * * adequately support [its] judgment concerning House District 23 as well as the balance of that judgment.

I, of course, agree that the election of one black candidate in each election since 1972 provides significant support for the State's position. The notion that this evidence creates some sort of a conclusive, legal presumption is not, however, supported by the language of the statute or by its legislative history. I therefore cannot agree with the Court's view that the District Court committed error by failing to apply a rule of law that emerges today without statutory support. The evidence of candidate success in District 23 is merely one part of an extremely large record which the District Court carefully considered before making its ultimate findings of fact, all of which should be upheld under a normal application of the "clearly erroneous" standard that the Court traditionally applies.

The Court identifies the reason why the success of one black candidate in the elections in 1978, 1980, and 1982 is not inconsistent with the District Court's ultimate finding concerning House District 23. The fact that one black candidate was also elected in the 1972, 1974, and 1976 elections is not sufficient, in my opinion, to overcome the additional findings that apply to House District 23, as well as to other districts in the State for each of those years. [Here JUSTICE STEVENS quoted the Court's reference, in Part V of its opinion, to racially polarized voting, a history of discrimination, and campaign appeals to racial prejudice.] * * * Accordingly, I concur in the Court's opinion except Part IV-B and except insofar as it explains why it reverses the judgment respecting House District 23.

Notes and Questions

1. What justification does the Court give for pegging the dilution inquiry to a minority group's potential electoral strength *in single-member districts*? Is the Court simply incorporating its own political theory into § 2 by preferring single-member to multimember districts?

2. As interpreted by the Court, did the amendment to § 2 simply replace the test applied by the plurality in *City of Mobile v. Bolden* with the one that had been applied in *Whitcomb v. Chavis* and *White v. Regester*? Is that what Congress intended to do?

3. Justice Brennan, writing for four Justices in Part III.C, concluded that § 2's inquiry into racially polarized voting was limited to the question whether voting patterns *correlated* with race, rather than the question whether groups voted as they did *because of* race. Is such an interpretation consistent with the text of § 2, which provides a right to be free from abridgment of the right to vote "on account of race or color"? What did the other five Justices conclude about the question Justice Brennan addressed in Part III.C?

4. Is there racially polarized voting in a jurisdiction where whites and minorities vote for different candidates, but where partisan affiliation and not race best explains those voting patterns? *Compare League of United Latin American Citizens v. Clements*, 999 F.2d 831 (5th Cir. 1994) (*en banc*), *with Goosby v. Town of Hempstead*, 180 F.3d 476 (2d Cir. 1999).

5. Is it appropriate to characterize a district as "racially polarized" if the majority prefers Candidate A to Candidate B by a 51%-49% margin, while the minority prefers Candidate B to Candidate A by the same margin? Would it be better to require, for example, 60% of the majority and the minority to support different candidates? *See United States v. City of Euclid*, 580 F. Supp. 2d 584, 603 (N.D. Ohio 2008).

6. One consequence of *Gingles*'s focus on *voter* preference and polarized voting, rather than on the races of *candidates*, is that it may be more difficult for a minority group to make out a claim under § 2 if the group itself is politically divided. Is such a result desirable? On the one hand, districting plans do not interfere with the ability to elect minority voters' preferred candidates if the minority voters do not, as a group, prefer particular candidates. On the other hand, however, a district controlled by a minority group may provide an increased opportunity to elect a member of that minority group, and therefore, recognizing a § 2 claim in such circumstances may enhance that group's opportunity for *descriptive* representation *i.e.*, representation by someone who shares important characteristics (in this case, racial characteristics) with the voters.

7. Did the Court (and Justice Brennan in those portions of his opinion that did not command a majority) appropriately make use of the legislative history surrounding the 1982 amendment to § 2, or did reliance on the Senate Report risk undermining the compromise that underlay the amendment? *See Holder v. Hall*, 512 U.S. 874, 931–36 (1994) [p. 343] (Thomas, J., concurring in the judgment) (criticizing *Gingles*'s reliance on legislative history).

8. From an ideological perspective, Justice Brennan's decision to overturn the district court's judgment with respect to District 23 is puzzling. Justice Brennan was one of the Court's leading liberals, and it may be surprising that he held the evidence of blacks' unequal electoral opportunity to be insufficient to make out a § 2 claim. What other reason might account for Justice Brennan's position?

9. The first *Gingles* precondition required a minority group to demonstrate that it was "sufficiently large and geographically compact to constitute a majority in a single-member district." Nevertheless, in footnote 12, the Court cautioned that it was not deciding "whether § 2 permits, and if it does, what standards should pertain to, a claim brought by a minority group, that is not sufficiently large and compact to constitute a majority in a single-member district, alleging that the use of a multi-member district impairs its ability *to influence* elections." The Court confronted § 2's applicability to single-member influence districts in *League of United Latin American Citizens (LULAC) v. Perry*, 548 U.S. 399 (2006) [p. 395], and held that § 2 does not require the creation of influence districts. *See id*. at 445 (opinion of Kennedy, J.).

Later, in *Bartlett v. Strickland*, 556 U.S. 1 (2009), a 3-2-4 decision, the Court held that § 2 contained no right to crossover districts, either. In a crossover district, the minority group is able to elect its preferred candidate—not a compromise candidate—because of majority voters who "crossover" and vote for the candidate supported by the minority.[b] The plurality opinion by Justice Kennedy, joined by Chief Justice Roberts and Justice Alito, reiterated *Gingles*'s first precondition that a minority group raising a § 2 claim must be able to show that it could constitute *a majority* in a reasonably compact district. *See id.* at 18. The remaining two members of the majority, Justice Thomas and Justice Scalia, would have held that § 2 did not permit vote-dilution claims at all. *See id.* at 26 (Thomas, J., concurring in the judgment).

The *Bartlett* standard may be intuitively attractive, because a majority group can always win an election, whereas a group constituting less than a majority will be dependent on support from (or coalitions with) others. But *Bartlett*'s 50% threshold unrealistically assumes either complete polarization (all minorities voting for one candidate and all other voters voting for a different candidate) or at least an identical number of "defectors"—minorities who vote for the majority-preferred candidate and members of the majority who vote for the minority-preferred candidate. In reality, of course, voting is rarely that polarized, and there is no reason to assume that the majority and the minority will vote equally as a bloc. In *Bartlett*, for example, the lower court found that the minority group could control the selection of representatives if it had slightly less than 40% of the voting-age population because of reliable crossover support from white voters. Further, the 50% threshold assumes equal voter turnout. In reality, however, a group constituting less than a majority can win elections without any crossover votes if the minority group turns out at a higher rate than the majority. Thus, as the dissenters charged, a 50% threshold in this context may be "arbitrary," *id.* at 33 (Souter, J., dissenting), because it does not address "the relevant question: Is the minority bloc large enough, is it cohesive enough, is the necessary majority crossover vote small enough, so that the minority (tending to vote cohesively) can likely vote its preferred candidate (rather than a consensus candidate) into office?" *Id.* at 45–46 (Breyer, J., dissenting).

The plurality responded that a group with less than a majority of a district's population has "no better or worse opportunity to elect a candidate than does any other group of voters with the same relative voting strength." *Id.* at 14 (plurality opinion); *see also id.* at 20 ("Minority groups in crossover districts cannot form a voting majority without crossover voters. In those districts minority voters have the same opportunity to elect their candidate as any other political group with the same relative voting strength."). Thus, according to the plurality, the electoral

---

b. Ordinarily, such crossover voting would defeat a § 2 claim for a separate reason: The majority would not be voting sufficiently as a bloc usually to defeat the minority's preferred candidate, and thus the third *Gingles* precondition would not be satisfied. 556 U.S. at 24 (plurality opinion). Yet "for some reason" the state in *Bartlett* conceded that there was majority bloc voting. *Id.* at 16.

power of the minority group was a function of its size, rather than the design of the district.

The plurality further touted the advantage of its 50% threshold in terms of its easy administrability and "straightforward guidance to courts and to those officials charged with drawing district lines," *id.* at 18, because of the threshold's "clear lines," *id.* at 17, and "objective, numerical test," *id.* at 18. Lastly, the plurality suggested that an alternative approach would "infuse race into virtually every redistricting, raising serious constitutional questions." *Id.* at 21 (quoting *LULAC v. Perry*, 548 U.S. at 446 (opinion of Kennedy, J.)).

10. The *Bartlett* plurality held that a minority group did not possess the opportunity to elect representatives of its choice unless it comprised more than 50% of the *voting-age* population in a district. Is that the appropriate denominator? Suppose, for example, that members of a particular minority group are registered to vote at a disproportionately low rate, either because of disqualifying felony convictions or simply because they have not completed the required paperwork. In such a situation, even if the minority group makes up a majority of a district's population, it may not be able to elect its chosen representative because not all of its members would actually be able to vote. Should courts instead ask whether a minority group is numerous enough as a percentage of registered voters? Total population? *Citizen* voting-age population? *See Reyes v. City of Farmers Branch, Tex.*, 586 F.3d 1019, 1023–25 (5th Cir. 2009).

11. *Bartlett v. Strickland* dealt with a minority group that was not sufficiently numerous to constitute a majority in a district. The plurality held that such a group could not satisfy the first prong of *Gingles*, even if it could be expected to receive crossover votes from other racial groups. What about the converse situation, where a minority group is sufficiently large to constitute a bare majority of a district's voting-age population, but where some members of that group would be expected to support an opposing candidate? In such a situation, would the minority group be sufficiently numerous to satisfy *Gingles*? *See Thompson v. Glades County Board of County Commissioners*, 2004 U.S. Dist. LEXIS 30989 (M.D. Fla. Aug. 27, 2004), *rev'd*, 493 F.3d 1253, 1262–65, *vacated en banc*, 508 F.3d 975 (2007), *district-court decision aff'd by an equally divided en banc court*, 532 F.3d 1179 (11th Cir. 2008), *cert. denied*, 556 U.S. 1126 (2009).

12. Apart from the question of the requirements of the VRA, *should* states create coalition, crossover, or influence districts? Many identifiable minority groups are not sufficiently numerous to amount to a majority in a single-member district, but a district may be drawn to provide such a group with an opportunity for political influence that would otherwise be lost. *See* Keith Aoki, *A Tale of Three Cities: Thoughts on Asian American Electoral and Political Power After 2000*, 8 UCLA Asian Pac. Am. L.J. 1 (2002).

13. *Gingles* was principally concerned with the dilutive effect of multimember districts on minority voting strength. *See* footnote 12. States can accomplish the

same result, however, without resorting to multimember districts. If a districting plan "cracks" a minority community into many single-member districts, it can split the votes of that minority community, so that those votes are ineffective. And if a plan "packs" a minority community into a small number of single-member districts, the minority group may lose its opportunity to exert influence over a greater number of legislators. Accordingly, as demonstrated in *Johnson v. De Grandy*, below, the Court has applied *Gingles* to claims that gerrymandering has diluted the effectiveness of minorities' votes even within a system of single-member districts. *See also Voinovich v. Quilter*, 507 U.S. 146, 153–54 (1993); *Growe v. Emison*, 507 U.S. 25, 37–42 (1993). As you read *De Grandy*, consider the ways in which application of *Gingles* should be modified in a challenge to the drawing of single-member districts.

14. In *Gingles*, Justice O'Connor charged that the Court's vote-dilution standard essentially created a right to proportional representation, in contravention of §2's proviso. Reread the proviso. Is a standard of proportionality inconsistent with the language of the statute? The proportionality baseline is at the forefront of the next case.

Johnson v. De Grandy

Supreme Court of the United States
512 U.S. 997, 114 S. Ct. 2647, 129 L. Ed. 2d 775 (1994)

JUSTICE SOUTER delivered the opinion of the Court [in which CHIEF JUSTICE REHNQUIST, JUSTICE BLACKMUN, JUSTICE STEVENS, JUSTICE O'CONNOR, and JUSTICE GINSBURG join, and in all but Parts III-B-2, III-B-4, and IV of which JUSTICE KENNEDY joins].

These consolidated cases are about the meaning of vote dilution and the facts required to show it, when §2 of the Voting Rights Act of 1965 is applied to challenges to single-member legislative districts. We hold that no violation of §2 can be found here, where, in spite of continuing discrimination and racial bloc voting, minority voters form effective voting majorities in a number of districts roughly proportional to the minority voters' respective shares in the voting-age population. While such proportionality is not dispositive in a challenge to single-member districting, it is a relevant fact in the totality of circumstances to be analyzed when determining whether members of a minority group have "less opportunity than other members of the electorate to participate in the political process and to elect representatives of their choice."

I * * *

[O]n April 10, 1992, the [Florida] legislature adopted Senate Joint Resolution 2-G (SJR 2-G), [which] called for dividing Florida into 40 single-member Senate, and 120 single-member House, districts based on population data from the 1990 census. * * *

[Plaintiffs, a group of Hispanic voters, sued,] claim[ing] that SJR 2-G "unlaw-fully fragments cohesive minority communities and otherwise impermissibly sub-merges their right to vote and to participate in the electoral process" [in violation of § 2,] and they pointed to areas around the State where black or Hispanic popu-lations could have formed a voting majority in a politically cohesive, reasonably compact district (or in more than one), if SJR 2-G had not fragmented each group among several districts or packed it into just a few. * * *

[T]he [District C]ourt reviewed the totality of circumstances as required by § 2 and *Thornburg* v. *Gingles*, 478 U.S. 30 (1986) [p. 316]. In explaining Dade County's "tripartite politics," in which "ethnic factors . . . predominate over all others," the court found political cohesion within each of the Hispanic and black populations but none between the two, and a tendency of non-Hispanic whites to vote as a bloc to bar minority groups from electing their chosen candidates except in a district where a given minority makes up a voting majority. The court further found that the nearly one million Hispanics in the Dade County area could be combined into 4 Senate and 11 House districts, each one relatively compact and with a functional majority of Hispanic voters, whereas SJR 2-G created fewer majority-Hispanic dis-tricts; and that one more Senate district with a black voting majority could have been drawn. Noting that Florida's minorities bore the social, economic, and politi-cal effects of past discrimination, the court concluded that SJR 2-G impermissibly diluted the voting strength of Hispanics in its House districts and of both Hispanics and blacks in its Senate districts. The findings of vote dilution in the senatorial dis-tricts had no practical effect, however, because the court held that remedies for the blacks and the Hispanics were mutually exclusive; it consequently deferred to the state legislature's work as the "fairest" accommodation of all the ethnic communi-ties in south Florida. * * *

III * * *

B

* * * The District Court found that the three *Gingles* preconditions were satis-fied, and that Hispanics had suffered historically from official discrimination, the social, economic, and political effects of which they generally continued to feel. Without more, and on the apparent assumption that what could have been done to create additional Hispanic supermajority districts should have been done, the Dis-trict Court found a violation of § 2. But the assumption was erroneous, and more is required, as a review of *Gingles* will show.

1 * * *

Gingles provided some structure to the statute's "totality of circumstances" test in a case challenging multimember legislative districts. The Court * * * summa-rized the three now-familiar *Gingles* factors (compactness/numerousness, minority cohesion or bloc voting, and majority bloc voting) as "necessary preconditions," 478 U.S., at 50, for establishing vote dilution by use of a multimember district.

But if *Gingles* so clearly identified the three as generally necessary to prove a § 2 claim, it just as clearly declined to hold them sufficient in combination, either in the sense that a court's examination of relevant circumstances was complete once the three factors were found to exist, or in the sense that the three in combination necessarily and in all circumstances demonstrated dilution. This was true not only because bloc voting was a matter of degree, with a variable legal significance depending on other facts, but also because the ultimate conclusions about equality or inequality of opportunity were intended by Congress to be judgments resting on comprehensive, not limited, canvassing of relevant facts. Lack of electoral success is evidence of vote dilution, but courts must also examine other evidence in the totality of circumstances, including the extent of the opportunities minority voters enjoy to participate in the political processes. 478 U.S., at 46, 79–80; 478 U.S., at 98–99 (O'CONNOR, J., concurring in judgment). To be sure, some § 2 plaintiffs may have easy cases, but although lack of equal electoral opportunity may be readily imagined and unsurprising when demonstrated under circumstances that include the three essential *Gingles* factors, that conclusion must still be addressed explicitly, and without isolating any other arguably relevant facts from the act of judgment.

2 * * *

* * * We think that in finding dilution here the District Court misjudged the relative importance of the *Gingles* factors and of historical discrimination, measured against evidence tending to show that in spite of these facts, SJR 2-G would provide minority voters with an equal measure of political and electoral opportunity. * * * The court failed to ask whether the totality of facts, including those pointing to proportionality,[11] showed that the new scheme would deny minority voters equal political opportunity.

Treating equal political opportunity as the focus of the enquiry, we do not see how these district lines, apparently providing political effectiveness in proportion to voting-age numbers, deny equal political opportunity. The record establishes that Hispanics constitute 50 percent of the voting-age population in Dade County and under SJR 2-G would make up supermajorities in 9 of the 18 House districts located primarily within the county. Likewise, if one considers the 20 House districts located at least in part within Dade County, the record indicates that Hispanics would be an effective voting majority in 45 percent of them (*i.e.*, nine), and would constitute 47 percent of the voting-age population in the area. In other words,

---

11. "Proportionality" as the term is used here links the number of majority-minority voting districts to minority members' share of the relevant population. The concept is distinct from the subject of the proportional representation clause of § 2, which provides that "nothing in this section establishes a right to have members of a protected class elected in numbers equal to their proportion in the population." [52 U.S.C. § 10301(b)]. This proviso speaks to the success of minority candidates, as distinct from the political or electoral power of minority voters. And the proviso also confirms what is otherwise clear from the text of the statute, namely, that the ultimate right of § 2 is equality of opportunity, not a guarantee of electoral success for minority-preferred candidates of whatever race.

under SJR 2-G Hispanics in the Dade County area would enjoy substantial proportionality. On this evidence, we think the State's scheme would thwart the historical tendency to exclude Hispanics, not encourage or perpetuate it. Thus in spite of that history and its legacy, including the racial cleavages that characterize Dade County politics today, we see no grounds for holding in these cases that SJR 2-G's district lines diluted the votes cast by Hispanic voters.

[P]laintiffs urge us to put more weight on the District Court's findings of packing and fragmentation, allegedly accomplished by the way the State drew certain specific lines * * *. We would agree that where a State has split (or lumped) minority neighborhoods that would have been grouped into a single district (or spread among several) if the State had employed the same line-drawing standards in minority neighborhoods as it used elsewhere in the jurisdiction, the inconsistent treatment might be significant evidence of a § 2 violation, even in the face of proportionality. The District Court, however, made no such finding. * * * [S]ome dividing by district lines and combining within them is virtually inevitable and befalls any population group of substantial size. Attaching the labels "packing" and "fragmenting" to these phenomena, without more, does not make the result vote dilution when the minority group enjoys substantial proportionality.

3

It may be that the significance of the facts under § 2 was obscured by the rule of thumb apparently adopted by the District Court, that anything short of the maximum number of majority-minority districts consistent with the *Gingles* conditions would violate § 2, at least where societal discrimination against the minority had occurred and continued to occur. But * * * reading § 2 to define dilution as any failure to maximize tends to obscure the very object of the statute and to run counter to its textually stated purpose. One may suspect vote dilution from political famine, but one is not entitled to suspect (much less infer) dilution from mere failure to guarantee a political feast. * * * Failure to maximize cannot be the measure of § 2.

4

While, for obvious reasons, the State agrees that a failure to leverage minority political strength to the maximum possible point of power is not definitive of dilution in bloc-voting societies, it seeks to impart a measure of determinacy by applying a definitive rule of its own: that as a matter of law no dilution occurs whenever the percentage of single-member districts in which minority voters form an effective majority mirrors the minority voters' percentage of the relevant population. Proportionality so defined would thus be a safe harbor for any districting scheme.

The safety would be in derogation of the statutory text and its considered purpose, however, and of the ideal that the Voting Rights Act of 1965 attempts to foster. An inflexible rule would run counter to the textual command of § 2, that the presence or absence of a violation be assessed "based on the totality of circumstances." [52 U.S.C. § 10301(b)]. * * * In modifying § 2, Congress thus endorsed our view in *White v. Regester*, 412 U.S. 755 (1973) [p. 288], that "whether the political processes are 'equally open' depends upon a searching practical evaluation of the 'past and present reality,'" Senate Report 30 (quoting 412 U.S., at 766, 770). In a substantial number of voting jurisdictions, that past reality has included such reprehensible practices as ballot box stuffing, outright violence, discretionary registration, property require-ments, the poll tax, and the white primary; and other practices censurable when the object of their use is discriminatory, such as at-large elections, runoff requirements, anti-single-shot devices, gerrymandering, the impeachment of officeholders, the annexation or deannexation of territory, and the creation or elimination of elective offices. Some of those expedients could occur even in a jurisdiction with numerically demonstrable proportionality; the harbor safe for States would thus not be safe for voters. It is, in short, for good reason that we have been, and remain, chary of enter-taining a simplification of the sort the State now urges upon us.

Even if the State's safe harbor were open only in cases of alleged dilution by the manipulation of district lines, however, it would rest on an unexplored premise of highly suspect validity: that in any given voting jurisdiction (or portion of that jurisdiction under consideration), the rights of some minority voters under § 2 may be traded off against the rights of other members of the same minority class. Under the State's view, the most blatant racial gerrymandering in half of a county's single-member districts would be irrelevant under § 2 if offset by political gerrymandering in the other half, so long as proportionality was the bottom line.

Finally, we reject the safe harbor rule because of a tendency the State would itself certainly condemn, a tendency to promote and perpetuate efforts to devise majority-minority districts even in circumstances where they may not be necessary to achieve equal political and electoral opportunity. Because in its simplest form the State's rule would shield from § 2 challenge a districting scheme in which the number of majority-minority districts reflected the minority's share of the relevant population, the conclusiveness of the rule might be an irresistible inducement to create such districts. It bears recalling, however, that for all the virtues of majority-minority districts as remedial devices, they rely on a quintessentially race-conscious calculus aptly described as the "politics of second best." If the lesson of *Gingles* is that society's racial and ethnic cleavages sometimes necessitate majority-minority districts to ensure equal political and electoral opportunity, that should not obscure the fact that there are communities in which minority citizens are able to form coalitions with voters from other racial and ethnic groups, having no need to be a majority within a single district in order to elect candidates of their choice. Those candidates may not represent perfection to every minority voter, but minority vot-ers are not immune from the obligation to pull, haul, and trade to find common political ground, the virtue of which is not to be slighted in applying a statute meant to hasten the waning of racism in American politics.

It is enough to say that, while proportionality in the sense used here is obviously an indication that minority voters have an equal opportunity, in spite of racial polar-ization, "to participate in the political process and to elect representatives of their choice," the degree of probative value assigned to proportionality may vary with other facts.[17] No single statistic provides courts with a shortcut to determine whether a set of single-member districts unlawfully dilutes minority voting strength. * * *

6

In sum, the District Court's finding of dilution did not address the statutory standard of unequal political and electoral opportunity, and reflected instead a misconstruction of § 2 that equated dilution with failure to maximize the number of reasonably compact majority-minority districts. Because the ultimate finding of dilution in districting for the Florida House was based on a misreading of the governing law, we hold it to be clearly erroneous.

IV

Having found insufficient evidence of vote dilution in the drawing of House districts in the Dade County area, we look now to the comparable districts for the state Senate. As in the case of House districts, we understand the District Court to have misapprehended the legal test for vote dilution when it found a violation of § 2 in the location of the Senate district lines. Because the court did not modify the State's plan, however, we hold the ultimate result correct in this instance. * * *

[Affirmed in part and reversed in part.]

Justice O'Connor, concurring.

The critical issue in these cases is whether § 2 of the Voting Rights Act of 1965 requires courts to "maximize" the number of districts in which minority voters may elect their candidates of choice. * * * The Court today makes clear that * * * the Voting Rights Act does not require maximization.

But today's opinion does more than reject the maximization principle. The opinion's central teaching is that proportionality—defined as the relationship between the number of majority-minority voting districts and the minority group's share of the relevant population—is *always* relevant evidence in determining vote dilution, but is *never* itself dispositive. * * *

* * * Lack of proportionality can never by itself prove dilution, for courts must always carefully and searchingly review the totality of the circumstances, including the extent to which minority groups have access to the political process. Nor does the presence of proportionality prove the absence of dilution. Proportionality is not a safe harbor for States; it does not immunize their election schemes from § 2 challenge.

---

17. So, too, the degree of probative value assigned to disproportionality, in a case where it is shown, will vary not only with the degree of disproportionality but with other factors as well. * * *

In sum, the Court's carefully crafted approach treats proportionality as relevant evidence, but does not make it the only relevant evidence. * * * With this understanding, I join the opinion of the Court.

JUSTICE KENNEDY, concurring in part and concurring in the judgment.

* * * I agree with the Court that the District Court's maximization theory was an erroneous application of § 2 [and that proportionality is relevant to the § 2 inquiry]. * * *

It is important to emphasize that [our precedents and] today's decision[] only construe the statute, and do not purport to assess its constitutional implications. Operating under the constraints of a statutory regime in which proportionality has some relevance, States might consider it lawful and proper to act with the explicit goal of creating a proportional number of majority-minority districts in an effort to avoid § 2 litigation. Likewise, a court finding a § 2 violation might believe that the only appropriate remedy is to order the offending State to engage in race-based redistricting and create a minimum number of districts in which minorities constitute a voting majority. The Department of Justice might require (in effect) the same as a condition of granting preclearance, under § 5 of the Act, 42 U.S.C. § 1973c [now 52 U.S.C. § 10304 — Eds.], to a State's proposed legislative redistricting. Those governmental actions, in my view, tend to entrench the very practices and stereotypes the Equal Protection Clause is set against. As a general matter, the sorting of persons with an intent to divide by reason of race raises the most serious constitutional questions. * * *

* * * But no constitutional claims were brought here, and the Court's opinion does not address any constitutional issues.

With these observations, I concur in all but Parts III-B-2, III-B-4, and IV of the Court's opinion and in its judgment.

JUSTICE THOMAS, with whom JUSTICE SCALIA joins, dissenting.

* * * In accordance with the views I express in *Holder* [v. *Hall*, 512 U.S. 891 (1994)] [p. 343], I would hold that an apportionment plan is not a "standard, practice, or procedure" that may be challenged under § 2. I therefore respectfully dissent.

Notes and Questions

1. Do you agree with the Court that a minority group may enjoy proportional representation and still make out a claim under § 2 that its members lack an equal opportunity "to participate in the political process and to elect representatives of their choice"? What would the plaintiffs in *De Grandy* have needed to show to succeed on such a claim?

Consider *Patino v. City of Pasadena, Texas*, 230 F. Supp. 3d 667 (S.D. Tex. 2017), *stay denied*, 677 Fed. Appx. 950 (5th Cir. 2017). Members of the city council had been elected in eight single-member districts, but the city changed that system and adopted a plan that contained six single-member districts and one two-member district. The district court found a dilution of Latinos' voting rights under VRA § 2, even though Latinos, who were just less than half the City's population, elected their preferred candidate to four of the eight council seats, including one of the two at-large seats. Furthermore, Latinos represented nearly 70% of the citizen voting-age population in one of the single-member districts that did not elect the Latinos' preferred candidate. Nevertheless, the district court discounted the importance of Latinos' success in the one election held under the new plan, because two of the successful Latino candidates had Anglo surnames and were incumbents. Do you think that Latino voters in Pasadena lacked an equal opportunity to elect representatives of their choice?

2. *De Grandy* expressed doubt that a state could make up for racial gerrymandering in part of the state by political gerrymandering elsewhere, even if the result would be proportional representation of the minority group. Why should it matter *where* the districts are that result in minorities having the opportunity to elect candidates of their choice?

3. Should retrogression play a role in the § 2 totality-of-the-circumstances inquiry? For different perspectives on that question, compare Ellen D. Katz, *Section 2 After Section 5: Voting Rights and the Race to the Bottom*, 59 Wm. & Mary L. Rev. 1561 (2018) (arguing that courts have considered past practices as part of the § 2 inquiry, and defending the practice to limit "backsliding" by states), with *Ohio Democratic Party v. Husted*, 843 F.3d 620, 623 (6th Cir. 2016) (arguing that such use would improperly create a "one-way ratchet" in § 2 litigation), and Derek T. Muller, *The Democracy Ratchet*, 94 Ind. L.J. 451 (2019) (surveying use of the ratchet argument in different voting-rights contexts and suggesting when it may and may not be appropriate).

4. Did the Court adequately distinguish its proportionality inquiry from the proviso in the amended § 2 ("[N]othing in this section establishes a right to have members of a protected class elected in numbers equal to their proportion in the population.")? Justice Thomas thought not:

> It should be clear that a system that gives a minority group proportional control effectively provides the "right" to elect a proportionate number of minority candidates that the Act disclaims. Whether that right is utilized by minority voters to elect minority candidates is a matter of the voters' choice. The *De Grandy* Court's position seems to be that the proviso is directed, not at a system intended to guarantee the *ability* to elect minority candidates in proportion to the minority's numbers, but only at a system that will *invariably guarantee* the election of a proportionate number of minority candidates. Only one system would fit that description: a system based on a racial register in which a quota of seats are [*sic*] set aside for members of a minority

group. I think it would be preposterous to suggest that the disclaimer in § 2(b) was intended solely to prohibit the use of such a system. * * * Moreover, to the extent that the decisions in *White* and *Whitcomb* can inform our understanding of § 2(b), they suggest that in expressing a concern that "proportionality" not be used as the measure of a voting rights violation, Congress was concerned with proportional electoral power, not merely proportional election of minority candidates. The proviso has been understood in the past simply as a disclaimer of a right to proportional representation, see, *e.g.*, *Gingles*, 478 U.S., at 84–86, 94 (O'CONNOR, J., concurring in judgment), and I think that understanding is correct.

Holder v. Hall, 512 U.S. 874, 928–29 n.26 (1994) [p. 343] (Thomas, J., concurring in the judgment). Should it matter that the legislative history relied upon in *Thornburg v. Gingles* stated that § 2(b) "does not establish a right to proportional representation"? S. Rep. No. 97-417, p.2 (1982), *quoted in Chisom v. Roemer*, 501 U.S. 380, 394 n.20 (1991).

5. In any democratic system of government, there must be some mechanism for resolving policy disagreement. If every group is represented in the legislature, then the legislature itself serves as the locus of democratic compromise — the place where different factions resolve their differences and where policy is determined. Where representation is less proportional, elections themselves serve as the locus of compromise; voters settle on representatives, with the policy more or less determined by the results of the elections. Section 2's goal of increasing minority voting power advances the first vision of democracy by increasing the opportunity for minority groups to access — and influence — legislative deliberations. Is that the best — or a realistic — way of conceptualizing democracy? Consider THE FEDERALIST No. 35, at 220 (Alexander Hamilton) (Jacob E. Cooke ed., 1961) ("It is said to be necessary that all classes of citizens should have some of their own number in the representative body, in order that their feelings and interests may be the better understood and attended to. But * * * this will never happen under any arrangement that leaves the votes of the people free.").

In attempting to control the negative effects of faction, should we draw districts that separate people with different interests into different districts, thereby giving minorities representation in the legislature? Or should we draw districts that resemble each other in their mix of people and interests? *See id.* No. 10, at 64 (James Madison) ("Extend the sphere [of a republic], and you take in a greater variety of parties and interests; you make it less probable that a majority of the whole will have a common motive to invade the rights of other citizens * * *."). Note that neither approach guarantees that minorities will succeed in getting the policies that they prefer; they may be outvoted either at the district level or in the legislature. Aside from policy outcomes, what are the advantages and disadvantages of a legislature comprised of members with diverse ideologies, compared to a legislature uniformly comprised of moderates?

D. "Standard, Practice, or Procedure" in Section 2

In Chapter 3, we examined the scope of § 5 of the Voting Rights Act, which requires covered jurisdictions to obtain preclearance of "any voting qualification or prerequisite to voting, or standard, practice, or procedure with respect to voting." 52 U.S.C. § 10304. Section 2 of the Act similarly applies to "standard[s], practice[s], [and] procedure[s]," 52 U.S.C. § 10301; accordingly, one might think that §§ 2 and 5 apply to the same laws. That intuition is generally correct, *see Chisom v. Roemer*, 501 U.S. 380, 401–02 (1991) (holding that § 2 applied to judicial elections, in part because the Court had already applied § 5 to them), but the complete answer is more complicated. Consider the next case.

Holder v. Hall

Supreme Court of the United States
512 U.S. 874, 114 S. Ct. 2581, 129 L. Ed. 2d 687 (1994)

JUSTICE KENNEDY announced the judgment of the Court and delivered an opinion, in which THE CHIEF JUSTICE [REHNQUIST] joined, and in all but Part II-B of which JUSTICE O'CONNOR joined.

This case presents the question whether the size of a governing authority is subject to a vote dilution challenge under § 2 of the Voting Rights Act of 1965, 42 U.S.C. § 1973 [now 52 U.S.C. § 10301 — Eds.].

I

The State of Georgia has 159 counties, one of which is Bleckley County, a rural county in central Georgia. Black persons make up nearly 20% of the eligible voting population in Bleckley County. Since its creation in 1912, the county has had a single-commissioner form of government for the exercise of "county governing authority." Under this system, the Bleckley County Commissioner performs all of the executive and legislative functions of the county government, including the levying of general and special taxes, the directing and controlling of all county property, and the settling of all claims. In addition to Bleckley County, about 10 other Georgia counties use the single-commissioner system; the rest have multimember commissions.

In 1985, the Georgia Legislature authorized Bleckley County to adopt a multimember commission consisting of five commissioners elected from single-member districts and a single chairman elected at large. In a referendum held in 1986, however, the electorate did not adopt the change to a multimember commission. (In a similar referendum four years earlier, county voters had approved a five-member district plan for the election of the county school board.)

In 1985, respondents (six black registered voters from Bleckley County and the Cochran/Bleckley County Chapter of the National Association for the

Advancement of Colored People) challenged the single-commissioner system [as violating § 2]. * * * Under the statute, the suit contended, Bleckley County must have a county commission of sufficient size that, with single-member election districts, the county's black citizens would constitute a majority in one of the single-member districts. * * *

II

A

Section 2 of the Voting Rights Act of 1965 provides that "[n]o voting qualification or prerequisite to voting, or standard, practice, or procedure shall be imposed or applied by any State or political subdivision in a manner which results in a denial or abridgement of the right of any citizen of the United States to vote on account of race or color." [52 U.S.C. § 10301(a)]. In a § 2 vote dilution suit, along with determining whether the *Gingles* preconditions are met and whether the totality of the circumstances supports a finding of liability [see *Thornburg* v. *Gingles*, 478 U.S. 30 (1986)] [p. 316]], a court must find a reasonable alternative practice as a benchmark against which to measure the existing voting practice. As JUSTICE O'CONNOR explained in *Gingles:* "The phrase vote dilution itself suggests a norm with respect to which the fact of dilution may be ascertained. . . . [I]n order to decide whether an electoral system has made it harder for minority voters to elect the candidates they prefer, a court must have an idea in mind of how hard it should be for minority voters to elect their preferred candidates under an acceptable system." 478 U.S., at 88 (opinion concurring in judgment).

In certain cases, the benchmark for comparison in a § 2 dilution suit is obvious. The effect of an anti-single-shot voting rule, for instance, can be evaluated by comparing the system with that rule to the system without that rule. But where there is no objective and workable standard for choosing a reasonable benchmark by which to evaluate a challenged voting practice, it follows that the voting practice cannot be challenged as dilutive under § 2.

As the facts of this case well illustrate, the search for a benchmark is quite problematic when a § 2 dilution challenge is brought to the size of a government body. There is no principled reason why one size should be picked over another as the benchmark for comparison. Respondents here argue that we should compare Bleckley County's sole commissioner system to a hypothetical five-member commission in order to determine whether the current system is dilutive. Respondents and the United States as *amicus curiae* give three reasons why the single-commissioner structure should be compared to a five-member commission (instead of, say, a 3-, 10-, or 15-member body): (1) because the five-member commission is a common form of governing authority in the State; (2) because the state legislature had authorized Bleckley County to adopt a five-member commission if it so chose (it did not); and (3) because the county had moved from a single superintendent of education to a school board with five members elected from single-member districts.

These referents do not bear upon dilution. It does not matter, for instance, how popular the single-member commission system is in Georgia in determining whether it dilutes the vote of a minority racial group in Bleckley County. That the single-member commission is uncommon in the State of Georgia, or that a five-member commission is quite common, tells us nothing about its effects on a minority group's voting strength. The sole commissioner system has the same impact regardless of whether it is shared by none, or by all, of the other counties in Georgia. It makes little sense to say (as do respondents and the United States) that the sole commissioner system should be subject to a dilution challenge if it is rare—but immune if it is common.

That Bleckley County was authorized by the State to expand its commission, and that it adopted a five-member school board, are likewise irrelevant considerations in the dilution inquiry. At most, those facts indicate that Bleckley County could change the size of its commission with minimal disruption. But the county's failure to do so says nothing about the effects the sole commissioner system has on the voting power of Bleckley County's citizens. Surely a minority group's voting strength would be no more or less diluted had the State not authorized the county to alter the size of its commission, or had the county not enlarged its school board. One gets the sense that respondents and the United States have chosen a benchmark for the sake of having a benchmark. But it is one thing to say that a benchmark can be found, quite another to give a convincing reason for finding it in the first place.

B

To bolster their argument, respondents point out that our § 5 cases may be interpreted to indicate that covered jurisdictions may not change the size of their government bodies without obtaining preclearance from the Attorney General or the federal courts. [S]ee *Presley* v. *Etowah County Comm'n*, 502 U.S. 491, 501–503 (1992); *City of Lockhart* v. *United States*, 460 U.S. 125, 131–132 (1983); *City of Rome* v. *United States*, 446 U.S. 156, 161 (1980). Respondents contend that these § 5 cases, together with the similarity in language between §§ 2 and 5 of the Act, compel the conclusion that the size of a government body must be subject to a dilution challenge under § 2. It is true that in *Chisom* v. *Roemer*, 501 U.S. 380, 401–402 (1991), we said that the coverage of §§ 2 and 5 is presumed to be the same (at least if differential coverage would be anomalous). We did not adopt a conclusive rule to that effect, however, and we do not think that the fact that a change in a voting practice must be precleared under § 5 necessarily means that the voting practice is subject to challenge in a dilution suit under § 2.

To be sure, if the structure and purpose of § 2 mirrored that of § 5, then the case for interpreting §§ 2 and 5 to have the same application in all cases would be convincing. But the two sections differ in structure, purpose, and application. Section 5 applies only in certain jurisdictions specified by Congress and "only to proposed changes in voting procedures." *Beer* v. *United States*, 425 U.S. 130, 138 (1976). In those covered jurisdictions, a proposed change in a voting practice must be approved in advance by the Attorney General or the federal courts. The purpose of this requirement "has always been to insure that no voting-procedure changes would be made that would lead to a retrogression in the position of racial minorities with respect to their effective exercise of the electoral franchise." 425 U.S., at 141. Under § 5, then, the proposed voting practice is measured against the existing voting practice to determine whether retrogression would result from the proposed change. See *id.* The baseline for comparison is present by definition; it is the existing status. While there may be difficulty in determining whether a proposed change would cause retrogression, there is little difficulty in discerning the two voting practices to compare to determine whether retrogression would occur.

Retrogression is not the inquiry in § 2 dilution cases. Unlike in § 5 cases, therefore, a benchmark does not exist by definition in § 2 dilution cases. And as explained above, with some voting practices, there in fact may be no appropriate benchmark to determine if an existing voting practice is dilutive under § 2. For that reason, a voting practice that is subject to the preclearance requirements of § 5 is not necessarily subject to a dilution challenge under § 2.

This conclusion is quite unremarkable. For example, in *Perkins v. Matthews*, 400 U.S. 379, 388 (1971), we held that a town's annexation of land was covered under § 5. Notwithstanding that holding, we think it quite improbable to suggest that a § 2 dilution challenge could be brought to a town's existing political boundaries (in an attempt to force it to annex surrounding land) by arguing that the current boundaries dilute a racial group's voting strength in comparison to the proposed new boundaries. Likewise, in *McCain v. Lybrand*, 465 U.S. 236 (1984), we indicated that a change from an appointive to an elected office was covered under § 5. Here, again, we doubt Congress contemplated that a racial group could bring a § 2 dilution challenge to an appointive office (in an attempt to force a change to an elective office) by arguing that the appointive office diluted its voting strength in comparison to the proposed elective office. We think these examples serve to show that a voting practice is not necessarily subject to a dilution challenge under § 2 even when a change in that voting practice would be subject to the preclearance requirements of § 5.

III

With respect to challenges to the size of a governing authority, respondents fail to explain where the search for reasonable alternative benchmarks should begin and end, and they provide no acceptable principles for deciding future cases. The wide range of possibilities makes the choice "inherently standardless," and we therefore conclude that a plaintiff cannot maintain a § 2 challenge to the size of a government body, such as the Bleckley County Commission. The judgment of the Court of Appeals is reversed, and the case is remanded * * *.

It is so ordered.

Justice O'Connor, concurring in part and concurring in the judgment.

I agree with Justices Kennedy and Thomas that a plaintiff cannot maintain a § 2 vote dilution challenge to the size of a governing authority, though I reach that conclusion by a somewhat different rationale. Justice Thomas rejects the notion that § 2 covers *any* dilution challenges, and would hold that § 2 is limited to "state enactments that regulate citizens' access to the ballot or the processes for counting a ballot." As Justice Stevens points out, however, *stare decisis* concerns weigh heavily here. These concerns require me to reject Justice Thomas' suggestion that we overhaul our established reading of § 2.

I also agree with Justice Blackmun that our precedents compel the conclusion that the size of the Bleckley County Commission is both a "standard, practice, or procedure" under § 2 and a "standard, practice, or procedure with respect to voting" under § 5.

As Justices Kennedy and Blackmun both recognize, in these cases we have consistently said that a change in size is a "standard, practice, or procedure with respect to voting" that is subject to § 5 preclearance. And though our cases involving size have concerned § 5, I do not think it possible to read the terms of § 2 more narrowly than the terms of § 5. * * * As a textual matter, I cannot see how a practice can be a "standard, practice, or procedure with respect to voting," yet not be a "standard, practice, or procedure." Indeed, the similarity in language led to our conclusion in *Chisom* v. *Roemer*, 501 U.S., [at] 401–402, that, at least for determining threshold coverage, §§ 2 and 5 have parallel scope.

But determining the threshold scope of coverage does not end the inquiry, at least so far as § 2 dilution challenges are concerned. * * * Section 2 vote dilution plaintiffs must establish that the challenged practice is dilutive. In order for an electoral system to dilute a minority group's voting power, there must be an alternative system that would provide greater electoral opportunity to minority voters. * * *

Accordingly, to determine whether voters possess the potential to elect representatives of choice in the absence of the challenged structure, courts must choose an objectively reasonable alternative practice as a benchmark for the dilution comparison. * * * We require preclearance of changes in size under § 5, because in a § 5 case the question of an alternative benchmark never arises—the benchmark is simply the former practice employed by the jurisdiction seeking approval of a change.

But § 2 dilution challenges raise more difficult questions. This case presents the question whether, in a § 2 dilution challenge to size, there can ever be an objective alternative benchmark for comparison. And I agree with Justice Kennedy that there cannot be. * * * In a dilution challenge to the size of a governing authority, choosing the alternative for comparison—a hypothetical larger (or smaller) governing authority—is extremely problematic. The wide range of possibilities makes the choice inherently standardless. Here, for example, respondents argued that the single-member commission structure was dilutive in comparison to a five-member structure, in which African-Americans would probably have been able to elect one representative of their choice. Some groups, however, will not be able to constitute a majority in one of five districts. Once a court accepts respondents' reasoning, it will have to allow a plaintiff group insufficiently large or geographically compact to form a majority in one of five districts to argue that the jurisdiction's failure to establish a 10-, 15-, or 25-commissioner structure is dilutive.

Respondents argue that this concern with arbitrary and standardless intrusions into the size of local governing authority is overstated. Respondents' principal support for this conclusion is that a five-member commission is the *most* common size for Georgia. But a five-member commission is not the *only* common size in Georgia: 22 Georgia counties have three-member commissions (and one county has an 11-member commission). Moreover, there is no good reason why the search for benchmarks should be limited to Georgia. Expanding the search nationwide produces many 20-person county commissions in Tennessee, and 40-member commissions in Wisconsin. In sum, respondents do not explain how common an alternative practice must be before it can be a reliable alternative benchmark for the dilution comparison, nor do they explain where the search for alternative benchmarks should begin and end.

Respondents' failure to provide any meaningful principles for deciding future cases demonstrates the difficulty with allowing dilution challenges to the size of a governing authority. Under respondents' open-ended test, a wide range of state governmental bodies may be subject to a dilution challenge. Within each State there are many forms of government, including county commissions that range dramatically in size. * * * Nor are deviations from the norm limited to counties. Statewide governing authorities also range dramatically in size, and often do not correlate to the size of the State. * * *

The discrepancies in size among state and local governing authorities reinforce my concern that the limiting principle offered by respondents will in practice limit very little. * * *

For these reasons, I concur in the conclusion that respondents' dilution challenge to the size of the Bleckley County Commission cannot be maintained under § 2 of the Voting Rights Act, and I join Parts I, II-A, and III of JUSTICE KENNEDY's opinion. * * *

JUSTICE THOMAS, with whom JUSTICE SCALIA joins, concurring in the judgment.

We are asked in this case to determine whether the size of a local governing body is subject to challenge under § 2 of the Voting Rights Act of 1965 as a "dilutive" practice. While I agree with JUSTICES KENNEDY and O'CONNOR that the size of a governing body cannot be attacked under § 2, I do not share their reasons for reaching that conclusion. * * * I would hold that the size of a government body is not a "standard, practice, or procedure" because, properly understood, those terms reach only state enactments that limit citizens' access to the ballot. * * *

As it was enforced in the years immediately following its enactment, the Voting Rights Act of 1965 was perceived primarily as legislation directed at eliminating literacy tests and similar devices that had been used to prevent black voter registration in the segregated South. * * *

The Act was immediately and notably successful in removing barriers to registration and ensuring access to the ballot. * * * By the end of 1967, black voter registration had reached at least 50% in every covered State.

The Court's decision in *Allen* v. *State Bd. of Elections*, 393 U.S. 544 (1969) [p. 252], however, marked a fundamental shift in the focal point of the Act. In an opinion dealing with four companion cases, the *Allen* Court determined that the Act should be given "the broadest possible scope." *Id.*, at 567. Thus, in *Fairley* v. *Patterson*, the Court decided that a covered jurisdiction's switch from a districting system to an at-large system for election of county supervisors was a "standard, practice, or procedure with respect to voting," subject to preclearance under § 5. *Id.*, at 569. Stating that the Act "was aimed at the subtle, as well as the obvious, state regulations which have the effect of denying citizens their right to vote because of their race," *id.*, at 565, the Court reasoned that § 5's preclearance provisions should apply, not only to changes in electoral laws that pertain to registration and access to the ballot, but to provisions that might "dilute" the force of minority votes that were duly cast and counted. See *id.*, at 569. The decision in *Allen* thus ensured that the terms "standard, practice, or procedure" would extend to encompass a wide array of electoral practices or voting systems that might be challenged for reducing the potential impact of minority votes.

As a consequence, *Allen* also ensured that courts would be required to confront a number of complex and essentially political questions in assessing claims of vote dilution under the Voting Rights Act. The central difficulty in any vote dilution case, of course, is determining a point of comparison against which dilution can be measured. As Justice Frankfurter observed several years before *Allen*, "[t]alk of 'debasement' or 'dilution' is circular talk. One cannot speak of 'debasement' or 'dilution' of the value of a vote until there is first defined a standard of reference as to what a vote should be worth." *Baker* v. *Carr*, 369 U.S. 186, 300 (1962) [p. 97] (dissenting opinion). See also *Thornburg* v. *Gingles*, 478 U.S., [at] 88 (O'CONNOR, J., concurring in judgment) ("[I]n order to decide whether an electoral system has made it harder for minority voters to elect the candidates they prefer, a court must have an idea in mind of how hard it 'should' be for minority voters to elect their preferred candidates under an acceptable system"). But in setting the benchmark of what "undiluted" or fully "effective" voting strength should be, a court must necessarily make some judgments based purely on an assessment of principles of political theory. As Justice Harlan pointed out in his dissent in *Allen*, the Voting Rights Act supplies no rule for a court to rely upon in deciding, for example, whether a multimember at-large system of election is to be preferred to a single-member district system; that is, whether one provides a more "effective" vote than another. * * * The choice is inherently a political one, and depends upon the selection of a theory for defining the fully "effective" vote—at bottom, a theory for defining effective participation in representative government. In short, what a court is actually asked to do in a vote dilution case is "to choose among competing bases of representation—ultimately, really, among competing theories of political philosophy." *Baker*, 369 U.S., at 300 (Frankfurter, J., dissenting).

Perhaps the most prominent feature of the philosophy that has emerged in vote dilution decisions since *Allen* has been the Court's preference for single-member districting schemes, both as a benchmark for measuring undiluted minority voting strength and as a remedial mechanism for guaranteeing minorities undiluted voting power.

It should be apparent, however, that there is no principle inherent in our constitutional system, or even in the history of the Nation's electoral practices, that makes single-member districts the "proper" mechanism for electing representatives to governmental bodies or for giving "undiluted" effect to the votes of a numerical minority. * * *

The obvious advantage the Court has perceived in single-member districts, of course, is their tendency to enhance the ability of any numerical minority in the electorate to gain control of seats in a representative body. But in choosing single-member districting as a benchmark electoral plan on that basis the Court has made a political decision and, indeed, a decision that itself depends on a prior political choice made in answer to Justice Harlan's question in *Allen*. Justice Harlan asked whether a group's votes should be considered more "effective" when they provide *influence* over a greater number of seats, or *control* over a lesser number of seats. In answering that query, the Court has determined that the purpose of the vote—or of the fully "effective" vote—is controlling seats. * * *

* * * Once one accepts the proposition that the effectiveness of votes is measured in terms of the control of seats, the core of any vote dilution claim is an assertion that the group in question is unable to control the "proper" number of seats—that is, the number of seats that the minority's percentage of the population would enable it to control in the benchmark "fair" system. The claim is inherently based on ratios between the numbers of the minority in the population and the numbers of seats controlled. * * * And once again, in selecting the proportion that will be used to define the undiluted strength of a minority—the ratio that will provide the principle for decision in a vote dilution case—a court must make a political choice. The ratio for which this Court has opted, and thus the mathematical principle driving the results in our cases, is undoubtedly direct proportionality. * * * While in itself that choice may strike us intuitively as the fairest or most just rule to apply, opting for proportionality is still a political choice, not a result required by any principle of law.

The dabbling in political theory that dilution cases have prompted, however, is hardly the worst aspect of our vote dilution jurisprudence. Far more pernicious has been the Court's willingness to accept the one underlying premise that must inform every minority vote dilution claim: the assumption that the group asserting dilution is not merely a racial or ethnic group, but a group having distinct political interests as well. Of necessity, in resolving vote dilution actions we have given credence to the view that race defines political interest. We have acted on the implicit assumption that members of racial and ethnic groups must all think alike on important matters of public policy and must have their own "minority preferred" representatives holding seats in elected bodies if they are to be considered represented at all.

It is true that in *Gingles* we stated that whether a racial group is "politically cohesive" may not be assumed, but rather must be proved in each case. See 478 U.S., at 51, 56. But the standards we have employed for determining political cohesion have proved so insubstantial that this "precondition" does not present much of a barrier to the assertion of vote dilution claims on behalf of any racial group. Moreover, it provides no test—indeed, it is not designed to provide a test—of whether race itself determines a distinctive political community of interest. According to the rule adopted in *Gingles*, plaintiffs must show simply that members of a racial group tend to prefer the same candidates. See 478 U.S., at 61–67 (opinion of Brennan, J.). There is no set standard defining how strong the correlation must be, and an inquiry into the cause for the correlation (to determine, for example, whether it might be the product of similar socioeconomic interests rather than some other factor related to race) is unnecessary. *Ibid.* See also *id.*, at 100 (O'CONNOR, J., concurring in judgment). Thus, whenever similarities in political preferences along racial lines exist, we proclaim that the cause of the correlation is irrelevant, but we effectively rely on the fact of the correlation to assume that racial groups have unique political interests. * * *

The assumptions upon which our vote dilution decisions have been based should be repugnant to any nation that strives for the ideal of a color-blind Constitution. * * * [O]ur voting rights decisions are rapidly progressing toward a system that is indistinguishable in principle from a scheme under which members of different racial groups are divided into separate electoral registers and allocated a proportion of political power on the basis of race. Under our jurisprudence, rather than requiring registration on racial rolls and dividing power purely on a population basis, we have simply resorted to the somewhat less precise expedient of drawing geographic district lines to capture minority populations and to ensure the existence of the "appropriate" number of "safe minority seats." * * * [F]ew devices could be better designed to exacerbate racial tensions than the consciously segregated districting system currently being constructed in the name of the Voting Rights Act.

As a practical political matter, our drive to segregate political districts by race can only serve to deepen racial divisions by destroying any need for voters or candidates to build bridges between racial groups or to form voting coalitions.

"Black-preferred" candidates are assured election in "safe black districts"; white-preferred candidates are assured election in "safe white districts." Neither group needs to draw on support from the other's constituency to win on election day. * * *

While the results we have already achieved under the Voting Rights Act might seem bad enough, we should recognize that our approach to splintering the electorate into racially designated single-member districts does not by any means mark a limit on the authority federal judges may wield to rework electoral systems under our Voting Rights Act jurisprudence. On the contrary, in relying on single-member districting schemes as a touchstone, our cases so far have been somewhat arbitrarily limited to addressing the interests of minority voters who are sufficiently geographically compact to form a majority in a single-member district. See *Gingles*, 478 U.S., at 49–50. There is no reason *a priori*, however, that our focus should be so constrained. The decision to rely on single-member geographic districts as a mechanism for conducting elections is merely a political choice—and one that we might reconsider in the future. * * * Already, some advocates have criticized the current strategy of creating majority-minority districts and have urged the adoption of other voting mechanisms—for example, cumulative voting[15] or a system using transferable votes[16]—that can produce proportional results without requiring division of the electorate into racially segregated districts. * * *

* * * Once we candidly recognize that geographic districting and other aspects of electoral systems that we have so far placed beyond question are merely political choices, those practices, too, may fall under suspicion of having a dilutive effect on minority voting strength. And when the time comes to put the question to the test, it may be difficult indeed for a Court that, under *Gingles*, has been bent on creating roughly proportional representation for geographically compact minorities to find a principled reason for holding that a geographically dispersed minority cannot challenge districting itself as a dilutive electoral practice. In principle, cumulative voting and other non-district-based methods of effecting proportional representation are simply more efficient and straightforward mechanisms for achieving what has already become our tacit objective: roughly proportional allocation of political power according to race. * * *

---

15. Under a cumulative voting scheme, * * * each voter has as many votes as there are posts to be filled, and the voter may cast as many of his votes as he wishes for a single candidate. The system thus allows a numerical minority to concentrate its voting power behind a given candidate without requiring that the minority voters themselves be concentrated into a single district.

16. * * * Under such a system, each voter rank orders his choices of candidates. To win, a candidate must receive a fixed quota of votes, which may be set by any of several methods. Ballots listing a given candidate as the voter's first choice are counted for that candidate until the candidate has secured the quota of votes necessary for election. Remaining first-choice ballots for that candidate are then transferred to another candidate, usually the one listed as the second choice on the ballot. Like cumulative voting, the system allows a minority group to concentrate its voting power without requiring districting, and it has the additional advantage of ensuring that "surplus" votes are transferred to support the election of the minority voters' next preference.

* * * [U]nder our constitutional system, this Court is not a centralized politburo appointed for life to dictate to the provinces the "correct" theories of democratic representation, the "best" electoral systems for securing truly "representative" government, the "fairest" proportions of minority political influence, or, as respondents would have us hold today, the "proper" sizes for local governing bodies. We should be cautious in interpreting any Act of Congress to grant us power to make such determinations. * * *

* * * Properly understood, the terms "standard, practice, or procedure" in §2(a) refer only to practices that affect minority citizens' access to the ballot. Districting systems and electoral mechanisms that may affect the "weight" given to a ballot duly cast and counted are simply beyond the purview of the Act.

* * * Under the plain terms of the Act, §2(a) covers only a defined category of state actions. Only "voting qualification[s]," "prerequisite[s] to voting," or "standard[s], practice[s], or procedure[s]" are subject to challenge under the Act. The first two items in this list clearly refer to conditions or tests applied to regulate citizens' access to the ballot. They would cover, for example, any form of test or requirement imposed as a condition on registration or on the process of voting on election day. * * *

* * * The general terms in the section are most naturally understood, therefore, to refer to any methods for conducting a part of the voting process that might similarly be used to interfere with a citizen's ability to cast his vote, and they are undoubtedly intended to ensure that the entire voting process — a process that begins with registration and includes the casting of a ballot and having the ballot counted — is covered by the Act. Simply by including general terms in §2(a) to ensure the efficacy of the restriction imposed, Congress should not be understood to have expanded the scope of the restriction beyond the logical limits implied in the specific terms of the statute.

Moreover, it is not only in the terms describing the practices regulated under the Act that §2(a) focuses on the individual voter. The section also speaks only in the singular of the right of "any citizen" to vote. Giving the terms "standard, practice, or procedure" an expansive interpretation to reach potentially dilutive practices, however, would distort that focus on the individual, for a vote dilution claim necessarily depends on the assertion of a group right. At the heart of the claim is the contention that the members of a group collectively have been unable to exert the influence that their numbers suggest they might under an alternative system. Such a group right, however, finds no grounding in the terms of §2(a). * * *

It is true that §14(c)(1) also states that the term "voting" "include[s] all action necessary to make a vote *effective*," and the Court has seized on this language as an indication that Congress intended the Act to reach claims of vote dilution. See *Allen*, 393 U.S., at 566. But if the word "effective" is not plucked out of context, the rest of §14(c)(1) makes clear that the actions Congress deemed necessary to make a vote "effective" were precisely the actions listed above: registering, satisfying other voting prerequisites, casting a ballot, and having it included in the final tally of votes cast. * * *

Reading the Act's prohibition of practices that may result in a "denial or abridgement of the right . . . to vote" as protecting only access to the ballot also yields an interpretation that is consistent with the Court's construction of virtually identical language in the Fifteenth Amendment. The use of language taken from the Amendment suggests that the section was intended to protect a "right to vote" with the same scope as the right secured by the Amendment itself; certainly, no reason appears from the text of the Act for giving the language a broader construction in the statute than we have given it in the Constitution. The Court has never decided, however, whether the Fifteenth Amendment should be understood to protect against vote "dilution."[20]

While the terms of §2(a) thus indicate that the section focuses only on securing access to the ballot, it might be argued that reenactment of §2 in 1982 should be understood as an endorsement of the interpretation contained in cases such as *Allen* that the terms "standard, practice, or procedure" were meant to reach potentially dilutive practices. It is true that we generally will assume that reenactment of specific statutory language is intended to include a "settled judicial interpretation" of that language. * * * But it was hardly well settled in 1982 that *Allen*'s broad reading of the terms "standard, practice, or procedure" in §5 would set the scope of §2 as a provision reaching claims of vote dilution.

On the contrary, in 1980 in *Mobile* v. *Bolden*, 446 U.S. 55 [p. 302], a plurality of the Court construed §2 in a manner flatly inconsistent with the understanding that those terms were meant to reach dilutive practices. Emphasizing that the section tracked the language of the Fifteenth Amendment by prohibiting the use of practices that might "deny or abridge the right . . . to vote," the *Bolden* plurality determined that §2 was "intended to have an effect no different from that of the Fifteenth Amendment itself." *Id.*, at 61. In the plurality's view, however, the Fifteenth Amendment did not extend to reach dilution claims; its protections were satisfied as long as members of racial minorities could "register and vote without hindrance." *Id.*, at 65. *Bolden* remained the last word from this Court interpreting §2 at the time the section was amended in 1982. Thus, the reenactment in the amended section of the same language covering any "standard, practice, or procedure" and the retention of virtually identical language protecting against the "denial or abridgement of

---

20. * * * *Gomillion* v. *Lightfoot*, 364 U.S. 339 (1960) [p. 279], does not indicate that the Fifteenth Amendment, in protecting the right to vote, incorporates a concern for anything beyond securing access to the ballot. The *Gomillion* plaintiffs' claims centered precisely on access: Their complaint was not that the weight of their votes had been diminished in some way, but that the boundaries of a city had been drawn to prevent blacks from voting in municipal elections altogether. *Gomillion* thus "maintains the distinction between an attempt to exclude Negroes totally from the relevant constituency, and a statute that permits Negroes to vote but which uses the gerrymander to contain the impact of Negro suffrage." *Allen*, 393 U.S., [at] 589 (Harlan, J., concurring in part and dissenting in part).

the right . . . to vote" can hardly be understood as an endorsement of a broad reading of the section as a provision reaching claims of vote dilution.[22] * * *

As the Court concluded in *Gingles*, the 1982 amendments incorporated into the Act, and specifically into § 2(b), a "results" test for measuring violations of § 2(a). * * * But the mere adoption of a "results" test, rather than an "intent" test, says nothing about the *type* of state laws that may be challenged using that test. * * * Thus, as an initial matter, there is no reason to think that § 2(b) could serve to expand the scope of the prohibition in § 2(a), which, as I described above, does not extend by its terms to electoral mechanisms that might have a dilutive effect on group voting power.

Even putting that concern aside for the moment, it should be apparent that the incorporation of a results test into the amended section does not necessarily suggest that Congress intended to allow claims of vote dilution under § 2. A results test is useful to plaintiffs whether they are challenging laws that restrict access to the ballot or laws that accomplish some diminution in the "proper weight" of a group's vote. Nothing about the test itself suggests that it is inherently tied to vote dilution claims. A law, for example, limiting the times and places at which registration can occur might be adopted with the purpose of limiting black voter registration, but it could be extremely difficult to prove the discriminatory intent behind such a facially neutral law. The results test would allow plaintiffs to mount a successful challenge to the law under § 2 without such proof.

Moreover, nothing in the language § 2(b) uses to describe the results test particularly indicates that the test was intended to be used under the Act for assessing claims of dilution. * * * The section speaks in terms of an opportunity—a chance—to participate and to elect, not an assured ability to attain any particular result. And since the ballot provides the formal mechanism for obtaining access to the political process and for electing representatives, it would seem that one who has had the same chance as others to register and to cast his ballot has had an equal opportunity to participate and to elect, whether or not any of the candidates he chooses is ultimately successful. * * *

It is true that the terms "standard, practice, or procedure" in § 5 of the Act have been construed to reach districting systems and other potentially dilutive electoral mechanisms, see, *e.g.*, *Allen*, 393 U.S., at 569, and Congress has reenacted § 5 subsequent to our decisions adopting that expansive interpretation. Nevertheless, the text of the section suggests precisely the same focus on measures that relate to access to the ballot that appears in § 2. * * *

---

22. If anything, * * * by reenacting virtually the same language derived from the Fifteenth Amendment to define the basic interest protected by the Act, Congress [might have] intended to preserve the limitation that the *Bolden* plurality found implicit in that language. It is clear from the terms of the amendments passed in 1982 that where Congress sought to alter the understanding of the Act announced in *Bolden*, it did so explicitly in the text of the statute. * * *

In my view, the tension between the terms of the Act and the construction we have placed on § 5 at the very least suggests that our interpretation of § 5 should not be adopted wholesale to supply the meaning of the terms "standard, practice, or procedure" under § 2. * * * Where a careful reading of the language of § 2 dictates a narrow interpretation of the section, there is no reason for transplanting our interpretation of the terms of § 5—an interpretation that I believe is in tension with the text of § 5 itself—to another section of the Act.[27] * * *

"*Stare decisis* is not an inexorable command," *Payne* v. *Tennessee*, 501 U.S. 808, 828 (1991). Indeed, "when governing decisions are unworkable or are badly reasoned, this Court has never felt constrained to follow precedent." *Id.*, at 827. [O]ur decision in *Gingles* interpreting the scope of § 2 was badly reasoned; it wholly substituted reliance on legislative history for analysis of statutory text. In doing so, it produced a far more expansive interpretation of § 2 than a careful reading of the language of the statute would allow.

Our interpretation of § 2 has also proved unworkable. As I outlined above, it has mired the federal courts in an inherently political task—one that requires answers to questions that are ill-suited to principled judicial resolution. Under § 2, we have assigned the federal judiciary a project that involves, not the application of legal standards to the facts of various cases or even the elaboration of legal principles on a case-by-case basis, but rather the creation of standards from an abstract evaluation of political philosophy.

Worse, our interpretation of § 2 has required us to distort our decisions to obscure the fact that the political choice at the heart of our cases rests on precisely the principle the Act condemns: proportional allocation of political power according to race. Continued adherence to a line of decisions that necessitates such dissembling cannot possibly promote what we have perceived to be one of the central values of the policy of *stare decisis:* the preservation of "the actual and perceived integrity of the judicial process." * * *

For the foregoing reasons, I agree with the Court's conclusion that the size of a governing body is not subject to challenge under § 2 of the Voting Rights Act. I therefore concur in the Court's judgment * * *.

---

27. I need not decide in this case whether I would overrule our decisions construing the terms "standard, practice, or procedure" in § 5; the challenge here involves only § 2. Although in my view our construction of § 5 may well be incorrect as a matter of first impression, *stare decisis* would suggest that such an error in prior decisions may not in itself justify overruling settled precedent. Determining whether to abandon prior decisions requires weighing a multitude of factors, one of the most important of which is the extent to which the decisions in question have proved unworkable. In that regard, while the practical differences in the application of §§ 2 and 5 that JUSTICE KENNEDY points out would not, in my view, suggest as an original matter that the same terms in the two sections should be read to have different meanings, JUSTICE KENNEDY's observations might suggest that different considerations would have a bearing on the question whether our past interpretations should be abandoned in the § 5 and § 2 contexts. Indeed, in the § 5 context they might suggest a contrary conclusion to the result I reach under § 2. That, however, is a question for another day.

JUSTICE BLACKMUN, with whom JUSTICE STEVENS, JUSTICE SOUTER, and JUSTICE GINSBURG join, dissenting. * * *

Consistent with the Act's remedial purposes, this Court has held that a wide variety of election- and voting-related practices fit within the term "standard, practice, or procedure." Among the covered practices are the annexation of land to enlarge city boundaries; a rule requiring employees to take leaves of absence while they campaign for elective office; candidate filing dates and other procedural requirements; and candidate residency requirements.

Specifically, this Court long has treated a change in the size of a governing authority as a change in a "standard, practice, or procedure" with respect to voting. In *City of Rome*, 446 U.S., at 161, it noted that it "is not disputed" that an expansion in the size of a board of education was "within the purview of the Act" and subject to preclearance under § 5. In *City of Lockhart* v. *United States*, it stated that a change from a three-member commission to a five-member commission was subject to § 5 preclearance. And, most recently, it said that the term "standard, practice, or procedure with respect to voting" included a change in the size of a governing authority or an increase or decrease in the number of elected offices. *Presley* v. *Etowah County Comm'n*, 502 U.S., [at] 500. * * *

To date, our precedent has dealt with § 5 challenges to a change in the size of a governing authority, rather than § 2 challenges to the existing size of a governing body. I agree with JUSTICE O'CONNOR that, as a textual matter, "standard, practice, or procedure" under § 2 is at least as broad as "standard, practice, or procedure with respect to voting" under § 5. In fact, because of the "close connection" between §§ 2 and 5, we interpret them similarly. See *Chisom* v. *Roemer*, 501 U.S., at 402. And in the context of § 2, the Court stated: "Section 2 protected the right to vote, and it did so without making any distinctions or imposing any limitations as to which elections would fall within its purview." *Id.*, at 392.

Congress repeatedly has endorsed the broad construction this Court has given the Act in general and § 5 in particular. Significantly, when Congress considered the 1982 amendments to the Voting Rights Act, it made no effort to curtail the application of § 5 to changes in size, in the face of the longstanding practice of submitting such changes for preclearance, and on the heels of this Court's recognition just two years earlier that it was "not disputed" that a change in the size of a governing body was covered under § 5. Similarly, the Attorney General, whose construction of the Act "is entitled to considerable deference," for years has required § 5 preclearance of the expansion or reduction of a governing body. It is not surprising that no party to this case argued that the size of a governing authority is not a "standard, practice, or procedure."

In light of this consistent and expansive interpretation of the Act by this Court, Congress, and the Attorney General, the Act's "all-inclusive" definition of "standard, practice, or procedure" cannot be read to exclude threshold coverage of challenges to the size of a governing authority. As five Members of the Court today agree, the size of a governing authority is a "standard, practice, or procedure" with respect to voting for purposes of § 2 as well as § 5 of the Voting Rights Act.

Although five Justices agree that the size of a governing body is a "standard, practice, or procedure" under § 2, a like number of Justices conclude [*sic*], under varying rationales, that Voting Rights plaintiffs nonetheless cannot bring size challenges under § 2. This conclusion is inconsistent with our precedent giving the Act "'the broadest possible scope' in combating racial discrimination," *Chisom*, 501 U.S., at 403, quoting *Allen*, 393 U.S., at 567, and with the vote-dilution analysis prescribed in *Thornburg v. Gingles.*

To prevail in a vote-dilution challenge, minority voters must show that they "possess the *potential* to elect representatives *in the absence of the challenged structure* or practice." [*Gingles*, 478 U.S.], at 50 n.17 (second emphasis supplied). [M]inority voters' potential "in the absence of" the allegedly dilutive mechanism must be measured against the benchmark of an alternative structure or practice that is reasonable and workable under the facts of the specific case.

By all objective measures, the proposed five-member Bleckley County Commission presents a reasonable, workable benchmark against which to measure the practice of electing a sole commissioner. First, the Georgia Legislature specifically authorized a five-member commission for Bleckley County. Moreover, a five-member commission is the most common form of governing authority in Georgia. Bleckley County, as one of a small and dwindling number of counties in Georgia still employing a sole commissioner, markedly departs from practices elsewhere in Georgia. * * * Finally, the county itself has moved from a single superintendent of education to a school board with five members elected from single-member districts, providing a workable and readily available model for commission districts. Thus, the proposed five-member baseline is reasonable and workable.

In this case, identifying an appropriate baseline against which to measure dilution is not difficult. In other cases, it may be harder. But the need to make difficult judgments does not "justify a judicially created limitation on the coverage of the broadly worded statute, as enacted and amended by Congress." *Chisom*, 501 U.S., at 403. Vote dilution is inherently a relative concept, requiring a highly "flexible, fact-intensive" inquiry, *Gingles*, 478 U.S., at 46, and calling for an exercise of the "court's overall judgment, based on the totality of circumstances and guided by those relevant factors in the particular case," as mandated by Congress. Certainly judges who engage in the complex task of evaluating reapportionment plans and examining district lines will be able to determine whether a proposed baseline is an appropriate one against which to measure a claim of vote dilution based on the size of a county commission.

There are, to be sure, significant constraints on size challenges. Minority plaintiffs, who bear the burden of demonstrating dilution, also bear the burden of demonstrating that their proposed benchmark is reasonable and workable. One indication of a benchmark's reasonableness is its grounding in history, custom, or practice. This consideration will discourage size challenges to traditional single-member executive offices, such as governors and mayors, or even sheriffs or clerks of court. By tradition and practice, these executive positions are occupied by one person, so plaintiffs could rarely point to an objectively reasonable alternative size that has any foundation in the past or present. The sole commissioner, by contrast, holds plenary legislative, as well as executive, power. A one-member legislature, far from being the norm, is an anomaly. * * *

Additionally, every successful vote-dilution challenge will be based on the "totality of the circumstances," often including the lingering effects of past discrimination. Not every racial or language minority that constitutes 5% of the population has a claim to have a governing authority expanded to 20 members in order to give them an opportunity to elect a representative. Instead, the voters would have to prove that a 20-member governing authority was a reasonable benchmark—which, of course, respondents could not do here—and that their claim satisfied the three *Gingles* preconditions and was warranted under the totality of the circumstances.

* * * These limitations protect against a proliferation of vote-dilution challenges premised on eccentric or impracticable alternative methods of redistricting.

* * * We have recognized over the years that seemingly innocuous and even well-intentioned election practices may impede minority voters' ability not only to vote, but to have their votes count. It is clear that the practice of electing a single-member county commission can be one such dilutive practice. It is equally clear that a five-member commission is an appropriate benchmark against which to measure the alleged dilutive effects of Bleckley County's practice of electing a sole commissioner. I respectfully dissent.

JUSTICE GINSBURG, dissenting. * * *

Section 2 of the Voting Rights Act of 1965 calls for an inquiry into "[t]he extent to which members of a protected class have been elected to office," but simultaneously disclaims any "right to have members of a protected class elected in numbers equal to their proportion in the population." [52 U.S.C. § 10301(b)]. "There is an inherent tension between what Congress wished to do and what it wished to avoid"—between Congress' "inten[t] to allow vote dilution claims to be brought under § 2" and its intent to avoid "creat[ing] a right to proportional representation for minority voters." *Gingles*, 478 U.S., [at] 84 (O'CONNOR, J., concurring in judgment). * * *

When courts are confronted with congressionally crafted compromises of this kind, it is "not an easy task" to remain "faithful to the balance Congress struck." [*Ibid.*] * * * However difficult this task may prove to be, it is one that courts must undertake because it is their mission to effectuate Congress' multiple purposes as best they can. See *Chisom* v. *Roemer*, 501 U.S., [at] 403 (1991) ("Even if serious problems lie ahead in applying the 'totality of the circumstances' [inquiry under § 2(b) of the Voting Rights Act], that task, difficult as it may prove to be, cannot justify a judicially created limitation on the coverage of the broadly worded statute[.]").

Separate opinion of JUSTICE STEVENS, in which JUSTICE BLACKMUN, JUSTICE SOUTER, and JUSTICE GINSBURG join. * * *

* * * [I]n 1969[,] the Court unequivocally rejected [a] narrow reading [of "standard, practice, or procedure"], relying heavily on a broad definition of the term "voting" as including "all action necessary to make a vote effective." *Allen* v. *State Bd. of Elections*, 393 U.S., [at] 565–566. * * * Congress one year later reenacted § 5 without in any way changing the operative words. During the next five years, the Court consistently adhered to *Allen*, and in 1975, Congress again reenacted § 5 without change. * * *

If the 1970 and 1975 reenactments had left any doubt as to congressional intent, that doubt would be set aside by the 1982 amendments to § 2[, which] * * * substituted a "results" test for an intent requirement. It is crystal clear that Congress intended the 1982 amendment to cover [more claims than just those alleging a lack of access to the ballot]. * * *

Throughout his opinion, JUSTICE THOMAS argues that this case is an exception to *stare decisis*, because *Allen* and its progeny have "immersed the federal courts in a hopeless project of weighing questions of political theory." There is no question that the Voting Rights Act has required the courts to resolve difficult questions, but that is no reason to deviate from an interpretation that Congress has thrice approved. Statutes frequently require courts to make policy judgments. The Sherman Act, for example, requires courts to delve deeply into the theory of economic organization. Similarly, Title VII of the Civil Rights Act has required the courts to formulate a theory of equal opportunity. Our work would certainly be much easier if every case could be resolved by consulting a dictionary, but when Congress has legislated in general terms, judges may not invoke judicial modesty to avoid difficult questions. * * *

Notes and Questions

1. As the opinions in *Holder v. Hall* made clear, §§ 2 and 5 use virtually identical language concerning the scope of their coverage ("standard, practice, or procedure" in § 2, and "standard, practice, or procedure with respect to voting" in § 5). Is it appropriate to interpret the language in the two sections in a different manner, as Justice Kennedy and perhaps Justice Thomas would? *Compare* Justice Scalia's opinion for the Court in *Reno v. Bossier Parish School Board*, 528 U.S. 320 (2000) (holding that "denying or abridging the right to vote on account of race or color" in VRA § 5 should be interpreted identically whether a law is challenged as having a discriminatory purpose or effect), *with* Pub. L. No. 109-246, 120 Stat. 577 (codified as amended at 52 U.S.C. § 10304(c) (2006)) (overturning *Bossier Parish*) (explicitly

adopting different meanings when applied to purpose and effect).[c] If §§ 2 and 5 should be interpreted together, does the lack of a baseline for § 2 claims suggest that *Allen v. State Board of Elections* was wrong to give § 5 such a broad reading?

2. Did Justice Thomas provide adequate reasons for departing from precedent?

3. In footnote 20 of his opinion, Justice Thomas characterized *Gomillion* not as a vote-dilution case, but rather as protecting blacks' ability to vote in municipal elections. Justice Stevens, in an omitted portion of his opinion, took issue with that characterization and argued that it undermined Justice Thomas's critique of *Allen*: "[If, as Justice Thomas argued, *Gomillion* involved a practice that interfered with access to the ballot] because some voters' ballots could not thereafter be cast for the same offices as before[,] * * * the substitution of an appointive office for an elective office, see *Bunton v. Patterson*, decided with *Allen*, 393 U.S., [at] 550–551, or a change in district boundaries that prevented voters from casting ballots for the reelection of their incumbent congressional Representatives, would also be covered practices." 512 U.S. at 959 n.1 (opinion of Stevens, J.). Must one accept *Allen*'s broad interpretation of "standard, practice, or procedure with respect to voting" if one accepts *Gomillion*?

4. Justices Kennedy and O'Connor appeared concerned that there was no logical stopping point to the plaintiffs' dilution theory. Future plaintiffs, they worried, might demand greater increases in the size of legislatures so as to provide representation to smaller and smaller minority groups. Did Justice Blackmun provide an adequate response to that criticism?

5. Justice O'Connor concluded that the size of a government body was a "standard, practice, or procedure," but that no benchmark existed against which to measure its dilutive effect. Is it reasonable to believe that Congress would include the size of government bodies within the scope of § 2 while making it impossible to succeed on claims alleging that the size of a government body has diluted the effectiveness of minority votes?

6. Justice Thomas criticized *Allen* for reading the Voting Rights Act to authorize the Court to choose a theory of "effective" representation. Would his approach solve the problem he identified, or did he merely replace *Allen*'s political theory with one of his own?

7. Justice Thomas alleged that one especially negative effect of the Court's § 2 jurisprudence was the racial segregation of voters into electoral districts. The next section examines the limitations that the Equal Protection Clause places on such race-conscious districting.

---

c. *See generally* Antonin Scalia & Bryan A. Garner, Reading Law: The Interpretation of Legal Texts 252 (2012) ("[L]aws dealing with the same subject—being *in pari materia* (translated as 'in a like manner')—should if possible be interpreted harmoniously.").

E. Constitutional Constraints on Majority-Minority Districting

The last two sections explored how § 2 of the Voting Rights Act can require states to draw districts to ensure that members of minority groups have the same opportunity as other members of the electorate to participate in the political process and to elect representatives of their choice. The Supreme Court has interpreted the Equal Protection Clause, however, to limit states' ability to take race into account in constructing electoral districts. In the Court's view, a districting scheme that subordinates traditional districting principles to considerations of race creates a racial classification and must pass strict scrutiny to be constitutional. This section examines the doctrine governing this type of racial gerrymandering, and the next section further examines the conflict that doctrine creates between the Equal Protection Clause and § 2 of the Voting Rights Act.

Shaw v. Reno

Supreme Court of the United States
509 U.S. 630, 113 S. Ct. 2816, 125 L. Ed. 2d 511 (1993)

JUSTICE O'CONNOR delivered the opinion of the Court [in which CHIEF JUSTICE REHNQUIST, JUSTICE SCALIA, JUSTICE KENNEDY, and JUSTICE THOMAS join].

This case involves two of the most complex and sensitive issues this Court has faced in recent years: the meaning of the constitutional "right" to vote, and the propriety of race-based state legislation designed to benefit members of historically disadvantaged racial minority groups. As a result of the 1990 census, North Carolina became entitled to a 12th seat in the United States House of Representatives. The General Assembly enacted a reapportionment plan that included one majority-black congressional district. After the Attorney General of the United States objected to the plan pursuant to § 5 of the Voting Rights Act of 1965, the General Assembly passed new legislation creating a second majority-black district. Appellants allege that the revised plan, which contains district boundary lines of dramatically irregular shape, constitutes an unconstitutional racial gerrymander. The question before us is whether appellants have stated a cognizable claim.

The voting age population of North Carolina is approximately 78% white, 20% black, and 1% Native American; the remaining 1% is predominantly Asian. The black population is relatively dispersed; blacks constitute a majority of the general population in only 5 of the State's 100 counties. Geographically, the State divides into three regions: the eastern Coastal Plain, the central Piedmont Plateau, and the western mountains. The largest concentrations of black citizens live in the Coastal Plain, primarily in the northern part. The General Assembly's first redistricting plan contained one majority-black district centered in that area of the State. * * *

The Attorney General, acting through the Assistant Attorney General for the Civil Rights Division, interposed a formal objection to the General Assembly's plan.

The Attorney General specifically objected to the configuration of boundary lines drawn in the south-central to southeastern region of the State. In the Attorney General's view, the General Assembly could have created a second majority-minority district "to give effect to black and Native American voting strength in this area" by using boundary lines "no more irregular than [those] found elsewhere in the proposed plan," but failed to do so for "pretextual reasons."

Under § 5, the State remained free to seek a declaratory judgment from the District Court for the District of Columbia notwithstanding the Attorney General's objection. It did not do so. Instead, the General Assembly enacted a revised redistricting plan that included a second majority-black district. The General Assembly located the second district not in the south-central to southeastern part of the State, but in the north-central region along Interstate 85.

The first of the two majority-black districts contained in the revised plan, District 1, is somewhat hook shaped. Centered in the northeast portion of the State, it moves southward until it tapers to a narrow band; then, with finger-like extensions, it reaches far into the southernmost part of the State near the South Carolina border. District 1 has been compared to a "Rorschach ink-blot test" and a "bug splattered on a windshield."

The second majority-black district, District 12, is even more unusually shaped. It is approximately 160 miles long and, for much of its length, no wider than the I-85 corridor. It winds in snakelike fashion through tobacco country, financial centers, and manufacturing areas "until it gobbles in enough enclaves of black neighborhoods." Northbound and southbound drivers on I-85 sometimes find themselves in separate districts in one county, only to "trade" districts when they enter the next county. Of the 10 counties through which District 12 passes, 5 are cut into 3 different districts; even towns are divided. At one point the district remains contiguous only because it intersects at a single point with two other districts before crossing over them. One state legislator has remarked that "if you drove down the interstate with both car doors open, you'd kill most of the people in the district." The district even has inspired poetry: "Ask not for whom the line is drawn; it is drawn to avoid thee." * * *

* * * Appellants are five residents of Durham County, North Carolina, all registered to vote in that county. Under the General Assembly's plan, two will vote for congressional representatives in District 12 and three will vote in neighboring District 2. * * * In their complaint, appellants did not claim that the General Assembly's reapportionment plan unconstitutionally "diluted" white voting strength. They did not even claim to be white. Rather, appellants' complaint alleged that the deliberate segregation of voters into separate districts on the basis of race violated their constitutional right to participate in a "color-blind" electoral process. Despite their invocation of the ideal of a "color-blind" Constitution, appellants appear to concede that race-conscious redistricting is not always unconstitutional. That concession is wise: This Court never has held that race-conscious state decision-making is

impermissible in *all* circumstances. What appellants object to is redistricting legislation that is so extremely irregular on its face that it rationally can be viewed only as an effort to segregate the races for purposes of voting, without regard for traditional districting principles and without sufficiently compelling justification. For the reasons that follow, we conclude that appellants have stated a claim upon which relief can be granted under the Equal Protection Clause. * * *

Appellants contend that redistricting legislation that is so bizarre on its face that it is "unexplainable on grounds other than race" demands the same close scrutiny that we give other state laws that classify citizens by race. Our voting rights precedents support that conclusion.

In *Guinn* v. *United States*, 238 U.S. 347 (1915), the Court invalidated under the Fifteenth Amendment a statute that imposed a literacy requirement on voters but contained a "grandfather clause" applicable to individuals and their lineal descendants entitled to vote "on [or prior to] January 1, 1866." The determinative consideration for the Court was that the law, though ostensibly race neutral, on its face "embodied no exercise of judgment and rested upon no discernible reason" other than to circumvent the prohibitions of the Fifteenth Amendment. *Id.*, at 363. In other words, the statute was invalid because, on its face, it could not be explained on grounds other than race.

The Court applied the same reasoning to the "uncouth twenty-eight-sided" municipal boundary line at issue in *Gomillion* [v. *Lightfoot*, 364 U.S. 339 (1960)] [p. 279]. Although the statute that redrew the city limits of Tuskegee was race neutral on its face, plaintiffs alleged that its effect was impermissibly to remove from the city virtually all black voters and no white voters. * * *

The Court extended the reasoning of *Gomillion* to congressional districting in *Wright* v. *Rockefeller*, 376 U.S. 52 (1964). At issue in *Wright* were four districts contained in a New York apportionment statute. The plaintiffs alleged that the statute excluded nonwhites from one district and concentrated them in the other three. Every Member of the Court assumed that the plaintiffs' allegation that the statute "segregated eligible voters by race and place of origin" stated a constitutional claim. The Justices disagreed only as to whether the plaintiffs had carried their burden of proof at trial. The dissenters thought the unusual shape of the district lines could "be explained only in racial terms." The majority, however, accepted the District Court's finding that the plaintiffs had failed to establish that the districts were in fact drawn on racial lines. * * *

Wright illustrates the difficulty of determining from the face of a single-member districting plan that it purposefully distinguishes between voters on the basis of race. A reapportionment statute typically does not classify persons at all; it classifies tracts of land, or addresses. Moreover, redistricting differs from other kinds of state decisionmaking in that the legislature always is *aware* of race when it draws district lines, just as it is aware of age, economic status, religious and political persuasion, and a variety of other demographic factors. That sort of race consciousness does not lead inevitably to impermissible race discrimination. As *Wright* demonstrates, when members of a racial group live together in one community, a reapportionment plan that concentrates members of the group in one district and excludes them from others may reflect wholly legitimate purposes. The district lines may be drawn, for example, to provide for compact districts of contiguous territory, or to maintain the integrity of political subdivisions.

The difficulty of proof, of course, does not mean that a racial gerrymander, once established, should receive less scrutiny under the Equal Protection Clause than other state legislation classifying citizens by race. Moreover, it seems clear to us that proof sometimes will not be difficult at all. In some exceptional cases, a reapportionment plan may be so highly irregular that, on its face, it rationally cannot be understood as anything other than an effort to "segregate . . . voters" on the basis of race. *Gomillion*, in which a tortured municipal boundary line was drawn to exclude black voters, was such a case. So, too, would be a case in which a State concentrated a dispersed minority population in a single district by disregarding traditional districting principles such as compactness, contiguity, and respect for political subdivisions. We emphasize that these criteria are important not because they are constitutionally required — they are not — but because they are objective factors that may serve to defeat a claim that a district has been gerrymandered on racial lines.

Put differently, we believe that reapportionment is one area in which appearances do matter. A reapportionment plan that includes in one district individuals who belong to the same race, but who are otherwise widely separated by geographical and political boundaries, and who may have little in common with one another but the color of their skin, bears an uncomfortable resemblance to political apartheid. It reinforces the perception that members of the same racial group — regardless of their age, education, economic status, or the community in which they live — think alike, share the same political interests, and will prefer the same candidates at the polls. * * * By perpetuating such notions, a racial gerrymander may exacerbate the very patterns of racial bloc voting that majority-minority districting is sometimes said to counteract.

The message that such districting sends to elected representatives is equally pernicious. When a district obviously is created solely to effectuate the perceived common interests of one racial group, elected officials are more likely to believe that their primary obligation is to represent only the members of that group, rather than their constituency as a whole. This is altogether antithetical to our system of representative democracy. * * *

For these reasons, we conclude that a plaintiff challenging a reapportionment statute under the Equal Protection Clause may state a claim by alleging that the legislation, though race neutral on its face, rationally cannot be understood as anything other than an effort to separate voters into different districts on the basis of race, and that the separation lacks sufficient justification. It is unnecessary for us to decide whether or how a reapportionment plan that, on its face, can be explained in nonracial terms successfully could be challenged. Thus, we express no view as to whether "the intentional creation of majority-minority districts, without more," always gives rise to an equal protection claim. We hold only that, on the facts of this case, appellants have stated a claim sufficient to defeat the state appellees' motion to dismiss. * * *

The dissenters * * * suggest that a racial gerrymander of the sort alleged here is functionally equivalent to gerrymanders for nonracial purposes, such as political gerrymanders. * * * But nothing in our case law compels the conclusion that racial and political gerrymanders are subject to precisely the same constitutional scrutiny. In fact, our country's long and persistent history of racial discrimination in voting—as well as our Fourteenth Amendment jurisprudence, which always has reserved the strictest scrutiny for discrimination on the basis of race—would seem to compel the opposite conclusion.

* * * JUSTICE STEVENS argues that racial gerrymandering poses no constitutional difficulties when district lines are drawn to favor the minority, rather than the majority. We have made clear, however, that equal protection analysis "is not dependent on the race of those burdened or benefited by a particular classification." Indeed, racial classifications receive close scrutiny even when they may be said to burden or benefit the races equally.

Finally, nothing in the Court's highly fractured decision in [*United Jewish Organizations of Williamsburgh, Inc.* v. *Carey*, 430 U.S. 144 (1977)] [p. 291] * * * forecloses the claim we recognize today. *UJO* concerned New York's revision of a reapportionment plan to include additional majority-minority districts in response to the Attorney General's denial of administrative preclearance under §5. In that regard, it closely resembles the present case. But the cases are critically different in another way. The plaintiffs in *UJO*—members of a Hasidic community split between two districts under New York's revised redistricting plan—did not allege that the plan, on its face, was so highly irregular that it rationally could be understood only as an effort to segregate voters by race. Indeed, the facts of the case would not have supported such a claim. Three Justices approved the New York statute, in part, precisely because it adhered to traditional districting principles:

> "We think it . . . permissible for a State, *employing sound districting principles such as compactness and population equality,* to attempt to prevent racial minorities from being repeatedly outvoted by creating districts that will afford fair representation to the members of those racial groups who are sufficiently numerous *and whose residential patterns afford the opportunity* of creating districts in which they will be in the majority." 430 U.S., at 168 (opinion of WHITE, J., joined by STEVENS and REHNQUIST, JJ.) (emphasis added). * * *

* * * *UJO*'s framework simply does not apply where, as here, a reapportionment plan is alleged to be so irrational on its face that it immediately offends principles

of racial equality. *UJO* set forth a standard under which white voters can establish unconstitutional vote dilution. But it did not purport to overrule *Gomillion* or *Wright*. Nothing in the decision precludes white voters (or voters of any other race) from bringing the analytically distinct claim that a reapportionment plan rationally cannot be understood as anything other than an effort to segregate citizens into separate voting districts on the basis of race without sufficient justification. Because appellants here stated such a claim, the District Court erred in dismissing their complaint. * * *

The state appellees suggest that a covered jurisdiction may have a compelling interest in creating majority-minority districts in order to comply with the Voting Rights Act. The States certainly have a very strong interest in complying with federal antidiscrimination laws that are constitutionally valid as interpreted and as applied. But in the context of a Fourteenth Amendment challenge, courts must bear in mind the difference between what the law permits and what it requires.

For example, on remand North Carolina might claim that it adopted the revised plan in order to comply with the §5 "nonretrogression" principle. * * * [But] covered jurisdictions [do not have] *carte blanche* to engage in racial gerrymandering in the name of nonretrogression. A reapportionment plan would not be narrowly tailored to the goal of avoiding retrogression if the State went beyond what was reasonably necessary to avoid retrogression. * * *

Before us, the state appellees contend that the General Assembly's revised plan was necessary not to prevent retrogression, but to avoid dilution of black voting strength in violation of §2[.] * * * Appellants maintain [however] * * * that the [*Gingles* preconditions are not met and so there can be no viable §2 claim]. * * * Appellants further argue that if §2 did require adoption of North Carolina's revised plan, §2 is to that extent unconstitutional. These arguments were not developed below, and the issues remain open for consideration on remand.

The state appellees alternatively argue that the General Assembly's plan advanced a compelling interest entirely distinct from the Voting Rights Act. We previously have recognized a significant state interest in eradicating the effects of past racial discrimination. But the State must have a "strong basis in evidence for [concluding] that remedial action [is] necessary."

* * * The state appellees assert that the deliberate creation of majority-minority districts is the most precise way—indeed the only effective way—to overcome the effects of racially polarized voting. This question also need not be decided at this stage of the litigation. We note, however, that only three Justices in *UJO* were prepared to say that States have a significant interest in minimizing the consequences of racial bloc voting apart from the requirements of the Voting Rights Act. And those three Justices specifically concluded that race-based districting, as a response to racially polarized voting, is constitutionally permissible only when the State "employ[s] sound districting principles," and only when the affected racial group's "residential patterns afford the opportunity of creating districts in which they will

be in the majority." 430 U.S., at 167–168 (opinion of WHITE, J., joined by STEVENS and REHNQUIST, JJ.).

Racial classifications of any sort pose the risk of lasting harm to our society. They reinforce the belief, held by too many for too much of our history, that individuals should be judged by the color of their skin. Racial classifications with respect to voting carry particular dangers. Racial gerrymandering, even for remedial purposes, may balkanize us into competing racial factions; it threatens to carry us further from the goal of a political system in which race no longer matters—a goal that the Fourteenth and Fifteenth Amendments embody, and to which the Nation continues to aspire. It is for these reasons that race-based districting by our state legislatures demands close judicial scrutiny.

* * * Today we hold only that appellants have stated a claim under the Equal Protection Clause by alleging that the North Carolina General Assembly adopted a reapportionment scheme so irrational on its face that it can be understood only as an effort to segregate voters into separate voting districts because of their race, and that the separation lacks sufficient justification. If the allegation of racial gerrymandering remains uncontradicted, the District Court further must determine whether the North Carolina plan is narrowly tailored to further a compelling governmental interest. Accordingly, we reverse the judgment of the District Court and remand the case for further proceedings consistent with this opinion.

It is so ordered.

JUSTICE WHITE, with whom JUSTICE BLACKMUN and JUSTICE STEVENS join, dissenting. * * *

The grounds for my disagreement with the majority are simply stated: Appellants have not presented a cognizable claim, because they have not alleged a cognizable injury. * * * As the majority recognizes, "redistricting differs from other kinds of state decisionmaking in that the legislature always is *aware* of race when it draws district lines, just as it is aware of age, economic status, religious and political persuasion, and a variety of other demographic factors." "Being aware," in this context, is shorthand for "taking into account," and it hardly can be doubted that legislators routinely engage in the business of making electoral predictions based on group characteristics—racial, ethnic, and the like. * * * Because extirpating such considerations from the redistricting process is unrealistic, the Court has not invalidated all plans that consciously use race, but rather has looked at their impact. * * *

* * * The State has made no mystery of its intent, which was to respond to the Attorney General's objections by improving the minority group's prospects of electing a candidate of its choice. I doubt that this constitutes a discriminatory purpose as defined in the Court's equal protection cases—*i.e.*, an intent to aggravate "the unequal distribution of electoral power." But even assuming that it does, there is no question that appellants have not alleged the requisite discriminatory effects.

Whites constitute roughly 76% of the total population and 79% of the voting age population in North Carolina. Yet, under the State's plan, they still constitute a voting majority in 10 (or 83%) of the 12 congressional districts. Though they might be dissatisfied at the prospect of casting a vote for a losing candidate—a lot shared by many, including a disproportionate number of minority voters—surely they cannot complain of discriminatory treatment.[6]

The majority attempts to distinguish *UJO* by imagining a heretofore unknown type of constitutional claim. * * * The logic of its theory appears to be that race-conscious redistricting that "segregates" by drawing odd-shaped lines is qualitatively different from race-conscious redistricting that affects groups in some other way.{[7]} The distinction is without foundation. * * * The consideration of race in "segregation" cases is no different than in other race-conscious districting; from the standpoint of the affected groups, moreover, the line-drawings all act in similar fashion. A plan that "segregates" being functionally indistinguishable from any of the other varieties of gerrymandering, we should be consistent in what we require from a claimant: proof of discriminatory purpose and effect.

The other part of the majority's explanation of its holding is related to its simultaneous discomfort and fascination with irregularly shaped districts. Lack of compactness or contiguity, like uncouth district lines, certainly is a helpful indicator that some form of gerrymandering (racial or other) might have taken place * * *.

But while district irregularities may provide strong indicia of a potential gerrymander, they do no more than that. In particular, they have no bearing on whether the plan ultimately is found to violate the Constitution. Given two districts drawn on similar, race-based grounds, the one does not become more injurious than the other simply by virtue of being snakelike, at least so far as the Constitution is concerned and absent any evidence of differential racial impact. The majority's contrary view is perplexing in light of its concession that "compactness or attractiveness has never been held to constitute an independent federal constitutional requirement for state legislative districts." It is shortsighted as well, for a regularly shaped district can just as effectively effectuate racially discriminatory gerrymandering as an odd-shaped one. By focusing on looks rather than impact, the majority "immediately casts attention in the wrong direction—toward superficialities of shape and size, rather than toward the political realities of district composition."

---

6. This is not to say that a group that has been afforded roughly proportional representation *never* can make out a claim of unconstitutional discrimination. Such districting might have both the intent and effect of "packing" members of the group so as to deprive them of any influence in other districts. Again, however, the equal protection inquiry should look at the group's overall influence over, and treatment by, elected representatives and the political process as a whole.

7. I borrow the term "segregate" from the majority, but, given its historical connotation, believe that its use is ill advised. Nor is it a particularly accurate description of what has occurred. The majority-minority district that is at the center of the controversy is, according to the State, 54.71% African-American. Even if racial distribution was a factor, no racial group can be said to have been "segregated"—*i.e.*, "set apart" or "isolated."

Limited by its own terms to cases involving unusually shaped districts, the Court's approach nonetheless will unnecessarily hinder to some extent a State's voluntary effort to ensure a modicum of minority representation. This will be true in areas where the minority population is geographically dispersed. It also will be true where the minority population is not scattered but, for reasons unrelated to race—for example incumbency protection—the State would rather not create the majority-minority district in its most "obvious" location. When, as is the case here, the creation of a majority-minority district does not unfairly minimize the voting power of any other group, the Constitution does not justify, much less mandate, such obstruction. * * *

* * * [Thus,] state efforts to remedy minority vote dilution are wholly unlike what typically has been labeled "affirmative action." To the extent that no other racial group is injured, remedying a Voting Rights Act violation does not involve preferential treatment. It involves, instead, an attempt to *equalize* treatment, and to provide minority voters with an effective voice in the political process. The Equal Protection Clause of the Constitution, surely, does not stand in the way. * * *

JUSTICE BLACKMUN, dissenting.

I join JUSTICE WHITE's dissenting opinion. * * * [T]he conscious use of race in redistricting does not violate the Equal Protection Clause unless the effect of the redistricting plan is to deny a particular group equal access to the political process or to minimize its voting strength unduly. It is particularly ironic that the case in which today's majority chooses to abandon settled law and to recognize for the first time this "analytically distinct" constitutional claim is a challenge by white voters to the plan under which North Carolina has sent black representatives to Congress for the first time since Reconstruction. I dissent.

JUSTICE STEVENS, dissenting. * * *

* * * I believe that the Equal Protection Clause is violated * * * when a group with power over the electoral process defines electoral boundaries solely to enhance its own political strength at the expense of any weaker group. That duty, however, is not violated when the majority acts to facilitate the election of a member of a group that lacks such power because it remains under-represented in the state legislature—whether that group is defined by political affiliation, by common economic interests, or by religious, ethnic, or racial characteristics. The difference between constitutional and unconstitutional gerrymanders has nothing to do with whether they are based on assumptions about the groups they affect, but whether their purpose is to enhance the power of the group in control of the districting process at the expense of any minority group, and thereby to strengthen the unequal distribution of electoral power. When an assumption that people in a particular minority group (whether they are defined by the political party, religion, ethnic group, or race to

which they belong) will vote in a particular way is used to *benefit* that group, no constitutional violation occurs. Politicians have always relied on assumptions that people in particular groups are likely to vote in a particular way when they draw new district lines, and I cannot believe that anything in today's opinion will stop them from doing so in the future.[3]

Finally, we must ask whether otherwise permissible redistricting to benefit an underrepresented minority group becomes impermissible when the minority group is defined by its race. The Court today answers this question in the affirmative, and its answer is wrong. If it is permissible to draw boundaries to provide adequate representation for rural voters, for union members, for Hasidic Jews, for Polish Americans, or for Republicans, it necessarily follows that it is permissible to do the same thing for members of the very minority group whose history in the United States gave birth to the Equal Protection Clause. A contrary conclusion could only be described as perverse.

Accordingly, I respectfully dissent.

JUSTICE SOUTER, dissenting. * * *

* * * Unlike other [affirmative-action] contexts * * *, electoral districting calls for decisions that nearly always require some consideration of race for legitimate reasons where there is a racially mixed population. As long as members of racial groups have the commonality of interest implicit in our ability to talk about concepts like "minority voting strength," and "dilution of minority votes," cf. *Thornburg* v. *Gingles*, and as long as racial bloc voting takes place, legislators will have to take race into account in order to avoid dilution of minority voting strength in the districting plans they adopt. One need look no further than the Voting Rights Act to understand that this may be required, and we have held that race may constitutionally be taken into account in order to comply with that Act. [*UJO*], 430 U.S., [at] 161–162 (plurality opinion of WHITE, J., joined by Brennan, BLACKMUN, and STEVENS, JJ.); *id.*, at 180 and n. (Stewart, J., joined by Powell, J., concurring in judgment).

A second distinction between districting and most other governmental decisions in which race has figured is that those other decisions using racial criteria characteristically occur in circumstances in which the use of race to the advantage of one person is necessarily at the obvious expense of a member of a different race. * * *

---

3. The majority does not acknowledge that we *require* such a showing from plaintiffs who bring a vote dilution claim under §2 of the Voting Rights Act. Under the three-part test established by *Thornburg* v. *Gingles*, a minority group must show that it could constitute the majority in a single-member district, "that it is politically cohesive," and "that the white majority votes sufficiently as a bloc to enable it . . . usually to defeat the minority's preferred candidate." At least the latter two of these three conditions depend on proving that what the Court today brands as "impermissible racial stereotypes" are true. * * *

In districting, by contrast, the mere placement of an individual in one district instead of another denies no one a right or benefit provided to others. All citizens may register, vote, and be represented. * * * It is true, of course, that one's vote may be more or less effective depending on the interests of the other individuals who are in one's district, and our cases recognize the reality that members of the same race often have shared interests. "Dilution" thus refers to the effects of districting decisions not on an individual's political power viewed in isolation, but on the political power of a group. This is the reason that the placement of given voters in a given district, even on the basis of race, does not, without more, diminish the effectiveness of the individual as a voter.

* * * Presumably because the legitimate consideration of race in a districting decision is usually inevitable under the Voting Rights Act when communities are racially mixed * * * and because, without more, it does not result in diminished political effectiveness for anyone, we have not taken the approach of applying the usual standard of such heightened "scrutiny" to race-based districting decisions. * * *

* * * If a cognizable harm like dilution or the abridgment of the right to participate in the electoral process is shown, the districting plan violates the Fourteenth Amendment. If not, it does not. Under this approach, in the absence of an allegation of such cognizable harm, there is no need for further scrutiny because a gerrymandering claim cannot be proven without the element of harm. Nor if dilution is proven is there any need for further constitutional scrutiny; there has never been a suggestion that such use of race could be justified under any type of scrutiny, since the dilution of the right to vote can not be said to serve any legitimate governmental purpose. * * *

* * * I would not respond to the seeming egregiousness of the redistricting now before us by untethering the concept of racial gerrymander in such a case from the concept of harm exemplified by dilution. In the absence of an allegation of such harm, I would affirm the judgment of the District Court. I respectfully dissent.

Notes and Questions

1. What is the constitutional right that *Shaw* recognized? In other words, how would you complete this sentence: "*Shaw* held that voters' constitutional rights are violated when . . ."? Now the hard part: *Why* is such a harm a constitutional violation?

2. Note that the Court did not declare that the use of race *per se* was unconstitutional. Rather, the Court focused on the question whether the *appearance* of a district was such that the districting plan could not "be understood as anything other than an effort to separate voters into different districts on the basis of race."

Should appearances matter? That is, is there a constitutional distinction between a districting plan that takes race into account and produces compact, pleasantly shaped districts, and a plan that takes race into account and produces sprawling districts such as North Carolina's District 12? If there is such a difference, what does it say about the character of the right that *Shaw* recognized?

3. Related to the meaning of the right established in *Shaw* is the question of standing: *Who* is permitted to sue to vindicate the right? In *United States v. Hays*, 515 U.S. 737 (1995), the Court held that only residents of gerrymandered districts — not neighboring districts or others in the state — have endured the particularized injury that permits them standing to sue. Here is the Court's explanation:

> We noted [in *Shaw*] that, in general, "[racial classifications] threaten to stigmatize individuals by reason of their membership in a racial group and to incite racial hostility." 509 U.S., at 643. We also noted "representational harms" the particular type of racial classification at issue in *Shaw* may cause: "When a district obviously is created solely to effectuate the perceived common interests of one racial group, elected officials are more likely to believe that their primary obligation is to represent only the members of that group, rather than their constituency as a whole." *Id.*, at 648. Accordingly, we held that "redistricting legislation that is so bizarre on its face that it is 'unexplainable on grounds other than race' demands the same close scrutiny that we give other state laws that classify citizens by race." *Id.*, at 644. Any citizen able to demonstrate that he or she, personally, has been injured by that kind of racial classification has standing to challenge the classification in federal court.
>
> Demonstrating the individualized harm our standing doctrine requires may not be easy in the racial gerrymandering context, as it will frequently be difficult to discern why a particular citizen was put in one district or another. Where a plaintiff resides in a racially gerrymandered district, however, the plaintiff has been denied equal treatment because of the legislature's reliance on racial criteria, and therefore has standing to challenge the legislature's action. Voters in such districts may suffer the special representational harms racial classifications can cause in the voting context. On the other hand, where a plaintiff does not live in such a district, he or she does not suffer those special harms, and any inference that the plaintiff has personally been subjected to a racial classification would not be justified absent specific evidence tending to support that inference. Unless such evidence is present, that plaintiff would be asserting only a generalized grievance against governmental conduct of which he or she does not approve. * * *
>
> Appellees insist that they challenged Act 1 [Louisiana's congressional redistricting plan] in its entirety, not District 4 in isolation. That is true. It is also irrelevant. The fact that Act 1 *affects* all Louisiana voters by classifying each of them as a member of a particular congressional district does not mean — even if Act 1 inflicts race-based injury on *some* Louisiana voters — that *every* Louisiana voter has standing to challenge Act 1 as

a racial classification. Only those citizens able to allege injury "as a direct result of having *personally* been denied equal treatment" may bring such a challenge, and citizens who do so carry the burden of proving their standing, as well as their case on the merits.

515 U.S. at 744–46. *See also Sinkfield v. Kelley*, 531 U.S. 28 (2000) (*per curiam*). Are you convinced that the "representational harm[s]" of race-conscious districting "personally" affect those within the gerrymandered district, and that they do not "personally" affect those outside the district?

As *Hays* implied, racial-gerrymandering claims under *Shaw* focus on particular districts; it is not sufficient to claim that a state's redistricting plan *as a whole* was infected with racial considerations. *Alabama Legislative Black Caucus v. Alabama*, 575 U.S. 254, 262–63 (2015). But does it even make sense to speak of "the" gerrymandered district, as *Hays* did, given that changes in district lines inevitably affect surrounding districts?

For further discussion of the standing issue, see John Hart Ely, *Standing to Challenge Pro-Minority Gerrymanders*, 111 HARV. L. REV. 576 (1997); Samuel Issacharoff & Pamela S. Karlan, *Standing and Misunderstanding in Voting Rights Law*, 111 HARV. L. REV. 2276 (1998).

4. As shown in the previous Note, standing turns on whether the plaintiff resides in the gerrymandered district. The plaintiff's race is not relevant to the question of standing. Should this be the law? Imagine four residents—one white and one black in each of two neighboring districts, one of which is majority-minority. Is the black person in the majority-minority district subject to any "representational harms"? Is the black person in the other district injured by the districting scheme? In what ways are the injuries of the white voters different depending on whether they reside in the challenged district?

5. Should *candidates* have standing to challenge racial gerrymanders? If so, what cognizable injury would they suffer? In *Wittman v. Personhuballah*, 578 U.S. __, 136 S. Ct. 1732 (2016), the Court considered a case where candidates complained that a racial gerrymander altered the partisan composition of their districts and made their election less likely. The Court held that the candidates lacked standing, because they had not even shown that the gerrymander would have the partisan effects to which they objected. The Court did not reach the question whether such a candidate would have standing if he showed that a racial gerrymander packed his district with voters unlikely to support him. *See also League of Women Voters v. Johnson*, 2018 WL 3861731 (E.D. Mich. 2018) (three-judge court) (denying legislators' motion to intervene); *Virginia House of Delegates v. Bethune-Hill*, 587 U.S. __, 139 S. Ct. 1945 (2019) (holding that the Virginia House of Delegates lacked standing in a racial-gerrymandering case).

6. The Court typically justifies its districting decisions—including its one-person, one-vote decisions as well as the racial-districting ones—as protecting the

rights of individual voters. But, as voices on and off the Court have pointed out, individual voters do not elect candidates. Thus, constitutional and statutory protections of voters' ability to elect candidates are difficult to conceive of as part of an individual-rights regime.

Rather, it may be more appropriate to imagine rights such as those contained in § 2 of the Voting Rights Act and in *Shaw* as group rights. Section 2, in other words, may be thought of as protecting a minority *group's* ability to elect its candidates of choice, rather than the negligible ability of any particular minority voter to elect his or her preferred candidate. Likewise, *Shaw* does not provide much protection against an individual voter's being placed in a district because of race, but provides some protection against the excessive concentration of racial groups in districts.

But if the right belongs to the group rather than an individual, the injury to the group is an inability to elect enough of its chosen representatives. The group right has nothing to do with the "representational harms" cited by the *Shaw* and *Hays* Courts. Accordingly, the injury is felt equally by all members of that group throughout the jurisdiction, and one's residence in a gerrymandered district should have no effect on one's standing.

Do you think potential plaintiffs challenging districting decisions are more likely to be upset by "representational harms" or by the overall distribution of legislative seats that results from the districting plan?

7. Do you view the use of race by the North Carolina legislature as "political apartheid"? Or is the use of race to create a district of diverse races laudable? Do you view North Carolina's adoption of majority-minority districts as segregating voters by race, or as its opposite—achieving diversity?

8. In this vein, *Shaw* should be considered with the Court's evolving attitude toward race-conscious measures to promote racial integration. In *Swann v. Charlotte-Mecklenburg Board of Education*, 402 U.S. 1 (1971), the Court unanimously approved a busing plan ordered by a district court to remedy the effects of state-imposed school segregation. *Swann* was limited by *Milliken v. Bradley*, 418 U.S. 717 (1974), however, which held that district courts could not order busing across school-district lines to remedy segregation by only one of the districts. In subsequent decades, as the effects of *de jure* segregation have waned, courts have withdrawn their control over schools' decisions. *See Freeman v. Pitts*, 503 U.S. 467 (1992).

States' *voluntary* decisions to pursue racial integration by race-conscious means have produced hard-to-reconcile constitutional rulings. The Court has invalidated set-asides for minority workers and students, *Adarand Constructors, Inc. v. Peña*, 515 U.S. 200 (1995); *City of Richmond v. J.A. Croson Co.*, 488 U.S. 469 (1989); *Regents of the University of California v. Bakke*, 438 U.S. 265 (1978), as well as policies that give a quantifiable benefit to minorities, *Gratz v. Bollinger*, 539 U.S. 244 (2003); *Wygant v. Jackson Board of Education*, 476 U.S. 267 (1986). On the other hand, the Court held in *Grutter v. Bollinger*, 539 U.S. 306 (2003), and *Fisher v. University of Texas at Austin*, 579 U.S. __, 136 S. Ct. 2198 (2016), that state universities could adopt racial preferences for students, provided that the preferences were simply one part of an assessment of how the students would improve the diversity and educational environment of the school.

In *Parents Involved in Community Schools v. Seattle School District No. 1*, 551 U.S. 701 (2007), the Court held unconstitutional two school districts' race-based K-12 school assignments. The controlling opinion of Justice Kennedy held that the particular methods employed in the assignment system did not adequately serve the interests in educational diversity accepted in *Grutter*. The other four Justices in the majority—Chief Justice Roberts and Justices Scalia, Thomas, and Alito—expressed greater skepticism concerning the use of race in school assignments, suggesting that "[t]he way to stop discrimination on the basis of race is to stop discriminating on the basis of race." *Id.* at 748 (plurality opinion).

9. Should *UJO* have controlled the outcome of this case? How did the Court distinguish *UJO*?

10. Should districters be more constrained in considering race than in considering other types of group membership? Is race any less "legitimate" of a districting consideration than compactness, incumbency protection, or other "traditional" districting criteria?

Miller v. Johnson

Supreme Court of the United States
515 U.S. 900, 115 S. Ct. 2475, 132 L. Ed. 2d 762 (1995)

JUSTICE KENNEDY delivered the opinion of the Court [in which CHIEF JUSTICE REHNQUIST, JUSTICE O'CONNOR, JUSTICE SCALIA, and JUSTICE THOMAS join]. * * *

Between 1980 and 1990, one of Georgia's 10 congressional districts was a majority-black district, that is, a majority of the district's voters were black. The 1990 Decennial Census indicated that Georgia's population of 6,478,216 persons, 27% of whom are black, entitled it to an additional eleventh congressional seat, prompting Georgia's General Assembly to redraw the State's congressional districts. Both the House and the Senate adopted redistricting guidelines which, among other things, required single-member districts of equal population, contiguous geography, nondilution of minority voting strength, fidelity to precinct lines where possible, and compliance with §§ 2 and 5 of the [Voting Rights] Act. Only after these requirements were met did the guidelines permit drafters to consider other ends, such as maintaining the integrity of political subdivisions, preserving the core of existing districts, and avoiding contests between incumbents.

[T]he General Assembly submitted a congressional redistricting plan to the Attorney General for preclearance on October 1, 1991. The legislature's plan contained two majority-minority districts, the Fifth and Eleventh, and an additional district, the Second, in which blacks comprised just over 35% of the voting age population. Despite the plan's increase in the number of majority-black districts from one to two and the absence of any evidence of an intent to discriminate against minority voters, the Department of Justice refused preclearance on January 21, 1992. The Department's objection letter noted a concern that Georgia had created only two majority-minority districts, and that the proposed plan did not "recognize" certain minority populations by placing them in a majority-black district.

The General Assembly returned to the drawing board. A new plan was enacted and submitted for preclearance. This second attempt assigned the black population in Central Georgia's Baldwin County to the Eleventh District and increased the black populations in the Eleventh, Fifth, and Second Districts. The Justice Department refused preclearance again, relying on alternative plans proposing three majority-minority districts. * * * The State did not seek a declaratory judgment from the District Court for the District of Columbia.

Twice spurned, the General Assembly set out to create three majority-minority districts to gain preclearance. [T]he General Assembly enacted a plan that "bore all the signs of [the Justice Department's] involvement * * * split[ting] 26 counties, 23 more than the existing congressional districts." * * * The Eleventh District lost the black population of Macon, but picked up Savannah, thereby connecting the black neighborhoods of metropolitan Atlanta and the poor black populace of coastal Chatham County, though 260 miles apart in distance and worlds apart in culture. In short, the social, political and economic makeup of the Eleventh District tells a tale of disparity, not community. * * *

Elections were held under the new congressional redistricting plan on November 4, 1992, and black candidates were elected to Congress from all three majority-black districts. On January 13, 1994, appellees, five white voters from the Eleventh District, filed this action * * * alleg[ing] that Georgia's Eleventh District was a racial gerrymander and so a violation of the Equal Protection Clause as interpreted in *Shaw v. Reno* [509 U.S. 630 (1993)] [p. 362]. * * *

A majority of the [three-judge] District Court panel agreed that the Eleventh District was invalid under *Shaw*, with one judge dissenting. * * *

Finding that the "evidence of the General Assembly's intent to racially gerrymander the Eleventh District is overwhelming, and practically stipulated by the parties involved," the District Court held that race was the predominant, overriding factor in drawing the Eleventh District. Appellants do not take issue with the court's factual finding of this racial motivation. Rather, they contend that evidence of a legislature's deliberate classification of voters on the basis of race cannot alone suffice to state a claim under *Shaw*. They argue that, regardless of the legislature's purposes, a plaintiff must demonstrate that a district's shape is so bizarre that it is unexplainable other than on the basis of race, and that appellees failed to make that showing here. Appellants' conception of the constitutional violation misapprehends our holding in *Shaw* and the Equal Protection precedent upon which *Shaw* relied.

Shaw recognized a claim "analytically distinct" from a vote dilution claim. 509 U.S., at 652; see *id.*, at 649–650. Whereas a vote dilution claim alleges that the State has enacted a particular voting scheme as a purposeful device "to minimize or cancel out the voting potential of racial or ethnic minorities," *Mobile* v. *Bolden*, 446 U.S. 55, 66 (1980) [p. 302], an action disadvantaging voters of a particular race, the essence of the equal protection claim recognized in *Shaw* is that the State has used race as a basis for separating voters into districts. Just as the State may not, absent extraordinary justification, segregate citizens on the basis of race in its public parks, buses, golf courses, beaches, and schools, so did we recognize in *Shaw* that it may not separate its citizens into different voting districts on the basis of race. The idea is a simple one: "At the heart of the Constitution's guarantee of equal protection lies the simple command that the Government must treat citizens 'as individuals, not "as simply components of a racial, religious, sexual or national class."'" When the State assigns voters on the basis of race, it engages in the offensive and demeaning assumption that voters of a particular race, because of their race, "think alike, share the same political interests, and will prefer the same candidates at the polls." *Shaw*, *supra*, at 647. Race-based assignments "embody stereotypes that treat individuals as the product of their race, evaluating their thoughts and efforts—their very worth as citizens—according to a criterion barred to the Government by history and the Constitution." They also cause society serious harm. As we concluded in *Shaw*:

> "Racial classifications with respect to voting carry particular dangers. Racial gerrymandering, even for remedial purposes, may balkanize us into competing racial factions; it threatens to carry us further from the goal of a political system in which race no longer matters—a goal that the Fourteenth and Fifteenth Amendments embody, and to which the Nation continues to aspire. It is for these reasons that race-based districting by our state legislatures demands close judicial scrutiny." *Shaw*, *supra*, at 657.

Our observation in *Shaw* of the consequences of racial stereotyping was not meant to suggest that a district must be bizarre on its face before there is a constitutional violation. Nor was our conclusion in *Shaw* that in certain instances a district's appearance (or, to be more precise, its appearance in combination with certain demographic evidence) can give rise to an equal protection claim a holding that bizarreness was a threshold showing, as appellants believe it to be. Our circumspect approach and narrow holding in *Shaw* did not erect an artificial rule barring accepted equal protection analysis in other redistricting cases. Shape is relevant not because bizarreness is a necessary element of the constitutional wrong or a threshold requirement of proof, but because it may be persuasive circumstantial evidence that race for its own sake, and not other districting principles, was the legislature's dominant and controlling rationale in drawing its district lines. The logical implication

* * * is that parties may rely on evidence other than bizarreness to establish race-based districting. * * *

Appellants and some of their *amici* argue that the Equal Protection Clause's general proscription on race-based decisionmaking does not obtain in the districting context because redistricting by definition involves racial considerations. Underlying their argument are the very stereotypical assumptions the Equal Protection Clause forbids. It is true that redistricting in most cases will implicate a political calculus in which various interests compete for recognition, but it does not follow from this that individuals of the same race share a single political interest. The view that they do is "based on the demeaning notion that members of the defined racial groups ascribe to certain 'minority views' that must be different from those of other citizens," the precise use of race as a proxy the Constitution prohibits. Nor can the argument that districting cases are excepted from standard equal protection precepts be resuscitated by *United Jewish Organizations of Williamsburgh, Inc.* v. *Carey*, 430 U.S. 144 (1977) [p. 291], where the Court addressed a claim that New York violated the Constitution by splitting a Hasidic Jewish community in order to include additional majority-minority districts. As we explained in *Shaw*, a majority of the Justices in *UJO* construed the complaint as stating a vote dilution claim, so their analysis does not apply to a claim that the State has separated voters on the basis of race. 509 U.S., at 652. To the extent any of the opinions in that "highly fractured decision," can be interpreted as suggesting that a State's assignment of voters on the basis of race would be subject to anything but our strictest scrutiny, those views ought not be deemed controlling.

In sum, we make clear that parties alleging that a State has assigned voters on the basis of race are neither confined in their proof to evidence regarding the district's geometry and makeup nor required to make a threshold showing of bizarreness. Today's case requires us further to consider the requirements of the proof necessary to sustain this equal protection challenge.

* * * Although race-based decisionmaking is inherently suspect, until a claimant makes a showing sufficient to support that allegation the good faith of a state legislature must be presumed. The courts, in assessing the sufficiency of a challenge to a districting plan, must be sensitive to the complex interplay of forces that enter a legislature's redistricting calculus. Redistricting legislatures will, for example, almost always be aware of racial demographics; but it does not follow that race predominates in the redistricting process. *Shaw, supra,* at 646. The distinction between being aware of racial considerations and being motivated by them may be difficult to make. This evidentiary difficulty, together with the sensitive nature of redistricting and the presumption of good faith that must be accorded legislative enactments, requires courts to exercise extraordinary caution in adjudicating claims that a state has drawn district lines on the basis of race. The plaintiff's burden is to show, either through circumstantial evidence of a district's shape and demographics or more direct evidence going to legislative purpose, that race was the predominant factor

motivating the legislature's decision to place a significant number of voters within or without a particular district. To make this showing, a plaintiff must prove that the legislature subordinated traditional race-neutral districting principles, including but not limited to compactness, contiguity, and respect for political subdivisions or communities defined by actual shared interests, to racial considerations. Where these or other race-neutral considerations are the basis for redistricting legislation, and are not subordinated to race, a State can "defeat a claim that a district has been gerrymandered on racial lines." *Shaw, supra*, at 647. * * *

In our view, the District Court applied the correct analysis, and its finding that race was the predominant factor motivating the drawing of the Eleventh District was not clearly erroneous. The court found it was "exceedingly obvious" from the shape of the Eleventh District, together with the relevant racial demographics, that the drawing of narrow land bridges to incorporate within the District outlying appendages containing nearly 80% of the district's total black population was a deliberate attempt to bring black populations into the district. * * * Although this evidence is quite compelling, we need not determine whether it was, standing alone, sufficient to establish a *Shaw* claim that the Eleventh District is unexplainable other than by race. The District Court had before it considerable additional evidence showing that the General Assembly was motivated by a predominant, overriding desire to assign black populations to the Eleventh District and thereby permit the creation of a third majority-black district in the Second.

The court found that "it became obvious," both from the Justice Department's objection letters and the three preclearance rounds in general, "that [the Justice Department] would accept nothing less than abject surrender to its maximization agenda." It further found that the General Assembly acquiesced and as a consequence was driven by its overriding desire to comply with the Department's maximization demands. * * * On this record, we fail to see how the District Court could have reached any conclusion other than that race was the predominant factor in drawing Georgia's Eleventh District; and in any event we conclude the court's finding is not clearly erroneous. * * *

* * * The evidence was compelling "that there are no tangible 'communities of interest' spanning the hundreds of miles of the Eleventh District." * * * It is apparent that it was not alleged shared interests but rather the object of maximizing the District's black population and obtaining Justice Department approval that in fact explained the General Assembly's actions. A State is free to recognize communities that have a particular racial makeup, provided its action is directed toward some common thread of relevant interests. "[W]hen members of a racial group live together in one community, a reapportionment plan that concentrates members of the group in one district and excludes them from others may reflect wholly legitimate purposes." *Shaw*, 509 U.S., at 646. But where the State assumes from a group of voters' race that they "think alike, share the same political interests, and will prefer the same candidates at the polls," it engages in racial stereotyping at odds with equal protection mandates. *Id.*, at 647.

Race was, as the District Court found, the predominant, overriding factor explaining the General Assembly's decision to attach to the Eleventh District various appendages containing dense majority-black populations. As a result, Georgia's congressional redistricting plan cannot be upheld unless it satisfies strict scrutiny, our most rigorous and exacting standard of constitutional review.

To satisfy strict scrutiny, the State must demonstrate that its districting legislation is narrowly tailored to achieve a compelling interest. There is a "significant state interest in eradicating the effects of past racial discrimination." *Shaw, supra*, at 656. The State does not argue, however, that it created the Eleventh District to remedy past discrimination, and with good reason: There is little doubt that the State's true interest in designing the Eleventh District was creating a third majority-black district to satisfy the Justice Department's preclearance demands. Whether or not in some cases compliance with the Voting Rights Act, standing alone, can provide a compelling interest independent of any interest in remedying past discrimination, it cannot do so here. As we suggested in *Shaw*, compliance with federal antidiscrimination laws cannot justify race-based districting where the challenged district was not reasonably necessary under a constitutional reading and application of those laws. See 509 U.S., at 653–655. * * *

Georgia's drawing of the Eleventh District was not required under the Act because there was no reasonable basis to believe that Georgia's earlier enacted plans violated § 5. Wherever a plan is "ameliorative," a term we have used to describe plans increasing the number of majority-minority districts, it "cannot violate § 5 unless the new apportionment itself so discriminates on the basis of race or color as to violate the Constitution." *Beer* [v. *United States*], 425 U.S. [130], 141 [(1976)]. Georgia's first and second proposed plans increased the number of majority-black districts from 1 out of 10 (10%) to 2 out of 11 (18.18%). These plans were "ameliorative" and could not have violated § 5's non-retrogression principle. * * *

The Voting Rights Act, and its grant of authority to the federal courts to uncover official efforts to abridge minorities' right to vote, has been of vital importance in eradicating invidious discrimination from the electoral process and enhancing the legitimacy of our political institutions. * * * Th[is] end is neither assured nor well served, however, by carving electorates into racial blocs. * * * It takes a shortsighted and unauthorized view of the Voting Rights Act to invoke that statute, which has played a decisive role in redressing some of our worst forms of discrimination, to demand the very racial stereotyping the Fourteenth Amendment forbids.

The judgment of the District Court is affirmed, and the cases are remanded for further proceedings consistent with this decision.

It is so ordered.

JUSTICE O'CONNOR, concurring.

I understand the threshold standard the Court adopts—"that the legislature subordinated traditional race-neutral districting principles . . . to racial consider-ations"—to be a demanding one. To invoke strict scrutiny, a plaintiff must show that the State has relied on race in substantial disregard of customary and tradi-tional districting practices. Those practices provide a crucial frame of reference and therefore constitute a significant governing principle in cases of this kind. The stan-dard would be no different if a legislature had drawn the boundaries to favor some other ethnic group; certainly the standard does not treat efforts to create majority-minority districts *less* favorably than similar efforts on behalf of other groups. Indeed, the driving force behind the adoption of the Fourteenth Amendment was the desire to end legal discrimination against blacks.

Application of the Court's standard does not throw into doubt the vast majority of the Nation's 435 congressional districts, where presumably the States have drawn the boundaries in accordance with their customary districting principles. That is so even though race may well have been considered in the redistricting process. See *Shaw* v. *Reno*, 509 U.S., [at] 646. But application of the Court's standard helps achieve *Shaw*'s basic objective of making extreme instances of gerrymandering sub-ject to meaningful judicial review. I therefore join the Court's opinion.

JUSTICE STEVENS, dissenting. * * *

Even assuming the validity of *Shaw,* I cannot see how respondents in these cases could [have standing to] assert the injury the Court attributes to them. Respondents, plaintiffs below, are white voters in Georgia's Eleventh Congressional District. The

Court's conclusion that they have standing to maintain a *Shaw* claim appears to rest on a theory that their placement in the Eleventh District caused them "representational harms." The *Shaw* Court explained the concept of "representational harms" as follows: "When a district obviously is created solely to effectuate the perceived common interests of one racial group, elected officials are more likely to believe that their primary obligation is to represent only the members of that group, rather than their constituency as a whole." *Shaw*, 509 U.S., at 648. Although the *Shaw* Court attributed representational harms solely to a message sent by the legislature's action, those harms can only come about if the message is received — that is, first, if all or most black voters support the same candidate, and, second, if the successful candidate ignores the interests of her white constituents. Respondents' standing, in other words, ultimately depends on the very premise the Court purports to abhor: that voters of a particular race "think alike, share the same political interests, and will prefer the same candidates at the polls." This generalization, as the Court recognizes, is "offensive and demeaning."

* * * [A vote dilution] claim allows voters to allege that gerrymandered district lines have impaired their ability to elect a candidate of their own race. The Court emphasizes, however, that a so-called *Shaw* claim is "'analytically distinct' from a vote dilution claim." [Nowhere] has the Court answered the question its analytic distinction raises: If the *Shaw* injury does not flow from an increased probability that white candidates will lose, then how can the increased probability that black candidates will win cause white voters, such as respondents, cognizable harm?

The Court attempts an explanation in these cases by equating the injury it imagines respondents have suffered with the injuries African Americans suffered under segregation. * * * This equation, however, fails to elucidate the elusive *Shaw* injury. Our desegregation cases redressed the *exclusion* of black citizens from public facilities reserved for whites. In this case, in contrast, any voter, black or white, may live in the Eleventh District. What respondents contest is the *inclusion* of too many black voters in the District as drawn. In my view, if respondents allege no vote dilution, that inclusion can cause them no conceivable injury. * * *

Equally distressing is the Court's equation of traditional gerrymanders, designed to maintain or enhance a dominant group's power, with a dominant group's decision to share its power with a previously underrepresented group. * * * I do not see how a districting plan that favors a politically weak group can violate equal protection. The Constitution does not mandate any form of proportional representation, but it certainly permits a State to adopt a policy that promotes fair representation of different groups. * * *

The Court's refusal to distinguish an enactment that helps a minority group from enactments that cause it harm is especially unfortunate at the intersection of race and voting, given that African Americans and other disadvantaged groups have struggled so long and so hard for inclusion in that most central exercise of our democracy. I have long believed that treating racial groups differently from other identifiable groups of voters, as the Court does today, is itself an invidious racial classification. Racial minorities should receive neither more nor less protection than other groups against gerrymanders. *A fortiori*, racial minorities should not be less eligible than other groups to benefit from districting plans the majority designs to aid them.

I respectfully dissent.

JUSTICE GINSBURG, with whom JUSTICE STEVENS and JUSTICE BREYER join, and with whom JUSTICE SOUTER joins except as to Part III-B, dissenting. * * *

II. * * *

In *Shaw*, the Court * * * wrote cautiously, emphasizing that judicial intervention is exceptional: "Strict [judicial] scrutiny" is in order, the Court declared, if a district is "so extremely irregular on its face that it rationally can be viewed only as an effort to segregate the races for purposes of voting." 509 U.S., at 642. * * * The problem in *Shaw* was not the plan architects' consideration of race as relevant in redistricting. Rather, in the Court's estimation, it was the virtual exclusion of other factors from the calculus. Traditional districting practices were cast aside, the Court concluded, with race alone steering placement of district lines.

The record before us does not show that race similarly overwhelmed traditional districting practices in Georgia. Although the Georgia General Assembly prominently considered race in shaping the Eleventh District, race did not crowd out all other factors, as the Court found it did in North Carolina's delineation of the *Shaw* district.

In contrast to the snake-like North Carolina district inspected in *Shaw*, Georgia's Eleventh District is hardly "bizarre," "extremely irregular," or "irrational on its face." Instead, the Eleventh District's design reflects significant consideration of "traditional districting factors (such as keeping political subdivisions intact) and the usual political process of compromise and trades for a variety of nonracial reasons." The District covers a core area in central and eastern Georgia, and its total land area of 6,780 square miles is about average for the State. The border of the Eleventh District runs 1,184 miles, in line with Georgia's Second District, which has a 1,243-mile border, and the State's Eighth District, with a border running 1,155 miles.

Nor does the Eleventh District disrespect the boundaries of political subdivisions. Of the 22 counties in the District, 14 are intact and 8 are divided. That puts the Eleventh District at about the state average in divided counties. * * * Seventy-one percent of the Eleventh District's boundaries track the borders of political subdivisions. Of the State's 11 districts, 5 score worse than the Eleventh District on this criterion, and 5 score better. Eighty-three percent of the Eleventh District's geographic area is composed of intact counties, above average for the State's congressional districts. And notably, the Eleventh District's boundaries largely follow precinct lines. * * * Georgia's Eleventh District, in sum, is not an outlier district shaped without reference to familiar districting techniques. * * *

Along with attention to size, shape, and political subdivisions, the Court recognizes as an appropriate districting principle, "respect for . . . communities defined by actual shared interests." The Court finds no community here, however, because a report in the record showed "fractured political, social, and economic interests within the Eleventh District's black population."

But ethnicity itself can tie people together, as volumes of social science literature have documented — even people with divergent economic interests. For this reason, ethnicity is a significant force in political life. * * * To accommodate the reality of ethnic bonds, legislatures have long drawn voting districts along ethnic lines. Our Nation's cities are full of districts identified by their ethnic character — Chinese, Irish, Italian, Jewish, Polish, Russian, for example. The creation of ethnic districts reflecting felt identity is not ordinarily viewed as offensive or demeaning to those included in the delineation.

III

To separate permissible and impermissible use of race in legislative apportionment, the Court orders strict scrutiny for districting plans "predominantly motivated" by race. No longer can a State avoid judicial oversight by giving — as in this case — genuine and measurable consideration to traditional districting practices. Instead, a federal case can be mounted whenever plaintiffs plausibly allege that other factors carried less weight than race. This invitation to litigate against the State seems to me neither necessary nor proper.

A

The Court derives its test from diverse opinions on the relevance of race in contexts distinctly unlike apportionment.[11] The controlling idea, the Court says, is "the

---

11. I would follow precedent directly on point. In [*UJO*], even though the State "deliberately used race in a purposeful manner" to create majority-minority districts, [430 U.S.], at 165 (opinion of White, J., joined by REHNQUIST and STEVENS, JJ.), seven of eight Justices participating voted to uphold the State's plan without subjecting it to strict scrutiny. Five Justices specifically agreed that the intentional creation of majority-minority districts does not give rise to an equal protection claim, absent proof that the districting diluted the majority's voting strength. See *ibid.* (opinion of White, J., joined by REHNQUIST and STEVENS, JJ.); *id.*, at 179–180 (Stewart, J., concurring in judgment, joined by Powell, J.).

Nor is *UJO* best understood as a vote dilution case. Petitioners' claim in *UJO* was that the State had "violated the Fourteenth and Fifteenth Amendments by *deliberately revising its reapportionment plan along racial lines.*" *Id.*, at 155 (opinion of White, J., joined by Brennan, Blackmun, and STEVENS, JJ.) (emphasis added). Petitioners themselves stated: "Our argument is . . . that the history of the area demonstrates that there could be — and in fact was — *no reason other than race* to divide the community at this time." *Id.*, at 154, n.14.

Though much like the claim in *Shaw*, the *UJO* claim failed because the *UJO* district adhered to traditional districting practices. See 430 U.S., at 168 (opinion of White, J., joined by REHNQUIST and STEVENS, JJ.) ("We think it . . . permissible for a State, *employing sound districting principles such as compactness and population equality*, . . . [to] create districts that will afford fair representation to the members of those racial groups who are sufficiently numerous *and whose residential patterns afford the opportunity of creating districts* in which they will be in the majority.") (emphasis added).

simple command [at the heart of the Constitution's guarantee of equal protection] that the Government must treat citizens as individuals, not as simply components of a racial, religious, sexual or national class."

In adopting districting plans, however, States do not treat people as individuals. Apportionment schemes, by their very nature, assemble people in groups. States do not assign voters to districts based on merit or achievement, standards States might use in hiring employees or engaging contractors. Rather, legislators classify voters in groups—by economic, geographical, political, or social characteristics—and then "reconcile the competing claims of [these] groups."

That ethnicity defines some of these groups is a political reality. Until now, no constitutional infirmity has been seen in districting Irish or Italian voters together, for example, so long as the delineation does not abandon familiar apportionment practices. If Chinese-Americans and Russian-Americans may seek and secure group recognition in the delineation of voting districts, then African-Americans should not be dissimilarly treated. Otherwise, in the name of equal protection, we would shut out "the very minority group whose history in the United States gave birth to the Equal Protection Clause." See *Shaw*, 509 U.S., at 679 (STEVENS, J., dissenting).

B

Under the Court's approach, judicial review of the same intensity, *i.e.*, strict scrutiny, is in order once it is determined that an apportionment is predominantly motivated by race. It matters not at all, in this new regime, whether the apportionment dilutes or enhances minority voting strength. As very recently observed, however, "there is no moral or constitutional equivalence between a policy that is designed to perpetuate a caste system and one that seeks to eradicate racial subordination." *Adarand Constructors, Inc. v. Peña*, [515 U.S. 200], 243 [(1995)] (STEVENS, J., dissenting).

Special circumstances justify vigilant judicial inspection to protect minority voters—circumstances that do not apply to majority voters. * * * White voters in Georgia do not lack means to exert strong pressure on their state legislators. The force of their numbers is itself a powerful determiner of what the legislature will do that does not coincide with perceived majority interests. * * *

Notes and Questions

1. The Court held in *Miller* that the shape of the district was *evidence* of an improper use of race, but that a district's irregular shape was not necessary to prove a constitutional violation. Rather, under *Miller*, the trigger for strict scrutiny is the use of race as the "predominant factor" in drawing district lines. Is that consistent with *Shaw v. Reno*?

In *Bethune-Hill v. Virginia State Board of Elections*, 580 U.S. __, 137 S. Ct. 788 (2017), the Supreme Court reinforced *Miller* and stressed that a racial gerrymander may be unconstitutional even if the state does not disregard traditional districting principles. The key is the "legislative purpose and intent," whether proven by circumstantial evidence (such as the districts' shape) or by direct evidence. If race predominates in the drawing of district lines, there is a racial gerrymander, whether or not the districts are misshapen. And if race does not predominate, states are free to have districts that have an uncouth shape. In the Court's words, "[t]he Equal Protection Clause does not prohibit misshapen districts. It prohibits unjustified racial classifications." 137 S. Ct. at 798.

2. Does the predominant-factor test make sense? Should the Constitution be interpreted to allow *some* consideration of race as long as other factors are more important? Or should the Court have to choose between forbidding all uses of race in redistricting and permitting states to consider race as they wish?

3. Districting plans are facially race-neutral; they divide people not by race *per se*, but by geography. As the cases in this Chapter illustrate, however, those plans can have a racially disparate effect because of racially identifiable residency patterns. Accordingly, one might think that the constitutionality of such districting plans would be evaluated according to the test established in *Washington v. Davis*, 426 U.S. 229 (1976), and *Village of Arlington Heights v. Metropolitan Housing Development Corp.*, 429 U.S. 252 (1977), under which strict scrutiny applies whenever race is "a motivating factor" in creating facially race-neutral laws. Consider the explanation provided in *Arlington Heights*:

> *Davis* does not require a plaintiff to prove that the challenged action rested solely on racially discriminatory purposes. Rarely can it be said that a legislature or administrative body operating under a broad mandate made a decision motivated solely by a single concern, or even that a particular purpose was the "dominant" or "primary" one. In fact, it is because legislators and administrators are properly concerned with balancing numerous competing considerations that courts refrain from reviewing the merits of their decisions, absent a showing of arbitrariness or irrationality. But racial discrimination is not just another competing consideration. When there is a proof that a discriminatory purpose has been a motivating factor in the decision, this judicial deference is no longer justified.

429 U.S. at 265–66 (footnote omitted). Why would *Davis* and *Arlington Heights* apply strict scrutiny whenever race is "a motivating factor" but *Miller v. Johnson* would reserve strict scrutiny for instances where race "predominates" in the formation of a districting plan?

4. Under *Miller v. Johnson*, race cannot be the "predominant factor" in drawing district lines. But "predominant" relative to what other factors? Suppose that a state redraws its districts and considers race, but the one consideration that is given the most consideration is the need to place equal numbers of voters in the districts. In such a situation, would equality of population be the factor that "predominates"? No. The Court held in *Alabama Legislative Black Caucus v. Alabama*, 575 U.S. 254, 272 (2015), that "an equal population goal is not one factor among others to be weighed against the use of race to determine whether race 'predominates'"—even

though, "in light of the Constitution's demands, th[e] role [of population equality] may often prove 'predominant' in the ordinary sense of that word." "Rather, it [population equality] is part of the redistricting background, taken as a given, when determining whether race, or other factors, predominate in a legislator's determination as to *how* equal population objectives will be met."

If population equality is not one of the considerations to be weighed against race to see which "predominated" in a legislature's redistricting decision, what considerations do qualify? *Alabama Legislative Black Caucus* listed several: "'compactness, contiguity, respect for political subdivisions or communities defined by actual shared interests,' incumbency protection, and political affiliation." *Id.* (quoting *Miller v. Johnson*, 515 U.S. at 916, and citing *Bush v. Vera*, 517 U.S. 952, 964, 968 (principal opinion by O'Connor, J.)). The difference with equality of population, according to *Alabama Legislative Black Caucus*, is that the question under *Shaw* is which factor or factors predominate "in determining *which* persons were placed *in appropriately apportioned districts*." 575 U.S. at 273 (quoting Brief of the United States as *amicus curiae* at 19) (some emphasis added by the Court).

5. After *Miller* established that strict scrutiny applied whenever race was the predominant factor in drawing district lines, two questions naturally presented themselves. First, how should a court determine when race predominates over politics in a legislature's districting decisions, especially when race correlates with political ideology? Second, what showing is necessary for a state to satisfy strict scrutiny? Both questions were at issue in *Bush v. Vera*, 517 U.S. 952 (1996).

As to the first issue, *Vera* held that the fact that a districting dispute involves concentrations of black voters

> would not, in and of itself, convert a political gerrymander into a racial gerrymander, no matter how conscious redistricters were of the correlation between race and party affiliation. If district lines merely correlate with race because they are drawn on the basis of political affiliation, which correlates with race, there is no racial classification to justify[.] * * *
>
> If the State's goal is otherwise constitutional political gerrymandering, it is free * * * to achieve that goal regardless of its awareness of its racial implications and regardless of the fact that it does so in the context of a majority-minority district. * * * But to the extent that race is used as a proxy for political characteristics, a racial stereotype requiring strict scrutiny is in operation.

Id. at 968 (plurality opinion). *See also id.* at 1001 (Thomas, J., concurring in the judgment) ("We have said that impermissible racial classifications do not follow inevitably from a legislature's mere awareness of racial demographics.").

6. As to the second issue in *Vera* (the application of strict scrutiny), both the plurality and the Justices concurring in the judgment assumed that compliance with §§ 2 and 5 of the Voting Rights Act would qualify as a compelling governmental interest, but held that the districting scheme at issue in that case was not narrowly

tailored to that interest. There was no need to comply with § 2 because the state could not create another *compact* majority-minority district, and § 2, as interpreted in *Gingles*, does not obligate states to create noncompact majority-minority districts. Accordingly, the state's creation of a noncompact majority-minority district was not necessary to remedy a § 2 violation. *See* 517 U.S. at 976–81 (plurality opinion); *id.* at 1003 (Thomas, J., concurring in the judgment). *See also Shaw v. Hunt*, 517 U.S. 899, 914–18 (1996) (*Shaw II*).

Nor did § 5 demand the drawing of the district lines at issue in *Vera*. The state contended that its decision to include more blacks in one district was necessary to satisfy § 5, but the new district did not simply maintain the minority voting strength in the district in question; rather, it augmented it. Accordingly, as in *Miller v. Johnson*, the use of race was not necessary to avoid § 5's prohibition on retrogression. *See Vera*, 517 U.S. at 982–83 (plurality opinion). *See also Shaw II*, 517 U.S. at 911–13. For an ambitious attempt to reformulate the judicial standards for § 2 cases, and to account for the constitutional difficulties raised by § 2 being applied when there is only disparate impact, see Nicholas O. Stephanopolous, *Disparate Impact, Unified Law*, 128 YALE L.J. 1566 (2019).

7. It follows from *Bush v. Vera* that a plaintiff may not prevail simply by demonstrating the irregularity of district lines, coupled with information about the demographic characteristics of the districts. In *Hunt v. Cromartie*, 526 U.S. 541 (1999), the Court held that summary judgment was inappropriate in such a case, where the state claimed that its districts were drawn for predominantly political — not racial — reasons. Citing *Vera*, among other cases, the Court noted that "a jurisdiction may engage in constitutional political gerrymandering, even if it so happens that the most loyal Democrats happen to be black Democrats and even if the State were *conscious* of that fact." 526 U.S. at 551. Accordingly, "[e]vidence that blacks constitute even a supermajority in one congressional district while amounting to less than a plurality in a neighboring district will not, by itself, suffice to prove that a jurisdiction was motivated by race in drawing its district lines when the evidence also shows a high correlation between race and party preference." *Id.* at 551–52.

8. Should strict scrutiny apply whenever a state consciously uses race to create a majority-minority district? *Bush v. Vera* presented that question, which divided the Justices who had formed a unified majority in *Shaw*. Justice O'Connor, Chief Justice Rehnquist, and Justice Kennedy concluded that strict scrutiny should not "apply to all cases of intentional creation of majority-minority districts." *Id.* at 958 (plurality opinion). Rather, a state could create a majority-minority district intentionally without triggering strict scrutiny, as long as other traditional districting criteria were not subordinated to the consideration of race.[d] Justices Thomas and Scalia, however,

---

d. In *Shaw v. Hunt*, 517 U.S. 899 (1996) (*Shaw II*), the Court concluded that North Carolina did predominantly consider race, subordinating other concerns: "That the legislature addressed [nonracial] interests does not in any way refute the fact that race was the legislature's predominant consideration. Race was the criterion that, in the State's view, could not be compromised; respecting communities of interest and protecting Democratic incumbents came into play only after the would have held that race necessarily predominates in a purposeful decision to create a majority-minority district. *See id.* at 1001 (Thomas, J., concurring in the judgment).

The Court's most recent discussion of the issue followed the lead of the *Vera* plurality and suggested (although it did not hold) that a state may intentionally create a majority-minority district without race being the predominant factor in the districting. In *Bethune-Hill v. Virginia Board of Elections, supra,* the Court considered a challenge to twelve majority-minority districts. It was "undisputed that the boundary lines for the 12 districts at issue were drawn with a goal of ensuring that each district would have a black voting-age population (BVAP) of at least 55%." 580 U.S. at __, 137 S. Ct. at 794. As to eleven of the districts, the district court nonetheless concluded that race was not the predominant factor in drawing the district lines, because the lines conformed to traditional districting principles. As discussed in Note 1, *supra,* the Supreme Court reversed, instructing the district court that "a conflict or inconsistency between the enacted plan and traditional redistricting criteria is not a threshold requirement or a mandatory precondition in order for a challenger to establish a claim of racial gerrymandering." *Id.* at 799. The Court remanded the case to the district court to determine whether, in fact, "race directed the shape of these 11 districts."

Because such a remand would not be necessary if race necessarily predominated in the creation of a majority-minority district, the Court's disposition likely means that a state could intentionally create such a district without using race as the predominant factor. Justice Kennedy wrote the opinion of the Court, which was joined by Chief Justice Roberts and Justices Ginsburg, Breyer, Sotomayor, and Kagan. Justices Thomas and Alito protested that strict scrutiny should apply to every intentionally created majority-minority district. *Id.* at 803 (Alito, J., concurring in part and concurring in the judgment); *id.* at 803 (Thomas, J., concurring in the judgment in part and dissenting in part). *But see Cooper v. Harris,* 581 U.S. __, 137 S. Ct. 1455, 1469 (2017) ("Faced with [a] body of evidence [] showing an announced racial target that subordinated other districting criteria and produced boundaries amplifying divisions between blacks and whites[,] the District Court did not clearly err in finding that race predominated in drawing [majority-minority] District 1. Indeed, as all three judges recognized, the court could hardly have concluded anything but.").

9. Does a district in which residents are connected only by a common ethnicity insult those residents by assuming that they "think alike, share the same political interests, and will prefer the same candidates at the polls," as the *Shaw* and *Miller* Courts alleged, or does such a district simply "accommodate the reality of ethnic bonds," as Justice Ginsburg argued? Is there a difference between the racial balancing underlying the intentional creation of majority-minority districts, and reliance on offensive stereotypes?

---

race-based decision had been made." *Id.* at 907. Is this analysis consistent with the *Vera* plurality's view that race does not necessarily predominate in the intentional creation of majority-minority districts?

The television comedy *All in the Family* famously explored the role of race and ethnicity in American society, including in elections. In the following scene, the main character, Archie Bunker, tries to explain to his son-in-law, Michael "Meathead" Stivic, his view that a candidate's ethnicity should be an important consideration for voters. Are his opinions more offensive than the assumption that minority voters should be grouped together in districts because they have the same political preferences? Why?

> Archie: I call this representative government. "Salvatore, Feldman, O'Reilly, Nelson." That's an Italian, a Jew, an Irishman, and a regular American there—what I call a "balanced ticket."
>
> Meathead: Why do you always have to label people by nationality?
>
> Archie: 'Cause how else are you going to get the right man for the right job? Take Feldman, there. He's up for treasurer. Well, that's perfect. Them people know how to handle money. Know what I mean?
>
> Meathead: No, I don't.
>
> Archie: Well, then you got Salvatore running for D.A. He can keep an eye on Feldman. You know, I want to tell you something about the Italians. When you do get an honest one, you really got something there.
>
> Meathead: Aw, come on, Arch.
>
> Archie: Well, here you got O'Reilly, the Mick. He can see that the graft is equally spread around. You got Nelson, the American guy. He's good for TV appearances—make the rest of them look respectable.

All in the Family: The Election Story (CBS television broadcast, Oct. 30, 1971).

10. Reconsider the justiciability questions discussed in Chapter 2. Are the standards for adjudicating racial-gerrymandering claims under *Miller* and *Shaw* any more judicially manageable than those for partisan-gerrymandering claims considered in *Rucho v. Common Cause*, 588 U.S. __, 139 S. Ct. 2484 (2019) [p. 180], *Vieth v. Jubelirer*, 541 U.S. 267 (2004), and *Davis v. Bandemer*, 478 U.S. 109 (1986)? *See* Michael R. Dimino, *You've Got (Political) Questions, We've Got No Answers*, 71 MERCER L. REV. 719, 726 (2020) ("[T]he Court regularly applies the predominant-factor test in evaluating claims of racial, rather than partisan, gerrymandering, so the test must be judicially manageable.") (footnote omitted).

11. In *Easley v. Cromartie*, 532 U.S. 234 (2001), the Court yet again confronted the constitutionality of North Carolina's District 12—the same district at issue in *Shaw I* and *Shaw II*, as well as in *Hunt v. Cromartie*. The district court in *Easley* held that race predominated in the North Carolina Legislature's drawing of the district lines, but the Supreme Court reversed in an opinion authored by Justice Breyer and joined by the rest of the Justices (Stevens, Souter, and Ginsburg) who had consistently dissented in the *Shaw* cases, as well as by Justice O'Connor. The district court's finding was "clearly erroneous," in the Supreme Court's view, because the

plaintiffs' evidence was insufficient to rebut the state's claim that it was motivated more by politics than by race.

The district court held that District 12 was drawn to include areas with high concentrations of blacks, passing over areas with higher concentrations of Democrats, even though the inclusion of the more highly Democratic precincts would have resulted in District 12 being far more compact. The district court reasoned that this evidence indicated that the state was attempting "to collect precincts with high racial identification rather than political identification." Nevertheless, the Supreme Court was not convinced:

> The problem with this evidence is that it focuses upon party registration, not upon voting behavior. [R]egistration figures do not accurately predict preference at the polls. In part this is because white voters registered as Democrats "cross-over" to vote for a Republican candidate more often than do African-Americans, who register and vote Democratic between 95% and 97% of the time. A legislature trying to secure a safe Democratic seat is interested in Democratic voting behavior. Hence, a legislature may, by placing reliable Democratic precincts within a district without regard to race, end up with a district containing more heavily African-American precincts, but the reasons would be political rather than racial.

Id. at 244–45. Is this rationale consistent with *Bush v. Vera* and *Hunt v. Cromartie*?

The district court in *Easley v. Cromartie* also had before it two pieces of direct evidence demonstrating the motives of some of the participants in the line-drawing. In the first, a state senator and "legislative redistricting leader" praised the districting plan as "provid[ing] for a fair, geographic, racial and partisan balance throughout the State of North Carolina." In the Supreme Court's view, the statement "shows that the legislature considered race, along with other partisan and geographic considerations; * * * it says little or nothing about whether race played a *predominant* role comparatively speaking." 532 U.S. at 253.

Similarly, the Court was not moved by an e-mail sent to two senators from a legislative staffer working on the redistricting. The e-mail stated that the staffer "moved Greensboro Black community into the 12th, and now need to take [about] 60,000 out of the 12th. I await your direction on this." The Court held that the e-mail was insufficient to support the district court's holding, in part because it did not explain "the point of the reference" to race — why the black voters were moved to the 12th District, or what would have been the "political consequences of failing to do so." *Id.* at 254.

Are you convinced that the North Carolina Legislature was predominantly motivated by politics? Was the district court's contrary finding "clearly erroneous"? Do you agree with the Court that a political motivation could cause the legislature to rely on race as the legislature did in drawing District 12? Justice Thomas, joined by Chief Justice Rehnquist and Justices Scalia and Kennedy, protested in dissent that the appropriate question in racial-gerrymandering cases is "*whether*, not *why*, race predominated. * * * It is not a defense that the legislature merely may have drawn the district based on the stereotype that blacks are reliable Democratic voters." *Id.* at 266–67 (Thomas, J., dissenting).

Note the conflict between the Court's approach in *Easley v. Cromartie* and the plurality's treatment of § 2 of the Voting Rights Act in *Thornburg v. Gingles*, 478 U.S. 30 (1986) [p. 316]. In *Easley v. Cromartie*, the Court found it crucial that politics, not race, was the most important factor in the drawing of district lines. In *Gingles*, however, the plurality disclaimed any interest in discerning whether race was the cause of polarized voting. Rather, the plurality focused on *whether*, not *why*, different races preferred different candidates. What explains the differing approaches?

In *Easley*, the Court was willing to explain the state's consideration of race as being for partisan ends. Indeed, the Court held that the lower court was clearly erroneous in finding that racial concerns predominated, because the state may have considered blacks to be more reliable Democratic voters than were white Democrats, and may therefore have created heavily black precincts for political reasons rather than racial ones. Consider the reverse situation. What if Republicans seek to entrench their power by diluting the power of the most reliable Democrats? If those dilutive measures purposely reduce the power of blacks—*not because they are black but because they are reliable Democrats*—is that racial discrimination? *Cf. North Carolina State Conference of the NAACP v. McCreary*, 831 F.3d 204, 233 (4th Cir. 2016) (striking down a law establishing a voter-ID requirement and restricting early voting and same-day registration) ("[T]he General Assembly used [the challenged law] to entrench itself. It did so by targeting voters who, based on race, were unlikely to vote for the majority party. Even if done for partisan ends, that constituted racial discrimination.").

12. North Carolina's District 12 was back before the Supreme Court yet again in *Cooper v. Harris*, 581 U.S. __, 137 S. Ct. 1455 (2017). Although *Harris* did not purport to undermine *Easley v. Cromartie*, the deference *Harris* showed to the district court's conclusions was in tension with the Court's approach in *Easley*. In *Easley*, the district court concluded that considerations of race predominated in the drawing of pro-Democratic district lines, but the Supreme Court reversed that finding as clearly erroneous and insisted that politics, not race, was the predominant factor. Legislators, in the opinion of the Court, manipulated the district's population of blacks, but they did so in order to draw districts favoring Democrats.

By the time of *Harris*, the North Carolina legislature was controlled by Republicans, and the districts they drew favored their party by packing blacks into majority-minority districts. The district court again held that race predominated, and this time the Supreme Court deferred to the district court's assessment of the motives of the line-drawers. As the Court explained, deference was appropriate so long as the lower court's factual finding was "'plausible'; we reverse only when 'left with the definite and firm conviction that a mistake has been committed.'" 137 S. Ct. at 1474 (quoting *Anderson v. Bessemer City*, 470 U.S. 564, 573–74 (1985)).

In confronting the problem of how to distinguish between racial and political motivations, *Harris* elaborated as follows:

> [I]f legislators use race as their predominant districting criterion with the end goal of advancing their partisan interests—perhaps thinking that a proposed district is more "sellable" as a race-based VRA compliance measure than as a political gerrymander and will accomplish much the same thing—their action still triggers strict scrutiny. See *Vera*, 517 U.S., at 968-970 (plurality opinion). In other words, the sorting of voters on the grounds of their race remains suspect even if race is meant to function as a proxy for other (including political) characteristics.

Id. at 1473 n.7. The Court appears to have believed that the Democratic legislators in *Easley* packed District 12 with reliable Democratic voters (who, incidentally, were black), whereas the Republican legislators in *Harris* packed District 12 with black voters (who, incidentally, were Democrats). *See id.* at 1478 (noting "that the districting plan's own architects had repeatedly described the influx of African-Americans into District 12 as a § 5 compliance measure, not a side-effect of political gerrymandering"). Is that analysis consistent with *Easley*?

13. There has been a vigorous debate on whether majority-minority legislative districts, like those at issue in the *Shaw* litigation and its progeny, help or hurt the representation of African Americans and their interests, and whether they help or hurt the interests of the Republican or Democratic Party. While these districts may increase the chance of electing black legislators, do they ultimately dilute the ability of black voters to influence non-African-American legislators? Do the districts lead to an increase in the number of conservative (often Republican) legislators in surrounding districts because majority-minority districts pull some reliable Democrats out of the neighboring districts and thereby limit their influence? As a matter of law or policy, is it, or should it be, possible to speak of one set of interests for all black (or other minority) voters that can be represented only by a member of that minority?[e]

---

e. For a sampling of the extensive scholarly literature offering differing perspectives on these questions, see Charles Cameron et al., *Do Majority-Minority Districts Maximize Substantive Black Representation in Congress?*, 90 Am. Pol. Sci. Rev. 794 (1996); Bernard Grofman et al., *Drawing Effective Minority Districts: A Conceptual Framework and Some Empirical Evidence*, 79 N.C. L. Rev. 1383 (2001); David Lublin, *The Election of African Americans and Latinos to the U.S. House of Representatives, 1972–1994*, 25 Am. Pol. Q. 269 (1997); Christine Leveaux Sharpe & James C. Garland, *Race, Roll Calls, and Redistricting: The Impact of Race-Based Redistricting on Congressional Roll-Call*, 54 Pol. Res. Q. 31 (2001); Kenneth W. Shotts, *Does Racial Redistricting Cause Conservative Policy Outcomes? Policy Preferences and Southern Representatives in the 1980s and 1990s*, 65 J. Pol. 216 (2003).

Likewise, there is ongoing discussion on the impact of the *Shaw* litigation itself. *See* Abigail Thernstrom, Voting Rights — and Wrongs: The Elusive Quest for Racially Fair Elections 155 (2009) (arguing that the *Shaw*-type litigation had little effect on the election of African-American representatives); Richard H. Pildes, *The Supreme Court, 2003 Term — Foreword: The Constitutionalization of Democratic Politics*, 118 Harv. L. Rev. 28, 67–68 (2004) (noting that there has been relatively little litigation raising *Shaw*-type issues, and attributing this to the drawing of districts by state legislators who have "internalized the vague constraints of *Shaw* in ways that generated a stable equilibrium").

14. For more information and background on the cases from *Shaw v. Reno* to *Easley v. Cromartie*, see Tinsley E. Yarbrough, Race and Redistricting: The *Shaw-Cromartie* Cases (2002); Melissa L. Saunders, *A Cautionary Tale:* Hunt v. Cromartie *and the Next Generation of* Shaw *Litigation*, 1 Election L.J. 173 (2002).

F. Resolving the *Shaw*/VRA Conflict

The Court's interpretation of the Equal Protection Clause in the racial-gerrymandering cases placed states in a difficult position. If they paid insufficient attention to race and failed to create enough districts in which minorities had the opportunity to elect their preferred representatives, they were vulnerable under § 2 or § 5 of the Voting Rights Act. If they took account of race, however, and drew district lines with the predominant purpose of conforming district lines to race, then they were vulnerable to a suit under the Constitution. This section explores the balance between those potentially (inevitably?) conflicting obligations.

League of United Latin American Citizens v. Perry

Supreme Court of the United States
548 U.S. 399, 126 S. Ct. 2594, 165 L. Ed. 2d 609 (2006)

Justice Kennedy announced the judgment of the Court and delivered the opinion of the Court with respect to Parts II-A and III [in which Justice Stevens, Justice Souter, Justice Ginsburg, and Justice Breyer join], an opinion with respect to Parts I and IV, in which The Chief Justice [Roberts] and Justice Alito join, an opinion with respect to Parts II-B and II-C [in which no other Justice joins], and an opinion with respect to Part II-D, in which Justice Souter and Justice Ginsburg join. * * *

Appellants contend [that Texas's 2003 congressional redistricting] plan is an unconstitutional partisan gerrymander and that the redistricting statewide violates § 2 of the Voting Rights Act of 1965, 42 U.S.C. § 1973 [now 52 U.S.C. § 10301 — Eds.]. Appellants also contend that the use of race and politics in drawing lines of specific districts violates the First Amendment and the Equal Protection Clause of the Fourteenth Amendment. * * *

I * * *

The 1990 census resulted in a 30-seat congressional delegation for Texas, an increase of 3 seats over the 27 representatives allotted to the State in the decade before. In 1991 the Texas Legislature drew new district lines. At the time, the Democratic Party controlled both houses in the state legislature, the governorship, and 19 of the State's 27 seats in Congress. Yet change appeared to be on the horizon. In the previous 30 years the Democratic Party's post-Reconstruction dominance over the Republican Party had eroded, and by 1990 the Republicans received 47% of the statewide vote, while the Democrats received 51%.

Faced with a Republican opposition that could be moving toward majority status, the state legislature drew a congressional redistricting plan designed to favor Democratic candidates. Using then-emerging computer technology to draw district lines with artful precision, the legislature enacted a plan later described as the "shrewdest gerrymander of the 1990s." * * *

Voters who considered this unfair and unlawful treatment sought to invalidate the 1991 plan as an unconstitutional partisan gerrymander, but to no avail. The 1991 plan realized the hopes of Democrats and the fears of Republicans with respect to the composition of the Texas congressional delegation. The 1990's were years of continued growth for the Texas Republican Party, and by the end of the decade it was sweeping elections for statewide office. Nevertheless, despite carrying 59% of the vote in statewide elections in 2000, the Republicans only won 13 congressional seats to the Democrats' 17.

These events likely were not forgotten by either party when it came time to draw congressional districts in conformance with the 2000 census and to incorporate two additional seats for the Texas delegation. The Republican Party controlled the governorship and the State Senate; it did not yet control the State House of Representatives, however. As so constituted, the legislature was unable to pass a redistricting scheme, resulting in litigation and the necessity of a court-ordered plan to comply with the Constitution's one-person, one-vote requirement. See *Balderas* v. *Texas*, [2001 U.S. Dist. LEXIS 25740] (E.D. Tex.) *(per curiam)*, summarily aff'd, 536 U.S. 919 (2002). The congressional districting map resulting from the *Balderas* litigation is known as Plan 1151C.

[T]wo members of the three-judge court that drew Plan 1151C later served on the three-judge court that issued the judgment now under review. Thus we have the benefit of their candid comments concerning the redistricting approach taken in the *Balderas* litigation. Conscious that the primary responsibility for drawing congressional districts is given to political branches of government, and hesitant to "und[o] the work of one political party for the benefit of another," the three-judge *Balderas* court sought to apply "only 'neutral' redistricting standards" when drawing Plan 1151C. Once the District Court applied these principles—such as placing the two new seats in high-growth areas, following county and voting precinct lines, and avoiding the pairing of incumbents—"the drawing ceased, leaving the map free of further change except to conform it to one-person, one-vote." Under Plan 1151C, the 2002 congressional elections resulted in a 17-to-15 Democratic majority in the Texas delegation, compared to a 59% to 40% Republican majority in votes for statewide office in 2000. * * *

The continuing influence of a court-drawn map that "perpetuated much of [the 1991] gerrymander" was not lost on Texas Republicans when, in 2003, they gained control of the State House of Representatives and, thus, both houses of the legislature. * * * After a protracted partisan struggle, during which Democratic legislators left the State for a time to frustrate quorum requirements, the legislature enacted a new congressional districting map in October 2003. It is called Plan 1374C. The 2004 congressional elections did not disappoint the plan's drafters. Republicans won 21 seats to the Democrats' 11, while also obtaining 58% of the vote in statewide races against the Democrats' 41%.

Soon after Texas enacted Plan 1374C, appellants challenged it in court, alleging a host of constitutional and statutory violations. [T]he District Court entered judgment against appellants on all their claims. * * *

II

[In Part II, JUSTICE KENNEDY's opinion (which was for the Court only in a small, inconsequential part) rejected the partisan-gerrymandering and one-person, one-vote attacks on Texas's mid-decade redistricting. The partisan-gerrymandering discussion has been overtaken by *Rucho v. Common Cause*, 588 U.S. __, 139 S. Ct. 2484 (2019) [p. 180]. The one-person, one-vote challenge was based on the argument that by the time of the mid-decade redistricting, the census data were outdated and thus the districts contained unequal numbers of people. Of course, that would also be true if the original districting plan were left in place, but the challengers argued that a mid-decade redistricting should be treated differently because it "unnecessarily" relied on the outdated data by drawing new districts when there was no legal compulsion to do so. A plurality of the Court rejected the argument, concluding that a ban on mid-decade redistricting would create hyper-partisanship at the outset of the decade. Further, it would discourage legislative compromise and result in courts drawing more districting plans, which could not then be undone by legislatures until the next census. Such a result would be unfortunate, in the view of the plurality, because it would invert the Constitution's decision to vest primary responsibility for drawing districts with state legislatures and Congress.]

III

Plan 1374C made changes to district lines in south and west Texas that appellants challenge as violations of §2 of the Voting Rights Act and the Equal Protection Clause of the Fourteenth Amendment. The most significant changes occurred to District 23, which—both before and after the redistricting—covers a large land area in west Texas, and to District 25, which earlier included Houston but now includes a different area, a north-south strip from Austin to the Rio Grande Valley.

After the 2002 election, it became apparent that District 23 as then drawn had an increasingly powerful Latino population that threatened to oust the incumbent Republican, Henry Bonilla. Before the 2003 redistricting, the Latino share of the citizen voting-age population was 57.5%, and Bonilla's support among Latinos had dropped with each successive election since 1996. In 2002, Bonilla captured only 8% of the Latino vote and 51.5% of the overall vote. Faced with this loss of voter support, the legislature acted to protect Bonilla's incumbency by changing the lines—and hence the population mix—of the district. * * * In the newly drawn district, the Latino share of the citizen voting-age population dropped to 46%, though the Latino share of the total voting-age population remained just over 50%.

These changes required adjustments elsewhere, of course, so the State inserted a third district between the two districts to the east of District 23, and extended all three of them farther north. New District 25 is a long, narrow strip that winds its way from McAllen and the Mexican-border towns in the south to Austin, in the center of the State and 300 miles away. * * * The Latino communities at the opposite ends of District 25 have divergent "needs and interests," owing to "differences in socio-economic status, education, employment, health, and other characteristics."

The District Court summed up the purposes underlying the redistricting in south and west Texas: "The change to Congressional District 23 served the dual goal of increasing Republican seats in general and protecting Bonilla's incumbency in particular, with the additional political nuance that Bonilla would be reelected in a district that had a majority of Latino voting age population—although clearly not a majority of citizen voting age population and certainly not an effective voting majority." The goal in creating District 25 was just as clear: "[t]o avoid retrogression under § 5" of the Voting Rights Act given the reduced Latino voting strength in District 23. * * *

Appellants argue that the changes to District 23 diluted the voting rights of Latinos who remain in the district. Specifically, the redrawing of lines in District 23 caused the Latino share of the citizen voting-age population to drop from 57.5% to 46%. The District Court recognized that "Latino voting strength in Congressional District 23 is, unquestionably, weakened under Plan 1374C." The question is whether this weakening amounts to vote dilution.

To begin the *Gingles* analysis [see *Thornburg v. Gingles*, 478 U.S. 30 (1986)] [p. 316], it is evident that the second and third *Gingles* preconditions—cohesion among the minority group and bloc voting among the majority population—are present in District 23. The District Court found "racially polarized voting" in south and west Texas, and indeed "throughout the State." The polarization in District 23 was especially severe: 92% of Latinos voted against Bonilla in 2002, while 88% of non-Latinos voted for him. Furthermore, the projected results in new District 23 show that the Anglo citizen voting-age majority will often, if not always, prevent

Latinos from electing the candidate of their choice in the district. For all these reasons, appellants demonstrated sufficient minority cohesion and majority bloc voting to meet the second and third *Gingles* requirements.

The first *Gingles* factor requires that a group be "sufficiently large and geographically compact to constitute a majority in a single-member district." 478 U.S., at 50. Latinos in District 23 could have constituted a majority of the citizen voting-age population in the district, and in fact did so under Plan 1151C. Though it may be possible for a citizen voting-age majority to lack real electoral opportunity, the Latino majority in old District 23 did possess electoral opportunity protected by § 2.

While the District Court stated that District 23 had not been an effective opportunity district under Plan 1151C, it recognized the district was "moving in that direction." Indeed, by 2002 the Latino candidate of choice in District 23 won the majority of the district's votes in 13 out of 15 elections for statewide officeholders. And in the congressional race, Bonilla could not have prevailed without some Latino support, limited though it was. State legislators changed District 23 specifically because they worried that Latinos would vote Bonilla out of office. * * * Since the redistricting prevented the immediate success of the emergent Latino majority in District 23, there was a denial of opportunity in the real sense of that term.

Plan 1374C's version of District 23, by contrast, "is unquestionably not a Latino opportunity district." Latinos, to be sure, are a bare majority of the voting-age population in new District 23, but only in a hollow sense, for the parties agree that the relevant numbers must include citizenship. This approach fits the language of § 2 because only eligible voters affect a group's opportunity to elect candidates. In sum, appellants have established that Latinos could have had an opportunity district in District 23 had its lines not been altered and that they do not have one now.

Considering the district in isolation, the three *Gingles* requirements are satisfied. The State argues, nonetheless, that it met its § 2 obligations by creating new District 25 as an offsetting opportunity district. * * * [But the State may] use one majority-minority district to compensate for the absence of another only when the racial group in each area had a § 2 right and both could not be accommodated. * * *

* * * To be sure, § 2 does not forbid the creation of a noncompact majority-minority district. The noncompact district cannot, however, remedy a violation elsewhere in the State. Simply put, the State's creation of an opportunity district for those without a § 2 right offers no excuse for its failure to provide an opportunity district for those with a § 2 right. And since there is no § 2 right to a district that is not reasonably compact, the creation of a noncompact district does not compensate for the dismantling of a compact opportunity district.

THE CHIEF JUSTICE claims compactness should be only a factor in the analysis, but his approach comports neither with our precedents nor with the nature of the right established by § 2. [*Johnson v.*] *De Grandy* expressly stated that the first *Gingles* prong looks only to the number of "reasonably compact districts." 512 U.S. [997], 1008 [(1994)] [p. 334]. *Shaw II*, moreover, refused to consider a noncompact district as a possible remedy for a §2 violation. [*Shaw v. Hunt*,] 517 U.S. [899], 916 [(1996)]. It is true *Shaw II* applied this analysis in the context of a State's using compliance with §2 as a defense to an equal protection challenge, but the holding was clear: A State cannot remedy a §2 violation through the creation of a noncompact district. * * *

Apart from its conflict with *De Grandy* and *Shaw II*, THE CHIEF JUSTICE's approach has the deficiency of creating a one-way rule whereby plaintiffs must show compactness but States need not (except, it seems, when using §2 as a defense to an equal protection challenge). THE CHIEF JUSTICE appears to accept that a plaintiff, to make out a §2 violation, must show he or she is part of a racial group that could form a majority in a reasonably compact district. If, however, a noncompact district cannot make up for the lack of a compact district, then this is equally true whether the plaintiff or the State proposes the noncompact district.

The District Court stated that Plan 1374C created "six *Gingles* Latino" districts, but it failed to decide whether District 25 was reasonably compact for §2 purposes. * * *

While no precise rule has emerged governing §2 compactness, the "inquiry should take into account 'traditional districting principles such as maintaining communities of interest and traditional boundaries.'" The recognition of nonracial communities of interest reflects the principle that a State may not "assum[e] from a group of voters' race that they 'think alike, share the same political interests, and will prefer the same candidates at the polls.'" *Miller* [v. *Johnson*, 515 U.S. 900], 920 [(1995)] [p. 376] (quoting *Shaw v. Reno*, 509 U.S. 630, 647 (1993) [p. 362]). In the absence of this prohibited assumption, there is no basis to believe a district that combines two far-flung segments of a racial group with disparate interests provides the opportunity that §2 requires or that the first *Gingles* condition contemplates. * * *

* * * [T]he District Court's findings regarding the different characteristics, needs, and interests of the Latino community near the Mexican border and the one in and around Austin are well supported and uncontested. Legitimate yet differing communities of interest should not be disregarded in the interest of race. The practical consequence of drawing a district to cover two distant, disparate communities is that one or both groups will be unable to achieve their political goals. * * * We do not question the District Court's finding that the groups' combined voting strength would enable them to elect a candidate each prefers to the Anglos' candidate of choice. We also accept that in some cases members of a racial group in different areas—for example, rural and urban communities—could share similar interests and therefore form a compact district if the areas are in reasonably close proximity. When, however, the only common index is race and the result will be to cause internal friction, the State cannot make this a remedy for a §2 violation elsewhere. We emphasize it is the enormous geographical distance separating the Austin and

Mexican-border communities, coupled with the disparate needs and interests of these populations — not either factor alone — that renders District 25 noncompact for § 2 purposes. The mathematical possibility of a racial bloc does not make a district compact.

Since District 25 is not reasonably compact, Plan 1374C contains only five reasonably compact Latino opportunity districts. Plan 1151C, by contrast, created six such districts. * * *

Appellants have thus satisfied all three *Gingles* requirements as to District 23, and the creation of new District 25 does not remedy the problem.

We proceed now to the totality of the circumstances, and first to the proportionality inquiry, comparing the percentage of total districts that are Latino opportunity districts with the Latino share of the citizen voting-age population. As explained in *De Grandy*, proportionality is "a relevant fact in the totality of circumstances." 512 U.S., at 1000. It does not, however, act as a "safe harbor" for States in complying with § 2. *Id.*, at 1017–1018. * * *

The State contends that proportionality should be decided on a regional basis, while appellants say their claim requires the Court to conduct a statewide analysis. * * * We conclude the answer in these cases is to look at proportionality statewide. * * * Appellants have alleged statewide vote dilution based on a statewide plan, so the electoral opportunities of Latinos across the State can bear on whether the lack of electoral opportunity for Latinos in District 23 is a consequence of Plan 1374C's redrawing of lines or simply a consequence of the inevitable "win some, lose some" in a State with racial bloc voting. Indeed, several of the other factors in the totality of circumstances have been characterized with reference to the State as a whole. *Gingles*, *supra*, at 44–45 (listing Senate Report factors). Particularly given the presence of racially polarized voting — and the possible submergence of minority votes — throughout Texas, it makes sense to use the entire State in assessing proportionality.

Looking statewide, there are 32 congressional districts. The five reasonably compact Latino opportunity districts amount to roughly 16% of the total, while Latinos make up 22% of Texas' citizen voting-age population. * * * Latinos are, therefore, two districts shy of proportional representation. There is, of course, no "magic parameter," *De Grandy*, 512 U.S., at 1017, n.14, and "rough proportionality," *id.*, at 1023, must allow for some deviations. We need not decide whether the two-district deficit in these cases weighs in favor of a § 2 violation. Even if Plan 1374C's disproportionality were deemed insubstantial, that consideration would not overcome the other evidence of vote dilution for Latinos in District 23. "[T]he degree of probative value assigned to proportionality may vary with other facts," *id.*, at 1020, and the other facts in these cases convince us that there is a § 2 violation.

District 23's Latino voters were poised to elect their candidate of choice. They were becoming more politically active, with a marked and continuous rise in

Spanish-surnamed voter registration. In successive elections Latinos were voting against Bonilla in greater numbers, and in 2002 they almost ousted him. * * * In response to the growing participation that threatened Bonilla's incumbency, the State divided the cohesive Latino community in Webb County, moving about 100,000 Latinos to District 28, which was already a Latino opportunity district, and leaving the rest in a district where they now have little hope of electing their candidate of choice.

The changes to District 23 undermined the progress of a racial group that has been subject to significant voting-related discrimination and that was becoming increasingly politically active and cohesive. * * *

Against this background, the Latinos' diminishing electoral support for Bonilla indicates their belief he was "unresponsive to the particularized needs of the members of the minority group." In essence the State took away the Latinos' opportunity because Latinos were about to exercise it. This bears the mark of intentional discrimination that could give rise to an equal protection violation. Even if we accept the District Court's finding that the State's action was taken primarily for political, not racial, reasons, the redrawing of the district lines was damaging to the Latinos in District 23. The State not only made fruitless the Latinos' mobilization efforts but also acted against those Latinos who were becoming most politically active * * *.

Furthermore, the reason for taking Latinos out of District 23, according to the District Court, was to protect Congressman Bonilla from a constituency that was increasingly voting against him. The Court has noted that incumbency protection can be a legitimate factor in districting, see *Karcher* v. *Daggett*, 462 U.S. [725], 740 [(1983)], but experience teaches that incumbency protection can take various forms, not all of them in the interests of the constituents. If the justification for incumbency protection is to keep the constituency intact so the officeholder is accountable for promises made or broken, then the protection seems to accord with concern for the voters. If, on the other hand, incumbency protection means excluding some voters from the district simply because they are likely to vote against the officeholder, the change is to benefit the officeholder, not the voters. By purposely redrawing lines around those who opposed Bonilla, the state legislature took the latter course. This policy, whatever its validity in the realm of politics, cannot justify the effect on Latino voters. The policy becomes even more suspect when considered in light of evidence suggesting that the State intentionally drew District 23 to have a nominal Latino voting-age majority (without a citizen voting-age majority) for political reasons. This use of race to create the façade of a Latino district also weighs in favor of appellants' claim. * * *

Based on the foregoing, the totality of the circumstances demonstrates a § 2 violation. Even assuming Plan 1374C provides something close to proportional representation for Latinos, its troubling blend of politics and race — and the resulting vote dilution of a group that was beginning to achieve § 2's goal of overcoming prior electoral discrimination — cannot be sustained.

Because we hold Plan 1374C violates §2 in its redrawing of District 23, we do not address appellants' claims that the use of race and politics in drawing that district violates the First Amendment and equal protection. We also need not confront appellants' claim of an equal protection violation in the drawing of District 25. The districts in south and west Texas will have to be redrawn to remedy the violation in District 23, and we have no cause to pass on the legitimacy of a district that must be changed. District 25, in particular, was formed to compensate for the loss of District 23 as a Latino opportunity district, and there is no reason to believe District 25 will remain in its current form once District 23 is brought into compliance with §2. We therefore vacate the District Court's judgment as to these claims.

IV

Appellants also challenge the changes to district lines in the Dallas area, alleging they dilute African-American voting strength in violation of §2 of the Voting Rights Act. Specifically, appellants contend that an African-American minority effectively controlled District 24 under Plan 1151C, and that §2 entitles them to this district.

Before Plan 1374C was enacted, District 24 had elected Anglo Democrat Martin Frost to Congress in every election since 1978. Anglos were the largest racial group in the district, with 49.8% of the citizen voting-age population, and third largest were Latinos, with 20.8%. African-Americans were the second-largest group, with 25.7% of the citizen voting-age population, and they voted consistently for Frost. The new plan broke apart this racially diverse district, assigning its pieces into several other districts.

Accepting that African-Americans would not be a majority of the single-member district they seek, and that African-Americans do not vote cohesively with Hispanics, appellants nonetheless contend African-Americans had effective control of District 24. As the Court has done several times before, we assume for purposes of this litigation that it is possible to state a §2 claim for a racial group that makes up less than 50% of the population. See *De Grandy*, 512 U.S., at 1009; *Voinovich v. Quilter*, 507 U.S. 146, 154 (1993); *Gingles*, 478 U.S., at 46–47 n.12. Even on the assumption that the first *Gingles* prong can accommodate this claim, however, appellants must show they constitute "a sufficiently large minority to elect their candidate of choice with the assistance of cross-over votes." *Voinovich, supra*, at 158. * * *

* * * In the absence of any contested Democratic primary in District 24 over the last 20 years, no obvious benchmark exists for deciding whether African-Americans could elect their candidate of choice. The fact that African-Americans voted for Frost—in the primary and general elections—could signify he is their candidate of choice. Without a contested primary, however, it could also be interpreted to show (assuming racial bloc voting) that Anglos and Latinos would vote in the Democratic primary in greater numbers if an African-American candidate of choice were to run, especially given Texas' open primary system. The District Court heard trial

testimony that would support both explanations, and we cannot say that it erred in crediting the testimony that endorsed the latter interpretation. * * *

That African-Americans had influence in the district does not suffice to state a § 2 claim in these cases. The opportunity "to elect representatives of their choice" requires more than the ability to influence the outcome between some candidates, none of whom is their candidate of choice. There is no doubt African-Americans preferred Martin Frost to the Republicans who opposed him. The fact that African-Americans preferred Frost to some others does not, however, make him their candidate of choice. Accordingly, the ability to aid in Frost's election does not make the old District 24 an African-American opportunity district for purposes of § 2. If § 2 were interpreted to protect this kind of influence, it would unnecessarily infuse race into virtually every redistricting, raising serious constitutional questions.

Appellants respond by pointing to *Georgia* v. *Ashcroft* [539 U.S. 461 (2003)] [p. 266], where the Court held that the presence of influence districts is a relevant consideration under § 5 of the Voting Rights Act. The inquiry under § 2, however, concerns the opportunity "to elect representatives of their choice," [52 U.S.C. § 10301(b)], not whether a change has the purpose or effect of "denying or abridging the right to vote," § [10304]. *Ashcroft* recognized the differences between these tests, 539 U.S., at 478, and concluded that the ability of racial groups to elect candidates of their choice is only one factor under § 5, *id.*, at 480. So while the presence of districts "where minority voters may not be able to elect a candidate of choice but can play a substantial, if not decisive, role in the electoral process" is relevant to the § 5 analysis, *id.*, at 482, the lack of such districts cannot establish a § 2 violation. The failure to create an influence district in these cases thus does not run afoul of § 2 of the Voting Rights Act. * * *

We reject the statewide challenge to Texas' redistricting as an unconstitutional political gerrymander and the challenge to the redistricting in the Dallas area as a violation of § 2 of the Voting Rights Act. We do hold that the redrawing of lines in District 23 violates § 2 of the Voting Rights Act. The judgment of the District Court is affirmed in part, reversed in part, and vacated in part, and the cases are remanded for further proceedings.

It is so ordered.

Justice Stevens, with whom Justice Breyer joins * * *, concurring in part and dissenting in part. * * *

* * * [A]ny decision to redraw district boundaries—like any other state action that affects the electoral process—must, at the very least, serve some legitimate governmental purpose. A purely partisan desire "to minimize or cancel out the voting strength of racial or political elements of the voting population," *Fortson* v. *Dorsey*, 379 U.S. 433, 439 (1965), is not such a purpose. Because a desire to minimize the strength of Texas Democrats was the sole motivation for the adoption of Plan 1374C, the plan cannot withstand constitutional scrutiny. * * *

* * * If, after finally achieving political strength in Texas, the Republicans had adopted a new plan in order to remove the excessively partisan Democratic gerrymander of the 1990's, the decision to do so would unquestionably have been supported by a neutral justification. But that is not what happened. Instead, * * * Texas Republicans abandoned a neutral apportionment map [drawn by the *Balderas* court] for the sole purpose of manipulating district boundaries to maximize their electoral advantage and thus create their own impermissible stranglehold on political power. * * *

* * * By taking an action for the sole purpose of advantaging Republicans and disadvantaging Democrats, the State of Texas violated its constitutional obligation to govern impartially. * * *

JUSTICE SOUTER, with whom JUSTICE GINSBURG joins, concurring in part and dissenting in part.

[JUSTICE SOUTER discussed the first *Gingles* precondition for §2 vote-dilution claims, which requires that a minority group demonstrate "that it is sufficiently large and geographically compact to constitute a majority in a single-member district." 478 U.S., at 50. He argued that a minority group should be able to satisfy that precondition if it would be able to elect its candidate of choice in a coalition district, even if the members of the minority group could not constitute an absolute majority of the population in the district. The Court confronted that issue, and rejected JUSTICE SOUTER's position, in *Bartlett* v. *Strickland*, 556 U.S. 1 (2009).]

JUSTICE BREYER, concurring in part and dissenting in part. * * *

[Plan 1374C's] effort "to maximize partisan advantage" encompasses an effort not only to exaggerate the favored party's electoral majority but also to produce a majority of congressional representatives even if the favored party receives only a *minority* of popular votes.

[B]ecause the plan entrenches the Republican Party, the State cannot successfully defend it as an effort simply to *neutralize* the Democratic Party's previous political gerrymander. Nor has the State tried to justify the plan on nonpartisan grounds, either as an effort to achieve legislative stability by avoiding legislative exaggeration of small shifts in party preferences or in any other way.

In sum, "the risk of entrenchment is demonstrated," "partisan considerations [have] render[ed] the traditional district-drawing compromises irrelevant," and "no justification other than party advantage can be found." The record reveals a plan that overwhelmingly relies upon the unjustified use of purely partisan line-drawing considerations and which will likely have seriously harmful electoral consequences. For these reasons, I believe the plan in its entirety violates the Equal Protection Clause.

CHIEF JUSTICE ROBERTS, with whom JUSTICE ALITO joins, concurring in part, concurring in the judgment in part, and dissenting in part.

I join Parts I and IV of the plurality opinion. With regard to Part II, I agree with the determination that appellants have not provided "a reliable standard for identifying unconstitutional political gerrymanders." * * *

I must, however, dissent from Part III of the Court's opinion. According to the District Court's factual findings, the State's drawing of district lines in south and west Texas caused the area to move from five out of seven effective Latino opportunity congressional districts, with an additional district "moving" in that direction, to *six* out of seven effective Latino opportunity districts. The end result is that while Latinos make up 58% of the citizen voting-age population in the area, they control 85% (six of seven) of the districts under the State's plan.

In the face of these findings, the majority nonetheless concludes that the State's plan somehow dilutes the voting strength of Latinos in violation of § 2 of the Voting Rights Act of 1965. The majority reaches its surprising result because it finds that Latino voters in one of the State's Latino opportunity districts—District 25— are insufficiently compact, in that they consist of two different groups, one from around the Rio Grande and another from around Austin. According to the majority, this may make it more difficult for certain Latino-preferred candidates to be elected from that district—*even though Latino voters make up 55% of the citizen voting-age population in the district and vote as a bloc.* The majority prefers old District 23, despite the District Court determination that new District 25 is "a more effective Latino opportunity district than Congressional District 23 had been." * * *

Unable to escape the District Court's factfinding, the majority is left in the awkward position of maintaining that its *theory* about compactness is more important under § 2 than the actual prospects of electoral success for Latino-preferred candidates under a State's apportionment plan. And that theory is a novel one to boot. Never before has this or any other court struck down a State's redistricting plan under § 2, on the ground that the plan achieves the maximum number of possible majority-minority districts, but loses on style points, in that the minority voters in one of those districts are not as "compact" as the minority voters would be in another district were the lines drawn differently. Such a basis for liability pushes voting rights litigation into a whole new area—an area far removed from the concern of the Voting Rights Act to ensure minority voters an equal opportunity "to elect representatives of their choice." [52 U.S.C. § 10301(b)]. * * *

The majority's only answer is to shift the focus to statewide proportionality. * * * [But t]he plaintiffs' § 2 claims concern "the impact of the legislative plan on Latino voting strength *in South and West Texas*," and that is the only area of the State in which they can satisfy the *Gingles* factors. That is accordingly the proper frame of reference in analyzing proportionality.

In any event, at a statewide level, 6 Latino opportunity districts out of 32, or 19% of the seats, would certainly seem to be "roughly proportional" to the Latino 22%

share of the population. The District Court accordingly determined that proportionality suggested the lack of vote dilution, even considered on a statewide basis. The majority avoids that suggestion by disregarding the District Court's factual finding that District 25 is an effective Latino opportunity district. That is not only improper, for the reasons given, but the majority's rejection of District 25 as a Latino opportunity district is also flatly inconsistent with its statewide approach to analyzing proportionality. Under the majority's view, the Latino voters in the northern end of District 25 cannot "count" along with the Latino voters at the southern end to form an effective majority, because they belong to different communities. But Latino voters from everywhere around the State of Texas—even those from areas where the *Gingles* factors are not satisfied—can "count" for purposes of calculating the proportion against which effective Latino electoral power should be measured. Heads the plaintiffs win; tails the State loses. * * *

Whatever the majority believes it is fighting with its holding, it is not vote dilution on the basis of race or ethnicity. I do not believe it is our role to make judgments about which *mixes* of minority voters should count for purposes of forming a majority in an electoral district, in the face of factual findings that the district is an effective majority-minority district. It is a sordid business, this divvying us up by race. When a State's plan already provides the maximum possible number of majority-minority effective opportunity districts, and the minority enjoys effective political power in the area well in *excess* of its proportion of the population, I would conclude that the courts have no further role to play in rejiggering the district lines under § 2.

Justice Scalia, with whom Justice Thomas joins, and with whom The Chief Justice and Justice Alito join as to Part III, concurring in the judgment in part and dissenting in part. * * *

II

I would dismiss appellants' vote-dilution claims premised on § 2 of the Voting Rights Act of 1965 for failure to state a claim, for the reasons set forth in Justice Thomas's opinion, which I joined, in *Holder* v. *Hall*, 512 U.S. 874, 891–946 (1994) [p. 343] (opinion concurring in judgment). * * *

III

* * * [The District Court found that the Texas Legislature removed 100,000 mostly Latino residents from District 23 not for racial reasons, but for political ones—specifically, ensuring Congressman Bonilla's continued reelection. That finding] dooms appellants' intentional-vote-dilution claim. * * *

* * * [In evaluating whether District 25 was an impermissible racial gerrymander,] the District Court applied the approach set forth in *Easley* [v. *Cromartie*, 532 U.S. 234, 241 (2001)], in which the Court held that race may be a motivation in redistricting as long as it is not the predominant one. See also *Bush* [v. *Vera*], 517 U.S. [952],

993 [(1996)] (O'Connor, J., concurring) ("[S]o long as they do not subordinate traditional districting criteria to the use of race for its own sake or as a proxy, States may intentionally create majority-minority districts, and may otherwise take race into consideration, without coming under strict scrutiny"). In my view, however, when a legislature intentionally creates a majority-minority district, race is necessarily its predominant motivation and strict scrutiny is therefore triggered. * * *

Texas must therefore show that its use of race was narrowly tailored to further a compelling state interest. Texas asserts that it created District 25 to comply with its obligations under § 5 of the Voting Rights Act. * * * Since its changes to District 23 had reduced Latino voting power in that district, Texas asserts that it needed to create District 25 as a Latino-opportunity district in order to avoid § 5 liability.

We have in the past left undecided whether compliance with federal antidiscrimination laws can be a compelling state interest. I would hold that compliance with § 5 of the Voting Rights Act can be such an interest. We long ago upheld the constitutionality of § 5 as a proper exercise of Congress's authority under § 2 of the Fifteenth Amendment to enforce that Amendment's prohibition on the denial or abridgment of the right to vote. See *South Carolina* v. *Katzenbach*, 383 U.S. 301 (1966) [p. 220]. If compliance with § 5 were not a compelling state interest, then a State could be placed in the impossible position of having to choose between compliance with § 5 and compliance with the Equal Protection Clause. Moreover, the compelling nature of the State's interest in § 5 compliance is supported by our recognition in previous cases that race may be used where necessary to remedy identified past discrimination. See, *e.g.*, *Shaw II*, at 909 (citing *Richmond* v. *J.A. Croson Co.*, 488 U.S. 469, 498–506 (1989)). Congress enacted § 5 for just that purpose, and that provision applies only to jurisdictions with a history of official discrimination. In the proper case, therefore, a covered jurisdiction may have a compelling interest in complying with § 5. * * *

* * * Appellants concede * * * that the changes made to District 23 "necessitated creating an additional effective Latino district elsewhere, in an attempt to avoid Voting Rights Act liability." This is, of course, precisely the State's position. Nor do appellants charge that in creating District 25 the State did more than what was required by § 5. In light of these concessions, * * * I would affirm the judgment of the District Court.

Notes and Questions

1. Why was District 25 not a sufficient remedy for the reduction of Latino voting strength in District 23? The Court's conclusion appears to rest on a conclusion that the right protected by § 2 is individual and personal; just as a state cannot deny person A the right to vote and instead give two votes to person B, a state cannot deny the voters in District 23 the right to equal electoral opportunity and instead grant special political opportunity to voters elsewhere. See *Shaw v. Hunt*, 517 U.S. 899, 917 (1996) (*Shaw II*) ("To accept that the [opportunity] district may be placed anywhere implies that the claim, and hence the coordinate right to an undiluted

vote (to cast a ballot equal among voters), belongs to the minority as a group and not to its individual members. It does not. See [52 U.S.C. § 10301] ('the right of any citizen').").

But the analogy may be flawed. The right protected by § 2 is not a conventional individual right, because the opportunity to elect representatives is possessed by groups of like-minded voters; an individual voter cannot elect representatives.[f] Likewise, an individual voter does not have the right to be placed into any particular district. Even if § 2 demands that a district be drawn to give members of a minority group an opportunity to elect a representative of their choice, the state need not place every member of that group in the opportunity district. *See Shaw II*, 517 U.S. at 917 n.9.[g] If § 2 protects a group right, however, should it matter whether Latinos are given the opportunity to elect a candidate in one part of the state rather than in another?

2. Should the Constitution be interpreted to bar mid-decade (re-)redistricting completely? Should the constitutionality of mid-decade redistricting depend on the legislature's motive for redrawing districts? If the Constitution places any greater limit on mid-decade redistricting than on beginning-of-the-decade redistricting, what provision of the Constitution has that effect?

3. Concerning District 24, the plurality accepted the district court's determination that blacks would not be able to elect their candidates of choice, even in the Democratic primary. If an alternative districting plan would have given blacks the ability to elect their preferred candidates in the primary, and if the Democratic nominee would be expected to win the general election, should a districting plan that deprived them of that power be a violation of § 2? In such a scenario, would an open-primary

---

f. *See Bush v. Vera*, 517 U.S. 952, 1049 n.3 (1996) (Souter, J., dissenting) (arguing that "any sophisticated right to genuinely meaningful electoral participation must be evaluated and measured as a group right") (quoting Samuel Issacharoff, *Groups and the Right to Vote*, 44 EMORY L.J. 869, 883 (1995)); T. Alexander Aleinikoff & Samuel Issacharoff, *Race and Redistricting: Drawing Constitutional Lines After* Shaw v. Reno, 92 MICH. L. REV. 588 (1993) (group right); Lani Guinier, *[E]racing Democracy: The Voting Rights Cases*, 108 HARV. L. REV. 109 (1994) (group right); Katherine Inglis Butler, *Affirmative Racial Gerrymandering: Rhetoric and Reality*, 26 CUMB. L. REV. 313 (1996) (individual right). *See also* Heather K. Gerken, *Understanding the Right to an Undiluted Vote*, 114 HARV. L. REV. 1663, 1684 (2001) ("[E]xamining the treatment of an individual voter * * * will reveal only whether that person had an equal opportunity to *cast* a vote. It will not tell us whether she had an equal opportunity to *aggregate* her vote.").

g. Viewing § 2 as conveying an individual right presents an additional problem when considering the rights of the voters selected to fill up a majority-minority district—the so-called "filler people." Aleinikoff & Issacharoff, *supra*, at 601. *See Gonzalez v. City of Aurora*, 535 F.3d 594, 598 (7th Cir. 2008) ("There is a serious problem with any proposal to employ black or Asian or white citizens of some other ethnic background as 'fill' in districts carefully drawn to ensure three 70%-Latino wards—wards in which the remaining 30% are (by design) never going to be able to elect a candidate of *their* choice."). If, however, the "filler people" can be "virtually represented" by legislators chosen in other districts—if § 2 is satisfied by the representation of the filler people's racial group in the legislature as a whole—then § 2's right appears to rest with the group and not the individual.

system, which would allow (mostly white) Republicans to vote in the Democratic primary, dilute black votes? *See Osburn v. Cox*, 369 F.3d 1283 (11th Cir. 2004).

4. The seemingly never-ending saga of Texas redistricting continued with *Abbott v. Perez*, 585 U.S. __, 138 S. Ct. 2305 (2018). *Perez* was the culmination of several years of litigation about redistricting following the 2010 census. The Texas legislature initially drafted a plan in 2011, but that plan was challenged in court and never implemented. Rather, a court-drawn plan was put into place for the 2012 elections, and the legislature adopted that court-drawn plan as its own (with only slight changes) in 2013. Despite the fact that the Texas legislature had adopted the court-drawn plan as a way of avoiding further litigation, the 2013 plan was challenged, and a three-judge district court in Texas struck it down. According to the district court, the 2011 plan had intentionally diluted the votes of minorities, and the 2013 plan had not sufficiently purged the "taint" of the earlier intentional discrimination.

The Supreme Court reversed in relevant part. It held that the intent of the 2013 legislature was "what matters," 138 S. Ct. at 2325, and that a legislature is not under an obligation to purge itself of any taint stemming from the intentional discrimination of its predecessors. Thus, even if the 2011 legislature had engaged in intentional discrimination, that did not prove the illegality of the 2013 plan, although "the intent of the 2011 Legislature . . . [is] relevant to the extent that [it] naturally give[s] rise to — or tend[s] to refute — inferences regarding the intent of the 2013 Legislature." *Id.* at 2327. Significantly, however, even accepting that there had been intentional discrimination in 2011, "it was the plaintiffs' burden to overcome the presumption of legislative good faith and show that the 2013 Legislature acted with invidious intent." 138 S. Ct. at 2325.

Abbott v. Perez struck down one district in the 2013 plan. House District 90, the Court concluded, was an unconstitutional racial gerrymander because of its predominant use of race in creating a district that could be controlled by Latinos. The state admitted that "race was the predominant factor in the design of" the district, but sought to defend on the ground that race was used to ensure that the plan could not be subject to a challenge under VRA §2. The Court disagreed, saying that the state had not carried its burden under the *Shaw* line of cases to demonstrate that it had "good reason" for thinking that it was necessary to use race to avoid a §2 violation. Texas pointed out that the Mexican-American Legal (or Legislative) Caucus (a group of Texas legislators representing majority-Hispanic constituencies) demanded that more Latinos be added to the district. The fact that such a group advocates for a broad reading of §2 does not, however, mean that such a reading actually describes the scope of §2. Texas also noted that the Democratic primary elections in 2012 and 2014 were very close, with the Latino candidate of choice narrowly losing in 2014 and narrowly winning in 2014. The Court concluded that these data, while they "may be suggestive," "were not enough to give the State good reason to conclude that it had to alter the district's lines solely on the basis of race." 138 S. Ct. at 2334.

Chapter 5

The Roles and Rights of Political Parties

A. Introduction

Political parties occupy an ambiguous position in the constitutional structure. On the one hand, the structure of government was believed to limit the influence of parties, and parties were seen at the time of the framing as obstacles to the pursuit of the public good. *See, e.g.*, Richard Hofstadter, The Idea of a Party System: The Rise of Legitimate Opposition in the United States, 1780–1840 (1969). On the other hand, the First Amendment's protections of "speech," "assembly," and "petition" seem to extend constitutional protection to associations, such as parties, that are vehicles for exercising all three of those rights. To complicate matters further, parties—and particularly the two major parties, which have been dominant in American politics for well over a century and whose members are the office-holders who create the statutes governing parties' place in government— are essential to the electoral machinery. For example, states depend on parties to winnow potential candidates to a small number whom the voters consider in the general election. If the parties did not perform that winnowing function, the state would have to do so, and our electoral structure would look very different from the way it does now.

The intertwinement between the two major parties and the state government has led to controversy concerning the degree to which the parties should be considered part of the state, and thus bound to abide by the constitutional limits on government action, and the degree to which parties should be considered private associations, whose autonomy from state control is constitutionally protected. This Chapter examines those issues.

In § B, we consider whether parties should be considered "state actors," such that they would be prohibited from discriminating on the ground of race against potential voters in primary elections. In a series of cases from *Nixon v. Herndon*, 273 U.S. 536 (1927), through *Terry v. Adams*, 345 U.S. 461 (1953) [p. 423], collectively referred to as the White Primary Cases, the Court held that neither states, nor the parties themselves, nor certain influential groups within the parties could exclude blacks from voting in primaries. As the fractured decision in *Terry* illustrated, however, it was unclear what principles motivated some of those conclusions. Accordingly, it is difficult to assess the extent to which those holdings extend to other sub-groups of parties, or whether parties should be considered state actors when engaged in activities other than primaries, such as advocating the election of particular candidates or establishing rules for participating in party conventions.

Section C considers whether the First Amendment guarantees parties the freedom to determine their membership, their nominees, and their policies separate from the influence of the state. The Supreme Court has granted parties considerable autonomy to determine, for example, rules governing internal party operations. Further, parties enjoy some ability to determine qualifications for participating in primaries and for seeking nominations, though parties' decisions in this regard are subject to some restrictions. As the White Primary Cases demonstrate, some of these restrictions are grounded in the Constitution; others, however, are imposed by state law. This section principally focuses on the question of which state-law restrictions are permissible and which abridge parties' First Amendment rights.

B. State Action

With the exception of the Thirteenth Amendment, which prohibits slavery, the Constitution regulates the conduct of only government and government officials—not private parties. For example, the First Amendment prohibits "Congress" from making laws abridging certain liberties, and the Fourteenth Amendment provides that "[n]o State" shall deprive persons of the equal protection of the laws.[a] If a private employer discriminates against job applicants who are racial minorities, such discrimination may well violate state and/or federal statutes, but it does not violate the Constitution.

Establishing that rule is easy enough in clear cases, but distinguishing between government action and the actions of private parties becomes difficult when government and the rest of society occupy less distinct spheres. Political parties, as we see in this section, are somewhere between state actors and private organizations. On the one hand, the very purpose of a party may be to change government policy, and therefore it may be anomalous to consider the party as part of the government whose policies the party opposes. Likewise, if all political parties were state actors, then the government would be acting in opposition to itself when those different parties criticized and campaigned against each other.

On the other hand, treating parties as strictly private entities would permit the parties to eviscerate constitutional protections. If primary elections, for example,

---

a. As you learned in Constitutional Law, the Supreme Court has held that the Fourteenth Amendment's Due Process Clause "incorporates" many of the provisions of the Bill of Rights against state infringement, even though those provisions by themselves apply only to the United States government. Thus today, for example, states, as well as the United States, are prohibited from abridging the freedom of speech. Whether a right has been incorporated or not, however, the Constitution protects that right only against government action.

were strictly private matters, then parties could effectively exclude racial minorities from the political process. Minorities could, of course, participate in the general election, but by that time their chance to influence politics might have passed. Moreover, the government is hardly a bystander concerning parties' affairs. Governmental regulation pervades the parties' business, and parties (especially major parties) benefit from special treatment granted by the government, such as the automatic placement of the parties' nominees on the general-election ballot. One might argue that it is wrong for parties to take these advantages while maintaining that they need not follow constitutional norms.

The following "White Primary Cases" examine the Supreme Court's attempt to reconcile the role of political parties with the state-action doctrine. The cases involve the Texas Democratic Party's attempt to exclude blacks during a period when the Party was by far the dominant political force in many Southern states, including Texas. Our first principal case is *Grovey v. Townsend*, 295 U.S. 45 (1935), but two cases decided before *Grovey* deserve mention here. In *Nixon v. Herndon*, 273 U.S. 536 (1927), the Court held that a state statute prohibiting blacks from participating in the Democratic primary election was a "direct and obvious violation of the Fourteenth [Amendment]." *Id.* at 541.

Texas legislators responded to *Nixon* by passing a new statute. The new statute did not *require* parties to exclude blacks or anyone else, but *permitted* them to do so: "every political party in this State through its State Executive Committee shall have the power to prescribe the qualifications of its own members and shall in its own way determine who shall be qualified to vote or otherwise participate in such political party." The Democratic State Executive Committee adopted a resolution excluding blacks from participation in primaries. This exclusion was challenged (by the same black man who had been excluded from voting in *Nixon v. Herndon*), and the Court struck it down in *Nixon v. Condon*, 286 U.S. 73 (1932) (*Nixon II*), by a vote of 5-4. Despite finding the exclusion unconstitutional, the Court in *Nixon II* did not hold that the party's discrimination could be attributed to the state simply because parties were state actors. Rather, the Court held that the state statute took power away from the party *convention* and placed it in the *executive committee*:

> Whatever our conclusion might be if the statute had remitted to the party the untrammeled power to prescribe the qualifications of its members, nothing of the kind was done. Instead, the statute lodged the power in a committee, which excluded the petitioner and others of his race, not by virtue of any authority delegated by the party, but by virtue of an authority originating or supposed to originate in the mandate of the law.

Id. at 84. Because the executive committee's power was granted by statute, the Court concluded that the actions of that committee could be attributed to the state.

As *Nixon II* noted, however, a different case would be presented if the limits on membership were decreed not by the executive committee, but by the convention, in which "resides" the power to "formulat[e] the party faith" as well as "[w]hatever inherent power a State political party has to determine the content of its membership." *Id.* at 84–85. It did not take long for that different case to make its way to the Court.

Grovey v. Townsend

Supreme Court of the United States
295 U.S. 45, 55 S. Ct. 622, 79 L. Ed. 1292 (1935)

MR. JUSTICE ROBERTS delivered the opinion of the Court [in which MR. CHIEF JUSTICE HUGHES, MR. JUSTICE VAN DEVANTER, MR. JUSTICE MCREYNOLDS, MR. JUSTICE BRANDEIS, MR. JUSTICE SUTHERLAND, MR. JUSTICE BUTLER, MR. JUSTICE STONE, and MR. JUSTICE CARDOZO join].

The petitioner, by complaint filed in the justice court of Harris county, Texas, alleged that, although he is a citizen of the United States and of the State and County, and a member of and believer in the tenets of the Democratic party, the respondent, the county clerk, a state officer, having as such only public functions to perform, refused him a ballot for a Democratic party primary election because he is of the negro race. * * * [The ballot] was refused him in virtue of a resolution of the state Democratic convention of Texas, adopted May 24, 1932, which is:

"Be it resolved that all white citizens of the State of Texas who are qualified to vote under the Constitution and laws of the state shall be eligible to membership in the Democratic party and as such entitled to participate in its deliberations."

The complaint charges that the respondent acted without legal excuse, and his wrongful and unlawful acts constituted a violation of the Fourteenth and Fifteenth Amendments of the Federal Constitution. [The lower court held against the would-be voter.] * * *

The charge is that respondent, a state officer, in refusing to furnish petitioner a ballot, obeyed the law of Texas, and the consequent denial of petitioner's right to vote in the primary election because of his race and color was state action forbidden by the Federal Constitution, and it is claimed that [*Nixon v. Herndon*, 273 U.S. 536 (1927), and *Nixon v. Condon*, 286 U.S. 73 (1932),] require us so to hold. The cited cases are, however, not in point. * * * Here, the qualifications of citizens to participate in party counsels and to vote at party primaries have been declared by the representatives of the party in convention assembled, and this action upon its face is not state action. * * *

[Petitioner argues] that the primary election was held under statutory compulsion; is wholly statutory in origin and incidents; those charged with its management have been deprived by statute and judicial decision of all power to establish qualifications for participation therein inconsistent with those laid down by the laws of the state, save only that the managers of such elections have been given the power to deny negroes the vote. It is further urged that, while the election is designated that of the Democratic party, the statutes not only require this method of selecting party nominees, but define the powers and duties of the party's representatives and of those who are to conduct the election so completely, and make them so thoroughly officers of the state that any action taken by them in connection with the qualifications of members of the party is in fact state action, and not party action.

In support of this view, petitioner refers to Title 50 of the Revised Civil Statutes of Texas of 1925, which requires that any party whose members cast more than 100,000 ballots at the previous election shall nominate candidates through primaries, and fixes the date at which they are to be held; requires primary election officials to be qualified voters; declares the same qualifications for voting in such an election as in the general elections; permits absentee voting as in a general election; requires that only an official ballot shall be used, as in a general election; specifies the form of ballot and how it shall be marked, as other sections do for general elections; fixes the number of ballots to be provided, as another article does for general elections; permits the use of voting booths, guard rails, and ballot boxes which by other statutes are provided for general elections; requires the officials of primary elections to take the same oath as officials at the general elections; defines the powers of judges at primary elections; provides elaborately for the purity of the ballot box; commands that the sealed ballot boxes be delivered to the county clerk after the election * * *; and confers jurisdiction of election contests upon district courts * * *. A perusal of these provisions, so it is said, will convince that the state has prescribed and regulated party primaries as fully as general elections, and has made those who manage the primaries state officers subject to state direction and control.

While it is true that Texas has, by its laws, elaborately provided for the expression of party preference as to nominees, has required that preference to be expressed in a certain form of voting, and has attempted in minute detail to protect the suffrage of the members of the organization against fraud, it is equally true that the primary is a party primary; the expenses of it are not borne by the state, but by members of the party seeking nomination; the ballots are furnished not by the state, but by the agencies of the party; the votes are counted and the returns made by instrumentalities created by the party; and the state recognizes the state convention as the organ of the party for the declaration of principles and the formulation of policies. * * *

In *Bell* v. *Hill*, 74 S.W.(2d) 113 [(Tex. 1934)], the [Supreme Court of Texas] concluded that [political] parties in the State of Texas arise from the exercise of the free will and liberty of the citizens composing them; that they are voluntary associations for political action, and are not the creatures of the state, and further decided that * * * the State Constitution guaranteed to citizens the liberty of forming political associations, and the only limitation upon this right to be found in that instrument is the clause which requires the maintenance of a republican form of government. The statutes regulating the nomination of candidates by primaries * * * were held not to extend to the denial of the right of citizens to form a political party and to determine who might associate with them as members thereof. The court declared that a proper view of the election laws of Texas, and their history, required the conclusion that the Democratic party in that state is a voluntary political association, and, by its representatives assembled in convention, has the power to determine who shall be eligible for membership and, as such, eligible to participate in the party's primaries. * * * In the light of the principles so announced, we are unable to characterize the managers of the primary election as state officers in such sense that any action taken by them in obedience to the mandate of the state convention respecting eligibility to participate in the organization's deliberations is state action. * * *

The complaint states that * * * in Texas, nomination by the Democratic party is equivalent to election. These facts (the truth of which the demurrer assumes) the petitioner insists, without more, make out a forbidden discrimination. * * * The argument is that, as a negro may not be denied a ballot at a general election on account of his race or color, if exclusion from the primary renders his vote at the general election insignificant and useless, the result is to deny him the suffrage altogether. So to say is to confuse the privilege of membership in a party with the right to vote for one who is to hold a public office. With the former, the state need have no concern; with the latter, it is bound to concern itself, for the general election is a function of the state government, and discrimination by the state as respects participation by negroes on account of their race or color is prohibited by the Federal Constitution. * * *

We find no ground for holding that the respondent has, in obedience to the mandate of the law of Texas, discriminated against the petitioner or denied him any right guaranteed by the Fourteenth and Fifteenth Amendments.

Judgment affirmed.

Notes and Questions

1. Consider the effect of Texas state law on the outcome of *Grovey*. The Supreme Court of the United States concluded that the Texas Democratic Party was not a state actor (itself a federal question) principally because the Supreme Court of Texas concluded that the state constitution and election laws allowed the Party to regulate its own membership.[b] Thus, under *Grovey*, a party's status as a state actor or private association appeared to be dependent on the control the state exercised over it. In other words, the opinion did not treat political parties as necessarily private entities; rather, the Texas Democratic Party was a private entity because Texas law allowed it to have the requisite autonomy.

2. Relatedly, it is important to recognize that *Grovey* did not establish a First Amendment right of parties to be free from state control. The Texas Democratic Party was a private entity not because it had a constitutional right to control its own membership, but because Texas state law allowed it to control its own membership.

---

b. Of course, parties' ostensible status in Texas as private associations did not stop the Texas Legislature from passing the 1923 statute at issue in *Nixon v. Herndon*, 273 U.S. 536 (1927). That statute, you will recall, prohibited blacks from participating in primary elections, whatever the desires of the party. It was struck down not because it violated the state constitution, but because it violated the Fourteenth Amendment.

We will discuss parties' constitutional rights to autonomy from state regulation later in this Chapter.

3. Between *Grovey* and *Smith v. Allwright*, 321 U.S. 649 (1944), the next case to consider Texas's white primary, the Court decided *United States v. Classic*, 313 U.S. 299 (1941). *Classic* was a criminal case, in which the defendants, commissioners of elections in Louisiana, were accused of fraudulently altering ballots and improperly certifying the results of a Democratic primary election for Congress. The fraud was alleged to have violated two federal statutes making it a crime to deprive a person of rights protected by the United States Constitution. The defendants argued that, because the primary election was a proceeding of a private voluntary association, no constitutional right was violated.

The Court rejected the argument in an opinion by then-Justice Stone, without so much as citing *Grovey*. In the Court's view, the right to vote for Congress was protected by the Constitution, and Congress could protect that right by ensuring that primaries were not tainted by fraud. As the Court explained,

> That the free choice by the people of representatives in Congress, subject only to the restrictions to be found in §§ 2 and 4 of Article I and elsewhere in the Constitution, was one of the great purposes of our constitutional scheme of government cannot be doubted. We cannot regard it as any the less the constitutional purpose, or its words as any the less guarantying the integrity of that choice, when a state, exercising its privilege in the absence of Congressional action, changes the mode of choice from a single step, a general election, to two, of which the first is the choice at a primary of those candidates from whom, as a second step, the representative in Congress is to be chosen at the election.

313 U.S. at 316–17. Further, the Court concluded that a contrary interpretation would enable states to undercut the constitutionally protected right to vote by placing important electoral decisions in the hands of "private" entities: "It is hardly the performance of the judicial function to construe a statute which, in terms, protects a right secured by the Constitution, here the right to choose a representative in Congress, as applying to an election whose only function is to ratify a choice already made at the primary, but as having no application to the primary which is the only effective means of choice." *Id.* at 324. Accordingly, the Court held that the defendants' fraud in a primary election interfered with voters' constitutional rights, within the meaning of the statutes, and that the statutes were themselves constitutional exercises of congressional power.

Did *Classic* undermine *Grovey*, or can the two cases be reconciled? The government, in arguing *Classic*, noted that the Louisiana primary, unlike the Texas primary at issue in *Grovey*, was conducted by state officials and at public expense. Do those differences suffice to explain the different outcomes? The following case, factually identical in all relevant respects to *Grovey*, relies on *Classic* in overruling the earlier case.

Smith v. Allwright

Supreme Court of the United States
321 U.S. 649, 64 S. Ct. 757, 88 L. Ed. 987 (1944)

MR. JUSTICE REED delivered the opinion of the Court [in which MR. CHIEF JUS-
TICE STONE, MR. JUSTICE BLACK, MR. JUSTICE DOUGLAS, MR. JUSTICE MURPHY, MR.
JUSTICE JACKSON, and MR. JUSTICE RUTLEDGE join].

This writ of certiorari brings here for review a claim for damages in the sum
of $5,000 on the part of petitioner, a Negro citizen of the 48th precinct of Harris
County, Texas, for the refusal of respondents, election and associate election judges,
respectively, of that precinct, to give petitioner a ballot or to permit him to cast a
ballot in the primary election of July 27, 1940, for the nomination of Democratic
candidates for the United States Senate and House of Representatives, and Governor
and other state officers. The refusal is alleged to have been solely because of the race
and color of the proposed voter. * * *

The Democratic party, on May 24, 1932, in a state convention adopted the following resolution, which has not since been "amended, abrogated, annulled or
avoided": "Be it resolved that all white citizens of the State of Texas who are qualified
to vote under the Constitution and laws of the State shall be eligible to membership
in the Democratic party and, as such, entitled to participate in its deliberations." It
was by virtue of this resolution that the respondents refused to permit the petitioner
to vote.

* * * Respondents * * * defended on the ground that the Democratic party of
Texas is a voluntary organization, with members banded together for the purpose
of selecting individuals of the group representing the common political beliefs as
candidates in the general election. As such a voluntary organization, it was claimed,
the Democratic party is free to select its own membership and limit to whites participation in the party primary. Such action, the answer asserted, does not violate
the Fourteenth, Fifteenth or Seventeenth Amendment, as officers of government
cannot be chosen at primaries, and the Amendments are applicable only to general
elections, where governmental officers are actually elected. Primaries, it is said, are
political party affairs, handled by party, not governmental, officers. * * *

Since *Grovey v. Townsend* [295 U.S. 45 (1935)] [p. 414] and prior to the present
suit, no case from Texas involving primary elections has been before this Court. We
did decide, however, *United States v. Classic*, 313 U.S. 299 [(1941)]. We there held
that § 4 of Article I of the Constitution authorized Congress to regulate primary, as
well as general, elections "where the primary is by law made an integral part of the
election machinery." 313 U.S., at 318. Consequently, in the *Classic* case, * * * corrupt acts of election officers were subjected to Congressional sanctions because that
body had power to protect rights of Federal suffrage secured by the Constitution
in primary as in general elections. This decision depended, too, on the determination that, under the Louisiana statutes, the primary was a part of the procedure for
choice of Federal officials. * * * The fusing by the *Classic* case of the primary and

general elections into a single instrumentality for choice of officers has a definite bearing on the permissibility under the Constitution of excluding Negroes from primaries. This is not to say that the *Classic* case cuts directly into the rationale of *Grovey* v. *Townsend*. This latter case was not mentioned in the opinion. *Classic* bears upon *Grovey* v. *Townsend* not because exclusion of Negroes from primaries is any more or less state action by reason of the unitary character of the electoral process, but because the recognition of the place of the primary in the electoral scheme makes clear that state delegation to a party of the power to fix the qualifications of primary elections is delegation of a state function that may make the party's action the action of the state. When *Grovey* v. *Townsend* was written, the Court looked upon the denial of a vote in a primary as a mere refusal by a party of party membership. As the Louisiana statutes for holding primaries are similar to those of Texas, our ruling in *Classic* as to the unitary character of the electoral process calls for a reexamination as to whether or not the exclusion of Negroes from a Texas party primary was state action.

The statutes of Texas relating to primaries and the resolution of the Democratic party of Texas extending the privileges of membership to white citizens only are the same in substance and effect today as they were when *Grovey* v. *Townsend* was decided by a unanimous Court. The question as to whether the exclusionary action of the party was the action of the State persists as the determinative factor. In again entering upon consideration of the inference to be drawn as to state action from a substantially similar factual situation, it should be noted that *Grovey* v. *Townsend* upheld exclusion of Negroes from primaries through the denial of party membership by a party convention. A few years before [in *Nixon* v. *Condon*, 286 U.S. 73 (1932)], this Court refused approval of exclusion by the State Executive Committee of the party. A different result was reached on the theory that the Committee action was state authorized, and the Convention action was unfettered by statutory control. Such a variation in the result from so slight a change in form influences us to consider anew the legal validity of the distinction which has resulted in barring Negroes from participating in the nominations of candidates of the Democratic party in Texas. * * *

We are thus brought to an examination of the qualifications for Democratic primary electors in Texas, to determine whether state action or private action has excluded Negroes from participation. * * * Texas requires electors in a primary to pay a poll tax. Every person who does so pay and who has the qualifications of age and residence is an acceptable voter for the primary. * * * Texas requires by the law the election of the county officers of a party. These compose the county executive committee. The county chairmen so selected are members of the district executive committee and choose the chairman for the district. Precinct primary election officers are named by the county executive committee. Statutes provide for the election by the voters of precinct delegates to the county convention of a party and the selection of delegates to the district and state conventions by the county convention. The state convention selects the state executive committee. No convention may place in platform or resolution any demand for specific legislation without endorsement of such legislation by the voters in a primary. Texas thus directs the selection of all party officers.

Primary elections are conducted by the party under state statutory authority. The county executive committee selects precinct election officials and the county, district or state executive committees, respectively, canvass the returns. These party committees or the state convention certify the party's candidates to the appropriate officers for inclusion on the official ballot for the general election. No name which has not been so certified may appear upon the ballot for the general election as a candidate of a political party. No other name may be printed on the ballot which has not been placed in nomination by qualified voters who must take oath that they did not participate in a primary for the selection of a candidate for the office for which the nomination is made.

The state courts are given exclusive original jurisdiction of contested elections and of mandamus proceedings to compel party officers to perform their statutory duties.

We think that this statutory system for the selection of party nominees for inclusion on the general election ballot makes the party which is required to follow these legislative directions an agency of the state in so far as it determines the participants in a primary election. The party takes its character as a state agency from the duties imposed upon it by state statutes; the duties do not become matters of private law because they are performed by a political party. The plan of the Texas primary follows substantially that of Louisiana, with the exception that, in Louisiana, the state pays the cost of the primary, while Texas assesses the cost against candidates. In numerous instances, the Texas statutes fix or limit the fees to be charged. Whether paid directly by the state or through state requirements, it is state action which compels. When primaries become a part of the machinery for choosing officials, state and national, as they have here, the same tests to determine the character of discrimination or abridgement should be applied to the primary as are applied to the general election. If the state requires a certain electoral procedure, prescribes a general election ballot made up of party nominees so chosen and limits the choice of the electorate in general elections for state offices, practically speaking, to those whose names appear on such a ballot, it endorses, adopts and enforces the discrimination against Negroes, practiced by a party entrusted by Texas law with the determination of the qualifications of participants in the primary. This is state action within the meaning of the Fifteenth Amendment.

The United States is a constitutional democracy. Its organic law grants to all citizens a right to participate in the choice of elected officials without restriction by any state because of race. This grant to the people of the opportunity for choice is not to be nullified by a state through casting its electoral process in a form which permits a private organization to practice racial discrimination in the election. Constitutional rights would be of little value if they could be thus indirectly denied.

The privilege of membership in a party may be, as this Court said in *Grovey* v. *Townsend*, 295 U.S., [at] 55, no concern of a state. But when, as here, that privilege is also the essential qualification for voting in a primary to select nominees for a general election, the state makes the action of the party the action of the state. In reaching this conclusion, we are not unmindful of the desirability of continuity of decision in constitutional questions. However, when convinced of former error, this Court has never felt constrained to follow precedent. In constitutional questions, where correction depends upon amendment, and not upon legislative action, this Court throughout its history has freely exercised its power to reexamine the basis of its constitutional decisions. This has long been accepted practice, and this practice has continued to this day. This is particularly true when the decision believed erroneous is the application of a constitutional principle, rather than an interpretation of the Constitution to extract the principle itself. Here, we are applying, contrary to the recent decision in *Grovey* v. *Townsend*, the well established principle of the Fifteenth Amendment, forbidding the abridgement by a state of a citizen's right to vote. *Grovey* v. *Townsend* is overruled.

Judgment reversed.

Mr. Justice Frankfurter concurs in the result [without opinion].

Mr. Justice Roberts [dissenting]. * * *

[*Grovey* v. *Townsend*] received the attention and consideration which the questions involved demanded, and the opinion represented the views of all the justices. It appears that those views do not now commend themselves to the court. I shall not restate them. They are exposed in the opinion, and must stand or fall on their merits. Their soundness, however, is not a matter which presently concerns me.

The reason for my concern is that the instant decision, overruling that announced about nine years ago, tends to bring adjudications of this tribunal into the same class as a restricted railroad ticket, good for this day and train only. I have no assurance, in view of current decisions, that the opinion announced today may not shortly be repudiated and overruled by justices who deem they have new light on the subject. * * *

It is regrettable that, in an era marked by doubt and confusion, an era whose greatest need is steadfastness of thought and purpose, this court, which has been looked to as exhibiting consistency in adjudication and a steadiness which would hold the balance even in the face of temporary ebbs and flows of opinion, should now itself become the breeder of fresh doubt and confusion in the public mind as to the stability of our institutions.

Notes and Questions

1. Consider the changes in the Court's membership between *Grovey* and *Smith*. Only Harlan Fiske Stone (who was elevated to Chief Justice by President Franklin Roosevelt) and Owen J. Roberts remained from 1935. The other seven Justices were

appointed to the Court by Roosevelt. Consider, too, the historical context of the case. *Smith* was argued in the midst of World War II, at a time when it might have been particularly troubling to permit American states to make racial distinctions in excluding people from the political process. *Cf. Shelley v. Kraemer*, 334 U.S. 1 (1948) (finding state action satisfied by judicial enforcement of a racially restrictive covenant governing the sale of real estate). For a discussion of *Smith v. Allwright's* practical success in granting blacks political power, see Michael J. Klarman, *The White Primary Rulings: A Case Study in the Consequences of Supreme Court Decision-making*, 29 Fla. St. U. L. Rev. 55 (2001) (arguing that *Smith* was more successful in altering societal practice than were the roughly contemporaneous decisions involving criminal procedure and school desegregation).

2. What difference is there between the regulation of state parties under Texas law, and the regulation of business corporations (which are generally not state actors) in every state's corporate law? *See Morse v. Republican Party of Virginia*, 517 U.S. 186, 274 n.15 (1996) (Thomas, J., dissenting); *see also Manhattan Community Access Corp. v. Halleck*, 587 U.S. __, 139 S. Ct. 1921 (2019) (holding that a privately operated public-access television channel was not a state actor); *Jackson v. Metropolitan Edison Co.*, 419 U.S. 345, 357–59 (1974) (holding that corporations are not state actors unless they enjoy a special relationship with the state, and further holding that a state-conferred utility monopoly does not qualify as such a relationship). Does the analogy indicate that the state-action question should be determined based on considerations other than the degree of state control over party procedures?

3. The state-action cases can be seen as trying to maintain two delicate distinctions. First, some nominally private entities carrying out functions related to elections should be considered state actors, but certainly not every group that holds political power can be a state actor. Otherwise, an influential group of friends might be a state actor only because of that influence. Second, as uncomfortable as most people are with parties' racial discrimination, a party's identity and membership are inextricably connected with its message. If a party cannot discriminate against people with an alternative message, then its ability to communicate its message will be compromised. For example, the mission of the Right to Life Party might be imperiled if it were obligated to accept abortion-rights advocates as members. Those twin concerns are at play in many of the cases in the remainder of this Chapter.

4. *Problem. Smith* held that a party is "an agency of the state *in so far as it determines the participants in a primary election*" (emphasis added). Does it make sense that a party might be considered an agency of the state for some purposes but not for others? In what actions other than selecting the qualifications for primary voters might a party be a state actor? In what actions might it be merely a private actor? Consider whether a party should be considered a state actor in carrying out the following functions:

a. Setting qualifications for party membership.

b. Setting qualifications for voting for party officials.

c. Setting qualifications for voting on the party platform.

d. Setting qualifications for voting in party elections to set any of the qualifications listed in (a)–(c).

5. Note 4 asks whether the party's status as a state actor might depend on the function it is performing. Might it depend also (or instead) on which provision of the Constitution it is alleged to have violated? Thus, might we be more inclined to treat a party as a state actor when it seeks to discriminate by race in violation of the Fourteenth or Fifteenth Amendment, as opposed to when it seeks to discriminate by viewpoint in alleged violation of the First Amendment (as incorporated through the Fourteenth Amendment for state parties)?

Terry v. Adams

Supreme Court of the United States
345 U.S. 461, 73 S. Ct. 809, 97 L. Ed. 1152 (1953)

Mr. Justice Black announced the judgment of the Court and an opinion in which Mr. Justice Douglas and Mr. Justice Burton join.

* * * This case raises questions concerning the constitutional power of a Texas county political organization called the Jaybird Democratic Association or Jaybird Party to exclude Negroes from its primaries on racial grounds. The Jaybirds deny that their racial exclusions violate the Fifteenth Amendment. They contend that the Amendment applies only to elections or primaries held under state regulation, that their association is not regulated by the state at all, and that it is not a political party, but a self-governing voluntary club. The District Court held the Jaybird racial discriminations invalid, and entered judgment accordingly. The Court of Appeals reversed, holding that there was no constitutional or congressional bar to the admitted discriminatory exclusion of Negroes, because Jaybird's primaries were not to any extent state controlled. We granted certiorari. * * *

The Jaybird Association or Party was organized in 1889. Its membership was then and always has been limited to white people; they are automatically members if their names appear on the official list of county voters. It has been run like other political parties, with an executive committee named from the county's voting precincts. Expenses of the party are paid by the assessment of candidates for office in its primaries. Candidates for county offices submit their names to the Jaybird Committee in accordance with the normal practice followed by regular political parties all over the country. Advertisements and posters proclaim that these candidates are running subject to the action of the Jaybird primary. While there is no legal compulsion on successful Jaybird candidates to enter Democratic primaries, they have nearly always done so, and, with few exceptions since 1889, have run and won without opposition in the Democratic primaries and the general elections that followed.{[1]} Thus, the party has been the dominant political group in the county since organization, having endorsed every county-wide official elected since 1889.

It is apparent that Jaybird activities follow a plan purposefully designed to exclude Negroes from voting and, at the same time, to escape the Fifteenth Amendment's command that the right of citizens to vote shall neither be denied nor abridged on account of race. These were the admitted party purposes according to the * * * testimony of the Jaybird's president[.] * * *

* * * The [Fifteenth] Amendment bans racial discrimination in voting by both state and nation. * * * Clearly the Amendment includes any election in which public issues are decided or public officials selected. Just as clearly, the Amendment excludes social or business clubs. And the statute shows the congressional mandate against discrimination whether the voting on public issues and officials is conducted in community, state or nation. Size is not a standard.

It is significant that precisely the same qualifications as those prescribed by Texas entitling electors to vote at county-operated primaries are adopted as the sole qualifications entitling electors to vote at the county-wide Jaybird primaries with a single proviso—Negroes are excluded. Everyone concedes that such a proviso in the county-operated primaries would be unconstitutional. The Jaybird Party thus brings into being and holds precisely the kind of election that the Fifteenth Amendment seeks to prevent. When it produces the equivalent of the prohibited election, the damage has been done.

For a state to permit such a duplication of its election processes is to permit a flagrant abuse of those processes to defeat the purposes of the Fifteenth Amendment. The use of the county-operated primary to ratify the result of the prohibited election merely compounds the offense. It violates the Fifteenth Amendment for a state, by such circumvention, to permit within its borders the use of any device that produces an equivalent of the prohibited election.

The only election that has counted in this Texas county for more than fifty years has been that held by the Jaybirds from which Negroes were excluded. The Democratic primary and the general election have become no more than the perfunctory ratifiers of the choice that has already been made in Jaybird elections from which Negroes have been excluded. It is immaterial that the state does not control that part of this elective process which it leaves for the Jaybirds to manage. The Jaybird primary has become an integral part, indeed the only effective part, of the elective process that determines who shall rule and govern in the county. The effect of

---

1. * * * Here, Jaybird nominees are not put on any ballot as Jaybird nominees; they enter their own names as candidates in the Democratic primary. This distinction is not one of substance, but of form, and a statement of this Court in *Smith* v. *Allwright*, [321 U.S. 649, 661 (1944)] [p. 418], seems appropriate: "*Such a variation in the result from so slight a change in form* influences us to consider anew the legal validity of the distinction which has resulted in barring Negroes from participating in the nominations of candidates of the Democratic party in Texas." (Emphasis supplied.) * * *

the whole procedure, Jaybird primary plus Democratic primary plus general election, is to do precisely that which the Fifteenth Amendment forbids—strip Negroes of every vestige of influence in selecting the officials who control the local county matters that intimately touch the daily lives of citizens. We reverse the Court of Appeals' judgment reversing that of the District Court. * * * The case is remanded to the District Court to enter such orders and decrees as are necessary and proper * * *. In exercising this jurisdiction, the Court is left free to hold hearings to consider and determine what provisions are essential to afford Negro citizens of Fort Bend County full protection from future discriminatory Jaybird-Democratic-general election practices which deprive citizens of voting rights because of their color.

Reversed and remanded.

Mr. Justice Frankfurter. * * *

This case is for me by no means free of difficulty. Whenever the law draws a line between permissive and forbidden conduct, cases are bound to arise which are not obviously on one side or the other. * * * To find a denial or abridgment of the [Fifteenth-Amendment-]guaranteed voting right to colored citizens of Texas solely because they are colored, one must find that the State has had a hand in it.

The State, in these situations, must mean not private citizens, but those clothed with the authority and the influence which official position affords. The application of the prohibition of the Fifteenth Amendment to "any State" is translated by legal jargon to read "state action." This phrase gives rise to a false direction in that it implies some impressive machinery or deliberative conduct normally associated with what orators call a sovereign state. The vital requirement is State responsibility—that somewhere, somehow, to some extent, there be an infusion of conduct by officials, panoplied with State power, into any scheme by which colored citizens are denied voting rights merely because they are colored.

As the action of the entire white voting community, the Jaybird primary is, as a practical matter, the instrument of those few in this small county who are politically active—the officials of the local Democratic party and, we may assume, the elected officials of the county. As a matter of practical politics, those charged by State law with the duty of assuring all eligible voters an opportunity to participate in the selection of candidates at the primary—the county election officials who are normally leaders in their communities—participate by voting in the Jaybird primary. They join the white voting community in proceeding with elaborate formality, in almost all respects parallel to the procedures dictated by Texas law for the primary itself, to express their preferences in a wholly successful effort to withdraw significance from the State-prescribed primary, to subvert the operation of what is formally the law of the State for primaries in this county. * * *

The State of Texas has entered into a comprehensive scheme of regulation of political primaries, including procedures by which election officials shall be chosen. The county election officials are thus clothed with the authority of the State to secure observance of the State's interest in "fair methods and a fair expression" of preferences in the selection of nominees. If the Jaybird Association, although not a political party, is a device to defeat the law of Texas regulating primaries, and if the electoral officials, clothed with State power in the county, share in that subversion, they cannot divest themselves of the State authority and help as participants in the scheme. [H]ere, the county election officials aid in this subversion of the State's official scheme of which they are trustees, by helping as participants in the scheme.

This is not a case of occasional efforts to mass voting strength. Nor is this a case of boss control, whether crudely or subtly exercised. Nor is this a case of spontaneous efforts by citizens to influence votes or even continued efforts by a fraction of the electorate in support of good government. This is a case in which county election officials have participated in and condoned a continued effort effectively to exclude Negroes from voting. Though the action of the Association as such may not be proscribed by the Fifteenth Amendment, its role in the entire scheme to subvert the operation of the official primary brings it "within reach of the law. . . . [T]hey are bound together as the parts of a single plan. The plan may make the parts unlawful."

The State here devised a process for primary elections. The right of all citizens to share in it, and not to be excluded by unconstitutional bars, is emphasized by the fact that, in Texas, nomination in the Democratic primary is tantamount to election. The exclusion of the Negroes from meaningful participation in the only primary scheme set up by the State was not an accidental, unsought consequence of the exercise of civic rights by voters to make their common viewpoint count. It was the design, the very purpose, of this arrangement that the Jaybird primary in May exclude Negro participation in July. That it was the action in part of the election officials charged by Texas law with the fair administration of the primaries, brings it within the reach of the law. The officials made themselves party to means whereby the machinery with which they are entrusted does not discharge the functions for which it was designed.

It does not follow, however, that the relief granted below was proper. * * * [A] federal court cannot require that petitioners be allowed to vote in the Jaybird primary. * * * To say that Negroes should be allowed to vote in the Jaybird primary would be to say that the State is under a duty to see to it that Negroes may vote in that primary. We cannot tell the State that it must participate in and regulate this primary; we cannot tell the State what machinery it will use. But a court of equity can free the lawful political agency from the combination that subverts its capacity to function. What must be done is that this county be rid of the means by which the unlawful "usage" in this case asserts itself.

Mr. Justice Clark, with whom The Chief Justice [Vinson], Mr. Justice Reed, and Mr. Justice Jackson join, concurring [in the judgment]. * * *

* * * Not every private club, association or league organized to influence public candidacies or political action must conform to the Constitution's restrictions on political parties. Certainly a large area of freedom permits peaceable assembly and concerted private action for political purposes to be exercised separately by white and colored citizens alike. More, however, is involved here.

The record discloses that the Jaybird Democratic Association operates as part and parcel of the Democratic Party, an organization existing under the auspices of Texas law. Each maintains the same basic qualification for membership: eligibility to vote under Texas law. Although the state Democratic Party in Texas, since *Smith* v. *Allwright*, no longer can restrict its membership to whites, the Jaybird Democratic Association bars Negroes from its ranks. In May of each election year, it conducts a full-scale white primary in which each candidate campaigns for his candidacy subject to the action of that primary *and the Democratic primary of July*, linking the two primaries together. After gaining the Jaybird Democratic Association's endorsement, the announced winners after full publicity then file in the July Democratic primary. * * * Significantly, since 1889, the winners of the Jaybird Democratic Association balloting, with but a single exception shown by this record, ran unopposed and invariably won in the Democratic July primary and the subsequent general elections for county-wide office.

Quite evidently, the Jaybird Democratic Association operates as an auxiliary of the local Democratic Party organization, selecting its nominees and using its machinery for carrying out an admitted design of destroying the weight and effect of Negro ballots in Fort Bend County. To be sure, the Democratic primary and the general election are nominally open to the colored elector. But his must be an empty vote cast after the real decisions are made. And because the Jaybird-indorsed nominee meets no opposition in the Democratic primary, the Negro minority's vote is nullified at the sole stage of the local political process where the bargaining and interplay of rival political forces would make it count.

The Jaybird Democratic Association device, as a result, strikes to the core of the electoral process in Fort Bend County. Whether viewed as a separate political organization or as an adjunct of the local Democratic Party, the Jaybird Democratic Association is the decisive power in the county's recognized electoral process. Over the years, its balloting has emerged as the locus of effective political choice. * * * [W]hen a state structures its electoral apparatus in a form which devolves upon a political organization the uncontested choice of public officials, that organization itself, in whatever disguise, takes on those attributes of government which draw the Constitution's safeguards in play.

In sum, we believe that the activities of the Jaybird Democratic Association fall within the broad principle laid down in *Smith* v. *Allwright*. For that reason we join the judgment of the Court.

Mr. Justice Minton, dissenting.

I am not concerned in the least as to what happens to the Jaybirds or their unworthy scheme. I am concerned about what this Court says is "state action" within the meaning of the Fifteenth Amendment to the Constitution. For, after all, this Court has power to redress a wrong under that Amendment only if the wrong is done by the State. * * *

As I understand Mr. Justice Black's opinion, he would have this Court redress the wrong even if it was individual action alone. I can understand that praiseworthy position, but it seems to me it is not in accord with the Constitution. State action must be shown.

Mr. Justice Frankfurter recognizes that it must be state action, but he seems to think it is enough to constitute state action if a state official participates in the Jaybird primary. That I cannot follow. For it seems clear to me that everything done by a person who is an official is not done officially, and as a representative of the State. However, I find nothing in this record that shows the state or county officials participating in the Jaybird primary.

Mr. Justice Clark seems to recognize that state action must be shown. He finds state action in assumption, not in facts. This record will be searched in vain for one iota of state action sufficient to support an anemic inference that the Jaybird Association is in any way associated with, or forms a part of or cooperates in any manner with, the Democratic Party of the County or State, or with the State. It calls itself the Jaybird Democratic Association because its interest is only in the candidates of the Democratic Party in the county, a position understandable in Texas. * * *

Neither is there any more evidence that the Jaybird Association avails itself of or conforms in any manner to any law of the State of Texas [regulating political parties]. * * *

However, its action is not forbidden by the law of the State of Texas. Does such failure of the State to act to prevent individuals from doing what they have the right as individuals to do amount to state action? I venture the opinion it does not. * * *

[T]he Jaybird Association * * * neither files, certifies, nor supplies anything for the primary or election. The winner of the poll in the Jaybird Association contest files in the Democratic primary, where he may and sometimes has received opposition, and successful opposition, in precinct contests for County Commissioner, Justice of the Peace, and Constable. There is no rule of the Jaybird Association that requires the successful party in its poll to file in the Democratic primary or elsewhere. It is all individual, voluntary action. Neither the State nor the Democratic Party avails itself of the action of or cooperates in any manner with the Jaybird Association. * * *

* * * What the Jaybird Association did here was to conduct as individuals, separate and apart from the Democratic Party or the State, a straw vote as to who should

receive the Association's endorsement for county and precinct offices. It has been successful in seeing that those who receive its endorsement are nominated and elected. That is true of concerted action by any group. In numbers there is strength. In organization there is effectiveness. * * *

I do not understand that concerted action of individuals which is successful somehow becomes state action. However, the candidates endorsed by the Jaybird Association have several times been defeated in primaries and elections. Usually, but not always, since 1938, only the Jaybird-endorsed candidate has been on the Democratic official ballot in the County.

In the instant case, the State of Texas has provided for elections and primaries. This is separate and apart and wholly unrelated to the Jaybird Association's activities. Its activities are confined to one County where a group of citizens have appointed themselves the censors of those who would run for public offices. Apparently, so far they have succeeded in convincing the voters of this County in most instances that their supported candidates should win. This seems to differ very little from situations common in many other places far north of the Mason-Dixon line, such as areas where a candidate must obtain the approval of a religious group. In other localities, candidates are carefully selected by both parties to give proper weight to Jew, Protestant, and Catholic, and certain posts are considered the sole possession of certain ethnic groups. The propriety of these practices is something the courts sensibly have left to the good or bad judgment of the electorate. It must be recognized that elections and other public business are influenced by all sorts of pressures from carefully organized groups. We have pressure from labor unions, from the National Association of Manufacturers, from the Silver Shirts, from the National Association for the Advancement of Colored People, from the Ku Klux Klan, and others. Far from the activities of these groups being properly labeled as state action, under either the Fourteenth or the Fifteenth Amendment, they are to be considered as attempts to influence or obtain state action.

The courts do not normally pass upon these pressure groups, whether their causes are good or bad, highly successful or only so-so. It is difficult for me to see how this Jaybird Association is anything but such a pressure group. Apparently it is believed in by enough people in Fort Bend County to obtain a majority of the votes for its approved candidates. This differs little from the situation in many parts of the "Bible Belt" where a church stamp of approval or that of the Anti-Saloon League must be put on any candidate who does not want to lose the election.

The State of Texas, in its elections and primaries, takes no cognizance of this Jaybird Association. The State treats its decisions apparently with the same disdain as it would the approval or condemnation of judicial candidates by a bar association poll of its members.

In this case, the majority have found that this pressure group's work does constitute state action. The basis of this conclusion is rather difficult to ascertain. Apparently it derives mainly from a dislike of the goals of the Jaybird Association. I share that dislike. I fail to see how it makes state action. I would affirm.

Notes and Questions

1. With no opinion commanding a majority of the Justices, making sense of the Court's decision in *Terry* requires one to assess the views of each individual Justice. What divided the eight Justices who voted to reverse? What test does each opinion employ to determine whether the Jaybirds' discrimination violated the Fifteenth Amendment?

2. During the Term when *Terry* was argued and decided, future Chief Justice William Rehnquist was one of Justice Jackson's law clerks. Consider the following memorandum that Rehnquist wrote to Jackson concerning the various draft opinions in *Terry*:

> Re: Opinions of Black and FF in <u>Terry</u> v. <u>Adams</u>

> If you are going to dissent, I should think you might combine the ideas which you expressed last week with an attack on the reasoning of the two "majority opinions."

> (1) <u>Black</u>—simply assumes the whole point in issue. The 15th Amendment requires state action, and certainly Congress under its power to "enforce" the amendment cannot drastically enlarge its scope. Yet the Black opinion utterly fails to face the problem of state action. He says rather that the effect of the Fifteenth Amendment is to prevent the states from discriminating against Negroes in official elections; the result here is to accomplish that result "by indirection;" therefore that result is bad. * * * Surely the justices of this Court do not sit here to ruthlessly frustrate results which they consider undesirable, regardless of the wording of the constitution.

> (2) <u>FF</u>—places the weight of the decision on the rather skimpy support to be found in his discovery of "state action": the county election officials voted in the Jaybird primary. In the first place, they voted not in their capacity as election officials, but as private citizens. Secondly, it was not their voting which effected the discrimination; it was the previously adopted rules, with which they may have had nothing to do. Thirdly, if this is the vice why not simply enjoin the officials from voting? When one must strain this hard to reach a result, the chances are that something is the matter with the result * * *.

> (3) Your ideas—the constitution does not prevent the majority from banding together, nor does it attaint success in the effort. It is about time the Court faced the fact that the white people in the South don't like the colored people; the constitution restrains them from effecting this dislike thru state action, but it most assuredly did not appoint the Court as a sociological watchdog to rear up every time private discrimination raises its admittedly ugly head. To the extent that this decision advances the frontier of state action and "social gain", it pushes back the frontier of freedom of association and majority rule. Liberals should be the first to realize, after the past twenty years, that it does not do to push blindly through towards

one constitutional goal without paying attention to other equally desirable values that are being trampled on in the process.

This is a position that I am sure ought to be stated; but if stated by Vinson, Minton, or Reed it just won't sound the same way as if you state it.

whr

William H. Rehnquist memo Re: Opinions of Black and Frankfurter, Robert Jackson Papers, Box 179, Library of Congress Manuscript Division (typographical errors corrected). Do you agree with the future Chief Justice's criticisms of Justice Black's and Justice Frankfurter's positions? Do you agree that an expansive interpretation of state action threatens associational freedoms? *Cf.* Herbert Wechsler, *Toward Neutral Principles of Constitutional Law*, 73 HARV. L. REV. 1, 33 (1959) (criticizing *Brown v. Board of Education*, 347 U.S. 483 (1954), as undermining whites' freedom not to associate with blacks).

3. The Rehnquist memo clearly indicates that Justice Jackson was considering dissenting in *Terry*, and the closing sentence suggests that Chief Justice Vinson and Justice Reed were considering dissenting as well. Each of those three Justices ended up joining Justice Clark's concurrence in the judgment, and their indecision may explain why Justice Black's opinion announced the Court's judgment, even though Justice Clark's opinion received more votes. Not only may it not have been clear until late in the decision-making process that Justice Clark's opinion would receive four votes, but if the Chief Justice was originally in dissent, the responsibility for assigning the opinion would belong to the senior Associate Justice in the majority—Justice Black.

4. What differentiated the Jaybirds from any other influential interest group? Do you agree with Justice Clark that the "decisive power" of the Jaybirds made the association a state actor? Under this view, the state-action question seems intermingled with the substantive right being protected. For example, Justice Clark noted that the Jaybird primary allowed a black person's vote to be "nullified at the sole stage of the local political process where the bargaining and interplay of rival political forces would make it count." Thus, in Justice Clark's view (as well as Justice Black's), state-action doctrine should not be interpreted to permit the purposes of the Fifteenth Amendment to be undermined. Or do you agree with Justice Minton that the actions of an interest group should not "somehow become[] state action" simply because of the group's "success[]"?

5. What did Justice Black mean when he concluded that a state must not "permit" the "duplication of its election processes"? If the state had no role in creating the duplicative process, why would the Fifteenth Amendment require its abolishment? What could the state have done to end that duplication without infringing the Jaybirds' First Amendment rights?

6. Does *Terry* have any applicability in a jurisdiction with competitive general elections? That is, if the Jaybirds exerted substantial influence over the nomination of Democrats, but Republicans presented a viable alternative in the general election,

would the Jaybirds still be state actors? What if the Democrats had been the minority party, and rarely or never won a general election?

7. *Problem.* Bluecollarville is a city of 50,000 people. Acme, Inc., is by far the biggest employer in the community, with virtually every Bluecollarville family having at least one member employed at the local plant. The plant is unionized, and the city council has been dominated by Democratic candidates approved by the local chapter of the union representing the workers at the plant. In fact, in the last fifty years, no candidate who has failed to win the endorsement of the union has won a seat on the council. The union makes its endorsement decisions by secret ballot after debating the candidates at a regular union meeting approximately one month before the Democratic primary. Should the union be considered a state actor when it restricts participation in its meetings and votes to union members? Would it make any difference if the union's membership policies were racially discriminatory? What if they discriminated on another ground, such as gender, age, or political viewpoint?

8. After the remand to the district court, blacks were permitted to vote in the Jaybird primary, and influenced the outcomes of some races in 1954, 1956, and 1958. Was it appropriate for the court to order the integration of the association? No longer able to serve its purpose once integrated, the primary was discontinued in 1959. *See* Pauline Yelderman, The Jaybird Democratic Association of Fort Bend County (1979).

9. Are party *conventions* equivalent to primaries for purposes of state action? In *Morse v. Republican Party of Virginia*, 517 U.S. 186 (1996), plaintiffs challenged the fee that the Party charged for taking part in the convention that would select the Republican nominee for United States Senate. All voters were permitted to participate as delegates to the convention, provided that they paid a registration fee of $35 or $45 (depending on the date of registration) and declared loyalty to the Party. In determining that the fee was subject to § 5 of the Voting Rights Act (constitutional claims were brought in the district court but were not at issue on appeal), the Court concluded that the Party qualified as a "State or political subdivision" within the meaning of the Act. The Court was severely split, however, and it is difficult to know what conclusions to draw from *Morse* about state action.

Justice Stevens, writing also for Justice Ginsburg, relied on the White Primary Cases and equated the "State or political subdivision" language with the Fifteenth Amendment's state-action requirement. Accordingly, for those two Justices, requiring a fee for participating in a convention would constitute state action, just as would the imposition of a poll tax or other discrimination in admitting voters to a primary election. *See id.* at 214–15 (opinion of Stevens, J.).

Justice Breyer, in an opinion expressing the views of Justices O'Connor and Souter, as well as his own, agreed with Justice Stevens that the language of the Voting Rights Act encompassed the action of the Party in charging the fee. Justice Breyer cautioned that parties may have First Amendment rights to be free from governmental regulation as to some aspects of "the workings of a political party convention," *id.* at 239 (Breyer, J., concurring in the judgment), but concluded that the fee in this particular case qualified as state action because the convention was open to any voter paying the fee, and therefore "resembles a primary about as closely as one could imagine." *Id.* at 238.

The four dissenting Justices concluded that the Party was not a "State or political subdivision." Justice Kennedy would have held that the statutory language did not include the Party, but was unwilling to discuss whether in his view the Constitution's state-action requirement reached further than the VRA, *see id.* at 250 (Kennedy, J., dissenting). Justice Thomas, however, speaking for himself as well as Chief Justice Rehnquist and Justice Scalia, argued that the Party was not a state actor under the Constitution. *See id.* at 266–76 (Thomas, J., dissenting). Justice Thomas distinguished *Terry* by noting that in that case "the Jaybird primary was the *de facto* general election and * * * Texas consciously permitted it to serve as such." *Id.* at 269. In *Morse*, by contrast, the state did not use the Republicans' convention to subvert constitutional requirements, and the Republican Party in no way dominated the state in the manner that the Democratic Party dominated Texas at the time of the White Primary Cases. *See id.* at 269–70.

Are you convinced by Justice Thomas's attempt to distinguish *Terry*? Is there any limiting principle in the analyses of Justice Stevens and Justice Breyer that would leave some party operations free of constitutional constraints?

10. *Problem.* Rule 6(C) of the Democratic Party's rules for selecting delegates to its National Convention provides that "[s]tate Delegate Selection Plans shall provide for equal division between delegate men and delegate women and alternate men and alternate women within the state's entire convention delegation." The United States Attorney for the District of West Dakota brings a declaratory-judgment action to bar the party from enforcing Rule 6(C), arguing that the rule violates the Equal Protection Clause. The national and state parties defend on the ground that they are not state actors, and therefore cannot violate the Equal Protection Clause. What result? *Cf. O'Brien v. Brown*, 409 U.S. 1, 5 (1972).

11. *Problem.* A group of Republicans favoring gay rights seeks to publicize its views by leasing a booth at the state party convention and taking out an advertisement in the convention program. The Party, however, refuses to permit the group to take either action because of the Party's opposition to the group's message. Is the Party violating the Constitution? (You may assume that such viewpoint-based action by the state would violate the First Amendment.) *See Republican Party of Texas v. Dietz*, 940 S.W.2d 86 (Tex. 1997).

12. *Problem.* New Jersey State Senator Alene Ammond was elected as a Democrat, but "the Terror of Trenton" was excluded from the Democratic Caucus in retaliation for public criticisms she made about the Caucus and its members. Does the exclusion violate the Constitution? Would the result change if Ammond were excluded because of her race? *See Ammond v. McGahn*, 390 F. Supp. 655 (D.N.J. 1975), *rev'd on other grounds*, 532 F.2d 325 (3d Cir. 1976). *See also Gewertz v. Jackman*, 467 F. Supp. 1047 (D.N.J. 1979) (denying a preliminary injunction where a state legislator

complained that he was removed from a committee in retaliation for his opposition to the party leadership, but stating in dicta that there was no constitutional barrier to granting such an injunction). *Cf. Vander Jagt v. O'Neill*, 699 F.2d 1166 (D.C. Cir. 1983) (refusing to require Congress to allocate committee seats proportionally by party); *Davids v. Akers*, 549 F.2d 120 (9th Cir. 1977) (same as applied to a state legislature).

13. *Problem*. The State of Metropolitana requires parties to choose their nominees for certain offices by primary election, and further provides that the winners of major parties' primaries receive automatic positions on the general-election ballot. Metropolitana also requires candidates seeking to appear on a party's primary ballot to submit petitions with a certain number of signatures. According to state law, both the petition-signers and the petition-witnesses must be registered members of the political party whose nomination the candidate is seeking. Petition-signers must be registered voters and residents of the political subdivision in which the office is being sought, but petition-witnesses are qualified as long as they are registered voters in the state. The Whig Party passes a rule, however, providing that candidates for that party's nomination must have their petitions witnessed by persons who are registered voters in the political subdivision in which the office is being sought.

The party rule is challenged by James Gordon, a candidate for district attorney of Gotham County who is seeking the nomination of the Whig Party, and by persons who live outside Gotham County but who are willing to witness petitions signed by registered voters in the county. The challengers argue that the rule interferes with their freedoms of speech, assembly, and petition, and additionally deprives them of the equal protection of the laws by treating them differently based on the political subdivision in which they live. The Party moves to dismiss on the ground that it is not a state actor. Should the motion be granted? *See Yassky v. Kings County Democratic County Committee*, 259 F. Supp. 2d 210 (E.D.N.Y. 2003).

14. *Problem*. In New York State, parties nominate judicial candidates at party conventions held in each judicial district. (For more details about this process, see *New York State Board of Elections v. López Torres*, 552 U.S. 196 (2008) [p. 487].) Kings County (Brooklyn) comprises one judicial district, and the Democratic Party is dominant within the County. The Party creates a screening committee to evaluate applicants for the Party's nominations in judicial races. The committee ranks applicants as "qualified" or "not qualified," and any candidate receiving a rating of "not qualified" is ineligible to receive the support of the Party's executive committee. Although the executive committee's endorsement is undoubtedly significant, it is possible for a candidate rated as "not qualified" to receive the nomination by convincing other convention delegates to support his candidacy. Are the members of the screening committee behaving as state actors in their evaluation of candidates? Does it matter if the committee is alleged to be discriminating against candidates on the basis of race? What about ideology? What if the candidate simply claims that

the committee has deprived her of the equal protection of the laws by rating her lower than other similarly qualified candidates? *See Jacobson v. Kings County Democratic Committee*, 788 Fed. Appx. 770 (2d Cir. 2019).

C. Associational Rights of Parties

An association's right to define itself extends not only to creating and advancing a mission, but also to establishing qualifications for taking part in its activities. The participation of those who do not share the association's goals can hinder the association's ability to achieve its goals and its ability to send a clear message concerning what its goals are. *See Boy Scouts of America v. Dale*, 530 U.S. 640, 653–59 (2000); *Hurley v. Irish-American Gay, Lesbian and Bisexual Group of Boston, Inc.*, 515 U.S. 557, 570, 580–81 (1995). On the other hand, as the state-action materials illustrate, parties' central role in the electoral process means that individuals excluded from participation in parties may be excluded from the most meaningful and consequential political debates and decisions.

The following materials concern challenges to state regulation of parties, and cases are presented largely in chronological order. This sequencing allows one more easily to track the Justices' developing approaches to questions of what a political party is and who should be able to speak on its behalf. Because the issues presented in each of the cases may appear only slightly different from each other, however, the doctrinal rules that result from these cases may appear confusing. In reading the cases, therefore, separate in your mind two types of challenges. In the first type, the state regulation has the effect of limiting the party's associations. Thus, in *Tashjian v. Republican Party of Connecticut*, 479 U.S. 208 (1986) [p. 443], and *Clingman v. Beaver*, 544 U.S. 581 (2005) [p. 460], the parties wished to allow more people to vote in their primaries than state law allowed.

In the second type of challenge, the state regulation expands the party's association beyond those with whom the party would prefer to associate. Thus, in *Democratic Party of the United States v. Wisconsin ex rel. La Follette*, 450 U.S. 107 (1981) [p. 436], *California Democratic Party v. Jones*, 530 U.S. 567 (2000) [p. 449], and *Washington State Grange v. Washington State Republican Party*, 552 U.S. 442 (2008) [p. 471], the parties wished to limit the class of persons eligible to vote in their primaries to a smaller group than provided for by state law. (Where both state law and the parties wish to exclude a non-member from voting in a primary, such individual's right to vote does not extend to such an election. *See Nader v. Schaffer*, 417 F. Supp. 837 (D. Conn.), *summarily aff'd*, 429 U.S. 989 (1976).)

Whether a party challenges a state law because it invites the participation of too many or too few primary voters, the basis for the challenge is the same. The parties claim that their right of association encompasses a right of self-definition, which is itself dependent on the ability to determine the persons with whom the party will associate. *See, e.g., Democratic Party*, 450 U.S. at 122.[c] As you read these cases, consider whether that claim is weaker or stronger depending on whether the party is attempting to expand or contract its associations, and whether the justifications for interfering with the party's choices are sufficiently weighty to overcome First Amendment objections.

Finally, also bear in mind the question of which bodies should be permitted to exercise the rights of the party. We might think of parties as distinct entities, but the parties themselves, like business corporations, take actions only through humans. The class of persons making up "the party" is the entire membership (*cf. Nixon v. Condon*, 286 U.S. 73, 84 (1932), discussed at pages 413–14, *supra*), but the entire membership is unlikely to be able to make many decisions concerning the way the party operates. Rather, decisions are often made by committees of the party, within the confines of state law that is created in large part by party members who hold office in government. But the committees and officeholders may not accurately represent the preferences of the party membership. Be wary, therefore, when you encounter claims that a certain law interferes with "the party's" rights.

Democratic Party of the United States v. Wisconsin ex rel. La Follette

Supreme Court of the United States
450 U.S. 107, 101 S. Ct. 1010, 67 L. Ed. 2d 82 (1981)

JUSTICE STEWART delivered the opinion of the Court [in which CHIEF JUSTICE BURGER, JUSTICE BRENNAN, JUSTICE WHITE, JUSTICE MARSHALL, and JUSTICE STEVENS join].

The charter of the appellant Democratic Party of the United States (National Party) provides that delegates to its National Convention shall be chosen through procedures in which only Democrats can participate. * * * The question on this appeal is whether Wisconsin may successfully insist that its delegates to the Convention be seated, even though those delegates are chosen through a process that includes a binding state preference primary election in which voters do not declare their party affiliation. * * *

Rule 2A of the Democratic Selection Rules for the 1980 National Convention states: "Participation in the delegate selection process in primaries or caucuses shall be restricted to Democratic voters only who publicly declare their party preference and have that preference publicly recorded." Under National Party rules, the "delegate selection process" includes any procedure by which delegates to the Convention are bound to vote for the nomination of particular candidates.

---

c. As we will see in *Eu v. San Francisco County Democratic Central Committee*, 489 U.S. 214 (1989) [p. 480], parties' right of self-definition extends beyond controlling their membership to controlling their own internal procedures and deliberations as well.

The election laws of Wisconsin allow non-Democrats—including members of other parties and independents—to vote in the Democratic primary without regard to party affiliation and without requiring a public declaration of party preference. The voters in Wisconsin's "open" primary express their choice among Presidential candidates for the Democratic Party's nomination; they do not vote for delegates to the National Convention. Delegates to the National Convention are chosen separately, after the primary, at caucuses of persons who have stated their affiliation with the Party. But these delegates, under Wisconsin law, are bound to vote at the National Convention in accord with the results of the open primary election. Accordingly, while Wisconsin's open Presidential preference primary does not itself violate National Party rules, the State's mandate that the results of the primary shall determine the allocation of votes cast by the State's delegates at the National Convention does.

In May, 1979, the Democratic Party of Wisconsin (State Party) submitted to the Compliance Review Commission of the National Party its plan for selecting delegates to the 1980 National Convention. The plan incorporated the provisions of the State's open primary laws, and, as a result, the Commission disapproved it as violating Rule 2A. Since compliance with Rule 2A was a condition of participation at the Convention, for which no exception could be made, the National Party indicated that Wisconsin delegates who were bound to vote according to the results of the open primary would not be seated.

The State Attorney General then brought an original action in the Wisconsin Supreme Court[, which] entered a judgment declaring that the State's system of selecting delegates to the Democratic National Convention is constitutional and binding on the appellants. * * * The National Party and the Democratic National Committee then brought this appeal[.] * * *

Rule 2A can be traced to efforts of the National Party to study and reform its nominating procedures and internal structure after the 1968 Democratic National Convention.[14] The Convention, the Party's highest governing authority, directed the Democratic National Committee (DNC) to establish a Commission on Party Structure and Delegate Selection (McGovern/Fraser Commission). This Commission concluded that a major problem faced by the Party was that rank-and-file Party members had been underrepresented at its Convention, and * * * expressed the concern that "a full opportunity for all Democrats to participate is diluted if members of other political parties are allowed to participate in the selection of delegates to the Democratic National Convention."

---

14. Wisconsin's open primary system * * * was adopted in 1903, and * * * is employed in Wisconsin not only to express preference for Presidential candidates, but to choose "partisan . . . state and local candidates . . . and an extensive array of nonpartisan officers" as well. * * *

* * * In 1974, the National Party adopted its charter[, according to which] "The National Convention shall be composed of delegates who are chosen through processes which * * * *restrict participation to Democrats only. . . .*" (emphasis added).

Rule 2A took its present form in 1976. Consistent with the charter, it restricted participation in the delegate selection process in primaries or caucuses to "Democratic voters only who publicly declare their party preference and have that preference publicly recorded." But the 1976 Delegate Selection Rules allowed for an exemption from any rule, including Rule 2A, that was inconsistent with state law if the state party was unable to secure changes in the law. * * *

[A] study, assessing the Wisconsin Democratic primaries from 1964 to 1972, found that crossover voters comprised 26% to 34% of the primary voters; that the voting patterns of crossover voters differed significantly from those of participants who identified themselves as Democrats; and that crossover voters altered the composition of the delegate slate chosen from Wisconsin.[18] [Relying in part on this study, another commission established by the Party in 1975] specifically recommended that "participation in the delegate selection process in primaries or caucuses . . . be restricted to Democratic voters only who publicly declare their party preference and have that preference publicly recorded." Accordingly, the text of Rule 2A was retained, but a new Rule, 2B, was added, prohibiting any exemptions from Rule 2A.

The question in this case is not whether Wisconsin may conduct an open primary election if it chooses to do so, or whether the National Party may require Wisconsin to limit its primary election to publicly declared Democrats. Rather, the question is whether, once Wisconsin has opened its Democratic Presidential preference primary to voters who do not publicly declare their party affiliation, it may then bind the National Party to honor the binding primary results, even though those results were reached in a manner contrary to National Party rules.

The Wisconsin Supreme Court considered the question before it to be the constitutionality of the "open" feature of the state primary election law, as such. Concluding that the open primary serves compelling state interests by encouraging voter participation, the court held the state open primary constitutionally valid. Upon this issue, the Wisconsin Supreme Court may well be correct. In any event, there is no need to question its conclusion here. For the rules of the National Party do not challenge the authority of a State to conduct an open primary, so long as it is not binding on the National Party Convention. The issue is whether the State may compel the National Party to seat a delegation chosen in a way that violates the rules of the Party. * * *

"[T]he National Democratic Party and its adherents enjoy a constitutionally protected right of political association." This First Amendment freedom to gather

---

18. A crossover primary is one that permits nonadherents of a party to "cross over" and vote in that party's primary.

in association for the purpose of advancing shared beliefs is protected by the Fourteenth Amendment from infringement by any State. And the freedom to associate for the "common advancement of political beliefs" necessarily presupposes the freedom to identify the people who constitute the association, and to limit the association to those people only. * * *

Here, the members of the National Party, speaking through their rules, chose to define their associational rights by limiting those who could participate in the processes leading to the selection of delegates to their National Convention. On several occasions, this Court has recognized that the inclusion of persons unaffiliated with a political party may seriously distort its collective decisions—thus impairing the party's essential functions—and that political parties may accordingly protect themselves "from intrusion by those with adverse political principles."[23] * * *

The State argues that its law places only a minor burden on the National Party. The National Party argues that the burden is substantial, because it prevents the Party from "screen[ing] out those whose affiliation is . . . slight, tenuous, or fleeting," and that such screening is essential to build a more effective and responsible Party. But it is not for the courts to mediate the merits of this dispute. For even if the State were correct,[25] a State, or a court, may not constitutionally substitute its own judgment for that of the Party. A political party's choice among the various ways of determining the makeup of a State's delegation to the party's national convention is protected by the Constitution. And as is true of all expressions of First Amendment freedoms, the courts may not interfere on the ground that they view a particular expression as unwise or irrational.

We must consider, finally, whether the State has compelling interests that justify the imposition of its will upon the appellants. * * * The State asserts a compelling interest in preserving the overall integrity of the electoral process, providing secrecy of the ballot, increasing voter participation in primaries, and preventing harassment of voters. But all those interests go to the conduct of the Presidential preference primary—not to the imposition of voting requirements upon those who, in a separate process, are eventually selected as delegates. Therefore, the interests advanced by the State do not justify its substantial intrusion into the associational freedom of members of the National Party.

The State has a substantial interest in the manner in which its elections are conducted, and the National Party has a substantial interest in the manner in which the delegates to its National Convention are selected. But these interests are not

---

23. The extent to which "raiding" is a motivation of Wisconsin voters matters not. * * * The concern of the National Party is, rather, with crossover voters in general, regardless of their motivation.

25. It may be the case, of course, that the public avowal of party affiliation required by Rule 2A provides no more assurance of party loyalty than does Wisconsin's requirement that a person vote in no more than one party's primary. But the stringency, and wisdom, of membership requirements is for the association and its members to decide—not the courts—so long as those requirements are otherwise constitutionally permissible.

incompatible, and, to the limited extent they clash in this case, both interests can be preserved. The National Party rules do not forbid Wisconsin to conduct an open primary. But if Wisconsin does open its primary, it cannot require that Wisconsin delegates to the National Party Convention vote there in accordance with the primary results if to do so would violate Party rules. Since the Wisconsin Supreme Court has declared that the National Party cannot disqualify delegates who are bound to vote in accordance with the results of the Wisconsin open primary, its judgment is reversed.

It so ordered.

JUSTICE POWELL, with whom JUSTICE BLACKMUN and JUSTICE REHNQUIST join, dissenting.

* * * Because I believe that this law does not impose a substantial burden on the associational freedom of the National Party, and actually promotes the free political activity of the citizens of Wisconsin, I dissent. * * *

* * * All that Wisconsin has done is to require the major parties to allow voters to affiliate with them—for the limited purpose of participation in a primary—*secretly*, in the privacy of the voting booth.[2] The Democrats remain free to require public affiliation from anyone wishing any greater degree of participation in party affairs. * * *

In evaluating the constitutional significance of this relatively minimal state regulation of party membership requirements, I am unwilling—at least in the context of a claim by one of the two major political parties—to conclude that every conflict between state law and party rules concerning participation in the nomination process creates a burden on associational rights. Instead, I would look closely at the nature of the intrusion, in light of the nature of the association involved, to see whether we are presented with a real limitation on First Amendment freedoms.

* * * If appellant National Party were an organization with a particular ideological orientation or political mission, perhaps this regulation would present a different question. In such a case, the state law might well open the organization to participation by persons with incompatible beliefs, and interfere with the associational rights of its founders.

---

2. It is not fully accurate to say, as the Court does, that the "election laws of Wisconsin allow non-Democrats—including members of other parties and independents—to vote in the Democratic primary." The Wisconsin statute [allows voters] "* * * to express their preference for the person to be the presidential candidate *of their party*" (emphasis added). Thus, the act of voting in the Democratic primary fairly can be described as an act of affiliation with the Democratic Party. The real issue in this case is whether the Party has the right to decide that only publicly affiliated voters may participate.

The situation might be different in those States with "blanket" primaries—*i.e.*, those where voters are allowed to participate in the primaries of more than one party on a single occasion, selecting the primary they wish to vote in with respect to each individual elective office.

The Democratic Party, however, is not organized around the achievement of defined ideological goals. Instead, the major parties in this country "have been characterized by a fluidity and overlap of philosophy and membership." *Rosario v. Rockefeller*, 410 U.S. 752, 769 (1973) (POWELL, J., dissenting). It can hardly be denied that this Party generally has been composed of various elements reflecting most of the American political spectrum.[4] The Party does take positions on public issues, but these positions vary from time to time, and there never has been a serious effort to establish for the Party a monolithic ideological identity by excluding all those with differing views. As a result, it is hard to see what the Democratic Party has to fear from an open primary plan. Wisconsin's law may influence to some extent the outcome of a primary contest by allowing participation by voters who are unwilling to affiliate with the Party publicly. It is unlikely, however, that this influence will produce a delegation with preferences that differ from those represented by a substantial number of delegates from other parts of the country. Moreover, it seems reasonable to conclude that, insofar as the major parties do have ideological identities, an open primary merely allows relatively independent voters to cast their lot with the party that speaks to their present concerns. By attracting participation by relatively independent-minded voters, the Wisconsin plan arguably may enlarge the support for a party at the general election. * * *

In sum, I would hold that the National Party has failed to make a sufficient showing of a burden on its associational rights.[9] * * *

Notes and Questions

1. If the rules of the Democratic Party had forbidden open primaries altogether, could the state demand that one be held? What if the party had decided to choose all its delegates by caucuses? Could the state require the party to hold some kind of primary? Would it make a difference if the party wanted to hold a primary, and the state demanded caucuses? *See American Party of Texas v. White*, 415 U.S. 767, 781 (1974) (stating that it was "too plain for argument" that states could require parties to select their nominees through either primaries or conventions, as the states chose). Could *Congress* require states to use primaries to select presidential nominees? *See* Richard L. Hasen, *"Too Plain for Argument?": The Uncertain Congressional*

---

4. The Charter of the National Democratic Party states that it is "open to all who desire to support the party and . . . be known as Democrats." This perception need not be taken as a criticism of the American party structure. The major parties have played a key role in forming coalitions and creating consensus on national issues. "Broad-based political parties supply an essential coherence and flexibility to the American political scene. They serve as coalitions of different interests that combine to seek national goals." * * *

9. Of course, the National Party could decide that it no longer wishes to be a relatively nonideological party, but it has not done so. Such a change might call into question the institutionalized status achieved by the two major parties in state and federal law. * * * Arguably, the special status of the major parties is an additional factor favoring state regulation of the electoral process even in the face of a claim by such a party that this regulation has interfered with its First Amendment rights.

Power to Require Parties to Choose Presidential Nominees Through Direct and Equal Primaries, 102 Nw. U. L. Rev. 2009 (2008).

2. The Court stated that Wisconsin's allegedly compelling interests "go to the conduct of the Presidential preference primary," rather than to the requirement that delegates vote in accordance with the primary results. But why would the state bother to hold an open primary (and why would voters bother to participate) if the delegates were entitled to disregard the results?

3. Should it matter that the Democratic Party is "relatively nonideological"? Is it? Do you think Justice Powell's view of the Party was a product of his background or of the behavior and commitments of the Party? Justice Powell was a Richmond, Virginia, Democrat, but politically moderate and nominated to the Court by a Republican President (Nixon) and confirmed by a Democratic Senate. (Then-Justice Rehnquist, however, who joined Justice Powell's opinion, was a lifelong conservative Republican.) Around the time of Justice Powell's nomination and of this case, the Democratic Party contained elements as disparate as George McGovern and James Eastland. Today, however, most observers believe the two major parties are much more ideologically homogenous. Should such a shift in ideological orientation affect the constitutionality of state laws mandating open primaries?

4. As noted in *Democratic Party*, the Party's rule excluding non-Democrats was prompted by the McGovern/Fraser Commission, which the Party formed after the tumultuous 1968 Democratic National Convention. The Commission found that the participation of non-Democrats in the nominating process lessened Democrats' influence in choosing the nominees of their own party, and led to the selection of nominees who were more moderate than the ones who would have been chosen by Democrats alone. Both Senator George McGovern and Representative Donald Fraser, the chairmen of the Commission, were quite liberal—which was to be expected because the Commission's members were chosen by the chairman of the Democratic National Committee. Not coincidentally, the rules championed by the Commission favored ideologically extreme candidates, and McGovern himself won the Democratic nomination for President in 1972, the first year under the new rules. Ideologically extreme candidates are at a disadvantage in the general election, however, as McGovern and the Democrats found out that fall when Richard Nixon won reelection by capturing 49 out of 50 states.

5. *Problem.* Recall from the Problem in Note 10 on page 433 that Rule 6(C) of the Democratic Party's rules for selecting delegates provides that "[s]tate Delegate Selection Plans shall provide for equal division between delegate men and delegate women and alternate men and alternate women within the state's entire convention delegation." East Dakota state law prohibits sex-based quotas, and the attorney general brings a declaratory-judgment action to ensure that the Party complies with the law. The Party argues that it has the right under the First Amendment to select delegates in the manner it chooses. Further, it argues, the tenets of the Democratic Party evince a commitment to gender equality such that Rule 6(C) is an important reflection of the Party's ideology. Does the First Amendment require the state to

exempt the Party from the anti-quota law? *See Bachur v. Democratic National Party*, 836 F.2d 837 (4th Cir. 1987); *cf. O'Brien v. Brown*, 409 U.S. 1, 5 (1972).

6. *Problem.* The Republican Party wishes to allocate delegates to its national convention not merely on the basis of state populations, but with "victory bonuses" that provide additional delegates to states voting Republican in past elections. Will the Party be able successfully to raise a First Amendment defense against a one-person, one-vote challenge? *See Ripon Society, Inc. v. National Republican Party*, 525 F.2d 567 (D.C. Cir. 1975) (*en banc*).

Tashjian v. Republican Party of Connecticut

Supreme Court of the United States
479 U.S. 208, 107 S. Ct. 544, 93 L. Ed. 2d 514 (1986)

JUSTICE MARSHALL delivered the opinion of the Court [in which JUSTICE BRENNAN, JUSTICE WHITE, JUSTICE BLACKMUN, and JUSTICE POWELL join].

Appellee Republican Party of the State of Connecticut in 1984 adopted a Party rule which permits independent voters—registered voters not affiliated with any political party—to vote in Republican primaries for federal and statewide offices. Appellant Julia Tashjian, the Secretary of the State of Connecticut, is charged with the administration of the State's election statutes, which include a provision requiring voters in any party primary to be registered members of that party. Conn. Gen. Stat. §9-431. Appellees * * * challenged this eligibility provision on the ground that it deprives the Party of its First Amendment right to enter into political association with individuals of its own choosing. The District Court granted summary judgment in favor of appellees. The Court of Appeals affirmed. We noted probable jurisdiction, and now affirm. * * *

The Party here contends that §9-431 impermissibly burdens the right of its members to determine for themselves with whom they will associate, and whose support they will seek, in their quest for political success. The Party's attempt to broaden the base of public participation in and support for its activities is conduct undeniably central to the exercise of the right of association. As we have said, the freedom to join together in furtherance of common political beliefs "necessarily presupposes the freedom to identify the people who constitute the association." *Democratic Party of United States* v. *Wisconsin ex rel. La Follette*, 450 U.S. 107, 122 (1981) [p. 436].

A major state political party necessarily includes individuals playing a broad spectrum of roles in the organization's activities. Some of the Party's members devote substantial portions of their lives to furthering its political and organizational goals, others provide substantial financial support, while still others limit their participation to casting their votes for some or all of the Party's candidates. Considered from the standpoint of the Party itself, the act of formal enrollment or public affiliation with the Party is merely one element in the continuum of participation in Party affairs, and need not be in any sense the most important.

Were the State to restrict by statute financial support of the Party's candidates to Party members, or to provide that only Party members might be selected as the Party's chosen nominees for public office, such a prohibition of potential association with nonmembers would clearly infringe upon the rights of the Party's members under the First Amendment to organize with like-minded citizens in support of common political goals. As we have said, "[a]ny interference with the freedom of a party is simultaneously an interference with the freedom of its adherents." *Democratic Party, supra*, at 122.[6] The statute here places limits upon the group of registered voters whom the Party may invite to participate in the "basic function" of selecting the Party's candidates. The State thus limits the Party's associational opportunities at the crucial juncture at which the appeal to common principles may be translated into concerted action, and hence to political power in the community.[7] * * *

* * * Appellant contends that the Party's rule would require the purchase of additional voting machines, the training of additional poll workers, and potentially the printing of additional ballot materials specifically intended for independents voting in the Republican primary. In essence, appellant claims that the administration of the system contemplated by the Party rule would simply cost the State too much.

[T]he possibility of future increases in the cost of administering the election system is not a sufficient basis here for infringing appellees' First Amendment rights. Costs of administration would likewise increase if a third major party should come

---

6. It is this element of potential interference with the rights of the Party's members which distinguishes the present case from others in which we have considered claims by nonmembers of a party seeking to vote in that party's primary despite the party's opposition. In this latter class of cases, the nonmember's desire to participate in the party's affairs is overborne by the countervailing and legitimate right of the party to determine its own membership qualifications. See *Rosario v. Rockefeller*, 410 U.S. 752 (1973); *Nader v. Schaffer*, 417 F. Supp. 837 (Conn.), summarily aff'd, 429 U.S. 989 (1976). Similarly, the Court has upheld the right of national political parties to refuse to seat at their conventions delegates chosen in state selection processes which did not conform to party rules. See *Democratic Party*; *Cousins v. Wigoda*, 419 U.S. 477 (1975). These situations are analytically distinct from the present case, in which the Party and its members seek to provide enhanced opportunities for participation by willing nonmembers. Under these circumstances, there is no conflict between the associational interests of members and nonmembers.

7. Appellant contends that any infringement of the associational right of the Party or its members is *de minimis*, because Connecticut law, as amended during the pendency of this litigation, provides that any previously unaffiliated voter may become eligible to vote in the Party's primary by enrolling as a Party member as late as noon on the last business day preceding the primary. Thus, appellant contends, any independent voter wishing to participate in any Party primary may do so.

This is not a satisfactory response to the Party's contentions for two reasons. First, * * * the formal affiliation process is one which individual voters may employ in order to associate with the Party, but it provides no means by which the members of the Party may choose to broaden opportunities for joining the association by their own act, without any intervening action by potential voters. Second, and more importantly, the requirement of public affiliation with the Party in order to vote in the primary conditions the exercise of the associational right upon the making of a public statement of adherence to the Party which the State requires regardless of the actual beliefs of the individual voter. * * *

into existence in Connecticut, thus requiring the State to fund a third major-party primary. Additional voting machines, poll workers, and ballot materials would all be necessary under these circumstances as well. But the State could not forever protect the two existing major parties from competition solely on the ground that two major parties are all the public can afford. While the State is of course entitled to take administrative and financial considerations into account in choosing whether or not to have a primary system at all, it can no more restrain the Republican Party's freedom of association for reasons of its own administrative convenience than it could on the same ground limit the ballot access of a new major party.

Appellant argues that § 9-431 is justified as a measure to prevent raiding, a practice "whereby voters in sympathy with one party designate themselves as voters of another party so as to influence or determine the results of the other party's primary." *Rosario* v. *Rockefeller*, 410 U.S., [at] 760. While we have recognized that "a State may have a legitimate interest in seeking to curtail 'raiding,' since that practice may affect the integrity of the electoral process," that interest is not implicated here. The statute as applied to the Party's rule prevents independents, who otherwise cannot vote in any primary, from participating in the Republican primary. Yet a raid on the Republican Party primary by independent voters * * * is not impeded by § 9-431; the independent raiders need only register as Republicans and vote in the primary. * * *

Appellant's next argument in support of § 9-431 is that the closed primary system avoids voter confusion. Appellant contends that "[t]he legislature could properly find that it would be difficult for the general public to understand what a candidate stood for who was nominated in part by an unknown amorphous body outside the party, while nevertheless using the party name." * * *

As we have said, "[t]here can be no question about the legitimacy of the State's interest in fostering informed and educated expressions of the popular will in a general election." *Anderson* v. *Celebrezze*, 460 U.S. [780], 796 [(1983)] [p. 517]. To the extent that party labels provide a shorthand designation of the views of party candidates on matters of public concern, the identification of candidates with particular parties plays a role in the process by which voters inform themselves for the exercise of the franchise. Appellant's argument depends upon the belief that voters can be "misled" by party labels. But "[o]ur cases reflect a greater faith in the ability of individual voters to inform themselves about campaign issues." *Id.*, at 797. * * *

In arguing that the Party rule interferes with educated decisions by voters, appellant also disregards the substantial benefit which the Party rule provides to the Party and its members in seeking to choose successful candidates. Given the numerical strength of independent voters in the State, one of the questions most likely to occur to Connecticut Republicans in selecting candidates for public office is how can the Party most effectively appeal to the independent voter? By inviting independents to assist in the choice at the polls between primary candidates selected at the Party convention, the Party rule is intended to produce the candidate and platform most likely to achieve that goal. The state statute is said to decrease voter confusion, yet it deprives the Party and its members of the opportunity to inform themselves as to the level of support for the Party's candidates among a critical group of electors. "A State's claim that it is enhancing the ability of its citizenry to make wise decisions by restricting the flow of information to them must be viewed with some skepticism." *Anderson* v. *Celebrezze, supra,* at 798. The State's legitimate interests in preventing voter confusion and providing for educated and responsible voter decisions in no respect "make it necessary to burden the [Party's] rights."

Finally, appellant contends that §9-431 furthers the State's compelling interest in protecting the integrity of the two-party system and the responsibility of party government. Appellant argues vigorously and at length that the closed primary system chosen by the state legislature promotes responsiveness by elected officials and strengthens the effectiveness of the political parties.

The relative merits of closed and open primaries have been the subject of substantial debate since the beginning of this century, and no consensus has as yet emerged. Appellant invokes a long and distinguished line of political scientists and public officials who have been supporters of the closed primary. But our role is not to decide whether the state legislature was acting wisely in enacting the closed primary system in 1955, or whether the Republican Party makes a mistake in seeking to depart from the practice of the past 30 years. * * *

* * * [We have upheld statutes that seek to protect the party against raiding by outsiders, but those cases are of little help to the State here, where] the state statute is defended on the ground that it protects the integrity of the Party against the Party itself.

Under these circumstances, the views of the State, which to some extent represent the views of the one political party transiently enjoying majority power, as to the optimum methods for preserving party integrity lose much of their force. The State argues that its statute is well designed to save the Republican Party from undertaking a course of conduct destructive of its own interests. But on this point "even if the State were correct, a State, or a court, may not constitutionally substitute its own judgment for that of the Party." *Democratic Party,* 450 U.S., at 123–124. The Party's determination of the boundaries of its own association, and of the structure which best allows it to pursue its political goals, is protected by the Constitution. "And as is true of all expressions of First Amendment freedoms, the courts may not interfere on the ground that they view a particular expression as unwise or irrational."[13]

---

13. Our holding today does not establish that state regulation of primary voting qualifications may never withstand challenge by a political party or its membership. A party seeking, for example, to open its primary to all voters, including members of other parties, would raise a different combination of considerations. Under such circumstances, the effect of one party's broadening of participation would threaten other parties with the disorganization effects which the statutes in *Storer* v. *Brown,* 415 U.S. 724 (1974) [p. 513], and *Rosario* v. *Rockefeller* were designed to prevent. * * *

We conclude that the State's enforcement, under these circumstances, of its closed primary system burdens the First Amendment rights of the Party. The interests which the appellant adduces in support of the statute are insubstantial, and accordingly the statute, as applied to the Party in this case, is unconstitutional. * * *

* * * The judgment of the Court of Appeals is

Affirmed.

Justice Stevens, with whom Justice Scalia joins, dissenting. * * *

[Justice Stevens noted that "the plain language of the Constitution requires that voters in congressional and senatorial elections 'shall have' the qualifications of voters in elections to the state legislature." Accordingly, he concluded that Connecticut could not constitutionally permit the Republicans to hold primaries for congressional elections in which independents were able to participate if a smaller class of voters (only Republicans) was eligible to participate in primaries for state legislative elections. In an omitted portion of the majority opinion, the Court held that the constitutional requirement did apply to primary elections, but was satisfied so long as every person qualified to vote for the state legislature was permitted to vote for Congress.]

Justice Scalia, with whom The Chief Justice [Rehnquist] and Justice O'Connor join, dissenting. * * *

In my view, the Court's opinion exaggerates the importance of the associational interest at issue, if indeed it does not see one where none exists. There is no question here of restricting the Republican Party's ability to recruit and enroll Party members by offering them the ability to select Party candidates; Conn. Gen. Stat. § 9-56 permits an independent voter to join the Party as late as the day before the primary. Nor is there any question of restricting the ability of the Party's members to select whatever candidate they desire. Appellees' only complaint is that the Party cannot leave the selection of its candidate to persons who are *not* members of the Party, and are unwilling to become members. It seems to me fanciful to refer to this as an interest in freedom of association between the members of the Republican Party and the putative independent voters. The Connecticut voter who, while steadfastly refusing to register as a Republican, casts a vote in the Republican primary, forms no more meaningful an "association" with the Party than does the independent or the registered Democrat who responds to questions by a Republican Party pollster. If the concept of freedom of association is extended to such casual contacts, it ceases to be of any analytic use.

The ability of the members of the Republican Party to select their own candidate, on the other hand, unquestionably implicates an associational freedom—but it can hardly be thought that that freedom is unconstitutionally impaired here. The Party is entirely free to put forward, if it wishes, that candidate who has the highest degree of support among Party members and independents combined. The State is under no obligation, however, to let its party primary be used, instead of a party-funded opinion poll, as the means by which the party identifies the relative popularity of its potential candidates among independents. Nor is there any reason apparent to me why the State cannot insist that this decision to support what might be called the independents' choice be taken *by the party membership in a democratic fashion*, rather than through a process that permits the members' votes to be diluted—and perhaps even absolutely outnumbered—by the votes of outsiders.

The Court's opinion characterizes this, disparagingly, as an attempt to "protec[t] the integrity of the Party against the Party itself." There are two problems with this characterization. The first, and less important, is that it is not true. We have no way of knowing that a majority of the Party's members is in favor of allowing ultimate selection of its candidates for federal and statewide office to be determined by persons outside the Party. That decision was not made by democratic ballot, but by the Party's state convention—which, for all we know, may have been dominated by officeholders and office seekers whose evaluation of the merits of assuring election of the Party's candidates, vis-à-vis the merits of proposing candidates faithful to the Party's political philosophy, diverged significantly from the views of the Party's rank and file. I had always thought it was a major purpose of state-imposed party primary requirements to protect the general party membership against this sort of minority control. Second and more important, however, *even if* it were the fact that the majority of the Party's members wanted its candidates to be determined by outsiders, there is no reason why the State is bound to honor that desire—any more than it would be bound to honor a party's democratically expressed desire that its candidates henceforth be selected by convention rather than by primary, or by the party's executive committee in a smoke-filled room. In other words, the validity of the state-imposed primary requirement itself, which we have hitherto considered "too plain for argument," *American Party of Texas* v. *White*, 415 U.S. 767, 781 (1974), presupposes that the State *has* the right "to protect the Party against the Party itself." Connecticut may lawfully require that significant elements of the democratic election process be democratic—whether the Party wants that or not. It is beyond my understanding why the Republican Party's delegation of its democratic choice to a Republican Convention can be proscribed, but its delegation of that choice to nonmembers of the Party cannot. * * *

I respectfully dissent.

Notes and Questions

1. The *Tashjian* Court frequently invoked the rights and interests of "the Party," but which individuals comprised the Party? Which individuals comprised the Party in the view of Justice Scalia?

2. Should an organization (or members of an organization) have a constitutional right to associate with non-members?

3. Did Connecticut law prevent the Party from associating with independents? Or did the state merely refuse to provide the Party with special assistance in associating with outsiders?

4. In Justice Scalia's view, the state's power to require parties to choose their nominees by primaries depends on the state having the right "to protect the Party against the Party itself." As such, it makes little sense to condemn closed primaries as paternalistic when the primary requirement itself is paternalistic. Is there a reason that a state would have the power to require primaries, but not have the power to determine the qualifications for voting in the primaries? What does *Democratic Party v. La Follette* say about that question?

5. The Court, in footnote 13, suggested that while a party has the right to invite independents to vote in its primary (in other words, selecting a "semiclosed" primary over the state's choice of a "closed" one), a party may not have the right to invite members of other parties to vote in its primary (which would make the primary an "open" one). Should a party have the right to invite members of other parties to vote in its primary? Should a party have the right to associate with members of other parties in different ways, such as by soliciting financial support, sending invitations to meetings, or the like? Reconsider those questions when you read *Clingman v. Beaver*, 544 U.S. 581 (2005) [p. 460], later in this section.

California Democratic Party v. Jones

Supreme Court of the United States
530 U.S. 567, 120 S. Ct. 2402, 147 L. Ed. 2d 502 (2000)

JUSTICE SCALIA delivered the opinion of the Court [in which CHIEF JUSTICE REHNQUIST, JUSTICE O'CONNOR, JUSTICE KENNEDY, JUSTICE SOUTER, JUSTICE THOMAS, and JUSTICE BREYER join].

This case presents the question whether the State of California may, consistent with the First Amendment to the United States Constitution, use a so-called "blanket" primary to determine a political party's nominee for the general election. * * *

Until 1996, to determine the nominees of qualified parties California held what is known as a "closed" partisan primary, in which only persons who are members of the political party—*i.e.*, who have declared affiliation with that party when they register to vote—can vote on its nominee. In 1996 the citizens of California adopted by initiative Proposition 198. Promoted largely as a measure that would "weaken" party "hard-liners" and ease the way for "moderate problem-solvers," ([quoting from a] ballot pamphlet distributed to voters), Proposition 198 changed California's partisan primary from a closed primary to a blanket primary. Under the new system, "all persons entitled to vote, including those not affiliated with any political party, shall have the right to vote . . . for any candidate regardless of the candidate's political affiliation." Whereas under the closed primary each voter received a ballot limited to candidates of his own party, as a result of Proposition 198 each voter's primary ballot now lists every candidate regardless of party affiliation and allows the voter to choose freely among them. It remains the case, however, that the candidate of each party who wins the greatest number of votes "is the nominee of that party at the ensuing general election."

Petitioners in this case are four political parties—the California Democratic Party, the California Republican Party, the Libertarian Party of California, and the Peace and Freedom Party—each of which has a rule prohibiting persons not members of the party from voting in the party's primary. Petitioners brought suit in the United States District Court for the Eastern District of California against respondent California Secretary of State, alleging, *inter alia*, that California's blanket primary violated their First Amendment rights of association, and seeking declaratory and injunctive relief. * * * [T]he District Court held that the burden on petitioners' rights of association was not a severe one, and was justified by state interests ultimately reducing to this: "enhancing the democratic nature of the election process and the representativeness of elected officials." The Ninth Circuit, adopting the District Court's opinion as its own, affirmed. We granted certiorari. * * *

We have recognized, of course, that States have a major role to play in structuring and monitoring the election process, including primaries. * * * What we have not held, however, is that the processes by which political parties select their nominees are, as respondents would have it, wholly public affairs that States may regulate freely. To the contrary, we have continually stressed that when States regulate parties' internal processes they must act within limits imposed by the Constitution. See, *e.g.*, *Eu v. San Francisco County Democratic Central Comm.*, 489 U.S. 214 (1989) [p. 480]; *Democratic Party of United States v. Wisconsin ex rel. La Follette*, 450 U.S. 107 (1981) [p. 436]. In this regard, respondents' reliance on *Smith v. Allwright*, 321 U.S. 649 (1944) [p. 418], and *Terry v. Adams*, 345 U.S. 461 (1953) [p. 423], is misplaced. In *Allwright*, we invalidated the Texas Democratic Party's rule limiting participation in its primary to whites; in *Terry*, we invalidated the same rule promulgated by the Jaybird Democratic Association, a "self-governing voluntary club." These cases held only that, when a State prescribes an election process that gives a special role to political parties, it "endorses, adopts and enforces the discrimination against Negroes," that the parties (or, in the case of the Jaybird Democratic Association, organizations that are "part and parcel" of the parties, see 345 U.S., at 482 (Clark, J., concurring)) bring into the process—so that the parties' discriminatory action becomes state action under the Fifteenth Amendment. *Allwright, supra*, at 664; see also *Terry*, 345 U.S., at 484 (Clark, J., concurring); 345 U.S., at 469 (opinion of Black, J.). They do not stand for the proposition that party affairs are public affairs, free of First Amendment protections—and our later holdings make that entirely clear.[5] See, *e.g.*, *Tashjian* [v. *Republican Party of Connecticut*, 479 U.S. 208 (1986)] [p. 443].

---

5. The dissent is therefore wrong to conclude that *Allwright* and *Terry* demonstrate that "the protections that the First Amendment affords to the internal processes of a political party do not encompass a right to exclude nonmembers from voting in a state-required, state-financed primary

Representative democracy in any populous unit of governance is unimaginable without the ability of citizens to band together in promoting among the electorate candidates who espouse their political views. * * * [T]he Court has recognized that the First Amendment protects "the freedom to join together in furtherance of common political beliefs," which "necessarily presupposes the freedom to identify the people who constitute the association, and to limit the association to those people only," *La Follette*, 450 U.S., at 122. That is to say, a corollary of the right to associate is the right not to associate. "Freedom of association would prove an empty guarantee if associations could not limit control over their decisions to those who share the interests and persuasions that underlie the association's being." 450 U.S., at 122 n.22.

In no area is the political association's right to exclude more important than in the process of selecting its nominee. That process often determines the party's positions on the most significant public policy issues of the day, and even when those positions are predetermined it is the nominee who becomes the party's ambassador to the general electorate in winning it over to the party's views. Some political parties—such as President Theodore Roosevelt's Bull Moose Party, the La Follette Progressives of 1924, the Henry Wallace Progressives of 1948, and the George Wallace American Independent Party of 1968—are virtually inseparable from their nominees (and tend not to outlast them).

Unsurprisingly, our cases vigorously affirm the special place the First Amendment reserves for, and the special protection it accords, the process by which a political party "selects a standard bearer who best represents the party's ideologies and preferences." *Eu*, 489 U.S., at 224. The moment of choosing the party's nominee, we have said, is "the crucial juncture at which the appeal to common principles may be translated into concerted action, and hence to political power in the community." *Tashjian*, 479 U.S., at 216.

In *La Follette*, the State of Wisconsin conducted an open presidential preference primary.[6] Although the voters did not select the delegates to the Democratic Party's National Convention directly—they were chosen later at caucuses of party

---

election." Those cases simply prevent exclusion that violates some independent constitutional proscription. The closest the dissent comes to identifying such a proscription in this case is its reference to "the First Amendment associational interests" of citizens to participate in the primary of a party to which they do not belong, and the "fundamental right" of citizens "to cast a meaningful vote for the candidate of their choice." As to the latter: Selecting a candidate is quite different from voting for the candidate of one's choice. If the "fundamental right" to cast a meaningful vote were really at issue in this context, Proposition 198 would be not only constitutionally permissible but constitutionally required, which no one believes. As for the associational "interest" in selecting the candidate of a group to which one does not belong, that falls far short of a constitutional right, if indeed it can even fairly be characterized as an interest. It has been described in our cases as a "desire"—and rejected as a basis for disregarding the First Amendment right to exclude.

6. An open primary differs from a blanket primary in that, although as in the blanket primary any person, regardless of party affiliation, may vote for a party's nominee, his choice is limited to that party's nominees *for all offices*. He may not, for example, support a Republican nominee for Governor and a Democratic nominee for attorney general.

members—Wisconsin law required these delegates to vote in accord with the primary results. Thus allowing nonparty members to participate in the selection of the party's nominee conflicted with the Democratic Party's rules. We held that, whatever the strength of the state interests supporting the open primary itself, they could not justify this "substantial intrusion into the associational freedom of members of the National Party."[7] 450 U.S., at 126.

California's blanket primary violates the principles set forth in these cases. Proposition 198 forces political parties to associate with—to have their nominees, and hence their positions, determined by—those who, at best, have refused to affiliate with the party, and, at worst, have expressly affiliated with a rival. In this respect, it is qualitatively different from a closed primary. Under that system, even when it is made quite easy for a voter to change his party affiliation the day of the primary, and thus, in some sense, to "cross over," at least he must formally *become a member of the party*; and once he does so, he is limited to voting for candidates of that party.[8]

The evidence in this case demonstrates that under California's blanket primary system, the prospect of having a party's nominee determined by adherents of an opposing party is far from remote—indeed, it is a clear and present danger. For example, in one 1997 survey of California voters 37 percent of Republicans said that they planned to vote in the 1998 Democratic gubernatorial primary, and 20 percent of Democrats said they planned to vote in the 1998 Republican United States Senate primary. Those figures are comparable to the results of studies in other States with blanket primaries. One expert testified, for example, that in Washington the number of voters crossing over from one party to another can rise to as high as 25 percent, and another that only 25 to 33 percent of all Washington voters limit themselves to candidates of one party throughout the ballot. The impact of voting

---

7. The dissent, in attempting to fashion its new rule—that the right not to associate does not exist with respect to primary elections—rewrites *La Follette* to stand merely for the proposition that a political party has a First Amendment right to "defin[e] the organization and composition of its governing units." In fact, however, the state-imposed burden at issue in *La Follette* was "the intrusion by those with adverse political principles" upon the selection of the party's nominee (in that case its presidential nominee). 450 U.S., at 122. * * *

Not only does the dissent's principle of no right to exclude conflict with our precedents, but it also leads to nonsensical results. In *Tashjian*, we held that the First Amendment protects a party's right to invite independents to participate in the primary. Combining *Tashjian* with the dissent's rule affirms a party's constitutional right to allow outsiders to select its candidates, but denies a party's constitutional right to reserve candidate selection to its own members. The First Amendment would thus guarantee a party's right to lose its identity, but not to preserve it.

8. In this sense, the blanket primary also may be constitutionally distinct from the open primary, in which the voter is limited to one party's ballot. See *La Follette, supra*, at 130, n.2 (Powell, J., dissenting) ("[T]he act of voting in the Democratic primary fairly can be described as an act of affiliation with the Democratic Party. . . . The situation might be different in those States with 'blanket' primaries—*i.e.*, those where voters are allowed to participate in the primaries of more than one party on a single occasion, selecting the primary they wish to vote in with respect to each individual elective office"). This case does not require us to determine the constitutionality of open primaries.

by nonparty members is much greater upon minor parties, such as the Libertarian Party and the Peace and Freedom Party. In the first primaries these parties conducted following California's implementation of Proposition 198, the total votes cast for party candidates in some races was more than *double* the total number of *registered party members.*

The record also supports the obvious proposition that these substantial numbers of voters who help select the nominees of parties they have chosen not to join often have policy views that diverge from those of the party faithful. The 1997 survey of California voters revealed significantly different policy preferences between party members and primary voters who "crossed over" from another party. One expert went so far as to describe it as "inevitable [under Proposition 198] that parties will be forced in some circumstances to give their official designation to a candidate who's not preferred by a majority or even plurality of party members." * * *

[T]he deleterious effects of Proposition 198 are not limited to altering the identity of the nominee. Even when the person favored by a majority of the party members prevails, he will have prevailed by taking somewhat different positions—and, should he be elected, will continue to take somewhat different positions in order to be renominated. As respondents' own expert concluded, "the policy positions of Members of Congress elected from blanket primary states are . . . more moderate, both in an absolute sense and relative to the other party, and so are more reflective of the preferences of the mass of voters at the center of the ideological spectrum." It is unnecessary to cumulate evidence of this phenomenon, since, after all, the whole *purpose* of Proposition 198 was to favor nominees with "moderate" positions. It encourages candidates—and officeholders who hope to be renominated—to curry favor with persons whose views are more "centrist" than those of the party base. In effect, Proposition 198 has simply moved the general election one step earlier in the process, at the expense of the parties' ability to perform the "basic function" of choosing their own leaders. * * *

In sum, Proposition 198 forces petitioners to adulterate their candidate-selection process—the "basic function of a political party"—by opening it up to persons wholly unaffiliated with the party. Such forced association has the likely outcome—indeed, in this case the *intended* outcome—of changing the parties' message. We can think of no heavier burden on a political party's associational freedom. Proposition 198 is therefore unconstitutional unless it is narrowly tailored to serve a compelling state interest. It is to that question which we now turn.

Respondents proffer seven state interests they claim are compelling. Two of them—producing elected officials who better represent the electorate and expanding candidate debate beyond the scope of partisan concerns—are simply circumlocution for producing nominees and nominee positions other than those the parties would choose if left to their own devices. [But requiring speakers to modify the content of their expression is impermissible.] * * *

Respondents' third asserted compelling interest is that the blanket primary is the only way to ensure that disenfranchised persons enjoy the right to an effective vote.

By "disenfranchised," respondents do not mean those who cannot vote; they mean simply independents and members of the minority party in "safe" districts. These persons are disenfranchised, according to respondents, because under a closed primary they are unable to participate in what amounts to the determinative election — the majority party's primary; the only way to ensure they have an "effective" vote is to force the party to open its primary to them. This also appears to be nothing more than reformulation of an asserted state interest we have already rejected — recharacterizing nonparty members' keen desire to participate in selection of the party's nominee as "disenfranchisement" if that desire is not fulfilled. We have said, however, that a "nonmember's desire to participate in the party's affairs is overborne by the countervailing and legitimate right of the party to determine its own membership qualifications." *Tashjian*, 479 U.S., at 215–216, n.6. The voter's desire to participate does not become more weighty simply because the State supports it. Moreover, even if it were accurate to describe the plight of the non-party-member in a safe district as "disenfranchisement," Proposition 198 is not needed to solve the problem. The voter who feels himself disenfranchised should simply join the party. That may put him to a hard choice, but it is not a state-imposed restriction upon *his* freedom of association, whereas compelling party members to accept his selection of their nominee *is* a state-imposed restriction upon theirs.

Respondents' remaining four asserted state interests — promoting fairness, affording voters greater choice, increasing voter participation, and protecting privacy — are not, like the others, automatically out of the running; but neither are they, *in the circumstances of this case*, compelling. That determination is not to be made in the abstract, by asking whether fairness, privacy, etc., are highly significant values; but rather by asking whether the *aspect* of fairness, privacy, etc., addressed by the law at issue is highly significant. And for all four of these asserted interests, we find it not to be.

The aspect of fairness addressed by Proposition 198 is presumably the supposed inequity of not permitting nonparty members in "safe" districts to determine the party nominee. If that is unfair at all (rather than merely a consequence of the eminently democratic principle that — except where constitutional imperatives intervene — the majority rules), it seems to us less unfair than permitting nonparty members to hijack the party. As for affording voters greater choice, it is obvious that the net effect of this scheme — indeed, its avowed purpose — is to *reduce* the scope of choice, by assuring a range of candidates who are all more "centrist." This may well be described as broadening the range of choices *favored by the majority* — but that is hardly a compelling state interest, if indeed it is even a legitimate one. The interest in increasing voter participation is just a variation on the same theme (more choices favored by the majority will produce more voters), and suffers from the same defect. As for the protection of privacy: The specific privacy interest at issue is not the confidentiality of medical records or personal finances, but confidentiality of one's party affiliation. Even if (as seems unlikely) a scheme for administering a closed primary could not be devised in which the voter's declaration of party affiliation would not be public information, we do not think that the State's interest in assuring the privacy of this piece of information in all cases can conceivably be considered a "compelling" one. If such information were generally so sacrosanct, federal statutes would not require a declaration of party affiliation as a condition of appointment to certain offices [including commissions for which no more than a certain number of members may be of the same party].

Finally, we may observe that even if all these state interests were compelling ones, Proposition 198 is not a narrowly tailored means of furthering them. Respondents could protect them all by resorting to a *nonpartisan* blanket primary. Generally speaking, under such a system, the State determines what qualifications it requires for a candidate to have a place on the primary ballot — which may include nomination by established parties and voter-petition requirements for independent candidates. Each voter, regardless of party affiliation, may then vote for any candidate, and the top two vote getters (or however many the State prescribes) then move on to the general election. This system has all the characteristics of the partisan blanket primary, save the constitutionally crucial one: Primary voters are not choosing a party's nominee. Under a nonpartisan blanket primary, a State may ensure more choice, greater participation, increased "privacy," and a sense of "fairness" — all without severely burdening a political party's First Amendment right of association.

* * * The burden Proposition 198 places on petitioners' rights of political association is both severe and unnecessary. The judgment for the Court of Appeals for the Ninth Circuit is reversed.

It is so ordered.

[JUSTICE KENNEDY joined the Court's opinion and wrote separately to argue that upholding the blanket primary would "compound[]" the interference with parties' First Amendment rights that he believed would result from the Court's acceptance of limits on parties' financial expenditures made in coordination with candidates. That doctrine is discussed in Chapter 8, *infra*.]

JUSTICE STEVENS, with whom JUSTICE GINSBURG joins * * *, dissenting. * * *

A State's power to determine how its officials are to be elected is a quintessential attribute of sovereignty. This case is about the State of California's power to decide who may vote in an election conducted, and paid for, by the State. The United States Constitution imposes constraints on the States' power to limit access to the polls, but we have never before held or suggested that it imposes any constraints on States' power to authorize additional citizens to participate in any state election for a state office. In my view, principles of federalism require us to respect the policy choice made by the State's voters in approving Proposition 198.

The blanket primary system instituted by Proposition 198 does not abridge "the ability of citizens to band together in promoting among the electorate candidates who espouse their political views." The Court's contrary conclusion rests on the premise that a political party's freedom of expressive association includes a "right not to associate," which in turn includes a right to exclude voters unaffiliated with the party from participating in the selection of that party's nominee in a primary election. In drawing this conclusion, however, the Court blurs two distinctions that are critical: (1) the distinction between a private organization's right to define itself and its messages, on the one hand, and the State's right to define the obligations of citizens and organizations performing public functions, on the other; and (2) the distinction between laws that abridge participation in the political process and those that encourage such participation.

When a political party defines the organization and composition of its governing units, when it decides what candidates to endorse, and when it decides whether and how to communicate those endorsements to the public, it is engaged in the kind of private expressive associational activity that the First Amendment protects.[3] * * *

[H]owever, the associational rights of political parties are neither absolute nor as comprehensive as the rights enjoyed by wholly private associations. I think it clear—though the point has never been decided by this Court—"that a State may require parties to use the primary format for selecting their nominees." The reason a State may impose this significant restriction on a party's associational freedoms is that both the general election and the primary are quintessential forms of state action. It is because the primary is state action that an organization—whether it calls itself a political party or just a "Jaybird" association—may not deny non-Caucasians the right to participate in the selection of its nominees. *Terry* v. *Adams*; *Smith* v. *Allwright*. The Court is quite right in stating that those cases "do not stand for the proposition that party affairs are [*wholly*] public affairs, free of First Amendment protections." They do, however, stand for the proposition that primary elections, unlike most "party affairs," are state action. The protections that the First Amendment affords to the "internal processes" of a political party do not encompass a right to exclude nonmembers from voting in a state-required, state-financed primary election.

The so-called "right not to associate" that the Court relies upon, then, is simply inapplicable to participation in a state election. A political party, like any other association, may refuse to allow non-members to participate in the party's decisions when it is conducting its own affairs; California's blanket primary system does not infringe this principle. But an election, unlike a convention or caucus, is a public affair. Although it is true that we have extended First Amendment protection to a party's right to invite independents to participate in its primaries, *Tashjian*, neither that case nor any other has held or suggested that the "right not to associate"

---

3. * * * *La Follette* is a case about state regulation of internal party processes, not about regulation of primary elections. State-mandated intrusion upon either delegate selection or delegate voting would surely implicate the affected party's First Amendment right to define the organization and composition of its governing units, but it is clear that California intrudes upon neither in this case. * * *

imposes a limit on the State's power to open up its primary elections to all voters eligible to vote in a general election. In my view, while state rules abridging participation in its elections should be closely scrutinized, the First Amendment does not inhibit the State from acting to broaden voter access to state-run, state-financed elections. When a State acts not to limit democratic participation but to expand the ability of individuals to participate in the democratic process, it is acting not as a foe of the First Amendment but as a friend and ally.

Although I would not endorse it, I could at least understand a constitutional rule that protected a party's associational rights by allowing it to refuse to select its candidates through state-regulated primary elections. A meaningful "right not to associate," if there is such a right in the context of limiting an electorate, ought to enable a party to insist on choosing its nominees at a convention or caucus where non-members could be excluded. In the real world, however, anyone can "join" a political party merely by asking for the appropriate ballot at the appropriate time or (at most) by registering within a state-defined reasonable period of time before an election; neither past voting history nor the voter's race, religion, or gender can provide a basis for the party's refusal to "associate" with an unwelcome new member. There is an obvious mismatch between a supposed constitutional right "not to associate" and a rule that turns on nothing more than the state-defined timing of the new associate's application for membership.

The Court's reliance on a political party's "right not to associate" as a basis for limiting a State's power to conduct primary elections will inevitably require it either to draw unprincipled distinctions among various primary configurations or to alter voting practices throughout the Nation in fundamental ways. [Three States presently have blanket primaries, while an additional 21 States have open primaries and 8 States have semi-closed primaries in which independents may participate.] * * * Given that open primaries are supported by essentially the same state interests that the Court disparages today and are not as "narrow" as nonpartisan primaries, there is surely a danger that open primaries will fare no better against a First Amendment challenge than blanket primaries have. * * *[8]

In my view, the First Amendment does not mandate that a putatively private association be granted the power to dictate the organizational structure of state-run, state-financed primary elections. It is not this Court's constitutional function

---

8. When coupled with our decision in *Tashjian* that a party may require a State to open up a closed primary, this intrusion has even broader implications. It is arguable that, under the Court's reasoning combined with *Tashjian*, the only nominating options open for the States to choose without party consent are: (1) not to have primary elections, or (2) to have what the Court calls a "nonpartisan primary"—a system presently used in Louisiana—in which candidates previously nominated by the various political parties and independent candidates compete. These two options are the same in practice because the latter is not actually a "primary" in the common, partisan sense of that term at all. Rather, it is a general election with a runoff that has few of the benefits of democratizing the party nominating process that led the Court to declare the State's ability to require nomination by primary "too plain for argument."

to choose between the competing visions of what makes democracy work — party autonomy and discipline versus progressive inclusion of the entire electorate in the process of selecting their public officials — that are held by the litigants in this case. That choice belongs to the people.

Even if the "right not to associate" did authorize the Court to review the State's policy choice, its evaluation of the competing interests at stake is seriously flawed. * * * The Court's glib rejection of the State's interest in increasing voter participation is particularly regrettable. In an era of dramatically declining voter participation, States should be free to experiment with reforms designed to make the democratic process more robust by involving the entire electorate in the process of selecting those who will serve as government officials. Opening the nominating process to all and encouraging voters to participate in any election that draws their interest is one obvious means of achieving this goal. I would also give some weight to the First Amendment associational interests of nonmembers of a party seeking to participate in the primary process, to the fundamental right of such nonmembers to cast a meaningful vote for the candidate of their choice, and to the preference of almost 60% of California voters — including a majority of registered Democrats and Republicans — for a blanket primary. In my view, a State is unquestionably entitled to rely on this combination of interests in deciding who may vote in a primary election conducted by the State. It is indeed strange to find that the First Amendment forecloses this decision. * * *

Notes and Questions

1. The Court suggested in footnote 8 that *open* primaries might be distinguishable from *blanket* primaries, such that the former might survive a First Amendment challenge. Do you find the distinction plausible?

2. The Court noted that the "forced association" effected by blanket primaries "has the likely outcome — indeed, in this case the *intended* outcome — of changing the parties' message." That effect, which occurs in open primaries as well as blanket ones, is sometimes subtle and sometimes dramatic. One of the dramatic episodes occurred in the 2014 Mississippi Republican primary for U.S. Senate. The incumbent, Thad Cochran, succeeded in narrowly defeating his more-conservative challenger, Chris McDaniel, by appealing to Democrats and in particular to black Democrats, who turned out in record numbers. *See* Jonathan Weisman & Campbell Robertson, *Blacks Regain Sway at Polls in Mississippi*, N.Y. TIMES (June 25, 2014), *at* http://www.nytimes.com/2014/06/26/us/politics/blacks-regain-sway-at-polls-in -mississippi.html?_r=0.

3. It appeared from *California Democratic Party v. Jones* that blanket primaries — and likely open primaries as well — posed substantial burdens on parties' associational rights as a matter of *law*. That is, there was no need to show that the blanket primary interfered with a party's selection of any particular nominee. The Court, recall, said that it was "unnecessary to cumulate evidence" of the blanket primary's burden on parties' rights, because the purpose of the blanket primary was to

nominate candidates different from the candidates the parties themselves would prefer to nominate.

But the Ninth Circuit has held that the associational burden presented by a state's primary laws is a question of *fact* to be decided in each individual case, with the party bearing the burden of proof. Therefore, in *Democratic Party of Hawaii v. Nago*, 833 F.3d 1119 (9th Cir. 2016), a case challenging the constitutionality of Hawaii's open primary, the court of appeals held that the Party could not succeed on its facial challenge because it had not proven that the open-primary system interfered with the Party's ability to select its nominees.

Should courts require evidence of the burden on parties' rights posed by primaries in which non-party members are invited to participate? Does it matter if, as in *Democratic Party of Hawaii v. Nago*, the ostensible purpose of an open primary is "to protect voter privacy and to encourage voter participation in elections," *id.* at 1121, rather than to encourage the selection of moderate nominees?

If evidence is required, what kind of evidence can a party be expected to produce? In *Democratic Party of Hawaii v. Nago*, the Party pointed out that even though there were only 65,000 members of the Party in Hawaii, a quarter of a million people participated in the Party's open primaries. Thus, among voters in the Democratic primary, non-members outnumbered Party members by a factor of three to one. Still, the court of appeals found that the Party had not presented sufficient evidence of the burden imposed on its associational freedom to select its nominees. As the Court explained, the non-members who voted in the party primary may have *identified* as Democrats even though they were not members.

4. *Problem.* Virginia permits parties to choose their nominees by a variety of methods, including primaries, caucuses, conventions, and unassembled caucuses known as "firehouse primaries." The parties themselves may select the method of nominating their candidates, except that an incumbent member of the state legislature may designate the method to be employed in determining the party's nominee for his or her seat. Thus, if a party wishes to nominate its state-legislative candidates by convention, but an incumbent legislator would prefer the party to hold a primary, there will be a primary and the party will nominate the winner of that primary. Does such a system violate the party's associational rights? Does it violate any other provision of the Constitution? *See Miller v. Brown*, 503 F.3d 360 (4th Cir. 2007).

5. What does *California Democratic Party* say about whether the constitutional right to vote extends to primaries?

6. Recall that *Tashjian v. Republican Party* involved the constitutionality of a state-mandated closed primary, *i.e.*, one as to which independents were barred, while *California Democratic Party* involved the constitutionality of a state-mandated blanket primary. Footnote 13 of *Tashjian* left open the constitutionality of state statutes mandating *semiclosed* primaries, *i.e.*, those as to which members of the party and independents may participate, but as to which members of *other* parties are barred. The next case considered that issue.

Clingman v. Beaver

Supreme Court of the United States
544 U.S. 581, 125 S. Ct. 2029, 161 L. Ed. 2d 920 (2005)

JUSTICE THOMAS delivered the opinion of the Court [in which CHIEF JUSTICE REHNQUIST, JUSTICE O'CONNOR, JUSTICE SCALIA, JUSTICE KENNEDY, and JUSTICE BREYER join], except as to Part II-A [in which CHIEF JUSTICE REHNQUIST, JUSTICE SCALIA, and JUSTICE KENNEDY join]. * * *

I

Oklahoma's election laws provide that only registered members of a political party may vote in the party's primary, unless the party opens its primary to registered Independents as well. In May 2000, the LPO [Libertarian Party of Oklahoma] notified the secretary of the Oklahoma State Election Board that it wanted to open its upcoming primary to all registered Oklahoma voters, without regard to their party affiliation. Pursuant to [Okla. Stat. Ann., Tit. 26] § 1-104, the secretary agreed as to Independent voters, but not as to voters registered with other political parties. The LPO and several Republican and Democratic voters then sued for declaratory and injunctive relief * * *, alleging that Oklahoma's semiclosed primary law unconstitutionally burdens their First Amendment right to freedom of political association. [The District Court held the semiclosed primary constitutional, but the Tenth Circuit reversed.] * * *

II

In *Tashjian* [v. *Republican Party of Connecticut*, 479 U.S. 208, 225 (1986)] [p. 443], this Court struck down, as inconsistent with the First Amendment, a closed primary system that prevented a political party from inviting Independent voters to vote in the party's primary. This case presents a question that *Tashjian* left open: whether a State may prevent a political party from inviting registered voters of other parties to vote in its primary. *Id.*, at 224, n.13. * * * We are persuaded that any burden Oklahoma's semiclosed primary imposes is minor and justified by legitimate state interests.

A

[T]he Republican and Democratic voters who have brought this action do not want to associate with the LPO, at least not in any formal sense. They wish to remain registered with the Republican, Democratic, or Reform parties, and yet to assist in selecting the Libertarian Party's candidates for the general election. Their interest is in casting a vote for a Libertarian candidate in a particular primary election, rather than in banding together with fellow citizens committed to the LPO's political goals and ideas. And the LPO is happy to have their votes, if not their membership on the party rolls.

However, a voter who is unwilling to disaffiliate from another party to vote in the LPO's primary forms little "association" with the LPO—nor the LPO with him.

See *Tashjian, supra,* at 235 (Scalia, J., dissenting). That same voter might wish to participate in numerous party primaries, or cast ballots for several candidates, in any given race. The issue is not "dual associations," [as Justice O'Connor claims], but seemingly boundless ones. * * *

Oklahoma's semiclosed primary system imposes an even slighter burden on voters than on the LPO. * * * In Oklahoma, registered members of the Republican, Democratic, and Reform Parties who wish to vote in the LPO primary simply need to file a form with the county election board secretary to change their registration. Voters are not "locked in" to an unwanted party affiliation because with only nominal effort they are free to vote in the LPO primary. For this reason, too, the registration requirement does not unduly hinder the LPO from associating with members of other parties. To attract members of other parties, the LPO need only persuade voters to make the minimal effort necessary to switch parties.

B

Respondents argue that this case is no different from *Tashjian.* According to respondents, the burden imposed by Oklahoma's semiclosed primary system is no less severe than the burden at issue in *Tashjian,* and hence we must apply strict scrutiny as we did in *Tashjian.* We disagree. * * * As an initial matter, *Tashjian* applied strict scrutiny with little discussion of the magnitude of the burdens imposed by Connecticut's closed primary on parties' and voters' associational rights. But not every electoral law that burdens associational rights is subject to strict scrutiny. Instead, as our cases since *Tashjian* have clarified, strict scrutiny is appropriate only if the burden is severe. In *Tashjian* itself, Independent voters could join the Connecticut Republican Party as late as the day before the primary. As explained above, requiring voters to register with a party prior to participating in the party's primary minimally burdens voters' associational rights.

Nevertheless, *Tashjian* is distinguishable. Oklahoma's semiclosed primary imposes an even less substantial burden than did the Connecticut closed primary at issue in *Tashjian.* In *Tashjian,* this Court identified two ways in which Connecticut's closed primary limited citizens' freedom of political association. The first and most important was that it required Independent voters to affiliate publicly with a party to vote in its primary. That is not true in this case. At issue here are voters who have *already* affiliated publicly with one of Oklahoma's political parties. These voters need not register as Libertarians to vote in the LPO's primary; they need only declare themselves Independents, which would leave them free to participate in any party primary that is open to registered Independents.

The second and less important burden imposed by Connecticut's closed primary system was that political parties could not "broaden opportunities for joining . . . by their own act, without any intervening action by potential voters." *Tashjian,* 479 U.S., at 216, n.7. Voters also had to act by registering themselves in a particular party. That is equally true of Oklahoma's semiclosed primary system: Voters must register as Libertarians or Independents to participate in the LPO's primary.

However, *Tashjian* did not characterize this burden alone as severe, and with good reason. Many electoral regulations, including voter registration generally, require that voters take some action to participate in the primary process. Election laws invariably "affect—at least to some degree—the individual's right to vote and his right to associate with others for political ends." *Anderson* v. *Celebrezze*, 460 U.S. 780, 788 (1983) [p. 517].

These minor barriers between voter and party do not compel strict scrutiny. To deem ordinary and widespread burdens like these severe would subject virtually every electoral regulation to strict scrutiny, hamper the ability of States to run efficient and equitable elections, and compel federal courts to rewrite state electoral codes. The Constitution does not require that result, for it is beyond question "that States may, and inevitably must, enact reasonable regulations of parties, elections, and ballots to reduce election- and campaign-related disorder." *Timmons* [v. *Twin Cities Area New Party*, 520 U.S. 351, 358 (1997)] [p. 526]; *Storer* v. *Brown*, 415 U.S. 724, 730 (1974)] [p. 513]. Oklahoma's semiclosed primary system does not severely burden the associational rights of the State's citizenry.

C

When a state electoral provision places no heavy burden on associational rights, "a State's important regulatory interests will usually be enough to justify reasonable, nondiscriminatory restrictions." *Timmons, supra,* at 358; *Anderson, supra,* at 788. Here, Oklahoma's semiclosed primary advances a number of regulatory interests that this Court recognizes as important: It "preserves [political] parties as viable and identifiable interest groups"; enhances parties' electioneering and party-building efforts; and guards against party raiding and "sore loser" candidacies by spurned primary contenders.

First, as Oklahoma asserts, its semiclosed primary "preserves the political parties as viable and identifiable interest groups, insuring that the results of a primary election, in a broad sense, accurately reflect the voting of the party members." The LPO wishes to open its primary to registered Republicans and Democrats, who may well vote in numbers that dwarf the roughly 300 registered LPO voters in Oklahoma. If the LPO is permitted to open its primary to all registered voters regardless of party affiliation, the candidate who emerges from the LPO primary may be "unconcerned with, if not . . . hostile to," the political preferences of the majority of the LPO's members. It does not matter that the LPO is willing to risk the surrender of its identity in exchange for electoral success. Oklahoma's interest is independent and concerns the integrity of its primary system. The State wants to "avoid primary election outcomes which would tend to confuse or mislead the general voting population to the extent [it] relies on party labels as representative of certain ideologies."

Moreover, this Court has found that "in facilitating the effective operation of [a] democratic government, a state might reasonably classify voters or candidates according to political affiliations." But for that classification to mean much,

Oklahoma must be allowed to limit voters' ability to roam among parties' primaries. * * * Opening the LPO's primary to all voters not only would render the LPO's *imprimatur* an unreliable index of its candidate's actual political philosophy, but it also "would make registered party affiliations significantly less meaningful in the Oklahoma primary election system." Oklahoma reasonably has concluded that opening the LPO's primary to all voters regardless of party affiliation would undermine the crucial role of political parties in the primary process.

Second, Oklahoma's semiclosed primary system, by retaining the importance of party affiliation, aids in parties' electioneering and party-building efforts. "It is common experience that direct solicitation of party members—by mail, telephone, or face-to-face contact, and by the candidates themselves or by their active supporters—is part of any primary election campaign." Yet parties' voter turnout efforts depend in large part on accurate voter registration rolls.

When voters are no longer required to disaffiliate before participating in other parties' primaries, voter registration rolls cease to be an accurate reflection of voters' political preferences. And without registration rolls that accurately reflect likely or potential primary voters, parties risk expending precious resources to turn out party members who may have decided to cast their votes elsewhere. If encouraging citizens to vote is an important state interest, then Oklahoma is entitled to protect parties' ability to plan their primaries for a stable group of voters.

Third, Oklahoma has an interest in preventing party raiding, or "the organized switching of blocs of voters from one party to another in order to manipulate the outcome of the other party's primary election." For example, if the outcome of the Democratic Party primary were not in doubt, Democrats might vote in the LPO primary for the candidate most likely to siphon off votes from the Republican candidate in the general election. Or a Democratic primary contender who senses defeat might launch a "sore loser" candidacy by defecting to the LPO primary, taking with him loyal Democratic voters, and thus undermining the Democratic Party in the general election. Oklahoma has an interest in "tempering the destabilizing effects" of precisely this sort of "party splintering and excessive factionalism." Oklahoma's semiclosed primary system serves that interest by discouraging voters from temporarily defecting from another party to vote in the LPO primary. While the State's interest will not justify "unreasonably exclusionary restrictions," *Timmons*, 520 U.S., at 367, we have "repeatedly upheld reasonable, politically neutral regulations" like Oklahoma's semiclosed primary law, *id.*, at 369. * * *

Oklahoma remains free to allow the LPO to invite registered voters of other parties to vote in its primary. But the Constitution leaves that choice to the democratic process, not to the courts. The judgment of the Court of Appeals is reversed, and the case is remanded for further proceedings.

It is so ordered.

JUSTICE O'CONNOR, with whom JUSTICE BREYER joins * * *, concurring in part and concurring in the judgment.

I join the Court's opinion except for Part II-A. * * *

The plurality questions whether the LPO and voters registered with another party have any constitutionally cognizable interest in associating with one another through the LPO's primary. Its doubts on this point appear to stem from two implicit premises: first, that a voter forms a cognizable association with a political party only by registering with that party; and second, that a voter can only form a cognizable association with one party at a time. Neither of these premises is sound, in my view. As to the first, registration with a political party surely may signify an important personal commitment, which may be accompanied by faithful voting and even activism beyond the polls. But for many voters, registration serves principally as a mandatory (and perhaps even ministerial) prerequisite to participation in the party's primaries. The act of casting a ballot in a given primary may, for both the voter and the party, constitute a form of association that is at least as important as the act of registering. The fact that voting is episodic does not, in my judgment, undermine its associational significance; it simply reflects the special character of the electoral process, which allows citizens to join together at regular intervals to shape government through the choice of public officials.

As to the question of dual associations, I fail to see why registration with one party should negate a voter's First Amendment interest in associating with a second party. We surely would not say, for instance, that a registered Republican or Democrat has no protected interest in associating with the Libertarian Party by attending meetings or making political contributions. The validity of voters' and parties' interests in dual associations seems particularly clear where minor parties are concerned. For example, a voter may have a longstanding affiliation with a major party that she wishes to maintain, but she may nevertheless have a substantial interest in associating with a minor party during particular election cycles or in elections for particular offices. The voter's refusal to disaffiliate from the major party may reflect her abiding commitment to that party (which is not necessarily inconsistent with her desire to associate with a second party), the objective costs of disaffiliation, or both. The minor party, for its part, may have a significant interest in augmenting its voice in the political process by associating with sympathetic members of the major parties.

None of this is to suggest that the State does not have a superseding interest in restricting certain forms of association. We have never questioned, for example, the States' authority to restrict voters' public registration to a single party or to limit each voter to participating in a single party's primary. But the fact that a State's regulatory authority may ultimately trump voters' or parties' associational interests in a particular context is no reason to dismiss the validity of those interests. As a more general matter, I question whether judicial inquiry into the genuineness, intensity, or duration of a given voter's association with a given party is a fruitful way to approach constitutional challenges to regulations like the one at issue here.

Primary voting is an episodic and sometimes isolated act of association, but it is a vitally important one and should be entitled to some level of constitutional protection. Accordingly, where a party invites a voter to participate in its primary and the voter seeks to do so, we should begin with the premise that there are significant associational interests at stake. From this starting point, we can then ask to what extent and in what manner the State may justifiably restrict those interests. * * *

* * * [A]ssuming the availability of reasonable reregistration procedures, a party's inability to persuade a voter to disaffiliate from a rival party would suggest not the presence of anticompetitive regulatory restrictions, but rather the party's failure to win the voter's allegiance. The semiclosed primary law, standing alone, does not impose a significant obstacle to participation in the LPO's primary, nor does it indicate partisan self dealing or a lockup of the political process that would warrant heightened judicial scrutiny.

For essentially the reasons explained by the Court, I agree that Oklahoma has a legitimate interest in requiring voters to disaffiliate from one party before participating in another party's primary. On the record before us, I also agree that the State's regulatory interests are adequate to justify the limited burden the semiclosed primary law imposes on respondents' freedom of association. And finally, I agree that this case is distinguishable from *Tashjian*. I joined the dissent in that case, and I think the Court's application of strict scrutiny there is difficult to square with the flexible standard of review articulated in our more recent cases. But *Tashjian* is entitled to respect under principles of *stare decisis*, and it can be fairly distinguished on the grounds that the closed primary law in that case imposed a greater burden on associational interests than does Oklahoma's semiclosed primary law, while the State's regulatory interests in *Tashjian* were weaker than they are here. * * *

JUSTICE STEVENS, with whom JUSTICE GINSBURG joins, and with whom JUSTICE SOUTER joins as to Parts I, II, and III, dissenting.

The Court's decision today diminishes the value of two important rights protected by the First Amendment: the individual citizen's right to vote for the candidate of her choice and a political party's right to define its own mission. No one would contend that a citizen's membership in either the Republican or the Democratic Party could disqualify her from attending political functions sponsored by another party, or from voting for a third party's candidate in a general election. If a third party invites her to participate in its primary election, her right to support the candidate of her choice merits constitutional protection, whether she elects to make a speech, to donate funds, or to cast a ballot. The importance of vindicating that individual right far outweighs any public interest in punishing registered Republicans or Democrats for acts of disloyalty. The balance becomes even more lopsided when the individual right is reinforced by the right of the Libertarian Party of Oklahoma (LPO) to associate with willing voters.

In concluding that the State's interests override those important values, the Court focuses on interests that are not legitimate. States do not have a valid interest in manipulating the outcome of elections, in protecting the major parties from competition, or in stunting the growth of new parties. While States do have a valid interest in conducting orderly elections and in encouraging the maximum participation of voters, neither of these interests overrides (or, indeed, even conflicts with) the valid interests of both the LPO and the voters who wish to participate in its primary.

In the final analysis, this case is simple. Occasionally, a political party's interest in defining its platform and its procedures for selecting and supporting its candidates conflicts with the voters' interest in participating in the selection of their elected representatives. If those values do conflict, we may be faced with difficult choices. But when, as in this case, those values reinforce one another a decision should be easy. Oklahoma has enacted a statute that impairs both; it denies a party the right to invite willing voters to participate in its primary elections. I would therefore affirm the Court of Appeals' judgment.

I

In rejecting the individual respondents' claims, the majority focuses on their associational interests. While the voters in this case certainly have an interest in associating with the LPO, they are primarily interested in voting for a particular candidate, who happens to be in the LPO. Indeed, I think we have lost sight of the principal purpose of a primary: to nominate a candidate for office.

Because our recent cases have focused on the associational interest of voters, rather than the right to vote itself, it is important to identify three basic precepts. First, it is clear that the right to vote includes the right to vote in a primary election. See *United States* v. *Classic*, 313 U.S. 299, 318 (1941); *Terry* v. *Adams*, 345 U.S. 461 (1953) [p. 423]. When the State makes the primary an "integral part of the procedure of choice," every eligible citizen's right to vote should receive the same protection as in the general election. Second, the right to vote, whether in the primary or the general election, is the right to vote "for the candidate of one's choice." Finally, in assessing burdens on that right—burdens that are not limited to absolute denial of the right—we should focus on the realities of the situation, not on empty formalism.

Here, the impact of the Oklahoma statute on the voters' right to vote for the candidate of their choosing is not a mere "burden"; it is a prohibition.[1] By virtue of the fact that their preferred candidate is a member of a different party, respondents are absolutely precluded from voting for him or her in the primary election. It is not an

---

1. It is not enough that registered members of other parties may simply change their registration. Changing one's political party is not simply a matter of filing a form with the State; for many individuals it can be a significant decision. A view that party membership is merely a label demeans for many the personal significance of party identification and illustrates what little weight the majority actually gives to the associational interests in this case.

answer that the voters could participate in another primary (*i.e.*, the primary for the party with which they are registered) since the individual for whom they wish to vote is not a candidate in that primary. If the so-called "white primary" cases make anything clear, it is that the denial of the right to vote cannot be cured by the ability to participate in a subsequent or different election. Just as the "only election that has counted" in *Terry* was the Jaybird primary, since it was there that the public official was selected in any meaningful sense, the only primary that counts here is the one in which the candidate respondents want to vote for is actually running.

This is not to say that voters have an absolute right to participate in whatever primary they desire. For instance, the parties themselves have a strong associational interest in determining which individuals may vote in their primaries, and that interest will normally outweigh the interest of the uninvited voter.[2] But in the ordinary case the State simply has no interest in classifying voters by their political party and in limiting the elections in which voters may participate as a result of that classification. * * *

II

In concluding that the Oklahoma statute is constitutional, the majority argues that associational interests between the LPO and registered members of other parties are either nonexistent or not heavily burdened by the Oklahoma scheme. * * * [O]ur decision in *Tashjian* rejected these arguments.

In *Tashjian* we held that the State could not prohibit Republicans from inviting voters who were not registered with a political party to participate in the Republican primary. We recognized that "the Party's attempt to broaden the base of public participation in and support for its activities is conduct undeniably central to the exercise of the right of association." 479 U.S., at 214. Importantly, we rejected the notion that the associational interest was somehow diminished because the voters the party sought to include were not formally registered as Republicans. *Id.*, at 215. * * *

Virtually identical interests are at stake in this case. It is the LPO's belief that attracting a more diverse group of voters in its primary would enable it to select a more mainstream candidate who would be more viable in the general election. Like the Republicans in *Tashjian*, the LPO is cognizant of the fact that in order to enjoy success at the voting booth it must have support from voters who identify themselves as independents, Republicans, or Democrats. * * *

---

2. The voters' interest may still prevail if, as was the case in *Terry* v. *Adams* and *Smith* v. *Allwright*, the party primary is the *de facto* election. In part because of this Court's refusal to intervene in political gerrymandering cases, *Davis* v. *Bandemer*, 478 U.S. 109 (1986), an increasing number of districts are becoming "safe districts" in which one party effectively controls the outcome of the election.

III

As justification for the State's abridgment of the constitutionally protected interests asserted by the LPO and the voters, the majority relies on countervailing state interests that are either irrelevant or insignificant. Neither separately nor in the aggregate do these interests support the Court's decision.

First, the Court makes the remarkable suggestion that by opening up its primary to Democrats and Republicans, the LPO will be saddled with so many nonlibertarian voters that the ultimate candidate will not be, in any sense, "libertarian." But the LPO is *seeking* the crossover voting of Republicans and Democrats. Rightly or wrongly, the LPO feels that the best way to produce a viable candidate is to invite voters from other parties to participate in its primary. That may dilute what the Court believes to be the core of the Libertarian philosophy, but it is no business of the State to tell a political party what its message should be, how it should select its candidates, or how it should form coalitions to ensure electoral success.

Second, the majority expresses concern that crossover voting may create voter confusion. This paternalistic concern is belied by the District Court's finding that no significant voter confusion would occur.

Third, the majority suggests that crossover voting will impair the State's interest in properly classifying candidates and voters. As an empirical matter, a crossover voter may have a lesser commitment to the party with which he is registered if he votes in another party's primary. Nevertheless, the State does not have a valid interest in defining what it means to be a Republican or a Democrat, or in attempting to ensure the political orthodoxy of party members simply for the convenience of those parties. Even if participation in the LPO's primary causes a voter to be a less committed "Democrat" or "Republican" (a proposition I reject[7]), the dilution of that commitment does not justify abridgment of the fundamental rights at issue in this case. While party identity is important in our political system, it should not be immunized from the risk of change.

Fourth, the majority argues that opening up the LPO primary to members of the Republican and Democratic Parties might interfere with electioneering and party-building efforts. It is clear, of course, that the majority here is concerned only with the Democratic and Republican Parties, since party building is precisely what the LPO is attempting to accomplish. Nevertheless, that concern is misplaced. Even if, as the majority claims, the Republican and Democratic voter rolls, mailing lists, and phone banks are not as accurate as they would otherwise be,[9] the administrative

---

7. Allowing a potential crossover voter to vote in the LPO primary would not change the level of commitment he has toward his party of registration; it would simply give him an outlet to express the views he already holds.

9. The majority's argument is that voters who would otherwise vote in the Republican or Democratic primaries would vote in the LPO primary, and that the Democratic and Republican lists would not be an accurate indicator of who is likely to vote in those primaries, and of which voters to spend party resources on. First, I find it doubtful that those voters who vote in the LPO primary

inconvenience of the major parties does not outweigh the right to vote or the associational interests of those voters and the LPO. At its core, this argument is based on a fear that the LPO might be successful in convincing Democratic or Republican voters to participate more fully in the LPO. Far from being a compelling interest, it is an impermissible one.

Finally, the majority warns against the possibility of raiding, by which voters of another party maliciously vote in a primary in order to change the outcome of the primary, either to nominate a particularly weak candidate, a "sore-loser" candidate, or a candidate who would siphon votes from another party. * * * [H]owever, * * * [i]f the LPO is willing to take the risk that its party may be "hijacked" by individuals who hold views opposite to their own, the State has little interest in second-guessing the LPO's decision. * * *

In the end, the balance of interests clearly favors the LPO and those voters who wish to participate in its primary. The associational interests asserted—the right to select a standard bearer that the party thinks has the best chance of success, the ability to associate at the crucial juncture of selecting a candidate, and the desire to reach out to voters of other parties—are substantial and undoubtedly burdened by Oklahoma's statutory scheme. Any doubt about that fact is clearly answered by *Tashjian*. On the other side, the interests asserted by the State are either entirely speculative or simply protectionist measures that benefit the parties in power. No matter what the standard, they simply do not outweigh the interests of the LPO and its voters. * * *

Notes and Questions

1. Was Justice Stevens correct that the Court's analysis was inconsistent with *Tashjian*, or do you agree with the Court that *Tashjian* was distinguishable? Note that zero members of the *Tashjian* majority remained on the Court at the time of *Beaver*, while each of the four *Tashjian* dissenters was still on the Court as of 2004. (Justice Stevens's *Tashjian* dissent, however, did not indicate disagreement with *Tashjian*'s First Amendment analysis, and as a result, it was not entirely surprising that he voted in *Beaver* to strike down Oklahoma's semiclosed primary.)

2. How significant a burden on the right to vote or the right to associate is a requirement that a primary voter affiliate with a party (as in a closed primary) or cancel his affiliation with a competing party (as in a semi-closed primary)? Even if a voter can register with or deregister from a party with a few clicks on the state's website (and then reverse that action immediately after the election), is there a potentially severe psychological burden in forcing a voter to cancel a registration with a beloved party or join a hated one? Cf. *Bullock v. Carter*, 405 U.S. 134, 146–47

---

would have voted in the Democratic or Republican primary; rather, they probably would not have been sufficiently motivated vote at all. Further, this would actually give Republicans and Democrats additional information as to which of their voters have Libertarian leanings.

(1972) [p. 507] ("[W]e can hardly accept as reasonable an alternative that requires candidates and voters to abandon their party affiliations in order to avoid the burdens of the filing fees imposed by state law [on candidates in primaries but not on independent candidates].").

3. In her concurrence, Justice O'Connor suggested that states may restrict voters' and parties' associational rights by prohibiting persons from being members of more than one party, or from voting in more than one primary. Why? If she is correct that parties and voters can form "dual associations," what justification does a state have in limiting the activities that can comprise that association? *See American Party of Texas v. White*, 415 U.S. 767, 786 (1974):

> We have previously held that to protect the integrity of party primary elections, States may establish waiting periods before voters themselves may be permitted to change their registration and participate in another party's primary. *Rosario* v. *Rockefeller*, 410 U.S. 752 (1973). Likewise, it seems to us that the State may determine that it is essential to the integrity of the nominating process to confine voters to supporting one party and its candidates in the course of the same nominating process. [W]e see nothing invidious in disqualifying those who have voted at a party primary from signing petitions for another party seeking ballot position for its candidates for the same offices.

To take examples offered by Justice O'Connor and Justice Stevens, could a state prohibit persons from attending meetings of multiple parties or from donating money to more than one party? If not, what difference explains Justice O'Connor's view that states may restrict party membership and primary voting?

4. Justice Stevens rested his analysis principally on the right to vote, rather than on parties' or voters' right of association. Why? Does the right to vote include a right to vote for the candidate of one's choice, as Justice Stevens claimed, regardless of the primary in which that candidate is competing? Should such a right extend to participation in party caucuses and conventions as well? Should there be a fundamental right to be a member of one's chosen political party? How might one balance those rights against the party's right *not* to associate with the individual?

5. *Problem*. Mississippi opens its primaries to those voters who "intend[] to support the nominations made in the primary in which [they] participate[]." It is not necessary, however, for voters to be members of the party in whose primary they wish to vote. The Mississippi Democratic Party challenges the law as creating the opportunity for non-Democrats to vote in its primary. Is the law unconstitutional? *See Mississippi State Democratic Party v. Barbour*, 491 F. Supp. 2d 641 (N.D. Miss. 2007), *vacated as unripe*, 529 F.3d 538 (5th Cir. 2008).

6. *Problem*. Until 2014, Utah law provided that candidates earn the right to appear on the primary ballot by competing in a caucus. If one candidate received 60% of the caucus vote, he or she would receive the party's nomination; otherwise, the top two candidates would run in a primary election. In that year, Utah changed its law

to provide an additional way of appearing on the primary ballot: In addition to the caucus route, candidates could earn a ballot position simply by collecting a certain number of signatures. The Republican Party, which prefers the old system, challenges this law, arguing that the law interferes with the Party's First Amendment rights by enabling the election of a candidate who did not succeed at the caucus. Is the Party correct? Does it matter whether the primary election is closed or open? *See Utah Republican Party v. Cox*, 885 F.3d 1219, *reh'g en banc denied*, 892 F.3d 1066 (10th Cir. 2018), *cert. denied*, 139 S. Ct. 1290 (2019).

7. *Problem*. State law provides that individuals eighteen years old and older may vote in primary and general elections. The major parties wish to permit those persons who are seventeen at the time of the primary but who will turn eighteen by the date of the general election to vote in the primaries. Must the state permit them to vote? What if the parties wished to permit sixteen-year-olds to vote in the primaries? What if the parties wish to exclude all persons under age 21? *See Board of Elections v. Snyder*, 76 A.3d 1110, 1113–14 (Md. 2013); Lisa Rein, *Pushing to Restore a Vote at 17*, Wash. Post Dec. 18, 2007, at B01.

8. After the Court held California's blanket primary unconstitutional, the State of Washington replaced its blanket primary with a "top-two" primary similar to the Louisiana system that *California Democratic Party* concluded would be constitutional. Under Louisiana's system, the candidates in the primary election were not identified by party, and the two candidates receiving the most votes, regardless of party, advanced to the general election. Washington's system added a twist: While the primary candidates were not identified as members of parties and were not running for the nomination of parties, each candidate was permitted to indicate on the ballot his or her party "preference." The next case explored whether that change tipped the constitutional balance.

Washington State Grange v. Washington State Republican Party

Supreme Court of the United States
552 U.S. 442, 128 S. Ct. 1184, 170 L. Ed. 2d 151 (2008)

Justice Thomas delivered the opinion of the Court [in which Chief Justice Roberts, Justice Stevens, Justice Souter, Justice Ginsburg, Justice Breyer, and Justice Alito join].

In 2004, voters in the State of Washington passed an initiative changing the State's primary election system. The People's Choice Initiative of 2004, or Initiative 872 (I-872), provides that candidates for office shall be identified on the ballot by their self-designated "party preference"; that voters may vote for any candidate; and that the top two votegetters for each office, regardless of party preference, advance to the general election. The Court of Appeals for the Ninth Circuit held I-872 facially invalid as imposing an unconstitutional burden on state political parties' First Amendment rights. Because I-872 does not on its face impose a severe burden on political parties' associational rights, and because respondents' arguments to the contrary rest on factual assumptions about voter confusion that can be evaluated only in the context of an as-applied challenge, we reverse. * * *

Under I-872, all elections for "partisan offices" are conducted in two stages: a primary and a general election. To participate in the primary, a candidate must file a "declaration of candidacy" form, on which he declares his "major or minor party preference, or independent status." Each candidate and his party preference (or independent status) is in turn designated on the primary election ballot. A political party cannot prevent a candidate who is unaffiliated with, or even repugnant to, the party from designating it as his party of preference. In the primary election, voters may select "any candidate listed on the ballot, regardless of the party preference of the candidates or the voter."

The candidates with the highest and second-highest vote totals advance to the general election, regardless of their party preferences. Thus, the general election may pit two candidates with the same party preference against one another. Each candidate's party preference is listed on the general election ballot, and may not be changed between the primary and general elections. * * *

* * * Respondents argue that I-872 is unconstitutional under [*California Democratic Party* v.] *Jones* [530 U.S. 567 (2000)] [p. 449] because it has the same "constitutionally crucial" infirmity that doomed California's blanket primary: it allows primary voters who are unaffiliated with a party to choose the party's nominee. Respondents claim that candidates who progress to the general election under I-872 will become the *de facto* nominees of the parties they prefer, thereby violating the parties' right to choose their own standard-bearers and altering their messages. * * *

The flaw in this argument is that, unlike the California primary, the I-872 primary does not, by its terms, choose parties' nominees. The essence of nomination—the choice of a party representative—does not occur under I-872. The law never refers to the candidates as nominees of any party, nor does it treat them as such. To the contrary, the election regulations specifically provide that the primary "does not serve to determine the nominees of a political party but serves to winnow the number of candidates to a final list of two for the general election." The top two candidates from the primary election proceed to the general election regardless of their party preferences. Whether parties nominate their own candidates outside the state-run primary is simply irrelevant. In fact, parties may now nominate candidates by whatever mechanism they choose because I-872 repealed Washington's prior regulations governing party nominations.[7]

---

7. It is true that parties may no longer indicate their nominees on the ballot, but that is unexceptionable: The First Amendment does not give political parties a right to have their nominees designated as such on the ballot. See *Timmons* v. *Twin Cities Area New Party*, 520 U.S. 351, 362–363 (1997) [p. 526]. Parties do not gain such a right simply because the State affords candidates the opportunity to indicate their party preference on the ballot. "Ballots serve primarily to elect candidates, not as forums for political expression." *Id.*, at 363.

Respondents counter that, even if the I-872 primary does not actually choose parties' nominees, it nevertheless burdens their associational rights because voters will assume that candidates on the general election ballot are the nominees of their preferred parties. This brings us to the heart of respondents' case—and to the fatal flaw in their argument. At bottom, respondents' objection to I-872 is that voters will be confused by candidates' party-preference designations. Respondents' arguments are largely variations on this theme. Thus, they argue that even if voters do not assume that candidates on the general election ballot are the nominees of their parties, they will at least assume that the parties associate with, and approve of, them. This, they say, compels them to associate with candidates they do not endorse, alters the messages they wish to convey, and forces them to engage in counterspeech to disassociate themselves from the candidates and their positions on the issues.

We reject each of these contentions for the same reason: They all depend, not on any facial requirement of I-872, but on the possibility that voters will be confused as to the meaning of the party-preference designation. But respondents' assertion that voters will misinterpret the party-preference designation is sheer speculation. * * * There is simply no basis to presume that a well-informed electorate will interpret a candidate's party-preference designation to mean that the candidate is the party's chosen nominee or representative or that the party associates with or approves of the candidate. This strikes us as especially true here, given that it was the voters of Washington themselves, rather than their elected representatives, who enacted I-872.

Of course, it is *possible* that voters will misinterpret the candidates' party-preference designations as reflecting endorsement by the parties. But these cases involve a facial challenge, and we cannot strike down I-872 on its face based on the mere possibility of voter confusion. Because respondents brought their suit as a facial challenge, we have no evidentiary record against which to assess their assertions that voters will be confused. Indeed, because I-872 has never been implemented, we do not even have ballots indicating how party preference will be displayed. It stands to reason that whether voters will be confused by the party-preference designations will depend in significant part on the form of the ballot. * * * [W]e must, in fairness to the voters of the State of Washington who enacted I-872 and in deference to the executive and judicial officials who are charged with implementing it, ask whether the ballot could conceivably be printed in such a way as to eliminate the possibility of widespread voter confusion and with it the perceived threat to the First Amendment.

It is not difficult to conceive of such a ballot. For example, petitioners propose that the actual I-872 ballot could include prominent disclaimers explaining that party preference reflects only the self-designation of the candidate and not an official endorsement by the party. They also suggest that the ballots might note preference in the form of a candidate statement that emphasizes the candidate's personal determination rather than the party's acceptance of the candidate, such as "my party preference is the Republican Party." Additionally, the State could decide to educate the public about the new primary ballots through advertising or explanatory materials mailed to voters along with their ballots. We are satisfied that there are a variety of ways in which the State could implement I-872 that would eliminate any real threat of voter confusion. And without the specter of widespread voter confusion, respondents' arguments about forced association and compelled speech fall flat. * * *

Because we have concluded that I-872 does not severely burden respondents, the State need not assert a compelling interest. The State's asserted interest in providing voters with relevant information about the candidates on the ballot is easily sufficient to sustain I-872.

* * * We accordingly hold that I-872 is facially constitutional. The judgment of the Court of Appeals is reversed.

It is so ordered.

CHIEF JUSTICE ROBERTS, with whom JUSTICE ALITO joins, concurring.

I share JUSTICE SCALIA's concern that permitting a candidate to identify his political party preference on an official election ballot — regardless of whether the candidate is endorsed by the party or is even a member — may effectively force parties to accept candidates they do not want, amounting to forced association in violation of the First Amendment.

* * * Voter perceptions matter, [however,] and if voters do not actually believe the parties and the candidates are tied together, it is hard to see how the parties' associational rights are adversely implicated. After all, individuals frequently claim to favor this or that political party; these preferences, without more, do not create an unconstitutional forced association. * * *

If the ballot is designed in such a manner that no reasonable voter would believe that the candidates listed there are nominees or members of, or otherwise associated with, the parties the candidates claimed to "prefer," the I-872 primary system would likely pass constitutional muster. I cannot say on the present record that it would be impossible for the State to design such a ballot. * * * On the other hand, if the ballot merely lists the candidates' preferred parties next to the candidates' names, or otherwise fails clearly to convey that the parties and the candidates are not necessarily associated, the I-872 system would not survive a First Amendment challenge.

JUSTICE SCALIA complains that * * * a particular candidate's "endorsement" of a party might alter the party's message, and this violates the party's freedom of association.

But there is no general right to stop an individual from saying, "I prefer this party," even if the party would rather he not. Normally, the party protects its message in such a case through responsive speech of its own. What makes this case different of course is that the State controls the content of the ballot, which we have never considered a public forum. Neither the candidate nor the party dictates the message conveyed by the ballot. In such a case, it is important to know what the ballot actually says—both about the candidate and about the party's association with the candidate. It is possible that no reasonable voter in Washington State will regard the listed candidates as members of, or otherwise associated with, the political parties the candidates claim to prefer. Nothing in my analysis requires the parties to produce studies regarding voter perceptions on this score, but I would wait to see what the ballot says before deciding whether it is unconstitutional.

Still, I agree with JUSTICE SCALIA that the history of the challenged law suggests the State is not particularly interested in devising ballots that meet these constitutional requirements. But this record simply does not allow us to say with certainty that the election system created by I-872 is unconstitutional. Accordingly, I agree with the Court that respondents' present challenge to the law must fail, and I join the Court's opinion.

JUSTICE SCALIA, with whom JUSTICE KENNEDY joins, dissenting.

The electorate's perception of a political party's beliefs is colored by its perception of those who support the party; and a party's defining act is the selection of a candidate and advocacy of that candidate's election by conferring upon him the party's endorsement. When the state-printed ballot for the general election causes a party to be associated with candidates who may not fully (if at all) represent its views, it undermines both these vital aspects of political association. The views of the self-identified party supporter color perception of the party's message, and that self-identification on the ballot, with no space for party repudiation or party identification of its own candidate, impairs the party's advocacy of its standard bearer. Because Washington has not demonstrated that this severe burden upon parties' associational rights is narrowly tailored to serve a compelling interest—indeed, because it seems to me Washington's only plausible interest is precisely to reduce the effectiveness of political parties—I would find the law unconstitutional. * * *

The State of Washington need not like, and need not favor, political parties. It is entirely free to decline running primaries for the selection of party nominees and to hold nonpartisan general elections in which party labels have no place on the ballot. Parties would then be left to their own devices in both selecting and publicizing their candidates. But Washington has done more than merely decline to make its electoral machinery available for party building. Recognizing that parties draw support for their candidates by giving them the party imprimatur, Washington seeks to reduce the effectiveness of that endorsement by allowing *any* candidate to use the ballot for drawing upon the goodwill that a party has developed, while preventing the party from using the ballot to reject the claimed association or to identify the genuine candidate of its choice. This does not merely place the ballot off limits for party building; it makes the ballot an instrument by which party building is impeded, permitting unrebutted associations that the party itself does not approve. * * *

The Court makes much of the fact that the party names shown on the Washington ballot may be billed as mere statements of candidate "preference." To be sure, the party is not *itself* forced to display favor for someone it does not wish to associate with, * * * as the political parties were arguably forced to do by lending their ballot endorsement as party nominee in *Jones*. But thrusting an unwelcome, self-proclaimed association upon the party on the election ballot itself is amply destructive of the party's associational rights. An individual's endorsement of a party shapes the voter's view of what the party stands for, no less than the party's endorsement of an individual shapes the voter's view of what the individual stands for. * * * And because the ballot is the only document voters are guaranteed to see, and the last thing they see before casting their vote, there is "no means of replying" that "would be equally effective with the voter."

Not only is the party's message distorted, but its goodwill is hijacked. There can be no dispute that candidate acquisition of party labels on Washington's ballot—even if billed as self-identification—is a means of garnering the support of those who trust and agree with the party. The "I prefer the D's" and "I prefer the R's" will not be on the ballot for esthetic reasons; they are designed to link candidates to unwilling parties (or at least parties who are unable to express their revulsion) and to encourage voters to cast their ballots based in part on the trust they place in the party's name and the party's philosophy. These harms will be present no matter how Washington's law is implemented. There is therefore "no set of circumstances" under which Washington's law would not severely burden political parties, and no good reason to wait until Washington has undermined its political parties to declare that it is forbidden to do so. * * *

* * * I assuredly do not share The Chief Justice's view that the First Amendment will be satisfied so long as the ballot "is designed in such a manner that no reasonable voter would believe that the candidates listed there are nominees or members of, or otherwise associated with, the parties the candidates claimed to 'prefer.'" To begin with, it seems to me quite impossible for the ballot to satisfy a reasonable voter that the candidate is not "associated with" the party for which he has expressed a preference. He has associated *himself* with the party by his very expression of a preference—and that indeed is the whole purpose of allowing the preference to be expressed. If all The Chief Justice means by "associated with" is that the candidate "does not speak on the party's behalf or with the party's approval," none of my analysis in this opinion relies upon that misperception, nor upon the misperception that the candidate is a member or the nominee of the party. Avoiding those misperceptions is far from enough. Is it enough to say on the ballot that a notorious and despised racist who says that the party is his choice does not speak with the party's approval? Surely not. His unrebutted association of that party with his views distorts the image of the party nonetheless. And the fact that the candidate who expresses a "preference" for one or another party is shown not to be the nominee of that party does not deprive him of the boost from the party's reputation which the party wishes to confer only on its nominee. * * *

The majority opinion and The Chief Justice's concurrence also endorse a wait-and-see approach on the grounds that it is not yet evident how the law will affect voter perception of the political parties. But contrary to the Court's suggestion, it is not incumbent on the political parties to adduce "evidence" that forced association affects their ability to advocate for their candidates and their causes. We have never put expressive groups to this perhaps-impossible task. Rather, we accept their own assessments of the matter. * * * [I]n *Jones*, * * * we [did not] require the political parties to demonstrate either that voters would incorrectly perceive the "nominee" labels on the ballot to be the products of party elections or that the labels would change voter perceptions of the party. It does not take a study to establish that when statements of party connection are the sole information listed next to candidate names on the ballot, those statements will affect voters' perceptions of what the candidate stands for, what the party stands for, and whom they should elect.

Since I conclude that Washington's law imposes a severe burden on political parties' associational rights, I would uphold the law only if it were "narrowly tailored" to advance "a compelling state interest." Neither the Court's opinion nor the State's submission claims that Washington's law passes such scrutiny. The State argues only that it "has a rational basis" for "providing voters with a modicum of relevant information about the candidates." This is the only interest the Court's opinion identifies as well.

But "rational basis" is the *least* demanding of our tests * * *. It falls far, far short of establishing the compelling state interest that the First Amendment requires. And to tell the truth, here even the existence of a rational basis is questionable. Allowing candidates to identify themselves with particular parties on the ballot displays the State's view that adherence to party philosophy is "an important—perhaps paramount—consideration in the citizen's choice." If that is so, however, it seems to me irrational not to allow the party to disclaim that self-association, or to identify its own endorsed candidate.

It is no mystery what is going on here. There is no state interest behind this law except the Washington Legislature's dislike for bright-colors partisanship, and its desire to blunt the ability of political parties with noncentrist views to endorse and advocate their own candidates. * * * I dissent from the Court's conclusion that the Constitution permits this sabotage.

Notes and Questions

1. Consider various forms the Washington ballot might take. If the ballot said simply "Joe Smith (R)" and "Sally Jones (D)," with a notation at the bottom of the ballot saying that the party indications were expressions of party preferences of candidates, and did not necessarily indicate party membership or the parties' endorsements, would such a ballot be constitutional? What if, as the Court suggested, the explanation were provided in a document provided with the ballot, but not on the ballot itself? After *Grange*, the Washington Secretary of State published a list of frequently asked questions for voters, which provided this explanation of the party preference: "Each candidate for partisan office may state a political party that he or

she prefers. A candidate's preference does not imply that the candidate is nominated or endorsed by the party, or that the party approves of or associates with that candidate." Should the document make any difference to the constitutional question?

2. If the disclaimer were to appear on the ballot, how detailed should the disclaimer have to be? If the ballot had a column next to the candidates' names that was labeled simply as "party preference," would that be constitutional? For the 2008 election, Washington chose to identify party preference on the ballot using this language:

JOHN SMITH (Prefers Example Party)

or

JOHN SMITH (States No Party Preference)

Sam Reed, Washington Secretary of State, *State Proposes Ballot Language for Top 2 Primary*, Apr. 16, 2008, *at* http://www.secstate.wa.gov/office/osos_ news.aspx?i=V 22ztlROa18W%2FvuTy7o2Mw%3D%3D. Does that language obviate the constitutional concern?

The Ninth Circuit upheld Washington's top-two primary against a constitutional challenge in *Washington State Republican Party v. Washington State Grange*, 676 F.3d 784 (9th Cir.), *cert. denied*, 568 U.S. 814 (2012); *see also Rubin v. Bowen*, No. RG11605301 (Cal. Super. Ct. 2013), *available at* http://electionlawblog.org/wp -content/uploads/11-Order-Amended-Corrected.pdf (upholding California's top-two primary). The court held that the manner in which Washington implemented the primary was unlikely to lead to widespread voter confusion. In addition to the ballot notation described above, the ballots contained the following notice: "READ: Each candidate for partisan office may state a political party that he or she prefers. A candidate's preference does not imply that the candidate is nominated or endorsed by the party, or that the party approves of or associates with that candidate." The state also mailed a notice to voters and aired advertisements explaining the new ballots.

3. How should a court assess a ballot's capacity to confuse voters? Chief Justice Roberts suggested the appropriate test should be whether "no reasonable voter would believe that the candidates listed [on the ballot] are nominees or members of, or otherwise associated with, the parties the candidates claimed to 'prefer.'" Is the level of confusion a factual question to be decided by a jury? Should the question be whether the ballot is likely to mislead a "reasonable voter"? Whether confusion of actual voters (how many?) is possible? Probable? Should we limit our assessment to the "well-informed electorate," to which the majority referred? Why? What kind of evidence would be sufficient to support an argument that the ballot is too confusing?

4. Justice Scalia argued that the Washington law would violate parties' right "not to associate" because the "very expression of a [candidate's] preference" on the ballot would associate the candidate with the party, regardless of the party's opinion of the candidate. Do parties have a right to be free from that kind of "association"?

Is Justice Scalia's broad conception of the right *not* to associate consistent with his narrow conception of the right to associate as seen in his *Tashjian* dissent and the majority opinion in *Beaver* (which he joined)?

5. Should states be able to use non-partisan ballots, which include no reference to the candidates' party affiliations? Should the state have to demonstrate an interest in promoting the image of the officeholder as non-partisan? Does it matter whether the election is for judicial office or for a "political" one? *See Ohio Council 8 American Federation of State, County, and Municipal Employees v. Husted*, 814 F.3d 329, 336 (6th Cir. 2016) (upholding Ohio's non-partisan ballot for judicial offices and holding that "a political party has no First Amendment right to use the general-election ballot for expressive activities").

6. *Problem.* Under Georgia law, "each person designated by the Secretary of State as a presidential candidate shall appear upon the ballot of the appropriate political party or body unless all committee members of the same political party or body as the candidate agree to delete such candidate's name from the ballot." The three-person committee (again, as dictated by state law) is comprised of the state party chair and the party's leaders in the state house and senate. A controversial candidate seeks the Republican Party's presidential nomination, but all three members of the committee agree to delete his name from the ballot. The committee believes that the candidate's views do not represent the views of the Party, and that association with the candidate will harm the Party. Does his exclusion violate his rights or the rights of voters who wish to vote for him? *See Duke v. Massey*, 87 F.3d 1226 (11th Cir. 1996). Would it matter if the statute permitted the committee to exclude a candidate by a majority vote, rather than requiring unanimity?

7. *Problem.* The Democratic Party's rules limit its presidential candidates to individuals who, "as determined by the Chairman of the Democratic National Committee, have established a bona fide record of public service, accomplishment, public writings and/or public statements affirmatively demonstrating that [they have] the interests, welfare and success of the Democratic Party of the United States at heart and will participate in the Convention in good faith." The DNC chair determines that one candidate's racist statements are "contrary to the fundamental beliefs of the Democratic Party." Accordingly, the chairperson exercises his authority under the quoted rule and prohibits any of the candidate's delegates from being seated at the convention. Is the Party a state actor? If so, is it constitutional for the Party to impose a viewpoint-based test for running for the party's nomination? Could a state constitutionally *prohibit* parties from imposing a viewpoint-based test on its candidates? *See LaRouche v. Fowler*, 152 F.3d 974 (D.C. Cir. 1998).

Suppose a party's by-laws provide that only members of the party may receive the party's nomination for public office. If the party nonetheless nominates a non-member, may the state refuse to certify the general-election ballot listing the candidate as the nominee of the party on the ground that the party violated its own by-laws? *See Ademiluyi v. Egbuonu*, 215 A.3d 329 (Md. 2019).

8. *Problem.* Texas law permits parties to determine which candidates shall appear on the primary ballot. May a party require candidates, as a condition of appearing on the primary ballot, to sign a statement pledging the candidate's full support of whichever candidate receives the nomination? *See Kucinich v. Texas Democratic Party*, 563 F.3d 161, 166 (5th Cir. 2009). *Cf. Chiafalo v. Washington*, 591 U.S. __, 140 S. Ct. 2316 (2020) (permitting states to punish presidential electors who fail to vote for the winner of the state's popular election); *Ray v. Blair*, 343 U.S. 214 (1952) (permitting parties to require potential presidential electors to pledge support for the parties' nominees). May the party enforce the same requirement as to persons wishing to *vote* in primaries or to participate in caucuses? May the state itself limit primary voting to persons who intend to support the party at the next election?[d]

9. Does a party have a First Amendment right to exclude potential voters on grounds other than viewpoint? If the Amazon Party wants to exclude men, or the Family Values Party wants to exclude gays, would it have the right to an exemption from a state's antidiscrimination law? *Cf. Boy Scouts of America v. Dale*, 530 U.S. 640 (2000) (holding that the Boy Scouts had a First Amendment right to bar a gay-rights activist from serving as a scout leader). If so, how do you distinguish the White Primary Cases?

10. Thus far, the cases in this section have dealt with parties' ability to set the qualifications for participating in their primaries. Leaving aside that question, do parties have a constitutional right to autonomy from state control in other aspects of their form and operation? For example, can the state prohibit parties' governing bodies from taking sides in primary elections? And can the state require parties to adopt a particular organizational structure? The next case considers those questions.

Eu v. San Francisco County Democratic Central Committee

Supreme Court of the United States
489 U.S. 214, 109 S. Ct. 1013, 103 L. Ed. 2d 271 (1989)

JUSTICE MARSHALL delivered the opinion of the Court [in which JUSTICE BRENNAN, JUSTICE WHITE, JUSTICE BLACKMUN, JUSTICE STEVENS, JUSTICE O'CONNOR, JUSTICE SCALIA, and JUSTICE KENNEDY join]. * * *

* * * The California Elections Code (Code) provides that the "official governing bodies" for [every "ballot-qualified"[1]] party are its "state convention," "state central

---

d. Two states have similar requirements on the books, although neither appears to enforce them. Indiana law provides that "A voter may vote at a primary election: (1) if the voter, at the last general election, voted for a majority of the regular nominees of the political party holding the primary election; or (2) if the voter did not vote at the last general election, but intends to vote at the next general election for a majority of the regular nominees of the political party holding the primary election." Ind. Code § 3-10-1-6. Tennessee law purports to require primary voters to declare their support for the party in whose primary the voter wishes to participate. *See* Tenn. Code Ann. § 2-7-115(b)(2).

1. A "ballot-qualified" party is eligible to participate in any primary election because: (a) during the last gubernatorial election, one of its candidates for state-wide office received two percent

committee," and "county central committees," and that these bodies are responsible for conducting the party's campaigns. At the same time, the Code provides that the official governing bodies "shall not endorse, support, or oppose, any candidate for nomination by that party for partisan office in the direct primary election." * * *

Although the official governing bodies of political parties are barred from issuing endorsements, other groups are not. Political clubs affiliated with a party, labor organizations, political action committees, other politically active associations, and newspapers frequently endorse primary candidates. With the official party organizations silenced by the ban, it has been possible for a candidate with views antithetical to those of her party nevertheless to win its primary.

In addition to restricting the primary activities of the official governing bodies of political parties, California also regulates their internal affairs. Separate statutory provisions dictate the size and composition of the state central committees; set forth rules governing the selection and removal of committee members; fix the maximum term of office for the chair of the state central committee; require that the chair rotate between residents of northern and southern California; specify the time and place of committee meetings; and limit the dues parties may impose on members. Violations of these provisions are criminal offenses punishable by fine and imprisonment.

Various [party members and committees] brought this action in federal court against state officials responsible for enforcing the Code. * * *

The District Court granted summary judgment for the plaintiffs * * *, ruling that the ban on primary endorsements * * * violated the First Amendment as applied to the States through the Fourteenth Amendment. * * * [T]he court [also] ruled that the laws prescribing the composition of state central committees, limiting the committee chairs' terms of office, and designating that the chair rotate between residents of northern and southern California violate the First Amendment. The court denied summary judgment with respect to the statutory provisions establishing the time and place of committee meetings and the amount of dues. The Court of Appeals for the Ninth Circuit affirmed. * * *

* * * To assess the constitutionality of a state election law, we first examine whether it burdens rights protected by the First and Fourteenth Amendments. If the challenged law burdens the rights of political parties and their members, it can survive constitutional scrutiny only if the State shows that it advances a compelling state interest and is narrowly tailored to serve that interest.

We first consider California's prohibition on primary endorsements by the official governing bodies of political parties. California concedes that its ban implicates the First Amendment, but contends that the burden is "miniscule." We disagree.

---

of the vote; (b) one percent of the State's voters are registered with the party; or (c) a petition establishing the party has been filed by ten percent of the State's voters.

  In the interest of simplicity, we use the terms "ballot-qualified party" and "political party" interchangeably.

The ban directly affects speech which "is at the core of our electoral process and of the First Amendment freedoms." * * *

California's ban on primary endorsements * * * prevents party governing bodies from stating whether a candidate adheres to the tenets of the party or whether party officials believe that the candidate is qualified for the position sought. This prohibition directly hampers the ability of a party to spread its message and hamstrings voters seeking to inform themselves about the candidates and the campaign issues. A "highly paternalistic approach" limiting what people may hear is generally suspect, but it is particularly egregious where the State censors the political speech a political party shares with its members.

Barring political parties from endorsing and opposing candidates not only burdens their freedom of speech but also infringes upon their freedom of association. * * * Freedom of association means not only that an individual voter has the right to associate with the political party of her choice, but also that a political party has a right to "identify the people who constitute the association" and to select a "standard bearer who best represents the party's ideologies and preferences."

Depriving a political party of the power to endorse suffocates this right. The endorsement ban prevents parties from promoting candidates "at the crucial juncture at which the appeal to common principles may be translated into concerted action, and hence to political power in the community." *Tashjian* [v. *Republican Party of Connecticut*], 479 U.S. [208], 216 [(1986)] [p. 443]. Even though individual members of the state central committees and county central committees are free to issue endorsements, imposing limitations "on individuals wishing to band together to advance their views on a ballot measure, while placing none on individuals acting alone, is clearly a restraint on the right of association." *Citizens Against Rent Control/Coalition for Fair Housing* v. *Berkeley*, 454 U.S. 290, 296 (1981).

Because the ban burdens appellees' rights to free speech and free association, it can only survive constitutional scrutiny if it serves a compelling governmental interest.[15] The State offers two: stable government and protecting voters from confusion and undue influence. Maintaining a stable political system is, unquestionably,

---

15. California contends that it need not show that its endorsement ban serves a compelling state interest, because the political parties have "consented" to it. In support of this claim, California observes that the legislators who could repeal the ban belong to political parties, that the bylaws of some parties prohibit primary endorsements, and that parties continue to participate in state-run primaries.

This argument is fatally flawed in several respects. We have never held that a political party's consent will cure a statute that otherwise violates the First Amendment. Even aside from this fundamental defect, California's consent argument is contradicted by the simple fact that the official governing bodies of various political parties have joined this lawsuit. * * *

There are other flaws in the State's argument. Simply because a legislator belongs to a political party does not make her at all times a representative of party interests. In supporting the endorsement ban, an individual legislator may be acting on her understanding of the public good or her interest in reelection. The independence of legislators from their parties is illustrated by the California Legislature's frequent refusal to amend the election laws in accordance with the wishes of a compelling state interest. California, however, never adequately explains how banning parties from endorsing or opposing primary candidates advances that interest. There is no showing, for example, that California's political system is any more stable now than it was in 1963, when the legislature enacted the ban. Nor does the State explain what makes the California system so peculiar that it is virtually the only State that has determined that such a ban is necessary.

The only explanation the State offers is that its compelling interest in stable government embraces a similar interest in party stability. The State relies heavily on *Storer* v. *Brown*, [415 U.S. 724, 730 (1974)] [p. 513], where we stated that because "splintered parties and unrestrained factionalism may do significant damage to the fabric of government," States may regulate elections to ensure that "some sort of order, rather than chaos . . . accompan[ies] the democratic processes." Our decision in *Storer*, however, does not stand for the proposition that a State may enact election laws to mitigate intraparty factionalism during a primary campaign. To the contrary, *Storer* recognized that "contending forces within the party employ the primary campaign and the primary election to finally settle their differences." *Id.*, at 735. A primary is not hostile to intraparty feuds; rather it is an ideal forum in which to resolve them. * * *

It is no answer to argue, as does the State, that a party that issues primary endorsements risks intraparty friction which may endanger the party's general election prospects. Presumably a party will be motivated by self-interest and not engage in acts or speech that run counter to its political success. However, even if a ban on endorsements saves a political party from pursuing self-destructive acts, that would not justify a State substituting its judgment for that of the party. Because preserving party unity during a primary is not a compelling state interest, we must look elsewhere to justify the challenged law.

The State's second justification for the ban on party endorsements and statements of opposition is that it is necessary to protect primary voters from confusion and undue influence. Certainly the State has a legitimate interest in fostering an informed electorate. However, "[a] State's claim that it is enhancing the ability of its citizenry to make wise decisions by restricting the flow of information to them must

---

political parties. Moreover, the State's argument ignores those parties with negligible, if any, representation in the legislature.

That the bylaws of some parties prohibit party primary endorsements also does not prove consent. These parties may have chosen to reflect state election law in their bylaws, rather than permit or require conduct prohibited by law. Nor does the fact that parties continue to participate in the state-run primary process indicate that they favor each regulation imposed upon that process. A decision to participate in state-run primaries more likely reflects a party's determination that ballot participation is more advantageous than the alternatives, that is, supporting independent candidates or conducting write-in campaigns. *See Storer* v. *Brown*, 415 U.S. 724, 745 (1974) [p. 513]; *Anderson* v. *Celebrezze*, 460 U.S. 780, 799, n.26 (1983) [p. 517].

Finally, the State's focus on the parties' alleged consent ignores the independent First Amendment rights of the parties' members. It is wholly undemonstrated that the members authorized the parties to consent to infringements of members' rights.

be viewed with some skepticism." *Tashjian, supra,* at 221. While a State may regulate the flow of information between political associations and their members when necessary to prevent fraud and corruption, there is no evidence that California's ban on party primary endorsements serves that purpose.[19]

Because the ban on primary endorsements by political parties burdens political speech while serving no compelling governmental interest, we hold that [it] violate[s] the First and Fourteenth Amendments.

We turn next to California's restrictions on the organization and composition of official governing bodies, the limits on the term of office for state central committee chair, and the requirement that the chair rotate between residents of northern and southern California. These laws directly implicate the associational rights of political parties and their members. As we noted in *Tashjian,* a political party's "determination . . . of the structure which best allows it to pursue its political goals, is protected by the Constitution." 479 U.S., at 224. Freedom of association also encompasses a political party's decisions about the identity of, and the process for electing, its leaders.

The laws at issue burden these rights. By requiring parties to establish official governing bodies at the county level, California prevents the political parties from governing themselves with the structure they think best. * * * Each restriction * * * limits a political party's discretion in how to organize itself, conduct its affairs, and select its leaders. Indeed, the associational rights at stake are much stronger than those we credited in *Tashjian.* There, we found that a party's right to free association embraces a right to allow registered voters who are not party members to vote in the party's primary. Here, party members do not seek to associate with nonparty members, but only with one another in freely choosing their party leaders.[21]

Because the challenged laws burden the associational rights of political parties and their members, the question is whether they serve a compelling state interest. A State indisputably has a compelling interest in preserving the integrity of its election process. Toward that end, a State may enact laws that interfere with a party's internal affairs when necessary to ensure that elections are fair and honest. *Storer* v. *Brown,* 415 U.S., at 730. For example, a State may impose certain eligibility requirements for voters in the general election even though they limit parties' ability to garner support and members. We have also recognized that a State may impose restrictions that promote the integrity of primary elections. None of these restrictions, however, involved direct regulation of a party's leaders. Rather, the infringement on the

---

19. The State suggested at oral argument that the endorsement ban prevents fraud by barring party officials from misrepresenting that they speak for the party. To the extent that the State suggests that only the primary election results can constitute a party endorsement, it confuses an endorsement from the official governing bodies that may influence election results with the results themselves. * * *

21. By regulating the identity of the parties' leaders, the challenged statutes may also color the parties' message and interfere with the parties' decisions as to the best means to promote that message.

associational rights of the parties and their members was the indirect consequence of laws necessary to the successful completion of a party's external responsibilities in ensuring the order and fairness of elections.

In the instant case, the State has not shown that its regulation of internal party governance is necessary to the integrity of the electoral process. Instead, it contends that the challenged laws serve a compelling "interest in the 'democratic management of the political party's internal affairs.'" This, however, is not a case where intervention is necessary to prevent the derogation of the civil rights of party adherents. Cf. *Smith* v. *Allwright*, 321 U.S. 649 (1944) [p. 418]. Moreover, as we have observed, the State has no interest in "protect[ing] the integrity of the Party against the Party itself." *Tashjian*, 479 U.S., at 224. The State further claims that limiting the term of the state central committee chair and requiring that the chair rotate between residents of northern and southern California helps "prevent regional friction from reaching a 'critical mass.'" However, a State cannot substitute its judgment for that of the party as to the desirability of a particular internal party structure, any more than it can tell a party that its proposed communication to party members is unwise.

In sum, a State cannot justify regulating a party's internal affairs without showing that such regulation is necessary to ensure an election that is orderly and fair. Because California has made no such showing here, the challenged laws cannot be upheld.

* * * Accordingly, the judgment of the Court of Appeals is

Affirmed.

CHIEF JUSTICE REHNQUIST took no part in the consideration or decision of this case.

[JUSTICE STEVENS joined the Court's opinion but wrote to express "reservations" about the Court's use of strict scrutiny, which he believed might be thought to foreordain a conclusion of unconstitutionality.]

Notes and Questions

1. *Whose* First Amendment rights were abridged by the ban on endorsements by parties' official governing bodies? The parties and their members certainly have the First Amendment right to endorse candidates, but was that right being abridged here? How do we know which candidates the members preferred? Likewise, the individual members of the governing bodies have a First Amendment right to endorse candidates, but the endorsements here were not those of any individuals, but of the collective bodies. Finally, the endorsements may be considered to reflect the views of the governing bodies. But it is unclear why the governing bodies as such should have a right to endorse primary candidates.

Consider, in this regard, a party whose members are torn between nominating Apollo and Bacchus. The membership prefers Apollo by a small margin, but the governing body prefers Bacchus and wishes to endorse him publicly. Is it permissible in such a case to view the governing body as acting for the party?

2. In holding that parties have a right to endorse candidates in primary elections, the Court necessarily conceived of parties of having an existence and a purpose independent of their candidates. Such a conception matters not only in identifying and defining a party's right of association, but also in assessing the place of parties within campaign-finance regulation. If parties have the right to create and disseminate a message independent of state interference—the basis of the right-of-association cases considered in this section—then we might expect to treat parties' campaign fund-raising and expenditures just as we would that of interest groups. On the other hand, parties exist largely, if not completely, to elect their candidates. Certainly, in the stage between nomination and general election, parties are focused most intently on electing their candidates, and so there is a great degree of overlap between the interests of the parties and those of their candidates.

In *Federal Election Commission v. Colorado Republican Federal Campaign Committee*, 533 U.S. 431 (2001), the Supreme Court considered the constitutionality of the federal limit on parties' coordinated expenditures—expenditures, that is, that are coordinated with their candidates. The Party argued that because the job of parties is to secure the election of its candidates, parties are "joined at the hip" with their candidates. Accordingly, the parties argued, coordinated expenditures should be viewed as appropriate and desirable, rather than as a source of corruption.

In a 5-4 decision, the Court disagreed. The Court held that parties' coordinated expenditures could be limited because such expenditures did raise the risk of corruption—specifically, the risk that parties would act as bagmen for special interests or wealthy donors who would give money to parties with the expectation that their contributions would be funneled to the grateful candidates. *See id.* at 452 ("[Parties] act as agents for spending on behalf of those who seek to produce obligated officeholders."). The Court noted that parties had the right to make unlimited *independent* expenditures in support of its candidates, but that coordinated expenditures by parties (like coordinated expenditures by other groups) could lead to the same kind of corruption sought to be prevented by limits on contributions. In permitting coordinated expenditures to be limited, did the Court place too little weight on parties' right to associate with their candidates?

3. *Eu* held unconstitutional California's attempt to regulate the internal governing structure of the Party. But did not *Smith v. Allwright*, 321 U.S. 649 (1944) [p. 418], *demand* that states regulate the internal governing structure of parties to ensure against racial discrimination? Did *Eu* adequately distinguish *Allwright*?

4. Does *Eu*, alone or in combination with *California Democratic Party v. Jones*, 530 U.S. 567 (2000) [p. 449], render state-mandated primary elections unconstitutional, on the ground that they interfere with the party's right to choose the process for selecting its leaders?

The final case in this Chapter—a First Amendment challenge to New York's convention method of selecting judicial candidates—involves several of the themes discussed in this Chapter. The case requires us to consider the parties' right of autonomy; individuals' rights to vote and run for office; the place of the two-party system in politics; and the appropriate roles of states, parties, judges, and the Constitution in establishing fair systems for selecting public officials.

New York State Board of Elections v. Lopez Torres

Supreme Court of the United States
552 U.S. 196, 128 S. Ct. 791, 169 L. Ed. 2d 665 (2008)

JUSTICE SCALIA delivered the opinion of the Court [in which CHIEF JUSTICE ROBERTS, JUSTICE STEVENS, JUSTICE SOUTER, JUSTICE THOMAS, JUSTICE GINSBURG, JUSTICE BREYER, and JUSTICE ALITO join].

The State of New York requires that political parties select their nominees for Supreme Court Justice at a convention of delegates chosen by party members in a primary election. We consider whether this electoral system violates the First Amendment rights of prospective party candidates.

The Supreme Court of New York is the State's trial court of general jurisdiction * * *. Under New York's current Constitution, the State is divided into 12 judicial districts, and Supreme Court Justices are elected to 14-year terms in each such district. * * *

Over the years, New York has changed the method by which Supreme Court Justices are selected several times. Under the New York Constitution of 1821, all judicial officers, except Justices of the Peace, were appointed by the Governor with the consent of the Senate. In 1846, New York amended its Constitution to require popular election of the Justices of the Supreme Court (and also the Judges of the New York Court of Appeals). In the early years under that regime, the State allowed political parties to choose their own method of selecting the judicial candidates who would bear their endorsements on the general-election ballot. The major parties opted for party conventions, the same method then employed to nominate candidates for other state offices.

In 1911, the New York Legislature enacted a law requiring political parties to select Supreme Court nominees * * * through direct primary elections. The primary system came to be criticized as a "device capable of astute and successful manipulation by professionals," and the Republican candidate for Governor in 1920 campaigned against it as "a fraud" that "offered the opportunity for two things, for the demagogue and the man with money." A law enacted in 1921 required parties to select their candidates for the Supreme Court by a convention composed of delegates elected by party members.

New York retains this system of choosing party nominees for Supreme Court Justice to this day. Section 6-106 of New York's election law sets forth its basic operation: "Party nominations for the office of justice of the supreme court shall be made by the judicial district convention." A "party" is any political organization whose candidate for Governor received 50,000 or more votes in the most recent election. In a September "delegate primary," party members elect delegates from each of New York's 150 assembly districts to attend the party's judicial convention for the judicial district in which the assembly district is located. An individual may run for delegate by submitting to the Board of Elections a designating petition signed by 500 enrolled party members residing in the assembly district, or by five percent of such enrolled members, whichever is less. These signatures must be gathered within a 37-day period preceding the filing deadline, which is approximately two months before the delegate primary. The delegates elected in these primaries are uncommitted; the primary ballot does not specify the judicial nominee whom they will support.

The nominating conventions take place one to two weeks after the delegate primary. Each of the 12 judicial districts has its own convention to nominate the party's Supreme Court candidate or candidates who will run at large in that district in the general election. The general election takes place in November. The nominees from the party conventions appear automatically on the general-election ballot. They may be joined on the general-election ballot by independent candidates and candidates of political organizations that fail to meet the 50,000 vote threshold for "party" status; these candidates gain access to the ballot by submitting timely nominating petitions with (depending on the judicial district) 3,500 or 4,000 signatures from voters in that district or signatures from five percent of the number of votes cast for Governor in that district in the prior election, whichever is less.

Respondent López Torres was elected in 1992 to the civil court for Kings County—a court with more limited jurisdiction than the Supreme Court—having gained the nomination of the Democratic Party through a primary election. She claims that soon after her election, party leaders began to demand that she make patronage hires, and that her consistent refusal to do so caused the local party to oppose her unsuccessful candidacy at the Supreme Court nominating conventions in 1997, 2002, and 2003. The following year, López Torres—together with other candidates who had failed to secure the nominations of their parties, voters who claimed to have supported those candidates, and the New York branch of a public-interest organization called Common Cause—brought suit in federal court against the New York Board of Elections, which is responsible for administering and enforcing the New York election law. They contended that New York's election law burdened the rights of challengers seeking to run against candidates favored by the party leadership, and deprived voters and candidates of their rights to gain access to the ballot and to associate in choosing their party's candidates. As relevant here, they sought a declaration that New York's convention system for selecting Supreme Court Justices violates their First Amendment rights, and an injunction mandating the establishment of a direct primary election to select party nominees for Supreme Court Justice.

The District Court issued a preliminary injunction granting the relief requested, [and a] unanimous panel of the United States Court of Appeals for the Second Circuit affirmed. * * *

A political party has a First Amendment right to limit its membership as it wishes, and to choose a candidate-selection process that will in its view produce the nominee who best represents its political platform. * * * In the present case, however, * * * [r]espondents are in no position to rely on the right that the First Amendment confers on political parties to structure their internal party processes and to select the candidate of the party's choosing. Indeed, both the Republican and Democratic state parties have intervened from the very early stages of this litigation to defend New York's electoral law. The weapon wielded by these plaintiffs is their *own* claimed associational right not only to join, but to have a certain degree of influence in, the party. They contend that New York's electoral system does not go far enough—does not go as far as the Constitution demands—in assuring that they will have a fair chance of prevailing in their parties' candidate-selection process.

This contention finds no support in our precedents. We have indeed acknowledged an individual's associational right to vote in a party primary without undue state-imposed impediment. [See *Kusper* v. *Pontikes*, 414 U.S. 51, 57 (1973).] [But] respondents do not claim that they have been excluded from voting in the primary. Moreover, even if we extended *Kusper* to cover not only the right to vote in the party primary but also the right to run, the requirements of the New York law (a 500-signature petition collected during a 37-day window in advance of the primary) are entirely reasonable. * * *

Respondents' real complaint is not that they cannot vote in the election for delegates, nor even that they cannot run in that election, but that the convention process that follows the delegate election does not give them a realistic chance to secure the party's nomination. The party leadership, they say, inevitably garners more votes for its slate of delegates (delegates uncommitted to any judicial nominee) than the unsupported candidate can amass for himself. And thus the leadership effectively determines the nominees. But this says nothing more than that the party leadership has more widespread support than a candidate not supported by the leadership. No New York law compels election of the leadership's slate—or, for that matter, compels the delegates elected on the leadership's slate to vote the way the leadership desires. And no state law prohibits an unsupported candidate from attending the convention and seeking to persuade the delegates to support her. * * * Here respondents complain not of the state law, but of the voters' (and their elected delegates') preference for the choices of the party leadership.

To be sure, we have * * * permitted States to set their faces against "party bosses" by requiring party-candidate selection through processes more favorable to insurgents, such as primaries. But to say that the State can require this is a far cry from saying that the Constitution demands it. None of our cases establishes an individual's constitutional right to have a "fair shot" at winning the party's nomination. And with good reason. What constitutes a "fair shot" is a reasonable enough question for legislative judgment, which we will accept so long as it does not too much infringe upon the party's associational rights. But it is hardly a manageable constitutional question for judges—especially for judges in our legal system, where traditional electoral practice gives no hint of even the existence, much less the content, of a constitutional requirement for a "fair shot" at party nomination. Party conventions, with their attendant "smoke-filled rooms" and domination by party leaders, have long been an accepted manner of selecting party candidates. * * * Selection by convention has never been thought unconstitutional, even when the delegates were not selected by primary but by party caucuses. * * *

Respondents put forward, as a special factor which gives them a First Amendment right to revision of party processes in the present case, the assertion that party loyalty in New York's judicial districts renders the general-election ballot "uncompetitive." They argue that the existence of entrenched "one-party rule" demands that the First Amendment be used to impose additional competition in the nominee-selection process of the parties. (The asserted "one-party rule," we may observe, is that of the Democrats in some judicial districts, and of the Republicans in others.) This is a novel and implausible reading of the First Amendment. * * *

The reason one-party rule is entrenched may be (and usually is) that voters approve of the positions and candidates that the party regularly puts forward. It is no function of the First Amendment to require revision of those positions or candidates. The States can, within limits (that is, short of violating the parties' freedom of association), discourage party monopoly—for example, by refusing to show party endorsement on the election ballot. But the Constitution provides no authority for federal courts to prescribe such a course. The First Amendment creates an open marketplace where ideas, most especially political ideas, may compete without government interference. It does not call on the federal courts to manage the market by preventing too many buyers from settling upon a single product.

Limiting respondents' court-mandated "fair shot at party endorsement" to situations of one-party entrenchment merely multiplies the impracticable lines courts would be called upon to draw. It would add to those alluded to earlier, the line at which mere party popularity turns into "one-party dominance." In the case of New York's election system for Supreme Court Justices, that line would have to be drawn separately for each of the 12 judicial districts—and in those districts that are "competitive" the current system would presumably remain valid. But why limit the remedy to *one*-party dominance? Does not the dominance of two parties similarly stifle competing opinions? Once again, we decline to enter the morass.

New York State has thrice (in 1846, 1911, and 1921) displayed a willingness to reconsider its method of selecting Supreme Court Justices. If it wishes to return to the primary system that it discarded in 1921, it is free to do so; but the First Amendment does not compel that. We reverse the Second Circuit's contrary judgment.

It is so ordered.

JUSTICE STEVENS, with whom JUSTICE SOUTER joins, concurring.

While I join JUSTICE SCALIA's cogent resolution of the constitutional issues raised by this case, I think it appropriate to emphasize the distinction between constitutionality and wise policy. Our holding with respect to the former should not be misread as endorsement of the electoral system under review, or disagreement with the findings of the District Court that describe glaring deficiencies in that system and even lend support to the broader proposition that the very practice of electing judges is unwise. But as I recall my esteemed former colleague, Thurgood Marshall, remarking on numerous occasions: "The Constitution does not prohibit legislatures from enacting stupid laws."

JUSTICE KENNEDY, * * * concurring in the judgment. * * *

* * * Were the state-mandated-and-designed nominating convention the sole means to attain access to the general election ballot there would be considerable force, in my view, to respondents' contention that the First Amendment prohibits the State from requiring a delegate selection mechanism with the rigidities and difficulties attendant upon this one. The system then would be subject to scrutiny from the standpoint of a "reasonably diligent independent candidate," *Storer* v. *Brown*, 415 U.S. 724, 742 (1974) [p. 513]. * * *

As the Court is careful to note, however, New York has a second mechanism for placement on the final election ballot. One who seeks to be a Justice of the New York Supreme Court may qualify by a petition process. The petition must be signed by the lesser of (1) 5 percent of the number of votes last cast for Governor in the judicial district or (2) either 3,500 or 4,000 voters (depending on the district). This requirement has not been shown to be an unreasonable one, a point respondents appear to concede. True, the candidate who gains ballot access by petition does not have a party designation; but the candidate is still considered by the voters.

The petition alternative changes the analysis.

This is not to say an alternative route to the general election exempts the delegate primary/nominating convention from all scrutiny. * * * But there is a dynamic relationship between, in this case, the convention system and the petition process; higher burdens at one stage are mitigated by lower burdens at the other. * * * On the particular facts and circumstances of this case, then, I reach the same conclusion the Court does.

Notes and Questions

1. Was the Court right to dismiss López Torres's argument that the convention system violated her rights because of the "one-party rule" that prevailed in many judicial districts? Suppose that the one-party domination of certain districts was the result, in part, of partisan gerrymandering. Would that fact undercut the Court's conclusion?

2. What constitutional constraints limit the capacity of state law to privilege the choices of party bosses?

3. In 2016, when Senator Bernie Sanders challenged former Secretary of State Hillary Clinton for the Democratic presidential nomination, Sanders's supporters objected to the influence of "superdelegates" at the Democratic National Convention. Because the superdelegates were uncommitted, meaning that they could vote for the candidate of their choice regardless of the results of any primary election, the superdelegates reduced the voting power of the delegates chosen through primary elections, and thereby undermined the power of the voters in primary elections. A Sanders supporter challenged the Democrats' use of superdelegates, arguing that it violated the First and Fourteenth Amendments. Relying on *López Torres*, however, the district court held that any right that the supporter had to participate in the nomination process did "not give him an absolute right to control the internal processes and priorities of" the Party and did not guarantee him a "fair shot" at influencing the Party's nomination. *Kurzon v. Democratic National Committee*, 197 F. Supp. 3d 638, 642–43 (S.D.N.Y. 2016). Furthermore, the court noted that prohibiting the Democratic Party from using superdelegates would "clearly infringe[]" the Party's "countervailing First Amendment rights." *Id.* at 643.

After the 2016 election, the Democrats changed their rules about superdelegates. The amendment reduced the number of superdelegates and provided that they would be ineligible to vote for the presidential nomination on the first ballot at the national convention. Thus, if a candidate receives a majority of "pledged" delegates, he or she will be the nominee. If no candidate receives a majority on the first ballot, however, the superdelegates may affect the outcome in the second and successive ballots.

Chapter 6

Ballot Access and Term Limits

A. Introduction

Denying someone access to the ballot—or using the ballot to handicap his or her candidacy—can be tantamount to keeping that person out of elective office, denying his or her supporters the ability to elect their favored candidate, and even keeping their views out of the public debate. For that reason, the Supreme Court has restricted states' ability to manipulate election results by controlling the ballot. For example, the Court has turned away states' attempts to use the ballot to signal voters to oppose a candidate, whether because the candidate belongs to a particular race or because he holds unpopular views on a controversial issue, such as term limits. Yet states retain substantial control over candidates' access to the ballot. States also have substantial control over ballot design, including the choice of which information to feature on ballots.

Because of the importance of ballot access, particularly for third parties and independent candidates, the Supreme Court has interpreted the Equal Protection Clause and the First Amendment to forbid states from using ballot-access laws and other regulations to stifle challenges to the existing political order. Accordingly, laws that leave all but the major-party candidates virtually no chance of appearing on the ballot are unconstitutional. On the other hand, the Court has also perceived a state interest in the orderly management of elections and has upheld certain regulations that have the effect of hindering third parties. Thus, minor parties and independent candidates may be required to demonstrate some showing of support, such as by collecting signatures on a petition, before being granted a spot on a ballot. If the requirement is too onerous, however, it will be held unconstitutional. Determining when a requirement is too onerous has proven to be a major difficulty, as we shall see.

Term limits—limits on the number of consecutive (or nonconsecutive) times a candidate may be reelected to the same office—can be found in both federal and state constitutions and statutes. Even without formal term limits, there have been various informal norms that certain political offices would be subject to rotation. For example, Abraham Lincoln served only one term in the U.S. House of Representatives in the 1840s due to such an informal agreement. Robert Struble, Jr., *House Turnover and the Principle of Rotation*, 94 POL. SCI. Q. 649 (1979–80) (discussing such norms in the U.S. House of Representatives in the nineteenth century). Until recently, most formal limits were restricted to executive offices. Most famously, the Twenty-Second Amendment to the U.S. Constitution limits Presidents to a maximum of two terms. The Amendment was adopted in 1951 after Franklin Roosevelt was elected four times, breaking the informal two-term tradition set by President Washington. Forty states place various term limits on their governors, and thirty-five percent of major cities place term limits on their mayors. Einer Elhauge, *Are Term Limits Undemocratic?*, 64 U. Chi. L. Rev. 83, 87 n.9 (1997).

Supporters of term limits have defended them by arguing that persons continually reelected to the same office unfairly or inappropriately aggrandize political power. Accordingly, the advantages of mandatory rotations have been thought by some to outweigh the greater experience and seniority possessed by long-serving representatives, as well as the right of voters to elect whom they want to office. This argument gained particular currency in the 1990s, when little turnover and high reelection rates led twenty-four states to adopt limits for state legislators, and led some to impose term limits on their members of Congress as well. Many people argued that limiting legislative terms would lead to, among other things, fewer professional politicians, greater devotion to the public good, less spending, and less capture by interest groups. Opponents of legislative term limits countered that such limits would degrade institutional memory and lead to the capture of less-experienced legislators by interest groups and bureaucrats, who are not affected by term limits. There was a lively popular and academic literature debating these points. *See, e.g.*, George F. Will, Restoration: Congress, Term Limits, and the Recovery of Deliberative Democracy (1992); Elizabeth Garrett, *Term Limitations and the Myth of the Citizen-Legislator*, 81 Cornell L. Rev. 623 (1996).

Inevitably, legal challenges were mounted to the new wave of legislative term limits, as §C of this Chapter describes. As you consider the legal and policy issues confronting the courts in these challenges, consider also the scholarly literature that has examined the efficacy of the new limits. That literature to date does not provide much comfort for supporters of term limits. For example, some studies show that states with term limits spend *more* than states without them. H. Abbie Erler, *Legislative Term Limits and State Spending*, 133 Pub. Choice 479 (2007) (offering speculations for this counterintuitive result, including that term limits open up the budgetary process in ways that lead to more participation by legislators and interest groups, which leads to more spending). Other studies suggest that term limits have had little effect on the type of people elected to office, but (at least in the opinion of surveyed legislators) have led to some of the ills forecast by critics of term limits, and to greater power for governors vis-à-vis legislatures. John M. Carey et al., *The Effects of Term Limits on State Legislators: A New Survey of the 50 States*, 31 Legis. Stud. Q. 105 (2006).[a] One term-limits sympathizer has described the empirical studies as a

---

a. For a sample of the large scholarly literature, see, e.g., Timothy Besley & Anne Case, *Does Electoral Accountability Affect Economic Policy Choices? Evidence from Gubernatorial Term Limits*, 110 Q. J. Econ. 769 (1995); Bruce E. Cain & Marc A. Levin, *Term Limits*, 2 Ann. Rev. Pol. Sci. 163 (1999); Andrew B. Hall, *Partisan Effects of Legislative Term Limits*, 39 Legis. Stud. Q. 407 (2014); Edward J. López, *Term Limits: Causes and Consequences*, 114 Pub. Choice 1 (2003); Susan M.

"mixed bag of positives and negatives." LARRY J. SABATO, A MORE PERFECT CONSTITUTION 51 (2007). To what extent, if at all, should federal and state judges take into account such studies when pondering challenges to term limits?

B. Third Parties, Independent Candidates, and Ballot Access

The constitutional law surrounding the regulation of minor parties and independent candidates presents a conflict between, on the one hand, states' interest in providing an orderly, stable election process that is easy for the public to understand and for voters to use; and, on the other hand, third parties' interest in challenging the existing political structure and public policies. The Supreme Court has recognized that "as a practical matter, there must be a substantial regulation of elections if they are to be fair and honest and if some sort of order, rather than chaos, is to accompany the democratic processes." *Storer v. Brown*, 415 U.S. 724, 730 (1974) [p. 513]. Nevertheless, politicians' self-interest suggests that, without constitutional constraints, the members of the two major parties who hold public office will use electoral regulations to continue the dominance of those parties. *See, e.g., Munro v. Socialist Workers Party*, 479 U.S. 189, 201 (1986) (Marshall, J., dissenting).

Williams v. Rhodes

Supreme Court of the United States
393 U.S. 23, 89 S. Ct. 5, 21 L. Ed. 2d 24 (1968)

MR. JUSTICE BLACK delivered the opinion of the Court [in which MR. JUSTICE DOUGLAS, MR. JUSTICE BRENNAN, MR. JUSTICE FORTAS, and MR. JUSTICE MARSHALL join].

The State of Ohio in a series of election laws has made it virtually impossible for a new political party, even though it has hundreds of thousands of members, or an old party, which has a very small number of members, to be placed on the state ballot to choose electors pledged to particular candidates for the Presidency and Vice Presidency of the United States.

Ohio Revised Code, § 3517.01, requires a new party to obtain petitions signed by qualified electors totaling 15% of the number of ballots cast in the last preceding gubernatorial election. The detailed provisions of other Ohio election laws result in the imposition of substantial additional burdens * * *.[1] Together these various

---

Miller et al., *Reexamining the Institutional Effects of Term Limits in U.S. State Legislatures*, 36 LEGIS. STUD. Q. 71 (2012).

1. Judge Kinneary describes, in his dissenting opinion below, the legal obstacles placed before a would-be third party even after the 15% signature requirement has been fulfilled:

"*First*, at the primary election, the new party, or any political party, is required to elect a state central committee consisting of two members from each congressional district restrictive provisions make it virtually impossible for any party to qualify on the ballot except the Republican and Democratic Parties. These two Parties face substantially smaller burdens because they are allowed to retain their positions on the ballot simply by obtaining 10% of the votes in the last gubernatorial election and need not obtain any signature petitions. Moreover, Ohio laws make no provision for ballot position for independent candidates as distinguished from political parties. * * *

* * * In determining whether or not a state law violates the Equal Protection Clause, we must consider the facts and circumstances behind the law, the interests which the State claims to be protecting, and the interests of those who are disadvantaged by the classification. In the present situation the state laws place burdens on two different, although overlapping, kinds of rights—the right of individuals to associate for the advancement of political beliefs, and the right of qualified voters, regardless of their political persuasion, to cast their votes effectively. * * *

No extended discussion is required to establish that the Ohio laws before us give the two old, established parties a decided advantage over any new parties struggling for existence and thus place substantially unequal burdens on both the right to vote and the right to associate. The right to form a party for the advancement of political goals means little if a party can be kept off the election ballot and thus denied an equal opportunity to win votes. So also, the right to vote is heavily burdened if that vote may be cast only for one of two parties at a time when other parties are clamoring for a place on the ballot. In determining whether the State has power to place such unequal burdens on minority groups where rights of this kind are at stake, the decisions of this Court have consistently held that "only a compelling state interest in the regulation of a subject within the State's constitutional power to regulate can justify limiting First Amendment freedoms."

The State has here failed to show any "compelling interest" which justifies imposing such heavy burdens on the right to vote and to associate.

---

and county central committees for each county in Ohio. *Second*, at the primary election the new party must elect delegates and alternates to a national convention. Since [an Ohio statute] prohibits a candidate from seeking the office of delegate to the national convention or committeeman if he voted as a member of a different party at a primary election in the preceding four year period, the new party would be required to have over twelve hundred members who had not previously voted in another party's primary, and who would be willing to serve as committeemen and delegates. *Third*, the candidates for nomination in the primary would have to file petitions signed by qualified electors. The term 'qualified electors' is not adequately defined in the Ohio Revised Code, but a related section provides that a qualified elector at a primary election of a political party is one who, (1) voted for a majority of that party's candidates at the last election, or, (2) has never voted in any election before. Since neither of the political party plaintiffs had any candidates at the last preceding regular state election, they would, of necessity, have to seek out members who had never voted before to sign the nominating petitions, and it would be only these persons who could vote in the primary election of the new party."

The State * * * claims that [it] may validly promote a two-party system in order to encourage compromise and political stability. The fact is, however, that the Ohio system does not merely favor a "two-party system"; it favors two particular parties—the Republicans and the Democrats—and in effect tends to give them a complete monopoly. There is, of course, no reason why two parties should retain a permanent monopoly on the right to have people vote for or against them. Competition in ideas and governmental policies is at the core of our electoral process and of the First Amendment freedoms. New parties struggling for their place must have the time and opportunity to organize in order to meet reasonable requirements for ballot position, just as the old parties have had in the past.

Ohio makes a variety of other arguments to support its very restrictive election laws. It points out, for example, that if three or more parties are on the ballot, it is possible that no one party would obtain 50% of the vote, and the runner-up might have been preferred to the plurality winner by a majority of the voters. Concededly, the State does have an interest in attempting to see that the election winner be the choice of a majority of its voters. But to grant the State power to keep all political parties off the ballot until they have enough members to win would stifle the growth of all new parties working to increase their strength from year to year. Considering these Ohio laws in their totality, this interest cannot justify the very severe restrictions on voting and associational rights which Ohio has imposed. * * *

The State also argues that its requirement of a party structure and an organized primary insures that those who disagree with the major parties and their policies "will be given a choice of leadership as well as issues" since any leader who attempts to capitalize on the disaffection of such a group is forced to submit to a primary in which other, possibly more attractive, leaders can raise the same issues and compete for the allegiance of the disaffected group. But while this goal may be desirable, Ohio's system cannot achieve it. Since the principal policies of the major parties change to some extent from year to year, and since the identity of the likely major party nominees may not be known until shortly before the election, this disaffected "group" will rarely if ever be a cohesive or identifiable group until a few months before the election. Thus, Ohio's burdensome procedures, requiring extensive organization and other election activities by a very early date, operate to prevent such a group from ever getting on the ballot and the Ohio system thus denies the "disaffected" not only a choice of leadership but a choice on the issues as well.

Finally Ohio claims that its highly restrictive provisions are justified because without them a large number of parties might qualify for the ballot, and the voters would then be confronted with a choice so confusing that the popular will could be frustrated. But the experience of many States, including that of Ohio prior to 1948, demonstrates that no more than a handful of parties attempts to qualify for ballot positions even when a very low number of signatures, such as 1% of the electorate, is required.[9] It is true that the existence of multitudinous fragmentary groups might justify some regulatory control but in Ohio at the present time this danger seems to us no more than "theoretically imaginable." No such remote danger can justify the immediate and crippling impact on the basic constitutional rights involved in this case.

* * * [T]he totality of the Ohio restrictive laws taken as a whole imposes a burden on voting and associational rights which we hold is an invidious discrimination, in violation of the Equal Protection Clause. * * *

MR. JUSTICE DOUGLAS. * * *

In our political life, third parties are often important channels through which political dissent is aired: "All political ideas cannot and should not be channeled into the programs of our two major parties. History has amply proved the virtue of political activity by minority, dissident groups, which innumerable times have been in the vanguard of democratic thought and whose programs were ultimately accepted.... The absence of such voices would be a symptom of grave illness in our society." *Sweezy* v. *New Hampshire*, 354 U.S. 234, 250–251 [(1957)] (opinion of WARREN, C.J.).

The Equal Protection Clause * * * protects voting rights and political groups, as well as economic units, racial communities, and other entities. When "fundamental rights and liberties" are at issue, a State has less leeway in making classifications than when it deals with economic matters. I would think that a State has precious little leeway in making it difficult or impossible for citizens to vote for whomsoever they please and to organize campaigns for any school of thought they may choose, whatever part of the spectrum it reflects.

Cumbersome election machinery can effectively suffocate the right of association, the promotion of political ideas and programs of political action, and the right to vote. The totality of Ohio's requirements has those effects. * * *

Hence I concur in today's decision; and, while my emphasis is different from the Court's, I join its opinion.

MR. JUSTICE HARLAN, concurring in the result.

* * * Ohio's statutory scheme violates the basic right of political association assured by the First Amendment which is protected against state infringement under the Due Process Clause of the Fourteenth Amendment. It is true that Ohio has not directly limited appellants' right to assemble or discuss public issues or solicit new members. Instead, by denying the appellants any opportunity to participate

---

9. Forty-two States require third parties to obtain the signatures of only 1% or less of the electorate in order to appear on the ballot. It appears that no significant problem has arisen in these States which have relatively lenient requirements for obtaining ballot position.

in the procedure by which the President is selected, the State has eliminated the basic incentive that all political parties have for conducting such activities, thereby depriving appellants of much of the substance, if not the form, of their protected rights. The right to have one's voice heard and one's views considered by the appropriate governmental authority is at the core of the right of political association. * * * Just as a political group has a right to organize effectively so that its position may be heard in court; so it has the right to place its candidate for the Presidency before whatever body has the power to make the State's selection of Electors. * * *

Of course, the State may limit the right of political association by invoking an impelling policy justification for doing so. But as my Brother BLACK's opinion demonstrates, Ohio has been able to advance no such justification for denying almost half a million of its citizens their fundamental right to organize effectively for political purposes. Consequently, it may not exclude them from the process by which Presidential Electors are selected.

In deciding this case of first impression, I think it unnecessary to draw upon the Equal Protection Clause [which is of dubious applicability to Presidential elections because of the inequalities the Constitution prescribes in the allocation of Presidential Electors]. * * *

A word should be added about the constitutional status of Ohio's requirement that a third party, to qualify for ballot position, must collect the signatures of eligible voters in a number equal to 15% of those voting at the last gubernatorial election. * * *

In my view, this requirement, even when regarded in isolation, must fall. As my Brother BLACK's opinion suggests, the only legitimate interest the State may invoke in defense of this barrier to third-party candidacies is the fear that, without such a barrier, candidacies will proliferate in such numbers as to create a substantial risk of voter confusion.[8] Ohio's requirement cannot be said to be reasonably related to this interest. Even in the unprecedented event of a complete and utter popular disaffection with the two established parties, Ohio law would permit as many as six additional party candidates to compete with the Democrats and Republicans only

---

8. My Brother STEWART is, of course, quite right in pointing out that the presence of third parties may on occasion result in the election of the major candidate who is in reality less preferred by the majority of the voters. It seems clear to me, however, that many constitutional electoral structures could be designed which would accommodate this valid state interest, without depriving other political organizations of the right to participate effectively in the political process. A runoff election may be mandated if no party gains a majority, or the decision could be left to the State Legislature in such a case. Alternatively, the voter could be given the right, at the general election, to indicate both his first and his second choice for the Presidency — if no candidate received a majority of first-choice votes, the second-choice votes could then be considered. Finally, Electors could be chosen on a district-by-district rather than an at-large basis, thereby apportioning the electoral vote in a way more nearly approximating the popular vote. I would conclude that, with the substantial variety of less restrictive alternatives that are available, this interest cannot support Ohio's 15% requirement.

if popular support should be divided relatively evenly among the new groups. And with fundamental freedoms at stake, such an unlikely hypothesis cannot support an incursion upon protected rights, especially since the presence of eight candidacies cannot be said, in light of experience, to carry a significant danger of voter confusion. As both Ohio's electoral history and the actions taken by the overwhelming majority of other States suggest, opening the ballot to this extent is perfectly consistent with the effective functioning of the electoral process. In sum, I think that Ohio has fallen far short of showing the compelling state interest necessary to overcome this otherwise protected right of political association.

Since Ohio's requirement is so clearly disproportionate to the magnitude of the risk that it may properly act to prevent, I need not reach the question of the size of the signature barrier a State may legitimately raise against third parties on this ground. This should be left to the Ohio Legislature in the first instance.

Mr. Justice Stewart, dissenting[.] * * *

* * * I concede that the Fourteenth Amendment imposes some limitations upon a state legislature's freedom to choose a method for the appointment of electors. A State may not, for example, adopt a system that discriminates on grounds of religious or political belief. But I cannot agree that Ohio's system violates the Fourteenth Amendment in any way. * * *

* * * By preventing parties that have not demonstrated timely and widespread support from gaining places on its ballot, Ohio's provisions tend to guard against the possibility that small-party candidates will draw enough support to prevent either of the major contenders from obtaining an absolute majority of votes—and against the consequent possibility that election may be secured by candidates who gain a plurality but who are, *vis-à-vis* their principal opponents, preferred by less than half of those voting. Surely the attainment of these objectives is well within the scope of a State's authority under our Constitution. One may perhaps disagree with the political theory on which the objectives are based, but it is inconceivable to me that the Constitution imposes on the States a political philosophy under which they must be satisfied to award election on the basis of a plurality rather than a majority vote.{[12]}

---

12. My Brother Harlan suggests that Ohio's interest may be protected in "less restrictive" ways. * * * [E]ach of the methods mentioned by Mr. Justice Harlan appears to me to entail consequences which arguably would frustrate other legitimate state interests. Nor do all of them serve as effectively to promote the interest in question here as does the statutory scheme the Ohio Legislature has in fact enacted. I do not think problems such as those raised in this case can be solved by means of facile and unelaborated suggestions of "less restrictive alternatives"; issues of legislative policy are too complex for such easy answers to be satisfactory.

In pursuing this interest Ohio has, at the same time, not completely prevented new parties from gaining access to that State's ballot. It has authorized ballot position for parties that can demonstrate by petition the support of 15% of the voting public 90 days before a primary election is to be held. My Brethren seem to suggest that the percentage figure is set too high, and the date too early. But I cannot join in this kind of second-guessing. While necessarily arbitrary, Ohio's standards can only be taken to represent reasonable attempts at accommodating the conflicting interests involved.[9]

Although Ohio's provisions do not freeze the Republican and Democratic Parties into the State's election structure by specific reference to those parties, it is true that established parties, once they become participants in the electoral process, continue to enjoy ballot position so long as they have polled 10% of the vote in the most recent Ohio gubernatorial election. It is suggested that the disparity between this figure and the 15% requirement applicable to new parties is invidiously discriminatory. But I cannot accept the theory that Ohio is constitutionally compelled to apply precisely the same numerical test in determining whether established parties enjoy widespread support as it applies in determining that question with regard to new parties. * * *

The Court's opinion appears to concede that the State's interest in attempting to ensure that a minority of voters do not thwart the will of the majority is a legitimate one, but summarily asserts that this legitimate interest cannot constitutionally be vindicated. That assertion seems to echo the claim of my concurring Brethren—a claim not made by the appellants—that Ohio's statutory requirements in some way infringe upon First Amendment rights. I cannot agree. * * *

* * * Ohio's ballot requirements have [no] substantial impact on the attempts of political dissidents to organize effectively. Such persons are entirely free to assemble, speak, write, and proselytize as they see fit. They are free either to attempt to modify the character of the established major parties or to go their own way and set up separate political organizations. And if they can timely demonstrate that they have substantial support within the State—according to Ohio's reasonable standards for deciding that question—they may secure ballot position for the candidates they support. Ohio has restricted only their ability to secure ballot position without demonstrating that support. To me the conclusion that that single disability in any way significantly impairs their First Amendment rights is sheer speculation. [T]he present two-party system in this country is the product of social and political forces rather than of legal restrictions on minority parties. This Court has been shown neither that in States with minimal ballot restrictions third parties have flourished, nor that in States with more difficult requirements they are moribund. Mere speculation ought not to suffice to strike down a State's duly enacted laws. * * *

---

9. The date specified, for instance, is related to Ohio's requirement that all political parties hold primary elections—another provision that is, it seems to me, well within the State's power to enact.

Mr. Justice White, dissenting * * *.

I agree with much of what my Brother Stewart says in his dissenting opinion[.] * * * Why a majority of the Court insists on holding the primary petition requirement impermissible, not on its own demerits, but because it appears in the statute books with more questionable provisions is the major mystery of the majority position. * * *

Mr. Chief Justice Warren, dissenting.

We have had but seven days to consider the important constitutional questions presented by these cases. * * * Appellants' belated requests for extraordinary relief have compelled all members of this Court to decide cases of this magnitude without the unhurried deliberation which is essential to the formulation of sound constitutional principles. * * *

Both the opinion of this Court and that of the District Court leave unresolved what restrictions, if any, a State can impose. Although both opinions treat the Ohio statutes as a "package," giving neither Ohio nor the courts any guidance, each contains intimations that a State can by reasonable regulation condition ballot position upon at least three considerations—a substantial showing of voter interest in the candidate seeking a place on the ballot, a requirement that this interest be evidenced sometime prior to the election, and a party structure demonstrating some degree of political organization. With each of these propositions I can agree. * * *

Whatever may be the applicable constitutional principles, appellants and the State of Ohio are entitled to know whether any of the various provisions attacked in this litigation do comport with constitutional standards. * * * Given the magnitude of the questions presented and the need for unhurried deliberation, I would dispose of appellants' request for declaratory relief * * * by a remand to the District Court for a clearer determination of the serious constitutional questions raised in these cases. * * *

Notes and Questions

1. Exactly what was the Court's holding? What was held unconstitutional? If you were advising the Ohio legislature about how to revise its statutes after *Williams*, what would you recommend?

2. *Williams* applied strict scrutiny, even though the Ohio laws did not explicitly favor any particular ideological view and did not discriminate against a suspect class. The laws certainly placed a greater burden on third parties than on major parties, but a law's disparate impact is not enough to trigger strict scrutiny, even where the harmed group is a racial minority. *See Washington v. Davis*, 426 U.S. 229 (1976). Should the Court have required the plaintiffs to prove Ohio's discriminatory *purpose* in passing these laws?

3. Justice Harlan argued that ballot access is constitutionally protected because it permits parties to make their views known to the electorate. How would such a conception of the First Amendment affect other cases we have confronted?

Jenness v. Fortson

Supreme Court of the United States
403 U.S. 431, 91 S. Ct. 1970, 29 L. Ed. 2d 554 (1971)

Mr. Justice Stewart delivered the opinion of the Court [in which Mr. Chief Justice Burger, Mr. Justice Douglas, Mr. Justice Brennan, Mr. Justice White, Mr. Justice Marshall, and Mr. Justice Blackmun join].

Under Georgia law a candidate for elective public office who does not enter and win a political party's primary election can have his name printed on the ballot at the general election only if he has filed a nominating petition signed by at least 5% of the number of registered voters at the last general election for the office in question. * * * [A]ppellants, who were prospective candidates and registered voters, [challenged the constitutionality of the petition requirement. The District Court held it valid.] * * *

The basic structure of the pertinent provisions of the Georgia Election Code is relatively uncomplicated. Any political organization whose candidate received 20% or more of the vote at the most recent gubernatorial or presidential election is a "political party." Any other political organization is a "political body." "Political parties" conduct primary elections, regulated in detail by state law, and only the name of the candidate for each office who wins this primary election is printed on the ballot at the subsequent general election, as his party's nominee for the office in question. A nominee of a "political body" or an independent candidate, on the other hand, may have his name printed on the ballot at the general election by filing a nominating petition. This petition must be signed by "a number of electors of not less than five per cent. of the total number of electors eligible to vote in the last election for the filling of the office the candidate is seeking." The total time allowed for circulating a nominating petition is 180 days, and it must be filed on the second Wednesday in June, the same deadline that a candidate filing in a party primary must meet.

It is to be noted that these procedures relate only to the right to have the name of a candidate or the nominee of a "political body" printed on the ballot. There is no limitation whatever, procedural or substantive, on the right of a voter to write in on the ballot the name of the candidate of his choice and to have that write-in vote counted.

In this litigation the appellants have mounted their attack upon Georgia's nominating-petition requirement on two different but related constitutional fronts. First, they say that to require a nonparty candidate to secure the signatures of a certain number of voters before his name may be printed on the ballot is to abridge the freedoms of speech and association guaranteed to that candidate and his supporters by the First and Fourteenth Amendments. Secondly, they say that when Georgia requires a nonparty candidate to secure the signatures of 5% of the voters before printing his name on the ballot, yet prints the names of those candidates who have won nomination in party primaries, it violates the Fourteenth Amendment by denying the nonparty candidate the equal protection of the laws. * * *

[*Williams* v. *Rhodes*, 393 U.S. 23 (1968)] [p. 495], it is clear, presented a statutory scheme vastly different from the one before us here. Unlike Ohio, Georgia freely provides for write-in votes. Unlike Ohio, Georgia does not require every candidate to be the nominee of a political party, but fully recognizes independent candidacies. Unlike Ohio, Georgia does not fix an unreasonably early filing deadline for candidates not endorsed by established parties. Unlike Ohio, Georgia does not impose upon a small party or a new party the Procrustean requirement of establishing elaborate primary election machinery. Finally, and in sum, Georgia's election laws, unlike Ohio's, do not operate to freeze the political status quo. In this setting we cannot say that Georgia's 5% petition requirement violates the Constitution.

Anyone who wishes, and who is otherwise eligible, may be an independent candidate for any office in Georgia. Any political organization, however new or however small, is free to endorse any otherwise eligible person as its candidate for whatever elective public office it chooses. So far as the Georgia election laws are concerned, independent candidates and members of small or newly formed political organizations are wholly free to associate, to proselytize, to speak, to write, and to organize campaigns for any school of thought they wish. They may confine themselves to an appeal for write-in votes. Or they may seek, over a six months' period, the signatures of 5% of the eligible electorate for the office in question. If they choose the latter course, the way is open. For Georgia imposes no suffocating restrictions whatever upon the free circulation of nominating petitions. A voter may sign a petition even though he has signed others, and a voter who has signed the petition of a nonparty candidate is free thereafter to participate in a party primary. The signer of a petition is not required to state that he intends to vote for that candidate at the election. A person who has previously voted in a party primary is fully eligible to sign a petition, and so, on the other hand, is a person who was not even registered at the time of the previous election. No signature on a nominating petition need be notarized.

The open quality of the Georgia system is far from merely theoretical. For the stipulation of facts in this record informs us that a candidate for Governor in 1966 and a candidate for President in 1968, gained ballot designation by nominating petitions, and each went on to win a plurality of the votes cast at the general election.

In a word, Georgia in no way freezes the status quo, but implicitly recognizes the potential fluidity of American political life. Thus, any political body that wins as much as 20% support at an election becomes a "political party" with its attendant ballot position rights and primary election obligations, and any "political party" whose support at the polls falls below that figure reverts to the status of a "political body" with its attendant nominating petition responsibilities and freedom from primary election duties. We can find in this system nothing that abridges the rights of free speech and association secured by the First and Fourteenth Amendments.

The appellants' claim under the Equal Protection Clause of the Fourteenth Amendment fares no better. * * * The fact is, of course, that from the point of view of one who aspires to elective public office in Georgia, alternative routes are available to getting his name printed on the ballot. He may enter the primary of a political party, or he may circulate nominating petitions either as an independent candidate or under the sponsorship of a political organization.[25] We cannot see how Georgia has violated the Equal Protection Clause of the Fourteenth Amendment by making available these two alternative paths, neither of which can be assumed to be inherently more burdensome than the other.

Insofar as we deal here with the claims of a "political body," as contrasted with those of an individual aspirant for public office or an individual voter, the situation is somewhat different. For it is true that a "political party" in Georgia is assured of having the name of its nominee—the primary election winner—printed on the ballot, whereas the name of the nominee of a "political body" will be printed only if nominating petitions have been filed that contain the requisite number of signatures. But we can hardly suppose that a small or a new political organization could seriously urge that its interests would be advanced if it were forced by the State to establish all of the elaborate statewide, county-by-county, organizational paraphernalia required of a "political party" as a condition for conducting a primary election. Indeed, a large reason for the Court's invalidation of the Ohio election laws in *Williams* v. *Rhodes* was precisely that Ohio *did* impose just such requirements on small and new political organizations.

The fact is that there are obvious differences in kind between the needs and potentials of a political party with historically established broad support, on the one hand, and a new or small political organization on the other. Georgia has not been guilty of invidious discrimination in recognizing these differences and providing different routes to the printed ballot. Sometimes the grossest discrimination can lie in treating things that are different as though they were exactly alike, a truism well illustrated in *Williams* v. *Rhodes*.

There is surely an important state interest in requiring some preliminary showing of a significant modicum of support before printing the name of a political organization's candidate on the ballot—the interest, if no other, in avoiding confusion, deception, and even frustration of the democratic process at the general election. The 5% figure is, to be sure, apparently somewhat higher than the percentage

---

25. The argument that the first alternative route is not realistically open to a candidate with unorthodox or "radical" views is hardly valid in the light of American political history. Time after time established political parties, at local, state, and national levels, have, while retaining their old labels, changed their ideological direction because of the influence and leadership of those with unorthodox or "radical" views.

of support required to be shown in many States as a condition for ballot position, but this is balanced by the fact that Georgia has imposed no arbitrary restrictions whatever upon the eligibility of any registered voter to sign as many nominating petitions as he wishes. Georgia in this case has insulated not a single potential voter from the appeal of new political voices within its borders.

The judgment is affirmed.

Mr. Justice Black and Mr. Justice Harlan concur in the result [without opinion].

Notes and Questions

1. Did *Jenness* do anything to clarify *Williams*'s holding? Are you satisfied with the Court's use of factors, rather than rules, in these cases? Is it possible to construct sensible rules for determining the constitutionality of ballot-access restrictions, or must such determinations be made on a case-by-case basis?

2. The Court explained that Georgia was not required to grant "political bodies" the automatic ballot access enjoyed by "political parties" at least in part because "political parties" were required to comply with additional burdens not faced by "political bodies." Do you believe the Constitution would allow states to require minor parties "to establish all of the elaborate statewide, county-by-county, organizational paraphernalia" that Georgia law required of "political parties"? *Cf. Eu v. San Francisco County Democratic Central Committee*, 489 U.S. 214 (1989) [p. 480]. If not, how could the state deny "political bodies" the automatic ballot position enjoyed by "political parties"? Should "political bodies" have the choice whether to establish the organizational structure of "parties" and gain the automatic ballot position that comes with that status, on the one hand, or to forego the organizational structure at the cost of having to endure the petition requirement, on the other?

3. In what circumstances might a 5% petition requirement be unconstitutional? Could a population be large enough that the number of people needed to reach 5% is unconstitutionally high *per se*? California has 19,978,449 registered voters. *See* California Secretary of State, *Odd-Numbered Year Report of Registration*, February 10, 2019, *available at* https://elections.cdn.sos.ca.gov/ror/ror-odd-year-2019 /historical-reg-stats.pdf. A 5% requirement applied to that population would mean the signatures of 998,923 people.

4. *Jenness* held that the state interest "in avoiding confusion, deception, and even frustration of the democratic process" sufficed to allow states to require "some preliminary showing of a significant modicum of support." The Court further discussed this authority in *Munro v. Socialist Workers Party*, 479 U.S. 189 (1986), in which it upheld a requirement that minor-party candidates receive 1% of the vote in

Washington's blanket primary to have their names appear on the general-election ballot. As against the claim that there had been no voter confusion necessitating such a limitation on ballot access, the Court (over a dissent by Justice Marshall, joined by Justice Brennan) responded as follows:

> To require States to prove actual voter confusion, ballot overcrowding, or the presence of frivolous candidacies as a predicate to the imposition of reasonable ballot access restrictions would invariably lead to endless court battles over the sufficiency of the "evidence" marshaled by a State to prove the predicate. Such a requirement would necessitate that a State's political system sustain some level of damage before the legislature could take corrective action. Legislatures, we think, should be permitted to respond to potential deficiencies in the electoral process with foresight rather than reactively, provided that the response is reasonable and does not significantly impinge on constitutionally protected rights.

Id. at 195–96. Is such a deferential approach appropriate?

5. Should a write-in alternative *by itself* be sufficient to insulate ballot-access restrictions from constitutional attack? *See Lubin v. Panish*, 415 U.S. 709, 719 n.5 (1974) (dictum) ("The realities of the electoral process * * * strongly suggest that 'access' via write-in votes falls far short of access in terms of having the name of the candidate on the ballot. * * * [A write-in candidate] would be forced to rest his chances solely upon those voters who would remember his name and take the affirmative step of writing it on the ballot."); *cf. U.S. Term Limits, Inc. v. Thornton*, 514 U.S. 779, 828–36 (1995) [p. 538] (holding unconstitutional a law indirectly imposing term limits by denying long-serving representatives a place on the ballot).

Bullock v. Carter

Supreme Court of the United States
405 U.S. 134, 92 S. Ct. 849, 31 L. Ed. 2d 92 (1972)

Mr. Chief Justice Burger delivered the opinion of the Court [in which Mr. Justice Douglas, Mr. Justice Brennan, Mr. Justice Stewart, Mr. Justice White, Mr. Justice Marshall, and Mr. Justice Blackmun join].

Under Texas law, a candidate must pay a filing fee as a condition to having his name placed on the ballot in a primary election. [Three candidates for different offices were denied places on the Democratic Party's primary ballots because they were unable to pay the filing fees. They challenged the constitutionality of the filing-fee requirement.] * * *

Under the Texas statute, payment of the filing fee is an absolute prerequisite to a candidate's participation in a primary election. There is no alternative procedure by which a potential candidate who is unable to pay the fee can get on the primary ballot by way of petitioning voters,[5] and write-in votes are not permitted in primary elections for public office. Any person who is willing and able to pay the filing fee and who meets the basic eligibility requirements for holding the office sought can run in a primary.

Candidates for most district, county, and precinct offices must pay their filing fee to the county executive committee of the political party conducting the primary; the committee also determines the amount of the fee. The party committee must make an estimate of the total cost of the primary and apportion it among the various candidates "as in their judgment is just and equitable." The committee's judgment is to be guided by "the importance, emolument, and term of office for which the nomination is to be made." In counties with populations of one million or more, candidates for offices of two-year terms can be assessed up to 10% of their aggregate annual salary, and candidates for offices of four-year terms can be assessed up to 15% of their aggregate annual salary. In smaller counties there are no such percentage limitations.

The record shows that the fees required of the candidates in this case are far from exceptional in their magnitude. The size of the filing fees is plainly a natural consequence of a statutory system that places the burden of financing primary elections on candidates rather than on the governmental unit, and that imposes a particularly heavy burden on candidates for local office. The filing fees required of candidates seeking nomination for state offices and offices involving statewide primaries are more closely regulated by statute and tend to be appreciably smaller. * * *

The filing-fee requirement is limited to party primary elections, but the mechanism of such elections is the creature of state legislative choice and hence is "state action" within the meaning of the Fourteenth Amendment. *Gray* v. *Sanders*, 372 U.S. 368 (1963) [p. 111]; *Nixon* v. *Herndon*, 273 U.S. 536 (1927). * * * The question presented in this case is whether a state law that prevents potential candidates for public office from seeking the nomination of their party due to their inability to pay a portion of the cost of conducting the primary election is state action that unlawfully discriminates against the candidates so excluded or the voters who wish to support them.

The threshold question to be resolved is whether the filing-fee system should be sustained if it can be shown to have some rational basis, or whether it must withstand a more rigid standard of review. * * *

The initial and direct impact of filing fees is felt by aspirants for office, rather than voters, and the Court has not heretofore attached such fundamental status to candidacy as to invoke a rigorous standard of review. However, the rights of voters

---

5. Texas law does permit the names of independent candidates to appear on the official ballot in the general election if a proper application containing a voter petition is submitted. * * * No fees are assessed against candidates in general elections.

and the rights of candidates do not lend themselves to neat separation; laws that affect candidates always have at least some theoretical, correlative effect on voters. Of course, not every limitation or incidental burden on the exercise of voting rights is subject to a stringent standard of review. Texas does not place a condition on the exercise of the right to vote, nor does it quantitatively dilute votes that have been cast. Rather, the Texas system creates barriers to candidate access to the primary ballot, thereby tending to limit the field of candidates from which voters might choose. The existence of such barriers does not of itself compel close scrutiny. In approaching candidate restrictions, it is essential to examine in a realistic light the extent and nature of their impact on voters.

Unlike a filing-fee requirement that most candidates could be expected to fulfill from their own resources or at least through modest contributions, the very size of the fees imposed under the Texas system gives it a patently exclusionary character. Many potential office seekers lacking both personal wealth and affluent backers are in every practical sense precluded from seeking the nomination of their chosen party, no matter how qualified they might be, and no matter how broad or enthusiastic their popular support. The effect of this exclusionary mechanism on voters is neither incidental nor remote. Not only are voters substantially limited in their choice of candidates, but also there is the obvious likelihood that this limitation would fall more heavily on the less affluent segment of the community, whose favorites may be unable to pay the large costs required by the Texas system. * * * Appellants do not dispute that this is endemic to the system. This disparity in voting power based on wealth cannot be described by reference to discrete and precisely defined segments of the community as is typical of inequities challenged under the Equal Protection Clause, and there are doubtless some instances of candidates representing the views of voters of modest means who are able to pay the required fee. But we would ignore reality were we not to recognize that this system falls with unequal weight on voters, as well as candidates, according to their economic status.

Because the Texas filing-fee scheme has a real and appreciable impact on the exercise of the franchise, and because this impact is related to the resources of the voters supporting a particular candidate, we conclude * * * that the laws must be "closely scrutinized" and found reasonably necessary to the accomplishment of legitimate state objectives in order to pass constitutional muster.

Appellants contend that the filing fees required by the challenged statutes are necessary both to regulate the ballot in primary elections and to provide a means for financing such elections.

The Court has recognized that a State has a legitimate interest in regulating the number of candidates on the ballot. In so doing, the State understandably and properly seeks to prevent the clogging of its election machinery, avoid voter confusion, and assure that the winner is the choice of a majority, or at least a strong plurality, of those voting, without the expense and burden of runoff elections. Although we have no way of gauging the number of candidates who might enter primaries in Texas if access to the ballot were unimpeded by the large filing fees in question here, we are bound to respect the legitimate objectives of the State in avoiding overcrowded ballots. Moreover, a State has an interest, if not a duty, to protect the integrity of its political processes from frivolous or fraudulent candidacies.

There is no escape from the conclusion that the imposition of filing fees ranging as high as $8,900 [approximately $56,000 in today's dollars — Eds.] tends to limit the number of candidates entering the primaries. However, even under conventional standards of review, a State cannot achieve its objectives by totally arbitrary means; the criterion for differing treatment must bear some relevance to the object of the legislation. To say that the filing-fee requirement tends to limit the ballot to the more serious candidates is not enough. There may well be some rational relationship between a candidate's willingness to pay a filing fee and the seriousness with which he takes his candidacy, but the candidates in this case affirmatively alleged that they were unable, not simply unwilling, to pay the assessed fees, and there was no contrary evidence. It is uncontested that the filing fees exclude legitimate as well as frivolous candidates. And even assuming that every person paying the large fees required by Texas law takes his own candidacy seriously, that does not make him a "serious candidate" in the popular sense. If the Texas fee requirement is intended to regulate the ballot by weeding out spurious candidates, it is extraordinarily ill-fitted to that goal; other means to protect those valid interests are available.

Instead of arguing for the reasonableness of the exclusion of some candidates, appellants rely on the fact that the filing-fee requirement is applicable only to party primaries, and point out that a candidate can gain a place on the ballot in the general election without payment of fees by submitting a proper application accompanied by a voter petition. Apart from the fact that the primary election may be more crucial than the general election in certain parts of Texas, we can hardly accept as reasonable an alternative that requires candidates and voters to abandon their party affiliations in order to avoid the burdens of the filing fees imposed by state law. Appellants have not demonstrated that their present filing-fee scheme is a necessary or reasonable tool for regulating the ballot.

In addition to the State's purported interest in regulating the ballot, the filing fees serve to relieve the State treasury of the cost of conducting the primary elections, and this is a legitimate state objective; in this limited sense it cannot be said that the fee system lacks a rational basis. But under the standard of review we consider applicable to this case, there must be a showing of necessity. * * *

We also reject the theory that since the candidates are availing themselves of the primary machinery, it is appropriate that they pay that share of the cost that they have occasioned. The force of this argument is diluted by the fact that candidates for offices requiring statewide primaries are generally assessed at a lower rate than candidates for local office, although the statewide primaries undoubtedly involve a greater expense.[29] More importantly, the costs do not arise because candidates decide to enter a primary or because the parties decide to conduct one, but because the State has, as a matter of legislative choice, directed that party primaries be held. The State has presumably chosen this course more to benefit the voters than the candidates.

Appellants seem to place reliance on the self-evident fact that if the State must assume the cost, the voters, as taxpayers, will ultimately be burdened with the expense of the primaries. But it is far too late to make out a case that the party primary is such a lesser part of the democratic process that its cost must be shifted away from the taxpayers generally. The financial burden for general elections is carried by all taxpayers and appellants have not demonstrated a valid basis for distinguishing between these two legitimate costs of the democratic process. It seems appropriate that a primary system designed to give the voters some influence at the nominating stage should spread the cost among all of the voters in an attempt to distribute the influence without regard to wealth. Viewing the myriad governmental functions supported from general revenues, it is difficult to single out any of a higher order than the conduct of elections at all levels to bring forth those persons desired by their fellow citizens to govern. Without making light of the State's interest in husbanding its revenues, we fail to see such an element of necessity in the State's present means of financing primaries as to justify the resulting incursion on the prerogatives of voters.

Since the State has failed to establish the requisite justification for this filing-fee system, we hold that it results in a denial of equal protection of the laws. It must be emphasized that nothing herein is intended to cast doubt on the validity of reasonable candidate filing fees or licensing fees in other contexts. By requiring candidates to shoulder the costs of conducting primary elections through filing fees and by providing no reasonable alternative means of access to the ballot, the State of Texas has erected a system that utilizes the criterion of ability to pay as a condition to being on the ballot, thus excluding some candidates otherwise qualified and denying an undetermined number of voters the opportunity to vote for candidates of their choice. These salient features of the Texas system are critical to our determination of constitutional invalidity.

Affirmed.

Mr. Justice Powell and Mr. Justice Rehnquist took no part in the consideration or decision of this case.

---

29. This would be a different case if the fees approximated the cost of processing a candidate's application for a place on the ballot, a cost resulting from the candidate's decision to enter a primary. The term *filing* fee has long been thought to cover the cost of filing, that is, the cost of placing a particular document on the public record.

Notes and Questions

1. In *Harper v. Virginia State Board of Elections*, 383 U.S. 663, 668 (1966) [p. 17], the Court concluded that poll taxes were "irrelevant" to "one's ability to participate intelligently in the electoral process." The Court therefore held that it was unconstitutional for a state to require voters to pay poll taxes, whether the voter was too poor to afford them or simply did not want to pay. In *Carter*, however, the Court acknowledged that the fee imposed on candidates was a "rational" — though very inexact — way of assessing "the seriousness with which [a candidate] takes his candidacy." *Carter* nonetheless struck down the fee after noting that "the candidates in this case affirmatively alleged that they were unable, not simply unwilling, to pay the assessed fees." Should that fact have made a difference?

2. *Problem.* A state statute requires each candidate for certain offices to pay a filing fee to participate in primary elections or to run as a write-in candidate at the general election. No candidate may win election unless he or she has paid the fee. The fee is 2% of the salary of the office sought. Sharon wants to run for County Supervisor, but is unable to pay the filing fee, which is $4300. Is the requirement constitutional? What if the statute required payment of the filing fee as a prerequisite to appearing on the ballot, but one could be a write-in candidate without paying the fee? What if potential candidates were permitted to obtain a certain number of signatures on a petition in lieu of paying the fee? *See Lubin v. Panish*, 415 U.S. 709 (1974).

3. If, in *Carter*, there had been no statute requiring a fee, and the parties themselves decided to impose an assessment on persons running for their endorsement, would such an assessment be unconstitutional? Is such a situation in fact any different from the one in *Carter* itself?

4. Would it be constitutional to impose a fee to seek a nomination in a party *caucus or convention*? Would it be constitutional for a state to *forbid* a party from imposing a fee on a candidate seeking a nomination in a party caucus or convention?

5. *Problem.* In order to appear on the general-election ballot, minor party candidates in Pencilonia must submit petitions with a number of signatures equal to two percent of the number of votes received by any elected candidate for statewide office in the most recent election (which has usually meant 20,000–25,000 signatures). Major-party candidates, by contrast, must compete in primary elections, which they can do by filing a certain number of signatures—two thousand for President, United States senator, and governor, or one thousand for state treasurer, auditor general, and attorney general.

In Pencilonia, the judiciary oversees challenges to the validity of minor-party candidates' petition signatures. (In all other states, such challenges are handled by an administrative agency in the executive branch.) In the event of a challenge, the court will require the challenger and the candidate to provide workers to review the signatures. Based on that review, the challenger and the candidate stipulate to the validity or invalidity of as many signatures as possible, and the court resolves any remaining disputes. The court may award costs "as it shall deem just," and some courts in recent years have required candidates to pay challengers' costs (totaling as much as $80,000) in cases where there has been extensive fraud and deception in gathering signatures.

Minor parties and candidates challenge the law, arguing that it places an unconstitutional burden on their ability to run for office, and on voters' correlative right to vote for them. They argue that the costs associated with defending their signatures are significant deterrents to running for office, and the threat of having to pay for challengers' costs is an even stronger deterrent. The state responds that the law is distinguishable from *Bullock v. Carter* in that there is no mandatory fee and candidates can avoid having to pay challengers' costs simply by not submitting improper signatures. Is it unconstitutional to force minor parties to defend their signatures in court?

Storer v. Brown

Supreme Court of the United States
415 U.S. 724, 94 S. Ct. 1274, 39 L. Ed. 2d 714 (1974)

Mr. Justice White delivered the opinion of the Court [in which Mr. Chief Justice Burger, Mr. Justice Stewart, Mr. Justice Blackmun, Mr. Justice Powell, and Mr. Justice Rehnquist join].

The California Elections Code forbids ballot position to an independent candidate for elective public office if he voted in the immediately preceding primary, §6830(c), or if he had a registered affiliation with a qualified political party at any time within one year prior to the immediately preceding primary election. §6830(d). * * *

Prior to the 1972 elections, appellants [including two independent candidates for Congress, Storer and Frommhagen, who had left the Democratic Party within a year of the 1972 primary elections] filed their actions to have the above sections of the Elections Code declared unconstitutional and their enforcement enjoined. * * *

A three-judge District Court concluded that the statutes served a sufficiently important state interest to sustain their constitutionality and dismissed the complaints. * * * We affirm[.] * * *

In challenging §6830(d), appellants rely on *Williams* v. *Rhodes* [393 U.S. 23 (1968)] [p. 495] and assert that under that case and subsequent cases dealing with exclusionary voting and candidate qualifications, *e.g., Dunn* v. *Blumstein*, 405 U.S. 330 (1972) [p. 74]; *Bullock* v. *Carter*, 405 U.S. 134 (1972) [p. 507]; *Kramer* v. *Union Free School District*, 395 U.S. 621 (1969) [p. 46], substantial burdens on the right to vote or to associate for political purposes are constitutionally suspect and invalid under the First and Fourteenth Amendments and under the Equal Protection Clause unless essential to serve a compelling state interest. These cases, however, do not necessarily condemn §6830(d). It has never been suggested that the *Williams-Kramer-Dunn* rule automatically invalidates every substantial restriction on the right to vote or to associate. Nor could this be the case under our Constitution where the States are given the initial task of determining the qualifications of voters who will elect members of Congress. Art. I, § 2, cl. 1. Also Art. I, § 4, cl. 1, authorizes the States to prescribe "the Times, Places and Manner of holding Elections for Senators and Representatives." Moreover, as a practical matter, there must be a substantial regulation of elections if they are to be fair and honest and if some sort of order, rather than chaos, is to accompany the democratic processes. In any event, the States have evolved comprehensive, and in many respects complex, election codes regulating in most substantial ways, with respect to both federal and state elections, the time, place, and manner of holding primary and general elections, the registration and qualifications of voters, and the selection and qualification of candidates.

It is very unlikely that all or even a large portion of the state election laws would fail to pass muster under our cases; and the rule fashioned by the Court to pass on constitutional challenges to specific provisions of election laws provides no litmus-paper test for separating those restrictions that are valid from those that are invidious under the Equal Protection Clause. The rule is not self-executing and is no substitute for the hard judgments that must be made. Decision in this context, as in others, is very much a "matter of degree," *Dunn* v. *Blumstein, supra,* at 348, very much a matter of "consider[ing] the facts and circumstances behind the law, the interests which the State claims to be protecting, and the interests of those who are disadvantaged by the classification." *Williams* v. *Rhodes, supra,* at 30; *Dunn* v. *Blumstein, supra,* at 335. What the result of this process will be in any specific case may be very difficult to predict with great assurance. * * *

[W]e have no hesitation in sustaining § 6830(d). In California, the independent candidacy route to obtaining ballot position is but a part of the candidate-nominating process, an alternative to being nominated in one of the direct party primaries. The independent candidate need not stand for primary election but must qualify for the ballot by demonstrating substantial public support in another way. Otherwise, the qualifications required of the independent candidate are very similar to, or identical with, those imposed on party candidates. Section 6401 imposes a flat disqualification upon any candidate seeking to run in a party primary if he has been "registered as affiliated with a political party other than that political party the nomination of which he seeks within 12 months immediately prior to the filing of the declaration." Moreover, §§ 6402 and 6611 provide that a candidate who has been defeated in a party primary may not be nominated as an independent or be a candidate of any other party; and no person may file nomination papers for a party nomination and an independent nomination for the same office, or for more than one office at the same election.

The requirement that the independent candidate not have been affiliated with a political party for a year before the primary is expressive of a general state policy aimed at maintaining the integrity of the various routes to the ballot. It involves no discrimination against independents. * * *

* * * The direct party primary in California is not merely an exercise or warm-up for the general election but an integral part of the entire election process, the initial stage in a two-stage process by which the people choose their public officers. It functions to winnow out and finally reject all but the chosen candidates. The State's general policy is to have contending forces within the party employ the primary campaign and primary election to finally settle their differences. The general election ballot is reserved for major struggles; it is not a forum for continuing intraparty feuds. The provision against defeated primary candidates running as independents effectuates this aim, the visible result being to prevent the losers from continuing the struggle and to limit the names on the ballot to those who have won the primaries and those independents who have properly qualified. The people, it is hoped, are presented with understandable choices and the winner in the general election with sufficient support to govern effectively.

Section 6830(d) carries very similar credentials. It protects the direct primary process by refusing to recognize independent candidates who do not make early plans to leave a party and take the alternative course to the ballot. It works against independent candidacies prompted by short-range political goals, pique, or personal quarrel. It is also a substantial barrier to a party fielding an "independent" candidate to capture and bleed off votes in the general election that might well go to another party.

A State need not take the course California has, but California apparently believes with the Founding Fathers that splintered parties and unrestrained factionalism may do significant damage to the fabric of government. See The Federalist, No. 10 (Madison). It appears obvious to us that the one-year disaffiliation provision furthers the State's interest in the stability of its political system. We also consider that interest as not only permissible, but compelling and as outweighing the interest the candidate and his supporters may have in making a late rather than an early decision to seek independent ballot status. Nor do we have reason for concluding that the device California chose, § 6830(d), was not an essential part of its overall mechanism to achieve its acceptable goals. [T]he Constitution does not require the State to choose ineffectual means to achieve its aims. To conclude otherwise might sacrifice the political stability of the system of the State, with profound consequences for the entire citizenry, merely in the interest of particular candidates and their supporters having instantaneous access to the ballot.

We conclude that § 6830(d) is not unconstitutional, and Storer and Frommhagen were properly barred from the ballot as a result of its application. * * *

[*Affirmed.*]

MR. JUSTICE BRENNAN, with whom MR. JUSTICE DOUGLAS and MR. JUSTICE MARSHALL concur, dissenting. * * *

The California statute absolutely denies ballot position to independent candidates who, at any time within 12 months prior to the immediately preceding primary election, were registered as affiliated with a qualified political party. Intertwined with [California's requirement that] primary elections [] be held five months before the general election, § 6830(d) plainly places a significant burden upon independent candidacy—and therefore effectively burdens as well the rights of potential supporters and voters to associate for political purposes and to vote—because potential independent candidates, currently affiliated with a recognized party, are required to take affirmative action toward candidacy fully *17 months* before the general election. Thus, such candidates must make that decision at a time when, as a matter of the realities of our political system, they cannot know either who will be the nominees of the major parties, or what the significant election issues may be. * * *

The Court acknowledges the burdens imposed by § 6830(d) upon fundamental personal liberties, but agrees with the State's assertion that the burdens are justified by the State's compelling interest in the stability of its political system. Without § 6830(d), the argument runs, the party's primary system, an integral part of the election process, is capable of subversion by a candidate who first opts to participate in that method of ballot access, and later abandons the party and its candidate-selection process, taking with him his party supporters. Thus, in sustaining the validity of § 6830(d), the Court finds compelling the State's interests in preventing splintered parties and unrestricted factionalism and protecting the direct-primary system.

But the identification of these compelling state interests, which I accept, does not end the inquiry. There remains the necessity of determining whether these vital state objectives "cannot be served equally well in significantly less burdensome ways." * * *

I have searched in vain for even the slightest evidence in the records of these cases of any effort on the part of the State to demonstrate the absence of reasonably less burdensome means of achieving its objectives. This crucial failure cannot be remedied by the Court's conjecture that other means "*might* sacrifice the political stability of the system of the State" (emphasis added). When state legislation burdens fundamental constitutional rights, as conceded here, we are not at liberty to speculate that the State might be able to demonstrate the absence of less burdensome means; the burden of affirmatively demonstrating this is upon the State.

Moreover, less drastic means—which would not require the State to give appellants "instantaneous access to the ballot"—seem plainly available to achieve California's objectives. First, requiring party disaffiliation 12 months before the primary elections is unreasonable on its face. There is no evidence that splintering and factionalism of political parties will result unless disaffiliation is effected that far in advance of the primaries. To the contrary, whatever threat may exist to party stability is more likely to surface only shortly before the primary, when the identities of the potential field of candidates and issues become known. Thus, the State's interests would be adequately served and the rights of the appellants less burdened if the date when disaffiliation must be effected were set significantly closer to the primaries. Second, the requirement of party disaffiliation could be limited to those independent candidates who actually run in a party primary. Section 6830(d) sweeps far too broadly in its application to potential independent candidates who, though registered as affiliated with a recognized party, do not run for the party's nomination. Such an independent candidate plainly poses no threat of utilizing the party machinery to run in the primary, and then declaring independent candidacy, thereby splitting the party. * * *

Anderson v. Celebrezze

Supreme Court of the United States
460 U.S. 780, 103 S. Ct. 1564, 75 L. Ed. 2d 547 (1983)

Justice Stevens delivered the opinion of the Court [in which Chief Justice Burger, Justice Brennan, Justice Marshall, and Justice Blackmun join].

On April 24, 1980, petitioner John Anderson announced that he was an independent candidate for the office of President of the United States. * * * On May 16, 1980, Anderson's supporters tendered a nominating petition containing approximately 14,500 signatures and a statement of candidacy to respondent Celebrezze, the Ohio Secretary of State. These documents would have entitled Anderson to a place on the ballot if they had been filed on or before March 20, 1980. Respondent refused to accept the petition solely because it had not been filed within the time required by § 3513.257 of the Ohio Revised Code.{2} Three days later Anderson and three voters * * * commenced this action * * *, challenging the constitutionality of Ohio's early filing deadline for independent candidates. The District Court granted petitioners' motion for summary judgment and ordered respondent to place Anderson's name on the general election ballot. * * *

[The Court of Appeals reversed, but t]he election was held while the appeal was pending. In Ohio Anderson received 254,472 votes, or 5.9 percent of the votes cast; nationally, he received 5,720,060 votes or approximately 6.6 percent of the total. * * *

After a date toward the end of March, even if intervening events create unanticipated political opportunities, no independent candidate may enter the Presidential race and seek to place his name on the Ohio general election ballot. Thus the direct impact of Ohio's early filing deadline falls upon aspirants for office. Nevertheless, as we have recognized, "the rights of voters and the rights of candidates do not lend themselves to neat separation; laws that affect candidates always have at least some theoretical, correlative effect on voters." Bullock v. Carter, 405 U.S. 134, 143 (1972) [p. 507]. Our primary concern is with the tendency of ballot access restrictions "to limit the field of candidates from which voters might choose." Therefore,

---

2. Anderson's name had been entered in the Republican primary in Ohio and 26 other States before he made his decision to run as an independent, and he actually competed unsuccessfully in nine Republican primaries. Nevertheless, the parties agree that his timely withdrawal from the Ohio primary avoided the application of the State's "sore loser" statute, which disqualifies a candidate who ran unsuccessfully in a party primary from running as an independent in the general election.

"[i]n approaching candidate restrictions, it is essential to examine in a realistic light the extent and nature of their impact on voters." *Ibid.*

The impact of candidate eligibility requirements on voters implicates basic constitutional rights.[7] * * * The right to vote is "heavily burdened" if that vote may be cast only for major-party candidates at a time when other parties or other candidates are "clamoring for a place on the ballot." The exclusion of candidates also burdens voters' freedom of association, because an election campaign is an effective platform for the expression of views on the issues of the day, and a candidate serves as a rallying-point for like-minded citizens.

Although these rights of voters are fundamental, not all restrictions imposed by the States on candidates' eligibility for the ballot impose constitutionally-suspect burdens on voters' rights to associate or to choose among candidates. We have recognized that, "as a practical matter, there must be a substantial regulation of elections if they are to be fair and honest and if some sort of order, rather than chaos, is to accompany the democratic processes." *Storer* v. *Brown*, 415 U.S. 724, 730 (1974) [p. 513]. To achieve these necessary objectives, States have enacted comprehensive and sometimes complex election codes. Each provision of these schemes, whether it governs the registration and qualifications of voters, the selection and eligibility of candidates, or the voting process itself, inevitably affects—at least to some degree—the individual's right to vote and his right to associate with others for political ends. Nevertheless, the State's important regulatory interests are generally sufficient to justify reasonable, nondiscriminatory restrictions.

Constitutional challenges to specific provisions of a State's election laws therefore cannot be resolved by any "litmus-paper test" that will separate valid from invalid restrictions. Instead, a court must * * * first consider the character and magnitude of the asserted injury to the rights protected by the First and Fourteenth Amendments that the plaintiff seeks to vindicate. It then must identify and evaluate the precise interests put forward by the State as justifications for the burden imposed by its rule. In passing judgment, the Court must not only determine the legitimacy and strength of each of those interests; it also must consider the extent to which those interests make it necessary to burden the plaintiff's rights. Only after weighing all these factors is the reviewing court in a position to decide whether the challenged provision is unconstitutional. The results of this evaluation will not be automatic; as we have recognized, there is "no substitute for the hard judgments that must be made."

---

7. In this case, we base our conclusions directly on the First and Fourteenth Amendments and do not engage in a separate Equal Protection Clause analysis. We rely, however, on the analysis in a number of our prior election cases resting on the Equal Protection Clause of the Fourteenth Amendment. These cases, applying the "fundamental rights" strand of equal protection analysis, have identified the First and Fourteenth Amendment rights implicated by restrictions on the eligibility of voters and candidates, and have considered the degree to which the State's restrictions further legitimate state interests.

An early filing deadline may have a substantial impact on independent-minded voters. In election campaigns, particularly those which are national in scope, the candidates and the issues simply do not remain static over time. Various candidates rise and fall in popularity; domestic and international developments bring new issues to center stage and may affect voters' assessments of national problems. Such developments will certainly affect the strategies of candidates who have already entered the race; they may also create opportunities for new candidacies. Yet Ohio's filing deadline prevents persons who wish to be independent candidates from entering the significant political arena established in the State by a Presidential election campaign — and creating new political coalitions of Ohio voters — at any time after mid-to-late March. At this point developments in campaigns for the major-party nominations have only begun, and the major parties will not adopt their nominees and platforms for another five months. Candidates and supporters within the major parties thus have the political advantage of continued flexibility; for independents, the inflexibility imposed by the March filing deadline is a correlative disadvantage because of the competitive nature of the electoral process.

If the State's filing deadline were later in the year, a newly-emergent independent candidate could serve as the focal point for a grouping of Ohio voters who decide, after mid-March, that they are dissatisfied with the choices within the two major parties. As we recognized in *Williams* v. *Rhodes*, 393 U.S. [23], 33 [(1968)] [p. 495], "[s]ince the principal policies of the major parties change to some extent from year to year, and since the identity of the likely major party nominees may not be known until shortly before the election, this disaffected 'group' will rarely if ever be a cohesive or identifiable group until a few months before the election." Indeed, several important third-party candidacies in American history were launched after the two major parties staked out their positions and selected their nominees at national conventions during the summer. But under § 3513.257, a late-emerging Presidential candidate outside the major parties, whose positions on the issues could command widespread community support, is excluded from the Ohio general election ballot.
* * *

It is clear, then, that the March filing deadline places a particular burden on an identifiable segment of Ohio's independent-minded voters. * * * A burden that falls unequally on new or small political parties or on independent candidates impinges, by its very nature, on associational choices protected by the First Amendment. It discriminates against those candidates and — of particular importance — against those voters whose political preferences lie outside the existing political parties. By limiting the opportunities of independent-minded voters to associate in the electoral arena to enhance their political effectiveness as a group, such restrictions threaten to reduce diversity and competition in the marketplace of ideas. Historically political figures outside the two major parties have been fertile sources of new ideas and new programs; many of their challenges to the status quo have in time made their way into the political mainstream. In short, the primary values protected by the First Amendment — "a profound national commitment to the principle that debate on public issues should be uninhibited, robust, and wide-open," *New York Times Co. v. Sullivan*, 376 U.S. 254, 270 (1964) — are served when election campaigns are not monopolized by the existing political parties. * * *

The State identifies three separate interests that it seeks to further by its early filing deadline for independent Presidential candidates: voter education, equal treatment for partisan and independent candidates, and political stability. * * *

There can be no question about the legitimacy of the State's interest in fostering informed and educated expressions of the popular will in a general election. * * * We are persuaded, however, that the State's important and legitimate interest in voter education does not justify the specific restriction on participation in a Presidential election that is at issue in this case.

* * * [T]oday even trivial details about national candidates are instantaneously communicated nationwide in both verbal and visual form[, and] the vast majority of the electorate not only is literate but is informed on a day-to-day basis about events and issues that affect election choices and about the ever-changing popularity of individual candidates. In the modern world it is somewhat unrealistic to suggest that it takes more than seven months to inform the electorate about the qualifications of a particular candidate simply because he lacks a partisan label. * * *

We also find no merit in the State's claim that the early filing deadline serves the interest of treating all candidates alike. It is true that a candidate participating in a primary election must declare his candidacy on the same date as an independent. But both the burdens and the benefits of the respective requirements are materially different, and the reasons for requiring early filing for a primary candidate are inapplicable to independent candidates in the general election.

The consequences of failing to meet the statutory deadline are entirely different for party primary participants and independents. The name of the nominees of the Democratic and Republican parties will appear on the Ohio ballot in November even if they did not decide to run until after Ohio's March deadline had passed, but the independent is simply denied a position on the ballot if he waits too long. Thus, under Ohio's scheme, the major parties may include all events preceding their national conventions in the calculus that produces their respective nominees and campaign platforms, but the independent's judgment must be based on a history that ends in March. The early filing deadline for a candidate in a party's primary election is adequately justified by administrative concerns. Seventy-five days appears to be a reasonable time for processing the documents submitted by candidates and preparing the ballot. The primary date itself must be set sufficiently in advance of the general election; furthermore, a Presidential preference primary must precede the national convention, which is regularly held during the summer. Finally, the successful participant in a party primary generally acquires the automatic support of an experienced political organization; in the Presidential contest, he obtains the support of convention delegates.

Neither the administrative justification nor the benefit of an early filing deadline is applicable to an independent candidate. Ohio does not suggest that the March deadline is necessary to allow petition signatures to be counted and verified or to permit November general election ballots to be printed. In addition, the early deadline does not correspond to a potential benefit for the independent, as it does for the party candidate. After filing his statement of candidacy, the independent does not participate in a structured intraparty contest to determine who will receive organizational support; he must develop support by other means. In short, "equal treatment" of partisan and independent candidates simply is not achieved by imposing the March filing deadline on both. As we have written, "[s]ometimes the grossest discrimination can lie in treating things that are different as though they were exactly alike." *Jenness* v. *Fortson*, 403 U.S. 431, 442 (1971) [p. 503]. * * *

Ohio's asserted interest in political stability amounts to a desire to protect existing political parties from competition — competition for campaign workers, voter support, and other campaign resources — generated by independent candidates who have previously been affiliated with the party. * * * [But] protecting the Republican and Democratic parties from external competition cannot justify the virtual exclusion of other political aspirants from the political arena. * * *

[T]he early filing deadline is not precisely drawn to protect the parties from "intraparty feuding," whatever legitimacy that state goal may have in a Presidential election. If the deadline is designed to keep intraparty competition within the party structure, its coverage is both too broad and too narrow. It is true that in this case § 3513.257 was applied to a candidate who had previously competed in party primaries and then sought to run as an independent. But the early deadline applies broadly to independent candidates who have not been affiliated in the recent past with any political party. On the other hand, as long as the decision to run is made before the March deadline, Ohio does not prohibit independent candidacies by persons formerly affiliated with a political party, or currently participating in intraparty competition in other States — regardless of the effect on the political party structure. * * *

We began our inquiry by noting that our primary concern is not the interest of candidate Anderson, but rather, the interests of the voters who chose to associate together to express their support for Anderson's candidacy and the views he espoused. Under any realistic appraisal, the "extent and nature" of the burdens Ohio has placed on the voters' freedom of choice and freedom of association, in an election of nationwide importance, unquestionably outweigh the State's minimal interest in imposing a March deadline.

The judgment of the Court of Appeals is

Reversed.

Justice Rehnquist, with whom Justice White, Justice Powell, and Justice O'Connor join, dissenting. * * *

On the record before us, the effect of the Ohio filing deadline is quite easily summarized: it requires that a candidate, who has already decided to run for President, decide by March 20 which route his candidacy will take. He can become a nonparty candidate by filing a nominating petition with 5,000 signatures and assure himself a place on the general election ballot. Or, he can become a party candidate and take his chances in securing a position on the general election ballot by seeking the nomination of a party's national convention. Anderson chose the latter route and submitted in a timely fashion his nominating petition for Ohio's Republican Primary. Then, realizing that he had no chance for the Republican nomination, Anderson sought to change the form of this candidacy. The Ohio filing deadline prevented him from making this change. Quite clearly, rather than prohibiting him from seeking the Presidency, the filing deadline only prevented Anderson from having two shots at it in the same election year. * * *

Underlying the Court's entire opinion is the idea that "independent candidates" are treated differently than candidates fielded by the "major parties." But this observation is no more productive than comparing apples and oranges and wondering at the difference between them.

[A]ny political party, major, minor, or otherwise, can qualify for a position on Ohio's general election ballot and have that position held open until later in the election year. * * * The Court suggests that if such a procedure is so important for political parties, then followers of a particular candidate should also have more time. This argument simply does not wash. Any group of like-minded voters, if they are of sufficient numbers, is free to form a political party and ensure more time in selecting a candidate to express their views. But followers of a particular candidate need no time to find such a representative; they are organized around that candidate. Such followers have no real organized existence in the absence of that particular candidate. * * *

* * * The Court's opinion draws no line; I presume that a State must wait until all party nominees are chosen and then allow all unsuccessful party candidates to refight their party battles by forming an "independent" candidacy. I find nothing in the Constitution which requires this result. * * *

Notes and Questions

1. Can *Anderson* be squared with *Jenness v. Fortson* and *Storer v. Brown*?

2. Did the Court's opinion imply that ballot-access restrictions would be evaluated under heightened scrutiny whether third parties and major parties were subject to the same or different rules?

3. Beyond its immediate ramifications for ballot access, *Anderson* has become important for establishing the approach used by the Court to evaluate the constitutionality of laws that burden voting. *See Burdick v. Takushi*, 504 U.S. 428, 433–34 (1992) [p. 990]; *Crawford v. Marion County Election Board*, 553 U.S. 181, 189–90

& n.8 (2008) [p. 999] (opinion of Stevens, J.); *id.* at 210–11 (Souter, J., dissenting). But while *Anderson* is much cited, it provides precious little guidance about how to decide cases. Professor Dan Lowenstein has suggested that *Anderson* represents "a sort of antidoctrine. It calls for judges to consider all of the factors that bear on a particular problem, giving each due weight under the particular circumstances." Daniel H. Lowenstein, *The Supreme Court Has No Theory of Politics — and Be Thankful for Small Favors, in* The U.S. Supreme Court and the Electoral Process 283, 295 (David K. Ryden ed., 2d ed. 2002). *See also Daunt v. Benson*, 956 F.3d 396, 424 (6th Cir. 2020) (Readler, J., concurring in the judgment) ("*Anderson-Burdick* is a dangerous tool. In sensitive policy-oriented cases, it affords far too much discretion to judges in resolving the dispute before them."); Edward B. Foley, *Voting Rules and Constitutional Law*, 81 Geo. Wash. L. Rev. 1836, 1859 (2013) (noting that *Anderson*'s test is "imprecise" and subject to differing application in the hands of different judges). Do you agree?

4. According to *Anderson*, "discriminatory" restrictions disadvantaging independent candidates trigger strict scrutiny as a matter of First Amendment law — not just as a matter of equal protection. *See* footnote 7. But as the *Anderson* dissent made clear, what one person views as discrimination, another may view as equity. Additionally, even where it is conceded that a regulation acts unequally on different people, reasonable arguments can often be constructed about whether such distinctions are justified. *Cf. Michael M. v. Superior Court*, 450 U.S. 464 (1981) (concluding that it was constitutional to distinguish between the sexes in the punishment of statutory rape). Indeed, as the Court in *Anderson* noted, the Constitution may *require* different treatment for groups that are in different circumstances. Do you believe Ohio treated independent candidates differently from party candidates? Do you think such treatment was appropriate?

5. *Problem.* Illinois requires independent candidates to obtain the signatures of 25,000 qualified voters and requires the submission of those signatures 134 days before the election — an earlier deadline than is imposed by every other state except Texas and Arizona. Are the two requirements constitutional when considered cumulatively? Is either requirement unconstitutional standing alone?

6. *Problem.* Independents wishing to appear on Hawaii's presidential-election ballot must obtain the signatures of 1% of the number of votes cast in the last presidential election. To form a new party, however, supporters must obtain signatures from only 0.1% of the state's registered voters. Is the disparity justified as compensating for earlier filing deadlines and primaries that party candidates must face? *See Nader v. Cronin*, 624 F.3d 1214 (9th Cir. 2010); *Peroutka v. Cronin*, 179 P.3d 1050 (Haw. 2008). What if the state required more signatures from supporters of the new party than from independent candidates? *See Green Party of Arkansas v. Daniels*, 445 F. Supp. 2d 1056 (D. Ark. 2006).

7. *Problem.* Ballots often contain information about candidates beside their names. Such information may include a candidate's party affiliation, current occupation, and status as an incumbent or challenger. States often limit the sort of

information that can appear on a ballot, however. Consider the following limitations. Do they unconstitutionally interfere with the right to vote?

A. Arkanzona permits each candidate to designate his or her political party affiliation, but only if the candidate is affiliated with a "recognized party." Recognized parties are those that polled at least 5% in the last gubernatorial election or that have filed a petition signed by registered voters numbering at least 1% of the number of voters in the last gubernatorial election. Candidates belonging to unrecognized parties and those belonging to no party must leave the space for party designation blank. The limitation is challenged by a candidate unaffiliated with a party who wishes to be identified as "Independent." *See Rosen v. Brown*, 970 F.2d 169 (6th Cir. 1992).

B. Bostonia permits candidates to designate their affiliations with "recognized parties," defined as in Arkanzona. Candidates who are unaffiliated, as well as candidates who are affiliated with an unrecognized party, are designated on the ballot as "Independent." The law is challenged by a candidate who is a member of an unrecognized party who wishes to have the ballot designate the name of his party. *See Schrader v. Blackwell*, 241 F.3d 783 (6th Cir. 2001); *Dart v. Brown*, 717 F.2d 1491 (5th Cir. 1983).

C. Connifornia permits candidates to designate their current occupations, but does not permit ballots to display "status" designations, except that incumbents may identify themselves as such. Charlie Candidate wishes to have the ballot identify him as a "peace activist." The state refuses to permit such a designation, citing the vagueness of the term and the potential for voter confusion. *See Rubin v. City of Santa Monica*, 308 F.3d 1008 (9th Cir. 2002).

8. *Problem.* West Vermont holds closed primaries, in which each party's primary is restricted to members of that party (subject to the requirement of *Tashjian v. Republican Party of Connecticut*, 479 U.S. 208 (1986) [p. 443], that parties have the option to invite independents to participate"). The state, however, imposes a deadline on persons wishing to register with a party. All such registrations must be filed at least thirty days before the general election, and take effect only after the election. (Exceptions are made, however, for those legally incapable of registering by the deadline, such as new residents and persons turning eighteen between the deadline and the election.) Thus, a person wishing to vote in the 2024 primary must register with that party no later than early October 2023. The state defends this deadline as justified by the interest in preventing party raiding. Is it constitutional? Should the deadline be evaluated under strict scrutiny? *See Rosario v. Rockefeller*, 410 U.S. 752 (1973).

What if the state forbids participation in a primary unless the voter refrains from participating in a different party's primary for the preceding twenty-three months? *See Kusper v. Pontikes*, 414 U.S. 51 (1973).

9. *Problem.* New York Election Law §§ 5-304(2) and 5-304(3) provide that a registered voter wishing to establish or change membership in a political party must do so at least twenty-five days before the general election to be eligible to vote in the following year's primary election. Sections 5-201(1) and 5-201(3), however, establish that a person *not* registered to vote may vote in the primary if he registers and joins a party as late as twenty-five days before the primary election itself. The state justifies the law on the ground that it encourages non-registered voters to register, without severely burdening the rights of voters who were already registered. Does the statutory scheme violate the Equal Protection Clause or the First Amendment rights of registered voters? Should a court apply strict or rational-basis scrutiny? *See Van Wie v. Pataki*, 87 F. Supp. 2d 148 (N.D.N.Y. 2000), *vacated as moot* 267 F.3d 109 (2d Cir. 2001).

10. In North Carolina, groups that wish to qualify as new parties and to have their nominees appear on the ballot must submit petitions by May 17 signed by 2% of the number of voters who voted for governor in the last election. In *Pisano v. Strech*, 743 F.3d 927 (4th Cir. 2014), the Fourth Circuit upheld North Carolina's May 17 petition deadline against a challenge that it unconstitutionally interfered with minor parties' ability to nominate presidential candidates. The court noted that the deadline left the parties with plenty of time—three and one-half years—in which to gather the signatures. Minor parties complained, arguing that the deadline was significantly in advance of the time when the major parties would choose their presidential nominees at their conventions in August and September. Accordingly, argued the minor parties, it was difficult to gather the signatures at such an early date because the public was not yet paying attention to politics. The court rejected this argument, explaining that North Carolina's deadline occurred *after* that state's primary, and so there was plenty of opportunity for the minor parties to take advantage of the citizens' political awareness during primary season.

11. Are constitutional rights implicated by the *ordering* of names on the ballot? Due to a phenomenon known as the "primacy effect," candidates listed first on a ballot have an advantage over later-listed candidates. If a state's law provides that ballot order will be determined by the votes that each party received in the previous gubernatorial election, does such a law violate the rights of candidates who are not the nominee of the governor's party? Does it violate the rights of third-party candidates who may not have any realistic chance of ever winning the governorship? *See Jacobson v. Lee*, 411 F. Supp. 3d 1249 (N.D. Fla. 2019) (holding the practice unconstitutional), *vacated for want of standing sub nom. Jacobson v. Florida Secretary of State*, 957 F.3d 1193 (11th Cir. 2020); *McLain v. Meier*, 637 F.2d 1159, 1165–67 (8th Cir. 1980) (striking down a similar law awarding preferential ballot position to the successful party in the previous congressional election).

What if a state gives preferential ballot position based on incumbency or seniority? *See Mann v. Powell*, 314 F. Supp. 677 (N.D. Ill. 1969), *aff'd*, 398 U.S. 955 (1970) (striking down such a law); *Netsch v. Lewis*, 344 F. Supp. 1280 (N.D. Ill.

1972) (same); *Gould v. Grubb*, 536 P.2d 1337 (Cal. 1975) (same); *Holtzman v. Power*, 313 N.Y.S.2d 904 (N.Y. Sup. Ct. 1970) (same). What if ballot position is determined by alphabetical order? *See Akins v. Secretary of State*, 904 A.2d 702 (N.H. 2006) (striking down such a law). *See also Sangmeister v. Woodard*, 565 F.2d 460 (7th Cir. 1977) (holding unconstitutional county clerks' practice of giving favorable ballot position to their own parties); Brett M. Pugach, *The County Line: The Law and Politics of Ballot Positioning in New Jersey*, 72 RUTGERS L. REV. __ (forthcoming 2020) (arguing that New Jersey's system of giving favorable ballot position to candidates endorsed by county party committees is unconstitutional).

12. One critical basis of disagreement concerning laws affecting third parties is the purpose served by their candidacies. Should minor parties have a First Amendment right of ballot access so they might "expand and affect political debate"? *Munro v. Socialist Workers Party*, 479 U.S. 189, 202 (1986) (Marshall, J., dissenting). *See also Williams v. Rhodes*, 393 U.S. 23, 39 (1968) [p. 495] (Douglas, J., concurring) (quoting *Sweezy v. New Hampshire*, 354 U.S. 234, 250–51 (1957) (opinion of Warren, C.J.)). Or should we think of the ballot as strictly a means to determine winners of elections? These questions have been in the background of the cases we have encountered so far. The next case brings them to the foreground.

Timmons v. Twin Cities Area New Party

Supreme Court of the United States
520 U.S. 351, 117 S. Ct. 1364, 137 L. Ed. 2d 589 (1997)

CHIEF JUSTICE REHNQUIST delivered the opinion of the Court [in which JUSTICE O'CONNOR, JUSTICE SCALIA, JUSTICE KENNEDY, JUSTICE THOMAS, and JUSTICE BREYER join].

Most States prohibit multiple-party, or "fusion," candidacies for elected office.[1] The Minnesota laws challenged in this case prohibit a candidate from appearing on the ballot as the candidate of more than one party. We hold that such a prohibition does not violate the First and Fourteenth Amendments to the United States Constitution.

* * * In April 1994, Minnesota State Representative Andy Dawkins was running unopposed in the Minnesota Democratic-Farmer-Labor Party's (DFL) primary. That same month, New Party members chose Dawkins as their candidate for the same office in the November 1994 general election. Neither Dawkins nor the DFL objected, and Dawkins signed the required affidavit of candidacy for the New Party. Minnesota, however, prohibits fusion candidacies. Because Dawkins had already filed as a candidate for the DFL's nomination, local election officials refused to accept the New Party's nominating petition.

---

1. "Fusion," also called "cross-filing" or "multiple-party nomination," is * * * "the nomination by more than one political party of the same candidate for the same office in the same general election."

The New Party filed suit in United States District Court, contending that Minnesota's antifusion laws violated the Party's associational rights under the First and Fourteenth Amendments. The District Court granted summary judgment for the state defendants * * *. The Court of Appeals reversed. * * * We granted certiorari, and now reverse.

Fusion was a regular feature of Gilded Age American politics * * * in part because political parties, rather than local or state governments, printed and distributed their own ballots. These ballots contained only the names of a particular party's candidates, and so a voter could drop his party's ticket in the ballot box without even knowing that his party's candidates were supported by other parties as well. But after the 1888 presidential election, which was widely regarded as having been plagued by fraud, many States moved to the "Australian ballot system." Under that system, an official ballot, containing the names of all the candidates legally nominated by all the parties, was printed at public expense and distributed by public officials at polling places. By 1896, use of the Australian ballot was widespread. During the same period, many States enacted other election-related reforms, including bans on fusion candidacies. Minnesota banned fusion in 1901. This trend has continued and, in this century, fusion has become the exception, not the rule. Today, multiple-party candidacies are permitted in just a few States, and fusion plays a significant role only in New York.

The First Amendment protects the right of citizens to associate and to form political parties for the advancement of common political goals and ideas. As a result, political parties' government, structure, and activities enjoy constitutional protection. On the other hand, it is also clear that States may, and inevitably must, enact reasonable regulations of parties, elections, and ballots to reduce election- and campaign-related disorder. * * *

When deciding whether a state election law violates First and Fourteenth Amendment associational rights, we weigh the "character and magnitude" of the burden the State's rule imposes on those rights against the interests the State contends justify that burden, and consider the extent to which the State's concerns make the burden necessary. *Burdick* [v. *Takushi*, 504 U.S. 428], 434 [(1992)] [p. 990] (quoting *Anderson* v. *Celebrezze*, 460 U.S. 780, 789 (1983) [p. 517]). Regulations imposing severe burdens on plaintiffs' rights must be narrowly tailored and advance a compelling state interest. Lesser burdens, however, trigger less exacting review, and a State's "important regulatory interests" will usually be enough to justify "reasonable, nondiscriminatory restrictions." *Burdick*, *supra*, at 434 (quoting *Anderson*, *supra*, at 788). No bright line separates permissible election-related regulation from unconstitutional infringements on First Amendment freedoms.

The New Party's claim that it has a right to select its own candidate is uncontroversial, so far as it goes. That is, the New Party, and not someone else, has the right to select the New Party's "standard bearer." It does not follow, though, that a party is absolutely entitled to have its nominee appear on the ballot as that party's candidate. A particular candidate might be ineligible for office, unwilling to serve, or, as here, another party's candidate. That a particular individual may not appear on the ballot as a particular party's candidate does not severely burden that party's associational rights.

* * * The ban, which applies to major and minor parties alike, simply precludes one party's candidate from appearing on the ballot, as that party's candidate, if already nominated by another party. Respondent is free to try to convince Representative Dawkins to be the New Party's, not the DFL's, candidate. Whether the Party still wants to endorse a candidate who, because of the fusion ban, will not appear on the ballot as the Party's candidate, is up to the Party. * * *

The Court of Appeals emphasized its belief that, without fusion-based alliances, minor parties cannot thrive. This is a predictive judgment which is by no means self-evident. But, more importantly, the supposed benefits of fusion to minor parties do not require that Minnesota permit it. Many features of our political system—e.g., single-member districts, "first past the post" elections, and the high costs of campaigning—make it difficult for third parties to succeed in American politics. But the Constitution does not require States to permit fusion any more than it requires them to move to proportional-representation elections or public financing of campaigns. * * *

It is true that Minnesota's fusion ban prevents the New Party from using the ballot to communicate to the public that it supports a particular candidate who is already another party's candidate. In addition, the ban shuts off one possible avenue a party might use to send a message to its preferred *candidate* because, with fusion, a candidate who wins an election on the basis of two parties' votes will likely know more—if the parties' votes are counted separately—about the particular wishes and ideals of his constituency. We are unpersuaded, however, by the Party's contention that it has a right to use the ballot itself to send a particularized message, to its candidate and to the voters, about the nature of its support for the candidate. Ballots serve primarily to elect candidates, not as forums for political expression. See *Burdick*, 504 U.S., at 438; *id.*, at 445 (KENNEDY, J., dissenting). Like all parties in Minnesota, the New Party is able to use the ballot to communicate information about itself and its candidate to the voters, so long as that candidate is not already someone else's candidate. The Party retains great latitude in its ability to communicate ideas to voters and candidates through its participation in the campaign, and Party members may campaign for, endorse, and vote for their preferred candidate even if he is listed on the ballot as another party's candidate.

In sum, Minnesota's laws do not restrict the ability of the New Party and its members to endorse, support, or vote for anyone they like. The laws do not directly limit the Party's access to the ballot. They are silent on parties' internal structure, governance, and policymaking. Instead, these provisions reduce the universe of potential candidates who may appear on the ballot as the Party's nominee only by ruling out those few individuals who both have already agreed to be another party's candidate and also, if forced to choose, themselves prefer that other party. They also limit, slightly, the Party's ability to send a message to the voters and to its preferred candidates. We conclude that the burdens Minnesota imposes on the Party's First and Fourteenth Amendment associational rights—though not trivial—are not severe. * * *

* * * [Accordingly], the State's asserted regulatory interests need only be "sufficiently weighty to justify the limitation" imposed on the Party's rights. * * * Minnesota argues here that its fusion ban is justified by its interests in avoiding voter confusion, promoting candidate competition (by reserving limited ballot space for opposing candidates), preventing electoral distortions and ballot manipulations, and discouraging party splintering and "unrestrained factionalism."

States certainly have an interest in protecting the integrity, fairness, and efficiency of their ballots and election processes as means for electing public officials. Petitioners contend that a candidate or party could easily exploit fusion as a way of associating his or its name with popular slogans and catchphrases. For example, members of a major party could decide that a powerful way of "sending a message" via the ballot would be for various factions of that party to nominate the major party's candidate as the candidate for the newly-formed "No New Taxes," "Conserve Our Environment," and "Stop Crime Now" parties. In response, an opposing major party would likely instruct its factions to nominate that party's candidate as the "Fiscal Responsibility," "Healthy Planet," and "Safe Streets" parties' candidate.

Whether or not the putative "fusion" candidates' names appeared on one or four ballot lines, such maneuvering would undermine the ballot's purpose by transforming it from a means of choosing candidates to a billboard for political advertising. The New Party responds to this concern, ironically enough, by insisting that the State could avoid such manipulation by adopting more demanding ballot-access standards rather than prohibiting multiple-party nomination. However, as we stated above, because the burdens the fusion ban imposes on the Party's associational rights are not severe, the State need not narrowly tailor the means it chooses to promote ballot integrity. The Constitution does not require that Minnesota compromise the policy choices embodied in its ballot-access requirements to accommodate the New Party's fusion strategy.

Relatedly, petitioners urge that permitting fusion would undercut Minnesota's ballot-access regime by allowing minor parties to capitalize on the popularity of another party's candidate, rather than on their own appeal to the voters, in order to secure access to the ballot. That is, voters who might not sign a minor party's nominating petition based on the party's own views and candidates might do so if they viewed the minor party as just another way of nominating the same person nominated by one of the major parties. Thus, Minnesota fears that fusion would enable minor parties, by nominating a major party's candidate, to bootstrap their way to major-party status in the next election and circumvent the State's nominating-petition requirement for minor parties. The State surely has a valid interest in making sure that minor and third parties who are granted access to the ballot are bona fide and actually supported, on their own merits, by those who have provided the statutorily required petition or ballot support.

States also have a strong interest in the stability of their political systems. This interest does not permit a State to completely insulate the two-party system from minor parties' or independent candidates' competition and influence, nor is it a paternalistic license for States to protect political parties from the consequences of their own internal disagreements. That said, the States' interest permits them to enact reasonable election regulations that may, in practice, favor the traditional two-party system, and that temper the destabilizing effects of party-splintering and excessive factionalism. The Constitution permits the Minnesota Legislature to decide that political stability is best served through a healthy two-party system. And while an interest in securing the perceived benefits of a stable two-party system will not justify unreasonably exclusionary restrictions, States need not remove all of the many hurdles third parties face in the American political arena today. * * *

We conclude that the burdens Minnesota's fusion ban imposes on the New Party's associational rights are justified by "correspondingly weighty" valid state interests in ballot integrity and political stability.[13] In deciding that Minnesota's fusion ban does not unconstitutionally burden the New Party's First and Fourteenth Amendment rights, we express no views on the New Party's policy-based arguments concerning the wisdom of fusion. It may well be that, as support for new political parties increases, these arguments will carry the day in some States' legislatures. But the Constitution does not require Minnesota, and the approximately 40 other States that do not permit fusion, to allow it. The judgment of the Court of Appeals is reversed.

It is so ordered.

JUSTICE STEVENS, with whom JUSTICE GINSBURG joins, and with whom JUSTICE SOUTER joins as to Parts I and II, dissenting. * * *

The Court's conclusion that the Minnesota statute prohibiting multiple-party candidacies is constitutional rests on three dubious premises: (1) that the statute imposes only a minor burden on the Party's right to choose and to support the candidate of its choice; (2) that the statute significantly serves the State's asserted interests in avoiding ballot manipulation and factionalism; and (3) that, in any event, the interest in preserving the two-party system justifies the imposition of the burden at issue in this case. I disagree with each of these premises.

---

13. * * * [The] supposed interest [in "avoiding voter confusion"] * * * plays no part in our analysis today.

I

The members of a recognized political party unquestionably have a constitutional right to select their nominees for public office and to communicate the identity of their nominees to the voting public. Both the right to choose and the right to advise voters of that choice are entitled to the highest respect.

The Minnesota statutes place a significant burden on both of those rights. The Court's recital of burdens that the statute does not inflict on the Party does nothing to minimize the severity of the burdens that it does impose. The fact that the Party may nominate its second choice surely does not diminish the significance of a restriction that denies it the right to have the name of its first choice appear on the ballot. Nor does the point that it may use some of its limited resources to publicize the fact that its first choice is the nominee of some other party provide an adequate substitute for the message that is conveyed to every person who actually votes when a party's nominees appear on the ballot.

As to the first point, the State contends that the fusion ban in fact limits by only a few candidates the range of individuals a party may nominate, and that the burden is therefore quite small. But the *number* of candidates removed from the Party's reach cannot be the determinative factor. The ban leaves the Party free to nominate any eligible candidate except the particular "standard bearer who best represents the party's ideologies and preferences." *Eu v. San Francisco County Democratic Central Comm.*, 489 U.S. 214, 224 (1989) [p. 480].

The Party could perhaps choose to expend its resources supporting a candidate who was not in fact the best representative of its members' views. But a party's choice of a candidate is the most effective way in which that party can communicate to the voters what the party represents and, thereby, attract voter interest and support.[1] * * *

The State next argues that—instead of nominating a second-choice candidate—the Party could remove itself from the ballot altogether, and publicly endorse the candidate of another party. But the right to be on the election ballot is precisely what separates a political party from any other interest group. The Court relies on the fact that the New Party remains free "to spread its message to all who will

---

1. The burden on the Party's right to nominate its first-choice candidate, by limiting the Party's ability to convey through its nominee what the Party represents, risks impinging on another core element of any political party's associational rights—the right to "broaden the base of public participation in and support for its activities." *Tashjian* v. *Republican Party of Conn.*, 479 U.S. 208, 214 (1986) [p. 443]. * * * A fusion ban burdens the right of a minor party to broaden its base of support because of the political reality that the dominance of the major parties frequently makes a vote for a minor party or independent candidate a "wasted" vote. When minor parties can nominate a candidate also nominated by a major party, they are able to present their members with an opportunity to cast a vote for a candidate who will actually be elected. Although this aspect of a party's effort to broaden support is distinct from the ability to nominate the candidate who best represents the party's views, it is important to note that the party's right to broaden the base of its support is burdened in both ways by the fusion ban.

listen," through fora other than the ballot. Given the limited resources available to most minor parties, and the less-than-universal interest in the messages of third parties, it is apparent that the Party's message will, in this manner, reach a much smaller audience than that composed of all voters who can read the ballot in the polling booth.

The majority rejects as unimportant the limits that the fusion ban may impose on the Party's ability to express its political views, relying on our decision in *Burdick* v. *Takushi*, in which we noted that "the purpose of casting, counting, and recording votes is to elect public officials, not to serve as a general forum for political expression." But * * * [o]ur conclusion that the ballot is not principally a forum for the individual expression of political sentiment through the casting of a vote does not justify the conclusion that the ballot serves no expressive purpose for the parties who place candidates on the ballot. Indeed, the long-recognized right to choose a "standard bearer who best represents the party's ideologies and preferences," *Eu*, 489 U.S., at 224, is inescapably an expressive right. * * *

II

Minnesota argues that the statutory restriction on the New Party's right to nominate the candidate of its choice is justified by the State's interests in avoiding voter confusion, preventing ballot clutter and manipulation, encouraging candidate competition, and minimizing intraparty factionalism. None of these rationales can support the fusion ban because the State has failed to explain how the ban actually serves the asserted interests.

I believe that the law significantly abridges First Amendment freedoms and that the State therefore must shoulder a correspondingly heavy burden of justification if the law is to survive judicial scrutiny. But even accepting the majority's view that the burdens imposed by the law are not weighty, the State's asserted interests must at least bear some plausible relationship to the burdens it places on political parties. * * *

* * * The possibility that members of the major parties will begin to create dozens of minor parties with detailed, issue-oriented titles for the sole purpose of nominating candidates under those titles is entirely hypothetical. * * * If the State wants to make it more difficult for any group to achieve the legal status of being a political party, it can do so within reason and still not run up against the First Amendment. * * * But once the State has established a standard for achieving party status, forbidding an acknowledged party from putting on the ballot its chosen candidate clearly frustrates core associational rights.

The State argues that the fusion ban promotes political stability by preventing intraparty factionalism and party raiding. States do certainly have an interest in maintaining a stable political system. But the State has not convincingly articulated how the fusion ban will prevent the factionalism it fears. * * * Indeed, the activity banned by Minnesota's law is the formation of coalitions, not the division and dissension of "splintered parties and unrestrained factionalism."

As for the State's argument that the fusion ban encourages candidate competition, this claim treats "candidates" as fungible goods, ignoring entirely each party's interest in nominating not just any candidate, but the candidate who best represents the party's views. Minnesota's fusion ban simply cannot be justified with reference to this or any of the above-mentioned rationales. I turn, therefore, to what appears to be the true basis for the Court's holding—the interest in preserving the two-party system.

III

* * * In most States, perhaps in all, there are two and only two major political parties. It is not surprising, therefore, that most States have enacted election laws that impose burdens on the development and growth of third parties. The law at issue in this case is undeniably such a law. The fact that the law was both intended to disadvantage minor parties and has had that effect is a matter that should weigh against, rather than in favor of, its constitutionality. * * *

Nothing in the Constitution prohibits the States from maintaining single-member districts with winner-take-all voting arrangements. And these elements of an election system do make it significantly more difficult for third parties to thrive. But these laws are different in two respects from the fusion bans at issue here. First, the method by which they hamper third-party development is not one that impinges on the associational rights of those third parties; minor parties remain free to nominate candidates of their choice, and to rally support for those candidates. The small parties' relatively limited likelihood of ultimate success on election day does not deprive them of the right to try. Second, the establishment of single-member districts correlates directly with the States' interests in political stability. Systems of proportional representation, for example, may tend toward factionalism and fragile coalitions that diminish legislative effectiveness. In the context of fusion candidacies, the risks to political stability are extremely attenuated. * * *

In some respects, the fusion candidacy is the best marriage of the virtues of the minor party challenge to entrenched viewpoints and the political stability that the two-party system provides. The fusion candidacy does not threaten to divide the legislature and create significant risks of factionalism, which is the principal risk proponents of the two-party system point to. But it does provide a means by which voters with viewpoints not adequately represented by the platforms of the two major parties can indicate to a particular candidate that—in addition to his support for the major party views—he should be responsive to the views of the minor party whose support for him was demonstrated where political parties demonstrate support—on the ballot. * * *

* * * I respectfully dissent.

JUSTICE SOUTER, dissenting.

I join parts I and II of JUSTICE STEVENS's dissent, agreeing as I do that none of the concerns advanced by the State suffices to justify the burden of the challenged statutes on petitioners' First Amendment interests. * * *

I am, however, unwilling to go the further distance of considering and rejecting the majority's "preservation of the two-party system" rationale. For while Minnesota has made no such argument before us, I cannot discount the possibility of a forceful one. There is considerable consensus that party loyalty among American voters has declined significantly in the past four decades, and that the overall influence of the parties in the political process has decreased considerably. In the wake of such studies, it may not be unreasonable to infer that the two-party system is in some jeopardy.

Surely the majority is right that States "have a strong interest in the stability of their political systems," that is, in preserving a political system capable of governing effectively. If it could be shown that the disappearance of the two-party system would undermine that interest, and that permitting fusion candidacies poses a substantial threat to the two-party scheme, there might well be a sufficient predicate for recognizing the constitutionality of the state action presented by this case. Right now, however, no State has attempted even to make this argument, and I would therefore leave its consideration for another day.

Notes and Questions

1. The greatest impediment to minor parties' electoral success is not ballot access. Rather, the prevalence in American jurisdictions of the plurality-winner, first-past-the-post system of elections all but ensures that over the long-term two parties representing views close to the political center will dominate. We discuss alternative election systems in Chapter 10, § E(2). For present purposes, it suffices to note that systems exist that would make it easier for minorities (including ideological minorities) to achieve representation in legislatures.

In light of the importance of vote-counting systems to third-party electoral chances, should courts be suspicious of states' decisions to adopt plurality-winner systems? Should an understanding of alternative voting structures affect courts' review of ballot-access restrictions?

2. Is a ban on fusion "nondiscriminatory," given that a candidate forced to choose between nominations of a major party and a minor party would be unlikely to choose the latter? The Court noted that Minnesota's ban "applie[d] to major and minor parties alike," but was this a situation where "the grossest discrimination can lie in treating things that are different as though they were exactly alike"? *Jenness v. Fortson*, 403 U.S. 431, 442 (1971) [p. 503].

3. Is the preservation of the two-party system a compelling interest? Is it a legitimate interest? If party loyalty weakened to the point where the two-party system were in "jeopardy" (to use Justice Souter's language), would that argue for upholding or striking down state laws designed to perpetuate the two-party system?

4. *Problem.* Maryland permits minor parties to nominate candidates for certain lower-court judgeships by whatever process is permitted by the parties' by-laws. Major parties must nominate candidates by running a primary election. When the Libertarian Party holds a meeting and nominates a candidate who is a member of the Democratic Party, the state refuses to certify the general-election ballot with the candidate listed as the nominee of the Libertarian Party. In the view of the state, the candidate evaded the law's demand that major-party candidates be nominated through a primary election. Does the refusal to certify the ballot violate the Libertarian Party's right to nominate a candidate of its choosing, given that the candidate was perfectly willing to accept the nomination? *See Ademiluyi v. Egbuonu*, 215 A.3d 329 (Md. 2019).

5. *Timmons* upheld a law limiting candidates to appearing on the ballot as the nominee of only one party. May states forbid candidates from appearing on the ballot for more than one *office*? Kentucky and Florida currently have such a law, *see* Fla. Stat. § 99.012; Ky. Rev. Stat. Ann. § 118.405, but it is relatively common for candidates to run for multiple offices. For example, Joe Biden was simultaneously elected to the vice presidency and reelected to the U.S. Senate in 2008, and Paul Ryan, who attempted to unseat Biden in 2012, was reelected to the House of Representatives despite losing his vice-presidential bid. Several states appear to have followed Texas's lead after the Lone Star State amended its law in 1960 to allow Lyndon Johnson to pursue the vice presidency and reelection to the U.S. Senate.

Should the government have the power to bar multiple candidacies? For example, should a state have the power to prohibit a state senator from simultaneously pursuing reelection and the governorship? Could it prohibit a sitting judge from simultaneously running for reelection and pursuing a higher judicial office? Could it prohibit a district attorney from simultaneously running for reelection and seeking to become a judge? Aside from the constitutional question, are such bans good policy?

C. Ballot Design, Term Limits, and Indirect Election Manipulation

In the last section, we explored ballot-access rules that made certain election outcomes (*e.g.*, the election of major-party candidates and therefore the maintenance of the two-party system) more likely. The ballot itself can also influence election outcomes. By choosing which information to include on ballots and how to present that information, government can encourage voters to focus on certain issues or characteristics, which may cause voters to choose certain candidates over others, or to vote differently on ballot questions. This section addresses the ability of the government to use the ballot to focus voters' attention in certain ways, most particularly with regard to the issue of candidates' support for term limits. We begin with a case that demonstrates very clearly that a ballot design that is neutral on its face can be employed to manipulate election results.

Anderson v. Martin

Supreme Court of the United States
375 U.S. 399, 84 S. Ct. 454, 11 L. Ed. 2d 430 (1964)

MR. JUSTICE CLARK delivered the opinion of the Court [in which MR. CHIEF JUSTICE WARREN, MR. JUSTICE BLACK, MR. JUSTICE DOUGLAS, MR. JUSTICE HARLAN, MR. JUSTICE BRENNAN, MR. JUSTICE STEWART, MR. JUSTICE WHITE, and MR. JUSTICE GOLDBERG join].

Louisiana Revised Statutes § 18:1174.1 provides that in all primary, general or special elections, the nomination papers and ballots shall designate the race of candidates for elective office. The question involved in this appeal is whether this requirement violates the Equal Protection and Due Process Clauses of the Fourteenth Amendment or the Fifteenth Amendment to the Constitution of the United States. * * *

At the outset it is well that we point out what this case does not involve. It has nothing whatever to do with the right of a citizen to cast his vote for whomever he chooses and for whatever reason he pleases or to receive all information concerning a candidate which is necessary to a proper exercise of his franchise. It has to do only with the right of a State to require or encourage its voters to discriminate upon the grounds of race. In the abstract, Louisiana imposes no restriction upon anyone's candidacy nor upon an elector's choice in the casting of his ballot. But by placing at racial label on a candidate at the most crucial stage in the electoral process—the instant before the vote is cast—the State furnishes a vehicle by which racial prejudice may be so aroused as to operate against one group because of race and for another. This is true because by directing the citizen's attention to the single consideration of race or color, the State indicates that a candidate's race or color is an important—perhaps paramount—consideration in the citizen's choice, which may decisively influence the citizen to cast his ballot along racial lines. Hence in a State or voting district where Negroes predominate, that race is likely to be favored by a racial designation on the ballot, while in those communities where other races are in the majority, they may be preferred. The vice lies not in the resulting injury but in the placing of the power of the State behind a racial classification that induces racial prejudice at the polls.

* * * Prior to [1960] the primary election ballot contained no information on the candidates other than their names; nor did the general election ballot, which only grouped the named candidates according to their respective political party. The 1960 amendment added "race" as the single item of information other than the name of the candidate. This addition to the statute in the light of "private attitudes and pressures" towards Negroes at the time of its enactment could only result in that "repressive effect" which "was brought to bear only after the exercise of governmental power." *Bates* v. *Little Rock*, 361 U.S. 516, 524 (1960).

Nor can the attacked provision be deemed to be reasonably designed to meet legitimate governmental interests in informing the electorate as to candidates. We see no relevance in the State's pointing up the race of the candidate as bearing upon his qualifications for office. Indeed, this factor in itself "underscores the purely racial character and purpose" of the statute. *Goss* v. *Board of Education*, 373 U.S. 683, 688 (1963).

The State contends that its Act is nondiscriminatory because the labeling provision applies equally to Negro and white. Obviously, Louisiana may not bar Negro citizens from offering themselves as candidates for public office, nor can it encourage its citizens to vote for a candidate solely on account of race. And that which cannot be done by express statutory prohibition cannot be done by indirection. Therefore, we view the alleged equality as superficial. Race is the factor upon which the statute operates and its involvement promotes the ultimate discrimination which is sufficient to make it invalid. *Goss* v. *Board of Education, supra*, at 688. The judgment is therefore

Reversed.

Notes and Questions

1. What was the holding of *Anderson*? Was the law unconstitutional because it "furnishe[d] a vehicle" for "arous[ing]" racial prejudice? But if it was not unconstitutional for voters to base their votes on racial prejudice, how could it be unconstitutional to "furnish[] a vehicle" for race-based voting? Cf. *Terry v. Adams*, 345 U.S. 461, 469 (1953) [p. 423] (opinion of Black, J.) ("For a state to permit * * * a duplication of its election processes [by an organization engaged in racial discrimination] is to permit a flagrant abuse of those processes to defeat the purposes of the Fifteenth Amendment."); *Shelley v. Kraemer*, 334 U.S. 1 (1948) (holding that judicial enforcement of racially restrictive real-estate covenants violates the Equal Protection Clause).

Should *Anderson* apply outside the racial context? If the state chose to include any other piece of information on the ballot—for example, incumbency status, current profession, party affiliation, age, county of residence, sex—would the result be different? If so, what would explain the difference?

2. Alternatively, was the problem in *Anderson* that race was the *only* characteristic highlighted on the ballot? The Court noted multiple times that race was the single characteristic that Louisiana chose to emphasize, signaling to the voters that it was especially important. Would it be constitutional for a ballot to indicate a candidate's race among several other pieces of information?

3. The Court noted that a candidate's status as a racial minority would be perceived as an advantage in some communities and as a disadvantage in others (although the Court specifically noted the anti-black prejudices common in Louisiana at the time). If a ballot made mention of a candidate's sex or race as a way of

promoting the candidacies of minorities or women, would that make a difference? Stated differently, how much does *Anderson* depend on assumptions about the purpose of the Louisiana legislature?

4. The Court asserted that actions "which cannot be done by express statutory prohibition cannot be done by indirection." In other words, Louisiana was constitutionally prohibited from barring blacks from public office, so it could not rig an election system to make it harder for blacks to win elections. But what are the limits of such a principle? Surely the government cannot reserve public offices for members of the major parties, but is it also unconstitutional for the government to adopt electoral rules, such as single-member-district elections and restrictive ballot-access laws, that achieve the same result "by indirection"?

––––––––––

The Constitution requires that members of the House of Representatives and of the Senate be at least twenty-five and thirty years old, respectively; citizens of the United States for seven and nine years, respectively; and inhabitants of the states from which they are elected. U.S. Const. art. I, § 2, cl. 2 (House); art. I, § 3, cl. 3 (Senate). For decades, states have added qualifications, including term limits, to those requirements. Throughout the twentieth century, federal and state courts routinely struck down these additional requirements. *See U.S. Term Limits, Inc. v. Thornton*, 514 U.S. 779, 798–800 (1995) (listing cases). The issue resurfaced in the 1990s and was resolved by the Supreme Court in the next case.

U.S. Term Limits, Inc. v. Thornton
Supreme Court of the United States
514 U.S. 779, 115 S. Ct. 1842, 131 L. Ed. 2d 881 (1995)

JUSTICE STEVENS delivered the opinion of the Court [in which JUSTICE KENNEDY, JUSTICE SOUTER, JUSTICE GINSBURG, and JUSTICE BREYER join]. * * *

At the general election on November 3, 1992, the voters of Arkansas adopted Amendment 73 to their State Constitution. Proposed as a "Term Limitation Amendment," its preamble stated:

> "The people of Arkansas find and declare that elected officials who remain in office too long become preoccupied with reelection and ignore their duties as representatives of the people. Entrenched incumbency has reduced voter participation and has led to an electoral system that is less free, less competitive, and less representative than the system established by the Founding Fathers. Therefore, the people of Arkansas, exercising their reserved powers, herein limit the terms of elected officials."

* * * Section 3 [of Amendment 73] applies to the Arkansas Congressional Delegation. It provides:

> "(a) Any person having been elected to three or more terms as a member of the United States House of Representatives from Arkansas shall not be

certified as a candidate and shall not be eligible to have his/her name placed on the ballot for election to the United States House of Representatives from Arkansas.

"(b) Any person having been elected to two or more terms as a member of the United States Senate from Arkansas shall not be certified as a candidate and shall not be eligible to have his/her name placed on the ballot for election to the United States Senate from Arkansas." * * *

[T]he constitutionality of Amendment 73 depends critically on the resolution of two distinct issues. The first is whether the Constitution forbids States to add to or alter the qualifications specifically enumerated in the Constitution. The second is, if the Constitution does so forbid, whether the fact that Amendment 73 is formulated as a ballot access restriction rather than as an outright disqualification is of constitutional significance. Our resolution of these issues draws upon our prior resolution of a related but distinct issue: whether Congress has the power to add to or alter the qualifications of its Members.

Twenty-six years ago, in *Powell* v. *McCormack*, 395 U.S. 486 (1969), we reviewed the history and text of the Qualifications Clauses in a case involving an attempted exclusion of a duly elected Member of Congress. The principal issue was whether the power granted to each House in Art. I, §5, cl. 1, to judge the "Qualifications of its own Members" includes the power to impose qualifications other than those set forth in the text of the Constitution. In an opinion by Chief Justice Warren for eight Members of the Court, we held that it does not. * * * We * * * conclude now, as we did in *Powell*, that history shows that, with respect to Congress, the Framers intended the Constitution to establish fixed qualifications. * * *

In *Powell*, of course, we did not rely solely on an analysis of the historical evidence, but instead complemented that analysis with "an examination of the basic principles of our democratic system." We noted that allowing Congress to impose additional qualifications would violate that "fundamental principle of our representative democracy . . . 'that the people should choose whom they please to govern them.'"

Our opinion made clear that this broad principle incorporated at least two fundamental ideas.[10] First, we emphasized the egalitarian concept that the opportunity to be elected was open to all. We noted in particular Madison's statement in The Federalist that "[u]nder these reasonable limitations [enumerated in the Constitution], the door of this part of the federal government is open to merit of every description, whether native or adoptive, whether young or old, and without regard to poverty or wealth, or to any particular profession of religious faith." *Powell*, 395 U.S., at 540, n.74, quoting The Federalist No. 52, at 326 [(C. Rossiter ed. 1961)]. Similarly, we

---

10. The principle also incorporated the more practical concern that reposing the power to adopt qualifications in Congress would lead to a self-perpetuating body to the detriment of the new Republic.

noted that Wilson Carey Nicholas defended the Constitution against the charge that it "violated democratic principles" by arguing: "It has ever been considered a great security to liberty, that very few should be excluded from the right of being chosen to the legislature. This Constitution has amply attended to this idea. We find no qualifications required except those of age and residence."

Second, we recognized the critical postulate that sovereignty is vested in the people, and that sovereignty confers on the people the right to choose freely their representatives to the National Government. * * * Thus, in *Powell*, we agreed * * * "[t]hat the right of the electors to be represented by men of their own choice, was so essential for the preservation of all their other rights, that it ought to be considered as one of the most sacred parts of our constitution." * * *

Our reaffirmation of *Powell* does not necessarily resolve the specific questions presented in these cases. For petitioners argue that whatever the constitutionality of additional qualifications for membership imposed by Congress, the historical and textual materials discussed in *Powell* do not support the conclusion that the Constitution prohibits additional qualifications imposed by States. In the absence of such a constitutional prohibition, petitioners argue, the Tenth Amendment and the principle of reserved powers require that States be allowed to add such qualifications. * * * We disagree for two independent reasons. First, we conclude that the power to add qualifications is not within the "original powers" of the States, and thus is not reserved to the States by the Tenth Amendment. Second, even if States possessed some original power in this area, we conclude that the Framers intended the Constitution to be the exclusive source of qualifications for Members of Congress, and that the Framers thereby "divested" States of any power to add qualifications. * * *

Contrary to petitioners' assertions, the power to add qualifications is not part of the original powers of sovereignty that the Tenth Amendment reserved to the States. Petitioners' Tenth Amendment argument misconceives the nature of the right at issue because that Amendment could only "reserve" that which existed before. As Justice Story recognized [in his *Commentaries on the Constitution of the United States*], "the states can exercise no powers whatsoever, which exclusively spring out of the existence of the national government, which the constitution does not delegate to them. . . . No state can say, that it has reserved, what it never possessed." [1 J. Story, Commentaries on the Constitution of the United States § 627 (3d ed. 1858).] * * *

With respect to setting qualifications for service in Congress, no such right existed before the Constitution was ratified. * * * [E]lecting representatives to the National Legislature was a new right, arising from the Constitution itself. The Tenth Amendment thus provides no basis for concluding that the States possess reserved power to add qualifications to those that are fixed in the Constitution. Instead, any state power to set the qualifications for membership in Congress must derive not from the reserved powers of state sovereignty, but rather from the delegated powers of national sovereignty. In the absence of any constitutional delegation to the

States of power to add qualifications to those enumerated in the Constitution, such a power does not exist.

Even if we believed that States possessed as part of their original powers some control over congressional qualifications, the text and structure of the Constitution, the relevant historical materials, and, most importantly, the "basic principles of our democratic system" all demonstrate that the Qualifications Clauses were intended to preclude the States from exercising any such power and to fix as exclusive the qualifications in the Constitution. * * *

As we noted earlier, the *Powell* Court recognized that an egalitarian ideal — that election to the National Legislature should be open to all people of merit — provided a critical foundation for the constitutional structure. This egalitarian theme echoes throughout the constitutional debates. In The Federalist No. 57, for example, Madison wrote:

> "Who are to be the objects of popular choice? Every citizen whose merit may recommend him to the esteem and confidence of his country. *No qualification of wealth, of birth, of religious faith, or of civil profession is permitted to fetter the judgment or disappoint the inclination of the people.*" The Federalist No. 57, at 351 (emphasis added).

* * * Additional qualifications pose the same obstacle to open elections whatever their source. The egalitarian ideal, so valued by the Framers, is thus compromised to the same degree by additional qualifications imposed by States as by those imposed by Congress.

Similarly, we believe that state-imposed qualifications, as much as congressionally imposed qualifications, would undermine the second critical idea recognized in *Powell*: that an aspect of sovereignty is the right of the people to vote for whom they wish. Again, the source of the qualification is of little moment in assessing the qualification's restrictive impact.

Finally, state-imposed restrictions, unlike the congressionally imposed restrictions at issue in *Powell*, violate a third idea central to this basic principle: that the right to choose representatives belongs not to the States, but to the people. From the start, the Framers recognized that the "great and radical vice" of the Articles of Confederation was "the principle of LEGISLATION for STATES or GOVERNMENTS, in their CORPORATE or COLLECTIVE CAPACITIES, and as contradistinguished from the INDIVIDUALS of whom they consist." The Federalist No. 15, at 108 (Hamilton). Thus the Framers, in perhaps their most important contribution, conceived of a Federal Government directly responsible to the people, possessed of direct power over the people, and chosen directly, not by States, but by the people. * * *

Consistent with these views, the constitutional structure provides for a uniform salary to be paid from the national treasury, allows the States but a limited role in federal elections, and maintains strict checks on state interference with the federal election process. The Constitution also provides that the qualifications of the representatives of each State will be judged by the representatives of the entire Nation. The Constitution thus creates a uniform national body representing the interests of a single people.

Permitting individual States to formulate diverse qualifications for their representatives would result in a patchwork of state qualifications, undermining the uniformity and the national character that the Framers envisioned and sought to ensure. * * * Such a patchwork would also sever the direct link that the Framers found so critical between the National Government and the people of the United States.[32] * * *

Petitioners argue that, even if States may not add qualifications, Amendment 73 is constitutional because it is not such a qualification, and because Amendment 73 is a permissible exercise of state power to regulate the "Times, Places and Manner of holding Elections." We reject these contentions.

[Amendment 73] merely provides that certain Senators and Representatives shall not be certified as candidates and shall not have their names appear on the ballot. They may run as write-in candidates and, if elected, they may serve. Petitioners contend that only a legal bar to service creates an impermissible qualification, and that Amendment 73 is therefore consistent with the Constitution. * * *

We need not decide whether petitioners' narrow understanding of qualifications is correct because, even if it is, Amendment 73 may not stand. As we have often noted, "[c]onstitutional rights would be of little value if they could be . . . indirectly denied." *Harman* v. *Forssenius*, 380 U.S. 528, 540 (1965), quoting *Smith* v. *Allwright*, 321 U.S. 649, 664 (1944) [p. 418]. The Constitution "nullifies sophisticated as well as simple-minded modes" of infringing on constitutional protections. *Lane* v. *Wilson*, 307 U.S. 268, 275 (1939).

In our view, Amendment 73 is an indirect attempt to accomplish what the Constitution prohibits Arkansas from accomplishing directly. * * * Indeed, it cannot be seriously contended that the intent behind Amendment 73 is other than to prevent the election of incumbents. * * *

Petitioners make the related argument that Amendment 73 merely regulates the "Manner" of elections, and that the amendment is therefore a permissible exercise of state power under Article I, § 4, cl. 1 (the Elections Clause), to regulate the "Times, Places and Manner" of elections. We cannot agree. * * *

The provisions at issue in *Storer* [v. *Brown*, 415 U.S. 724 (1974)] [p. 513] and our other Elections Clause cases [such as *Burdick* v. *Takushi*, 504 U.S. 428 (1992) [p. 990],

---

32. There is little significance to the fact that Amendment 73 was adopted by a popular vote, rather than as an Act of the state legislature. In fact, none of the petitioners argues that the constitutionality of a state law would depend on the method of its adoption. This is proper, because the voters of Arkansas, in adopting Amendment 73, were acting as citizens of the State of Arkansas, and not as citizens of the National Government. The people of the State of Arkansas have no more power than does the Arkansas Legislature to supplement the qualifications for service in Congress. * * *

Munro v. Socialist Workers Party, 479 U.S. 189 (1986), and *Roudebush* v. *Hartke*, 405 U.S. 15 (1972),] were thus constitutional because they regulated election *procedures* and did not even arguably impose any substantive qualification rendering a class of potential candidates ineligible for ballot position. They served the state interest in protecting the integrity and regularity of the election process, an interest independent of any attempt to evade the constitutional prohibition against the imposition of additional qualifications for service in Congress. And they did not involve measures that exclude candidates from the ballot without reference to the candidates' support in the electoral process. Our cases upholding state regulations of election procedures thus provide little support for the contention that a state-imposed ballot access restriction is constitutional when it is undertaken for the twin goals of disadvantaging a particular class of candidates and evading the dictates of the Qualifications Clauses. * * *

The merits of term limits, or "rotation," have been the subject of debate since the formation of our Constitution, when the Framers unanimously rejected a proposal to add such limits to the Constitution. The cogent arguments on both sides of the question that were articulated during the process of ratification largely retain their force today. Over half the States have adopted measures that impose such limits on some offices either directly or indirectly, and the Nation as a whole, notably by constitutional amendment, has imposed a limit on the number of terms that the President may serve. Term limits, like any other qualification for office, unquestionably restrict the ability of voters to vote for whom they wish. On the other hand, such limits may provide for the infusion of fresh ideas and new perspectives, and may decrease the likelihood that representatives will lose touch with their constituents. It is not our province to resolve this longstanding debate.

We are, however, firmly convinced that allowing the several States to adopt term limits for congressional service would effect a fundamental change in the constitutional framework. Any such change must come not by legislation adopted either by Congress or by an individual State, but rather—as have other important changes in the electoral process—through the amendment procedures set forth in Article V. The Framers decided that the qualifications for service in the Congress of the United States be fixed in the Constitution and be uniform throughout the Nation. That decision reflects the Framers' understanding that Members of Congress are chosen by separate constituencies, but that they become, when elected, servants of the people of the United States. They are not merely delegates appointed by separate, sovereign States; they occupy offices that are integral and essential components of a single National Government. In the absence of a properly passed constitutional amendment, allowing individual States to craft their own qualifications for Congress would thus erode the structure envisioned by the Framers, a structure that was designed, in the words of the Preamble to our Constitution, to form a "more perfect Union."

The judgment is affirmed.

It is so ordered.

JUSTICE KENNEDY, concurring. * * *

Federalism was our Nation's own discovery. The Framers split the atom of sovereignty. It was the genius of their idea that our citizens would have two political capacities, one state and one federal, each protected from incursion by the other. The resulting Constitution created a legal system unprecedented in form and design, establishing two orders of government, each with its own direct relationship, its own privity, its own set of mutual rights and obligations to the people who sustain it and are governed by it. * * *

Of course, because the Framers recognized that state power and identity were essential parts of the federal balance, the Constitution is solicitous of the prerogatives of the States, even in an otherwise sovereign federal province. The Constitution uses state boundaries to fix the size of congressional delegations, Art. I, § 2, cl. 3, ensures that each State shall have at least one representative, *ibid.*, grants States certain powers over the times, places, and manner of federal elections (subject to congressional revision), Art. I, § 4, cl. 1, requires that when the President is elected by the House of Representatives, the delegations from each State have one vote, Art. II, § 1, cl. 3, and Amdt. 12, and allows States to appoint electors for the President, Art. II, § 1, cl. 2. Nothing in the Constitution or The Federalist Papers, however, supports the idea of state interference with the most basic relation between the National Government and its citizens, the selection of legislative representatives. * * *

Not the least of the incongruities in the position advanced by Arkansas is the proposition, necessary to its case, that it can burden the rights of resident voters in federal elections by reason of the manner in which they earlier had exercised it. If the majority of the voters had been successful in selecting a candidate, they would be penalized from exercising that same right in the future. Quite apart from any First Amendment concerns, see *Williams* v. *Rhodes*, 393 U.S. 23, 30 (1968) [p. 495]; *Anderson* v. *Celebrezze*, 460 U.S. 780, 786–88 (1983) [p. 517], neither the law nor federal theory allows a State to burden the exercise of federal rights in this manner. * * *

* * * There can be no doubt, if we are to respect the republican origins of the Nation and preserve its federal character, that there exists a federal right of citizenship, a relationship between the people of the Nation and their National Government, with which the States may not interfere. Because the Arkansas enactment intrudes upon this federal domain, it exceeds the boundaries of the Constitution.

JUSTICE THOMAS, with whom THE CHIEF JUSTICE [REHNQUIST], JUSTICE O'CONNOR, and JUSTICE SCALIA join, dissenting.

It is ironic that the Court bases today's decision on the right of the people to "choose whom they please to govern them." Under our Constitution, there is only one State whose people have the right to "choose whom they please" to represent

Arkansas in Congress. The Court holds, however, that neither the elected legislature of that State nor the people themselves (acting by ballot initiative) may prescribe any qualifications for those representatives. The majority therefore defends the right of the people of Arkansas to "choose whom they please to govern them" by invalidating a provision that won nearly 60% of the votes cast in a direct election and that carried every congressional district in the State.

I dissent. Nothing in the Constitution deprives the people of each State of the power to prescribe eligibility requirements for the candidates who seek to represent them in Congress. The Constitution is simply silent on this question. And where the Constitution is silent, it raises no bar to action by the States or the people.

Because the majority fundamentally misunderstands the notion of "reserved" powers, I start with some first principles. Contrary to the majority's suggestion, the people of the States need not point to any affirmative grant of power in the Constitution in order to prescribe qualifications for their representatives in Congress, or to authorize their elected state legislators to do so. * * *

* * * The Federal Government and the States * * * face different default rules: Where the Constitution is silent about the exercise of a particular power—that is, where the Constitution does not speak either expressly or by necessary implication—the Federal Government lacks that power and the States enjoy it.

These basic principles are enshrined in the Tenth Amendment, which declares that all powers neither delegated to the Federal Government nor prohibited to the States "are reserved to the States respectively, or to the people." With this careful last phrase, the Amendment avoids taking any position on the division of power between the state governments and the people of the States: It is up to the people of each State to determine which "reserved" powers their state government may exercise. But the Amendment does make clear that powers reside at the state level except where the Constitution removes them from that level. All powers that the Constitution neither delegates to the Federal Government nor prohibits to the States are controlled by the people of each State. * * *

* * * If we are to invalidate Arkansas' Amendment 73, we must point to something in the Federal Constitution that deprives the people of Arkansas of the power to enact such measures. The majority disagrees that it bears this burden. But its arguments are unpersuasive.

The majority begins by announcing an enormous and untenable limitation on the principle expressed by the Tenth Amendment. According to the majority, the States possess only those powers that the Constitution affirmatively grants to them or that they enjoyed before the Constitution was adopted; the Tenth Amendment "could only 'reserve' that which existed before." From the fact that the States had not previously enjoyed any powers over the particular institutions of the Federal Government established by the Constitution, the majority derives a rule precisely opposite to the one that the Amendment actually prescribes. * * *

The majority's essential logic is that the state governments could not "reserve" any powers that they did not control at the time the Constitution was drafted. But it was not the state governments that were doing the reserving. The Constitution derives its authority instead from the consent of *the* people of the States. Given the fundamental principle that all governmental powers stem from the people of the States, it would simply be incoherent to assert that the people of the States could not reserve any powers that they had not previously controlled. * * *

* * * Whatever one might think of the wisdom of [Amendment 73], we may not override the decision of the people of Arkansas unless something in the Federal Constitution deprives them of the power to enact such measures.

The majority settles on "the Qualifications Clauses" as the constitutional provisions that Amendment 73 violates. Because I do not read those provisions to impose any unstated prohibitions on the States, it is unnecessary for me to decide whether the majority is correct to identify Arkansas' ballot-access restriction with laws fixing true term limits or otherwise prescribing "qualifications" for congressional office. [T]he Qualifications Clauses are merely straightforward recitations of the minimum eligibility requirements that the Framers thought it essential for every Member of Congress to meet. They restrict state power only in that they prevent the States from abolishing all eligibility requirements for membership in Congress. * * *

* * * This restriction on state power reflects the fact that when the people of one State send immature, disloyal, or unknowledgeable representatives to Congress, they jeopardize not only their own interests but also the interests of the people of other States. Because Congress wields power over all the States, the people of each State need some guarantee that the legislators elected by the people of other States will meet minimum standards of competence. The Qualifications Clauses provide that guarantee: They list the requirements that the Framers considered essential to protect the competence of the National Legislature.

If the people of a State decide that they would like their representatives to possess additional qualifications, however, they have done nothing to frustrate the policy behind the Qualifications Clauses. Anyone who possesses all of the constitutional qualifications, plus some qualifications required by state law, still has all of the federal qualifications. Accordingly, the fact that the Constitution specifies certain qualifications that the Framers deemed necessary to protect the competence of the National Legislature does not imply that it strips the people of the individual States of the power to protect their own interests by adding other requirements for their own representatives. * * *

The majority responds that "a patchwork of state qualifications" would "undermin[e] the uniformity and the national character that the Framers envisioned and sought to ensure." Yet the Framers thought it perfectly consistent with the "national character" of Congress for the Senators and Representatives from each State to be chosen by the legislature or the people of that State. The majority never explains why Congress' fundamental character permits this state-centered system, but nonetheless prohibits the people of the States and their state legislatures from setting any eligibility requirements for the candidates who seek to represent them.

As for the majority's related assertion that the Framers intended qualification requirements to be uniform, this is a conclusion, not an argument. Indeed, it is a conclusion that the Qualifications Clauses themselves contradict. At the time of the framing, and for some years thereafter, the Clauses' citizenship requirements incorporated laws that varied from State to State. Thus, the Qualifications Clauses themselves made it possible that a person would be qualified to represent State A in Congress even though a similarly situated person would not be qualified to represent State B. * * *

Although the Qualifications Clauses neither state nor imply the prohibition that it finds in them, the majority infers from the Framers' "democratic principles" that the Clauses must have been generally understood to preclude the people of the States and their state legislatures from prescribing any additional qualifications for their representatives in Congress. But the majority's evidence on this point establishes only two more modest propositions: (1) the Framers did not want the Federal Constitution itself to impose a broad set of disqualifications for congressional office, and (2) the Framers did not want the Federal Congress to be able to supplement the few disqualifications that the Constitution does set forth. The logical conclusion is simply that the Framers did not want the people of the States and their state legislatures to be constrained by too many qualifications imposed at the national level. The evidence does not support the majority's more sweeping conclusion that the Framers intended to bar the people of the States and their state legislatures from adopting additional eligibility requirements to help narrow their own choices. * * *

* * * One reason why the Framers decided not to let Congress prescribe the qualifications of its own Members was that incumbents could have used this power to perpetuate themselves or their ilk in office. As Madison pointed out at the Philadelphia Convention, Members of Congress would have an obvious conflict of interest if they could determine who may run against them. But neither the people of the States nor the state legislatures would labor under the same conflict of interest when prescribing qualifications for Members of Congress, and so the Framers would have had to use a different calculus in determining whether to deprive them of this power. * * *

Congressional power over qualifications would have enabled the representatives from some States, acting collectively in the National Legislature, to prevent the people of another State from electing their preferred candidates. * * *

Yet this is simply to say that qualifications should not be set at the national level for offices whose occupants are selected at the state level. The majority never identifies the democratic principles that would have been violated if a state legislature, in the days before the Constitution was amended to provide for the direct election of Senators, had imposed some limits of its own on the field of candidates that it would consider for appointment. Likewise, the majority does not explain why democratic principles prohibit the people of a State from adopting additional eligibility require-ments to help narrow their choices among candidates seeking to represent them in the House of Representatives. Indeed, the invocation of democratic principles to invalidate Amendment 73 seems particularly difficult in the present case, because Amendment 73 remains fully within the control of the people of Arkansas. If they wanted to repeal it (despite the 20-point margin by which they enacted it less than three years ago), they could do so by a simple majority vote. * * * When the people of a State themselves decide to restrict the field of candidates whom they are willing to send to Washington as their representatives, they simply have not violated the principle that "the people should choose whom they please to govern them." * * *

It is radical enough for the majority to hold that the Constitution implicitly pre-cludes the people of the States from prescribing any eligibility requirements for the congressional candidates who seek their votes. This holding, after all, does not stop with negating the term limits that many States have seen fit to impose on their Sena-tors and Representatives.[39] Today's decision also means that no State may disqualify congressional candidates whom a court has found to be mentally incompetent, who are currently in prison, or who have past vote-fraud convictions. Likewise, after today's decision, the people of each State must leave open the possibility that they will trust someone with their vote in Congress even though they do not trust him with *a* vote in the election for Congress.

In order to invalidate § 3 of Amendment 73, however, the majority must go fur-ther. The bulk of the majority's analysis * * * addresses the issues that would be raised if Arkansas had prescribed "genuine, unadulterated, undiluted term limits." But as the parties have agreed, Amendment 73 does not actually create this kind of disqualification. It does not say that covered candidates may not serve any more terms in Congress if reelected, and it does not indirectly achieve the same result by barring those candidates from seeking reelection. It says only that if they are to win reelection, they must do so by write-in votes. * * *

The majority suggests that this does not matter, because Amendment 73 itself says that it has the purpose of "evading the requirements of the Qualifications Clauses." * * * (I am not sure why the intent behind a law should affect our analysis under the Qualifications Clauses. If a law does not in fact add to the constitutional qualifications, the mistaken expectations of the people who enacted it would not seem to affect whether it violates the alleged exclusivity of those Clauses.) In any event, inquiries into legislative intent are even more difficult than usual when the

---

39. Going into the November 1994 elections, eight States [(Colorado, Michigan, Missouri, Montana, Ohio, Oregon, South Dakota, and Utah)] had adopted "pure" term limits of one sort or another. Eight other States [(Arizona, Arkansas, California, Florida, North Dakota, Okla-homa, Washington, and Wyoming)] had enacted "ballot access" provisions triggered by long-term incumbency or multiple prior terms in Congress. In the 1994 elections, six more States—Alaska, Idaho, Maine, Massachusetts, Nebraska, and Nevada—enacted term-limit or ballot-access mea-sures, bringing to 22 the total number of States with such provisions. In 21 of these States, the mea-sures have been enacted by direct vote of the people.

legislative body whose unified intent must be determined consists of 825,162 Arkansas voters.

The majority nonetheless thinks it clear that the goal of [Amendment 73] is "to prevent the election of incumbents." * * * [But o]ne of petitioners' central arguments is that congressionally conferred advantages have artificially inflated the pre-existing electoral chances of the covered candidates, and that Amendment 73 is merely designed to level the playing field on which challengers compete with them. * * * For instance, federal law gives incumbents enormous advantages in building name recognition and good will in their home districts [citing the ability to send "franked" mail free of charge, taxpayer-funded staffs, and access to House and Senate recording studios]. At the same time that incumbent Members of Congress enjoy these in-kind benefits, Congress imposes spending and contribution limits in congressional campaigns that "can prevent challengers from spending more . . . to overcome their disadvantage in name recognition." * * *The voters of Arkansas evidently believe that incumbents would not enjoy [astonishingly high reelection rates] if electoral contests were truly fair—that is, if the government did not put its thumb on either side of the scale. The majority offers no reason to question the accuracy of this belief. Given this context, petitioners portray § 3 of Amendment 73 as an effort at the state level to offset the electoral advantages that congressional incumbents have conferred upon themselves at the federal level.

* * * [T]oday's decision reads the Qualifications Clauses to impose substantial implicit prohibitions on the States and the people of the States. I would not draw such an expansive negative inference * * *. Rather, I would read the Qualifications Clauses to do no more than what they say. I respectfully dissent.

Notes and Questions

1. Both the majority and dissenting opinions in *U.S. Term Limits* spent a considerable amount of time discussing democratic principles to place their legal analyses in context. Einer Elhauge, in his article *Are Term Limits Undemocratic?*, 64 U. CHI. L. REV. 83 (1997), revisited those principles and confronted the apparent paradox that the same voters who frequently support term limits nonetheless also frequently vote to keep incumbent officeholders. There is no contradiction, Elhauge argued, because voters who—at least sometimes—wish to oust incumbents (keeping with the ethos of term limits) face a collective-action problem. Any individual political jurisdiction that has term limits is at a disadvantage to jurisdictions that do not, since the latter keep seniority and other political advantages for their incumbents. In contrast, he suggested, the justification for the more established term limits for Presidents, governors, and mayors may reflect the need to deal with high barriers of political entry to run for such positions. He concluded that these rationales provided the better reasons to find term limits to be prodemocratic. How persuasive are Elhauge's arguments? Do they provide a better basis to support term limits at the state (and sub-state) level than at the federal level, or vice-versa?

2. The majority in *U.S. Term Limits* took pains to distinguish "procedural" regulations that protect the "integrity and regularity of the election process" from "substantive" restrictions such as those enacted by Arkansas. In other contexts, the Supreme Court has upheld various state-imposed ballot-access qualifications, including ones that fell more onerously on independent candidates than on major-party candidates. *See, e.g., Storer v. Brown*, 415 U.S. 724 (1974) [p. 513] (upholding provisions of California law that made independent candidates ineligible for placement on the general-election ballot if they had been members of an existing political party in the past primary season). Could these and similar state restrictions be attacked under *U.S. Term Limits*, at least for elections to federal offices? In *Campbell v. Davidson*, 233 F.3d 1229 (10th Cir. 2000), the court struck down provisions of Colorado law that required seekers of federal office to be registered voters in that state before the beginning of the term of office. Following *U.S. Term Limits* and distinguishing cases like *Storer*, the court concluded that the requirements did not merely winnow candidates for the ballot but impermissibly excluded certain types of candidates.

3. Is there a constitutional difference between the people of a state acting collectively to add to the constitutionally specified qualifications—the effort struck down in *U.S. Term Limits*—and the people acting individually by voting against any candidate not possessing the additional qualifications? If a state legislature were to choose presidential electors (or, before the Seventeenth Amendment, United States senators), could it constitutionally restrict its choice to those candidates with certain experience, or who were members of the majority party in the legislature?

4. While *U.S. Term Limits* placed considerable weight on the Qualifications Clauses of the Constitution, do the broader principles applied by the Court suggest that term limits for *state* officials also violate the Constitution? One court answered in the negative, concluding that lifetime term limits in California were constitutional, and that *U.S. Term Limits* was limited to congressional offices. *Bates v. Jones*, 131 F.3d 843, 847 n.1 (9th Cir. 1997) (*en banc*). In contrast, the dissent argued that the broader analysis of *U.S. Term Limits* suggested that it had implications for attacks on state term limits. *Id.* at 868–72 (Fletcher, J., dissenting).

5. The vast majority of legislative term limits enacted in the 1990s were adopted by popular initiative or referendum, not by state legislatures. Michael J. Klarman, *Majoritarian Judicial Review: The Entrenchment Problem*, 85 Geo. L.J. 491, 510 (1997). Why have state legislatures largely not enacted these limits? To what extent, if at all, should the method of enactment of term limits affect judicial review of such provisions? *Compare* Julian N. Eule, *Judicial Review of Direct Democracy*, 93 Yale L.J. 1503 (1990) (arguing that products of direct democracy are sufficiently different from ordinary legislation to justify heightened judicial scrutiny, at least on most issues), *with* Michael E. Solimine, *Judicial Review of Direct Democracy: A Reappraisal*, 104 Ky. L.J. 671 (2016) (arguing that the Supreme Court has not been clear on this issue, and that most products of direct and representative democracy are similar enough to warrant ordinary judicial review).

6. Term limits are themselves sometimes limited or repealed, as support for the measures ebbs despite initial enthusiasm. For example, since the widespread adoption of such limits for state legislatures in the 1990s, two have been repealed by legislatures (Idaho and Utah), and others have been ruled unconstitutional by state supreme courts (Massachusetts, Oregon, Washington, and Wyoming). For other examples, see David W. Chen & Michael Barbaro, *Across Country, New Challenges to Term Limits*, N.Y. TIMES, Sept. 10, 2008, at A1. A high-profile example of the controversy that continues to surround term limits was the extension of the two-term limit for New York City's mayor to three terms in 2008. The extension survived a legal challenge, *Molinari v. Bloomberg*, 564 F.3d 587 (2d Cir. 2009), but it proved a political liability for incumbent Mayor Michael Bloomberg, the beneficiary of the change. Michael Barbaro, *Change to Term Limits Dogs Mayor*, N.Y. TIMES, Oct. 4, 2009, at A17. He nonetheless won reelection.

7. How does *U.S. Term Limits* apply to other state regulations of the election process for federal office? For example, should it invalidate state laws that permit the recall of members of Congress? For an affirmative answer, see *Committee to Recall Robert Menendez v. Wells*, 7 A.3d 720 (N.J. 2010). The court struck down a state constitutional provision permitting the recall of any elected official representing the state in Congress on the basis of *U.S. Term Limits*. While many state provisions—a few explicitly, and more implicitly—appeared to permit the recall of members of Congress, the court noted that the consensus of scholarly authority, and the opinions of many state attorneys general, was that such provisions were unenforceable.

8. *Problem.* In 2019, California passed a law forbidding the secretary of state from "print[ing] the name of a candidate for President of the United States on a primary election ballot, unless the candidate, at least 98 days before the presidential primary election, files with the Secretary of State copies of every income tax return the candidate filed with the Internal Revenue Service in the five most recent taxable years." Once filed with the secretary, the returns would be posted online, with some private information redacted. The government claimed that the law advanced its "strong interest in ensuring that its voters make informed, educated choices in the voting booth." Specifically, the government averred that "a Presidential candidate's income tax returns provide voters with essential information regarding the candidate's potential conflicts of interest, business dealings, financial status and charitable donations." The timing of the law's passage, as well as statements in the legislative history, suggest that the law was an attempt to force President Trump to disclose his tax returns. Did the law violate the Presidential Qualifications Clause by imposing additional qualifications for the presidency? Did it interfere with the parties' right to choose their nominees based on the qualities that they think most important? Or was the law distinguishable from *Term Limits* because it advanced voters' interest in having "essential information" about the candidates? See *Griffin v. Padilla*, 408 F. Supp. 3d 1169 (E.D. Cal.), *vacated as moot*, 2019 WL 7557783 (9th Cir. 2019).

Cook v. Gralike

Supreme Court of the United States
531 U.S. 510, 121 S. Ct. 1029, 149 L. Ed. 2d 44 (2001)

JUSTICE STEVENS delivered the opinion of the Court [in which JUSTICE SCALIA, JUSTICE KENNEDY, JUSTICE SOUTER, JUSTICE THOMAS, JUSTICE GINSBURG, and JUSTICE BREYER join]. * * *

Article VIII [of the Missouri Constitution] "instruct[s]" each Member of Missouri's congressional delegation "to use all of his or her delegated powers to pass the Congressional Term Limits Amendment" set forth in § 16 of the Article. That proposed amendment would limit service in the United States Congress to three terms in the House of Representatives and two terms in the Senate.

Three provisions in Article VIII combine to advance its purpose. Section 17 prescribes that the statement "DISREGARDED VOTERS' INSTRUCTION ON TERM LIMITS" be printed on all primary and general ballots adjacent to the name of a Senator or Representative who fails to take any one of eight legislative acts in support of the proposed amendment. Section 18 provides that the statement "DECLINED TO PLEDGE TO SUPPORT TERM LIMITS" be printed on all primary and general election ballots next to the name of every nonincumbent congressional candidate who refuses to take a "Term Limit" pledge that commits the candidate, if elected, to performing the legislative acts enumerated in § 17. And § 19 directs the Missouri Secretary of State to determine and declare, pursuant to §§ 17 and 18, whether either statement should be printed alongside the name of each candidate for Congress.

Respondent Don Gralike was a nonincumbent candidate for election in 1998 to the United States House of Representatives from Missouri's Third Congressional District. A month after Article VIII was amended, Gralike brought suit * * * to enjoin petitioner, the Secretary of State of Missouri, from implementing the Article, which the complaint alleges violates several provisions of the Federal Constitution. * * *

* * * Through the Elections Clause, the Constitution delegated to the States the power to regulate the "Times, Places and Manner of holding Elections for Senators and Representatives," subject to a grant of authority to Congress to "make or alter such Regulations." Art. I, § 4, cl. 1. * * *

[P]etitioner argues that Article VIII "merely regulates the manner in which elections are held by disclosing information about congressional candidates." As such, petitioner concludes, Article VIII is a valid exercise of Missouri's delegated power.

We disagree. * * * As we made clear in U.S. Term Limits[, Inc. v. Thornton, 514 U.S. 779 (1995)] [p. 538], "the Framers understood the Elections Clause as a grant of authority to issue procedural regulations, and not as a source of power to dictate electoral outcomes, to favor or disfavor a class of candidates, or to evade important constitutional restraints." 514 U.S., at 833–834. Article VIII is not a procedural regulation. It does not regulate the time of elections; it does not regulate the place of elections; nor, we believe, does it regulate the manner of elections. As to the last point, Article VIII bears no relation to the "manner" of elections as we understand it, for in our commonsense view that term encompasses matters like "notices, registration, supervision of voting, protection of voters, prevention of fraud and corrupt practices, counting of votes, duties of inspectors and canvassers, and making and publication of election returns." *Smiley* [v. *Holm*], 285 U.S. [355,] 366 [(1932)]; see also *U.S. Term Limits, Inc.* v. *Thornton*, 514 U.S., at 833. In short, Article VIII is not among "the numerous requirements as to procedure and safeguards which experience shows are necessary in order to enforce the fundamental right involved," *Smiley*, 285 U.S., at 366, ensuring that elections are "fair and honest," and that "some sort of order, rather than chaos, is to accompany the democratic process," *Storer* v. *Brown*, 415 U.S. 724, 730 (1974) [p. 513].

Rather, Article VIII is plainly designed to favor candidates who are willing to support the particular form of a term limits amendment set forth in its text and to disfavor those who either oppose term limits entirely or would prefer a different proposal. As noted, the state provision does not just "instruct" each member of Missouri's congressional delegation to promote in certain ways the passage of the specified term limits amendment. It also attaches a concrete consequence to noncompliance—the printing of the statement "DISREGARDED VOTERS' INSTRUCTIONS ON TERM LIMITS" by the candidate's name on all primary and general election ballots. Likewise, a nonincumbent candidate who does not pledge to follow the instruction receives the ballot designation "DECLINED TO PLEDGE TO SUPPORT TERM LIMITS."

In describing the two labels, the courts below have employed terms such as "pejorative," "negative," "derogatory," "intentionally intimidating," "particularly harmful," "politically damaging," "a serious sanction," "a penalty," and "official denunciation." The general counsel to petitioner's office, no less, has denominated the labels as "the Scarlet Letter." We agree with the sense of these descriptions. They convey the substantial political risk the ballot labels impose on current and prospective congressional members who, for one reason or another, fail to comply with the conditions set forth in Article VIII for passing its term limits amendment. Although petitioner now claims that the labels "merely" inform Missouri voters about a candidate's compliance with Article VIII, she has acknowledged under oath that the ballot designations would handicap candidates for the United States Congress. To us, that is exactly the intended effect of Article VIII.

Indeed, it seems clear that the adverse labels handicap candidates "at the most crucial stage in the election process—the instant before the vote is cast." *Anderson* v. *Martin*, 375 U.S. 399, 402 (1964) [p. 536]. At the same time, "by directing the citizen's attention to the single consideration" of the candidates' fidelity to term limits, the labels imply that the issue "is an important—perhaps paramount—consideration in the citizen's choice, which may decisively influence the citizen to cast his ballot" against candidates branded as unfaithful. *Ibid.* While the precise damage the labels may exact on candidates is disputed between the parties, the labels surely place their targets at a political disadvantage to unmarked candidates for congressional office. Thus, far from regulating the procedural mechanisms of elections, Article VIII attempts to "dictate electoral outcomes." *U.S. Term Limits, Inc. v. Thornton*, 514 U.S., at 833–834. Such "regulation" of congressional elections simply is not authorized by the Elections Clause.

Accordingly, the judgment of the Court of Appeals is affirmed.

It is so ordered.

JUSTICE KENNEDY, concurring. * * *

A State is not permitted to interpose itself between the people and their National Government as it seeks to do here. Whether a State's concern is with the proposed enactment of a constitutional amendment or an ordinary federal statute it simply lacks the power to impose any conditions on the election of Senators and Representatives, save neutral provisions as to the time, place, and manner of elections pursuant to Article I, § 4. * * * The Court rules, as it must, that the amendments to Article VIII of the Missouri Constitution do not regulate the time or place of federal elections; rather, those provisions are an attempt to control the actions of the State's congressional delegation.

The dispositive principle in this case is fundamental to the Constitution, to the idea of federalism, and to the theory of representative government. The principle is that Senators and Representatives in the National Government are responsible to the people who elect them, not to the States in which they reside. The Constitution was ratified by Conventions in the several States, not by the States themselves, U.S. Const., Art. VII, a historical fact and a constitutional imperative which underscore the proposition that the Constitution was ordained and established by the people of the United States. U.S. Const., preamble. The idea of federalism is that a National Legislature enacts laws which bind the people as individuals, not as citizens of a State; and, it follows, freedom is most secure if the people themselves, not the States as intermediaries, hold their federal legislators to account for the conduct of their office. If state enactments were allowed to condition or control certain actions of federal legislators, accountability would be blurred, with the legislators having the excuse of saying that they did not act in the exercise of their best judgment but simply in conformance with a state mandate. As noted in the concurring opinion in *Thornton*, "[n]othing in the Constitution or The Federalist Papers . . . supports the idea of state interference with the most basic relation between the National Government and its citizens, the selection of legislative representatives." 514 U.S., at 842. Yet that is just what Missouri seeks to do through its law—to wield the power granted to it by the Elections Clause to handicap those who seek federal office by affixing pejorative labels next to their names on the ballot if they do not pledge to support the State's preferred position on a certain issue. Neither the design of the Constitution nor sound principles of representative government are consistent with the right or power of a State to inter-fere with the direct line of accountability between the National Legislature and the people who elect it. For these reasons Article VIII is void.

This said, it must be noted that when the Constitution was enacted, respectful petitions to legislators were an accepted mode of urging legislative action. This right is preserved to individuals (the people) in the First Amendment. Even if a State, as an entity, is not itself protected by the Petition Clause, there is no principle prohibiting a state legislature from following a parallel course and by a memorial resolution requesting the Congress of the United States to pay heed to certain state concerns. From the earliest days of our Republic to the present time, States have done so in the context of federal legislation. Indeed, the situation was even more complex in the early days of our Nation, when Senators were appointed by state legislatures rather than directly elected. At that time, it appears that some state leg-islatures followed a practice of instructing the Senators whom they had appointed to pass legislation, while only requesting that the Representatives, who had been elected by the people, do so. * * * The fact that the Members of the First Congress decided not to codify a right to instruct legislative representatives does not, in my view, prove that they intended to prohibit nonbinding petitions or memorials by the State as an entity.

If there are to be cases in which a close question exists regarding whether the State has exceeded its constitutional authority in attempting to influence congres-sional action, this case is not one of them. In today's case the question is not close. Here the State attempts to intrude upon the relationship between the people and their congressional delegates by seeking to control or confine the discretion of those delegates, and the interference is not permissible.

With these observations, I concur in the Court's opinion.

Justice Thomas, concurring * * *.

I continue to believe that, because they possess "reserved" powers, "the people of the States need not point to any affirmative grant of power in the Constitution in order to prescribe qualifications for their representatives in Congress, or to autho-rize their elected state legislators to do so." *U.S. Term Limits, Inc.* v. *Thornton*, 514 U.S., [at] 846 (Thomas, J., dissenting). For this reason, I disagree with the Court's premise, derived from *U.S. Term Limits*, that the States have no authority to regulate congressional elections except for the authority that the Constitution expressly del-egates to them. Nonetheless, the parties conceded the validity of this premise, and I therefore concur.

Chief Justice Rehnquist, with whom Justice O'Connor joins, concurring in the judgment.

I would affirm the judgment of the Court of Appeals, but on the ground that Missouri's Article VIII violates the First Amendment to the United States Constitution. Specifically, I believe that Article VIII violates the First Amendment right of a political candidate, once lawfully on the ballot, to have his name appear unaccompanied by pejorative language required by the State. * * * *

Article I, § 4, provides that "[t]he Times, Places and Manner of holding Elections for Senators and Representatives, shall be prescribed in each State by the Legislature thereof." Missouri justifies Article VIII as a "time, place, and manner" regulation of election. Restrictions of this kind are valid "provided that they are justified without reference to the content of the regulated speech, that they are narrowly tailored to serve a significant governmental interest, and that they leave open ample alternative channels for communication of the information." *Clark* v. *Community for Creative Non-Violence*, 468 U.S. 288, 293 (1984). Missouri's Article VIII flunks two of these three requirements. Article VIII is not only not content neutral, but it actually discriminates on the basis of viewpoint because only those candidates who fail to conform to the State's position receive derogatory labels. The result is that the State injects itself into the election process at an absolutely critical point — the composition of the ballot, which is the last thing the voter sees before he makes his choice — and does so in a way that is not neutral as to issues or candidates. The candidates who are thus singled out have no means of replying to their designation which would be equally effective with the voter.

In *Anderson* v. *Martin*, we held that a Louisiana statute requiring the designation of a candidate's race on the ballot violated the Equal Protection Clause. In describing the effect of such a designation, the Court said: "[B]y directing the citizen's attention to the single consideration of race or color, the State indicates that a candidate's race or color is an important — perhaps paramount — consideration in the citizen's choice, which may decisively influence the citizen to cast his ballot along racial lines." *Id.*, at 402. So, too, here the State has chosen one and only one issue to comment on the position of the candidates. During the campaign, they may debate tax reform, Social Security, national security, and a host of other issues; but when it comes to the ballot on which one or the other of them is chosen, the State is saying that the issue of term limits is paramount. Although uttered in a different context, what we said in *Police Dept. of Chicago* v. *Mosley*, 408 U.S. 92, 96 (1972), is equally

---

* The Court of Appeals upheld their First Amendment claim, but based its reasoning on the view that the ballot statements were "compelled speech" by the candidate, and therefore ran afoul of cases such as *Wooley* v. *Maynard*, 430 U.S. 705 (1977). I do not agree with the reasoning of the Court of Appeals. I do not believe a reasonable voter, viewing the ballot labeled as Article VIII requires, would think that the candidate in question chose to characterize himself as having "disregarded voters' instructions" or as "having declined to pledge" to support term limits.

applicable here: "[Government] may not select which issues are worth discussing or debating."

If other Missouri officials feel strongly about the need for term limits, they are free to urge rejection of candidates who do not share their view and refuse to "take the pledge." Such candidates are able to respond to that sort of speech with speech of their own. But the State itself may not skew the ballot listings in this way without violating the First Amendment.

Notes and Questions

1. How does *Gralike* apply to other state regulations of federal elections? Justice Kennedy said that *Gralike* itself was not a close case, but how should close cases be evaluated? For example, states frequently list the political parties of candidates on ballots for federal office. Others list each candidate's county of residence. Such a practice can be a significant disadvantage for candidates in statewide races who live in low-population areas because, in the absence of more information, voters will tend to vote for candidates who live near them. May a candidate disadvantaged by such a procedure object under *Gralike*? For a general discussion of other ballot restrictions in light of *Gralike*, see Matthew M. Mannix, Comment, *Opening Ballot Access to Political Outsiders: How Third Parties Could Use* Cook v. Gralike *to Challenge the Dominance of America's Two-Party System*, 11 ROGER WILLIAMS U. L. REV. 273 (2005).

2. Does or should *Gralike* apply to *state* elections? How would the authors of the concurring opinions resolve that issue?

3. Why do you think Justice Scalia joined the majority opinion in *Gralike* after dissenting in *U.S. Term Limits*?

4. It has been argued that even without the Qualifications Clauses and the First Amendment, the result in *Gralike* should be the same because the structural provisions of "a representative democracy—plainly contemplated by the Constitution's provisions for the federal legislature and federal elections—is dependent on the operation of elections unbiased by the existing government." Vicki C. Jackson, Cook v. Gralike: *Easy Cases and Structural Reasoning*, 2001 SUP. CT. REV. 299, 300; *cf. National Endowment for the Arts v. Finley*, 524 U.S. 569, 598 n.3 (1998) (Scalia, J., concurring in the judgment) ("I suppose it would be unconstitutional for the government to give money to an organization devoted to the promotion of candidates nominated by the Republican party—but it would be just as unconstitutional for the government itself to promote candidates nominated by the Republican party, and I do not think that that unconstitutionality has anything to do with the First Amendment."). But if Article VIII of the Missouri Constitution did not violate the Qualifications Clauses or the First Amendment, by what authority could the Supreme Court invalidate it?

Chapter 7

Political Speech

A. Introduction

The First Amendment "has its fullest and most urgent application * * * to the conduct of campaigns for political office." *Monitor Patriot Co. v. Roy*, 401 U.S. 265, 272 (1971). Accordingly, the constitutional protections of "the freedom of speech, [and] of the press" are particularly important in election law. Elections provide the clearest opportunity for the people to exercise the power of self-governance in a republic, and the power of the vote can be effective only if, and to the extent that, voters can inform themselves about the candidates and issues to be considered at elections. *See, e.g.*, ALEXANDER MEIKLEJOHN, FREE SPEECH AND ITS RELATIONSHIP TO SELF GOVERNMENT (1948).

Yet the importance of elections to the democratic process, and of speech to elections, means that disinformation can produce particularly severe negative consequences. Additionally, free-speech protections allow persons to exert influence commensurate with their ability to articulate a persuasive message and to distribute it to an audience. Because some people are better than others at producing and distributing speech, and because some people can devote more resources to the effort than can others, free speech can result in inequality of political influence. Thus, ironically, elections present both a compelling context for protecting free speech, and a compelling context for limiting it.

This summary seeks to provide sufficient background to enable students to appreciate the First Amendment issues raised by campaign activity, but the coverage in this Chapter leaves undiscussed many important areas of First Amendment doctrine, including some that relate to the expression of political speech and the communication of ideas that have the potential to shape politics. Thus, the Supreme Court's treatment of subversive speech and symbolic expression, for example, are not analyzed here. Students seeking a more comprehensive presentation of First Amendment doctrine should consult RUSSELL L. WEAVER, UNDERSTANDING THE FIRST AMENDMENT (7th ed. 2020) or DANIEL A. FARBER, THE FIRST AMENDMENT (5th ed. 2020).

The First Amendment applies by its terms only to congressional laws that abridge the listed freedoms, but the other branches of the federal government are also required to respect its strictures. Further, the Court has long considered First Amendment rights to be fundamental, and accordingly has interpreted the Fourteenth Amendment as extending the First Amendment's protections to the states. *See Everson v. Board of Education,* 330 U.S. 1, 5, 15 (1947) (incorporating the Establishment Clause); *Fiske v. Kansas,* 274 U.S. 380, 386–87 (1927) (incorporating the Free Speech Clause); *Gitlow v. New York,* 268 U.S. 652, 666 (1925) (announcing the same principle in dictum).

As a general matter, "content-based" regulations trigger strict scrutiny, meaning that the regulations must be narrowly tailored to a compelling governmental interest, while "content-neutral" regulations concerning the time, place, or manner of speech are evaluated under a more forgiving test resembling intermediate scrutiny. Regulations that are justified by a purpose unrelated to the content of the speech will be upheld if "they are narrowly tailored to serve a significant governmental interest, and * * * they leave open ample alternative channels for communication of the information." *McCullen v. Coakley,* 573 U.S. 464, 477 (2014) (quoting *Ward v. Rock Against Racism,* 491 U.S. 781, 791 (1989), in turn quoting *Clark v. Community for Creative Non-Violence,* 468 U.S. 288, 293 (1984)). Although the tests for content-based and content-neutral laws ostensibly require narrow tailoring, the narrow tailoring applicable to content-neutral laws is more forgiving than in other contexts, such as equal-protection law. *See* EUGENE VOLOKH, THE FIRST AMENDMENT AND RELATED STATUTES: PROBLEMS, CASES AND POLICY ARGUMENTS 354 (7th ed. 2020) (citing *Ward, supra,* and *Members of the City Council v. Taxpayers for Vincent,* 466 U.S. 789 (1984), for the propositions that content-neutral time, place, and manner restrictions need not be the least restrictive means of achieving the governmental interest and may be underinclusive).

A content-based restriction is one where the harm the government seeks to prevent is related to the message of the speaker; the government must assess the content of the message to ascertain whether it risks the harm the government is trying to avoid. A content-neutral restriction, by contrast, seeks to achieve a result unrelated to the message of a given speaker. A ban on sound trucks, for example, limits the expression of speech, but does so in a content-neutral way because the harm the government seeks to prevent—the disturbances caused by noise—are unrelated to the message conveyed by the sound truck. Whether the sound truck carries a speech by a mayoral candidate, an advertisement about a ballot issue, a commercial advertisement, or a public-service announcement, the harm is the same. Content-neutral regulations are more apt to be constitutional than are content-based restrictions, but they must still meet the intermediate-scrutiny standard. The government cannot simply ban all speech within a certain area and defend on the ground that the ban is content-neutral. *See Board of Airport Commissioners v. Jews for Jesus, Inc.,* 482 U.S. 569 (1987).

"Viewpoint-based" restrictions are a subset of content-based ones. *Rosenberger v. Rector and Visitors of the University of Virginia,* 515 U.S. 819, 829 (1995) ("Viewpoint discrimination is . . . an egregious form of content discrimination."). Viewpoint-based restrictions not only distinguish between types of speech depending on the message that is conveyed by the speech, but use the power of the government to advantage one side in a debate. Thus, a regulation applying to speech "about the National Football League" would be content-based because the government would need to assess the speech to determine if the NFL were the subject of the speech. A regulation applying to speech "promoting the National Football League," however, would not only be content-based but would be viewpoint-based as well, because it would leave unregulated speech denigrating the League. Viewpoint-based regulations are almost always unconstitutional. *See, e.g., Iancu v. Brunetti*, 588 U.S. ___, 139 S. Ct. 2294 (2019) (striking down, as viewpoint-based, a law barring the registration of "immoral" or "scandalous" trademarks); *Matal v. Tam*, 582 U.S. ___, 137 S. Ct. 1744 (2017) (striking down a law prohibiting the registration of any trademark that might "disparage . . . or bring . . . into contemp[t] or disrepute" any "persons, living or dead").

A good, real-life example of the distinction between "content-based" and "viewpoint-based" restrictions can be seen in *Reed v. Town of Gilbert*, 576 U.S. 155 (2015). There, a local ordinance distinguished between types of signs posted by private parties, and provided greater protection to some types than to others. For example, the ordinance imposed greater restrictions on "ideological signs" (a category for signs "communicating a message or ideas" and not covered by any of twenty-three other categories), "political signs" (any "temporary sign designed to influence the outcome of an election called by a public body"), and "temporary directional" signs (signs directing the public to an event), than it imposed on other classes of signs. "Political signs," for example, were restricted to a period close to an election; "directional signs" could be displayed no more than twelve hours before the event and one hour after. The Court of Appeals had upheld the ordinance on the grounds that the town "did not adopt its regulation of speech [based on] disagree[ment] with the message conveyed." *Reed v. Town of Gilbert*, 707 F.3d 1057, 1071 (9th Cir. 2013). The Supreme Court disagreed. While the lack of animus toward the message meant that the ordinance was not "viewpoint-based," it was nonetheless still "content-based" because it placed heavier burdens on "political" signs than on, *e.g.*, garage-sale signs, specifically because of the former's political content. The Supreme Court applied strict scrutiny and found the ordinance unconstitutional. *See also Barr v. American Association of Political Consultants, Inc.*, 591 U.S. ___, 140 S. Ct. 2335 (2020) (applying strict scrutiny and striking down a content-based exception that permitted robocalls to collect government debt but otherwise banned such calls); *Victory Processing, LLC v. Fox*, 937 F.3d 1218 (9th Cir. 2019) (applying strict scrutiny and striking down a content-based ban on robocalls "related to a political campaign").

When the power of the government is used to privilege or punish speech based on content, the First Amendment is obviously implicated. But even regulations that apply to speech regardless of content can violate the First Amendment. As noted above, content-neutral regulations must satisfy intermediate scrutiny: They must be narrowly tailored to serve an important or substantial government interest, but they need not be the least-restrictive means of serving that interest. *See Ward*, *supra*, at 798–99. Content-neutral speech restrictions may also be unconstitutional if they simply restrict too much speech. For example, in *City of Ladue v. Gilleo*, 512 U.S. 43 (1994), the Supreme Court struck down a content-neutral city ordinance that banned homeowners from displaying signs on their property. As the Court explained, the City had

> almost completely foreclosed a venerable means of communication that is both unique and important. It has totally foreclosed that medium to political, religious, or personal messages. Signs that react to a local happening or express a view on a controversial issue both reflect and animate change in the life of a community. Often placed on lawns or in windows, residential signs play an important part in political campaigns, during which they are displayed to signal the resident's support for particular candidates, parties, or causes. They may not afford the same opportunities for conveying complex ideas as do other media, but residential signs have long been an important and distinct medium of expression.

Our prior decisions have voiced particular concern with laws that foreclose an entire medium of expression. Thus, we have held invalid ordinances that completely banned the distribution of pamphlets within the municipality, *Lovell v. City of Griffin*, 303 U.S. 444, 451–452 (1938); handbills on the public streets, *Jamison v. Texas*, 318 U.S. 413, 416 (1943); the door-to-door distribution of literature, *Martin v. City of Struthers*, 319 U.S. 141, 145–149 (1943); *Schneider v. State (Town of Irvington)*, 308 U.S. 147, 164–165 (1939), and live entertainment, *Schad v. Mount Ephraim*, 452 U.S. 61, 75–76 (1981). Although prohibitions foreclosing entire media may be completely free of content or viewpoint discrimination, the danger they pose to the freedom of speech is readily apparent—by eliminating a common means of speaking, such measures can suppress too much speech.

Ladue contends, however, that its ordinance is a mere regulation of the "time, place, or manner" of speech because residents remain free to convey their desired messages by other means, such as hand-held signs, "letters, handbills, flyers, telephone calls, newspaper advertisements, bumper stickers, speeches, and neighborhood or community meetings." However, even regulations that do not foreclose an entire medium of expression, but merely shift the time, place, or manner of its use, must "leave open ample alternative channels for communication." *Clark v. Community for Creative Non–Violence*, 468 U.S. 288, 293 (1984). In this case, we are not persuaded that adequate substitutes exist for the important medium of speech that Ladue has closed off. * * *

Residential signs are an unusually cheap and convenient form of communication. Especially for persons of modest means or limited mobility, a yard or window sign may have no practical substitute. Even for the affluent, the added costs in money or time of taking out a newspaper advertisement, handing out leaflets on the street, or standing in front of one's house with a handheld sign may make the difference between participating and not participating in some public debate. Furthermore, a person who puts up a sign at her residence often intends to reach *neighbors*, an audience that could not be reached nearly as well by other means.

512 U.S. at 54–57. Stay-at-home orders that were put in place to limit the spread of COVID-19 challenged the limits of this doctrine. In some states, stay-at-home orders prevented people from assembling in large numbers in the summer and fall of 2020, *i.e.*, in the months preceding the election. In Pennsylvania, for example, the governor issued an order forbidding indoor gatherings of more than twenty-five people and outdoor gatherings of more than 250 people. Even if those orders were content-neutral, would they be narrowly tailored? Under *Gilleo*, would they limit too much valuable political speech to be constitutional? What alternative avenues of communication would be available to a candidate or political party that was prevented from holding a rally? Would those alternatives be "ample"? *See County of Butler v. Wolf*, __ F. Supp. 3d __, __-__, 2020 WL 5510690, *10-*15 (W.D. Pa. 2020) (striking down Pennsylvania's attendance limits on in-person assemblies after concluding that the limits, which applied statewide, were not narrowly tailored to account for different risks of transmitting the virus); *Benner v. Wolf*, __ F. Supp. 3d __, __, 2020 WL 2564920, *7–*8 (M.D. Pa. 2020) (in a challenge to Pennsylvania's limitation on in-person assemblies, denying a temporary restraining order after concluding that there were ample alternatives available, to wit, telephone and video-conference communications, "speaking on television and radio," "sending out direct mailings," "putting up yard signs," and "protesting"); *Illinois Republican Party v. Pritzker*, __ F. Supp. 3d __, 2020 WL 3604106 (N.D. Ill. 2020) (refusing to enjoin Illinois's similar limitation).

Certain categories of language have traditionally not been considered to be part of "the freedom of speech," and therefore the government can limit the use of such language without triggering the strict-scrutiny test. These categories include obscenity, fighting words, and libel. *See Chaplinsky v. New Hampshire*, 315 U.S. 568, 571–72 (1942). Even as to such "low-value speech," however, the Constitution may provide some protection—especially if a regulation is motivated by disagreement with the speaker's message, *see R.A.V. v. City of St. Paul, Minnesota*, 505 U.S. 377 (1992), or if the regulation may in practice chill not only unprotected speech, but other expression as well. In *New York Times Co v. Sullivan*, 376 U.S. 254 (1964), for example, the Court struck down a libel judgment against a newspaper as inconsistent with the First Amendment. The Court reasoned that even though libel is constitutionally unprotected, speakers would refrain from exercising their rights if they knew that a false statement would subject them to liability. Accordingly, the Court held that a state may award damages for libel only where the defendant's false statements were made with knowledge of their falsity, or with reckless disregard for whether they were false or not. *See id.* at 280.

Libel prohibitions are only one kind of regulation affecting speech about public affairs and public figures. Media outlets have occasionally been targets of governmental "fairness" regulation when regulators fear that media coverage has the capacity to slant the public's perception of candidates or issues. For the most part, such restrictions have failed to survive constitutional review. An exception exists, however, for regulation of broadcast media. Whereas regulation of newspapers' editorializing has been held flatly unconstitutional, *see Miami Herald Publishing Co. v. Tornillo*, 418 U.S. 241 (1974) [p. 593], the Supreme Court upheld the FCC's (since-repealed) requirement that radio and television broadcasters provide criticized persons an opportunity to respond to attacks. *See Red Lion Broadcasting Co. v. Federal Communications Commission*, 395 U.S. 367 (1969). Broadcast media were different, the Court concluded, because the scarcity of available broadcast frequencies prevented each potential speaker from having access to the airwaves. Accordingly, broadcasters could constitutionally be considered to hold their licenses in the public interest, and be obligated to grant members of the public access to their stations when necessary to provide a balanced presentation of issues.

Government is usually prohibited from imposing civil or criminal penalties for political speech, and may not interfere with the speech of candidates for public office. *See Brown v. Hartlage*, 456 U.S. 45 (1982) [p. 568]. Where a state's electoral process incorporates a role for petitions (often as a prerequisite to ballot-access for third parties or initiatives), the circulation of such petitions involves "core political speech." *See Meyer v. Grant*, 486 U.S. 414, 420–22 (1986) [p. 647]. Even judicial candidates possess a First Amendment right to announce their views in campaigns, though states may be able to restrict judicial campaign speech (particularly fundraising) more than they can restrict speech in other types of campaigns. *See Republican Party of Minnesota v. White*, 536 U.S. 765, 783 (2002) [p. 605]; *Williams-Yulee v. Florida Bar*, 575 U.S. 433 (2015) [p. 622].

Sometimes the government attempts to limit speech only in certain locations owned or controlled by the government. For example, the government might impose no restrictions on individuals' speech on their own property, but might seek to limit their speech in public schools, prisons, sidewalks, public squares, or government offices. The constitutionality of such limitations on speech depends on the character of the place where the speech is restricted. Where the place is a traditional forum for private individuals' speech—streets, parks, and sidewalks are the principal, if not exclusive, examples—the government may not limit speech unless the limit passes strict scrutiny. If the government creates a non-traditional forum for private parties' speech, speech within that "designated public forum" may not be limited unless the limits pass strict scrutiny. The government may also designate a nontraditional forum for private speech while limiting the speech to the discussion of certain topics, thus creating a "limited [or limited-purpose] public forum." The government may enforce those limits (even though those limits are based on the content of the expression) as long as the limits are reasonable and viewpoint-neutral. The same requirements of reasonableness and viewpoint-neutrality apply in non-public fora, which are government-controlled areas or resources, such as airports, that are designed for a purpose other than speech. Lastly, there are government-owned or government-controlled places that are used for communication of the government's own message. These areas are not fora at all, and the government is free to decide not only the content of the speech but the viewpoint as well. A government's website that contains only the government's own messages, for example, is used for communication, but is not a forum for private speech, and the government can choose the messages it expresses without having to open the website to messages with differing points of view. By contrast, if the website contained a public-comment section, that section would be a designated public forum and the government could not make content-based distinctions without satisfying strict scrutiny. For more on the public-forum doctrine, see FARBER, THE FIRST AMENDMENT, *supra*, at 185–207; VOLOKH, THE FIRST AMENDMENT AND RELATED STATUTES, *supra*, at 619–90.

When government acts not as a regulator of speech by the general public but as an employer, it may sometimes condition employment on an employee's agreement not to engage in political speech — provided that the employee's speech would adversely affect job performance. Where an individual's job performance is unaffected by the speech, government may not discipline an employee for speech that opposes the government's viewpoint. *See Pickering v. Board of Education*, 391 U.S. 563 (1968). In a series of cases upholding limitations on government employees' political activity, however, the Court has indicated that the government may impose limits on employees' First Amendment freedoms where public confidence in government demands that workers not be seen as having their jobs depend on their support for the party or politicians in power. *See Broadrick v. Oklahoma*, 413 U.S. 601 (1973); *Civil Service Commission v. National Association of Letter Carriers*, 413 U.S. 548 (1973) [p. 679]; *United Public Workers v. Mitchell*, 330 U.S. 75 (1947) [p. 668].

The dangers of a partisan government workforce are so acute that the Court has not only authorized limits on employees' speech, but has also held that the First Amendment itself requires government to refrain from making certain employment decisions on a patronage basis. Patronage persists to some degree, of course, but the Court has stated that party loyalty may be the basis for personnel decisions relating only to those positions for which "party affiliation is an appropriate requirement for the effective performance of the public office involved." *Branti v. Finkel*, 445 U.S. 507, 518–20 (1980).

Two types of political speech — campaign finance and anonymous speech — are the subjects of their own Chapters. As you read the materials in this one, however, you should consider how the principles developed here should apply in evaluating the constitutionality of restrictions on raising or spending money in campaigns, as well as laws that require the disclosure of one's identity if one chooses to speak on political matters or to make political donations.

B. False Statements

The freedom of speech is central not only to our Constitution, but to any system of democratic self-government. Without the ability to discuss public issues and candidates free of government coercion, we could not hold government officials accountable. The ability of the people to exercise political power effectively depends on their ability to educate themselves and to persuade others about the issues of the day. In addition to aiding self-governance, free speech advances society's interest in finding truth. Without the ability to offer and critique ideas, society would not be able to discover new truths about science, politics, economics, or indeed any field of inquiry. Literature, too, by allowing us to understand the human condition, allows us to learn truths that can make our society (and us as individuals) better.

Yet unrestrained speech can be damaging. In fact, unrestrained speech can undermine the very values that free speech is meant to protect. *See Dun & Bradstreet, Inc. v. Greenmoss Builders*, 472 U.S. 749, 767–69 (1985) (White, J., concurring in the judgment). False statements, for example, can make it harder for society to identify (and base policy on) the truth, and can make it harder for people to vote in ways that advance the interests of themselves and the country. As a consequence, the Supreme Court has never treated the right to free speech as absolute. In *Chaplinsky v. New Hampshire*, 315 U.S. 568, 571–72 (1942), the Supreme Court identified "certain well defined and narrowly limited classes of speech, the prevention and punishment of which have never been thought to raise any Constitutional problem. These include the lewd and obscene, the profane, the libelous, and the insulting or 'fighting' words — those which, by their very utterance, inflict injury or tend to incite an immediate breach of the peace."

Of those categories of unprotected expression, libel is the one most directly relevant to election law. English common law permitted libeled persons to recover in tort for the damage to their reputations. Such a suit, however, has obvious and profound consequences for society's ability to engage in a "debate on public issues [that is] uninhibited, robust, and wide-open." *New York Times Co. v. Sullivan*, 376 U.S. 254, 270 (1964). Accordingly, the Supreme Court has interpreted the First Amendment to limit the instances in which a defamed plaintiff may recover for libel. Among the most important limitations is the following: Recovery may be had only for false statements of fact. Statements of opinion and true statements of fact may not lead to liability, regardless of the damage they may do to the plaintiff's reputation. While "there is no such thing as a false *idea*," *Gertz v. Robert Welch, Inc.*, 418 U.S. 323, 339 (1974) (emphasis added), "there is no constitutional value in false statements of fact. Neither the intentional lie nor the careless error materially advances society's interest in 'uninhibited, robust, and wide-open' debate on public issues." *Id.* at 340.

The Court has recognized, however, that "erroneous statement is inevitable in free debate." *New York Times*, 376 U.S. at 217; *see also Gertz*, 418 U.S. at 340 ("Although the erroneous statement of fact is not worthy of constitutional protection, it is nevertheless inevitable in free debate."). That is, speakers and publishers will make some false statements regardless of how careful they are to check their facts. Accordingly, if speakers and publishers could be sued whenever they made a mistake that damaged someone's reputation, very few people would have the wherewithal to speak about public officials and public affairs, and society would be harmed by the reduced discussion about public issues. The Court therefore determined that it was essential to protect some false statements so that speakers and publishers would not be "chilled" from bringing potentially important matters to public attention.

The Court's answer to this quandary was the "actual malice" standard. *New York Times* held that the First Amendment prohibited states from awarding tort damages to public officials and public figures for libelous statements unless the defendant knew the statements were false, or unless the defendant acted with reckless disregard for whether the statements were false or not. *See* 376 U.S. at 280. Thus, libeled public officials and public figures can recover for the knowing or reckless lie, but not for the merely negligent false statement. *See St. Amant v. Thompson*, 390 U.S. 727 (1968); *Gertz*, 418 U.S. at 347. Public officials (relatively high-level officeholders and candidates) and public figures (celebrities) have a large effect on public affairs, so the Court was especially keen on ensuring that discussions about them not be chilled. On the other hand, the Court was more comfortable with a negligence standard for private figures, because they have little access to the media to correct damaging falsehoods, and there is less of a need to encourage "uninhibited, robust, and wide-open" discussions concerning ordinary members of the general public. *See Gertz*, 418 U.S. at 347.

New York Times and its progeny have had a tremendous influence on political discourse because of the protection they provide to even some false and damaging speech. It is important to recognize, though, that *New York Times* did not protect false speech because of an absolutist desire to protect all expression; rather, it protected false speech primarily because of its fear that penalizing false speech would result in the communication of less true speech. *United States v. Alvarez*, 567 U.S. 709 (2012) [p. 575], which appears as a principal case in this Chapter, expanded the *Times* holding to protect even knowingly false statements in situations where the statements caused no identifiable harm. It is unclear, however, whether *Alvarez* will insulate misinformation that might disrupt the electoral process. As you read the cases in this section, consider how to balance the harms caused by false speech against the harms caused by chilling valuable speech, and ask yourself whether you trust the government or juries to decide the truth of political speech.

Brown v. Hartlage

Supreme Court of the United States
456 U.S. 45, 102 S. Ct. 1523, 71 L. Ed. 2d 732 (1982)

Justice Brennan delivered the opinion of the Court [in which Justice White, Justice Marshall, Justice Blackmun, Justice Powell, Justice Stevens, and Justice O'Connor join]. * * *

I

This case involves a challenge to an application of the Kentucky Corrupt Practices Act. The parties were opposing candidates in the 1979 general election for the office of Jefferson County Commissioner, "C" District. Petitioner, Carl Brown, was the challenger; respondent, Earl Hartlage, was the incumbent. On August 15, 1979, in the course of the campaign, Brown held a televised press conference together with Bill Creech, the "B" District candidate on the same party ticket. * * *

On behalf of himself and his running mate, Creech pledged the taxpayers some relief:

> "We abhor the commissioners' outrageous salaries. And to prove the strength of our convictions, one of our first official acts as county commissioners will be to lower our salary to a more realistic level. We will lower our salaries, saving the taxpayers $36,000 during our first term of office, by $3,000 each year."

[Brown himself reiterated the pledge.]

Shortly after the press conference, Brown and Creech learned that their commitment to lower their salaries arguably violated the Kentucky Corrupt Practices Act [because it was akin to buying votes with the resulting tax savings]. On August 19, 1979, they issued a joint statement retracting their earlier pledge:

> "We are men enough to admit when we've made a mistake.
>
> "We have discovered that there are Kentucky court decisions and Attorney General opinions which indicate that our pledge to reduce our salaries if elected may be illegal. . . .
>
> ". . . [We] do hereby formally rescind our pledge to reduce the County Commissioner's salary if elected and instead pledge to seek corrective legislation in the next session of the General Assembly, to correct this silly provision of State Law."

In the November 6, 1979, election, Brown defeated Hartlage by 10,151 votes. Creech was defeated.

Hartlage then filed this action * * *, alleging that Brown had violated the Corrupt Practices Act and seeking to have the election declared void and the office of Jefferson County Commissioner, "C" District, vacated by Brown. [Ky. Rev. Stat. § 121.055], upon which Hartlage based his claim, provides:

"Candidates prohibited from making expenditure, loan, promise, agreement, or contract as to action when elected, in consideration for vote. — No candidate for nomination or election to any state, county, city or district office shall * * * promise, agree or make a contract with any person to vote for or support any particular individual, thing or measure, in consideration for the vote or the financial or moral support of that person in any election, primary or nominating convention, and no person shall require that any candidate make such a promise, agreement or contract."

[The Kentucky Court of Appeals held that Brown violated the Corrupt Practices Act, and, imposing the statutorily prescribed remedy, ordered a new election.]

II

We begin our analysis of § 121.055 by acknowledging that the States have a legitimate interest in preserving the integrity of their electoral processes. Just as a State may take steps to ensure that its governing political institutions and officials properly discharge public responsibilities and maintain public trust and confidence, a State has a legitimate interest in upholding the integrity of the electoral process itself. But when a State seeks to uphold that interest by restricting speech, the limitations on state authority imposed by the First Amendment are manifestly implicated. * * *

The free exchange of ideas provides special vitality to the process traditionally at the heart of American constitutional democracy—the political campaign. "[If] it be conceded that the First Amendment was 'fashioned to assure the unfettered interchange of ideas for the bringing about of political and social changes desired by the people,' then it can hardly be doubted that the constitutional guarantee has its fullest and most urgent application precisely to the conduct of campaigns for political office." *Monitor Patriot Co.* v. *Roy,* 401 U.S. 265, 271–272 (1971). The political candidate does not lose the protection of the First Amendment when he declares himself for public office. Quite to the contrary:

"The candidate, no less than any other person, has a First Amendment right to engage in the discussion of public issues and vigorously and tirelessly to advocate his own election and the election of other candidates. Indeed, it is of particular importance that candidates have the unfettered opportunity to make their views known so that the electorate may intelligently evaluate the candidates' personal qualities and their positions on vital public issues before choosing among them on election day. * * *" *Buckley* v. *Valeo* 424 U.S. 1, 52–53 (1976) *(per curiam)* [p. 728].

When a State seeks to restrict directly the offer of ideas by a candidate to the voters, the First Amendment surely requires that the restriction be demonstrably supported by not only a legitimate state interest, but a compelling one, and that the restriction operate without unnecessarily circumscribing protected expression.

III

* * * We discern three bases upon which the application of the statute to Brown's promise might conceivably be justified: first, as a prohibition on buying votes;

second, as facilitating the candidacy of persons lacking independent wealth; and third, as an application of the State's interests and prerogatives with respect to factual misstatements. We consider these possible justifications in turn.

A

* * * No body politic worthy of being called a democracy entrusts the selection of leaders to a process of auction or barter. And as a State may prohibit the giving of money or other things of value to a voter in exchange for his support, it may also declare unlawful an agreement embodying the intention to make such an exchange. Although agreements to engage in illegal conduct undoubtedly possess some element of association, the State may ban such illegal agreements without trenching on any right of association protected by the First Amendment. The fact that such an agreement necessarily takes the form of words does not confer upon it, or upon the underlying conduct, the constitutional immunities that the First Amendment extends to speech. * * *

It is thus plain that *some* kinds of promises made by a candidate to voters, and *some* kinds of promises elicited by voters from candidates, may be declared illegal without constitutional difficulty. But it is equally plain that there are constitutional limits on the State's power to prohibit candidates from making promises in the course of an election campaign. Some promises are universally acknowledged as legitimate, indeed "indispensable to decisionmaking in a democracy"; and the "maintenance of the opportunity for free political discussion to the end that government may be responsive to the will of the people and that changes may be obtained by lawful means . . . is a fundamental principle of our constitutional system." Candidate commitments enhance the accountability of government officials to the people whom they represent, and assist the voters in predicting the effect of their vote. The fact that some voters may find their self-interest reflected in a candidate's commitment does not place that commitment beyond the reach of the First Amendment. We have never insisted that the franchise be exercised without taint of individual benefit; indeed, our tradition of political pluralism is partly predicated on the expectation that voters will pursue their individual good through the political process, and that the summation of these individual pursuits will further the collective welfare.[7] So long as the hoped-for personal benefit is to be achieved through the normal processes of government, and not through some private arrangement, it has always been, and remains, a reputable basis upon which to cast one's ballot.

It remains to determine the standards by which we might distinguish between those "private arrangements" that are inconsistent with democratic government, and those candidate assurances that promote the representative foundation of our political system. We hesitate before attempting to formulate some test of constitutional legitimacy: the precise nature of the promise, the conditions upon which it is given, the circumstances under which it is made, the size of the audience, the nature

---

7. See The Federalist No. 10. * * *

and size of the group to be benefited, all might, in some instance and to varying extents, bear upon the constitutional assessment. But acknowledging the difficulty of rendering a concise formulation, or recognizing the possibility of borderline cases, does not disable us from identifying cases far from any troublesome border.

It is clear that the statements of petitioner Brown in the course of the August 15 press conference were very different in character from the corrupting agreements and solicitations historically recognized as unprotected by the First Amendment. Notably, Brown's commitment to serve at a reduced salary was made openly, subject to the comment and criticism of his political opponent and to the scrutiny of the voters. We think the fact that the statement was made in full view of the electorate offers a strong indication that the statement contained nothing fundamentally at odds with our shared political ethic.

The Kentucky Court of Appeals analogized Brown's promise to a bribe. But however persuasive that analogy might be as a matter of state law, there is no *constitutional* basis upon which Brown's pledge to reduce his salary might be equated with a candidate's promise to pay voters for their support from his own pocketbook. * * * [D]espite the Kentucky courts' characterization of the promise to serve at a reduced salary as an offer "to reduce pro tanto the amount of taxes each individual taxpayer must pay, and thus . . . an offer to the voter of pecuniary gain," it is impossible to discern in Brown's generalized commitment any invitation to enter into an agreement that might place the statement outside the realm of unequivocal protection that the Constitution affords to political speech. Not only was the source of the promised benefit the public fisc, but that benefit was to extend beyond those voters who cast their ballots for Brown, to all taxpayers and citizens. Even if Brown's commitment could in some sense have been deemed an "offer," it scarcely contemplated a particularized acceptance or a *quid pro quo* arrangement. It was to be honored, "if elected"; it was conditioned not on any particular vote or votes, but entirely on the *majority's* vote.

In sum, Brown did not offer some private payment or donation in exchange for voter support; Brown's statement can only be construed as an expression of his intention to exercise public power in a manner that he believed might be acceptable to some class of citizens. If Brown's expressed intention had an individualized appeal to some taxpayers who felt themselves the likely beneficiaries of his form of fiscal restraint, that fact is of little constitutional significance. The benefits of most public policy changes accrue not only to the undifferentiated "public," but more directly to particular individuals or groups. Like a promise to lower taxes, to increase efficiency in government, or indeed to increase taxes in order to provide some group with a desired public benefit or public service, Brown's promise to reduce his salary cannot be deemed beyond the reach of the First Amendment, or considered as inviting the kind of corrupt arrangement the appearance of which a State may have a compelling interest in avoiding.

A State may insist that candidates seeking the approval of the electorate work within the framework of our democratic institutions, and base their appeal on assertions of fitness for office and statements respecting the means by which they intend to further the public welfare. But a candidate's promise to confer some ultimate benefit on the voter, *qua* taxpayer, citizen, or member of the general public, does not lie beyond the pale of First Amendment protection.

B

* * * The State might legitimately fear that [an] emphasis on free public service might result in persons of independent wealth but less ability being chosen over those who, though better qualified, could not afford to serve at a reduced salary.{[8]} But if § 121.055 was designed to further this interest, it chooses a means unacceptable under the First Amendment.[9] In barring certain public statements with respect to this issue, the State ban runs directly contrary to the fundamental premises underlying the First Amendment as the guardian of our democracy. That Amendment embodies our trust in the free exchange of ideas as the means by which the people are to choose between good ideas and bad, and between candidates for political office. The State's fear that voters might make an ill-advised choice does not provide the State with a compelling justification for limiting speech. It is simply not the function of government to "select which issues are worth discussing or debating" in the course of a political campaign.

C

[Section] 121.055 * * * bars promises to serve at a reduced salary only when the salary of the official has been "fixed by law," and where the promise cannot, therefore, be delivered. Of course, demonstrable falsehoods are not protected by the First Amendment in the same manner as truthful statements. But "erroneous statement is inevitable in free debate, and . . . it must be protected if the freedoms of expression are to have the 'breathing space' that they 'need . . . to survive,'" *New York Times Co.* v. *Sullivan*, 376 U.S. 254, 271–272 (1964), quoting *NAACP* v. *Button*, 371 U.S. 415, 433 (1963). Section 121.055, as applied in this case, has not afforded the requisite "breathing space."

The Commonwealth of Kentucky has provided that a candidate for public office forfeits his electoral victory if he errs in announcing that he will, if elected, serve at a reduced salary. As the Kentucky courts have made clear in this case, a candidate's liability under § 121.055 for such an error is absolute: His election victory

---

8. [The Kentucky Court of Appeals feared that allowing candidates to promise to serve without remuneration]

"* * * would permit the various elective public offices to become filled by those who would purchase their election thereto by making the most extravagant bid. The auction method of choosing a public officer would supplant the personal fitness test. Eventually most of the public offices would be occupied by the opulent, who could afford to serve without pay, or by the ambitious, who would serve only for the pittance of honor attached to the office, or by the designing grafter, who would surely obtain his remuneration by methods which would not bear scrutiny. Under such a system good government would certainly vanish from every subdivision of the state." * * *

9. A State could address this concern by prohibiting the reduction of a public official's salary during his term of office, as Kentucky has done here. * * *

must be voided even if the offending statement was made in good faith and was quickly repudiated. The chilling effect of such absolute accountability for factual misstatements in the course of political debate is incompatible with the atmosphere of free discussion contemplated by the First Amendment in the context of political campaigns. Although the state interest in protecting the political process from distortions caused by untrue and inaccurate speech is somewhat different from the state interest in protecting individuals from defamatory falsehoods, the principles underlying the First Amendment remain paramount. Whenever compatible with the underlying interests at stake, under the regime of that Amendment "we depend for . . . correction not on the conscience of judges and juries but on the competition of other ideas." In a political campaign, a candidate's factual blunder is unlikely to escape the notice of, and correction by, the erring candidate's political opponent. The preferred First Amendment remedy of "more speech, not enforced silence," thus has special force. There has been no showing in this case that petitioner made the disputed statement other than in good faith and without knowledge of its falsity, or that he made the statement with reckless disregard as to whether it was false or not. Moreover, petitioner retracted the statement promptly after discovering that it might have been false. Under these circumstances, nullifying petitioner's election victory was inconsistent with the atmosphere of robust political debate protected by the First Amendment.

[*Reversed and remanded.*]

The Chief Justice [Burger] concurs in the judgment [without opinion].

Justice Rehnquist, concurring in the result.

I agree that the provision of the Kentucky Corrupt Practices Act discussed by the Court in its opinion impermissibly limits freedom of speech on the part of political candidates in violation of the First and Fourteenth Amendments to the United States Constitution. Because on different facts I think I would give more weight to the State's interest in preventing corruption in elections, I am unable to join the Court's analogy between such laws and state defamation laws. * * *

Notes and Questions

1. *Problem.* Hawaii enacts a "Code of Fair Campaign Practices" establishing rules for conducting campaigns. Among the rules are that candidates "shall not use campaign material relating to any candidate's election which misrepresents, distorts, or otherwise falsifies the facts regarding the candidate," and that candidates "shall refrain from the use of personal vilification, character defamation, or any other form of scurrilous personal attacks on any candidate or his family." Candidates need not sign the Code, but a list of candidates endorsing the Code and a list of candidates refusing to endorse the Code are made public at a website maintained by the

state's Campaign Spending Commission. Candidates who sign the Code and then breach it are subject to censure.

A candidate challenging the incumbent state senator signs the pledge and, during the campaign, distributes a flyer containing a cartoon depicting his opponent in a pocket labeled "Special Interests." The flyer also alleges that the incumbent's law firm had received one million dollars from one particular interest, and cited a newspaper story. The Commission censures the candidate, reasoning that he had no facts upon which to allege that the incumbent's position in the senate resulted in any gain for the incumbent or his firm. Is the censure constitutional? If the statement is protected under *New York Times* and *Brown v. Hartlage*, may the candidate waive that First Amendment protection by signing the Code? Would the result change if the state did not publicize the names of the non-signatories by maintaining the website? *See Ancheta v. Watada*, 135 F. Supp. 2d 1114 (D. Haw. 2001).

2. *Problem.* Roy Cooper, candidate for North Carolina Attorney General, sponsors a television advertisement, in which he criticizes his opponent, Dan Boyce. The audio portion of the advertisement is as follows:

> Dan Boyce—his law firm sued the state, charging $28,000 an hour in lawyer fees to the taxpayers. The Judge said it shocks the conscience. Dan Boyce's law firm wanted more than a police officer's salary for each hour's work. Dan Boyce, wrong for Attorney General.

In reality, the law firm carrying Boyce's name, Boyce & Isley, did not come into existence until after the institution of the suit, so the advertisement was arguably deceptive and defamatory in that it alleged that Boyce's law firm "sued the state." Further, the attorneys' fee was requested—not "charged"—by Boyce and was a contingency fee for successfully prosecuting a $150 million class-action suit.

Boyce, his partners, and the firm sued Cooper for defamation. Does the First Amendment permit the plaintiffs to recover? *See Boyce & Isley, PLLC v. Cooper*, 568 S.E.2d 893 (N.C. Ct. App. 2002).

3. Proclaiming that campaigning for public office is "not for the thin-skinned or the faint-hearted, to use two apropos clichés," the court in *Schatz v. Republican State Leadership Committee*, 669 F.3d 50 (1st Cir. 2012), held that an unsuccessful candidate who filed a defamation action against the opposing political party, based on allegedly false statements in political ads, failed to allege actual malice by the defendants. The ads accused Schatz, a town selectman, of voting to give $10,000 of taxpayers' money to a "political organization." The charge was true, but left out details—such as the fact that voters had authorized the expenditure, which was for the purpose of countering a school-consolidation measure—that would have made the expenditure appear less sinister. Similarly, the ads accused Schatz of voting to cancel an Independence Day fireworks display. The selectmen did in fact cancel the display, but Schatz voted the other way—a fact not disclosed in the newspaper report on which the ad was based. The court conceded that the complaint "used actual malice buzzwords," *id.* at 56, but failed adequately to allege facts to back

up those legal conclusions. *See id.* at 57–58. Given the rigor with which cases like *Schatz* apply the actual-malice standard, how likely is this sort of defamation claim to succeed?

4. *Problem.* A candidate running for state office in the 2006 Republican primary publicizes some complimentary remarks other public officials made about him in 2004. In the campaign advertisement, the candidate reprints the text of the remarks accurately, and also notes in small print that they were made in 2004. Nevertheless, he is fined by a state agency charged with administering a law barring the use of endorsements without the approval of the endorsing party. Here, because the candidate never received permission from the public officials who made the statements, he violated the statute. Is the statute constitutional as applied to him? Would the statute be constitutional as applied to a candidate who accurately reprinted the text of the remarks, but nowhere indicated the date the remarks were made? Would the statute be constitutional as applied to a candidate who materially misrepresented the remarks that were made? The next case may prove useful in answering the last question.

United States v. Alvarez

Supreme Court of the United States
567 U.S. 709, 132 S. Ct. 2537, 183 L. Ed. 2d 574 (2012)

JUSTICE KENNEDY announced the judgment of the Court and delivered an opinion, in which THE CHIEF JUSTICE [ROBERTS], JUSTICE GINSBURG, and JUSTICE SOTOMAYOR join.

Lying was his habit. Xavier Alvarez, the respondent here, lied when he said that he played hockey for the Detroit Red Wings and that he once married a starlet from Mexico. But when he lied in announcing he held the Congressional Medal of Honor, respondent ventured onto new ground; for that lie violates a federal criminal statute, the Stolen Valor Act of 2005. 18 U.S.C. §704. [Under the Act, anyone who "falsely represents himself or herself, verbally or in writing, to have been awarded any decoration or medal authorized by Congress for the Armed Forces of the United States" may be punished by a fine, six months' imprisonment, or both. Violators who claim to have won the Congressional Medal of Honor are subject to a heightened penalty—a fine, one year's imprisonment, or both.]

In 2007, respondent attended his first public meeting as a board member of the Three Valley Water District Board. The board is a governmental entity with headquarters in Claremont, California. He introduced himself as follows: "I'm a retired marine of 25 years. I retired in the year 2001. Back in 1987, I was awarded the Congressional Medal of Honor. I got wounded many times by the same guy." None of this was true. For all the record shows, respondent's statements were but a pathetic attempt to gain respect that eluded him. The statements do not seem to have been made to secure employment or financial benefits or admission to privileges reserved for those who had earned the Medal.

Respondent was indicted under the Stolen Valor Act for lying about the Congressional Medal of Honor at the meeting. The United States District Court for the Central District of California rejected his claim that the statute is invalid under the First Amendment. Respondent pleaded guilty to one count, reserving the right to appeal on his First Amendment claim. The United States Court of Appeals for the Ninth Circuit, in a decision by a divided panel, found the Act invalid under the First Amendment and reversed the conviction. * * *

* * * [C]ontent-based restrictions on speech have been permitted, as a general matter, only when confined to the few "historic and traditional categories [of expression] long familiar to the bar." Among these categories are advocacy intended, and likely, to incite imminent lawless action; obscenity; defamation; speech integral to criminal conduct; so-called "fighting words"; child pornography; fraud; true threats; and speech presenting some grave and imminent threat the government has the power to prevent, although a restriction under the last category is most difficult to sustain. These categories have a historical foundation in the Court's free speech tradition. The vast realm of free speech and thought always protected in our tradition can still thrive, and even be furthered, by adherence to those categories and rules.

Absent from those few categories where the law allows content-based regulation of speech is any general exception to the First Amendment for false statements. This comports with the common understanding that some false statements are inevitable if there is to be an open and vigorous expression of views in public and private conversation, expression the First Amendment seeks to guarantee.

The Government disagrees with this proposition. It cites language from some of this Court's precedents to support its contention that false statements have no value and hence no First Amendment protection. * * * These quotations all derive from cases discussing defamation, fraud, or some other legally cognizable harm associated with a false statement, such as an invasion of privacy or the costs of vexatious litigation. In those decisions the falsity of the speech at issue was not irrelevant to our analysis, but neither was it determinative. The Court has never endorsed the categorical rule the Government advances: that false statements receive no First Amendment protection. Our prior decisions have not confronted a measure, like the Stolen Valor Act, that targets falsity and nothing more.

Even when considering some instances of defamation and fraud, moreover, the Court has been careful to instruct that falsity alone may not suffice to bring the speech outside the First Amendment. The statement must be a knowing or reckless falsehood. The Government thus seeks * * * to convert a rule that limits liability even in defamation cases where the law permits recovery for tortious wrongs into a rule that expands liability in a different, far greater realm of discourse and expression. That inverts the rationale for the exception. The requirements [sic] of a knowing falsehood or reckless disregard for the truth as the condition for recovery in certain defamation cases exists to allow more speech, not less. A rule designed to tolerate certain speech ought not blossom to become a rationale for a rule restricting it. * * *

The Act by its plain terms applies to a false statement made at any time, in any place, to any person. * * * Here the lie was made in a public meeting, but the statute would apply with equal force to personal, whispered conversations within a home. The statute seeks to control and suppress all false statements on this one subject in almost limitless times and settings. And it does so entirely without regard to whether the lie was made for the purpose of material gain.

Permitting the government to decree this speech to be a criminal offense, whether shouted from the rooftops or made in a barely audible whisper, would endorse government authority to compile a list of subjects about which false statements are punishable. That governmental power has no clear limiting principle. * * * Were this law to be sustained, there could be an endless list of subjects the National Government or the States could single out. Where false claims are made to effect a fraud or secure moneys or other valuable considerations, say offers of employment, it is well established that the Government may restrict speech without affronting the First Amendment. But the Stolen Valor Act is not so limited in its reach. Were the Court to hold that the interest in truthful discourse alone is sufficient to sustain a ban on speech, absent any evidence that the speech was used to gain a material advantage, it would give government a broad censorial power unprecedented in this Court's cases or in our constitutional tradition. The mere potential for the exercise of that power casts a chill, a chill the First Amendment cannot permit if free speech, thought, and discourse are to remain a foundation of our freedom. * * *

* * * The Government's interest in protecting the integrity of the Medal of Honor is beyond question. But to recite the Government's compelling interests is not to end the matter. The First Amendment requires that the Government's chosen restriction on the speech at issue be "actually necessary" to achieve its interest. There must be a direct causal link between the restriction imposed and the injury to be prevented. * * * The Government points to no evidence to support its claim that the public's general perception of military awards is diluted by false claims such as those made by Alvarez. * * *

[Further, t]he Government has not shown, and cannot show, why counterspeech would not suffice to achieve its interest. The facts of this case indicate that the dynamics of free speech, of counterspeech, of refutation, can overcome the lie. Respondent lied at a public meeting. Even before the FBI began investigating him for his false statements "Alvarez was perceived as a phony." Once the lie was made public, he was ridiculed online, his actions were reported in the press, and a fellow board member called for his resignation. There is good reason to believe that a similar fate would befall other false claimants. See Brief for Reporters Committee for Freedom of the Press et al. as *Amici Curiae* 30–33 (listing numerous examples of public exposure of false claimants). Indeed, the outrage and contempt expressed for respondent's lies can serve to reawaken and reinforce the public's respect for the Medal, its recipients, and its high purpose. The acclaim that recipients of the Congressional Medal of Honor receive also casts doubt on the proposition that the public will be misled by the claims of charlatans or become cynical of those whose heroic deeds earned them the Medal by right.

The remedy for speech that is false is speech that is true. This is the ordinary course in a free society. The response to the unreasoned is the rational; to the uninformed, the enlightened; to the straight-out lie, the simple truth. * * * The First Amendment itself ensures the right to respond to speech we do not like, and for good reason. Freedom of speech and thought flows not from the beneficence of the state but from the inalienable rights of the person. And suppression of speech by the government can make exposure of falsity more difficult, not less so. Society has the right and civic duty to engage in open, dynamic, rational discourse. These ends are not well served when the government seeks to orchestrate public discussion through content-based mandates. * * *

It is a fair assumption that any true holders of the Medal who had heard of Alvarez's false claims would have been fully vindicated by the community's expression of outrage, showing as it did the Nation's high regard for the Medal. The same can be said for the Government's interest. The American people do not need the assistance of a government prosecution to express their high regard for the special place that military heroes hold in our tradition. Only a weak society needs government protection or intervention before it pursues its resolve to preserve the truth. Truth needs neither handcuffs nor a badge for its vindication.

In addition, when the Government seeks to regulate protected speech, the restriction must be the "least restrictive means among available, effective alternatives." There is, however, at least one less speech-restrictive means by which the Government could likely protect the integrity of the military awards system. A Government-created database could list Congressional Medal of Honor winners. Were a database accessible through the Internet, it would be easy to verify and expose false claims. * * *

The judgment of the Court of Appeals is affirmed.

It is so ordered.

JUSTICE BREYER, with whom JUSTICE KAGAN joins, concurring in the judgment. * * *

In determining whether a statute violates the First Amendment, this Court * * * has taken account of the seriousness of the speech-related harm the provision will likely cause, the nature and importance of the provision's countervailing objectives, the extent to which the provision will tend to achieve those objectives, and whether there are other, less restrictive ways of doing so. Ultimately the Court has had to determine whether the statute works speech-related harm that is out of proportion to its justifications. * * *

The statute before us * * * creates a significant risk of First Amendment harm. As written, it applies in family, social, or other private contexts, where lies will often cause little harm. It also applies in political contexts, where although such lies are more likely to cause harm, the risk of censorious selectivity by prosecutors is also high. Further, given the potential haziness of individual memory along with the large number of military awards covered (ranging from medals for rifle marksmanship to the Congressional Medal of Honor), there remains a risk of chilling that is not completely eliminated by *mens rea* requirements; a speaker might still be worried about being *prosecuted* for a careless false statement, even if he does not have the intent required to render him liable. And so the prohibition may be applied where it should not be applied, for example, to bar stool braggadocio or, in the political arena, subtly but selectively to speakers that the Government does not like. These considerations lead me to believe that the statute as written risks significant First Amendment harm.

Like both the plurality and the dissent, I believe the statute nonetheless has substantial justification. * * * To permit those who have not earned [military] honors to claim otherwise dilutes the value of the awards. Indeed, the Nation cannot fully honor those who have sacrificed so much for their country's honor unless those who claim to have received its military awards tell the truth. Thus, the statute risks harming protected interests but only in order to achieve a substantial countervailing objective.

We must therefore ask whether it is possible substantially to achieve the Government's objective in less burdensome ways. In my view, the answer to this question is "yes." * * * For example, not all military awards are alike. Congress might determine that some warrant greater protection than others. And a more finely tailored statute might, as other kinds of statutes prohibiting false factual statements have done, insist upon a showing that the false statement caused specific harm or at least was material, or focus its coverage on lies most likely to be harmful or on contexts where such lies are most likely to cause harm.

* * * And an accurate, publicly available register of military awards, easily obtainable by political opponents, may well adequately protect the integrity of an award against those who would falsely claim to have earned it. And so it is likely that a more narrowly tailored statute combined with such information-disseminating devices will effectively serve Congress' end.

The Government has provided no convincing explanation as to why a more finely tailored statute would not work. In my own view, such a statute could significantly reduce the threat of First Amendment harm while permitting the statute to achieve its important protective objective. That being so, I find the statute as presently drafted works disproportionate constitutional harm. It consequently fails intermediate scrutiny, and so violates the First Amendment.

For these reasons, I concur in the Court's judgment.

JUSTICE ALITO, with whom JUSTICE SCALIA and JUSTICE THOMAS join, dissenting. * * *

As Congress recognized, the lies proscribed by the Stolen Valor Act inflict substantial harm. In many instances, the harm is tangible in nature: Individuals often falsely represent themselves as award recipients in order to obtain financial or other material rewards, such as lucrative contracts and government benefits. An investigation of false claims in a single region of the United States, for example, revealed that 12 men had defrauded the Department of Veterans Affairs out of more than $1.4 million in veteran's benefits. In other cases, the harm is less tangible, but nonetheless significant. The lies proscribed by the Stolen Valor Act tend to debase the distinctive honor of military awards. * * *

It is well recognized in trademark law that the proliferation of cheap imitations of luxury goods blurs the "'signal' given out by the purchasers of the originals." In much the same way, the proliferation of false claims about military awards blurs the signal given out by the actual awards by making them seem more common than they really are, and this diluting effect harms the military by hampering its efforts to foster morale and esprit de corps. Surely it was reasonable for Congress to conclude that the goal of preserving the integrity of our country's top military honors is at least as worthy as that of protecting the prestige associated with fancy watches and designer handbags.

Both the plurality and JUSTICE BREYER argue that Congress could have preserved the integrity of military honors by means other than a criminal prohibition, but Congress had ample reason to believe that alternative approaches would not be adequate. The chief alternative that is recommended is the compilation and release of a comprehensive list or database of actual medal recipients. If the public could readily access such a resource, it is argued, imposters would be quickly and easily exposed, and the proliferation of lies about military honors would come to an end. This remedy, unfortunately, will not work. The Department of Defense has explained that the most that it can do is to create a database of recipients of certain top military honors awarded since 2001.[13] * * *

The plurality and the concurrence also suggest that Congress could protect the system of military honors by enacting a narrower statute. The plurality recommends a law that would apply only to lies that are intended to "secure moneys or other valuable considerations." In a similar vein, the concurrence comments that "a more finely tailored statute might . . . insist upon a showing that the false statement caused specific harm." But much damage is caused, both to real award recipients and to the system of military honors, by false statements that are not linked to any financial or other tangible reward. Unless even a small financial loss—say, a dollar given to a homeless man falsely claiming to be a decorated veteran—is more important in the eyes of the First Amendment than the damage caused to the very integrity of the military awards system, there is no basis for distinguishing between the Stolen Valor Act and the alternative statutes that the plurality and concurrence appear willing to sustain. * * *

---

13. In addition, since the Department may not disclose the Social Security numbers or birthdates of recipients, this database would be of limited use in ascertaining the veracity of a claim involving a person with a common name.

Time and again, this Court has recognized that as a general matter false factual statements possess no intrinsic First Amendment value. Consistent with this recognition, many kinds of false factual statements have long been proscribed without "rais[ing] any Constitutional problem." Laws prohibiting fraud, perjury, and defamation, for example, were in existence when the First Amendment was adopted, and their constitutionality is now beyond question.

We have also described as falling outside the First Amendment's protective shield certain false factual statements that were neither illegal nor tortious at the time of the Amendment's adoption. The right to freedom of speech has been held to permit recovery for the intentional infliction of emotional distress by means of a false statement, see [*Hustler Magazine, Inc.* v.] *Falwell*, [485 U.S. 46,] 56 [(1988)], even though that tort did not enter our law until the late 19th century. And in [*Time, Inc.* v.] *Hill*, [385 U.S. 374,] 390 [(1967)], the Court concluded that the free speech right allows recovery for the even more modern tort of false-light invasion of privacy.

In line with these holdings, it has long been assumed that the First Amendment is not offended by prominent criminal statutes with no close common-law analog. The most well known of these is probably 18 U.S.C. § 1001, which makes it a crime to "knowingly and willfully" make any "materially false, fictitious, or fraudulent statement or representation" in "any matter within the jurisdiction of the executive, legislative, or judicial branch of the Government of the United States." Unlike perjury, § 1001 is not limited to statements made under oath or before an official government tribunal. Nor does it require any showing of "pecuniary or property loss to the government." Instead, the statute is based on the need to protect "agencies from the perversion which *might* result from the deceptive practices described."

Still other statutes make it a crime to falsely represent that one is speaking on behalf of, or with the approval of, the Federal Government. See, *e.g.*, 18 U.S.C. § 912 (making it a crime to falsely impersonate a federal officer); § 709 (making it a crime to knowingly use, without authorization, the names of enumerated federal agencies, such as "Federal Bureau of Investigation," in a manner reasonably calculated to convey the impression that a communication is approved or authorized by the agency). We have recognized that § 912, like § 1001, does not require a showing of pecuniary or property loss and that its purpose is to "maintain the general good repute and dignity" of Government service. All told, there are more than 100 federal criminal statutes that punish false statements made in connection with areas of federal agency concern.

These examples amply demonstrate that false statements of fact merit no First Amendment protection in their own right. It is true, as Justice Breyer notes, that many in our society either approve or condone certain discrete categories of false statements, including false statements made to prevent harm to innocent victims and so-called "white lies." But respondent's false claim to have received the Medal of Honor did not fall into any of these categories. * * * Respondent's claim, like all those covered by the Stolen Valor Act, served no valid purpose. * * *

In stark contrast to hypothetical laws prohibiting false statements about history, science, and similar matters, the Stolen Valor Act presents no risk at all that valuable speech will be suppressed. The speech punished by the Act is not only verifiably false and entirely lacking in intrinsic value, but it also fails to serve any instrumental purpose that the First Amendment might protect. Tellingly, when asked at oral argument what truthful speech the Stolen Valor Act might chill, even respondent's counsel conceded that the answer is none.

Notes and Questions

1. Note that the plurality and the dissent started from different premises. Justice Kennedy treated categories of unprotected speech as limited exceptions to the general rule banning content-based suppression of speech. Justice Alito, by contrast, treated those categories as establishing the principle that false speech is worthy of protection only when attempts to ban it would also suppress truthful speech. Which approach was more faithful to the Court's precedents?

2. Justice Breyer argued that the Stolen Valor Act chilled some "careless" speech, despite its (imputed) *mens rea* requirement, because speakers might fear *prosecution* even if a *conviction* would be impossible. (The plurality likewise cited the Act's potential to chill speech as a reason for striking it down.) If such a concern were taken seriously, would that require that we protect defamatory speech made with "actual malice"?

3. Do you agree with Justice Breyer that the statute's coverage was constitutionally problematic because it applied "in family, social, or other private contexts, where lies will often cause little harm"? When *Alvarez* was denied rehearing *en banc* by the Ninth Circuit, Chief Judge Kozinski wrote a concurring opinion arguing that it was necessary to provide constitutional protection for "the white lies, exaggerations and deceptions that are an integral part of human intercourse." *United States v. Alvarez*, 638 F.3d 666, 673 (9th Cir. 2011) (denying reh'g *en banc*) (Kozinski, C.J., concurring). He then provided examples of such untruths:

> We lie to protect our privacy ("No, I don't live around here"); to avoid hurt feelings ("Friday is my study night"); to make others feel better ("Gee you've gotten skinny"); to avoid recriminations ("I only lost $10 at poker"); to prevent grief ("The doc says you're getting better"); to maintain domestic tranquility ("She's just a friend"); to avoid social stigma ("I just haven't met the right woman"); for career advancement ("I'm sooo lucky to have a smart boss like you"); to avoid being lonely ("I love opera"); to eliminate a rival ("He has a boyfriend"); to achieve an objective ("But I love you so much"); to defeat an objective ("I'm allergic to latex"); to make an exit ("It's not you, it's me"); to delay the inevitable ("The check is in the mail"); to communicate displeasure ("There's nothing wrong"); to get someone off your back ("I'll call you about lunch"); to escape a nudnik ("My mother's on the other line"); to namedrop ("We go way back"); to set up a surprise

party ("I need help moving the piano"); to buy time ("I'm on my way"); to keep up appearances ("We're not talking divorce"); to avoid taking out the trash ("My back hurts"); to duck an obligation ("I've got a headache"); to maintain a public image ("I go to church every Sunday"); to make a point ("Ich bin ein Berliner"); to save face ("I had too much to drink"); to humor ("Correct as usual, King Friday"); to avoid embarrassment ("That wasn't me"); to curry favor ("I've read all your books"); to get a clerkship ("You're the greatest living jurist"); to save a dollar ("I gave at the office"); or to maintain innocence ("There are eight tiny reindeer on the rooftop").

Id. at 674–75. Are these statements harmless? After *Alvarez*, is there anything the legal system can do to punish one who, for example, uses "she's just a friend" to conceal a long-running affair from his wife? More generally, should false campaign speech be entitled to any more—or any less—protection than false speech about other topics?

4. The *Alvarez* plurality accepted longstanding limitations on political speech, including the law of defamation approved by *New York Times Co. v. Sullivan* and its progeny. Should the Court treat lies about ballot measures as analogous to defamation, or are they akin to the law struck down in *Alvarez*? On the one hand, lies about ballot measures do not harm any individual in the way that defamation harms the person defamed. On the other hand, perhaps statements about ballot measures are unlikely to trigger the "counterspeech" that could inform the public about the truth. *See Rickert v. Public Disclosure Comm'n*, 168 P.3d 826 (Wash. 2007) (striking down a false-statements prohibition in candidate elections); *Washington ex rel. Public Disclosure Comm'n v. 119 Vote No! Comm.*, 957 P.2d 691 (Wash. 1998) (striking down a false-statements prohibition concerning ballot measures).

In *281 Care Committee v. Arneson*, 766 F.3d 774, 785 (8th Cir. 2014), the Eighth Circuit struck down Minnesota's political false-statements law, which prohibited knowingly or recklessly false statements about ballot questions. Do *281 Care Committee* and *Alvarez* grant constitutional protection to campaign "dirty tricks"?

5. *Problem.* Because Justice Kennedy's opinion garnered only four votes, Justice Breyer's opinion stated the controlling rule. Thus, it is important to consider what other, narrower, statutes banning false or misleading speech might survive Justice Breyer's test of proportionality. Consider the following questions, the first two of which were raised by Justice Breyer in a portion of his opinion not reprinted here:

A. May a political organization be punished for infringing the trademark of a different organization? *See United We Stand America, Inc. v. United We Stand America New York, Inc.*, 128 F.3d 86 (2d Cir. 1997).

B. May a state prohibit candidates from falsely claiming to be incumbents? *See Hoy v. Fox*, 389 N.W.2d 446 (Mich. Ct. App. 1986).

C. May a state criminalize lies about the voting process that are designed to trick people into staying away from the polls? *See* Richard L. Hasen, *A*

Constitutional Right to Lie in Campaigns and Elections?, 74 MONT. L. REV. 53 (2013); Eugene Volokh, *Freedom of Speech and Knowing Falsehoods*, VOLOKH CONSPIRACY, June 28, 2012, http://www.volokh.com/2012/06/28/freedom -of-speech-and-knowing-falsehoods/. *See also* Joshua S. Sellers, *Legislating Against Lying in Campaigns and Elections*, 71 OKLA. L. REV. 141 (2018) (arguing that *Alvarez* and *Susan B. Anthony List v. Driehaus* (immediately below) permit governments to sanction false statements in mandatory campaign-disclosure filings or those involving election administration). The Supreme Court has indicated in dictum that the government "may prohibit messages intended to mislead voters about voting requirements and procedures." *Minnesota Voters Alliance v. Mansky*, 585 U.S. __, 138 S. Ct. 1876, 1889 n.4 (2018) [p. 1033].

D. May the government penalize the Republican National Committee for mailing fundraising appeals resembling official census forms? The letters are labeled as being from the RNC, but also say, among other things, "OFFICIAL DOCUMENT" and "2020 Congressional District Census." *See* Andrew Sheeler, *This 'Census' Form in Your Mailbox Isn't from the Government. Here's Who Sent It Out and Why,* SACRAMENTO BEE (Feb. 5, 2020), at https://www.sacbee.com/news/politics-government/capitol-alert /article239951158.html.

E. A state has a professional-licensing statute prohibiting anyone other than licensed professionals from identifying themselves as members of those professions. Bob Hartley runs for the state legislature, and identifies himself on his campaign website as a psychologist. In truth, he is not a psychologist and does not have a Ph.D. in psychology (which is a requirement to be a licensed psychologist). He did, however, complete a four-year post-doctoral fellowship in psychology at Yale, and the dissertation for his Ph.D. in education was published in *Genetic Psychology Monographs*. Hartley was a professor in the psychology departments at Yale University and Vassar College, studied under leading psychologists, and was a member of the American Psychological Association for several years.

May the state constitutionally prosecute Hartley for using the title "psychologist" on his campaign website? What if Hartley identified himself as a "psychologist" on his professional website, rather than on his campaign website? *See Serafine v. Branaman*, 810 F.3d 354, 361 (5th Cir. 2016). *Cf. National Institute of Family and Life Advocates v. Becerra*, 585 U.S. __, 138 S. Ct. 2361, 2371–72 (2018) ("Speech is not unprotected merely because it is uttered by 'professionals.'").

Would it make any difference if the state prosecuted a candidate for identifying himself as an "interior designer" when he lacked the license that would have enabled him to use that title, or for identifying himself as a "realtor" when he was a real-estate agent but not a member of the National

Association of Realtors? *See Byrum v. Landreth*, 566 F.3d 442 (5th Cir. 2009). *Cf. Lee v. Weisman*, 505 U.S. 577, 636 (1992) (Scalia, J., dissenting) ("[I]nterior decorating is a rock-hard science compared to psychology practiced by amateurs.").

Susan B. Anthony List v. Driehaus

United States Court of Appeals for the Sixth Circuit
814 F.3d 466 (2016)

COLE, CHIEF JUDGE [with whom SUTTON, CIRCUIT JUDGE, and BELL, DISTRICT JUDGE (sitting by designation), join]. * * *

Ohio's political false-statements laws [Ohio Rev. Code § 3517.21(B)(9)–(10)] prohibit persons from disseminating false information about a political candidate in campaign materials during the campaign season "knowing the same to be false or with reckless disregard of whether it was false or not, if the statement is designed to promote the election, nomination, or defeat of the candidate." The statutes specifically prohibit false statements about a candidate's voting record, but are not limited to that. "Campaign materials" are broadly defined as, but not limited to, "sample ballots, an advertisement on radio or television or in a newspaper or periodical, a public speech, [or] press release."

Any person, including the Secretary of State or a Board of Elections official, may file a complaint with the Commission alleging a violation of the political false-statements laws. For a complaint filed shortly before an election, there is a three-step process to be convicted of the crime of making a political false statement. First, a panel of the Commission conducts a preliminary probable cause hearing based on the complaint and issues a public finding. If the panel finds probable cause, the complaint proceeds to an adjudicatory hearing before the full Commission. If, after the adjudicatory hearing, the Commission finds by clear and convincing evidence that a party violated the political false-statements laws, it may refer the case to a prosecutor. If convicted in subsequent state court proceedings, first-time violators may be sentenced up to six months in prison or fined up to $5,000. For complaints filed after an election, more than sixty days before a primary election, or more than ninety days before a general election, there is no probable cause hearing and the complaint proceeds directly to an adjudicatory hearing.

In 2010, then-Congressman Steven Driehaus filed a complaint with the Commission alleging that SBA List violated Ohio's political false-statements laws by issuing a press release accusing him of voting for "taxpayer-funded abortion" by voting for the Affordable Care Act.[a] A panel of the Commission issued a probable cause find-

---

a. The statement was literally true, as the Affordable Care Act does use tax dollars to pay for certain abortions, such as those that are the result of rape. The statement might have been thought to be misleading, however, as some people reading the statement might have inferred that the Act provided money for elective abortions. —Eds.

ing that SBA List violated the law. SBA List responded by filing suit against Driehaus and various state officials in the Southern District of Ohio. * * * [T]he district court "str[uck] down the laws as unconstitutional and permanently enjoin[ed] the Ohio Elections Commission and its members from enforcing Ohio's political false-statements laws." The Commission appeals. * * *

[Because the false-statements laws are content-based restrictions on core political speech, they are subject to strict scrutiny.] * * * Ohio's laws reach not only defamatory and fraudulent remarks, but *all* false speech regarding a political candidate, even that which may not be material, negative, defamatory, or libelous. Accordingly, strict scrutiny is appropriate. * * *

Laws subject to strict scrutiny are presumptively unconstitutional and can only survive if they (1) serve a compelling state interest and (2) are narrowly tailored to achieve that interest. * * * Here, Ohio's interests in preserving the integrity of its elections, protecting "voters from confusion and undue influence," and "ensuring that an individual's right to vote is not undermined by fraud in the election process" are compelling. *Burson v. Freeman*, 504 U.S. 191, 199 (1992) [p. 1024] (plurality opinion); *see also McIntyre* [*v. Ohio Elections Commission*], 514 U.S. [334,] 349 [(1995)] [p. 922] (Ohio's interest in preventing fraud and libel "carries special weight during election campaigns when false statements, if credited, may have serious adverse consequences for the public at large."). But Ohio's laws * * * are not narrowly tailored in their (1) timing, (2) lack of a screening process for frivolous complaints, (3) application to non-material statements, (4) application to commercial intermediaries, and (5) over-inclusiveness and under-inclusiveness.

First, the timing of Ohio's administrative process does not necessarily promote fair elections. While the laws provide an expedited timeline for complaints filed within a certain number of days before an election, complaints filed outside this timeframe are free to linger for six months. Even when a complaint is expedited, there is no guarantee the administrative or criminal proceedings will conclude before the election or within time for the candidate's campaign to recover from any false information that was disseminated. Indeed, candidates filing complaints against their political opponents count on the fact that "an ultimate decision on the merits will be deferred until after the relevant election." [*Susan B. Anthony List v.*] *Driehaus*, 134 S. Ct. [2334,] 2346 [(2014)] (quoting Br. of Amicus Curiae Ohio Att'y Gen. Michael DeWine in Supp. of Neither Party).[b] A final finding that occurs *after* the election does not preserve the integrity of the election. On the other hand, in many cases, "a preelection probable-cause finding . . . itself may be viewed [by the electorate] as a sanction by the State" that "triggers 'profound' political damage,

---

b. The cited 2014 Supreme Court decision held that the plaintiffs' pre-enforcement challenge to Ohio's false-statements laws was justiciable, because the challengers had presented a credible threat that the statute would be enforced against them. The Supreme Court remanded the case, resulting in this decision on the merits. — Eds.

even before a final [Commission] adjudication." The timing of Ohio's process is not narrowly tailored to promote fair elections.

Second, Ohio fails to screen out frivolous complaints prior to a probable cause hearing. While this permits a panel of the Commission to review and reach a probable cause conclusion on complaints as quickly as possible, it also provides frivolous complainants an audience and requires purported violators to respond to a potentially frivolous complaint. "Because the universe of potential complainants is not restricted to state officials who are constrained by explicit guidelines or ethical obligations, there is a real risk of complaints from, for example, political opponents." *Driehaus*, 134 S. Ct. at 2345. There is no process for screening out frivolous complaints or complaints that, on their face, only complain of non-actionable statements, such as opinions. Indeed, some complainants use the law's process "to gain a campaign advantage without ever having to prove the falsity of a statement . . . tim[ing] their submissions to achieve maximum disruption . . . forc[ing political opponents] to divert significant time and resources . . . in the crucial days leading up to an election." [*Id.*] at 2346 (quoting DeWine Amicus Br.). The potential for attorney's fees and the costs for frivolous complaints does not save the law because this finding of frivolity does not occur until *after* a probable cause finding or a full adjudicatory hearing. The process of designating a panel, permitting parties to engage in motion practice, and having a panel conduct a probable cause review for plainly frivolous or non-actionable complaints is not narrowly tailored to preserve fair elections.

Third, Ohio's laws apply to *all* false statements, including non-material statements. * * * Thus, influencing an election by lying about a political candidate's shoe size or vote on whether to continue a congressional debate is just as actionable as lying about a candidate's party affiliation or vote on an important policy issue, such as the Affordable Care Act. Further, the law prohibits false statements regarding a political candidate—even outside the political arena—so long as the statement is "designed to promote the election, nomination, or defeat of the candidate," and is made in broadly defined "campaign materials." Penalizing non-material statements, particularly those made outside the political arena, is not narrowly tailored to preserve fair elections.

Fourth, Ohio's laws apply to anyone who advertises, "post[s], publish[es], circulate[s], distribute[s], or otherwise disseminate[s]" false political speech. Such a broad prohibition "applies not only to the speaker of the false statement but also to commercial intermediaries like the company that was supposed to erect SBA List's billboard in 2010." Conducting hearings against or prosecuting a billboard company executive, who was simply the messenger, is not narrowly tailored to preserve fair elections.

Fifth, the law is both over-inclusive and underinclusive. Causing damage to a campaign that ultimately may not be in violation of the law, through a preliminary probable cause ruling, does not preserve the integrity of the elections and in fact undermines the state's interest in promoting fair elections. At the same time, the law may not timely penalize those who violate it, nor does it provide for campaigns that are the victim of potentially damaging false statements. "[A] law cannot be regarded as protecting an interest of the highest order, and thus as justifying a restriction on truthful speech, when it leaves appreciable damage to that supposedly vital interest unprohibited." *Reed* [*v. Town of Gilbert*, 576 U.S. 155, __, 135 S. Ct. 2218, 2232 (2015) (quoting *Republican Party of Minnesota v. White*, 536 U.S. 765, 780 (2002))] [p. 605]. Though Ohio's interests "are assuredly legitimate, we are not persuaded that they justify [such an] extremely broad prohibition." Indeed, courts have consistently erred on the side of permitting more political speech than less. *See, e.g.,* [*United States v.*] *Alvarez*, [567 U.S. 709, 727–28 (2012)] [p. 575]. * * *

Other courts to evaluate similar laws post-*Alvarez* have reached the same conclusion. *See 281 Care Comm. v. Arneson*, 766 F.3d 774, 785 (8th Cir. 2014) ("[N]o amount of narrow tailoring succeeds because [Minnesota's political false-statements law] is not necessary, is simultaneously overbroad and underinclusive, and is not the least restrictive means of achieving any stated goal."); *Commonwealth v. Lucas*, 34 N.E.3d 1242, 1257 (Mass. 2015) (striking down Massachusetts' law, which was similar to Ohio's); *see also Rickert v. State Pub. Disclosure Comm'n*, 168 P.3d 826, 829–31 (Wash. 2007) (striking down Washington's political false-statements law, which required proof of actual malice, but not defamatory nature).

Ohio's political false-statements laws are content-based restrictions targeting core political speech that are not narrowly tailored to serve the state's admittedly compelling interest in conducting fair elections. Accordingly, we affirm the district court's judgment finding the laws unconstitutional.

Notes and Questions

1. *SBA List* was one of the first cases to apply *Alvarez* in the context of campaign speech. The Sixth Circuit identified five reasons that the Ohio laws were not narrowly tailored to the compelling interest in protecting voters from confusion, fraud, and undue influence. Was each of those reasons independently sufficient to render the laws unconstitutional? Or were the laws insufficiently tailored only because they had all of those defects in combination?

2. Suppose that Ohio amended its laws to address all the procedural flaws identified by the court: complaints would be fast-tracked; frivolous complaints would be screened out; the prohibition would be restricted to statements that are both false and material; the punishments would apply only to the speakers of false statements; and there would be no probable-cause announcement. If those problems were fixed, would *Alvarez* still prohibit a government's attempt to punish false campaign speech? Is there a difference between the government's attempt to declare the truth of political statements and the government's pronouncement of other truths, such as the rate of inflation, the unemployment rate, or any of the determinations of truth made by courts and juries?

3. *Problem.* California's "Truth in Political Advertising Act," Cal. Elec. Code § 20010, prohibits a person, acting with actual malice, from superimposing an image of a candidate on another photograph, or superimposing another image on a photo of a candidate, unless accompanied by a disclaimer stating, "This picture is not an accurate representation of fact." If the Act were applied to punish the speech in the following examples, would it violate the First Amendment?

A. Karo Tarossian, a candidate for Los Angeles City Council, distributes campaign mailers showing the head of Tarossian's opponent, Monica Rodriguez, superimposed on a photo of a woman in front of an oil-drilling operation. The woman is holding a sign that says, "I am funded by Chevron." *See* Dakota Smith, *Campaign Mailer with Photoshopped Images Draws Accusations in L.A. City Council Race for Valley Seat*, L.A. Times, Apr. 10, 2017, *at* http://www.latimes.com/local/lanow/la-me-ln-mailer-council -race-20170410-story.html.

B. The same Monica Rodriguez distributes a campaign advertisement featuring the head of her opponent superimposed on the image of a cartoon frog, so as to make the point that the opponent hopped from job to job. *See id.*

C. A candidate doctors a photo to make it appear as if his opponent marched in a gay-pride parade, and then sends the photo to conservative voters.

4. The 2016 election brought to the fore the phenomenon of what quickly became known as "fake news." Narrowly defined, "fake news" refers to false stories online, presented as if coming from authentic news sources so as to deceive readers about their truthfulness. For example, one site purports to be the on-line site of the "Boston Tribune," a non-existent newspaper. Others closely copy the name and appearance of authentic news organizations, such as the fake news website ABCNews.com .co. More broadly, the term now is often used to refer to any news story with incorrect facts, or even lacking proper context. Thus, President Trump has sometimes labeled traditional media outlets as "fake news."

In one well publicized incident, a North Carolina man read a "fake news" story that a child-prostitution ring was being run out of a pizza parlor in Washington, D.C., by associates of Democratic presidential candidate Hillary Clinton. Angered, the man drove to Washington and was arrested after firing a shot inside the restaurant (no one was hurt). *See* Cecilia Kang & Adam Goldman, *In Washington Pizzeria Attack, Fake News Brought Real Guns*, N.Y. Times, Dec. 5, 2016, *available at* https:// www.nytimes.com/2016/12/05/business/media/comet-ping-pong-pizza-shooting -fake-news-consequences.html.

Do *Alvarez* and *Susan B. Anthony List* allow room for the government to regulate "fake news"? What would be some of the pros and cons of allowing the government to regulate "fake news"? *See* Cass R. Sunstein, *Falsehoods and the First Amendment* (July 25, 2019), *available at* https://ssrn.com/abstract=3426765.

5. Senator (and 2020 presidential candidate) Elizabeth Warren has urged that there be "civil and criminal penalties for knowingly disseminating false information about when and how to vote in U.S. elections." She has also called on "[s]ocial media platforms [to] ban accounts that knowingly disseminate false information about the time, place, and manner of voting." Elizabeth Warren, *Fighting Digital Disinformation, at* https://elizabethwarren.com/plans/fighting-digital-disinformation?source =soc-WB-ew-tw-rollout-20200129. Are those proposals constitutional? (While the actions of social-media companies themselves would not be state action, the companies might be subject to the First Amendment if their action is taken as a result of pressure from the government.) Is it relevant that Senator Warren's proposal aims to combat disinformation campaigns that, in her words, "sought to polarize and disenfranchise particular groups—chiefly Black voters"?

C. Media Coverage

The First Amendment's protection of "the freedom of speech, [and] of the press" extends not just to candidates, but to the institutional media as well, and, indeed, everyone else. The press has been viewed as fulfilling a watchdog function, informing the public about candidates and public officials, among other issues of the day. Accordingly, the Court has been reluctant to permit government oversight of this institution, which is supposed to oversee government. *Mills v. Alabama*, which follows this introduction, is an excellent example of the Court's protective treatment of the press. Nevertheless, First Amendment rights are not absolute. As a general matter, the freedom of the press protects media entities from laws that subject them to special harms (a special tax on newspaper ink, for example), but it does not entitle them to an exemption from the obligations of the rest of society. *See Branzburg v. Hayes*, 408 U.S. 665 (1972) (rejecting a reporter's claimed immunity from testifying before a grand jury). The permissible scope of government regulation depends on the medium and the policies pursued by the regulation.

The Supreme Court has refused to permit states to limit the editorial discretion of newspapers, reasoning that people upset with the policies of existing papers can start their own. *See Miami Herald Publishing Co. v. Tornillo*, 418 U.S. 241 (1974) [p. 593]. Broadcast media, however, present a different picture, so to speak. Because the broadcast spectra are necessarily limited (and thus not everyone who wants a broadcast station can have one), the Court has treated broadcasters as fulfilling a public function and has permitted far more government intervention in the editorial policies of broadcasters than would be permissible in the case of newspapers. The Court upheld the so-called "fairness doctrine" in *Red Lion Broadcasting Co. v. FCC*, 395 U.S. 367 (1969), but the decision has been subject to criticism since then—in part due to technological innovations that many see as weakening the distinction the Court drew between print and broadcast media. The FCC's repeal of the doctrine in 1987, *see In re Syracuse Peace Council*, 2 F.C.C. Rcd. 5043 (1987), *upheld* 867 F.2d 654 (D.C. Cir. 1989), has made it unnecessary for the Court to revisit *Red Lion* head-on, but it has been limited by decisions such as *Federal Communications Commission v. League of Women Voters*, 468 U.S. 364 (1984), which held that the government could not impose a ban on editorializing by broadcasters — even ones receiving money from the government.

Mills v. Alabama

Supreme Court of the United States
384 U.S. 214, 86 S. Ct. 1434, 16 L. Ed. 2d 484 (1966)

Mr. Justice Black delivered the opinion of the Court [in which Mr. Chief Justice Warren, Mr. Justice Douglas, Mr. Justice Clark, Mr. Justice Brennan, Mr. Justice Stewart, Mr. Justice White, and Mr. Justice Fortas join].

The question squarely presented here is whether a State, consistently with the United States Constitution, can make it a crime for the editor of a daily newspaper to write and publish an editorial *on election day* urging people to vote a certain way on issues submitted to them.

On November 6, 1962, Birmingham, Alabama, held an election for the people to decide whether they preferred to keep their existing city commission form of government or replace it with a mayor-council government. On election day the Birmingham Post-Herald, a daily newspaper, carried an editorial written by its editor, appellant, James E. Mills, which strongly urged the people to adopt the mayor-council form of government. Mills was later arrested on a complaint charging that by publishing the editorial *on election day* he had violated § 285 of the Alabama Corrupt Practices Act, which makes it a crime "to do any electioneering or to solicit any votes * * * in support of or in opposition to any proposition that is being voted on on the day on which the election affecting such candidates or propositions is being held." * * *

Whatever differences may exist about interpretations of the First Amendment, there is practically universal agreement that a major purpose of that Amendment was to protect the free discussion of governmental affairs. This of course includes discussions of candidates, structures and forms of government, the manner in which government is operated or should be operated, and all such matters relating to political processes. The Constitution specifically selected the press, which includes not only newspapers, books, and magazines, but also humble leaflets and circulars, to play an important role in the discussion of public affairs. Thus the press serves and was designed to serve as a powerful antidote to any abuses of power by governmental officials and as a constitutionally chosen means for keeping officials elected by the people responsible to all the people whom they were selected to serve. Suppression of the right of the press to praise or criticize governmental agents and to clamor and contend for or against change, which is all that this editorial did, muzzles one of the very agencies the Framers of our Constitution thoughtfully and deliberately selected to improve our society and keep it free. The Alabama Corrupt

Practices Act by providing criminal penalties for publishing editorials such as the one here silences the press at a time when it can be most effective. It is difficult to conceive of a more obvious and flagrant abridgment of the constitutionally guaranteed freedom of the press.

Admitting that the state law restricted a newspaper editor's freedom to publish editorials on election day, the Alabama Supreme Court nevertheless sustained the constitutionality of the law on the ground that the restrictions on the press were only "reasonable restrictions" or at least "within the field of reasonableness." The court reached this conclusion because it thought the law imposed only a minor limitation on the press—restricting it only on election days—and because the court thought the law served a good purpose. It said:

> "It is a salutary legislative enactment that protects the public from confusive last-minute charges and countercharges and the distribution of propaganda in an effort to influence voters on an election day; when as a practical matter, because of lack of time, such matters cannot be answered or their truth determined until after the election is over."

This argument, even if it were relevant to the constitutionality of the law, has a fatal flaw. The state statute leaves people free to hurl their campaign charges up to the last minute of the day before election. The law held valid by the Alabama Supreme Court then goes on to make it a crime to answer those "last-minute" charges on election day, the only time they can be effectively answered. Because the law prevents any adequate reply to these charges, it is wholly ineffective in protecting the electorate "from confusive last-minute charges and countercharges." We hold that no test of reasonableness can save a state law from invalidation as a violation of the First Amendment when that law makes it a crime for a newspaper editor to do no more than urge people to vote one way or another in a publicly held election.

The judgment of the Supreme Court of Alabama is reversed and the case is remanded for further proceedings not inconsistent with this opinion.

It is so ordered.

MR. JUSTICE DOUGLAS, concurring. [Omitted.]

Separate opinion of MR. JUSTICE HARLAN. * * *

* * * I agree with the Court that the decision below cannot stand. But I would rest reversal on the ground that the relevant provision of the Alabama statute—"to do any electioneering or to solicit any votes [on election day] * * * in support of or in opposition to any proposition that is being voted on on the day on which the election affecting such candidates or propositions is being held"—did not give the appellant * * * fair warning that the publication of an editorial of this kind was reached by the foregoing provisions of the Alabama Corrupt Practices Act. I deem a broader holding unnecessary.

Notes and Questions

1. *Problem.* A Virgin Islands statute prohibits candidates and their campaign staffs from engaging in political activity after 2:00 a.m. on election day. Is such a prohibition distinguishable from *Mills*? *See Abiff v. Virgin Islands Legislature*, 216 F. Supp. 2d 455 (D.V.I. 2002).

2. *Problem.* An Arizona statute requires any PAC wishing to promote the election or defeat of a candidate within ten days before an election to mail a copy of the advertisement to the opposition candidate twenty-four hours before its publication. The state defends the statute as "necessary to an informed electorate because it affords candidates an opportunity to respond to last-minute negative 'hit pieces' that may confuse or misinform voters." Is the statute constitutional? *See Arizona Right to Life Political Action Committee v. Bayless*, 320 F.3d 1002 (9th Cir. 2003). Would it make any difference if, instead of requiring PACs to mail advertisements to the opposition candidate, the statute required PACs to mail advertisements to a government agency, which would then investigate the accuracy of the advertisements' claims and issue press releases correcting any misleading or false assertions?

3. *Problem.* May a state ban exit polling within three hundred feet of a polling place? *See Daily Herald Co. v. Munro*, 758 F.2d 350 (9th Cir. 1984); *American Broadcasting Co. v. Blackwell*, 479 F. Supp. 2d 719 (S.D. Ohio 2006); *CBS v. Smith*, 681 F. Supp. 794 (S.D. Fla. 1988); *National Broadcasting Co. v. Colburg*, 699 F. Supp. 241 (D. Mont. 1988); *National Broadcasting Co. v. Cleland*, 697 F. Supp. 1204 (N.D. Ga. 1988); *Firestone v. News-Press Publishing Co.*, 538 So. 2d 457 (Fla. 1989). What if a state permitted the media to *conduct* exit polls, but prohibited the *announcement of the results* until the polls closed, reasoning that potential voters would be dissuaded from voting if they believed the election had, for practical purposes, been decided? *See CBS, Inc. v. Growe*, 15 MEDIA L. REP. 2275 (D. Minn. 1988).

Miami Herald Publishing Co. v. Tornillo

Supreme Court of the United States
418 U.S. 241, 94 S. Ct. 2831, 41 L. Ed. 2d 730 (1974)

MR. CHIEF JUSTICE BURGER delivered the opinion of the Court [in which MR. JUSTICE DOUGLAS, MR. JUSTICE BRENNAN, MR. JUSTICE STEWART, MR. JUSTICE WHITE, MR. JUSTICE MARSHALL, MR. JUSTICE BLACKMUN, MR. JUSTICE POWELL, and MR. JUSTICE REHNQUIST join].

The issue in this case is whether a state statute granting a political candidate a right to equal space to reply to criticism and attacks on his record by a newspaper violates the guarantees of a free press.

* * * Florida Statute § 104.38 [is] a "right of reply" statute which provides that if a candidate for nomination or election is assailed regarding his personal character or official record by any newspaper, the candidate has the right to demand that the newspaper print, free of cost to the candidate, any reply the candidate may make to the newspaper's charges. The reply must appear in as conspicuous a place

and in the same kind of type as the charges which prompted the reply, provided it does not take up more space than the charges. Failure to comply with the statute constitutes a first-degree misdemeanor. [The *Miami Herald* published editorials critical of Tornillo's candidacy for the Florida House of Representatives. Tornillo demanded that the *Herald* print his replies, but the newspaper refused.] * * *

The appellee and supporting advocates of an enforceable right of access to the press vigorously argue that government has an obligation to ensure that a wide variety of views reach the public. * * * It is urged that at the time the First Amendment to the Constitution was ratified in 1791 as part of our Bill of Rights the press was broadly representative of the people it was serving. While many of the newspapers were intensely partisan and narrow in their views, the press collectively presented a broad range of opinions to readers. Entry into publishing was inexpensive; pamphlets and books provided meaningful alternatives to the organized press for the expression of unpopular ideas and often treated events and expressed views not covered by conventional newspapers. A true marketplace of ideas existed in which there was relatively easy access to the channels of communication.

Access advocates submit that although newspapers of the present are superficially similar to those of 1791 the press of today is in reality very different from that known in the early years of our national existence. * * * Newspapers have become big business and there are far fewer of them to serve a larger literate population. Chains of newspapers, national newspapers, national wire and news services, and one-newspaper towns, are the dominant features of a press that has become noncompetitive and enormously powerful and influential in its capacity to manipulate popular opinion and change the course of events. * * *

The result of these vast changes has been to place in a few hands the power to inform the American people and shape public opinion. Much of the editorial opinion and commentary that is printed is that of syndicated columnists distributed nationwide and, as a result, we are told, on national and world issues there tends to be a homogeneity of editorial opinion, commentary, and interpretive analysis. The abuses of bias and manipulative reportage are, likewise, said to be the result of the vast accumulations of unreviewable power in the modern media empires. In effect, it is claimed, the public has lost any ability to respond or to contribute in a meaningful way to the debate on issues. The monopoly of the means of communication allows for little or no critical analysis of the media except in professional journals of very limited readership. * * *

The obvious solution, which was available to dissidents at an earlier time when entry into publishing was relatively inexpensive, today would be to have additional newspapers. But the same economic factors which have caused the disappearance of vast numbers of metropolitan newspapers, have made entry into the marketplace of ideas served by the print media almost impossible. It is urged that the claim of newspapers to be "surrogates for the public" carries with it a concomitant fiduciary obligation to account for that stewardship. From this premise it is reasoned that the only effective way to insure fairness and accuracy and to provide for some accountability is for government to take affirmative action. The First Amendment interest of the public in being informed is said to be in peril because the "market-place of ideas" is today a monopoly controlled by the owners of the market. * * *

* * * The clear implication [of our prior cases] has been that any such a com-pulsion to publish that which "'reason' tells them should not be published" is unconstitutional. A responsible press is an undoubtedly desirable goal, but press responsibility is not mandated by the Constitution and like many other virtues it cannot be legislated.

Appellee's argument that the Florida statute does not amount to a restriction of appellant's right to speak because "the statute in question here has not prevented the *Miami Herald* from saying anything it wished" begs the core question. Compelling editors or publishers to publish that which "'reason' tells them should not be pub-lished" is what is at issue in this case. The Florida statute operates as a command in the same sense as a statute or regulation forbidding appellant to publish specified matter. Governmental restraint on publishing need not fall into familiar or tradi-tional patterns to be subject to constitutional limitations on governmental powers. The Florida statute exacts a penalty on the basis of the content of a newspaper. The first phase of the penalty resulting from the compelled printing of a reply is exacted in terms of the cost in printing and composing time and materials and in taking up space that could be devoted to other material the newspaper may have preferred to print. It is correct, as appellee contends, that a newspaper is not subject to the finite technological limitations of time that confront a broadcaster but it is not correct to say that, as an economic reality, a newspaper can proceed to infinite expansion of its column space to accommodate the replies that a government agency determines or a statute commands the readers should have available.

Faced with the penalties that would accrue to any newspaper that published news or commentary arguably within the reach of the right-of-access statute, edi-tors might well conclude that the safe course is to avoid controversy. Therefore, under the operation of the Florida statute, political and electoral coverage would be blunted or reduced. Government-enforced right of access inescapably "dampens the vigor and limits the variety of public debate," *New York Times Co.* v. *Sullivan*, 376 U.S. 254, 279 (1964). * * *

Even if a newspaper would face no additional costs to comply with a compulsory access law and would not be forced to forgo publication of news or opinion by the inclusion of a reply, the Florida statute fails to clear the barriers of the First Amend-ment because of its intrusion into the function of editors. A newspaper is more than a passive receptacle or conduit for news, comment, and advertising. The choice of material to go into a newspaper, and the decisions made as to limitations on the size and content of the paper, and treatment of public issues and public officials — whether fair or unfair — constitute the exercise of editorial control and judgment. It has yet to be demonstrated how governmental regulation of this crucial process can be exercised consistent with First Amendment guarantees of a free press as they have evolved to this time. Accordingly, the judgment of the Supreme Court of Florida is reversed.

It is so ordered.

MR. JUSTICE BRENNAN, with whom MR. JUSTICE REHNQUIST joins, concurring.

I join the Court's opinion which, as I understand it, addresses only "right of reply" statutes and implies no view upon the constitutionality of "retraction" statutes affording plaintiffs able to prove defamatory falsehoods a statutory action to require publication of a retraction.

MR. JUSTICE WHITE, concurring.

* * * We have learned, and continue to learn, from what we view as the unhappy experiences of other nations where government has been allowed to meddle in the internal editorial affairs of newspapers. * * *

Of course, the press is not always accurate, or even responsible, and may not present full and fair debate on important public issues. But the balance struck by the First Amendment with respect to the press is that society must take the risk that occasionally debate on vital matters will not be comprehensive and that all viewpoints may not be expressed. * * * Any other accommodation—any other system that would supplant private control of the press with the heavy hand of government intrusion—would make the government the censor of what the people may read and know. * * * Whatever power may reside in government to influence the publishing of certain narrowly circumscribed categories of material, we have never thought that the First Amendment permitted public officials to dictate to the press the contents of its news columns or the slant of its editorials. * * *

Notes and Questions

1. Tornillo argued that the "communications revolution" in the half-century before 1974 had changed the media in such a way as to make right-of-reply statutes necessary to ensure that a wide variety of views were made available to the public. In making this argument, Tornillo focused on the consolidation of media ownership, including the diminution in the number of newspapers produced in many markets and cross-ownership between media, as well as the tendency of media to focus on national news and to report it in a similar way. Nevertheless, other developments in the "communications revolution" arguably cut the other way, demonstrating that modern technology was making it easier to publicize diverse views without the assistance of right-of-reply statutes. Do you see how?

2. In the years since 1974, communications technology has continued to improve, and ownership of media conglomerates has continued to become more centralized. How should such developments affect the attitude of the courts to right-of-reply statutes?

3. Does the majority opinion affect laws requiring newspapers to print retractions to correct misstatements of fact? Would a state be able to require that such retractions "appear in as conspicuous a place and in the same kind of type as the" misstatements? Would it matter if the misstatements were made negligently, recklessly, intentionally, or through no fault of the newspaper?

4. As mentioned in the introduction, the Supreme Court has been far more accepting of government interference with broadcasters' messages. Before its repeal by the FCC in 1987, *see In re Syracuse Peace Council*, 2 F.C.C. Rcd. 5043 (1987), *upheld*, 867 F.2d 654 (D.C. Cir. 1989), the fairness doctrine required broadcasters to provide for the equal airing of differing views. Thus, the fairness doctrine gave persons an opportunity to respond to attacks on them by the station.

A separate "equal-time" requirement, found at 47 U.S.C. § 315, requires broadcasters to provide "equal opportunities" to the station's facilities for all candidates for any public office. For example, if a radio station sells a thirty-second advertisement to Candidate X for $200, it must be willing to sell a thirty-second advertisement to Candidate Y for $200. Broadcasters do not, however, have to provide equal time to balance coverage of a news event or an interview.

The Supreme Court has justified the disparity in treatment between print publishers and broadcasters by focusing on "spectrum scarcity." The broadcast spectrum is limited. If multiple broadcasters attempt to broadcast on the same frequency in the same area, their signals will interfere with each other. For that reason, the Federal Communications Commission licenses broadcasters, assigning each a frequency and imposing other limitations to prevent signal interference. And because the number of broadcasters in any given area is limited by the physics of the electromagnetic broadcast spectrum, the government has the power to ensure that the people who do have licenses use them to serve the "public interest." If only a handful of people will have the ability to use the public's broadcast spectrum, the government can require its licensees to operate their stations to serve the public rather than merely as a means of proselytizing their own messages. *See Red Lion Broadcasting Co. v. Federal Communications Commission*, 395 U.S. 367 (1969). Broadcasters are thus akin to a utility monopoly: Where there is limited opportunity for customers to choose competitors, government regulation insists that each provider adhere to public-interest restrictions that would not be imposed in a perfectly functioning market.

By contrast, there is no physical (as distinct from economic or practical) limitation on the number of print publications that may reach an audience, and so a system of government licensing of the print media would be about as clear a violation of the Free Press Clause as could be imagined. *See Lovell v. City of Griffin*, 303 U.S. 444 (1938) (striking down a ban on the distribution of literature without permission). As *Tornillo* held, people upset with the content of a newspaper can get their news elsewhere; the government has no authority to ensure the fairness of the print media. Spectrum scarcity continues to justify limitations on over-the-air broadcasters' freedom, but the development of cable made scarcity much less of a problem for television. It is no concern at all for Internet publishers. Accordingly, online publications have the freedom of *Tornillo*; government oversight of the Internet to ensure fairness would be unconstitutional.

Suppose a broadcaster decides to adhere to a policy of strict neutrality: *Nobody* may use the facilities to discuss public issues. Does that satisfy the broadcaster's obligations? The statute is clear that "[n]o obligation is imposed upon any licensee to allow the use of its station by any * * * candidate," §315(a), but broadcasters do have an obligation to act in the public interest. In *Columbia Broadcasting System, Inc. v. Democratic National Committee*, 412 U.S. 94 (1973), the Court upheld a Federal Communications Commission ruling that broadcasters need not accept any editorial advertisements, *if* they are otherwise satisfying their obligation to act in the "public interest" by providing full and fair coverage of public issues.

Arkansas Educational Television Commission v. Forbes

Supreme Court of the United States
523 U.S. 666, 118 S. Ct. 1633, 140 L. Ed. 2d 875 (1998)

JUSTICE KENNEDY delivered the opinion of the Court [in which CHIEF JUSTICE REHNQUIST, JUSTICE O'CONNOR, JUSTICE SCALIA, JUSTICE THOMAS, and JUSTICE BREYER join].

A state-owned public television broadcaster sponsored a candidate debate from which it excluded an independent candidate with little popular support. The issue before us is whether, by reason of its state ownership, the station had a constitutional obligation to allow every candidate access to the debate. We conclude that, unlike most other public television programs, the candidate debate was subject to constitutional constraints applicable to nonpublic fora under our forum precedents. Even so, the broadcaster's decision to exclude the candidate was a reasonable, viewpoint-neutral exercise of journalistic discretion.

Petitioner, the Arkansas Educational Television Commission (AETC), is an Arkansas state agency owning and operating a network of five noncommercial television stations. * * * In the spring of 1992, AETC staff began planning a series of debates between candidates for federal office in the November 1992 elections. AETC decided to televise a total of five debates, scheduling one for the Senate election and one for each of the four congressional elections in Arkansas. Working in close consultation with Bill Simmons, Arkansas Bureau Chief for the Associated Press, AETC staff developed a debate format allowing about 53 minutes during each 1-hour debate for questions to and answers by the candidates. Given the time constraint, the staff and Simmons "decided to limit participation in the debates to the major party candidates or any other candidate who had strong popular support."

On June 17, 1992, AETC invited the Republican and Democratic candidates for Arkansas' Third Congressional District to participate in the AETC debate for that seat. Two months later, after obtaining the 2,000 signatures required by Arkansas law, respondent Ralph Forbes was certified as an independent candidate qualified to appear on the ballot for the seat. Forbes was a perennial candidate who had sought, without success, a number of elected offices in Arkansas. On August 24, 1992, he wrote to AETC requesting permission to participate in the debate for his district, scheduled for October 22, 1992. On September 4, AETC Executive Director Susan Howarth denied Forbes' request, explaining that AETC had "made a bona fide journalistic judgement that our viewers would best be served by limiting the debate" to the candidates already invited.

On October 19, 1992, Forbes filed suit against AETC, seeking injunctive and declaratory relief as well as damages. * * * At trial, AETC professional staff testified Forbes was excluded because he lacked any campaign organization, had not generated appreciable voter support, and was not regarded as a serious candidate by the press covering the election. The jury made express findings that AETC's decision to exclude Forbes had not been influenced by political pressure or disagreement with his views. The District Court entered judgment for AETC.

The Court of Appeals * * * reversed. * * * The court asserted * * * that AETC had "opened its facilities to a particular group — candidates running for the Third District Congressional seat." AETC's action, the court held, made the debate a public forum, to which all candidates "legally qualified to appear on the ballot" had a presumptive right of access. Applying strict scrutiny, the court determined that AETC's assessment of Forbes' "political viability" was neither a "compelling nor [a] narrowly tailored" reason for excluding him from the debate. * * * We now reverse. * * *

As a general rule, the nature of editorial discretion counsels against subjecting broadcasters to claims of viewpoint discrimination. Programming decisions would be particularly vulnerable to claims of this type because even principled exclusions rooted in sound journalistic judgment can often be characterized as viewpoint based. To comply with their obligation to air programming that serves the public interest, broadcasters must often choose among speakers expressing different viewpoints. * * * Much like a university selecting a commencement speaker, a public institution selecting speakers for a lecture series, or a public school prescribing its curriculum, a broadcaster by its nature will facilitate the expression of some viewpoints instead of others. Were the judiciary to require, and so to define and approve, pre-established criteria for access, it would risk implicating the courts in judgments that should be left to the exercise of journalistic discretion.

When a public broadcaster exercises editorial discretion in the selection and presentation of its programming, it engages in speech activity. Although programming decisions often involve the compilation of the speech of third parties, the decisions nonetheless constitute communicative acts. * * *

Although public broadcasting as a general matter does not lend itself to scrutiny under the forum doctrine, candidate debates present the narrow exception to the rule. For two reasons, a candidate debate like the one at issue here is different from other programming. First, unlike AETC's other broadcasts, the debate was by design a forum for political speech by the candidates. Consistent with the long tradition of candidate debates, the implicit representation of the broadcaster was that the views expressed were those of the candidates, not its own. The very purpose of the debate was to allow the candidates to express their views with minimal intrusion by the broadcaster. In this respect the debate differed even from a political talk show, whose host can express partisan views and then limit the discussion to those ideas.

Second, in our tradition, candidate debates are of exceptional significance in the electoral process. "[I]t is of particular importance that candidates have the . . . opportunity to make their views known so that the electorate may intelligently evaluate the candidates' personal qualities and their positions on vital public issues before choosing among them on election day." *CBS, Inc. v. FCC*, 453 U.S. 367, 396 (1981). Deliberation on the positions and qualifications of candidates is integral to our system of government, and electoral speech may have its most profound and widespread impact when it is disseminated through televised debates. * * *

The special characteristics of candidate debates support the conclusion that the AETC debate was a forum of some type. * * * Forbes argues, and the Court of Appeals held, that the debate was a public forum to which he had a First Amendment right of access. Under our precedents, however, the debate was a nonpublic forum, from which AETC could exclude Forbes in the reasonable, viewpoint-neutral exercise of its journalistic discretion.

For our purposes, it will suffice to employ the categories of speech fora already established and discussed in our cases. "[T]he Court [has] identified three types of fora: the traditional public forum, the public forum created by government designation, and the nonpublic forum." * * * [T]raditional public fora are open for expressive activity regardless of the government's intent. The objective characteristics of these properties require the government to accommodate private speakers. The government is free to open additional properties for expressive use by the general public or by a particular class of speakers, thereby creating designated public fora. Where the property is not a traditional public forum and the government has not chosen to create a designated public forum, the property is either a nonpublic forum or not a forum at all.

The parties agree the AETC debate was not a traditional public forum. The Court has rejected the view that traditional public forum status extends beyond its historic confines; and even had a more expansive conception of traditional public fora been adopted, the almost unfettered access of a traditional public forum would be incompatible with the programming dictates a television broadcaster must follow. The issue, then, is whether the debate was a designated public forum or a nonpublic forum.

Under our precedents, the AETC debate was not a designated public forum. To create a forum of this type, the government must intend to make the property "generally available" to a class of speakers. * * * A designated public forum is not created when the government allows selective access for individual speakers rather than general access for a class of speakers. * * *

* * * By recognizing the distinction [between the "general access" characteristic of a designated public forum and the "selective access" of a nonpublic forum], we encourage the government to open its property to some expressive activity in cases where, if faced with an all-or-nothing choice, it might not open the property at all. That this distinction turns on governmental intent does not render it unprotective of speech. Rather, it reflects the reality that, with the exception of traditional public fora, the government retains the choice of whether to designate its property as a forum for specified classes of speakers.

Here, the debate did not have an open-microphone format. * * * AETC made candidate-by-candidate determinations as to which of the eligible candidates would participate in the debate. "Such selective access, unsupported by evidence of a purposeful designation for public use, does not create a public forum." Thus the debate was a nonpublic forum.

[T]he Court of Appeals' holding would result in less speech, not more. In ruling that the debate was a public forum open to all ballot-qualified candidates, the Court of Appeals would place a severe burden upon public broadcasters who air candidates' views. In each of the 1988, 1992, and 1996 Presidential elections, for example, no fewer than 19 candidates appeared on the ballot in at least one State. In the 1996 congressional elections, it was common for 6 to 11 candidates to qualify for the ballot for a particular seat. On logistical grounds alone, a public television editor might, with reason, decide that the inclusion of all ballot-qualified candidates would "actually undermine the educational value and quality of debates."

Were it faced with the prospect of cacophony, on the one hand, and First Amendment liability, on the other, a public television broadcaster might choose not to air candidates' views at all. * * * These concerns are more than speculative. As a direct result of the Court of Appeals' decision in this case, the Nebraska Educational Television Network canceled a scheduled debate between candidates in Nebraska's 1996 United States Senate race. A First Amendment jurisprudence yielding these results does not promote speech but represses it.

The debate's status as a nonpublic forum, however, did not give AETC unfettered power to exclude any candidate it wished. * * * To be consistent with the First Amendment, the exclusion of a speaker from a nonpublic forum must not be based on the speaker's viewpoint and must otherwise be reasonable in light of the purpose of the property.

In this case, the jury found Forbes' exclusion was not based on "objections or opposition to his views." The record provides ample support for this finding, demonstrating as well that AETC's decision to exclude him was reasonable. AETC Executive Director Susan Howarth testified Forbes' views had "absolutely" no role in the decision to exclude him from the debate. She further testified Forbes was excluded because (1) "the Arkansas voters did not consider him a serious candidate"; (2) "the news organizations also did not consider him a serious candidate"; (3) "the Associated Press and a national election result reporting service did not plan to run his name in results on election night"; (4) Forbes "apparently had little, if any, financial support, failing to report campaign finances to the Secretary of State's office or to the Federal Election Commission"; and (5) "there [was] no 'Forbes for Congress' campaign headquarters other than his house." Forbes himself described his campaign organization as "bedlam" and the media coverage of his campaign as "zilch." It is, in short, beyond dispute that Forbes was excluded not because of his viewpoint but because he had generated no appreciable public interest. * * *

Nor did AETC exclude Forbes in an attempted manipulation of the political process. The evidence provided powerful support for the jury's express finding that AETC's exclusion of Forbes was not the result of "political pressure from anyone inside or outside [AETC]." There is no serious argument that AETC did not act in good faith in this case. AETC excluded Forbes because the voters lacked interest in his candidacy, not because AETC itself did.

The broadcaster's decision to exclude Forbes was a reasonable, viewpoint-neutral exercise of journalistic discretion consistent with the First Amendment. The judgment of the Court of Appeals is

Reversed.

JUSTICE STEVENS, with whom JUSTICE SOUTER and JUSTICE GINSBURG join, dissenting.

The Court has decided that a state-owned television network has no "constitutional obligation to allow every candidate access to" political debates that it sponsors. I do not challenge that decision. The judgment of the Court of Appeals should nevertheless be affirmed. * * *

No written criteria cabined the discretion of the AETC staff. Their subjective judgment about a candidate's "viability" or "newsworthiness" allowed them wide latitude either to permit or to exclude a third participant in any debate.[14] Moreover, in exercising that judgment they were free to rely on factors that arguably should favor inclusion as justifications for exclusion. Thus, the fact that Forbes had little financial support was considered as evidence of his lack of viability when that factor might have provided an independent reason for allowing him to share a free forum with wealthier candidates.[15] * * *

The reasons that support the need for narrow, objective, and definite standards to guide licensing decisions apply directly to the wholly subjective access decisions

---

14. It is particularly troubling that AETC excluded the only independent candidate but invited all the major-party candidates to participate in the planned debates, regardless of their chances of electoral success. As this Court has recognized, "political figures outside the two major parties have been fertile sources of new ideas and new programs; many of their challenges to the status quo have in time made their way into the political mainstream." *Anderson v. Celebrezze*, 460 U.S. 780, 794 (1983) [p. 517].

15. Lack of substantial financial support apparently was not a factor in the decision to invite a major-party candidate with even less financial support than Forbes.

made by the staff of AETC.[18] The importance of avoiding arbitrary or viewpoint-based exclusions from political debates militates strongly in favor of requiring the controlling state agency to use (and adhere to) preestablished, objective criteria to determine who among qualified candidates may participate. * * * A constitutional duty to use objective standards—i.e., "neutral principles"—for determining whether and when to adjust a debate format would impose only a modest requirement that would fall far short of a duty to grant every multiple-party request. Such standards would also have the benefit of providing the public with some assurance that state-owned broadcasters cannot select debate participants on arbitrary grounds. * * *

Notes and Questions

1. The Court essentially held that there is no requirement that public entities sponsoring debates adhere to preexisting criteria in inviting candidates to participate; as long as the decision to exclude a certain candidate is not motivated by disagreement with the candidate's viewpoint and is otherwise reasonable, the exclusion is constitutional. Justice Stevens argued that such a rule created too much opportunity for abuse, and that the public entity should not be permitted to limit participation in debates through an *ad hoc* process. Despite the Court's holding that preexisting criteria are not constitutional necessities, would you advise such entities to adopt them? Why or why not?

2. Is Justice Stevens's approach workable in other contexts? Would he require a state university to adhere to preexisting criteria in selecting a commencement speaker? What constitutional constraints would apply to such a situation under the Court's analysis?

3. Because the debate in *Forbes* was open only on a selective basis, the Court held it to be a nonpublic forum. Where a station is broadcasting its own views, however, and not the views of candidates or others, it is not operating as a forum at all. As discussed in the Notes following *Tornillo*, broadcasters—in contrast to print media—have an obligation to act in the public interest, but that does not mean that the government is free to control the content of their broadcasting. In *Federal Communications Commission v. League of Women Voters*, 468 U.S. 364 (1984), for example, the Supreme Court held unconstitutional a law that prohibited editorializing by any station receiving funds from the Corporation for Public Broadcasting. The government argued that the ban was necessary to ensure stations' independence. As

---

18. Ironically, it is the standardless character of the decision to exclude Forbes that provides the basis for the Court's conclusion that the debates were a nonpublic forum rather than a limited public forum. The Court explains that "[a] designated public forum is not created when the government allows selective access for individual speakers rather than general access for a class of speakers." If, as AETC claims, it did invite either the entire class of "viable" candidates, or the entire class of "newsworthy" candidates, under the Court's reasoning, it created a designated public forum.

with *United Public Workers v. Mitchell*, 330 U.S. 75 (1947) [p. 668], the ban on editorializing protected the recipient of the government benefit from being pressured to engage in political speech supporting those distributing the benefit. Further, the government argued that it was entitled to decide to spend the public's money on stations that did not editorialize. The Court rejected both arguments, concluding that there were less restrictive ways of achieving both interests while protecting broadcasters' liberty to engage in editorials—a core element of political speech.

D. Speech in Judicial Campaigns

Thirty-nine states elect some or all of their judges, either in contested elections or "retention" elections (described below). Within the former category, some states use partisan elections, in which the candidates' parties are identified on the ballot, while other states use nonpartisan elections. *See generally, e.g.*, Robert N. Hunter, Jr., *Do Nonpartisan, Publicly Financed Judicial Elections Enhance Relative Judicial Independence?* 93 N.C. L. Rev. 1825 (2015). Even in states with nonpartisan ballots, however, parties (just like every other private association) may endorse and campaign for candidates. *See Geary v. Renne*, 911 F.2d 280 (9th Cir. 1990) *(en banc)*. The remainder of the states select their judges by appointment—usually, but not always, in a process that resembles the federal model of nomination by the executive and confirmation by part or all of the legislature. *See* U.S. Const. art. II, § 2, cl. 2.

Some of the thirty-nine states with elective judiciaries use a hybrid judicial-selection system known alternately as the Missouri Plan, after the state that first implemented it, or, misleadingly, as "merit selection." *See* Michael R. Dimino, *The Futile Quest for a System of Judicial "Merit" Selection*, 67 Alb. L. Rev. 803, 803 (2004) (calling "merit selection" "a propagandistic misnomer [because] nothing ensures that judges chosen under that plan will be better than judges [selected] under any other system"). Appointments under the Missouri Plan are made by the governor from a list of candidates approved by a judicial nominating commission. The appointees then run in retention elections to stay in office for additional terms. In a retention election, a sitting judge appears on the ballot unopposed, and voters are asked to decide only whether that judge should be retained in office. Unsurprisingly, and by design, incumbents win retention at extremely high rates.

Despite the fact that the vast majority of state judges must face the voters to continue in office, state codes of judicial conduct restrict the speech and campaign activities of judicial candidates. Drafters and supporters of the codes reason that judicial candidates' appeals to voters are inconsistent with the judicial function; judges should seek to apply the law rather than to achieve results that will be popular with the electorate. Opponents see the restrictions not only as paternalistic and inconsistent with the very idea of electing judges, but as a means to promote the continuance in office of judges with unpopular views. The following case struck down one limitation on judicial campaign speech, but the constitutionality of other speech restrictions remains to be decided.

Republican Party of Minnesota v. White

Supreme Court of the United States
536 U.S. 765, 122 S. Ct. 2528, 153 L. Ed. 2d 694 (2002)

JUSTICE SCALIA delivered the opinion of the Court [in which CHIEF JUSTICE REHNQUIST, JUSTICE O'CONNOR, JUSTICE KENNEDY, and JUSTICE THOMAS join].

The question presented in this case is whether the First Amendment permits the Minnesota Supreme Court to prohibit candidates for judicial election in that State from announcing their views on disputed legal and political issues.

I

Since Minnesota's admission to the Union in 1858, the State's Constitution has provided for the selection of all state judges by popular election. Since 1912, those elections have been nonpartisan. Since 1974, they have been subject to a legal restriction which states that a "candidate for a judicial office, including an incumbent judge," shall not "announce his or her views on disputed legal or political issues." This prohibition, promulgated by the Minnesota Supreme Court and based on Canon 7(B) of the 1972 American Bar Association (ABA) Model Code of Judicial Conduct, is known as the "announce clause." Incumbent judges who violate it are subject to discipline, including removal, censure, civil penalties, and suspension without pay. Lawyers who run for judicial office also must comply with the announce clause. Those who violate it are subject to, *inter alia*, disbarment, suspension, and probation. * * *

[Gregory] Wersal [a candidate for the Minnesota Supreme Court in 1996 and 1998] filed this lawsuit * * *, seeking, *inter alia*, a declaration that the announce clause violates the First Amendment and an injunction against its enforcement. Wersal alleged that he was forced to refrain from announcing his views on disputed issues during the 1998 campaign, to the point where he declined response to questions put to him by the press and public, out of concern that he might run afoul of the announce clause. Other plaintiffs in the suit, including the Minnesota Republican Party, alleged that, because the clause kept Wersal from announcing his views, they were unable to learn those views and support or oppose his candidacy accordingly. The parties filed cross-motions for summary judgment, and the District Court found in favor of respondents, holding that the announce clause did not violate the First Amendment. [T]he United States Court of Appeals for the Eighth Circuit affirmed. We granted certiorari.

II

Before considering the constitutionality of the announce clause, we must be clear about its meaning. * * * We know that "announcing . . . views" on an issue covers much more than *promising* to decide an issue a particular way. The prohibition extends to the candidate's mere statement of his current position, even if he does not bind himself to maintain that position after election. All the parties agree this is the case, because the Minnesota Code contains a so-called "pledges or promises" clause, which *separately* prohibits judicial candidates from making "pledges or promises of conduct in office other than the faithful and impartial performance of the duties of the office"—a prohibition that is not challenged here and on which we express no view.

There are, however, some limitations that the Minnesota Supreme Court has placed upon the scope of the announce clause that are not (to put it politely) immediately apparent from its text. * * * [J]udicial candidates may criticize past [court] decisions, [even where such criticism touches on disputed legal or political issues]. * * *

There are yet further limitations upon the apparent plain meaning of the announce clause: In light of the constitutional concerns, the [Minnesota Supreme] Court construed the clause to reach only disputed issues that are likely to come before the candidate if he is elected judge [and] to allow general discussions of case law and judicial philosophy. * * *

It seems to us, however, that—like the text of the announce clause itself—these limitations upon the text of the announce clause are not all that they appear to be. First, respondents acknowledged at oral argument that statements critical of past judicial decisions are *not* permissible if the candidate also states that he is against *stare decisis*. Thus, candidates must choose between stating their views critical of past decisions and stating their views in opposition to *stare decisis*. Or, to look at it more concretely, they may state their view that prior decisions were erroneous only if they do not assert that they, if elected, have any power to eliminate erroneous decisions. Second, limiting the scope of the clause to issues likely to come before a court is not much of a limitation at all. One would hardly expect the "disputed legal or political issues" raised in the course of a state judicial election to include such matters as whether the Federal Government should end the embargo of Cuba. Quite obviously, they will be those legal or political disputes that are the proper (or by past decisions have been made the improper) business of the state courts. And within that relevant category, "there is almost no legal or political issue that is unlikely to come before a judge of an American court, state or federal, of general jurisdiction." Third, construing the clause to allow "general" discussions of case law and judicial philosophy turns out to be of little help in an election campaign. At oral argument, respondents gave, as an example of this exception, that a candidate is free to assert that he is a "strict constructionist." But that, like most other philosophical generalities, has little meaningful content for the electorate unless it is exemplified by application to a particular issue of construction likely to come before a court—for example, whether a particular statute runs afoul of any provision of the Constitution. Respondents conceded that the announce clause would prohibit the candidate from exemplifying his philosophy in this fashion. Without such application to real-life issues, all candidates can claim to be "strict constructionists" with equal (and unhelpful) plausibility.

In any event, it is clear that the announce clause prohibits a judicial candidate from stating his views on any specific nonfanciful legal question within the province of the court for which he is running, except in the context of discussing past decisions—and in the latter context as well, if he expresses the view that he is not bound by *stare decisis*.[5] * * *

III

As the Court of Appeals recognized, the announce clause both prohibits speech on the basis of its content and burdens a category of speech that is "at the core of our First Amendment freedoms"—speech about the qualifications of candidates for public office. The Court of Appeals concluded that the proper test to be applied to determine the constitutionality of such a restriction is what our cases have called strict scrutiny; the parties do not dispute that this is correct. Under the strict-scrutiny test, respondents have the burden to prove that the announce clause is (1) narrowly tailored, to serve (2) a compelling state interest. *E.g., Eu v. San Francisco County Democratic Central Comm.*, 489 U.S. 214, 222 (1989) [p. 480]. In order for respondents to show that the announce clause is narrowly tailored, they must demonstrate that it does not "unnecessarily circumscribe protected expression." *Brown v. Hartlage*, 456 U.S. 45, 54 (1982) [p. 568].

The Court of Appeals concluded that respondents had established two interests as sufficiently compelling to justify the announce clause: preserving the impartiality of the state judiciary and preserving the appearance of the impartiality of the state judiciary. Respondents reassert these two interests before us, arguing that the first is compelling because it protects the due process rights of litigants, and that the second is compelling because it preserves public confidence in the judiciary. Respondents are rather vague, however, about what they mean by "impartiality." * * *

A

One meaning of "impartiality" in the judicial context—and of course its root meaning—is the lack of bias for or against either *party* to the proceeding. Impartiality in this sense assures equal application of the law. That is, it guarantees a party that the judge who hears his case will apply the law to him in the same way he applies it to any other party. This is the traditional sense in which the term is used. It is also the sense in which it is used in the cases cited by respondents and *amici* for the proposition that an impartial judge is essential to due process. *Tumey v. Ohio*, 273 U.S. 510, 523, 531–534 (1927) (judge violated due process by sitting in a case in

---

5. In 1990, in response to concerns that its 1972 Model Canon—which was the basis for Minnesota's announce clause—violated the First Amendment, the ABA replaced that canon with a provision that prohibits a judicial candidate from making "statements that commit or appear to commit the candidate with respect to cases, controversies or issues that are likely to come before the court." ABA Model Code of Judicial Conduct, Canon 5(A)(3)(d)(ii) (2000). At oral argument, respondents argued that the limiting constructions placed upon Minnesota's announce clause * * * by the Minnesota Supreme Court[] render the scope of the clause no broader than the ABA's 1990 canon. * * * We do not know whether the announce clause (as interpreted by state authorities) and the 1990 ABA canon are one and the same. No aspect of our constitutional analysis turns on this question.

which it would be in his financial interest to find against one of the parties); *Aetna Life Ins. Co.* v. *Lavoie*, 475 U.S. 813, 822–825 (1986) (same); *Ward* v. *Monroeville*, 409 U.S. 57, 58–62 (1972) (same).

We think it plain that the announce clause is not narrowly tailored to serve impartiality (or the appearance of impartiality) in this sense. Indeed, the clause is barely tailored to serve that interest *at all*, inasmuch as it does not restrict speech for or against particular *parties*, but rather speech for or against particular *issues*. To be sure, when a case arises that turns on a legal issue on which the judge (as a candidate) had taken a particular stand, the party taking the opposite stand is likely to lose. But not because of any bias against that party, or favoritism toward the other party. *Any* party taking that position is just as likely to lose. The judge is applying the law (as he sees it) evenhandedly.

B

It is perhaps possible to use the term "impartiality" in the judicial context (though this is certainly not a common usage) to mean lack of preconception in favor of or against a particular *legal view*. This sort of impartiality would be concerned, not with guaranteeing litigants equal application of the law, but rather with guaranteeing them an equal chance to persuade the court on the legal points in their case. Impartiality in this sense may well be an interest served by the announce clause, but it is not a *compelling* state interest, as strict scrutiny requires. A judge's lack of predisposition regarding the relevant legal issues in a case has never been thought a necessary component of equal justice, and with good reason. For one thing, it is virtually impossible to find a judge who does not have preconceptions about the law. As then-JUSTICE REHNQUIST observed of our own Court: "Since most Justices come to this bench no earlier than their middle years, it would be unusual if they had not by that time formulated at least some tentative notions that would influence them in their interpretation of the sweeping clauses of the Constitution and their interaction with one another. It would be not merely unusual, but extraordinary, if they had not at least given opinions as to constitutional issues in their previous legal careers." *Laird* v. *Tatum*, 409 U.S. 824, 835 (1972) (memorandum opinion). Indeed, even if it were possible to select judges who did not have preconceived views on legal issues, it would hardly be desirable to do so. "Proof that a Justice's mind at the time he joined the Court was a complete *tabula rasa* in the area of constitutional adjudication would be evidence of lack of qualification, not lack of bias." *Ibid.* * * * And since avoiding judicial preconceptions on legal issues is neither possible nor desirable, pretending otherwise by attempting to preserve the "appearance" of that type of impartiality can hardly be a compelling state interest either.

C

A third possible meaning of "impartiality" (again not a common one) might be described as openmindedness. This quality in a judge demands, not that he have no preconceptions on legal issues, but that he be willing to consider views that oppose his preconceptions, and remain open to persuasion, when the issues arise in a pending case. This sort of impartiality seeks to guarantee each litigant, not an *equal* chance to win the legal points in the case, but at least *some* chance of doing so. It may well be that impartiality in this sense, and the appearance of it, are desirable in the judiciary, but we need not pursue that inquiry, since we do not believe the Minnesota Supreme Court adopted the announce clause for that purpose.

Respondents argue that the announce clause serves the interest in openminded-ness, or at least in the appearance of openmindedness, because it relieves a judge from pressure to rule a certain way in order to maintain consistency with state-ments the judge has previously made. The problem is, however, that statements in election campaigns are such an infinitesimal portion of the public commitments to legal positions that judges (or judges-to-be) undertake, that this object of the prohibition is implausible. Before they arrive on the bench (whether by election or otherwise) judges have often committed themselves on legal issues that they must later rule upon. More common still is a judge's confronting a legal issue on which he has expressed an opinion while on the bench. Most frequently, of course, that prior expression will have occurred in ruling on an earlier case. But judges often state their views on disputed legal issues outside the context of adjudication—in classes that they conduct, and in books and speeches. Like the ABA Codes of Judi-cial Conduct, the Minnesota Code not only permits but encourages this. That is quite incompatible with the notion that the need for openmindedness (or for the appearance of openmindedness) lies behind the prohibition at issue here.

The short of the matter is this: In Minnesota, a candidate for judicial office may not say "I think it is constitutional for the legislature to prohibit same-sex mar-riages." He may say the very same thing, however, up until the very day before he declares himself a candidate, and may say it repeatedly (until litigation is pending) after he is elected. As a means of pursuing the objective of openmindedness that respondents now articulate, the announce clause is so woefully underinclusive as to render belief in that purpose a challenge to the credulous.

Justice Stevens asserts that statements made in an election campaign pose a special threat to openmindedness because the candidate, when elected judge, will have a *particular* reluctance to contradict them. That might be plausible, perhaps, with regard to campaign *promises*. A candidate who says "If elected, I will vote to uphold the legislature's power to prohibit same-sex marriages" will positively be breaking his word if he does not do so (although one would be naive not to recog-nize that campaign promises are—by long democratic tradition—the least bind-ing form of human commitment). But, as noted earlier, the Minnesota Supreme Court has adopted a separate prohibition on campaign "pledges or promises," which is not challenged here. The proposition that judges feel significantly greater compulsion, or appear to feel significantly greater compulsion, to maintain consis-tency with *nonpromissory* statements made during a judicial campaign than with such statements made before or after the campaign is not self-evidently true. * * * In any event, it suffices to say that respondents have not carried the burden imposed by our strict-scrutiny test to establish this proposition (that campaign statements are uniquely destructive of openmindedness) on which the validity of the announce clause rests.

Moreover, the notion that the special context of electioneering justifies an *abridgment* of the right to speak out on disputed issues sets our First Amendment jurisprudence on its head. "Debate on the qualifications of candidates" is "at the core of our electoral process and of the First Amendment freedoms," not at the edges. *Eu*, 489 U.S., at 222–223. "The role that elected officials play in our society makes it all the more imperative that they be allowed freely to express themselves on matters of current public importance." "It is simply not the function of government to select which issues are worth discussing or debating in the course of a political campaign." *Brown*, 456 U.S., at 60. We have never allowed the government to prohibit candidates from communicating relevant information to voters during an election.

JUSTICE GINSBURG would do so—and much of her dissent confirms rather than refutes our conclusion that the purpose behind the announce clause is not openmindedness in the judiciary, but the undermining of judicial elections. She contends that the announce clause must be constitutional because due process would be denied if an elected judge sat in a case involving an issue on which he had previously announced his view. She reaches this conclusion because, she says, such a judge would have a "direct, personal, substantial, and pecuniary interest" in ruling consistently with his previously announced view, in order to reduce the risk that he will be "voted off the bench and thereby lose [his] salary and emoluments." But elected judges—regardless of whether they have announced any views beforehand—*always* face the pressure of an electorate who might disagree with their rulings and therefore vote them off the bench. Surely the judge who frees Timothy McVeigh places his job much more at risk than the judge who (horror of horrors!) reconsiders his previously announced view on a disputed legal issue. So if, as JUSTICE GINSBURG claims, it violates due process for a judge to sit in a case in which ruling one way rather than another increases his prospects for reelection, then—quite simply—the practice of electing judges is itself a violation of due process. It is not difficult to understand how one with these views would approve the election-nullifying effect of the announce clause. They are not, however, the views reflected in the Due Process Clause of the Fourteenth Amendment, which has coexisted with the election of judges ever since it was adopted.

JUSTICE GINSBURG devotes the rest of her dissent to attacking arguments we do not make. For example, * * * we neither assert nor imply that the First Amendment requires campaigns for judicial office to sound the same as those for legislative office. What we do assert, and what JUSTICE GINSBURG ignores, is that, *even if* the First Amendment allows greater regulation of judicial election campaigns than legislative election campaigns, the announce clause still fails strict scrutiny because it is woefully underinclusive, prohibiting announcements by judges (and would-be judges) only at certain times and in certain forms. We rely on the cases involving speech during elections only to make the obvious point that this underinclusiveness cannot be explained by resort to the notion that the First Amendment provides less protection during an election campaign than at other times.[11]

But in any case, JUSTICE GINSBURG greatly exaggerates the difference between judicial and legislative elections. She asserts that "the rationale underlying unconstrained speech in elections for political office—that representative government depends on the public's ability to choose agents who will act at its behest—does not carry over to campaigns for the bench." This complete separation of the judiciary from the enterprise of "representative government" might have some truth in those countries where judges neither make law themselves nor set aside the laws enacted by the legislature. It is not a true picture of the American system. Not only do state-court judges possess the power to "make" common law, but they have the immense power to shape the States' constitutions as well. Which is precisely why the election of state judges became popular.[12]

IV

There is an obvious tension between the article of Minnesota's popularly approved Constitution which provides that judges shall be elected, and the Minnesota Supreme Court's announce clause which places most subjects of interest to the voters off limits. (The candidate-speech restrictions of all the other States that have them are also the product of judicial fiat.) The disparity is perhaps unsurprising, since the ABA, which originated the announce clause, has long been an opponent of judicial elections. That opposition may be well taken (it certainly had the support of the Founders of the Federal Government), but the First Amendment does not permit it to achieve its goal by leaving the principle of elections in place while preventing candidates from discussing what the elections are about. "The greater power to dispense with elections altogether does not include the lesser power to conduct elections under conditions of state-imposed voter ignorance. If the State chooses to tap the energy and the legitimizing power of the democratic process, it must accord the participants in that process . . . the First Amendment rights that attach to their roles." *Renne* v. *Geary*, 501 U.S. 312, 349 (1991) (Marshall, J., dissenting).

The Minnesota Supreme Court's canon of judicial conduct prohibiting candidates for judicial election from announcing their views on disputed legal and political issues violates the First Amendment. Accordingly, we reverse the grant of

---

11. Nor do we assert that candidates for judicial office should be *compelled* to announce their views on disputed legal issues. Thus, JUSTICE GINSBURG's repeated invocation of instances in which nominees to this Court declined to announce such views during Senate confirmation hearings is pointless. [T]he practice of *voluntarily* demurring does not establish the legitimacy of *legal compulsion* to demur * * *.

12. * * * Even if the policymaking capacity of judges were limited to courts of last resort, that would only prove that the announce clause fails strict scrutiny [because] the announce clause * * * applies to high- and low-court candidates alike. In fact, however, the judges of inferior courts *often* "make law," since the precedent of the highest court does not cover every situation, and not every case is reviewed. * * *

summary judgment to respondents and remand the case for proceedings consistent with this opinion.

It is so ordered.

JUSTICE O'CONNOR, concurring.

I join the opinion of the Court but write separately to express my concerns about judicial elections generally. Respondents claim that "the Announce Clause is necessary . . . to protect the State's compelling governmental interest in an actual and perceived . . . impartial judiciary." I am concerned that, even aside from what judicial candidates may say while campaigning, the very practice of electing judges undermines this interest.

* * * Elected judges cannot help being aware that if the public is not satisfied with the outcome of a particular case, it could hurt their reelection prospects. Even if judges were able to suppress their awareness of the potential electoral consequences of their decisions and refrain from acting on it, the public's confidence in the judiciary could be undermined simply by the possibility that judges would be unable to do so.

Moreover, contested elections generally entail campaigning. And campaigning for a judicial post today can require substantial funds. * * * Yet relying on campaign donations may leave judges feeling indebted to certain parties or interest groups. Even if judges were able to refrain from favoring donors, the mere possibility that judges' decisions may be motivated by the desire to repay campaign contributors is likely to undermine the public's confidence in the judiciary. * * *

Minnesota has chosen to select its judges through contested popular elections instead of through an appointment system or a combined appointment and retention election system along the lines of the Missouri Plan. In doing so the State has voluntarily taken on the risks to judicial bias described above. As a result, the State's claim that it needs to significantly restrict judges' speech in order to protect judicial impartiality is particularly troubling. If the State has a problem with judicial impartiality, it is largely one the State brought upon itself by continuing the practice of popularly electing judges.

JUSTICE KENNEDY, concurring.

I agree with the Court that Minnesota's prohibition on judicial candidates' announcing their legal views is an unconstitutional abridgment of the freedom of speech. There is authority for the Court to apply strict scrutiny analysis to resolve some First Amendment cases, and the Court explains in clear and forceful terms why the Minnesota regulatory scheme fails that test. So I join its opinion.

I adhere to my view, however, that content-based speech restrictions that do not fall within any traditional exception should be invalidated without inquiry into narrow tailoring or compelling government interests. * * * The political speech of candidates is at the heart of the First Amendment, and direct restrictions on the content of candidate speech are simply beyond the power of government to impose. * * *

Minnesota may choose to have an elected judiciary. It may strive to define those characteristics that exemplify judicial excellence. It may enshrine its definitions in a code of judicial conduct. It may adopt recusal standards more rigorous than due process requires, and censure judges who violate these standards. What Minnesota may not do, however, is censor what the people hear as they undertake to decide for themselves which candidate is most likely to be an exemplary judicial officer. Deciding the relevance of candidate speech is the right of the voters, not the State. See *Brown* v. *Hartlage*, 456 U.S., [at] 60. The law in question here contradicts the principle that unabridged speech is the foundation of political freedom. * * *

* * * The State may not regulate the content of candidate speech merely because the speakers are candidates. This case does not present the question whether a State may restrict the speech of judges because they are judges—for example, as part of a code of judicial conduct; the law at issue here regulates judges only when and because they are candidates. Whether the rationale of [cases concerning the speech of government employees] could be extended to allow a general speech restriction on sitting judges—regardless of whether they are campaigning—in order to promote the efficient administration of justice, is not an issue raised here.

Petitioner Gregory Wersal was not a sitting judge but a challenger; he had not voluntarily entered into an employment relationship with the State or surrendered any First Amendment rights. His speech may not be controlled or abridged in this manner. Even the undoubted interest of the State in the excellence of its judiciary does not allow it to restrain candidate speech by reason of its content. Minnesota's attempt to regulate campaign speech is impermissible.

JUSTICE STEVENS, with whom JUSTICE SOUTER, JUSTICE GINSBURG, and JUSTICE BREYER join, dissenting. * * *

There is a critical difference between the work of the judge and the work of other public officials. In a democracy, issues of policy are properly decided by majority vote; it is the business of legislators and executives to be popular. But in litigation, issues of law or fact should not be determined by popular vote; it is the business of judges to be indifferent to unpopularity. * * *

Consistent with that fundamental attribute of the office, countless judges in countless cases routinely make rulings that are unpopular and surely disliked by at least 50 percent of the litigants who appear before them. It is equally common for them to enforce rules that they think unwise, or that are contrary to their personal predilections. For this reason, opinions that a lawyer may have expressed before becoming a judge, or a judicial candidate, do not disqualify anyone for judicial service because every good judge is fully aware of the distinction between the law and a personal point of view. It is equally clear, however, that such expressions after a lawyer has been nominated to judicial office shed little, if any, light on his capacity for judicial service. Indeed, to the extent that such statements seek to enhance the popularity of the candidate by indicating how he would rule in specific cases if elected, they evidence a lack of fitness for the office.

Of course, any judge who faces reelection may believe that he retains his office only so long as his decisions are popular. Nevertheless, the elected judge, like the lifetime appointee, does not serve a constituency while holding that office. He has a duty to uphold the law and to follow the dictates of the Constitution. If he is not a judge on the highest court in the State, he has an obligation to follow the precedent of that court, not his personal views or public opinion polls.[2] He may make common law, but judged on the merits of individual cases, not as a mandate from the voters.

By recognizing a conflict between the demands of electoral politics and the distinct characteristics of the judiciary, we do not have to put States to an all or nothing choice of abandoning judicial elections or having elections in which anything goes. * * * [A] judicial candidate, who announces his views in the context of a campaign, is effectively telling the electorate: "Vote for me because I believe X, and I will judge cases accordingly." Once elected, he may feel free to disregard his campaign statements, but that does not change the fact that the judge announced his position on an issue likely to come before him *as a reason to vote for him.* Minnesota has a compelling interest in sanctioning such statements. * * *

The Court boldly asserts that respondents have failed to carry their burden of demonstrating "that campaign statements are uniquely destructive of openmindedness." But the very purpose of most statements prohibited by the announce clause is to convey the message that the candidate's mind is not open on a particular issue. The lawyer who writes an article advocating harsher penalties for polluters surely does not commit to that position to the same degree as the candidate who says "vote for me because I believe all polluters deserve harsher penalties." At the very least, such statements obscure the appearance of openmindedness. More importantly, like the reasoning in the Court's opinion, they create the false impression that the standards for the election of political candidates apply equally to candidates for judicial office.[4] * * *

---

2. The Court largely ignores the fact that judicial elections are not limited to races for the highest court in the State. Even if announcing one's views in the context of a campaign for the State Supreme Court might be permissible, the same statements are surely less appropriate when one is running for an intermediate or trial court judgeship. * * *

4. JUSTICE KENNEDY would go even further and hold that no content-based restriction of a judicial candidate's speech is permitted under the First Amendment. While he does not say so explicitly, this extreme position would preclude even Minnesota's prohibition against "pledges or promises" by a candidate for judicial office. A candidate could say "vote for me because I promise to never reverse a rape conviction," and the Board could do nothing to formally sanction that

Justice Ginsburg, with whom Justice Stevens, Justice Souter, and Justice Breyer join, dissenting.

Whether state or federal, elected or appointed, judges perform a function fundamentally different from that of the people's elected representatives. Legislative and executive officials act on behalf of the voters who placed them in office; "judges represent the Law." *Chisom v. Roemer*, 501 U.S. 380, 411 (1991) (Scalia, J., dissenting). * * *

The speech restriction must fail, in the Court's view, because an electoral process is at stake; if Minnesota opts to elect its judges, the Court asserts, the State may not rein in what candidates may say. I do not agree with this unilocular, "an election is an election," approach. * * *

* * * Even when they develop common law or give concrete meaning to constitutional text, judges act only in the context of individual cases, the outcome of which cannot depend on the will of the public. Thus, the rationale underlying unconstrained speech in elections for political office—that representative government depends on the public's ability to choose agents who will act at its behest—does not carry over to campaigns for the bench. * * *

All parties to this case agree that, whatever the validity of the Announce Clause, the State may constitutionally prohibit judicial candidates from pledging or promising certain results. The reasons for this agreement are apparent. Pledges or promises of conduct in office, however commonplace in races for the political branches, are inconsistent "with the judge's obligation to decide cases in accordance with his or her role." This judicial obligation to avoid prejudgment corresponds to the litigant's right, protected by the Due Process Clause of the Fourteenth Amendment, to "an impartial and disinterested tribunal in both civil and criminal cases." * * *

* * * When a judicial candidate promises to rule a certain way on an issue that may later reach the courts, the potential for due process violations is grave and manifest. If successful in her bid for office, the judicial candidate will become a judge, and in that capacity she will be under pressure to resist the pleas of litigants who advance positions contrary to her pledges on the campaign trail. If the judge fails to honor her campaign promises, she will not only face abandonment by supporters of her professed views, she will also "risk being assailed as a dissembler," willing to say one thing to win an election and to do the opposite once in office. A judge in this position therefore may be thought to have a "direct, personal, substantial, [and] pecuniary interest" in ruling against certain litigants, for she may be voted off the bench and thereby lose her salary and emoluments unless she honors the pledge that secured her election. * * *

---

candidate. The unwisdom of this proposal illustrates why the same standards should not apply to speech in campaigns for judicial and legislative office.

In addition to protecting litigants' due process rights, * * * [p]rohibiting a judicial candidate from pledging or promising certain results if elected directly promotes the State's interest in preserving public faith in the bench. When a candidate makes such a promise during a campaign, the public will no doubt perceive that she is doing so in the hope of garnering votes. And the public will in turn likely conclude that when the candidate decides an issue in accord with that promise, she does so at least in part to discharge her undertaking to the voters in the previous election and to prevent voter abandonment in the next. The perception of that unseemly *quid pro quo* — a judicial candidate's promises on issues in return for the electorate's votes at the polls — inevitably diminishes the public's faith in the ability of judges to administer the law without regard to personal or political self-interest.[4] * * *

Uncoupled from the Announce Clause, the ban on pledges or promises is easily circumvented. By prefacing a campaign commitment with the caveat, "although I cannot promise anything," or by simply avoiding the language of promises or pledges altogether, a candidate could declare with impunity how she would decide specific issues. Semantic sanitizing of the candidate's commitment would not, however, diminish its pernicious effects on actual and perceived judicial impartiality. * * *

By targeting statements that do not technically constitute pledges or promises but nevertheless "publicly make known how [the candidate] would decide" legal issues, the Announce Clause prevents this end run around the letter and spirit of its companion provision. No less than the pledges or promises clause itself, the Announce Clause is an indispensable part of Minnesota's effort to maintain the health of its judiciary, and is therefore constitutional for the same reasons. * * *

Notes and Questions

1. The Court avoided addressing whether judicial openmindedness and the appearance of judicial openmindedness were compelling state interests because, the Court concluded, Minnesota did not adopt the announce clause for those purposes. Why should it matter whether the state had the purpose of achieving certain compelling interests, if the statute did in fact serve them? In the Court's view, the prohibition was "so woefully underinclusive" that it would fail the narrow-tailoring portion of the strict-scrutiny analysis even if openmindedness and its appearance were compelling interests. Could a speech limitation be drafted so as to advance judicial openmindedness in a narrowly tailored way?

---

4. The author of the Court's opinion declined on precisely these grounds to tell the Senate whether he would overrule a particular case: "Let us assume that I have people arguing before me to do it or not to do it. I think it is quite a thing to be arguing to somebody who you know has made a representation in the course of his confirmation hearings, and that is, by way of condition to his being confirmed, that he will do this or do that. I think I would be in a very bad position to adjudicate the case without being accused of having a less than impartial view of the matter." (hearings before the Senate Judiciary Committee on the nomination of then-Judge Scalia).

2. *Is* openmindedness a compelling interest? Is it of compelling importance for judges to remain open to persuasion by the most frivolous arguments? *See* Michael R. Dimino, *Pay No Attention to that Man Behind the Robe: Judicial Elections, the First Amendment, and Judges as Politicians*, 21 YALE L. & POL'Y REV. 301, 343–46 (2003).

3. The Court in *Republican Party v. White* proclaimed that it was not taking any position on the constitutionality of bans on judicial candidates' pledging and promising particular conduct in office. Are such restrictions constitutional? Is it possible to distinguish "pledges or promises" from announcements of legal or political views without chilling the exercise of protected speech?

4. Would it be constitutional for a state (taking a cue from the 1990 ABA Model Code of Judicial Conduct) to ban judicial candidates from making statements that "commit or appear to commit" them with respect to issues likely to come before the court? Is there any way for a candidate to announce his views on a "disputed legal or political issue" without "appearing to commit" himself to such a view?

5. Restrictions on judicial conduct and campaign speech do not prevent judges or judicial candidates from *holding* views on legal or political issues; rather, they prevent others from *discovering* those views. Accordingly, the principal benefit of such restrictions is not in promoting judicial neutrality, but in promoting an *image* of judicial neutrality. Is that interest compelling? *Compare* Charles Gardner Geyh, *Straddling the Fence Between Truth and Pretense: The Role of Law and Preference in Judicial Decision Making and the Future of Judicial Independence*, 22 NOTRE DAME J.L., ETHICS & PUB. POL'Y 435, 448 (2008), *with* Dimino, *Pay No Attention, supra*, at 346. Does respect for the courts depend on the public's belief that judges do not have views on such matters? *See* James L. Gibson, *Challenges to the Impartiality of State Supreme Courts: Legitimacy Theory and "New-Style" Judicial Campaigns*, 102 AM. POL. SCI. REV. 59 (2008). If promoting respect for the courts is a compelling state interest, would promoting respect for other branches of government justify restrictions on speech in, say, legislative or presidential campaigns? *Cf.* Sedition Act, 1 Stat. 596 (1798) (forbidding the publication of "any false, scandalous and malicious writing or writings against the government of the United States, or either house of the Congress of the United States, or the President of the United States, with intent to defame the[m] * * *, or to bring them, or either of them, into contempt or disrepute * * *").

6. Why do you suppose that Justice Souter, who usually was quite solicitous of First Amendment claims, and Chief Justice Rehnquist, who usually was not, flipped sides in this case? *See* Michael R. Dimino, *Counter-Majoritarian Power and Judges' Political Speech*, 58 FLA. L. REV. 53 (2006).

7. Should the Court have treated elected judges as government employees, with restrictions on their political activities evaluated under *United Public Workers v. Mitchell*, 330 U.S. 75 (1947) [p. 668]? May states restrict the speech of *appointed* judges on a government-employment theory? May states restrict the speech of

lawyers on the theory that the license to practice law is a state-conferred benefit that may be conditioned on maintaining public respect for the legal system?

8. The dissenters argued that states should be able to adopt a middle road between fully competitive elections and appointive systems. Thus, in Justice Stevens's words, the Court unwisely "put States to an all or nothing choice of abandoning judicial elections or having elections in which anything goes." 536 U.S. at 800 (Stevens, J., dissenting). The majority, by contrast, adopted the view that "the greater power to dispense with elections altogether does not include the lesser power to conduct elections under conditions of state-imposed voter ignorance." Throughout this course you have seen and will see many variants of the greater-includes-the-lesser argument. Usually the argument runs into difficulty where the "lesser" power isn't really part of the greater one, but is instead a different power. For example, a state need not have elected school boards, but if it chooses to have them, the elections must comply with the constitutional guarantee of equality. *See Kramer v. Union Free School District No. 15*, 395 U.S. 621, 628–30 & n.11 (1969) [p. 46]. Likewise here, the power to appoint judges may not be the same as the power to limit speech by or about judges.

Do you agree with the dissenters that a middle road is possible? Do you think that a state could adopt such a middle approach for presidential elections, on the rationale that the state legislature need not have popular elections for presidential electors at all? *See McPherson v. Blacker*, 146 U.S. 1, 27 (1892) [p. 1065]. Would it be constitutional for a state to hold judicial elections, but to deviate from the requirements of one-person, one-vote? *See Wells v. Edwards*, 347 F. Supp. 453 (M.D. La. 1972), *aff'd* 409 U.S. 1095 (*per curiam*) (holding judicial elections immune from one person, one vote).

9. If you agree with the dissenters in *White*, how much freedom do you believe states should be given to define the independence of state offices? Edmund Burke famously argued in his Speech to the Electors of Bristol that representatives should act as fiduciaries and not simply serve public opinion: "Your representative owes you, not his industry only, but his judgment; and he betrays, instead of serving you, if he sacrifices it to your opinion." EDMUND BURKE, SPEECHES OF THE RIGHT HON. EDMUND BURKE 130 (J. Burke ed. 1867). Should states be able to restrict campaign speech in legislative or executive races by reasoning that unrestrained campaigning encourages representatives to "betray" their constituents by pandering to voters and "sacrific[ing] judgment to [popular] opinion"? Officials in the executive and legislative branches—not only the judicial branch—have an obligation to apply the law irrespective of public opinion." *See, e.g.*, U.S. CONST. art VI, cl. 3 ("The Senators and Representatives before mentioned, and the Members of the several State Legislatures, and all executive and judicial Officers, both of the United States and of the several States, shall be bound by Oath or Affirmation, to support this Constitution. . . ."); *United States v. Nixon*, 418 U.S. 683 (1974) (requiring the President to comply with a subpoena); *Cooper v. Aaron*, 358 U.S. 1, 18–19 (1959) (requiring states to abide by the Court's decision in *Brown v. Board of Education*, 347 U.S. 483 (1954));

Marbury v. Madison, 5 U.S. (1 Cranch) 137, 168 (1803) (stating that the Jefferson administration's refusal to provide Marbury his commission "is a plain violation" of Marbury's right to the document, "for which the laws of his country afford him a remedy"). Would the *White* dissenters uphold restrictions on campaign speech in elections for district attorney, secretary of state, or coroner?

10. Underlying the dissenters' argument is the conviction that states are entitled to treat judicial offices differently from "political" ones because of the differences in their respective duties. Should states be able to make this choice for the people? That is, should a state be able to restrict speech in judicial elections because it wants the judicial function to be (and to be recognized as) non-political, if the people want to vote based on campaign statements? *See generally* Dimino, *Pay No Attention, supra.*

11. As you will see in Chapter 8, Justice Ginsburg's argument that the announce clause was necessary to prevent evasion of the pledges-and-promises clause is analogous to the argument that stringent campaign-finance restrictions are necessary to ensure that other limits are not evaded. Such house-that-Jack-built arguments are not limited to election law. *Cf. Wickard v. Filburn*, 317 U.S. 111, 127–29 (1942); *McCulloch v. Maryland*, 17 U.S. (4 Wheat.) 316, 417 (1819).

12. Is the entire enterprise of electing judges inconsistent with the ideal of an independent judiciary that can defend the rule of law? *See, e.g.,* Steven P. Croley, *The Majoritarian Difficulty: Elective Judiciaries and the Rule of Law*, 62 U. Chi. L. Rev. 689 (1995); Michael R. Dimino, Sr., *Accountability Before the Fact*, 22 Notre Dame J.L., Ethics & Pub. Pol'y 451 (2008); Charles Gardner Geyh, *Why Judicial Elections Stink*, 64 Ohio St. L.J. 43 (2003); David E. Pozen, *The Irony of Judicial Elections*, 108 Colum. L. Rev. 265 (2008). Consider *New York Board of Elections v. López Torres*, 552 U.S. 196, 212 (2008) [p. 487] (Kennedy, J., joined by Breyer, J., concurring in the judgment):

> When one considers that elections require candidates to conduct campaigns and to raise funds in a system designed to allow for competition among interest groups and political parties, the persisting question is whether that process is consistent with the perception and the reality of judicial independence and judicial excellence. The rule of law, which is a foundation of freedom, presupposes a functioning judiciary respected for its independence, its professional attainments, and the absolute probity of its judges. And it may seem difficult to reconcile these aspirations with elections.
>
> Still, though the Framers did not provide for elections of federal judges, most States have made the opposite choice, at least to some extent. In light of this longstanding practice and tradition in the States, the appropriate practical response is not to reject judicial elections outright but to find ways to use elections to select judges with the highest qualifications. A judicial election system presents the opportunity, indeed the civic obligation, for voters and the community as a whole to become engaged in the legal

process. Judicial elections, if fair and open, could be an essential forum for society to discuss and define the attributes of judicial excellence and to find ways to discern those qualities in the candidates. The organized bar, the legal academy, public advocacy groups, a principled press, and all the other components of functioning democracy must engage in this process.

Justice Stevens more bluntly suggested that problems observed in judicial elections "lend support to the * * * proposition that the very practice of electing judges is unwise." *Id.* at 209 (Stevens, J., joined by Souter, J., concurring). Ultimately, however, Justice Stevens concluded that "[t]he Constitution does not prohibit legislatures from enacting stupid laws." *Id.*

For additional commentary on state judicial elections, from a variety of perspectives, see CHRIS W. BONNEAU & MELINDA GANN HALL, IN DEFENSE OF JUDICIAL ELECTIONS (1999), *reviewed in* Michael E. Solimine, *Independence, Accountability, and the Case for State Judicial Elections*, 9 ELECTION L.J. 215 (2010); JED HANDELSMAN SHUGERMAN, THE PEOPLE'S COURTS: PURSUING JUDICIAL INDEPENDENCE IN AMERICA (2012); James J. Sample, *Retention Elections 2.010*, 46 U.S.F. L. REV. 383 (2011); and Rebecca D. Gill, *Beyond High Hopes and Unmet Expectations: Judicial Selection Reforms in the States*, 96 JUDICATURE 278 (2013).

13. Despite the Court's apparently unanimous view in *López Torres* that states may constitutionally select their judges by popular elections, *Caperton v. A.T. Massey Coal Co.*, 556 U.S. 868 (2009), decided the following year by a 5-4 margin, may indicate that there are constitutional concerns surrounding the election of judges. In *Caperton*, the Court held that the Due Process Clause required the recusal of an elected state-supreme-court justice in a case reviewing the legality of a $50 million judgment. The CEO of the company against which the judgment was entered had spent $3 million in support of the judge's election. Almost all of the $3 million was spent independently of the judge's campaign, however, and the company itself spent nothing. The Court held that due process was compromised, but was careful to state that the "extreme" facts of *Caperton* distinguished that case from more common instances in which litigants have supported the selection of judges hearing their cases. The Court's test for determining when the Due Process Clause has been violated, however, was vague:

> We conclude that there is a serious risk of actual bias—based on objective and reasonable perceptions—when a person with a personal stake in a particular case had a significant and disproportionate influence in placing the judge on the case by raising funds or directing the judge's election campaign when the case was pending or imminent. The inquiry centers on the contribution's relative size in comparison to the total amount of money contributed to the campaign, the total amount spent in the election, and the apparent effect such contribution had on the outcome of the election.

556 U.S. at 884. Are you satisfied that judicial elections can continue after *Caperton*, or will recusal motions hamper the effective operation of elected courts?

14. Does recusal unconstitutionally burden the First Amendment rights of a candidate's supporters? *Nevada Commission on Ethics v. Carrigan*, 564 U.S. 117 (2011), involved a state law requiring legislators to recuse themselves from voting on measures when their private relationships would call into question their "independence of judgment." The Supreme Court held that the First Amendment right of free speech did not extend to casting a legislative vote, but did not address whether the recusal provision unconstitutionally burdened campaign speech.

In a concurring opinion, Justice Kennedy suggested that legislative recusal provisions may well violate the constitutional rights of persons who offer their support to candidates:

> As a general matter, citizens voice their support and lend their aid because they wish to confer the powers of public office on those whose positions correspond with their own. That dynamic, moreover, links the principles of participation and representation at the heart of our democratic government. Just as candidates announce positions in exchange for citizens' votes, *Brown* v. *Hartlage*, 456 U.S. 45, 55–56 (1982) [p. 568], so too citizens offer endorsements, advertise their views, and assist political campaigns based upon bonds of common purpose. These are the mechanisms that sustain representative democracy.

564 U.S. at 131–32 (Kennedy, J., concurring).

Nevertheless, Justice Kennedy suggested that requiring recusal of *judges* might be different:

> The differences between the role of political bodies in formulating and enforcing public policy, on the one hand, and the role of courts in adjudicating individual disputes according to law, on the other, may call for a different understanding of the responsibilities attendant upon holders of those respective offices and of the legitimate restrictions that may be imposed upon them.

Id. at 132. *See also id.* at 124 & n.3 (opinion of the Court) (noting that "[t]here are of course differences between a legislator's vote and a judge's, and thus between legislative and judicial recusal rules," and contrasting a judge's vote while on the bench (which is not part of the freedom of speech protected by the First Amendment) to his or her "speech during elections" (which was held in *Republican Party of Minnesota v. White* to be protected)).

Is Justice Kennedy's proposed distinction between judges and legislators consistent with the reasoning of *Republican Party of Minnesota v. White*?

15. In 2015, the Supreme Court revisited the First Amendment's applicability to judicial campaigns, emphatically concluding that judicial elections are *not* exactly like those for "political" offices. This time the issue was the constitutionality of an ethical canon prohibiting judicial candidates from personally soliciting campaign funds.

Williams-Yulee v. Florida Bar

Supreme Court of the United States
575 U.S. 433, 135 S. Ct. 1656, 191 L. Ed. 2d 570 (2015)

CHIEF JUSTICE ROBERTS delivered the opinion of the Court, except as to Part II.[c]

* * * In an effort to preserve public confidence in the integrity of their judiciaries, many * * * States prohibit judges and judicial candidates from personally soliciting funds for their campaigns. We must decide whether the First Amendment permits such restrictions on speech.

We hold that it does. Judges are not politicians, even when they come to the bench by way of the ballot. And a State's decision to elect its judiciary does not compel it to treat judicial candidates like campaigners for political office. A State may assure its people that judges will apply the law without fear or favor—and without having personally asked anyone for money. * * *

I * * *

Canon 7C(1) [of the Florida Code of Judicial Conduct] governs fundraising in judicial elections. The Canon, which is based on a provision in the American Bar Association's Model Code of Judicial Conduct, provides:

> "A candidate, including an incumbent judge, for a judicial office that is filled by public election between competing candidates shall not personally solicit campaign funds, or solicit attorneys for publicly stated support, but may establish committees of responsible persons to secure and manage the expenditure of funds for the candidate's campaign and to obtain public statements of support for his or her candidacy. Such committees are not prohibited from soliciting campaign contributions and public support from any person or corporation authorized by law."

Florida statutes impose additional restrictions on campaign fundraising in judicial elections. Contributors may not donate more than $1,000 per election to a trial court candidate or more than $3,000 per retention election to a Supreme Court justice. Campaign committee treasurers must file periodic reports disclosing the names of contributors and the amount of each contribution.

Judicial candidates can seek guidance about campaign ethics rules from the Florida Judicial Ethics Advisory Committee. The Committee has interpreted Canon 7 to allow a judicial candidate to serve as treasurer of his own campaign committee, learn the identity of campaign contributors, and send thank you notes to donors.

Like Florida, most other States prohibit judicial candidates from soliciting campaign funds personally, but allow them to raise money through committees.

---

c. JUSTICES BREYER, SOTOMAYOR, and KAGAN join this opinion in its entirety. JUSTICE GINSBURG joins all except Part II. — Eds.

According to the American Bar Association, 30 of the 39 States that elect trial or appellate judges have adopted restrictions similar to Canon 7C(1).

Lanell Williams-Yulee, who refers to herself as Yulee, has practiced law in Florida since 1991. In September 2009, she decided to run for a seat on the county court for Hillsborough County, a jurisdiction of about 1.3 million people that includes the city of Tampa. Shortly after filing paperwork to enter the race, Yulee drafted a letter announcing her candidacy. The letter described her experience and desire to "bring fresh ideas and positive solutions to the Judicial bench." The letter then stated:

> "An early contribution of $25, $50, $100, $250, or $500, made payable to 'Lanell Williams-Yulee Campaign for County Judge', will help raise the initial funds needed to launch the campaign and get our message out to the public. I ask for your support [i]n meeting the primary election fund raiser goals. Thank you in advance for your support."

Yulee signed the letter and mailed it to local voters. She also posted the letter on her campaign Web site.

Yulee's bid for the bench did not unfold as she had hoped. She lost the primary to the incumbent judge. Then the Florida Bar filed a complaint against her [for violating] the ban on personal solicitation of campaign funds in Canon 7C(1).

Yulee admitted that she had signed and sent the fundraising letter. But she argued that the Bar could not discipline her for that conduct because the First Amendment protects a judicial candidate's right to solicit campaign funds in an election. The Florida Supreme Court * * * publicly reprimanded [Yulee] and ordered [her] to pay the costs of the proceeding ($1,860).

II

* * * The parties agree that Canon 7C(1) restricts Yulee's speech on the basis of its content by prohibiting her from soliciting contributions to her election campaign. The parties disagree, however, about the level of scrutiny that should govern our review.

* * * As we have long recognized, speech about public issues and the qualifications of candidates for elected office commands the highest level of First Amendment protection. See *Eu* v. *San Francisco County Democratic Central Comm.*, 489 U.S. 214, 223 (1989) [p. 480]. Indeed, in our only prior case concerning speech restrictions on a candidate for judicial office, this Court and both parties assumed that strict scrutiny applied. *Republican Party of Minn.* v. *White*, 536 U.S. 765, 774 (2002) [p. 605]. * * * [W]e hold today what we assumed in *White*: A State may restrict the speech of a judicial candidate only if the restriction is narrowly tailored to serve a compelling interest.

III

* * * Canon 7C(1) advances the State's compelling interest in preserving public confidence in the integrity of the judiciary, and it does so through means narrowly

tailored to avoid unnecessarily abridging speech. This is therefore one of the rare cases in which a speech restriction withstands strict scrutiny.

A

The Florida Supreme Court adopted Canon 7C(1) to promote the State's interests in "protecting the integrity of the judiciary" and "maintaining the public's confidence in an impartial judiciary." The way the Canon advances those interests is intuitive: Judges, charged with exercising strict neutrality and independence, cannot supplicate campaign donors without diminishing public confidence in judicial integrity. * * * Simply put, Florida and most other States have concluded that the public may lack confidence in a judge's ability to administer justice without fear or favor if he comes to office by asking for favors.

The interest served by Canon 7C(1) has firm support in our precedents. We have recognized the "vital state interest" in safeguarding "public confidence in the fairness and integrity of the nation's elected judges." *Caperton* v. *A.T. Massey Coal Co.*, 556 U.S. 868, 889 (2009). The importance of public confidence in the integrity of judges stems from the place of the judiciary in the government. Unlike the executive or the legislature, the judiciary "has no influence over either the sword or the purse; . . . neither force nor will but merely judgment." The Federalist No. 78, p. 465 (C. Rossiter ed. 1961) (A. Hamilton) (capitalization altered). The judiciary's authority therefore depends in large measure on the public's willingness to respect and follow its decisions. * * * It follows that public perception of judicial integrity is "a state interest of the highest order." *Caperton*, 556 U.S., at 889. * * *

The parties devote considerable attention to our cases analyzing campaign finance restrictions in political elections. But a State's interest in preserving public confidence in the integrity of its judiciary extends beyond its interest in preventing the appearance of corruption in legislative and executive elections. As we explained in *White*, States may regulate judicial elections differently than they regulate political elections, because the role of judges differs from the role of politicians. 536 U.S., at 783; *id.*, at 805 (GINSBURG, J., dissenting). Politicians are expected to be appropriately responsive to the preferences of their supporters. Indeed, such "responsiveness is key to the very concept of self-governance through elected officials." The same is not true of judges. In deciding cases, a judge is not to follow the preferences of his supporters, or provide any special consideration to his campaign donors. * * * As in *White*, therefore, our precedents applying the First Amendment to political elections have little bearing on the issues here. * * *

* * * Moreover, personal solicitation by a judicial candidate "inevitably places the solicited individuals in a position to fear retaliation if they fail to financially support that candidate." Potential litigants then fear that "the integrity of the judicial system has been compromised, forcing them to search for an attorney in part based upon the criteria of which attorneys have made the obligatory contributions." A State's decision to elect its judges does not require it to tolerate these risks. The Florida Bar's interest is compelling.

B

Yulee acknowledges the State's compelling interest in judicial integrity. She argues, however, that the Canon's failure to restrict other speech equally damaging to judicial integrity and its appearance undercuts the Bar's position. In particular, she notes that Canon 7C(1) allows a judge's campaign committee to solicit money, which arguably reduces public confidence in the integrity of the judiciary just as much as a judge's personal solicitation. Yulee also points out that Florida permits judicial candidates to write thank you notes to campaign donors, which ensures that candidates know who contributes and who does not. * * *

* * * Canon 7C(1) raises no fatal underinclusivity concerns. The solicitation ban aims squarely at the conduct most likely to undermine public confidence in the integrity of the judiciary: personal requests for money by judges and judicial candidates. The Canon applies evenhandedly to all judges and judicial candidates, regardless of their viewpoint or chosen means of solicitation. And unlike some laws that we have found impermissibly underinclusive, Canon 7C(1) is not riddled with exceptions. Indeed, the Canon contains zero exceptions to its ban on personal solicitation.

Yulee relies heavily on the provision of Canon 7C(1) that allows solicitation by a candidate's campaign committee. But Florida, along with most other States, has reasonably concluded that solicitation by the candidate personally creates a categorically different and more severe risk of undermining public confidence than does solicitation by a campaign committee. The identity of the solicitor matters, as anyone who has encountered a Girl Scout selling cookies outside a grocery store can attest. When the judicial candidate himself asks for money, the stakes are higher for all involved. The candidate has personally invested his time and effort in the fundraising appeal; he has placed his name and reputation behind the request. The solicited individual knows that, and also knows that the solicitor might be in a position to singlehandedly make decisions of great weight: The same person who signed the fundraising letter might one day sign the judgment. This dynamic inevitably creates pressure for the recipient to comply, and it does so in a way that solicitation by a third party does not. Just as inevitably, the personal involvement of the candidate in the solicitation creates the public appearance that the candidate will remember who says yes, and who says no.

In short, personal solicitation by judicial candidates implicates a different problem than solicitation by campaign committees. However similar the two solicitations may be in substance, a State may conclude that they present markedly different appearances to the public. Florida's choice to allow solicitation by campaign committees does not undermine its decision to ban solicitation by judges.

Likewise, allowing judicial candidates to write thank you notes to campaign donors does not detract from the State's interest in preserving public confidence in the integrity of the judiciary. Yulee argues that permitting thank you notes heightens the likelihood of actual bias by ensuring that judicial candidates know who supported their campaigns, and ensuring that the supporter knows that the candidate knows. Maybe so. But the State's compelling interest is implicated most directly by the candidate's personal solicitation itself. A failure to ban thank you notes for contributions not solicited by the candidate does not undercut the Bar's rationale. * * *

Taken to its logical conclusion, the position advanced by Yulee and the principal dissent is that Florida may ban the solicitation of funds by judicial candidates only if the State bans *all* solicitation of funds in judicial elections. The First Amendment does not put a State to that all-or-nothing choice. We will not punish Florida for leaving open more, rather than fewer, avenues of expression, especially when there is no indication that the selective restriction of speech reflects a pretextual motive.

C * * *

* * * Yulee concedes—and the principal dissent seems to agree—that Canon 7C(1) is valid in numerous applications. Yulee acknowledges that Florida can prohibit judges from soliciting money from lawyers and litigants appearing before them. In addition, she says the State "might" be able to ban "direct one-to-one solicitation of lawyers and individuals or businesses that could reasonably appear in the court for which the individual is a candidate." She also suggests that the Bar could forbid "in person" solicitation by judicial candidates. But Yulee argues that the Canon cannot constitutionally be applied to her chosen form of solicitation: a letter posted online and distributed via mass mailing. No one, she contends, will lose confidence in the integrity of the judiciary based on personal solicitation to such a broad audience.

This argument misperceives the breadth of the compelling interest that underlies Canon 7C(1). Florida has reasonably determined that personal appeals for money by a judicial candidate inherently create an appearance of impropriety that may cause the public to lose confidence in the integrity of the judiciary. That interest may be implicated to varying degrees in particular contexts, but the interest remains whenever the public perceives the judge personally asking for money.

Moreover, the lines Yulee asks us to draw are unworkable. Even under her theory of the case, a mass mailing would create an appearance of impropriety if addressed to a list of all lawyers and litigants with pending cases. So would a speech soliciting contributions from the 100 most frequently appearing attorneys in the jurisdiction. Yulee says she might accept a ban on one-to-one solicitation, but is the public impression really any different if a judicial candidate tries to buttonhole not one prospective donor but two at a time? Ten? Yulee also agrees that in person solicitation creates a problem. But would the public's concern recede if the request for money came in a phone call or a text message?

We decline to wade into this swamp. The First Amendment requires that Canon 7C(1) be narrowly tailored, not that it be "perfectly tailored." The impossibility of perfect tailoring is especially apparent when the State's compelling interest is as intangible as public confidence in the integrity of the judiciary. Yulee is of course correct that some personal solicitations raise greater concerns than others. A judge who passes the hat in the courthouse creates a more serious appearance of impropriety than does a judicial candidate who makes a tasteful plea for support on the radio. But most problems arise in greater and lesser gradations, and the First Amendment does not confine a State to addressing evils in their most acute form. Here, Florida has concluded that all personal solicitations by judicial candidates create a public appearance that undermines confidence in the integrity of the judiciary; banning all personal solicitations by judicial candidates is narrowly tailored to address that concern. * * *

Finally, Yulee contends that Florida can accomplish its compelling interest through the less restrictive means of recusal rules and campaign contribution limits. We disagree. A rule requiring judges to recuse themselves from every case in which a lawyer or litigant made a campaign contribution would disable many jurisdictions. And a flood of postelection recusal motions could "erode public confidence in judicial impartiality" and thereby exacerbate the very appearance problem the State is trying to solve. Moreover, the rule that Yulee envisions could create a perverse incentive for litigants to make campaign contributions to judges solely as a means to trigger their later recusal—a form of peremptory strike against a judge that would enable transparent forum shopping.

As for campaign contribution limits, Florida already applies them to judicial elections. A State may decide that the threat to public confidence created by personal solicitation exists apart from the amount of money that a judge or judicial candidate seeks. Even if Florida decreased its contribution limit, the appearance that judges who personally solicit funds might improperly favor their campaign donors would remain. Although the Court has held that contribution limits advance the interest in preventing *quid pro quo* corruption and its appearance in political elections, we have never held that adopting contribution limits precludes a State from pursuing its compelling interests through additional means. And in any event, a State has compelling interests in regulating judicial elections that extend beyond its interests in regulating political elections, because judges are not politicians.

In sum, because Canon 7C(1) is narrowly tailored to serve a compelling government interest, the First Amendment poses no obstacle to its enforcement in this case. As a result of our decision, Florida may continue to prohibit judicial candidates from personally soliciting campaign funds, while allowing them to raise money through committees and to otherwise communicate their electoral messages in practically any way. The principal dissent faults us for not answering a slew of broader questions, such as whether Florida may cap a judicial candidate's spending or ban independent expenditures by corporations. Yulee has not asked these questions, and for good reason—they are far afield from the narrow regulation actually at issue in this case. * * *

* * * Judicial candidates have a First Amendment right to speak in support of their campaigns. States have a compelling interest in preserving public confidence in their judiciaries. When the State adopts a narrowly tailored restriction like the

one at issue here, those principles do not conflict. A State's decision to elect judges does not compel it to compromise public confidence in their integrity.

The judgment of the Florida Supreme Court is

Affirmed.

JUSTICE BREYER, concurring.

As I have previously said, I view this Court's doctrine referring to tiers of scrutiny as guidelines informing our approach to the case at hand, not tests to be mechanically applied. On that understanding, I join the Court's opinion.

JUSTICE GINSBURG, * * * concurring in part and concurring in the judgment.

I join the Court's opinion save for Part II. As explained in my dissenting opinion in *Republican Party of Minnesota* v. *White*, I would not apply exacting scrutiny to a State's endeavor sensibly to "differentiate elections for political offices . . . , from elections designed to select those whose office it is to administer justice without respect to persons." * * *

JUSTICE SCALIA, with whom JUSTICE THOMAS joins, dissenting.

An ethics canon adopted by the Florida Supreme Court bans a candidate in a judicial election from asking anyone, under any circumstances, for a contribution to his campaign. Faithful application of our precedents would have made short work of this wildly disproportionate restriction upon speech. Intent upon upholding the Canon, however, the Court flattens one settled First Amendment principle after another.

I * * *

* * * I do not for a moment question the Court's conclusion that States have different compelling interests when regulating judicial elections than when regulating political ones. Unlike a legislator, a judge must be impartial—without bias for or against any party or attorney who comes before him. I accept for the sake of argument that States have a compelling interest in ensuring that its judges are *seen* to be impartial. I will likewise assume that a judicial candidate's request to a litigant or attorney presents a danger of coercion that a political candidate's request to a constituent does not. But Canon 7C(1) does not narrowly target concerns about impartiality or its appearance; it applies even when the person asked for a financial contribution has no chance of ever appearing in the candidate's court. And Florida does not invoke concerns about coercion, presumably because the Canon bans solicitations regardless of whether their object is a lawyer, litigant, or other person vulnerable to judicial pressure. So Canon 7C(1) fails exacting scrutiny and infringes the First Amendment. This case should have been just that straightforward.

II * * *

A

The first sign that mischief is afoot comes when the Court describes Florida's compelling interest. The State must first identify its objective with precision before one can tell whether that interest is compelling and whether the speech restriction narrowly targets it. In *White*, for example, the Court did not allow a State to invoke hazy concerns about judicial impartiality in justification of an ethics rule against judicial candidates' announcing their positions on legal issues. The Court instead separately analyzed the State's concerns about judges' bias against parties, preconceptions on legal issues, and openmindedness, and explained why each concern (and each for a different reason) did not suffice to sustain the rule. [536 U.S.,] at 775–780.

In stark contrast to *White*, the Court today relies on Florida's invocation of an ill-defined interest in "public confidence in judicial integrity." The Court at first suggests that "judicial integrity" involves the "ability to administer justice without fear or favor." * * * When the Court explains how solicitation undermines confidence in judicial integrity, integrity starts to sound like saintliness. It involves independence from any "*possible* temptation" that "*might* lead" the judge, "even unknowingly," to favor one party. When the Court turns to distinguishing in-person solicitation from solicitation by proxy, the any-possible-temptation standard no longer helps and thus drops out. The critical factors instead become the "pressure" a listener feels during a solicitation and the "appearance that the candidate will remember who says yes, and who says no." But when it comes time to explain Florida's decision to allow candidates to write thank-you notes, the "appearance that the candidate ... remember[s] who says yes" gets nary a mention. And when the Court confronts Florida's decision to prohibit mass-mailed solicitations, concern about pressure fades away. More outrageous still, the Court at times molds the interest in the perception that judges have integrity into an interest in the perception that judges do not solicit — for example when it says, "all personal solicitations by judicial candidates create a public appearance that undermines confidence in the integrity of the judiciary; banning all personal solicitations by judicial candidates is narrowly tailored to address that concern." This is not strict scrutiny; it is sleight of hand.

B

The Court's twistifications have not come to an end; indeed, they are just beginning. In order to uphold Canon 7C(1) under strict scrutiny, Florida must do more than point to a vital public objective brooding overhead. The State must also meet a difficult burden of demonstrating that the speech restriction substantially advances the claimed objective. * * *

* * * The Court announces, on the basis of its "intuiti[on]," that allowing personal solicitations will make litigants worry that "judges' decisions may be motivated by the desire to repay campaign contributions." But this case is not about

whether Yulee has the right to receive campaign contributions. It is about whether she has the right to *ask* for campaign contributions that Florida's statutory law already allows her to receive. Florida bears the burden of showing that banning *requests* for lawful contributions will improve public confidence in judges—not just a little bit, but significantly, because "the Government does not have a compelling interest in each marginal percentage point by which its goals are advanced."

Neither the Court nor the State identifies the slightest evidence that banning requests for contributions will substantially improve public trust in judges. Nor does common sense make this happy forecast obvious. [J]udicial elections in America date back more than two centuries—but rules against personal solicitations date back only to 1972. The peaceful coexistence of judicial elections and personal solicitations for most of our history calls into doubt any claim that allowing personal solicitations would imperil public faith in judges. Many States allow judicial candidates to ask for contributions even today, but nobody suggests that public confidence in judges fares worse in these jurisdictions than elsewhere. And in any event, if candidates' appeals for money are "characteristically intertwined" with discussion of qualifications and views on public issues, how can the Court be so sure that the public will regard them as improprieties rather than as legitimate instances of campaigning? In the final analysis, Florida comes nowhere near making the convincing demonstration required by our cases that the speech restriction in this case substantially advances its objective.

C

But suppose we play along with the premise that prohibiting solicitations will significantly improve the public reputation of judges. Even then, Florida must show that the ban restricts no more speech than necessary to achieve the objective.

Canon 7C(1) falls miles short of satisfying this requirement. The Court seems to accept Florida's claim that solicitations erode public confidence by creating the perception that judges are selling justice to lawyers and litigants. Yet the Canon prohibits candidates from asking for money from *anybody*—even from someone who is neither lawyer nor litigant, even from someone who (because of recusal rules) cannot possibly appear before the candidate as lawyer or litigant. Yulee thus may not call up an old friend, a cousin, or even her parents to ask for a donation to her campaign. The State has not come up with a plausible explanation of how soliciting someone who has no chance of appearing in the candidate's court will diminish public confidence in judges.

No less important, Canon 7C(1) bans candidates from asking for contributions even in messages that do not target any listener in particular—mass-mailed letters, flyers posted on telephone poles, speeches to large gatherings, and Web sites addressed to the general public. Messages like these do not share the features that lead the Court to pronounce personal solicitations a menace to public confidence in the judiciary. Consider online solicitations. They avoid "the spectacle of lawyers or potential litigants directly handing over money to judicial candidates." People who come across online solicitations do not feel "pressure" to comply with the request. Nor does the candidate's signature on the online solicitation suggest "that the candidate will remember who says yes, and who says no." Yet Canon 7C(1) prohibits these and similar solicitations anyway. This tailoring is as narrow as the Court's scrutiny is strict.

Perhaps sensing the fragility of the initial claim that *all* solicitations threaten public confidence in judges, the Court argues that "the lines Yulee asks [it] to draw are unworkable." That is a difficulty of the Court's own imagination. In reality, the Court could have chosen from a whole spectrum of workable rules. It could have held that States may regulate no more than solicitation of participants in pending cases, or solicitation of people who are likely to appear in the candidate's court, or even solicitation of any lawyer or litigant. And it could have ruled that candidates have the right to make fundraising appeals that are not directed to any particular listener (like requests in mass-mailed letters), or at least fundraising appeals plainly directed to the general public (like requests placed online). The Supreme Court of Florida has made similar accommodations in other settings. It allows sitting judges to solicit memberships in civic organizations if (among other things) the solicitee is not "likely ever to appear before the court on which the judge serves." And it allows sitting judges to accept gifts if (among other things) "the donor is not a party or other person . . . whose interests have come or are likely to come before the judge." It is not too much to ask that the State show election speech similar consideration.

The Court's accusation of unworkability also suffers from a bit of a pot-kettle problem. Consider the many real-world questions left open by today's decision. Does the First Amendment permit restricting a candidate's appearing at an event where somebody *else* asks for campaign funds on his behalf? Does it permit prohibiting the candidate's *family* from making personal solicitations? Does it allow prohibiting the candidate from participating in the creation of a Web site that solicits funds, even if the candidate's name does not appear next to the request? More broadly, could Florida ban thank-you notes to donors? Cap a candidate's campaign spending? Restrict independent spending by people other than the candidate? Ban independent spending by corporations? And how, by the way, are judges supposed to decide whether these measures promote public confidence in judicial integrity, when the Court does not even have a consistent theory about what it means by "judicial integrity"? For the Court to wring its hands about workability under these circumstances is more than one should have to bear.

D * * *

* * * The Court tells us that "all personal solicitations by judicial candidates create a public appearance that undermines confidence in the integrity of the judiciary." But Canon 7C(1) does not restrict *all* personal solicitations; it restricts only personal solicitations related to campaigns. The part of the Canon challenged here prohibits personal pleas for "campaign funds," and the Canon elsewhere prohibits personal appeals to attorneys for "publicly stated support." So although Canon

7C(1) prevents Yulee from asking a lawyer for a few dollars to help her buy campaign pamphlets, it does not prevent her asking the same lawyer for a personal loan, access to his law firm's luxury suite at the local football stadium, or even a donation to help her fight the Florida Bar's charges. What could possibly justify these distinctions? Surely the Court does not believe that requests for campaign favors erode public confidence in a way that requests for favors unrelated to elections do not. Could anyone say with a straight face that it looks *worse* for a candidate to say "please give my campaign $25" than to say "please give *me* $25"?

* * * Canon 7C(1)'s scope suggests that it has nothing to do with the appearances created by judges' asking for money, and everything to do with hostility toward judicial campaigning. How else to explain the Florida Supreme Court's decision to ban *all* personal appeals for campaign funds (even when the solicitee could never appear before the candidate), but to tolerate appeals for other kinds of funds (even when the solicitee will surely appear before the candidate)? It should come as no surprise that the ABA, whose model rules the Florida Supreme Court followed when framing Canon 7C(1), opposes judicial elections — preferring instead a system in which (surprise!) a committee of lawyers proposes candidates from among whom the Governor must make his selection.

The Court tries to strike a pose of neutrality between appointment and election of judges, but no one should be deceived. A Court that sees impropriety in a candidate's request for *any* contributions to his election campaign does not much like judicial selection by the people. One cannot have judicial elections without judicial campaigns, and judicial campaigns without funds for campaigning, and funds for campaigning without asking for them. When a society decides that its judges should be elected, it necessarily decides that selection by the people is more important than the oracular sanctity of judges, their immunity from the (shudder!) indignity of begging for funds, and their exemption from those shadows of impropriety that fall over the proletarian public officials who must run for office. * * * The prescription that judges be elected probably springs from the people's realization that their judges can become their rulers — and (it must be said) from just a deep-down feeling that members of the Third Branch will profit from a hearty helping of humble pie, and from a severe reduction of their great remove from the (ugh!) People. (It should not be thought that I myself harbor such irreverent and revolutionary feelings; but I think it likely — and year by year more likely — that those who favor the election of judges do so.) In any case, hostility to campaigning by judges entitles the people of Florida to amend their Constitution to replace judicial elections with the selection of judges by lawyers' committees; it does not entitle the Florida Supreme Court to adopt, or this Court to endorse, a rule of judicial conduct that abridges candidates' speech in the judicial elections that the Florida Constitution prescribes. * * *

I respectfully dissent.

JUSTICE KENNEDY, dissenting. * * *

With all due respect for the Court, it seems fair and necessary to say its decision rests on two premises, neither one correct. One premise is that in certain elections—here an election to choose the best qualified judge—the public lacks the necessary judgment to make an informed choice. Instead, the State must protect voters by altering the usual dynamics of free speech. The other premise is that since judges should be accorded special respect and dignity, their election can be subject to certain content-based rules that would be unacceptable in other elections. In my respectful view neither premise can justify the speech restriction at issue here. Although States have a compelling interest in seeking to ensure the appearance and the reality of an impartial judiciary, it does not follow that the State may alter basic First Amendment principles in pursuing that goal. * * *

It is not within our Nation's First Amendment tradition to abridge speech simply because the government believes a question is too difficult or too profound for voters. If the State is concerned about unethical campaign practices, it need not revert to the assumption that voters themselves are insensitive to ethics. Judicial elections were created to enable citizens to decide for themselves which judges are best qualified and which are most likely to "stand by the constitution of the State against the encroachment of power." The Court should not now presume citizens are unequipped for that task when it comes to judging for themselves who should judge them. * * *

* * * This law comes nowhere close to being narrowly tailored. And by saying that it survives that vital First Amendment requirement, the Court now writes what is literally a casebook guide to eviscerating strict scrutiny any time the Court encounters speech it dislikes. On these premises, and for the reasons explained in more detail by JUSTICE SCALIA, it is necessary for me to file this respectful dissent.

JUSTICE ALITO, dissenting.

I largely agree with what I view as the essential elements of the dissents filed by JUSTICES SCALIA and KENNEDY. * * * Florida has a compelling interest in making sure that its courts decide cases impartially and in accordance with the law and that its citizens have no good reason to lack confidence that its courts are performing their proper role. But the Florida rule is not narrowly tailored to serve that interest.

Indeed, this rule is about as narrowly tailored as a burlap bag. It applies to all solicitations made in the name of a candidate for judicial office—including, as was the case here, a mass mailing. It even applies to an ad in a newspaper. It applies to requests for contributions in any amount, and it applies even if the person solicited is not a lawyer, has never had any interest at stake in any case in the court in question, and has no prospect of ever having any interest at stake in any litigation in that court. If this rule can be characterized as narrowly tailored, then narrow tailoring has no meaning, and strict scrutiny, which is essential to the protection of free speech, is seriously impaired.

Notes and Questions

1. Are there sufficient reasons to distinguish between the First Amendment protection given to financing judicial campaigns, on the one hand, and financing legislative or executive campaigns, on the other? In both instances, restrictions on the funding would be justified by the need to prevent the actuality or appearance of impropriety. But the Court appears to have a different vision of impropriety for those different offices, as you will learn in the next Chapter. The Court seems to accept that "political" officials will show a certain favoritism for their supporters, while *Williams-Yulee* found a compelling interest in avoiding even the appearance that judges would favor theirs.

2. *Problem.* In the years since *Republican Party of Minnesota v. White* struck down the announce clause, there has been much controversy about the constitutionality of other restrictions on judicial campaign activity. *Williams-Yulee* is unlikely to resolve those controversies. Are the following restrictions narrowly tailored to serve a compelling interest?

A. Laws prohibiting judicial candidates from identifying themselves as members of political parties. *See Carey v. Wotnitzek*, 614 F.3d 189 (6th Cir. 2010); *Siefert v. Alexander*, 608 F.3d 974 (7th Cir. 2010), *cert. denied*, 131 S. Ct. 2872 (2011); *Republican Party of Minnesota v. White*, 416 F.3d 738 (8th Cir. 2005) (*en banc*) (on remand from the Supreme Court).

B. Laws prohibiting judicial candidates from seeking, accepting, or using party endorsements. *See French v. Jones*, 876 F.3d 1228 (9th Cir. 2017), *cert. denied*, 138 S. Ct. 1598 (2018); *Republican Party v. White, supra*.

C. Laws prohibiting judicial candidates from attending political gatherings. *See id.*

D. Laws prohibiting judicial candidates from speaking at political gatherings or speaking on behalf of political organizations. *See Bauer v. Shepard*, 620 F.3d 704 (7th Cir. 2010), *cert. denied*, 563 U.S. 974 (2011).

E. Laws prohibiting judicial candidates from holding party office.

F. Laws prohibiting judicial candidates from endorsing or opposing candidates for public office. *See Wersal v. Sexton*, 613 F.3d 821 (8th Cir. 2010); *Siefert, supra*; *Bauer, supra*.

G. Laws prohibiting judicial candidates from soliciting or receiving campaign contributions except during a fundraising window beginning four months before a primary election. *See Platt v. Board of Commissioners on Grievances and Discipline of the Ohio Supreme Court*, 894 F.3d 235 (6th Cir. 2018); *cf. Jones v. Jegley*, 947 F.3d 1100 (8th Cir. 2020) (enjoining a similar prohibition as applied to a candidate for non-judicial office).

3. *Problem.* Michconsota prohibits judicial candidates from "misrepresent[ing] the identity, qualifications, present position, or other fact concerning the candidate or an opponent." The canon further provides that a judicial candidate "should not knowingly make representations that, although true, are misleading, or knowingly make statements that are likely to confuse the public with respect to the proper role of judges and lawyers in the American adversary system."

A. Is the prohibition unconstitutional on its face?

B. Is the prohibition constitutional as applied to the following example? Candidate A, a former district attorney, runs against Candidate B, a former public defender. In one of his campaign advertisements, Candidate A charges that Candidate B "worked to put criminals on the street. Like Reuben Rapist, who raped an 11-year-old girl with learning disabilities. Candidate B found a loophole. Rapist went on to molest another child."

> Each of those statements is, literally, true. As a criminal defense attorney, Candidate B did work to put criminals on the street. Candidate B did represent Rapist on appeal of his rape conviction. Candidate B achieved a reversal of Rapist's conviction by pointing to an error at Rapist's trial, although Rapist did commit the rape. And, after being released from prison, Rapist did rape another child.

> What the advertisement did not mention, however, was that the reversal of Rapist's conviction was itself reversed by the state supreme court because the trial error was harmless. Rapist thus served his full sentence, and raped the second child after serving the entire sentence imposed after his trial. None of Candidate B's efforts did anything to increase the likelihood that the second rape would occur.

As to both (a) and (b), is it constitutional to discipline a judicial candidate on the ground that his campaign statements, while literally true, are misleading? *See In re Judicial Disciplinary Proceedings Against Gableman*, 784 N.W.2d 631 (Wis. 2010) (opinion of three justices concluding that candidates may not be disciplined for such statements); *In re Judicial Disciplinary Proceedings Against Gableman*, 784 N.W.2d 605 (Wis. 2010) (statement of three other justices concluding that candidates may be disciplined for such statements).

Should the constitutional standard be any different for a candidate running for a judicial office than for a candidate running for a legislative or executive office? *See Susan B. Anthony List v. Driehaus*, 814 F.3d 466 (6th Cir. 2016) [p. 585] (striking down false-statements ban applicable to non-judicial races); *Rickert v. Public Disclosure Comm'n*, 168 P.3d 826 (Wash. 2007) (striking down a law banning false statements, and overturning a penalty imposed on a legislative candidate for making false statements about an opponent). *Cf. United States v. Alvarez*, 567 U.S. 709 (2012) [p. 575] (overturning the conviction of a water-district board member for lying about having received the Congressional Medal of Honor); *Central Hudson Gas & Electric Co. v. Public Service Comm'n*, 447 U.S. 557 (1980) (holding that commercial advertising is protected by the First Amendment, but requiring that the advertising relate to a lawful activity and not be misleading).

4. A committee of the Judicial Conference of the United States (the policymaking body for the federal courts) proposed an ethics rule prohibiting federal judges from being members of the Federalist Society or the American Constitution Society because of those organizations' "political" associations. *See* Committee on Codes of Conduct, Judicial Conference of the United States, *Advisory Opinion No. 117: Judges' Involvement with the American Constitution Society, the Federalist Society, and the American Bar Association, available at* http://eppc.org/wp-content/uploads/2020 /01/Guide-Vol02B-Ch02-AdvOp11720OGC-ETH-2020-01-20-EXP-1.pdf. The proposal was withdrawn after being met with strong opposition. Would a rule like the proposed one be constitutional as applied to elected state judges?

If judges have no right to be members of "political" groups, what qualifies such a group as "political"? According to its website, the Federalist Society was "founded on the principles that the state exists to preserve freedom, that the separation of governmental powers is central to our Constitution, and that it is emphatically the province and duty of the judiciary to say what the law is, not what it should be." Advancing those principles, according to the Society, "entails reordering priorities within the legal system to place a premium on individual liberty, traditional values, and the rule of law." The Federalist Society for Law and Public Policy Studies, *About Us: Our Purpose, at* https://fedsoc.org/about-us. The Society does not, however, take official positions about particular controversies. Is it properly labeled as "political"? Would a reasonable person question the impartiality of a judge who belongs to the Federalist Society and who is asked to decide a constitutional question implicating any of those values?

If membership in the Federalist Society and the American Constitution Society raises the appearance of partiality, should judges also be barred from being members of the American Bar Association, which regularly takes positions on public issues and which has been criticized for its perceived liberal bias? *See id.* at 11 (concluding that membership in the ABA is not problematic because its policy agenda is "ancillary to the ABA's core, neutral, and appropriate" objectives of "improvement of the law in general and advocacy for the legal profession as a whole.").

5. In 2014 (before *Williams-Yulee*), the Ninth Circuit invalidated several provisions of the Arizona Code of Judicial Conduct that restricted the speech of judicial candidates. *Wolfson v. Concannon*, 750 F.3d 1145 (9th Cir. 2014). The court held that the provisions—which banned the personal solicitation of campaign funds, as well as making speeches, raising funds, or otherwise supporting or opposing another's campaign—were not narrowly tailored to serve the compelling interests in the actuality and appearance of an impartial judiciary. Interestingly, the court invalidated several of the provisions only as applied to persons who were running for judicial office but who were not incumbent judges. The court reasoned that the speech prohibitions were not narrowly tailored ways of protecting the impartiality of the judiciary

when they applied to people who were not, and might never be, judges. The plaintiff, Wolfson, was such a candidate, and the court held that he could not challenge the rules as applied to incumbent judges. *See Wolfson v. Brammer*, 616 F.3d 1045, 1064 (9th Cir. 2010). Are such speech restrictions constitutional as applied to incumbent judges running for re-election? After *Williams-Yulee* was decided, the Ninth Circuit reheard the case *en banc* and upheld the restrictions, in part because *Williams-Yulee* required only that the restrictions be narrowly, not "perfectly," tailored. *Wolfson v. Concannon*, 811 F.3d 1176 (9th Cir. 2016) (*en banc*).

6. Ohio statutes, dating to the Progressive Era, prohibit the inclusion of judicial candidates' political party affiliations on Ohio's nonpartisan general-election ballot. Does that prohibition violate the First Amendment rights of the candidate or of the party? A recent attack on the statute was rejected in *Ohio Council 8 American Federation of State, County & Municipal Employees v. Husted*, 814 F.3d 329 (6th Cir. 2016). Is there a constitutional difference between (a) laws prohibiting judicial candidates from announcing their partisan affiliations, (b) laws prohibiting parties from endorsing their preferred judicial candidates, *see Sanders County Republican Central Comm. v. Bullock*, 698 F.3d 741 (9th Cir. 2012), and (c) laws prohibiting judicial candidates' partisan affiliations from appearing on the ballot?

For one lower court's attempt to decide some of the questions raised by *Williams-Yulee* and *White*, consider the following case:

Winter v. Wolnitzek

United States Court of Appeals for the Sixth Circuit
834 F.3d 681 (2016)

Sutton, Circuit Judge [with whom Cole, Chief Judge, and Cook, Circuit Judge, join].

* * * A growing line of cases grapples with the States' authority to create a system of judicial elections on the one hand and regulate judicial campaign speech on the other. *See Williams-Yulee v. Fla. Bar*, [575 U.S. 433], 135 S. Ct. 1656 (2015) [p. 622]; *Republican Party of Minn. v. White*, 536 U.S. 765 (2002) [p. 605]; *Carey v. Wolnitzek*, 614 F.3d 189 (6th Cir. 2010). At issue today are several clauses in Kentucky's judicial canons—from prohibitions on "campaign[ing] as a member of a political organization," to "endors[ing] . . . a candidate for public office," to "mak[ing] a contribution to a political organization," to making any "commitments" with respect to "cases, controversies, or issues" likely to come before the court, to making "false" or "misleading" statements. * * *

Robert Winter's campaign literature identified him as a "lifelong Republican" and informed voters that his opponents were registered Democrats. The Judicial Conduct Commission, which enforces the Code, sent him a "probable cause" letter, stating that his mailers may have violated the canon prohibiting "campaign[ing] as a member of a political organization."

Incumbent Allison Jones asked voters to "re-elect" her, even though she was initially appointed to her seat, and she promised to "work with the legislative and executive branches to ensure that the law provides stiff penalties for heroin dealers and that the judiciary has the tools necessary to reduce recidivism among heroin addicts that are arrested and sentenced." Her "re-elect" statement, the Commission wrote in its probable cause letter, potentially violated the canon prohibiting "false and misleading statements." And her "stiff penalties" comment potentially constituted an impermissible "commitment" on an issue likely to come before her court.

Cameron Blau, an aspiring judge, wants to give speeches supporting the Republican Party, to hold Republican fundraisers, to seek and receive endorsements from Republican candidates, and to donate to candidates and to the party. The Code bans all of that, which left Blau "fear[ful] [to] engag[e]" in any of it due to the risk of public reprimand, disbarment from the practice of law, or eventual suspension without pay and removal from office. * * *

The plaintiffs challenge eight features of the Commonwealth's Code of Judicial Conduct.

(1) *Campaigning clause.* "Except as permitted by law," Canon 5(A)(1)(a) says, "a judge or a candidate for election to judicial office shall not[] campaign as a member of a political organization." The Kentucky Supreme Court * * * held that this clause prohibits candidates from "portray[ing] themselves, either directly or by implication, as the official nominee of a political party." Interpreted that way, the district court held, the canon is vague and unconstitutionally overbroad. We agree.

The problem with this canon is that it's unclear when candidates go from permissibly affiliating with a party to illegally implying that they are the nominee of a party. On the one hand, the First Amendment establishes that a State may not prevent judicial candidates from publicly taking a stance on "matters of current public importance." *White*, 536 U.S. at 781–82 (quoting *Wood v. Georgia*, 370 U.S. 375, 395 (1962)). Saying "I am a Republican" is shorthand for just that, which means candidates have a constitutional right to portray themselves as a member of a political party. *Carey*, 614 F.3d at 201–02. On the other hand, Kentucky has a right to prevent candidates from identifying themselves as *the* nominee of a political party for a judicial seat. That's because Kentucky runs its judicial elections on a nonpartisan basis. There is no Democratic or Republican nominee for each seat because political parties don't officially endorse Kentucky judicial candidates, and indeed the two candidates vying in a general election for the same seat could each support the same party.

[T]he Kentucky Supreme Court construed the canon to prohibit "suggesting to the voters that the candidate is *the* endorsed nominee of a political party." A candidate for judicial office, it explained, may say that he is "a Republican" or "a Democrat," or "the only Republican" or "the only Democrat," because those phrases don't imply an endorsement. Those claims merely portray a candidate as a member of a party. So far so good. But claiming to be "the Liberal Democrat" or "the Conservative Republican," it added, implies an endorsement—due to the definite article—and therefore violates the canon.

This last point makes the canon, as construed by Kentucky's highest court, too vague to tightly regulate the problem and too vague to avoid scaring off permissible electoral speech. It's unclear when a candidate crosses the line from exercising his constitutional right to portray himself as a member of a political party to impermissibly implying the endorsement of that party. A few examples illustrate the uncertainty. Could a candidate truthfully claim to have "the endorsement of leaders of the Republican Party"? What if a candidate says, quite accurately, that "the Republicans support my campaign"? We are not sure whether this would violate Kentucky law, making us doubt whether judicial candidates would know either. The Kentucky Supreme Court said that claiming to be "*the* Conservative Republican" would violate the canon by implying an endorsement; it thought the use of "the" was the key, while the word "conservative" was mere "surplusage." But how about claiming to be "the moderate Republican candidate" or "the most experienced conservative Republican candidate"? After reading those phrases, some might infer an endorsement, but others might infer that there are other Republicans in the race. It's hard to know when a candidate has portrayed himself as an official nominee "by implication." Because the canon (as interpreted by the Kentucky Supreme Court) gives judicial candidates little confidence about when they exercise their right to affiliate with a party or when they violate the law, the campaigning clause is vague and unconstitutionally overbroad. The district court rightly struck it in its entirety.

(2) *Speeches clause.* Suffering from a related problem is the infelicitously named speeches clause, which bans judicial candidates from "mak[ing] speeches for or against a political organization or candidate." A candidate has a free-speech right to say in a campaign speech that she is "a Republican," yet this clause by its terms bars a speech in which she says she is "for the Republican party." Because this clause does too much in one sense and too little in another, it does not narrowly address the problem at hand and thus is facially invalid.

In one sense, the speeches clause "does too little to advance the State's interest in impartiality and the avoidance of partisan influence." Kentucky allows "a judicial candidate [to] identify himself to the public as a member of a political party" in many ways. The candidate may tell any audience, no matter how big, that he is a Republican or a Democrat. He may give a speech for any political interest group, from the National Rifle Association to Planned Parenthood. And he may email, tweet, write, or say in an interview that he is for a political party. Banning him from giving a *speech* to the same effect creates serious under-inclusivity problems.

In another sense, the clause "suppresses too much speech to advance the government's interest." By banning speech functionally identical to the speech permitted by *Carey*—that he supports a particular party—the clause suffers from debilitating over-inclusivity problems. Both problems establish a fit defect and preclude the canon from running the gauntlet of strict scrutiny.

True, other circuits have upheld speeches clauses in other States' judicial codes. But they did so while reviewing more narrowly written canons. *See Wolfson v. Concannon*, 811 F.3d 1176, 1179 n.2 (9th Cir. 2016) (*en banc*) (prohibiting candidates from making "speeches *on behalf of* a political organization" (emphasis added)); *Bauer v. Shepard*, 620 F.3d 704, 711 (7th Cir. 2010) (same). The prohibitions at issue did not "prevent judicial candidates from announcing their views on disputed legal and political subjects." *Wolfson*, 811 F.3d at 1185. This one does. It is unconstitutional.

(3) *Contributions clause.* This clause prohibits judicial candidates from "mak[ing] a contribution to a political organization or candidate." As the plaintiffs see it, the provision suffers from a patent defect: If a candidate may declare "the party [he] support[s]," it also must be the case that he can "put his money where his mouth is" by contributing to that party. It is not that easy.

There is a distinction between speech-limiting regulations that limit all judges (elected or not) and those that hamstring judges in their efforts to run for election. * * * The campaigning and speeches clauses, invalidated above, restrict what judicial candidates may say in their own campaigns and thus violate the First Amendment. The lesson is straightforward: A State may not hold judicial elections, then prevent candidates from explaining what makes them qualified for that office.

But * * * [a] contribution to a political organization or a candidate in a different campaign "is less a judge's communication about his qualifications and beliefs than an effort to affect a separate political campaign, or even more problematically, assume a role as political powerbroker." *Siefert v. Alexander*, 608 F.3d 974, 984 (7th Cir. 2010). While "[j]udicial candidates have a First Amendment right to speak in support of their campaigns," *Williams-Yulee*, 135 S. Ct. at 1673, they do not have an unlimited right to contribute money to someone else's campaign. Otherwise, the Code of Conduct for United States Judges—which bans judges from "mak[ing] a contribution to a political organization or candidate"—is unconstitutional. That would come as a surprise. The "distance between" a contribution to someone else's campaign "and speech about a judge's own campaign justifies a more deferential approach to government prohibition" of contributions. *Siefert*, 608 F.3d at 984.

Financial contributions, we realize, amount to speech. *See Buckley v. Valeo*, 424 U.S. 1, 17–18 (1976) [p. 728]. But the alignment between speech and money makes a difference only with respect to Janus-faced regulations that tell judicial candidates to run for office but deny them the tools for doing so. That is not what this regulation does. A contribution of time, money, or reputation to a political organization or a candidate in a separate election, whether judicial or not, differs in kind and degree from a judicial candidate contributing the same to his own campaign. * * * The contributions clause narrowly serves the Commonwealth's compelling interest in preventing the appearance that judicial candidates are no different from other elected officials when it comes to quid pro quo politics. It is constitutional.

(4) *Endorsements clause.* The endorsements clause is of a piece. It prohibits judicial candidates from "publicly endors[ing] or oppos[ing] a candidate for public office." * * * Endorsements differ from a candidate's own expressions of agreement with a political party's platform or another candidate's views. When a judicial candidate endorses a particular candidate, he "support[s] or aid[s]" the other candidate, rather than supporting himself[.] * * * Because endorsements often are "exchanged between political actors on a quid pro quo basis," *id.*, the endorsements clause is narrowly tailored to Kentucky's compelling interest in preventing judges from becoming (or being perceived as becoming) part of partisan political machines. As long as Kentucky "does not regulate speech with regard to any underlying issues," it may target "the act of endorsement itself, which . . . is a direct expression of bias in favor of or against potential parties to a case, or at the very least, damages the appearance of impartiality." *Wersal v. Sexton*, 674 F.3d 1010, 1026 (8th Cir. 2012). A ban on such endorsements also guards against the risk that, once a judge is elected, he will not be able to (and he will not be perceived as being able to) referee disputes involving elected officials he did or did not endorse.

The clause does not suffer from the too-much and too-little coverage problems that the speeches and contributions clauses do. The plaintiffs have not identified any protected speech banned by the endorsements clause that makes it over-inclusive. It does not prohibit speech in opposition to one's *own* opponent any more than it prohibits "endorsing" oneself. Yet it does ban the endorsement of a candidate in a different race, an act that, like the personal solicitations in *Williams-Yulee*, signals the judicial candidate's "active[] engage[ment] in political campaigns." *Wolfson*, 811 F.3d at 1184 (upholding Arizona's endorsement clause).

While the clause is narrowly drawn, it is not perfectly drawn. It has a modest under-inclusivity problem because * * * a judicial candidate may "privately express[] his or her views on judicial candidates or other candidates for public office." True enough. But private expressions of approval or disapproval create far fewer quid pro quo appearance problems than the candidate formally putting his name and reputation behind another. The endorsements clause "aims squarely at the conduct most likely to undermine" non-partisanship in judicial elections and is thus narrowly tailored to that interest. *Williams-Yulee*, 135 S. Ct. at 1668.

(5) *Acting as a leader clause.* Kentucky prohibits a judge from "act[ing] as a leader or hold[ing] any office in a political organization." This clause does all that the First Amendment asks of it when it comes to Blau's facial challenge. The Commonwealth targets an admirable goal (preserving public confidence in its judges, *Williams-Yulee*, 135 S. Ct. at 1666) and uses permissible means in doing so ("diminishing reliance on political parties in judicial selection," *Carey*, 614 F.3d at 201). A judge who heads up a political party entrenches, rather than diminishes, political parties in judicial selection. Whether the candidate wishes to act as a leader of a political

organization or hold office in a political organization, she cannot do so without directly undermining Kentucky's legitimate policy choice to hold nonpartisan elections for judges.

The difficulty comes in resolving Blau's as-applied challenge to the clause. The Kentucky Supreme Court read this clause broadly, interpreting it to include not just leading a political party or holding a formal office but also "hosting a political event." And that, it turns out, is one of the things Blau wants to do. There are many types of political events, and it's not clear how many this canon covers.

Happily for us, Blau identifies the one he wants to host: a "fundraiser[]." And the State, it seems to us, can comfortably ban that kind of event. *Williams-Yulee* tells us the rule when it comes to fundraising for oneself. Judicial candidates do not have a constitutional right to "supplicate campaign donors." 135 S. Ct. at 1666. And fundraising for others is controlled by our reasoning on the endorsements clause. As with endorsements, fundraisers "may be exchanged between political actors on a quid pro quo basis" and are thus less about a judge's "qualifications and beliefs than [they are] an effort to affect a separate political campaign, or even more problematically, assume a role as political powerbroker." *Siefert*, 608 F.3d at 984. Both types of fundraisers bring "a judge's impartiality . . . into question" and can cause "the public [to] lose faith" in the promise of neutral and apolitical judging. *Wolfson*, 811 F.3d at 1184; *see also Bauer*, 620 F.3d at 712–13. Kentucky's ban on judges and judicial candidates hosting political fundraisers, together with its ban on their holding a political office or leading a political party, does not impermissibly infringe Blau's free-speech rights.

(6) *False statements clause.* This clause prohibits a judge or judicial candidate from "knowingly" or "with reckless disregard for the truth" making any "false[] statements" during a campaign. The Kentucky Supreme Court interpreted it to prohibit "untrue utterance[s]" that are "material[]" to a campaign, and to apply to Jones' request for voters to "re-elect" her even though she was initially appointed to her post.

The clause is constitutional on its face. The narrowest way to keep judges honest during their campaigns is to prohibit them from consciously making false statements about matters material to the campaign. This canon does that, and does it clearly. In the words of the district court: "Don't want to violate the Canon? Don't tell a lie on purpose or recklessly." Given the mens rea requirement, a judicial candidate will necessarily be conscious of violating this canon. *Cf. Weaver v. Bonner*, 309 F.3d 1312, 1319–20 (11th Cir. 2002).

This court, it is true, recently invalidated a false-statement ban that covered all non-judicial candidates for political office in Ohio. *See Susan B. Anthony List v. Driehaus*, 814 F.3d 466, 473–76 (6th Cir. 2016) [p. 585]. But the Ohio law swept more broadly than Kentucky's: It applied to all false statements, not just material ones, and it imposed liability on publishers of false statements, not just speakers, *Susan B. Anthony List*, 814 F.3d at 475. Kentucky's narrower interest in preserving public confidence in the honesty and integrity of its judiciary also is more compelling than Ohio's purported interest in protecting voters in other elected races from misinformation. *See id.* at 475. However much or however little truth-bending the public has come to expect from candidates for political jobs, "[j]udges are not politicians," and a "State's decision to elect its judiciary does not compel it to treat judicial candidates like campaigners for political office." *Williams-Yulee*, 135 S. Ct. at 1662. Kentucky has a "vital state interest" in safeguarding the public's confidence in the honesty of its judiciary, *see id.* at 1666 (quoting *Caperton v. A.T. Massey Coal Co.*, 556 U.S. 868, 889 (2009)), and the State's ban on materially false statements by judicial candidates survives strict scrutiny—at least facially.

As applied to Jones, however, the State's ban does not. The headwater of this problem is the Kentucky Supreme Court's ruling that Jones' "re-elect" statement qualified as a "materially false statement . . . calculated to mislead and deceive the voters." Yes, "re-elect" *could* mean what the court thought it meant: elect someone to the same position to which she was previously elected. And that was not true for Jones. The Governor had appointed her to the position; she had not been elected to it. But the term fairly could also mean "to elect for another term in office," precisely what Jones was seeking. *Webster's Third New International Dictionary* 1907. Applied to a statement such as "re-elect," readily capable of a true interpretation here, the ban outstrips the Commonwealth's interest in ensuring candidates don't tell knowing lies and thus fails to give candidates the "breathing space" necessary to free debate. *Brown v. Hartlage*, 456 U.S. 45, 60–61 (1982); *see Weaver*, 309 F.3d at 1319–20.

(7) *Misleading statements clause.* [Kentucky]'s ban on misleading statements fails across the board. If "misleading" adds anything to "false," it is to include statements that, while technically true or ambiguous, create false implications or give rise to false inferences. But only a ban on conscious falsehoods satisfies strict scrutiny. *See Weaver*, 309 F.3d at 1319. "[E]rroneous statement is inevitable in free debate," and "[t]he chilling effect of . . . absolute accountability for factual misstatements in the course of political debate is incompatible with [an] atmosphere of free discussion." *Brown*, 456 U.S. at 60–61 (quotation omitted). "Negligent misstatements," in contrast to knowing misstatements, "must be protected in order to give protected speech the 'breathing space' it requires," even in judicial elections. *Weaver*, 309 F.3d at 1320. Unknowing lies do not undermine the integrity of the judiciary in the same way that knowing lies do, and the ability of an opponent to correct a misstatement "more than offsets the danger of a misinformed electorate." *Id.* This clause adds little to the permissible ban on false statements, and what it adds cannot be squared with the First Amendment.

(8) *Commits clause.* Judicial candidates may not, "in connection with cases, controversies, or issues that are likely to come before the court, make pledges, promises or commitments that are inconsistent with the impartial performance of the adjudicative duties of judicial office." * * *

[N]o one questions that Kentucky may prohibit judges from making commitments to decide specific cases in a certain way. "The First Amendment," after all, "permits a State to limit speech when the Due Process Clause demands nothing less." [H]owever, the canon does more than that by forbidding a judge from making "a promise with respect to 'issues' as well." * * *

Kentucky has * * * narrowed the commits clause to cover only a commitment "that [is] inconsistent with the impartial performance of the adjudicative duties of judicial office." * * * What appears to narrow the clause, the plaintiffs respond, makes it unconstitutionally vague. It is impossible to know, they contend, what is (and what is not) an issue-based commitment that is "inconsistent with the impartial performance of the adjudicative duties of judicial office."

There is something to the point, and we can understand why the district court agreed with it. * * * We doubt, for example, that Jones' promise to "continue to work with the legislative and executive branches to ensure that the law provides stiff penalties for heroin dealers" is "inconsistent with [] impartiality" and thus anticipate that it could not be constitutionally proscribed. But we don't know if that's how the Commonwealth will construe the provision. Our inability to know how much protected speech the canon sweeps in means we could hold, as the district court did, that the clause is vague and unconstitutionally overbroad.

But again, "discretion, to say nothing of respect for a co-equal sovereign, is the better part of valor." *Carey*, 614 F.3d at 209. If Kentucky interprets "impartiality" to mean solely "impartiality as to parties," the clause may well advance a compelling interest and do so narrowly. *See White*, 536 U.S. at 775–77. [W]e think it wise to "remand this aspect of the case to the district court," which will allow the defendants to "obtain authority to remove the 'issues' language"; to adopt "an acceptable narrowing construction of the 'issues' language along with a modification to the commentary"; or to "suggest certification to the Kentucky Supreme Court." 614 F.3d at 209. * * *

Regulating campaign speech is not easy. It's not supposed to be. But treating elections for the courts just like elections for the political branches does not make sense either. Candidates for judicial office, if elected, are supposed to follow the rule of law—no matter current public opinion, no matter the views of the political branches, no matter the views of the parties that support them. But candidates for the other offices are permitted to, indeed often expected to, listen to the views of their constituents and parties. Navigating these cross-currents is no simple task— and for that we have considerable sympathy for the efforts of the Commission. At the same time Kentucky has the right to elect its judges on a nonpartisan basis, however, it has no right to suspend the First Amendment in the process. If the Commission wishes to impose mandatory sanctions on the speech of judicial candidates for office, as opposed to non-enforceable guidelines or best practices, it must satisfy the rigors of the First Amendment in doing so.

We affirm the district court's judgment as to the campaigning, speeches, endorsements, acting as a leader, and misleading statements clauses, and as to the facial challenge to the false statements clause. We reverse the court's judgment on the contributions clause and the as-applied challenge to the false statements clause. And we vacate the court's judgment on the commits clause and remand for further consideration of that clause's meaning and validity.

Notes and Questions

1. In *Winter*, the Sixth Circuit struck down laws that limited judges' ability to campaign, but the court was far more accepting of laws that sought to remove judges from participating in, or supporting, others' campaigns. Is that line the appropriate one? What compelling interest is advanced by speech restrictions that treat judges as political actors—but only during their own campaigns?

2. The court said that the state had "a right" to prevent a judicial candidate from claiming to be the nominee of a party, because Kentucky's judicial elections were non-partisan. But parties have the right to endorse candidates whether or not the ballot features the parties' names. Could Kentucky prohibit judicial candidates from accurately stating that they were endorsed in a non-partisan race? Would there be any difference if the candidate claimed to be "nominated" rather than "endorsed"? After all, "nominate" means only to propose for appointment or election to an office—a definition that might apply to partisan and non-partisan races.

3. What kinds of "political events" could a state prevent its judicial candidates from hosting? If a candidate hosts an event featuring candidates for other offices, wouldn't that present an "endorsement"?

4. The *Winter* court upheld the false-statements clause even though it had struck down a similar ban on false statements applicable to non-judicial races. *See Susan B. Anthony List v. Driehaus*, 814 F.3d 466, 473–76 (6th Cir. 2016) [p. 585]. Was *Winter* correct that the interest in promoting "public confidence in the honesty and integrity of [the] judiciary" was more compelling than the interest in protecting the public from misinformation in other elections? Does *United States v. Alvarez*, 567 U.S. 709 (2012) [p. 575], not apply to judges campaigning for election?

5. What kinds of commitments are "inconsistent with the impartial performance of the adjudicative duties of judicial office"? Certainly a commitment to decide a case in favor of one party is inconsistent with impartial judging, but what about commitments to impose harsh sentences on convicted criminals, to protect the interests of crime victims, or to protect the rights of tenants in cases against landlords?

6. Normatively, the court may well be right that judges "are supposed to follow the rule of law—no matter current public opinion, no matter the views of the political branches, no matter the views of the parties that support them." Descriptively, however, we know that judges are influenced by their ideologies, their backgrounds,

and the societies in which they live. Should it be permissible for states to restrict judicial candidates' speech based on an ideal of judicial behavior when the reality is something else?

Put another way, does the compelling interest in avoiding the appearance of judicial impartiality depend on how well judges adhere to judicial impartiality in reality? One might conclude, as one recent court did in striking down a ban on judicial candidates' soliciting money, that "[a] scrupulously independent judiciary means little, after all, if the public does not view it as such." *Platt v. Board of Commissioners on Grievances and Discipline of the Ohio Supreme Court*, 894 F.3d 235 (6th Cir. 2018). *Platt* noted that Ohio "presume[s] . . . that judges are able to set aside any partisan interests once they have assumed judicial office and have taken an oath to decide cases on the facts and the law before them." Still, the court held that the ban "serve[d] the state's interest . . . in the public's *perception* of impartiality." *Id.* at 262 (quoting *In re Disqualification of Bryant*, 885 N.E.2d 246, 246 (Ohio 2006)). Does the state have a compelling interest in ensuring that the public views the state judiciary as "scrupulously independent" of politics if the judiciary is not in actuality so independent? If not, who decides whether the judiciary is actually as independent of politics as its image would have it seem?

7. President Trump has complained that his administration has been treated unfairly by "Obama judges," prompting a rebuke by Chief Justice Roberts, who responded that "We do not have Obama judges or Trump judges, Bush judges or Clinton judges. What we have is an extraordinary group of dedicated judges doing their level best to do equal right to those appearing before them." It is undeniable, however, that judicial philosophy affects judicial decisions, and that there are some observable differences between the overall jurisprudence of Democrat-appointed judges and that of Republican-appointed judges. Is there a compelling interest that would permit the government to suppress speech that would undermine Chief Justice Roberts's idealistic message of judges' political neutrality?

E. Circulation of Petitions

We encountered petition circulation in Chapter 6 when we studied the obstacles facing a third-party or independent candidate seeking to appear on the ballot. Petitions are a common requirement for the placement of initiatives on the ballot as well.

The simplest type of burden presented by petition requirements is the number of signatures that must be obtained. But, as *Williams v. Rhodes*, 393 U.S. 23 (1968) [p. 495], well illustrated, that is not the only hurdle for petitioners to surmount. Restrictions on *how*, *when*, and *by whom* signatures may be collected, as well as limits or bans on compensating signature-gatherers can have a significant impact on a petition's chances of meeting the signature threshold. Those burdens will be our primary concerns in this section.

Meyer v. Grant

Supreme Court of the United States
486 U.S. 414, 108 S. Ct. 1886, 100 L. Ed. 2d 425 (1988)

JUSTICE STEVENS delivered the opinion of the Court [in which CHIEF JUSTICE REHNQUIST, JUSTICE BRENNAN, JUSTICE WHITE, JUSTICE MARSHALL, JUSTICE BLACKMUN, JUSTICE O'CONNOR, JUSTICE SCALIA, and JUSTICE KENNEDY join]. * * *

Colorado is one of several States that permits its citizens to place propositions on the ballot through an initiative process. * * * State law requires that the persons who circulate the approved drafts of the petitions for signature be registered voters. Before the signed petitions are filed with the Secretary of State, the circulators must sign affidavits attesting that each signature is the signature of the person whose name it purports to be and that, to the best of their knowledge and belief, each person signing the petition is a registered voter. The payment of petition circulators is punished as a felony.

Appellees are proponents of an amendment to the Colorado Constitution that would remove motor carriers from the jurisdiction of the Colorado Public Utilities Commission. * * * Based on their own experience as petition circulators, as well as that of other unpaid circulators, appellees concluded that they would need the assistance of paid personnel to obtain the required number of signatures within the allotted time. They then brought this action under 42 U.S.C. § 1983 against the Secretary of State and the Attorney General of Colorado seeking a declaration that the statutory prohibition against the use of paid circulators violates their rights under the First Amendment. [The District Court upheld the prohibition, but the en banc Court of Appeals reversed.] * * *

We fully agree with the Court of Appeals' conclusion that this case involves a limitation on political expression subject to exacting scrutiny. *Buckley* v. *Valeo*, 424 U.S. 1, 45 (1976) [p. 728]. * * * The circulation of an initiative petition of necessity involves both the expression of a desire for political change and a discussion of the merits of the proposed change. Although a petition circulator may not have to persuade potential signatories that a particular proposal should prevail to capture their signatures, he or she will at least have to persuade them that the matter is one deserving of the public scrutiny and debate that would attend its consideration by the whole electorate. This will in almost every case involve an explanation of the nature of the proposal and why its advocates support it. Thus, the circulation of a petition involves the type of interactive communication concerning political change that is appropriately described as "core political speech."

The refusal to permit appellees to pay petition circulators restricts political expression in two ways: First, it limits the number of voices who will convey appellees' message and the hours they can speak and, therefore, limits the size of the audience they can reach. Second, it makes it less likely that appellees will garner the number of signatures necessary to place the matter on the ballot, thus limiting their ability to make the matter the focus of statewide discussion. * * *

Appellants argue that even if the statute imposes some limitation on First Amendment expression, the burden is permissible because other avenues of expression remain open to appellees and because the State has the authority to impose limitations on the scope of the state-created right to legislate by initiative. Neither of these arguments persuades us that the burden imposed on appellees' First Amendment rights is acceptable.

That appellees remain free to employ other means to disseminate their ideas does not take their speech through petition circulators outside the bounds of First Amendment protection. Colorado's prohibition of paid petition circulators restricts access to the most effective, fundamental, and perhaps economical avenue of political discourse, direct one-on-one communication. That it leaves open "more burdensome" avenues of communication, does not relieve its burden on First Amendment expression. The First Amendment protects appellees' right not only to advocate their cause but also to select what they believe to be the most effective means for so doing.

* * * Colorado contends that because the power of the initiative is a state-created right, it is free to impose limitations on the exercise of that right. [But] the power to ban initiatives entirely [does not] include[] the power to limit discussion of political issues raised in initiative petitions. * * * We agree with the Court of Appeals' conclusion that the statute trenches upon an area in which the importance of First Amendment protections is "at its zenith." For that reason the burden that Colorado must overcome to justify this criminal law is well-nigh insurmountable.

We are not persuaded by the State's arguments that the prohibition is justified by its interest in making sure that an initiative has sufficient grass roots support to be placed on the ballot, or by its interest in protecting the integrity of the initiative process. As the Court of Appeals correctly held, the former interest is adequately protected by the requirement that no initiative proposal may be placed on the ballot unless the required number of signatures has been obtained.[7]

The State's interest in protecting the integrity of the initiative process does not justify the prohibition because the State has failed to demonstrate that it is necessary to burden appellees' ability to communicate their message in order to meet its concerns. The Attorney General has argued that the petition circulator has the duty to verify the authenticity of signatures on the petition and that compensation

---

7. Colorado also seems to suggest that it is permissible to mute the voices of those who can afford to pay petition circulators. "But the concept that government may restrict the speech of some elements of our society in order to enhance the relative voice of others is wholly foreign to the First Amendment." *Buckley* v. *Valeo*, 424 U.S., [at] 48–49. The concern that persons who can pay petition circulators may succeed in getting measures on the ballot when they might otherwise have failed cannot defeat First Amendment rights. As we said in *First National Bank of Boston* v. *Bellotti*, 435 U.S. 765, 790–791 (1978), paid advocacy "may influence the outcome of the vote; this would be its purpose. But the fact that advocacy may persuade the electorate is hardly a reason to suppress it. * * * [T]he people in our democracy are entrusted with the responsibility for judging and evaluating the relative merits of conflicting arguments."

might provide the circulator with a temptation to disregard that duty. No evidence has been offered to support that speculation, however, and we are not prepared to assume that a professional circulator—whose qualifications for similar future assignments may well depend on a reputation for competence and integrity—is any more likely to accept false signatures than a volunteer who is motivated entirely by an interest in having the proposition placed on the ballot.

Other provisions of the Colorado statute deal expressly with the potential danger that circulators might be tempted to pad their petitions with false signatures. It is a crime to forge a signature on a petition, to make false or misleading statements relating to a petition, or to pay someone to sign a petition. Further, the top of each page of the petition must bear a statement printed in red ink warning potential signatories that it is a felony to forge a signature on a petition or to sign the petition when not qualified to vote and admonishing signatories not to sign the petition unless they have read and understand the proposed initiative. These provisions seem adequate to the task of minimizing the risk of improper conduct in the circulation of a petition, especially since the risk of fraud or corruption, or the appearance thereof, is more remote at the petition stage of an initiative than at the time of balloting.

* * * The Colorado statute prohibiting the payment of petition circulators imposes a burden on political expression that the State has failed to justify. The Court of Appeals correctly held that the statute violates the First and Fourteenth Amendments. Its judgment is therefore affirmed.

It is so ordered.

Buckley v. American Constitutional Law Foundation, Inc.

Supreme Court of the United States
525 U.S. 182, 119 S. Ct. 636, 142 L. Ed. 2d 599 (1999)

JUSTICE GINSBURG delivered the opinion of the Court [in which JUSTICE STEVENS, JUSTICE SCALIA, JUSTICE KENNEDY, and JUSTICE SOUTER join].

Colorado allows its citizens to make laws directly through initiatives placed on election ballots. We review in this case three conditions Colorado places on the ballot-initiative process: (1) the requirement that initiative-petition circulators be registered voters; (2) the requirement that they wear an identification badge bearing the circulator's name; and (3) the requirement that proponents of an initiative report the names and addresses of all paid circulators and the amount paid to each circulator. * * *

III

By constitutional amendment in 1980, and corresponding statutory change the next year, Colorado added to the requirement [not challenged in this action] that petition circulators be residents, the further requirement that they be registered voters. Registration, Colorado's Attorney General explained at oral argument, demonstrates "commit[ment] to the Colorado law-making process," and facilitates verification of the circulator's residence. Beyond question, Colorado's registration requirement drastically reduces the number of persons, both volunteer and paid, available to circulate petitions. We must therefore inquire whether the State's concerns warrant the reduction.

When this case was before the District Court, registered voters in Colorado numbered approximately 1.9 million. At least 400,000 persons eligible to vote were not registered. * * *

The Tenth Circuit reasoned that the registration requirement placed on Colorado's voter-eligible population produces a speech diminution of the very kind produced by the ban on paid circulators at issue in *Meyer* [v. *Grant*, 486 U.S. 414 (1988)] [p. 647]. We agree. The requirement that circulators be not merely voter eligible, but registered voters * * * decreases the pool of potential circulators as certainly as that pool is decreased by the prohibition of payment to circulators.[16] Both provisions "limi[t] the number of voices who will convey [the initiative proponents'] message" and, consequently, cut down "the size of the audience [proponents] can reach." In this case, as in *Meyer*, the requirement "imposes a burden on political expression that the State has failed to justify."

Colorado acknowledges that the registration requirement limits speech, but not severely, the State asserts, because "it is exceptionally easy to register to vote." The ease with which qualified voters may register to vote, however, does not lift the burden on speech at petition circulation time. Of course there are individuals who fail to register out of ignorance or apathy. But there are also individuals for whom, as the trial record shows, the choice not to register implicates political thought and expression. A lead plaintiff in this case, long active in ballot-initiative support — a party no doubt "'able and willing' to convey a political message" — testified that his refusal to register is a "form of . . . private and public protest." Another initiative proponent similarly stated that some circulators refuse to register because "they don't believe that the political process is responsive to their needs." For these voter-eligible circulators, the ease of registration misses the point.

The State's dominant justification appears to be its strong interest in policing lawbreakers among petition circulators. Colorado seeks to ensure that circulators will be amenable to the Secretary of State's subpoena power, which in these matters does not extend beyond the State's borders. The interest in reaching law violators, however, is served by the requirement, upheld below, that each circulator submit an affidavit setting out, among several particulars, the "address at which he or she

---

16. Persons eligible to vote, we note, would not include "convicted drug felons who have been denied the franchise as part of their punishment," and could similarly be barred from circulating petitions. The dissent's concern that hordes of "convicted drug dealers," will swell the ranks of petition circulators, unstoppable by legitimate state regulation, is therefore undue. Even more imaginary is the dissent's suggestion that if the merely voter eligible are included among petition circulators, children and citizens of foreign lands will not be far behind. * * *

resides, including the street name and number, the city or town, [and] the county." This address attestation, we note, has an immediacy, and corresponding reliability, that a voter's registration may lack. The attestation is made at the time a petition section is submitted; a voter's registration may lack that currency.

ACLF did not challenge Colorado's right to require that all circulators be residents, a requirement that, the Tenth Circuit said, "more precisely achieved" the State's subpoena service objective. Nor was any eligible-to-vote qualification in contest in this lawsuit. Colorado maintains that it is more difficult to determine who is a state resident than it is to determine who is a registered voter. The force of that argument is diminished, however, by the affidavit attesting to residence that each circulator must submit with each petition section.

In sum, assuming that a residence requirement would be upheld as a needful integrity-policing measure — a question we * * * have no occasion to decide because the parties have not placed the matter of residence at issue — the added registration requirement is not warranted. That requirement cuts down the number of message carriers in the ballot-access arena without impelling cause.

IV

Colorado enacted the provision requiring initiative-petition circulators to wear identification badges in 1993, five years after our decision in *Meyer*. The Tenth Circuit held the badge requirement invalid insofar as it requires circulators to display their names. The Court of Appeals did not rule on the constitutionality of other elements of the badge provision, namely, the "requirements that the badge disclose whether the circulator is paid or a volunteer, and if paid, by whom." Nor do we.

Evidence presented to the District Court, that court found, "demonstrated that compelling circulators to wear identification badges inhibits participation in the petitioning process." The badge requirement, a veteran ballot-initiative-petition organizer stated, "very definitely limited the number of people willing to work for us and the degree to which those who were willing to work would go out in public." Another witness told of harassment he personally experienced as circulator of a hemp initiative petition. He also testified to the reluctance of potential circulators to face the recrimination and retaliation that bearers of petitions on "volatile" issues sometimes encounter: "[W]ith their name on a badge, it makes them afraid." Other petition advocates similarly reported that "potential circulators were not willing to wear personal identification badges."

Colorado urges that the badge enables the public to identify, and the State to apprehend, petition circulators who engage in misconduct. Here again, the affidavit requirement, unsuccessfully challenged below, is responsive to the State's concern; as earlier noted, each petition section must contain, along with the collected signatures of voters, the circulator's name, address, and signature. This notarized submission, available to law enforcers, renders less needful the State's provision for personal names on identification badges.

While the affidavit reveals the name of the petition circulator and is a public rec-ord, it is tuned to the speaker's interest as well as the State's. Unlike a name badge worn at the time a circulator is soliciting signatures, the affidavit is separated from the moment the circulator speaks. As the Tenth Circuit explained, the name badge requirement "forces circulators to reveal their identities at the same time they deliver their political message"; it operates when reaction to the circulator's message is immediate and "may be the most intense, emotional, and unreasoned." The affi-davit, in contrast, does not expose the circulator to the risk of "heat of the moment" harassment.

Our decision in *McIntyre* v. *Ohio Elections Comm'n*, 514 U.S. 334 (1995) [p. 922], is instructive here. The complainant in *McIntyre* challenged an Ohio law that prohib-ited the distribution of anonymous campaign literature. * * * "Circulating a petition is akin to distributing a handbill," the Tenth Circuit observed in the decision now before us. Both involve a one-on-one communication. But the restraint on speech in this case is more severe than was the restraint in *McIntyre*. Petition circulation is the less fleeting encounter, for the circulator must endeavor to persuade electors to sign the petition. That endeavor, we observed in *Meyer*, "of necessity involves both the expression of a desire for political change and a discussion of the merits of the proposed change."

The injury to speech is heightened for the petition circulator because the badge requirement compels personal name identification at the precise moment when the circulator's interest in anonymity is greatest. For this very reason, the name badge requirement does not qualify for inclusion among the "more limited [election pro-cess] identification requirement[s]" to which we alluded in *McIntyre*. In contrast, the affidavit requirement * * *, which must be met only after circulators have com-pleted their conversations with electors, exemplifies the type of regulation for which *McIntyre* left room.

In sum, we conclude * * * that Colorado's current badge requirement discour-ages participation in the petition circulation process by forcing name identification without sufficient cause. * * *

V

* * * Colorado requires ballot-initiative proponents who pay circulators to file both a final report when the initiative petition is submitted to the Secretary of State, and monthly reports during the circulation period. The Tenth Circuit invalidated the final report provision only insofar as it compels disclosure of information spe-cific to each paid circulator, in particular, the circulators' names and addresses and the total amount paid to each circulator. As modified by the Court of Appeals deci-sion, the final report will reveal the amount paid per petition signature, and thus, effectively, the total amount paid to petition circulators. * * *

Mindful of *Buckley* [v. *Valeo*, 424 U.S. 1 (1976)] [p. 933], which upheld disclosure provisions of the Federal Election Campaign Act], the Tenth Circuit * * * upheld the State's requirements for disclosure of *payors*, in particular, proponents' names and the total amount they have spent to collect signatures for their petitions. In this regard, the State and supporting *amici* stress the importance of disclosure as a control or check on domination of the initiative process by affluent special interest groups. Disclosure of the names of initiative sponsors, and of the amounts they have spent gathering support for their initiatives, responds to that substantial state interest.

Through the disclosure requirements that remain in place, voters are informed of the source and amount of money spent by proponents to get a measure on the ballot; in other words, voters will be told "who has proposed [a measure]," and "who has provided funds for its circulation." The added benefit of revealing the names of paid circulators and amounts paid to each circulator, the lower courts fairly determined from the record as a whole, is hardly apparent and has not been demonstrated.[22]

We note, furthermore, that ballot initiatives do not involve the risk of "*quid pro quo*" corruption present when money is paid to, or for, candidates. * * *

In sum, we agree with the Court of Appeals [*sic*] appraisal: Listing paid circulators and their income from circulation "forc[es] paid circulators to surrender the anonymity enjoyed by their volunteer counterparts"; no more than tenuously related to the substantial interests disclosure serves, Colorado's reporting requirements, to the extent that they target paid circulators, "fai[l] exacting scrutiny." * * *

Affirmed.

JUSTICE THOMAS, concurring in the judgment.

When considering the constitutionality of a state election regulation that restricts core political speech or imposes "severe burdens" on speech or association, we have generally required that the law be narrowly tailored to serve a compelling state interest. But if the law imposes "lesser burdens," we have said that the State's important regulatory interests are generally sufficient to justify reasonable, nondiscriminatory restrictions. The Court today appears to depart from this now-settled approach. In my view, Colorado's badge, registration, and reporting requirements each must be evaluated under strict scrutiny. Judged by that exacting standard, I agree with the majority that each of the challenged regulations violates the First and Fourteenth Amendments, and accordingly concur only in the judgment. * * *

---

22. JUSTICE O'CONNOR states that "[k]nowing the names of paid circulators and the amounts paid to them [will] allo[w] members of the public to evaluate the sincerity or, alternatively, the potential bias of any circulator that approaches them." It is not apparent why or how this is so, for the reports containing the names of paid circulators would be filed with the Secretary of State and would not be at hand at the moment the circulators "approac[h]."

Colorado argues that its badge, registration, and reporting requirements impose "lesser" burdens, and consequently, each ought to be upheld as serving important state interests. I cannot agree.

The challenged badge requirement directly regulates the content of speech. The State requires that all petition circulators disclose, at the time they deliver their political message, their names and whether they were paid or unpaid. Therefore, the regulation must be evaluated under strict scrutiny. Moreover, the category of burdened speech is defined by its content—Colorado's badge requirement does not apply to those who circulate candidate petitions, only to those who circulate initiative or referendum proposals. Content-based regulation of speech typically must be narrowly tailored to a compelling state interest. The State's dominant justification for its badge requirement is that it helps the public to identify, and the State to apprehend, petition circulators who perpetrate fraud. Even assuming that this is a compelling interest, plainly, this requirement is not narrowly tailored. It burdens all circulators, whether they are responsible for committing fraud or not. In any event, the State has failed to satisfy its burden of demonstrating that fraud is a real, rather than a conjectural, problem.

Although Colorado's registration requirement does not *directly* regulate speech, it operates in the same fashion that Colorado's prohibition on paid circulators did in *Meyer*—the requirement reduces the voices available to convey political messages. We unanimously concluded in *Meyer* that initiative petition circulation was core political speech. * * * I see no reason to revisit our earlier conclusion. The aim of a petition is to secure political change, and the First Amendment, by way of the Fourteenth Amendment, guards against the State's efforts to restrict free discussions about matters of public concern.

Colorado primarily defends its registration requirement on the ground that it ensures that petition circulators are residents, which permits the State to more effectively enforce its election laws against those who violate them. The Tenth Circuit assumed, and so do I, that the State has a compelling interest in ensuring that all circulators are residents. Even so, it is clear, as the Court of Appeals decided, that the registration requirement is not narrowly tailored. A large number of Colorado's residents are not registered voters, as the majority points out, and the State's asserted interest could be more precisely achieved through a residency requirement. * * *

In my view, the burdens that the reporting requirement imposes on circulation are too attenuated to constitute a "severe burden" on core political speech. However, "compelled disclosure, in itself, can seriously infringe on privacy of association and belief guaranteed by the First Amendment." *Buckley* v. *Valeo*, 424 U.S., [at] 64 (*per curiam*). In *Buckley*, because the disclosure requirements of the Federal Election Campaign Act of 1971 encroached on associational rights, we required that they pass a "strict test." *Id.*, at 66. The same associational interests are burdened by the State's reporting requirements here, and they must be evaluated under strict scrutiny.

* * * Even assuming that Colorado has a compelling interest in identifying circulators, its law does not serve that interest. The State requires that proponents identify only the names of *paid* circulators, not *all* circulators. The interest in requiring a report as to the money paid to each circulator by name, as the majority points out, has not been demonstrated.

The State contends that its asserted interest in providing the press and the electorate with information as to how much money is spent by initiative proponents to advance a particular measure is similar to the governmental interests in providing the electorate with information about how money is spent by a candidate and where it comes from, and in deterring actual corruption and avoiding the appearance of corruption that we recognized in *Buckley*. However, we have suggested that ballot initiatives and candidate elections involve different considerations. [*First National Bank of Boston* v. *Bellotti*, 435 U.S. 765, 787 n.26 (1978); *Citizens Against Rent Control* v. *Berkeley*, 454 U.S. 290, 296–300 (1981).] Indeed, we recognized in *Meyer* that "the risk of improper conduct . . . is more remote at the petition stage of an initiative." Similarly, I would think, at the very least, the State's interest in informing the public of the financial interests behind an initiative proposal is not compelling during the petitioning stage. * * *

JUSTICE O'CONNOR, with whom JUSTICE BREYER joins, concurring in the judgment in part and dissenting in part.

Petition circulation undoubtedly has a significant political speech component. * * * [W]e held in [*Meyer* v. *Grant*] that regulations directly burdening the one-on-one, communicative aspect of petition circulation are subject to strict scrutiny.

Not all circulation-related regulations target this aspect of petition circulation, however. Some regulations govern the electoral process by directing the manner in which an initiative proposal qualifies for placement on the ballot. These latter regulations may indirectly burden speech but are a step removed from the communicative aspect of petitioning and are necessary to maintain an orderly electoral process. Accordingly, these regulations should be subject to a less exacting standard of review. * * *

I agree with the Court that requiring petition circulators to wear identification badges, specifically name badges, should be subject to, and fails, strict scrutiny. * * *

Unlike the majority, however, I believe that the requirement that initiative petition circulators be registered voters is a permissible regulation of the electoral process. It is indeed a classic example of this type of regulation * * * [that] only indirectly and incidentally burdens the communicative aspects of petition circulation. By its terms, the requirement does not directly prohibit otherwise qualified initiative petition circulators from circulating petitions. Moreover, * * * this requirement can be satisfied quite easily. * * *

Because the registration requirement indirectly and incidentally burdens the one-on-one, communicative aspect of petition circulation, [it must] advance [only] a legitimate state interest to be a reasonable regulation of the electoral process. Colorado maintains that the registration requirement is necessary to enforce its laws prohibiting circulation fraud and to guarantee the State's ability to exercise its subpoena power over those who violate these laws, two patently legitimate interests. In the past, Colorado has had difficulty enforcing its prohibition on circulation fraud, in particular its law against forging petition signatures, because violators fled the State. Colorado has shown that the registration requirement is an easy and a verifiable way to ensure that petition circulators fall under the State's subpoena power. For these reasons, I would uphold the requirement as a reasonable regulation of Colorado's electoral process.

Most disturbing is the Court's holding that Colorado's disclosure provisions are partially unconstitutional. * * * Colorado's disclosure provision is a step removed from the one-on-one, communicative aspects of petition circulation, and it burdens this communication in only an incidental manner. Like the mandatory affidavit that must accompany every set of signed petitions, the required disclosure reports "revea[l] the name of the petition circulator and [are] public record[s] . . . [, but are] separated from the moment the circulator speaks." This characteristic indeed makes the disclosure reports virtually indistinguishable from the affidavit requirement, which the Court suggests is a permissible regulation of the electoral process, and similarly lessens any chilling effect the reports might have on speech. If anything, the disclosure reports burden speech less directly than the affidavits because the latter are completed by the petition circulator, while the former are completed by the initiative proponent and thus are a step removed from petition circulation. In fact, the Court does not suggest that there is any record evidence tending to show that such remote disclosure will deter the circulation of initiative petitions. To the extent the disclosure requirements burden speech, the burden must be viewed as incremental and insubstantial in light of the affidavit requirement, which also reveals the identity of initiative petition circulators.

As a regulation of the electoral process with an indirect and insignificant effect on speech, the disclosure provision should be upheld so long as it advances a legitimate government interest. Colorado's asserted interests in combating fraud and providing the public with information about petition circulation are surely sufficient to survive this level of review. * * * Disclosure deters circulation fraud and abuse by encouraging petition circulators to be truthful and self-disciplined. The disclosure required here advances Colorado's interest in law enforcement by enabling the State to detect and to identify on a timely basis abusive or fraudulent circulators. Moreover, like election finance reporting generally, Colorado's disclosure reports provide facts useful to voters who are weighing their options. Members of the public deciding whether to sign a petition or how to vote on a measure can discover who has proposed it, who has provided funds for its circulation, and to whom these funds have been provided. Knowing the names of paid circulators and the amounts paid to them also allows members of the public to evaluate the sincerity or, alternatively, the potential bias of any circulator that approaches them. In other words, if one knows a particular circulator is well paid, one may be less likely to believe the sincerity of the circulator's statements about the initiative proposal. The monthly disclosure reports are public records available to the press and public, are "contemporaneous with circulation," and are more accessible than the other "masses of papers filed with the petitions."

It is apparent from the preceding discussion that, to combat fraud and to inform potential signatories in a timely manner, disclosure must be made at the time people are being asked to sign petitions and before any subsequent vote on a measure that qualifies for the ballot. * * * Accordingly, the monthly reports, which are disseminated during the circulation period and are available to the press, uniquely advance Colorado's interests. The affidavit requirement is not an effective substitute because the affidavits are not completed until after all signatures have been collected and thus after the time that the information is needed. In addition, the public's access to the affidavits is generally more restricted than its access to monthly disclosure reports, for as the District Court found, the public will have "greater difficulty in finding [the] names and addresses [of petition circulators] in the masses of papers filed with the petitions as compared with the monthly reports."

To be sure, Colorado requires disclosure of financial information about only paid circulators. But, contrary to the Court's assumption, this targeted disclosure is permissible because the record suggests that paid circulators are more likely to commit fraud and gather false signatures than other circulators. The existence of occasional fraud in Colorado's petitioning process is documented in the record. An elections officer for the State of Colorado testified that only paid circulators have been involved in recent fraudulent activity. Likewise, respondent William C. Orr, the executive director of the American Constitutional Law Foundation, Inc., while examining a witness, explained to the trial court that "volunteer organizations, they're self-policing and there's not much likelihood of fraud. . . . Paid circulators are perhaps different."

Because the legitimate interests asserted by Colorado are advanced by the disclosure provision and outweigh the incidental and indirect burden that disclosure places on political speech, I would uphold the provision as a reasonable regulation of the electoral process. Colorado's interests are more than legitimate, however. We have previously held that they are substantial. See *Buckley* v. *Valeo*, at 67, 68. Therefore, even if I thought more exacting scrutiny were required, I would uphold the disclosure requirements.

Because I feel the Court's decision invalidates permissible regulations that are vitally important to the integrity of the political process, and because the decision threatens the enforceability of other important and permissible regulations, I concur in the judgment only in part and dissent in part.

CHIEF JUSTICE REHNQUIST, dissenting. * * *

* * * [T]he Court today holds that a State cannot require that those who circulate the petitions to get initiatives on the ballot be electors, and that a State is constitutionally required to instead allow those who make no effort to register to vote—political dropouts—and convicted drug dealers [denied the franchise as part of their punishment] to engage in this electoral activity.{[1]} Although the Court argues that only those eligible to vote may now circulate candidate petitions, there is no Colorado law to this effect. Such a law would also be even harder to administer than one which limited circulation to residents, because eligible Colorado voters are that subset of Colorado residents who have fulfilled the requirements for registration, and have not committed a felony or been otherwise disqualified from the franchise. A State would thus have to perform a background check on circulators to determine if they are not felons. And one of the reasons the State wished to limit petition circulation to electors in the first place was that it is far easier to determine who is an elector from who is a resident, much less who is "voter eligible." * * *

State ballot initiatives are a matter of state concern, and a State should be able to limit the ability to circulate initiative petitions to those people who can ultimately vote on those initiatives at the polls. If eligible voters make the conscious decision not to register to vote on the grounds that they reject the democratic process, they should have no right to complain that they cannot circulate initiative petitions to people who *are* registered voters. And the idea that convicted drug felons who have lost the right to vote under state law nonetheless have a constitutional right to circulate initiative petitions scarcely passes the "laugh test."

But the implications of today's holding are even more stark than its immediate effect. Under the Court's interpretation of *Meyer*, any ballot initiative regulation is unconstitutional if it either diminishes the pool of people who can circulate petitions or makes it more difficult for a given issue to ultimately appear on the ballot. Thus, while today's judgment is ostensibly circumscribed in scope, it threatens to invalidate a whole host of historically established state regulations of the electoral process in general. Indeed, while the Court is silent with respect to whether a State can limit initiative petition circulation to state residents, the implication of its reading of *Meyer* * * * is that under today's decision, a State cannot limit the ability to circulate issues of local concern to its own residents.

May a State prohibit children or foreigners from circulating petitions, where such restrictions would also limit the number of voices who could carry the proponents' message and thus cut down on the size of the audience the initiative proponents could reach? And if initiative petition circulation cannot be limited to electors, it would seem that a State can no longer impose an elector or residency requirement on those who circulate petitions to place candidates on ballots, either. At least 19

---

1. The respondents also presented the example of children who wished to circulate petitions. * * * Because the Court of Appeals held that the age restriction on petition circulation was constitutional, it is unnecessary to point out the absurdity of the respondents' minority argument.

States plus the District of Columbia explicitly require that candidate petition circulators be electors, and at least one other State requires that its petition circulators be state residents. Today's decision appears to place each of these laws in serious constitutional jeopardy. * * *

As to the other two laws struck down by the Court, I agree that the badge requirement for petition circulators is unconstitutional. * * * I disagree, however, that the First Amendment renders the disclosure requirements unconstitutional. The Court affirms the Court of Appeals' invalidation of only the portion of the law that requires final reports to disclose information specific to each paid circulator — the name, address, and amount paid to each. Important to the Court's decision is the idea that there is no risk of "*quid pro quo*" corruption when money is paid to ballot initiative circulators, and that paid circulators should not have to surrender the anonymity enjoyed by their volunteer counterparts. I disagree with this analysis because, under Colorado law, *all* petition circulators must surrender their anonymity under the affidavit requirement. Colorado law requires that each circulator must submit an affidavit which must include the circulator's "name, the address at which he or she resides, including the street name and number, the city or town, [and] the county." This affidavit requirement was upheld by the Tenth Circuit as not significantly burdening political expression, and is relied upon by the Court in holding that the registered voter requirement is unconstitutional. The only additional piece of information for which the disclosure requirement asks is thus the amount paid to each circulator. Since even after today's decision the identity of the circulators as well as the total amount of money paid to circulators will be a matter of public record, I do not believe that this additional requirement is sufficient to invalidate the disclosure requirements as a whole. They serve substantial interests and are sufficiently narrowly tailored to satisfy the First Amendment. * * *

Notes and Questions

1. The Court repeatedly noted that ACLF did not challenge residency requirements for signature-gatherers, but only the further requirement that signature-gatherers be registered voters. Was this a sign that the residency requirement, too, would be unconstitutional? Or was the registration requirement unconstitutional because the residency requirement was a less restrictive means of satisfying the state's interests? *See Yes on Term Limits, Inc. v. Savage,* 550 F.3d 1023 (10th Cir. 2008); *Nader v. Brewer,* 531 F.3d 1028 (9th Cir. 2008); *Chandler v. City of Arvada,* 292 F.3d 1236 (10th Cir. 2002); *Initiative & Referendum Institute v. Jaeger,* 241 F.3d 614 (8th Cir. 2001); *Krislov v. Rednour,* 226 F.3d 851 (7th Cir. 2000). Could a state ban other election-related speech, such as television advertising, by out-of-staters concerning state-law issues?

2. Suppose that the speech at issue related to a national matter and not a state one. For example, imagine that Congress proposes a Twenty-Eighth Amendment to the Constitution, and the states are considering whether to ratify it. May a state

prohibit citizens of other states from speaking about the matter? What if the state prohibited election-related speech by citizens of foreign countries?

3. Might out-of-state-resident petition-circulators have claims under the Privileges and Immunities Clause, Art. IV, § 2, cl. 1, and the dormant Commerce Clause, Art I, § 8, cl. 3, in addition to claims under the First Amendment? The Clauses generally operate to prevent states from privileging their own citizens as to fundamental liberties and economic opportunities (such as the opportunity to work as a petition-circulator), respectively. Nevertheless, states are permitted to favor their own citizens if they have a good enough reason for doing so.[5] *See generally Supreme Court v. Piper*, 470 U.S. 274, 282 & n.13 (1985) (noting that the Privileges and Immunities Clause does not require states to forfeit their identities as sovereign political bodies, and that accordingly a state may restrict the privileges of voting and holding elective office to state residents); *Corfield v. Coryell*, 4 Wash. C.C. 371, Fed. Cas. No. 3,230 (1823).

4. Should one's ability to speak, or the state's ability to require registration or disclosure, differ depending on whether the election is a ballot initiative or a candidate election?

5. Chief Justice Rehnquist characterized the proposition that minors have a constitutional right to circulate petitions as "absurd[]," and the Court seemed to agree, saying that the suggestion was "imaginary." But why should minors not have such a right? Certainly minors generally possess a right to engage in expressive activity. *See, e.g., Tinker v. Des Moines Independent Community School District*, 393 U.S. 503 (1969). One of the few points on which a clear majority of the Court was able to agree in *McConnell v. Federal Election Commission*, 540 U.S. 93 (2003) [p. 829], was that the Bipartisan Campaign Reform Act's prohibition of contributions by minors, 2 U.S.C. § 441k, was unconstitutional. *See* 540 U.S. at 231–32. Should the same result obtain in the case of petition circulation?

6. More broadly, why should a state be able to tie the ability to engage in election-related *speech* to the ability to *vote*? Are you comfortable calling petition circulation "speech," or should it receive less protection under the First Amendment than, for example, distributing leaflets? In *Empower Our Neighborhoods v. Guadagno*, 2014 N.J. Super. Unpub. LEXIS 764 (N.J. Super. Ct. Law Div. Mar. 31, 2014), the court noted that "circulating petitions is primarily a freedom of speech issue and does not necessarily implicate the right to vote," *id.* at *74, but nonetheless required, at least temporarily, that petition-circulators be eligible to vote—*i.e.*, that they be at least age 18 and state residents. The court argued that such a requirement might be based on the need to have confidence in petition-circulators when they certify that they witnessed

---

5. Discrimination in favor of state residents will be upheld against a Privileges-and-Immunities-Clause challenge if it is "closely related to the advancement of a substantial state interest." *Supreme Court v. Friedman*, 487 U.S. 59, 65 (1988). The test under the dormant Commerce Clause is whether the state law "serves a legitimate local purpose" that "could not be served as well by nondiscriminatory means." *Maine v. Taylor*, 477 U.S. 131, 138 (1986).

the signatures on the petition and that they believe that the signatories are registered voters in the district. The court struck down requirements that petition-circulators themselves be registered voters and that they reside in the district.

7. Does it abridge the First Amendment right of petition-circulators to require that each section of an initiative petition contain the circulator's name? In *Chula Vista Citizens for Jobs and Fair Competition v. Norris*, 755 F.3d 671 (9th Cir. 2014), a divided panel of the Ninth Circuit struck down such a requirement. The court held that the requirement failed exacting scrutiny, noting that initiative proponents were already required to disclose their identities twice: in filing with the city clerk a notice of intent to circulate a petition, and in publishing that notice in a newspaper.

8. *Problem.* May a state prohibit initiative supporters from paying signature-gatherers by the signature? The state argues that the prohibition guards against fraud; the opponents argue that the prohibition makes it more expensive and inefficient to gather signatures. *See Citizens for Tax Reform v. Deters*, 518 F.3d 375 (6th Cir. 2008); *Prete v. Bradbury*, 438 F.3d 949 (9th Cir. 2006); *Initiative & Referendum Inst. v. Jaeger*, 241 F.3d 614 (8th Cir. 2001).

9. *Problem.* Many New England towns employ the "open town-hall meeting" style of governing, according to which all registered voters are empowered to legislate, in an exercise of direct, rather than representative, democracy. Debate at town-hall meetings is presided over by a moderator, who is elected by the voters of the town. All registered voters may speak at the meetings, but non-registered voters may speak only if the moderator permits them to do so. Does such a system abridge the First Amendment rights of non-registered voters who reside in the town? *See Curnin v. Town of Egremont*, 510 F.3d 24 (1st Cir. 2007). What if non-registered voters were absolutely barred from speaking, leaving the moderator without discretion? What if non-registered voters were prohibited from speaking at a public-comment portion of a representative body's meeting? *See Mesa v. White*, 197 F.3d 1041 (10th Cir. 1999); *Piscottano v. Town of Somers*, 396 F. Supp. 2d 187 (D. Conn. 2005); *Scroggins v. City of Topeka*, 2 F. Supp. 2d 1362 (D. Kan. 1998); *Pesek v. City of Brunswick*, 794 F. Supp. 768 (N.D. Ohio 1992).

F. Government Speech

The government can, and often does, speak to us. From statutory directives to agency web sites, and from "Just Say No" campaigns to town newsletters, we are confronted daily with government speech. Such speech rarely raises a constitutional question, even if the government is discriminating on the basis of viewpoint in creating its message—after all, the expression of a viewpoint is often the whole purpose of speaking. *See, e.g., Rust v. Sullivan*, 500 U.S. 173 (1991). Government speech in the context of elections, however, raises more serious questions. The next case explores whether the First Amendment, or any other portion of the Constitution, prohibits the government from taking sides in an electoral contest.

Kidwell v. City of Union

United States Court of Appeals for the Sixth Circuit
462 F.3d 620 (6th Cir. 2006), *cert. denied*, 550 U.S. 935 (2007)

GIBBONS, CIRCUIT JUDGE [with whom GRIFFIN, CIRCUIT JUDGE, joins]. * * *

This case arises from a series of disputed ballot initiatives beginning in 1997 relating to the creation and funding of a fire department in the City of Union[, Ohio]. In 1997, Union's fire and emergency services (along with those of other neighboring communities) were provided by the neighboring township of Randolph. The combination of the restructuring of the townships and the perceived inadequacy in Union's emergency services led to changes in the fire department structure. The Union Council * * * ultimately passed an emergency resolution establishing a town fire department. The new fire department became effective on January 1, 1998.

The resolution establishing a Union fire department was challenged by the plaintiffs via a ballot initiative requiring a referendum. The referendum was preceded by a lively campaign in which the plaintiffs organized a "Vote Yes" campaign to retain the extant fire districts. The Council supported the opposite position and used public funds to disseminate information supporting its position to citizens [by] the hanging of "Vote No" banners, mailing of leaflets to residents, advertising in local newspapers, and using the town newsletter to support the Council's position. The referendum occurred in November 1997, and the Council's decision was ratified. Voters funded the new fire department in a May 1998 referendum. [Plaintiffs brought suit under 42 U.S.C. § 1983, arguing that the City's advocacy violated the First and Fourteenth Amendments. The District Court granted summary judgment to the defendants.] * * *

[P]laintiffs argue that Union unconstitutionally denied them access to two public fora—the town newsletter and the town treasury—to which others had been granted access. A government abridges "equality in the field of ideas" when it grants "the use of a [public] forum to people whose views it finds acceptable, but [denies its] use to those wishing to express less favored or more controversial views." *Police Dept. of City of Chicago v. Mosley*, 408 U.S. 92, 96 (1972).

Plaintiffs assert that they were denied access to the town newsletter, but * * * they provide no evidence that they asked for or were refused access to that forum, even if it was public. Plaintiffs have similarly failed to present evidence that any other private group was given access to the newsletter other than a single quote about the contested issue that was responsive to another quote advocating the contrary position. "[W]hen government property is not dedicated to open communication the government may—without further justification—restrict use to those who participate in the forum's official business." *Perry Educ. Ass'n v. Perry Local Educators' Ass'n*, 460 U.S. 37, 53 (1983). The single quotation cannot be construed as opening the newsletter as a public forum. Further, "when the government determines an overarching message and retains power to approve every word disseminated at its behest, the message must be attributed to the government for First Amendment purposes."

Here, Union approved the message delivered in the town newsletter, so its content must be considered that of the city itself, not that of the quoted private citizen. Plaintiffs thus cannot prevail on their public forum claim relating to the newsletter.

The town treasury is not a public forum; it is not "by tradition or designation a forum for public communication." *Perry,* 460 U.S. at 46. Nor is the treasury a limited purpose public forum; Union has not opened that treasury to the public by making any town funds available to private individuals or groups. Union has used the treasury for its own speech—a use that has no effect on the treasury as a public forum. To hold that Union's advocacy converts its treasury to a public forum would severely limit the town's ability to self-regulate and would be tantamount to a heckler's veto, where the government could not speak for fear of opening its treasury to the public. This argument is therefore baseless, and the plaintiffs' public forum challenge cannot succeed.

[The plaintiffs also argue that they were unconstitutionally compelled] to support positions with which they disagree. This case, however, presents a compelled subsidy—not a compelled speech—claim because the plaintiffs were not themselves required to speak in any manner. * * *

The Supreme Court has held in several instances that compelled subsidies may violate the First Amendment rights of citizens. *See Abood v. Detroit Bd. of Ed.,* 431 U.S. 209 (1977) (labor union political action); *Keller v. State Bar of Cal.,* 496 U.S. 1 (1990) (bar dues for political action); *Board of Regents of Univ. of Wis. Sys. v. Southworth,* 529 U.S. 217 (2000) (student activities fund for extracurricular activity). All of the cases in which the Supreme Court has held a compelled subsidy to be a First Amendment violation have involved subsidies of speech by private organizations rather than by the government itself. Governmental subsidies are distinguishable from the labor union, state bar, and state university contexts because it is imperative that government be free to make unpopular decisions without opening the public fisc to opposing views. The Supreme Court recognized this distinction in *Southworth*: "The government, as a general rule, may support valid programs and policies by taxes or other exactions binding on protesting parties. Within this broader principle it seems inevitable that funds raised by the government will be spent for speech and other expression to defend its own policies." 529 U.S. at 229. More recently, in *Johanns v. Livestock Mktg. Ass'n,* 544 U.S. [550,] 559 [(2005)], the Court addressed a compelled subsidy directly in the governmental context:

> Our compelled-subsidy cases have consistently respected the principle that "[c]ompelled support of a private association is fundamentally different from compelled support of government." "Compelled support of government"—even those programs of government one does not approve—is of course perfectly constitutional, as every taxpayer must attest. And some government programs involve, or entirely consist of, advocating a position.

Here, the plaintiffs have challenged the expenditure of tax dollars by a governmental entity to advocate a position—a case that the Supreme Court deemed "perfectly constitutional" in *Johanns*. Though the plaintiffs acknowledge that the speech in this case is attributable to the government, they argue that the power of the government to compel subsidies for its speech is not as broad as the Supreme Court suggested in *Johanns*. Because the asserted subsidy arose in the context of an election, the plaintiffs argue that this court should find Union's speech to be unconstitutionally compulsive.

As the dissent recognizes, elections raise unique constitutional issues because they are the very foundation of a democratic system: where the government uses its official voice in an attempt to affect the identity of the people's elected representatives, it can undermine its legitimacy as a champion of the people's will and thereby subvert one of the principles underlying democratic society. Although these principles require some limit on the government's power to advocate during elections, they do not support a bright line rule barring such speech, at least where the government speaks within the scope of its governance functions. Governments must serve their citizens in myriad ways, including by provision of emergency services, and these activities require funding through taxation. Union's speech related to emergency service and tax initiatives thus fits squarely within its competence as governor and was made in the context of "advocat[ing] and defend[ing] its own policies." The issues on which the city advocated were thus germane to the mechanics of its function, and are clearly distinguishable from the hypothetical cases of government speech in support of particular candidates suggested by the dissent. Where speech is not so directed, the result may be different: in *Mountain States Legal Foundation v. Denver School District No. 1*, by contrast, the court ruled illegal a *local* school board's use of public funds for advocacy in a *statewide* initiative regarding education funding. 459 F. Supp. 357, 361 (D. Colo. 1978). Unlike Union's actions, the school board's advocacy in *Mountain States* was not directly related to its governance functions and was struck down.

In this case, Ohio's home rule system made Union's policies subject to acceptance or rejection by ballot. In this context, a limit on government speech during elections would allow hecklers to silence the government on issues in which it has an interest and expertise—and on which citizens have an interest in hearing their government's perspective. Because Union's speech in this case was germane to its role as governor, plaintiffs have failed to show that democratic legitimacy is threatened or that Union's compelled subsidy of its speech violates the Constitution.

The natural outcome of government speech is that some constituents will be displeased by the stance their government has taken. Displeasure does not necessarily equal unconstitutional compulsion, however, and in most cases the electoral process—not First Amendment litigation—is the appropriate recourse for such displeasure. The needs of effective governance command that the bar limiting government speech be high. The plaintiffs in this case have failed to show that the City of Union's expenditures crossed the line separating a valid compelled subsidy from an unconstitutional one, and valid advocacy from prescription of orthodoxy.

For the foregoing reasons, we affirm the district court decision.

MARTIN, CIRCUIT JUDGE, dissenting.

* * * Although local governmental expenditures to advocate in an election may seem commonplace and uninspiring, I take the position that governmental campaigning in elections is implicitly prohibited by our constitutional design and republican form of government. "Free and honest elections are the very foundation of our republican form of government," and when the government uses tax dollars to enter an electoral contest and advocate in favor of a position or candidate, it distorts the very check on governmental power so central to our constitutional design—the next election—that I must conclude such activity is unconstitutional. * * *

* * * I concede that the government may ordinarily speak to advocate and defend its own policies. The caveat, however, is always that the citizens' remedy is at the ballot box in the next election. [Here], however, the government is distorting the *only* check on its power. I am not sure I would limit this argument to the confines of the First Amendment; rather, to me, it is more of a structural argument regarding democratic principles and the structure and purpose of the [C]onstitution. * * *

I believe that the Constitution properly prohibits the government from having a horse in the race when it comes to elections. When government advocates on one side of an issue, the ultimate source of governing power is shifted away from the people and the threat of official doctrine exists. Of course, the threat is not as omnipresent today in the United States as it is in some other countries. There is no real evidence in any of these cases on point that the government as speaker crowded out private speech. There is no evidence that the government sought to suppress or in any way discourage other speech of a contrary nature. The absence of this evidence, however, does not in my opinion cure the underlying evil—that is, ordinary democratic controls are insufficient as a remedy in situations where governmental influence threatens to undermine the independent political process. Governmental advocacy and campaign expenditures could arguably threaten to undermine free and fair elections, could be coercive, and could reasonably undermine the reliability and outcome of elections where the government acts as a participant.

Moreover, it could be argued that when the government takes sides in an election, it gives a content or viewpoint based subsidy to those advocating the position the government chooses to side with. In the ordinary case of governmental action outside of an election, political controls can remedy citizen disagreement with governmental actions. Citizens can make their voices known at the ballot box in the next election by voting current officeholders out. Governmental electioneering, however, diminishes the effectiveness of the political response and threatens underlying constitutional values and democratic principles. The outcome of elections ideally should reflect the pure will of the people unpolluted by government electioneering. Where the political response cannot provide an adequate remedy, it can be argued that courts must step in.

Thus, I would hold that the Constitution requires governmental neutrality in elections—that is, the Constitution permits the government to educate and inform the public, but it may not cross the line into advocacy. Thus, government could provide factual information in newsletters and other forms of communication with the electorate. [I]t would not always be easy finding the line of demarcation between informing and advocacy, but courts should look closely at the facts of each case, including the words used, the tone of the communication, the timing, and any other relevant factors. Moreover, government may provide equal access to a forum (as it does in so many other contexts) allowing both sides of the debate to advance their positions. Thus, a governmental newsletter such as the one at issue in this case could grant equal space to competing factions to make their best case to the electorate. This position, I think, would more appropriately reflective [*sic*] of the balance the Framers sought to strike in our democratic structure and goes a long way to ensuring that the true power remains with the people.

For these reasons, I must respectfully dissent from today's majority opinion.

Notes and Questions

1. Should this case have been resolved on the basis of the First Amendment or the general "structural" features of the Constitution referenced in Judge Martin's dissent? *Cf. National Endowment for the Arts v. Finley*, 524 U.S. 569, 598 n.3 (1998) (Scalia, J., concurring in the judgment) ("I suppose it would be unconstitutional for the government to give money to an organization devoted to the promotion of candidates nominated by the Republican Party—but it would be just as unconstitutional for the government itself to promote candidates nominated by the Republican Party, and I do not think that that unconstitutionality has anything to do with the First Amendment."). Are there judicially manageable standards for enforcing these "structural" features? Are there other reasons courts should not enforce guarantees not protected by (relatively) specific constitutional text?[d] In a portion of the dissent not reprinted here, Judge Martin suggested that "[p]erhaps th[e] day has come" to revisit the Supreme Court's conclusion that the Guarantee Clause is nonjusticiable. *See* 462 F.3d at 635 n.5 (Martin, J., dissenting). Was his invocation of an undefined "structural" protection against governmental electoral advocacy simply a ruse to evade binding precedent?

2. Is there an administrable line between government speech that governs, informs and educates, on the one hand, and that which advocates electoral results, on the other? Is there an administrable line between advocacy of government policies, which Judge Martin conceded is permissible, and advocacy of electoral results,

---

d. If you believe that courts are without power to enforce the structural guarantee of democracy without a clause in the Constitution specifically protecting it, do you reach the same conclusion with regard to the Court's holdings enforcing implicit constitutional limitations on governmental structure stemming from concerns about federalism and the separation of powers? *See, e.g., Alden v. Maine*, 527 U.S. 706 (1999); *Seminole Tribe v. Florida*, 517 U.S. 44 (1996); *National League of Cities v. Usery*, 426 U.S. 833 (1976), *overruled by Garcia v. San Antonio Metropolitan Transportation Authority*, 469 U.S. 528 (1985); *United States v. Nixon*, 418 U.S. 683 (1974); *Myers v. United States*, 272 U.S. 52 (1926).

which he argued is not? How would you classify stickers distributed to voters that say, "Vote in Honor of a Veteran"? What if the stickers also include the name of the Secretary of State? What if the secretary of state is expected to run in the next election for lieutenant governor? *See* Geoff Pender, *Campaigning on Your Dime? Complaint over Hosemann Stickers Raises Long-Running Issue*, CLARION-LEDGER (Jackson, Miss.), June 7, 2018, *available at* https://www.clarionledger.com/story /news/politics/2018/06/06/candidate-questions-hosemanns-vote-veteran-stickers -polls/677963002/.

3. In Chapter 8, we will address the constitutionality of certain restrictions on the financing of "electioneering communications." Under the bright-line definition adopted in the Bipartisan Campaign Reform Act and upheld in *McConnell v. Federal Election Commission*, 540 U.S. 93 (2003) [p. 829], (but called into some question by *Federal Election Commission v. Wisconsin Right to Life, Inc.*, 551 U.S. 449 (2007)) all advertisements that (1) referred to a "clearly identified candidate for Federal office"; (2) were made within sixty days before a general election or thirty days before a primary election; and (3) could be received by 50,000 or more persons in the district, were subject to the restrictions. Before BCRA, the law placed more importance on the distinction between express advocacy, which could be regulated, and issue advocacy, which was not subject to as many limitations. The bright-line definition was adopted to avoid perceived problems of "sham" issue advocacy, where advertisements would ostensibly discuss issues, but would in reality encourage voters to support or oppose certain candidates.

Do Judge Martin's proposed distinctions create the same potential for subterfuge? How would he address the constitutionality of a governmentally sponsored advertisement discussing the advantages of "the Smith-Jones Health Care Act"? What about the commonplace signs at state borders that welcome travelers and gratuitously include the name of the incumbent governor? Suppose a legislator were to use his privilege to send free mail to his constituents telling of all the great things he has accomplished during his term—just in case any of the voters were to find such information relevant in deciding whom to support in the election the following month. Is such action unconstitutional?

4. What limits are there on the majority's willingness to tolerate governmentally sponsored electoral speech? The majority says that perhaps a government could not speak on a matter that is far afield from its governing role, but doesn't government speech pose the greatest threat to democracy when it *is* directly related to its governing function?

5. The court argued that restricting government's electoral speech would deprive citizens of the ability to "hear[] their government's perspective." Are you troubled by the implication that the government has a perspective independent of the citizenry?

6. Are you concerned that government speech can overwhelm opposing messages, or do you believe that government speech will affect elections only if the voters agree with it? In other words, does government speech honor the public's

capacity to reason or seek to subvert it? We will return to the issue of the persuasive power of campaign speech in Chapter 8.

G. Public Employees

Government employees may be particularly interested in public affairs, and their knowledge may be invaluable to the rest of us in assessing the performance of government. As a result, the political participation of those employees may be especially valuable both for them and for everyone else. On the other hand, there are also more pressing reasons to restrict the political activities of government workers than those of the rest of us. We want to be sure that civil servants will apply the law impartially, and if we think that they are using the law to their political advantage, our confidence in government will be undermined. Additionally, we may view restrictions on workers' political activity as protection for the workers themselves — if an employee is forbidden from taking part in a political campaign, then we can be sure that a supervisor will not pressure the employee to work on behalf of the supervisor's (or the governing administration's) preferred candidate. The cases in this section explore the extent to which public employment can limit employees' First Amendment right to participate in politics.

United Public Workers of America (C.I.O.) v. Mitchell

Supreme Court of the United States
330 U.S. 75, 67 S. Ct. 556, 91 L. Ed. 754 (1947)

Mr. Justice Reed delivered the opinion of the Court [in which Mr. Chief Justice Vinson, Mr. Justice Frankfurter, and Mr. Justice Burton join]. * * *

[Appellants brought this constitutional challenge to the second sentence of § 9(a) of the Hatch Act, which] reads, "No officer or employee in the executive branch of the Federal Government * * * shall take any active part in political management or in political campaigns."{2}

---

2. 18 U.S.C. § 61h, as amended:

"(a) It shall be unlawful for any person employed in the executive branch of the Federal Government, or any agency or department thereof, to use his official authority or influence for the purpose of interfering with an election or affecting the result thereof. No officer or employee in the executive branch of the Federal Government, or any agency or department thereof, except a part-time officer or part-time employee without compensation * * * shall take any active part in political management or in political campaigns. All such persons shall retain the right to vote as they may choose and to express their opinions on all political subjects and candidates. * * *

"(b) Any person violating the provisions of this section shall be immediately removed from the position or office held by him, and thereafter no part of the funds appropriated by any Act of Congress for such position or office shall be used to pay the compensation of such person."

* * * It is alleged that the individuals desire to engage in acts of political management and in political campaigns. * * *[11] From the affidavits it is plain, and we so
assume, that these activities will be carried on completely outside of the hours of
employment. Appellants challenge the second sentence of §9(a) as [violating the
First Amendment's protections of freedom of speech, of the press, and of assembly;
the Ninth and Tenth Amendments; and the Fifth Amendment's Due Process Clause,
this last owing to the Act's alleged vagueness and its allegedly arbitrary distinctions
between the employees subject to the restrictions of the Act and the employees not
so restricted]. * * *

* * * The District Court * * * determined that the questioned provision of the
Hatch Act was valid * * *. It accordingly dismissed the complaint and granted summary judgment to defendants. * * *

[Appellant George Poole] was a ward executive committeeman of a political
party and was politically active on election day as a worker at the polls and a paymaster for the services of other party workers. * * * We accept appellants' contention that the nature of political rights reserved to the people by the Ninth and Tenth
Amendments are involved. The right claimed as inviolate may be stated as the right
of a citizen to act as a party official or worker to further his own political views. * * *
And, if we look upon due process as a guarantee of freedom in those fields, there is
a corresponding impairment of that right under the Fifth Amendment. Appellants'
objections under the Amendments are basically the same.

We do not find persuasion in appellants' argument that such activities during free
time are not subject to regulation even though admittedly political activities cannot
be indulged in during working hours. The influence of political activity by government employees, if evil in its effects on the service, the employees or people dealing
with them, is hardly less so because that activity takes place after hours. Of course,
the question of the need for this regulation is for other branches of government

---

[Note that the Hatch Act, including the penalty provision, has been amended. It now permits the offending employee to be suspended without pay for no less than thirty days. 5 U.S.C.
§7326. —Eds.]

11. "In discharge of their duties of citizenship, of their right to vote, and in exercise of their constitutional rights of freedom of speech, of the press, of assembly, and the right to engage in political
activity, the individual plaintiffs desire to engage in the following acts: write for publication letters
and articles in support of candidates for office; be connected editorially with publications which
are identified with the legislative program of UFWA [former name of the present union appellant]
and candidates who support it; solicit votes, aid in getting out voters, act as accredited checker,
watcher, or challenger; transport voters to and from the polls without compensation therefor; participate in and help in organizing political parades; initiate petitions, and canvass for the signatures of others on such petitions; serve as party ward committeeman or other party official; and
perform any and all acts not prohibited by any provision of law other than the second sentence of
Section 9(a) and Section 15 of the Hatch Act, which constitute taking an active part in political
management and political campaigns."

rather than the courts. Our duty in this case ends if the Hatch Act provision under examination is constitutional.

Of course, it is accepted constitutional doctrine that these fundamental human rights are not absolutes. * * * The essential rights of the First Amendment in some instances are subject to the elemental need for order without which the guarantees of civil rights to others would be a mockery. * * * Again this Court must balance the extent of the guarantees of freedom against a congressional enactment to protect a democratic society against the supposed evil of political partisanship by classified employees of government. * * *

* * * Congress and the President are responsible for an efficient public service. If, in their judgment, efficiency may be best obtained by prohibiting active participation by classified employees in politics as party officers or workers, we see no constitutional objection.

Another Congress may determine that on the whole, limitations on active political management by federal personnel are unwise. The teaching of experience has evidently led Congress to enact the Hatch Act provisions. To declare that the present supposed evils of political activity are beyond the power of Congress to redress would leave the nation impotent to deal with what many sincere men believe is a material threat to the democratic system. Congress is not politically naive or regardless of public welfare or that of the employees. It leaves untouched full participation by employees in political decisions at the ballot box and forbids only the partisan activity of federal personnel deemed offensive to efficiency. With that limitation only, employees may make their contributions to public affairs or protect their own interests, as before the passage of the act.

The argument that political neutrality is not indispensable to a merit system for federal employees may be accepted. But because it is not indispensable does not mean that it is not desirable or permissible. Modern American politics involves organized political parties. Many classifications of Government employees have been accustomed to work in politics—national, state and local—as a matter of principle or to assure their tenure. Congress may reasonably desire to limit party activity of federal employees so as to avoid a tendency toward a one-party system. It may have considered that parties would be more truly devoted to the public welfare if public servants were not overactive politically.

Appellants urge that federal employees are protected by the Bill of Rights and that Congress may not "enact a regulation providing that no Republican, Jew or Negro shall be appointed to federal office, or that no federal employee shall attend Mass or take any active part in missionary work." None would deny such limitations on Congressional power but because there are some limitations it does not follow that a prohibition against acting as ward leader or worker at the polls is invalid. A reading of the Act * * * shows the wide range of public activities with which there is no interference by the legislation. It is only partisan political activity that is interdicted. It is active participation in political management and political campaigns. Expressions, public or private, on public affairs, personalities and matters of public interest, not an objective of party action, are unrestricted by law so long as the Government employee does not direct his activities toward party success.

It is urged, however, that Congress has gone further than necessary in prohibiting political activity to all types of classified employees. It is pointed out by appellants "that the impartiality of many of these is a matter of complete indifference to the effective performance" of their duties. Mr. Poole would appear to be a good illustration for appellants' argument. The complaint states that he is a roller in the Mint. We take it this is a job calling for the qualities of a skilled mechanic and that it does not involve contact with the public. Nevertheless, if in free time he is engaged in political activity, Congress may have concluded that the activity may promote or retard his advancement or preferment with his superiors. Congress may have thought that Government employees are handy elements for leaders in political policy to use in building a political machine. For regulation of employees it is not necessary that the act regulated be anything more than an act reasonably deemed by Congress to interfere with the efficiency of the public service. There are hundreds of thousands of United States employees with positions no more influential upon policy determination than that of Mr. Poole. Evidently what Congress feared was the cumulative effect on employee morale of political activity by all employees who could be induced to participate actively. It does not seem to us an unconstitutional basis for legislation.

There is a suggestion that administrative workers may be barred, constitutionally, from political management and political campaigns while the industrial workers may not be barred, constitutionally, without an act "narrowly drawn to define and punish specific conduct." A ready answer, it seems to us, lies in the fact that * * * Congress has determined that the presence of government employees, whether industrial or administrative, in the ranks of political party workers is bad. Whatever differences there may be between administrative employees of the Government and industrial workers in its employ are differences in detail so far as the constitutional power under review is concerned. Whether there are such differences and what weight to attach to them, are all matters of detail for Congress. We do not know whether the number of federal employees will expand or contract; whether the need for regulation of their political activities will increase or diminish. The use of the constitutional power of regulation is for Congress, not for the courts.

We have said that Congress may regulate the political conduct of Government employees "within reasonable limits," even though the regulation trenches to some extent upon unfettered political action. The determination of the extent to which political activities of governmental employees shall be regulated lies primarily with Congress. Courts will interfere only when such regulation passes beyond the general existing conception of governmental power. That conception develops from practice, history, and changing educational, social and economic conditions. The regulation of such activities as Poole carried on has the approval of long practice by the Commission, court decisions upon similar problems and a large body of informed public opinion. Congress and the administrative agencies have authority over the discipline and efficiency of the public service. When actions of civil servants in the judgment of Congress menace the integrity and the competency of the service, legislation to forestall such danger and adequate to maintain its usefulness is required. The Hatch Act is the answer of Congress to this need. We cannot say with such a background that these restrictions are unconstitutional.

* * * The activities of Mr. Poole, as ward executive committeeman and a worker at the polls, obviously fall within the prohibitions of § 9 of the Hatch Act against taking an active part in political management and political campaigns. * * * We need to examine no further at this time into the validity of the definition of political activity * * *.

The judgment of the District Court is accordingly affirmed.

Affirmed.

Mr. Justice Murphy and Mr. Justice Jackson took no part in the consideration or decision of this case.

Mr. Justice Rutledge dissents as to Poole for the reasons stated by Mr. Justice Black. He does not pass upon the constitutional questions presented by the other appellants for the reason that he feels the controversy as to them is not yet appropriate for the discretionary exercise of declaratory judgment jurisdiction.

Mr. Justice Frankfurter, concurring.

[T]his case should be dismissed for want of jurisdiction [because the appeal was not timely docketed]. * * * But under compulsion of the Court's assumption of jurisdiction, I reach the merits and join in Mr. Justice Reed's opinion.

Mr. Justice Black, dissenting. * * *

* * * Legislation which muzzles several million citizens threatens popular government, not only because it injures the individuals muzzled, but also, because of its harmful effect on the body politic in depriving it of the political participation and interest of such a large segment of our citizens. * * *

It is argued that it is in the interest of clean politics to suppress political activities of federal and state employees. It would hardly seem to be imperative to muzzle millions of citizens because some of them, if left their constitutional freedoms, might corrupt the political process. All political corruption is not traceable to state and federal employees. Therefore, it is possible that other groups may later be compelled to sacrifice their right to participate in political activities for the protection of the purity of the Government of which they are a part.

It may be true, as contended, that some higher employees, unless restrained, might coerce their subordinates or that Government employees might use their official position to coerce other citizens. But is such a possibility of coercion of a subordinate by his employer limited to governmental employer-employee relationships? The same quality of argument would support a law to suppress the political freedom of all employees of private employers, and particularly of employers who borrow money or draw subsidies from the Government. * * * If the possibility exists that some * * * public employees may, by reason of their more influential positions, coerce other public employees or other citizens, laws can be drawn to punish the coercers. It hardly seems consistent with our system of equal justice to all to suppress the political and speaking freedom of millions of good citizens because a few bad citizens might engage in coercion.

It may also be true, as contended, that if public employees are permitted to exercise a full freedom to express their views in political campaigns, some public officials will discharge some employees and grant promotion to others on a political rather than on a merit basis. For the same reasons other public officials, occupying positions of influence, may use their influence to have their own political supporters appointed or promoted. But here again, if the practice of making discharges, promotions or recommendations for promotions on a political basis is so great an evil as to require legislation, the law could punish those public officials who engage in the practice. To punish millions of employees and to deprive the nation of their contribution to public affairs, in order to remove temptation from a proportionately small number of public officials, seems at the least to be a novel method of suppressing what is thought to be an evil practice. * * *

Mr. Justice Douglas, dissenting in part. * * *

If [civil servants] are beneficiaries of political patronage rather than professional careerists, serious results might follow—or so Congress could reasonably believe. Public confidence in the objectivity and integrity of the civil service system might be so weakened as to jeopardize the effectiveness of administrative government. Or it might founder on the rocks of incompetency, if every change in political fortunes turned out the incumbents, broke the continuity of administration, and thus interfered with the development of expert management at the technical levels. Or if the incumbents were political adventurers or party workers, partisanship might color or corrupt the processes of administration of law with which most of the administrative agencies are entrusted.

The philosophy is to develop a civil service which can and will serve loyally and equally well any political party which comes into power.

Those considerations might well apply to the entire group of civil servants in the administrative category—whether they are those in the so-called expert classification or are clerks, stenographers and the like. They are the ones who have access to the files, who meet the public, who arrange appointments, who prepare the basic data on which policy decisions are made. Each may be a tributary, though perhaps a small one, to the main stream which we call policy making or administrative action. If the element of partisanship enters into the official activities of any member of the group it may have its repercussions or effect throughout the administrative process. Thus in that type of case there would be much to support the view of the Court that Congress need not undertake to draw the line to include only the more important offices but can take the precaution of protecting the whole by insulating even the lowest echelon from partisan activities.

So, I think that if the issues tendered by Poole were tendered by an administrative employee, we would have quite a different case. For Poole claims the right to work as a ward executive committeeman, *i.e.*, as an officeholder in a political party.

But Poole, being an industrial worker, is as remote from contact with the public or from policy making or from the functioning of the administrative process as a charwoman. The fact that he is in the classified civil service is not, I think, relevant to the question of the degree to which his political activities may be curtailed. He is in a position not essentially different from one who works in the machine shop of a railroad or steamship which the Government runs, or who rolls aluminum in a manufacturing plant which the Government owns and operates. Can all of those categories of industrial employees constitutionally be insulated from American political life? If at some future time it should come to pass in this country, as it has in England, that a broad policy of state ownership of basic industries is inaugurated, does this decision mean that all of the hundreds of thousands of industrial workers affected could be debarred from the normal political activity which is one of our valued traditions?

The evils of the "spoils" system do not, of course, end with the administrative group of civil servants. History shows that the political regimentation of government industrial workers produces its own crop of abuses. Those in top policy posts or others in supervisory positions might seek to knit the industrial workers in civil service into a political machine. As a weapon they might seek to make the advancement of industrial workers dependent on political loyalty, on financial contributions, or on other partisan efforts. Or political activities of these workers might take place on government premises, on government time, or otherwise at government expense. These are specific evils which would require a specific treatment.

There is, however, no showing of any such abuse here. What Poole did, he did on his own without compulsion or suggestion or invitation from any one higher up. Nor does it appear that what he did was done on government time or on government premises. Moreover, as Mr. Justice Black points out, laws can be drawn to punish those who use such coercion. * * * Absent coercion, improper use of government position or government funds, or neglect or inefficiency in the performance of duty, federal employees have the same rights as other citizens under the Constitution. They are not second class citizens. If, in exercise of their rights, they find common political interests and join with each other or other groups in what they conceive to be their interests or the interests of the nation, they are simply doing what any other group might do. In other situations where the balance was between constitutional rights of individuals and a community interest which sought to qualify those rights, we have insisted that the statute be "narrowly drawn to define and punish specific conduct as constituting a clear and present danger to a substantial interest" of government.

That seems to me the proper course to follow here. The prohibition in § 9(a) of the Hatch Act against government employees taking an "active part in political management or in political campaigns" applies without discrimination to all employees whether industrial or administrative. The same is true of the Civil Service Rules. But the supposed evils are both different and narrower in case of industrial workers than they are in the case of the administrative group. The public interest in the political activity of a machinist or elevator operator or charwoman is a distinct and different problem. In those cases the public concern is in the preservation of an unregimented industrial group, in a group free from political pressures of superiors who use their official power for a partisan purpose. Then official power is misused, perverted. The Government is corrupted by making its industrial workers political captives, victims of bureaucratic power, agents for perpetuating one party in power.

Offset against that public concern are the interests of the employees in the exercise of cherished constitutional rights. * * * If those rights are to be qualified by the larger requirements of modern democratic government, the restrictions should be narrowly and selectively drawn to define and punish the specific conduct which constitutes a clear and present danger to the operations of government. It seems plain to me that that evil has its roots in the coercive activity of those in the hierarchy who have the power to regiment the industrial group or who undertake to do so. To sacrifice the political rights of the industrial workers goes far beyond any demonstrated or demonstrable need. Those rights are too basic and fundamental in our democratic political society to be sacrificed or qualified for anything short of a clear and present danger to the civil service system. No such showing has been made in the case of these industrial workers,[14] which justifies their political sterilization as distinguished from selective measures aimed at the coercive practices on which the spoils system feeds.

Notes and Questions

1. Who is protected, and who is harmed, by the Hatch Act? If you believe that the employees themselves are helped (by removing pressure to conform to supervisors' political preferences), do you think the First Amendment permits such paternalism?

---

14. Whether the Act, being unconstitutional as applied to Poole, could be separably applied to civil service employees in other categories is a question I do not reach.

2. As a consumer of government services, would you fear unfair treatment if your postal carrier was wearing a button supporting a political candidate you opposed? What if the IRS agent auditing your tax return did the same thing? What if you appeared before a judge who was supporting a candidate you opposed?

3. In any of the above examples, do you worry about bias because the employee *holds* a political opinion, or because the employee has made his political opinion *known*? In other words, if the postal carrier, the IRS agent, or the judge held the same political views, but kept those views to himself or herself, would the threat of bias be any less significant? Note that similar questions arise when considering the free-speech rights of judicial candidates. We considered those questions in connection with *Republican Party of Minnesota v. White*, 536 U.S. 765 (2002) [p. 605], in §D of this Chapter.

4. Between *Mitchell* and *Civil Service Commission v. National Association of Letter Carriers*, 413 U.S. 548 (1973) [p. 679], in which the Court again considered the constitutionality of the Hatch Act, the Court significantly expanded the First Amendment protections of government employees. In 1892, Justice Holmes, then serving on the Massachusetts Supreme Judicial Court, famously wrote that an individual fired from the police force because of his membership in a political committee "may have a constitutional right to talk politics, but he has no constitutional right to be a policeman." *McAuliffe v. Mayor of New Bedford*, 29 N.E. 517, 517 (Mass. 1892). The Court has since rejected that view, and has extended First Amendment protections to public employees, although the Court has maintained that certain restrictions on the rights of employees are necessary to the employment relationship, and are therefore constitutional.

The seminal case concerning the free-speech rights of public employees is *Pickering v. Board of Education*, 391 U.S. 563 (1968). *Pickering* involved a schoolteacher who was fired for writing a letter to the editor critical of the Board of Education's funding priorities. The Court noted that the Board's use of money was obviously a matter of public concern—one on which school employees were likely to be particularly knowledgeable, and so the public had an interest in hearing the teacher's perspective. But because the government, like all employers, has an interest in the efficient operation of its offices that might be undermined by employee speech, it was necessary to balance the interests. As the Court phrased the inquiry, courts must "arrive at a balance between the interests of the teacher, as a citizen, in commenting upon matters of public concern and the interest of the State, as an employer, in promoting the efficiency of the public services it performs through its employees." *Id.* at 568.

Three points in that formulation are worth special attention. First, the employee's interest is "as a citizen." That is, if the employee's job duties include speaking—if the employee's job is to be a spokesman, for example—then the government employer is fully entitled to fire the employee if the employee does not speak in the way that the government wants. The employee has no right to speak his mind "as" a representative of the government. Second, the government's interest that must be balanced is its interest "as an employer." The only government interest that counts in the *Pickering* balance is in the effective functioning of the government office—not the wide range of government interests that might be considered in applying the usual tiers of scrutiny. The reason is that the question in these cases is whether the employment relationship gives the government more power to restrict the speech of the employee than the government would have to restrict the speech of a non-employee. Therefore, the only additional interests that the government has in regulating employees' speech is in combating the potential disruption that the speech could cause to the functioning of the government office. Third, the government employer cannot justify a firing solely on the basis that the employee's speech is critical of his superiors. Obviously there is a limit to this principle—poor relations with co-workers and supervisors can have a negative impact on the functioning of any workplace—but Pickering's speech was protected even though it might have lessened public esteem for the Board of Education.

Subsequent decisions have upheld the firing of an assistant district attorney who, upset about a transfer, distributed a questionnaire to other employees seeking their opinion about "transfer policy, office morale, the need for a grievance committee, the level of confidence in supervisors, and whether employees felt pressured to work in political campaigns," *Connick v. Myers*, 461 U.S. 138 (1983), and upheld the firing of a nurse who made critical comments about a supervisor, *Waters v. Churchill*, 511 U.S. 661 (1994), but held unconstitutional the firing of a clerical employee in a county constable's office who, upon hearing of an assassination attempt on President Reagan, remarked, "if they go for him again, I hope they get him," *Rankin v. McPherson*, 483 U.S. 378 (1987).

More recently, in *Garcetti v. Ceballos*, 547 U.S. 410 (2006), the Court upheld the imposition of discipline against a deputy district attorney who became involved in a confrontation with employees of the sheriff's department and ultimately testified for the defense in a case where he believed the investigation had been improperly conducted. The Court applied a two-part test drawn from *Pickering* to determine whether the discipline was constitutionally imposed. First, the employee's speech must be on a matter of public concern. Private matters—such as complaints about most internal office policies—do not give rise to First Amendment protection against discipline. Second, if the speech is about a matter of public concern, discipline may be imposed only where the speech has the potential to interfere with the operations of the office. In other words, government may restrict the speech of employees on matters of public concern only if there is a justification for treating their speech differently from the speech of nonemployees. *Id.* at 418. The Court in *Ceballos* held that because the deputy was acting pursuant to his official duties, his speech could not be considered to be "on a matter of public concern." *Id.* at 421. In *Lane v. Franks*, 573 U.S. 228 (2014), the Court held that under *Pickering* and *Ceballos*, a public employee's sworn testimony under subpoena, outside the scope of his ordinary job duties, was entitled to First Amendment protection.

5. If challenges such as *Mitchell* were to be evaluated under this two-part test, an individual's speech at political conventions or contributions to political candidates, etc., would satisfy the "public concern" part of the test. The controversial part of the analysis would be in assessing whether the interests of the government employer outweighed the interests of the speaker. In that vein, consider *McPherson*'s rationale for holding that the county constable was prohibited from firing the employee who professed hope for the President's assassination:

> While McPherson's statement was made at the workplace, there is no evidence that it interfered with the efficient functioning of the office. The Constable was evidently not afraid that McPherson had disturbed or interrupted other employees—he did not inquire to whom respondent had made the remark and testified that he "was not concerned who she had made it to." * * *

> Nor was there any danger that McPherson had discredited the office by making her statement in public. McPherson's speech took place in an area to which there was ordinarily no public access; her remark was evidently made in a private conversation with another employee. There is no suggestion that any member of the general public was present or heard McPherson's statement. * * *

> * * * Evidently because McPherson had made the statement, and because the Constable believed that she "meant it," he decided that she was not a suitable employee to have in a law enforcement agency. But in weighing the State's interest in discharging an employee based on any claim that the content of a statement made by the employee somehow undermines the mission of the public employer, some attention must be paid to the responsibilities of the employee within the agency. The burden of caution employees bear with respect to the words they speak will vary with the extent of authority and public accountability the employee's role entails. Where, as here, an employee serves no confidential, policymaking, or public contact role, the danger to the agency's successful functioning from that employee's private speech is minimal. We cannot believe that every employee in Constable Rankin's office, whether computer operator, electrician, or file clerk, is equally required, on pain of discharge, to avoid any statement susceptible of being interpreted by the Constable as an indication that the employee may be unworthy of employment in his law enforcement agency. At some point, such concerns are so removed from the effective functioning of the public employer that they cannot prevail over the free speech rights of the public employee.

> This is such a case. McPherson's employment-related interaction with the Constable was apparently negligible. Her duties were purely clerical * * *. There is no indication that she would ever be in a position to further—or indeed to have any involvement with—the minimal law enforcement activity engaged in by the Constable's office. Given the function of the

agency, McPherson's position in the office, and the nature of her statement, we are not persuaded that Rankin's interest in discharging her outweighed her rights under the First Amendment.

483 U.S. at 388–92. Justice Scalia, joined by Chief Justice Rehnquist and Justices White and O'Connor, dissented, arguing that "no law enforcement agency is required by the First Amendment to permit one of its employees to 'ride with the cops and cheer for the robbers.'" *Id.* at 394 (Scalia, J., dissenting). He further argued that the Court's distinction between policymaking employees and others was misguided: "Nonpolicymaking employees * * * can hurt working relationships and undermine public confidence in an organization every bit as much as policymaking employees." *Id.* at 400 (Scalia, J., dissenting).

6. Do decisions such as *Pickering* and its progeny indicate that *Mitchell*'s understanding of the First Amendment is out of step with modern jurisprudence? The following case thought not.

United States Civil Service Commission v. National Association of Letter Carriers, AFL-CIO

Supreme Court of the United States
413 U.S. 548, 93 S. Ct. 2880, 37 L. Ed. 2d 796 (1973)

Mr. Justice White delivered the opinion of the Court [in which Mr. Chief Justice Burger, Mr. Justice Stewart, Mr. Justice Blackmun, Mr. Justice Powell, and Mr. Justice Rehnquist join].

[This case] present[s] the single question whether the prohibition in § 9(a) of the Hatch Act, now codified in 5 U.S.C. § 7324(a)(2), against federal employees taking "an active part in political management or in political campaigns," is unconstitutional on its face. * * *

[Plaintiffs—the National Association of Letter Carriers, six individual federal employees and certain local Democratic and Republican political committees—filed a complaint, claiming that the Act prevented them from engaging in certain political activity, including running for public office, holding office in a political club, campaigning for others, and writing letters to newspapers.]

We unhesitatingly reaffirm the [*United Public Workers* v.] *Mitchell* [330 U.S. 75 (1947)] [p. 668] holding that Congress had, and has, the power to prevent Mr. Poole and others like him from holding a party office, working at the polls, and acting as party paymaster for other party workers. An Act of Congress going no farther would in our view unquestionably be valid. So would it be if, in plain and understandable language, the statute forbade activities such as organizing a political party or club; actively participating in fund-raising activities for a partisan candidate or political party; becoming a partisan candidate for, or campaigning for, an elective public office; actively managing the campaign of a partisan candidate for public office; initiating or circulating a partisan nominating petition or soliciting votes for a partisan candidate for public office; or serving as a delegate, alternate or proxy to a political party convention. Our judgment is that neither the First Amendment nor any other provision of the Constitution invalidates a law barring this kind of partisan political conduct by federal employees. * * *

It seems fundamental in the first place that employees in the Executive Branch of the Government, or those working for any of its agencies, should administer the law in accordance with the will of Congress, rather than in accordance with their own or the will of a political party. They are expected to enforce the law and execute the programs of the Government without bias or favoritism for or against any political party or group or the members thereof. A major thesis of the Hatch Act is that to serve this great end of Government—the impartial execution of the laws—it is essential that federal employees, for example, not take formal positions in political parties, not undertake to play substantial roles in partisan political campaigns, and not run for office on partisan political tickets. Forbidding activities like these will reduce the hazards to fair and effective government.

There is another consideration in this judgment: it is not only important that the Government and its employees in fact avoid practicing political justice, but it is also critical that they appear to the public to be avoiding it, if confidence in the system of representative Government is not to be eroded to a disastrous extent.

Another major concern of the restriction against partisan activities by federal employees was perhaps the immediate occasion for enactment of the Hatch Act in 1939. That was the conviction that the rapidly expanding Government work force should not be employed to build a powerful, invincible, and perhaps corrupt political machine. The experience of the 1936 and 1938 campaigns convinced Congress that these dangers were sufficiently real that substantial barriers should be raised against the party in power—or the party out of power, for that matter—using the thousands or hundreds of thousands of federal employees, paid for at public expense, to man its political structure and political campaigns.

A related concern, and this remains as important as any other, was to further serve the goal that employment and advancement in the Government service not depend on political performance, and at the same time to make sure that Government employees would be free from pressure and from express or tacit invitation to vote in a certain way or perform political chores in order to curry favor with their superiors rather than to act out their own beliefs. It may be urged that prohibitions against coercion are sufficient protection; but for many years the joint judgment of the Executive and Congress has been that to protect the rights of federal employees with respect to their jobs and their political acts and beliefs it is not enough merely to forbid one employee to attempt to influence or coerce another.[12] * * * Perhaps

---

12. In the 1940 debate over amendments to the Hatch Act, it was frequently stated that the only objectionable provisions were those restrictions in § 9 and the proposed § 12 against voluntary political activity. In response to the inquiry whether he was condemning those "who, without any coercion, voluntarily desire to take a part in politics," Senator Hatch replied that he "would draw the line if it could be drawn; but I defy . . . [anyone] to draw that line."

Congress at some time will come to a different view of the realities of political life and Government service; but that is its current view of the matter, and we are not now in any position to dispute it. Nor, in our view, does the Constitution forbid it.

Neither the right to associate nor the right to participate in political activities is absolute in any event. Nor are the management, financing, and conduct of political campaigns wholly free from governmental regulation. We agree with the basic holding of *Mitchell* that plainly identifiable acts of political management and political campaigning on the part of federal employees may constitutionally be prohibited. * * *

[The Court lastly concluded that the challenged prohibitions were not unconstitutionally vague or overbroad, relying on administrative regulations specifying the prohibited activities. The Court also noted that employees in doubt as to the legality of certain activities may request and receive advisory opinions from the Commission.]

For the foregoing reasons, the judgment of the District Court is reversed.

So ordered.

Mr. Justice Douglas, with whom Mr. Justice Brennan and Mr. Justice Marshall concur, dissenting.

The Hatch Act by § 9(a) prohibits federal employees from taking "an active part in political management or in political campaigns." * * * There is no definition of what "an active part . . . in political campaigns" means. The Act incorporates over 3,000 rulings of the Civil Service Commission between 1886 and 1940, and many hundreds of rulings since 1940. But even with that gloss on the Act, the critical phrases lack precision. In 1971, the Commission published a three-volume work entitled Political Activities Reporter which contains over 800 of its decisions since the enactment of the Hatch Act. One can learn from studying those volumes that it is not "political activity" to march in a band during a political parade or to wear political badges or to "participate fully in public affairs, except as prohibited by law, in a manner which does not materially compromise his efficiency or integrity as an employee or the neutrality, efficiency, or integrity of his agency." 5 CFR § 733.111(a)(13).

That is to say, some things, like marching in a band, are clear. Others are pregnant with ambiguity as "participate fully in public affairs, except as prohibited by law, in a manner which does not materially compromise," etc. * * *

The chilling effect of these vague and generalized prohibitions is so obvious as not to need elaboration. That effect would not be material to the issue of constitutionality if only the normal contours of the police power were involved. On the run of social and economic matters the "rational basis" standard which *United Public Workers* v. *Mitchell* applied would suffice. But what may have been unclear to some in *Mitchell* should be now be abundantly clear to all. We deal here with a First Amendment right to speak, to propose, to publish, to petition Government, to assemble. Time and place are obvious limitations. Thus no one could object if employees were barred from using office time to engage in outside activities whether political or otherwise. But it is of no concern of Government what an employee does in his spare time, whether religion, recreation, social work, or politics is his hobby—unless what he does impairs efficiency or other facets of the merits of his job. Some things, some activities do affect or may be thought to affect the employee's job performance. But his political creed, like his religion, is irrelevant. In the areas of speech, like religion, it is of no concern what the employee says in private to his wife or to the public in Constitution Hall. If Government employment were only a "privilege," then all sorts of conditions might be attached. But it is now settled that Government employment may not be denied or penalized "on a basis that infringes [the employee's] constitutionally protected interests—especially, his interest in freedom of speech." If Government, as the majority stated in *Mitchell*, may not condition public employment on the basis that the employee will not "take any active part in missionary work," it is difficult to see why it may condition employment on the basis that the employee not take "an active part . . . in political campaigns." For speech, assembly, and petition are as deeply embedded in the First Amendment as proselytizing a religious cause.

Free discussion of governmental affairs is basic in our constitutional system. Laws that trench on that area must be narrowly and precisely drawn to deal with precise ends. * * * The present Act cannot be appropriately narrowed to meet the need for narrowly drawn language not embracing First Amendment speech or writing without substantial revision. * * *

The Commission, on a case-by-case approach, has listed 13 categories of prohibited activities, starting with the catch-all "include but are not limited to." So the Commission ends up with open-end discretion to penalize X or not to penalize him. For example, a "permissible" activity is the employee's right to "[e]xpress his opinion as an individual privately and publicly on political subjects and candidates." Yet "soliciting votes" is prohibited. Is an employee safe from punishment if he expresses his opinion that candidate X is the best and candidate Y the worst? Is that crossing the forbidden line of soliciting votes?

A nursing assistant at a veterans' hospital put an ad in a newspaper reading:

> "To All My Many Friends of Poplar Bluff and Butler County I want to take this opportunity to ask your vote and support in the election, TUESDAY, AUGUST 7th. A very special person is seeking the Democratic nomination for Sheriff. I do not have to tell you of his qualifications, his past records stand.
>
> "This person is my dad, Lester (Less) Massingham.
>
> "THANK YOU
>
> "WALLACE (WALLY) MASSINGHAM"

He was held to have violated the Act.

Is a letter a permissible "expression" of views or a prohibited "solicitation?" The Solicitor General says it is a "permissible" expression; but the Commission ruled otherwise. For an employee who does not have the Solicitor General as counsel great consequences flow from an innocent decision. He may lose his job. Therefore the most prudent thing is to do nothing. Thus is self-imposed censorship imposed on many nervous people who live on narrow economic margins.

I would strike this provision of the law down as unconstitutional so that a new start may be made on this old problem that confuses and restricts nearly five million federal, state, and local public employees today that live under the present Act.

Notes and Questions

1. *Letter Carriers* involved the constitutionality of restrictions on federal employees. On the day *Letter Carriers* was decided, the Court upheld similar restrictions on state employees as well. *Broadrick v. Oklahoma*, 413 U.S. 601 (1973).

2. Reconsider Note 1 on page 675, which asked whether employees are helped or harmed by restrictions on their political activity. In striking down a ban on honoraria for low-level employees' speeches and articles that applied even when the speeches and articles had nothing to do with the employees' work, the Court relied on the characterization of the Hatch Act as protecting employees from pressure to participate in politics. The Court distinguished the honoraria ban from the Hatch Act's ban on political activity by arguing that the honoraria ban did nothing to protect "employees' morale or liberty." *United States v. National Treasury Employees Union*, 513 U.S. 454, 471 (1995).

Would it be constitutional to ban government employees from accepting honoraria for speeches or articles directly related to the individual's official duties? Would it be constitutional to apply such a statute to employees hired after the effective date of the amendment, *even after they have left government service?*

3. *Problem.* May the following governmental officials be banned from taking honoraria? In each, assume that a statute prohibits payment for such endeavors.

A. Oliver Wendell Douglas, an accomplished author and farmer before his appointment to the Eighth Circuit, wishes to write books and give speeches about the law, literature, and life on the prairie.

B. Miss Teri Story, a Supreme Court Justice, wishes to publish a treatise on constitutional law and to teach a course on the subject at the Harvard Law School.

C. Sandy Beach, a member of Congress and a former college professor of government, wishes to write about the power of interest groups and the influence they have with legislators.

D. Marvin Pickering, a schoolteacher, wishes to give lectures concerning the expenditure of funds in the school system.

4. *Treasury Employees* held not only that certain government employees must be permitted to speak, but that they must be permitted to receive payment for speaking. Yet under *Mitchell* and *Letter Carriers*, employees may be prohibited from speaking or taking actions that have too close a connection with partisan politics. Is the line between those two types of cases too fuzzy? Suppose an employee wishes to give lectures on black history and in the course of those lectures mentions his view of President Obama or the historical significance of his election? Would such speech fall within the constitutional protection established by *Treasury Employees*? Should it?

5. In 1993, the Hatch Act was amended to permit government employees to engage in more political activity. The current version of the Act, 5 U.S.C. §§ 7321–7326, permits most employees to "take an active part in political management or in political campaigns" when off duty, but employees may not solicit or receive political contributions, and may not run for "a partisan political office." 5 U.S.C. §§ 7323(a), 7324(a)(1). While the employee is on duty, however, he or she "may not engage in political activity." 5 U.S.C. § 7324(a)(1). Employees' political activity is also forbidden in government buildings and vehicles, as well as when the employees are wearing government uniforms. 5 U.S.C. §§ 7324(a)(2)–(4).

6. *Problem.* May this amended statute be applied constitutionally to forbid grade-school teachers from wearing political buttons while working? *See Weingarten v. Board of Education*, 591 F. Supp. 2d 511 (S.D.N.Y. 2008). May a public university apply the same prohibition to its faculty? Would the ban on political buttons be constitutional as applied to an industrial worker, like Mr. Poole, who has little or no contact with the public? *See* 5 C.F.R. § 734.306.

7. *Problem.* Does the amended statute forbid a postal worker from attaching a political poster to the employee union bulletin board in a non-public area of a post office? *See Burrus v. Vegliante*, 336 F.3d 82 (2d Cir. 2003). If so, it is constitutional? May a teacher be forbidden from posting political material on a bulletin board in an area closed to students? *See Weingarten, supra.*

8. *Problem.* Lisa Guffey and Christine Smith are employed by the Administrative Office of U.S. Courts. Respectively, Guffey and Smith administer court-appointed-attorney programs and provide information-technology support. They have no contact with the public and they interact with federal judges a handful of times per year. They do not work on individual cases and do not work in courthouses. The government argues that it is necessary to ban them from engaging in political activity for two reasons: First, restrictions on political activity should apply uniformly to the entire judicial branch. Second, the "public's confidence in an impartial judiciary will be tainted if it believes that the employees who work for the judicial branch are driven by partisan political interests." Is it constitutional to prohibit them from speaking on political matters (for example, using social media, bumper stickers, and yard signs) and donating to campaigns? *See Guffey v. Duff*, 2020 WL 2065274 (D.D.C. April 29, 2020).

9. Should a speech's constitutional protection depend on the location where it is delivered? Would, for example, a government employee's speech be protected if given on a street corner but not if given at a political convention? Would such a result violate the speaker's, or the party's, constitutional rights?

10. So-called "resign-to-run" statutes prohibit an officeholder from pursuing a different position unless he or she resigns the first office. Such statutes, like the Hatch Act and the employment discipline at issue in *Pickering*, discourage government employees from participating in politics. Resign-to-run statutes, however, impose restrictions on persons already holding office (rather than on unelected employees) and do not interfere with officeholders' right to speak. These differences caused the Court, in *Clements v. Fashing*, 457 U.S. 957 (1982), to conclude that resign-to-run statutes do not severely interfere with First Amendment rights, and to uphold them under the rational-basis test.

Are resign-to-run statutes good policy? Would it be a good idea to institute them on the national level, requiring, for example, members of Congress to resign their offices before running for President, or requiring representatives to resign before running for the Senate? Should sitting senators be ineligible for judicial nominations?

Suppose that instead of requiring an officeholder to resign his or her office before running for a different post, a state law made an office-holder ineligible for any other office until the expiry of his or her term. *Cf.* U.S. Const. art. I, § 6, cl. 2 ("No Senator or Representative shall, during the Time for which he was elected, be appointed to any civil Office under the Authority of the United States, which shall have been created, or the Emoluments whereof shall have been encreased during such time; and no Person holding any Office under the United States, shall be a Member of either House during his Continuance in Office."). Does a state have a sufficiently important interest in requiring ambitious officeholders to complete their terms so as to overcome the impact such a law has on the First Amendment rights of such would-be candidates and the voters who would support them? *See Fashing*, 457 U.S. at 966–69 (plurality opinion). What if the disqualification continued for a period *after* the term of office expired?

H. Patronage

In the *Divine Comedy*'s Eighth Circle of Hell, Dante finds the Simoniacs, who had sold Church offices. He speaks to one, Pope Nicholas III, who is stuck upside-down in a rock, with only his feet and legs up to the calf visible and the soles of his feet afire. Nicholas admits to using his power to advance his family and his own wealth, provoking Dante's condemnation:

> *Well, tell me now: what was the sum of money that holy Peter had to pay our*
> *Lord before He gave the keys into his keeping? Certainly He asked no more*

*than "Follow me." Nor did Peter or the rest extort gold coins or silver from Matthias when he was picked to fill the place the evil one [Judas Iscariot] had lost. So stay stuck there, for you are rightly punished * * *.*

Inferno, Canto XIX (Mark Musa trans., Penguin Books 1971). The following cases also condemn the dispensation of offices according to considerations other than merit, though the punishment is considerably less severe.

Elrod v. Burns

Supreme Court of the United States
427 U.S. 347, 96 S. Ct. 2673, 49 L. Ed. 2d 547 (1976)

MR. JUSTICE BRENNAN announced the judgment of the Court and delivered an opinion in which MR. JUSTICE WHITE and MR. JUSTICE MARSHALL joined.

This case presents the question whether public employees who allege that they were discharged or threatened with discharge solely because of their partisan political affiliation or nonaffiliation state a claim for deprivation of constitutional rights secured by the First and Fourteenth Amendments. * * *

In December 1970, the Sheriff of Cook County, [Illinois,] a Republican, was replaced by Richard Elrod, a Democrat. At that time, respondents, all Republicans, were employees of the Cook County Sheriff's Office. They were non-civil-service employees and, therefore, not covered by any statute, ordinance, or regulation protecting them from arbitrary discharge. One respondent, John Burns, was Chief Deputy of the Process Division and supervised all departments of the Sheriff's Office working on the seventh floor of the building housing that office. Frank Vargas was a bailiff and security guard at the Juvenile Court of Cook County. Fred L. Buckley was employed as a process server in the office. Joseph Dennard was an employee in the office.

It has been the practice of the Sheriff of Cook County, when he assumes office from a Sheriff of a different political party, to replace non-civil-service employees of the Sheriffs' Office with members of his own party when the existing employees lack or fail to obtain requisite support from, or fail to affiliate with, that party. Consequently, subsequent to Sheriff Elrod's assumption of office, respondents * * * were discharged from their employment solely because they did not support and were not members of the Democratic Party and had failed to obtain the sponsorship of one of its leaders. * * *

The Cook County Sheriff's practice of dismissing employees on a partisan basis is but one form of the general practice of political patronage. The practice also includes placing loyal supporters in government jobs that may or may not have been made available by political discharges. Nonofficeholders may be the beneficiaries of lucrative government contracts for highway construction, buildings, and supplies. Favored wards may receive improved public services. Members of the judiciary may even engage in the practice through the appointment of receiverships, trusteeships, and refereeships. Although political patronage comprises a broad range of activities, we are here concerned only with the constitutionality of dismissing public employees for partisan reasons.

Patronage practice is not new to American politics. It has existed at the federal level at least since the Presidency of Thomas Jefferson, although its popularization and legitimation primarily occurred later, in the Presidency of Andrew Jackson. The practice is not unique to American politics. It has been used in many European countries, and in darker times, it played a significant role in the Nazi rise to power in Germany and other totalitarian states. More recent times have witnessed a strong decline in its use, particularly with respect to public employment. Indeed, only a few decades after Andrew Jackson's administration, strong discontent with the corruption and inefficiency of the patronage system of public employment eventuated in the Pendleton Act, the foundation of modern civil service. And on the state and local levels, merit systems have increasingly displaced the practice. * * * [But t]he decline of patronage employment is not, of course, relevant to the question of its constitutionality. * * *

The cost of the practice of patronage is the restraint it places on freedoms of belief and association. In order to maintain their jobs, respondents were required to pledge their political allegiance to the Democratic Party, work for the election of other candidates of the Democratic Party, contribute a portion of their wages to the Party, or obtain the sponsorship of a member of the Party, usually at the price of one of the first three alternatives. Regardless of the incumbent party's identity, Democratic or otherwise, the consequences for association and belief are the same. An individual who is a member of the out-party maintains affiliation with his own party at the risk of losing his job. He works for the election of his party's candidates and espouses its policies at the same risk. The financial and campaign assistance that he is induced to provide to another party furthers the advancement of that party's policies to the detriment of his party's views and ultimately his own beliefs, and any assessment of his salary is tantamount to coerced belief. See *Buckley* v. *Valeo*, 424 U.S. 1, 19 (1976) [p. 728]. Even a pledge of allegiance to another party, however ostensible, only serves to compromise the individual's true beliefs. Since the average public employee is hardly in the financial position to support his party and another, or to lend his time to two parties, the individual's ability to act according to his beliefs and to associate with others of his political persuasion is constrained, and support for his party is diminished.

It is not only belief and association which are restricted where political patronage is the practice. The free functioning of the electoral process also suffers. Conditioning public employment on partisan support prevents support of competing political interests. Existing employees are deterred from such support, as well as the multitude seeking jobs. As government employment, state or federal, becomes more pervasive, the greater the dependence on it becomes, and therefore the greater becomes the power to starve political opposition by commanding partisan support, financial and otherwise. Patronage thus tips the electoral process in favor of the incumbent party, and where the practice's scope is substantial relative to the size of the electorate, the impact on the process can be significant.

Our concern with the impact of patronage on political belief and association does not occur in the abstract, for political belief and association constitute the core of those activities protected by the First Amendment. * * * Patronage, therefore, to the extent it compels or restrains belief and association, is inimical to the process which undergirds our system of government and is "at war with the deeper traditions of democracy embodied in the First Amendment." As such, the practice unavoidably confronts decisions by this Court either invalidating or recognizing as invalid government action that inhibits belief and association through the conditioning of public employment on political faith.

The Court recognized in *United Public Workers* v. *Mitchell*, 330 U.S. 75, 100 (1947) [p. 668], that "Congress may not 'enact a regulation providing that no Republican, Jew or Negro shall be appointed to federal office. . . .'" This principle was reaffirmed in *Wieman* v. *Updegraff*, 344 U.S. 183 (1952), which held that a State could not require its employees to establish their loyalty by extracting an oath denying past affiliation with Communists. And in *Cafeteria Workers* v. *McElroy*, 367 U.S. 886, 898 (1961), the Court recognized again that the government could not deny employment because of previous membership in a particular party.

Particularly pertinent to the constitutionality of the practice of patronage dismissals are *Keyishian* v. *Board of Regents*, 385 U.S. 589 (1967), and *Perry* v. *Sindermann*, 408 U.S. 593 (1972). In *Keyishian*, the Court invalidated New York statutes barring employment merely on the basis of membership in "subversive" organizations. *Keyishian* squarely held that political association alone could not, consistently with the First Amendment, constitute an adequate ground for denying public employment. In *Perry*, the Court broadly rejected the validity of limitations on First Amendment rights as a condition to the receipt of a governmental benefit, stating that the government "may not deny a benefit to a person on a basis that infringes his constitutionally protected interests—especially, his interest in freedom of speech. For if the government could deny a benefit to a person because of his constitutionally protected speech or associations, his exercise of those freedoms would in effect be penalized and inhibited. This would allow the government to 'produce a result which [it] could not command directly.' Such interference with constitutional rights is impermissible."

Patronage practice falls squarely within the prohibitions of *Keyishian* and *Perry*. Under that practice, public employees hold their jobs on the condition that they provide, in some acceptable manner, support for the favored political party. The threat of dismissal for failure to provide that support unquestionably inhibits protected belief and association, and dismissal for failure to provide support only penalizes its exercise. The belief and association which government may not ordain directly are achieved by indirection.[13] And regardless of how evenhandedly these restraints may operate in the long run, after political office has changed hands several times, protected interests are still infringed and thus the violation remains. * * *

Although the practice of patronage dismissals clearly infringes First Amendment interests, our inquiry is not at an end, for the prohibition on encroachment of First Amendment protections is not an absolute. Restraints are permitted for appropriate reasons. [Petitioners suggest] that because there is no right to a government benefit, such as public employment, the benefit may be denied for any reason. *Perry*, however, emphasized that "[f]or at least a quarter-century, this Court has made clear that even though a person has no 'right' to a valuable governmental benefit and even though the government may deny him the benefit for any number of reasons, there are some reasons upon which the government may not rely." *Perry* and *Keyishian* properly recognize one such impermissible reason: The denial of a public benefit may not be used by the government for the purpose of creating an incentive enabling it to achieve what it may not command directly. "[T]he theory that public employment which may be denied altogether may be subjected to any conditions, regardless of how unreasonable, has been uniformly rejected." "It is too late in the day to doubt that the liberties of religion and expression may be infringed by the denial of or placing of conditions upon a benefit or privilege." *Sherbert* v. *Verner*, 374 U.S. 398, 404 (1963). "[T]his Court now has rejected the concept that constitutional rights turn upon whether a governmental benefit is characterized as a 'right' or as a 'privilege.'" *Sugarman* v. *Dougall*, 413 U.S. 634, 644 (1973).

* * * It is firmly established that a significant impairment of First Amendment rights must survive exacting scrutiny. * * * Thus encroachment "cannot be justified upon a mere showing of a legitimate state interest." The interest advanced must be paramount, one of vital importance, and the burden is on the government to show the existence of such an interest. In the instant case, care must be taken not to confuse the interest of partisan organizations with governmental interests. Only the latter will suffice. Moreover, it is not enough that the means chosen in furtherance of the interest be rationally related to that end. The gain to the subordinating

---

13. The increasingly pervasive nature of public employment provides officials with substantial power through conditioning jobs on partisan support, particularly in this time of high unemployment. Since the government, however, may not seek to achieve an unlawful end either directly or indirectly, the inducement afforded by placing conditions on a benefit need not be particularly great in order to find that rights have been violated. Rights are infringed both where the government fines a person a penny for being a Republican and where it withholds the grant of a penny for the same reason. Petitioners contend that even though the government may not provide that public employees may retain their jobs only if they become affiliated with or provide support for the in-party, respondents here have waived any objection to such requirements. The difficulty with this argument is that it completely swallows the rule. Since the qualification may not be constitutionally imposed absent an appropriate justification, to accept the waiver argument is to say that the government may do what it may not do. A finding of waiver in this case, therefore, would be contrary to our view that a partisan job qualification abridges the First Amendment.

interest provided by the means must outweigh the incurred loss of protected rights, and the government must "emplo[y] means closely drawn to avoid unnecessary abridgment. . . ." * * * In short, if conditioning the retention of public employment on the employee's support of the in-party is to survive constitutional challenge, it must further some vital government end by a means that is least restrictive of freedom of belief and association in achieving that end, and the benefit gained must outweigh the loss of constitutionally protected rights.

One interest which has been offered in justification of patronage is the need to insure effective government and the efficiency of public employees. It is argued that employees of political persuasions not the same as that of the party in control of public office will not have the incentive to work effectively and may even be motivated to subvert the incumbent administration's efforts to govern effectively. We are not persuaded. The inefficiency resulting from the wholesale replacement of large numbers of public employees every time political office changes hands belies this justification. And the prospect of dismissal after an election in which the incumbent party has lost is only a disincentive to good work. Further, it is not clear that dismissal in order to make room for a patronage appointment will result in replacement by a person more qualified to do the job since appointment often occurs in exchange for the delivery of votes, or other party service, not job capability. More fundamentally, however, the argument does not succeed because it is doubtful that the mere difference of political persuasion motivates poor performance; nor do we think it legitimately may be used as a basis for imputing such behavior. * * * At all events, less drastic means for insuring government effectiveness and employee efficiency are available to the State. Specifically, employees may always be discharged for good cause, such as insubordination or poor job performance, when those bases in fact exist.

Even if the first argument that patronage serves effectiveness and efficiency be rejected, it still may be argued that patronage serves those interests by giving the employees of an incumbent party the incentive to perform well in order to insure their party's incumbency and thereby their jobs. Patronage, according to the argument, thus makes employees highly accountable to the public. But the ability of officials more directly accountable to the electorate to discharge employees for cause and the availability of merit systems, growth in the use of which has been quite significant, convince us that means less intrusive than patronage still exist for achieving accountability in the public work force and, thereby, effective and efficient government. The greater effectiveness of patronage over these less drastic means, if any, is at best marginal, a gain outweighed by the absence of intrusion on protected interests under the alternatives.

The lack of any justification for patronage dismissals as a means of furthering government effectiveness and efficiency distinguishes this case from *CSC* v. *Letter Carriers*, 413 U.S. 548 (1973) [p. 679], and *United Public Workers* v. *Mitchell*. In both of those cases, legislative restraints on political management and campaigning by public employees were upheld despite their encroachment on First Amendment rights because, *inter alia*, they did serve in a necessary manner to foster and protect efficient and effective government. Interestingly, the activities that were restrained by the legislation involved in those cases are characteristic of patronage practices. As the Court observed in *Mitchell*: "The conviction that an actively partisan governmental personnel threatens good administration has deepened since [1882]. Congress recognizes danger to the service in that political rather than official effort may earn advancement and to the public in that governmental favor may be channeled through political connections."

A second interest advanced in support of patronage is the need for political loyalty of employees, not to the end that effectiveness and efficiency be insured, but to the end that representative government not be undercut by tactics obstructing the implementation of policies of the new administration, policies presumably sanctioned by the electorate. The justification is not without force, but is nevertheless inadequate to validate patronage wholesale. Limiting patronage dismissals to policymaking positions is sufficient to achieve this governmental end. Nonpolicymaking individuals usually have only limited responsibility and are therefore not in a position to thwart the goals of the in-party.

No clear line can be drawn between policymaking and nonpolicymaking positions. While nonpolicymaking individuals usually have limited responsibility, that is not to say that one with a number of responsibilities is necessarily in a policymaking position. The nature of the responsibilities is critical. Employee supervisors, for example, may have many responsibilities, but those responsibilities may have only limited and well-defined objectives. An employee with responsibilities that are not well defined or are of broad scope more likely functions in a policymaking position. In determining whether an employee occupies a policymaking position, consideration would also be given to whether the employee acts as an adviser or formulates plans for the implementation of broad goals. Thus, the political loyalty "justification is a matter of proof, or at least argument, directed at particular kinds of jobs." Since, as we have noted, it is the government's burden to demonstrate an overriding interest in order to validate an encroachment on protected interests, the burden of establishing this justification as to any particular respondent will rest on the petitioners on remand, cases of doubt being resolved in favor of the particular respondent.

It is argued that a third interest supporting patronage dismissals is the preservation of the democratic process. According to petitioners, "we have contrived no system for the support of party that does not place considerable reliance on patronage. The party organization makes a democratic government work and charges a price for its services." The argument is thus premised on the centrality of partisan politics to the democratic process.

Preservation of the democratic process is certainly an interest protection of which may in some instances justify limitations on First Amendment freedoms. But however important preservation of the two-party system or any system involving a fixed number of parties may or may not be, we are not persuaded that the elimination of patronage practice or, as is specifically involved here, the interdiction of patronage dismissals, will bring about the demise of party politics. Political parties existed in the absence of active patronage practice prior to the administration of Andrew Jackson, and they have survived substantial reduction in their patronage power through the establishment of merit systems.

Patronage dismissals thus are not the least restrictive alternative to achieving the contribution they may make to the democratic process. The process functions as well without the practice, perhaps even better, for patronage dismissals clearly also retard that process. Patronage can result in the entrenchment of one or a few parties to the exclusion of others. And most indisputably, as we recognized at the outset, patronage is a very effective impediment to the associational and speech freedoms which are essential to a meaningful system of democratic government. Thus, if patronage contributes at all to the elective process, that contribution is diminished by the practice's impairment of the same. Indeed, unlike the gain to representative government provided by the Hatch Act in *CSC* v. *Letter Carriers* and *United Public Workers* v. *Mitchell*, the gain to representative government provided by the practice of patronage, if any, would be insufficient to justify its sacrifice of First Amendment rights.

To be sure, *Letter Carriers* and *Mitchell* upheld Hatch Act restraints sacrificing political campaigning and management, activities themselves protected by the First Amendment. But in those cases it was the Court's judgment that congressional subordination of those activities was permissible to safeguard the core interests of individual belief and association. Subordination of some First Amendment activity was permissible to protect other such activity. Today, we hold that subordination of other First Amendment activity, that is, patronage dismissals, not only is permissible, but also is mandated by the First Amendment. And since patronage dismissals fall within the category of political campaigning and management, this conclusion irresistibly flows from *Mitchell* and *Letter Carriers*. For if the First Amendment did not place individual belief and association above political campaigning and management, at least in the setting of public employment, the restraints on those latter activities could not have been judged permissible in *Mitchell* and *Letter Carriers*.[27] * * *

In summary, patronage dismissals severely restrict political belief and association. Though there is a vital need for government efficiency and effectiveness, such dismissals are on balance not the least restrictive means for fostering that end. There is also a need to insure that policies which the electorate has sanctioned are

---

27. The judgment that the First Amendment interests in political campaigning and management must, in the setting of public employment, give way to the First Amendment interests in individual belief and association does not necessarily extend to other contexts. Restraining political campaigning and management in the area of public employment leaves it free to continue in other settings. The consequence of no such restraint, however, is the complete restriction of individual belief and association for each public employee affected.

effectively implemented. That interest can be fully satisfied by limiting patronage dismissals to policymaking positions. Finally, patronage dismissals cannot be justified by their contribution to the proper functioning of our democratic process through their assistance to partisan politics since political parties are nurtured by other, less intrusive and equally effective methods. More fundamentally, however, any contribution of patronage dismissals to the democratic process does not suffice to override their severe encroachment on First Amendment freedoms. We hold, therefore, that the practice of patronage dismissals is unconstitutional under the First and Fourteenth Amendments, and that respondents thus stated a valid claim for relief. * * *

The judgment of the Court of Appeals is

Affirmed.

MR. JUSTICE STEVENS did not participate in the consideration or decision of this case.

MR. JUSTICE STEWART, with whom MR. JUSTICE BLACKMUN joins, concurring in the judgment. * * *

This case does not require us to consider the broad contours of the so-called patronage system, with all its variations and permutations. In particular, it does not require us to consider the constitutional validity of a system that confines the hiring of some governmental employees to those of a particular political party, and I would intimate no views whatever on that question.

The single substantive question involved in this case is whether a nonpolicymaking, nonconfidential government employee can be discharged or threatened with discharge from a job that he is satisfactorily performing upon the sole ground of his political beliefs. I agree with the plurality that he cannot.

MR. CHIEF JUSTICE BURGER, dissenting.

The Court's decision today represents a significant intrusion into the area of legislative and policy concerns[.] * * * Constant inroads on the powers of the States to manage their own affairs cannot fail to complicate our system and centralize more power in Washington. * * *

MR. JUSTICE POWELL, with whom THE CHIEF JUSTICE and MR. JUSTICE REHNQUIST join, dissenting.

The Court holds unconstitutional a practice as old as the Republic, a practice which has contributed significantly to the democratization of American politics. This decision is urged on us in the name of First Amendment rights, but in my view the judgment neither is constitutionally required nor serves the interest of a representative democracy. It also may well disserve rather than promote core values of the First Amendment. I therefore dissent. * * *

Partisan politics, as we now know them, did not assume a prominent role in national politics immediately after the adoption of the Constitution. Nonetheless, [President] Washington tended to confine appointments even of customs officials and postmasters to Federalists, as opposed to anti-Federalists. As the role of parties expanded, partisan considerations quickly influenced employment decisions. John Adams removed some Republicans from minor posts, and Jefferson, the first President to succeed a President of an opposing party, made significant patronage use of the appointment and removal powers. The administrations of Madison, Monroe, and John Quincy Adams provided no occasion for conspicuous patronage practice in employment, as each succeeded a copartisan. Jackson, of course, used patronage extensively when he became the first President since Jefferson to succeed an antagonistic administration.

It thus appears that patronage employment practices emerged on the national level at an early date, and that they were conspicuous during Jackson's Presidency largely because of their necessary dormancy during the long succession of Republican Presidents. During that period, however, patronage in hiring was practiced widely in the States, especially in New York and Pennsylvania. This afforded a theoretical and popular legitimacy to patronage, helping to lay the groundwork for acceptance of Jackson's actions on the national level.

It is recognized that patronage in employment played a significant role in democratizing American politics. Before patronage practices developed fully, an "aristocratic" class dominated political affairs, a tendency that persisted in areas where patronage did not become prevalent. Patronage practices broadened the base of political participation by providing incentives to take part in the process, thereby increasing the volume of political discourse in society. Patronage also strengthened parties, and hence encouraged the development of institutional responsibility to the electorate on a permanent basis. * * *

In many situations patronage employment practices also entailed costs to government efficiency. These costs led eventually to reforms placing most federal and state civil service employment on a nonpatronage basis. But the course of such reform is of limited relevance to the task of constitutional adjudication in this case. It is pertinent to note, however, that a perceived impingement on employees' political beliefs by the patronage system was not a significant impetus to such reform. * * *

[Petitioners] apparently accepted patronage jobs knowingly and willingly, while fully familiar with the "tenure" practices long prevailing in the Sheriff's Office. Such employees have benefited from their political beliefs and activities; they have not been penalized for them. In these circumstances, I am inclined to [believe] that beneficiaries of a patronage system may not be heard to challenge it when it comes their turn to be replaced. * * * In any event, I am forced to turn to the question addressed by the plurality * * *.

* * * In concluding that patronage hiring practices are unconstitutional, the plurality seriously underestimates the strength of the government interest especially at the local level in allowing some patronage hiring practices, and it exaggerates the perceived burden on First Amendment rights.

As indicated above, patronage hiring practices have contributed to American democracy by stimulating political activity and by strengthening parties, thereby helping to make government accountable.[6] It cannot be questioned seriously that these contributions promote important state interests. * * *

We also have recognized the strong government interests in encouraging stable political parties and avoiding excessive political fragmentation. Through the medium of established parties the "people . . . are presented with understandable choices and the winner in the general election with sufficient support to govern effectively," *Storer* v. *Brown*, 415 U.S. 724, 735 (1974) [p. 513], while "splintered parties and unrestrained factionalism [might] do significant damage to the fabric of government."

Without analysis, however, the plurality opinion disparages the contribution of patronage hiring practices in advancing these state interests. * * * In my view, this thinking reflects a disturbing insensitivity to the political realities relevant to the disposition of this case.

The complaining parties are or were employees of the Sheriff. In many communities, the sheriff's duties are as routine as process serving, and his election attracts little or no general public interest. * * * Long experience teaches that at this local level traditional patronage practices contribute significantly to the democratic process. The candidates for these offices derive their support at the precinct level, and their modest funding for publicity, from cadres of friends and political associates who hope to benefit if their "man" is elected. The activities of the latter are often the principal source of political information for the voting public. The "robust" political discourse that the plurality opinion properly emphasizes is furthered — not restricted — by the time-honored system.

Patronage hiring practices also enable party organizations to persist and function at the local level. Such organizations become visible to the electorate at large only at election time, but the dull periods between elections require ongoing activities: precinct organizations must be maintained; new voters registered; and minor political "chores" performed for citizens who otherwise may have no practical means of access to officeholders. In some communities, party organizations and clubs also render helpful social services.

---

6. Some commentators have believed that patronage hiring practices promote other social interests as well: "Patronage is peculiarly important for minority groups, involving much more than the mere spoils of office. Each first appointment given a member of any underdog element is a boost in that element's struggle for social acceptance. It means that another barrier to their advance has been lifted, another shut door has swung open." S. Lubell, The Future of American Politics 76–77 (1952).

It is naive to think that these types of political activities are motivated at these levels by some academic interest in "democracy" or other public service impulse. For the most part, as every politician knows, the hope of some reward generates a major portion of the local political activity supporting parties. It is difficult to over-estimate the contributions to our system by the major political parties, fortunately limited in number compared to the fractionalization that has made the continued existence of democratic government doubtful in some other countries. Parties gen-erally are stable, high-profile, and permanent institutions. When the names on a long ballot are meaningless to the average voter, party affiliation affords a guidepost by which voters may rationalize a myriad of political choices. Voters can and do hold parties to long-term accountability, and it is not too much to say that, in their absence, responsive and responsible performance in low-profile offices, particularly, is difficult to maintain.

It is against decades of experience to the contrary, then, that the plurality opinion concludes that patronage hiring practices interfere with the "free functioning of the electoral process." This *ad hoc* judicial judgment runs counter to the judgments of the representatives of the people in state and local governments, representatives who have chosen, in most instances, to retain some patronage practices in combination with a merit-oriented civil service. One would think that elected representatives of the people are better equipped than we to weigh the need for some continuation of patronage practices in light of the interests above identified, and particularly in view of local conditions.[10] Against this background, the assertion in the plurality opinion that "[p]atronage dismissals . . . are not the least restrictive alternative to achieving [any] contribution they may make to the democratic process" is uncon-vincing, especially since no alternative to some continuation of patronage practices is suggested.

I thus conclude that patronage hiring practices sufficiently serve important state interests, including some interests sought to be advanced by the First Amendment, to justify a tolerable intrusion on the First Amendment interests of employees or potential employees.

* * * This case differs materially from previous cases involving the imposi-tion of political conditions on employment, see, *e.g., Garner* v. *Los Angeles Board of Public Works,* 341 U.S. 716 (1951), cases where there was an attempt to exclude "a minority group . . . odious to the majority." In that context there was a danger

---

10. The judgment today is limited to nonpolicymaking positions. A "policy-making" excep-tion, however, will not allow substantial advancement of the state interests undercut by the Court's holding, as it is doubtful that any significant number of employees can be identified as policymak-ers in a sheriff's office. States have chosen to provide for the election of many local officials who have little or no genuine policymaking functions, and the subordinates of such officials are even less likely to have such functions. It thus is predictable that the holding today will terminate almost completely the contributions of patronage hiring practices to the democratic process. The proba-bility of this result is increased to the extent that the needs of efficiency in local government require that policymaking positions be included in a merit-oriented, nonpolitical civil service.

that governmental action was directed toward the elimination of political beliefs by penalizing adherents to them. But patronage hiring practices have been consistent historically with vigorous ideological competition in the political "marketplace." And even after one becomes a beneficiary, the system leaves significant room for individual political expression. Employees, regardless of affiliation, may vote freely[11] and express themselves on some political issues. The principal intrusion of patronage hiring practices on First Amendment interests thus arises from the coercion on associational choices that may be created by one's desire initially to obtain employment. This intrusion, while not insignificant, must be measured in light of the limited role of patronage hiring in most government employment. The pressure to abandon one's beliefs and associations to obtain government employment—especially employment of such uncertain duration—does not seem to me to assume impermissible proportions in light of the interests to be served. * * *[12]

Notes and Questions

1. Who is in a better position to assess the wisdom of patronage hiring practices—elected officials, as Justice Powell argued, or electorally unaccountable judges, as the plurality implied?

2. Four years after *Elrod*, the Court was presented with the question whether assistant public defenders could be discharged because of their political affiliations or sympathies. The Court held that they could not, but in so doing the Court appeared to revise the *Elrod* standard for determining which employees could be dismissed on political grounds. While *Elrod* had focused on whether the position had "policymaking" responsibilities or required confidentiality, *Branti v. Finkel*, 445 U.S. 507, 518–20 (1980), asked whether "party affiliation is an appropriate requirement for the effective performance of the public office involved":

---

11. It appears that before the adoption of the Australian ballot, one's access to or retention of a government job sometimes could depend on voting "correctly." Today this ultimate core of political expression is beyond the reach of any coercive effects of the patronage system.

12. In concluding that the Constitution does not require the invalidation of state and local patronage systems, I wish to make clear that approval of any particular type of system or of the practice in any particular State, city, or community is not implied. I believe that the prevailing practice is to establish a broad base of merit-oriented civil service, but to leave some room for the operation of traditional patronage. I must say that the "mix" in Cook County (where only about half of the employees in the Sheriff's Office are within the merit system) seems disproportionate. On the other hand, there are smaller communities—*e.g.*, where nonpartisan, council-manager forms of government exist—in which the merit system embraces the vast majority of public employees. Political scientists and students of government differ, and their views also have varied from time to time, as to the best means of structuring state and local government employment in the public interest. Nor is the answer necessarily the same for every community without regard to its size, form of government, or other local conditions. My conviction, as indicated in the opinion above, is that we should not foreclose local options in the name of a constitutional right perceived to be applicable for the first time after nearly two centuries.

[I]t is not always easy to determine whether a position is one in which political affiliation is a legitimate factor to be considered. Under some circumstances, a position may be appropriately considered political even though it is neither confidential nor policymaking in character. As one obvious example, if a State's election laws require that precincts be supervised by two election judges of different parties, a Republican judge could be legitimately discharged solely for changing his party registration. That conclusion would not depend on any finding that the job involved participation in policy decisions or access to confidential information. Rather, it would simply rest on the fact that party membership was essential to the discharge of the employee's governmental responsibilities.

It is equally clear that party affiliation is not necessarily relevant to every policymaking or confidential position. The coach of a state university's football team formulates policy, but no one could seriously claim that Republicans make better coaches than Democrats, or vice versa, no matter which party is in control of the state government. On the other hand, it is equally clear that the Governor of a State may appropriately believe that the official duties of various assistants who help him write speeches, explain his views to the press, or communicate with the legislature cannot be performed effectively unless those persons share his political beliefs and party commitments. In sum, the ultimate inquiry is not whether the label "policymaker" or "confidential" fits a particular position; rather, the question is whether the hiring authority can demonstrate that party affiliation is an appropriate requirement for the effective performance of the public office involved.

Having thus framed the issue, it is manifest that the continued employment of an assistant public defender cannot properly be conditioned upon his allegiance to the political party in control of the county government. The primary, if not the only, responsibility of an assistant public defender is to represent individual citizens in controversy with the State. * * *

Thus, whatever policymaking occurs in the public defender's office must relate to the needs of individual clients and not to any partisan political interests. Similarly, although an assistant is bound to obtain access to confidential information arising out of various attorney-client relationships, that information has no bearing whatsoever on partisan political concerns. Under these circumstances, it would undermine, rather than promote, the effective performance of an assistant public defender's office to make his tenure dependent on his allegiance to the dominant political party.

Justice Powell, in a dissent joined by then-Justice Rehnquist and in part by Justice Stewart, criticized the Court for going beyond *Elrod* in holding that even some policymaking officials would be insulated from patronage dismissals if their political affiliation was not relevant to the job. He further argued that the "appropriate[ness]" standard was so vague as to raise the possibility of litigation over a wide range of jobs, making the judiciary the "final arbiters as to who federal, state, and local governments may employ." *Id.* at 525 (Powell, J., dissenting). In a portion of the dissent joined only by then-Justice Rehnquist, Justice Powell reiterated the view he expressed in *Elrod* that patronage was valuable in supporting the two-party system. He further argued that "[b]ecause voters certainly may elect governmental officials [including public defenders and their assistants] on the basis of party ties, it is difficult to perceive a constitutional reason for prohibiting them from delegating that same authority to legislators and appointed officials." *Id.* at 533–34 (Powell, J., dissenting). Justice Stewart also filed a dissenting opinion, in which he argued that the "confidential" nature of the job of an assistant public defender distinguished *Branti* from *Elrod. See id.* at 520–21 (Stewart, J., dissenting).

3. What explains Chief Justice Burger's switch from dissenting in *Elrod* to joining the *Branti* majority?

4. Lower courts have consistently held that in evaluating whether an employee may be dismissed for political reasons, the responsibilities specified in the job description, rather than the duties that the employee customarily performed, are controlling. As explained in *Sanders v. Montoya*, 982 P.2d 1064 (N.M. Ct. App. 1999), focusing on the job description lessens the burden on courts by making it unnecessary to reevaluate every job whenever there is a shift in the way office administration is handled. Further, the job-description approach provides certainty to litigants and allows the new administration to fill certain positions with political allies, regardless of the ways in which the prior administration had been using its employees.

5. Should the First Amendment provide protection against dismissal for an employee who is running for election against her boss? In *Carver v. Dennis*, 104 F.3d 847 (6th Cir. 1997), the plaintiff was a deputy county clerk. She was fired because she planned to run against the incumbent county clerk. The court held that there is a distinction between dismissals based on one's political affiliation, political beliefs, or the expression of those beliefs, on the one hand, and one's political candidacy, on the other. The court concluded that only the first category received protection under *Elrod* and *Branti*: "This was not a patronage dismissal. It was not a dismissal because of political beliefs or affiliations. It was not a dismissal based on politics at all, except to the extent that running for public office is a political exercise in its broad sense." *Id.* at 850. *See also Wilbur v. Mahan*, 3 F.3d 214 (7th Cir. 1993); *Bart v. Telford*, 677 F.2d 622 (7th Cir. 1982). Does this explanation understate the importance to democracy of running for office? *See Click v. Copeland*, 970 F.2d 106, 112 (5th Cir. 1992). Is there a constitutional difference between firing the employee and subjecting him or her to retaliatory harassment? *See Wallace v. Benware*, 67 F.3d 655, 661 (7th Cir. 1995) (holding that a sheriff could dismiss or demote a deputy who had run against him, but could not subject him to "a campaign of petty harassment").

6. Judge Easterbrook of the Seventh Circuit has argued that the Supreme Court's decisions upholding the Hatch Act and resign-to-run statutes, *see supra* § G, mean that public employees may be dismissed if they run for office. *See Wilbur*, 3 F.3d at 219–21 (Easterbrook, J., concurring in the judgment). The majority, in an opinion by Judge Posner, responded that "it would be rather a stretch of the Hatch Act cases to interpret them as authorizing a public official selectively to apply a 'resign to run' provision to his political enemies." *Id.* at 216 (opinion of the court). Judge Easterbrook countered that a public official is not behaving selectively when he discharges every employee who runs against him — "[a]nyone running for his seat is an incumbent's enemy" — and that it would be ironic to encourage, in the name of the First Amendment, a policy *mandating* dismissal of employees who run for office. *Id.* at 220 (Easterbrook, J., concurring in judgment). Who has the better of the argument?

7. Would the result change if the employee were running for Congress, rather than for the boss's position? *See Newcomb v. Brennan*, 558 F.2d 825 (7th Cir. 1977).

What if the candidate were not the employee herself, but her son? Would the employee receive protection from being fired because of her son's candidacy? *See Smith v. Frye*, 488 F.3d 263 (4th Cir.), *cert. denied*, 552 U.S. 1039 (2007). What if an employee is subject to retaliation neither for her political affiliation nor for her relative's candidacy *per se*, but for her campaigning on behalf of her relative who was running against a candidate supported by her superiors? *See Riddell v. Gordon*, 2008 WL 4766952, 2008 U.S. Dist. LEXIS 88410 (D. Del. Oct. 31, 2008).

Suppose instead that after an election for county clerk in which the incumbent is defeated, the new office-holder fires an employee who is the wife of his former opponent. *See Lowe v. Padgett*, 740 F. Supp. 481 (E.D. Tenn. 1989), *aff'd* 897 F.2d 529 (6th Cir. 1990). *Cf. McCabe v. Sharrett*, 12 F.3d 1558 (11th Cir. 1994) (holding that a police chief acted constitutionally when he transferred his secretary because he feared the secretary's marriage to another police officer might compromise her loyalty and her ability to keep confidences).

8. *Problem.* Barney Fife, deputy sheriff of Mayberry, decides to challenge incumbent sheriff Andy Taylor in the next election. Another deputy, Floyd Barber, and jailer Otis Campbell decide to support Fife, and spend off-duty time distributing leaflets and otherwise campaigning for him. Taylor is upset at the challenge, and fires Fife as well as Barber and Campbell. Should the Constitution be interpreted to provide all three employees with the same protection, or are there significant distinctions owing to their positions or their activities? *See Jantzen v. Hawkins*, 188 F.3d 1247 (10th Cir. 1999).

Rutan v. Republican Party of Illinois

Supreme Court of the United States
497 U.S. 62, 110 S. Ct. 2729, 111 L. Ed. 2d 52 (1990)

JUSTICE BRENNAN delivered the opinion of the Court [in which JUSTICE WHITE, JUSTICE MARSHALL, JUSTICE BLACKMUN, and JUSTICE STEVENS join].

To the victor belong only those spoils that may be constitutionally obtained. *Elrod* v. *Burns*, 427 U.S. 347 (1976) [p. 686], and *Branti* v. *Finkel*, 445 U.S. 507 (1980), decided that the First Amendment forbids government officials to discharge or threaten to discharge public employees solely for not being supporters of the political party in power, unless party affiliation is an appropriate requirement for the position involved. Today we are asked to decide the constitutionality of several related political patronage practices—whether promotion, transfer, recall, and hiring decisions involving low-level public employees may be constitutionally based on party affiliation and support. We hold that they may not.

The petition and cross-petition before us arise from a lawsuit protesting certain employment policies and practices instituted by Governor James Thompson of Illinois. On November 12, 1980, the Governor issued an executive order proclaiming a hiring freeze for every agency, bureau, board, or commission subject to his control. The order prohibits state officials from hiring any employee, filling any vacancy, creating any new position, or taking any similar action. It affects approximately 60,000 state positions. More than 5,000 of these become available each year as a result of resignations, retirements, deaths, expansions, and reorganizations. The order proclaims that "*no* exceptions" are permitted without the Governor's "express permission after submission of appropriate requests to [his] office."

Requests for the Governor's "express permission" have allegedly become routine. Permission has been granted or withheld through an agency expressly created for this purpose, the Governor's Office of Personnel (Governor's Office). Agencies have been screening applicants under Illinois' civil service system, making their personnel choices, and submitting them as requests to be approved or disapproved by the Governor's Office. Among the employment decisions for which approvals have been required are new hires, promotions, transfers, and recalls after layoffs.

By means of the freeze, according to petitioners and cross-respondents, the Governor has been using the Governor's Office to operate a political patronage system to limit state employment and beneficial employment-related decisions to those who are supported by the Republican Party. In reviewing an agency's request that a particular applicant be approved for a particular position, the Governor's Office has looked at whether the applicant voted in Republican primaries in past election years, whether the applicant has provided financial or other support to the Republican Party and its candidates, whether the applicant has promised to join and work for the Republican Party in the future, and whether the applicant has the support of Republican Party officials at state or local levels. * * *

* * * We granted certiorari to decide the important question whether the First Amendment's proscription of patronage dismissals recognized in *Elrod* and *Branti* extends to promotion, transfer, recall, or hiring decisions involving public employment positions for which party affiliation is not an appropriate requirement.

* * * Respondents urge us to view *Elrod* and *Branti* as inapplicable because the patronage dismissals at issue in those cases are different in kind from failure to promote, failure to transfer, and failure to recall after layoff. Respondents initially contend that the employee[s'] First Amendment rights have not been infringed because they have no entitlement to promotion, transfer, or rehire. We rejected just such an argument in *Elrod* and *Branti*, as both cases involved state workers who were employees at will with no legal entitlement to continued employment. * * *

Respondents next argue that the employment decisions at issue here do not violate the First Amendment because the decisions are not punitive, do not in any way adversely affect the terms of employment, and therefore do not chill the exercise of protected belief and association by public employees. This is not credible. * * *

The same First Amendment concerns that underlay our decisions in *Elrod* and *Branti* are implicated here. Employees who do not compromise their beliefs stand to lose the considerable increases in pay and job satisfaction attendant to promotions, the hours and maintenance expenses that are consumed by long daily commutes, and even their jobs if they are not rehired after a "temporary" layoff. These are significant penalties and are imposed for the exercise of rights guaranteed by the First Amendment. Unless these patronage practices are narrowly tailored to further vital government interests, we must conclude that they impermissibly encroach on First Amendment freedoms.

We find, however, that our conclusions in *Elrod* and *Branti* are equally applicable to the patronage practices at issue here. A government's interest in securing effective employees can be met by discharging, demoting, or transferring staff members whose work is deficient. A government's interest in securing employees who will loyally implement its policies can be adequately served by choosing or dismissing certain high-level employees on the basis of their political views. Likewise, the "preservation of the democratic process" is no more furthered by the patronage promotions, transfers, and rehires at issue here than it is by patronage dismissals. First, "political parties are nurtured by other, less intrusive and equally effective methods." Political parties have already survived the substantial decline in patronage employment practices in this century. Second, patronage decidedly impairs the elective process by discouraging free political expression by public employees. Respondents, who include the Governor of Illinois and other state officials, do not suggest any other overriding government interest in favoring Republican Party supporters for promotion, transfer, and rehire.

We therefore determine that promotions, transfers, and recalls after layoffs based on political affiliation or support are an impermissible infringement on the First

Amendment rights of public employees. * * * The First Amendment is not a tenure provision, protecting public employees from actual or constructive discharge. [But it] prevents the government, except in the most compelling circumstances, from wielding its power to interfere with its employees' freedom to believe and associate, or to not believe and not associate. * * *

* * * Patronage hiring places burdens on free speech and association similar to those imposed by the patronage practices discussed above. A state job is valuable. Like most employment, it provides regular paychecks, health insurance, and other benefits. In addition, there may be openings with the State when business in the private sector is slow. There are also occupations for which the government is a major (or the only) source of employment, such as social workers, elementary school teachers, and prison guards. Thus, denial of a state job is a serious privation.

Nonetheless, respondents contend that the burden imposed is not of constitutional magnitude. Decades of decisions by this Court belie such a claim. We premised *Torcaso* v. *Watkins*, 367 U.S. 488 (1961), on our understanding that loss of a job opportunity for failure to compromise one's convictions states a constitutional claim. We held that Maryland could not refuse an appointee a commission for the position of notary public on the ground that he refused to declare his belief in God, because the required oath "unconstitutionally invades the appellant's freedom of belief and religion." *Id.*, at 496. In *Keyishian* v. *Board of Regents of Univ. of New York*, 385 U.S. 589, 609–610 (1967), we held a law affecting appointment and retention of teachers invalid because it premised employment on an unconstitutional restriction of political belief and association. In *Elfbrandt* v. *Russell*, 384 U.S. 11, 19 (1966), we struck down a loyalty oath which was a prerequisite for public employment.

Almost half a century ago, this Court made clear that the government "may not enact a regulation providing that no Republican . . . shall be appointed to federal office." *Public Workers* v. *Mitchell*, 330 U.S. 75, 100 (1947) [p. 668]. What the First Amendment precludes the government from commanding directly, it also precludes the government from accomplishing indirectly. Under our sustained precedent, conditioning hiring decisions on political belief and association plainly constitutes an unconstitutional condition, unless the government has a vital interest in doing so. We find no such government interest here, for the same reasons that we found that the government lacks justification for patronage promotions, transfers, or recalls. * * *

We hold that the rule of *Elrod* and *Branti* extends to promotion, transfer, recall, and hiring decisions based on party affiliation and support * * *.

[Affirmed in part, reversed in part, and remanded.]

[The concurring opinion of JUSTICE STEVENS, responding to JUSTICE SCALIA'S dissent, is omitted.]

JUSTICE SCALIA, with whom THE CHIEF JUSTICE [REHNQUIST] and JUSTICE KENNEDY join, and with whom JUSTICE O'CONNOR joins [except as to the first paragraph reprinted here], dissenting. * * *

* * * The provisions of the Bill of Rights were designed to restrain transient majorities from impairing long-recognized personal liberties. They did not create by implication novel individual rights overturning accepted political norms. Thus, when a practice not expressly prohibited by the text of the Bill of Rights bears the endorsement of a long tradition of open, widespread, and unchallenged use that dates back to the beginning of the Republic, we have no proper basis for striking it down. Such a venerable and accepted tradition is not to be laid on the examining table and scrutinized for its conformity to some abstract principle of First Amendment adjudication devised by this Court. To the contrary, such traditions are themselves the stuff out of which the Court's principles are to be formed. They are, in these uncertain areas, the very points of reference by which the legitimacy or illegitimacy of *other* practices are to be figured out. When it appears that the latest "rule," or "three-part test," or "balancing test" devised by the Court has placed us on a collision course with such a landmark practice, it is the former that must be recalculated by us, and not the latter that must be abandoned by our citizens. I know of no other way to formulate a constitutional jurisprudence that reflects, as it should, the principles adhered to, over time, by the American people, rather than those favored by the personal (and necessarily shifting) philosophical dispositions of a majority of this Court. * * *

Even accepting the Court's own mode of analysis, however, and engaging in "balancing" a tradition that ought to be part of the scales, *Elrod, Branti,* and today's extension of them seem to me wrong.

The Court limits patronage on the ground that the individual's interest in uncoerced belief and expression outweighs the systemic interests invoked to justify the practice. The opinion indicates that the government may prevail only if it proves that the practice is "narrowly tailored to further vital government interests."

That strict-scrutiny standard finds no support in our cases. * * * When dealing with its own employees, the government may not act in a manner that is "patently arbitrary or discriminatory," but its regulations are valid if they bear a "rational connection" to the governmental end sought to be served, *Kelley* v. *Johnson,* 425 U.S. 238, 247 (1976).

In particular, restrictions on speech by public employees are not judged by the test applicable to similar restrictions on speech by nonemployees. We have said that "[a] governmental employer may subject its employees to such special restrictions on free expression as are reasonably necessary to promote effective government." *Brown* v. *Glines,* 444 U.S. 348, 356, n.13 (1980). In *Public Workers* v. *Mitchell,* 330 U.S., at 101, upholding provisions of the Hatch Act which prohibit political activities by federal employees, we said that "it is not necessary that the act regulated be anything more than an act reasonably deemed by Congress to interfere with the efficiency of the public service." * * *

Since the government may dismiss an employee for political *speech* "reasonably deemed by Congress to interfere with the efficiency of the public service," *Public Workers* v. *Mitchell*, it follows, *a fortiori*, that the government may dismiss an employee for political *affiliation* if "reasonably necessary to promote effective government." * * * For purposes of my ensuing discussion, however, I will apply a less permissive standard that seems more in accord with our general "balancing" test: Can the governmental advantages of this employment practice reasonably be deemed to outweigh its "coercive" effects? * * *

* * * The Court holds that the governmental benefits of patronage cannot reasonably be thought to outweigh its "coercive" effects (even the lesser "coercive" effects of patronage hiring as opposed to patronage firing) not merely in 1990 in the State of Illinois, but at any time in any of the numerous political subdivisions of this vast country. It seems to me that that categorical pronouncement reflects a naive vision of politics and an inadequate appreciation of the systemic effects of patronage in promoting political stability and facilitating the social and political integration of previously powerless groups.

The whole point of my dissent is that the desirability of patronage is a policy question to be decided by the people's representatives; I do not mean, therefore, to endorse that system. But in order to demonstrate that a legislature could reasonably determine that its benefits outweigh its "coercive" effects, I must describe those benefits as the proponents of patronage see them: As Justice Powell discussed at length in his *Elrod* dissent, patronage stabilizes political parties and prevents excessive political fragmentation—both of which are results in which States have a strong governmental interest. Party strength requires the efforts of the rank and file, especially in "the dull periods between elections," to perform such tasks as organizing precincts, registering new voters, and providing constituent services. Even the most enthusiastic supporter of a party's program will shrink before such drudgery, and it is folly to think that ideological conviction alone will motivate sufficient numbers to keep the party going through the off years. * * *

The Court simply refuses to acknowledge the link between patronage and party discipline, and between that and party success. * * * It is unpersuasive to claim, as the Court does, that party workers are obsolete because campaigns are now conducted through media and other money-intensive means. Those techniques have supplemented but not supplanted personal contacts. Certainly they have not made personal contacts unnecessary in campaigns for the lower level offices that are the foundations of party strength, nor have they replaced the myriad functions performed by party regulars not directly related to campaigning. And to the extent such techniques have replaced older methods of campaigning (partly in response to the limitations the Court has placed on patronage), the political system is not clearly better off. Increased reliance on money-intensive campaign techniques tends to entrench those in power much more effectively than patronage—but without the attendant benefit of strengthening the party system. A challenger can more easily obtain the support of party workers (who can expect to be rewarded even if the candidate loses—if not this year, then the next) than the financial support of political action committees (which will generally support incumbents, who are likely to prevail).

It is self-evident that eliminating patronage will significantly undermine party discipline; and that as party discipline wanes, so will the strength of the two-party system. But, says the Court, "[p]olitical parties have already survived the substantial decline in patronage employment practices in this century." This is almost verbatim what was said in *Elrod.* Fourteen years later it seems much less convincing. Indeed, now that we have witnessed, in 18 of the last 22 years, an Executive Branch of the Federal Government under the control of one party while the Congress is entirely or (for two years) partially within the control of the other party; now that we have undergone the most recent federal election, in which 98% of the incumbents, of whatever party, were returned to office; and now that we have seen elected officials changing their political affiliation with unprecedented readiness, the statement that "political parties have already survived" has a positively whistling-in-the-graveyard character to it. Parties have assuredly survived—but as what? As the forges upon which many of the essential compromises of American political life are hammered out? Or merely as convenient vehicles for the conducting of national Presidential elections?

The patronage system does not, of course, merely foster political parties in general; it fosters the two-party system in particular. When getting a job, as opposed to effectuating a particular substantive policy, is an available incentive for party workers, those attracted by that incentive are likely to work for the party that has the best chance of displacing the "ins," rather than for some splinter group that has a more attractive political philosophy but little hope of success. Not only is a two-party system more likely to emerge, but the differences between those parties are more likely to be moderated, as each has a relatively greater interest in appealing to a majority of the electorate and a relatively lesser interest in furthering philosophies or programs that are far from the mainstream. The stabilizing effects of such a system are obvious. In the context of electoral laws we have approved the States' pursuit of such stability, and their avoidance of the "splintered parties and unrestrained factionalism [that] may do significant damage to the fabric of government." *Storer* v. *Brown*, 415 U.S. 724, 736 (1974) [p. 513] (upholding law disqualifying persons from running as independents if affiliated with a party in the past year).

Equally apparent is the relatively destabilizing nature of a system in which candidates cannot rely upon patronage-based party loyalty for their campaign support, but must attract workers and raise funds by appealing to various interest groups. * * *

Patronage, moreover, has been a powerful means of achieving the social and political integration of excluded groups. By supporting and ultimately dominating a particular party "machine," racial and ethnic minorities have—on the basis of their politics rather than their race or ethnicity—acquired the patronage awards the machine had power to confer. No one disputes the historical accuracy of this observation, and there is no reason to think that patronage can no longer serve that function. The abolition of patronage, however, prevents groups that have only recently obtained political power, especially blacks, from following this path to economic and social advancement. * * *

While the patronage system has the benefits argued for above, it also has undoubted disadvantages. It facilitates financial corruption, such as salary kickbacks and partisan political activity on government-paid time. It reduces the efficiency of government, because it creates incentives to hire more and less-qualified workers and because highly qualified workers are reluctant to accept jobs that may only last until the next election. And, of course, it applies some greater or lesser inducement for individuals to join and work for the party in power.

To hear the Court tell it, this last is the greatest evil. That is not my view, and it has not historically been the view of the American people. Corruption and inefficiency, rather than abridgment of liberty, have been the major criticisms leading to enactment of the civil service laws—for the very good reason that the patronage system does not have as harsh an effect upon conscience, expression, and association as the Court suggests. As described above, it is the nature of the pragmatic, patronage-based, two-party system to build alliances and to suppress rather than foster ideological tests for participation in the division of political "spoils." What the patronage system ordinarily demands of the party worker is loyalty to, and activity on behalf of, the organization itself rather than a set of political beliefs. He is generally free to urge *within the organization* the adoption of any political position; but if that position is rejected he must vote and work for the party nonetheless. The diversity of political expression (other than expression of party loyalty) is channeled, in other words, to a different stage—to the contests for party endorsement rather than the partisan elections. It is undeniable, of course, that the patronage system entails some constraint upon the expression of views, particularly at the partisan-election stage, and considerable constraint upon the employee's right to associate with the other party. It greatly exaggerates these, however, to describe them as a general "coercion of belief." Indeed, it greatly exaggerates them to call them "coercion" at all, since we generally make a distinction between inducement and compulsion. The public official offered a bribe is not "coerced" to violate the law, and the private citizen offered a patronage job is not "coerced" to work for the party. In sum, I do not deny that the patronage system influences or redirects, perhaps to a substantial degree, individual political expression and political association. But like the many generations of Americans that have preceded us, I do not consider that a significant impairment of free speech or free association.

In emphasizing the advantages and minimizing the disadvantages (or at least minimizing one of the disadvantages) of the patronage system, I do not mean to suggest that that system is best. It may not always be; it may never be. To oppose our *Elrod-Branti* jurisprudence, one need not believe that the patronage system is *necessarily* desirable; nor even that it is always and everywhere *arguably* desirable; but merely that it is a political arrangement that may sometimes be a reasonable choice, and should therefore be left to the judgment of the people's elected representatives. The choice in question, I emphasize, is not just between patronage and a merit-based civil service, but rather among various combinations of the two that may suit different political units and different eras: permitting patronage hiring, for example, but prohibiting patronage dismissal; permitting patronage in most municipal agencies but prohibiting it in the police department; or permitting it in the mayor's office but prohibiting it everywhere else. I find it impossible to say that, always and everywhere, all of these choices fail our "balancing" test.

The last point explains why *Elrod* and *Branti* should be overruled, rather than merely not extended. Even in the field of constitutional adjudication, where the pull of *stare decisis* is at its weakest, one is reluctant to depart from precedent. But when that precedent is not only wrong, not only recent, not only contradicted by a long prior tradition, but also has proved unworkable in practice, then all reluctance ought to disappear. In my view that is the situation here. Though unwilling to leave it to the political process to draw the line between desirable and undesirable patronage, the Court has neither been prepared to rule that no such line exists (*i.e.*, that *all* patronage is unconstitutional) nor able to design the line itself in a manner that judges, lawyers, and public employees can understand. *Elrod* allowed patronage dismissals of persons in "policymaking" or "confidential" positions. *Branti* retreated from that formulation, asking instead "whether the hiring authority can demonstrate that party affiliation is an appropriate requirement for the effective performance of the public office involved." What that means is anybody's guess. * * *

Since the current doctrine leaves many employees utterly in the dark about whether their jobs are protected, they are likely to play it safe. On the other side, the exception was designed to permit the government to implement its electoral mandate. But unless the government is fairly sure that dismissal is permitted, it will leave the politically uncongenial official in place, since an incorrect decision will expose it to lengthy litigation and a large damages award, perhaps even against the responsible officials personally.

This uncertainty and confusion are not the result of the fact that *Elrod*, and then *Branti*, chose the wrong "line." My point is that there is no right line — or at least no right line that can be nationally applied and that is known by judges. Once we reject as the criterion a long political tradition showing that party-based employment is entirely permissible, yet are unwilling (as any reasonable person must be) to replace it with the principle that party-based employment is entirely impermissible, we have left the realm of law and entered the domain of political science, seeking to ascertain when and where the undoubted benefits of political hiring and firing are worth its undoubted costs. The answer to that will vary from State to State, and indeed from city to city, even if one rejects out of hand (as the *Branti* line does) the benefits associated with party stability. Indeed, the answer will even vary from year to year. During one period, for example, it may be desirable for the manager of a municipally owned public utility to be a career specialist, insulated from the political system. During another, when the efficient operation of that utility or even its very existence has become a burning political issue, it may be desirable that he be hired and fired on a political basis. The appropriate "mix" of party-based employment is a political question if there ever was one, and we should give it back to the voters of the various political units to decide, through civil service legislation crafted to suit the time and place, which mix is best.

Even were I not convinced that *Elrod* and *Branti* were wrongly decided, I would hold that they should not be extended beyond their facts, viz., actual discharge of employees for their political affiliation. Those cases invalidated patronage firing in order to prevent the "restraint it places on freedoms of belief and association." The loss of one's current livelihood is an appreciably greater constraint than such other disappointments as the failure to obtain a promotion or selection for an uncongenial transfer. * * *

Notes and Questions

1. Justices Brennan, Powell, and Scalia engaged in a lively debate in *Elrod*, *Branti*, and *Rutan* over the importance of patronage for the well-being of political parties. Who had the better of that argument? In that regard, consider Cynthia Grant Bowman, *"We Don't Want Anybody Anybody Sent": The Death of Patronage Hiring in Chicago*, 86 Nw. U. L. Rev. 57 (1991), which contends that in practice, political patronage has not been generally beneficial to political parties. For example, Bowman argues that, in many cities, political patronage often did not aid disadvantaged immigrant and minority groups, in part due to the limited number of jobs that could be filled by such patronage.

2. In their dissenting opinions, Justice Powell and Justice Scalia made much of the capacity of patronage to promote the two-party system. How significant do you think the government interest is in limiting the number of competing parties? *See* Chapter 6, § B, *supra*.

3. Assuming it is proper for the government to promote a stable two-party system, is patronage necessary to achieve that end? Duverger's Law holds that an electoral structure of single-member districts with plurality winners itself encourages the development of two (and only two) centrist parties. The "Law" is not universal—regional parties have been successful in nations that use single-member, first-past-the-post systems—but perhaps it indicates that the viability of the two-party system is not jeopardized by the *Elrod/Branti/Rutan* holdings. *See generally* William H. Riker, *The Two-Party System and Duverger's Law: An Essay on the History of Political Science*, 76 Am. Pol. Sci. Rev. 753 (1982); Maurice Duverger, *Factors in a Two-Party and Multiparty System*, in Party Politics and Pressure Groups 23 (1972).

4. In the latter part of the twentieth century, many political campaigns at the national, state, and local levels have been characterized as candidate-driven with regard to strategy, fund-raising, and the mobilization of workers, with the party

itself taking a largely secondary role. Is it fair to attribute, even in part, this decline of the power of political parties to cases like *Elrod* and its progeny? Or did these cases mainly follow rather than cause this trend? For an argument in favor of the latter view, see Richard L. Hasen, *Patronage*, in 4 ENCYCLOPEDIA OF THE AMERICAN CONSTITUTION 1885, 1886 (Leonard W. Levy & Kenneth L. Karst eds., 2d ed. 2000).

5. Whatever the precise linkage between patronage and the health of political parties, one apparent effect of *Elrod* and its progeny was to route patronage away from government jobs and toward government contracts with private firms. This trend was exacerbated by stagnation or declines in public employment, and increasing efforts to privatize certain traditionally governmental functions. *See* Cynthia Grant Bowman, *The Supreme Court's Patronage Decisions and the Theory and Practice of Politics*, in THE U.S. SUPREME COURT AND THE ELECTORAL PROCESS 126, 140–42 (David K. Ryden ed., 2d ed. 2002). Should patronage in contracting be treated the same way as patronage in employment?

The Supreme Court confronted this issue in the companion cases of *Board of County Commissioners, Wabaunsee County v. Umbehr*, 518 U.S. 668 (1996), and *O'Hare Truck Service v. City of Northlake*, 518 U.S. 712 (1996). In *Umbehr*, the Court held that when a county canceled a trash-hauling contract, allegedly because of the hauler's criticism of the county, the hauler had a cause of action for a violation of his First Amendment rights. In *O'Hare*, the Court held that an independent contractor, allegedly dropped from a regularly used list due to the failure to make campaign contributions to the mayor, also had a cause of action for a violation of free-speech rights. In both cases, the Court balanced the interests of the government to contract against the free-speech rights of contractors, drawing in part on cases such as *Pickering v. Board of Education*, 391 U.S. 563 (1968), involving public employees. Such a balancing approach had not been used in *Elrod*, *Branti*, or *Rutan*; *O'Hare* explained that in *Elrod*, *Branti*, and *Rutan*, the employment decisions had been based on a "raw test of political affiliation," rather than on free speech. Justice Scalia, joined by Justice Thomas, dissented in both *Umbehr* and *O'Hare*. Chief Justice Rehnquist, Justice Kennedy, and Justice O'Connor, each of whom had dissented in *Rutan*, were in the majority in both cases; the latter two Justices wrote the majority opinions in *O'Hare* and *Umbehr*, respectively. In his dissent, Justice Scalia approved of the use of a *Pickering*-type balancing test to resolve those cases, but argued that *Umbehr* and *O'Hare* were incoherent in attempting to distinguish intrusions on rights of "free speech" (to which balancing applied) and of political affiliation (to which the *Elrod/Branti/Rutan* rules applied).

6. In *Rutan*, Justice Scalia pointed out the difficulties in determining the jobs for which political affiliation would be a relevant qualification. Consider how one court has grappled with this issue. The United States Court of Appeals for the Sixth Circuit considered the following government jobs to fall within the exception: (1) positions specifically named in law to which discretionary authority is granted concerning law enforcement or policy "of political concern"; (2) positions to which a significant

amount of such discretionary authority has been explicitly or implicitly delegated; (3) confidential advisors to such position-holders; or (4) positions that are filled by balancing out political party representation or by balancing out selections made by government parties. *McCloud v. Testa*, 97 F.3d 1536, 1557 (6th Cir. 1996). The Sixth Circuit later clarified that a court should consider the inherent duties of a position, rather than the actual tasks undertaken by an employee, and a position need not fit perfectly into one of these categories in order to fit under the exception. *Silberstein v. City of Dayton*, 440 F.3d 306, 319 (6th Cir. 2006). How easy or difficult is it to apply these multi-factor tests?

7. *Problem.* Analyze whether persons holding the following government positions should receive First Amendment protection against patronage-based dismissals:

A. Assistant county attorneys, charged with "representing the County in court cases and in the performance of other legal work." *See Gordon v. County of Rockland*, 110 F.3d 886 (2d Cir. 1997); *Fazio v. City and County of San Francisco*, 125 F.3d 1328 (9th Cir. 1997); *Finkelstein v. Bergna*, 924 F.2d 1449 (9th Cir. 1991). *See also Shade v. Rackauckas*, 2004 Cal. App. Unpub. LEXIS 7691 (Cal. Ct. App. 2004) (drawing a distinction between "assistant district attorneys" and "senior deputy district attorneys" and characterizing only the former as possessing policymaking responsibilities).

B. An attorney employed by a private firm that does work for the city attorney, fired after public officials told the firm that it would lose City work unless the plaintiff's political opposition to the mayor ceased. *See Biggs v. Best*, 189 F.3d 989 (9th Cir. 1999).

C. Deputy sheriff. *Compare Hall v. Tollett*, 128 F.3d 418 (6th Cir. 1997) (granting protection), *with Cutcliffe v. Cochran*, 117 F.3d 1353 (11th Cir. 1997), *and Upton v. Thompson*, 930 F.2d 1209 (7th Cir. 1991) (denying it). *See also DiRuzza v. County of Tehama*, 206 F.3d 1304 (9th Cir. 2000).

D. Chief deputy sheriff, which differs from the position of deputy sheriff only in that the chief deputy would assume the responsibilities of the sheriff if the sheriff were unable to perform. *See Hall*, 128 F.3d at 425–26.

E. Correctional officer. *See Flenner v. Sheahan*, 107 F.3d 459 (7th Cir. 1997).

F. Administrative assistant to the mayor. *Faughender v. City of North Olmsted*, 927 F.2d 909 (6th Cir. 1991).

G. Administrative assistants in the county prosecutor's office. *See Hobler v. Brueher*, 325 F.3d 1145 (9th Cir. 2003).

H. Administrative assistant to the county engineer or the state department of transportation. *See Smith v. Sushka*, 117 F.3d 965 (6th Cir. 1997); *Rice v. Ohio Department of Transportation*, 14 F.3d 1133 (6th Cir. 1994).

I. Director of administrative services for the state treasurer's office. *See Garcia-Montoya v. State Treasurer's Office*, 16 P.3d 1084 (N.M. 2001).

8. *United Public Workers v. Mitchell* opined that "a regulation providing that no Republican . . . shall be appointed to federal office" would be unconstitutional. 330 U.S. at 100. If you think the Court was wrong in *Elrod*, *Branti*, and *Rutan* to construct a constitutional right against the use of patronage as a qualification for certain types of government service, do you also disagree with *Mitchell's* dictum?

9. In a portion of his *Rutan* dissent not reprinted here, Justice Scalia wryly observed that federal judges, many of whom were nominated by Presidents based on political affiliation, were now holding that public officials could not hire or fire based on such affiliations. If *state* judges are chosen based, in whole or in part, on their political affiliation, does that violate the rights of lawyers who are excluded from judicial appointments because they do not share such affiliations? In many states, for example, judicial vacancies are filled by gubernatorial appointment, even in states that hold judicial elections at the end of a judge's term. Governors often fill such vacancies based on political affiliation, that is, restricting consideration to lawyers from their parties.

In *Newman v. Voinovich*, 986 F.2d 159 (6th Cir. 1993), a Republican Ohio governor refused to consider Democratic applicants to fill a judicial vacancy. (Disclosure: One of the authors of this Casebook served as co-counsel for the plaintiff.) The court held that this practice did not state a claim under *Elrod* and *Branti*. State judges, the court held, fell under the exception of those cases. The court reasoned that "judges are policymakers because their political beliefs influence and dictate their decisions on important jurisprudential matters." *Id.* at 163. *See also Kurowski v. Krajewski*, 848 F.2d 767, 770 (7th Cir. 1988) (holding that judicial appointments may be based on party affiliation because "[a] judge both makes and implements governmental policy"). Did *Newman* properly apply the exception as described in *Branti*? Is "party affiliation * * * an appropriate requirement for the effective performance" of a judicial office? Should it matter that judges work in a branch of government separate from the appointing authority? Or that the state has, in effect, chosen to permit the governor to take political considerations into account in filling judicial vacancies? Or that, under Ohio law, judicial elections are officially nonpartisan? For discussion, see Michael E. Solimine, *Constitutional Restrictions on the Partisan Appointment of Federal and State Judges*, 61 U. Cin. L. Rev. 955 (1993).

A similar controversy arose in a challenge to provisions of the Delaware Constitution. Those provisions mandated that certain courts with even numbers of judges be comprised of equal numbers of judges from the two major parties, and that other courts with odd numbers of judges be comprised of a bare majority from one major party and the remainder from the other major party. Thus, members of the "wrong" political party were ineligible to fill certain vacancies, and both independents and members of third parties were ineligible for all of the judgeships. The Third Circuit, in *Adams v. Governor of Delaware*, 922 F.3d 166 (3d Cir.), *cert. granted sub nom. Carney v. Adams*, 140 S. Ct. 602 (2019), held the provisions invalid. The *Adams* court, expressly disagreeing with *Newman* and *Kurowski*, held that state judges "are not policymakers because whatever decisions judges make in a given case relates [*sic*] to the case under review and not to partisan political interests." 922 F.3d at 169. According to the Third Circuit, the policymaking exception under *Elrod* and *Branti* applies only to those "employees whose jobs cannot be performed effectively except by someone who shares the political beliefs of the appointing authority." *Id.* at 180 (internal quotation marks and brackets omitted). Because judges were capable of performing their functions despite a political disagreement with the appointing governor, the court struck down the partisan-balance provisions. Did the court apply the proper standard for determining whether partisan affiliation was an appropriate criterion for appointment? If the Third Circuit was right that partisanship is an unconstitutional criterion on which to evaluate judges, is it unconstitutional for governors and presidents to appoint judges based in part on their commitment to the party in power? Or is there some basis for saying that the Delaware provision violated the First Amendment because it rendered some people ineligible for a judgeship based solely on their party membership, even if they would not have been appointed anyway?

Several agencies (the Federal Election Commission among them) are subject to statutory restrictions on the party affiliations of their members. The FEC's statute, for example, provides that "[n]o more than 3 members of the Commission * * * may be affiliated with the same political party." 52 U.S.C. § 30106(a)(1). Note, however, that such a statute does not restrict the appointments to Republicans and Democrats (and, in fact, as of April 2020, one current member of the FEC, Steven Walther, is an independent). Even if it is constitutional to forbid one party from having more than a bare majority on an agency or a court, does the Delaware Constitution violate the First Amendment because it completely bars independents and members of third parties from becoming judges?

If independents and third parties are guaranteed seats in a government body, does that violate the rights of people who choose to affiliate with a major party? In *Daunt v. Benson*, 956 F.3d 396 (6th Cir. 2020), an amendment to the Michigan Constitution established an independent redistricting commission comprised of four Republicans, four Democrats, and five members unaffiliated with either major party. The court upheld the commission's structure over a claim that excluding people from certain positions because of their party affiliation violated the First Amendment. *See also Hechinger v. Martin*, 411 F. Supp. 650 (D.D.C. 1976) (three-judge court) (upholding a law guaranteeing at least some representation on the D.C. Council to political minorities), *summarily aff'd*, 429 U.S. 1030 (1977); *LoFrisco v. Schaffer*, 341 F. Supp. 743 (D. Conn.) (similarly upholding a law guaranteeing representation for political minorities by limiting the number of candidates a party may nominate), *summarily aff'd*, 409 U.S. 972 (1972).

10. Relatedly, does the First Amendment protect administrative-law judges from dismissal based on political ideology or affiliation? *See Roldan-Plumey v. Cerezo-Suarez*, 115 F.3d 58 (1st Cir. 1997). What about domestic-relations-court referees? *See Mumford v. Zieba*, 4 F.3d 429 (6th Cir. 1993).

Chapter 8

Campaign Finance

A. Introduction

Perhaps no issue in the field of election law has been so contentious for so long as that of campaign finance.

In a 1997 interview, former House Minority Leader Richard Gephardt (D-Mo.) stated, "What we have is two important values in direct conflict: freedom of speech, and our desire for healthy campaigns in a healthy democracy." Nancy Gibbs, *The Wake Up Call*, Time, Feb. 3, 1997, at 22. Although Gephardt was often criticized for suggesting that these values were in conflict, in fact his comment well summed up the debate. There is virtually unanimous agreement that the purpose of the First Amendment is to "protect the free discussion of governmental affairs," *Mills v. Alabama*, 384 U.S. 214, 218 (1966). Yet many Americans are deeply concerned when politicians must solicit large sums of cash to finance their political campaigns. This system of campaign funding is often perceived to foster political corruption and to create political inequality inconsistent with the principles behind one person, one vote.

As you read through the cases in this Chapter, you should see that the tension between free speech, on the one hand, and anti-corruption and equality concerns, on the other, is a constant theme. The opinions often carry an edge rarely found in judicial writing. Perhaps this is because campaign finance brings to the surface deep disagreements not only about the proper mode of constitutional interpretation, but about theories of democratic representation, about the meaning of political equality, and about our fundamental attitudes towards government.

Further confusing the debate is that the goals Americans set for their campaign-finance system are often at cross-purposes. For example, caps on campaign spending free officeholders from the burden of fundraising, but can also reduce the flow of communication needed for a well informed electorate. Disclosure of campaign contributions provides information to the electorate but compromises privacy and perhaps even the notion of a secret ballot. And partisan politics always hovers in the background, for few areas of law so directly affect partisan prospects. Is it best, then, to leave balancing of these concerns to the legislature, which claims particular familiarity with campaigns and elections? Or does the unique opportunity for self-interested legislators to manipulate the law for partisan or personal advantage suggest a particularly strong need for judicial skepticism of legislative enactments?

B. Basic Principles

At the core of most campaign-finance regulation systems are restrictions on contributions to political campaigns. Although there have been some proposals to address political inequality, and even corruption, through public-financing plans that do not rely on limitations on contributions and spending, these are the exception. *See* Joel Fleishman & Pope McCorkle, *Level Up Rather than Level Down: Towards a New Theory of Campaign Finance*, 52 J.L. & Pol. 211 (1984); Bruce Ackerman & Ian Ayres, Voting with Dollars: A New Paradigm for Campaign Finance (2002). Most proposals for reform and, more importantly, virtually all laws in the United States, have been built around restrictions on contributions to candidates, parties, campaigns, or other political organizations, and in some cases, around limits on expenditures.

For many years, the Supreme Court avoided the First Amendment issues raised by campaign-finance regulations. In *United States v. Newberry*, 256 U.S. 232 (1921), a lower court convicted Truman Newberry, a candidate in Michigan's Republican primary for the U.S. Senate, of violating the Corrupt Practices Act by contributing $100,000 (approximately $1.7 million in 2020 dollars) to his own campaign, in violation of limits existing in Michigan state law.[a] A divided Supreme Court reversed on the ground that the constitutional authority to regulate the "Times, Places and Manner" of elections did not extend to primaries, which it viewed as private affairs. (This holding would be overruled in *United States v. Classic*, 313 U.S. 299 (1941), one of the "White Primary Cases." *See* Chapter 5, § B.)

In *United States v. Congress of Industrial Organizations*, 335 U.S. 106 (1948), the lower court held that a provision of the Taft-Hartley Act prohibiting corporations and unions from making political contributions or expenditures was unconstitutional insofar as it applied to political commentary, editorials, and endorsements in a newspaper published by a union for its members' benefit. The Supreme Court affirmed without reaching the constitutional issue. While four members of the Court—Justices Rutledge, Black, Douglas, and Murphy—would have found that the law did cover the publication in question and that it was unconstitutional, the majority, in an opinion authored by Justice Reed, concluded that the statute did not clearly prohibit "a trade journal, a house organ, or a newspaper published by a corporation, from expressing views on candidates or political proposals in the regular course of its publication."

In the following case, commonly referred to as *Auto Workers*, the Supreme Court again avoided ruling on the constitutionality of limitations on contributions and

---

a. Newberry, a founder of the Packard Automobile Company, defeated Ford Motor Company founder Henry Ford for the Republican nomination. Ford, however, also entered and won the Democratic primary, and Newberry defeated him a second time in the general election. Newberry was represented in the Supreme Court by former Justice and presidential candidate, and future Chief Justice, Charles Evans Hughes. Ford was a political ally of President Woodrow Wilson, who had defeated Hughes in the 1916 presidential race.

expenditures. However, the opinion, written by Justice Frankfurter, is important for the extensive history it presents of campaign-finance law. This history has been relied on by the Supreme Court in numerous later cases, although, as discussed in the Notes that follow, it has fallen into some disrepute in recent years.

United States v. International Union United Automobile, Aircraft and Agricultural Implement Workers of America (UAW-CIO)
Supreme Court of the United States
352 U.S. 567, 77 S. Ct. 529, 1 L. Ed. 2d 563 (1957)

Mr. Justice Frankfurter delivered the opinion of the Court [in which Mr. Justice Burton, Mr. Justice Clark, Mr. Justice Harlan, and Mr. Justice Brennan join].[b]

The issues tendered in this case are the construction and, ultimately, the constitutionality of 18 U.S.C. §610, an Act of Congress that prohibits corporations and labor organizations from making "a contribution or expenditure in connection with" any election for federal office. * * *

Appreciation of the circumstances that begot this statute is necessary for its understanding, and understanding of it is necessary for adjudication of the legal problems before us. Speaking broadly, what is involved here is the integrity of our electoral process, and, not less, the responsibility of the individual citizen for the successful functioning of that process. This case thus raises issues not less than basic to a democratic society.

The concentration of wealth consequent upon the industrial expansion in the post-Civil War era had profound implications for American life. The impact of the abuses resulting from this concentration gradually made itself felt by a rising tide of reform protest in the last decade of the nineteenth century. The Sherman Law was a response to the felt threat to economic freedom created by enormous industrial combines. The income tax law of 1894 reflected congressional concern over the growing disparity of income between the many and the few.

No less lively, although slower to evoke federal action, was popular feeling that aggregated capital unduly influenced politics, an influence not stopping short of corruption. * * *

In the [18]90's many States passed laws requiring candidates for office and their political committees to make public the sources and amounts of contributions to their campaign funds and the recipients and amounts of their campaign expenditures. The theory behind these laws was that the spotlight of publicity would discourage corporations from making political contributions and would thereby end their control over party policies. But these state publicity laws either became dead

---

b. This case was decided on March 11, 1957, before the Senate had confirmed Charles Whittaker to fill the seat vacated by Stanley Reed. Accordingly, only eight Justices participated. —Eds.

letters or were found to be futile. As early as 1894, the sober-minded Elihu Root saw the need for more effective legislation. He urged the Constitutional Convention of the State of New York to prohibit political contributions by corporations:

> "The idea is to prevent . . . the great railroad companies, the great insurance companies, the great telephone companies, the great aggregations of wealth from using their corporate funds, directly or indirectly, to send members of the legislature to these halls in order to vote for their protection and the advancement of their interests as against those of the public. It strikes at a constantly growing evil which has done more to shake the confidence of the plain people of small means of this country in our political institutions than any other practice which has ever obtained since the foundation of our Government. And I believe that the time has come when something ought to be done to put a check to the giving of $50,000 or $100,000 by a great corporation toward political purposes upon the understanding that a debt is created from a political party to it."

Concern over the size and source of campaign funds so actively entered the presidential campaign of 1904 that it crystallized popular sentiment for federal action to purge national politics of what was conceived to be the pernicious influence of "big money" campaign contributions. * * * President Theodore Roosevelt quickly responded to this national mood. In his annual message to Congress on December 5, 1905, he recommended that:

> "All contributions by corporations to any political committee or for any political purpose should be forbidden by law; directors should not be permitted to use stockholders' money for such purposes; and, moreover, a prohibition of this kind would be, as far as it went, an effective method of stopping the evils aimed at in corrupt practices acts."

Grist was added to the reformers' mill by the investigation of the great life insurance companies conducted by the Joint Committee of the New York Legislature, the Armstrong Committee, under the guidance of Charles Evans Hughes. The Committee's report, filed early in 1906, revealed that one insurance company alone had contributed almost $50,000 to a national campaign committee in 1904 and had given substantial amounts in preceding presidential campaigns. The Committee concluded:

> "Contributions by insurance corporations for political purposes should be strictly forbidden. Neither executive officers nor directors should be allowed to use the moneys paid for purposes of insurance in support of political candidates or platforms. . . . Whether made for the purpose of supporting political views or with the desire to obtain protection for the corporation, these contributions have been wholly unjustifiable. * * * The frank admission that moneys have been obtained for use in State campaigns upon the expectation that candidates thus aided in their election would support the

interests of the companies, has exposed both those who solicited the contributions and those who made them to severe and just condemnation."

Less than a month later the Committee on Elections of the House of Representatives began considering a number of proposals designed to cleanse the political process. Some bills prohibited political contributions by certain classes of corporations; some merely required disclosure of contributions; and others made bribery at elections a federal crime. The feeling of articulate reform groups was reflected at a public hearing held by the Committee. Perry Belmont, leader of a nation-wide organization advocating a federal publicity bill, stated:

"... this thing has come to the breaking point. We have had enough of it. We don't want any more secret purchase of organizations, which nullifies platforms, nullifies political utterances and the pledges made by political leaders in and out of Congress."

This view found strong support in the testimony of Samuel Gompers, President of the American Federation of Labor, who said, with respect to the publicity bill:

"* * * It is doubtful to my mind if the contributions and expenditures of vast sums of money in the nominations and elections for our public offices can continue to increase without endangering the endurance of our Republic in its purity and in its essence.

"... If the interests of any people are threatened by corruption in our public life or corruption in elections, surely it must of necessity be those, that large class of people, whom we for convenience term the wageworkers.

"[O]ne of the reasons for the absence of legislation of a liberal or sympathetic or just character, so far as it affects the interest of the wage-earners of America, can be fairly well traced with the growth of the corruption funds and the influences that are in operation during elections and campaigns. . . . I am under the impression that the patience of the American workingmen is about exhausted—

"... [If] we are really determined that our elections shall be free from the power of money and its lavish use and expenditure without an accounting to the conscience and the judgment of the people of America, we will have to pass some measure of this kind."

President Roosevelt's annual message of 1906 listed as the first item of congressional business a law prohibiting political contributions by corporations. Shortly thereafter, in 1907, Congress provided:

"That it shall be unlawful for any national bank, or any corporation organized by authority of any laws of Congress, to make a money contribution in connection with any election to any political office. It shall also be unlawful for any corporation whatever to make a money contribution in connection with any election at which Presidential and Vice-Presidential electors or a Representative in Congress is to be voted for or any election by any State legislature of a United States Senator."

As the historical background of this statute indicates, its aim was not merely to prevent the subversion of the integrity of the electoral process. Its underlying philosophy was to sustain the active, alert responsibility of the individual citizen in a democracy for the wise conduct of government.

This Act of 1907 was merely the first concrete manifestation of a continuing congressional concern for elections "free from the power of money." The 1909 Congress witnessed unsuccessful attempts to amend the Act to proscribe the contribution of anything of value and to extend its application to the election of state legislatures. The Congress of 1910 translated popular demand for further curbs upon the political power of wealth into a publicity law that required committees operating to influence the results of congressional elections in two or more States to report all contributions and disbursements and to identify contributors and recipients of substantial sums. That law also required persons who spent more than $50 annually for the purpose of influencing congressional elections in more than one State to report those expenditures if they were not made through a political committee. At the next session that Act was extended to require all candidates for the Senate and the House of Representatives to make detailed reports with respect to both nominating and election campaigns. The amendment also placed maximum limits on the amounts that congressional candidates could spend in seeking nomination and election, and forbade them from promising employment for the purpose of obtaining support. And in 1918 Congress made it unlawful either to offer or to solicit anything of value to influence voting.

This Court's decision in *Newberry* v. *United States*, 256 U.S. 232 [(1921)], invalidating federal regulation of Senate primary elections, led to the Federal Corrupt Practices Act of 1925, a comprehensive revision of existing legislation. The debates preceding that Act's passage reveal an attitude important to an understanding of the course of this legislation. Thus, Senator Robinson, one of the leaders of the Senate, said:

> "We all know . . . that one of the great political evils of the time is the apparent hold on political parties which business interests and certain organizations seek and sometimes obtain by reason of liberal campaign contributions. Many believe that when an individual or association of individuals makes large contributions for the purpose of aiding candidates of political parties in winning the elections, they expect, and sometimes demand, and occasionally, at least, receive, consideration by the beneficiaries of their contributions which not infrequently is harmful to the general public interest. It is unquestionably an evil which ought to be dealt with, and dealt with intelligently and effectively."

One of the means chosen by Congress to deal with this evil was § 313 of the 1925 Act, which strengthened the 1907 statute (1) by changing the phrase "money contribution" to "contribution" * * *; (2) by extending the prohibition on corporate contributions to the election to Congress of Delegates and Resident Commissioners; and (3) by penalizing the recipient of any forbidden contribution as well as the contributor.

When, in 1940, Congress moved to extend the Hatch Act, which was designed to free the political process of the abuses deemed to accompany the operation of a vast civil administration, its reforming zeal also led Congress to place further restrictions upon the political potentialities of wealth. Section 20 of the law amending the Hatch Act made it unlawful for any "political committee," as defined in the Act of 1925, to receive contributions of more than $3,000,000 or to make expenditures of more than that amount in any calendar year. And § 13 made it unlawful "for any person, directly or indirectly, to make contributions in an aggregate amount in excess of $5,000, during any calendar year, or in connection with any campaign for nomination or election, to or on behalf of any candidate for an elective Federal office" or any committee supporting such a candidate. The term "person" was defined to include any committee, association, organization or other group of persons. In offering § 13 from the Senate floor Senator Bankhead said:

> "We all know that money is the chief source of corruption. We all know that large contributions to political campaigns not only put the political party under obligation to the large contributors, who demand pay in the way of legislation, but we also know that large sums of money are used for the purpose of conducting expensive campaigns through the newspapers and over the radio; in the publication of all sorts of literature, true and untrue; and for the purpose of paying the expenses of campaigners sent out into the country to spread propaganda, both true and untrue."

The need for unprecedented economic mobilization propelled by World War II enormously stimulated the power of organized labor and soon aroused consciousness of its power outside its ranks. Wartime strikes gave rise to fears of the new concentration of power represented by the gains of trade unionism. And so the belief grew that, just as the great corporations had made huge political contributions to influence governmental action or inaction, whether consciously or unconsciously, the powerful unions were pursuing a similar course, and with the same untoward consequences for the democratic process. Thus, in 1943, when Congress passed the Smith-Connally Act to secure defense production against work stoppages, contained therein was a provision extending to labor organizations, for the duration of the war, § 313 of the Corrupt Practices Act. The testimony of Congressman Landis, author of this measure, before a subcommittee of the House Committee on Labor makes plain the dominant concern that evoked it:

> "[P]ublic opinion toward the conduct of labor unions is rapidly undergoing a change. The public thinks, and has a right to think, that labor unions, as public institutions should be granted the same rights and no greater rights than any other public group. My bill seeks to put labor unions on exactly the same basis, insofar as their financial activities are concerned, as corporations have been on for many years.

"... One of the matters upon which I sensed that the public was taking a stand opposite to that of labor leaders was the question of the handling of funds of labor organizations. The public was aroused by many rumors of huge war chests being maintained by labor unions, of enormous fees and dues being extorted from war workers, of political contributions to parties and candidates which later were held as clubs over the head of high Federal officials. * * *

Despite § 313's wartime application to labor organizations, Congress was advised of enormous financial outlays said to have been made by some unions in connection with the national elections of 1944. The Senate's Special Committee on Campaign Expenditures investigated, *inter alia*, the role of the Political Action Committee of the Congress of Industrial Organizations. The Committee found "no clear-cut violation of the Corrupt Practices Act on the part of the Political Action Committee" on the ground that it had made direct contributions only to candidates and political committees involved in state and local elections and federal primaries, to which the Act did not apply, and had limited its participation in federal elections to political "expenditures," as distinguished from "contributions" to candidates or committees. The Committee also investigated, on complaint of Senator Taft, the Ohio C.I.O. Council's distribution to the public at large of 200,000 copies of a pamphlet opposing the re-election of Senator Taft and supporting his rival. In response to the C.I.O.'s assertion that this was not a proscribed "contribution" but merely an "expenditure of its own funds to state its position to the world, exercising its right of free speech," ... the Committee requested the Department of Justice to bring a test case on these facts. It also recommended extension of § 313 to cover primary campaigns and nominating conventions. A minority of the Committee, Senators Ball and Ferguson, advocated further amendment of § 313 to proscribe "expenditures" as well as "contributions" in order to avoid the possibility of emasculation of the statutory policy through a narrow judicial construction of "contributions."

The 1945 Report of the House Special Committee to Investigate Campaign Expenditures expressed concern over the vast amounts that some labor organizations were devoting to politics[.] * * * Like the Senate Committee, it advocated extension of § 313 to primaries and nominating conventions, and noted the existence of a controversy over the scope of "contribution." The following year the House Committee made a further study of the activities of organizations attempting to influence the outcome of federal elections. It found that the Brotherhood of Railway Trainmen and other groups employed professional political organizers, sponsored partisan radio programs and distributed campaign literature. It concluded that:

"The intent and purpose of the provision of the act prohibiting any corporation or labor organization making any contribution in connection with any election would be wholly defeated if it were assumed that the term 'making any contribution' related only to the donating of money directly to a candidate, and excluded the vast expenditures of money in the activities herein shown to be engaged in extensively. Of what avail would a law be to prohibit the contributing direct to a candidate and yet permit the expenditure of large sums in his behalf?

"The committee is firmly convinced, after a thorough study of the provisions of the act, the legislative history of the same, and the debates on the said provisions when it was pending before the House, that the act was intended to prohibit such expenditures."

Accordingly, to prevent further evasion of the statutory policy, the Committee attached to its recommendation that the prohibition of contributions by labor organizations be made permanent the additional proposal that the statute

"be clarified so as to specifically provide that expenditures of money for salaries to organizers, purchase of radio time, and other expenditures by the prohibited organizations in connection with elections, constitute violations of the provisions of said section, whether or not said expenditures are with or without the knowledge or consent of the candidates."

Early in 1947 the Special Committee to Investigate Senatorial Campaign Expenditures in the 1946 elections, the Ellender Committee, urged similar action to "plug the existing loophole." * * *

Shortly thereafter, Congress again acted to protect the political process from what it deemed to be the corroding effect of money employed in elections by aggregated power. Section 304 of the labor bill introduced into the House by Representative Hartley in 1947, like the Ellender bill, embodied the changes recommended in the reports of the Senate and House Committees on Campaign Expenditures. It sought to amend § 313 of the Corrupt Practices Act to proscribe any "expenditure" as well as "any contribution," to make permanent § 313's application to labor organizations and to extend its coverage to federal primaries and nominating conventions. * * * In explaining § 304 to his colleagues, Senator Taft * * * said:

"* * * In this instance the words of the Smith-Connally Act have been somewhat changed in effect so as to plug up a loophole which obviously developed, and which, if the courts had permitted advantage to be taken of it, as a matter of fact, would absolutely have destroyed the prohibition against political advertising by corporations. If 'contribution' does not mean 'expenditure,' then a candidate for office could have his corporation friends publish an advertisement for him in the newspapers every day for a month before election. I do not think the law contemplated such a thing, but it was claimed that it did, at least when it applied to labor organizations. So, all we are doing here is plugging up the hole which developed, following the recommendation by our own Elections Committee, in the Ellender bill."

* * * [T]he bill subsequently became law despite the President's veto. It is this section of the statute that the District Court held did not reach the activities alleged in the indictment. * * *

[T]he indictment charged appellee with having used union dues to sponsor commercial television broadcasts designed to influence the electorate to select certain candidates for Congress in connection with the 1954 elections.

To deny that such activity, either on the part of a corporation or a labor organization, constituted an "expenditure in connection with any [federal] election" is to deny the long series of congressional efforts calculated to avoid the deleterious influences on federal elections resulting from the use of money by those who exercise control over large aggregations of capital. More particularly, this Court would have to ignore the history of the statute from the time it was first made applicable to labor organizations. As indicated by the reports of the Congressional Committees that investigated campaign expenditures, it was to embrace precisely the kind of indirect contribution alleged in the indictment that Congress amended § 313 to proscribe "expenditures." It is open to the Government to prove under this indictment activity by appellee that, except for an irrelevant difference in the medium of communication employed, is virtually indistinguishable from the Brotherhood of Railway Trainmen's purchase of radio time to sponsor candidates or the Ohio C.I.O.'s general distribution of pamphlets to oppose Senator Taft. Because such conduct was claimed to be merely "an expenditure [by the union] of its own funds to state its position to the world," the Senate and House Committees recommended and Congress enacted, as we have seen, the prohibition of "expenditures" as well as "contributions" to "plug the existing loophole." * * *

Appellee urges that if, as we hold, 18 U.S.C. § 610 embraces the activity alleged in the indictment, it offends several rights guaranteed by the Constitution.[2] The Government replies that the actual restraint upon union political activity imposed by the statute is so narrowly limited that Congress did not exceed its powers to protect the political process from undue influence of large aggregations of capital and to promote individual responsibility for democratic government. * * *

The wisdom of refraining from avoidable constitutional pronouncements * * * is peculiarly appropriate in the circumstances of this case. First of all, these questions come to us unillumined by the consideration of a single judge—we are asked to decide them in the first instance. [O]nly an adjudication on the merits can provide the concrete factual setting that sharpens the deliberative process especially demanded for constitutional decision. Finally, by remanding the case for trial it may well be that the Court will not be called upon to pass on the questions now raised. * * *

---

2. ". . . if such an expenditure is prohibited by 18 U.S.C. § 610, * * * the statute (i) abridges freedom of speech and of the press and the right peaceably to assemble and to petition; (ii) abridges the right to choose senators and representatives guaranteed by Article I, § 2 and the Seventeenth Amendment; (iii) creates an arbitrary and unlawful classification and discriminates against labor organizations in violation of the Fifth Amendment, and (iv) is vague and indefinite and fails to provide a reasonably ascertainable standard of guilt in violation of the Fifth and Sixth Amendments." Brief for appellee, pp. 2–3.

Because the District Court's erroneous interpretation of the statute led it to stop the prosecution prematurely, its judgment must be reversed and the case must be remanded to it for further proceedings not inconsistent with this opinion.

Reversed and remanded.

MR. JUSTICE DOUGLAS, with whom THE CHIEF JUSTICE [WARREN] and MR. JUSTICE BLACK join, dissenting.

We deal here with a problem that is fundamental to the electoral process and to the operation of our democratic society. It is whether a union can express its views on the issues of an election and on the merits of the candidates, unrestrained and unfettered by the Congress. The principle at stake is not peculiar to unions. It is applicable as well to associations of manufacturers, retail and wholesale trade groups, consumers' leagues, farmers' unions, religious groups and every other association representing a segment of American life and taking an active part in our political campaigns and discussions. It is as important an issue as has come before the Court, for it reaches the very vitals of our system of government.

Under our Constitution it is We The People who are sovereign. The people have the final say. The legislators are their spokesmen. The people determine through their votes the destiny of the nation. It is therefore important—vitally important—that all channels of communication be open to them during every election, that no point of view be restrained or barred, and that the people have access to the views of every group in the community.

In *United States* v. *C.I.O.*, 335 U.S. 106, 144 [(1948)], Mr. Justice Rutledge spoke of the importance of the First Amendment rights—freedom of expression and freedom of assembly—to the integrity of our elections. "The most complete exercise of those rights," he said, "is essential to the full, fair and untrammeled operation of the electoral process. To the extent they are curtailed the electorate is deprived of information, knowledge and opinion vital to its function."

What the Court does today greatly impairs those rights. It sustains an indictment charging no more than the use of union funds for broadcasting television programs that urge and endorse the selection of certain candidates for the Congress of the United States. The opinion of the Court places that advocacy in the setting of corrupt practices. The opinion generates an environment of evil-doing and points to the oppressions and misdeeds that have haunted elections in this country.

Making a speech endorsing a candidate for office does not, however, deserve to be identified with antisocial conduct. Until today political speech has never been considered a crime. The making of a political speech up to now has always been one of the preferred rights protected by the First Amendment. It usually costs money to communicate an idea to a large audience. But no one would seriously contend that the expenditure of money to print a newspaper deprives the publisher of freedom of the press. Nor can the fact that it costs money to make a speech—whether it be hiring a hall or purchasing time on the air—make the speech any the less an exercise of First Amendment rights. Yet this statute, as construed and applied in this indictment, makes criminal any "expenditure" by a union for the purpose of expressing its views on the issues of an election and the candidates. * * *

I would affirm the judgment dismissing the indictment.

Notes and Questions

1. For many years, the Supreme Court and lower courts uncritically quoted from Justice Frankfurter's history of campaign-finance laws. *See, e.g., McConnell v. Federal Election Commission*, 540 U.S. 93, 115–16, 136–37 (2003) [p. 829]. In recent years, however, legal scholars have challenged Justice Frankfurter's "heroic" account of the development of campaign-finance law. The most direct analysis of Frankfurter's opinion has come from Professor Allison Hayward, who has argued that Justice Frankfurter's opinion "avoided political context and truncated political and legislative history. What emerges from a more complete account is a messy, complicated record, dictated by political opportunism. At each step, reform was a way to capitalize on public sentiment and restrict political rivals' access to financial resources, using little debated legislative vehicles and parliamentary skill." Allison R. Hayward, *Revisiting the Fable of Reform*, 45 Harv. J. on Legis. 421, 422 (2008). In *Citizens United v. Federal Election Commission*, 558 U.S. 310 (2010) [p. 844], the Supreme Court, relying on Hayward's scholarship and an amicus brief filed by several campaign-finance scholars, declared the *United Auto Workers'* history "flawed." *Id.* at 363.

Others have similarly argued that most reform is best explained by efforts to gain partisan or ideological advantage and to protect incumbent legislators. *See* John Samples, The Fallacy of Campaign Finance Reform 189–232 (2006); Raymond J. La Raja, Small Change: Money, Political Parties, and Campaign Finance Reform 43–80 (2008). Professor Adam Winkler has argued that the primary motivation for the Tillman Act and early publicity acts had little to do with battling political corruption or inequality, but rather with protecting the rights of corporate shareholders and the reserves of insurance companies. Adam Winkler, *Other People's Money: Corporations, Agency Costs, and Campaign Finance Law*, 92 Geo. L.J. 871 (2004).

Should the motivations of legislators matter when determining the constitutionality of campaign-finance laws? Should it matter if the history of the law in question demonstrates concern for the "wise conduct of government" (Frankfurter), or the absence of "any exercise of reasoned policy judgment"? Hayward, *supra*, at 454. Does the legislative motive affect your attitude toward legislation in this area?

2. At the close of *Auto Workers*, Justice Frankfurter raised several issues that, he suggested, might be clarified by allowing the prosecution to continue:

> [W]as the broadcast paid for out of the general dues of the union membership or may the funds be fairly said to have been obtained on a voluntary

basis? Did the broadcast reach the public at large or only those affiliated with appellee? Did it constitute active electioneering or simply state the record of particular candidates on economic issues? Did the union sponsor the broadcast with the intent to affect the results of the election? * * *

352 U.S. at 592.

Do you agree that these issues could, or should, make a difference in determining the law's constitutionality? Why or why not?

3. Was Justice Frankfurter's cautious approach of avoiding constitutional adjudication the right choice? *Auto Workers* did not return to the Supreme Court. On November 6, 1957, a federal jury found the defendants not guilty on all counts. Hayward, *supra*, at 463. The failure of the prosecution in *Auto Workers* was, in fact, not atypical—in fact, between 1925 and 1971, there was not a single successful prosecution under the Federal Corrupt Practices Act. Frank Sorauf, Inside Campaign Finance: Myths and Realities 6 (1992).

In 1972, Congress completely revamped federal campaign-finance law with the passage of the Federal Election Campaign Act ("FECA").[c] In its original form, FECA relied primarily on disclosure of, rather than limits on, contributions. However, the law had scarcely taken effect before the Watergate scandal broke. Although the new disclosure requirements of FECA actually helped to break key parts of the Watergate scandal, *see* Herbert E. Alexander, Financing Politics: Money, Elections and Political Reform 30–32 (1992), the scandal provided the impetus for a more far-reaching law. The 1974 amendments to FECA effectively re-wrote the law from the ground up, including new limits on contributions and expenditures, new disclosure requirements, public financing of presidential campaigns, and the creation of a new, independent federal agency, the Federal Election Commission, to oversee enforcement.

The law was immediately challenged by a conglomeration of plaintiffs from across the political spectrum, including former Democratic presidential candidate Eugene McCarthy, Conservative Party U.S. Senator James Buckley, the Libertarian Party, the Mississippi Republican Party, the New York branch of the American Civil Liberties Union, the American Conservative Union, and many others. The Court of Appeals upheld all major parts of the Act. *Buckley v. Valeo*, 519 F.2d 821 (D.C. Cir. 1975). The ambitious scope of the law and the creation of a new enforcement commission made it difficult, if not impossible, for the Supreme Court to avoid the issues it had sidestepped in *Newberry*, *CIO*, and *Auto Workers*. The resulting decision, *Buckley v. Valeo*, 424 U.S. 1 (1976) (*per curiam*), is by some measures the

---

c. FECA was passed in February 1972, but is normally referred to as the Federal Election Campaign Act of 1971, when the bill was introduced.

longest Supreme Court opinion ever, and certainly the longest *per curiam* opinion.[d] More than forty years later, it remains the touchstone of campaign-finance law, and the starting point for virtually every Supreme Court or lower-court opinion on campaign finance. Below are substantial portions of the *Buckley* opinion, setting forth general principles and dealing with contribution and expenditure limits. Later in this Chapter, we will look at portions of *Buckley* dealing with public financing of campaigns, and in Chapter 9 we will examine disclosure of contributions and expenditures.

Buckley v. Valeo

Supreme Court of the United States
424 U.S. 1, 96 S. Ct. 612, 46 L. Ed. 2d 659 (1976)

PER CURIAM. [MR. JUSTICE BRENNAN, MR. JUSTICE STEWART, and MR. JUSTICE POWELL join this opinion in full, and MR. JUSTICE REHNQUIST joins all portions of the opinion excerpted here. MR. JUSTICE MARSHALL joins all but Part I-C-2. MR. JUSTICE BLACKMUN joins all but Part I-B. MR. CHIEF JUSTICE BURGER joins Part I-C.]

These appeals present constitutional challenges to the key provisions of the Federal Election Campaign Act of 1971 (Act), and related provisions of the Internal Revenue Code of 1954, all as amended in 1974. * * *

I. Contribution and Expenditure Limitations

The intricate statutory scheme adopted by Congress to regulate federal election campaigns includes restrictions on political contributions and expenditures that apply broadly to all phases of and all participants in the election process. The major contribution and expenditure limitations in the Act prohibit individuals from contributing more than $25,000 in a single year or more than $1,000 to any single candidate for an election campaign and from spending more than $1,000 a year "relative to a clearly identified candidate." Other provisions restrict a candidate's use of personal and family resources in his campaign and limit the overall amount that can be spent by a candidate in campaigning for federal office. * * *

A. General Principles

The Act's contribution and expenditure limitations operate in an area of the most fundamental First Amendment activities. Discussion of public issues and debate on the qualifications of candidates are integral to the operation of the system of government established by our Constitution. The First Amendment affords the broadest protection to such political expression in order "to assure [the] unfettered interchange of ideas for the bringing about of political and social changes desired by the people." *Roth* v. *United States*, 354 U.S. 476, 484 (1957). Although

---

d. For insight into the writing of the *Buckley* opinion, including information about which Justices were principally responsible for drafting which portions of the *per curiam* opinion, see Richard L. Hasen, *The Untold Drafting History of* Buckley v. Valeo, 2 ELECTION L.J. 241 (2003).

First Amendment protections are not confined to "the exposition of ideas," "there is practically universal agreement that a major purpose of that Amendment was to protect the free discussion of governmental affairs, . . . of course includ[ing] discussions of candidates." *Mills* v. *Alabama*, 384 U.S. 214, 218 (1966). This no more than reflects our "profound national commitment to the principle that debate on public issues should be uninhibited, robust, and wide-open," *New York Times Co.* v. *Sullivan*, 376 U.S. 254, 270 (1964). In a republic where the people are sovereign, the ability of the citizenry to make informed choices among candidates for office is essential, for the identities of those who are elected will inevitably shape the course that we follow as a nation. As the Court observed in *Monitor Patriot Co.* v. *Roy*, 401 U.S. 265, 272 (1971), "it can hardly be doubted that the constitutional guarantee has its fullest and most urgent application precisely to the conduct of campaigns for political office."

The First Amendment protects political association as well as political expression. The constitutional right of association explicated in *NAACP* v. *Alabama*, 357 U.S. 449, 460 (1958) [p. 919], stemmed from the Court's recognition that "[e]ffective advocacy of both public and private points of view, particularly controversial ones, is undeniably enhanced by group association." Subsequent decisions have made clear that the First and Fourteenth Amendments guarantee "freedom to associate with others for the common advancement of political beliefs and ideas," a freedom that encompasses "[t]he right to associate with the political party of one's choice."

It is with these principles in mind that we consider the primary contentions of the parties with respect to the Act's limitations upon the giving and spending of money in political campaigns. Those conflicting contentions could not more sharply define the basic issues before us. Appellees contend that what the Act regulates is conduct, and that its effect on speech and association is incidental at most. Appellants respond that contributions and expenditures are at the very core of political speech, and that the Act's limitations thus constitute restraints on First Amendment liberty that are both gross and direct.

In upholding the constitutional validity of the Act's contribution and expenditure provisions on the ground that those provisions should be viewed as regulating conduct, not speech, the Court of Appeals relied upon *United States* v. *O'Brien*, 391 U.S. 367 (1968). The *O'Brien* case involved a defendant's claim that the First Amendment prohibited his prosecution for burning his draft card because his act was "symbolic speech" engaged in as a "demonstration against the war and against the draft." On the assumption that "the alleged communicative element in O'Brien's conduct [was] sufficient to bring into play the First Amendment," the Court sustained the conviction because it found "a sufficiently important governmental interest in regulating the nonspeech element" that was "unrelated to the suppression of free expression" and that had an "incidental restriction on alleged First Amendment freedoms . . . no greater than [was] essential to the furtherance of that interest." *Id.*, at 376–377. The Court expressly emphasized that *O'Brien* was not a case "where the alleged governmental interest in regulating conduct arises in some measure because the communication allegedly integral to the conduct is itself thought to be harmful." *Id.*, at 382.

We cannot share the view that the present Act's contribution and expenditure limitations are comparable to the restrictions on conduct upheld in *O'Brien*. The expenditure of money simply cannot be equated with such conduct as destruction of a draft card. Some forms of communication made possible by the giving and spending of money involve speech alone, some involve conduct primarily, and some involve a combination of the two. Yet this Court has never suggested that the dependence of a communication on the expenditure of money operates itself to introduce a nonspeech element or to reduce the exacting scrutiny required by the First Amendment. For example, in *Cox* v. *Louisiana*, 379 U.S. 559 (1965), the Court contrasted picketing and parading with a newspaper comment and a telegram by a citizen to a public official. The parading and picketing activities were said to constitute conduct "intertwined with expression and association," whereas the newspaper comment and the telegram were described as a "pure form of expression" involving "free speech alone" rather than "expression mixed with particular conduct." *Id.*, at 563–564.

Even if the categorization of the expenditure of money as conduct were accepted, the limitations challenged here would not meet the *O'Brien* test because the governmental interests advanced in support of the Act involve "suppressing communication." The interests served by the Act include restricting the voices of people and interest groups who have money to spend and reducing the overall scope of federal election campaigns. Although the Act does not focus on the ideas expressed by persons or groups subjected to its regulations, it is aimed in part at equalizing the relative ability of all voters to affect electoral outcomes by placing a ceiling on expenditures for political expression by citizens and groups. Unlike *O'Brien*, where the Selective Service System's administrative interest in the preservation of draft cards was wholly unrelated to their use as a means of communication, it is beyond dispute that the interest in regulating the alleged "conduct" of giving or spending money "arises in some measure because the communication allegedly integral to the conduct is itself thought to be harmful."

Nor can the Act's contribution and expenditure limitations be sustained * * * [as] reasonable time, place, and manner regulations, which do not discriminate among speakers or ideas, in order to further an important governmental interest unrelated to the restriction of communication. * * * [T]he present Act's contribution and expenditure limitations impose direct quantity restrictions on political communication and association by persons, groups, candidates, and political parties in addition to any reasonable time, place, and manner regulations otherwise imposed.[17]

---

17. The nongovernmental appellees argue that just as the decibels emitted by a sound truck can be regulated consistently with the First Amendment, the Act may restrict the volume of dollars in political campaigns without impermissibly restricting freedom of speech. This comparison

A restriction on the amount of money a person or group can spend on political communication during a campaign necessarily reduces the quantity of expression by restricting the number of issues discussed, the depth of their exploration, and the size of the audience reached.[18] This is because virtually every means of communicating ideas in today's mass society requires the expenditure of money. The distribution of the humblest handbill or leaflet entails printing, paper, and circulation costs. Speeches and rallies generally necessitate hiring a hall and publicizing the event. The electorate's increasing dependence on television, radio, and other mass media for news and information has made these expensive modes of communication indispensable instruments of effective political speech.

The expenditure limitations contained in the Act represent substantial rather than merely theoretical restraints on the quantity and diversity of political speech. The $1,000 ceiling on spending "relative to a clearly identified candidate" would appear to exclude all citizens and groups except candidates, political parties, and the institutional press from any significant use of the most effective modes of communication.[20] Although the Act's limitations on expenditures by campaign organizations and political parties provide substantially greater room for discussion and debate, they would have required restrictions in the scope of a number of past congressional and Presidential campaigns and would operate to constrain campaigning by candidates who raise sums in excess of the spending ceiling.

By contrast with a limitation upon expenditures for political expression, a limitation upon the amount that any one person or group may contribute to a candidate or political committee entails only a marginal restriction upon the contributor's ability to engage in free communication. A contribution serves as a general expression of support for the candidate and his views, but does not communicate the underlying basis for the support. The quantity of communication by the contributor does not increase perceptibly with the size of his contribution, since the expression rests solely on the undifferentiated, symbolic act of contributing. At most, the size of the contribution provides a very rough index of the intensity of the contributor's support for the candidate. A limitation on the amount of money a person may give to a candidate or campaign organization thus involves little direct restraint on his political communication, for it permits the symbolic expression of support evidenced by a contribution but does not in any way infringe the contributor's freedom

---

underscores a fundamental misconception. [A] decibel restriction * * * limit[s] the manner of operating a soundtruck, but not the extent of its proper use. By contrast, the Act's dollar ceilings restrict the extent of the reasonable use of virtually every means of communicating information. * * *

18. Being free to engage in unlimited political expression subject to a ceiling on expenditures is like being free to drive an automobile as far and as often as one desires on a single tank of gasoline.

20. The record indicates that, as of January 1, 1975, one full-page advertisement in a daily edition of a certain metropolitan newspaper cost $6,971.04—almost seven times the annual limit on expenditures "relative to" a particular candidate imposed on the vast majority of individual citizens and associations.

to discuss candidates and issues. While contributions may result in political expression if spent by a candidate or an association to present views to the voters, the transformation of contributions into political debate involves speech by someone other than the contributor.

Given the important role of contributions in financing political campaigns, contribution restrictions could have a severe impact on political dialogue if the limitations prevented candidates and political committees from amassing the resources necessary for effective advocacy. There is no indication, however, that the contribution limitations imposed by the Act would have any dramatic adverse effect on the funding of campaigns and political associations.[23] The overall effect of the Act's contribution ceilings is merely to require candidates and political committees to raise funds from a greater number of persons and to compel people who would otherwise contribute amounts greater than the statutory limits to expend such funds on direct political expression, rather than to reduce the total amount of money potentially available to promote political expression.

The Act's contribution and expenditure limitations also impinge on protected associational freedoms. Making a contribution, like joining a political party, serves to affiliate a person with a candidate. In addition, it enables like-minded persons to pool their resources in furtherance of common political goals. The Act's contribution ceilings thus limit one important means of associating with a candidate or committee, but leave the contributor free to become a member of any political association and to assist personally in the association's efforts on behalf of candidates. And the Act's contribution limitations permit associations and candidates to aggregate large sums of money to promote effective advocacy. By contrast, the Act's $1,000 limitation on independent expenditures "relative to a clearly identified candidate" precludes most associations from effectively amplifying the voice of their adherents, the original basis for the recognition of First Amendment protection of the freedom of association. See *NAACP* v. *Alabama*, 357 U.S., at 460. The Act's constraints on the ability of independent associations and candidate campaign organizations to expend resources on political expression "is simultaneously an interference with the freedom of [their] adherents," *Sweezy* v. *New Hampshire*, 354 U.S. 234, 250 (1957) (plurality opinion).

In sum, although the Act's contribution and expenditure limitations both implicate fundamental First Amendment interests, its expenditure ceilings impose significantly more severe restrictions on protected freedoms of political expression and association than do its limitations on financial contributions.

---

23. Statistical findings agreed to by the parties reveal that approximately 5.1% of the $73,483,613 raised by the 1,161 candidates for Congress in 1974 was obtained in amounts in excess of $1,000. In 1974, two major-party senatorial candidates, Ramsey Clark and Senator Charles Mathias, Jr., operated large-scale campaigns on contributions raised under a voluntarily imposed $100 contribution limitation.

B. Contribution Limitations

1. The $1,000 Limitation on Contributions by Individuals and Groups to Candidates and Authorized Campaign Committees

Section 608(b) provides, with certain limited exceptions, that "no person shall make contributions to any candidate with respect to any election for Federal office which, in the aggregate, exceed $1,000." The statute defines "person" broadly to include "an individual, partnership, committee, association, corporation or any other organization or group of persons." The limitation reaches a gift, subscription, loan, advance, deposit of anything of value, or promise to give a contribution, made for the purpose of influencing a primary election, a Presidential preference primary, or a general election for any federal office.[24] The $1,000 ceiling applies regardless of whether the contribution is given to the candidate, to a committee authorized in writing by the candidate to accept contributions on his behalf, or indirectly via earmarked gifts passed through an intermediary to the candidate.[25] The restriction applies to aggregate amounts contributed to the candidate for each election—with primaries, run-off elections, and general elections counted separately and all Presidential primaries held in any calendar year treated together as a single election campaign. * * *

Appellants contend that the $1,000 contribution ceiling unjustifiably burdens First Amendment freedoms, employs overbroad dollar limits, and discriminates against candidates opposing incumbent officeholders and against minor-party candidates in violation of the Fifth Amendment. We address each of these claims of invalidity in turn.

(a)

As the general discussion in Part I-A indicated, the primary First Amendment problem raised by the Act's contribution limitations is their restriction of one aspect of the contributor's freedom of political association. * * * In view of the fundamental nature of the right to associate, governmental "action which may have the effect of curtailing the freedom to associate is subject to the closest scrutiny." Yet, it is clear that "[n]either the right to associate nor the right to participate in political activities is absolute." *CSC* v. *Letter Carriers*, 413 U.S. 548, 567 (1973) [p. 679]. Even a "'significant interference' with protected rights of political association" may be sustained if the State demonstrates a sufficiently important interest and employs means closely drawn to avoid unnecessary abridgment of associational freedoms.

Appellees argue that the Act's restrictions on large campaign contributions are justified by three governmental interests. According to the parties and *amici*, the

---

24. The Act exempts from the contribution ceiling the value of all volunteer services provided by individuals to a candidate or a political committee and excludes the first $500 spent by volunteers on certain categories of campaign-related activities. * * *

25. Expenditures by persons and associations that are "authorized or requested" by the candidate or his agents are treated as contributions under the Act.

primary interest served by the limitations and, indeed, by the Act as a whole, is the prevention of corruption and the appearance of corruption spawned by the real or imagined coercive influence of large financial contributions on candidates' positions and on their actions if elected to office. Two "ancillary" interests underlying the Act are also allegedly furthered by the $1,000 limits on contributions. First, the limits serve to mute the voices of affluent persons and groups in the election process and thereby to equalize the relative ability of all citizens to affect the outcome of elections. Second, it is argued, the ceilings may to some extent act as a brake on the skyrocketing cost of political campaigns and thereby serve to open the political system more widely to candidates without access to sources of large amounts of money.

It is unnecessary to look beyond the Act's primary purpose—to limit the actuality and appearance of corruption resulting from large individual financial contributions—in order to find a constitutionally sufficient justification for the $1,000 contribution limitation. Under a system of private financing of elections, a candidate lacking immense personal or family wealth must depend on financial contributions from others to provide the resources necessary to conduct a successful campaign. The increasing importance of the communications media and sophisticated mass-mailing and polling operations to effective campaigning make the raising of large sums of money an ever more essential ingredient of an effective candidacy. To the extent that large contributions are given to secure a political *quid pro quo* from current and potential office holders, the integrity of our system of representative democracy is undermined. Although the scope of such pernicious practices can never be reliably ascertained, the deeply disturbing examples surfacing after the 1972 election demonstrate that the problem is not an illusory one.

Of almost equal concern as the danger of actual *quid pro quo* arrangements is the impact of the appearance of corruption stemming from public awareness of the opportunities for abuse inherent in a regime of large individual financial contributions. In *CSC* v. *Letter Carriers*, the Court found that the danger to "fair and effective government" posed by partisan political conduct on the part of federal employees charged with administering the law was a sufficiently important concern to justify broad restrictions on the employees' right of partisan political association. Here, as there, Congress could legitimately conclude that the avoidance of the appearance of improper influence "is also critical . . . if confidence in the system of representative Government is not to be eroded to a disastrous extent."

Appellants contend that the contribution limitations must be invalidated because bribery laws and narrowly drawn disclosure requirements constitute a less restrictive means of dealing with "proven and suspected *quid pro quo* arrangements." But laws making criminal the giving and taking of bribes deal with only the most blatant and specific attempts of those with money to influence governmental action. And while disclosure requirements serve the many salutary purposes discussed elsewhere in this opinion, Congress was surely entitled to conclude that disclosure was only a partial measure, and that contribution ceilings were a necessary legislative concomitant to deal with the reality or appearance of corruption inherent in a system permitting unlimited financial contributions, even when the identities of the contributors and the amounts of their contributions are fully disclosed.

The Act's $1,000 contribution limitation focuses precisely on the problem of large campaign contributions— the narrow aspect of political association where the actuality and potential for corruption have been identified—while leaving persons free to engage in independent political expression, to associate actively through volunteering their services, and to assist to a limited but nonetheless substantial extent in supporting candidates and committees with financial resources.[31] Significantly, the Act's contribution limitations in themselves do not undermine to any material degree the potential for robust and effective discussion of candidates and campaign issues by individual citizens, associations, the institutional press, candidates, and political parties.

We find that, under the rigorous standard of review established by our prior decisions, the weighty interests served by restricting the size of financial contributions to political candidates are sufficient to justify the limited effect upon First Amendment freedoms caused by the $1,000 contribution ceiling.

(b)

Appellants' first overbreadth challenge to the contribution ceilings rests on the proposition that most large contributors do not seek improper influence over a candidate's position or an officeholder's action. Although the truth of that proposition may be assumed, it does not undercut the validity of the $1,000 contribution limitation. Not only is it difficult to isolate suspect contributions but, more importantly, Congress was justified in concluding that the interest in safeguarding against the appearance of impropriety requires that the opportunity for abuse inherent in the process of raising large monetary contributions be eliminated.

A second, related overbreadth claim is that the $1,000 restriction is unrealistically low because much more than that amount would still not be enough to enable an unscrupulous contributor to exercise improper influence over a candidate or officeholder, especially in campaigns for statewide or national office. While the contribution limitation provisions might well have been structured to take account of the

---

31. While providing significant limitations on the ability of all individuals and groups to contribute large amounts of money to candidates, the Act's contribution ceilings do not foreclose the making of substantial contributions to candidates by some major special-interest groups through the combined effect of individual contributions from adherents or * * * political funds * * * authorized under the Act to contribute to candidates. As a prime example, § 610 permits corporations and labor unions to establish segregated funds to solicit voluntary contributions to be utilized for political purposes. Corporate and union resources without limitation may be employed to administer these funds and to solicit contributions from employees, stockholders, and union members. Each separate fund may contribute up to $5,000 per candidate per election so long as the fund qualifies as a political committee under § 608(b)(2). * * *

graduated expenditure limitations for Congressional and Presidential campaigns, Congress' failure to engage in such fine tuning does not invalidate the legislation. As the Court of Appeals observed, "[i]f it is satisfied that some limit on contributions is necessary, a court has no scalpel to probe, whether, say, a $2,000 ceiling might not serve as well as $1,000." Such distinctions in degree become significant only when they can be said to amount to differences in kind.

(c)

Apart from these First Amendment concerns, appellants argue that the contribution limitations work such an invidious discrimination between incumbents and challengers that the statutory provisions must be declared unconstitutional on their face. In considering this contention, it is important at the outset to note that the Act applies the same limitations on contributions to all candidates regardless of their present occupations, ideological views, or party affiliations. Absent record evidence of invidious discrimination against challengers as a class, a court should generally be hesitant to invalidate legislation which on its face imposes evenhanded restrictions.

There is no such evidence to support the claim that the contribution limitations in themselves discriminate against major-party challengers to incumbents. Challengers can and often do defeat incumbents in federal elections. Major-party challengers in federal elections are usually men and women who are well known and influential in their community or State. Often such challengers are themselves incumbents in important local, state, or federal offices. Statistics in the record indicate that major-party challengers as well as incumbents are capable of raising large sums for campaigning. Indeed, a small but nonetheless significant number of challengers have in recent elections outspent their incumbent rivals. And, to the extent that incumbents generally are more likely than challengers to attract very large contributions, the Act's $1,000 ceiling has the practical effect of benefiting challengers as a class.[e] Contrary to the broad generalization drawn by the appellants, the practical impact of the contribution ceilings in any given election will clearly depend upon the amounts in excess of the ceilings that, for various reasons, the candidates in that election would otherwise have received and the utility of these additional amounts to the candidates. To be sure, the limitations may have a significant effect on particular challengers or incumbents, but the record provides no basis for predicting that such adventitious factors will invariably and invidiously benefit incumbents as a class. Since the danger of corruption and the appearance of corruption apply with equal force to challengers and to incumbents, Congress had ample justification for imposing the same fundraising constraints upon both.

---

e. In fact, data made available by FECA's disclosure requirements have consistently shown that House challengers receive a higher percentage of their total funds in contributions of $1000 or more. *See, e.g.,* Michael J. Malbin & Brendan Galvin, *CFI's Guide to Money in Federal Elections* 64, Table 2–8 (2020), *available at* http://cfinst.org/pdf/federal/2018Report/CFIGuide _MoneyinFederalElections_2018upd.pdf. —Eds.

The charge of discrimination against minor-party and independent candidates is more troubling, but the record provides no basis for concluding that the Act invidiously disadvantages such candidates. As noted above, the Act on its face treats all candidates equally with regard to contribution limitations. And the restriction would appear to benefit minor-party and independent candidates relative to their major-party opponents because major-party candidates receive far more money in large contributions. * * * [T]he record is virtually devoid of support for the claim that the $1,000 contribution limitation will have a serious effect on the initiation and scope of minor-party and independent candidacies. Moreover, any attempt to exclude minor parties and independents *en masse* from the Act's contribution limitations overlooks the fact that minor-party candidates may win elective office or have a substantial impact on the outcome of an election.

In view of these considerations, we conclude that the impact of the Act's $1,000 contribution limitation on major-party challengers and on minor-party candidates does not render the provision unconstitutional on its face.

2. The $5,000 Limitation on Contributions by Political Committees

Section 608(b)(2) permits certain committees, designated as "political committees," to contribute up to $5,000 to any candidate with respect to any election for federal office. In order to qualify for the higher contribution ceiling, a group must have been registered with the Commission as a political committee for not less than six months, have received contributions from more than 50 persons and, except for state political party organizations, have contributed to five or more candidates for federal office. Appellants argue that these qualifications unconstitutionally discriminate against *ad hoc* organizations in favor of established interest groups and impermissibly burden free association. The argument is without merit. Rather than undermining freedom of association, the basic provision enhances the opportunity of *bona fide* groups to participate in the election process, and the registration, contribution, and candidate conditions serve the permissible purpose of preventing individuals from evading the applicable contribution limitations by labeling themselves committees.

3. Limitations on Volunteers' Incidental Expenses

The Act excludes from the definition of contribution "the value of services provided without compensation by individuals who volunteer a portion or all of their time on behalf of a candidate or political committee." Certain expenses incurred by persons in providing volunteer services to a candidate are exempt from the $1,000 ceiling only to the extent that they do not exceed $500. These expenses are expressly limited to (1) "the use of real or personal property and the cost of invitations, food, and beverages, voluntarily provided by an individual to a candidate in rendering voluntary personal services on the individual's residential premises for candidate-related activities"; "the sale of any food or beverage by a vendor for use in a candidate's campaign at a charge [at least equal to cost but] less than the normal comparable charge"; and (3) "any unreimbursed payment for travel expenses made by an individual who on his own behalf volunteers his personal services to a candidate."

If, as we have held, the basic contribution limitations are constitutionally valid, then surely these provisions are a constitutionally acceptable accommodation of Congress' valid interest in encouraging citizen participation in political campaigns while continuing to guard against the corrupting potential of large financial contributions to candidates. The expenditure of resources at the candidate's direction for a fundraising event at a volunteer's residence or the provision of in-kind assistance in the form of food or beverages to be resold to raise funds or consumed by the participants in such an event provides material financial assistance to a candidate. The ultimate effect is the same as if the person had contributed the dollar amount to the candidate and the candidate had then used the contribution to pay for the fundraising event or the food. Similarly, travel undertaken as a volunteer at the direction of the candidate or his staff is an expense of the campaign and may properly be viewed as a contribution if the volunteer absorbs the fare. Treating these expenses as contributions when made to the candidate's campaign or at the direction of the candidate or his staff forecloses an avenue of abuse without limiting actions voluntarily undertaken by citizens independently of a candidate's campaign.

4. The $25,000 Limitation on Total Contributions During any Calendar Year

In addition to the $1,000 limitation on the nonexempt contributions that an individual may make to a particular candidate for any single election, the Act contains an overall $25,000 limitation on total contributions by an individual during any calendar year. * * * The overall $25,000 ceiling does impose an ultimate restriction upon the number of candidates and committees with which an individual may associate himself by means of financial support. But this quite modest restraint upon protected political activity serves to prevent evasion of the $1,000 contribution limitation by a person who might otherwise contribute massive amounts of money to a particular candidate through the use of unearmarked contributions to political committees likely to contribute to that candidate, or huge contributions to the candidate's political party. The limited, additional restriction on associational freedom imposed by the overall ceiling is thus no more than a corollary of the basic individual contribution limitation that we have found to be constitutionally valid.

C. Expenditure Limitations

The Act's expenditure ceilings impose direct and substantial restraints on the quantity of political speech. The most drastic of the limitations restricts individuals and groups, including political parties that fail to place a candidate on the ballot, to an expenditure of $1,000 "relative to a clearly identified candidate during a calendar year." Other expenditure ceilings limit spending by candidates, their campaigns, and political parties in connection with election campaigns. It is clear that a primary effect of these expenditure limitations is to restrict the quantity of campaign speech by individuals, groups, and candidates. The restrictions, while neutral as to the ideas expressed, limit political expression "at the core of our electoral process and of the First Amendment freedoms."

1. The $1,000 Limitation on Expenditures "Relative to a Clearly Identified Candidate"

Section 608(e)(1) provides that "[n]o person may make any expenditure . . . relative to a clearly identified candidate during a calendar year which, when added to all other expenditures made by such person during the year advocating the election or defeat of such candidate, exceeds $1,000."[45] The plain effect of § 608(e)(1) is to prohibit all individuals, who are neither candidates nor owners of institutional press facilities, and all groups, except political parties and campaign organizations, from voicing their views "relative to a clearly identified candidate" through means that entail aggregate expenditures of more than $1,000 during a calendar year. The provision, for example, would make it a federal criminal offense for a person or association to place a single one-quarter page advertisement "relative to a clearly identified candidate" in a major metropolitan newspaper.

Before examining the interests advanced in support of § 608(e)(1)'s expenditure ceiling, consideration must be given to appellants' contention that the provision is unconstitutionally vague. * * * The test is whether the language of § 608(e)(1) affords the "[p]recision of regulation [that] must be the touchstone in an area so closely touching our most precious freedoms."

The key operative language of the provision limits "any expenditure . . . relative to a clearly identified candidate." Although "expenditure," "clearly identified," and "candidate" are defined in the Act, there is no definition clarifying what expenditures are "relative to" a candidate. The use of so indefinite a phrase as "relative to" a candidate fails to clearly mark the boundary between permissible and impermissible speech, unless other portions of § 608(e)(1) make sufficiently explicit the range of expenditures covered by the limitation. The section prohibits "any expenditure . . . relative to a clearly identified candidate during a calendar year which, *when added to all other expenditures . . . advocating the election or defeat of such candidate*, exceeds $1,000." (Emphasis added.) This context clearly permits, if indeed it does not require, the phrase "relative to" a candidate to be read to mean "advocating the election or defeat of" a candidate.

---

45. * * * The statute provides some limited exceptions through various exclusions from the otherwise comprehensive definition of "expenditure." The most important exclusions are: (1) "any news story, commentary, or editorial distributed through the facilities of any broadcasting station, newspaper, magazine, or other periodical publication, unless such facilities are owned or controlled by any political party, political committee, or candidate," and (2) "any communication by any membership organization or corporation to its members or stockholders, if such membership organization or corporation is not organized primarily for the purpose of influencing the nomination for election, or election, of any person to Federal office." * * *

But while such a construction of §608(e)(1) refocuses the vagueness question, [it does not] eliminate[] the problem of unconstitutional vagueness altogether. For the distinction between discussion of issues and candidates and advocacy of election or defeat of candidates may often dissolve in practical application. Candidates, especially incumbents, are intimately tied to public issues involving legislative proposals and governmental actions. Not only do candidates campaign on the basis of their positions on various public issues, but campaigns themselves generate issues of public interest. In an analogous context, this Court in *Thomas* v. *Collins*, 323 U.S. 516 (1945), observed:

> "[W]hether words intended and designed to fall short of invitation would miss that mark is a question both of intent and of effect. No speaker, in such circumstances, safely could assume that anything he might say upon the general subject would not be understood by some as an invitation. In short, the supposedly clear-cut distinction between discussion, laudation, general advocacy, and solicitation puts the speaker in these circumstances wholly at the mercy of the varied understanding of his hearers and consequently of whatever inference may be drawn as to his intent and meaning.
>
> "Such a distinction offers no security for free discussion. In these conditions it blankets with uncertainty whatever may be said. It compels the speaker to hedge and trim." *Id.* at 535.

The constitutional deficiencies described in *Thomas* v. *Collins* can be avoided only by reading §608(e)(1) as limited to communications that include explicit words of advocacy of election or defeat of a candidate, much as the definition of "clearly identified" in §608(e)(2) requires that an explicit and unambiguous reference to the candidate appear as part of the communication.[51] * * * [I]n order to preserve the provision against invalidation on vagueness grounds, §608(e)(1) must be construed to apply only to expenditures for communications that in express terms advocate the election or defeat of a clearly identified candidate for federal office.[52]

We turn then to the basic First Amendment question—whether §608(e)(1) even as thus narrowly and explicitly construed, impermissibly burdens the constitutional right of free expression. * * *

The discussion in Part I-A, *supra*, explains why the Act's expenditure limitations impose far greater restraints on the freedom of speech and association than do its

---

51. Section 608(e)(2) defines "clearly identified" to require that the candidate's name, photograph or drawing, or other unambiguous reference to his identity appear as part of the communication. Such other unambiguous reference would include use of the candidate's initials (*e.g.*, FDR), the candidate's nickname (*e.g.*, Ike), his office (*e.g.*, the President or the Governor of Iowa), or his status as a candidate (*e.g.*, the Democratic Presidential nominee, the senatorial candidate of the Republican Party of Georgia).

52. This construction would restrict the application of §608(e)(1) to communications containing express words of advocacy of election or defeat, such as "vote for," "elect," "support," "cast your ballot for," "Smith for Congress," "vote against," "defeat," "reject."

contribution limitations. The markedly greater burden on basic freedoms caused by §608(e)(1) thus cannot be sustained simply by invoking the interest in maximizing the effectiveness of the less intrusive contribution limitations. Rather, the constitutionality of §608(e)(1) turns on whether the governmental interests advanced in its support satisfy the exacting scrutiny applicable to limitations on core First Amendment rights of political expression.

We find that the governmental interest in preventing corruption and the appearance of corruption is inadequate to justify §608(e)(1)'s ceiling on independent expenditures. First, assuming, *arguendo*, that large independent expenditures pose the same dangers of actual or apparent *quid pro quo* arrangements as do large contributions, §608(e)(1) does not provide an answer that sufficiently relates to the elimination of those dangers. Unlike the contribution limitations' total ban on the giving of large amounts of money to candidates, §608(e)(1) prevents only some large expenditures. So long as persons and groups eschew expenditures that in express terms advocate the election or defeat of a clearly identified candidate, they are free to spend as much as they want to promote the candidate and his views. The exacting interpretation of the statutory language necessary to avoid unconstitutional vagueness thus undermines the limitation's effectiveness as a loophole-closing provision by facilitating circumvention by those seeking to exert improper influence upon a candidate or officeholder. It would naively underestimate the ingenuity and resourcefulness of persons and groups desiring to buy influence to believe that they would have much difficulty devising expenditures that skirted the restriction on express advocacy of election or defeat but nevertheless benefited the candidate's campaign. Yet no substantial societal interest would be served by a loophole-closing provision designed to check corruption that permitted unscrupulous persons and organizations to expend unlimited sums of money in order to obtain improper influence over candidates for elective office.

Second, quite apart from the shortcomings of §608(e)(1) in preventing any abuses generated by large independent expenditures, the independent advocacy restricted by the provision does not presently appear to pose dangers of real or apparent corruption comparable to those identified with large campaign contributions. The parties defending §608(e)(1) * * * argue that expenditures controlled by or coordinated with the candidate and his campaign might well have virtually the same value to the candidate as a contribution and would pose similar dangers of abuse. Yet such controlled or coordinated expenditures are treated as contributions rather than expenditures under the Act. Section 608(b)'s contribution ceilings rather than §608(e)(1)'s independent expenditure limitation prevent attempts to circumvent the Act through prearranged or coordinated expenditures amounting to disguised contributions. By contrast, §608(e)(1) limits expenditures for express advocacy of candidates made totally independently of the candidate and his campaign. Unlike contributions, such independent expenditures may well provide little assistance to the candidate's campaign and indeed may prove counterproductive. The absence of prearrangement and coordination of an expenditure with the candidate or his agent not only undermines the value of the expenditure to the candidate, but also alleviates the danger that expenditures will be given as a *quid pro quo* for improper commitments from the candidate. Rather than preventing circumvention of the contribution limitations, §608(e)(1) severely restricts all independent advocacy despite its substantially diminished potential for abuse.

While the independent expenditure ceiling thus fails to serve any substantial governmental interest in stemming the reality or appearance of corruption in the electoral process, it heavily burdens core First Amendment expression. * * * Advocacy of the election or defeat of candidates for federal office is no less entitled to protection under the First Amendment than the discussion of political policy generally or advocacy of the passage or defeat of legislation.

It is argued, however, that the ancillary governmental interest in equalizing the relative ability of individuals and groups to influence the outcome of elections serves to justify the limitation on express advocacy of the election or defeat of candidates imposed by §608(e)(1)'s expenditure ceiling. But the concept that government may restrict the speech of some elements of our society in order to enhance the relative voice of others is wholly foreign to the First Amendment, which was designed "to secure 'the widest possible dissemination of information from diverse and antagonistic sources,'" and "to assure unfettered interchange of ideas for the bringing about of political and social changes desired by the people." The First Amendment's protection against governmental abridgment of free expression cannot properly be made to depend on a person's financial ability to engage in public discussion. * * *

For the reasons stated, we conclude that §608(e)(1)'s independent expenditure limitation is unconstitutional under the First Amendment.

2. Limitation on Expenditures by Candidates from Personal or Family Resources

The Act also sets limits on expenditures by a candidate from his personal funds or his immediate family. * * * The ceiling on personal expenditures by candidates on their own behalf, like the limitations on independent expenditures contained in §608(e)(1), imposes a substantial restraint on the ability of persons to engage in protected First Amendment expression. The candidate, no less than any other person, has a First Amendment right to engage in the discussion of public issues and vigorously and tirelessly to advocate his own election and the election of other candidates. Indeed, it is of particular importance that candidates have the unfettered opportunity to make their views known so that the electorate may intelligently evaluate the candidates' personal qualities and their positions on vital public issues before choosing among them on election day. Mr. Justice Brandeis' observation that in our country "public discussion is a political duty," *Whitney* v. *California*, 274 U.S. 357, 375 (concurring opinion), applies with special force to candidates for public office. Section 608(a)'s ceiling on personal expenditures by a candidate in furtherance of his own candidacy thus clearly and directly interferes with constitutionally protected freedoms.

The primary governmental interest served by the Act—the prevention of actual and apparent corruption of the political process—does not support the limitation on the candidate's expenditure of his own personal funds. As the Court of Appeals concluded: "Manifestly, the core problem of avoiding undisclosed and undue influence on candidates from outside interests has lesser application when the monies involved come from the candidate himself or from his immediate family." Indeed, the use of personal funds reduces the candidate's dependence on outside contributions and thereby counteracts the coercive pressures and attendant risks of abuse to which the Act's contribution limitations are directed.

The ancillary interest in equalizing the relative financial resources of candidates competing for elective office, therefore, provides the sole relevant rationale for §608(a)'s expenditure ceiling. That interest is clearly not sufficient to justify the provision's infringement of fundamental First Amendment rights. First, the limitation may fail to promote financial equality among candidates. A candidate who spends less of his personal resources on his campaign may nonetheless outspend his rival as a result of more successful fundraising efforts. Indeed, a candidate's personal wealth may impede his efforts to persuade others that he needs their financial contributions or volunteer efforts to conduct an effective campaign. Second, and more fundamentally, the First Amendment simply cannot tolerate §608(a)'s restriction upon the freedom of a candidate to speak without legislative limit on behalf of his own candidacy. We therefore hold that §608(a)'s restriction on a candidate's personal expenditures is unconstitutional.

3. Limitations on Campaign Expenditures

Section 608(c) places limitations on overall campaign expenditures by candidates seeking nomination for election and election to federal office. * * *

No governmental interest that has been suggested is sufficient to justify the restriction on the quantity of political expression imposed by §608(c)'s campaign expenditure limitations. The major evil associated with rapidly increasing campaign expenditures is the danger of candidate dependence on large contributions. The interest in alleviating the corrupting influence of large contributions is served by the Act's contribution limitations and disclosure provisions rather than by §608(c)'s campaign expenditure ceilings. The Court of Appeals' assertion that the expenditure restrictions are necessary to reduce the incentive to circumvent direct contribution limits is not persuasive. There is no indication that the substantial criminal penalties for violating the contribution ceilings combined with the political repercussion of such violations will be insufficient to police the contribution provisions. Extensive reporting, auditing, and disclosure requirements applicable to both contributions and expenditures by political campaigns are designed to facilitate the detection of illegal contributions. Moreover, * * * the Act permits an officeholder or successful candidate to retain contributions in excess of the expenditure ceiling and to use these funds for "any other lawful purpose." This provision undercuts whatever marginal role the expenditure limitations might otherwise play in enforcing the contribution ceilings.

The interest in equalizing the financial resources of candidates competing for federal office is no more convincing a justification for restricting the scope of federal election campaigns. Given the limitation on the size of outside contributions, the financial resources available to a candidate's campaign, like the number of volunteers recruited, will normally vary with the size and intensity of the candidate's support. There is nothing invidious, improper, or unhealthy in permitting such funds to be spent to carry the candidate's message to the electorate. Moreover, the equalization of permissible campaign expenditures might serve not to equalize the opportunities of all candidates but to handicap a candidate who lacked substantial name recognition or exposure of his views before the start of the campaign.

The campaign expenditure ceilings appear to be designed primarily to serve the governmental interests in reducing the allegedly skyrocketing costs of political campaigns. * * * [T]he mere growth in the cost of federal election campaigns in and of itself provides no basis for governmental restrictions on the quantity of campaign spending and the resulting limitation on the scope of federal campaigns. The First Amendment denies government the power to determine that spending to promote one's political views is wasteful, excessive, or unwise. In the free society ordained by our Constitution it is not the government but the people—individually as citizens and candidates and collectively as associations and political committees—who must retain control over the quantity and range of debate on public issues in a political campaign.

For these reasons we hold that § 608(c) is constitutionally invalid.

In sum, the provisions of the Act that impose a $1,000 limitation on contributions to a single candidate, a $5,000 limitation on contributions by a political committee to a single candidate, and a $25,000 limitation on total contributions by an individual during any calendar year, are constitutionally valid. These limitations, along with the disclosure provisions, constitute the Act's primary weapons against the reality or appearance of improper influence stemming from the dependence of candidates on large campaign contributions. The contribution ceilings thus serve the basic governmental interest in safeguarding the integrity of the electoral process without directly impinging upon the rights of individual citizens and candidates to engage in political debate and discussion. By contrast, the First Amendment requires the invalidation of the Act's independent expenditure ceiling, its limitation on a candidate's expenditures from his own personal funds, and its ceilings on overall campaign expenditures. These provisions place substantial and direct restrictions on the ability of candidates, citizens, and associations to engage in protected political expression, restrictions that the First Amendment cannot tolerate. * * *

Mr. Justice Stevens took no part in the consideration or decision of these cases.

Mr. Chief Justice Burger, concurring in part and dissenting in part.

* * * [T]he Court's result does violence to the intent of Congress in this comprehensive scheme of campaign finance. By dissecting the Act bit by bit, and casting off vital parts, the Court fails to recognize that the whole of this Act is greater than the sum of its parts. Congress intended to regulate all aspects of federal campaign finances, but what remains after today's holding leaves no more than a shadow of what Congress contemplated. I question whether the residue leaves a workable program. * * *

I agree fully with that part of the Court's opinion that holds unconstitutional the limitations the Act puts on campaign expenditures, which "place substantial and direct restrictions on the ability of candidates, citizens, and associations to engage in protected political expression, restrictions that the First Amendment cannot tolerate." Yet when it approves similarly stringent limitations on contributions, the Court ignores the reasons it finds so persuasive in the context of expenditures. For me contributions and expenditures are two sides of the same First Amendment coin.

* * * Limiting contributions, as a practical matter, will limit expenditures and will put an effective ceiling on the amount of political activity and debate that the Government will permit to take place. The argument that the ceiling is not, after all, very low as matters now stand gives little comfort for the future, since the Court elsewhere notes the rapid inflation in the cost of political campaigning.[5]

The Court attempts to separate the two communicative aspects of political contributions—the "moral" support that the gift itself conveys, which the Court suggests is the same whether the gift is $10 or $10,000,[6] and the fact that money translates into communication. The Court dismisses the effect of the limitations on the second aspect of contributions: "[T]he transformation of contributions into political debate involves speech by someone other than the contributor." On this premise—that contribution limitations restrict only the speech of "someone other than the contributor"—rests the Court's justification for treating contributions differently from expenditures. The premise is demonstrably flawed; the contribution

---

5. The Court notes that 94.9% of the funds raised by congressional candidates in 1974 came in contributions of less than $1,000, and suggests that the effect of the contribution limitations will be minimal. This logic ignores the disproportionate influence large contributions may have when made early in a campaign; "seed money" can be essential, and the inability to obtain it may effectively end some candidacies before they begin. * * *

6. Whatever the effect of the limitation, it is clearly arbitrary—Congress has imposed the same ceiling on contributions to a New York or California senatorial campaign that it has put on House races in Alaska or Wyoming. Both the strength of support conveyed by the gift of $1,000 and the gift's potential for corruptly influencing the recipient will vary enormously from place to place. * * *

limitations will, in specific instances, limit exactly the same political activity that the expenditure ceilings limit, and at least one of the "expenditure" limitations the Court finds objectionable [*i.e.*, limits on a candidate's contributions to his own campaign] operates precisely like the "contribution" limitations.

The Court's attempt to distinguish the communication inherent in political contributions from the speech aspects of political expenditures simply "will not wash." We do little but engage in word games unless we recognize that people—candidates and contributors—spend money on political activity because they wish to communicate ideas, and their constitutional interest in doing so is precisely the same whether they or someone else utters the words.

The Court attempts to make the Act seem less restrictive by casting the problem as one that goes to freedom of association rather than freedom of speech. I have long thought freedom of association and freedom of expression were two peas from the same pod. The contribution limitations of the Act impose a restriction on certain forms of associational activity that are for the most part, as the Court recognizes, harmless in fact. And the restrictions are hardly incidental in their effect upon particular campaigns. Judges are ill-equipped to gauge the precise impact of legislation, but a law that impinges upon First Amendment rights requires us to make the attempt. It is not simply speculation to think that the limitations on contributions will foreclose some candidacies.[9] The limitations will also alter the nature of some electoral contests drastically.[10]

* * * If such restraints can be justified at all, they must be justified by the very strongest of state interests. With this much the Court clearly agrees; the Court even goes so far as to note that legislation cutting into these important interests must employ "means closely drawn to avoid unnecessary abridgment of associational freedoms."

After a bow to the "weighty interests" Congress meant to serve, the Court then forsakes this analysis in one sentence: "Congress was surely entitled to conclude that disclosure was only a partial measure, and that contribution ceilings were a necessary legislative concomitant to deal with the reality or appearance of corruption." In striking down the limitations on campaign expenditures, the Court relies in part on its conclusion that other means—namely, disclosure and contribution ceilings—will adequately serve the statute's aim. It is not clear why the same analysis is not also appropriate in weighing the need for contribution ceilings in addition

---

9. Candidates who must raise large initial contributions in order to appeal for more funds to a broader audience will be handicapped. It is not enough to say that the contribution ceilings "merely ... require candidates ... to raise funds from a greater number of persons," where the limitations will effectively prevent candidates without substantial personal resources from doing just that.

10. Under the Court's holding, candidates with personal fortunes will be free to contribute to their own campaigns as much as they like, since the Court chooses to view the Act's provisions in this regard as unconstitutional "expenditure" limitations rather than "contribution" limitations.

to disclosure requirements. Congress may well be entitled to conclude that disclosure was a "partial measure," but I had not thought until today that Congress could enact its conclusions in the First Amendment area into laws immune from the most searching review by this Court.

Finally, it seems clear to me that in approving these limitations on contributions the Court must rest upon the proposition that "pooling" money is fundamentally different from other forms of associational or joint activity. I see only two possible ways in which money differs from volunteer work, endorsements, and the like. Money can be used to buy favors, because an unscrupulous politician can put it to personal use; second, giving money is a less visible form of associational activity. With respect to the first problem, the Act does not attempt to do any more than the bribery laws to combat this sort of corruption. In fact, the Act does not reach at all, and certainly the contribution limits do not reach, forms of "association" that can be fully as corrupt as a contribution intended as a *quid pro quo*—such as the eleventh-hour endorsement by a former rival, obtained for the promise of a federal appointment. This underinclusiveness is not a constitutional flaw, but it demonstrates that the contribution limits do not clearly focus on this first distinction. To the extent Congress thought that the second problem, the lesser visibility of contributions, required that money be treated differently from other forms of associational activity, disclosure laws are the simple and wholly efficacious answer; they make the invisible apparent. * * *

Mr. Justice White, concurring in part and dissenting in part.

I am * * * in agreement with the Court's judgment upholding the limitations on contributions. I dissent, however, from the Court's view that the expenditure limitations violate the First Amendment.

Concededly, neither the limitations on contributions nor those on expenditures directly or indirectly purport to control the content of political speech by candidates or by their supporters or detractors. What the Act regulates is giving and spending money, acts that have First Amendment significance not because they are themselves communicative with respect to their qualifications of the candidate, but because money may be used to defray the expenses of speaking or otherwise communicating about the merits or demerits of federal candidates for election. The act of giving money to political candidates, however, may have illegal or other undesirable consequences: it may be used to secure the express or tacit understanding that the giver will enjoy political favor if the candidate is elected. Both Congress and this Court's cases have recognized this as a mortal danger against which effective preventive and curative steps must be taken. * * *

It would make little sense to me and apparently made none to Congress, to limit the amounts an individual may give to a candidate or spend with his approval but fail to limit the amounts that could be spent on his behalf. Yet the Court permits the former while striking down the latter limitation. No more than $1,000 may be given to a candidate or spent at his request or with his approval or cooperation; but otherwise, apparently, a contributor is to be constitutionally protected in spending unlimited amounts of money in support of his chosen candidate or candidates.

Let us suppose that each of two brothers spends $1 million on TV spot announcements that he has individually prepared and in which he appears, urging the election of the same named candidate in identical words. One brother has sought and obtained the approval of the candidate; the other has not. The former may validly be prosecuted under § 608(e); under the Court's view, the latter may not, even though the candidate could scarcely help knowing about and appreciating the expensive favor. For constitutional purposes it is difficult to see the difference between the two situations. * * *

As an initial matter, the argument that money is speech and that limiting the flow of money to the speaker violates the First Amendment proves entirely too much. Compulsory bargaining and the right to strike, both provided for or protected by federal law, inevitably have increased the labor costs of those who publish newspapers, which are in turn an important factor in the recent disappearance of many daily papers. Federal and state taxation directly removes from company coffers large amounts of money that might be spent on larger and better newspapers. The antitrust laws are aimed at preventing monopoly profits and price fixing, which gouge the consumer. It is also true that general price controls have from time to time existed and have been applied to the newspapers or other media. But it has not been suggested, nor could it be successfully, that these laws, and many others, are invalid because they siphon off or prevent the accumulation of large sums that would otherwise be available for communicative activities. * * *

[E]xpenditure ceilings reinforce the contribution limits and help eradicate the hazard of corruption. The Court upholds the overall limit of $25,000 on an individual's political contributions in a single election year on the ground that it helps reinforce the limits on gifts to a single candidate. By the same token, the expenditure limit imposed on candidates plays its own role in lessening the chance that the contribution ceiling will be violated. Without limits on total expenditures, campaign costs will inevitably and endlessly escalate. Pressure to raise funds will constantly build and with it the temptation to resort in "emergencies" to those sources of large sums, who, history shows, are sufficiently confident of not being caught to risk flouting contribution limits. Congress would save the candidate from the predicament by establishing a reasonable ceiling on all candidates. This is a major consideration in favor of the limitation. It should be added that many successful candidates will also be saved from large, over-hanging campaign debts which must be paid off with money raised while holding public office and at a time when they are already preparing or thinking about the next campaign. The danger to the public interest in such situations is self-evident.

Besides backing up the contribution provisions, which are aimed at preventing untoward influence on candidates that are elected, expenditure limits have their own potential for preventing the corruption of federal elections themselves. For many years the law has required the disclosure of expenditures as well as contributions. * * * [T]he corrupt use of money by candidates is as much to be feared as the corrosive influence of large contributions. There are many illegal ways of spending money to influence elections. One would be blind to history to deny that unlimited money tempts people to spend it on *whatever* money can buy to influence an election. On the assumption that financing illegal activities is low on the campaign organization's priority list, the expenditure limits could play a substantial role in preventing unethical practices. There just would not be enough of "that kind of money" to go around.

I have little doubt in addition that limiting the total that can be spent will ease the candidate's understandable obsession with fundraising, and so free him and his staff to communicate in more places and ways unconnected with the fundraising function. There is nothing objectionable—indeed it seems to me a weighty interest in favor of the provision—in the attempt to insulate the political expression of federal candidates from the influence inevitably exerted by the endless job of raising increasingly large sums of money. * * *

It is also important to restore and maintain public confidence in federal elections. It is critical to obviate or dispel the impression that federal elections are purely and simply a function of money, that federal offices are bought and sold or that political races are reserved for those who have the facility—and the stomach—for doing whatever it takes to bring together those interests, groups, and individuals that can raise or contribute large fortunes in order to prevail at the polls. * * *

I also disagree with the Court's judgment that § 608(a), which limits the amount of money that a candidate or his family may spend on his campaign, violates the Constitution. Although it is true that this provision does not promote any interest in preventing the corruption of candidates, the provision does, nevertheless, serve salutary purposes related to the integrity of federal campaigns. By limiting the importance of personal wealth, § 608(a) helps to assure that only individuals with a modicum of support from others will be viable candidates. * * *

Notes and Questions

1. Congress's authority to regulate campaign finance is well established in the Court's jurisprudence and generally assumed in *Buckley*. 424 U.S. at 14, n.16. Article I, § 4 of the Constitution, on which the Court relied, gives Congress the power to regulate the "Times, Places and Manner of holding Elections for Senators and Representatives." Is "holding [an] Election[]" the same as campaigning, or has the Court wrongfully conflated "campaign" with "election"? *See* Robert G. Natelson, *The Original Scope of Congressional Power to Regulate Elections*, 13 U. Pa. J. Const. L. 1 (2010). Natelson argued that the Elections Clause was limited to provisions of public notice, establishing the time and place for voting, supervision of officers and election judges, management of poll lists, and similar voting mechanics—not campaigning for office. *Id.* at 9–20.

One of the difficulties in regulating "campaigns" is that there are no set boundaries to a "campaign." In some sense, everything an officeholder, or would-be officeholder, does is "campaigning": shaping an image, promoting issues, getting to know potential allies and voters. All speech about public affairs is, in some sense, campaign-related. Whenever some speech or activity is prohibited or limited by the campaign-finance system, candidates, donors, and voters will adjust their activities to take advantage of unregulated speech and political activities. To prevent this "circumvention" of the laws, the regulatory system must expand to include more speech and political activity. Is such expansion compatible with the First Amendment? In a portion of his separate opinion concerning FECA's public-financing system for presidential campaigns, Chief Justice Burger noted that the government was not "polic[ing] the integrity of the electoral process" but instead was policing "political debate itself." 424 U.S. at 248. Note that this theory, if adopted, would invalidate almost all campaign-finance regulation.

2. What are the constitutional interests at stake in campaign-finance regulation? Read *Buckley* carefully: Does it say, as some have suggested, say that "money is speech," *see* J. Skelly Wright, *Politics and the Constitution: Is Money Speech?*, 85 YALE L.J. 1001, 1005 (1976), or is its message slightly but significantly different — that money is necessary to speak widely, and that preventing dissemination of speech is a First Amendment problem? In either case, virtually everyone agrees that campaign-finance laws, in the Court's words, "operate in an area of the most fundamental First Amendment activities." Since *Buckley*, twenty-one men and women have sat on the Court, and only Justice Stevens has argued that for constitutional purposes, campaign-contribution and campaign-expenditure limitations should be treated as restrictions on property rather than on speech and association. *See Nixon v. Shrink Missouri Government PAC*, 528 U.S. 377, 398–99 [p. 768] (Stevens, J., concurring). What fundamental First Amendment activities are at stake?

3. The controversial issues in the courts have not been whether the First Amendment is at issue, but how much regulation can be justified under the First Amendment and whether or not, in the words of Justice Breyer, "constitutionally protected interests lie on both sides of the legal equation," *id*. at 400 (Breyer, J., concurring); *see also* STEPHEN BREYER, ACTIVE LIBERTY 49 (2005); Burt Neuborne, *Toward a Democracy Centered Reading of the First Amendment*, 93 NW. U. L. REV. 1055, 1058–59 (1999) (arguing that constitutional "values" support campaign finance limitations); Harold Leventhal, *Courts and Political Thickets*, 77 COLUM. L. REV. 345, 373 (1977). Justice Breyer has argued that restrictions can enhance First Amendment interests. As a result, "a presumption against constitutionality is out of place." *Nixon*, 528 U.S. at 401 (Breyer, J., concurring). In what ways might campaign-finance regulations enhance free speech or other constitutional values? For arguments that "constitutionally protected interests" or "constitutional values" are poor substitutes for traditional First Amendment analysis, see Daniel D. Polsby, Buckley v. Valeo: *The Special Nature of Political Speech*, 1976 SUP. CT. REV. 1 (1976); Bradley A. Smith, *The*

John Roberts Salvage Company: After McConnell, *a New Court Looks to Repair the Constitution*, 68 Ohio St. L.J. 891, 904–907 (2007).

The dispute over the role of constitutional values and interests is not merely one of theory, but of empirical analysis as well. Critics of campaign-finance regulation have not only disputed whether there are constitutionally protected interests on both sides of the legal equation, but whether regulation in fact protects or enhances any such interest that might exist. *See* Rodney A. Smith, Money, Power & Elections: How Campaign Finance Reform Subverts American Democracy (2006); Bradley A. Smith, Unfree Speech: The Folly of Campaign Finance Reform 144–45 (2001).

4. For the most part, *Buckley* seems to recognize just one compelling government interest: prevention of "corruption or its appearance." The extent to which campaign contributions are truly a source of political corruption is hotly disputed in professional literature. *Compare* Stephen D. Ansolabehere et al., *Why Is There So Little Money in American Politics*, 17 J. Econ. Perspectives 105, 113–17 (2003) (compiling and reviewing thirty-six peer-reviewed studies between 1977 and 2002 and concluding, "after controlling for legislator ideology, [campaign] contributions have no detectable effects on the behavior of legislators"), *with* Daniel H. Lowenstein, *On Campaign Finance Reform: The Root of All Evil Is Deeply Rooted*, 18 Hofstra L. Rev. 301, 313–35 (1989) (recognizing the difficulty of establishing direct causation between campaign contributions and legislative activity, but noting the difficulty in studying and measuring corruption through econometric studies; and arguing that large contributions create inherent conflicts of interest: "[T]he corrupt element is intermingled with the entire process, in a way that cannot be isolated."). Either way, there is no question that the public perceives contributions as corrupting. *See, e.g.*, Nathaniel Persily & Kelli Lammi, *Perceptions of Corruption and Campaign Finance: When Public Opinion Determines Constitutional Law*, 153 U. Pa. L. Rev. 119 (2004).

But what did the Court mean by "corruption"? In a portion of the opinion joined by all Justices except Justice Blackmun, who would have struck down contribution limits, *Buckley* defined "corruption" as "large contributions * * * given to secure a political *quid pro quo*." 424 U.S. at 26. In *Federal Election Commission v. National Conservative Political Action Committee*, 470 U.S. 480 (1985), then-Justice Rehnquist wrote for a seven-member majority:

> Corruption is a subversion of the political process. Elected officials are influenced to act contrary to their obligations of office by the prospect of financial gain to themselves or infusions of money into their campaigns. The hallmark of corruption is the financial *quid pro quo*: dollars for political favors.

How satisfied are you with that definition?

In recent years, a number of scholars have attempted to expand the meaning of "corruption" to include broader themes of disconnection between voters and officeholders. Professor Larry Lessig has argued that large amounts of private money in campaigns break the "dependence" of the legislature on the will of the people and lead to "dependence corruption" that justifies new restraints on political speech. *See* Lawrence Lessig, *A Reply to Professor Hasen*, 126 HARV. L. REV. F. 61 (2012). Indeed, Lessig went so far as to argue that this lack of dependence on the will of the people constitutes "corruption" as the term would have been used at the Founding. Larry Lessig, *What an Originalist Would Understand 'Corruption' to Mean*, 102 CAL. L. REV. 1 (2014). Professor Zephyr Teachout has made similar arguments, suggesting that the Constitution includes an inherent "anti-corruption" principle, which can be understood to authorize sweeping government regulation of political campaigns. Zephyr Teachout, *The Anti-Corruption Principle*, 94 CORNELL L. REV. 341 (2009). For doubts that the Framers' views on corruption can be shoehorned into modern analysis, see Bruce E. Cain, *Is 'Dependence Corruption' the Solution to America's Campaign Finance Problems?*, 102 CAL. L. REV. 37 (2014). But assume that the Founders would have understood "corruption" along the lines of Lessig's "dependence corruption" or Teachout's broad, overpowering "anti-corruption principle": Would that substantially alter the constitutional analysis, which is based, at least in part, on the principle that regulation suppresses speech and thereby undermines First Amendment rights? In other words, is the First Amendment merely a broad, aspirational statement of concern for free speech and prevention of corruption, or is it better understood as a constitutional constraint that purposefully defines and limits the approaches that government may take to try to stamp out corruption?

Professor Robert Post refashioned the problem as one not of "corruption," but the loss of "electoral integrity"—the citizenry's "trust[] that representatives will be attentive to public opinion." ROBERT C. POST, CITIZENS DIVIDED: CAMPAIGN FINANCE REFORM AND THE CONSTITUTION (2014). How, if at all, would a regime based on "electoral integrity" look different from the doctrine established by *Buckley*? How would judges determine if "electoral integrity" had been violated? *See* Pamela S. Karlan, *Citizens Deflected: Electoral Integrity and Political Reforms, in* CITIZENS DIVIDED, *supra*, at 141; Justin Levitt, *Electoral Integrity: The Confidence Game*, 89 N.Y.U. L. REV. ONLINE 70 (2014).

As we will see, the Court itself has sometimes wavered on its formulation of a corruption interest sufficient to justify restrictions on First Amendment activity. In *Austin v. Michigan State Chamber of Commerce*, 494 U.S. 652, 660 (1990), a six-Justice majority suggested another definition: "the corrosive and distorting effects of immense aggregation of wealth that are accumulated with the corporate form and that have little or no correlation to the public's support for the corporation's political ideas." What does this mean? Is it important that political ideas be disseminated only in proportion to their pre-existing levels of support in the larger public? And in *McConnell v. Federal Election Commission*, 540 U.S. 93, 150 (2003) [p. 829] the Court suggested that "access to high-level government officials" that might come with campaign contributions or expenditures constituted "corruption." However, both of these definitions were later rejected by the Court in *Citizens United v. Federal Election*

Commission, 558 U.S. 310 (2010) [p. 844]. Is "access" corrupting? Officeholders must divide their time—does it not make sense that they would meet with those who supported their election? Even the *McConnell* Court agreed that access did not necessarily "secure actual influence," let alone policy results. 540 U.S. at 150.

5. What is meant by "the appearance of corruption"? If there is actual corruption, why isn't that enough? If the "appearance of corruption" refers to fears unsupported by evidence, should such unsupported fears provide sufficient justification to restrict free speech? Persily & Lammi, *supra*, at 124, note that irrational fears, in other contexts, are one of the few reasons insufficient to pass the Court's lowest level of scrutiny, rational basis. *See Romer v. Evans*, 517 U.S. 620 (1996); *City of Cleburne v. Cleburne Living Center*, 473 U.S. 432 (1985). Should the "appearance of corruption" be a broad justification for campaign-finance regulation, given that it is always easy to find people dissatisfied with the quality or actions of government, who will define such unsatisfactory results as "corruption"? Or should it be more tightly tied to what the Court has held to be actual corruption and require the appearance of *quid pro quo* exchanges? Is the "appearance of corruption" merely a way to deal with the difficulty of proving bribery or other *quid pro quo* exchanges, and thus limited to narrow situations, as when money passes from a donor to a politician's campaign? *See* Bradley A. Smith, *Super PACs and the Role of 'Coordination' in Campaign Finance Law*, 49 WILLAMETTE L. REV. 603, 615–616 (2013).

6. One of the most oft-quoted passages of *Buckley* is its quick dismissal of the equality interest proffered by the government as "wholly foreign to the First Amendment." However, many scholars believe that the equality rationale is the more compelling reason to support limitations and restrictions on campaign activity. *See, e.g.,* J. Skelly Wright, *Money and the Pollution of Politics: Is the First Amendment an Obstacle to Political Equality?*, 82 COLUM. L. REV. 611 (1982); Owen Fiss, *Free Speech and Social Structure*, 71 IOWA L. REV. 1405, 1425 (1986); Cass R. Sunstein, *Political Equality and Unintended Consequences*, 94 COLUM. L. REV. 1390, 1398–99 (1994). The result of *Buckley*, however, is that arguments to the courts favoring campaign-finance regulation, regardless of their motivation, must be shoehorned into an anti-corruption rationale. *See* Elizabeth Garrett, *Justice Marshall's Jurisprudence on Law and Politics*, 52 How. L.J. 655, 665–679 (2009).

Did the Court err in rejecting the equality rationale? *Compare* Fiss, *supra*, at 1416, 1425 ("We should learn to recognize the state not only as an enemy, but also as a friend of speech. * * * [W]e may sometimes find it necessary to restrict the speech of some elements of our society in order to enhance the relative influence of others."), *with* Polsby, *supra*, at 43 ("Almost every country in the world, including those behind the iron curtain, can display a constitution that guarantees freedom of expression to the people—to the extent, of course, that the people's representatives deem proper. With *Buckley v. Valeo* in hand, we can boast that our Constitution protects something far scarcer in history than that sort of freedom. And with the knowledge of the caliber of people who sometimes get their hands on our government, it is well that this is so."). *See also* David A. Strauss, *What Is the Goal of*

Campaign Finance Reform, 1995 U. CHI. LEGAL F. 141; Bruce E. Cain, *Moralism & Realism in Campaign Finance Reform*, 1995 U. CHI. LEGAL F. 111; Daniel H. Lowenstein, *Campaign Contributions and Corruption*, 1995 U. CHI. LEGAL F. 163.

Buckley did recognize other state interests in the context of disclosure, which will be discussed in Chapter 9.

7. What is the level of scrutiny that *Buckley* applied to expenditure limits? To limits on contributions? Read again *Buckley*'s standard for contribution limits: A regulation "may be sustained if the State demonstrates a sufficiently important interest and employs means closely drawn to avoid unnecessary abridgment of associational freedoms." What does this mean? How does it compare to the "exacting scrutiny" that the Court declared to be the standard for reviewing expenditure limits? *See* Marlene A. Nicholson, *Political Campaign Expenditure Limitations and the Unconstitutional Conditions Doctrine*, 10 HASTINGS CONST. L.Q. 601, 607–08 (1983). Is "exacting scrutiny" the same as "strict scrutiny"? Note that the term "strict scrutiny" as a phrase for describing a heightened degree of judicial review only began to see regular use in the 1960s, and at the time of *Buckley* the Justices on the Court still used a variety of terms to convey the concept of heightened scrutiny that today is generally referenced as "strict scrutiny." *See* Richard H. Fallon, Jr., *Strict Judicial Scrutiny*, 54 UCLA L. REV. 1267, 1273–85 (2007).

A concern voiced in *Buckley* that has resurfaced regularly in the Court's later cases is whether or not restrictions primarily serve to benefit incumbent officeholders seeking re-election. *Compare* John R. Lott, Jr., *Campaign Finance Reform and Electoral Competition*, 129 PUB. CHOICE 263, 292 (2006) (finding that campaign-finance contribution limits advantage incumbents and depress electoral competition), *with* Thomas Stratmann & Francisco J. Aparicio-Castillo, Comment, *Campaign Finance Reform and Electoral Competition*, 133 PUB. CHOICE 107, 108–10 (2007) (criticizing Lott's findings), *and* Thomas Stratmann & Francisco J. Aparicio-Castillo, *Competition Policy for Elections: Do Campaign Contribution Limits Matter?*, 127 PUB. CHOICE 177, 199 (2006) (finding that contribution limits increase electoral competition by making incumbents more vulnerable). *See also* Michael S. Kang, *To Here from Theory in Election Law*, 87 TEX. L. REV. 787, 802–06 (2009); Richard Briffault, *On Dejudicializing American Campaign Finance Law*, 29 GA. ST. U. L. REV. 887, 925–28 (2011).

Does this concern about incumbents' self-dealing go to the level of scrutiny to be applied, or to the Court's analysis under whatever level of scrutiny is applied?

8. Does *Buckley*'s distinction between contributions and expenditures make sense? What are some of the consequences of that distinction? Perhaps the most obvious consequence of the Court's decision to uphold contribution limits while striking down expenditure limits is that the distinction leaves an unlimited demand for campaign money, while limiting the supply of campaign money available. Joel M. Gora, *No Law . . . Abridging*, 24 HARV. J.L. & PUB. POL'Y 841, 859 (2001) (book review). What are some of the predictable results of constricting supply

while leaving demand unlimited? *See* Samuel Issacharoff & Pamela S. Karlan, *The Hydraulics of Campaign Finance Reform*, 77 Tex. L. Rev. 1705, 1710–11 (1999). Other commentators argue that the distinction is fundamentally flawed as a matter of constitutional law: The commentators include those both those who would allow limits on spending, Burt Neuborne, *The Supreme Court and Free Speech: Love and a Question*, 42 St. Louis U. L. Rev. 789, 796–97 (1996); William P. Marshall, *The Last Best Chance for Campaign Finance Reform*, 94 Nw. U. L. Rev. 335, 350–51 (2000), and those who would abolish limits on contributions, *see* Lillian R. BeVier, *Money & Politics: A Perspective on the First Amendment and Campaign Finance Reform*, 73 Cal. L. Rev. 1045 (1985); Bradley A. Smith, *Money Talks: Speech, Corruption, Equality and Campaign Finance*, 86 Geo. L.J. 45 (1997).

Despite these criticisms, the contribution/expenditure distinction has remained remarkably durable. Professor Daniel Lowenstein has argued that "[c]ontribution limits address the conflict of interest problem more directly * * * than campaign spending limits, whereas spending limits restrict speech more directly than contribution limits." Also, "[a]lthough the jury of social scientists is still out, there is reason to believe that to the extent spending limits reduce spending more than contribution limits, this will tend to make spending limits more detrimental to electoral competition." Lowenstein concluded, however, that these distinctions are insufficient to "support a general principle that expenditure limits are nearly always unconstitutional while contribution limits are nearly always valid." Daniel H. Lowenstein, *A Patternless Mosaic: Campaign Finance and the First Amendment After Austin*, 21 Cap. U. L. Rev. 381, 401–402 (1992). Eugene Volokh has offered a more vigorous defense, arguing that the distinction offers a realistic compromise between the public's concerns about corruption and equality and First Amendment demands that speakers retain "considerable opportunities to speak." Eugene Volokh, *Freedom of Speech and Speech About Political Candidates: The Unintended Consequences of Three Proposals*, 24 Harv. J.L. & Pub. Pol'y 47, 65 (2000); *see also* Eugene Volokh, *Why* Buckley v. Valeo *Is Basically Right*, 34 Ariz. St. L.J. 1095 (2002). For a readable introduction to the complexities of campaign-finance regulation, together with a measured and skeptical appraisal of reforms, see Peter H. Schuck, *Campaign Finance Reform Revisited*, Nat'l Affairs, Winter 2019, at 76–93.

Note on the "Express Advocacy"/"Issue Advocacy" Distinction

Re-read *Buckley*'s footnote 52 and the accompanying text (p. 740, *supra*). Here the Court distinguished between what became commonly known as "express advocacy," that is, explicit exhortations for voters to vote for or against specific candidates, and "issue advocacy," the discussion of candidates and issues that stopped short of such explicit exhortations to vote in particular ways. In the decades after *Buckley*, this distinction would come to dominate many of the legal debates over the reach and propriety of campaign-finance laws.

Buckley limited the definition of "expenditure" to "express advocacy." But why does this limitation matter, and why did the Court bother to make the distinction, given that *Buckley* went on to hold that independent expenditures—whether issue speech or express advocacy—could not be constitutionally limited? The reasons are a bit complex, but very helpful to understanding the development of campaign-finance law.

First, although *Buckley* struck down limits on expenditures by individuals and campaigns, it did not specifically address 52 U.S.C. §30118, which prohibited expenditures by corporations. After *Buckley* and until the Supreme Court decision in *Citizens United v. Federal Election Commission*, 558 U.S. 310 (2010) [p. 844], the FEC and many states continued to hold that corporate expenditures were illegal, at least in candidate races. *See Austin v. Michigan State Chamber of Commerce*, 494 U.S. 652 (1990). Thus, corporate- and union-funded independent expenditures were barred if they included "express advocacy," but not if they avoided "express advocacy."

Second, "political committees," a term defined by FECA, are much more heavily regulated than other entities are, and the *Buckley* Court indicated that this was a matter of constitutional limitation as well as statutory law. 424 U.S. at 79–80. As explained in the immediately following Note on Political Committees (pp. 759–61), *Buckley* held that political committee status would only accrue to "organizations that are under the control of a candidate or the major purpose of which is the nomination or election of a candidate." *Id.* at 79. But *Buckley* did not indicate how one might establish the "major purpose" of an organization. A narrow interpretation might limit the definition to candidate committees, political parties, and PACs formed to contribute directly to candidates—that is, to organizations formed explicitly to engage in candidate elections. This approach would obviously leave many organizations making expenditures outside the ambit of political committee. Another approach would focus on the organization's overall intent. But determining "intent" would seem to raise exactly the type of vagueness problem and chilling effect that the Court sought to avoid with the express advocacy standard in the first place. The FEC eventually adopted an approach of measuring primary purpose by expenditures—if a group devoted more than half its resources to "express advocacy" expenditures and contributions to candidates, it would be deemed a "political committee," subject to the full array of registration and reporting requirements, and also to limitations on the size and sources of contributions it could receive, including no corporate or labor funding. If it did not devote more than half its resources to a combination of making contributions to political committees and express advocacy, it was free of such requirements. *See Akins v. Federal Election Commission*, 101 F.3d 731, 734 (D.C. Cir. 1996), *vacated on other grounds*, 524 U.S. 11 (1998).

Even if an organization did not qualify as a political committee, if it ran an ad expressly advocating the election or defeat of a candidate, it still had to report that particular expenditure to the FEC. But if the ad did not expressly advocate for or against a candidate, the organization or spender had no reporting or disclosure obligations.

As a practical matter, this meant that large organizations such as the United States Chamber of Commerce or the Sierra Club, both of which are incorporated, could not pay for advertisements expressly advocating the election or defeat of a candidate, but they could pay for what became generically known as "issue" ads. These ads could praise or damn a candidate or officeholder's positions on issues, past acts, or even character, if they avoided "express advocacy." *Buckley* actually anticipated this result. Having determined that "expenditure" had to be defined as express advocacy in order to avoid constitutional vagueness problems, the Court then struck down expenditure limits, in part because "[i]t would naively underestimate the ingenuity and resourcefulness of persons and groups desiring to buy influence to believe that they would have much difficulty devising expenditures that skirted the restriction on express advocacy of election or defeat but nevertheless benefited the candidate's campaign." 424 U.S. at 45. Given this, "no substantial societal interest would be served" by limiting expenditures. *Id.*

As a result of these various rulings, whether or not an organization was engaged in "express advocacy" was a very important issue. The FEC sought to expand the scope of what qualified as "express advocacy," and was therefore subject to regulation, while citizens' organizations fought against such expansion. The FEC and these advocacy groups engaged in an ongoing guerrilla war in the appellate courts through the 1990s over the definition of "express advocacy," with the FEC generally getting the worst of the battle. Consider the following three cases, which both typified and framed the battle:

• In *Federal Election Commission v. Central Long Island Tax Reform Immediately Committee*, 616 F.2d 45 (2d Cir. 1980) (*CLITRIM*), CLITRIM, a local group loosely affiliated with Tax Reform Immediately (TRIM), a project of the national John Birch Society, spent $135 to hand out a four-page pamphlet at local shopping malls, commuter railway stations, and a local political meeting. The pamphlet

> furnished information on the general views of the organizations, identified the officers of the Committee, furnished information about the CLITRIM members and invited others to join. The remaining pages reported the voting record of Congressman Jerome A. Ambro, a local representative of central Long Island. These pages included a photograph of Congressman Ambro and a chart of 24 votes cast by him, 21 of which were characterized as for "Higher Taxes and More Government" and 3 as for "Lower Taxes and Less Government." CLITRIM's stand against higher taxes and "Big Government" in favor of lower taxes and "Less Government" was made clear by slogans and commentaries. However, the leaflet did not refer to any federal election, to Congressman Ambro's political affiliation or candidacy, or to any electoral opponent of the Congressman.

Id. at 51. The pamphlet also stated, "[i]f your Representative consistently votes for measures that increase taxes, let him know how you feel. And thank him when he votes for lower taxes and less government." *Id.* at 53. Various complaints were filed against CLITRIM and other local TRIM affiliates, and the FEC investigated. The Court of Appeals held that the leaflets did not constitute "express advocacy."

• In *Federal Election Commission v. Furgatch*, 807 F. 2d 857 (9th Cir.), *cert denied*, 484 U.S. 850 (1987), the FEC scored a rare victory in the express-advocacy wars — but the circumstances of the win, and the narrowness of the court's opinion, show how little success the FEC had. Harvey Furgatch purchased a full-page ad in the *Boston Globe* three days before the 1980 presidential election, headlined "Don't let him do it." The ad then provided a long list of allegations about the behavior of President Jimmy Carter. The ad concluded that Carter was "attempt[ing] to hide his own record, or lack of it. If he succeeds the country will be burdened with four more years of incoherencies, ineptness and illusion, as he leaves a legacy of low-level campaigning. DON'T LET HIM DO IT." *Id.* at 858. The Court of Appeals held that Furgatch's ad did amount to "express advocacy," because it included a "clear plea for action" and that at that point the only act a reader could take to "not let him do it" was to vote against Carter. But the Court stressed, "[w]e emphasize that if any reasonable alternative reading of speech can be suggested, it cannot be express advocacy." *Id* at 864–65. The case was, said the Court, "a close call." *Id.* at 861.

• The FEC's efforts to use *Furgatch* to broaden the definition of "express advocacy" beyond the type of examples described in *Buckley* were almost wholly unsuccessful, reaching a denouement in *Federal Election Commission v. Christian Action Network*, 110 F.3d 1049 (4th Cir. 1997) (*CAN*). In that case, CAN ran a TV ad with the following text:

> Bill Clinton's vision for America includes job quotas for homosexuals, giving homosexuals special civil rights, allowing homosexuals in the armed forces. Al Gore supports homosexual couples' adopting children and becoming foster parents. Is this your vision for a better America? For more information on traditional family values, contact the Christian Action Network.

Id. at 1058. The ad can be viewed at https://www.youtube.com/watch?v =NSJhhKwWhWo. The FEC conceded that the ad did not urge the defeat of Bill Clinton in the 1992 presidential race, but argued that it could still be deemed express advocacy because, "considered as a whole with the imagery, music, film footage, and voice intonations, the advertisements' nonprescriptive language unmistakably conveyed a message expressly advocating the defeat of Governor Clinton." String-citing numerous defeats the FEC had suffered in court on the express-advocacy question, the court held that the FEC's argument lacked "substantial justification" and could not be "made in good faith." *Id.* at 1064. The Court took the unusual step of awarding attorney's fees against the FEC. *Id.*

These three cases illustrate how unwilling lower courts have been to extend the definition of "express advocacy" beyond the types of explicit phrases — "vote for," "elect," "support," "cast your ballot for," "Smith for Congress," "vote against," "defeat," "reject"—found in *Buckley.* 424 U.S. at 44 n.52.

As you will see, a pair of decisions in 2010—the Supreme Court's decision in *Citizens United* [p. 844] (striking down prohibitions on independent expenditures by corporations), and the U.S. Court of Appeals for the District of Columbia Circuit's decision in *SpeechNow.org v. Federal Election Commission*, 599 F.3d 686 (D.C. Cir. 2010) (*en banc*) (striking down limits on the size and source of contributions to political committees that make only independent expenditures)—have greatly reduced the importance of the "express advocacy"/"issue advocacy" distinction. But the "express advocacy" standard remains important for determining political committee status under federal law, with its added reporting and organizational requirements, and it remains embedded as well in many state laws. *See, e.g.*, Mich. Stat. Ann. 169.206(j); *State ex rel. Two Unnamed Petitioners v. Peterson*, 866 N.W.2d 165 (Wis. 2015). Understanding the distinction—as well as the narrow definition that the courts have given to "express advocacy"—remains valuable both for understanding many of the cases that follow in this Chapter, and for understanding ongoing issues in campaign-finance law.

Note on Political Committees

The Federal Election Campaign Act amendments of 1974, in addition to placing limits on contributions and expenditures, defined a "political committee" as "any committee, club, association, or other group of persons which receives contributions aggregating in excess of $1,000 during a calendar year or which makes expenditures aggregating in excess of $1,000 during a calendar year." 52 U.S.C. § 30101(4).

This definition is critically important, because once an organization or group is deemed to be a "political committee" under FECA, it is subject to a broad array of regulatory requirements. It must register with the FEC, and further

> it must appoint a treasurer; ensure that contributions are forwarded to the treasurer within 10 or 30 days of receipt, depending on the amount of contribution; see that its treasurer keeps an account of every contribution regardless of amount, the name and address of any person who makes a contribution in excess of $50, all contributions received from political committees, and the name and address of any person to whom a disbursement is made regardless of amount; and preserve receipts for all disbursements over $200 and all records for three years. [It] must file a statement of organization containing its name, address, the name of its custodian of records, and its banks, safety deposit boxes, or other depositories; must report any change in the above information within 10 days; and may dissolve only upon filing a written statement that it will no longer receive any contributions nor make disbursements, and that it has no outstanding debts or obligations.

Federal Election Commission v. Massachusetts Citizens for Life, 479 U.S. 238, 253 (1986). On top of these organizational and record-keeping requirements, a political committee has to report to the FEC, for public disclosure, the name, address, and employer of all donors in excess of $200. Additionally, prior to the decision in *SpeechNow.org v. Federal Election Commission*, 599 F.3d 686 (D.C. Cir. 2010) (*en banc*), all political committees were subject to limitations on the size of contributions they could accept, as well as the sources of those contributions.

In another part of the *Buckley* opinion that appears in Chapter 9 at pages 937–39, *infra*, the Court held that FECA's broad definition of "political committee" was unconstitutionally vague for the same reasons it held that the definition of "expenditure" was unconstitutionally vague. Because "'political committee' is defined only in terms of amount of annual 'contributions' and 'expenditures,' [it] could be interpreted to reach groups engaged purely in issue discussion. * * * To fulfill the purposes of the Act [the definition of 'political committee'] need only encompass organizations that are under the control of a candidate or the major purpose of which is the nomination or election of a candidate." *Buckley*, 424 U.S. at 79.

By narrowing the definition of "political committee" to organizations with a major purpose of nominating or electing candidates, the Court protected groups such as the American Civil Liberties Union, the U.S. Chamber of Commerce, the Sierra Club, and literally thousands of small citizens' groups around the country from having to register as political committees if they spent a small amount on direct political advocacy. But how would the "major purpose" of a group be ascertained? As a practical matter, the FEC held that a group had a "major purpose" of electing candidates if more than half of its activity consisted of making "contributions" or "expenditures" under FECA, as those terms were narrowly construed in *Buckley*. See *Akins v. Federal Election Commission*, 101 F.3d 731, 734 (D.C. Cir. 1996), *vacated on other grounds*, 524 U.S. 11 (1998).

FECA and FEC regulations provide for several types of political committees. An "authorized committee" is a campaign committee specifically authorized by a candidate for office to conduct the campaign. Every candidate must designate at least one authorized committee, and at least one "principal campaign committee" responsible for the campaign (typically these are one and the same). Political parties, including state and local party organizations, are designated as "party committees."

Political committees that are not party committees or candidate committees are generally referred to as PACs, an acronym for "political action committee." A PAC is a method for like-minded individuals to pool their resources to support candidates they favor. Basically, there are two types of PACs, "connected" and "unconnected." Connected PACs include PACs established by a corporation or labor union. The Act calls these PACs "separate segregated funds" (or "SSFs"), because the union or corporation must keep the funds separate from its general treasury. A "connected PAC" may also be established by a membership association (such as the Sierra Club or the National Rifle Association) or trade association (such as the National Association of Realtors). Though the rules governing these PACs, including how and from whom they can solicit contributions, are complex, a simplified explanation is that these SSFs and other connected PACs can solicit contributions only from individuals associated with the connected or sponsoring organization. Unions can solicit members and their families for contributions; corporations can solicit PAC contributions from shareholders, officers, and management and their families; connected PACs solicit from members of the sponsoring organization. A "non-connected committee"—as the name suggests—is not sponsored by or connected to any such entity, and is free to solicit contributions from the general public. The big advantage of a connected PAC is that the sponsoring organization can pay to organize and provide administrative support for the PAC. These costs—organizing the PAC, arranging fundraising events, maintaining mailing lists, complying with legal accounting and reporting requirements, and soliciting contributions—are often quite substantial, and can easily eat up 40 to 50% or more of a PAC's revenues. A non-connected PAC must absorb these costs from contributions given to it. But it has the advantage of being able to solicit contributions from anyone.

PACs are also designated as multi-candidate committees or non-multi-candidate committees. Non-multi-candidate committees are limited to contributing $1000 to a federal candidate, whereas multi-candidate committees can contribute up to $5000. A committee becomes a multi-candidate committee by being registered with the Federal Election Commission for at least six months, receiving donations from at least 51 contributors, and contributing to at least 5 candidates.

Finally, there are independent-expenditure committees, commonly known as "Super PACs." These are discussed at length *infra* at pages 882–85. In a nutshell, they make only independent expenditures, and are free from limitations on the size and sources of contributions to the PAC. They must comply with the usual political committee filing, reporting, and disclosure requirements.

As you read the following sections on contribution limits and especially expenditure limits, consider that in many cases, what is at stake is not merely the ability of a group to make such contributions or expenditures—as we have just seen, *Buckley* makes clear that the government cannot limit expenditures—but whether the disbursements by the group will be deemed to be "contributions" or "expenditures" under the Act, thus counting toward the group's "major purpose," and triggering political-committee status, with the accompanying regulatory burdens and restrictions on fundraising.

C. Limits on Contributions

A key distinction in *Buckley* is between limits on contributions, which are subject to a lower standard of review and generally held constitutional, and limits on expenditures, which are given more rigorous scrutiny and were found unconstitutional in *Buckley*. Understanding this paradigm is basic to any understanding of campaign-finance law. In this section and the following two sections, we will see how the case law regulating contributions and expenditures has developed, and consider the effects of this dichotomy on regulation.

Limits on contributions take two basic forms: source limitations and amount limitations. For example, under the Federal Election Campaign Act, direct union and corporate contributions to candidates are prohibited. 52 U.S.C. § 30118. This is a source limitation. Contributions by individuals are allowed, but limited. 52 U.S.C. § 30117. This is an amount limitation. These limits on individual contributions are adjusted each election cycle for inflation, and published by the FEC. This all sounds simple enough, but the law provides a variety of often-confusing limits for contributions to—and by—different types of entities. The limits for the 2019–20 election cycle are shown in the figure below:

CONTRIBUTION LIMITS FOR 2019–2020

DONORS	RECIPIENTS				
	Candidate Committee	PAC[1] (SSF and Nonconnected)	State/District/ Local Party Committee	National Party Committee	Additional National Party Committee Accounts[2]
Individual	$2,800* per election	$5,000 per year	$10,000 per year (combined)	$35,500* per year	$106,500* per account, per year
Candidate Committee	$2,000 per election	$5,000 per year	Unlimited Transfers	Unlimited Transfers	
PAC Multicandidate	$5,000 per election	$5,000 per year	$5,000 per year (combined)	$15,000 per year	$45,000 per account, per year
PAC Nonmulticandidate	$2,800* per election	$5,000 per year	$10,000 per year (combined)	$35,500* per year	$106,500* per account, per year
State/District/Local Party Committee	$5,000 per election (combined)	$5,000 per year (combined)	Unlimited Transfers		
National Party Committee	$5,000 per election[3]	$5,000 per year			

*– Indexed for inflation in odd-numbered years.

[1] "PAC" here refers to a committee that makes contributions to other federal political committees. Independent-expenditure-only political committees (sometimes called "super PACs") may accept unlimited contributions, including from corporations and labor organizations.

[2] The limits in this column apply to a national party committee's accounts for: (i) the presidential nominating convention; (ii) election recounts and contests and other legal proceedings; and (iii) national party headquarters buildings. A party's national committee, Senate campaign committee and House campaign committee are each considered separate national party committees with separate limits. Only a national party committee, not the parties' national congressional campaign committees, may have an account for the presidential nominating convention.

[3] Additionally, a national party committee and its Senatorial campaign committee may contribute up to $49,600 combined per campaign to each Senate candidate.

This publication provides guidance on certain aspects of federal campaign finance law. This publication is not intended to replace the law or to change its meaning, nor does this publication create or confer any rights for or on any person or bind the Federal Election Commission (Commission) or the public. The reader is encouraged also to consult the Federal Election Campaign Act of 1971, as amended, Commission regulations, Commission advisory opinions, and applicable court decisions.

For further information, please contact:
Federal Election Commission
Washington, DC 20463
(800) 424-9530; (202) 694-1100
info@fec.gov

Issued February 2019

Notes and Questions

1. In *California Medical Association v. Federal Election Commission*, 453 U.S. 182 (1981), the California Medical Association (CMA), an unincorporated association of physicians, formed the California Medical Political Action Committee, a federal political action committee (PAC) governed by the Federal Election Campaign Act. The CMA wanted to spend more than $5,000 to pay the administrative cost of operating the PAC. But while the Federal Election Campaign Act allows corporations and unions to pay these administrative and compliance costs without limit, thus increasing the amounts that can be spent on political races, the Act makes no such provision for an unincorporated organization such as CMA to do so. Thus, CMA's payment of PAC expenses would exceed the legally allowable limit for contributions to a political committee.

CMA argued that it could hardly "corrupt" its own PAC, and also that it violated equal protection that a corporation could pay the administrative expenses of its separate segregated fund without counting it as a "contribution" to the PAC, but an unincorporated organization could not. The Court rejected both arguments, noting that if an unincorporated organization could pay all of a PAC's administrative expenses, that would free up other dollars to go to candidates, with the effect that the sponsoring organization would be circumventing the limits on contributions. As to the fact that corporations could pay those expenses, the Court noted that, that fact aside, corporations faced far more restrictions on their political activity than did an unincorporated entity, such as the CMA.

Does the result in *California Medical Association* do anything to prevent corruption or its appearance? If so, how? The California Medical Association's desire to provide administrative support for its PAC from its general treasury was undoubtedly prompted by the cost of operating and maintaining a PAC. For many PACs, the administrative and compliance costs can equal or even exceed the amount raised by the PAC for the purpose of making contributions to candidates. *See* John M. de Figueiredo & Elizabeth Garrett, *Paying for Politics*, 78 S. CAL. L. REV. 591, 603 (2005). Does the limit on the administrative support that an unincorporated organization such as CMA can give to its PAC increase the potential for corruption from PAC giving, given that PACs are still limited to contributing $5,000 to any one candidate?

2. In another early post-*Buckley* decision, *Federal Election Commission v. National Right to Work Committee*, 459 U.S. 197 (1982), the Court addressed the ability of a connected PAC to solicit contributions from the public. The National Right to Work Committee (NRWC) was a non-profit, non-stock corporation. The organization's articles of incorporation provided that the corporation "shall not have members." As an educational organization, NRWC regularly mailed millions of individuals from lists it had compiled or purchased, and such mailings typically included requests for financial support. Persons who responded to NRWC surveys and "action alerts," but who did not contribute financially, were considered "supporting members." Those

who contributed financially were called "active members." Both groups received acknowledgements and a membership card. However, such status gave them no voting rights or control over the organization, and there were no membership meetings or other member activities.

After FECA was passed, NRWC established a separate segregated fund, or PAC, to receive donations and to make contributions to candidates for federal office who shared the organization's goals. In accordance with FEC regulations, NRWC paid for the administration of the PAC from its general treasury. As a connected PAC (*see* Note on Political Committees, *supra*, pp. 759–61), it was limited to soliciting contributions from "members." NRWC solicited contributions for the PAC from some 267,000 recent donors/"active members." The FEC argued that the persons solicited by NRWC were not actually "members" of the organization, and therefore were ineligible to contribute to the group's PAC. The Supreme Court, in a unanimous opinion, ruled that the solicited individuals were not "members" within the meaning of the statute, and thus could not be solicited to contribute to NRWC's PAC. The Court went on to dismiss NRWC's claim that the membership requirement violated its freedom of association, citing two justifications:

> The first purpose of § 441b, the government states, is to ensure that substantial aggregations of wealth amassed by the special advantages which go with the corporate form of organization should not be converted into political "war chests" which could be used to incur political debts from legislators who are aided by the contributions. * * * The second purpose of the provisions, petitioners argue, is to protect the individuals who have paid money into a corporation or union for purposes other than the support of candidates from having that money used to support political candidates to whom they may be opposed. * * *
>
> We agree with petitioners that these purposes are sufficient to justify the regulation at issue.

459 U.S. at 207–08. Did either of the purposes cited by the Court actually apply to NRWC?

As to the first, was NRWC amassing "substantial aggregations of wealth" from market activity? The Court expressed concern that large war chests might "be used to incur debts from legislators." But NRWC's "war chest" came from donations from members of the public. Was this a problem, given that limitations on contributions to the PAC ensured that any "war chest" so accumulated would be the result of large numbers of people voluntarily making small contributions, and that NRWC's PAC itself was limited to contributing no more than $5,000 to any candidate in an election? Or, to put it differently, should it matter if the candidate feels a debt to a group when that debt is incurred because the group represents large numbers of people who care about an issue? Don't those large numbers reflect the popularity of the group's ideas?

The Court also said that the "war chest" was accumulated thanks to "special advantages which go with the corporate form." What "special advantages" did NRWC gain from the corporate form that it could convert into a "political 'war chest'"? One might suggest limited liability as the most important advantage of the corporate form, but in fact NRWC would still be liable to the full extent of its members' contributions (that is to say, to the full extent of its budget and retained capital, since its income came from contributions). Further, contributions to NRWC were made from after-tax income and were not tax deductible, so while NRWC, as a non-profit, was not directly taxed, its income had already been taxed at the donor level. Was there some other special benefit it obtained from the corporate form, other than ease in managing its affairs? Isn't that why corporations are created—to make it easier for groups of people to manage their joint affairs?

The Court's acceptance of the second interest offered by the state—protecting persons who have "paid money into a corporation or union" from having their "money used to support political candidates to whom they may be opposed"— is even more puzzling. Whatever the merits of that concern where members are required to join unions by law, *see Janus v. American Federation of State, County, and Municipal Employees*, 585 U.S. __, 138 S. Ct. 2448 (2018), or are unable to sell corporate stock without significant sacrifice, *see* Stuart Taylor, Jr., *Congress Can Help Repair Ruling's Damage*, NAT'L J., Jan. 30, 2010, *available at* https://www.stuarttaylorjr.com /content-congress-can-help-repair-rulings-damage/, does it apply in the case of the National Right to Work Committee? Wouldn't most people who "paid money into the corporation" do so precisely because they favored the organization's political goals and trusted NRWC to make sound judgments in advancing those goals? (Note that the NRWC did not have capital stock, only members and donors.) Of course, donors may not agree with every decision of NRWC to endorse a candidate. But is it any more likely that a typical NRWC supporter would be upset if his money supported the occasional candidate the donor did not support, than a shareholder of a for-profit company might be with dozens of individual corporate decisions, such as lobbying for or against legislation? In short, when you give to any organization, don't you always run some risk that you may not agree with some future action the organization takes?

3. In the wake of *NRWC*, a good deal of an organization's ability to solicit and raise PAC funds will depend on the definition of "member." The Court suggested that to be considered "members" for purposes of PAC solicitations, individuals would need to have some ability to exercise control over an organization's administration and finance. How much control is enough? In 1993, the FEC adopted a regulation that limited the definition of "member" to those who either (i) had a "significant financial attachment" to the organization beyond "merely the payment of dues," (ii) paid regular dues and had the right to vote directly for at least one member of the organization's board, or (iii) had the right to vote directly for all members of the organization's board. 11 C.F.R. § 114.1(e) (1993). The United States Chamber of Commerce and the American Medical Association sued. The plaintiffs noted that

under the FEC regulation, over 220,000 dues-paying members of the Chamber (all but 63 of their total membership) and approximately 44,500 of the AMA's 290,000 dues-paying physicians would not qualify as "members," meaning that the organization could not solicit them for PAC contributions or communicate with them on political matters, other than by using its PAC. The Court of Appeals held that the definition violated the First Amendment rights of the plaintiffs to communicate with their members. *United States Chamber of Commerce v. Federal Election Commission*, 69 F.3d 600 (D.C. Cir. 1995). The FEC then amended its rule to provide that anyone paying regular dues qualified as a "member" for purposes of the Act. 11 C.F.R. § 100.134(f).

4. *Buckley* upheld limits on contributions, but can a donation be limited merely because it is a "contribution" to a political organization? In *Citizens Against Rent Control/Coalition for Fair Housing v. City of Berkeley*, 454 U.S. 290 (1981), the City of Berkeley, California, had enacted an ordinance prohibiting contributions in excess of $250 to any political committee, including those formed solely to support or to oppose ballot measures. The Court declined to adopt a rigid, formalistic application of *Buckley* in which a contribution could be limited merely because it was called a "contribution." Rather, the Court insisted that the limit must have a functional relationship to the state's anti-corruption interest.

> *Buckley* identified a single narrow exception to the rule that limits on political activity were contrary to the First Amendment. The exception relates to the perception of undue influence of large contributors to a *candidate.* * * * "Referenda are held on issues, not candidates for public office. The risk of corruption perceived in cases involving candidate elections * * * simply is not present in a popular vote on a public issue."

454 U.S. at 296–298 (emphasis in original). The Court thus held unconstitutional a contribution limit applied to ballot committees.

5. *Problem.* City Alderman Conrad Sweat nearly lost his seat in the last election when his opponent, a political neophyte and wealthy auto-dealership owner, spent $100,000 of his own money on his campaign. This shattered the previous record for spending in a race for alderman, which had been just $54,000. The dealer has publicly indicated that he may seek the office again in the near future. The City's campaign-finance ordinance imposes a $500 limit on contributions to a campaign. Alderman Sweat has proposed an amendment to the ordinance, which would redefine an expenditure by a candidate as a "contribution" to his own campaign, thus subjecting it to the $500 limit. Is the amendment constitutional? *See Nixon v. Shrink Missouri Government PAC*, 528 U.S. 377, 405 (2000) [p. 768] (Breyer, J., concurring).

6. Decisions in *California Medical Association*, *National Right to Work Committee*, and *Citizens Against Rent Control* aside, the first two decades of post-*Buckley* litigation largely concerned expenditures, rather than contributions. This was not surprising, given that *Buckley* clearly upheld limits on contributions to candidate committees and political parties. Recall that the *Buckley* plaintiffs argued that the

law was overbroad because the $1,000 limit—approximately $4,800 in inflation-adjusted dollars in 2020—was set at a level far below that creating any meaningful threat of corruption. The Court's response—"a court has no scalpel to probe, whether, say, a $2,000 ceiling might not serve as well as $1,000"—seemed to foreclose most challenges to limits. But *Buckley* did suggest that contribution limits could be challenged if it were shown that "the limitations prevented candidates and political committees from amassing the resources necessary for effective advocacy." As inflation gradually eroded the relative purchasing power of $1,000, it seemed only a matter of time before new challenges were brought to the level of limits on campaign contributions. Such a challenge reached the Supreme Court in 2000, in the following case. The case is also important for its discussion of the level of evidence that the state must put forth to justify the infringements contribution limits impose on First Amendment rights.

Nixon v. Shrink Missouri Government PAC

Supreme Court of the United States
528 U.S. 377, 120 S. Ct. 897, 145 L. Ed. 2d 886 (2000)

JUSTICE SOUTER delivered the opinion of the Court [in which CHIEF JUSTICE REHNQUIST, JUSTICE STEVENS, JUSTICE O'CONNOR, JUSTICE GINSBURG, and JUSTICE BREYER join].

The principal issues in this case are whether *Buckley* v. *Valeo*, 424 U.S. 1 (1976) [p. 728], is authority for state limits on contributions to state political candidates and whether the federal limits approved in *Buckley*, with or without adjustment for inflation, define the scope of permissible state limitations today. We hold *Buckley* to be authority for comparable state regulation, which need not be pegged to *Buckley*'s dollars.

In 1994, the Legislature of Missouri enacted Senate Bill 650 to restrict the permissible amounts of contributions to candidates for state office. * * *

The statutory dollar amounts are baselines for an adjustment [for inflation] each even-numbered year * * *. When this suit was filed, the limits ranged from a high of $1,075 for contributions to candidates for statewide office (including state auditor) and for any office where the population exceeded 250,000, down to $275 for contributions to candidates for state representative or for any office for which there were fewer than 100,000 people represented.

Respondents Shrink Missouri Government PAC, a political action committee, and Zev David Fredman, a candidate for the 1998 Republican nomination for state auditor, sought to enjoin enforcement of the contribution statute as violating their First and Fourteenth Amendment rights (presumably those of free speech, association, and equal protection, although the complaint did not so state). Shrink Missouri gave $1,025 to Fredman's candidate committee in 1997, and another $50 in 1998. Shrink Missouri represented that, without the limitation, it would contribute more to the Fredman campaign. Fredman alleged he could campaign effectively only with more generous contributions than [the law] allowed.

[T]he District Court sustained the statute. * * * The Court of Appeals for the Eighth Circuit nonetheless enjoined enforcement of the law pending appeal and ultimately reversed. * * *

Precision about the relative rigor of the standard to review contribution limits was not a pretense of the *Buckley per curiam* opinion. To be sure, in addressing the speech claim, we explicitly rejected both *O'Brien* intermediate scrutiny for communicative action, see *United States* v. *O'Brien*, 391 U.S. 367 (1968), and the similar standard applicable to merely time, place, and manner restrictions. * * * In distinguishing these tests, the discussion referred generally to "the exacting scrutiny required by the First Amendment," and added that "the constitutional guarantee has its fullest and most urgent application precisely to the conduct of campaigns for political office." * * *

We then, however, drew a line between expenditures and contributions, treating expenditure restrictions as direct restraints on speech, which nonetheless suffered little direct effect from contribution limits. * * * We thus said, in effect, that limiting contributions left communication significantly unimpaired.

We flagged a similar difference between expenditure and contribution limitations in their impacts on the association right. * * * "We have consistently held that restrictions on contributions require less compelling justification than restrictions on independent spending." It has, in any event, been plain ever since *Buckley* that contribution limits would more readily clear the hurdles before them. * * * Thus, under *Buckley*'s standard of scrutiny, a contribution limit involving "significant interference" with associational rights could survive if the Government demonstrated that contribution regulation was "closely drawn" to match a "sufficiently important interest," though the dollar amount of the limit need not be "fine tun[ed]."

While we did not attempt to parse distinctions between the speech and association standards of scrutiny for contribution limits, we did make it clear that those restrictions bore more heavily on the associational right than on freedom to speak. We consequently proceeded on the understanding that a contribution limitation surviving a claim of associational abridgment would survive a speech challenge as well, and we held the standard satisfied by the contribution limits under review. * * *

In speaking of "improper influence" and "opportunities for abuse" in addition to "*quid pro quo* arrangements," we recognized a concern not confined to bribery of public officials, but extending to the broader threat from politicians too compliant with the wishes of large contributors. These were the obvious points behind our recognition that the Congress could constitutionally address the power of money "to influence governmental action" in ways less "blatant and specific" than bribery.

In defending its own statute, Missouri espouses those same interests of preventing corruption and the appearance of it that flows from munificent campaign contributions. Even without the authority of *Buckley*, there would be no serious question about the legitimacy of the interests claimed, which, after all, underlie bribery and antigratuity statutes. While neither law nor morals equate all political contributions, without more, with bribes, we spoke in *Buckley* of the perception of corruption "inherent in a regime of large individual financial contributions" to candidates for public office, as a source of concern "almost equal" to *quid pro quo* improbity. The public interest in countering that perception was, indeed, the entire answer to the overbreadth claim raised in the *Buckley* case. This made perfect sense. Leave the perception of impropriety unanswered, and the cynical assumption that large donors call the tune could jeopardize the willingness of voters to take part in democratic governance. Democracy works "only if the people have faith in those who govern, and that faith is bound to be shattered when high officials and their appointees engage in activities which arouse suspicions of malfeasance and corruption." *United States v. Mississippi Valley Generating Co.*, 364 U.S. 520 (1961).

Although respondents neither challenge the legitimacy of these objectives nor call for any reconsideration of *Buckley*, they take the State to task * * * for failing to justify the invocation of those interests with empirical evidence of actually corrupt practices or of a perception among Missouri voters that unrestricted contributions must have been exerting a covertly corrosive influence. The state statute is not void, however, for want of evidence.

The quantum of empirical evidence needed to satisfy heightened judicial scrutiny of legislative judgments will vary up or down with the novelty and plausibility of the justification raised. *Buckley* demonstrates that the dangers of large, corrupt contributions and the suspicion that large contributions are corrupt are neither novel nor implausible. * * *

* * * [T]his case does not present a close call requiring further definition of whatever the State's evidentiary obligation may be. * * * Although Missouri does not preserve legislative history, the State presented an affidavit from State Senator Wayne Goode, the co-chair of the state legislature's Interim Joint Committee on Campaign Finance Reform at the time the State enacted the contribution limits, who stated that large contributions have "the real potential to buy votes." The District Court cited newspaper accounts of large contributions supporting inferences of impropriety. One report questioned the state treasurer's decision to use a certain bank for most of Missouri's banking business after that institution contributed $20,000 to the treasurer's campaign. Another made much of the receipt by a candidate for state auditor of a $40,000 contribution from a brewery and one for $20,000 from a bank. * * * [T]he Eighth Circuit itself * * * identified a $420,000 contribution to candidates in northern Missouri from a political action committee linked to an investment bank, and three scandals, including one in which a state representative was "accused of sponsoring legislation in exchange for kickbacks," and another in which Missouri's former attorney general pleaded guilty to charges of conspiracy to misuse state property, after being indicted for using a state workers' compensation fund to benefit campaign contributors. And although majority votes do not,

as such, defeat First Amendment protections, the statewide vote on Proposition A [which imposed even stricter contribution limits than the ones enacted by the Missouri Legislature] certainly attested to the perception relied upon here: "[A]n overwhelming 74 percent of the voters of Missouri determined that contribution limits are necessary to combat corruption and the appearance thereof."

There might, of course, be need for a more extensive evidentiary documentation if respondents had made any showing of their own to cast doubt on the apparent implications of *Buckley*'s evidence and the record here, but the closest respondents come to challenging these conclusions is their invocation of academic studies said to indicate that large contributions to public officials or candidates do not actually result in changes in candidates' positions. Smith, *Money Talks: Speech, Corruption, Equality, and Campaign Finance*, 86 Geo. L.J. 45, 58 (1997); Smith, *Faulty Assumptions and Undemocratic Consequences of Campaign Finance Reform*, 105 Yale L.J. 1049, 1067–1068 (1995). Other studies, however, point the other way. F. Sorauf, Inside Campaign Finance 169 (1992); Hall & Wayman, *Buying Time: Moneyed Interests and the Mobilization of Bias in Congressional Committees*, 84 Am. Pol. Sci. Rev. 797 (1990); D. Magleby & C. Nelson, The Money Chase 78 (1990). Given the conflict among these publications, and the absence of any reason to think that public perception has been influenced by the studies cited by respondents, there is little reason to doubt that sometimes large contributions will work actual corruption of our political system, and no reason to question the existence of a corresponding suspicion among voters.

Nor do we see any support for respondents' various arguments that in spite of their striking resemblance to the limitations sustained in *Buckley*, those in Missouri are so different in kind as to raise essentially a new issue about the adequacy of the Missouri statute's tailoring to serve its purposes. Here, as in *Buckley*, "[t]here is no indication . . . that the contribution limitations imposed by the [law] would have any dramatic[ally] adverse effect on the funding of campaigns and political associations," and thus no showing that "the limitations prevented the candidates and political committees from amassing the resources necessary for effective advocacy." 424 U.S., at 21. The District Court found here that in the period since the Missouri limits became effective, "candidates for state elected office [have been] quite able to raise funds sufficient to run effective campaigns," and that "candidates for political office in the state are still able to amass impressive campaign war chests." * * *

These conclusions of the District Court and the supporting evidence also suffice to answer respondents' variant claim that the Missouri limits today differ in kind from *Buckley*'s owing to inflation since 1976. Respondents seem to assume that *Buckley* set a minimum constitutional threshold for contribution limits, which in dollars adjusted for loss of purchasing power are now well above the lines drawn by Missouri. But this assumption is a fundamental misunderstanding of what we held.

In *Buckley*, we specifically rejected the contention that $1,000, or any other amount, was a constitutional minimum below which legislatures could not regulate.

As indicated above, we referred instead to the outer limits of contribution regulation by asking whether there was any showing that the limits were so low as to impede the ability of candidates to "amas[s] the resources necessary for effective advocacy." We asked, in other words, whether the contribution limitation was so radical in effect as to render political association ineffective, drive the sound of a candidate's voice below the level of notice, and render contributions pointless. Such being the test, the issue in later cases cannot be truncated to a narrow question about the power of the dollar, but must go to the power to mount a campaign with all the dollars likely to be forthcoming. [T]he dictates of the First Amendment are not mere functions of the Consumer Price Index.

* * * The judgment of the Court of Appeals is, accordingly, reversed, and the case is remanded for proceedings consistent with this opinion.

It is so ordered.

JUSTICE STEVENS, concurring.

* * * Money is property; it is not speech.

Speech has the power to inspire volunteers to perform a multitude of tasks on a campaign trail, on a battleground, or even on a football field. Money, meanwhile, has the power to pay hired laborers to perform the same tasks. It does not follow, however, that the First Amendment provides the same measure of protection to the use of money to accomplish such goals as it provides to the use of ideas to achieve the same results.

* * * The right to use one's own money to hire gladiators, or to fund "speech by proxy," certainly merits significant constitutional protection. These property rights, however, are not entitled to the same protection as the right to say what one pleases.

JUSTICE BREYER, with whom JUSTICE GINSBURG joins, concurring.

The dissenters accuse the Court of weakening the First Amendment. They believe that failing to adopt a "strict scrutiny" standard "balance[s] away First Amendment freedoms." But the principal dissent oversimplifies the problem faced in the campaign finance context. It takes a difficult constitutional problem and turns it into a lopsided dispute between political expression and government censorship. Under the cover of this fiction and its accompanying formula, the dissent would make the Court absolute arbiter of a difficult question best left, in the main, to the political branches. * * *

[T]his is a case where constitutionally protected interests lie on both sides of the legal equation. For that reason there is no place for a strong presumption against constitutionality, of the sort often thought to accompany the words "strict scrutiny." Nor can we expect that mechanical application of the tests associated with "strict scrutiny"—the tests of "compelling interests" and "least restrictive means"—will properly resolve the difficult constitutional problem that campaign finance statutes pose. * * *

On the one hand, a decision to contribute money to a campaign is a matter of First Amendment concern—not because money *is* speech (it is not); but because it *enables* speech. Through contributions the contributor associates himself with the candidate's cause, helps the candidate communicate a political message with which the contributor agrees, and helps the candidate win by attracting the votes of similarly minded voters. * * * Both political association and political communication are at stake.

On the other hand, restrictions upon the amount any one individual can contribute to a particular candidate seek to protect the integrity of the electoral process—the means through which a free society democratically translates political speech into concrete governmental action. * * * Moreover, by limiting the size of the largest contributions, such restrictions aim to democratize the influence that money itself may bring to bear upon the electoral process. Cf. *Reynolds* v. *Sims*, 377 U.S. 533, 565 (1964) [p. 122] (in the context of apportionment, the Constitution "demands" that each citizen have "an equally effective voice"). In doing so, they seek to build public confidence in that process and broaden the base of a candidate's meaningful financial support, encouraging the public participation and open discussion that the First Amendment itself presupposes.

In service of these objectives, the statute imposes restrictions of degree. It does not deny the contributor the opportunity to associate with the candidate through a contribution, though it limits a contribution's size. Nor does it prevent the contributor from using money (alone or with others) to pay for the expression of the same views in other ways. Instead, it permits all supporters to contribute the same amount of money, in an attempt to make the process fairer and more democratic.

Under these circumstances, a presumption against constitutionality is out of place. I recognize that *Buckley* used language that could be interpreted to the contrary. It said, for example, that it rejected "the concept that government may restrict the speech of some elements of our society in order to enhance the relative voice of others." But those words cannot be taken literally. The Constitution often permits restrictions on the speech of some in order to prevent a few from drowning out the many—in Congress, for example, where constitutionally protected debate is limited to provide every Member an equal opportunity to express his or her views. Or in elections, where the Constitution tolerates numerous restrictions on ballot access, limiting the political rights of some so as to make effective the political rights of the entire electorate. See, *e.g.*, *Storer* v. *Brown*, 415 U.S. 724, 736 (1974) [p. 513]. Regardless, as the result in *Buckley* made clear, the statement does not automatically invalidate a statute that seeks a fairer electoral debate through contribution limits, nor should it forbid the Court to take account of the competing constitutional interests just mentioned.

In such circumstances — where a law significantly implicates competing consti-tutionally protected interests in complex ways — the Court has closely scrutinized the statute's impact on those interests, but refrained from employing a simple test that effectively presumes unconstitutionality. Rather, it has balanced interests. And in practice that has meant asking whether the statute burdens any one such interest in a manner out of proportion to the statute's salutary effects upon the others (perhaps, but not necessarily, because of the existence of a clearly superior, less restrictive alternative). Where a legislature has significantly greater institu-tional expertise, as, for example, in the field of election regulation, the Court in practice defers to empirical legislative judgments — at least where that deference does not risk such constitutional evils as, say, permitting incumbents to insulate themselves from effective electoral challenge. * * * Applying this approach to the present case, I would uphold the statute essentially for the reasons stated by the Court. * * *

JUSTICE KENNEDY, dissenting. * * *

* * * Whether our officeholders can discharge their duties in a proper way when they are beholden to certain interests both for reelection and for campaign support is, I should think, of constant concern not alone to citizens but to conscientious officeholders themselves. There are no easy answers, but the Constitution relies on one: open, robust, honest, unfettered speech that the voters can examine and assess in an ever-changing and more complex environment.

* * * It suffices here to say that the law in question does not come even close to passing any serious scrutiny. * * *

JUSTICE THOMAS, with whom JUSTICE SCALIA joins, dissenting.

In the process of ratifying Missouri's sweeping repression of political speech, the Court today adopts the analytic fallacies of our flawed decision in *Buckley* v. *Valeo*. Unfortunately, the Court is not content to merely adhere to erroneous prece-dent. Under the guise of applying *Buckley*, the Court proceeds to weaken the already enfeebled constitutional protection that *Buckley* afforded campaign contributions. In the end, the Court employs a *sui generis* test to balance away First Amendment freedoms.

Because the Court errs with each step it takes, I dissent. [O]ur decision in *Buckley* was in error, and I would overrule it. I would subject campaign contribution limi-tations to strict scrutiny, under which Missouri's contribution limits are patently unconstitutional.

I begin with a proposition that ought to be unassailable: Political speech is the primary object of First Amendment protection. * * * The Founders sought to pro-tect the rights of individuals to engage in political speech because a self-governing people depends upon the free exchange of political information. And that free exchange should receive the most protection when it matters the most—during campaigns for elective office. * * *

I do not start with these foundational principles because the Court openly disagrees with them. * * * Instead, I start with them because the Court today abandons them. For nearly half a century, this Court has extended First Amendment protection to a multitude of forms of "speech," such as making false defamatory statements, filing lawsuits, dancing nude, exhibiting drive-in movies with nudity, burning flags, and wearing military uniforms. Not surprisingly, the Courts of Appeals have followed our lead and concluded that the First Amendment protects, for example, begging, shouting obscenities, erecting tables on a sidewalk, and refusing to wear a necktie. In light of the many cases of this sort, today's decision is a most curious anomaly. Whatever the proper status of such activities under the First Amendment, I am confident that they are less integral to the functioning of our Republic than campaign contributions. Yet the majority today, rather than going out of its way to *protect* political speech, goes out of its way to *avoid* protecting it. [C]ontributions to political campaigns generate essential political speech. And contribution caps, which place a direct and substantial limit on core speech, should be met with the utmost skepticism and should receive the strictest scrutiny.

To justify its decision upholding contribution limitations while striking down expenditure limitations, the Court in *Buckley* explained that expenditure limits "represent substantial rather than merely theoretical restraints on the quantity and diversity of political speech," while contribution limits "entai[l] only a marginal restriction upon the contributor's ability to engage in free communication." In drawing this distinction, the Court in *Buckley* relied on the premise that contributing to a candidate differs qualitatively from directly spending money. It noted that "[w]hile contributions may result in political expression if spent by a candidate or an association to present views to the voters, the transformation of contributions into political debate involves speech by someone other than the contributor." * * *

But this was a faulty distinction *ab initio* because it ignored the reality of how speech of all kinds is disseminated:

> "Even in the case of a direct expenditure, there is usually some go-between that facilitates the dissemination of the spender's message—for instance, an advertising agency or a television station. To call a contribution 'speech by proxy' thus does little to differentiate it from an expenditure. The only possible difference is that contributions involve an extra step in the proxy chain. But again, that is a difference in form, not substance."

And, inasmuch as the speech-by-proxy argument was disconnected from the realities of political speech to begin with, it is not surprising that we have firmly rejected it since *Buckley*. In *Federal Election Comm'n* v. *National Conservative Political Action Comm.*, 470 U.S. 480 (1985), we cast aside the argument that a contribution does not represent the constitutionally protected speech of a contributor, recognizing "that the contributors obviously like the message they are hearing from these organizations and want to add their voices to that message; otherwise they would not part with their money." * * * Through contributing, citizens see to it that their views on policy and politics are articulated. In short, "they are aware that however great the confidence they may justly feel in their own good sense, their interests can be more effectually promoted by [another] than by themselves." The Federalist No. 35, p. 214 (C. Rossiter ed. 1961) (A. Hamilton). * * *

The decision of individuals to speak through contributions rather than through independent expenditures is entirely reasonable. Political campaigns are largely candidate focused and candidate driven. Citizens recognize that the best advocate for a candidate (and the policy positions he supports) tends to be the candidate himself. And candidate organizations also offer other advantages to citizens wishing to partake in political expression. Campaign organizations offer a ready-built, convenient means of communicating for donors wishing to support and amplify political messages. Furthermore, the leader of the organization—the candidate—has a strong self-interest in efficiently expending funds in a manner that maximizes the power of the messages the contributor seeks to disseminate. Individual citizens understandably realize that they "may add more to political discourse by giving rather than spending, if the donee is able to put the funds to more productive use than can the individual." *Colorado Republican* [*Federal Campaign Comm.* v. *Federal Election Comm'n*, 518 U.S. 604,] 636 [(1996)] [p. 886] (Thomas, J., concurring in judgment and dissenting in part). * * *

In the end, *Buckley*'s claim that contribution limits "d[o] not in any way infringe the contributor's freedom to discuss candidates and issues," ignores the distinct role of candidate organizations as a means of individual participation in the Nation's civic dialogue. The result is simply the suppression of political speech. By depriving donors of their right to speak through the candidate, contribution limits relegate donors' points of view to less effective modes of communication. Additionally, limiting contributions curtails individual participation. "Even for the affluent, the added costs in money or time of taking out a newspaper advertisement, handing out leaflets on the street, or standing in front of one's house with a hand-held sign may make the difference between participating and not participating in some public debate." *Buckley* completely failed in its attempt to provide a basis for permitting government to second-guess the individual choices of citizens partaking in quintessentially democratic activities. "The First Amendment mandates that we presume that speakers, not the government, know best both what they want to say and how to say it."

The Court in *Buckley* denigrated the speech interests not only of contributors, but also of candidates. * * *

[T]he right to free speech is a right held by each American, not by Americans en masse. The Court in *Buckley* provided no basis for suppressing the speech of an individual candidate simply because other candidates (or candidates in the aggregate) may succeed in reaching the voting public. And any such reasoning would fly in the face of the premise of our political system—liberty vested in individual hands safe-guards the functioning of our democracy. In the case at hand, the Missouri scheme has a clear and detrimental effect on a candidate such as respondent Fredman, who lacks the advantages of incumbency, name recognition, or substantial personal wealth, but who has managed to attract the support of a relatively small number of dedicated supporters: It forbids his message from reaching the voters. * * *

In my view, the Constitution leaves it entirely up to citizens and candidates to determine who shall speak, the means they will use, and the amount of speech sufficient to inform and persuade. *Buckley*'s ratification of the government's attempt to wrest this fundamental right from citizens was error. * * *

After ignoring these shortcomings, the Court proceeds to apply something less—much less—than strict scrutiny. Just how much less the majority never says. The Court in *Buckley* at least purported to employ a test of "closest scrutiny." The Court's words were belied by its actions, however, and it never deployed the test in the fashion that the superlative instructs. * * * The Court today abandons even that pretense and reviews contributions under the *sui generis* "*Buckley*'s standard of scrutiny," which fails to obscure the Court's ad hoc balancing away of First Amendment rights. * * *

After hiding behind *Buckley*'s discredited reasoning and invoking "*Buckley*'s standard of scrutiny," the Court proceeds to significantly extend the holding in that case. The Court's substantive departure from *Buckley* begins with a revision of our compelling-interest jurisprudence. In *Buckley*, the Court indicated that the only interest that could qualify as "compelling" in this area was the government's interest in reducing actual and apparent corruption. And the Court repeatedly used the word "corruption" in the narrow *quid pro quo* sense, meaning "[p]erversion or destruction of integrity in the discharge of public duties by bribery or favour." 3 Oxford English Dictionary 974 (2d ed. 1989). * * *

The majority today, by contrast, separates "corruption" from its *quid pro quo* roots and gives it a new, far-reaching (and speech-suppressing) definition, something like "[t]he perversion of anything from an original state of purity." 3 Oxford English Dictionary, *supra*, at 974. * * * And the Court proceeds to define that state of purity, casting aspersions on "politicians too compliant with the wishes of large contributors." "But precisely what the 'corruption' may consist of we are never told with assurance." Presumably, the majority does not mean that politicians should be free of attachments to constituent groups.[9] * * * [W]ithout bothering to offer any elaboration, much less justification, the majority permits vague and unenumerated

---

9. The Framers, of course, thought such attachments inevitable in a free society and that faction would infest the political process. As to controlling faction, James Madison explained, "There are again two methods of removing the causes of faction: the one, by destroying the liberty which is essential to its existence; the other, by giving to every citizen the same opinions, the same passions, and the same interests." The Federalist No. 10, p.78 (C. Rossiter ed. 1961). Contribution caps are an example of the first method, which Madison contemptuously dismissed:

harms to suffice as a compelling reason for the government to smother political speech. * * *

Missouri does assert that its contribution caps are aimed at preventing actual and apparent corruption. * * * But the State's contribution limits are not narrowly tailored to that harm. The limits directly suppress the political speech of both contributors and candidates, and only clumsily further the governmental interests that they allegedly serve. They are crudely tailored because they are massively overinclusive, prohibiting all donors who wish to contribute in excess of the cap from doing so and restricting donations without regard to whether the donors pose any real corruption risk. * * * Moreover, the government has less restrictive means of addressing its interest in curtailing corruption. Bribery laws bar precisely the *quid pro quo* arrangements that are targeted here. And disclosure laws "deter actual corruption and avoid the appearance of corruption by exposing large contributions and expenditures to the light of publicity." * * *

In the end, contribution limitations find support only in the proposition that other means will not be as effective at rooting out corruption. But when it comes to a significant infringement on our fundamental liberties, that some undesirable conduct may not be deterred is an insufficient justification to sweep in vast amounts of protected political speech. * * *

* * * States are free to enact laws that directly punish those engaged in corruption and require the disclosure of large contributions, but they are not free to enact generalized laws that suppress a tremendous amount of protected speech along with the targeted corruption. * * *

I respectfully dissent.

Notes and Questions

1. *Shrink PAC*, as this decision is often called, was the first in a series of cases from the early 2000s reflecting an approach that one commentator dubbed "the new deference." Richard L. Hasen, *Rethinking the Unconstitutionality of Contribution and Expenditure Limits in Ballot Measure Campaigns*, 78 S. CAL. L. REV. 885, 886 (2005). These cases—*Shrink PAC*; *Federal Election Commission v. Colorado Republican Federal Campaign Committee* (*Colorado Republican II*), 533 U.S. 431 (2001);

"It could never be more truly said than of the first remedy that it was worse than the disease. Liberty is to faction what air is to fire, an aliment without which it instantly expires. But it could not be a less folly to abolish liberty, which is essential to political life, because it nourishes faction than it would be to wish the annihilation of air, which is essential to animal life, because it imparts to fire its destructive agency." *Ibid.*
The Framers preferred a political system that harnessed such faction for good, preserving liberty while also ensuring good government. Rather than adopting the repressive "cure" for faction that the majority today endorses, the Framers armed individual citizens with a remedy. "If a faction consists of less than a majority, relief is supplied by the republican principle, which enables the majority to defeat its sinister views by regular vote." *Id.*, at 80.

Federal Election Commission v. Beaumont, 539 U.S. 146 (2003); and *McConnell v. Federal Election Commission*, 540 U.S. 93 (2003) [p. 829]—are marked by a high degree of deference to legislative judgment and expertise atypical of the Court's earlier campaign-finance decisions.

Consider the level of evidence that the Court found acceptable to justify Missouri's statute in *Shrink PAC*: a handful of newspaper editorial and affidavits submitted by supporters of the legislation opining, without examples of *quid pro quo* exchanges, on the potential harmful effects if the legislation were not passed. The Court held that the quantity of "empirical evidence needed to satisfy heightened judicial scrutiny of legislative judgments will vary up or down with the novelty and plausibility of the justification raised." Some have suggested, in the words of one scholar, that in *Shrink PAC*, "since contribution limits do not seem to be narrowly tailored to the problem of eliminating corruption, the Court simply lowered the bar." J. Clark Kelso, Book Review, *Mr. Smith Goes to Washington*, 1 ELECTION L.J. 75, 78 (2002). Do you think that the evidence described in the Court's opinion should be sufficient to carry the government's burden? Compare the Court's approach here to its approach in non-political-speech cases, *e.g.*, *Greater New Orleans Broadcasting Association v. United States*, 527 U.S. 173, 188 (1999) ("[A] governmental body seeking to sustain a restriction on commercial speech must demonstrate that the harms it recites are real and that its restriction will in fact alleviate them to a material degree.") (quoting *Edenfield v. Fane*, 507 U.S. 761, 768 (1993)); *Rubin v. Coors Brewing Co.*, 514 U.S. 476, 487 (1995) ("[T]his requirement [is] critical.").

2. *Shrink PAC* was the first challenge to the size of a contribution limit to reach the Supreme Court since *Buckley*. Missouri's 1998 limit of $1075 was the equivalent of approximately $355 in 1975, when *Buckley* was heard. Upholding contribution limits generally, the *Buckley* Court suggested that limits could nevertheless be unconstitutional if they "prevented candidates and political committees from amassing the resources necessary for effective advocacy." How would a court decide when or if this point were reached? Is there a realistic alternative to the posture of deference taken by the majority in *Shrink PAC*?

The majority relied on the District Court's finding that "candidates for political office in the state are still able to amass impressive campaign war chests." Justice Thomas's dissent focused specifically on the plaintiff, Zev Fredman, and his inability to compete under the Missouri limits. Which is more important to the First Amendment analysis—that most candidates can raise the funds needed to compete, or that some candidates cannot? Is free speech an aggregate right, or an individual right?

3. Justice Breyer suggested that the Court "in practice" has deferred to the legislature where it has "significantly greater institutional expertise, as, for example, in the field of election regulation." Is this true? Compare this to many of the cases that appear elsewhere in this book, *e.g.*, *Reynolds v. Sims*, 377 U.S. 533 (1964) [p. 122] (population criteria for redistricting); *Shaw v. Reno*, 509 U.S. 630 (1993) [p. 362]

(consideration of race in redistricting); *Tashjian v. Republican Party of Connecticut*, 479 U.S. 208 (1986) [p. 443] (closed primaries); *California Democratic Party v. Jones*, 530 U.S. 567 (2000) [p. 449] (blanket primaries); *Meyer v. Grant*, 486 U.S. 414 (1988) [p. 647] (gathering petition signatures); *Williams v. Rhodes*, 393 U.S. 23 (1968) [p. 495] (independent ballot access); *Republican Party of Minnesota v. White*, 536 U.S. 765 (2002) [p. 605] (speech in judicial elections), or *Buckley v. Valeo*, 424 U.S. 1 (1976) [p. 728] (independent expenditures in campaigns).

Justice Breyer did qualify his position by adding that deference has been accorded "at least where that deference does not risk such constitutional evils as, say, permitting incumbents to insulate themselves from effective electoral challenge." Do the cases listed above, and others in this book where the Court has not deferred to the legislature, hinge on incumbents insulating themselves from effective challenge? Or are there other evils, and if so, which evils should qualify as triggering a higher level of scrutiny, *i.e.*, less deference? In their separate *Shrink PAC* dissents, Justices Thomas and Kennedy both noted that Zev Fredman needed to accept larger contributions because he lacked the advantages of some other candidates, mainly incumbents. How is a Justice to tell, then, if a law allows incumbents to insulate themselves from challenge? One way might be through increased reliance on social-science research. *See* Richard L. Hasen, *The Newer Incoherence: Competition, Social Science, and Balancing in Campaign Finance Law after* Randall v. Sorrell, 68 Ohio St. L.J. 849 (2007). But does relying on social-science research merely put the judge exactly in the position of second-guessing legislative judgments? For a response to Professor Hasen, see Bradley A. Smith, *The John Roberts Salvage Company: After* McConnell, *a New Court Looks to Repair the Constitution*, 68 Ohio St. L.J. 891, 907–909 (2007).

4. *Shrink PAC* revealed deep divisions among the Justices in their approaches to campaign-finance restrictions. Beginning with *Buckley*, every Justice to serve on the Court had agreed that these were properly considered First Amendment cases. In *Shrink PAC*, Justice Stevens became the first Justice to disavow that paradigm. *See* Bradley A. Smith, McCutcheon v. Federal Election Commission: *An Unlikely Blockbuster*, 9 NYU J.L. & Liberty 48, 50 (2015). Justices Thomas and Scalia, meanwhile, broke firmly in the other direction. They renounced *Buckley*'s expenditure/contribution distinction and would have held limits on both unconstitutional, while Justice Kennedy stopped just short of joining them. Meanwhile, Justice Breyer staked out his position that there "is no place for a strong presumption of unconstitutionality, of the sort often thought to accompany the words 'strict scrutiny,'" thus rejecting the *Buckley* test in his own way. Since *Shrink PAC*, 5-4 decisions have been the norm in campaign-finance cases heard by the Court. *See* Smith, McCutcheon: *An Unlikely Blockbuster, supra*, at 53 n.10.

———————

In 2002, Congress passed the Bipartisan Campaign Reform Act, commonly known by its acronym "BCRA," or as "McCain-Feingold," after its primary sponsors in the Senate. BCRA was a wide-ranging statute that purported to address numerous campaign-finance issues, including contributions by minors, the definition of "coordinated" expenditures, and more, but its core provisions dealt with two perceived problems: "soft money" and "issue advocacy." The issue-advocacy provisions attempted to limit certain types of expenditures close to an election, and are discussed in § D of this Chapter.

The Federal Election Campaign Act limited contributions to candidate committees, parties, and PACs, when the contributions were made for the purpose of influencing federal elections. States, of course, remained free to set their own limits on contributions in connection with campaigns for state office. In an early advisory opinion, the Federal Election Commission permitted state political parties to accept contributions outside of FECA's source and amount limitations to be used in state and local elections. Advisory Opinion 1978-10, FEDERAL ELECTION CAMPAIGN FINANCING GUIDE (CCH) ¶ 5340. Later the FEC ruled that national parties could pay for activities affecting both state and federal elections, such as get-out-the-vote drives and generic party advertising (*e.g.*, "Vote Republican") with a mix of both federal and non-federal money, Advisory Opinion 1979-17, FEDERAL ELECTION CAMPAIGN FINANCING GUIDE (CCH) ¶ 5416. Money raised under the limitations of FECA gradually became known as "federal" or "hard" money. Money raised outside of FECA's limits became known as "non-federal" or "soft" money. In 1995, the Commission determined that soft money could be used to fund ads that mentioned federal candidates, so long as they did not expressly advocate the election or defeat of a candidate. Advisory Opinion 1995-25, FEDERAL ELECTION CAMPAIGN FINANCING GUIDE (CCH) ¶ 6162. As the permissible uses of soft money expanded, so did the amount raised and spent. By the election of 2000, soft money accounted for roughly 42% of the spending by the national political parties. Much of this money was raised in very large amounts — 800 donors contributed almost $300 million to the national parties in the 2000 election cycle.

BCRA prohibited national parties from receiving or spending soft money, prohibited national parties from soliciting or directing soft-money contributions to other organizations, and sharply limited the ability of state and local parties to use non-federal funds to pay for activities that might affect a federal election — such as voter registration and get-out-the-vote drives. All of these provisions and others in BCRA were challenged in *McConnell v. Federal Election Commission*, 540 U.S. 93 (2003) [p. 829]. In a lengthy, sprawling opinion, a 5-4 Court majority upheld all key provisions of the Act.

In a joint opinion by Justices O'Connor and Stevens, joined by Justices Souter, Ginsburg, and Breyer, the Court brushed aside claims that the statute was unconstitutionally overbroad. Particularly important was the Court's view of the anti-corruption interest at stake:

> Plaintiffs argue that without concrete evidence of an instance in which a federal officeholder has actually switched a vote (or, presumably, evidence of a specific instance where the public believes a vote was switched), Congress has not shown that there exists real or apparent corruption. But the record

is to the contrary. The evidence connects soft money to manipulations of the legislative calendar, leading to Congress' failure to enact, among other things, generic drug legislation, tort reform, and tobacco legislation. * * *

More importantly, plaintiffs conceive of corruption too narrowly. Our cases have firmly established that Congress' legitimate interest extends beyond preventing simple cash-for-votes corruption to curbing "undue influence on an officeholder's judgment, and the appearance of such influence." Many of the "deeply disturbing examples" of corruption cited by this Court in *Buckley* to justify FECA's contribution limits were not episodes of vote buying, but evidence that various corporate interests had given substantial donations to gain access to high-level government officials. Even if that access did not secure actual influence, it certainly gave the "appearance of such influence." * * *

JUSTICE KENNEDY [the author of the principal dissent] would limit Congress' regulatory interest *only* to the prevention of the actual or apparent *quid pro quo* corruption "inherent in" contributions made directly to, contributions made at the express behest of, and expenditures made in coordination with, a federal officeholder or candidate. Regulation of any other donation or expenditure—regardless of its size, the recipient's relationship to the candidate or officeholder, its potential impact on a candidate's election, its value to the candidate, or its unabashed and explicit intent to purchase influence—would, according to Justice Kennedy, simply be out of bounds. This crabbed view of corruption, and particularly of the appearance of corruption, ignores precedent, common sense, and the realities of political fundraising exposed by the record in this litigation.

JUSTICE KENNEDY's interpretation of the First Amendment would render Congress powerless to address more subtle but equally dispiriting forms of corruption. Just as troubling to a functioning democracy as classic *quid pro quo* corruption is the danger that officeholders will decide issues not on the merits or the desires of their constituencies, but according to the wishes of those who have made large financial contributions valued by the officeholder. Even if it occurs only occasionally, the potential for such undue influence is manifest. And unlike straight cash-for-votes transactions, such corruption is neither easily detected nor practical to criminalize. The best means of prevention is to identify and to remove the temptation. * * *

JUSTICE KENNEDY likewise takes too narrow a view of the appearance of corruption. He asserts that only those transactions with "inherent corruption potential," which he again limits to contributions directly to candidates, justify the inference "that regulating the conduct will stem the appearance of real corruption." In our view, however, Congress is not required to ignore historical evidence regarding a particular practice or to view conduct in isolation from its context. To be sure, mere political favoritism or opportunity for influence alone is insufficient to justify regulation. As the record demonstrates, it is the manner in which parties have *sold* access to federal candidates and officeholders that has given rise to the appearance of undue influence. Implicit (and, as the record shows, sometimes explicit) in the sale of access is the suggestion that money buys influence. It is no surprise then that purchasers of such access unabashedly admit that they are seeking to purchase just such influence. It was not unwarranted for Congress to conclude that the selling of access gives rise to the appearance of corruption. * * *

540 U.S. at 149–153.

The *McConnell* Court also rejected the plaintiffs' claim that BCRA violated the equal protection component of the Due Process Clause of the Fifth Amendment by subjecting parties to restrictions on activities and fund-raising that did not apply to interest groups:

Congress is fully entitled to consider the real-world differences between political parties and interest groups when crafting a system of campaign finance regulation. * * * Interest groups do not select slates of candidates for elections. Interest groups do not determine who will serve on legislative committees, elect congressional leadership, or organize legislative caucuses. Political parties have influence and power in the legislature that vastly exceeds that of any interest group. As a result, it is hardly surprising that party affiliation is the primary way by which voters identify candidates, or that parties in turn have special access to and relationships with federal officeholders. Congress' efforts at campaign finance regulation may account for these salient differences.

Id. at 188.

Notes and Questions

1. Perhaps the most significant element of the *McConnell* opinion was its definition of the corruption interest that the government may seek to address through reform. The Court held that mere preferential access to contributors was enough to justify the ban on party soft money. Richard Briffault, McConnell v. FEC *and the Transformation of Campaign Finance Law*, 3 ELECTION L.J. 147, 162–63 (2004), noted the effect:

By focusing on special access, *McConnell* reframed the corruption analysis from the consideration of contributions on formal decisions to their effect on the opportunity to influence government actions. * * * [T]he Court treated preferential access as a problem in itself, and found that Congress could take steps to eliminate a campaign finance device that created special incentives to officeholders to give special access to donors.

The *McConnell* Court determined that contributions to parties could be limited, "[e]ven if that access did not secure actual influence." Since *Buckley*, of course, the Court had recognized a legitimate state interest that went beyond preventing *quid pro quo* corruption to include preventing the "appearance of corruption." But in *McConnell*, the Court moved one step further, holding that the state may limit access that creates the opportunity for the appearance of corruption. See Lillian R. BeVier, McConnell v. FEC: *Not Senator Buckley's First Amendment*, 3 ELECTION L.J. 127 (2004), for a critique of this conclusion and other elements of the decision.

2. How big a problem is access? Consider the folowing scenario:

> You get back from lunch. You've got fourteen phone messages on your desk. Thirteen of them are from constituents you've never heard of, and one of them is from a guy who just came to your fundraiser two weeks earlier and gave you $2,000. Which phone call are you going to return first?

PHILIP M. STERN, THE BEST CONGRESS MONEY CAN BUY 101 (1988) (quoting former Congressman Michael Barnes). Certainly the idea that money buys access has a common-sense appeal, and the *McConnell* Court relied heavily on anecdotal tales from BCRA's congressional supporters about money and access. *See also* MARTIN SCHRAM, SPEAKING FREELY (1995).

Several scholars, however, have challenged whether this common-sense notion is empirically true. While there are no doubt anecdotal stories of access, these researchers argue that in fact constituents are more likely to gain access to members of Congress than are contributors. *See* John Samples, *Against Deference*, 12 NEXUS J. OP. 21, 28–31 (2007); Marie Hojnakni & David Kimball, *PAC Contributions and Lobbying Contacts in Congressional Committees*, 54 POL. RES. Q. 176 (2001); Michelle L. Chin et al., *A Foot in the Door: An Experimental Study of PAC and Constituency Influence on Access*, 62 J. POL. 543 (2000). *But see* Richard Hall & Frank Wyman, *Buying Time: Moneyed Interests and the Mobilization of Bias in Congressional Committees*, 84 AMER. POL. SCI. REV. 797 (1990). *See also* Bradley A. Smith, *Money Talks: Speech, Corruption, Equality, and Campaign Finance*, 86 GEO. L.J. 45, 92–93 (1997) (arguing that eliminating access based on campaign contributions would not increase political equality or decrease the appearance of corruption).

3. Contrary to many expectations, the national political parties were largely able to replace the soft money lost due to BCRA. Gary Jacobson, *A Collective Dilemma Solved: The Distribution of Party Campaign Resources in the 2006 and 2008 Congressional Elections* (paper presented at UCLA Election Law Symposium, Jan. 29, 2010). Nevertheless, the effect of BCRA on the parties remains hotly disputed. Supporters of BCRA argued that even if party fundraising were curtailed, parties would benefit because they would be weaned from their addiction to television advertising and forced to work harder to recruit volunteers and small donors. *See* Nathaniel Persily, *The Law of American Party Finance*, *in* PARTY FUNDING AND CAMPAIGN FINANCING IN INTERNATIONAL PERSPECTIVE, 212, 237–238 (Keith Ewing & Samuel Issacharoff eds., 2006) (citing *McConnell* defendants' expert). Others, however, have argued

that parties have indeed lost influence to non-party interest groups. *See, e.g.*, Jeff Brindle, *Real Reform Means Repealing BCRA and Strengthening Parties*, Campaigns and Elections (Sept. 30, 2012); Peter J. Wallison & Joel M. Gora, Better Parties, Better Government: A Realistic Program for Campaign Finance Reform (2009); Raymond J. La Raja, Small Change: Money, Political Parties, and Campaign Finance Reform (2008).

4. *McConnell*, following close on the heels of *Shrink PAC* [p. 768], *Federal Election Commission v. Colorado Republican Federal Campaign Committee*, 533 U.S. 431 (2001), and *Federal Election Commission v. Beaumont*, 539 U.S. 146 (2003), marks the apogee of judicial deference to congressional decision making. The majority argued that given Congress's particular expertise in elections and in witnessing the effects of money on legislative behavior, judicial deference to congressional decisions in this area was particularly appropriate. Justice Scalia, dissenting, argued that given Congress's particular vested interest in elections, and thus the potential for witting or unwitting self-dealing, judicial deference to congressional decisions in this area was particularly inappropriate. Which view do you find more persuasive?

Do legislators really know more about campaign-finance issues than they do about the issues involved in other bills? If so, should this lead to increased deference? BCRA was passed after nearly a decade of vote-trading and revisions aimed at attracting the votes of specific legislators. *See* John Samples, The Fallacy of Campaign Finance Reform 238–54 (2006). Does this history simply illustrate the usual horse-trading involved in the legislative process? Is horse-trading particularly problematic in the campaign-finance area, given the particular interest legislators might have in the rules governing their—and their competitors'—campaigns? Do they really know more about the legislation itself? Eleven months after BCRA took effect, members of the House Committee on Rules and Administration, which has jurisdiction over campaign-finance legislation, inquired as to whether the FEC might develop a program to explain the Act to members of Congress. Jennifer Yachnin, *House Admin Requests BCRA Symposium*, Roll Call, Oct. 30, 2003.

5. The *McConnell* opinions constitute one of the longest Supreme Court cases—by some measures *the* longest Supreme Court case—ever reported. The opinion's strongly deferential tone suggested that the Court was prepared to accept campaign-finance regulation going far beyond that upheld in *McConnell* itself. Thus, *McConnell* looked like a blockbuster case that could soon replace *Buckley* as the lodestar of campaign-finance jurisprudence. But *McConnell* did not hold up well. The majority opinion was heavily criticized, even by many who agreed with the judgment, *see, e.g.*, Richard L. Hasen, Buckley *Is Dead, Long Live* Buckley: *The New Campaign Finance Incoherence of* McConnell v. Federal Election Commission, 153 U. Pa. L. Rev. 31, 32–33 (2004), and before long, the Court itself began to back away from some of *McConnell*'s potential implications.

McConnell's holding on the soft-money ban, however, has held up against challenges. *See Republican National Committee v. Federal Election Commission*, 698 F.

Supp. 2d 150 (D.D.C.), *cert. denied*, 561 U.S. 1040 (2010); *In re Cao*, 619 F.3d 410 (5th Cir. 2010), *cert. denied*, 562 U.S. 1286 (2011). That fact notwithstanding, within months, litigation was underway that would cause the *McConnell* paradigm to begin to unravel.

By February 2006, when the Court heard *Randall v. Sorrell*, Chief Justice Roberts had replaced Chief Justice Rehnquist (who was in the majority in *Shrink PAC*, but dissented in *McConnell*), and Justice Alito had replaced Justice O'Connor (who was in the majority in both cases and co-authored the opinion of the Court in *McConnell*). *Randall* again presented the Court with the question of when, if ever, a contribution limit could be too low to withstand constitutional scrutiny. The Court was also asked to revisit *Buckley*'s holding concerning the constitutionality of spending limitations.

Randall v. Sorrell

Supreme Court of the United States
548 U.S. 230, 126 S. Ct. 2479, 165 L. Ed. 2d 482 (2006)

Justice Breyer announced the judgment of the Court and delivered an opinion, in which The Chief Justice [Roberts] joins, and in which Justice Alito joins except as to Parts II-B-1 and II-B-2.

We here consider the constitutionality of a Vermont campaign finance statute that limits both (1) the amounts that candidates for state office may spend on their campaigns (expenditure limitations) and (2) the amounts that individuals, organizations, and political parties may contribute to those campaigns (contribution limitations). We hold that both sets of limitations are inconsistent with the First Amendment. Well-established precedent makes clear that the expenditure limits violate the First Amendment. *Buckley v. Valeo*, 424 U.S. 1, 54–58 (1976) (*per curiam*) [p. 728]. The contribution limits are unconstitutional because in their specific details (involving low maximum levels and other restrictions) they fail to satisfy the First Amendment's requirement of careful tailoring. That is to say, they impose burdens upon First Amendment interests that (when viewed in light of the statute's legitimate objectives) are disproportionately severe.

I * * *

In 1997, Vermont enacted * * * [Act 64], the statute at issue here. Act 64, which took effect immediately after the 1998 elections, imposes mandatory expenditure limits on the total amount a candidate for state office can spend during a "two-year general election cycle," *i.e.*, the primary plus the general election, in approximately the following amounts: governor, $300,000; lieutenant governor, $100,000; other statewide offices, $45,000; state senator, $4,000 (plus an additional $2,500 for each additional seat in the district); state representative (two-member district), $3,000; and state representative (single member district), $2,000. These limits are adjusted for inflation in odd-numbered years * * *. Incumbents seeking reelection * * * may spend no more than 90% of the above amounts. * * *

With certain minor exceptions, expenditures over $50 made on a candidate's behalf by others count against the candidate's expenditure limit if those expenditures are "intentionally facilitated by, solicited by or approved by" the candidate's campaign. These provisions apply so as to count against a campaign's expenditure limit any spending by political parties or committees that is coordinated with the campaign and benefits the candidate. And any party expenditure that "primarily benefits six or fewer candidates who are associated with the political party" is "presumed" to be coordinated with the campaign and therefore to count against the campaign's expenditure limit.

Act 64 also imposes strict contribution limits. The amount any single individual can contribute to the campaign of a candidate for state office during a "two-year general election cycle" is limited as follows: governor, lieutenant governor, and other statewide offices, $400; state senator, $300; and state representative, $200. Unlike its expenditure limits, Act 64's contribution limits are not indexed for inflation.

A political committee is subject to these same limits. So is a political party, defined broadly to include "any subsidiary, branch or local unit" of a party, as well as any "national or regional affiliates" of a party (taken separately or together). Thus, for example, the statute treats the local, state, and national affiliates of the Democratic Party as if they were a single entity and limits their total contribution to a single candidate's campaign for governor (during the primary and the general election together) to $400.

The Act also imposes a limit of $2,000 upon the amount any individual can give to a political party during a 2-year general election cycle.

The Act defines "contribution" broadly in approximately the same way it defines "expenditure." Any expenditure made on a candidate's behalf counts as a contribution to the candidate if it is "intentionally facilitated by, solicited by or approved by" the candidate. And a party expenditure that "primarily benefits six or fewer candidates who are associated with the" party is "presumed" to count against the party's contribution limits.

There are a few exceptions. A candidate's own contributions to the campaign and those of the candidate's family fall outside the contribution limits. Volunteer services do not count as contributions. Nor does the cost of a meet-the-candidate function, provided that the total cost for the function amounts to $100 or less. * * *

II

[The Court determined that Vermont's limitations on expenditures were unconstitutional, and that it was not appropriate in this case to reconsider "so well established a precedent" as *Buckley*.]

III

We turn now to a more complex question, namely, the constitutionality of Act 64's contribution limits. The parties, while accepting *Buckley*'s approach, dispute whether, despite *Buckley*'s general approval of statutes that limit campaign contributions, Act 64's contribution limits are so severe that in the circumstances its particular limits violate the First Amendment. * * *

Following *Buckley*, we must determine whether Act 64's contribution limits prevent candidates from "amassing the resources necessary for effective [campaign] advocacy"; whether they magnify the advantages of incumbency to the point where they put challengers to a significant disadvantage; in a word, whether they are too low and too strict to survive First Amendment scrutiny. In answering these questions, we recognize, as *Buckley* stated, that we have "no scalpel to probe" each possible contribution level. We cannot determine with any degree of exactitude the precise restriction necessary to carry out the statute's legitimate objectives. In practice, the legislature is better equipped to make such empirical judgments, as legislators have "particular expertise" in matters related to the costs and nature of running for office. Thus ordinarily we have deferred to the legislature's determination of such matters.

Nonetheless, as *Buckley* acknowledged, we must recognize the existence of some lower bound. At some point the constitutional risks to the democratic electoral process become too great. After all, the interests underlying contribution limits, preventing corruption and the appearance of corruption, "directly implicate the integrity of our electoral process." Yet that rationale does not simply mean "the lower the limit, the better." That is because contribution limits that are too low can also harm the electoral process by preventing challengers from mounting effective campaigns against incumbent officeholders, thereby reducing democratic accountability. Were we to ignore that fact, a statute that seeks to regulate campaign contributions could itself prove an obstacle to the very electoral fairness it seeks to promote. Thus, we see no alternative to the exercise of independent judicial judgment as a statute reaches those outer limits. And, where there is strong indication in a particular case, *i.e.*, danger signs, that such risks exist (both present in kind and likely serious in degree), courts, including appellate courts, must review the record independently and carefully with an eye toward assessing the statute's "tailoring," that is, toward assessing the proportionality of the restrictions. * * *

We find those danger signs present here. As compared with the contribution limits upheld by the Court in the past, and with those in force in other States, Act 64's limits are sufficiently low as to generate suspicion that they are not closely drawn. The Act sets its limits per election cycle, which includes both a primary and a general election. Thus, in a gubernatorial race with both primary and final election contests, the Act's contribution limit amounts to $200 per election per candidate (with significantly lower limits for contributions to candidates for State Senate and House of Representatives). These limits apply both to contributions from individuals and to contributions from political parties, whether made in cash or in expenditures coordinated (or presumed to be coordinated) with the candidate.

These limits are well below the limits this Court upheld in *Buckley*. Indeed, in terms of real dollars (*i.e.*, adjusting for inflation), the Act's $200 per election limit on individual contributions to a campaign for governor is slightly more than one-twentieth of the limit on contributions to campaigns for federal office before the Court in *Buckley*. Adjusted to reflect its value in 1976 (the year *Buckley* was decided), Vermont's contribution limit on campaigns for statewide office (including governor) amounts to $113.91 per 2-year election cycle, or roughly $57 per election, as compared to the $1,000 per election limit on individual contributions at issue in *Buckley*. (The adjusted value of Act 64's limit on contributions from political parties to candidates for statewide office, again $200 per candidate per election, is just over one one-hundredth of the comparable limit before the Court in *Buckley*, $5,000 per election.) Yet Vermont's gubernatorial district—the entire State—is no smaller than the House districts to which *Buckley*'s limits applied. In 1976, the average congressional district contained a population of about 465,000. * * * Indeed, Vermont's population is 621,000—about one-third *larger*. * * *

Moreover, considered as a whole, Vermont's contribution limits are the lowest in the Nation. Act 64 limits contributions to candidates for statewide office (including governor) to $200 per candidate per election. We have found no State that imposes a lower per election limit. Indeed, we have found only seven States that impose limits on contributions to candidates for statewide office at or below $500 per election, more than twice Act 64's limit. * * * We are aware of no State that imposes a limit on contributions from political parties to candidates for statewide office lower than Act 64's $200 per candidate per election limit. Similarly, we have found only three States that have limits on contributions to candidates for state legislature below Act 64's $150 and $100 per election limits. And we are aware of no State that has a lower limit on contributions from political parties to state legislative candidates.

Finally, Vermont's limit is well below the lowest limit this Court has previously upheld, the limit of $1,075 per election (adjusted for inflation every two years) for candidates for Missouri state auditor. [*Nixon v. Shrink Missouri Government PAC*, 528 U.S. 377, 386 (2000) (*Shrink*) [p. 768].] The comparable Vermont limit of roughly $200 per election, not adjusted for inflation, is less than one-sixth of Missouri's current inflation-adjusted limit ($1,275).

We recognize that Vermont's population is much smaller than Missouri's. Indeed, Vermont is about one-ninth of the size of Missouri. Thus, *per citizen*, Vermont's limit is slightly more generous. As of 2006, the ratio of the contribution limit to the size of the constituency in Vermont is .00064, while Missouri's ratio is .00044, 31% lower.

But this does not necessarily mean that Vermont's limits are less objectionable than the limit upheld in *Shrink*. A campaign for state auditor is likely to be less costly than a campaign for governor; campaign costs do not automatically increase or decrease in precise proportion to the size of an electoral district. Moreover, Vermont's limits, unlike Missouri's limits, apply in the same amounts to contributions made by political parties. And, as we have said, Missouri's (current) $1,275 per election limit, unlike Vermont's $200 per election limit, is indexed for inflation.

The factors we have mentioned offset any neutralizing force of population differences. At the very least, they make it difficult to treat *Shrink*'s (then) $1,075 limit as providing affirmative support for the lawfulness of Vermont's far lower levels. *Cf.* 528 U.S., at 404 (BREYER, J., concurring) (the *Shrink* "limit . . . is low enough to raise . . . a [significant constitutional] question"). And even were that not so, Vermont's failure to index for inflation means that Vermont's levels would soon be far lower than Missouri's regardless of the method of comparison.

In sum, Act 64's contribution limits are substantially lower than both the limits we have previously upheld and comparable limits in other States. These are danger signs that Act 64's contribution limits may fall outside tolerable First Amendment limits. We consequently must examine the record independently and carefully to determine whether Act 64's contribution limits are "closely drawn" to match the State's interests.

Our examination of the record convinces us that, from a constitutional perspective, Act 64's contribution limits are too restrictive. We reach this conclusion based not merely on the low dollar amounts of the limits themselves, but also on the statute's effect on political parties and on volunteer activity in Vermont elections. *Taken together*, Act 64's substantial restrictions on the ability of candidates to raise the funds necessary to run a competitive election, on the ability of political parties to help their candidates get elected, and on the ability of individual citizens to volunteer their time to campaigns show that the Act is not closely drawn to meet its objectives. In particular, five factors together lead us to this decision.

First, the record suggests, though it does not conclusively prove, that Act 64's contribution limits will significantly restrict the amount of funding available for challengers to run competitive campaigns. For one thing, the petitioners' expert, Clark Bensen, conducted a race-by-race analysis of the 1998 legislative elections (the last to take place before Act 64 took effect) and concluded that Act 64's contribution limits would have reduced the funds available in 1998 to Republican challengers in competitive races in amounts ranging from 18% to 53% of their total campaign income. * * *

For another thing, the petitioners' expert witnesses produced evidence and analysis showing that Vermont political parties (particularly the Republican Party) "target" their contributions to candidates in competitive races, that those contributions represent a significant amount of total candidate funding in such races, and that the contribution limits will cut the parties' contributions to competitive races dramatically. Their statistics showed that the party contributions accounted for a significant percentage of the total campaign income in those races. And their studies showed that Act 64's contribution limits would cut the party contributions by between 85% (for the legislature on average) and 99% (for governor).

More specifically, Bensen pointed out that in 1998, the Republican Party made contributions to 19 Senate campaigns in amounts that averaged $2,001, which on average represented 16% of the recipient campaign's total income. Act 64 would reduce these contributions to $300 per campaign, an average reduction of about 85%. The party contributed to 50 House campaigns in amounts averaging $787, which on average represented 28% of the recipient campaign's total income. Act 64 would reduce these contributions to $200 per campaign, an average reduction of 74.5%. And the party contributed $40,600 to its gubernatorial candidate, an amount that accounted for about 16% of the candidate's funding. The Act would have reduced that contribution by 99%, to $400.

Bensen added that 57% of all 1998 Senate campaigns and 30% of all House campaigns exceeded Act 64's expenditure limits, which were enacted along with the statute's contribution limits. Moreover, 27% of all Senate campaigns and 10% of all House campaigns spent more than double those limits.

The respondents did not contest these figures. Rather, they presented evidence that focused, not upon *strongly contested* campaigns, but upon the funding amounts available for the *average* campaign. * * *

The respondents' evidence leaves the petitioners' evidence unrebutted in certain key respects. That is because the critical question concerns not simply the *average* effect of contribution limits on fundraising but, more importantly, the ability of a candidate running against an incumbent officeholder to mount an effective *challenge*. And information about *average* races, rather than *competitive* races, is only distantly related to that question, because competitive races are likely to be far more expensive than the average race. We concede that the record does contain some anecdotal evidence supporting the respondents' position, namely, testimony about a post-Act-64 competitive mayoral campaign in Burlington, which suggests that a challenger can "amas[s] the resources necessary for effective advocacy." But the facts of that particular election are not described in sufficient detail to offer a convincing refutation of the implication arising from the petitioners' experts' studies.

Rather, the petitioners' studies, taken together with low *average* Vermont campaign expenditures and the typically higher costs that a challenger must bear to overcome the name-recognition advantage enjoyed by an incumbent, raise a reasonable inference that the contribution limits are so low that they may pose a significant obstacle to candidates in competitive elections. Information about average races does not rebut that inference. Consequently, the inference amounts to one factor (among others) that here counts against the constitutional validity of the contribution limits.

Second, Act 64's insistence that political parties abide by *exactly* the same low contribution limits that apply to other contributors threatens harm to a particularly important political right, the right to associate in a political party. * * *

The Act applies its $200 to $400 limits—precisely the same limits it applies to an individual—to virtually all affiliates of a political party taken together as if they were a single contributor. That means, for example, that the Vermont Democratic Party, taken together with all its local affiliates, can make one contribution of at most $400 to the Democratic gubernatorial candidate, one contribution of at most $300 to a Democratic candidate for State Senate, and one contribution of at most $200 to a Democratic candidate for the State House of Representatives. The Act includes within these limits not only direct monetary contributions but also expenditures in kind: stamps, stationery, coffee, doughnuts, gasoline, campaign buttons, and so forth. Indeed, it includes all party expenditures "intended to promote the election of a specific candidate or group of candidates" as long as the candidate's campaign "facilitate[s]," "solicit[s]," or "approve[s]" them. And a party expenditure that "primarily benefits six or fewer candidates who are associated with the" party is "presumed" to count against the party's contribution limits.

In addition to the negative effect on "amassing funds" that we have described, the Act would severely limit the ability of a party to assist its candidates' campaigns by engaging in coordinated spending on advertising, candidate events, voter lists, mass mailings, even yard signs. And, to an unusual degree, it would discourage those who wish to contribute small amounts of money to a party, amounts that easily comply with individual contribution limits. Suppose that many individuals do not know Vermont legislative candidates personally, but wish to contribute, say, $20 or $40, to the State Republican Party, with the intent that the party use the money to help elect whichever candidates the party believes would best advance its ideals and interests—the basic object of a political party. Or, to take a more extreme example, imagine that 6,000 Vermont citizens each want to give $1 to the State Democratic Party because, though unfamiliar with the details of the individual races, they would like to make a small financial contribution to the goal of electing a Democratic state legislature. And further imagine that the party believes control of the legislature will depend on the outcome of three (and only three) House races. The Act prohibits the party from giving $2,000 (of the $6,000) to each of its candidates in those pivotal races. Indeed, it permits the party to give no more than $200 to each candidate, thereby thwarting the aims of the 6,000 donors from making a meaningful contribution to state politics by giving a small amount of money to the party they support. Thus, the Act would severely inhibit collective political activity by preventing a political party from using contributions by small donors to provide meaningful assistance to any individual candidate. * * *

Third, the Act's treatment of volunteer services aggravates the problem. Like its federal statutory counterpart, the Act excludes from its definition of "contribution" all "services provided without compensation by individuals volunteering their time on behalf of a candidate." But the Act does not exclude the expenses those volunteers incur, such as travel expenses, in the course of campaign activities. The Act's broad definitions would seem to count those expenses against the volunteer's contribution limit, at least where the spending was facilitated or approved by campaign

officials. And, unlike the Federal Government's treatment of comparable requirements, the State has not (insofar as we are aware) created an exception excluding
such expenses. * * *

The absence of some such exception may matter in the present context, where
contribution limits are very low. That combination, low limits and no exceptions,
means that a gubernatorial campaign volunteer who makes four or five round trips
driving across the State performing volunteer activities coordinated with the campaign can find that he or she is near, or has surpassed, the contribution limit. So
too will a volunteer who offers a campaign the use of her house along with cof-
fee and doughnuts for a few dozen neighbors to meet the candidate, say, two or
three times during a campaign. Such supporters will have to keep careful track of
all miles driven, postage supplied (500 stamps equals $200), pencils and pads used,
and so forth. And any carelessness in this respect can prove costly, perhaps generating a headline, "Campaign laws violated," that works serious harm to the candidate.

These sorts of problems are unlikely to affect the constitutionality of a limit that
is reasonably high. * * * But Act 64's contribution limits are so low, and its definition
of "contribution" so broad, that the Act may well impede a campaign's ability effectively to use volunteers, thereby making it more difficult for individuals to associate
in this way. * * * Again, the very low limits at issue help to transform differences in
degree into difference in kind. And the likelihood of unjustified interference in the
present context is sufficiently great that we must consider the lack of tailoring in the
Act's definition of "contribution" as an added factor counting against the constitutional validity of the contribution limits before us.

Fourth, unlike the contribution limits we upheld in *Shrink*, Act 64's contribution
limits are not adjusted for inflation. Its limits decline in real value each year. Indeed,
in real dollars the Act's limits have already declined by about 20% ($200 in 2006
dollars has a real value of $160.66 in 1997 dollars). A failure to index limits means
that limits which are already suspiciously low will almost inevitably become too
low over time. It means that future legislation will be necessary to stop that almost
inevitable decline, and it thereby imposes the burden of preventing the decline upon
incumbent legislators who may not diligently police the need for changes in limit
levels to ensure the adequate financing of electoral challenges.

Fifth, we have found nowhere in the record any special justification that might
warrant a contribution limit so low or so restrictive as to bring about the serious
associational and expressive problems that we have described. Rather, the basic
justifications the State has advanced in support of such limits are those present
in *Buckley*. The record contains no indication that, for example, corruption (or
its appearance) in Vermont is significantly more serious a matter than elsewhere.
Indeed, other things being equal, one might reasonably believe that a contribution
of, say, $250 (or $450) to a candidate's campaign was less likely to prove a corruptive
force than the far larger contributions at issue in the other campaign finance cases
we have considered.

These five sets of considerations, taken together, lead us to conclude that Act 64's contribution limits are not narrowly tailored. * * *

IV

We conclude that * * * Act 64's contribution limits * * * violate the First Amendment, for they burden First Amendment interests in a manner that is disproportionate to the public purposes they were enacted to advance. * * *

JUSTICE ALITO, concurring in part and concurring in the judgment. [Omitted.]

JUSTICE KENNEDY, concurring in the judgment. [Omitted.]

JUSTICE THOMAS, with whom JUSTICE SCALIA joins, concurring in the judgment. [Omitted.]

JUSTICE STEVENS, dissenting. [This opinion appears at pages 816–18.]

JUSTICE SOUTER, with whom JUSTICE GINSBURG joins, and with whom JUSTICE STEVENS joins as to Parts II and III, dissenting. * * *

[In Part I, JUSTICE SOUTER argued that *Buckley* did not "categorically foreclose the possibility that some spending limits might comport with the First Amendment" and that the case should be remanded for further development of the record. That portion appears at page 818.]

II

Although I would defer judgment on the merits of the expenditure limitations, I believe the Court of Appeals correctly rejected the challenge to the contribution limits. Low though they are, one cannot say that "the contribution limitation[s are] so radical in effect as to render political association ineffective, drive the sound of a candidate's voice below the level of notice, and render contributions pointless." *Shrink*, 528 U.S., [at] 397.

The limits set by Vermont are not remarkable departures either from those previously upheld by this Court or from those lately adopted by other States. The plurality concedes that on a per-citizen measurement Vermont's limit for state-wide elections "is slightly more generous" than the one set by the Missouri statute approved by this Court in *Shrink*. Not only do those dollar amounts get more generous the smaller the district, they are consistent with limits set by the legislatures of many other States, all of them with populations larger than Vermont's, some significantly so. The point is not that this Court is bound by judicial sanctions of those numbers; it is that the consistency in legislative judgment tells us that Vermont is not an eccentric party of one, and that this is a case for the judicial deference that our own precedents say we owe here. * * *

To place Vermont's contribution limits beyond the constitutional pale, therefore, is to forget not only the facts of *Shrink*, but also our self-admonition against second-guessing legislative judgments about the risk of corruption to which contribution limits have to be fitted. And deference here would surely not be overly complaisant. Vermont's legislators themselves testified at length about the money that gets their special attention, *see* Act 64, H. 28, Legislative Findings and Intent (finding that "[s]ome candidates and elected officials, particularly when time is limited, respond and give access to contributors who make large contributions in preference to those who make small or no contributions"); testimony of Elizabeth Ready: "If I have only got an hour at night when I get home to return calls, I am much more likely to return [a donor's] call than I would [a non-donor's]. . . . [W]hen you only have a few minutes to talk, there are certain people that get access." * * * And testimony identified the amounts high enough to pay for effective campaigning in a State where the cost of running tends to be on the low side. * * *

Still, our cases do not say deference should be absolute. We can all imagine dollar limits that would be laughable, and per capita comparisons that would be meaningless because aggregated donations simply could not sustain effective campaigns. The plurality thinks that point has been reached in Vermont, and in particular that the low contribution limits threaten the ability of challengers to run effective races against incumbents. * * * [But t]he petitioners offered, and the plurality invokes, no evidence that the risk of a pro-incumbent advantage has been realized; in fact, * * * the experience of the Burlington race [where, the plurality concedes, a mayoral challenger was able to run a competitive campaign] is confirmed by recent empirical studies addressing this issue of incumbent's advantage. See, *e.g.*, Eom & Gross, *Contribution Limits and Disparity in Contributions Between Gubernatorial Candidates*, 59 Pol. Research Q. 99 (2006) ("Analyses of both the number of contributors and the dollar amount of contributions [to gubernatorial candidates] suggest no support for an increased bias in favor of incumbents resulting from the presence of campaign contribution limits. If anything, contribution limits can work to reduce the bias that traditionally works in favor of incumbents. Also, contribution limits do not seem to increase disparities between gubernatorial candidates in general") (emphasis deleted); Bardwell, *Money and Challenger Emergence in Gubernatorial Primaries*, 55 Pol. Research Q. 653 (2002) (finding that contribution limits favor neither incumbents nor challengers); Hogan, *The Costs of Representation in State Legislatures: Explaining Variations in Campaign Spending*, 81 Soc. Sci. Q. 941, 952 (2000) (finding that contribution limits reduce incumbent spending but have no effect on challenger or open-seat candidate spending). The Legislature of Vermont evidently tried to account for the realities of campaigning in Vermont, and I see no evidence of constitutional miscalculation sufficient to dispense with respect for its judgments.

III

* * * [I]ssues of detail call for some attention, the first being the requirement that a volunteer's expenses count against the person's contribution limit. The plurality certainly makes out the case that accounting for these expenses will be a colossal nuisance, but there is no case here that the nuisance will noticeably limit volunteering, or that volunteers whose expenses reach the limit cannot continue with their efforts subject to charging their candidates for the excess. Granted, if the provisions for contribution limits were teetering on the edge of unconstitutionality, Act 64's treatment of volunteers' expenses might be the finger-flick that gives the fatal push, but it has no greater significance than that.

Second, the failure of the Vermont law to index its limits for inflation is even less important. This challenge is to the law as it is, not to a law that may have a different impact after future inflation if the state legislature fails to bring it up to economic date.

Third, subjecting political parties to the same contribution limits as individuals does not condemn the Vermont scheme. What we said in *Federal Election Comm'n* v. *Colorado Republican Federal Campaign Comm.*, 533 U.S. 431, 454–455 (2001), dealing with regulation of coordinated expenditures, goes here, too. The capacity and desire of parties to make large contributions to competitive candidates with uphill fights are shared by rich individuals, and the risk that large party contributions would be channels to evade individual limits cannot be eliminated. Nor are these reasons to support the party limits undercut by claims that the restrictions render parties impotent, for the parties are not precluded from uncoordinated spending to benefit their candidates. That said, I acknowledge the suggestions in the petitioners' briefs that such restrictions in synergy with other influences weakening party power would justify a wholesale reexamination of the situation of party organization today. But whether such a comprehensive reexamination belongs in courts or only in legislatures is not an issue presented by these cases. * * *

IV

Because I do not see the contribution limits as depressed to the level of political inaudibility, I respectfully dissent.

Notes and Questions

1. In campaign-finance cases, it is rare for Justice Thomas and Justice Souter to agree, but the two agreed (Justice Thomas in an opinion not reprinted above) that *Randall*'s plurality opinion was not faithful to *Shrink PAC*. Indeed, Justice Souter seemed rather appropriately vexed at the near disappearance of *Shrink PAC* from the plurality opinion in *Randall*. Do you agree that *Randall* turned its back on *Shrink PAC*? Contrast, for example, *Shrink PAC*'s rejection of the plaintiff's claim that limits should be adjusted for inflation, with the emphasis the *Randall* plurality placed on the lack of inflation indexing in Vermont, and contrast the value of Vermont's limits with the limits in *Buckley* adjusted for inflation and population.

2. What is a contribution? One factor the Court considered in finding Vermont's contribution limits unconstitutionally low was the strict limit on volunteer activity. What types of volunteer activity can or should be considered contributions at all? Most citizens who volunteer for a campaign devote only a few hours to the effort. However, consider a law student who spends the summer volunteering for a campaign, devoting 10 weeks of full-time work. As a summer clerk at a local law firm, the student could earn $1000 per week. How should his volunteer work be valued? Similarly, the FEC's regulations on volunteer activity permit a major music artist to perform at a campaign rally on behalf of a candidate without charging a fee. *See* FEC Advisory Opinion 1980-42 (June 25, 1980). The value of such an appearance, of course, might normally be many thousands of dollars.

Under the equality rationale for campaign finance, rejected by the Supreme Court in *Buckley* but favored by many academics and activists, does it make sense to exclude volunteer activity from the definition of "contribution"? Certainly, such a construction allows a small number of people, mainly celebrities, to make contributions of enormous value that other citizens cannot match. Bradley A. Smith, *Faulty Assumptions and Undemocratic Consequences of Campaign Finance Reform*, 105 YALE L.J. 1049, 1078–81 (1996).

3. The ability of more and more people to create and upload videos for public viewing on the Internet, or to devote blog sites to political activity, has created new dilemmas for the government's regulatory apparatus. In Advisory Opinion 1998-22 (Nov. 12, 1998), the FEC determined that a web site set up by an individual to support President Clinton had to be reported as an independent expenditure. By 2002, the FEC had changed its tune; writing regulations to implement the Bipartisan Campaign Reform Act, the Agency wrote a broad exemption for Internet activity—so broad that a federal court struck it down as contrary to the Act. *See Shays v. Federal Election Commission*, 337 F. Supp. 2d 28 (D.D.C. 2004). The Agency's second effort at an Internet regulation also exempted a substantial amount of Internet activity, a decision that remains at once popular and controversial. *See* 71 Fed. Reg. 18589 (Apr. 12, 2006); Daniel W. Butrymowicz, *Loophole.com: How the FEC's Failure to Fully Regulate the Internet Undermines Campaign Finance Law*, 109 COLUM. L. REV. 1708 (2009).

4. The Federal Election Campaign Act and most state campaign-finance laws specifically exempt press editorializing and reporting from the definitions of contribution and expenditure. Is such an exemption constitutionally required? In 2005, voters in Washington State were asked to consider Initiative 912 (I-912), repealing a statewide gas tax enacted by the legislature. Two Seattle area radio hosts, Kirby Wilbur and John Carlson, were strongly critical of the gas tax, and began devoting substantial portions of their programs to advocating for repeal of the tax. They also encouraged listeners to contribute to No New Gas Tax (NNGT), the organization formed to support I-912, to circulate petitions to qualify the initiative for the ballot, and to visit NNGT's website and offices to obtain petitions. Officials in San Juan County and three Washington cities (all of whom stood to benefit from the gas-tax

revenue) filed a complaint with the state's Public Disclosure Commission, which enforced the state's campaign-finance laws. The local governments complained that the on-air activities of Wilbur and Carlson constituted "contributions" to NNGT that were required to be publicly reported under state law. (The prosecutors also hired a private law firm—the bond counsel for the State of Washington, and thus a firm that stood to benefit from bonds issued on the strength of the gas-tax revenues—to prosecute the matter.) A trial court held for the local governments, agreeing with the complainants that the activity of the radio hosts and their station constituted political contributions rather than "commentary." The Washington Supreme Court reversed, holding that the activities were not a "contribution" under the Washington statute, but declining to rule on the question of whether such activities were constitutionally protected. *San Juan County v. No New Gas Tax*, 157 P.3d 831 (Wash. 2007).

Does the Constitution mandate a media exemption? If so, who is entitled to the exemption? Talk radio or television hosts, such as Wilbur and Carlson, or Rush Limbaugh and Rachel Maddow? Politically oriented comedians such as Stephen Colbert? What about bloggers? Newspapers? *See* Clifford A. Jones, *The Stephen Colbert Problem: The Media Exemption for Corporate Political Advocacy and the "Hail to the Cheese Stephen Colbert Nacho Cheese Doritos 2008 Presidential Campaign Coverage,"* 19 U. Fla. J. L. & Pub. Pol'y 295 (2008) (exploring the breakdown of traditional media categories in the modern era). *See also* Richard L. Hasen, *Campaign Finance Laws and the Rupert Murdoch Problem*, 77 Tex. L. Rev. 1627 (1999) (arguing that the media exemption is "unjustifiable" and that limits on the press should be acceptable); Allison R. Hayward, *Regulation of Blog Campaign Advocacy on the Internet: Comparing U.S., German, and E.U. Approaches*, 16 Cardozo J. Int'l & Comp. L. 379 (2008) (comparing and evaluating various approaches).

Should the activities of the radio commentators have been considered a contribution at all, any media exemption aside? Do you think their activities were a "contribution" to the I-912 campaign? The Washington state law defined contribution, in pertinent part, as "(i) A loan, gift, deposit, subscription, forgiveness of indebtedness, donation, advance, pledge, payment, transfer of funds between political committees, or *anything of value, including personal and professional services* for less than full consideration; * * *. (iii) The *financing* by a person of the dissemination, distribution, or republication, in whole or in part, *of broadcast*, written, graphic, or other form of *political advertising* or electioneering communication *prepared by a candidate, a political committee, or its authorized agent.*" Had Wilber and Carlson made "contributions" within the meaning of the statute? If so, was the statute constitutional under *Buckley v. Valeo*?

5. Federal law similarly defines a "contribution" as "anything of value" that is given "for the purpose of influencing any election for Federal office." 52 U.S.C. § 30101(8)(A)(i). The definition was at issue in a controversy relating to Donald

Trump's 2016 presidential campaign. Shortly before the election, Russian citizens offered to provide the Trump campaign with information that would place Trump's opponent, Hillary Clinton, in a bad light. Although campaign officials met with the Russians, none of the promised information was ever delivered. Because foreigners are prohibited from making contributions, and because it is illegal to solicit an illegal contribution (whether or not the contribution actually takes place), some argued that the campaign officials who arranged for the meeting violated the law. While opposition research is certainly a "[]thing of value" in a general sense, should the statute be read so broadly as to treat information as a contribution? If information is included as a type of contribution, what would be the effect on First Amendment rights of American citizens? *See* Michael R. Dimino, *The Value of Information to Election Campaigns, in* Ellen S. Podgor et al., The Mueller Investigation and Beyond 157–63 (2020).

6. *Randall* remains the only case in which the Supreme Court has overturned a contribution limit as unconstitutionally low. But the case is not a dead letter. In *Thompson v. Hebdon*, 509 F.3d 1027, 1037 (9th Cir. 2018), *rev'd*, 140 S. Ct. 348 (2019), the Ninth Circuit did not apply *Randall* to a challenge to Alaska's contribution limits, noting the lack of a majority opinion in *Randall*. The Supreme Court unanimously reversed and remanded with instructions to apply *Randall.*

7. *Problem.* Does *Randall* provide a meaningful set of criteria for lower courts to apply in determining if a limit is unconstitutionally low? You are the legislative aide to a state senator in Colorado, population 4.9 million. Concerned about heavy spending in state races, the senator wants to propose a bill reducing the maximum contribution in state races to $400 in all state races. Contributions to parties would be capped at $500 and parties would be limited to contributing $500 to candidates. Individuals would be subject to an overall contributions cap of $2,500 per election cycle. Limits would not be indexed for inflation, but all volunteer services would be exempt. Following *Buckley*, independent expenditures are unlimited. The Senator wants your opinion as to whether the contribution limits are constitutional under *Randall*.

8. Although *Randall* is unique in holding a contribution limit to be too low, a few years later, the Supreme Court struck down a certain type of contribution limit in its entirety. In *McCutcheon v. Federal Election Commission*, which is set forth immediately below, the Court held that the limit in question—a restriction on the aggregate amount that an individual could contribute to all candidates in an election cycle—failed to address the government's anti-corruption interest in any meaningful way.

McCutcheon v. Federal Election Commission

Supreme Court of the United States
572 U.S. 185, 134 S. Ct. 1434, 188 L. Ed. 2d 468 (2014)

CHIEF JUSTICE ROBERTS announced the judgment of the Court and delivered an opinion, in which JUSTICE SCALIA, JUSTICE KENNEDY, and JUSTICE ALITO join. * * *

In a series of cases over the past 40 years, we have spelled out how to draw the constitutional line between the permissible goal of avoiding corruption in the political process and the impermissible desire simply to limit political speech. We have said that government regulation may not target the general gratitude a candidate may feel toward those who support him or his allies, or the political access such support may afford. "Ingratiation and access . . . are not corruption." *Citizens United* v. *Federal Election Comm'n*, 558 U.S. 310, 360 (2010) [p. 844]. They embody a central feature of democracy—that constituents support candidates who share their beliefs and interests, and candidates who are elected can be expected to be responsive to those concerns.

Any regulation must instead target what we have called "*quid pro quo*" corruption or its appearance. See *id.*, at 359. That Latin phrase captures the notion of a direct exchange of an official act for money. * * * "The hallmark of corruption is the financial *quid pro quo*: dollars for political favors." *Federal Election Comm'n v. National Conservative Political Action Comm.*, 470 U.S. 480, 497 (1985). Campaign finance restrictions that pursue other objectives, we have explained, impermissibly inject the Government "into the debate over who should govern." [*Arizona Free Enterprise Club's Freedom Club PAC v. Bennett*, 564 U.S. 721, 750 (2011) [p. 904].] And those who govern should be the *last* people to help decide who *should* govern.

The statute at issue in this case imposes two types of limits on campaign contributions. The first, called base limits, restricts how much money a donor may contribute to a particular candidate or committee. 2 U.S.C. § 441a(a)(1). The second, called aggregate limits, restricts how much money a donor may contribute in total to all candidates or committees. § 441a(a)(3). This case does not involve any challenge to the base limits, which we have previously upheld as serving the permissible objective of combatting corruption. The Government contends that the aggregate limits also serve that objective, by preventing circumvention of the base limits. We conclude, however, that the aggregate limits do little, if anything, to address that concern, while seriously restricting participation in the democratic process. The aggregate limits are therefore invalid under the First Amendment.

For the 2013–2014 election cycle, the base limits in the Federal Election Campaign Act of 1971 (FECA), as amended by the Bipartisan Campaign Reform Act of 2002 (BCRA), permit an individual to contribute up to $2,600 per election to a candidate ($5,200 total for the primary and general elections); $32,400 per year to a national party committee; $10,000 per year to a state or local party committee; and $5,000 per year to a political action committee, or "PAC." 2 U.S.C. § 441a(a)(1); 78 Fed. Reg. 8532 (2013). * * *

For the 2013–2014 election cycle, the aggregate limits in BCRA permit an individual to contribute a total of $48,600 to federal candidates and a total of $74,600 to other political committees. Of that $74,600, only $48,600 may be contributed to state or local party committees and PACs, as opposed to national party committees. § 441a(a)(3); 78 Fed. Reg. 8532. All told, an individual may contribute up to $123,200 to candidate and noncandidate committees during each two-year election cycle.

The base limits thus restrict how much money a donor may contribute to any particular candidate or committee; the aggregate limits have the effect of restricting how many candidates or committees the donor may support, to the extent permitted by the base limits. * * *

* * * *Buckley* held that the Government's interest in preventing *quid pro quo* corruption or its appearance was "sufficiently important," [424 U.S.,] at 26–27; we have elsewhere stated that the same interest may properly be labeled "compelling," see *National Conservative Political Action Comm.*, 470 U.S., at 496–497, so that the interest would satisfy even strict scrutiny. Moreover, regardless whether we apply strict scrutiny or *Buckley*'s "closely drawn" test, we must assess the fit between the stated governmental objective and the means selected to achieve that objective. Or to put it another way, if a law that restricts political speech does not "avoid unnecessary abridgement" of First Amendment rights, *Buckley*, 424 U.S., at 25, it cannot survive "rigorous" review.

Because we find a substantial mismatch between the Government's stated objective and the means selected to achieve it, the aggregate limits fail even under the "closely drawn" test. * * *

[In upholding a $25,000 aggregate contribution limit, *Buckley*] characterized that restriction as a "quite modest restraint upon protected political activity." [*Id.*, at 38.] We cannot agree with that characterization. An aggregate limit on *how many* candidates and committees an individual may support through contributions is not a "modest restraint" at all. The Government may no more restrict how many candidates or causes a donor may support than it may tell a newspaper how many candidates it may endorse.

To put it in the simplest terms, the aggregate limits prohibit an individual from fully contributing to the primary and general election campaigns of ten or more candidates, even if all contributions fall within the base limits Congress views as adequate to protect against corruption. The individual may give up to $5,200 each to nine candidates, but the aggregate limits constitute an outright ban on further contributions to any other candidate (beyond the additional $1,800 that may be spent before reaching the $48,600 aggregate limit). At that point, the limits deny the individual all ability to exercise his expressive and associational rights by contributing to someone who will advocate for his policy preferences. A donor must limit the number of candidates he supports, and may have to choose which of several policy concerns he will advance—clear First Amendment harms that the dissent never acknowledges.

It is no answer to say that the individual can simply contribute less money to more people. To require one person to contribute at lower levels than others because he wants to support more candidates or causes is to impose a special burden on broader participation in the democratic process. And as we have recently admonished, the Government may not penalize an individual for "robustly exercis[ing]" his First Amendment rights.

The First Amendment burden is especially great for individuals who do not have ready access to alternative avenues for supporting their preferred politicians and policies. In the context of base contribution limits, *Buckley* observed that a supporter could vindicate his associational interests by personally volunteering his time and energy on behalf of a candidate. Such personal volunteering is not a realistic alternative for those who wish to support a wide variety of candidates or causes. Other effective methods of supporting preferred candidates or causes without contributing money are reserved for a select few, such as entertainers capable of raising hundreds of thousands of dollars in a single evening. * * *

[W]hile preventing corruption or its appearance is a legitimate objective, Congress may target only a specific type of corruption—"*quid pro quo*" corruption. As *Buckley* explained, Congress may permissibly seek to rein in "large contributions [that] are given to secure a political *quid pro quo* from current and potential office holders." 424 U.S., at 26. In addition to "actual *quid pro quo* arrangements," Congress may permissibly limit "the appearance of corruption stemming from public awareness of the opportunities for abuse inherent in a regime of large individual financial contributions" to particular candidates. *Id.*, at 27; see also *Citizens United*, 558 U.S., at 359 ("When *Buckley* identified a sufficiently important governmental interest in preventing corruption or the appearance of corruption, that interest was limited to *quid pro quo* corruption").

Spending large sums of money in connection with elections, but not in connection with an effort to control the exercise of an officeholder's official duties, does not give rise to such *quid pro quo* corruption. Nor does the possibility that an individual who spends large sums may garner "influence over or access to" elected officials or political parties. *Id.*, at 359. And because the Government's interest in preventing the appearance of corruption is equally confined to the appearance of *quid pro quo* corruption, the Government may not seek to limit the appearance of mere influence or access. * * *

The Government has a strong interest * * * in combatting corruption and its appearance. We have, however, held that this interest must be limited to a specific kind of corruption—*quid pro quo* corruption—in order to ensure that the Government's efforts do not have the effect of restricting the First Amendment right of citizens to choose who shall govern them. For the reasons set forth, we conclude that the aggregate limits on contributions do not further the only governmental interest this Court accepted as legitimate in *Buckley*. They instead intrude without justification on a citizen's ability to exercise "the most fundamental First Amendment activities." *Buckley*, 424 U.S., at 14.

The judgment of the District Court is reversed.

JUSTICE THOMAS concurring in the judgment.

* * * Contributions and expenditures are simply "two sides of the same First Amendment coin," and our efforts to distinguish the two have produced mere "word games" rather than any cognizable principle of constitutional law. *Buckley, supra*, at 241, 244, (Burger, C.J., concurring in part and dissenting in part). For that reason, I would overrule *Buckley* and subject the aggregate limits in BCRA to strict scrutiny, which they would surely fail. * * *

JUSTICE BREYER, with whom JUSTICE GINSBURG, JUSTICE SOTOMAYOR, and JUSTICE KAGAN join, dissenting.

* * * The plurality's first claim—that large aggregate contributions do not "give rise" to "corruption"—is plausible only because the plurality defines "corruption" too narrowly. The plurality describes the constitutionally permissible objective of campaign finance regulation as follows: "Congress may target only a specific type of corruption—'quid pro quo' corruption." It then defines *quid pro quo* corruption to mean no more than "a direct exchange of an official act for money"—an act akin to bribery. It adds specifically that corruption does *not* include efforts to "garner 'influence over or access to' elected officials or political parties." Moreover, the Government's efforts to prevent the "appearance of corruption" are "equally confined to the appearance of *quid pro quo* corruption," as narrowly defined. In the plurality's view, a federal statute could not prevent an individual from writing a million dollar check to a political party (by donating to its various committees), because the rationale for any limit would "dangerously broade[n] the circumscribed definition of *quid pro quo* corruption articulated in our prior cases."

This critically important definition of "corruption" is inconsistent with the Court's prior case law (with the possible exception of *Citizens United*). It is virtually impossible to reconcile with this Court's decision in *McConnell* [v. *Federal Election Commission*, 540 U.S. 93 (2003)] [p. 829], upholding the Bipartisan Campaign Reform Act of 2002 (BCRA). And it misunderstands the constitutional importance of the interests at stake. In fact, constitutional interests—indeed, First Amendment interests—lie on both sides of the legal equation.

In reality, as the history of campaign finance reform shows and as our earlier cases on the subject have recognized, the anticorruption interest that drives Congress to regulate campaign contributions is a far broader, more important interest than the plurality acknowledges. It is an interest in maintaining the integrity of our public governmental institutions. And it is an interest rooted in the Constitution and in the First Amendment itself.

Consider at least one reason why the First Amendment protects political speech. Speech does not exist in a vacuum. Rather, political communication seeks to secure government action. A politically oriented "marketplace of ideas" seeks to form a public opinion that can and will influence elected representatives. * * * Accordingly, the First Amendment advances not only the individual's right to engage in political speech, but also the public's interest in preserving a democratic order in which collective speech *matters.*

What has this to do with corruption? It has everything to do with corruption. Corruption breaks the constitutionally necessary "chain of communication" between the people and their representatives. It derails the essential speech-to-government-action tie. Where enough money calls the tune, the general public will not be heard. Insofar as corruption cuts the link between political thought and political action, a free marketplace of political ideas loses its point.

That is one reason why the Court has stressed the constitutional importance of Congress' concern that a few large donations not drown out the voices of the many. * * *

That is also why the Court has used the phrase "subversion of the political process" to describe circumstances in which "[e]lected officials are influenced to act contrary to their obligations of office by the prospect of financial gain to themselves or infusions of money into their campaigns." *NCPAC*, 470 U.S., at 497.

The "appearance of corruption" can make matters worse. It can lead the public to believe that its efforts to communicate with its representatives or to help sway public opinion have little purpose. And a cynical public can lose interest in political participation altogether. Democracy, the Court has often said, cannot work unless "the people have faith in those who govern." *United States* v. *Mississippi Valley Generating Co.*, 364 U.S. 520, 562 (1961).

The upshot is that the interests the Court has long described as preventing "corruption" or the "appearance of corruption" are more than ordinary factors to be weighed against the constitutional right to political speech. Rather, they are interests rooted in the First Amendment itself. They are rooted in the constitutional effort to create a democracy responsive to the people—a government where laws reflect the very thoughts, views, ideas, and sentiments, the expression of which the First Amendment protects. Given that end, we can and should understand campaign finance laws as resting upon a broader and more significant constitutional rationale than the plurality's limited definition of "corruption" suggests. We should see these laws as seeking in significant part to strengthen, rather than weaken, the First Amendment. * * *

Notes and Questions

1. During the 2014 election cycle, the aggregate limits faced by McCutcheon, a self-employed engineer from Alabama, were $48,600 in contributions to all federal candidates, and $74,600 to all other political committees, of which no more than $48,600 could be contributed to PACs and state and local party committees, for a total of $123,200 in contributions. Obviously, only a very small number of Americans can afford to contribute so much to candidates in an election. Indeed, during the 2012 election cycle, fewer than 600 contributors bumped up against the cap. For this and other reasons, the immediate effects of *McCutcheon* are likely to be less than earthshattering:

> The inevitable result * * * [of *McCutcheon* is] that a small number of wealthy donors would take money that is currently not spent on politics, or used for independent expenditures, and contribute it directly to candidates and parties. This would, at the margin, positively address two longstanding concerns of regulatory advocates. First, by making more money available from proven donors, it would provide slight relief from the burdens of fundraising for officeholders. Second, it could be expected to bring a small percentage of independent expenditure dollars currently going to organizations with fewer disclosure obligations back to candidates and parties, which have the greatest disclosure obligations.

Bradley A. Smith, McCutcheon v. Federal Election Commission: *An Unlikely Blockbuster*, 9 N.Y.U. J. L. & LIB. 48, 51–52 (2015). Yet *McCutcheon*, like so many recent campaign-finance decisions on the Court, was a 5-4 decision, with very lengthy opinions and a heated dissent. Why? Consider the concept of corruption used by the majority in *McConnell* (discussed at pages 780–84, *supra*) versus the concept of corruption employed by the *McCutcheon* plurality. What will be the impact of this difference on future cases?

2. Notice that Justice Breyer's dissent attempted to shift the paradigm: For Justice Breyer, the First Amendment is not about preserving individual liberty from government encroachment, but about enabling the government to create a more efficient "marketplace of ideas" that will "secure government action." This conception of the Amendment as a "collective" right is radically different from the conception held by the majority. The majority saw the First Amendment as protecting an individual right to speak and as protecting the integrity of the electoral system from politicians themselves: Incumbent officeholders are "the last people" we should trust to regulate political speech. What ramifications flow from each view? Who has the better argument?

3. The district court in *McCutcheon* offered

> a hypothetical scenario that might occur in a world without aggregate limits. A single donor might contribute the maximum amount under the base limits to nearly 50 separate committees, each of which might then transfer

the money to the same single committee. That committee, in turn, might use all the transferred money for coordinated expenditures on behalf of a particular candidate, allowing the single donor to circumvent the base limit on the amount he may contribute to that candidate. The District Court acknowledged that "it may seem unlikely that so many separate entities would willingly serve as conduits" for the single donor's interests, but it concluded that such a scenario "is not hard to imagine."

572 U.S. at 195–96 (plurality opinion) (quoting 893 F. Supp. 2d 133, 140 (D.D.C. 2012) (three-judge court)).

The *McCutcheon* dissent went much further down this path than the District Court did, offering a series of hypothetical scenarios such as one in which over 500 candidate and party committees would coordinate all their activities, allowing a donor to write a single check for over $3.6 million (which would then be redistributed to all the various candidate and party committees participating subject to the base limits on each committee), and then having each of the 500-plus recipient committees transfer money to a single candidate. *Id.* at 247–48, 268, Appendix B, Table 2(b). Such hypotheticals were dismissed by the plurality as, in some cases, "illegal under current campaign finance laws," *id.* at 216, and in others as "highly implausible," "speculation," and "divorced from reality," *id.* at 213, 216–17. *See also* Allen Dickerson, McCutcheon v. FEC *and the Supreme Court's Pivot to* Buckley, 2014 CATO SUP. CT. REV. 95, 121–25 (2014); *id.* at 123 ("Notably, even in a world with aggregate limits, it would be possible for an individual conspiring with 15 PACs to funnel $74,600 to a single candidate. Yet, perhaps unsurprisingly, nobody appears to do this—because it would involve breaking an astounding number of federal laws."); *see also* Zac Morgan, McCutcheon's *Wild Hypotheticals*, INST. FOR FREE SPEECH, Dec. 11, 2013, *available at* https://www.ifs.org/news/mccutcheons-wild-hypotheticals/ (analyzing hypotheticals raised by Justices Kagan and Breyer at oral argument and discussing how those hypotheticals would violate the law even after a victory for the *McCutcheon* plaintiffs). Notice again the contrasting approaches of the two camps. In *Shrink Missouri Government PAC* [p. 768], the majority, upholding the regulation in question, had argued that the plausibility of the government's rationale effectively lowered the evidentiary bar needed to justify the regulation. The *McCutcheon* plurality effectively flipped that standard. Under *McCutcheon*, claims of possible "circumvention" by the government must be plausible and backed by some actual evidence or experience before they will be given credence as an important state interest by the Court. The plurality also rejected what it called a "prophylaxis-upon-prophylaxis" approach to preventing "circumvention" of the law. 572 U.S at 221. What is the importance of this change, going forward?

4. The dissent also objected to the plurality's claim that the aggregate limits were not closely drawn to address the government's concerns: "The plurality concludes that even if circumvention were a threat, the aggregate limits are 'poorly tailored' to address it * * * because there are several alternative ways Congress could prevent

evasion of the base limits. * * * The plurality, however, does not show, or try to show, that these hypothetical alternatives could effectively replace aggregate contribution limits." 572 U.S. at 257–58. Implicit in the plurality's approach was the assumption that it is up to the government to prove that its means are narrowly tailored—not up to the plaintiffs to prove that they are not. Who should have this burden? Why does it matter? How is it likely to affect future cases?

5. *Problems.* Consider the following scenarios in light of the foregoing case law on contributions:

A. A state legislator has discovered that a handful of children, some as young as age seven, have made contributions of $500 or more to candidates. In each case, the child's parents had already contributed the legal maximum to a candidate. The legislator believes that these donations are really controlled by the parents, who use the children to circumvent the limits on contributions. He proposes a law prohibiting anyone under the age of sixteen from contributing to a candidate. Is the law constitutional? *See McConnell v. Federal Election Commission*, 540 U.S. 93, 231–32 (2003).

B. State law allows an individual to contribute up to $5,000 to a candidate for the primary election, and up to $5,000 for the general election. This is true even if the candidate has no primary opponent. State law also allows a candidate to transfer funds left over from past races to his current campaign account. Thus, a candidate can transfer leftover primary funds to his general election account. Plaintiff Morgan Justice is running for state senate. A first-time candidate for office, he has just survived a difficult and expensive primary to win his party's nomination, and now faces an incumbent in the general election. The incumbent had no primary opposition. Plaintiff Guy Rich did not contribute to any candidate in the primary because he had no strong preference between the three candidates in the primary, but he now wishes to contribute $10,000 to Justice for the general election, as he strongly dislikes the incumbent and considers the race particularly important to his party's chances to gain a majority in the legislature. Justice and Rich have challenged the law. They do not challenge the total election cycle limit of $10,000, but argue that it is unconstitutional as a violation of the First Amendment and the Equal Protection Clause of the Fourteenth Amendment to force Rich to divide his contributions between the primary and general election. They argue that because the incumbent has no primary opposition, donors can effectively contribute $10,000 for the general election to the incumbent, but not to Justice. They also argue that if the incumbent is not "corrupted" by receiving $10,000 from a donor in an election year, neither is Justice. The state argues that the limits are per election, not per year or per candidate. It argues that while some candidates are unopposed in primaries, others are not. Further, in some races the primary may be hotly contested, but the winner of a particular party primary is almost certain to win the general election. Allowing a donor to contribute a full $10,000 in a hotly contested race may be enough to sway a legislator unduly and lead to *quid pro quo* corruption. What should be the result? *See Holmes v. Federal Election Commission*, 99 F. Supp. 3d 123 (D.D.C. 2015).

6. As part of the Bipartisan Campaign Reform Act of 2002 (BCRA), Congress enacted what became known as the "millionaire's amendment." The workings of the provision were exceedingly complex, but basically it provided that when a candidate was outspending his opponent by at least $350,000, owing to the candidate's spending his personal funds on the race, contribution limits for the outspent candidate would be trebled (from $2,300 to $6,900 at the time the provision was challenged). In *Davis v. Federal Election Commission*, 554 U.S. 724 (2008), the Court held the scheme unconstitutional. Justice Alito, writing for a 5-4 majority that included Chief Justice Roberts and Justices Scalia, Kennedy, and Thomas, argued that "while the [Amendment] does not impose a cap on a candidate's expenditure of personal funds, * * * it imposes an unprecedented penalty on any candidate who robustly exercises his First Amendment right. [The Millionaire's Amendment] requires a candidate to choose between the First Amendment right to engage in unfettered political speech and subjection to discriminatory fundraising limits." 554 U.S. at 738–39. The Court saw no anti-corruption interest served by the Amendment. Justice Stevens, writing in dissent for himself and Justices Souter, Ginsburg, and Breyer, argued, "Davis cannot show that the Millionaire's Amendment causes him * * * any First Amendment injury whatsoever. The Millionaire's Amendment quiets no speech at all." *Id.* at 753.

What class of candidates do you think is most likely to benefit from the Millionaire's Amendment? (Hint: Of the top dozen self-funded candidates for U.S. House and Senate in 2018, all were challengers. Center for Responsive Politics, https://www.opensecrets.org/overview/topself.php.) Historically, challengers are more reliant on large contributions than are incumbents, and the incumbent spending advantage more than doubled after passage of FECA's contribution limits in 1974. Most self-funded candidates are challengers. Why do you think this is so?

Was the *Davis* dissent correct in suggesting that no one was silenced by the Millionaire's Amendment? After all, challenger Davis was still free to spend his money. Is there some other problem with the state attempting to equalize the race by imposing different contribution limits on different candidates?

7. One longstanding feature of federal law and many state laws is a ban on political contributions by government contractors. Is such a complete ban overbroad, at least as applied to individuals who hold small research or consulting contracts with the government? *See Wagner v. Federal Election Commission*, 793 F.3d 1 (D.C. Cir. 2015) (*en banc*) (upholding the federal ban), *cert. denied*, 136 S. Ct. 895 (2016). The plaintiffs in the case were two consultants earning approximately $600/day when consulting with the government, and a researcher with a $12,000 work contract.

8. Do special circumstances exist that may justify bans on contributions for other classes of persons? *See* 17 C.F.R. § 275.206(4)–5 (barring an investment adviser who makes a political contribution to an elected official in a position to influence the selection of the adviser from providing any advisory services to the government for compensation, either directly or through a fund, for two years).

9. For many years, the constitutionality of contribution limits seemed to be one of the more settled questions in campaign-finance law. However, with the decisions in *Randall v. Sorrell*, 548 U.S. 230 (2006) [p. 786] and *McCutcheon*, it is no longer clear that this is the case. Justice Thomas has clearly stated his view that *Buckley* should be overruled on contribution limits, and that contribution limits should be held unconstitutional. Justice Alito has suggested, in a concurrence in *Randall*, that he would be open to reconsidering *Buckley* if the issue were placed squarely before the Court. 548 U.S. at 263–64 (Alito, J., concurring in part and concurring in the judgment). Meanwhile, Chief Justice Roberts wrote the plurality opinions in both *Randall* and *McCutcheon*. Justices Gorsuch and Kavanaugh have not been called on to consider contribution limits during their brief tenures, though both joined the *per curiam* opinion in *Thompson v. Hebdon*, 589 U.S. __, 140 S. Ct. 348 (2019), requiring the Ninth Circuit to evaluate Alaska's contribution limits under *Randall*. Are there possibly five votes to overturn *Buckley*'s holding on contribution limits?

Regardless of how you count the votes for possibly overruling *Buckley*, do you think *Buckley*'s distinction between contributions and expenditures can be justified, or are they truly, as Chief Justice Burger said, "two sides of the same First Amendment coin"? And if the latter, is the Court too easy on contribution limits, or too hard on expenditure limits? How rigorous should the Court be in its examination of campaign-contribution limits? And what is a sufficiently important state interest to overcome the language of the First Amendment, which is written in absolutist terms? As we turn to the constitutional treatment of expenditure limits, you might keep these questions in mind. You might also consider whether, constitutional issues aside, it makes sense to maintain contribution limits in a world of unlimited expenditures. Do they serve a purpose when expenditures are unlimited? What do you think would be the effect of removing—or dramatically raising—contribution limits? Consider that eleven states still have either no limits on contributions at all, or no general limits on the size of individual contributions in state races. Those states are Alabama, Indiana, Iowa, Mississippi, Nebraska, North Dakota, Oregon, Pennsylvania, Texas, Utah, and Virginia. *See* National Conference of State Legislatures, *State Limits on Contributions to Candidates, 2019–2020 Election Cycle* (2019), *at* https://www.ncsl.org/Portals/1/Documents/Elections/Contribution-Limits-to-Candidates-2019-2020.pdf?ver=2019-10-02-132802-117. Are you prepared to say that those states are better or more poorly governed than other states? That corruption is more or less of a problem than in other states? Are there any particular patterns or common traits in those states that seem relevant?

D. Limitations on Expenditures

1. *From* Buckley *to* Randall

Recall that in *Buckley v. Valeo*, 424 U.S. 1 (1976) (*per curiam*) [p. 728], the Supreme Court subjected limitations on expenditures to an apparently higher degree of scrutiny than it applied to limitations on contributions, and ultimately struck down limitations on total spending by candidates and political committees, on candidates' expenditures on their own campaigns, and on the amounts that could be spent by individuals or groups acting independently of a campaign. Before reading further, you may find it useful to review that section of the *Buckley* opinion.

Limitations on expenditures raise many of the same big-picture issues as do limitations on contributions: What role, if any, should the First Amendment leave for government to try to equalize political influence or campaign expenditures? What is meant by "corruption" and "the appearance of corruption"? To what extent can we trust government actors to make and to enforce fair rules governing political participation? Does the legislature merit more than the usual deference from the judiciary, due to its "particular expertise" in the field, or less, due to its apparent self-interest? What should be the standard of review? What is the empirical effect of money in campaigns—does it "drown out" voices, or does it allow voices to be heard?

While these and many other questions cut across the regulation of both contributions and expenditures (as well as the constitutional questions raised by those regulations), and while many cases discussed in this Chapter involve both contribution and expenditure limits, we believe it is useful to separate the analysis. There are two principal reasons for separating our consideration of contributions and expenditures. First, that has been the approach taken by the Court ever since *Buckley*. Second, understanding the distinction *Buckley* made between contributions and expenditures, and how that distinction has shaped regulatory efforts, is crucial to understanding campaign-finance law at a practical—and practitioner's—level.

As you consider the materials that follow, ask yourself whether the Court's constitutional distinction between contributions and expenditures makes sense, and perhaps more importantly, why it might make sense to a Court that has often been pulled in two very different directions. Note that in the cases in this section, the presumption is that the spending is either by the candidate, or independent of a candidate—that is, it is not done by a third party at the request of a candidate or after conferring with the candidate about the expenditure, its message, audience, timing, etc. In § E, we will discuss such "coordinated" expenditures.

Buckley struck down the limits on independent spending in the Federal Election Campaign Act "because we found no tendency in such expenditures, uncoordinated with the candidate or his campaign, to corrupt or to give the appearance of corruption." *Federal Election Commission v. National Conservative Political Action Committee*, 470 U.S. 480, 497 (1985). Expenditures made independently of a candidate's campaign did not present the opportunity for *quid pro quo* exchange—the "hallmark of corruption." *Id.* And unlike contribution limits, which did not necessarily reduce spending by candidates or campaign, expenditure limits "impose[d] direct and substantial restraints on the quantity of political speech." *Buckley*, 424 U.S. at 39. Similarly, limits on spending by campaigns themselves fell because "the interest in alleviating the corrupting influence of large contributions [wa]s served by * * * contribution limitations and disclosure provisions." *Id.* at 55.

Not quite three years after deciding *Buckley*, the Court re-emphasized that only the prevention of *quid pro quo* corruption could justify limitations on campaign contributions and expenditures. *First National Bank of Boston v. Bellotti*, 435 U.S. 765 (1978). The question at issue in *Bellotti* was the constitutionality of a Massachusetts statute that prohibited corporations from making expenditures regarding ballot initiatives. The Court struck down the prohibition, noting that "[t]he risk of corruption perceived in cases involving candidate elections simply is not present in a popular vote on a public issue." 435 U.S. at 790.

The FEC made another stab at defending expenditure limits after the 1980 presidential campaign. The Presidential Election Campaign Fund Act offers presidential candidates of major political parties the option of receiving public financing for their general-election campaigns. At the time of the 1980 campaign, if a presidential candidate accepted public financing, it was a criminal offense for independent political committees to expend more than $1,000 to further that candidate's election. The FEC sued two organizations, the National Conservative Political Action Committee ("NCPAC") and the Fund for a Conservative Majority ("FCM"), that had spent far in excess of $1000 urging the election of Ronald Reagan. The Court again rejected the effort to limit independent expenditures:

> On the record before us, these expenditures were "independent" in that they were not made at the request of or in coordination with the official Reagan election campaign committee or any of its agents. Indeed, there are indications that the efforts of these organizations were at times viewed with disfavor by the official campaign as counterproductive to its chosen strategy. NCPAC and FCM expressed their intention to conduct similar activities in support of President Reagan's reelection in 1984, and we may assume that they did so. * * *

> There can be no doubt that the expenditures at issue in this case produce speech at the core of the First Amendment. * * * The PACs in this case, of course, are not lone pamphleteers or street corner orators in the Tom Paine mold; they spend substantial amounts of money in order to communicate their political ideas through sophisticated media advertisements. And of course the criminal sanction in question is applied to the expenditure of money to propagate political views, rather than to the propagation of those views unaccompanied by the expenditure of money. But for purposes of presenting political views in connection with a nationwide Presidential

election, allowing the presentation of views while forbidding the expenditure of more than $1,000 to present them is much like allowing a speaker in a public hall to express his views while denying him the use of an amplifying system. * * *

We also reject the notion that the PACs' form of organization or method of solicitation diminishes their entitlement to First Amendment protection. The First Amendment freedom of association is squarely implicated in these cases. NCPAC and FCM are mechanisms by which large numbers of individuals of modest means can join together in organizations which serve to "[amplify] the voice of their adherents." *Buckley* v. *Valeo*, 424 U.S., at 22. It is significant that in 1979–1980 approximately 101,000 people contributed an average of $75 each to NCPAC and in 1980 approximately 100,000 people contributed an average of $25 each to FCM.

* * * [T]he contributors obviously like the message they are hearing from these organizations and want to add their voices to that message; otherwise they would not part with their money. To say that their collective action in pooling their resources to amplify their voices is not entitled to full First Amendment protection would subordinate the voices of those of modest means as opposed to those sufficiently wealthy to be able to buy expensive media ads with their own resources.

Justices Brennan and Marshall, who had joined the *Buckley* majority finding that limits on independent expenditures were unconstitutional, this time joined Justice White in dissent. Justice White reiterated his belief that *Buckley* was wrongly decided on the question of independent expenditures, but also took issue with the Court's empirical observations:

The credulous acceptance of the formal distinction between coordinated and independent expenditures blinks political reality. That the PACs' expenditures are not formally "coordinated" is too slender a reed on which to distinguish them from actual contributions to the campaign. The candidate cannot help but know of the extensive efforts "independently" undertaken on his behalf. In this realm of possible tacit understandings and implied agreements, I see no reason not to accept the congressional judgment that so-called independent expenditures must be closely regulated.

The PACs do not operate in an anonymous vacuum. There are significant contacts between an organization like NCPAC and candidates for, and holders of, public office. In addition, personnel may move between the staffs of candidates or officeholders and those of PACs.

Writing separately, Justice Marshall added, "an eager supporter will be able to discern a candidate's needs and desires; similarly, a willing candidate will notice the supporter's efforts." But is that really corruption? If the possibility that a candidate, once elected, will reward his supporters is enough to limit an activity, is there any political activity that cannot be limited by the government? Isn't the reason people participate in politics because they expect to be rewarded, if only by enactment of public policies that they favor? Should an officeholder be required to abandon the priorities of those who voted for him on the basis of his campaign platform?

A 2014 study of campaign staff, candidates, and other political players found considerable frustration among campaign staff "at not being able to coordinate with the outside groups. For example, there was a common experience of being on the receiving end of an attack and wanting to respond with a particular message but lacking the resources. Meanwhile, an outside group wanting to support the campaign has the resources to respond but lacks the critical information or, from the campaign's perspective, gets the message wrong." Daniel P. Tokaji & Renata E.B. Strause, *The New Soft Money: Outside Spending in Congressional Elections*, ELECTION LAW @ MORITZ 64 (2014). Respondents generally found it difficult to maximize efficiency with independent expenditures because of the lack of information. *Id.* at 62–68. Note also that federal law guarantees candidate expenditures the "lowest unit rate" from broadcasters. Independent spenders get no such favoritism, but must pay market rates for their ads. *See* 47 U.S.C. § 315(b).

The potential negative ramifications of the majority's view are generally well known and often voiced: large independent expenditures; a fear that these expenditures warp the electoral process and ultimately public policy; a loss of public confidence in government; the possibility of official action being taken in gratitude for large independent expenditures or in the hope of future independent expenditures; and actual *quid pro quo* exchanges that are simply difficult to prove without an obvious "victim" to report the crime. Less discussed are the potential negative ramifications of the dissent. What are some of the implications of the dissent's view? The limit on independent expenditures in both *Buckley* and *NCPAC* was just $1,000. Does such a limit effectively shut down most public participation in campaigns, except through direct (and limited) financial support of the candidates? Can citizens and the organizations to which they belong really be forced to choose (or to have the choice made for them by law) between contact with officeholders, which Justice White saw as destroying independence, and the right to speak and campaign for or against officeholders? What would such a political system look like? If access alone were enough to justify limits, how would the government decide who had enough access, and who needed more? Would there be constraints on government's ability to try to reallocate political power by limiting the ability of some to speak? What might that regime look like? *Cf.* Kurt Vonnegut, Jr., *Harrison Bergeron* (1961), *reprinted in* LAW IN LITERATURE: LEGAL THEMES IN SHORT STORIES 54 (Elizabeth Villiers Gemmette ed., 1992).

Support for spending limits did not die with *Buckley*, *Bellotti*, and *NCPAC*. In 1997, Vermont enacted Proposition 64, which included both new contribution limits and spending limitations. After a long, tortuous journey through the lower courts, Proposition 64 reached the Supreme Court in 2006. As we have already seen, *see* pp. 787–93, *supra*, the Supreme Court, in Part III of *Randall v. Sorrell*, held that the new contribution limits were unconstitutionally low. The Court first, however, discussed the question of expenditure limits.

Randall v. Sorrell

Supreme Court of the United States
548 U.S. 230, 126 S. Ct. 2479, 165 L. Ed. 2d 482 (2006)

JUSTICE BREYER announced the judgment of the Court and delivered an opinion, in which THE CHIEF JUSTICE [ROBERTS] joins, and in which JUSTICE ALITO joins except as to Parts II-B-1 and II-B-2.

We here consider the constitutionality of a Vermont campaign finance statute that limits * * * the amounts that candidates for state office may spend on their campaigns (expenditure limitations). * * *

II * * *

B

1

The respondents recognize that, in respect to expenditure limits, *Buckley* [v. *Valeo*, 424 U.S. 1 (1976)] [p. 728] appears to be a controlling—and unfavorable—precedent. They seek to overcome that precedent in two ways. First, they ask us in effect to overrule *Buckley*. Post-*Buckley* experience, they believe, has shown that contribution limits (and disclosure requirements) alone cannot effectively deter corruption or its appearance; hence experience has undermined an assumption underlying that case. Indeed, the respondents have devoted several pages of their briefs to attacking *Buckley*'s holding on expenditure limits.

Second, in the alternative, they ask us to limit the scope of *Buckley* significantly by distinguishing *Buckley* from the present case. They advance as a ground for distinction a justification for expenditure limitations that, they say, *Buckley* did not consider, namely, that such limits help to protect candidates from spending too much time raising money rather than devoting that time to campaigning among ordinary voters. We find neither argument persuasive.

2

The Court has often recognized the "fundamental importance" of *stare decisis*, the basic legal principle that commands judicial respect for a court's earlier decisions and the rules of law they embody. * * * [T]he rule of law demands that adhering to our prior case law be the norm. Departure from precedent is exceptional, and requires "special justification." * * * This is especially true where, as here, the principle has become settled through iteration and reiteration over a long period of time.

We can find here no such special justification that would require us to overrule *Buckley*. Subsequent case law has not made *Buckley* a legal anomaly or otherwise undermined its basic legal principles. * * * We cannot find in the respondents' claims any demonstration that circumstances have changed so radically as to undermine *Buckley*'s critical factual assumptions. The respondents have not shown, for example, any dramatic increase in corruption or its appearance in Vermont; nor have they shown that expenditure limits are the only way to attack that problem. * * * At the same time, *Buckley* has promoted considerable reliance. Congress and state legislatures have used *Buckley* when drafting campaign finance laws. And, as we have said, this Court has followed *Buckley*, upholding and applying its reasoning in later cases. Overruling *Buckley* now would dramatically undermine this reliance on our settled precedent.

For all these reasons, we find this a case that fits the *stare decisis* norm. And we do not perceive the strong justification that would be necessary to warrant overruling so well established a precedent. We consequently decline the respondents' invitation to reconsider *Buckley*.

3

The respondents also ask us to distinguish these cases from *Buckley*. But we can find no significant basis for that distinction. Act 64's expenditure limits are not substantially different from those at issue in *Buckley*. In both instances the limits consist of a dollar cap imposed upon a candidate's expenditures. Nor is Vermont's primary justification for imposing its expenditure limits significantly different from Congress' rationale for the *Buckley* limits: preventing corruption and its appearance.

The sole basis on which the respondents seek to distinguish *Buckley* concerns a further supporting justification. They argue that expenditure limits are necessary in order to reduce the amount of time candidates must spend raising money. Increased campaign costs, together with the fear of a better-funded opponent, mean that, without expenditure limits, a candidate must spend too much time raising money instead of meeting the voters and engaging in public debate. *Buckley*, the respondents add, did not fully consider this justification. Had it done so, they say, the Court would have upheld, not struck down, FECA's expenditure limits.

In our view, it is highly unlikely that fuller consideration of this time protection rationale would have changed *Buckley*'s result. The *Buckley* Court was aware of the connection between expenditure limits and a reduction in fundraising time. In a section of the opinion dealing with FECA's public financing provisions, it wrote that Congress was trying to "free candidates from the rigors of fundraising." * * * The Court of Appeals' opinion and the briefs filed in this Court pointed out that a natural consequence of higher campaign expenditures was that "candidates were compelled to allow to fund raising increasing and extreme amounts of money and energy." And, in any event, the connection between high campaign expenditures and increased fundraising demands seems perfectly obvious.

Under these circumstances, the respondents' argument amounts to no more than an invitation so to limit *Buckley*'s holding as effectively to overrule it. For the reasons set forth above, we decline that invitation as well. And, given *Buckley*'s continued authority, we must conclude that Act 64's expenditure limits violate the First Amendment. * * *

JUSTICE ALITO, concurring in part and concurring in the judgment. [JUSTICE ALITO argued that was not necessary to re-examine *Buckley* to decide this case.]

JUSTICE KENNEDY, concurring in the judgment. [Omitted.]

JUSTICE THOMAS, with whom JUSTICE SCALIA joins, concurring in the judgment. [Omitted.]

JUSTICE STEVENS, dissenting.

I am convinced that *Buckley*'s holding on expenditure limits is wrong, and that the time has come to overrule it.

I have not reached this conclusion lightly. As JUSTICE BREYER correctly observes, *stare decisis* is a principle of "fundamental importance." But it is not an inexorable command, and several factors, taken together, provide special justification for revisiting the constitutionality of statutory limits on candidate expenditures. * * *

As Justice White recognized, it is quite wrong to equate money and speech. *Buckley*, 424 U.S., at 263 (opinion concurring in part and dissenting in part). To the contrary:

> "The burden on actual speech imposed by limitations on the spending of money is minimal and indirect. All rights of direct political expression and advocacy are retained. Even under the campaign laws as originally enacted, everyone was free to spend as much as they chose to amplify their views on general political issues, just not specific candidates. The restrictions, to the extent they do affect speech, are viewpoint-neutral and indicate no hostility to the speech itself or its effects." *National Conservative Political Action Comm.*, 470 U.S., at 508–509 (White, J., dissenting).

Accordingly, these limits on expenditures are far more akin to time, place, and manner restrictions than to restrictions on the content of speech. Like Justice White, I would uphold them "so long as the purposes they serve are legitimate and sufficiently substantial."

Buckley's conclusion to the contrary relied on the following oft-quoted metaphor: "Being free to engage in unlimited political expression subject to a ceiling on expenditures is like being free to drive an automobile as far and as often as one desires on a single tank of gasoline."

But, of course, while a car cannot run without fuel, a candidate can speak without spending money. And while a car can only travel so many miles per gallon, there is no limit on the number of speeches or interviews a candidate may give on a limited budget. Moreover, provided that this budget is above a certain threshold, a candidate can exercise due care to ensure that her message reaches all voters. Just as a driver need not use a Hummer to reach her destination, so a candidate need not flood the airways with ceaseless sound-bites of trivial information in order to provide voters with reasons to support her.

* * * Not only do these limits serve as an important complement to corruption-reducing contribution limits, * * * but they also "protect equal access to the political arena, [and] free candidates and their staffs from the interminable burden of fund-raising." *Colorado Republican Federal Campaign Comm. v. Federal Election Comm'n*, 518 U.S. 604, 649–650 (1996) [p. 886] (STEVENS, J., dissenting). These last two interests are particularly acute. When campaign costs are so high that only the rich have the reach to throw their hats into the ring, we fail "to protect the political process from undue influence of large aggregations of capital and to promote individual responsibility for democratic government." States have recognized this problem, but *Buckley*'s perceived ban on expenditure limits severely limits their options in dealing with it.

The interest in freeing candidates from the fundraising straitjacket is even more compelling. Without expenditure limits, fundraising devours the time and attention of political leaders, leaving them too busy to handle their public responsibilities effectively. That fact was well recognized by backers of the legislation reviewed in *Buckley*, by the Court of Appeals judges who voted to uphold the expenditure limitations in that statute, and by Justice White—who not incidentally had personal experience as an active participant in a Presidential campaign. * * * The validity of their judgment has surely been confirmed by the mountains of evidence that has been accumulated in recent years concerning the time that elected officials spend raising money for future campaigns and the adverse effect of fundraising on the performance of their official duties.

Additionally, there is no convincing evidence that these important interests favoring expenditure limits are fronts for incumbency protection. *Buckley*'s cursory suggestion to the contrary failed to take into account the mixed evidence before it on this issue. * * * And only by "permit[ting] States nationwide to experiment with these critically needed reforms"—as 18 States urge us to do—will we enable further research on how expenditure limits relate to our incumbent reelection rates.[4]

---

4. Indeed, the example of the city of Albuquerque suggests that concerns about incumbent entrenchment are unfounded. In 1974, the city set expenditure limits on municipal elections. A 2-year interlude aside, these limits applied until 2001, when they were successfully challenged by municipal candidates. *Homans v. Albuquerque*, 217 F. Supp. 2d 1197, aff'd, 366 F.3d 900 (CA 10), cert. denied, 543 U.S. 1002 (2004). In its findings of fact, the Federal District Court determined that "[n]ationwide, eighty-eight percent (88%) of incumbent Mayors successfully sought reelection in

In the meantime, a legislative judgment that "enough is enough" should command the greatest possible deference from judges interpreting a constitutional provision that, at best, has an indirect relationship to activity that affects the quantity—rather than the quality or the content—of repetitive speech in the marketplace of ideas. * * *

JUSTICE SOUTER, with whom JUSTICE GINSBURG joins, * * * dissenting.

We said in *Buckley* that "expenditure limitations impose far greater restraints on the freedom of speech and association than do . . . contribution limitations," but the *Buckley* Court did not categorically foreclose the possibility that some spending limit might comport with the First Amendment. Instead, *Buckley* held that the constitutionality of an expenditure limitation "turns on whether the governmental interests advanced in its support satisfy the [applicable] exacting scrutiny." In applying that standard in *Buckley* itself, the Court gave no indication that it had given serious consideration to an aim that Vermont's statute now pursues: to alleviate the drain on candidates' and officials' time caused by the endless fundraising necessary to aggregate many small contributions to meet the opportunities for ever more expensive campaigning. * * *

The legislature's findings are surely significant enough to justify the Court of Appeals's remand to the District Court to decide whether Vermont's spending limits are the least restrictive means of accomplishing what the court unexceptionably found to be worthy objectives. * * *

Notes and Questions

1. Act 64 was passed, in part, specifically "to provoke a test case to overrule *Buckley* with regard to expenditure limitations." *Landell v. Sorrell*, 382 F.3d 91, 156 (2d Cir. 2002) (Winter, J., dissenting), *rev'd sub nom. Randall v. Sorrell*. To strengthen the case for overruling *Buckley*, the Vermont Legislature relied extensively on the interest cited by Justice Souter—saving the candidates (and hence frequently incumbent officeholders) the time involved in raising campaign funds. For a fuller explication of the "time-protection rationale" offered by Vermont in support of spending limits, *see* Mark C. Alexander, *Let Them Do Their Jobs: The Compelling Government Interest in Protecting the Time of Candidates and Elected Officials*, 37 LOY. U. CHI. L.J. 669 (2006); Vincent Blasi, *Free Speech and the Widening Gyre of Fund-Raising: Why Campaign Spending Limits May Not Violate the First Amendment After All*, 94 COLUM. L. REV. 1281 (1994).

One author of this casebook has argued that the state's evidence in *Randall* was "a fraud." *See* Bradley A. Smith, *Fooling the Court*, ELECTIONLAW@MORITZ, Mar. 1, 2006, *available at* http://moritzlaw.osu.edu/electionlaw/etable06/060301-smith01

1999. In contrast, since 1974, the City has had a zero percent (0%) success rate for Mayors seeking reelection." 217 F. Supp. 2d, at 1200. * * *

.php (noting that none of the Vermont lawmakers supporting the legislation either admitted to or identified any specific acts of corruption; that the state's attorney general admitted he had never prosecuted a politician for corruption in over a decade on the job; and that Vermont's legislators earned $8,000 annually for their part-time service, while the average cost of running for a two-year term in the legislature was $4,000—thus, assuming the part-time legislators had other sources of income, a typical legislator could completely fund an average campaign using just one-quarter of his salary, and never spend any time fundraising).

2. After *Randall*, is *Buckley* "superprecedent"? *See* Allison R. Hayward, *The Per Curiam Opinion of Steel:* Buckley v. Valeo *as Superprecedent?: Clues from Wisconsin and Vermont*, 2005–06 Cato Sup. Ct. Rev. 195 (2006).[f] Justice Breyer's plurality opinion put little effort into rebutting the state's time-protection argument, or into arguments that contribution limits alone are insufficient to deter corruption or its appearance. Rather, it dealt with the question of the constitutionality of spending limits primarily by clinging to precedent. Why do you think this was? Think about the Justices as strategic and repeat players, and consider the shift in the make-up of the Court after the decision in *McConnell v. Federal Election Commission*, 540 U.S. 93 (2003) [p. 829].

3. In arguing for not disturbing the *Buckley* precedent on expenditure limitations, Justice Breyer suggested that states have relied on *Buckley* when drafting legislation. Does this argument make sense? Would you have encouraged, or expected, more states to act as Vermont did and pass laws in direct defiance of the Court's constitutional ruling in *Buckley*? If the Court had reversed *Buckley* on expenditure limits, in what way would states have been harmed by their past reliance?

4. Justice Stevens argued that unlimited spending merely encourages "ceaseless sound-bites of trivial information." Compare Justice Stevens's view to Justice Thomas's in *Nixon v. Shrink Missouri Government PAC*, 528 U.S. 377, 411 (2000) [p. 768] (Thomas, J., dissenting): "[A] self-governing people depends upon the free exchange of political information." Do these differing views of the value of campaign speech explain the Court's divisions?

———————

f. *See* Bryan A. Garner et al., The Law of Judicial Precedent 802 (2016) (defining "superprecedent" as, *inter alia*, "A precedent that has become so well established in the law by a long life of reaffirmations that it is very difficult to overturn it; specif., a precedent that has been reaffirmed many times and whose rationale has been extended to cover cases in which the facts are dissimilar, even wholly unrelated, to those of the precedent. For example, *Roe v. Wade* [410 U.S. 113 (1973)] has been called a superprecedent because it has survived more than three dozen attempts to overturn it and has been relied on in decisions protecting gay rights and the right to die."). Garner et al. cross-reference "super stare decisis," which is in turn defined as "[t]he supposed doctrine that courts must follow earlier court decisions without considering whether those decisions were correct. Critics argue that strict adherence to old decisions can result in grave injustices and cite as an example the repudiation of *Plessy v. Ferguson*, 163 U.S. 537 (1896), by *Brown v. Board of Education*, 347 U.S. 483 (1954)." Garner et al., *supra*, at 807.

2. Restraints on Corporate and Union Expenditures

If general limits on expenditures are unconstitutional, may the characteristics of certain entities justify a limit or prohibition on expenditures by a particular class of speakers? And in particular, may corporate speech be limited?

The earliest state laws regulating campaign expenditures were prohibitions on corporate contributions that were passed in the 1890s. The first federal campaign-finance law was the Tillman Act, passed in 1907 and named for its primary Senate sponsor, the fiery, controversial South Carolina Senator "Pitchfork" Ben Tillman. ROBERT MUTCH, CAMPAIGNS, CONGRESSES AND COURTS: THE MAKING OF FEDERAL CAMPAIGN FINANCE LAW 2–6 (1988). Corporations soon learned, however, that they could escape the effects of the ban simply by making "expenditures" rather than "contributions." In 1947, Congress extended the ban to prohibit corporations (and unions) from using general-treasury funds for campaign expenditures. Enforcement of these laws was lax, however, and they were readily circumvented in any case. *See* BRADLEY A. SMITH, UNFREE SPEECH: THE FOLLY OF CAMPAIGN FINANCE REFORM 24–30 (2001). The prohibition on corporate and union spending from general-treasury funds was renewed as part of the 1974 amendments to FECA. 2 U.S.C. § 441b.

As we noted at the outset of this Chapter, the Supreme Court sidestepped the substantive issue in early challenges to prohibitions on corporate and union contributions. *See United States v. Auto Workers* (UAW-CIO) 352 U.S. 567 (1957) [p. 717]; *United States v. C.I.O.*, 335 U.S. 106 (1948). Several of the *Buckley* plaintiffs, such as the American Civil Liberties Union, were incorporated entities, but although *Buckley* struck down general limits on expenditures, this targeted, anti-corporate provision was not explicitly challenged in *Buckley*.

In 1978, the Supreme Court took up a Massachusetts statute that prohibited corporate expenditures intended to influence the public vote on ballot initiatives. The specific case involved a proposed amendment to the Massachusetts Constitution allowing for the imposition of a graduated income tax on individual income. In *First National Bank of Boston v. Bellotti*, 435 U.S. 765 (1978), the Court held the Massachusetts law unconstitutional, with an opinion that emphasized the rights of listeners as much as those of speakers. Justice Powell wrote for a 5-4 majority:

> The court below framed the principal question in this case as whether and to what extent corporations have First Amendment rights. We believe that the court posed the wrong question. The Constitution often protects interests broader than those of the party seeking their vindication. The First Amendment, in particular, serves significant societal interests. The proper question therefore is not whether corporations "have" First Amendment rights and, if so, whether they are coextensive with those of natural persons. Instead, the question must be whether [the Massachusetts statute] abridges expression that the First Amendment was meant to protect. * * *

If the speakers here were not corporations, no one would suggest that the State could silence their proposed speech. It is the type of speech indispensable to decisionmaking in a democracy, and this is no less true because the speech comes from a corporation rather than an individual. The inherent worth of the speech in terms of its capacity for informing the public does not depend upon the identity of its source, whether corporation, association, union, or individual. * * *

Referenda are held on issues, not candidates for public office. The risk of corruption perceived in cases involving candidate elections simply is not present in a popular vote on a public issue. To be sure, corporate advertising may influence the outcome of the vote; this would be its purpose. But the fact that advocacy may persuade the electorate is hardly a reason to suppress it: The Constitution "protects expression which is eloquent no less than that which is unconvincing." * * * [T]he people in our democracy are entrusted with the responsibility for judging and evaluating the relative merits of conflicting arguments.

435 U.S. at 775–76, 777, 790–91.

Bellotti seemed to settle the constitutional question of limiting corporate spending on ballot initiatives. But it left open the question of whether different compelling reasons might justify limits on corporate (and union) independent expenditures in candidate races. *See id.* at 787 n.26 ("[O]ur consideration of a corporation's right to speak on issues of general public interest implies no comparable right in the quite different context of participation in a political campaign for election to public office."). Such restrictions were common. The federal government had passed a prohibition on corporate and union expenditures in candidate races in 1947, and by 2010, twenty-three states also had bans on corporate spending in candidate races. National Conference of State Legislatures, *Life After Citizens United*, Jan. 28, 2010, *available at* http://www.ncsl.org/default.aspx?tabid=19607.

In *Federal Election Commission v. Massachusetts Citizens for Life, Inc.*, 479 U.S. 238 (1986), the Supreme Court held that such prohibitions on corporate political expenditures in candidate races were unconstitutional as applied to Massachusetts Citizens for Life ("MCFL"), a small, non-profit corporation. The Court stressed three features "essential to our holding": 1) the corporation was formed to promote political ideas, and did not engage in business activities; 2) it had no shareholders or others with a claim on its earnings; and 3) it was not established by another corporation, and accepted no corporate funds. The criteria in *MCFL* suggested that the harmful consequences of corporate speech did not attach to the corporate form; rather, only certain corporations' speech implicated the government's interests in preventing corporations from making independent expenditures. After all, MCFL was very different from Exxon or IBM, and those differences seemed to be at the core of the Court's opinion.

Four years after *MCFL*, the Court addressed a challenge to a Michigan ban on corporate expenditures in candidate races. The challenge was brought by an organization, the Michigan Chamber of Commerce, that in most ways seemed closer to an organization such as MCFL than to for-profit corporations, but which was funded almost entirely by for-profit corporations. In *Austin v. Michigan State Chamber of Commerce*, 494 U.S. 652 (1990), the Court upheld the constitutionality of the law. Writing for a 6-3 majority, Justice Marshall redefined the meaning of "corruption" that had guided the Court since *Buckley*:

> Regardless of whether [the] danger of "financial *quid pro quo*" corruption may be sufficient to justify a restriction on independent expenditures, Michigan's regulation aims at a different type of corruption in the political arena: the corrosive and distorting effects of immense aggregations of wealth that are accumulated with the help of the corporate form and that have little or no correlation to the public's support for the corporation's political ideas. The Act does not attempt "to equalize the relative influence of speakers on elections"; rather, it ensures that expenditures reflect actual public support for the political ideas espoused by corporations.

494 U.S. at 659–60.

The Court also rejected the Chamber's argument that the law violated the Fourteenth Amendment's Equal Protection Clause because it did not apply to unions and other aggregations of wealth:

> Whereas unincorporated unions, and indeed individuals, may be able to amass large treasuries, they do so without the significant state-conferred advantages of the corporate structure. * * * As a result, the funds available for a union's political activities more accurately reflect members' support for the organization's political views than does a corporation's general treasury.

In a concurrence, Justice Brennan emphasized that the Michigan law prevented dissenting members of the Chamber, and dissenting shareholders of supportive member corporations, from having their money used for political causes they did not support. The law also prevented the Chamber from "serving as a conduit for corporate political spending." *Id.* at 672–73 (Brennan, J., concurring).

Dissenting, Justice Scalia made the following argument:

> The Court does not try to defend the proposition that independent advocacy poses a substantial risk of political "corruption," as English speakers understand that term. Rather, it asserts that that concept (which it defines as "'financial *quid pro quo*' corruption") is really just a narrow subspecies of a hitherto unrecognized genus of political corruption. "Michigan's regulation," we are told, "aims at a different type of corruption in the political arena: the corrosive and distorting effects of immense aggregations of wealth that are accumulated with the help of the corporate form and that have little or no correlation to the public's support for the

corporation's political ideas." Under this mode of analysis, virtually anything the Court deems politically undesirable can be turned into political corruption—by simply describing its effects as politically "corrosive," which is close enough to "corruptive" to qualify. It is sad to think that the First Amendment will ultimately be brought down not by brute force but by poetic metaphor.

The Court's opinion ultimately rests upon that proposition whose violation constitutes the "New Corruption": Expenditures must "reflect actual public support for the political ideas espoused." This illiberal free-speech principle of "one man, one minute" was proposed and soundly rejected in *Buckley.* * * * But it can be said that I have not accurately quoted today's decision. It does not endorse the proposition that government may ensure that expenditures "reflect actual public support for the political ideas espoused," but only the more limited proposition that government may ensure that expenditures "reflect actual public support for the political ideas espoused *by corporations.*" The limitation is of course entirely irrational. Why is it perfectly all right if advocacy by an individual billionaire is out of proportion with "actual public support" for his positions? * * *

JUSTICE BRENNAN's concurrence would have us believe that the prohibition adopted by Michigan and approved by the Court is a paternalistic measure to protect the corporate shareholders of America. It is designed, we are told, "to avert [the] danger" that "corporate funds drawn from the general treasury—which represents, after all, [the shareholders'] money," might be used on behalf of a political candidate he opposes. But such solicitude is a most implausible explanation for the Michigan statute, inasmuch as it permits corporations to take as many ideological and political positions as they please, so long as they are not "in assistance of, or in opposition to, the nomination or election of a candidate." That is indeed the Court's sole basis for distinguishing *First National Bank of Boston* v. *Bellotti*, which invalidated restriction of a corporation's general political speech. The Michigan law appears to be designed, in other words, neither to protect shareholders, nor even (impermissibly) to "balance" general political debate, but to protect political candidates.

Id. at 684–86 (Scalia, J., dissenting).

Notes and Questions

1. Do corporations have First Amendment rights? *Bellotti* argued that that was not the proper question; rather, it focused on the public's right to hear, perhaps in an effort to avoid abstract questions of corporate personhood and First Amendment rights. What individuals have a right to hear, said the Court, cannot be denied them simply due to the identity of the speaker. This reasoning has been criticized; after all, the people of Massachusetts, through their legislature, decided

they did not wish to hear from corporations. *See* Carl E. Schneider, *Free Speech and Corporate Freedom: A Comment on First National Bank of Boston v. Bellotti*, 59 S. Cal. L. Rev. 1227, 1235 (1986). But the constitution protects minority rights—even if only a minority of Massachusetts citizens want to hear from corporations, are they not entitled, under the First Amendment, to do so? How, if at all, would the Court's treatment of campaign finance in particular, and the First Amendment more generally, change, depending on whether courts focus on the speakers or on the listeners?

2. Justice White suggested in his *Bellotti* dissent that if corporate speech were prohibited, the individual shareholders, employees, and customers "could even form associations for the very purpose of promoting political or ideological causes." Suppose that the shareholders of a corporation agreed that the income-tax proposal opposed by First National Bank was, indeed, a bad idea, because it was bad for their investments in the Bank. If they joined together, how might they organize? Might they form a corporation? A great many, if not most, political-advocacy groups are incorporated. Should that be prohibited? If not, why force the First National Bank shareholders to form a second corporation to speak about the public policies that might affect their original corporation?

Justice White also suggested that the board of directors of a corporation could endorse a view and publicize it at their individual expense. Suppose that a state has placed on a ballot an initiative that a corporation's directors have concluded will cost the corporation $400 million over ten years. They wish to spend $500,000 to try to defeat the initiative. Is that a good use of corporate funds? Is it realistic to ask the corporate president to pay that personally? If it were the rule that officers and directors had to pay for political advocacy to benefit the corporation from their personal funds, wouldn't such anticipated expenses simply be included in future compensation packages?

Would your answer to the question above change if independent economists determined that the proposition would cost the state 50,000 jobs, throwing those workers onto the unemployment rolls?

3. The background to *Bellotti* is instructive. In 1962, the Massachusetts state legislature put a proposal on the ballot to amend the state constitution to provide for a graduated individual income tax. Lytron, Inc., intended to contribute $500 to a group opposing the amendment, and was one of several corporations that sought to oppose the amendment. It was claimed that the expenditure would be *ultra vires* under a state statute prohibiting corporate expenditures that did not "materially affect[] any of the property, business or assets of the corporation," but the Massachusetts Supreme Court held that the expenditure was not barred by the statute. *Lustwerk v. Lytron, Inc.*, 183 N.E.2d 871 (Mass. 1962). The proposed amendment was defeated by voters.

The legislature amended the statute to provide that "No question submitted to the voters concerning the taxation of the income, property or transactions of individuals shall be deemed materially to affect the property, business or assets of the corporation," and again put the question of a graduated-income-tax amendment — this time placing such a tax on both individuals and corporations — before the voters. The amended statute prohibiting corporate expenditures on the ballot issue was again challenged, and held inapplicable because the proposed constitutional amendment included both individual and corporate taxes. *First National Bank of Boston v. Attorney General*, 290 N.E.2d 526 (Mass. 1972). The proposed amendment was again defeated by the voters.

Flummoxed, the legislature again amended the statute on corporate spending, and then again proposed a constitutional amendment to permit a graduated income tax — setting the stage for *Bellotti*. *See* 435 U.S. at 769 n.3. Is this background relevant to the constitutional question decided by the Supreme Court? How so?

4. Look at the ad in question in *Austin v. Michigan State Chamber of Commerce*, reproduced below from Justice Kennedy's dissent in the case. Is the information of the type that could be valuable to voters? Would the ad have the same impact if funded by an individual business executive? Or is the sponsor part of the message and what gives it salience?

Michigan Needs Richard Bandstra To Help Us Be Job Competitive Again

The Michigan State Chamber of Commerce, an organization of over 8,000 member companies, associations and local chambers of commerce, is committed to making Michigan more competitive for business investment and job creation. With that goal in mind, we'd like to share some facts with the electors in the 93rd House District before they vote in tomorrow's special election.

To be job competitive, Michigan needs to have fair regulatory policies on business regarding such important issues as workers' compensation and we need to encourage greater efficiency in state government by lowering the state personal income tax.

Currently, workers' compensation costs are 20% higher in Michigan than those in neighboring states. Why? Our eligibility standards are not the same as most other states. Too many people are allowed to quality for too long a period of a time.

Many Grand Rapids businesses are competing with firms in other states having lower regulatory costs. Unless checked, this disadvantage may continue to cost Michigan jobs . . . jobs that are lost when businesses leave Michigan, expand out of state, or when out-state companies seeking to expand don't locate here in Michigan.

To ensure that Michigan is job competitive, we need legislators at the State Capitol who will show courage and stand up to special interests that advocate greater regulation and taxes.

The Michigan State Chamber of Commerce believes Richard Bandstra has the background and training to do the best job in Lansing for the people of the 93rd House District. We believe he will work to reduce workers' compensation costs and for an early rollback of the personal income tax rate.

The State Chamber is committed to job development in Michigan. We believe Richard Bandstra shares that commitment.

On Monday June 10th, Elect Richard Bandstra State Representative 93rd House District Special Election

Not authorized by the Candidate Committee of Richard Bandstra
Paid for by the Michigan Chamber of Commerce • Suite 400, 200 N. Washington Square • Lansing, Michigan 48933

5. *Austin* found that the state ban on corporate expenditures was, in accordance with *Buckley*, attempting to address corruption. The Court referred to the harm addressed by the ban as a "different type of corruption": "the corrosive and distortive effects of immense aggregations of wealth * * *." What does that mean? When people refer to government "corruption," do you think this is usually what they have in mind?

6. The *Austin* Court suggested that there was something wrong when political spending had "little or no correlation to the to the public's support for the corporation's political ideas." Is there any reason to think political spending should regularly correlate with the public's support for the donors' ideas? *See* Bradley A. Smith, *Searching for Corruption in All the Wrong Places*, 2002–2003 Cato Sup. Ct. Rev. 187, 204 (2003) ("Such an assertion misconstrues the entire purpose of the political campaign, which is to persuade and change minds. Political fund raisers have long noticed that a group's fund raising often increases after a political defeat, as members and supporters devote more resources to promoting their vision to recapture lost ground or stave off further defeat. Certainly the mere disequilibrium between the determination of a speaker to speak and the level of preexisting support for the ideas expressed does not amount to [corruption]."). Historically, unpopular causes and new approaches to public policy have typically been most reliant on large contributions. Bradley A. Smith, Unfree Speech: The Folly of Campaign Finance Reform 66–67 (2001). Why would that be?

As of May 2020, the Idaho legislature was dominated by Republicans, 56-14 in the State House and 28-7 in the State Senate. It has been twenty-eight years since a Democrat received as much as 45% of the vote in a race for Governor. No Democrat has been elected to the U.S. Senate since 1974, or carried the state in a presidential race since 1964. In 2018, Republicans swept all statewide offices, winning the offices of Governor, Lieutenant Governor, Attorney General, Secretary of State, Treasurer, and Controller, and both of the state's congressional seats, with at least 59.7% of the vote. Suppose the state adopted a public-funding program for campaigns, which provided each major-party candidate with the same amount of funds to spend on the election. Would this be problematic on the grounds that the funds did not correspond to the public's demonstrated support for the two parties' political ideas?

7. Elizabeth Garrett, a clerk for Justice Marshall at the time of *Austin* and later President of Cornell University, wrote in 2009 that Justice Marshall approved of the equality rationale rejected in *Buckley*. Justice Marshall's majority opinion in *Austin*, according to Professor Garrett, "appropriated the language used to describe an egalitarian justification for campaign finance regulation, but * * * expressed that state interest in the acceptable corruption terminology." Elizabeth Garrett, *Influence and Legacy: The Future of the Post-Marshall Court: New Voices in Politics: Justice Marshall's Jurisprudence on Law and Politics*, 52 How. L.J. 655, 670–71, 675 (2009).

8. Was the Court's distinction in *Austin* between unions and corporations for equal-protection purposes persuasive? The majority argued that while unions may amass large treasuries, they do so "without the significant state-conferred advantages of the corporate structure." 494 U.S. at 665. Is that true? Consider the legislatively imposed rules governing labor relations that have, since the 1930s, replaced many common-law doctrines in an open effort to confer advantages on unions. Examples include the statutory prohibition on "yellow dog" contracts, which required a worker to agree not to join a union as a condition of employment; limits on the use of injunctions against picketing that threatens violence; and requirements that corporations recognize unions, refrain from retaliation against or dismissal of employees for union activity, and negotiate with unions. *See* Richard A. Epstein, *A Common Law for Labor Relations: A Critique of the New Deal Labor Legislation*, 92 YALE L.J. 1357 (1983).

9. Only about 40% of firms in the Fortune 500 maintain PACs. Does this shed any light on the perceived value of corporate political spending? *See* Stephen D. Ansolabehere et al., *Why is There So Little Money in American Politics*, 17 J. ECON. PERSPECTIVES 105 (2003).

Recall that while *Buckley* prohibited limitations on expenditures, it reached that holding only after it first narrowed FECA's definition of "expenditure" to apply only to "expenditures for communications that in express terms advocate the election or defeat of a clearly identified candidate for federal office." 424 U.S. at 44. As the Court further explained in its famous footnote 52, by this it meant "communications containing express words of advocacy of election or defeat, such as 'vote for,' 'elect,' 'support,' 'cast your ballot for,' 'Smith for Congress,' 'vote against,' 'defeat,' 'reject.'" *Id.* at 44 n.52. [*See* Note on the "Express Advocacy" / "Issue Advocacy" Distinction, pp. 755–59, *supra*.] Coupled with *Bellotti's* holding that corporations had a clear right to engage in issue speech, this meant that even after *Austin*, corporations remained free to fund ads about issues—and to mention candidates in those ads so long as they avoided "express advocacy."

By the mid-1990s, the Republican and Democratic Parties were raising substantial funds from corporations, unions, and wealthy individuals in order to fund "issue ads" that glowed with praise for their party's candidates (or searing criticism of their opponent's), but which avoided "express advocacy" of "election or defeat." Because they avoided "express advocacy," such ad buys were not considered "expenditures" under the law, and contributions to fund them, which became known as "soft money," were not considered "contributions" under the law. Additionally, non-party advocacy groups such as Planned Parenthood, the NAACP, the Club for Growth, and the National Rifle Association, often themselves incorporated, used money from corporate and union donations to fund similar issue ads. *See* ANNENBERG PUBLIC POLICY CENTER, ISSUE ADVERTISING IN THE 1999–2000 ELECTION CYCLE (2001). Perhaps the most famous such "issue ad" was the "Bill Yellowtail" ad, the text of which is set forth in footnote 78 of the Court's opinion in *McConnell v. Federal Election Commission*, 540 U.S. 93, 193 (2003), below.

In 2002, Congress passed the Bipartisan Campaign Reform Act (BCRA), commonly known as "McCain-Feingold" for its principal Senate sponsors. Although the bill covered a broad array of perceived abuses, the core provisions dealt with "soft money." Title I of BCRA prohibited political parties from funding operations with "soft money." Title II made it illegal to use corporate or union funds for "electioneering communications," which were defined as broadcast ads that mentioned a candidate for office and aired within thirty days of a primary election or caucus, or sixty days of a general election, with the potential to reach 50,000 or more voters. Note that Title II thus sought to regulate speech that would not qualify as "express advocacy" under *Buckley*'s footnote 52. We have already seen how the Supreme Court in *McConnell v. FEC* resolved the challenge to the party soft-money provision of Title I [*see* p. 767–72]. Below is an excerpt from the Court's opinions dealing with Title II.

McConnell v. Federal Election Commission

Supreme Court of the United States
540 U.S. 93, 124 S. Ct. 619, 157 L. Ed. 2d 491 (2003)

JUSTICE STEVENS and JUSTICE O'CONNOR delivered the opinion of the Court with respect to BCRA Titles I and II.* * * *

[T]he term "electioneering communication" * * * is defined to encompass any "broadcast, cable, or satellite communication" that

"(I) refers to a clearly identified candidate for Federal office;

"(II) is made within—

"(aa) 60 days before a general, special, or runoff election for the office sought by the candidate; or

"(bb) 30 days before a primary or preference election, or a convention or caucus of a political party that has authority to nominate a candidate, for the office sought by the candidate; and

"(III) in the case of a communication which refers to a candidate other than President or Vice President, is targeted to the relevant electorate." 2 U.S.C. § 434(f)(3)(A)(i).

New FECA § 304(f)(3)(C) further provides that a communication is "targeted to the relevant electorate" if it "can be received by 50,000 or more persons" in the district or State the candidate seeks to represent. 2 U.S.C. § 434(f)(3)(C). * * *

The major premise of plaintiffs' challenge to BCRA's use of the term "electioneering communication" is that *Buckley* drew a constitutionally mandated line between

---

* JUSTICE SOUTER, JUSTICE GINSBURG, and JUSTICE BREYER join this opinion in its entirety.

express advocacy and so-called issue advocacy, and that speakers possess an invio-
lable First Amendment right to engage in the latter category of speech. Thus, plaintiffs maintain, Congress cannot constitutionally require disclosure of, or regulate
expenditures for, "electioneering communications" without making an exception for those "communications" that do not meet *Buckley*'s definition of express
advocacy.

That position misapprehends our prior decisions, for the express advocacy
restriction was an endpoint of statutory interpretation, not a first principle of constitutional law. In *Buckley* we began by examining then-18 U.S.C. § 608(e)(1), which
restricted expenditures "relative to a clearly identified candidate," and we found that
the phrase "relative to" was impermissibly vague. We concluded that the vagueness
deficiencies could "be avoided only by reading § 608(e)(1) as limited to communications that include explicit words of advocacy of election or defeat of a candidate."
We provided examples of words of express advocacy, such as "'vote for,' 'elect,' 'support,' . . . 'defeat,' [and] 'reject,'" and those examples eventually gave rise to what is
now known as the "magic words" requirement.

We then considered FECA's disclosure provisions, * * * which defined
"expenditur[e]" to include the use of money or other assets "for the purpose of . . .
influencing" a federal election. Finding that the "ambiguity of this phrase" posed
"constitutional problems," we noted our "obligation to construe the statute, if that
can be done consistent with the legislature's purpose, to avoid the shoals of vagueness." "To insure that the reach" of the disclosure requirement was "not impermissibly broad, we construe[d] 'expenditure' for purposes of that section in the same
way we construed the terms of § 608(e) — to reach only funds used for communications that expressly advocate the election or defeat of a clearly identified candidate."

Thus, a plain reading of *Buckley* makes clear that the express advocacy limitation, in both the expenditure and the disclosure contexts, was the product of statutory interpretation rather than a constitutional command. In narrowly reading the
FECA provisions in *Buckley* to avoid problems of vagueness and overbreadth, we
nowhere suggested that a statute that was neither vague nor overbroad would be
required to toe the same express advocacy line. * * *

Nor are we persuaded, independent of our precedents, that the First Amendment erects a rigid barrier between express advocacy and so-called issue advocacy.
That notion cannot be squared with our longstanding recognition that the presence or absence of magic words cannot meaningfully distinguish electioneering
speech from a true issue ad. Indeed, the unmistakable lesson from the record in
this litigation * * * is that *Buckley*'s magic-words requirement is functionally meaningless. * * * Not only can advertisers easily evade the line by eschewing the use of
magic words, but they would seldom choose to use such words even if permitted.
And although the resulting advertisements do not urge the viewer to vote for or
against a candidate in so many words, they are no less clearly intended to influence

the election.[78] *Buckley*'s express advocacy line, in short, has not aided the legislative effort to combat real or apparent corruption, and Congress enacted BCRA to correct the flaws it found in the existing system.

Finally we observe that new FECA § 304(f)(3)'s definition of "electioneering communication" raises none of the vagueness concerns that drove our analysis in *Buckley*. The term "electioneering communication" applies only (1) to a broadcast (2) clearly identifying a candidate for federal office, (3) aired within a specific time period, and (4) targeted to an identified audience of at least 50,000 viewers or listeners. These components are both easily understood and objectively determinable. * * * Thus, the constitutional objection that persuaded the Court in *Buckley* to limit FECA's reach to express advocacy is simply inapposite here. * * *

Since our decision in *Buckley*, Congress' power to prohibit corporations and unions from using funds in their treasuries to finance advertisements expressly advocating the election or defeat of candidates in federal elections has been firmly embedded in our law. * * *

Section 203 of BCRA amends FECA § 316(b)(2) to extend this rule, which previously applied only to express advocacy, to all "electioneering communications" covered by the definition of that term in amended FECA § 304(f)(3), discussed above. Thus, under BCRA, corporations and unions may not use their general treasury funds to finance electioneering communications, but they remain free to organize and administer segregated funds, or PACs, for that purpose. Because corporations can still fund electioneering communications with PAC money, it is "simply wrong" to view the provision as a "complete ban" on expression rather than a regulation. * * *

* * * [P]laintiffs argue that the justifications that adequately support the regulation of express advocacy do not apply to significant quantities of speech encompassed by the definition of electioneering communications.

This argument fails to the extent that the issue ads broadcast during the 30- and 60-day periods preceding federal primary and general elections are the functional equivalent of express advocacy. The justifications for the regulation of express advocacy apply equally to ads aired during those periods if the ads are intended to influence the voters' decisions and have that effect. The precise percentage of

---

78. One striking example is an ad that a group called "Citizens for Reform" sponsored during the 1996 Montana congressional race, in which Bill Yellowtail was a candidate. The ad stated:

"Who is Bill Yellowtail? He preaches family values but took a swing at his wife. And Yellowtail's response? He only slapped her. But 'her nose was not broken.' He talks law and order . . . but is himself a convicted felon. And though he talks about protecting children, Yellowtail failed to make his own child support payments—then voted against child support enforcement. Call Bill Yellowtail. Tell him to support family values."

The notion that this advertisement was designed purely to discuss the issue of family values strains credulity.

issue ads that clearly identified a candidate and were aired during those relatively brief preelection time spans but had no electioneering purpose is a matter of dispute between the parties and among the judges on the District Court. Nevertheless, the vast majority of ads clearly had such a purpose. Moreover, whatever the precise percentage may have been in the past, in the future corporations and unions may finance genuine issue ads during those time frames by simply avoiding any specific reference to federal candidates, or in doubtful cases by paying for the ad from a segregated fund.

In addition * * * some plaintiffs contend that [BCRA § 316(b)(2)] unconstitutionally discriminates in favor of media companies. FECA § 304(f)(3)(B)(i) excludes from the definition of electioneering communications any "communication appearing in a news story, commentary, or editorial distributed through the facilities of any broadcasting station, unless such facilities are owned or controlled by any political party, political committee, or candidate." 2 U.S.C. § 434(f)(3)(B) (i). Plaintiffs argue this provision gives free rein to media companies to engage in speech without resort to PAC money. Section 304(f)(3)(B)(i)'s effect, however, is much narrower than plaintiffs suggest. The provision excepts news items and commentary only; it does not afford *carte blanche* to media companies generally to ignore FECA's provisions. The statute's narrow exception is wholly consistent with First Amendment principles. "A valid distinction . . . exists between corporations that are part of the media industry and other corporations that are not involved in the regular business of imparting news to the public." *Austin* [v. *Michigan Chamber of Commerce*], 494 U.S. [652], 668 [(1990)]. Numerous federal statutes have drawn this distinction to ensure that the law "does not hinder or prevent the institutional press from reporting on, and publishing editorials about, newsworthy events." * * *

We affirm the District Court's judgment to the extent that it upheld the constitutionality of FECA § 316(b)(2). * * *

JUSTICE SCALIA, concurring in part and dissenting in part. * * *

I wish to address three fallacious propositions that might be thought to justify some or all of the provisions of this legislation—only the last of which is explicitly embraced by the principal opinion for the Court, but all of which underlie, I think, its approach to these cases.

(a) Money is Not Speech * * *

In any economy operated on even the most rudimentary principles of division of labor, effective public communication requires the speaker to make use of the services of others. An author may write a novel, but he will seldom publish and distribute it himself. A freelance reporter may write a story, but he will rarely edit, print, and deliver it to subscribers. To a government bent on suppressing speech, this mode of organization presents opportunities: Control any cog in the machine, and you can halt the whole apparatus. License printers, and it matters little whether authors are still free to write. Restrict the sale of books, and it matters little who prints them. Predictably, repressive regimes have exploited these principles by attacking all levels of the production and dissemination of ideas. In response to this threat, we have interpreted the First Amendment broadly.

Division of labor requires a means of mediating exchange, and in a commercial society, that means is supplied by money. The publisher pays the author for the right to sell his book; it pays its staff who print and assemble the book; it demands payments from booksellers who bring the book to market. This, too, presents opportunities for repression: Instead of regulating the various parties to the enterprise individually, the government can suppress their ability to coordinate by regulating their use of money. What good is the right to print books without a right to buy works from authors? Or the right to publish newspapers without the right to pay deliverymen? The right to speak would be largely ineffective if it did not include the right to engage in financial transactions that are the incidents of its exercise.

* * * [A] law limiting the amount a person can spend to broadcast his political views is a direct restriction on speech. That is no different from a law limiting the amount a newspaper can pay its editorial staff or the amount a charity can pay its leafletters. It is equally clear that a limit on the amount a candidate can *raise* from any one individual for the purpose of speaking is also a direct limitation on speech. That is no different from a law limiting the amount a publisher can accept from any one shareholder or lender, or the amount a newspaper can charge any one advertiser or customer.

(b) Pooling Money is Not Speech

Another proposition which could explain at least some of the results of today's opinion is that the First Amendment right to spend money for speech does not include the right to combine with others in spending money for speech. Such a proposition fits uncomfortably with the concluding words of our Declaration of Independence: "And for the support of this Declaration, . . . we mutually pledge to each other our Lives, *our Fortunes* and our sacred Honor." (Emphasis added.) The freedom to associate with others for the dissemination of ideas—not just by singing or speaking in unison, but by pooling financial resources for expressive purposes— is part of the freedom of speech. * * *

If it were otherwise, Congress would be empowered to enact legislation requiring newspapers to be sole proprietorships, banning their use of partnership or corporate form. That sort of restriction would be an obvious violation of the First Amendment, and it is incomprehensible why the conclusion should change when what is at issue is the pooling of funds for the most important (and most perennially threatened) category of speech: electoral speech. The principle that such financial association does not enjoy full First Amendment protection threatens the existence of all political parties.

(c) Speech by Corporations Can Be Abridged

The last proposition that might explain at least some of today's casual abridgment of free-speech rights is this: that the particular form of association known as a corporation does not enjoy full First Amendment protection. Of course the text of the First Amendment does not limit its application in this fashion, even though "[b]y the end of the eighteenth century the corporation was a familiar figure in American economic life." C. Cooke, Corporation, Trust and Company 92 (1951). Nor is there any basis in reason why First Amendment rights should not attach to corporate associations—and we have said so. [*See, e.g., First Nat. Bank of Boston* v. *Bellotti*, 435 U.S. 765 (1978)]. * * *

* * * In the modern world, giving the government power to exclude corporations from the political debate enables it effectively to muffle the voices that best represent the most significant segments of the economy and the most passionately held social and political views. People who associate—who pool their financial resources—for purposes of economic enterprise overwhelmingly do so in the corporate form; and with increasing frequency, incorporation is chosen by those who associate to defend and promote particular ideas—such as the American Civil Liberties Union and the National Rifle Association, parties to these cases. Imagine, then, a government that wished to suppress nuclear power—or oil and gas exploration, or automobile manufacturing, or gun ownership, or civil liberties—and that had the power to prohibit corporate advertising against its proposals. To be sure, the individuals involved in, or benefited by, those industries, or interested in those causes, could (given enough time) form political action committees or other associations to make their case. But the organizational form in which those enterprises already *exist*, and in which they can most quickly and most effectively get their message across, is the corporate form. The First Amendment does not in my view permit the restriction of that political speech. And the same holds true for corporate electoral speech: A candidate should not be insulated from the most effective speech that the major participants in the economy and major incorporated interest groups can generate.

* * * But let us not be deceived. While the Government's briefs and arguments before this Court focused on the horrible "appearance of corruption," the most passionate floor statements during the debates on this legislation pertained to so-called attack ads, which the Constitution surely protects, but which Members of Congress analogized to "crack cocaine," 144 Cong. Rec. S868 (Feb. 24, 1998) (remarks of Sen. Daschle), "drive-by shooting[s]," *id.*, at S879 (remarks of Sen. Durbin), and "air pollution," 143 Cong. Rec. 20505 (1997) (remarks of Sen. Dorgan). There is good reason to believe that the ending of negative campaign ads was the principal attraction of the legislation. A Senate sponsor said, "I hope that we will not allow our attention to be distracted from the real issues at hand—how to raise the tenor of the debate in our elections and give people real choices. No one benefits from negative ads. They don't aid our Nation's political dialog." *Id.*, at 20521–20522 (remarks of Sen. McCain). He assured the body that "[y]ou cut off the soft money, you are going to see a lot less of that [attack ads]. Prohibit unions and corporations, and you will see

a lot less of that. If you demand full disclosure for those who pay for those ads, you are going to see a lot less of that." 147 Cong. Rec. S3116 (Mar. 29, 2001) (remarks of Sen. McCain). See also, *e.g.*, 148 Cong. Rec. S2117 (Mar. 20, 2002) (remarks of Sen. Cantwell) ("This bill is about slowing the ad war. . . . It is about slowing political advertising and making sure the flow of negative ads by outside interest groups does not continue to permeate the airwaves"); 143 Cong. Rec. 20746 (1997) (remarks of Sen. Boxer) ("These so-called issues ads are not regulated at all and mention candidates by name. They directly attack candidates without any accountability. It is brutal. . . . We have an opportunity in the McCain-Feingold bill to stop that."); 145 Cong. Rec. S12606–S12607 (Oct. 14, 1999) (remarks of Sen. Wellstone) ("I think these issue advocacy ads are a nightmare. I think all of us should hate them. . . . [By passing the legislation], [w]e could get some of this poison politics off television").

Another theme prominent in the legislative debates was the notion that there is too much money spent on elections. * * *

> "Despite the ever-increasing sums spent on campaigns, we have not seen an improvement in campaign discourse, issue discussion or voter education. More money does not mean more ideas, more substance or more depth. Instead, it means more of what voters complain about most. More 30-second spots, more negativity and an increasingly longer campaign period." *Id.* at S2150 (Mar. 20, 2002) (remarks of Sen. Kerry).

Perhaps voters do detest these 30-second spots—though I suspect they detest even more hour-long campaign-debate interruptions of their favorite entertainment programming. Evidently, however, these ads *do persuade* voters, or else they would not be so routinely used by sophisticated politicians of all parties. The point, in any event, is that it is not the proper role of those who govern us to judge which campaign speech has "substance" and "depth" (do you think it might be that which is least damaging to incumbents?) and to abridge the rest.

* * * This litigation is about preventing criticism of the government. I cannot say for certain that many, or some, or even any, of the Members of Congress who voted for this legislation did so not to produce "fairer" campaigns, but to mute criticism of their records and facilitate reelection. Indeed, I will stipulate that all those who voted for the Act believed they were acting for the good of the country. There remains the problem of the Charlie Wilson Phenomenon, named after Charles Wilson, former president of General Motors, who is supposed to have said during the Senate hearing on his nomination as Secretary of Defense that "what's good for General Motors is good for the country." Those in power, even giving them the benefit of the greatest good will, are inclined to believe that what is good for them is good for the country. Whether in prescient recognition of the Charlie Wilson Phenomenon, or out of fear of good old-fashioned, malicious, self-interested manipulation, "[t]he fundamental approach of the First Amendment . . . was to assume the worst, and to rule the regulation of political speech 'for fairness' sake' simply out of bounds." * * *

The first instinct of power is the retention of power, and, under a Constitution that requires periodic elections, that is best achieved by the suppression of election-time speech. * * * The federal election campaign laws, which are already (as today's opinions show) so voluminous, so detailed, so complex, that no ordinary citizen dare run for office, or even contribute a significant sum, without hiring an expert adviser in the field, can be expected to grow more voluminous, more detailed, and more complex in the years to come—and always, always, with the objective of reducing the excessive amount of speech.

JUSTICE THOMAS * * * concurring in the judgment in part and dissenting in part[.]

* * * Today's holding continues a disturbing trend: the steady decrease in the level of scrutiny applied to restrictions on core political speech. Although this trend is most obvious in the review of contribution limits, it has now reached what even this Court today would presumably recognize as a direct restriction on core political speech: limitations on independent expenditures. * * *

The chilling endpoint of the Court's reasoning is not difficult to foresee: outright regulation of the press. None of the rationales offered by the defendants, and none of the reasoning employed by the Court, exempts the press. * * * Media companies can run pro-candidate editorials as easily as non-media corporations can pay for advertisements. Candidates can be just as grateful to media companies as they can be to corporations and unions. In terms of "the corrosive and distorting effects" of wealth accumulated by corporations that has "little or no correlation to the public's support for the corporation's political ideas," *Austin*, 494 U.S. at 660, there is no distinction between a media corporation and a non-media corporation. Media corporations are influential. There is little doubt that the editorials and commentary they run can affect elections. Nor is there any doubt that media companies often wish to influence elections. One would think that the New York Times fervently hopes that its endorsement of Presidential candidates will actually influence people. What is to stop a future Congress from determining that the press is "too influential," and that the "appearance of corruption" is significant when media organizations endorse candidates or run "slanted" or "biased" news stories in favor of candidates or parties? Or, even easier, what is to stop a future Congress from concluding that the availability of unregulated media corporations creates a loophole that allows for easy "circumvention" of the limitations of the current campaign finance laws? * * *

Although today's opinion does not expressly strip the press of First Amendment protection, there is no principle of law or logic that would prevent the application of the Court's reasoning in that setting. The press now operates at the whim of Congress.

Justice Kennedy, [with whom Chief Justice Rehnquist and Justice Scalia join], dissenting in part[.] * * *

The Court * * * in effect interprets the anticorruption rationale to allow regulation not just of "actual or apparent *quid pro quo* arrangements," but of any conduct that wins goodwill from or influences a Member of Congress. * * * Access, in the Court's view, has the same legal ramifications as actual or apparent corruption of officeholders. This new definition of corruption sweeps away all protections for speech that lie in its path.

* * * Access in itself * * * shows only that in a general sense an officeholder favors someone or that someone has influence on the officeholder. There is no basis, in law or in fact, to say favoritism or influence in general is the same as corrupt favoritism or influence in particular. By equating vague and generic claims of favoritism or influence with actual or apparent corruption, the Court adopts a definition of corruption that dismantles basic First Amendment rules, permits Congress to suppress speech in the absence of a *quid pro quo* threat, and moves beyond the rationale that is *Buckley*'s very foundation.

The generic favoritism or influence theory articulated by the Court is at odds with standard First Amendment analyses because it is unbounded and susceptible to no limiting principle. Any given action might be favored by any given person, so by the Court's reasoning political loyalty of the purest sort can be prohibited. There is no remaining principled method for inquiring whether a campaign finance regulation does in fact regulate corruption in a serious and meaningful way. We are left to defer to a congressional conclusion that certain conduct creates favoritism or influence.

Though the majority cites common sense as the foundation for its definition of corruption, in the context of the real world only a single definition of corruption has been found to identify political corruption successfully and to distinguish good political responsiveness from bad—that is *quid pro quo*. Favoritism and influence are not, as the Government's theory suggests, avoidable in representative politics. It is in the nature of an elected representative to favor certain policies, and, by necessary corollary, to favor the voters and contributors who support those policies. It is well understood that a substantial and legitimate reason, if not the only reason, to cast a vote for, or to make a contribution to, one candidate over another is that the candidate will respond by producing those political outcomes the supporter favors. Democracy is premised on responsiveness. *Quid pro quo* corruption has been, until now, the only agreed upon conduct that represents the bad form of responsiveness and presents a justiciable standard with a relatively clear limiting principle: Bad responsiveness may be demonstrated by pointing to a relationship between an official and a *quid*. * * *

These regulations are more than minor clerical requirements. Rather, they create major disincentives for speech, with the effect falling most heavily on smaller entities that often have the most difficulty bearing the costs of compliance. Even worse, for an organization that has not yet set up a PAC, spontaneous speech that "refers to a clearly identified candidate for Federal office" becomes impossible, even if the group's vital interests are threatened by a piece of legislation pending before Congress on the eve of a federal election. Couple the litany of administrative burdens with the categorical restriction limiting PACs' solicitation activities to "members," and it is apparent that PACs are inadequate substitutes for corporations in their ability to engage in unfettered expression.

Even if the newly formed PACs manage to attract members and disseminate their messages against these heavy odds, they have been forced to assume a false identity while doing so. * * * Forcing speech through an artificial "secondhand endorsement structure . . . debases the value of the voice of nonprofit corporate speakers . . . [because] PAC's are interim, ad hoc organizations with little continuity or responsibility." In contrast, their sponsoring organizations "have a continuity, a stability, and an influence" that allows "their members and the public at large to evaluate their . . . credibility." * * *

Once we turn away from the distraction of the PAC option, the provision cannot survive strict scrutiny. * * *

The prohibition, with its crude temporal and geographic proxies, is a severe and unprecedented ban on protected speech. * * * Suppose a few Senators want to show their constituents in the logging industry how much they care about working families and propose a law, 60 days before the election, that would harm the environment by allowing logging in national forests. Under § 203, a nonprofit environmental group would be unable to run an ad referring to these Senators in their districts. The suggestion that the group could form and fund a PAC in the short time required for effective participation in the political debate is fanciful. For reasons already discussed, moreover, an ad hoc PAC would not be as effective as the environmental group itself in gaining credibility with the public. Never before in our history has the Court upheld a law that suppresses speech to this extent. * * *

We are supposed to find comfort in the knowledge that the ad is banned under § 203 only if it "is targeted to the relevant electorate," defined as communications that can be received by 50,000 or more persons in the candidate's district. This Orwellian criterion, however, is analogous to a law, unconstitutional under any known First Amendment theory, that would allow a speaker to say anything he chooses, so long as his intended audience could not hear him. * * * A central purpose of issue ads is to urge the public to pay close attention to the candidate's platform on the featured issues. By banning broadcast in the very district where the candidate is standing for election, § 203 shields information at the heart of the First Amendment from precisely those citizens who most value the right to make a responsible judgment at the voting booth.

* * * The mere fact that an ad may, in one fashion or another, influence an election is an insufficient reason for outlawing it. I should have thought influencing elections to be the whole point of political speech. Neither strict scrutiny nor any other standard the Court has adopted to date permits outlawing speech on the

ground that it might influence an election, which might lead to greater access to politicians by the sponsoring organization, which might lead to actual corruption or the appearance of corruption. Settled law requires a real and close connection between end and means. The attenuated causation the majority endorses today is antithetical to the concept of narrow tailoring. * * *

For the foregoing reasons, with respect, I dissent * * *.

Notes and Questions

1. *McConnell* upheld the restrictions on "electioneering communications" in part on the ground that the distinction between "express advocacy" and "issue advocacy" was "functionally meaningless." Recall, however, that one reason the *Buckley* Court struck down limits on independent expenditures was that, having held that the term "expenditure" should be interpreted as applying only to express advocacy, the state had no interest in limiting expenditures, because "[i]t would naively underestimate the ingenuity and resourcefulness of persons and groups * * * to believe that they would have much difficulty devising expenditures that skirted the restriction on express advocacy * * * but nevertheless benefitted a candidate's campaign." 424 U.S. at 45. So, was the *Buckley* Court right?

McConnell's description of the distinction between issue advocacy and express advocacy as "functionally meaningless" is one of the opinion's most notable phrases, appearing twice in the opinion. The second appearance of the phrase, however, includes a qualifier: "the line between express advocacy and issue advocacy is, *for Congress's purposes*, functionally meaningless." 540 U.S. at 217 (emphasis added). Did the distinction serve any purpose for persons other than Congress? Imagine that you are a lawyer, seeking to advise your client as to whether a particular ad is subject to regulation under FECA. Would the express-advocacy standard be functionally meaningless, or would it be very meaningful in helping you advise your client?

Buckley drew the distinction between issue advocacy and express advocacy in order to remove the vagueness problem for the speaker. BCRA handled this vagueness problem by establishing a bright line based on the number of days prior to an election that an ad was run, and whether it clearly identified a candidate. This standard shifted the question from one of vagueness to one of overbreadth. The litigants hotly debated the meaning of two studies relied on by the government: Craig B. Holman & Luke P. McLoughlin, Buying Time 2000: Television Advertisements in the 2000 Federal Elections (Brennan Center for Justice 2001), and Jonathan S. Krasno & Daniel E. Seltz, Buying Time 1998: Television Advertisements in the 1998 Congressional Elections (Brennan Center for Justice 2000), but in the end the Court was comfortable that most issue ads run within BCRA's electioneering-communications time frame "clearly had such [an electioneering] purpose." The plaintiffs' expert has criticized the Court for "ignor[ing] the data and empirical issues." James L. Gibson, *BCRA's Assault on the First Amendment: The Death of the Overbreadth Doctrine?*, 3 Election L.J. 245, 249 (2004). Professor

David Magleby, who served as an expert for the government, counters that *McConnell* was unique in the attention paid by the Court to the record evidence. David B. Magleby, *The Importance of the Record in* McConnell v. FEC, 3 ELECTION L.J. 285 (2004).

Did *McConnell* underestimate the scope of BCRA's electioneering-communications prohibitions? While the law's electioneering-communications window appears to be limited to 90 days (30 days before the primary, 60 days before the general election), the fact that many media markets lap into multiple states means that, at the presidential level, in many metropolitan areas the prohibition extends far beyond those time frames. *See* Bradley A. Smith & Jason Robert Owen, *Boundary-Based Restrictions in Boundless Broadcast Media Markets:* McConnell v. FEC's *Underinclusive Overbreadth Analysis*, 18 STAN. L. & POL'Y REV. 240 (2007) (studying numerous multi-state media markets and finding that in presidential elections the electioneering-communications limitations applied for more than 120 days in all markets, and upwards of 200 days in many).

2. Note that the distinction between express advocacy and issue advocacy remained an important part of the law after *McConnell*, because it continued to determine the level of regulation of speech outside the "electioneering-communications" windows of BCRA. Even after *Citizens United v. Federal Election Commission*, 558 U.S. 310 (2010) [p. 844], upheld the right of corporations to make independent expenditures on express advocacy, the distinction remains important for purposes of reporting and disclosure, as we will see in Chapter 9.

3. Are limits on corporate speech content-neutral? Or do they reflect certain assumptions about the positions that corporations might take on public issues and campaigns?

4. Justice Scalia suggested that much of the impetus for BCRA was to protect incumbent lawmakers from criticism, and he cited numerous quotes from the Congressional Record. Is it appropriate for judges to question the motives of lawmakers in this way? Is such criticism relevant to the constitutionality of a law, if the law can be supported on more neutral grounds? Is the possibility that incumbents will use campaign-finance laws to help keep themselves in power a reason to maintain a high level of judicial scrutiny and skepticism about the ostensible purposes of campaign-finance regulations?

5. At the time it was decided, *McConnell* was thought to mark the triumph of judicial deference in the realm of campaign finance. However, the Court's decision in *Randall v. Sorrell*, 548 U.S. 230 (2006) [pp. 786, 814], just two Terms later marked a return to judicial skepticism, and just three and a half years after being announced, *McConnell's* holding on independent expenditures was sharply trimmed back in *Federal Election Commission v. Wisconsin Right to Life, Inc.* (WRTL II), 551 U.S. 449 (2007). *WRTL II* was an as-applied challenge to the very electioneering-communications provisions of BCRA that were upheld against a facial challenge in *McConnell*. WRTL, a non-profit corporation that accepted contributions from

for-profit corporations, sought to run a trio of radio ads urging senators to oppose filibusters of President George W. Bush's judicial nominees. Here is the script of one of the ads, called "Wedding":

> "PASTOR: And who gives this woman to be married to this man?

> "BRIDE'S FATHER: Well, as father of the bride, I certainly could. But instead, I'd like to share a few tips on how to properly install drywall. Now you put the drywall up. . . .

> "VOICE-OVER: Sometimes it's just not fair to delay an important decision.

> "But in Washington it's happening. A group of Senators is using the filibuster delay tactic to block federal judicial nominees from a simple 'yes' or 'no' vote. So qualified candidates don't get a chance to serve.

> "It's politics at work, causing gridlock and backing up some of our courts to a state of emergency.

> "Contact Senators Feingold and Kohl and tell them to oppose the filibuster.

> "Visit: BeFair.org

> "Paid for by Wisconsin Right to Life (befair.org), which is responsible for the content of this advertising and not authorized by any candidate or candidate's committee."

Id. at 458. Two other ads, "Loan" and "Waiting" were similar. The ads were prohibited by BCRA because they were to air within the thirty-day pre-primary election window proscribed by BCRA for corporate funded ads naming a candidate. WRTL argued that the ads were not the "functional equivalent of express advocacy" as upheld in *McConnell*. The government argued that an ad should be considered the "functional equivalent of express advocacy" if it was intended to influence elections and could have that effect. The Court disagreed. Chief Justice Roberts wrote the lead opinion:

> Far from serving the values the First Amendment is meant to protect, an intent-based test would chill core political speech by opening the door to a trial on every ad within the terms of § 203, on the theory that the speaker actually intended to affect an election, no matter how compelling the indications that the ad concerned a pending legislative or policy issue. No reasonable speaker would choose to run an ad covered by BCRA if its only defense to a criminal prosecution would be that its motives were pure. An intent-based standard "blankets with uncertainty whatever may be said," and "offers no security for free discussion." * * *

> [A] court should find that an ad is the functional equivalent of express advocacy only if the ad is susceptible of no reasonable interpretation other than as an appeal to vote for or against a specific candidate. Under this test, WRTL's three ads are plainly not the functional equivalent of express advocacy. First, their content is consistent with that of a genuine issue ad:

The ads focus on a legislative issue, take a position on the issue, exhort the public to adopt that position, and urge the public to contact public officials with respect to the matter. Second, their content lacks indicia of express advocacy: The ads do not mention an election, candidacy, political party, or challenger; and they do not take a position on a candidate's character, qualifications, or fitness for office. * * *

BCRA § 203 can be constitutionally applied to WRTL's ads only if it is narrowly tailored to further a compelling interest. * * * This Court has never recognized a compelling interest in regulating ads, like WRTL's, that are neither express advocacy nor its functional equivalent.{9} * * *

This Court has long recognized "the governmental interest in preventing corruption and the appearance of corruption" in election campaigns. This interest has been invoked as a reason for upholding *contribution* limits. We have suggested that this interest might also justify limits on electioneering *expenditures* because it may be that, in some circumstances, "large independent expenditures pose the same dangers of actual or apparent *quid pro quo* arrangements as do large contributions."

McConnell arguably applied this interest—which this Court had only assumed could justify regulation of express advocacy—to ads that were the "functional equivalent" of express advocacy. But to justify regulation of WRTL's ads, this interest must be stretched yet another step to ads that are *not* the functional equivalent of express advocacy. Enough is enough. Issue ads like WRTL's are by no means equivalent to contributions, and the *quid-pro-quo* corruption interest cannot justify regulating them. To equate WRTL's ads with contributions is to ignore their value as political speech.

Appellants argue that an expansive definition of "functional equivalent" is needed to ensure that issue advocacy does not circumvent the rule against express advocacy, which in turn helps protect against circumvention of

---

9. The dissent stresses a number of points that, while not central to our decision, nevertheless merit a response. First, the dissent overstates its case when it asserts that the "PAC alternative" gives corporations a constitutionally sufficient outlet to speak. PACs impose well-documented and onerous burdens, particularly on small nonprofits. * * * Second, the response that a speaker should just take out a newspaper ad, or use a website, rather than complain that it cannot speak through a broadcast communication, is too glib. Even assuming for the sake of argument that the possibility of using a different medium of communication has relevance in determining the permissibility of a limitation on speech, newspaper ads and websites are not reasonable alternatives to broadcast speech in terms of impact and effectiveness. Third, we disagree with the dissent's view that corporations can still speak by changing what they say to avoid mentioning candidates. That argument is akin to telling Cohen that he cannot wear his jacket because he is free to wear one that says "I disagree with the draft," cf. *Cohen* v. *California*, 403 U.S. 15 (1971), or telling 44 Liquormart that it can advertise so long as it avoids mentioning prices, cf. *44 Liquormart, Inc.* v. *Rhode Island*, 517 U.S. 484 (1996). Such notions run afoul of "the fundamental rule of protection under the First Amendment, that a speaker has the autonomy to choose the content of his own message." *Hurley* v. *Irish-American Gay, Lesbian and Bisexual Group of Boston, Inc.*, 515 U.S. 557, 573 (1995).

the rule against contributions. But such a prophylaxis-upon-prophylaxis approach to regulating expression is not consistent with strict scrutiny. * * *

[W]hen it comes to defining what speech qualifies as the functional equivalent of express advocacy subject to such a ban * * * we give the benefit of the doubt to speech, not censorship. The First Amendment's command that "Congress shall make no law . . . abridging the freedom of speech" demands at least that.

Id. at 468–482. Chief Justice Roberts's opinion was joined only by Justice Alito. Justices Scalia, Kennedy, and Thomas concurred in the judgment, and would have used the case to reconsider (and presumably overrule) *McConnell*. The dissenting Justices, in an opinion by Justice Souter, argued that the Chief Justice's opinion was a *de facto* overruling of *McConnell* (an opinion shared by the three Justices concurring in the judgment). Not surprisingly (at least in retrospect), much of Justice Souter's dissent foreshadowed arguments that the dissent would make three years later in *Citizens United*.

6. *WRTL II* not only limited the reach of *McConnell*, but the lead opinion struck a remarkably different tone from that in *McConnell*. The *McConnell* majority concluded by stating the Court expected that more regulation would be needed in the future. In contrast, Chief Justice Roberts's controlling opinion in *WRTL II* conspicuously concluded with a recitation of the First Amendment and the simple exclamation, "enough is enough."

Professor Hasen has noted the different tone of the two opinions:

The *McConnell* opinion was full of language about legislative deference, flexibility, political reality, and the need to give Congress the room to address campaign finance problems step-by-step. It gave a long and fawning history tracing congressional efforts to limit big money, and especially corporate election spending, in the federal electoral process. It spoke of the ease of evading campaign finance laws, and the need for courts to take a functional, not formal, view of what counts as election-related speech. It minimized First Amendment concerns by noting alternative means for corporate influence over the electoral process, including PAC requirements, alternative means of communications, or even changing the content of the electoral message such as by omitting the name of the candidate mentioned in the advertisement.

The tone of the principal opinion in *WRTL II* is the polar opposite of *McConnell*. There is no nod to legislative deference or recognition of Congress's need to react to the "hydraulic" effect of money. Rather than talk of a PAC alternative, the *WRTL II* principal opinion mentions a free speech "ban" (or variations on the word "ban") twelve times and a speech "blackout" seventeen times. It refers to corporate election broadcasting paid for from treasury funds as a "crime" twice. * * *

The *WRTL II* principal opinion makes no mention of congressional deference (nor does it use the term "loophole," a term appearing ten times in the *McConnell* joint majority opinion), but the term "First Amendment" appears eighteen times and variations on the word "censor" three times. In contrast, the discussion of section 203 in *McConnell*'s joint majority opinion mentioned the First Amendment merely three times, and never to celebrate the free speech principles behind the Amendment."

Richard L. Hasen, *Beyond Incoherence: The Roberts Court's Deregulatory Turn in* FEC v. Wisconsin Right to Life, 92 MINN. L. REV. 1064, 1086–87 (2008). By the time of *WRTL*, the tone of the Justices' opinions in campaign-finance cases seemed, to at least some observers, to be growing sharper and more bitter.

[T]he nub of the controversy lies in this: the majority and the dissents in *WRTL II* (or in any of the campaign finance cases that the Court has decided since *Austin*) occupy *no* common First Amendment ground. Though they disagree in good faith, both of their points of view cannot be right, and the differences that exist between them are at such a fundamental level that they leave scant room for compromise * * *

[O]ne finds the justices talking past one another. They share neither empirical assumptions nor theoretical premises.

Lillian R. BeVier, *First Amendment Basics Redux:* Buckley v. Valeo *to* FEC v. Wisconsin Right to Life, 2006–07 CATO SUP. CT. REV. 77, 105 (2007).

Thus, *McConnell* and *WRTL* shaped the battlefield for the Court's blockbuster decision in *Citizens United v. Federal Election Commission*, which overruled key portions of *McConnell* and *Austin v. Michigan State Chamber of Commerce*.

Citizens United v. Federal Election Commission

Supreme Court of the United States
558 U.S. 310, 130 S. Ct. 876, 175 L. Ed. 2d 753 (2010)

JUSTICE KENNEDY delivered the opinion of the Court [in the entirety of which CHIEF JUSTICE ROBERTS, JUSTICE SCALIA, and JUSTICE ALITO join; in which JUSTICE THOMAS joins except as to Part IV; and in which JUSTICE STEVENS, JUSTICE GINSBURG, JUSTICE BREYER, and JUSTICE SOTOMAYOR join as to Part IV].

Federal law prohibits corporations and unions from using their general treasury funds to make independent expenditures for speech defined as an "electioneering communication" or for speech expressly advocating the election or defeat of a candidate. 2 U.S.C. § 441b. Limits on electioneering communications were upheld in *McConnell v. Federal Election Comm'n*, 540 U.S. 93, 203–209 (2003) [p. 829]. The holding of *McConnell* rested to a large extent on an earlier case, *Austin v. Michigan Chamber of Commerce*, 494 U.S. 652 (1990). *Austin* had held that political speech may be banned based on the speaker's corporate identity.

In this case we are asked to reconsider *Austin* and, in effect, *McConnell*.

I

Citizens United is a nonprofit corporation. It * * * has an annual budget of about $12 million. Most of its funds are from donations by individuals; but, in addition, it accepts a small portion of its funds from for-profit corporations.

In January 2008, Citizens United released a film entitled *Hillary: The Movie.* We refer to the film as *Hillary.* It is a 90-minute documentary about then-Senator Hillary Clinton, who was a candidate in the Democratic Party's 2008 Presidential primary elections. *Hillary* mentions Senator Clinton by name and depicts interviews with political commentators and other persons, most of them quite critical of Senator Clinton. *Hillary* was released in theaters and on DVD, but Citizens United wanted to increase distribution by making it available through video-on-demand.

* * * In December 2007, a cable company offered, for a payment of $1.2 million, to make *Hillary* available on a video-on-demand channel called "Elections '08." * * *

To implement the proposal, Citizens United was prepared to pay for the video-on-demand; and to promote the film, it produced two 10-second ads and one 30-second ad for *Hillary.* Each ad includes a short (and, in our view, pejorative) statement about Senator Clinton, followed by the name of the movie and the movie's Website address. Citizens United desired to promote the video-on-demand offering by running advertisements on broadcast and cable television.

Before the Bipartisan Campaign Reform Act of 2002 (BCRA), federal law prohibited—and still does prohibit—corporations and unions from using general treasury funds to make direct contributions to candidates or independent expenditures that expressly advocate the election or defeat of a candidate, through any form of media, in connection with certain qualified federal elections. 2 U.S.C. § 441b; BCRA § 203 amended § 441b to prohibit any "electioneering communication" as well. An electioneering communication is defined as "any broadcast, cable, or satellite communication" that "refers to a clearly identified candidate for Federal office" and is made within 30 days of a primary or 60 days of a general election. § 434(f)(3)(A). * * * Corporations and unions * * * may establish, however, a "separate segregated fund" (known as a political action committee, or PAC) for [express advocacy or electioneering communications]. The moneys received by the segregated fund are limited to donations from stockholders and employees of the corporation or, in the case of unions, members of the union.

Citizens United wanted to make *Hillary* available through video-on-demand within 30 days of the 2008 primary elections. It feared, however, that both the film and the ads would be covered by § 441b's ban on corporate-funded independent expenditures, thus subjecting the corporation to civil and criminal penalties * * *. In December 2007, Citizens United sought declaratory and injunctive relief against the FEC. It argued that (1) § 441b is unconstitutional as applied to *Hillary*; and (2)

BCRA's disclaimer and disclosure requirements, are unconstitutional as applied to *Hillary* and to the three ads for the movie. * * *

II * * *

[In Part II, the Court determined that the ads for *Hillary* were covered by the statute, and did not fall within any statutory exemption; the Court further determined that an as-applied exemption was unavailable.]

As the foregoing analysis confirms, the Court cannot resolve this case on a narrower ground without chilling political speech, speech that is central to the meaning and purpose of the First Amendment. * * *

III * * *

* * * Section 441b makes it a felony for all corporations—including nonprofit advocacy corporations—either to expressly advocate the election or defeat of candidates or to broadcast electioneering communications within 30 days of a primary election and 60 days of a general election. Thus, the following acts would all be felonies under §441b: The Sierra Club runs an ad, within the crucial phase of 60 days before the general election, that exhorts the public to disapprove of a Congressman who favors logging in national forests; the National Rifle Association publishes a book urging the public to vote for the challenger because the incumbent U.S. Senator supports a handgun ban; and the American Civil Liberties Union creates a Web site telling the public to vote for a Presidential candidate in light of that candidate's defense of free speech. These prohibitions are classic examples of censorship.

Section 441b is a ban on corporate speech notwithstanding the fact that a PAC created by a corporation can still speak. A PAC is a separate association from the corporation. So the PAC exemption from §441b's expenditure ban does not allow corporations to speak. Even if a PAC could somehow allow a corporation to speak—and it does not—the option to form PACs does not alleviate the First Amendment problems with §441b. PACs are burdensome alternatives; they are expensive to administer and subject to extensive regulations. For example, every PAC must appoint a treasurer, forward donations to the treasurer promptly, keep detailed records of the identities of the persons making donations, preserve receipts for three years, and file an organization statement and report changes to this information within 10 days.

And that is just the beginning. PACs must file detailed monthly reports with the FEC, which are due at different times depending on the type of election that is about to occur:

> "These reports must contain information regarding the amount of cash on hand; the total amount of receipts, detailed by 10 different categories; the identification of each political committee and candidate's authorized or affiliated committee making contributions, and any persons making loans, providing rebates, refunds, dividends, or interest or any other offset to operating expenditures in an aggregate amount over $200; the

total amount of all disbursements, detailed by 12 different categories; the names of all authorized or affiliated committees to whom expenditures aggregating over $200 have been made; persons to whom loan repayments or refunds have been made; the total sum of all contributions, operating expenses, outstanding debts and obligations, and the settlement terms of the retirement of any debt or obligation." [*McConnell,*] 540 U.S., at 331–332 [(opinion of Kennedy, J.)].

PACs have to comply with these regulations just to speak. This might explain why fewer than 2,000 of the millions of corporations in this country have PACs. PACs, furthermore, must exist before they can speak. Given the onerous restrictions, a corporation may not be able to establish a PAC in time to make its views known regarding candidates and issues in a current campaign.

Section 441b's prohibition on corporate independent expenditures is thus a ban on speech. As a "restriction on the amount of money a person or group can spend on political communication during a campaign," that statute "necessarily reduces the quantity of expression by restricting the number of issues discussed, the depth of their exploration, and the size of the audience reached." *Buckley* v. *Valeo*, 424 U.S. 1, 19 (1976) [p. 728]. * * * If § 441b applied to individuals, no one would believe that it is merely a time, place, or manner restriction on speech. Its purpose and effect are to silence entities whose voices the Government deems to be suspect.

Speech is an essential mechanism of democracy, for it is the means to hold officials accountable to the people. The right of citizens to inquire, to hear, to speak, and to use information to reach consensus is a precondition to enlightened self-government and a necessary means to protect it. * * *

For these reasons, political speech must prevail against laws that would suppress it, whether by design or inadvertence. Laws that burden political speech are "subject to strict scrutiny," which requires the Government to prove that the restriction "furthers a compelling interest and is narrowly tailored to achieve that interest." * * * Premised on mistrust of governmental power, the First Amendment stands against attempts to disfavor certain subjects or viewpoints. Prohibited, too, are restrictions distinguishing among different speakers, allowing speech by some but not others. As instruments to censor, these categories are interrelated: Speech restrictions based on the identity of the speaker are all too often simply a means to control content.

Quite apart from the purpose or effect of regulating content, moreover, the Government may commit a constitutional wrong when by law it identifies certain preferred speakers. By taking the right to speak from some and giving it to others, the Government deprives the disadvantaged person or class of the right to use speech to strive to establish worth, standing, and respect for the speaker's voice. The Government may not by these means deprive the public of the right and privilege to determine for itself what speech and speakers are worthy of consideration. The First Amendment protects speech and speaker, and the ideas that flow from each.

The Court has upheld a narrow class of speech restrictions that operate to the disadvantage of certain persons, but these rulings were based on an interest in allowing governmental entities [such as schools, prisons, the military, and the civil service] to perform their functions. The corporate independent expenditures at issue in this case, however, would not interfere with governmental functions, so these cases are inapposite. These precedents stand only for the proposition that there are certain governmental functions that cannot operate without some restrictions on particular kinds of speech. By contrast, it is inherent in the nature of the political process that voters must be free to obtain information from diverse sources in order to determine how to cast their votes. At least before *Austin*, the Court had not allowed the exclusion of a class of speakers from the general public dialogue.

We find no basis for the proposition that, in the context of political speech, the Government may impose restrictions on certain disfavored speakers. Both history and logic lead us to this conclusion.

The Court has recognized that First Amendment protection extends to corporations. [The Court here cited twenty-three cases, including *First National Bank of Boston v. Bellotti*, 435 U.S. 765, 778 n.14 (1978), involving corporations' free-speech rights.]

This protection has been extended by explicit holdings to the context of political speech. See, *e.g.*, [*NAACP v.*] *Button*, 371 U.S. [415], 428–429 [(1963)]; *Grosjean* v. *American Press Co.*, 297 U.S. 233, 244 (1936). Under the rationale of these precedents, political speech does not lose First Amendment protection "simply because its source is a corporation." *Bellotti, supra*, at 784; see *Pacific Gas & Elec. Co. v. Public Util. Comm'n of Cal.*, 475 U.S. 1, 8 (1986) (plurality opinion) ("The identity of the speaker is not decisive in determining whether speech is protected. Corporations and other associations, like individuals, contribute to the 'discussion, debate, and the dissemination of information and ideas' that the First Amendment seeks to foster" (quoting *Bellotti*, 435 U.S., at 783)). The Court has thus rejected the argument that political speech of corporations or other associations should be treated differently under the First Amendment simply because such associations are not "natural persons." *Id.*, at 776; see *id.*, at 780, n.16. * * *

The *Buckley* Court explained that the potential for *quid pro quo* corruption distinguished direct contributions to candidates from independent expenditures. The Court emphasized that "the independent expenditure ceiling . . . fails to serve any substantial governmental interest in stemming the reality or appearance of corruption in the electoral process," *id.*, at 47–48, because "[t]he absence of prearrangement and coordination . . . alleviates the danger that expenditures will be given as a *quid pro quo* for improper commitments from the candidate," *id.*, at 47. *Buckley* invalidated § 608(e)'s restrictions on independent expenditures, with only one Justice dissenting.

Buckley did not consider § 610's separate ban on corporate and union independent expenditures * * *. Had § 610 [of the Federal Election Campaign Act] been challenged in the wake of *Buckley*, however, it could not have been squared with the reasoning and analysis of that precedent. The expenditure ban invalidated in *Buckley*, §608(e), applied to corporations and unions; and some of the prevailing plaintiffs in *Buckley* were corporations, *id.*, at 8. * * *

Notwithstanding this precedent, Congress recodified §610's corporate and union expenditure ban at 2 U.S.C. §441b four months after *Buckley* was decided. Section 441b is the independent expenditure restriction challenged here.

Less than two years after *Buckley*, *Bellotti* reaffirmed the First Amendment principle that the Government cannot restrict political speech based on the speaker's corporate identity. *Bellotti* could not have been clearer when it struck down a state-law prohibition on corporate independent expenditures related to referenda issues:

> "We thus find no support in the First . . . Amendment, or in the decisions of this Court, for the proposition that speech that otherwise would be within the protection of the First Amendment loses that protection simply because its source is a corporation that cannot prove, to the satisfaction of a court, a material effect on its business or property. * * *

> "In the realm of protected speech, the legislature is constitutionally disqualified from dictating the subjects about which persons may speak and the speakers who may address a public issue." *Id.*, at 784–785.

It is important to note that the reasoning and holding of *Bellotti* did not rest on the existence of a viewpoint-discriminatory statute. It rested on the principle that the Government lacks the power to ban corporations from speaking.

Bellotti did not address the constitutionality of the State's ban on corporate independent expenditures to support candidates. In our view, however, that restriction would have been unconstitutional under *Bellotti*'s central principle: that the First Amendment does not allow political speech restrictions based on a speaker's corporate identity.

Thus the law stood until *Austin*. * * * There, the Michigan Chamber of Commerce sought to use general treasury funds to run a newspaper ad supporting a specific candidate. Michigan law, however, prohibited corporate independent expenditures that supported or opposed any candidate for state office. A violation of the law was punishable as a felony. The Court sustained the speech prohibition.

To bypass *Buckley* and *Bellotti*, the *Austin* Court identified a new governmental interest in limiting political speech: an antidistortion interest. *Austin* found a compelling governmental interest in preventing "the corrosive and distorting effects of immense aggregations of wealth that are accumulated with the help of the corporate form and that have little or no correlation to the public's support for the corporation's political ideas." 494 U.S., at 660.

The Court is thus confronted with conflicting lines of precedent: a pre-*Austin* line that forbids restrictions on political speech based on the speaker's corporate identity and a post-*Austin* line that permits them. No case before *Austin* had held that Congress could prohibit independent expenditures for political speech based on the speaker's corporate identity. * * *

In its defense of the corporate-speech restrictions in § 441b, the Government notes the antidistortion rationale on which *Austin* and its progeny rest in part, yet it all but abandons reliance upon it. It argues instead that two other compelling interests support *Austin*'s holding that corporate expenditure restrictions are con-stitutional: an anticorruption interest and a shareholder-protection interest. We consider the three points in turn.

As for *Austin*'s antidistortion rationale, the Government does little to defend it. And with good reason, for the rationale cannot support § 441b.

If the First Amendment has any force, it prohibits Congress from fining or jailing citizens, or associations of citizens, for simply engaging in political speech. If the antidistortion rationale were to be accepted, however, it would permit Government to ban political speech simply because the speaker is an association that has taken on the corporate form. The Government contends that *Austin* permits it to ban cor-porate expenditures for almost all forms of communication stemming from a cor-poration. If *Austin* were correct, the Government could prohibit a corporation from expressing political views in media beyond those presented here, such as by printing books. The Government responds "that the FEC has never applied this statute to a book," and if it did, "there would be quite [a] good as-applied challenge." This troubling assertion of brooding governmental power cannot be reconciled with the confidence and stability in civic discourse that the First Amendment must secure.

* * * *Austin* sought to defend the antidistortion rationale as a means to prevent corporations from obtaining "an unfair advantage in the political marketplace" by using "resources amassed in the economic marketplace." 494 U.S., at 659. But *Buck-ley* rejected the premise that the Government has an interest "in equalizing the rela-tive ability of individuals and groups to influence the outcome of elections." 424 U.S., at 48; see *Bellotti*, 435 U.S., at 791, n.30. * * * The rule that political speech can-not be limited based on a speaker's wealth is a necessary consequence of the premise that the First Amendment generally prohibits the suppression of political speech based on the speaker's identity.

Either as support for its antidistortion rationale or as a further argument, the *Austin* majority undertook to distinguish wealthy individuals from corporations on the ground that "[s]tate law grants corporations special advantages—such as limited liability, perpetual life, and favorable treatment of the accumulation and distribution of assets." 494 U.S., at 658–659. This does not suffice, however, to allow laws prohibiting speech. "It is rudimentary that the State cannot exact as the price of those special advantages the forfeiture of First Amendment rights." *Id.*, at 680 (SCALIA, J., dissenting).

It is irrelevant for purposes of the First Amendment that corporate funds may "have little or no correlation to the public's support for the corporation's political ideas." *Id.*, at 660 (majority opinion). All speakers, including individuals and the media, use money amassed from the economic marketplace to fund their speech. The First Amendment protects the resulting speech, even if it was enabled by economic transactions with persons or entities who disagree with the speaker's ideas. See *id.*, at 707 (KENNEDY, J., dissenting) ("Many persons can trace their funds to corporations, if not in the form of donations, then in the form of dividends, interest, or salary").

Austin's antidistortion rationale would produce the dangerous, and unacceptable, consequence that Congress could ban political speech of media corporations. Media corporations are now exempt from §441b's ban on corporate expenditures. Yet media corporations accumulate wealth with the help of the corporate form, the largest media corporations have "immense aggregations of wealth," and the views expressed by media corporations often "have little or no correlation to the public's support" for those views. Thus, under the Government's reasoning, wealthy media corporations could have their voices diminished to put them on par with other media entities. There is no precedent for permitting this under the First Amendment.

The media exemption discloses further difficulties with the law now under consideration. There is no precedent supporting laws that attempt to distinguish between corporations which are deemed to be exempt as media corporations and those which are not. "We have consistently rejected the proposition that the institutional press has any constitutional privilege beyond that of other speakers." *Id.*, at 691 (SCALIA, J., dissenting). With the advent of the Internet and the decline of print and broadcast media, moreover, the line between the media and others who wish to comment on political and social issues becomes far more blurred.

The law's exception for media corporations is, on its own terms, all but an admission of the invalidity of the antidistortion rationale. And the exemption results in a further, separate reason for finding this law invalid: Again by its own terms, the law exempts some corporations but covers others, even though both have the need or the motive to communicate their views. The exemption applies to media corporations owned or controlled by corporations that have diverse and substantial investments and participate in endeavors other than news. So even assuming the most doubtful proposition that a news organization has a right to speak when others do not, the exemption would allow a conglomerate that owns both a media business and an unrelated business to influence or control the media in order to advance its overall business interest. At the same time, some other corporation, with an identical business interest but no media outlet in its ownership structure, would be forbidden to speak or inform the public about the same issue. This differential treatment cannot be squared with the First Amendment.

There is simply no support for the view that the First Amendment, as originally understood, would permit the suppression of political speech by media corporations. The Framers may not have anticipated modern business and media corporations. Yet television networks and major newspapers owned by media corporations have become the most important means of mass communication in modern times. The First Amendment was certainly not understood to condone the suppression of political speech in society's most salient media. It was understood as a response to the repression of speech and the press that had existed in England and the heavy taxes on the press that were imposed in the colonies. The great debates between the Federalists and the Anti-Federalists over our founding document were published and expressed in the most important means of mass communication of that era—newspapers owned by individuals. At the founding, speech was open, comprehensive, and vital to society's definition of itself; there were no limits on the sources of speech and knowledge. The Framers may have been unaware of certain types of speakers or forms of communication, but that does not mean that those speakers and media are entitled to less First Amendment protection than those types of speakers and media that provided the means of communicating political ideas when the Bill of Rights was adopted.

Austin interferes with the "open marketplace" of ideas protected by the First Amendment. It permits the Government to ban the political speech of millions of associations of citizens. Most of these are small corporations without large amounts of wealth. See Congressional Research Service Report for Congress, Business Organizational Choices 10 (2009) (more than 75% of corporations whose income is taxed under federal law have less than $1 million in receipts per year). This fact belies the Government's argument that the statute is justified on the ground that it prevents the "distorting effects of immense aggregations of wealth." *Austin*, 494 U.S., at 660. It is not even aimed at amassed wealth.

The censorship we now confront is vast in its reach. The Government has "muffle[d] the voices that best represent the most significant segments of the economy." *McConnell*, *supra*, at 257–258 (opinion of (SCALIA, J.). And "the electorate [has been] deprived of information, knowledge and opinion vital to its function." By suppressing the speech of manifold corporations, both for-profit and nonprofit, the Government prevents their voices and viewpoints from reaching the public and advising voters on which persons or entities are hostile to their interests. Factions will necessarily form in our Republic, but the remedy of "destroying the liberty" of some factions is "worse than the disease." The Federalist No. 10, p. 130 (B. Wright ed. 1961) (J. Madison). Factions should be checked by permitting them all to speak, see *ibid.*, and by entrusting the people to judge what is true and what is false. * * *

Even if § 441b's expenditure ban were constitutional, wealthy corporations could still lobby elected officials, although smaller corporations may not have the resources to do so. And wealthy individuals and unincorporated associations can spend unlimited amounts on independent expenditures. Yet certain disfavored associations of citizens—those that have taken on the corporate form—are penalized for engaging in the same political speech.

When Government seeks to use its full power, including the criminal law, to command where a person may get his or her information or what distrusted source he or she may not hear, it uses censorship to control thought. This is unlawful. The First Amendment confirms the freedom to think for ourselves.

What we have said also shows the invalidity of other arguments made by the Government. For the most part relinquishing the antidistortion rationale, the Government falls back on the argument that corporate political speech can be banned in order to prevent corruption or its appearance. In *Buckley*, the Court found this interest "sufficiently important" to allow limits on contributions but did not extend that reasoning to expenditure limits. 424 U.S., at 25. * * *

* * * Limits on independent expenditures, such as § 441b, have a chilling effect extending well beyond the Government's interest in preventing *quid pro quo* corruption. The anticorruption interest is not sufficient to displace the speech here in question. Indeed, 26 States do not restrict independent expenditures by for-profit corporations. The Government does not claim that these expenditures have corrupted the political process in those States.

A single footnote in *Bellotti* purported to leave open the possibility that corporate independent expenditures could be shown to cause corruption. 435 U.S., at 788, n.26. For the reasons explained above, we now conclude that independent expenditures, including those made by corporations, do not give rise to corruption or the appearance of corruption. * * *

When *Buckley* identified a sufficiently important governmental interest in preventing corruption or the appearance of corruption, that interest was limited to *quid pro quo* corruption. The fact that speakers may have influence over or access to elected officials does not mean that these officials are corrupt:

> "Favoritism and influence are not . . . avoidable in representative politics. It is in the nature of an elected representative to favor certain policies, and, by necessary corollary, to favor the voters and contributors who support those policies. It is well understood that a substantial and legitimate reason, if not the only reason, to cast a vote for, or to make a contribution to, one candidate over another is that the candidate will respond by producing those political outcomes the supporter favors. Democracy is premised on responsiveness." *McConnell*, 540 U.S., at 297 (opinion of KENNEDY, J.).

Reliance on a "generic favoritism or influence theory . . . is at odds with standard First Amendment analyses because it is unbounded and susceptible to no limiting principle." *Id.*, at 296.

The appearance of influence or access, furthermore, will not cause the electorate to lose faith in our democracy. By definition, an independent expenditure is political speech presented to the electorate that is not coordinated with a candidate. The fact that a corporation, or any other speaker, is willing to spend money to try to persuade voters presupposes that the people have the ultimate influence over elected officials. This is inconsistent with any suggestion that the electorate will refuse "to take part in democratic governance" because of additional political speech made by a corporation or any other speaker. * * *

The *McConnell* record was "over 100,000 pages" long, yet it "does not have any direct examples of votes being exchanged for . . . expenditures." This confirms *Buckley's* reasoning that independent expenditures do not lead to, or create the appearance of, *quid pro quo* corruption. In fact, there is only scant evidence that independent expenditures even ingratiate. Ingratiation and access, in any event, are not corruption. The BCRA record establishes that certain donations to political parties, called "soft money," were made to gain access to elected officials. This case, however, is about independent expenditures, not soft money. When Congress finds that a problem exists, we must give that finding due deference; but Congress may not choose an unconstitutional remedy. If elected officials succumb to improper influences from independent expenditures; if they surrender their best judgment; and if they put expediency before principle, then surely there is cause for concern. We must give weight to attempts by Congress to seek to dispel either the appearance or the reality of these influences. The remedies enacted by law, however, must comply with the First Amendment; and, it is our law and our tradition that more speech, not less, is the governing rule. An outright ban on corporate political speech during the critical preelection period is not a permissible remedy. Here Congress has created categorical bans on speech that are asymmetrical to preventing *quid pro quo* corruption.

The Government contends further that corporate independent expenditures can be limited because of its interest in protecting dissenting shareholders from being compelled to fund corporate political speech. This asserted interest, like *Austin's* antidistortion rationale, would allow the Government to ban the political speech even of media corporations. Assume, for example, that a shareholder of a corporation that owns a newspaper disagrees with the political views the newspaper expresses. Under the Government's view, that potential disagreement could give the Government the authority to restrict the media corporation's political speech. The First Amendment does not allow that power. There is, furthermore, little evidence of abuse that cannot be corrected by shareholders "through the procedures of corporate democracy." *Bellotti*, 435 U.S., at 794; see *id.*, at 794, n.34.

Those reasons are sufficient to reject this shareholder-protection interest; and, moreover, the statute is both underinclusive and overinclusive. As to the first, if Congress had been seeking to protect dissenting shareholders, it would not have banned corporate speech in only certain media within 30 or 60 days before an election. A dissenting shareholder's interests would be implicated by speech in any media at any time. As to the second, the statute is overinclusive because it covers all corporations, including nonprofit corporations and for-profit corporations with only single shareholders. As to other corporations, the remedy is not to restrict speech but to consider and explore other regulatory mechanisms. The regulatory mechanism here, based on speech, contravenes the First Amendment.

We need not reach the question whether the Government has a compelling interest in preventing foreign individuals or associations from influencing our Nation's political process. Cf. 2 U.S.C. § 441e (contribution and expenditure ban applied to "foreign national[s]"). Section 441b is not limited to corporations or associations that were created in foreign countries or funded predominately by foreign shareholders. Section 441b therefore would be overbroad even if we assumed, *arguendo*, that the Government has a compelling interest in limiting foreign influence over our political process. * * *

Due consideration leads to this conclusion: *Austin* should be and now is overruled. We return to the principle established in *Buckley* and *Bellotti* that the Government may not suppress political speech on the basis of the speaker's corporate identity. No sufficient governmental interest justifies limits on the political speech of nonprofit or for-profit corporations. * * * Section 441b's restrictions on corporate independent expenditures are therefore invalid and cannot be applied to *Hillary*.

Given our conclusion we are further required to overrule the part of *McConnell* that upheld BCRA § 203's extension of § 441b's restrictions on corporate independent expenditures. See 540 U.S., at 203–209. The *McConnell* Court relied on the antidistortion interest recognized in *Austin* to uphold a greater restriction on speech than the restriction upheld in *Austin*, see 540 U.S., at 205, and we have found this interest unconvincing and insufficient. This part of *McConnell* is now overruled.

IV

[Part IV, upholding BCRA's disclosure requirements for electioneering communications, is reprinted in Chapter 9, *infra*.]

V * * *

The judgment of the District Court is reversed with respect to the constitutionality of 2 U.S.C. § 441b's restrictions on corporate independent expenditures. * * * The case is remanded for further proceedings consistent with this opinion.

It is so ordered.

CHIEF JUSTICE ROBERTS, with whom JUSTICE ALITO joins, concurring. * * *

This is the first case in which we have been asked to overrule *Austin*, and thus it is also the first in which we have had reason to consider how much weight to give *stare decisis* in assessing its continued validity. The dissent erroneously declares that the Court "reaffirmed" *Austin*'s holding in subsequent cases — namely, *Federal Election Comm'n v. Beaumont*, 539 U.S. 146 (2003); *McConnell*; and *WRTL*. Not so. Not a single party in any of those cases asked us to overrule *Austin*, and as the dissent points out, the Court generally does not consider constitutional arguments that have not properly been raised. *Austin*'s validity was therefore not directly at issue in the cases the dissent cites. The Court's unwillingness to overturn *Austin* in those cases cannot be understood as a *reaffirmation* of that decision. * * *

[The policies behind *stare decisis*] weigh against retaining our decision in *Austin*. First, as the majority explains, that decision was an "aberration" insofar as it departed from the robust protections we had granted political speech in our earlier cases. *Austin* undermined the careful line that *Buckley* drew to distinguish limits on contributions to candidates from limits on independent expenditures on speech. *Buckley* rejected the asserted government interest in regulating independent expenditures, concluding that "restrict[ing] the speech of some elements of our society in order to enhance the relative voice of others is wholly foreign to the First Amendment." 424 U.S., at 48–49. *Austin*, however, allowed the Government to prohibit these same expenditures out of concern for "the corrosive and distorting effects of immense aggregations of wealth" in the marketplace of ideas. 494 U.S., at 660. *Austin's* reasoning was—and remains—inconsistent with *Buckley's* explicit repudiation of any government interest in "equalizing the relative ability of individuals and groups to influence the outcome of elections." 424 U.S., at 48–49.

Austin was also inconsistent with *Bellotti's* clear rejection of the idea that "speech that otherwise would be within the protection of the First Amendment loses that protection simply because its source is a corporation." 435 U.S., at 784. The dissent correctly points out that *Bellotti* involved a referendum rather than a candidate election, and that *Bellotti* itself noted this factual distinction. But this distinction does not explain why corporations may be subject to prohibitions on speech in candidate elections when individuals may not.

Second, the validity of *Austin's* rationale—itself adopted over two "spirited dissents"—has proved to be the consistent subject of dispute among Members of this Court ever since. The simple fact that one of our decisions remains controversial is, of course, insufficient to justify overruling it. But it does undermine the precedent's ability to contribute to the stable and orderly development of the law. In such circumstances, it is entirely appropriate for the Court—which in this case is squarely asked to reconsider *Austin's* validity for the first time—to address the matter with a greater willingness to consider new approaches capable of restoring our doctrine to sounder footing.

Third, the *Austin* decision is uniquely destabilizing because it threatens to subvert our Court's decisions even outside the particular context of corporate express advocacy. The First Amendment theory underlying *Austin's* holding is extraordinarily broad. *Austin's* logic would authorize government prohibition of political speech by a category of speakers in the name of equality—a point that most scholars acknowledge (and many celebrate), but that the dissent denies.

It should not be surprising, then, that Members of the Court have relied on *Austin's* expansive logic to justify greater incursions on the First Amendment, even outside the original context of corporate advocacy on behalf of candidates running for office. See, *e.g.*, *Davis* v. *Federal Election Comm'n*, 554 U.S. 724, 756 (2008) (STEVENS, J., concurring in part and dissenting in part) (relying on *Austin* and other cases to justify restrictions on campaign spending by individual candidates, explaining that "there is no reason that their logic—specifically, their concerns about the corrosive and distorting effects of wealth on our political process—is not equally applicable in the context of individual wealth"); *McConnell, supra,* at 203–209 (extending *Austin* beyond its original context to cover not only the "functional equivalent" of express advocacy by corporations, but also electioneering speech conducted by labor unions). The dissent in this case succumbs to the same temptation, suggesting that *Austin* justifies prohibiting corporate speech because such speech might unduly influence "the market for legislation." The dissent reads *Austin* to permit restrictions on corporate speech based on nothing more than the fact that the corporate form may help individuals coordinate and present their views more effectively. A speaker's ability to persuade, however, provides no basis for government regulation of free and open public debate on what the laws should be.

If taken seriously, *Austin*'s logic would apply most directly to newspapers and other media corporations. They have a more profound impact on public discourse than most other speakers. These corporate entities are, for the time being, not subject to § 441b's otherwise generally applicable prohibitions on corporate political speech. But this is simply a matter of legislative grace. The fact that the law currently grants a favored position to media corporations is no reason to overlook the danger inherent in accepting a theory that would allow government restrictions on their political speech.

These readings of *Austin* do no more than carry that decision's reasoning to its logical endpoint. In doing so, they highlight the threat *Austin* poses to First Amendment rights generally, even outside its specific factual context of corporate express advocacy. Because *Austin* is so difficult to confine to its facts—and because its logic threatens to undermine our First Amendment jurisprudence and the nature of public discourse more broadly—the costs of giving it *stare decisis* effect are unusually high.

Finally and most importantly, the Government's own effort to defend *Austin*—or, more accurately, to defend something that is not quite *Austin*—underscores its weakness as a precedent of the Court. The Government concedes that *Austin* "is not the most lucid opinion," yet asks us to reaffirm its holding. But while invoking *stare decisis* to support this position, the Government never once even *mentions* the compelling interest that *Austin* relied upon in the first place: the need to diminish "the corrosive and distorting effects of immense aggregations of wealth that are accumulated with the help of the corporate form and that have little or no correlation to the public's support for the corporation's political ideas." 494 U.S., at 660.

Instead of endorsing *Austin* on its own terms, the Government urges us to reaffirm *Austin*'s specific holding on the basis of two new and potentially expansive interests—the need to prevent actual or apparent *quid pro quo* corruption, and the need to protect corporate shareholders. Those interests may or may not support the *result* in *Austin*, but they were plainly not part of the *reasoning* on which *Austin* relied.

To its credit, the Government forthrightly concedes that *Austin* did not embrace either of the new rationales it now urges upon us. * * *

To the extent that the Government's case for reaffirming *Austin* depends on radically reconceptualizing its reasoning, that argument is at odds with itself. *Stare decisis* is a doctrine of preservation, not transformation. It counsels deference to past mistakes, but provides no justification for making new ones. There is therefore no basis for the Court to give precedential sway to reasoning that it has never accepted, simply because that reasoning happens to support a conclusion reached on different grounds that have since been abandoned or discredited. * * *

JUSTICE SCALIA, with whom JUSTICE ALITO joins, and with whom JUSTICE THOMAS joins in [relevant] part, concurring. * * *

I write separately to address JUSTICE STEVENS' discussion of "*Original Understandings.*" This section of the dissent purports to show that today's decision is not supported by the original understanding of the First Amendment. The dissent attempts this demonstration, however, in splendid isolation from the text of the First Amendment. It never shows why "the freedom of speech" that was the right of Englishmen did not include the freedom to speak in association with other individuals, including association in the corporate form.

Instead of taking this straightforward approach to determining the Amendment's meaning, the dissent embarks on a detailed exploration of the Framers' views about the "role of corporations in society." The Framers didn't like corporations, the dissent concludes, and therefore it follows (as night the day) that corporations had no rights of free speech. Of course the Framers' personal affection or disaffection for corporations is relevant only insofar as it can be thought to be reflected in the understood meaning of the text they enacted—not, as the dissent suggests, as a freestanding substitute for that text. But the dissent's distortion of proper analysis is even worse than that. Though faced with a constitutional text that makes no distinction between types of speakers, the dissent feels no necessity to provide even an isolated statement from the founding era to the effect that corporations are *not* covered, but places the burden on petitioners to bring forward statements showing that they *are* ("there is not a scintilla of evidence to support the notion that anyone believed [the First Amendment] would preclude regulatory distinctions based on the corporate form").

Despite the corporation-hating quotations the dissent has dredged up, it is far from clear that by the end of the 18th century corporations were despised. If so, how came there to be so many of them? The dissent's statement that there were few business corporations during the eighteenth century—"only a few hundred during all of the 18th century"—is misleading. There were approximately 335 charters issued to business corporations in the United States by the end of the 18th century. * * * [W]hat seems like a small number by today's standards surely does not indicate the relative importance of corporations when the Nation was considerably smaller. * * *

Even if we thought it proper to apply the dissent's approach of excluding from First Amendment coverage what the Founders disliked, and even if we agreed that the Founders disliked founding-era corporations; modern corporations might not qualify for exclusion. Most of the Founders' resentment towards corporations was directed at the state-granted monopoly privileges that individually chartered corporations enjoyed. Modern corporations do not have such privileges, and would probably have been favored by most of our enterprising Founders—excluding, perhaps, Thomas Jefferson and others favoring perpetuation of an agrarian society. Moreover, if the Founders' specific intent with respect to corporations is what matters, why does the dissent ignore the Founders' views about other legal entities that have more in common with modern business corporations than the founding-era corporations? At the time of the founding, religious, educational, and literary corporations were incorporated under general incorporation statutes, much as business corporations are today.[4] There were also small unincorporated business associations, which some have argued were the "true progenitors" of today's business corporations. Were all of these silently excluded from the protections of the First Amendment?

The lack of a textual exception for speech by corporations cannot be explained on the ground that such organizations did not exist or did not speak. To the contrary, colleges, towns and cities, religious institutions, and guilds had long been organized as corporations at common law and under the King's charter, and * * * the practice of incorporation only expanded in the United States. Both corporations and voluntary associations actively petitioned the Government and expressed their views in newspapers and pamphlets. For example: An antislavery Quaker corporation petitioned the First Congress, distributed pamphlets, and communicated through the press in 1790. The New York Sons of Liberty sent a circular to colonies farther south in 1766. And the Society for the Relief and Instruction of Poor Germans circulated a biweekly paper from 1755 to 1757. The dissent offers no evidence—none whatever—that the First Amendment's unqualified text was originally understood to exclude such associational speech from its protection.

Historical evidence relating to the textually similar clause "the freedom of . . . the press" also provides no support for the proposition that the First Amendment excludes conduct of artificial legal entities from the scope of its protection. The freedom of "the press" was widely understood to protect the publishing activities of individual editors and printers. But these individuals often acted through newspapers, which (much like corporations) had their own names, outlived the individuals who had founded them, could be bought and sold, were sometimes owned by more

---

4. At times (though not always) the dissent seems to exclude such non-"business corporations" from its denial of free speech rights. Finding in a seemingly categorical text a distinction between the rights of business corporations and the rights of non-business corporations is even more imaginative than finding a distinction between the rights of *all* corporations and the rights of other associations.

than one person, and were operated for profit. Their activities were not stripped of First Amendment protection simply because they were carried out under the banner of an artificial legal entity. And the notion which follows from the dissent's view, that modern newspapers, since they are incorporated, have free-speech rights only at the sufferance of Congress, boggles the mind.[6] * * *

The dissent says that when the Framers "constitutionalized the right to free speech in the First Amendment, it was the free speech of individual Americans that they had in mind." That is no doubt true. All the provisions of the Bill of Rights set forth the rights of individual men and women—not, for example, of trees or polar bears. But the individual person's right to speak includes the right to speak *in association with other individual persons.* Surely the dissent does not believe that speech by the Republican Party or the Democratic Party can be censored because it is not the speech of "an individual American." It is the speech of many individual Americans, who have associated in a common cause, giving the leadership of the party the right to speak on their behalf. The association of individuals in a business corporation is no different—or at least it cannot be denied the right to speak on the simplistic ground that it is not "an individual American."[7]

But to return to, and summarize, my principal point, which is the conformity of today's opinion with the original meaning of the First Amendment. The Amendment is written in terms of "speech," not speakers. Its text offers no foothold for excluding any category of speaker, from single individuals to partnerships of individuals, to unincorporated associations of individuals, to incorporated associations of individuals—and the dissent offers no evidence about the original meaning of the text to support any such exclusion. We are therefore simply left with the question whether the speech at issue in this case is "speech" covered by the First Amendment. No one says otherwise. A documentary film critical of a potential Presidential candidate is core political speech, and its nature as such does not change simply because it was funded by a corporation. Nor does the character of that funding produce

---

6. The dissent seeks to avoid this conclusion (and to turn a liability into an asset) by interpreting the Freedom of the Press Clause to refer to the institutional press (thus demonstrating, according to the dissent, that the Founders "did draw distinctions—explicit distinctions—between types of 'speakers,' or speech outlets or forms"). It is passing strange to interpret the phrase "the freedom of speech, or of the press" to mean, not everyone's right to speak or publish, but rather everyone's right to speak or the institutional press's right to publish. No one thought that is what it meant. Patriot Noah Webster's 1828 dictionary contains, under the word "press," the following entry: "*Liberty of the press*, in civil policy, is the free right of publishing books, pamphlets, or papers without previous restraint; or the unrestrained right which every citizen enjoys of publishing his thoughts and opinions, subject only to punishment for publishing what is pernicious to morals or to the peace of the state." * * *

7. The dissent says that "speech" refers to oral communications of human beings, and since corporations are not human beings they cannot speak. This is sophistry. The authorized spokesman of a corporation is a human being, who speaks on behalf of the human beings who have formed that association—just as the spokesman of an unincorporated association speaks on behalf of its members. The power to publish thoughts, no less than the power to speak thoughts, belongs only to human beings * * *.

any reduction whatever in the "inherent worth of the speech" and "its capacity for informing the public." Indeed, to exclude or impede corporate speech is to muzzle the principal agents of the modern free economy. We should celebrate rather than condemn the addition of this speech to the public debate.

JUSTICE STEVENS, with whom JUSTICE GINSBURG, JUSTICE BREYER, and JUSTICE SOTOMAYOR join, concurring in part and dissenting in part.

The real issue in this case concerns how, not if, the appellant may finance its electioneering. Citizens United is a wealthy nonprofit corporation that runs a political action committee (PAC) with millions of dollars in assets. Under the Bipartisan Campaign Reform Act of 2002 (BCRA), it could have used those assets to televise and promote *Hillary: The Movie* wherever and whenever it wanted to. It also could have spent unrestricted sums to broadcast *Hillary* at any time other than the 30 days before the last primary election. Neither Citizens United's nor any other corporation's speech has been "banned." All that the parties dispute is whether Citizens United had a right to use the funds in its general treasury to pay for broadcasts during the 30-day period. The notion that the First Amendment dictates an affirmative answer to that question is, in my judgment, profoundly misguided. * * *

The So-Called "Ban"

Pervading the Court's analysis is the ominous image of a "categorical ba[n]" on corporate speech. * * * This characterization is highly misleading, and needs to be corrected.

* * * For starters, [the] statutes [upheld in *Austin* and *McConnell*] provide exemptions for PACs, separate segregated funds established by a corporation for political purposes. * * * A significant and growing number of corporations avail themselves of this option; during the most recent election cycle, corporate and union PACs raised nearly a billion dollars. Administering a PAC entails some administrative burden, but so does complying with the disclaimer, disclosure, and reporting requirements that the Court today upholds, and no one has suggested that the burden is severe for a sophisticated for-profit corporation. * * * Like all other natural persons, every shareholder of every corporation remains entirely free under *Austin* and *McConnell* to do however much electioneering she pleases outside of the corporate form. The owners of a "mom & pop" store can simply place ads in their own names, rather than the store's. If ideologically aligned individuals wish to make unlimited expenditures through the corporate form, they may utilize an *MCFL* organization that has policies in place to avoid becoming a conduit for business or union interests. [See *Federal Election Commission v. Massachusetts Citizens for Life, Inc.*, 479 U.S. 238 (1986) (*MCFL*).]

The laws upheld in *Austin* and *McConnell* leave open many additional avenues for corporations' political speech. Consider the statutory provision we are ostensibly evaluating in this case, BCRA §203. It has no application to genuine issue advertising—a category of corporate speech Congress found to be far more substantial than election-related advertising—or to Internet, telephone, and print advocacy. Like numerous statutes, it exempts media companies' news stories, commentaries, and editorials from its electioneering restrictions, in recognition of the unique role played by the institutional press in sustaining public debate. It also allows corporations to spend unlimited sums on political communications with their executives and shareholders, to fund additional PAC activity through trade associations, to distribute voting guides and voting records, to underwrite voter registration and voter turnout activities, to host fundraising events for candidates within certain limits, and to publicly endorse candidates through a press release and press conference. * * *

In many ways, then, § 203 functions as a source restriction or a time, place, and manner restriction. It applies in a viewpoint-neutral fashion to a narrow subset of advocacy messages about clearly identified candidates for federal office, made during discrete time periods through discrete channels. In the case at hand, all Citizens United needed to do to broadcast *Hillary* right before the primary was to abjure business contributions or use the funds in its PAC, which by its own account is "one of the most active conservative PACs in America."

So let us be clear: Neither *Austin* nor *McConnell* held or implied that corporations may be silenced; the FEC is not a "censor"; and in the years since these cases were decided, corporations have continued to play a major role in the national dialogue. Laws such as § 203 target a class of communications that is especially likely to corrupt the political process, that is at least one degree removed from the views of individual citizens, and that may not even reflect the views of those who pay for it. Such laws burden political speech, and that is always a serious matter, demanding careful scrutiny. But the majority's incessant talk of a "ban" aims at a straw man.

Identity-Based Distinctions

The second pillar of the Court's opinion is its assertion that "the Government cannot restrict political speech based on the speaker's . . . identity." * * * Like its paeans to unfettered discourse, the Court's denunciation of identity-based distinctions may have rhetorical appeal but it obscures reality.

* * * The Government routinely places special restrictions on the speech rights of students, prisoners, members of the Armed Forces, foreigners, and its own employees. When such restrictions are justified by a legitimate governmental interest, they do not necessarily raise constitutional problems.

* * * It is fair to say that our First Amendment doctrine has "frowned on" certain identity-based distinctions, particularly those that may reflect invidious discrimination or preferential treatment of a politically powerful group. But it is simply incorrect to suggest that we have prohibited all legislative distinctions based on identity or content. Not even close.

The election context is distinctive in many ways, and the Court, of course, is right that the First Amendment closely guards political speech. But in this context, too, the authority of legislatures to enact viewpoint-neutral regulations based on content and identity is well settled. We have, for example, allowed state-run broadcasters to exclude independent candidates from televised debates. *Arkansas Ed. Television Comm'n* v. *Forbes*, 523 U.S. 666 (1998) [p. 598]. We have upheld statutes that prohibit the distribution or display of campaign materials near a polling place. *Burson* v. *Freeman*, 504 U.S. 191 (1992) [p. 1024]. Although we have not reviewed them directly, we have never cast doubt on laws that place special restrictions on campaign spending by foreign nationals. And we have consistently approved laws that bar Government employees, but not others, from contributing to or participating in political activities. These statutes burden the political expression of one class of speakers, namely, civil servants. Yet we have sustained them on the basis of longstanding practice and Congress' reasoned judgment that certain regulations which leave "untouched full participation . . . in political decisions at the ballot box," *Civil Service Comm'n* v. *Letter Carriers*, 413 U.S. 548, 556 (1973) [p. 679], help ensure that public officials are "sufficiently free from improper influences," *id.*, at 564, and that "confidence in the system of representative Government is not . . . eroded to a disastrous extent."

The same logic applies to this case with additional force because it is the identity of corporations, rather than individuals, that the Legislature has taken into account. As we have unanimously observed, legislatures are entitled to decide "that the special characteristics of the corporate structure require particularly careful regulation" in an electoral context. [*Federal Election Comm'n* v. *National Right to Work Comm.*], 459 U.S. [197], 209–210 [(1982) (*NRWC*)].[50] Not only has the distinctive potential of corporations to corrupt the electoral process long been recognized, but within the area of campaign finance, corporate spending is also "furthest from the core of political expression, since corporations' First Amendment speech and association interests are derived largely from those of their members and of the public in receiving information," *Beaumont*, 539 U.S., at 161, n.8. Campaign finance distinctions based on corporate identity tend to be less worrisome, in other words, because the "speakers" are not natural persons, much less members of our political community, and the governmental interests are of the highest order. Furthermore, when corporations, as a class, are distinguished from noncorporations, as a class, there is a lesser risk that regulatory distinctions will reflect invidious discrimination or political favoritism.

If taken seriously, our colleagues' assumption that the identity of a speaker has *no* relevance to the Government's ability to regulate political speech would lead to some remarkable conclusions. Such an assumption would have accorded the propaganda broadcasts to our troops by "Tokyo Rose" during World War II the same protection as speech by Allied commanders. More pertinently, it would appear to afford the same protection to multinational corporations controlled by foreigners

---

50. They are likewise entitled to regulate media corporations differently from other corporations "to ensure that the law 'does not hinder or prevent the institutional press from reporting on, and publishing editorials about, newsworthy events.'" *McConnell*, 540 U.S., at 208 (quoting *Austin*, 494 U.S., [at] 668).

as to individual Americans: To do otherwise, after all, could "enhance the relative voice" of some (*i.e.*, humans) over others (*i.e.*, nonhumans). Under the majority's view, I suppose it may be a First Amendment problem that corporations are not permitted to vote, given that voting is, among other things, a form of speech.

In short, the Court dramatically overstates its critique of identity-based distinctions, without ever explaining why corporate identity demands the same treatment as individual identity. Only the most wooden approach to the First Amendment could justify the unprecedented line it seeks to draw.

Our First Amendment Tradition

A third fulcrum of the Court's opinion is the idea that *Austin* and *McConnell* are radical outliers, "aberration[s]" in our First Amendment tradition. The Court has it exactly backwards. It is today's holding that is the radical departure from what had been settled First Amendment law. To see why, it is useful to take a long view.

1. *Original Understandings*

Let us start from the beginning. The Court invokes "ancient First Amendment principles" and original understandings to defend today's ruling, yet it makes only a perfunctory attempt to ground its analysis in the principles or understandings of those who drafted and ratified the Amendment. Perhaps this is because there is not a scintilla of evidence to support the notion that anyone believed it would preclude regulatory distinctions based on the corporate form. To the extent that the Framers' views are discernible and relevant to the disposition of this case, they would appear to cut strongly against the majority's position.

This is not only because the Framers and their contemporaries conceived of speech more narrowly than we now think of it, see Bork, Neutral Principles and Some First Amendment Problems, 47 Ind. L.J. 1, 22 (1971), but also because they held very different views about the nature of the First Amendment right and the role of corporations in society. Those few corporations that existed at the founding were authorized by grant of a special legislative charter. * * * Corporations were created, supervised, and conceptualized as quasi-public entities, "designed to serve a social function for the state." It was "assumed that [they] were legally privileged organizations that had to be closely scrutinized by the legislature because their purposes had to be made consistent with public welfare."

* * * General incorporation statutes, and widespread acceptance of business corporations as socially useful actors, did not emerge until the 1800's.

The Framers thus took it as a given that corporations could be comprehensively regulated in the service of the public welfare. Unlike our colleagues, they had little trouble distinguishing corporations from human beings, and when they constitutionalized the right to free speech in the First Amendment, it was the free speech of individual Americans that they had in mind. * * * In light of these background practices and understandings, it seems to me implausible that the Framers believed "the freedom of speech" would extend equally to all corporate speakers, much less that it would preclude legislatures from taking limited measures to guard against corporate capture of elections. * * *

2. *Legislative and Judicial Interpretation*

A century of more recent history puts to rest any notion that today's ruling is faithful to our First Amendment tradition. At the federal level, the express distinction between corporate and individual political spending on elections stretches back to 1907, when Congress passed the Tillman Act, banning all corporate contributions to candidates. * * *

Over the years, the limitations on corporate political spending have been modified in a number of ways, as Congress responded to changes in the American economy and political practices that threatened to displace the commonweal. * * * The Taft-Hartley Act of 1947 is of special significance for this case. In that Act passed more than 60 years ago, Congress extended the prohibition on corporate support of candidates to cover not only direct contributions, but independent expenditures as well. * * *

By the time Congress passed FECA in 1971, the bar on corporate contributions and expenditures had become such an accepted part of federal campaign finance regulation that when a large number of plaintiffs, including several nonprofit corporations, challenged virtually every aspect of the Act in *Buckley*, no one even bothered to argue that the bar as such was unconstitutional. *Buckley* famously (or infamously) distinguished direct contributions from independent expenditures, but its silence on corporations only reinforced the understanding that corporate expenditures could be treated differently from individual expenditures. * * *

Thus, it was unremarkable, in a 1982 case holding that Congress could bar nonprofit corporations from soliciting nonmembers for PAC funds, that then-Justice Rehnquist wrote for a unanimous Court that Congress' "careful legislative adjustment of the federal electoral laws, in a cautious advance, step by step, to account for the particular legal and economic attributes of corporations . . . warrants considerable deference" and "reflects a permissible assessment of the dangers posed by those entities to the electoral process." *NRWC*, 459 U.S., at 209. * * *

The corporate/individual distinction was not questioned by the Court's disposition, in 1986, of a challenge to the expenditure restriction as applied to a distinctive type of nonprofit corporation. In *MCFL*, we * * * held by a 5-to-4 vote was that a limited class of corporations must be allowed to use their general treasury funds for independent expenditures, because Congress' interests in protecting shareholders and "restrict[ing] 'the influence of political war chests funneled through the corporate form'" did not apply to corporations that were structurally insulated from those concerns. * * *

Four years later, in *Austin*, we considered whether corporations falling outside the *MCFL* exception could be barred from using general treasury funds to make independent expenditures in support of, or in opposition to, candidates. We held they could be. * * * In light of the corrupting effects such spending might have on the political process, we permitted the State of Michigan to limit corporate expenditures on candidate elections to corporations' PACs, which rely on voluntary contributions and thus "reflect actual public support for the political ideals espoused by corporations," *ibid.* * * *

In the 20 years since *Austin*, we have reaffirmed its holding and rationale a number of times, see, *e.g.*, *Beaumont*, 539 U.S., at 153–156, most importantly in *McConnell*, where we upheld the provision challenged here, § 203 of BCRA.[62] * * *

When we asked in *McConnell* "whether a compelling governmental interest justifie[d]" § 203, we found the question "easily answered": "We have repeatedly sustained legislation aimed at 'the corrosive and distorting effects of immense aggregations of wealth that are accumulated with the help of the corporate form and that have little or no correlation to the public's support for the corporation's political ideas.'" 540 U.S., at 205 (quoting *Austin*, 494 U.S., at 660). These precedents "represent respect for the legislative judgment that the special characteristics of the corporate structure require particularly careful regulation." 540 U.S., at 205. * * * What made the answer even easier than it might have been otherwise was the option to form PACs, which give corporations, at the least, "a constitutionally sufficient opportunity to engage in" independent expenditures. 540 U.S., at 203.

3. *Buckley and Bellotti* * * *

The majority emphasizes *Buckley's* statement that "[t]he concept that government may restrict the speech of some elements of our society in order to enhance the relative voice of others is wholly foreign to the First Amendment." But this elegant phrase cannot bear the weight that our colleagues have placed on it. For one thing, the Constitution does, in fact, permit numerous "restrictions on the speech of some in order to prevent a few from drowning out the many": for example, restrictions on ballot access and on legislators' floor time. * * * The majority suggests that *Austin* rests on the foreign concept of speech equalization, but we made it clear in *Austin* (as in several cases before and since) that a restriction on the way corporations spend their money is no mere exercise in disfavoring the voice of some elements of our society in preference to others. Indeed, we *expressly* ruled that the compelling interest supporting Michigan's statute was not one of "equaliz[ing] the relative influence of speakers on elections," but rather the need to confront the distinctive corrupting potential of corporate electoral advocacy financed by general treasury dollars. * * *

The case on which the majority places even greater weight than *Buckley*, however, is *Bellotti*, claiming it "could not have been clearer" that *Bellotti's* holding

---

62. According to THE CHIEF JUSTICE, we are "erroneou[s]" in claiming that *McConnell* and *Beaumont* "reaffirmed" *Austin*. In both cases, the Court explicitly relied on *Austin* and quoted from it at length. The *McConnell* Court did so in the teeth of vigorous protests by Justices in today's majority that *Austin* should be overruled. Both Courts also heard criticisms of *Austin* from parties or *amici*. If this does not qualify as reaffirmation of a precedent, then I do not know what would.

forbade distinctions between corporate and individual expenditures like the one at issue here. The Court's reliance is odd. The only thing about *Bellotti* that could not be clearer is that it declined to adopt the majority's position. *Bellotti* ruled, in an explicit limitation on the scope of its holding, that "our consideration of a corporation's right to speak on issues of general public interest implies no comparable right in the quite different context of participation in a political campaign for election to public office." 435 U.S., at 788, n.26. *Bellotti*, in other words, did not touch the question presented in *Austin* and *McConnell*, and the opinion squarely disavowed the proposition for which the majority cites it.

The majority attempts to explain away the distinction *Bellotti* drew—between general corporate speech and campaign speech intended to promote or prevent the election of specific candidates for office—as inconsistent with the rest of the opinion and with *Buckley*. Yet the basis for this distinction is perfectly coherent: The anticorruption interests that animate regulations of corporate participation in candidate elections * * * do not apply equally to regulations of corporate participation in referenda. A referendum cannot owe a political debt to a corporation, seek to curry favor with a corporation, or fear the corporation's retaliation. * * *

Austin and *McConnell*, then, sit perfectly well with *Bellotti*. * * * The difference between the cases is not that *Austin* and *McConnell* rejected First Amendment protection for corporations whereas *Bellotti* accepted it. The difference is that the statute at issue in *Bellotti* smacked of viewpoint discrimination, targeted one class of corporations, and provided no PAC option; and the State has a greater interest in regulating independent corporate expenditures on candidate elections than on referenda, because in a functioning democracy the public must have faith that its representatives owe their positions to the people, not to the corporations with the deepest pockets. * * *

The Anticorruption Interest

* * * Corruption can take many forms. Bribery may be the paradigm case. But the difference between selling a vote and selling access is a matter of degree, not kind. And selling access is not qualitatively different from giving special preference to those who spent money on one's behalf. Corruption operates along a spectrum, and the majority's apparent belief that *quid pro quo* arrangements can be neatly demarcated from other improper influences does not accord with the theory or reality of politics. It certainly does not accord with the record Congress developed in passing BCRA, a record that stands as a remarkable testament to the energy and ingenuity with which corporations, unions, lobbyists, and politicians may go about scratching each other's backs—and which amply supported Congress' determination to target a limited set of especially destructive practices.

* * * As summarized [by one District Judge in the *McConnell* litigation]:

> The factual findings of the Court illustrate that corporations and labor unions routinely notify Members of Congress as soon as they air electioneering communications relevant to the Members' elections. The record also indicates that Members express appreciation to organizations for the airing

of these election-related advertisements. Indeed, Members of Congress are particularly grateful when negative issue advertisements are run by these organizations, leaving the candidates free to run positive advertisements and be seen as 'above the fray.' Political consultants testify that campaigns are quite aware of who is running advertisements on the candidate's behalf, when they are being run, and where they are being run. Likewise, a prominent lobbyist testifies that these organizations use issue advocacy as a means to influence various Members of Congress. * * *

* * * [This] analysis shows the great difficulty in delimiting the precise scope of the *quid pro quo* category, as well as the adverse consequences that *all* such arrangements may have. There are threats of corruption that are far more destructive to a democratic society than the odd bribe. Yet the majority's understanding of corruption would leave lawmakers impotent to address all but the most discrete abuses. * * *

Quid Pro Quo Corruption

The majority appears to think it decisive that the BCRA record does not contain "direct examples of votes being exchanged for . . . expenditures." It would have been quite remarkable if Congress had created a record detailing such behavior by its own Members. Proving that a specific vote was exchanged for a specific expenditure has always been next to impossible: Elected officials have diverse motivations, and no one will acknowledge that he sold a vote. Yet, even if "[i]ngratiation and access . . . are not corruption" themselves, they are necessary prerequisites to it; they can create both the opportunity for, and the appearance of, *quid pro quo* arrangements. The influx of unlimited corporate money into the electoral realm also creates new opportunities for the mirror image of *quid pro quo* deals: threats, both explicit and implicit. Starting today, corporations with large war chests to deploy on electioneering may find democratically elected bodies becoming much more attuned to their interests. * * *

Austin and Corporate Expenditures * * *

1. *Antidistortion*

* * * Unlike natural persons, corporations have "limited liability" for their owners and managers, "perpetual life," separation of ownership and control, "and favorable treatment of the accumulation and distribution of assets . . . that enhance their ability to attract capital and to deploy their resources in ways that maximize the return on their shareholders' investments." 494 U.S., at 658–659. Unlike voters in U.S. elections, corporations may be foreign controlled.[70] Unlike other interest groups, business corporations have been "effectively delegated responsibility for ensuring society's economic welfare"; they inescapably structure the life of every

---

70. In state elections, even domestic corporations may be "foreign"-controlled in the sense that they are incorporated in another jurisdiction and primarily owned and operated by out-of-state residents.

citizen. "[T]he resources in the treasury of a business corporation," furthermore, "are not an indication of popular support for the corporation's political ideas." *Id.,* at 659 (quoting *MCFL,* 479 U.S., at 258). "They reflect instead the economically motivated decisions of investors and customers. The availability of these resources may make a corporation a formidable political presence, even though the power of the corporation may be no reflection of the power of its ideas." 494 U.S., at 659 (quoting *MCFL,* 479 U.S., at 258). * * *

[S]ome corporations have affirmatively urged Congress to place limits on their electioneering communications. These corporations fear that officeholders will shake them down for supportive ads, that they will have to spend increasing sums on elections in an ever-escalating arms race with their competitors, and that public trust in business will be eroded. A system that effectively forces corporations to use their shareholders' money both to maintain access to, and to avoid retribution from, elected officials may ultimately prove more harmful than beneficial to many corporations. It can impose a kind of implicit tax. * * *

* * * Corporate "domination" of electioneering, *Austin,* 494 U.S., at 659, can generate the impression that corporations dominate our democracy. When citizens turn on their televisions and radios before an election and hear only corporate electioneering, they may lose faith in their capacity, as citizens, to influence public policy. A Government captured by corporate interests, they may come to believe, will be neither responsive to their needs nor willing to give their views a fair hearing. The predictable result is cynicism and disenchantment * * *. To the extent that corporations are allowed to exert undue influence in electoral races, the speech of the eventual winners of those races may also be chilled. Politicians who fear that a certain corporation can make or break their reelection chances may be cowed into silence about that corporation. * * *

* * * All of the majority's theoretical arguments turn on a proposition with undeniable surface appeal but little grounding in evidence or experience, "that there is no such thing as too much speech." If individuals in our society had infinite free time to listen to and contemplate every last bit of speech uttered by anyone, anywhere; and if broadcast advertisements had no special ability to influence elections apart from the merits of their arguments (to the extent they make any); and if legislators always operated with nothing less than perfect virtue; then I suppose the majority's premise would be sound. In the real world, we have seen, corporate domination of the airwaves prior to an election may decrease the average listener's exposure to relevant viewpoints, and it may diminish citizens' willingness and capacity to participate in the democratic process.

* * * *Austin*'s "concern about corporate domination of the political process" reflects more than a concern to protect governmental interests outside of the First Amendment. It also reflects a concern to *facilitate* First Amendment values by preserving some breathing room around the electoral "marketplace" of ideas, the marketplace in which the actual people of this Nation determine how they will govern themselves. The majority seems oblivious to the simple truth that laws such as § 203

do not merely pit the anticorruption interest against the First Amendment, but also pit competing First Amendment values against each other. There are, to be sure, serious concerns with any effort to balance the First Amendment rights of speakers against the First Amendment rights of listeners. But when the speakers in question are not real people and when the appeal to "First Amendment principles" depends almost entirely on the listeners' perspective, it becomes necessary to consider how listeners will actually be affected. * * *

2. *Shareholder Protection*

There is yet another way in which laws such as § 203 can serve First Amendment values. Interwoven with *Austin*'s concern to protect the integrity of the electoral process is a concern to protect the rights of shareholders from a kind of coerced speech: electioneering expenditures that do not "reflec[t] [their] support." 494 U.S., at 660–661. When corporations use general treasury funds to praise or attack a particular candidate for office, it is the shareholders, as the residual claimants, who are effectively footing the bill. Those shareholders who disagree with the corporation's electoral message may find their financial investments being used to undermine their political convictions.

The PAC mechanism, by contrast, helps assure that those who pay for an electioneering communication actually support its content and that managers do not use general treasuries to advance personal agendas. * * *

The Court dismisses this interest on the ground that abuses of shareholder money can be corrected "through the procedures of corporate democracy," and, it seems, through Internet-based disclosures. I fail to understand how this addresses the concerns of dissenting union members, who will also be affected by today's ruling, and I fail to understand why the Court is so confident in these mechanisms. By "corporate democracy," presumably the Court means the rights of shareholders to vote and to bring derivative suits for breach of fiduciary duty. In practice, however, many corporate lawyers will tell you that "these rights are so limited as to be almost nonexistent," given the internal authority wielded by boards and managers and the expansive protections afforded by the business judgment rule.[g] Modern technology may help make it easier to track corporate activity, including electoral advocacy, but it is utopian to believe that it solves the problem. Most American households that own stock do so through intermediaries such as mutual funds and pension plans, which makes it more difficult both to monitor and to alter particular holdings. Studies show that a majority of individual investors make no trades at all during a given year. Moreover, if the corporation in question operates a PAC, an investor who sees the company's ads may not know whether they are being funded through the PAC or through the general treasury.

---

g. The business-judgment rule insulates corporate directors from suit by presuming that corporate transactions have been undertaken with due care, in good faith, and in the belief that they are in the corporation's best interest. —Eds.

If and when shareholders learn that a corporation has been spending general treasury money on objectionable electioneering, they can divest. Even assuming that they reliably learn as much, however, this solution is only partial. The injury to the shareholders' expressive rights has already occurred; they might have preferred to keep that corporation's stock in their portfolio for any number of economic reasons; and they may incur a capital gains tax or other penalty from selling their shares, changing their pension plan, or the like. The shareholder protection rationale has been criticized as underinclusive, in that corporations also spend money on lobbying and charitable contributions in ways that any particular shareholder might disapprove. But those expenditures do not implicate the selection of public officials, an area in which "the interests of unwilling . . . corporate shareholders [in not being] forced to subsidize that speech" "are at their zenith." * * *

* * * At bottom, the Court's opinion is * * * a rejection of the common sense of the American people, who have recognized a need to prevent corporations from undermining self-government since the founding, and who have fought against the distinctive corrupting potential of corporate electioneering since the days of Theodore Roosevelt. It is a strange time to repudiate that common sense. While American democracy is imperfect, few outside the majority of this Court would have thought its flaws included a dearth of corporate money in politics.

I would affirm the judgment of the District Court.

Notes and Questions

1. Comparing the *Citizens United* majority and concurring opinions with the dissent, it is almost as if one is reading two different cases. The majority told of a nonprofit making a documentary about a presidential candidate; Justice Stevens's dissent talked of a "wealthy" corporation "with millions in assets." Justice Scalia focused on "mom and pop" stores; the dissent on "large war chests" and "corporate domination." The dissent talked of corporations as "different from human beings"; the majority (and Justice Scalia's concurrence in particular) saw them as associations of human beings. The two sides didn't agree on original understandings, or even the meaning of their own recent precedents. The dissent saw corporate speech as potentially dangerous to democracy, while the majority viewed uninhibited speech—from corporations as well as individuals—as essential to democratic debate.[h]

---

h. Can these fault lines be reconciled? Can you see others in the debate, not just in *Citizens United* but in *McConnell* and earlier opinions? On the question of original understandings, James Madison's career may shed some light on how he would have interpreted the First Amendment in this area. *See* Anthony J. Gaughan, *James Madison,* Citizens United, *and the Constitutional Problem of Corruption,* 69 AMER. U. L. REV. 101, 140 (2020) (arguing that Madison's early career suggested a distrust of money in politics, but that most of his career showed strong "support for a broad and sweeping freedom of expression [that] extended to all speakers, including politicians, business leaders, journalists, voters, and ordinary citizens alike").

The one thing on which the majority and the dissent agreed was that expenditure limits implicate the First Amendment. Should the characteristics of the corporate speaker affect the First Amendment interests that are involved? Corporations vary widely, from mom-and-pop stores to Fortune 500 companies, from non-profits to for-profit businesses, from highly to lightly regulated industries, and from start-ups to established players. Does the fact that corporations are so different in purpose, size, and operation suggest that a flat ban on all corporations' political expeditures must necessarily fail the type of "narrow tailoring" normally required when a statute impinges on a fundamental right? *See R.A.V. v. City of St. Paul*, 505 U.S. 377 (1992). Or does any amount of political spending by any type of corporation pose a threat of corruption?

Would a statute barring expenditures only by for-profit corporations be constitutional? What about one limiting the *amount* of expenditures by corporations?

2. In *Western Tradition Partnership v. Bullock*, 271 P.3d 1 (Mont. 2011), the Montana Supreme Court, post-*Citizens United*, upheld Montana's ban on independent corporate expenditures. The court interpreted *Citizens United* not to hold that a prohibition on independent expenditures was *per se* unconstitutional, but only that such a prohibition must be justified by a record of corruption. The court then relied on the following history as establishing a sufficiently compelling state interest to justify the ban:

> Examples of well-financed corruption abound. In the fight over mineral rights between entrepreneur F. Augustus Heinze and the Anaconda Company, then controlled by Standard Oil, Heinze managed to control the two State judges in Butte, who routinely decided cases in his favor. The Butte judges denied being bribed, but one of them admitted that Anaconda representatives had offered him $250,000 cash to sign an affidavit that Heinze had bribed him.

> In response to the legal conflicts with Heinze, in 1903 Anaconda/Standard closed down all its industrial and mining operations (but not the many newspapers it controlled), throwing 4/5 of the labor force of Montana out of work. Its price for sending its employees back to work was that the Governor call a special session of the Legislature to enact a measure that would allow Anaconda to avoid having to litigate in front of the Butte judges. The Governor and Legislature capitulated and the statute survives.

> W.A. Clark, who had amassed a fortune from the industrial operations in Butte, set his sights on the United States Senate. In 1899, in the wake of a large number of suddenly affluent members, the Montana Legislature elected Clark to the U.S. Senate. Clark admitted to spending $272,000 in the effort and the estimated expense was over $400,000. Complaints of Clark's bribery of the Montana Legislature led to an investigation by the U.S. Senate in 1900. The Senate investigating committee concluded that Clark had won his seat through bribery and unseated him. The Senate committee

"expressed horror at the amount of money which had been poured into politics in Montana elections * * * and expressed its concern with respect to the general aura of corruption in Montana." * * *

After the Anaconda Company cleared itself of opposition from Heinze and others, it controlled 90% of the press in the state and a majority of the legislature. By 1915 the company, after having acquired all of Clark's holdings as well as many others, "clearly dominated the Montana economy and political order . . . [and] local folks now found themselves locked in the grip of a corporation controlled from Wall Street and insensitive to their concerns." Even at that time it was evident that industrial corporations controlled the state "thus converting the state government into a political instrument for the furthering and accomplishment of legislation and the execution of laws favorable to the absentee stockholders of the large corporations and inimical to the economic interests of the wage earning and farming classes who constitute by far the larger percentage of the population in Montana."

In 1900 Clark himself testified in the United States Senate that "[m]any people have become so indifferent to voting" in Montana as a result of the "large sums of money that have been expended in the state. * * * "This naked corporate manipulation of the very government (Governor and Legislature) of the State ultimately resulted in populist reforms that are still part of Montana law. In 1906 the people voted to amend the state Constitution to allow for voter initiatives. Not long thereafter, in 1906 this new initiative power was used to enact reforms including * * * the Corrupt Practices Act, part of which survives as [the statute] at issue in this case.

271 P.3d at 23–28 (citations omitted).

Read this history closely. How relevant is it to the constitutionality of the ban on independent corporate expenditures? Do its examples—bribery of judges and legislators, control of newspapers (which were exempt from the Montana prohibition on corporate expenditures), use of economic power to close factories, and allegations of legislative dominance a decade after the state prohibited corporate expenditures—support a ban on independent campaign expenditures as necessary to prevent corruption? Consider that Senator Clark and other senators at the time were chosen by the state legislature, not by popular vote. When referencing "the amount of money which had been poured into politics in Montana elections," was the Court even talking about campaign expenditures of the type covered by *Citizens United*? Do these examples demonstrate that corporate spending poses a threat of corruption, or do they fail to support the notion that independent corporate spending in campaigns corrupts the legislature? Does it make a difference to your thinking that during this period of alleged corporate domination, the state passed the reforms mentioned in the last quoted paragraph, including the ban on corporate political spending?

Could the early Montana statute be interpreted as an effort to by anti-Anaconda forces to improve their political position by limiting opposition speech? *See* Robert G. Natelson, *Montana's Supreme Court Relies on Erroneous History in Rejecting* Citizens United 8 (Center for Competitive Politics 2012), *available at* ifs.org/wp-content/uploads/2012/06/2012-06-Natelson-Montanas-Supreme-Court-Relies-on-Errroneous-History.pdf. According to Natelson:

> Montana activists have a long history of adopting campaign finance "reforms"—even obviously unconstitutional ones—to promote their political agendas. [Montana's 1906 ban on corporate expenditures] was just one example. Another arose in 1975, when "progressives" successfully banned corporate spending on ballot issues. A federal appeals court struck down the ban as unconstitutional. In 1996, they convinced the voters to pass I-125—yet another ban on corporate spending in ballot issue campaigns. The purpose was to prevent mining companies from defending themselves against an anti-mining initiative (I-137), to be offered at the following general election. Two federal courts invalidated I-125.

> During oral argument on the *Western Tradition* case, the Montana justices communicated that they were deeply concerned about how corporate contributions might change electoral results—particularly in their own elections, where corporate money has heretofore been locked out and financing dominated by trial lawyers.

The U.S. Supreme Court, in a one-page *per curiam* opinion, summarily reversed, 5-4. *American Tradition Partnership v. Bullock*, 567 U.S. 516 (2012). The Justices split along the same lines as in *Citizens United*, with Justice Kagan, who joined Justice Breyer's dissent, having succeeded Justice Stevens.

Recall that in *Citizens United*, the Supreme Court wrote, "independent expenditures, including those made by corporations, do not give rise to corruption or the appearance of corruption." In *American Tradition Partnership*, the Court did not even discuss any of the evidence that the Montana court found persuasive, writing only, "[t]he question presented in this case is whether the holding of *Citizens United* applies to the Montana state law. There can be no serious doubt that it does. Montana's arguments in support of the judgment below either were already rejected in *Citizens United* or fail to meaningfully distinguish that case." 567 U.S. at 516–17. After *American Tradition Partnership*, should the language from *Citizens United* be viewed as an evidentiary judgment by the Court, or rather as a statement of what type of spending constitutes "corruption" as a matter of law, and hence defines the "compelling government interest" for purposes of the First Amendment?

3. Does *Citizens United* undercut the rationale for restricting direct corporate contributions to candidates? The case that it does is at least superficially appealing. If, as *Citizens United* says, "government cannot restrict political speech based on the speaker's corporate identity," then one might question the justification for the outright prohibition on corporate contributions to candidates. Does a $2,600

contribution from a corporation really offer more opportunity for *quid pro quo* exchange than a $2,600 contribution from that corporation's CEO does? Similarly, *Citizens United* noted that due to the costs and burdens of maintaining a political action committee, "fewer than 2000 of the millions of corporations in this country have PACs." If PACs are an inadequate substitute for corporate expenditures, should the Court extend this reasoning to hold that PACs are an inadequate substitute for most corporations to make contributions?

Apparently not. William Danielczyk was criminally prosecuted for, *inter alia*, using straw donors to contribute corporate funds to a campaign. Danielczyk argued that after *Citizens United*, a complete ban on corporate contributions was unconstitutional. The Court of Appeals, however, upheld the ban, and the Supreme Court denied certiorari. *United States v. Danielczyk*, 683 F.3d 611 (4th Cir. 2012), *cert. denied*, 568 U.S. 1193 (2013).

Are there justifications for banning corporate contributions that are not present in considering corporate expenditures? Recall that *Buckley* held that a limit on independent expenditures imposed a greater First Amendment burden than did a limit on contributions, and that contributions posed a greater danger of corruption than did independent expenditures. Are these considerations enough to justify the difference? Is there an equal-protection claim? Should Congress have to treat all potential donors and spenders alike? Consider *Austin v. Michigan State Chamber of Commerce*, 494 U.S. 652 (1990), which held that the state could regulate corporations and unions differently; and *California Medical Association v. FEC*, 453 U.S. 182 (1981), which upheld distinctions in the treatment of partnerships and corporations.

4. Does a ban on corporate electioneering actually benefit corporations, in that it protects them from being pressured to support candidates? Compare the discussion of restrictions on the political activities of government employees in Chapter 7, §G.

5. One of the dividing lines between the majority and the dissent in *Citizens United* was whether the "state-conferred advantages" of the corporate form justified a ban on contributions and expenditures. What, exactly, are the state-conferred advantages of corporate status, and how do they affect this calculus?

The dissenters cited three advantages, the first of which was limited liability. Does limited liability really help companies amass large sums that can be used for political purposes?

> [M]anagers who divert corporate resources from profitmaking activities towards funding political campaigns on such a grand level as to warrant the characterization "corrosive and distorting" will find their firm's "large treasuries" shrinking as the firm becomes less competitive in its product and the capital markets. * * *

> True, limited liability does help managers obtain capital. But it does so only by capping investors' personal liability to creditors of the corporation at the amount of the investors' investment. Limited liability does not shield

the corporation itself from liability for its debts. So to suppose that limited liability will help an incorporated firm amass a huge treasury for use in electoral campaigns is to suppose investor irrationality. Who would invest in a company that, rather than promising handsome returns, merely hands over the corporate treasury to political candidates?

Robert H. Sitkoff, *Corporate Political Speech, Political Extortion, and the Competition for Corporate Charters*, 69 U. Chi. L. Rev. 1103, 1109–10 (2002).

A second cited benefit is perpetual life. But the law, of course, does not prohibit inherited wealth from being spent on political activity, nor does it prevent unincorporated businesses from being sold or passed down over generations. But, in fact, corporate scholar Robert Sitkoff has argued that "perpetual life cuts in precisely the opposite direction than * * * supposed * * * [because] managers must always look forward to tomorrow's product and capital market competition." *Id.* at 1109.

The third "state-conferred advantage" is general benefits in taxation and the retention and distribution of assets. Doctors, lawyers, and other learned professionals gain protection from competition through state licensing systems. Many of these professionals make a great deal of money. Can the state limit their political expenditures because of the benefits they receive from the state?[i] By registering their homes' deeds with the state, homeowners gain certain advantages. Homeowners also receive favorable federal tax treatment through the home-mortgage-interest deduction and the one-time exclusion of capital gains on the sale of a home. May the government compel homeowners to give up their right to make political contributions or expenditures in exchange for these benefits?

> Those individuals who form that type of voluntary association known as a corporation are, to be sure, given special advantages—notably, the immunization of their personal fortunes from liability for the actions of the association—that the State is under no obligation to confer. But so are other associations and private individuals given all sorts of special advantages that the State need not confer, ranging from tax breaks to contract awards to public employment to outright cash subsidies. It is rudimentary that the State cannot exact as the price of those special advantages the forfeiture of First Amendment rights.

Austin v. Michigan State Chamber of Commerce, 494 U.S. 652, 680 (1990) (Scalia, J., dissenting). The doctrine of "unconstitutional conditions" was first named in *Doyle v. Continental Insurance Company*, 94 U.S. 535, 543 (1876) (Bradley, J., dissenting) ("Though a State may have the power, if it sees fit to subject its citizens to the inconvenience, of prohibiting * * * corporations from transacting business within its jurisdiction, it has no power to impose unconstitutional conditions upon their

---

i. *See generally, e.g.,* W. Bradley Wendel, *Free Speech for Lawyers*, 28 Hastings Const. L.Q. 305 (2001); Kathleen M. Sullivan, *The Intersection of Free Speech and the Legal Profession: Constraints on Lawyers' First Amendment Rights*, 67 Fordham L. Rev. 569 (1998).

doing so."); *see also, e.g., Matal v. Tam*, 582 U.S. __, __-__, 137 S. Ct. 1744, 1760–61 (2017) (holding that the benefits of trademark registration do not permit the government to restrict the speech of the holders of trademarks); *Elrod v. Burns*, 427 U.S. 347 (1976) [p. 686]. For two academic views seeking to make sense of the doctrine of unconstitutional conditions, see Kathleen M. Sullivan, *Unconstitutional Conditions*, 102 HARV. L. REV. 1413 (1989), and Richard A. Epstein, *The Supreme Court, 1987 Term—Forward: Unconstitutional Conditions, State Power, and the Limits of Consent*, 102 HARV. L. REV. 4 (1988).

The competing views of the majority and dissent were substantially shaped by differing theories of what a corporation is. The dissenters in *Bellotti* and *Citizens United* (and the majority in *Austin*) appeared to adhere to some version of the concession theory, in which the state retains presumptive authority to regulate the corporate entity. The majority in *Bellotti* and *Citizens United* (and the dissent in *Austin*) appeared to adhere to what is generally called contractarian theory, in which corporations are seen not as "creatures of the state" but as creations of the individuals who found, own, and manage them. These individuals are bound in an extensive web of express and implied contracts embodied in the corporation; to regulate the corporation is to regulate the individuals who make up the corporation. For an overview of relevant corporate theory, see Anne Tucker, *Flawed Assumptions: A Corporate Law Analysis of Free Speech and Corporate Personhood in* Citizens United, 61 CASE W. RES. L. REV. 497, 501–506 (2010). For a small sampling of the literature on corporate governance, theory, and speech rights, see Stefan J. Padfeld, *The Silent Role of Corporate Theory in the Supreme Court's Campaign Finance Cases*, 15 U. PA. J. CONST. L. 831 (2013); Roger Coffin, *A Responsibility to Speak:* Citizens United, *Corporate Governance, and Managing Risks*, 8 HASTINGS BUS. L.J. 103 (2012); Larry E. Ribstein, *The First Amendment and Corporate Governance*, 27 GA. ST. U. L. REV. 1019, 1021 (2011).

6. Consider that much of what the media do in commenting or reporting on political campaigns meets the core definition of "expenditure" in the Federal Election Campaign Act. Publication, after all, involves spending money for "the purpose of influencing an election." 52 U.S.C. § 30101(9)(A). At a minimum, it would be easy to allege an intent to influence an election, thus allowing complaints to be filed, discovery to ensue, and so forth. Recall that the potential chilling effect of that type of enforcement caused the Court in *Buckley* to limit the statutory definition of "expenditure" to what became known as "express advocacy." Further, media expenditures routinely meet the definition of "coordinated" activity—for example, when an editorial board meets with a candidate and promotes its endorsement on facts and themes gleaned from the meeting—and would therefore qualify as direct "contributions" to the campaign.

The Act contains an exemption, however, for "any news story, commentary, or editorial distributed through the facilities of any broadcasting station, newspaper, magazine, or other periodical publication, unless such facilities are owned or controlled by a political party, political committee, or candidate." 52 U.S.C. § 30101(9)

(B)(i). The exemption does not, on its face, cover items such as newsletters, books, on-line publications, or even cable television, but in fact it has been construed liberally. *See, e.g., Federal Election Commission v. Phillips Publishing, Inc.*, 517 F. Supp. 1308 (D.D.C. 1981).

Statutory exemption aside, if it is constitutional to limit expenditures merely because of the advantages of the corporate form, or because corporations have large assets and influence, would it be constitutional to regulate media corporations? And would it be constitutional, under the Equal Protection Clause, to exempt media corporations from campaign-finance laws? Consider Justice Scalia's dissenting opinion in *Austin*:

> [A] few words are in order concerning the Court's approval of the Michigan law's exception for "media corporations." This is all right, we are told, because of "the unique role that the press plays in 'informing and educating the public, offering criticism, and providing a forum for discussion and debate.'" But if one believes in the Court's rationale of "compelling state need" to prevent amassed corporate wealth from skewing the political debate, surely that "unique role" of the press does not give Michigan justification for *excluding* media corporations from coverage, but provides especially strong reason to *include* them. Amassed corporate wealth that regularly sits astride the ordinary channels of information is much more likely to produce the New Corruption (too much of one point of view) than amassed corporate wealth that is generally busy making money elsewhere. Such media corporations not only have vastly greater power to perpetrate the evil of overinforming, they also have vastly greater opportunity. General Motors, after all, will risk a stockholder suit if it makes a political endorsement that is not plausibly tied to its ability to make money for its shareholders. But media corporations make money *by* making political commentary, including endorsements. For them, unlike any other corporations, the whole world of politics and ideology is fair game. Yet the Court tells us that it is reasonable to *exclude* media corporations, rather than target them specially.

> Members of the institutional press, despite the Court's approval of their illogical exemption from the Michigan law, will find little reason for comfort in today's decision. The theory of New Corruption it espouses is a dagger at their throats. The Court today holds merely that media corporations *may* be excluded from the Michigan law, not that they *must* be. We have consistently rejected the proposition that the institutional press has any constitutional privilege beyond that of other speakers.

Austin, 494 U.S. 690–91 (Scalia, J., dissenting) (emphases in original).

Whether the "press exemption" is statutory or constitutional, who is entitled to claim its benefits? In 2004, the National Rifle Association launched its own satellite radio station, "NRA News," specifically to take advantage of the exemption for the press. Many overtly political magazines are published with little intent ever to make a profit, and are subsidized by wealthy individuals, foundations (which sometimes accept corporate contributions), or corporations. Would the exemption extend to a book or movie published or produced by a pro-life or pro-choice organization? What about on-line bloggers, web sites, and tweets? *See* Bradley A. Smith, *The John Roberts Salvage Company: After* McConnell, *A New Court Looks to Repair the Constitution*, 68 Ohio St. L.J. 891, 895–899 (2007). Does the press exemption cover activities outside of direct publication, such as paid advertising by the publisher about the publication? *See Readers Digest Association v. Federal Election Commission*, 509 F. Supp. 1210 (S.D.N.Y. 1981) (yes). In 2014, Citizens United itself was recognized as falling under the press exemption contained in Colorado's state campaign-finance statute, thus relieving it from disclosure obligations. *Citizens United v. Gessler*, 773 F.3d 200 (10th Cir. 2014).

7. One argument for preserving a ban on corporate spending is the protection of minority shareholders, who may not want their funds spent to support candidates with whom they disagree. While this issue was discussed in the opinions in *Bellotti*, *MCFL*, *Austin*, and *WRTL II*, it received an unusual amount of attention in the immediate aftermath of *Citizens United*. One view holds that unhappy shareholders can simply sell their stock. Others argue that divestment is not always a viable alternative. Consider, for example, that selling stock at a particular time may result in a major tax liability or a loss on the sale; or consider a public employee whose retirement contributions are invested in the state retirement system, which then invests in a company making political expenditures in support of candidates he opposes. Should such individuals be protected from such corporate expenditures?

Consider that corporations frequently make charitable contributions and other expenditures with which some stockholders disagree. For example, some corporations may opt to increase profits by skimping on pollution-control equipment, or to decrease profits by spending more on safety or green energy. Generally speaking, under the business-judgment rule, corporate directors have broad discretion to make decisions that may offend some shareholders, such as which charitable contributions to make and which themes to use in corporate advertising. Does *limiting* that discretion as to political expeditures interfere with the rights of *majority* shareholders, either by muzzling their speech or by creating management inefficiencies that would detract from shareholder value?

One leading corporate scholar has argued that consideration of minority shareholders should not affect the First Amendment rights of corporations:

> [T]he shareholder-protection rationale for the current scheme of restrictions on corporate political activity depends on a showing that (1) shareholders incur agency costs from permitting corporate political activity * * * (2) that these costs outweigh benefits of permitting the managers to engage in corporate speech through the corporation * * *; and (3) that the costs of leaving such protection to shareholder choice outweigh the benefits of doing so. Such a showing would be extraordinarily difficult to make.

Larry E. Ribstein, *Corporate Political Speech*, 49 WASH. & LEE L. REV. 109 (1992); *see also* Robert H. Sitkoff, *Corporate Political Speech, Political Extortion, and the Competition for Corporate Charters*, 69 U. CHI. L. REV. 1103 (2002) (arguing that the theory of shareholder protection "assumes that shareholders are locked into their investment, and further that in the absence of regulation all corporations will engage in political speech. But these assumptions depend on a paucity of investment opportunities and/or opaque securities markets. These assumptions are dubious."). For an opposing view that argues exactly those assumptions, *see* Victor Brudney, *Business Corporations and Stockholders' Rights under the First Amendment*, 91 YALE L.J. 235, 235–37 (1981). *See also* Adam Winkler, *Corporate Personhood and the Rights of Corporate Speech*, 30 SEA. U. L. REV. 863 (2007).

8. After *Citizens United*, is it constitutional for Congress to ban foreign-owned U.S. corporations from making independent expenditures? (Note that another section of FECA already prohibits foreign corporations from making contributions or expenditures, 2 U.S.C. § 441e, 11 C.F.R. § 110.20.)

In *Bluman v. Federal Election Commission*, 800 F. Supp. 2d 281 (D.D.C. 2011) (three-judge court), *summarily aff'd*, 565 U.S. 1104 (2012), a suit instituted shortly after *Citizens United* was decided, the plaintiffs were a Canadian citizen who had resided in the U.S. for four years on student and work visas, and was eligible to remain for as long as five more years; and a dual Canadian-Israeli citizen living in the United States and working temporarily as a medical resident, with eligibility to remain in the U.S. for as much as seven more years. Each sought to contribute to various U.S. politicians, parties, and PACs that supported their views on a variety of issues, but was forbidden to do so by federal law, which prohibits non-permanent-resident aliens from making contributions in connection with United States elections.

A three-judge panel of the federal district court (in an opinion by then-Judge Brett Kavanaugh) upheld the prohibition and was summarily affirmed by the Supreme Court. Although critics have argued that the result in *Bluman* was in tension with *Citizens United*'s statement that the constitutional protection for speech did not depend on "the identity of the speaker," the district court held that *Bluman* "d[id] not implicate those debates." *Id.* at 286. Rather, the district court viewed the case as raising "a preliminary and foundational question about the definition of the American political community and, in particular, the role of foreign citizens in the U.S. electoral process." *Id.* In other words, in cases such as *Citizens United* and *Buckley v. Valeo*, where the question is the constitutionality of restraints on U.S. citizens, the identity of the speaker is insignificant. Foreign citizens, however, are not always granted the same rights. The court cited a long list of areas in which the Supreme Court has upheld limitations on foreign citizens' participation in American political life, including the rights to vote, to serve as jurors, and to hold certain public offices. *Id.* at 287. "The government may reserve 'participation in its democratic political institutions' for citizens of this country. * * * [T]he 'exclusion of aliens from basic governmental processes is not a deficiency in the democratic system

Table 2

Committee Type	Contribution Limits	May Contribute Directly to Candidates	May Make Independent Expenditures	May Make Electioneering Communication	Disclosure
Traditional PAC	No corporate or union funds; $5000 individual limit	Yes, up to $5000	Yes	Yes	Yes—full FEC disclosure
Super PAC	None	No	Yes	Yes	Yes—full FEC disclosure
527	None	No	Yes, if not primary purpose	Yes	Limited disclosure to IRS
501(c)(4), 501(c)(6)	None	No	Yes, if not primary purpose	Yes	Disclosure to FEC of independent expenditure; disclosure of donors only if specific contribution

but *a necessary consequence of the community's process of political self-definition.'"* *Id.* (citations omitted) (emphasis in original). Are you convinced? For a discussion of this aspect of *Bluman, see* Todd E. Pettys, *Campaign Finance, Federalism, and the Case of the Long-Armed Donor,* 81 U. Chi. L. Rev. Dialogue 77 (2014).

9. *Problem.* Consider the constitutionality of the following proposals:

A. A state imposes a ban on independent expenditures by corporations chartered in other states, or by corporations having a majority of shares owned by out-of-state residents.

B. A state limits a candidate's out-of-state contributions to $100,000.

C. A state limits a candidate's out-of-state contributions to a percentage of total contributions.

D. Congress limits the amount a candidate can receive from persons living outside the candidate's district.

E. Congress prohibits contributions from persons living outside the district.

See Thompson v. Hebdon, 909 F.3d 1027, 1040–43 (9th Cir. 2018), *vacated and remanded on other grounds,* 589 U.S. __, 140 S. Ct. 348 (2019). *See also* Eugene D. Mazo, *Our Campaign Finance Nationalism,* 46 Pepp. L. Rev. 759 (2019).

10. Some have argued that *Citizens United* should be overruled, by constitutional amendment if necessary. For an argument against an amendment, by a critic of the *Citizens United* decision, see Richard L. Hasen, *Three Wrong Progressive Approaches (and One Right One) to Campaign Finance Reform*, 8 Harv. L. & Pol'y Rev. 21 (2014) (noting that even after such an amendment, individuals could still spend; corporations could presumably—depending on the amendment's language—still spend on issues; and it would not be clear how or if an amendment could exclude media companies).

Note on "Super PACs" After *Citizens United*

Citizens United is often credited (or blamed) for the creation of what the Federal Election Commission recognizes as "Independent Expenditure Committees" but what have become colloquially known as "Super PACs." A Super PAC is simply a PAC, subject to the same organizational and reporting requirements as any other PAC. However, Super PACs make only independent expenditures—they do not contribute to parties, candidates, or traditional PACs. As a result, Super PACs are permitted to receive contributions from any source, including corporations and unions, in any amount, without limit.

Super PACs are actually not a direct creation of *Citizens United*, but rather of a Court of Appeals case, *SpeechNow.org v. Federal Election Commission*, 599 F.3d 686 (D.C. Cir. 2010) (*en banc*). In *SpeechNow*, an unincorporated group of individuals challenged the $5,000 personal limit on contributions to a political committee as applied to a committee that made only independent expenditures. The plaintiffs argued that if it were not corrupting for a single individual to finance independent expenditures without limit, then it could not be corrupting if that same individual joined with others to make such expenditures. The Court of Appeals, sitting *en banc*, relied heavily on *Citizens United* (decided just six days before oral argument in *SpeechNow*) to rule 9-0 for the plaintiffs, and the government chose not to appeal. Thus the two cases are interlocking: *Citizens United* held that, as a matter of law, independent expenditures are not corrupting; *SpeechNow*, relying on that ruling, allowed speakers to pool their resources, without limit, to make independent expenditures; and *Citizens United* in turn permitted corporations and unions to join in those pooling efforts.

SpeechNow was quickly followed by several other courts and is generally treated as the law nationwide. *See Republican Party of New Mexico v. King*, 741 F.3d 1089 (10th Cir. 2013); *New York Progress and Protection PAC v. Walsh*, 733 F.3d 483 (2nd Cir. 2013); *Texans for Free Enterprise v. Texas Ethics Commission*, 732 F.3d 535 (5th Cir. 2013); *Thalheimer v. City of San Diego*, 645 F.3d 1109 (9th Cir. 2011); *Wisconsin Right to Life State Political Action Committee v. Barland*, 664 F.3d 139 (7th Cir. 2011); *Long Beach Area Chamber of Commerce v. City of Long Beach*, 603 F.3d 684 (9th Cir. 2010); *Michigan Chamber of Commerce v. Land*, 725 F. Supp. 2d 665 (W.D. Mich. 2010). Nevertheless, in the fall of 2016, a group, including three members of Congress and represented by Harvard law professor Laurence Tribe, filed suit seeking to reverse the FEC's acquiescence in these decisions. The district court dismissed the complaint, because it held the FEC's action to be consistent with law. *See Lieu v. Federal Election Commission*, 370 F. Supp. 3d 175 (D.D.C. 2019).

Despite some popular perception to the contrary, a substantial majority of contributions to Super PACs has come from individuals, not corporations or unions. *See* Nathaniel Persily et al., *Campaign Finance in the United States: Assessing an Era of Fundamental Change*, BIPARTISAN POLICY CENTER, Jan. 2018, at 38, *at* https://bipartisanpolicy.org/wp-content/uploads/2019/03/BPC-Democracy-Campaign-Finance-in-the-United-States.pdf.

Super PACs, however, are not the only way that persons can join together to speak. Non-profit "social welfare" organizations, such as the NAACP Voter Education Fund, the Sierra Club, and the National Rifle Association, which operate under § 501(c)(4) of the Internal Revenue Code, may also make independent expenditures. The same is true for trade associations, such as the U.S. Chamber of Commerce, which are organized under § 501(c)(6) of the Code. These organizations can accept corporate and union contributions as well as individual contributions.

If political contributions and expenditures become the primary activity of such an organization, however, two consequences result. First, the group or organization could become a "political committee" as defined by the Federal Election Campaign Act, *see* Note on Political Committees, pp. 759–61, *supra*, and thus subject to the full organizational and reporting requirements of the Act. Second, the group would jeopardize or lose its tax status — it would presumably be forced to reorganize under § 527 of the Internal Revenue Code, the section used by political organizations. For political purposes, the major consequence of being reclassified under § 527 is that such a group must publicly disclose its donors, either through the FEC reporting system (if it qualifies as a "political committee" under the Federal Election Campaign Act, meaning it makes $1,000 or more in express-advocacy expenditures or takes in more than $1,000 in contributions for that purpose) or otherwise through the IRS. Non-profits and trade associations operating under § 501(c) can keep the identity of their donors and members confidential. Alternatively, the organization may simply be taxed as a for-profit corporation.

What constitutes an organization's "primary purpose" has never been clearly resolved. Generally, most experts in the field assume an organization must simply devote less than half its resources to political activity to avoid that designation. But note further that, for purposes of making this determination, lobbying does not count as political activity. Thus a group can devote substantial sums to campaigning, and most or all the rest of its budget to lobbying. For a concise introduction to these issues, see Donald B. Tobin, *The Rise of 501(c)(4)'s in Campaign Activity: Are They as Clever as They Think?*, Election Law@Moritz, Oct. 5, 2010, *at* http://moritzlaw.osu.edu/electionlaw/comments/index.php?ID=7667.

The end result after *Citizens United* and various other decisions and statutes was that there were several types of organizations available to people wishing to engage in political activity:

A. Traditional PACs: Traditional PACs register with the FEC and report all donors over $200. They may make contributions to candidates and party committees, or make independent expenditures. They may be (and at the federal level are) subject to limits on the size of contributions they may receive, and the sources of those contributions (no corporate or union money). Examples include Emily's List Political Action Committee and Microsoft Political Action Committee.

B. Independent Expenditure Committees, or Super PACs: Super PACs are subject to the same registration and reporting requirements as traditional PACs, but may make only independent expenditures. They may accept contributions without limit from individuals, corporations, and unions. Examples include American Crossroads, formed by Republican strategist Karl Rove, and Priorities USA, a Super PAC formed to help re-elect President Obama.

C. Non-PAC 527s: A non-PAC 527 is an organization that is deemed by the IRS to have political activity as its primary purpose, but that does not qualify as a "political committee" under FEC regulations. This comes about when the organization engages in "electioneering communications" or other political messages that do not include "express advocacy" (which is needed to trigger "committee" status under FECA, per *Buckley*) but are deemed sufficiently political by the IRS, which uses a broader definition of "political activity," to be ineligible for § 501(c)(4) status. The organizations are not subject to contribution restrictions but must publicly disclose their donors through the Internal Revenue Service, and cannot engage in "express advocacy" communications. They may not contribute directly to parties or candidates. Such organizations, including Swift Boat Veterans for Truth and MoveOn.org in the 2004 presidential campaign, were popular in the past, but have declined in use since the advent of Super PACs. MoveOn has in recent years disbanded its 527 arm.

D. Section 501(c)(4) and (c)(6) organizations: These organizations may not make direct contributions to candidates, but may make independent expenditures so long as those expenditures do not become their primary purpose. They do not have to disclose their donors to the public unless those donors contribute specifically to fund political advertising. The NAACP Voter Education Fund and the National Rifle Association are examples of non-profits operating under § 501(c)(4); the U.S. Chamber of Commerce is an example of a trade association operating under § 501(c)(6).

It is possible for one umbrella organization to operate any combination of the above forms of organizations. For example, a § 501(c)(4) non-profit group may establish a traditional PAC to contribute to directly to candidates, a Super PAC to make independent expenditures, and may also make limited expenditures from its general treasury, allowing some donors to remain confidential, provided it keeps the various funds separate. *See Carey v. Federal Election Commission*, 791 F. Supp. 2d 121 (D.D.C. 2011).

In the 2015–16 presidential-election cycle, the Federal Election Commission reported that independent expenditures and electioneering communications accounted for approximately 26.8% of total federal political spending, or $1.72 billion of $6.4 billion. Federal Election Commission, *Summary of Campaign Activity of 2015–16 Election Cycle*, Mar. 23, 2017, https://www.fec.gov/updates/statistical -summary-24-month-campaign-activity-2015-2016-election-cycle/. Super PACs accounted for approximately 16% of total spending. Persily et al., *supra*, at 15, Table 1.

Table 2 shows the regulatory regimes governing each form of political organization at the federal level.

Problem: Dick and Jane have approached you on behalf of an informal group of fifteen or so anti-war activists who gather each weekend to picket and to pass out anti-war literature. The group wants to buy radio ads and put up billboards urging the defeat of their incumbent congressman, Hank Manley, whom they believe has been too supportive of the war. "We don't want to pull any punches," they tell you. "We want these ads to be hard hitting." To be effective, they believe they need to raise at least $100,000. The members of their informal group are middle-class professionals — teachers, college professors, a yoga instructor, some small business owners and a few stay-at-home parents, and they doubt they can raise the $100,000 from within the group. But Jane has talked about their plans with her friend Joe Rich, a wealthy entrepreneur. Rich told Jane he would be willing to contribute up to $150,000 to help defeat Manley. However, since one of his companies has a number of government contracts, he doesn't want to upset Manley, who, if re-elected, might use his office to try to harm his government business. For tax purposes, he would also prefer to make the contribution through one of his corporations, if possible. (All his companies are privately held.) How would you advise Dick and Jane to proceed? What are the pluses and minuses of each form of organization?

E. Coordinated Expenditures

Recall that in *Buckley v. Valeo* the Supreme Court held that expenditures are entitled to greater protection than are contributions. It then struck down both limitations on expenditures made by candidates, and limitations on expenditures made independently of candidates. But the Court also noted that expenditures that are "controlled by or coordinated with" a campaign are treated under the Act as contributions to the campaign and, accordingly, are subject to limitation. The treatment of coordinated expenditures as contributions creates a tremendously important issue for political advocates, candidates, and the lawyers who advise them: What does it mean to "coordinate," such that what would otherwise be an "expenditure" not subject to limits becomes a "contribution" subject to limits? Somewhat surprisingly, there is remarkably little judicial guidance on the subject, and what there is has largely involved coordination between parties and candidates; there is even less guidance about what other organizations can do. The FEC, for its part, has wrestled for years with several different definitions of "coordination." We begin this section with what little direction has been provided by the Supreme Court.

Colorado Republican Federal Campaign Committee v. Federal Election Commission (*Colorado Republican I*)

Supreme Court of the United States
518 U.S. 604, 116 S. Ct. 2309, 135 L. Ed. 2d 795 (1996)

Justice Breyer announced the judgment of the Court and delivered an opinion, in which Justice O'Connor and Justice Souter join.

In April 1986, before the Colorado Republican Party had selected its senatorial candidate for the fall's election, that party's Federal Campaign Committee bought radio advertisements attacking Timothy Wirth, the Democratic Party's likely candidate. The Federal Election Commission (FEC) charged that this "expenditure" exceeded the dollar limits that a provision of the Federal Election Campaign Act of 1971 (FECA or Act) imposes upon political party "expenditure[s] in connection with" a "general election campaign" for congressional office. 2 U.S.C. § 441a(d)(3). This case focuses upon the constitutionality of those limits as applied to this case. We conclude that the First Amendment prohibits the application of this provision to the kind of expenditure at issue here — an expenditure that the political party has made independently, without coordination with any candidate. * * *

* * * [W]ithout special treatment, political parties ordinarily would be subject to the general limitation on contributions by a "multicandidate political committee" * * * See § 441a(a)(4). That provision * * * limits annual contributions by a "multicandidate political committee" to no more than $5,000 to any candidate. * * * This contribution limit governs not only direct contributions but also indirect contributions that take the form of coordinated expenditures, defined as "expenditures made . . . in cooperation, consultation, or concert, with, or at the request or suggestion of, a candidate, his authorized political committees, or their agents." § 441a(a)(7)(B)(i). Thus, ordinarily, a party's coordinated expenditures would be subject to the $5,000 limitation.

However, FECA's special provision, which we shall call the "Party Expenditure Provision," creates a *general exception* from this contribution limitation, and from any other limitation on expenditures. * * * After exempting political parties from the general contribution and expenditure limitations of the statute, the Party Expenditure Provision then imposes a *substitute limitation* upon party "expenditures" in a senatorial campaign equal to the greater of $20,000 or "2 cents multiplied by the voting age population of the State," adjusted for inflation since

1974. The provision permitted a political party in Colorado in 1986 to spend about $103,000 in connection with the general election campaign of a candidate for the United States Senate. * * *

In January 1986, Timothy Wirth, then a Democratic Congressman, announced that he would run for an open Senate seat in November. In April, before either the Democratic primary or the Republican convention, the Colorado Republican Federal Campaign Committee (Colorado Party or Party), a petitioner here, bought radio advertisements attacking Congressman Wirth. The State Democratic Party complained to the FEC. It pointed out that the Colorado Party had previously assigned its $103,000 general election allotment to the National Republican Senatorial Committee, leaving it without any permissible spending balance. See *Federal Election Comm'n* v. *Democratic Senatorial Campaign Comm.*, 454 U.S. 27 (1981) (state party may appoint national senatorial campaign committee as agent to spend its Party Expenditure Provision allotment). It argued that the purchase of radio time was an "expenditure in connection with the general election campaign of a candidate for Federal office," which, consequently, exceeded the Party Expenditure Provision limits. * * *

The summary judgment record indicates that the expenditure in question is what this Court in *Buckley* called an "independent" expenditure, not a "coordinated" expenditure that other provisions of FECA treat as a kind of campaign "contribution." See *Buckley* [v. *Valeo*, 424 U.S. 1], 36–37, 46–47, 78 [(1978) (*per curiam*)] [p. 728]; [*Federal Election Comm'n* v. *National Conservative Political Action Comm.*, 470 U.S. 480, 498 (1985)]. * * * In a deposition, the Colorado Party's Chairman, Howard Callaway, pointed out that, at the time of the expenditure, the Party had not yet selected a senatorial nominee from among the three individuals vying for the nomination. He added that he arranged for the development of the script at his own initiative, that he, and no one else, approved it, that the only other politically relevant individuals who might have read it were the Party's executive director and political director, and that all relevant discussions took place at meetings attended only by Party staff.

* * * [Callaway stated] that it was the practice of the Party to "coordinate with the candidate" "campaign strategy," and for Callaway to be "as involved as [he] could be" with the individuals seeking the Republican nomination, by making available to them "all of the assets of the party." These latter statements, however, are general descriptions of Party practice. They do not refer to the advertising campaign at issue here or to its preparation. Nor do they conflict with, or cast significant doubt upon, the uncontroverted direct evidence that this advertising campaign was developed by the Colorado Party independently and not pursuant to any general or particular understanding with a candidate. We can find no "genuine" issue of fact in this respect. * * * And we therefore treat the expenditure, for constitutional purposes, as an "independent" expenditure, not an indirect campaign contribution.

So treated, the expenditure falls within the scope of the Court's precedents that extend First Amendment protection to independent expenditures. Beginning with *Buckley*, the Court's cases have found a "fundamental constitutional difference between money spent to advertise one's views independently of the candidate's campaign and money contributed to the candidate to be spent on his campaign." *NCPAC, supra*, at 497. * * *

Given these established principles, we do not see how a provision that limits a political party's independent expenditures can escape their controlling effect. A political party's independent expression not only reflects its members' views about the philosophical and governmental matters that bind them together, it also seeks to convince others to join those members in a practical democratic task, the task of creating a government that voters can instruct and hold responsible for subsequent success or failure. The independent expression of a political party's views is "core" First Amendment activity no less than is the independent expression of individuals, candidates, or other political committees. See, *e.g.*, *Eu* v. *San Francisco County Democratic Central Comm.*, 489 U.S. 214 (1989) [p. 480].

We are not aware of any special dangers of corruption associated with political parties that tip the constitutional balance in a different direction. * * *

* * * If anything, an independent expenditure made possible by a $20,000 donation, but controlled and directed by a party rather than the donor, would seem less likely to corrupt than the same (or a much larger) independent expenditure made directly by that donor. In any case, the constitutionally significant fact, present equally in both instances, is the lack of coordination between the candidate and the source of the expenditure. This fact prevents us from assuming, absent convincing evidence to the contrary, that a limitation on political parties' independent expenditures is necessary to combat a substantial danger of corruption of the electoral system. * * *

[T]he Government and supporting *amici* argue that the expenditure is "coordinated" because a party and its candidate are identical, *i.e.*, the party, in a sense, "is" its candidates. We cannot assume, however, that this is so. See, *e.g.*, W. Keefe, Parties, Politics, and Public Policy in America 59–74 (5th ed. 1988) (describing parties as "coalitions" of differing interests). Congress chose to treat candidates and their parties quite differently under the Act, for example, by regulating contributions from one to the other. And we are not certain whether a metaphysical identity would help the Government, for in that case one might argue that the absolute identity of views and interests eliminates any potential for corruption, as would seem to be the case in the relationship between candidates and their campaign committees. * * *

For these reasons, the judgment of the Court of Appeals is vacated, and the case is remanded for further proceedings.

Justice Kennedy, with whom The Chief Justice [Rehnquist] and Justice Scalia join, concurring in the judgment and dissenting in part. [Omitted.]

Justice Thomas, with whom The Chief Justice [Rehnquist] and Justice Scalia join * * * concurring in the judgment and dissenting in part. * * *

Were I convinced that the *Buckley* framework rested on a principled distinction between contributions and expenditures, which I am not, I would nevertheless conclude that § 441a(d)(3)'s limits on political parties violate the First Amendment. * * *

The Government asserts that the purpose of § 441a(d)(3) is to prevent the corruption of candidates and elected representatives by party officials. * * * As applied in the specific context of campaign funding by political parties, the anti-corruption rationale loses its force. What could it mean for a party to "corrupt" its candidate or to exercise "coercive" influence over him? The very aim of a political party is to influence its candidate's stance on issues and, if the candidate takes office or is reelected, his votes. When political parties achieve that aim, that achievement does not, in my view, constitute "a subversion of the political process." For instance, if the Democratic Party spends large sums of money in support of a candidate who wins, takes office, and then implements the Party's platform, that is not corruption; that is successful advocacy of ideas in the political marketplace and representative government in a party system. * * *

The structure of political parties is such that the theoretical danger of those groups actually engaging in *quid pro quos* with candidates is significantly less than the threat of individuals or other groups doing so. American political parties, generally speaking, have numerous members with a wide variety of interests, features necessary for success in majoritarian elections. Consequently, the influence of any one person or the importance of any single issue within a political party is significantly diffused. * * *

In sum, there is only a minimal threat of "corruption," as we have understood that term, when a political party spends to support its candidate or to oppose his competitor, whether or not that expenditure is made in concert with the candidate. Parties and candidates have traditionally worked together to achieve their common goals, and when they engage in that work, there is no risk to the Republic. To the contrary, the danger to the Republic lies in Government suppression of such activity. Under *Buckley* and our subsequent cases, § 441a(d)(3)'s heavy burden on First Amendment rights is not justified by the threat of corruption at which it is assertedly aimed.

To conclude, I would find § 441a(d)(3) unconstitutional not just as applied to petitioners, but also on its face. * * *

JUSTICE STEVENS, with whom JUSTICE GINSBURG joins, dissenting.

In my opinion, all money spent by a political party to secure the election of its candidate for the office of United States Senator should be considered a "contribution" to his or her campaign. * * *

[T]hree interests provide a constitutionally sufficient predicate for federal limits on spending by political parties. First, such limits serve the interest in avoiding both the appearance and the reality of a corrupt political process. A party shares a unique relationship with the candidate it sponsors because their political fates are inextricably linked. That interdependency creates a special danger that the party—or the persons who control the party—will abuse the influence it has over the candidate by virtue of its power to spend. The provisions at issue are appropriately aimed at reducing that threat. The fact that the party in this case had not yet chosen its nominee at the time it broadcast the challenged advertisements is immaterial to the analysis. Although the Democratic and Republican nominees for the 1996 Presidential race will not be selected until this summer, current advertising expenditures by the two national parties are no less contributions to the campaigns of the respective frontrunners than those that will be made in the fall.

Second, these restrictions supplement other spending limitations embodied in the Federal Election Campaign Act of 1971, which are likewise designed to prevent corruption. Individuals and certain organizations are permitted to contribute up to $1,000 to a candidate. Since the same donors can give up to $5,000 to party committees, if there were no limits on party spending, their contributions could be spent to benefit the candidate and thereby circumvent the $1,000 cap. * * *

Finally, I believe the Government has an important interest in leveling the electoral playing field by constraining the cost of federal campaigns. * * * It is quite wrong to assume that the net effect of limits on contributions and expenditures—which tend to protect equal access to the political arena, to free candidates and their staffs from the interminable burden of fund-raising, and to diminish the importance of repetitive 30-second commercials—will be adverse to the interest in informed debate protected by the First Amendment.

Congress surely has both wisdom and experience in these matters that is far superior to ours. I would therefore accord special deference to its judgment on questions related to the extent and nature of limits on campaign spending. Accordingly, I would affirm the judgment of the Court of Appeals.

Notes and Questions

1. The importance of "coordination" should not be underestimated, especially in a post-*Citizens United* world. While independent spending, including by corporations and unions, is not subject to limits, expenditures that are coordinated with a candidate or political party are treated as "contributions," and hence subject to strict limits, including a complete ban on corporate and union contributions. Thus,

an organization that crosses the "coordination" line could suddenly find that it has engaged in substantial illegal spending.

Yet coordination is an elusive concept, made more difficult by the fact that most major interest groups have regular contacts with their advocates and supporters in the legislature. For example, a major interest group such as the Sierra Club or the National Association of Manufacturers will meet frequently with allies in Congress to discuss legislation. In doing so, they may discuss the status of public opinion on issues of mutual concern, ways to move public opinion, and the general political climate as it relates to their issues. Later, when these candidates seek reelection or election to a higher office, these same interest groups may wish to support their candidacies. At what point does their general political knowledge about the plans and messages of the candidates rise to the level of "coordination"?

This determination is made still more difficult by the fluidity of staffing in politics, and the relatively small number of skilled vendors. For example, it would not be uncommon for the legislative director of a pro-environmental-protection congressman to accept a job with the Sierra Club; and then to leave the Sierra Club later to serve as campaign manager for her former boss's re-election effort, which the Sierra Club will seek to support. Given the staffer's knowledge of both the Sierra Club and the candidate's campaign, does this create coordination *per se*? Furthermore, there are a relatively small number of political consultants who handle most major campaigns. Suppose that Senator Jones has hired Political Admen, Inc., to handle media for her campaign, and that the Club for Growth, a group that lobbies for lower taxes and reduced government spending, also uses Political Admen, Inc., for its media needs. If the Club decides to make expenditures in support of Senator Jones, Political Admen will have access to the media and messaging strategies of both the Club and Senator Jones, as it advises each on how to spend campaign dollars. Does this constitute coordination?

Making this inquiry even more difficult is what some have called "independent coordination." That is, it is not generally difficult for political junkies to know which states, congressional districts, or portions of districts are particularly important. Similarly, it is relatively easy, simply by paying attention to the news, to learn of the key issues in a campaign, and to follow the speeches and pronouncements of the candidates. Moreover, campaigns will usually publicize upcoming campaign appearances, and the campaign may speak openly in the press about its strategies for winning. Indeed, because the law now requires ad buys to be made public, groups can even know of a candidate's advertising plans. Thus, an organization can typically gather all the information it needs to run a "coordinated" campaign without ever speaking to the candidate.

2. Prior to *Colorado Republican I*, the FEC considered all party expenditures to be *per se* coordinated with their candidates. Is it possible for a party to make expenditures to influence a race without coordinating those expenditures with its candidates? Remember that the expenditures in *Colorado Republican I* were made

before the Party had even selected its candidate. Yet both the opinions concurring in the judgment and dissenting seemed to consider parties and candidates, in Justice Stevens's words, "inextricably linked." For the dissenters, that linkage suggested that party spending is not much different from, or perhaps even potentially more corrupting than, other spending, and thus was an argument for regulation. For the concurring Justices, the linkage between parties and candidates suggested that the regulation was unconstitutional because it limited political speech even in the absence of any threat of corruption and made it impossible for the party to achieve the goals for which its members associated. The plurality opinion, meanwhile, treated the parties much like any other spenders, and like any other spender, parties can act independently of candidates. Which view of coordination do you think is most correct, and which set of consequences would you draw from that view? Is it possible that all three views expressed can be correct, depending on time and place?

3. *Problem:* Jeb Clinton, a former governor, senator, cabinet member, and member of a prominent political family, is widely expected to seek his party's nomination for President in 2024. Throughout 2022 and the winter and spring of 2023, Clinton makes several speeches around the country, travels extensively to meet with state party leaders, and actively raises money for the party and various PACs that generally support his party. Public-opinion surveys consistently show him to be a leading presidential contender. The party, meanwhile, runs advertisements promoting issues generally associated with Clinton. Clinton and party officials have numerous discussions about the party's messaging and attempt to coordinate party activities with Clinton's visits to different states. Clinton has not declared himself a candidate for President. The first caucuses and primaries are eight months in the future, with the general election over eighteen months away. Leaders of the opposing party have come to you, as counsel for that party, asking if it is worthwhile to file a complaint with the Federal Election Commission alleging illegal coordination between Clinton and the Party. If it is not possible to file a complaint immediately, they wonder if a complaint could be filed when and if Clinton declares his candidacy. Your advice?

4. While *Colorado Republican I* tells us, in one particular situation, what coordination is *not*, it tells us very little about what coordination *is*. Perhaps surprisingly, the courts have made very few forays into the discussion. One of the few federal-court decisions to examine the concept of coordination in depth is *Federal Election Commission v. Christian Coalition*, 52 F. Supp. 2d 45 (D.D.C. 1999). District Judge Joyce Hens Green described the standard advocated by the FEC as one in which "any consultation between a potential spender and a federal candidate's campaign organization about the candidate's plans, projects, or needs renders any subsequent expenditures made for the purpose of influencing the election 'coordinated,' i.e., contributions." *Id.* at 89. The court found this standard, which it called the "insider trading" standard, to be unconstitutionally overbroad:

> To be sure, the scenario the FEC paints to support its approach is plausible: A corporate or union representative meets with campaign staff on one or more occasions and receives non-public information about the

campaign's strategy; the corporate or union representative learns that the campaign seeks to highlight one or more of the candidate's policy positions before a specific constituency; acting on the "tip," the corporation or union expends or "invests" considerable sums from its "war chest" to pay for communications highlighting said policy position(s) before said constituency; after the candidate is elected, the corporation or union seeks to profit from its investment by demanding special access to the elected official or a legislative *quid pro quo*. * * *

Nonetheless, while this plausible scenario demonstrates that the potential for corruption flowing from coordinated expenditures is non-speculative, the prohibition on such expenditures must be narrowly tailored to meet this danger. An "insider trading" or conspiracy approach also sweeps in all attempts by corporations and unions to discuss policy matters with the candidate while these groups are contemporaneously funding communications directed at the same policy matters. *Cf. Clifton* [*v. Maine Right to Life Committee,*] 114 F.3d [1309], 1313 [(1st Cir. 1997) (holding that inquiries about a candidate's position for the purpose of producing a non-partisan voter guide do not constitute "coordination")]. The FEC believes that its concept of coordination is narrowly tailored to the anti-corruption interest because its definition "reaches only those expenditures that are made after consultation with a candidate concerning campaign strategy or activities, not mere lobbying or asking a candidate or incumbent where she stands on a particular policy issue or proposed legislation."

But as the facts of this case demonstrate, discussion of campaign strategy and discussion of policy issues are hardly two easily distinguished subjects. *See Buckley,* 424 U.S. at 249 ("Candidates, especially incumbents, are intimately tied to public issues involving legislative proposals and governmental actions."). The FEC's tidy distinction between discussion of campaign strategy and mere lobbying is cold comfort for those who seek to discuss with a candidate an issue that is at the time dominating the campaign. Indeed, the record in this case demonstrates that a candidate's decision when to take a stand, where to stand, and how to communicate the stand on a policy issue often are integral parts of campaign strategy. The facts further demonstrate that a candidate frequently listens to the concerns of sympathetic constituencies or factions before making those important strategic decisions. While the FEC's approach would certainly address the potential for corruption in the above-described scenario, it would do so only by heavily burdening the common, probably necessary, communications between candidates and constituencies during an election campaign.

Id. at 89–90.

The court noted that it had pressed each party to provide its proposed legal standard for defining the activities that would amount to "coordination" of expenditures, but "neither party was particularly responsive." *Id.* at 91. The court thus supplied its own definition:

> In the absence of a request or suggestion from the campaign, an expressive expenditure becomes "coordinated" where the candidate or her agents can exercise control over, or where there has been substantial discussion or negotiation between the campaign and the spender over, a communication's: (1) contents; (2) timing; (3) location, mode, or intended audience (e.g., choice between newspaper or radio advertisement); or (4) "volume" (e.g., number of copies of printed materials or frequency of media spots). Substantial discussion or negotiation is such that the candidate and spender emerge as partners or joint venturers in the expressive expenditure, but the candidate and spender need not be equal partners.

Id. at 92. Applying that definition, the court found that on the facts of the case no coordination had occurred.

5. In response to *Colorado Republican I* and *Christian Coalition* (which it did not appeal), the FEC adopted a new definition of coordination in 2000, essentially adopting the standard used by Judge Green in *Christian Coalition*. 65 Fed. Reg. 76138 (Dec. 6, 2000). Campaign-finance-reform groups were concerned that this new FEC definition allowed too many opportunities for "coordinated" activities to pass unregulated. Thus, extensive efforts were made to write a new statutory definition of coordination into the Bipartisan Campaign Reform Act of 2002. Ultimately, however, Congress could not agree on a definition, and settled for repealing the existing FEC regulation and ordering the agency to write a new definition. Pub. L. No. 107-155, § 214 (2002). Accordingly, the FEC adopted a new definition in 2002. But the lead House sponsors of BCRA challenged the FEC's regulations in court as insufficiently rigorous and contrary to the statute, and a federal district court agreed in *Shays v. Federal Election Commission*, 337 F. Supp. 2d 28 (D.D.C. 2004), *aff'd*, 414 F. 3d 76 (D.C. Cir. 2005) (*Shays I*). The Commission tried again, passing new rules in 2006, which were again successfully challenged in Court as insufficiently rigorous, *Shays v. FEC*, 508 F. Supp. 2d 10 (D.D.C. 2007), *aff'd*, 528 F. 3d 914 (D.C. Cir. 2008) (*Shays II*). The FEC opened yet another rulemaking in the fall of 2009, seven years after passage of BCRA. *See* 74 Fed. Reg. 53893 (Oct. 21, 2009). Due to disagreements among the commissioners, no new final rule had been issued as of May 2020. Pursuant to the order in *Shays II*, the FEC's 2003 regulations remain in effect while the FEC works to promulgate new regulations.

For a concise history of the effort to develop workable coordination rules from *Christian Coalition* through the FEC's first post-BCRA rulemaking, see Robert F. Bauer, *The McCain-Feingold Coordination Rules: The Ongoing Program to Keep Politics Under Control*, 32 Fordham Urb. L.J. 507 (2005).

6. In *Clifton v. Maine Right to Life Committee*, 114 F.3d 1309 (1st Cir. 1997), the Court of Appeals found the FEC's coordination rules invalid in the context of an interest group's preparation of a "voter scorecard." The FEC rule provided that a

person or organization preparing a voter scorecard (a summary of a candidate's votes or positions on various public issues) "must have no contact at all with any candidate or political committee," except for written questions and responses; that each candidate must be given the same prominence and space in the guide; and that there must be no "electioneering message" conveyed by any scoring or rating system used. *Id.* at 1311. Basing its decision on the organization's right to control how it presents its non-electoral message, and its right to communicate with officeholders and candidates in its chosen form, the court held that the FEC rules were invalid "insofar as the FEC may purport to prohibit mere inquiries to candidates, and * * * insofar as it limits any contact with candidates to written inquiries and replies and imposes an equal space and prominence restriction." *Id.* at 1317.

7. The FEC coordination rule adopted in 2003, 11 C.F.R. § 109, includes both "conduct" and "content" standards. Conduct standards regulate the types of contacts and conduct that constitute "coordination." Under the conduct prong of the regulation, a communication is coordinated if it "is created, produced, or distributed at the request or suggestion of a candidate, * * * political party committee," or their agents, or if the spender is

materially involved in decisions regarding:

 i. The content of the communication;

 ii. The intended audience for the communication;

 iii. The means or mode of the communication;

 iv. The specific media outlet used for the communication;

 v. The timing or frequency of the communication; or

 vi. The size or prominence of a printed communication, or duration of a communication by means of broadcast, cable, or satellite.

Id. This coordination can occur through "substantial discussion" or the use of a common vendor, contractor, or former employee who shares material information between the two parties. The complicated regulations do not, however, require "agreement or formal collaboration." The regulations provide a safe harbor for discussion of legislative issues, but not if those discussions include "campaign plans, projects, activities, or needs." *Id.* The regulations defining "coordination" take up over five pages of fine print in the Code of Federal Regulations, and are well worth reviewing in their entirety, if only to appreciate their complexity.

The content requirement limits coordination to only certain communications— specifically, to communications including "express advocacy"; "electioneering communications" as defined in BCRA (essentially broadcast ads made within 30 days of a primary or caucus or 60 days of a general election, *see McConnell v. Federal Election Commission*, *supra* p. 828); republication or distribution of a candidate's own campaign material; and certain other "public communications" that reference a candidate or party close to an election.

What is the purpose of including a "content" standard? Investigations into alleg-edly coordinated actions are among the most intrusive undertaken by the FEC. In order to determine if the coordination has taken place, the FEC typically probes into the number and content of communications between the candidate and his campaign staff, and between the staff and the leadership of the group alleged to be illegally coordinating its activities. This inquiry frequently involves substantial probing into the political strategy and tactics of both entities. *See* James Bopp, Jr. & Richard E. Colestrom, *The First Amendment Needs No Reform: Protecting Liberty from Campaign Finance Reformers*, 51 CATH. U. L. REV. 785, 833 (2002). *See generally* Bradley A. Smith & Stephen M. Hoersting, *A Toothless Anaconda: Innovation, Impo-tence, and Overenforcement at the Federal Election Commission*, 1 ELECTION L.J. 145, 167–169 (2002). Then consider the Supreme Court's decision in *Buckley*, narrowing the definition of "expenditure" to "express advocacy":

> [The Act contains] no definition clarifying what expenditures are "rel-ative to" a candidate. The use of so indefinite a phrase as "relative to" a candidate fails to clearly mark the boundary between permissible and impermissible speech * * *.

> "[W]hether words intended and designed to fall short of invitation would miss that mark is a question both of intent and of effect. No speaker, in such circumstances, safely could assume that anything he might say upon the general subject would not be understood by some as an invitation. In short, the supposedly clear-cut distinction between discussion, laudation, general advocacy, and solicitation puts the speaker in these circumstances wholly at the mercy of the varied understanding of his hearers and conse-quently of whatever inference may be drawn as to his intent and meaning.

> "Such a distinction offers no security for free discussion. In these con-ditions it blankets with uncertainty whatever may be said. It compels the speaker to hedge and trim."

Buckley v. Valeo, 424 U.S. 1, 41–43 (1976) (*per curiam*) [p. 728] (citations omitted). Does the vagueness problem go away merely because an expenditure is coordinated? Try answering the following problem:

Problem: Senator Workman has made support for organized labor a major theme throughout his political career. Over the course of his term, representatives of the AFL-CIO meet regularly with Mr. Workman, whom they consider a key legislative ally, on a wide variety of issues of concern to labor. At times, the AFL-CIO runs advertisements attempting to build public support on matters of importance to organized labor, such as opposition to free-trade agreements and support for work-place-safety standards. In planning such campaigns, they often meet with Senator Workman to discuss the Senate's legislative agenda, which senators' votes might be swayed by shifts in public opinion or by greater publicity, and other issues of strat-egy. Unions are prohibited from making direct contributions to a candidate's cam-paign. Has the AFL-CIO met the "conduct" standards for coordination? How about the content standard? As a lawyer for the AFL-CIO, advise your client as to whether its activities constitute coordinated expenditures, and hence illegal contributions to the campaign.

8. In *Wisconsin ex rel. Two Unnamed Petitioners v. Peterson*, 866 N.W.2d 165 (Wis. 2015), *cert. denied*, 137 S. Ct. 77 (2016), the plaintiffs were subject to a criminal investigation under a Wisconsin statute that limited coordinated speech for "political purposes." The plaintiffs had allegedly coordinated various public messages with the state's governor to promote the latter's policy agenda. In accordance with Wisconsin state law, a special prosecutor was appointed to investigate. The investigation proved controversial and intrusive. As described by the Wisconsin Supreme Court majority,

> search warrants were executed at approximately 6:00 a.m. on October 3, in pre-dawn, armed, paramilitary-style raids in which bright floodlights were used to illuminate the targets' homes.

> The breadth of the documents gathered pursuant to subpoenas and seized pursuant to search warrants is amazing. Millions of documents, both in digital and paper copy, were subpoenaed and/or seized. Deputies seized business papers, computer equipment, phones, and other devices, while their targets were restrained under police supervision and denied the ability to contact their attorneys. The special prosecutor obtained virtually every document possessed by the Unnamed Movants relating to every aspect of their lives, both personal and professional, over a five-year span (from 2009 to 2013). Such documents were subpoenaed and/or seized without regard to content or relevance to the alleged violations. . . . As part of this dragnet, the special prosecutor also had seized wholly irrelevant information, such as retirement income statements, personal financial account information, personal letters, and family photos.

866 N.W.2d at 183. The court, in a 4-3 decision, terminated the investigation and held that the phrase "political purposes" in the Wisconsin statute was unconstitutionally vague and overbroad under both the United States and Wisconsin Constitutions. To save the statute, the Court narrowed its application to speech that met the *Buckley* definition of "express advocacy." *See* pp. 755–59, *supra*.

9. In the wake of *Citizens United v. Federal Election Commission*, 558 U.S. 310 (2010) [p. 844], *SpeechNow.org v. Federal Election Commission*, 599 F.3d 686 (D.C. Cir. 2010), and the ensuing creation of "Super PACs," there has been a good deal of criticism that Super PACs are not, as required by law, operating independently of the candidates they support. The concern is typically voiced that Super PACs are run by party operatives, former staffers, supporters, or friends of the candidate supported. *See, e.g.*, Richard Briffault, *Coordination Reconsidered*, 113 Colum. L. Rev. Sidebar 88 (2013); Kyle Langvardt, *The Sorry Case for* Citizens United, 6 Charleston L. Rev. 569, 574 (2012); Taylor Lincoln, *Super Connected: Outside Groups' Devotion to Individual Candidates and Political Parties Disproves the Supreme Court's Key*

Assumption in Citizens United *That Unregulated Outside Spenders Would Be 'Independent'* (Public Citizen 2012). But whom would you expect to run a political organization that supported a candidate? Wouldn't it always be at least a "supporter"? For an argument as to why such contacts cannot constitutionally justify regulation as "coordinated" communications, see Bradley A. Smith, *Super PACs and the Role of 'Coordination' in Campaign Finance Law,* 49 WILLAMETTE L. REV. 603, 630–635 (2013).

10. Is it possible to draw a coordination standard that does not unduly limit protected independent expenditures, yet at the same time protects against corruption? Michael Gilbert and Brian Barnes have argued that it is impossible to draw a coordination standard that is not both wildly underinclusive (failing to capture much corrupting behavior) and wildly overinclusive (prohibiting much non-corrupting speech), and that this is true regardless of the definition one gives to corruption. They concluded that "coordination [does not] relate[] in any operational way to corruption." Michael D. Gilbert & Brian Barnes, *The Coordination Fallacy,* 4 FLA. ST. U. L. REV. 399 (2016). Does this conclusion go too far? Note that if Gilbert and Barnes are correct, the implications are enormous. Absent some anti-coordination rule, contribution limits (at least so long as private expenditures are allowed) become all but meaningless—the candidate can simply ask someone else to pay the bills. Would a coordination rule that merely prohibited republication of campaign materials, direct payment of campaign bills, or expenditures made at a candidate's request, be workable?

11. You may have suspected that *Colorado Republican I* would be followed by *Colorado Republican II,* and indeed it was. On remand from the Supreme Court, it was determined that the Party really did intend to engage in coordinated spending, and so the question the parties to the suit had originally raised—did limits on party coordinated spending violate the Constitution—finally returned to the Supreme Court in 2001. In *Federal Election Commission v. Colorado Republican Federal Campaign Committee,* 533 U.S. 431 (2001), the Supreme Court ruled, 5-4, that limits on party coordinated expenditures did not violate the Constitution. Since there was no question that the Party's expenditures were coordinated, the case did not say much about the standard for coordination.

Rather, *Colorado Republican II* was most remarkable for the majority's searing assessment of the role of parties. The majority, per Justice Souter, described political parties as "instruments of some contributors whose object is * * * to support any candidate who will be obliged to the contributors"; "agents for spending on behalf of those who seek to produce obligated officeholders"; and vehicles used to "circumvent contribution limits * * * and thereby exacerbate the threat of corruption." *Id.* at 452–53. The dissenters (Justice Thomas, joined by Chief Justice Rehnquist and Justices Scalia and Kennedy), not surprisingly, offered a much more benign and indeed salutary assessment of the role of parties. The two sides also engaged in a lengthy battle over the quantum and type of evidence the government should have to produce, mirroring the debate of *Nixon v. Shrink Missouri Government PAC,* 528 U.S.

377 (2000) [p. 768], one year earlier. For a book-length defense of the proposition that parties ought to receive favored status under the law, *see* PETER J. WALLISON & JOEL M. GORA, BETTER PARTIES, BETTER GOVERNMENT: A REALISTIC PROGRAM FOR CAMPAIGN FINANCE REFORM 87–111 (2009). They see parties as buffers between donors and the ultimate recipients of funds, as mediators between candidates and interest groups, and as sources that can direct funds to those races and candidates where they can be used most efficiently.

12. "The * * * result of this pair of cases [*Colorado Republican I* and *Colorado Republican II*] is to drive a wedge between parties and candidates. Parties can spend unlimited sums to help their candidates, but only if they do so independently of the candidates—that is, without sharing information on the candidate's strengths and weaknesses, strategies, plans, polling data, and so forth." Bradley A. Smith, *A Moderate, Modern Campaign Finance Reform Agenda*, 12 NEXUS J. OP. 3, 16 (2007). As a matter of policy, does this make sense?

F. Government Financing of Campaigns

Over the years, many observers have sought to cut the Gordian Knot of campaign-finance reform by having the government pay for, or at least subsidize, campaigns, thus reducing the importance of private contributions. In 1907, President Theodore Roosevelt, dogged by his own campaign-finance scandals, proposed "a very radical measure." Congress should provide "an appropriation for the proper and legitimate expenses of each of the great national parties, an appropriation ample enough to meet the necessity for thorough organization and machinery," coupled with limits on private contributions. Theodore Roosevelt, Seventh Annual Message (Dec. 3, 1907) (transcript available at http://www.presidency.ucsb.edu/ws/index.php?pid=29548). *See also* ROBERT E. MUTCH, CAMPAIGNS, CONGRESS AND COURTS: THE MAKING OF FEDERAL CAMPAIGN FINANCE LAW 6–8 (1988).

Roosevelt predicted that "it will take some time for people so to familiarize themselves with such a proposal as to be willing to consider its adoption," *id.*, and he was quite right—not until 1971 did Congress take steps to enact such a plan. For a description of the operation, rise, and fall of the federal public-financing system, see James Sample, *The Last Rites of Public Campaign Finance*, 92 NEB. L. REV. 349 (2013); *see also* Joel M. Gora, *Don't Feed the Alligators: Government Funding of Political Speech and the Unyielding Vigilance of the First Amendment*, 2011 CATO SUP. CT. REV. 81 (2011).

But while the notion of having the government pay for campaigns sounds simple, in fact, like so much of campaign-finance law, it, too, raises difficult constitutional and policy questions, as the materials below show. The federal law, enacted in 1971 and reinforced with the 1974 Federal Election Campaign Act amendments, was first challenged in our old friend, *Buckley v. Valeo*.

Buckley v. Valeo

Supreme Court of the United States
424 U.S. 1, 96 S. Ct. 612, 46 L. Ed. 2d 659 (1976)

PER CURIAM. [MR. JUSTICE BRENNAN, MR. JUSTICE STEWART, and MR. JUSTICE POWELL join this opinion in full, and MR. JUSTICE MARSHALL and MR. JUSTICE BLACKMUN join all portions of the opinion excerpted here. MR. JUSTICE REHNQUIST joins in the portions excerpted here, except to the extent that Section III finds the treatment of minor parties and independent candidates to be constitutional.] * * *

* * * In the free society ordained by our Constitution it is not the government but the people—individually as citizens and candidates and collectively as associations and political committees—who must retain control over the quantity and range of debate on public issues in a political campaign.[65] * * *

III. Public Financing of Presidential Election Campaigns

[The Act] establishes a Presidential Election Campaign Fund (Fund), financed from general revenues in the aggregate amount designated by individual taxpayers, * * * who on their income tax returns may authorize payment to the Fund of one dollar of their tax liability in the case of an individual return or two dollars in the case of a joint return.[j] The Fund consists of three separate accounts to finance (1) party nominating conventions, (2) general election campaigns, and (3) primary campaigns. * * *

For expenses in the general election campaign, [26 U.S.C.] § 9004(a)(1) entitles each major-party [Presidential] candidate to $20,000,000. This amount is * * * adjusted for inflation. To be eligible for funds the candidate must pledge not to incur expenses in excess of the entitlement under § 9004(a)(1) and not to accept private contributions except to the extent that the fund is insufficient to provide the full entitlement. * * * New-party candidates receive no money prior to the general election, but any candidate receiving 5% or more of the popular vote in the election is entitled to post-election payments according to [a] formula applicable to minor-party candidates. * * *

[T]he Presidential Primary Matching Payment Account * * * is intended to aid campaigns by candidates seeking Presidential nomination "by a political party," in "primary elections." The threshold eligibility requirement is that the candidate raise at least $5,000 in each of 20 States, counting only the first $250 from each person contributing to the candidate. In addition, the candidate must agree to abide by the

---

65. For the reasons discussed in Part III, *infra*, Congress may engage in public financing of election campaigns and may condition acceptance of public funds on an agreement by the candidate to abide by specified expenditure limitations. Just as a candidate may voluntarily limit the size of the contributions he chooses to accept, he may decide to forgo private fundraising and accept public funding.

j. Now $3 and $6, respectively. —Eds.

spending limits. Funding is provided according to a matching formula: each qualified candidate is entitled to a sum equal to the total private contributions received, disregarding contributions from any person to the extent that total contributions to the candidate by that person exceed $250. Payments to any candidate under Chapter 96 [of Title 26] may not exceed 50% of the overall expenditure ceiling accepted by the candidate. * * *

Appellants * * * argue that "by analogy" to the Religion Clauses of the First Amendment public financing of election campaigns, however meritorious, violates the First Amendment. * * * [T]he analogy is patently inapplicable to our issue here. Although "Congress shall make no law . . . abridging the freedom of speech, or of the press," [the public-financing provision] is a congressional effort, not to abridge, restrict, or censor speech, but rather to use public money to facilitate and enlarge public discussion and participation in the electoral process, goals vital to a self-governing people. Thus, [the provision] furthers, not abridges, pertinent First Amendment values. * * *

It cannot be gainsaid that public financing as a means of eliminating the improper influence of large private contributions furthers a significant governmental interest. In addition, the limits on contributions necessarily increase the burden of fund-raising, and Congress properly regarded public financing as an appropriate means of relieving major-party Presidential candidates from the rigors of soliciting private contributions. * * *

Mr. Justice Stevens took no part in the consideration or decision of these cases.

Mr. Chief Justice Burger, concurring in part and dissenting in part.

Since the turn of this century when the idea of Government subsidies for political campaigns first was broached, there has been no lack of realization that the use of funds from the public treasury to subsidize political activity of private individuals would produce substantial and profound questions about the nature of our democratic society. The Majority Leader of the Senate, although supporting such legislation in 1967, said that "the implications of these questions . . . go to the very heart and structure of the Government of the Republic." The Solicitor General in his amicus curiae brief states that "the issues involved here are of indisputable moment." He goes on to express his view that public financing will have "profound effects in the way candidates approach issues and each other." Public financing, he notes, "affects the role of the party in campaigns for office, changes the role of the incumbent government vis-a-vis all parties, and affects the relative strengths and strategies of candidates vis-a-vis each other and their party's leaders."

* * * The public monies at issue here are not being employed simply to police the integrity of the electoral process or to provide a forum for the use of all participants in the political dialogue, as would, for example, be the case if free broadcast time

were granted. Rather, we are confronted with the Government's actual financing, out of general revenues, a segment of the political debate itself. * * *

* * * [T]he inappropriateness of subsidizing, from general revenues, the actual political dialogue of the people—the process which begets the Government itself—is as basic to our national tradition as the separation of church and state also deriving from the First Amendment, or the separation of civilian and military authority, neither of which is explicit in the Constitution but both of which have developed through case-by-case adjudication of express provisions of the Constitution. * * *

"[V]arying measures of control * * *" *Lemon* v. *Kurtzman*, 403 U.S. [602], 621 [(1971)] * * * usually accompany grants from Government * * *. Up to now, the Court has always been extraordinarily sensitive, when dealing with First Amendment rights, to the risk that the "flag tends to follow the dollars." * * *

Notes and Questions

1. Were Chief Justice Burger's fears well grounded? The system of government financing for presidential campaigns has been in effect for more than four decades, although in 2012, for the first time, both major-party candidates chose to raise private funds rather than to participate in the public-financing system. In 2016, no significant candidate accepted the government subsidies, and the same was true in 2020, at least through the primaries. Have Chief Justice Burger's worries come true? Can you think of ways that government financing might change candidate and party behavior? Consider the following: Candidates have long been entitled to the "lowest unit rate"—that is, the lowest charge made to other advertisers for similar broadcast time—by federal law. 47 U.S.C. § 315(b). As part of the Bipartisan Campaign Reform Act of 2002, federal candidates must appear in their broadcast ads, identify themselves, and state that they approve the message. 52 U.S.C. § 30120(d). Such a statement usually consumes 10% or more of the typical television ad, forcing the candidate to forego saying something else. The provision is enforced not by penalizing the campaign directly but instead by depriving the non-complying candidate of the right to the lowest unit rate. A law passed in Arizona provides another example of an attempt by government to influence campaign speech by offering a benefit to campaigns—with strings attached. The Arizona Law required recipients of public funding to participate in at least one public debate. Do these restrictions suggest that Chief Justice Burger was right, or that his worries were relatively trivial? If Congress sought to place too many restrictions on campaigns, could the courts step in on a case-by-case basis? For an elaboration of Chief Justice Burger's concerns, *see* Bradley A. Smith, *Separation of Campaign & State*, 81 Geo. Wash. L. Rev. 2038 (2013).

2. Prior to 2014, the law also provided for public funds to subsidize the parties' presidential nominating conventions. That feature was repealed in 2014. Pub. L. 113–94 (2014).

3. Notice the mysterious footnote 65. Remember that *Buckley* struck down limits on independent expenditures and on candidate expenditures. Thus, Congress may not impose spending limits on campaigns. Footnote 65, however, said that Congress may "condition" the receipt of government subsidies on a candidate's agreeing to limit expenditures. It promised to explain why in § III of the opinion, but, in fact, it never did. Explanation or no, *Buckley* held that candidate participation in a public-funding system that places limits on expenditures must be voluntary and not compelled.

One of the rationales offered in favor of prohibitions on corporate campaign spending is the protection of dissenting shareholders. *See Austin v. Michigan State Chamber of Commerce*, 494 U.S. 652, 673–75 (1990). *See also Janus v. American Federation of State, County, and Municipal Employees*, 585 U.S. __, 138 S. Ct. 2448 (2018) (holding that a requirement that non-union members pay fees to a union constituted unconstitutionally compelled political speech). The Presidential Election Campaign Fund avoided the problem of forcing taxpayers to fund candidates with opposing views by earmarking funds designated for that purpose by taxpayers. Should states be permitted to adopt public-financing systems that use general tax revenues — necessarily meaning that taxpayers are required to fund candidates with whom they disagree?

4. *Problem.* The City of Portlandia has launched a program in which residents receive vouchers, valued at $50 each, that they can donate to political candidates of their choice. The program is funded not from general levies, but by a special property-tax assessment levied on homeowners in the city. Some of the vouchers are, of course, contributed to candidates with whom some of the homeowners disagree. Is the program constitutional? *See Elster v. City of Seattle*, 444 P.3d 590 (Wash. 2019).

5. *Problem.* Jim Chambers is running for state senate. Jim was born in Peru and became a naturalized U.S. citizen twenty-three years ago. His name had been passed down from his paternal great-grandfather, an American who immigrated to Peru in 1917. Jim is seven-eighths Hispanic in his lineage, is of dark complexion, and speaks English with a slight accent. Jim is an accomplished physician, highly respected by his peers, and has served in several appointed, policy-making positions in state government, generally receiving high marks for his service. His voice, however, is high pitched and not always commanding. And Jim is not, shall we say gently, especially handsome. Jim fears that he does not do well on camera because of his appearance and voice. His district is one of the least racially diverse in the state, and for both ideological and electoral reasons Jim wishes to downplay race in the campaign. For all these reasons, Jim appears only briefly, if at all, in his campaign's television advertisements.

The state has a system of public funding of campaigns. Jim believes that the incentives developed to encourage candidates to participate in the public financing system, including particularly burdensome reporting requirements and very low contribution limits placed on non-participating candidates, make it impossible for him to compete financially in the race if he does not participate in the public-funding program. However, the program also requires candidates accepting public funds to participate in a series of three one-hour, televised debates, which Jim thinks could also doom his candidacy, given the electorate's superficial attraction to on-camera appearance and his concerns that some voters will voter against him on account of race. If Jim challenges the public-funding law as coercive, what should be the result? *See* Ariz. Rev. Stat. Ann. § 16-956 (A).

6. Assuming that government can provide incentives to a candidate to participate in a voluntary system of public funding, at what point do those incentives become unconstitutionally coercive? For example, could a state set a contribution limit of just $25, but offer the opportunity to participate in a generous public funding system as an alternative? With the notable exception of *Day v. Holahan*, 34 F.3d 1356 (8th Cir. 1994), most federal courts upheld incentive plans for participation in government-financing systems prior to 2010. *See North Carolina Right to Life v. Leake*, 524 F.3d 427 (4th Cir.), *cert. denied*, 555 U.S. 994 (2008); *Daggett v. Commission on Governmental Ethics and Election Practices*, 205 F.3d 445 (1st Cir. 2000); *Gable v. Patton*, 142 F.3d 940 (6th Cir. 1998); *Rosenstiel v. Rodriguez*, 101 F.3d 1544 (8th Cir. 1996); *Vote Choice, Inc. v. DiStefano*, 4 F.3d 26 (1st Cir. 1993). However, the Supreme Court's decision in *Davis v. Federal Election Commission*, 554 U.S. 724 (2008) [discussed at pp. 807–09, *supra*], cast considerable doubt on the ability of government to treat candidates differently for fundraising purposes, and in particular to "penalize" a candidate for raising or spending money by relaxing fundraising rules for that candidate's opponent. The Supreme Court's decision in the next case seemed to have confirmed those doubts, and either overruled or raised serious questions about the validity of several of the Courts of Appeals' decisions cited above.

Arizona Free Enterprise Club's Freedom Club PAC v. Bennett

Supreme Court of the United States
564 U.S. 721, 131 S. Ct. 2806, 180 L. Ed. 2d 664 (2011)

CHIEF JUSTICE ROBERTS delivered the opinion of the Court [in which JUSTICE SCALIA, JUSTICE KENNEDY, JUSTICE THOMAS, and JUSTICE ALITO join]. * * *

The Arizona Citizens Clean Elections Act, passed by initiative in 1998, created a voluntary public financing system to fund the primary and general election campaigns of candidates for state office. All eligible candidates for Governor, secretary of state, attorney general, treasurer, superintendent of public instruction, the corporation commission, mine inspector, and the state legislature (both the House and Senate) may opt to receive public funding. Eligibility is contingent on the collection of a specified number of five-dollar contributions from Arizona voters, and the acceptance of certain campaign restrictions and obligations. Publicly funded candidates must agree, among other things, to limit their expenditure of personal funds to $500; * * * [and] adhere to an overall expenditure cap. * * *

In exchange for accepting these conditions, participating candidates are granted public funds to conduct their campaigns. In many cases, this initial allotment may be the whole of the State's financial backing of a publicly funded candidate. But when certain conditions are met, publicly funded candidates are granted additional "equalizing" or matching funds.

* * * [M]atching funds are triggered when a privately financed candidate's expenditures, combined with the expenditures of independent groups made in support of the privately financed candidate or in opposition to a publicly financed candidate, exceed the * * * allotment of state funds to the publicly financed candidate. * * * A privately financed candidate's expenditures of his personal funds are counted as contributions for purposes of calculating matching funds during a general election.

Once matching funds are triggered, each additional dollar that a privately financed candidate spends during the primary results in one dollar in additional state funding to his publicly financed opponent (less a 6% reduction meant to account for fundraising expenses). During a general election, every dollar that a candidate receives in contributions—which includes any money of his own that a candidate spends on his campaign—results in roughly one dollar in additional state funding to his publicly financed opponent. In an election where a privately funded candidate faces multiple publicly financed candidates, one dollar raised or spent by the privately financed candidate results in an almost one dollar increase in public funding to each of the publicly financed candidates.

Once the public financing cap is exceeded, * * * [s]pending by independent groups on behalf of a privately funded candidate, or in opposition to a publicly funded candidate, results in matching funds. Independent expenditures made in support of a publicly financed candidate can result in matching funds for other publicly financed candidates in a race. The matching funds provision is not activated, however, when independent expenditures are made in opposition to a privately financed candidate. Matching funds top out at two times the initial authorized grant of public funding to the publicly financed candidate. * * *

An example may help clarify how the Arizona matching funds provision operates. Arizona is divided into 30 districts for purposes of electing members to the State's House of Representatives. Each district elects two representatives to the House biannually. In the last general election, the number of candidates competing for the two available seats in each district ranged from two to seven. Arizona's Fourth District had three candidates for its two available House seats. Two of those candidates opted to accept public funding; one candidate chose to operate his campaign with private funds.

In that election, if the total funds contributed to the privately funded candidate, added to that candidate's expenditure of personal funds and the expenditures of supportive independent groups, exceeded $21,479—the allocation of public funds for the general election in a contested State House race—the matching funds provision would be triggered. At that point, a number of different political activities could result in the distribution of matching funds. For example:

- If the privately funded candidate spent $1,000 of his own money to conduct a direct mailing, each of his publicly funded opponents would receive $940 ($1,000 less the 6% offset).

- If the privately funded candidate held a fundraiser that generated $1,000 in contributions, each of his publicly funded opponents would receive $940.

- If an independent expenditure group spent $1,000 on a brochure expressing its support for the privately financed candidate, each of the publicly financed candidates would receive $940 directly.

- If an independent expenditure group spent $1,000 on a brochure opposing one of the publicly financed candidates, but saying nothing about the privately financed candidate, the publicly financed candidates would receive $940 directly.

- If an independent expenditure group spent $1,000 on a brochure supporting one of the publicly financed candidates, the other publicly financed candidate would receive $940 directly, but the privately financed candidate would receive nothing.

- If an independent expenditure group spent $1,000 on a brochure opposing the privately financed candidate, no matching funds would be issued.

A publicly financed candidate would continue to receive additional state money in response to fundraising and spending by the privately financed candidate and independent expenditure groups until that publicly financed candidate received a total of $64,437 in state funds (three times the initial allocation for a State House race).

Petitioners * * * filed suit challenging the constitutionality of the matching funds provision. The candidates and independent expenditure groups argued that the matching funds provision unconstitutionally penalized their speech and burdened their ability to fully exercise their First Amendment rights. * * *

Although the speech of the candidates and independent expenditure groups that brought this suit is not directly capped by Arizona's matching funds provision, those parties contend that their political speech is substantially burdened by the state law in the same way that speech was burdened by the law we recently found invalid in *Davis* v. *Federal Election Comm'n*, 554 U.S. 724 (2008). In *Davis*, we considered a First Amendment challenge to the so-called "Millionaire's Amendment" of the Bipartisan Campaign Reform Act of 2002. Under that Amendment, if a candidate for the United States House of Representatives spent more than $350,000 of his personal funds, [his opponent] was permitted to collect individual contributions up to $6,900 per contributor—three times the normal contribution limit of $2,300. The candidate who spent more than the personal funds limit remained subject to the original contribution cap. * * *

In addressing the constitutionality of the Millionaire's Amendment, we acknowledged that the provision did not impose an outright cap on a candidate's personal expenditures. We nonetheless concluded that the Amendment was unconstitutional because it forced a candidate "to choose between the First Amendment right to engage in unfettered political speech and subjection to discriminatory fundraising limitations." *Id.*, at 739. * * *

The logic of *Davis* largely controls our approach to this case. Much like the burden placed on speech in *Davis*, the matching funds provision "imposes an unprecedented penalty on any candidate who robustly exercises [his] First Amendment right[s]." Under that provision, "the vigorous exercise of the right to use personal funds to finance campaign speech" leads to "advantages for opponents in the competitive context of electoral politics." *Ibid.*

* * * If the law at issue in *Davis* imposed a burden on candidate speech, the Arizona law unquestionably does so as well.

The penalty imposed by Arizona's matching funds provision is different in some respects from the penalty imposed by the law we struck down in *Davis*. But those differences make the Arizona law *more* constitutionally problematic, not less. First, the penalty in *Davis* consisted of raising the contribution limits for one of the candidates. The candidate who benefited from the increased limits still had to go out and raise the funds. He may or may not have been able to do so. The other candidate, therefore, faced merely the possibility that his opponent would be able to raise additional funds, through contribution limits that remained subject to a cap. * * * Here the benefit to the publicly financed candidate is the direct and automatic release of public money. That is a far heavier burden than in *Davis*.

Second, * * * the matching funds provision can create a multiplier effect. In the Arizona Fourth District House election previously discussed, if the spending cap were exceeded, each dollar spent by the privately funded candidate would result in an additional dollar of campaign funding to each of that candidate's publicly financed opponents. In such a situation, the matching funds provision forces privately funded candidates to fight a political hydra of sorts. Each dollar they spend generates two adversarial dollars in response, * * * a markedly more significant burden than in *Davis*.

Third, unlike the law at issue in *Davis*, all of this is to some extent out of the privately financed candidate's hands. Even if that candidate opted to spend less than the initial public financing cap, any spending by independent expenditure groups to promote the privately financed candidate's election — regardless whether such support was welcome or helpful — could trigger matching funds. What is more, that state money would go directly to the publicly funded candidate to use as he saw fit. That disparity in control — giving money directly to a publicly financed candidate, in response to independent expenditures that cannot be coordinated with the privately funded candidate — is a substantial advantage for the publicly funded candidate. That candidate can allocate the money according to his own campaign strategy, which the privately financed candidate could not do with the independent group expenditures that triggered the matching funds.

The burdens that this regime places on independent expenditure groups are akin to those imposed on the privately financed candidates themselves. * * * [T]he more money spent on [a] candidate's behalf or in opposition to a publicly funded candidate, the more money the publicly funded candidate receives from the State. * * * [T]he effect of a dollar spent on election speech is a guaranteed financial payout to the publicly funded candidate the group opposes. Moreover, spending one dollar can result in the flow of dollars to multiple candidates the group disapproves of, dollars directly controlled by the publicly funded candidate or candidates.

In some ways, the burden the Arizona law imposes on independent expenditure groups is worse than the burden it imposes on privately financed candidates, and thus substantially worse than the burden we found constitutionally impermissible in *Davis*. If a candidate contemplating an electoral run in Arizona surveys the campaign landscape and decides that the burdens imposed by the matching funds regime make a privately funded campaign unattractive, he at least has the option of taking public financing. Independent expenditure groups, of course, do not.

Once the spending cap is reached, an independent expenditure group that wants to support a particular candidate—because of that candidate's stand on an issue of concern to the group—can only avoid triggering matching funds in one of two ways. The group can either opt to change its message from one addressing the merits of the candidates to one addressing the merits of an issue, or refrain from speaking altogether. * * * [F]orcing that choice—trigger matching funds, change your message, or do not speak—certainly contravenes "the fundamental rule of protection under the First Amendment, that a speaker has the autonomy to choose the content of his own message."[6] * * *

The State argues that the matching funds provision actually results in more speech by "increas[ing] debate about issues of public concern" in Arizona elections and "promot[ing] the free and open debate that the First Amendment was intended to foster." * * * Any increase in speech resulting from the Arizona law is of one kind and one kind only—that of publicly financed candidates. The burden imposed on privately financed candidates and independent expenditure groups reduces their speech. * * * Thus, even if the matching funds provision did result in more speech by publicly financed candidates and more speech in general, it would do so at the expense of impermissibly burdening (and thus reducing) the speech of privately

---

6. The dissent sees *"chutzpah"* in candidates exercising their right not to participate in the public financing scheme, while objecting that the system violates their First Amendment rights. The charge is unjustified, but, in any event, it certainly cannot be leveled against the independent expenditure groups. The dissent barely mentions such groups in its analysis, and fails to address not only the distinctive burdens imposed on these groups—as set forth above—but also the way in which privately financed candidates are particularly burdened when matching funds are triggered by independent group speech.

financed candidates and independent expenditure groups. This sort of "beggar thy neighbor" approach to free speech—"restrict[ing] the speech of some elements of our society in order to enhance the relative voice of others" is "wholly foreign to the First Amendment." *Id.*, at 48–49.[7] * * *

The State also argues * * * that any burden on privately financed candidates and independent expenditure groups is more analogous to the burden placed on speakers by the disclosure and disclaimer requirements we recently upheld in *Citizens United* than to direct restrictions on candidate and independent expenditures. This analogy is not even close. A political candidate's disclosure of his funding resources does not result in a cash windfall to his opponent, or affect their respective disclosure obligations.

The State * * * reasons that if providing all the money up front would not burden speech, providing it piecemeal does not do so either. And the State further argues that such incremental administration is necessary to ensure that public funding is not under- or over-distributed.

These arguments miss the point. It is not the amount of funding that the State provides to publicly financed candidates that is constitutionally problematic in this case. It is the manner in which that funding is provided—in direct response to the political speech of privately financed candidates and independent expenditure groups. And the fact that the State's matching mechanism may be more efficient than other alternatives * * * is of no moment; "the First Amendment does not permit the State to sacrifice speech for efficiency."

The United States as *amicus* contends that "[p]roviding additional funds to petitioners' opponents does not make petitioners' own speech any less effective" and thus does not substantially burden speech. Of course it does. One does not have to subscribe to the view that electoral debate is zero sum to see the flaws in the United States' perspective. All else being equal, an advertisement supporting the election of a candidate that goes without a response is often more effective than an advertisement that is directly controverted. And even if the publicly funded candidate decides to use his new money to address a different issue altogether, the end goal of that spending is to claim electoral victory over the opponent that triggered the additional state funding. * * *

There is a debate between the parties in this case as to what state interest is served by the matching funds provision. The privately financed candidates and independent expenditure groups contend that the provision works to "level[] electoral

---

7. The dissent also repeatedly argues that the Arizona matching funds regime results in "*more* political speech," but—given the logic of the dissent's position—that is only as a step to *less* speech. If the matching funds provision achieves its professed goal and causes candidates to switch to public financing, there will be less speech: no spending above the initial state-set amount by formerly privately financed candidates, and no associated matching funds for anyone. Not only that, the level of speech will depend on the State's judgment of the desirable amount, an amount tethered to available (and often scarce) state resources.

opportunities" by equalizing candidate "resources and influence." The State and the Clean Elections Institute counter that the provision "furthers Arizona's interest in preventing corruption and the appearance of corruption." * * *

We have repeatedly rejected the argument that the government has a compelling state interest in "leveling the playing field" that can justify undue burdens on political speech.

"Leveling electoral opportunities means making and implementing judgments about which strengths should be permitted to contribute to the outcome of an election," *Davis, supra*, at 742 — a dangerous enterprise and one that cannot justify burdening protected speech. * * * [S]uch basic intrusion by the government into the debate over who should govern goes to the heart of First Amendment values.

"Leveling the playing field" can sound like a good thing. But in a democracy, campaigning for office is not a game. It is a critically important form of speech. The First Amendment embodies our choice as a Nation that, when it comes to such speech, the guiding principle is freedom — the "unfettered interchange of ideas" — not whatever the State may view as fair.

* * * But even if the ultimate objective of the matching funds provision is to combat corruption — and not "level the playing field" — the burdens that the matching funds provision imposes on protected political speech are not justified.

Burdening a candidate's expenditure of his own funds on his own campaign does not further the State's anticorruption interest. Indeed, we have said that * * * "the use of personal funds reduces the candidate's dependence on outside contributions and thereby counteracts the coercive pressures and attendant risks of abuse" of money in politics. * * *

We have also held that "independent expenditures . . . do not give rise to corruption or the appearance of corruption." * * *

* * * Arizona already has some of the most austere contribution limits in the United States. * * * In the face of such ascetic contribution limits, strict disclosure requirements, and the general availability of public funding, it is hard to imagine what marginal corruption deterrence could be generated by the matching funds provision.

Perhaps recognizing that the burdens the matching funds provision places on speech cannot be justified in and of themselves, * * * the State and the Clean Elections Institute offer another argument: They contend that the provision indirectly serves the anticorruption interest, by ensuring that enough candidates participate in the State's public funding system, which in turn helps combat corruption. * * *

The flaw in the State's argument is apparent in what its reasoning would allow. By the State's logic it could grant a publicly funded candidate five dollars in matching funds for every dollar his privately financed opponent spent, or force candidates who wish to run on private funds to pay a $10,000 fine in order to encourage participation in the public funding regime. Such measures might well promote participation in public financing, but would clearly suppress or unacceptably alter political speech. How the State chooses to encourage participation in its public funding sys-tem matters, and we have never held that a State may burden political speech—to the extent the matching funds provision does—to ensure adequate participation in a public funding system. Here the State's chosen method is unduly burdensome and not sufficiently justified to survive First Amendment scrutiny. * * *

The judgment of the Court of Appeals for the Ninth Circuit is reversed.

JUSTICE KAGAN, with whom JUSTICE GINSBURG, JUSTICE BREYER, and JUSTICE SOTOMAYOR join, dissenting. * * *

* * * Arizona's matching funds provision does not restrict, but instead subsidizes, speech. The law "impose[s] no ceiling on [speech] and do[es] not prevent anyone from speaking." *Citizens United*. By enabling participating candidates to respond to their opponents' expression, the statute expands public debate, in adherence to "our tradition that more speech, not less, is the governing rule." *Id.* What the law does—all the law does—is fund more speech. * * *

[Petitioners] are making a novel argument: that Arizona violated *their* First Amendment rights by disbursing funds to *other* speakers even though they could have received (but chose to spurn) the same financial assistance. Some people might call that *chutzpah*.

Indeed, what petitioners demand is essentially a right to quash others' speech through the prohibition of a (universally available) subsidy program. Petitioners are able to convey their ideas without public financing—and they would prefer the field to themselves, so that they can speak free from response. * * *

* * * According to the Court, the special problem here lies in Arizona's matching funds mechanism, which the majority claims imposes a "substantia[l] burde[n]" on a privately funded candidate's speech. Sometimes, the majority suggests that this "burden" lies in the way the mechanism "diminish[es] the effectiveness" of the privately funded candidate's expression by enabling his opponent to respond. At other times, the majority indicates that the "burden" resides in the deterrent effect of the mechanism: The privately funded candidate "might not spend money" because doing so will trigger matching funds. Either way, the majority is wrong to see a substantial burden on expression.[5]

* * * [H]as the majority shown that the burden resulting from the Arizona stat-ute is "substantial"? I will not quarrel with the majority's assertion that responsive

---

5. The majority's error on this score extends both to candidates and to independent expendi-ture groups. Contrary to the majority's suggestion, nearly all of my arguments showing that the Clean Elections Act does not impose a substantial burden apply to both sets of speakers (and apply regardless of whether independent or candidate expenditures trigger the matching funds). That is also true of every one of my arguments demonstrating the State's compelling interest in this legislation. But perhaps the best response to the majority's view that the Act inhibits independent expenditure groups lies in an empirical fact already noted: Expenditures by these groups have risen by 253% since Arizona's law was enacted. * * *

speech by one candidate may make another candidate's speech less effective; that, after all, is the whole idea of the First Amendment, and a *benefit* of having more responsive speech. * * * And I will assume that the operation of this statute may on occasion deter a privately funded candidate from spending money, and conveying ideas by that means. * * * Still, does that effect count as a severe burden on expression? By the measure of our prior decisions—which have upheld campaign reforms with an equal or greater impact on speech—the answer is no.

Number one: *Any* system of public financing, including the lump-sum model upheld in *Buckley*, imposes a similar burden on privately funded candidates. Suppose Arizona were to do what all parties agree it could under *Buckley*—provide a single upfront payment (say, $150,000) to a participating candidate, rather than an initial payment (of $50,000) plus 94% of whatever his privately funded opponent spent, up to a ceiling (the same $150,000). That system would "diminis[h] the effectiveness" of a privately funded candidate's speech at least as much, and in the same way: It would give his opponent, who presumably would not be able to raise that sum on his own, more money to spend. And so too, a lump-sum system may deter speech. A person relying on private resources might well choose not to enter a race at all, because he knows he will face an adequately funded opponent. And even if he decides to run, he likely will choose to speak in different ways— for example, by eschewing dubious, easy-to-answer charges—because his opponent has the ability to respond. Indeed, privately funded candidates may well find the lump-sum system *more* burdensome than Arizona's (assuming the lump is big enough). Pretend you are financing your campaign through private donations. Would you prefer that your opponent receive a guaranteed, upfront payment of $150,000, or that he receive only $50,000, with the *possibility*—a possibility that you mostly get to control—of collecting another $100,000 somewhere down the road? Me too. * * *

Number two: Our decisions about disclosure and disclaimer requirements show the Court is wrong. Starting in *Buckley* and continuing through last Term, the Court has repeatedly declined to view these requirements as a substantial First Amendment burden, even though they discourage some campaign speech. * * * Like a disclosure rule, the matching funds provision may occasionally deter, but "impose[s] no ceiling" on electoral expression.

The majority breezily dismisses this comparison, labeling the analogy "not even close" because disclosure requirements result in no payment of money to a speaker's opponent. * * * But the majority does not tell us why this difference matters. Nor could it. The majority strikes down the matching funds provision because of its ostensible *effect*—most notably, that it may deter a person from spending money in an election. But this Court has acknowledged time and again that disclosure obligations have the selfsame effect. * * *

Number three: Any burden that the Arizona law imposes does not exceed the burden associated with contribution limits, which we have also repeatedly upheld. * * * Rather than potentially deterring or "diminish[ing] the effectiveness" of expressive activity, these limits stop it cold. Yet we have never subjected these restrictions to the most stringent review. * * *

For all these reasons, the Court errs in holding that the government action in this case substantially burdens speech and so requires the State to offer a compelling interest. But in any event, Arizona has come forward with just such an interest, explaining that the Clean Elections Act attacks corruption and the appearance of corruption in the State's political system. * * *

* * * The Clean Elections Act, the State avers, "deters *quid pro quo* corruption and the appearance of corruption by providing Arizona candidates with an option to run for office without depending on outside contributions." And so Arizona, like many state and local governments, has implemented public financing on the theory (which this Court has previously approved), that the way to reduce political corruption is to diminish the role of private donors in campaigns.[11]

And that interest justifies the matching funds provision at issue because it is a critical facet of Arizona's public financing program. The provision is no more than a disbursement mechanism; but it is also the thing that makes the whole Clean Elections Act work. [P]ublic financing has an Achilles heel—the difficulty of setting the subsidy at the right amount. Too small, and the grant will not attract candidates to the program; and with no participating candidates, the program can hardly decrease corruption. Too large, and the system becomes unsustainable, or at the least an unnecessary drain on public resources. But finding the sweet-spot is near impossible because of variation, across districts and over time, in the political system. Enter the matching funds provision, which takes an ordinary lump-sum amount, divides it into thirds, and disburses the last two of these (to the extent necessary) via a self-calibrating mechanism. That provision is just a fine-tuning of the lump-sum program approved in *Buckley*—a fine-tuning, it bears repeating, that prevents no one from speaking and discriminates against no message. But that fine-tuning can make the difference between a wholly ineffectual program and one that removes corruption from the political system. * * *

I respectfully dissent.

---

11. The majority briefly suggests that the State's "austere contribution limits" lessen the need for public financing, but provides no support for that dubious claim. As Arizona and other jurisdictions have discovered, contribution limits may not eliminate the risk of corrupt dealing between candidates and donors[;] * * * *Buckley* upheld *both* limits on contributions to federal candidates *and* public financing of presidential campaigns. Arizona, like Congress, was "surely entitled to conclude" that contribution limits were only a "partial measure," and that a functional public financing system was also necessary to eliminate political corruption. * * *

Notes and Questions

1. Was the Court correct that "[t]he logic of *Davis*" controlled the outcome of this case? Why or why not?

2. Did the majority adequately address the dissent's principal argument—that no one's speech was being limited, and the government was merely providing more avenues for speech?

3. If, as the dissent argued, it would be legal for the government simply to provide a larger grant to participating candidates at the outset, why was it problematic to start participating candidates with a small grant and then raise the amount only if the participating candidate was being outspent? Isn't the latter actually a better situation for the non-participating candidate (as well as for the taxpayers)?

Did the problem relate to the horserace nature of elections and the trigger for added matching funds? A candidate must decide at the outset whether or not to participate. Once a candidate has decided to forego the subsidy, however, his calculation may be upset not by his own spending, but by the independent spending of others that may be of little advantage to him, or even harmful. Similarly, in a multi-candidate primary or race in which only one candidate was privately funded, independent expenditures supporting that candidate could trigger matching funds for each of his participating opponents, thus releasing more money against the favored candidate than the amount of the expenditure for that candidate. If you were advising a grassroots organization, would you urge it to make an independent expenditure in such a race?

4. Justice Kagan argued that Arizona's interest in distributing matching funds was not the equalization of resources *per se*, but rather encouraging candidates to opt-in to the public-financing system. Encouraging participation in the public-financing system, in turn, was tied to the traditional anti-corruption interest. Is this argument meaningfully different from the equality argument, or is it simply a back-door way of promoting equality in anti-corruption garb?

5. One co-author of this Casebook, noting Justice Kagan's point that Arizona could simply have awarded the entire matching-fund amount at the outset of the campaign, has argued that what truly disturbed the majority was not that speech was discouraged but that government financing generally requires the government to take sides in elections. If the government-financing system is not effective because not enough candidates (particularly those most likely to win and eventually hold office) participate, then the government must try to ensure that publicly financed candidates win a substantial portion of elections. Nor is such a commitment "content-neutral."

> The very act of subsidizing candidates who choose to raise funds in a particular manner is a way of choosing favorites. The plan in Arizona was referred to as "clean elections" and administered by the Citizens Clean

Elections Commission. Participating candidates were, therefore, regularly referred to as "clean" candidates. It is hard to see this as anything but the "scarlet letter" approach properly rejected in [*Cook v.*] *Gralike* [531 U.S. 510, 525–526 (2001) [p. 552] (striking down a state law that required ballots to state that a candidate had "disregarded voters' instruction" by refusing to support particular legislation)]. Even without this "scarlet letter," the government's decision to subsidize some candidates acts as an implicit endorsement of the candidates' means of financing the campaign. Campaign fundraising is part of the campaign itself. Campaigns craft messages with great care and follow a myriad of strategies. Some seek large numbers of small contributions, hoping to use the psychological commitment of having donated to assure strong support. Others rely on large contributions to save time and expense that would go into fundraising. Telling a campaign how to raise funds interferes with campaign strategy as much as if the government were to subsidize candidates for advertising in some media but not others. Giving to some the seal of approval— "clean"—while denying it to others is not neutral.

Furthermore, the propriety of spending tax money is itself an issue in a campaign. Once the government has decided it has an interest in drawing candidates into the government financing system, it has a vested interest in increasing their odds of winning. Of course, some candidates will nonetheless choose to stay out of the system, often for ideological reasons—most probably that they favor lower levels of spending or limited government power to dispense subsidies. Which type of candidate do you believe is most likely to turn down government funding: a candidate who believes, on ideological grounds, in small, limited government, or a candidate who believes in larger, more activist government? As Justice Kagan might answer, "me too."

See Bradley A. Smith, *Separation of Campaign & State*, 81 Geo. Wash. L. Rev. 2038, 2094 (2013).

6. Although most government-financing systems are accompanied by restrictions on contributions and expenditures, the government could simply provide funds to candidates with no strings attached. What would be some of the advantages or disadvantages of such an approach? *See* Joel Fleishman & Pope McCorkle, *Level Up Rather than Level Down: Towards a New Theory of Campaign Finance*, 52 J.L. & Pol. 211 (1984).

7. Not surprisingly, there is voluminous literature about whether or not public financing addresses the problems it is intended to resolve. To a substantial extent, the many authors' views of public funding depend on the extent to which they see the present system as "corrupt" or "unequal," on their understandings of how politics does or should work in practice, and on their normative philosophical views

about equality and freedom. For a small taste of this literature, consider John Samples, *The Failure of Taxpayer Financing of Political Campaigns*, *in* WELFARE FOR POLITICIANS?: TAXPAYER FINANCING OF CAMPAIGNS 213 (John Samples ed., 2005); Patrick Basham, *Taxpayer Financing in Comparative Perspective*, *in* WELFARE FOR POLITICIANS?, *supra*, at 275; BRUCE ACKERMAN & IAN AYRES, VOTING WITH DOLLARS: A NEW PARADIGM FOR CAMPAIGN FINANCE (2002); Richard Briffault, *Public Funding and Democratic Elections*, 148 U. PA. L. REV. 563 (1999); Bradley A. Smith, *Some Problems with Taxpayer Funded Political Campaigns*, 148 U. PA. L. REV. 591 (1999).

Chapter 9

Anonymous Speech

A. Introduction

The right to speak may mean very little in practical terms if one will suffer negative consequences for speaking. It is for that reason that modern First Amendment doctrine forbids not only "prior restraints," but also the imposition of *ex post* punishments on protected speech, whether those punishments are criminal or civil. *See, e.g.*, *Brandenburg v. Ohio*, 395 U.S. 444 (1969) (striking down a criminal conviction for the advocacy of violence as violating the First Amendment); *New York Times Co. v. Sullivan*, 376 U.S. 254 (1964) (holding that a libel judgment against a newspaper violated the publisher's First Amendment rights). Further, even the *possibility* of subsequent punishment might produce a "chilling effect" by causing would-be speakers to censor themselves rather than risk negative consequences for speaking. The effect of chilling speech is not only to interfere with the free-speech rights of the speaker, but to deprive the rest of society of the benefits that come with the free exchange of ideas. Therefore, the Court has attempted to counter this chilling effect by protecting speech that might otherwise be suppressed through the prospect of future sanctions.[a]

Yet one may be dissuaded from speaking even if there is no risk of criminal or civil punishment imposed by government. Speech can be chilled because it might cause someone to lose a job, a contract, or a friend, even if the speech won't lead to imprisonment or a fine. If society is really interested in ensuring that everyone receives the benefit of the free exchange of ideas, perhaps we should try to ensure that speech isn't chilled from any of those sources.

While many speakers are eager to be publicly identified, or to endorse candidates or causes publicly, others are not. People may be reticent to speak if their words might upset a spouse, a boss, a friend, or a neighbor. Business executives may wish to speak in a personal capacity and not have their thoughts tied to the business, which might lead some consumers to boycott the enterprise, thus harming

---

a. For example, the overbreadth doctrine allows free-speech challenges to be raised by people whose own rights would not be implicated by a given restriction. *See, e.g.*, *Washington State Grange v. Washington State Republican Party*, 552 U.S. 442, 449 (2008) [p. 471]. Such a rule is contrary to the usual procedure, which requires that one assert his or her own claims. *See, e.g.*, *United States v. Salerno*, 481 U.S. 739, 745 (1987). Justice Thomas, noting the unusual nature of the overbreadth doctrine, has suggested that it be reexamined. *See United States v. Sineneng-Smith*, 590 U.S. __, __-__, 140 S. Ct. 1575, 1583–88 (2020) (Thomas, J., concurring).

employees and stockholders of the company. Proponents of civic and charitable organizations may not want their personal political views to create problems for their charitable endeavors. Others may wish to protect family, friends, or business associates from controversy.

One way of promoting that speech would be to protect speakers' anonymity. If speakers are able to keep their identities secret, then they will be less likely to face consequences for their speech, and as a result, they will be less likely to censor themselves. Further, speakers may wish to encourage the audience to focus on the merits of the speech itself, uncolored by whatever feelings the audience might have for the speaker. (The *Federalist Papers* were published anonymously primarily for that reason.) Thus, anonymity permits the speech to reach the public even when the speaker would not be willing to associate himself or herself publicly with the speech.

On the other hand, permitting speakers to be anonymous might lead to harmful results. If an anonymous speaker falsifies a story and defames someone, the victim of the defamation might have a hard time recovering. Likewise, if speech is obscene or reveals national-security secrets, perhaps the speaker should not be immune from the consequences of making the speech. Furthermore, anonymity itself might make it harder to evaluate the speech. Readers might find an argument more or less persuasive depending on the knowledge and biases of its author; if the readers do not know who the author is, they may have a more difficult time gauging the argument. Lastly, disclosure of a speaker's identity might provide useful information to society. If a politician is being supported by people aligned with a certain industry or interest group, perhaps the identity of the supporters is important information that can be used by voters in deciding whether to vote for that politician.

This Chapter considers the conflict between the interests in promoting speech and encouraging people to participate in politics, on the one hand, and, on the other, giving the public information about the identities of people who are attempting to influence politics. Because people can try to influence politics in different ways (as we have explored in Chapters 7 and 8), speakers may wish to remain anonymous when they are engaged in a variety of different tasks, from writing and publishing to contributing to campaigns and signing petitions. Accordingly, the following materials address not only disclosure of the actual physical speakers, but of the funders of speech as well.

To what extent should speakers and funders be permitted to remain anonymous, or, better put, what government interests are sufficient to justify forcing involuntary disclosure of the identities of speakers and funders? As you read the materials that follow, consider whether the speaker's interest in remaining anonymous and the government's interest in disclosure differ depending on the kind of speech that is involved.

B. The First Amendment Interest in Anonymity

National Association for the Advancement of Colored People v. Alabama ex rel. Patterson

Supreme Court of the United States

357 U.S. 449, 78 S. Ct. 1163, 2 L. Ed. 2d 1488 (1958)

Mr. Justice Harlan delivered the opinion of the Court [in which Mr. Chief Justice Warren, Mr. Justice Black, Mr. Justice Frankfurter, Mr. Justice Douglas, Mr. Justice Burton, Mr. Justice Clark, Mr. Justice Brennan, and Mr. Justice Whittaker join].

* * * The question presented is whether Alabama, consistently with the Due Process Clause of the Fourteenth Amendment, can compel petitioner to reveal to the State's Attorney General the names and addresses of all its Alabama members and agents, without regard to their positions or functions in the Association. * * *

Alabama has a statute similar to those of many other States which requires a foreign corporation, except as exempted, to qualify before doing business by filing its corporate charter with the Secretary of State and designating a place of business and an agent to receive service of process. The statute imposes a fine on a corporation transacting intrastate business before qualifying and provides for criminal prosecution of officers of such a corporation. The National Association for the Advancement of Colored People is a nonprofit membership corporation organized under the laws of New York. * * *

In 1956 the Attorney General of Alabama brought an equity suit in the State Circuit Court, Montgomery County, to enjoin the Association from conducting further activities within, and to oust it from, the State [on the ground that it was doing business in the State without complying with the qualification statute]. * * *

Petitioner * * * contended that its activities did not subject it to the qualification requirements of the statute and that in any event what the State sought to accomplish by its suit would violate rights to freedom of speech and assembly guaranteed under the Fourteenth Amendment to the Constitution of the United States. Before the date set for a hearing on this motion, the State moved for the production of a large number of the Association's records and papers, including bank statements, leases, deeds, and records containing the names and addresses of all Alabama "members" and "agents" of the Association. It alleged that all such documents were necessary for adequate preparation for the hearing, in view of petitioner's denial of the conduct of intrastate business within the meaning of the qualification statute. Over petitioner's objections, the court ordered the production of a substantial part of the requested records, including the membership lists, and postponed the hearing on the restraining order to a date later than the time ordered for production.

* * * [P]etitioner did not comply with the production order, and for this failure was adjudged in civil contempt and fined $10,000. The contempt judgment provided

that the fine would be subject to reduction or remission if compliance were forthcoming within five days but otherwise would be increased to $100,000.

At the end of the five-day period petitioner produced substantially all the data called for by the production order except its membership lists, as to which it contended that Alabama could not constitutionally compel disclosure, and moved to modify or vacate the contempt judgment, or stay it execution pending appellate review. This motion was denied. * * *

* * * Petitioner argues that in view of the facts and circumstances shown in the record, the effect of compelled disclosure of the membership lists will be to abridge the rights of its rank-and-file members to engage in lawful association in support of their common beliefs. It contends that governmental action which, although not directly suppressing association, nevertheless carries this consequence, can be justified only upon some overriding valid interest of the State.

Effective advocacy of both public and private points of view, particularly controversial ones, is undeniably enhanced by group association, as this Court has more than once recognized by remarking upon the close nexus between the freedoms of speech and assembly. It is beyond debate that freedom to engage in association for the advancement of beliefs and ideas is an inseparable aspect of the "liberty" assured by the Due Process Clause of the Fourteenth Amendment, which embraces freedom of speech. Of course, it is immaterial whether the beliefs sought to be advanced by association pertain to political, economic, religious or cultural matters, and state action which may have the effect of curtailing the freedom to associate is subject to the closest scrutiny.

The fact that Alabama, so far as is relevant to the validity of the contempt judgment presently under review, has taken no direct action to restrict the right of petitioner's members to associate freely, does not end inquiry into the effect of the production order. In the domain of these indispensable liberties, whether of speech, press, or association, the decisions of this Court recognize that abridgement of such rights, even though unintended, may inevitably follow from varied forms of governmental action. * * *

It is hardly a novel perception that compelled disclosure of affiliation with groups engaged in advocacy may constitute * * * a restraint on freedom of association[.] * * * Inviolability of privacy in group association may in many circumstances be indispensable to preservation of freedom of association, particularly where a group espouses dissident beliefs.

We think that the production order, in the respects here drawn in question, must be regarded as entailing the likelihood of a substantial restraint upon the exercise by petitioner's members of their right to freedom of association. Petitioner has made an uncontroverted showing that on past occasions revelation of the identity of its rank-and-file members has exposed these members to economic reprisal, loss of employment, threat of physical coercion, and other manifestations of public hostility. Under these circumstances, we think it apparent that compelled disclosure of petitioner's Alabama membership is likely to affect adversely the ability of petitioner and its members to pursue their collective effort to foster beliefs which they admittedly have the right to advocate, in that it may induce members to withdraw from the Association and dissuade others from joining it because of fear of exposure of their beliefs shown through their associations and of the consequences of this exposure.

It is not sufficient to answer, as the State does here, that whatever repressive effect compulsory disclosure of names of petitioner's members may have upon participation by Alabama citizens in petitioner's activities follows not from state action but from private community pressures. The crucial factor is the interplay of governmental and private action, for it is only after the initial exertion of state power represented by the production order that private action takes hold.

We turn to the final question whether Alabama has demonstrated an interest in obtaining the disclosures it seeks from petitioner which is sufficient to justify the deterrent effect which we have concluded these disclosures may well have on the free exercise by petitioner's members of their constitutionally protected right of association. Such a "subordinating interest of the State must be compelling," *Sweezy* v. *New Hampshire*, 354 U.S. 234, 265 [(1957)] (concurring opinion). It is not of moment that the State has here acted solely through its judicial branch, for whether legislative or judicial, it is still the application of state power which we are asked to scrutinize.

It is important to bear in mind that petitioner asserts no right to absolute immunity from state investigation, and no right to disregard Alabama's laws. As shown by its substantial compliance with the production order, petitioner does not deny Alabama's right to obtain from it such information as the State desires concerning the purposes of the Association and its activities within the State. Petitioner has not objected to divulging the identity of its members who are employed by or hold official positions with it. It has urged the rights solely of its ordinary rank-and-file members. This is therefore not analogous to a case involving the interest of a State in protecting its citizens in their dealings with paid solicitors or agents of foreign corporations by requiring identifications.

* * * The issues in the litigation commenced by Alabama by its bill in equity were whether the character of petitioner and its activities in Alabama had been such as to make petitioner subject to the registration statute, and whether the extent of petitioner's activities without qualifying suggested its permanent ouster from the State. Without intimating the slightest view upon the merits of these issues, we are unable to perceive that the disclosure of the names of petitioner's rank-and-file members has a substantial bearing on either of them. * * *

We hold that the immunity from state scrutiny of membership lists which the Association claims on behalf of its members is here so related to the right of the members to pursue their lawful private interests privately and to associate freely with others in so doing as to come within the protection of the Fourteenth Amendment.

And we conclude that Alabama has fallen short of showing a controlling justification for the deterrent effect on the free enjoyment of the right to associate which disclosure of membership lists is likely to have. Accordingly, the judgment of civil contempt and the $100,000 fine which resulted from petitioner's refusal to comply with the production order in this respect must fall. * * *

For the reasons stated, the judgment of the Supreme Court of Alabama must be reversed and the case remanded for proceedings not inconsistent with this opinion.

Reversed.

McIntyre v. Ohio Elections Commission

Supreme Court of the United States
514 U.S. 334, 115 S. Ct. 1511, 131 L. Ed. 2d 426 (1995)

JUSTICE STEVENS delivered the opinion of the Court [in which JUSTICE O'CONNOR, JUSTICE KENNEDY, JUSTICE SOUTER, JUSTICE GINSBURG, and JUSTICE BREYER join].

The question presented is whether an Ohio statute that prohibits the distribution of anonymous campaign literature is a "law . . . abridging the freedom of speech" within the meaning of the First Amendment.

On April 27, 1988, Margaret McIntyre distributed leaflets to persons attending a public meeting at the Blendon Middle School in Westerville, Ohio. At this meeting, the superintendent of schools planned to discuss an imminent referendum on a proposed school tax levy. The leaflets expressed Mrs. McIntyre's opposition to the levy. There is no suggestion that the text of her message was false, misleading, or libelous. She had composed and printed it on her home computer and had paid a professional printer to make additional copies. Some of the handbills identified her as the author; others merely purported to express the views of "CONCERNED PARENTS AND TAX PAYERS." Except for the help provided by her son and a friend, who placed some of the leaflets on car windshields in the school parking lot, Mrs. McIntyre acted independently.

While Mrs. McIntyre distributed her handbills, an official of the school district, who supported the tax proposal, advised her that the unsigned leaflets did not conform to the Ohio election laws. Undeterred, Mrs. McIntyre appeared at another meeting on the next evening and handed out more of the handbills.

The proposed school levy was defeated at the next two elections, but it finally passed on its third try in November 1988. Five months later, the same school official filed a complaint with the Ohio Elections Commission charging that Mrs. McIntyre's distribution of unsigned leaflets violated § 3599.09(A) of the Ohio Code.[3] The commission agreed and imposed a fine of $100. * * *

---

3. [The statute prohibits, *inter alia*, the printing or distribution of "any * * * publication which is designed to promote the nomination or election or defeat of a candidate, or to promote the adoption or defeat of any issue, or to influence the voters in any election, or make an expenditure for the purpose of financing political communications * * * unless there appears on such form of

Ohio maintains that the statute under review is a reasonable regulation of the electoral process. The State does not suggest that all anonymous publications are pernicious or that a statute totally excluding them from the marketplace of ideas would be valid. This is a wise (albeit implicit) concession, for the anonymity of an author is not ordinarily a sufficient reason to exclude her work product from the protections of the First Amendment.

"Anonymous pamphlets, leaflets, brochures and even books have played an important role in the progress of mankind." Great works of literature have frequently been produced by authors writing under assumed names.[4] Despite readers' curiosity and the public's interest in identifying the creator of a work of art, an author generally is free to decide whether or not to disclose his or her true identity. The decision in favor of anonymity may be motivated by fear of economic or official retaliation, by concern about social ostracism, or merely by a desire to preserve as much of one's privacy as possible. Whatever the motivation may be, at least in the field of literary endeavor, the interest in having anonymous works enter the marketplace of ideas unquestionably outweighs any public interest in requiring disclosure as a condition of entry. Accordingly, an author's decision to remain anonymous, like other decisions concerning omissions or additions to the content of a publication, is an aspect of the freedom of speech protected by the First Amendment.

The freedom to publish anonymously extends beyond the literary realm. In *Talley* [v. *California*, 362 U.S. 60 (1960)], the Court held that the First Amendment protects the distribution of unsigned handbills urging readers to boycott certain Los Angeles merchants who were allegedly engaging in discriminatory employment practices. Writing for the Court, Justice Black noted that "[p]ersecuted groups and sects from time to time throughout history have been able to criticize oppressive practices and laws either anonymously or not at all." *Id.*, at 64. * * * On occasion, quite apart from any threat of persecution, an advocate may believe her ideas will be more persuasive if her readers are unaware of her identity. Anonymity thereby provides a way for a writer who may be personally unpopular to ensure that readers will not prejudge her message simply because they do not like its proponent. Thus, even in the field of political rhetoric, where "the identity of the speaker is an important component of many attempts to persuade," *City of Ladue* v. *Gilleo*, 512 U.S. 43, 56 (1994), the most effective advocates have sometimes opted for anonymity. The specific holding in *Talley* related to advocacy of an economic boycott, but the Court's

---

publication in a conspicuous place or is contained within said statement the name and residence or business address of the chairman, treasurer, or secretary of the organization issuing the same, or the person who issues, makes, or is responsible therefor."]

4. American names such as Mark Twain (Samuel Langhorne Clemens) and O. Henry (William Sydney Porter) come readily to mind. Benjamin Franklin employed numerous different pseudonyms. Distinguished French authors such as Voltaire (Francois Marie Arouet) and George Sand (Amandine Aurore Lucie Dupin), and British authors such as George Eliot (Mary Ann Evans), Charles Lamb (sometimes wrote as "Elia"), and Charles Dickens (sometimes wrote as "Boz"), also published under assumed names. Indeed, some believe the works of Shakespeare were actually written by the Earl of Oxford rather than by William Shaksper of Stratford-on-Avon.

reasoning embraced a respected tradition of anonymity in the advocacy of political causes. This tradition is perhaps best exemplified by the secret ballot, the hard-won right to vote one's conscience without fear of retaliation.

California had defended the Los Angeles ordinance at issue in *Talley* as a law "aimed at providing a way to identify those responsible for fraud, false advertising and libel." We rejected that argument because nothing in the text or legislative history of the ordinance limited its application to those evils. * * * The Ohio statute likewise contains no language limiting its application to fraudulent, false, or libelous statements; to the extent, therefore, that Ohio seeks to justify § 3599.09(A) as a means to prevent the dissemination of untruths, its defense must fail for the same reason given in *Talley*. As the facts of this case demonstrate, the ordinance plainly applies even when there is no hint of falsity or libel.

Ohio's statute does, however, contain a different limitation: It applies only to unsigned documents designed to influence voters in an election. In contrast, the Los Angeles ordinance prohibited all anonymous handbilling "in any place under any circumstances." For that reason, Ohio correctly argues that *Talley* does not necessarily control the disposition of this case. We must, therefore, decide whether and to what extent the First Amendment's protection of anonymity encompasses documents intended to influence the electoral process.

Ohio places its principal reliance on cases such as *Anderson* v. *Celebrezze*, 460 U.S. 780 (1983) [p. 517]; *Storer v. Brown*, 415 U.S. 724 (1974) [p. 513]; and *Burdick* v. *Takushi*, 504 U.S. 428 (1992) [p. 990], in which we reviewed election code provisions governing the voting process itself. In those cases we * * * considered the relative interests of the State and the injured voters, and we evaluated the extent to which the State's interests necessitated the contested restrictions. * * *

* * * Unlike the statutory provisions challenged in *Storer* and *Anderson*, § 3599.09(A) of the Ohio Code does not control the mechanics of the electoral process. It is a regulation of pure speech. Moreover, even though this provision applies evenhandedly to advocates of differing viewpoints,[8] it is a direct regulation of the content of speech. * * * Furthermore, the category of covered documents is defined by their content—only those publications containing speech designed to influence the voters in an election need bear the required markings. Consequently, we are not faced with an ordinary election restriction; this case "involves a limitation on political expression subject to exacting scrutiny." * * *

* * * Indeed, the speech in which Mrs. McIntyre engaged—handing out leaflets in the advocacy of a politically controversial viewpoint—is the essence of First Amendment expression. That this advocacy occurred in the heat of a controversial referendum vote only strengthens the protection afforded to Mrs. McIntyre's

---

8. Arguably, the disclosure requirement places a more significant burden on advocates of unpopular causes than on defenders of the status quo. For purposes of our analysis, however, we assume the statute evenhandedly burdens all speakers who have a legitimate interest in remaining anonymous.

expression: Urgent, important, and effective speech can be no less protected than impotent speech, lest the right to speak be relegated to those instances when it is least needed. No form of speech is entitled to greater constitutional protection than Mrs. McIntyre's.

When a law burdens core political speech, we apply "exacting scrutiny," and we uphold the restriction only if it is narrowly tailored to serve an overriding state interest. * * * Ohio judges its interest in preventing fraudulent and libelous statements and its interest in providing the electorate with relevant information to be sufficiently compelling to justify the anonymous speech ban. * * *

Insofar as the interest in informing the electorate means nothing more than the provision of additional information that may either buttress or undermine the argument in a document, we think the identity of the speaker is no different from other components of the document's content that the author is free to include or exclude. * * * The simple interest in providing voters with additional relevant information does not justify a state requirement that a writer make statements or disclosures she would otherwise omit. Moreover, in the case of a handbill written by a private citizen who is not known to the recipient, the name and address of the author add little, if anything, to the reader's ability to evaluate the document's message. Thus, Ohio's informational interest is plainly insufficient to support the constitutionality of its disclosure requirement.

The state interest in preventing fraud and libel stands on a different footing. We agree with Ohio's submission that this interest carries special weight during election campaigns when false statements, if credited, may have serious adverse consequences for the public at large. Ohio does not, however, rely solely on § 3599.09(A) to protect that interest. Its Election Code includes detailed and specific prohibitions against making or disseminating false statements during political campaigns. These regulations apply both to candidate elections and to issue-driven ballot measures. * * *

As this case demonstrates, the prohibition encompasses documents that are not even arguably false or misleading. It applies not only to the activities of candidates and their organized supporters, but also to individuals acting independently and using only their own modest resources. It applies not only to elections of public officers, but also to ballot issues that present neither a substantial risk of libel nor any potential appearance of corrupt advantage. It applies not only to leaflets distributed on the eve of an election, when the opportunity for reply is limited, but also to those distributed months in advance. It applies no matter what the character or strength of the author's interest in anonymity. Moreover, as this case also demonstrates, the absence of the author's name on a document does not necessarily protect either that person or a distributor of a forbidden document from being held responsible for compliance with the Election Code. Nor has the State explained why it can more easily enforce the direct bans on disseminating false documents against anonymous authors and distributors than against wrongdoers who might use false names and addresses in an attempt to avoid detection. We recognize that a State's enforcement interest might justify a more limited identification requirement, but Ohio has shown scant cause for inhibiting the leafletting at issue here. * * *

Under our Constitution, anonymous pamphleteering is not a pernicious, fraudulent practice, but an honorable tradition of advocacy and of dissent. Anonymity is a shield from the tyranny of the majority. It thus exemplifies the purpose behind the Bill of Rights, and of the First Amendment in particular: to protect unpopular individuals from retaliation—and their ideas from suppression—at the hand of an intolerant society. The right to remain anonymous may be abused when it shields fraudulent conduct. But political speech by its nature will sometimes have unpalatable consequences, and, in general, our society accords greater weight to the value of free speech than to the dangers of its misuse. Ohio has not shown that its interest in preventing the misuse of anonymous election-related speech justifies a prohibition of all uses of that speech. The State may, and does, punish fraud directly. But it cannot seek to punish fraud indirectly by indiscriminately outlawing a category of speech, based on its content, with no necessary relationship to the danger sought to be prevented. One would be hard pressed to think of a better example of the pitfalls of Ohio's blunderbuss approach than the facts of the case before us.

The judgment of the Ohio Supreme Court is reversed.

It is so ordered.

JUSTICE GINSBURG, concurring. * * *

In for a calf is not always in for a cow. The Court's decision finds unnecessary, overintrusive, and inconsistent with American ideals the State's imposition of a fine on an individual leafleteer who, within her local community, spoke her mind, but sometimes not her name. We do not thereby hold that the State may not in other, larger circumstances require the speaker to disclose its interest by disclosing its identity. Appropriately leaving open matters not presented by McIntyre's handbills, the Court recognizes that a State's interest in protecting an election process "might justify a more limited identification requirement." But the Court has convincingly explained why Ohio lacks "cause for inhibiting the leafletting at issue here."

JUSTICE THOMAS, concurring in the judgment.

I agree with the majority's conclusion that Ohio's election law is inconsistent with the First Amendment. I would apply, however, a different methodology to this case. Instead of asking whether "an honorable tradition" of anonymous speech has existed throughout American history, or what the "value" of anonymous speech might be, we should determine whether the phrase "freedom of speech, or of the press," as originally understood, protected anonymous political leafletting. I believe that it did. * * *

Unfortunately, we have no record of discussions of anonymous political expression either in the First Congress, which drafted the Bill of Rights, or in the state ratifying conventions. Thus, our analysis must focus on the practices and beliefs held by the Founders concerning anonymous political articles and pamphlets. * * *

There is little doubt that the Framers engaged in anonymous political writing. The essays in the Federalist Papers, published under the pseudonym of "Publius," are only the most famous example of the outpouring of anonymous political writing that occurred during the ratification of the Constitution. Of course, the simple fact that the Framers engaged in certain conduct does not necessarily prove that they forbade its prohibition by the government. In this case, however, the historical evidence indicates that Founding-era Americans opposed attempts to require that anonymous authors reveal their identities on the ground that forced disclosure violated the "freedom of the press."

For example, the earliest and most famous American experience with freedom of the press, the 1735 Zenger trial, centered around anonymous political pamphlets. The case involved a printer, John Peter Zenger, who refused to reveal the anonymous authors of published attacks on the Crown Governor of New York. When the Governor and his council could not discover the identity of the authors, they prosecuted Zenger himself for seditious libel. Although the case set the Colonies afire for its example of a jury refusing to convict a defendant of seditious libel against Crown authorities, it also signified at an early moment the extent to which anonymity and the freedom of the press were intertwined in the early American mind.

During the Revolutionary and Ratification periods, the Framers' understanding of the relationship between anonymity and freedom of the press became more explicit. In 1779, for example, the Continental Congress attempted to discover the identity of an anonymous article in the Pennsylvania Packet signed by the name "Leonidas." Leonidas, who actually was Dr. Benjamin Rush, had attacked the Members of Congress for causing inflation throughout the States and for engaging in embezzlement and fraud. Elbridge Gerry, a delegate from Massachusetts, moved to haul the printer of the newspaper before Congress to answer questions concerning Leonidas. Several Members of Congress then rose to oppose Gerry's motion on the ground that it invaded the freedom of the press. * * * In the end, these arguments persuaded the assembled delegates, who "sat mute" in response to Gerry's motion. Neither the printer nor Dr. Rush ever appeared before Congress to answer for their publication.

At least one of the state legislatures shared Congress' view that the freedom of the press protected anonymous writing. Also in 1779, the upper house of the New Jersey State Legislature attempted to punish the author of a satirical attack on the Governor and the College of New Jersey (now Princeton) who had signed his work "Cincinnatus." Attempting to enforce the crime of seditious libel, the State Legislative Council ordered Isaac Collins—the printer and editor of the newspaper in which the article had appeared—to reveal the author's identity. Refusing, Collins declared: "Were I to comply . . . I conceive I should betray the trust reposed in me, and be far from acting as a faithful guardian of the Liberty of the Press." Apparently, the State Assembly agreed that anonymity was protected by the freedom of the press, as it voted to support the editor and publisher by frustrating the council's orders. * * *

To be sure, there was some controversy among newspaper editors over publishing anonymous articles and pamphlets. But this controversy was resolved in a manner that indicates that the freedom of the press protected an author's anonymity. The tempest began when a Federalist, writing anonymously himself, expressed fear that "emissaries" of "foreign enemies" would attempt to scuttle the Constitution by "fill[ing] the press with objections" against the proposal. He called upon printers to refrain from publishing when the author "chooses to remain concealed." Benjamin Russell, the editor of the prominent Federalist newspaper the Massachusetts Centinel, immediately adopted a policy of refusing to publish Anti-Federalist pieces unless the author provided his identity to be "handed to the publick, if required." A few days later, the Massachusetts Gazette announced that it would emulate the example set by the Massachusetts Centinel. * * * Federalists expressed similar thoughts in Philadelphia.

Ordinarily, the fact that some founding-era editors as a matter of policy decided not to publish anonymous articles would seem to shed little light upon what the Framers thought the *government* could do. The widespread criticism raised by the Anti-Federalists, however, who were the driving force behind the demand for a Bill of Rights, indicates that they believed the freedom of the press to include the right to author anonymous political articles and pamphlets. That most other Americans shared this understanding is reflected in the Federalists' hasty retreat before the withering criticism of their assault on the liberty of the press [with the Centinel publishing anonymous Anti-Federalist essays and the Gazette refusing to release the names of Anti-Federalist authors]. * * *

The controversy over Federalist attempts to prohibit anonymous political speech is significant for several reasons. First, the Anti-Federalists clearly believed the right to author and publish anonymous political articles and pamphlets was protected by the liberty of the press. Second, although printers' editorial policies did not constitute state action, the Anti-Federalists believed that the Federalists were merely flexing the governmental powers they would fully exercise upon the Constitution's ratification. Third, and perhaps most significantly, it appears that the Federalists agreed with the Anti-Federalist critique. * * * When Federalist attempts to ban anonymity are followed by a sharp, widespread Anti-Federalist defense in the name of the freedom of the press, and then by an open Federalist retreat on the issue, I must conclude that both Anti-Federalists and Federalists believed that the freedom of the press included the right to publish without revealing the author's name. * * *

The large quantity of newspapers and pamphlets the Framers produced during the various crises of their generation show the remarkable extent to which the Framers relied upon anonymity. During the break with Great Britain, the revolutionaries employed pseudonyms both to conceal their identity from Crown authorities and to impart a message. * * *

[A]fter the Ratification, * * * anonymous political pamphlets and newspaper articles remained the favorite media for expressing views on candidates [and issues].

* * * James Madison and Alexander Hamilton, for example, resorted to pseudonyms in the famous "Helvidius" and "Pacificus" debates over President Washington's declaration of neutrality in the war between the British and French. Anonymous writings continued in such Republican papers as the Aurora and Federalists [*sic*] organs such as the Gazette of the United States at least until the election of Thomas Jefferson. * * *

While, like JUSTICE SCALIA, I am loath to overturn a century of practice shared by almost all of the States, I believe the historical evidence from the framing outweighs recent tradition. * * * Because the majority has adopted an analysis that is largely unconnected to the Constitution's text and history, I concur only in the judgment.

JUSTICE SCALIA, with whom THE CHIEF JUSTICE [REHNQUIST] joins, dissenting. * * *

* * * Anonymous electioneering was not prohibited by law in 1791 or in 1868. In fact, it was widely practiced at the earlier date, an understandable legacy of the revolutionary era in which political dissent could produce governmental reprisal. * * * The practice of anonymous electioneering may have been less general in 1868, when the Fourteenth Amendment was adopted, but at least as late as 1837 it was respectable enough to be engaged in by Abraham Lincoln.

But to prove that anonymous electioneering was used frequently is not to establish that it is a constitutional right. Quite obviously, not every restriction upon expression that did not exist in 1791 or in 1868 is *ipso facto* unconstitutional, or else modern election laws such as those involved in *Burson* v. *Freeman*, 504 U.S. 191 (1992) [p. 1024] [limiting electioneering within a certain distance of polling places], and *Buckley* v. *Valeo* would be prohibited, as would (to mention only a few other categories) modern antinoise regulation * * * and modern parade-permitting regulation[.] * * *

[JUSTICE THOMAS's] concurrence recounts * * * pre- and post-Revolution examples of defense of anonymity in the name of "freedom of the press," but not a single one involves the context of restrictions imposed in connection with a free, democratic election, which is all that is at issue here. For many of them, moreover, * * * the issue of anonymity was incidental to the (unquestionably free-speech) issue of whether criticism of the government could be *punished* by the state.

Thus, the sum total of the historical evidence marshaled by the concurrence for the principle of *constitutional entitlement* to anonymous electioneering is partisan claims in the debate on ratification (which was *almost* like an election) that a viewpoint-based restriction on anonymity by newspaper editors violates freedom of speech. * * *

What we have, then, is the most difficult case for determining the meaning of the Constitution. No accepted existence of governmental restrictions of the sort at issue here demonstrates their constitutionality, but neither can their nonexistence clearly be attributed to constitutional objections. In such a case, constitutional adjudication necessarily involves not just history but judgment: judgment as to whether the government action under challenge is consonant with the concept of the protected freedom (in this case, the freedom of speech and of the press) that existed when the constitutional protection was accorded. In the present case, *absent other indication*, I would be inclined to agree with the concurrence that a society which used anonymous political debate so regularly would not regard as constitutional even moderate restrictions made to improve the election process. (I would, however, want further evidence of common practice in 1868, since I doubt that the Fourteenth Amendment time-warped the post-Civil War States back to the Revolution.)

But there *is* other indication, of the most weighty sort: the widespread and long-standing traditions of our people. Principles of liberty fundamental enough to have been embodied within constitutional guarantees are not readily erased from the Nation's consciousness. A governmental practice that has become general throughout the United States, and particularly one that has the validation of long, accepted usage, bears a strong presumption of constitutionality. And that is what we have before us here. Ohio Rev. Code Ann. § 3599.09(A) was enacted by the General Assembly of the State of Ohio almost 80 years ago. Even at the time of its adoption, there was nothing unique or extraordinary about it. The earliest statute of this sort was adopted by Massachusetts in 1890, little more than 20 years after the Fourteenth Amendment was ratified. No less than 24 States had similar laws by the end of World War I, and today every State of the Union except California has one, as does the District of Columbia, and as does the Federal Government where advertising relating to candidates for federal office is concerned. Such a universal and long-established American legislative practice must be given precedence, I think, over historical and academic speculation regarding a restriction that assuredly does not go to the heart of free speech. * * *

The Court says that the State has not explained "why it can more easily enforce the direct bans on disseminating false documents against anonymous authors and distributors than against wrongdoers who might use false names and addresses in an attempt to avoid detection." I am not sure what this complicated comparison means. I am sure, however, that (1) a person who is required to put his name to a document is much less likely to lie than one who can lie anonymously, and (2) the distributor of a leaflet which is unlawful because it is anonymous runs much more risk of immediate detection and punishment than the distributor of a leaflet which is unlawful because it is false. Thus, people will be more likely to observe a signing requirement than a naked "no falsity" requirement; and, having observed that requirement, will then be significantly less likely to lie in what they have signed.

But the usefulness of a signing requirement lies not only in promoting observance of the law against campaign falsehoods (though that alone is enough to sustain it). It lies also in promoting a civil and dignified level of campaign debate—which the State has no power to command, but ample power to encourage by such undemanding measures as a signature requirement. Observers of the past few national elections have expressed concern about the increase of character assassination—"mudslinging" is the colloquial term—engaged in by political candidates and their supporters to the detriment of the democratic process. Not all of this, in fact not much of it, consists of actionable untruth; most is innuendo, or demeaning characterization, or mere disclosure of items of personal life that have no bearing upon suitability for office. Imagine how much all of this would increase if it could be done anonymously. The principal impediment against it is the reluctance of most individuals and organizations to be publicly associated with uncharitable and uncivil expression. Consider, moreover, the increased potential for "dirty tricks." It is not unheard-of for campaign operatives to circulate material over the name of their opponents or their opponents' supporters (a violation of election laws) in order to attract or alienate certain interest groups. How much easier—and sanction free!—it would be to circulate anonymous material (for example, a *really* tasteless, though not actionably false, attack upon one's own candidate) with the hope and expectation that it will be attributed to, and held against, the other side. * * *

We have approved much more onerous disclosure requirements in the name of fair elections. In *Buckley* v. *Valeo*, we upheld provisions of the Federal Election Campaign Act that required private individuals to report to the Federal Election Commission independent expenditures made for communications advocating the election or defeat of a candidate for federal office. Our primary rationale for upholding this provision was that it served an "informational interest" by "increas[ing] the fund of information concerning those who support the candidates." The provision before us here serves the same informational interest, as well as more important interests, which I have discussed above. * * *

I respectfully dissent.

Notes and Questions

1. *Problem.* Mac Marga, a successful local businessman, has asked your advice. His state has a law identical to that in *McIntyre*. The school district covering his city of 200,000 people has placed a proposed school tax levy on the ballot. Marga believes that the District does not really need the money, and that high taxes are destroying the city's economic base and could force his company to relocate. He wants his corporation, the Marga Corporation, to spend $70,000 on radio, television, and newspaper ads to help defeat the levy. Marga's children attend public schools in the District, however, and he is concerned that if he is associated with efforts to defeat the levy, his children will be discriminated against by teachers and administrators when competing for spots on athletic teams, in other extra-curricular activities, and in grades. He wants to know if he can simply list the ads as having been paid for by "Concerned Taxpayers." What do you tell him? What if Marga makes the expenditures as an individual, rather than through his corporation?

2. *Problem.* Tony Teacher has announced his candidacy for school board. A former president of the local teachers union affiliate, he has the support of most of the teachers in the district. He strongly supports higher taxes to improve the school district's educational programs. Sally, a small-business owner, thinks taxes are already

too high. She wishes to spend $2,500 on leaflets urging Teacher's defeat, but she is concerned about having her name on the leaflets, as required by state law, because her husband is a teacher in the same school where Tony Teacher works. She wants to know if she must comply with the law requiring all campaign material to include the name of the person paying for it. What do you advise?

3. Why do you think the school officials might have waited until after the levy had passed to file a complaint against Ms. McIntyre? What interest were they attempting to vindicate? What harm, if any, was caused by listing the flyers as paid for by "Concerned Parents and Taxpayers" (which McIntyre and her husband were) rather than by "Margaret McIntyre"?

4. Even as it ruled for McIntyre, the Supreme Court suggested that the state had a legitimate interest in preventing fraudulent speech. Does this interest still exist after *United States v. Alvarez*, 567 U.S. 709 (2012) [p. 575]?

5. As the Problems in Notes 1 and 2 demonstrate, *McIntyre* leaves many unanswered questions about its scope. Is it limited to its particular facts? Does it apply only to individuals? To individuals, such as McIntyre, engaged in small scale activities? How small? Does it apply in candidate races, or only in ballot-issue campaigns?

C. Reporting and Disclosure of Campaign Contributions and Expenditures

In 1890, New York passed the nation's first law requiring disclosure of campaign contributions and expenditures. The first federal "publicity act" was passed in 1910. *See* EARL R. SIKES, STATE AND FEDERAL CORRUPT PRACTICES LEGISLATION 122, 284–291 (1928). Mandatory disclosure of campaign contributions and expenditures has been a mainstay of campaign-finance law, both in the United States and internationally, ever since. *See* Joel W. Johnson, *Democracy and Disclosure: Electoral Systems and the Regulation of Political Finance*, 7 ELECTION L.J. 325 (2008).

As of 2020, every U.S. state has laws requiring disclosure of at least some campaign contributions, and most also require some disclosure of both candidate expenditures and independent expenditures. *See* National Conference of State Legislatures, *Campaign Finance Laws: An Overview* (2015). Even many of the staunchest opponents of campaign-contribution and -expenditure regulation favor disclosure as an acceptable alternative to greater regulation. *See e.g.* JOHN SAMPLES, THE FALLACY OF CAMPAIGN FINANCE REFORM 272–86 (2006); Kathleen M. Sullivan, *Political Money and Freedom and Speech*, 30 U. C. DAVIS LAW REV. 1663, 1668 (1997). Indeed, so firmly rooted are disclosure laws in the regulatory landscape that one congressional reform advocate is reported to have declared that disclosure was "not regulation." *See* Bradley A. Smith, *In Defense of Political Ano-nymity*, 20 CITY J. 74, 75 (2010).

Yet disclosure laws are not free from controversy. As seen in the previous sec-tion, the Supreme Court has a long tradition of protecting anonymous speech, *see Thomas v. Collins*, 323 U.S. 516 (1945); *Talley v. California*, 362 U.S. 60 (1960); *McIntyre v. Ohio Elections Commission*, 514 U.S. 334 (1995) [p. 922]; *Watchtower Bible & Tract Society v. Village of Stratton*, 536 U.S. 150 (2002). It is not surprising then, that both *Buckley v. Valeo*, 424 U.S. 1 (1976), below, and *McConnell v. Federal Election Commission*, 540 U.S. 93 (2003) [p. 941], involved challenges to disclosure provisions of the Federal Election Campaign Act.

Buckley v. Valeo

Supreme Court of the United States

424 U.S. 1, 96 S. Ct. 612, 46 L. Ed. 2d 659 (1976)

PER CURIAM. [The portions of the opinion reprinted here are joined by MR. JUSTICE BRENNAN, MR. JUSTICE STEWART, MR. JUSTICE MARSHALL, MR. JUSTICE BLACKMUN, MR. JUSTICE POWELL, and MR. JUSTICE REHNQUIST.] * * *

II. Reporting and Disclosure Requirements

Unlike the limitations on contributions and expenditures imposed by 18 U.S.C. §608, the disclosure requirements of the Act, 2 U.S.C. §431 *et seq.*, are not chal-lenged by appellants as *per se* unconstitutional restrictions on the exercise of First Amendment freedoms of speech and association. Indeed, appellants argue that "narrowly drawn disclosure requirements are the proper solution to virtually all of the evils Congress sought to remedy." The particular requirements embodied in the Act are attacked as overbroad—both in their application to minor-party and inde-pendent candidates and in their extension to contributions as small as $11 or $101. Appellants also challenge the provision for disclosure by those who make inde-pendent contributions and expenditures, §434(e). The Court of Appeals found no constitutional infirmities in the provisions challenged here. We affirm the determi-nation on overbreadth and hold that §434(e), if narrowly construed, also is within constitutional bounds. * * *

The Act presently under review replaced all prior disclosure laws. Its primary disclosure provisions impose reporting obligations on "political committees" and candidates. "Political committee" is defined in §431(d) as a group of persons that receives "contributions" or makes "expenditures" of over $1,000 in a calendar year. * * *

Each political committee is required to register with the Commission and to keep detailed records of both contributions and expenditures. These records must include the name and address of everyone making a contribution in excess of $10, along with the date and amount of the contribution. If a person's contributions aggregate more than $100, his occupation and principal place of business are also to be included.[b] These files are subject to periodic audits and field investigations by the Commission.

Each committee and each candidate also is required to file quarterly reports. The reports are to contain detailed financial information, including the full name, mailing address, occupation, and principal place of business of each person who has contributed over $100[c] in a calendar year, as well as the amount and date of the contributions. They are to be made available by the Commission "for public inspection and copying." Every candidate for federal office is required to designate a "principal campaign committee," which is to receive reports of contributions and expenditures made on the candidate's behalf from other political committees and to compile and file these reports, together with its own statements, with the Commission.

Every individual or group, other than a political committee or candidate, who makes "contributions" or "expenditures" of over $100[d] in a calendar year "other than by contribution to a political committee or candidate" is required to file a statement with the Commission. Any violation of these recordkeeping and reporting provisions is punishable by a fine * * * or a prison term * * *, or both.

A. General Principles

Unlike the overall limitations on contributions and expenditures, the disclosure requirements impose no ceiling on campaign-related activities. But we have repeatedly found that compelled disclosure, in itself, can seriously infringe on privacy of association and belief guaranteed by the First Amendment. *E.g., Gibson* v. *Florida Legislative Comm.*, 372 U.S. 539 (1963); *NAACP* v. *Button*, 371 U.S. 415 (1963); *Shelton* v. *Tucker*, 364 U.S. 479 (1960); *Bates* v. *Little Rock*, 361 U.S. 516 (1960); *NAACP* v. *Alabama*, 357 U.S. 449 (1958) [p. 919].

We long have recognized that significant encroachments on First Amendment rights of the sort that compelled disclosure imposes cannot be justified by a mere showing of some legitimate governmental interest. Since *NAACP* v. *Alabama* we have required that the subordinating interests of the State must survive exacting scrutiny. We also have insisted that there be a "relevant correlation" or "substantial relation" between the governmental interest and the information required to be disclosed. This type of scrutiny is necessary even if any deterrent effect on the exercise of First Amendment rights arises, not through direct government action, but indirectly as an unintended but inevitable result of the government's conduct in requiring disclosure.

Appellees argue that the disclosure requirements of the Act differ significantly from those at issue in *NAACP* v. *Alabama* and its progeny because the Act only

---

b. The thresholds in this paragraph are, as of 2020, $50 and $200, respectively. *See* 52 U.S.C. §§ 30102(c)(2), (3). In inflation-adjusted terms, the 1974 limits of $10 and $100 would be $55 and $550 today. Accordingly, in "real" dollars, the current $50 limit is almost equivalent to the limit in 1974, while the current $200 limit is less than 40% of the limit in 1974. —Eds.

c. $200 as of 2020. *See* 52 U.S.C. § 30104(b)(3). —Eds.

d. $250 as of 2020. *See* 52 U.S.C. § 30104(c)(1). —Eds.

requires disclosure of the names of contributors and does not compel political organizations to submit the names of their members.

[G]roup association is protected because it enhances "[e]ffective advocacy." The right to join together "for the advancement of beliefs and ideas" is diluted if it does not include the right to pool money through contributions, for funds are often essential if "advocacy" is to be truly or optimally "effective." Moreover, the invasion of privacy of belief may be as great when the information sought concerns the giving and spending of money as when it concerns the joining of organizations, for "[f]inancial transactions can reveal much about a person's activities, associations, and beliefs." Our past decisions have not drawn fine lines between contributors and members but have treated them interchangeably. In *Bates*, for example, we applied the principles of *NAACP* v. *Alabama* and reversed convictions for failure to comply with a city ordinance that required the disclosure of "dues, assessments, and contributions paid, by whom and when paid."

The strict test established by *NAACP* v. *Alabama* is necessary because compelled disclosure has the potential for substantially infringing the exercise of First Amendment rights. But we have acknowledged that there are governmental interests sufficiently important to outweigh the possibility of infringement, particularly when the "free functioning of our national institutions" is involved.

The governmental interests sought to be vindicated by the disclosure requirements are of this magnitude. They fall into three categories. First, disclosure provides the electorate with information "as to where political campaign money comes from and how it is spent by the candidate" in order to aid the voters in evaluating those who seek federal office. It allows voters to place each candidate in the political spectrum more precisely than is often possible solely on the basis of party labels and campaign speeches. The sources of a candidate's financial support also alert the voter to the interests to which a candidate is most likely to be responsive and thus facilitate predictions of future performance in office.

Second, disclosure requirements deter actual corruption and avoid the appearance of corruption by exposing large contributions and expenditures to the light of publicity. This exposure may discourage those who would use money for improper purposes either before or after the election. A public armed with information about a candidate's most generous supporters is better able to detect any post-election special favors that may be given in return. And * * * Congress could reasonably conclude that full disclosure during an election campaign tends "to prevent the corrupt use of money to affect elections." In enacting these requirements, it may have been mindful of Mr. Justice Brandeis' advice: "Publicity is justly commended as a remedy for social and industrial diseases. Sunlight is said to be the best of disinfectants; electric light the most efficient policeman."

Third, and not least significant, recordkeeping, reporting, and disclosure requirements are an essential means of gathering the data necessary to detect violations of the contribution limitations described [in Part I of the opinion, reprinted in Chapter 8].

The disclosure requirements, as a general matter, directly serve substantial governmental interests. In determining whether these interests are sufficient to justify the requirements we must look to the extent of the burden that they place on individual rights.

It is undoubtedly true that public disclosure of contributions to candidates and political parties will deter some individuals who otherwise might contribute. In some instances, disclosure may even expose contributors to harassment or retaliation. These are not insignificant burdens on individual rights, and they must be weighed carefully against the interests which Congress has sought to promote by this legislation. In this process, we note and agree with appellants' concession that disclosure requirements—certainly in most applications—appear to be the least restrictive means of curbing the evils of campaign ignorance and corruption that Congress found to exist. Appellants argue, however, that the balance tips against disclosure when it is required of contributors to certain parties and candidates. We turn now to this contention.

B. Application to Minor Parties and Independents

Appellants contend that the Act's requirements are overbroad insofar as they apply to contributions to minor parties and independent candidates because the governmental interest in this information is minimal and the danger of significant infringement on First Amendment rights is greatly increased.

In *NAACP* v. *Alabama*, the organization had "made an uncontroverted showing that on past occasions revelation of the identity of its rank-and-file members [had] exposed these members to economic reprisal, loss of employment, threat of physical coercion, and other manifestations of public hostility," and the State was unable to show that the disclosure it sought had a "substantial bearing" on the issues it sought to clarify. Under those circumstances, the Court held that "whatever interest the State may have in [disclosure] has not been shown to be sufficient to overcome petitioner's constitutional objections." * * * [However], *NAACP* v. *Alabama* is inapposite where, as here, any serious infringement on First Amendment rights brought about by the compelled disclosure of contributors is highly speculative.

It is true that the governmental interest in disclosure is diminished when the contribution in question is made to a minor party with little chance of winning an election. As minor parties usually represent definite and publicized viewpoints, there may be less need to inform the voters of the interests that specific candidates represent. Major parties encompass candidates of greater diversity. In many situations the label "Republican" or "Democrat" tells a voter little. The candidate who bears it may be supported by funds from the far right, the far left, or any place in between on the political spectrum. It is less likely that a candidate of, say, the Socialist Labor Party will represent interests that cannot be discerned from the party's ideological position.

The Government's interest in deterring the "buying" of elections and the undue influence of large contributors on officeholders also may be reduced where contributions to a minor party or an independent candidate are concerned, for it is less likely that the candidate will be victorious. But a minor party sometimes can play a significant role in an election. Even when a minor-party candidate has little or no chance of winning, he may be encouraged by major-party interests in order to divert votes from other major-party contenders.

We are not unmindful that the damage done by disclosure to the associational interests of the minor parties and their members and to supporters of independents could be significant. These movements are less likely to have a sound financial base and thus are more vulnerable to falloffs in contributions. In some instances, fears of reprisal may deter contributions to the point where the movement cannot survive. The public interest also suffers if that result comes to pass, for there is a consequent reduction in the free circulation of ideas both within and without the political arena.

There could well be a case, similar to those before the Court in *NAACP* v. *Alabama* and *Bates*, where the threat to the exercise of First Amendment rights is so serious and the state interest furthered by disclosure so insubstantial that the Act's requirements cannot be constitutionally applied. But no appellant in this case has tendered record evidence of the sort proffered in *NAACP* v. *Alabama*. * * * On this record, the substantial public interest in disclosure identified by the legislative history of this Act outweighs the harm generally alleged. * * *

C. Section 434(e)

Section 434(e) requires "[e]very person (other than a political committee or candidate) who makes contributions or expenditures" aggregating over $100 in a calendar year "other than by contribution to a political committee or candidate" to file a statement with the Commission. Unlike the other disclosure provisions, this section does not seek the contribution list of any association. Instead, it requires direct disclosure of what an individual or group contributes or spends. * * *

* * * Section 434(e) is part of Congress' effort to achieve "total disclosure" by reaching "every kind of political activity" in order to insure that the voters are fully informed and to achieve through publicity the maximum deterrence to corruption and undue influence possible. The provision is responsive to the legitimate fear that efforts would be made, as they had been in the past, to avoid the disclosure requirements by routing financial support of candidates through avenues not explicitly covered by the general provisions of the Act.

In its effort to be all-inclusive, however, the provision raises serious problems of vagueness, particularly treacherous where, as here, the violation of its terms carries criminal penalties and fear of incurring these sanctions may deter those who seek to exercise protected First Amendment rights.

Section 434(e) applies to "[e]very person . . . who makes contributions or expenditures." "Contributions" and "expenditures" are defined in parallel provisions in terms of the use of money or other valuable assets "for the purpose of . . . influenc-ing" the nomination or election of candidates for federal office. It is the ambiguity of this phrase that poses constitutional problems. * * *

* * * The general requirement that "political committees" and candidates disclose their expenditures could raise * * * vagueness problems, for "political committee" is defined only in terms of amount of annual "contributions" and "expenditures," and could be interpreted to reach groups engaged purely in issue discussion. * * * To fulfill the purposes of the Act, ["political committee"] need only encompass organizations that are under the control of a candidate or the major purpose of which is the nomination or election of a candidate. Expenditures of candidates and of "political committees" so construed can be assumed to fall within the core area sought to be addressed by Congress. They are, by definition, campaign related.

But when the maker of the expenditure is not within these categories—when it is an individual other than a candidate or a group other than a "political commit-tee"—the relation of the information sought to the purposes of the Act may be too remote. To insure that the reach of § 434(e) is not impermissibly broad, we construe "expenditure" for purposes of that section in the same way we construed the terms of § 608(e)[e]—to reach only funds used for communications that expressly advocate the election or defeat of a clearly identified candidate. This reading is directed pre-cisely to that spending that is unambiguously related to the campaign of a particu-lar federal candidate.

In summary, § 434(e) as construed, imposes independent reporting require-ments on individuals and groups that are not candidates or political committees only in the following circumstances: (1) when they make contributions earmarked for political purposes or authorized or requested by a candidate or his agent, to some person other than a candidate or political committee, and (2) when they make expenditures for communications that expressly advocate the election or defeat of a clearly identified candidate.

[Section] 434(e), as construed, bears a sufficient relationship to a substantial governmental interest. As narrowed, § 434(e) * * * does not reach all partisan dis-cussion for it only requires disclosure of those expenditures that expressly advo-cate a particular election result. This might have been fatal if the only purpose of § 434(e) were to stem corruption or its appearance by closing a loophole in the general disclosure requirements. But the disclosure provisions, including § 434(e), serve another, informational interest, and even as construed § 434(e) increases the fund of information concerning those who support the candidates. It goes beyond

e. As discussed in Chapter 8, § 608(e) imposed a $1000 limit on expenditures "relative to a clearly identified candidate." The Court held that "in order to preserve the provision against inval-idation on vagueness grounds, § 608(e)(1) must be construed to apply only to expenditures for communications that in express terms advocate the election or defeat of a clearly identified candi-date for federal office." 424 U.S. at 44; *see also id.* n.52. —Eds.

the general disclosure requirements to shed the light of publicity on spending that is unambiguously campaign related but would not otherwise be reported because it takes the form of independent expenditures or of contributions to an individual or group not itself required to report the names of its contributors. * * * [I]t is not fatal that § 434(e) encompasses purely independent expenditures uncoordinated with a particular candidate or his agent. The corruption potential of these expenditures may be significantly different, but the informational interest can be as strong as it is in coordinated spending, for disclosure helps voters to define more of the candidates' constituencies.

D. Thresholds

Appellants' third contention, based on alleged overbreadth, is that the monetary thresholds in the record-keeping and reporting provisions lack a substantial nexus with the claimed governmental interests, for the amounts involved are too low even to attract the attention of the candidate, much less have a corrupting influence.

The provisions contain two thresholds. Records are to be kept by political committees of the names and addresses of those who make contributions in excess of $10, § 432(c)(2), and these records are subject to Commission audit, § 438(a)(8). If a person's contributions to a committee or candidate aggregate more than $100, his name and address, as well as his occupation and principal place of business, are to be included in reports filed by committees and candidates with the Commission, § 434(b)(2), and made available for public inspection, § 438(a)(4). * * *

The $10 and $100 thresholds are indeed low. Contributors of relatively small amounts are likely to be especially sensitive to recording or disclosure of their political preferences. These strict requirements may well discourage participation by some citizens in the political process, a result that Congress hardly could have intended. Indeed, there is little in the legislative history to indicate that Congress focused carefully on the appropriate level at which to require recording and disclosure. Rather, it seems merely to have adopted the thresholds existing in similar disclosure laws since 1910. But we cannot require Congress to establish that it has chosen the highest reasonable threshold. The line is necessarily a judgmental decision, best left in the context of this complex legislation to congressional discretion. We cannot say, on this bare record, that the limits designated are wholly without rationality. * * *

In summary, we find no constitutional infirmities in the recordkeeping, reporting, and disclosure provisions of the Act.

Mr. Justice Stevens took no part in the consideration or decision of these cases.

Mr. Chief Justice Burger, concurring in part and dissenting in part. * * *

Disclosure is, in principle, the salutary and constitutional remedy for most of the ills Congress was seeking to alleviate. I therefore agree fully with the broad proposition that public disclosure of contributions by individuals and by entities—particularly corporations and labor unions—is an effective means of revealing the type of political support that is sometimes coupled with expectations of special favors or rewards. That disclosure impinges on First Amendment rights is conceded by the Court, but given the objectives to which disclosure is directed, I agree that the need for disclosure outweighs individual constitutional claims.

* * * The Court's theory, however, goes beyond permissible limits. Under the Court's view, disclosure serves broad informational purposes, enabling the public to be fully informed on matters of acute public interest. Forced disclosure of one aspect of a citizen's political activity, under this analysis, serves the public right to know. This open-ended approach is the only plausible justification for the otherwise irrationally low ceilings of $10 and $100 for anonymous contributions. The burdens of these low ceilings seem to me obvious, and the Court does not try to question this. With commendable candor, the Court acknowledges: "It is undoubtedly true that public disclosure of contributions to candidates and political parties will deter some individuals who otherwise might contribute."

Examples come readily to mind. Rank-and-file union members or rising junior executives may now think twice before making even modest contributions to a candidate who is disfavored by the union or management hierarchy. Similarly, potential contributors may well decline to take the obvious risks entailed in making a reportable contribution to the opponent of a well-entrenched incumbent. This fact of political life did not go unnoticed by the Congress: "The disclosure provisions really have in fact made it difficult for challengers to challenge incumbents." 120 Cong. Rec. 34392 (1974) (remarks of Sen. Long). * * *

The public right to know ought not be absolute when its exercise reveals private political convictions. Secrecy, like privacy, is not *per se* criminal. On the contrary, secrecy and privacy as to political preferences and convictions are fundamental in a free society. For example, one of the great political reforms was the advent of the secret ballot as a universal practice. Similarly, the enlightened labor legislation of our time has enshrined the secrecy of choice of a bargaining representative for workers. * * *

* * * I would therefore hold unconstitutional the provisions requiring reporting of contributions of more than $10 and to make a public record of the name, address, and occupation of a contributor of more than $100.

McConnell v. Federal Election Commission

Supreme Court of the United States
540 U.S. 93, 124 S. Ct. 619, 157 L. Ed. 2d 491 (2003)

JUSTICE STEVENS and JUSTICE O'CONNOR delivered the opinion of the Court [in relevant part, in which JUSTICE SOUTER, JUSTICE GINSBURG, and JUSTICE BREYER join]. * * *

[Under FECA § 304, as amended by BCRA § 201], whenever any person makes disbursements totaling more than $10,000 during any calendar year for the direct costs of producing and airing electioneering communications, he must file a statement with the FEC identifying the pertinent elections and all persons sharing the costs of the disbursements. If the disbursements are made from a corporation's or labor union's segregated account, or by a single individual who has collected contributions from others, the statement must identify all persons who contributed $1,000 or more to the account or the individual during the calendar year. The statement must be filed within 24 hours of each "disclosure date"—a term defined to include the first date and all subsequent dates on which a person's aggregate undisclosed expenses for electioneering communications exceed $10,000 for that calendar year. Another subsection further provides that the execution of a contract to make a disbursement is itself treated as a disbursement for purposes of FECA's disclosure requirements.

[P]laintiffs challenge amended FECA § 304's disclosure requirements as unnecessarily (1) requiring disclosure of the names of persons who contributed $1,000 or more to the individual or group that paid for a communication, and (2) mandating disclosure of executory contracts for communications that have not yet aired. * * *

[T]he important state interests that prompted the *Buckley* Court to uphold FECA's disclosure requirements—providing the electorate with information, deterring actual corruption and avoiding any appearance thereof, and gathering the data necessary to enforce more substantive electioneering restrictions—apply in full to BCRA. Accordingly, *Buckley* amply supports application of FECA § 304's disclosure requirements to the entire range of "electioneering communications." * * *

* * * *Buckley* forecloses a facial attack on the new provision in § 304 that requires disclosure of the names of persons contributing $1,000 or more to segregated funds or individuals that spend more than $10,000 in a calendar year on electioneering communications. Like our earlier decision in *NAACP* v. *Alabama*, 357 U.S. 449 (1958) [p. 919], *Buckley* recognized that compelled disclosures may impose an unconstitutional burden on the freedom to associate in support of a particular cause. Nevertheless, *Buckley* rejected the contention that FECA's disclosure requirements could not constitutionally be applied to minor parties and independent candidates because the Government's interest in obtaining information from such parties was minimal and the danger of infringing their rights substantial. In *Buckley*, unlike *NAACP*, we found no evidence that any party had been exposed to economic reprisals or physical threats as a result of the compelled disclosures. We

acknowledged that such a case might arise in the future, however, and addressed the standard of proof that would then apply:

"We recognize that unduly strict requirements of proof could impose a heavy burden, but it does not follow that a blanket exemption for minor parties is necessary. Minor parties must be allowed sufficient flexibility in the proof of injury to assure a fair consideration of their claim. The evidence offered need show only a reasonable probability that the compelled disclosure of a party's contributors' names will subject them to threats, harassment, or reprisals from either Government officials or private parties."

In this litigation the District Court applied *Buckley*'s evidentiary standard and found * * * that the evidence did not establish the requisite "reasonable probability" of harm to any plaintiff group or its members. The District Court noted that some parties had expressed such concerns, but it found a "lack of specific evidence about the basis for these concerns." We agree, but we note that, like our refusal to recognize a blanket exception for minor parties in *Buckley*, our rejection of plaintiffs' facial challenge to the requirement to disclose individual donors does not foreclose possible future challenges to particular applications of that requirement.

We also are unpersuaded by plaintiffs' challenge to new FECA § 304(f)(5), which requires disclosure of executory contracts for electioneering communications. * * *

* * * BCRA's amendments to FECA § 304 mandate disclosure only if and when a person makes disbursements totaling more than $10,000 in any calendar year to pay for electioneering communications. Plaintiffs do not take issue with the use of a dollar amount, rather than the number or dates of the ads, to identify the time when a person paying for electioneering communications must make disclosures to the FEC. Nor do they question the need to make the contents of parties' disclosure statements available to curious voters in advance of elections. Given the relatively short time frames in which electioneering communications are made, the interest in assuring that disclosures are made promptly and in time to provide relevant information to voters is unquestionably significant. Yet fixing the deadline for filing disclosure statements based on the date when aggregate disbursements exceed $10,000 would open a significant loophole * * *. [P]olitical supporters could avoid preelection disclosures concerning ads slated to run during the final week of a campaign simply by making a preelection downpayment of less than $10,000, with the balance payable after the election. * * *

The record contains little evidence identifying any harm that might flow from the enforcement of § 304(f)(5)'s "advance" disclosure requirement. * * * It is no doubt true that § 304(f)(5) will sometimes require the filing of disclosure statements in advance of the actual broadcast of an advertisement. But the same would be true in the absence of an advance disclosure requirement, if a television station insisted on advance payment for all of the ads covered by a contract. * * *

[A]mended FECA § 304's disclosure requirements are constitutional because they "d[o] not prevent anyone from speaking." Moreover, the required disclosures "would not have to reveal the specific content of the advertisements, yet they would perform an important function in informing the public about various candidates' supporters *before* election day." Accordingly, we * * * [uphold] the disclosure requirements in amended FECA § 304. * * *

JUSTICE KENNEDY, [with whom THE CHIEF JUSTICE [REHNQUIST] and JUSTICE SCALIA join,] concurring in the judgment in part and dissenting in part[.] * * *

[BCRA §] 201's advance disclosure requirement — the aspect of the provision requiring those who have contracted to speak to disclose their speech in advance — is, in my view, unconstitutional. Advance disclosure imposes real burdens on political speech that *post hoc* disclosure does not. It forces disclosure of political strategy by revealing where ads are to be run and what their content is likely to be (based on who is running the ad). It also provides an opportunity for the ad buyer's opponents to dissuade broadcasters from running ads. Against those tangible additional burdens, the Government identifies no additional interest uniquely served by advance disclosure. If Congress intended to ensure that advertisers could not flout these disclosure laws by running an ad before the election, but paying for it afterwards, then Congress should simply have required the disclosure upon the running of the ad. Burdening the First Amendment further by requiring advance disclosure is not a constitutionally acceptable alternative. To the extent § 201 requires advance disclosure, it finds no justification in its subordinating interests and imposes greater burdens than the First Amendment permits.

JUSTICE THOMAS, * * * dissenting in part[.]* * *

I must now address an issue on which I differ from all of my colleagues: the disclosure provisions in BCRA § 201, now contained in new FECA § 304(f). * * * [T]his Court has explicitly recognized that "the interest in having anonymous works enter the marketplace of ideas unquestionably outweighs any public interest in requiring disclosure as a condition of entry," and thus that "an author's decision to remain anonymous . . . is an aspect of the freedom of speech protected by the First Amendment." [*McIntyre* v. *Ohio Elections Comm'n*, 514 U.S. 334, 342 (1995)] [p. 922.] The Court now backs away from this principle, allowing the established right to anonymous speech to be stripped away based on the flimsiest of justifications.

The only plausible interest asserted by the defendants to justify the disclosure provisions is the interest in providing "information" about the speaker to the public. But we have already held that "[t]he simple interest in providing voters with additional relevant information does not justify a state requirement that a writer make statements or disclosures she would otherwise omit." *Id.*, at 348. Of course, *Buckley* upheld the disclosure requirement on expenditures for communications using words of express advocacy based on this informational interest. And admittedly, *McIntyre* purported to distinguish *Buckley*. But the two ways *McIntyre* distinguished *Buckley* — one, that the disclosure of "an expenditure and its use, without more, reveals far less information [than a forced identification of the author of a pamphlet]"; and two, that in candidate elections, the "Government can identify a compelling state interest in avoiding the corruption that might result from campaign expenditures"—are inherently implausible. The first is simply wrong. The revelation of one's political expenditures for independent communications about candidates can be just as revealing as the revelation of one's name on a pamphlet for a noncandidate election. The second was outright rejected in *Buckley* itself, where the Court concluded that independent expenditures did not create any substantial risk of real or apparent corruption. Hence, the only reading of *McIntyre* that remains consistent with the principles it contains is that it overturned *Buckley* to the extent that *Buckley* upheld a disclosure requirement solely based on the governmental interest in providing information to the voters.

The right to anonymous speech cannot be abridged based on the interests asserted by the defendants. I would thus hold that the disclosure requirements of BCRA § 201 are unconstitutional. Because of this conclusion, the so-called advance disclosure requirement of § 201 necessarily falls as well. * * *

Citizens United v. Federal Election Commission

Supreme Court of the United States
558 U.S. 310, 130 S. Ct. 876, 175 L. Ed. 2d 753 (2010)

Justice Kennedy delivered the opinion of the Court [in which Chief Justice Roberts, Justice Stevens, Justice Scalia, Justice Ginsburg, Justice Breyer, Justice Alito and Justice Sotomayor join as to the portion excerpted here.] * * *

Under BCRA § 311, televised electioneering communications funded by anyone other than a candidate must include a disclaimer that "_____ is responsible for the content of this advertising." 2 U.S.C. § 441d(d)(2). The required statement must be made in a "clearly spoken manner," and displayed on the screen in a "clearly readable manner" for at least four seconds. *Ibid.* It must state that the communication "is not authorized by any candidate or candidate's committee"; it must also display the name and address (or Web site address) of the person or group that funded the advertisement. § 441d(a)(3). Under BCRA § 201, any person who spends more than $10,000 on electioneering communications within a calendar year must file a disclosure statement with the FEC. 2 U.S.C. § 434(f)(1). That statement must identify the person making the expenditure, the amount of the expenditure, the election to which the communication was directed, and the names of certain contributors. § 434(f)(2).

Disclaimer and disclosure requirements may burden the ability to speak, but they "impose no ceiling on campaign-related activities" and "do not prevent anyone from speaking." The Court has subjected these requirements to "exacting scrutiny," which requires a "substantial relation" between the disclosure requirement and a "sufficiently important" governmental interest.

In *Buckley* [v. *Valeo*, 424 U.S. 1 (1976)] [p. 933], the Court explained that disclosure could be justified based on a governmental interest in "provid[ing] the electorate with information" about the sources of election-related spending. The *McConnell* [v. *Federal Election Commission*, 540 U.S. 93 (2003)] [p. 941] Court applied this interest in rejecting facial challenges to BCRA §§ 201 and 311. * * *

Citizens United sought to broadcast one 30-second and two 10-second ads to promote [its movie] *Hillary*. * * * Citizens United argues that the disclaimer requirements in § 311 are unconstitutional as applied to its ads. It contends that the governmental interest in providing information to the electorate does not justify requiring disclaimers for any commercial advertisements, including the ones at issue here. We disagree. * * * At the very least, the disclaimers avoid confusion by making clear that the ads are not funded by a candidate or political party. * * *

* * * Citizens United argues that disclosure requirements can chill donations to an organization by exposing donors to retaliation. Some *amici* point to recent events in which donors to certain causes were blacklisted, threatened, or otherwise targeted for retaliation. In *McConnell*, the Court recognized that § 201 would be unconstitutional as applied to an organization if there were a reasonable probability that the group's members would face threats, harassment, or reprisals if their names were disclosed. The examples cited by *amici* are cause for concern. Citizens United, however, has offered no evidence that its members may face similar threats or reprisals. To the contrary, Citizens United has been disclosing its donors for years and has identified no instance of harassment or retaliation.

Shareholder objections raised through the procedures of corporate democracy can be more effective today because modern technology makes disclosures rapid and informative. A campaign finance system that pairs corporate independent expenditures with effective disclosure has not existed before today. * * * With the advent of the Internet, prompt disclosure of expenditures can provide shareholders and citizens with the information needed to hold corporations and elected officials accountable for their positions and supporters. Shareholders can determine whether their corporation's political speech advances the corporation's interest in making profits, and citizens can see whether elected officials are "'in the pocket' of so-called moneyed interests." The First Amendment protects political speech; and disclosure permits citizens and shareholders to react to the speech of corporate entities in a proper way. This transparency enables the electorate to make informed decisions and give proper weight to different speakers and messages.

For the same reasons we uphold the application of BCRA §§ 201 and 311 to the ads, we affirm their application to *Hillary*. We find no constitutional impediment to the application of BCRA's disclaimer and disclosure requirements to a movie broadcast via video-on-demand. And there has been no showing that, as applied in this case, these requirements would impose a chill on speech or expression.

JUSTICE THOMAS, concurring in part and dissenting in part. * * *

* * * The disclosure, disclaimer, and reporting requirements in BCRA §§ 201 and 311 are * * * unconstitutional.

[JUSTICE THOMAS related examples provided by *amici* of threats against persons whose support for a California ballot proposition was disclosed because of a California law similar to §§ 201 and 311.] These instances of retaliation sufficiently demonstrate why this Court should invalidate mandatory disclosure and reporting requirements. But *amici* present evidence of yet another reason to do so — the threat of retaliation from *elected officials*. As *amici*'s submissions make clear, this threat extends far beyond a single ballot proposition in California. For example, a candidate challenging an incumbent state attorney general reported that some members of the State's business community feared donating to his campaign because they did not want to cross the incumbent; in his words, "I go to so many people and hear the same thing: 'I sure hope you beat [the incumbent], but I can't afford to have my name on your records. He might come after me next.'" The incumbent won reelection in 2008.

My point is not to express any view on the merits of the political controversies I describe. Rather, it is to demonstrate — using real-world, recent examples — the fallacy in the Court's conclusion that "[d]isclaimer and disclosure requirements . . . impose no ceiling on campaign-related activities, and do not prevent anyone from speaking." Of course they do. Disclaimer and disclosure requirements enable private citizens and elected officials to implement political strategies *specifically calculated* to curtail campaign-related activity and prevent the lawful, peaceful exercise of First Amendment rights. * * *

I cannot endorse a view of the First Amendment that subjects citizens of this Nation to death threats, ruined careers, damaged or defaced property, or preemptive and threatening warning letters as the price for engaging in "core political speech, the 'primary object of First Amendment protection.'" Accordingly, I respectfully dissent from the Court's judgment upholding BCRA §§ 201 and 311.

Notes and Questions

1. *Buckley* and *McConnell* are two of the longest sets of opinions in Supreme Court history. Yet the discussion of disclosure is relatively brief in each case, with very little consideration of the evidence and arguments offered by the parties. How sound are the opinions?

The *Buckley* Court identified three government interests served by mandatory disclosure. The first government interest was in preventing corruption that fell short of bribery. The theory was that disclosure would embarrass both large donors and the candidates who accepted the donations. *See* Perry Belmont, *Publicity of Election*

Expenditures, 180 N. Amer. Rev. 166, 182 (1905). Is such a theory realistic? According to two skeptics,

> [t]he theory of disclosure insists that voters will reject candidates at the polls when disclosure shows too much spending, misdirected spending, unsavory or disfavored financial sources, or excessive contributions. In elections, however, a citizen cannot express himself solely on campaign finance practices; his vote for a candidate is a decision about many other issues as well * * *. Voters do not and should not give campaign finance practices heavy weight in making ballot choices, and therefore candidates rarely need fear that disclosure of such practices will result in political penalties at the polls.

David W. Adamany & George E. Agree, Political Money: A Strategy for Campaign Financing in America 103–12 (1975). In 2000, before the Bipartisan Campaign Reform Act prohibited unlimited soft-money donations to parties, 800 individuals contributed an average of $375,000 to the national political parties. Richard Briffault, *The Future of Reform: Campaign Finance After the Bipartisan Campaign Reform Act of 2002*, 34 Ariz. St. L.J. 1179, 1183 (2002). Does this prove that Adamany and Agree were correct?

Even if some voters punish candidates for accepting large contributions, is it justifiable to require disclosure of modest contributions? Some analysts have expressed the concern, voiced by Chief Justice Burger in *Buckley*, that many laws set the disclosure threshold so low as to capture contributions that are highly unlikely to have any improper influence on a candidate or officeholder. *See, e.g.*, William McGeveran, *Mrs. McIntyre's Checkbook: Privacy Costs of Political Contribution Disclosure*, 6 U. Pa. J. Const. L. 1, 30 (2003).

The second government interest recognized in *Buckley* was in providing the electorate with information. Do mandated disclosures serve this interest? Certainly public endorsements by interest groups and prominent individuals have value to voters. Does disclosure of information about contributions and expenditures add to that knowledge? Low disclosure thresholds may inhibit the effectiveness of disclosure laws in meeting the government's information interest, by drowning voters with data of little informational value. *See id.* at 28–29; *see also* Richard Briffault, *Campaign Finance Disclosure 2.0*, 9 Election L.J. 273 (2010). And voters, in fact, rarely seek out such information. Raymond J. LaRaja, *Sunshine Laws and the Press: The Effect of Campaign Disclosure on News Reporting*, 6 Election L.J. 236, 237 (2007). Others casting doubt on the informational benefits of disclosure include Benjamin Barr & Stephen R. Klein, *Publius Was Not a PAC: Reconciling Anonymous Political Speech, The First Amendment, and Campaign Finance Disclosure*, 14 Wyo. L. Rev. 253 (2014); and Dick Carpenter & Jeffrey Milyo, *The Public's Right to Know Versus Compelled Speech: What Does Social Science Research Tell Us About the Benefits and Costs of Campaign Finance Disclosure in Non-Candidate Elections*, 40 Fordham Urb. L.J. 101 (2012).

How far does the informational interest of voters extend? In *Independence Institute v. Federal Election Commission*, 216 F. Supp. 3d 176 (D.D.C. 2016), *summarily aff'd*, 137 S. Ct. 1204 (2017), a three-judge district-court panel upheld donor-disclosure provisions of the Federal Election Campaign Act. The Independence Institute, a think tank organized under § 501(c)(3) of the Internal Revenue Code (and therefore prohibited from political-campaign activity), had, for some years, through studies and papers, advocated for federal sentencing reform. It thus sought to air the following radio advertisement:

> Let the punishment fit the crime. But for many federal crimes, that's no longer true. Unfair laws tie the hands of judges, with huge increases in prison costs that help drive up the debt. And for what purpose? Studies show that these laws don't cut crime. In fact, the soaring costs from these laws make it harder to prosecute and lock up violent felons. Fortunately, there is a bipartisan bill to help fix the problem — the Justice Safety Valve Act, bill number S. 619. It would allow judges to keep the public safe, provide rehabilitation, and deter others from committing crimes.

> Call Senators Michael Bennet and Mark Udall at 202-224-3121. Tell them to support S. 619, the Justice Safety Valve Act. Tell them it's time to let the punishment fit the crime.

Because Senator Bennet was up for re-election, the ad fell under the donor-disclosure provisions of the Bipartisan Campaign Reform Act. The Institute argued that the mandated disclosure was unconstitutional notwithstanding *McConnell*, but the court rejected the argument.

Is the ad above, in your opinion, a campaign ad, an "issue ad," or something else? After *Citizens United* and *Independence Institute*, is there any limit to what the government can designate as an "electioneering communication" requiring disclosure of donors, so long as the speech mentions a candidate? Has the Court *sub silentio* overruled *Buckley*'s "exacting scrutiny" requirement for compulsory donor disclosure? *See Buckley*, 424 U.S. at 64 (*per curiam*) (quoted *supra* at page 933). Is compulsory donor disclosure now subject to a *de facto* rational-basis test?

Other studies suggest that compulsory disclosure discourages political participation. *See* Alexandre Courture Gagnon & Filip Palda, *The Price of Transparency: Do Campaign Finance Disclosure Laws Discourage Political Participation by Citizens' Groups*, 146 Pub. Choice 353 (2011).

The third and final government interest recognized in *Buckley* for requiring the reporting of campaign contributions was in aiding the enforcement of other limitations, such as those on contributions. Assuming that this interest is valid, does it justify public disclosure of the information so reported?

2. Another interest? Bob Bauer, a prominent practitioner who served as General Counsel to the Obama for President campaign and later as White House Counsel, has suggested that, in practice, the primary purpose of disclosure has become to

generate news stories and press releases justifying further restrictions on contributions, spending, and other activity. Robert F. Bauer, *Not Just a Private Matter: The Purposes of Disclosure in an Expanded Regulatory System*, 6 ELECTION L.J. 38 (2007). Bauer expressed skepticism that disclosure served the government interests identified in *Buckley*.

3. As recently as 1996, researchers and others interested in learning about donors to federal campaigns typically had to visit the office of the Federal Election Commission and manually view the records, often on microfiche. Disclosure was overwhelmingly, therefore, a Washington, D.C., activity, with distribution of the information to the broader public mediated by reporters and a small number of public-interest groups that sought to organize and publish the information. The rise of the Internet, electronic filing, and online publication of reports has dramatically changed the nature of disclosure, making it possible for anyone with Internet access to pull up filing information at virtually zero cost, often within hours of contributions being made. Some prominent web sites, such as the Huffington Post and EightMaps.com, have linked the required disclosure information to mapping services, so that an interested person can find, within seconds, not only the names and addresses of donors, but maps to their homes. Forty-nine states now post information about campaign contributors on the Internet, with forty states doing so within two days of filing.

As donor information has become widely available, tales of abuse of the information, including lost employment, commercial boycotts, physical threats, vandalism, and even death threats have surfaced with increasing frequency. *See ProtectMarriage .com v. Bowen*, 599 F. Supp. 2d 1197 (E.D. Cal. 2009); Elian Dashev, *Economic Boycotts as Harassment: The Threat to First Amendment Protected Speech in the Aftermath of* Doe v. Reed, 45 LOY. L.A. L. REV. 207 (2011); Bradley A. Smith, *In Defense of Political Anonymity*, 20 CITY J. 74, 76–77 (2010). Does this development change the calculus from that set forth by the Court in *Buckley* and *McConnell*?

For more sanguine views on the costs and benefits of disclosure, see, *e.g.*, Lloyd Hitoshi Mayer, *Politics and the Public's Right to Know*, 13 ELECTION L.J. 138 (2014); Michael Kang, *Campaign Disclosure in Direct Democracy*, 97 MINN. L. REV. 1700 (2013); and Jonathan C. Zellner, *Artificial Grassroots Advocacy and the Constitutionality of Legislative Identification and Control Measures*, 43 CONN. L. REV. 357 (2010).

4. Although one longstanding justification for disclosure laws is that they assist in preventing corruption, some commentators have noted that it is the very ability of candidates and officeholders to identify contributors (and non-contributors) that creates many of the public concerns about campaign contributions. Without the ability to identify donors (and non-donors), officeholders can neither be influenced by donations, nor can they abuse their office to extract, through threats of adverse government action, contributions from unwilling donors. *See* Michael D. Gilbert, *Transparency and Corruption: A General Analysis*, 2018 U. CHI. LEG. F. 117. In a much-discussed book, Yale Law School Professors Bruce Ackerman and Ian

Ayres argued that rather than compel disclosure of contributor information, the government should establish a system, similar to a blind trust, that prevents candidates from knowing who their donors are. Bruce Ackerman & Ian Ayres, Voting With Dollars: A New Paradigm for Campaign Finance (2002). Two law reviews held symposia, featuring many of the country's leading campaign-finance and election-law scholars, dedicated specifically to discussing the Ackerman/Ayres book. *See* 91 Cal. L. Rev. 641–768 (2003); 37 U. Rich. L. Rev. 935–1184 (2003). A strong critique of the Ackerman/Ayres proposal is Lillian R. BeVier, *What Ails Us?* (Book Review), 112 Yale L.J. 1135 (2003).

5. In the wake of *Citizens United*, there has been a great deal of confusion about what campaign spending must be disclosed. Of course, disclosure rules for candidate and party committees and ballot committees will vary from state to state. However, most states follow the basic contours of federal law, with the major difference typically being the thresholds that trigger mandatory disclosure.

The information that a group or organization must disclose largely depends on its form of organization and the nature of its activities.

A. *Candidate committees, political parties, and political action committees ("PACs").* These overt campaign organizations are subject to the greatest disclosure requirements. At the federal level, they must disclose all donors in excess of $200 in aggregate giving. Many states have much lower thresholds. *See, e.g.,* Florida Stat. Title IX § 106.7(4)(a)(1) (2011) (requiring reporting of all contributions regardless of size). They also must file detailed reports on expenditures, by category and vendor. Reports are typically filed monthly during election years, although expenditures or contributions close to the election can trigger added reporting requirements, often demanding reporting within forty-eight hours. *See* 2 U.S.C. §§ 432–434.

B. *Super PACs.* Super PACs are subject to the same organizational and reporting requirements as regular PACs. It has been argued, however, that if a non-profit membership corporation contributes to a Super PAC, voters would know that the non-profit funded the Super PAC, but may not know who funded the non-profit. *See* Trevor Potter, *Five Myths About Super PACs*, Wash. Post, p. B2, Apr. 15, 2012. It is unclear, however, how great a concern this should be. Many non-profits that engage in politically oriented messaging, such as the NAACP Voter Education Fund, the National Rifle Association, and the National Association of Realtors, are well known to voters. How much more is gained by knowing the identities of their specific members?

One example that is suggested as demonstrating the need for greater disclosure by Super PACs is the case of W. Spann, LLC. The corporation was formed in March of 2011 and dissolved in July of that year. In between, its only business appears to have been donating $1 million to a Super PAC. Dan Eggen, *Mystery Firm's $1M Donation to Pro-Romney PAC Raises*

Concern Over Transparency, WASH. POST, p. A2, Aug. 4, 2011. However, within three days, the creator of W. Spann, LLC—Edward Conard, a long-time supporter of presidential candidate Mitt Romney—was identified. Conard was apparently advised by his estate-planning attorney to fund the donation through the short-lived LLC. Michael Isikoff, *Firm Gives $1 Million to Pro-Romney Group, Then Dissolves*, MSNBC, Aug. 4, 2011, *available at* http://www.msnbc.msn.com/id/44011308/. Federal law prohibits contributions in the name of another, which has been interpreted to include reimbursing or advancing the money for a contribution. 2 U.S.C. § 441f; 11 C.F.R. § 110.4. Knowing this, was the contribution from W. Spann, LLC, legal? Based on what you have heard about *Citizens United*, why would an attorney not experienced in campaign-finance law think that this was legal? Consider this passage from a leading reform organization blog: "*Citizens United* created an environment in which it is perfectly legal for a shell non-profit corporation to engage in election-related spending on behalf of a hidden interest." Lisa Rosenberg, *Citizens United Decision Could Lead to Foreign Interests Influencing US Elections*, Sunlight Foundation Blog, Mar. 13, 2012, *available at* http://sunlightfoundation.com/blog/2012/03/13 /citizens-united-decision-could-lead-to-foreign-interests-influencing-us -elections/. In light of 2 U.S.C. § 441f, is that a correct statement of the law? Could such comments create incorrect public perceptions of what the law allows?

For a review of some problems with trying to increase Super PAC disclosure to include donors to non-profits that then contribute to Super PACs, see Bradley A. Smith, *Disclosure in a Post-*Citizens United *Real World*, 6 U. St. THOMAS J. L. & PUB. POL'Y 257 (2012).

C. *Non-PAC 527s.* Buckley v. Valeo narrowed the definition of "political committee" to organizations with a primary purpose of engaging in electoral advocacy, which it defined as "express advocacy." *See* pp. 755–59, *supra*. The Internal Revenue Service, however, uses a broader definition of what constitutes political advocacy. *See* David S. Karp, *Taxing Issues: Reexamining the Regulation of Issue Advocacy by Tax-Exempt Organizations*, 77 N.Y.U. L. REV. 1805 (2002). By devoting most of its resources to political activity, as defined by the IRS, but avoiding express advocacy, a group qualifies as a Non-PAC 527, named for § 527 of the Internal Revenue Code, under which political committees operate. These "527s" were a popular vehicle for campaign organizers in the 1990s through the election of 2004 because they could raise unlimited contributions from individuals, corporations, and unions. The PAC limits were inapplicable because they did not make direct campaign contributions or engage in "express advocacy," and so they were exempt from FECA's political-committee limits and disclosure provisions, per *Buckley*. In 2000, Congress required these organizations to disclose their donors to the Internal Revenue Service, or else pay taxes on undisclosed receipts. Pub. L. No. 06t-230 (2000). Non-PAC 527s have declined dramatically in use since *SpeechNow.org. v. Federal Election Commission*, 559 F.3d 686 (D.C. Cir. 2010) (*en banc*), permitted the creation of Super PACs, and *Citizens United* made it possible for unions and corporations to fund express-advocacy communications.

D. *Non-Profit Organizations.* Non-profit organizations operating under 26 U.S.C. §§ 501(c)(4) ("social welfare organizations") and (c)(6) ("business leagues") may engage in political activity so long as such activity does not become their primary purpose. Even if political activity is their primary purpose, they may escape regulation as political committees under FECA pursuant to *Federal Election Commission v. Massachusetts Citizens for Life, Inc.*, 479 U.S. 238 (1986) (discussed at page 821, *supra*). These groups still must file reports with the FEC when they make political expenditures, but they do not need to disclose who contributed to the organization unless the contributions were made to fund specific ads, which is rare. *See* 2 U.S.C. § 434(c)(1). Due to a quirk in the law, however, even though they do not need to disclose donors when making independent expenditures (*i.e.*, expenditures for express advocacy), these non-profits must disclose the names of individual donors when making "electioneering communications" (broadcast ads mentioning a candidate without express advocacy within sixty days of a general election or thirty days of a primary). *See* 2 U.S.C. § 434(f); *Van Hollen v. Federal Election Commission*, 811 F.3d 486 (D.C. Cir. 2016).

6. Note that in addition to the disclosures mentioned above, every broadcast ad and most print ads must also contain a disclosure notice stating the name of the individual or organization paying for the ad. Furthermore, Federal Communication Commission regulations require broadcasters to maintain a "political file," available for public inspection, that tracks all political ad buys. 47 C.F.R. § 73.1212. While these disclosures reveal who bought an ad, they do not necessarily inform the listener or viewer as to who contributed the funds used by the organization to purchase the ad. Is this added level of disclosure necessary? Does it rise to the level of a "compelling government interest"?

7. In addition to theoretical and constitutional issues about who should be compelled to disclose political spending, and when such disclosure should occur, there are practical issues that make it much easier to call for disclosure than to devise a system that effectively informs the public. Consider the following Problem, which is based on a real-world model of political activity.

Problem. In December 2016, the Acme Widget Company made a $200,000 dues payment to the North American Chamber of Business ("NACB"). It made another such payment in December of 2017. The NACB had a budget of $50 million annually, with thousands of member companies that paid dues based on their size and desired level of participation in the group. In March 2014, the NACB transferred $600,000 to the State Chamber of Business. The State Chamber of Business is independent from NACB, but NACB often worked with various state groups. It transferred the $600,000 as part of a program in which it agreed to match money raised by state organizations to help elect pro-business candidates. The State Chamber of Business had raised another $600,000 for political activity from 157 member companies over the previous six months. In raising the money, it did not state any specific races in which it planned to spend money or to make endorsements, and of course, donors gave up all rights to the money contributed. In June 2018, the State Chamber of Business transferred $1.1 million to Moving Our State Forward, a 501(c)(4) established by the State Chamber in 2005 to conduct lobbying, public education, and political activity. The State Chamber normally used Moving Our State Forward as its primary vehicle for political action. In July 2018, Moving Our State Forward transferred $500,000 to the State Business Alliance, a Super PAC organized in February 2018 by various business groups in the state. The State Business Alliance received donations from other trade and business associations and corporations, and had a total budget for 2018 of $2.8 million. In September 2018, the State Business Alliance made a $250,000 television ad buy attacking a member of Congress. What disclosures were required?

8. As we have seen, the Supreme Court has consistently upheld mandatory disclosure of donors to candidate committees, albeit with an exception for minor parties facing harassment. *See Brown v. Socialist Workers Party '74 Campaign Committee*, 459 U.S. 87 (1982) [p. 962]. However, the law is much more mixed when disclosure laws are applied to persons who contribute to organizations that discuss candidates and issues without specifically advocating the election or defeat of a candidate, or who make only occasional expenditures advocating the election or defeat of a candidate.

McIntyre presented one such case. There, you will recall, the challenged Ohio law required speakers to identify themselves on the face of an ad. Though typically called "disclaimers"—presumably from their similar positioning to the various legal limitations included in advertisements for commercial products—these provisions require the speaker to "claim" the ad in question. The best known "disclaimer" requirement is probably the "stand by your ad" provision of BCRA, which requires candidates for federal office to state in broadcast ads that they "approve this message." 52 U.S.C. § 30120.

The Supreme Court's protection of anonymity in *NAACP v. Alabama, McIntyre,* and similar cases[f] is difficult to square with its acceptance in *Buckley, McConnell,*

---

f. Such cases include *Thomas v. Collins*, 323 U.S. 516 (1945) (union organizer could not be required to obtain license before speaking); *Bates v. City of Little Rock*, 361 U.S. 516 (1960) (NAACP could not be required to turn over donor and member information as a condition of doing business in the city); *Talley v. California*, 362 U.S. 60 (1960) (picketers could not be required to put names and *Citizens United* of laws requiring the disclosure of the identity of those who make political expenditures. What factors might explain the different directions in the Court's jurisprudence? What reasons might there be to treat campaign-finance cases differently from other political-speech cases? In the long run, will the tendency toward more disclosure in campaign-finance cases undercut the Court's commitment to protecting anonymity for other speakers?

The *McIntyre* Court attempted to distinguish the Ohio law from the disclosure laws that had earlier been held constitutional in *Buckley* and *First National Bank of Boston v. Bellotti*, 435 U.S. 765 (1978):

> * * * In *Bellotti*, * * * although we commented in dicta on the prophylactic effect of requiring identification of the source of corporate advertising ["so that the people will be able to evaluate the arguments to which they are being subjected," 435 U.S., at 792 n.32], that footnote did not necessarily apply to independent communications by an individual like Mrs. McIntyre.

> Our * * * comments concerned contributions to the candidate or expenditures authorized by the candidate or his responsible agent. They had no reference to the kind of independent activity pursued by Mrs. McIntyre. Required disclosures about the level of financial support a candidate has received from various sources are supported by an interest in avoiding the appearance of corruption that has no application to this case.

> True, in another portion of the *Buckley* opinion we expressed approval of a requirement that even "independent expenditures" in excess of a threshold level be reported to the Federal Election Commission. But that requirement entailed nothing more than an identification to the Commission of the amount and use of money expended in support of a candidate. Though such mandatory reporting undeniably impedes protected First Amendment activity, the intrusion is a far cry from compelled self-identification on all election-related writings. A written election-related document — particularly a leaflet — is often a personally crafted statement of a political viewpoint. Mrs. McIntyre's handbills surely fit that description. As such, identification of the author against her will is particularly intrusive; it reveals unmistakably the content of her thoughts on a controversial issue. Disclosure of an expenditure and its use, without more, reveals far less information. It may be information that a person prefers to keep secret, and undoubtedly it often gives away something about the spender's political views. Nonetheless, even though money may "talk," its speech is less specific, less personal, and less provocative than a handbill — and as a result,

---

and addresses of funders on handbills); and *Watchtower Bible & Tract Society v. Village of Stratton*, 536 U.S. 150 (2002) (door-to-door religious canvassers could not be required to register with the government).

when money supports an unpopular viewpoint it is less likely to precipitate retaliation. * * *

Are you convinced by the distinctions made by the Court? In the next case, Richard Posner and Frank Easterbrook, two of the most respected judges on the U.S. Courts of Appeals, were presented with a challenge to a disclosure law that required them to confront some of the apparent conflicts in the law of anonymous speech.

Majors v. Abell

United States Court of Appeals for the Seventh Circuit
361 F.3d 349 (7th Cir. 2004)

POSNER, CIRCUIT JUDGE [with whom BAUER, CIRCUIT JUDGE, joins].

An Indiana statute, challenged in this suit as an infringement of free speech, requires that political advertising that "expressly advocat[es] the election or defeat of a clearly identified candidate" contain "a disclaimer that appears and is presented in a clear and conspicuous manner to give the reader or observer adequate notice of the identity of persons who paid for . . . the communication," and makes violation a misdemeanor. "Disclaimer" is a misnomer; the correct word would be "disclosure"—but as we'll see, that word has been appropriated to describe a reporting requirement. * * *

The constitutional issue * * * is difficult because it entails a balancing of imponderables. On the one hand, forbidding anonymous political advertising reduces the amount of political advertising because some would-be advertisers are unwilling to reveal their identity. On the other hand, the quality of the political advertising that continues to be produced and disseminated under such a regime is enhanced because the advertising contains additional information useful to the consumer. The avidity with which candidates for public office seek endorsements is evidence (as if any were needed) that the identity of a candidate's supporters—and opponents—is information that the voting public values highly. In areas of inquiry where logic or exact observation is unavailing, a speaker's credibility often depends crucially on who he is. As Aristotle said, "persuasion is achieved by the speaker's personal character when the speech is so spoken as to make us think him credible. We believe good men more fully and more readily than others: this is true generally whatever the question is, and absolutely true where exact certainty is impossible and opinions are divided." Aristotle, *Rhetoric*, in 2 *The Complete Works of Aristotle* 2152, 2155 (Jonathan Barnes ed. 1984). "Where exact certainty is impossible and opinions are divided" is a pretty good description of politics.

Can we get help in answering the thorny question presented by this appeal from the case law, and in particular from the Supreme Court's recent and very lengthy opinions in [*McConnell v. Federal Election Comm'n*, 540 U.S. 93 (2003)] [p. 941]? The provision of the Bipartisan Campaign Reform Act that is analogous to the Indiana statute [required i]ndividuals who spend more than $10,000 producing such communications, or contribute at least $1,000 to an organization that produces them, [to] report (in the case of the contributions it is the recipient who must report) their identities to the Federal Election Commission. 2 U.S.C. §§ 434(f)(1)–(2). Without attempting to narrow the class of covered "individuals," the Supreme Court upheld this provision on the ground that it served "important state interests . . . [in] providing the electorate with information, deterring actual corruption and avoiding any appearance thereof, and gathering the data necessary to enforce more substantive electioneering restrictions." * * *

True, what is required is disclosure to an agency rather than disclosure in the political ad itself, though, as is apparent from the Court's reference to "providing the electorate with information," the identity of the contributor is available to the public rather than secreted by the FEC. 2 U.S.C. §§ 434(a)(11)–(12), (d)(2). That may not seem a big difference from the standpoint of protecting the advertiser from retaliation, but the Court had earlier indicated that having to identify itself to the entire audience for the ad has as a practical matter a greater inhibiting effect than just a reporting requirement does because it broadcasts the advertiser's name to the entire electoral community. *Buckley v. American Constitutional Law Foundation, Inc.,* 525 U.S. 182, 197–200 (1999) [p. 649]. The reaction may not be "retaliation" in any strong sense, but there is a weak sense as well; there may be a degree of social ostracism, some dirty looks, a few snide comments, and such, and we and other courts have long recognized that mild forms of retaliation can be effective in deterring the exercise of free speech.

The Court in *McIntyre* [v. *Ohio Elections Commission,* 514 U.S. 334 (1995)] [p. 922] thought "the intrusion" on freedom of political advocacy brought about by a reporting requirement was "a far cry from compelled self-identification on all election-related writings," 514 U.S. at 355, which is what we have here—and what the Bipartisan Campaign Reform Act does not have; it does not even require identifying the specific ads financed by the reporting contributor. But of course the very thing that makes reporting less inhibiting than notice in the ad itself—fewer people are likely to see the report than the notice—makes reporting a less effective method of conveying information that by hypothesis the voting public values. It's as if cigarette companies, instead of having to disclose the hazards of smoking in their ads, had only to file a disclosure statement with the Food and Drug Administration.

The only reference to *McIntyre* by the majority in *McConnell* appears in a footnote that distinguishes "genuine issue ads" from "regulation of campaign speech" and assumes that restrictions constitutionally applicable to the latter, such as the restrictions both in the Bipartisan Campaign Reform Act and in the Indiana statute, might not be applicable to the former; *McIntyre* is cited noncommittally as having invalidated a "statute banning the distribution of anonymous campaign literature." 540 U.S. at 206 n.88. Remember that *McIntyre* had only been about issue referenda, where there are no candidates and so, it might be thought, "campaign literature" is more likely to consist of "genuine issue ads." Thus the Court may have so far narrowed *McIntyre* (one of the dissenting opinions said the Court had overruled it) that it no longer overlaps the Indiana statute.

An alternative interpretation, however, is that because the Bipartisan Campaign Reform Act and therefore the *McConnell* decision are about campaign financing, the decision is inapplicable to people who pay for political ads themselves, since they are not engaged in fund-raising. On that reading, *McIntyre*, which was such a case, is unaffected by *McConnell*, and so the Indiana statute, which is also about requiring self-financiers to identify themselves, is condemned by *McIntyre*'s holding. But campaign financing and fund-raising are not synonyms, as the argument assumes; and the Bipartisan Campaign Reform Act is not just about fund-raising—the relevant provision that the Court upheld applies equally to self-financed and other-financed ads. * * * And the first governmental interest that the Court recited in upholding the provision—that it would provide the electorate with information—is applicable to self-financed ads. An ad might seem disinterested, but if the voting public knew who had paid for it—maybe it was an interest group that the candidate was known to have done favors for—the existence of an interest might be revealed. To draw the constitutional line between self- and other-financed campaign ads would be to deliver a gratuitous benefit to wealthy candidates and wealthy supporters of candidates. * * *

* * * [T]o require only the reporting of the advertiser's name to a public agency, while it would as a practical matter allay some of the anxieties of potential advertisers, would at the same time reduce the amount of information possessed by voters. Both sides of the First Amendment balance would be depressed. We cannot say that the net effect of invalidating the Indiana statute would be to promote political speech.

As an original matter it could be objected that speech and the press would no longer be free if the government could insist that every speaker and every writer add to his message information that the government deems useful to the intended audience for the message, and that it is arbitrary for the government to single out the identity of the writer or speaker and decree that that information, though no other that potential voters might value as much or more, must be disclosed. But the Supreme Court crossed that Rubicon in *McConnell*. Reluctant, without clearer guidance from the Court, to interfere with state experimentation in the baffling and conflicted field of campaign finance law without guidance from authoritative precedent, we hold that the Indiana statute is constitutional.

The decision of the district court * * * is Affirmed.

EASTERBROOK, CIRCUIT JUDGE, dubitante.[g]

Four decisions of the Supreme Court hold or strongly imply that the ability to speak anonymously—and thus with less concern for repercussions—is part of the "freedom of speech" protected by the first amendment against governmental interference. *Talley v. California*, 362 U.S. 60 (1960); *McIntyre v. Ohio Elections Commission*; *Buckley v. American Constitutional Law Foundation*; *Watchtower Bible & Tract Society of New York, Inc. v. Stratton*, 536 U.S. 150, 166–67 (2002). See Jonathan Turley, *Registering Publius: The Supreme Court and the Right to Anonymity*, 2001-02 Cato Sup. Ct. Rev. 57. * * *

There have been times and places in the United States when opposing elected political officials risked both wealth and health. Decisions such as *O'Hare Truck Service, Inc. v. Northlake*, 518 U.S. 712 (1996), and *Rutan v. Republican Party of Illinois*, 497 U.S. 62 (1990) [p. 701], hold that government is not entitled to retaliate, but what people do in fact often differs from what they should do, and litigation after the fact is no cure-all. It is no cure at all for retaliation by private actors, who are free to penalize those whose political views they do not accept, provided only that they do not cross the line into violence—and that line has not always been observed; think of persons whose candidates were the "wrong" race. Anonymity thus may be especially valuable when opposing entrenched actors. Disclosure also makes it easier to see who has not done his bit for the incumbents, so that arms may be twisted and pockets tapped. Labor law deems it improper for employers to nose out union adherents' names; judges and members of the NLRB perceive that knowledge may facilitate retaliation and that fear of this outcome will stifle speech. Yet although union organizers may operate in secret, and everyone may vote in secret (our adoption of the Australian ballot came from awareness that disclosure could affect political support), political advocates must disclose their identities. Today the court holds that a state may require persons engaged in core political speech to identify themselves so that the officeholders and their allies can pinpoint their critics. How can this be?

According to my colleagues, the answer lies in the fact that *McConnell v. Federal Election Commission* rejected a constitutional challenge to § 201 of the Bipartisan Campaign Reform Act of 2002, which amended § 304 of the Federal Election Campaign Act. Section 304 as amended requires any person who makes disbursements exceeding $10,000 in any year for speech in federal campaigns, or who donates $1,000 or more to another person or group engaged in advocacy, to disclose his identity to the Federal Election Commission. Indiana's law differs—it starts from a lower threshold (100 sheets of paper) and requires disclosure to the public in the electioneering literature rather than to an agency—but once it is settled that speakers must reveal their identities directly to the political establishment, five Justices may think that everything else is mere detail.

---

g. "Dubitante" is a rarely used label by a judge who expresses doubt but does not dissent from the Court's opinion. —Eds.

Still, the Justices' failure to discuss *McIntyre*, or even to cite *Talley, American Constitutional Law Foundation*, or *Watchtower*, makes it impossible for courts at our level to make an informed decision—for the Supreme Court has not told us what principle to apply. Does *McConnell* apply to all electioneering? All speakers? To primary communications (as opposed to notices sent to agencies)? The Supreme Court wrote that §304 is valid because it is (in the view of five Justices) a wise balance among competing interests. Yet the function of the first amendment is to put the regulation of speech off limits to government *even if* regulation is deemed wise. For the judiciary to say that a law is valid to the extent that it is good is to operate as a council of revision and to deny the power of a written constitution to constrain contemporary legislation supported by the social class from which judges are drawn. And when, as in *McConnell*, the judgment is supported by a one-vote margin, any Justice's conclusion that a particular extension is unwise will reverse the constitutional outcome. How can legislators or the judges of other courts determine what is apt to tip the balance?

Footnote 88 to the lead opinion in *McConnell* hints that one or more members of the majority may believe that the validity of the federal statute depends on its entire complement of rules. This footnote—the only place in which a majority opinion discusses *McIntyre* (though not when dealing with §304!)—says that "BCRA's fidelity to those imperatives" sets it apart from the law held invalid in *McIntyre*. This treats the statute as a unit. It is difficult to say that the Indiana legislation at issue today displays "fidelity" to the "imperatives" of curtailing public corruption while allowing room for expression. As far as I can see, it has nothing to do with the risk of subtle bribery, and it attaches no weight to the risks borne by supporters of unpopular candidates. The majority in *McConnell* emphasized that the disclosure to the agency did *not* include the content of the advertisement. In Indiana the disclosure is affixed to the speech; the association is unavoidable; does this make a difference? My colleagues think not; I am not so sure.

Doubtless "a speaker's credibility often depends crucially on who he is." But how does this support *obligatory* disclosure? Speakers who prefer concealment in order to reduce their personal risks, and who accept the discount that readers attach to advocacy from unnamed sources, do not impose burdens on strangers. What then is the justification for regulation? "People are intelligent enough to evaluate the source of an anonymous writing. They can see it is anonymous. They know it is anonymous. They can evaluate its anonymity along with its message, as long as they are permitted, as they must be, to read that message." *McIntyre*, 514 U.S. at 348 n.11. Arguments that speech may be regulated to protect the audience from misunderstanding should fare poorly and outside of electioneering *have* fared poorly. See, e.g., *Virginia State Board of Pharmacy v. Virginia Citizens Consumer Council, Inc.*, 425 U.S. 748, 769–70 (1976). Anyway, we must consider the possibility that anonymity promotes a focus on the strength of the argument rather than the identity of the speaker; this is a reason why Madison, Hamilton, and Jay chose to publish *The Federalist* anonymously. Instead of having to persuade New Yorkers that his roots in Virginia should be overlooked, Madison could present the arguments and let the reader evaluate them on merit.

Trade associations and other interest groups will have little difficulty complying with Indiana's law. Factions that hope to secure political favors enjoy legal counsel who specialize in election matters. Professionals in the field not only will assure compliance but also will exploit the inevitable loopholes. The identity of these interest groups is no mystery; many operate from marble-clad buildings and deploy full-time lobbyists. Statutes such as Indiana's have their real bite when flushing small groups, political clubs, or solitary speakers into the limelight, or reducing them to silence. Indiana's statute, which requires disclosure from the first dollar of speech, bears especially heavily on political outsiders. Indiana has essentially forbidden *all* spontaneous political speech, perhaps all electioneering by individuals and small groups. Before favoring or opposing any candidate, a would-be speaker must navigate a thicket of rules. * * *

Often the Supreme Court says that even a small fee or tax, or a short delay in obtaining a free license (as in *Watchtower*), is an unacceptable burden on speech. Yet in *McConnell* the Court was sanguine about the delays, and non-trivial legal expenses, entailed in complying with complex rules for campaign speech. These outlays come on top of the costs that must be borne by persons who back the wrong horse and incur the enmity of elected officials—for the winners now are entitled to learn all of their vocal opponents' identities. Maybe these effects can be justified with respect to electioneering at the national level by deep-pocket interest groups—though I think that the Justices have been too ready to equate political support to bribery—but for local elections the equation is impossible to sustain.

Indiana does not contend that requiring disclosure by plaintiffs Carol Antun, Perry Metzger, and Bruce Martin—who want to use their own resources to speak on behalf of candidates of the Libertarian Party (and oppose incumbents, for libertarians do not occupy any major office in Indiana)—is essential to avert a material risk of underground favor-trading or bribery. Nor does the state try to justify mandatory disclosure by any truly independent speaker. Instead Indiana contends that it is entitled to regulate *all* electioneering by *every* speaker in order to avoid drawing lines. Given *McConnell*, I cannot be confident that my colleagues are wrong in thinking that five Justices will go along. But I also do not understand how that position can be reconciled with established principles of constitutional law.

Notes and Questions

1. If Aristotle, quoted in Judge Posner's opinion for the court, is correct, and "we believe good men more fully and more readily," is that an argument against permitting anonymous speech? Or does it suggest that voters will discount anonymous speech accordingly, leaving no need for mandated disclosure?

2. At the close of his opinion, Judge Easterbrook noted that the speakers in *Majors* wished to oppose incumbent officeholders. What was the relevance of this

observation? Is there a reason speakers might be more reluctant to be publicly associated with opposition to incumbents than to challengers?

3. How much detail can a state require in a "disclaimer"? Under federal law, for example, if an organization—we'll call it Citizens for Democratic Socialism—independently funds a radio advertisement supporting a candidate's election, the advertisement must include the following disclaimer:

> "Paid for by Citizens for Democratic Socialism, www.citizensfordemocrat icsocialism.org, not authorized by any candidate or candidate's committee. Citizens for Democratic Socialism is responsible for the content of this advertising."

See 52 U.S.C. §30120; 11 C.F.R. §§110.11(b)-(c). How fast can you say this disclaimer? For most people, speaking quickly, it takes at least six seconds, or twenty percent of a thirty-second ad. Six seconds may not seem like a lot, but consider what else an ad might say in six seconds: "Give me liberty, or give me death"; "We have nothing to fear but fear itself"; "It's time we start caring about one another—this year, vote for Joe Smith, Democratic Socialist."

Is all of the required disclaimer really necessary? How much is redundant? Could the disclaimer be unconstitutionally overinclusive, in that it interferes with the speaker's message more than necessary to serve the government's interests? In *National Institute of Family and Life Advocates v. Becerra*, 585 U.S. __, 138 S. Ct. 2361 (2018), the Supreme Court considered a California statute requiring crisis-pregnancy centers to provide specific notices to pregnant women. In finding the statute unconstitutional, the Court noted that the statute "imposes a government-scripted, speaker-based disclosure requirement that is wholly disconnected from California's informational interest." 138 S. Ct. at 2377. The California statute would have, in certain circumstances, required a government notice much longer than the speaker's own message, thus, "drown[ing] out the facility's own message." *Id.* at 2377–78. Political-disclaimer laws do not require so lengthy a message, but is there a lesser point at which the disclaimer notice could effectively harm a speaker's ability to communicate its desired message? *Cf. Pacific Gas & Electric Co. v. Public Utilities Commission of California*, 475 U.S. 1 (1986) (striking down a law requiring a utility to place a third party's speech in its billing envelopes); *Miami Herald Publishing Co. v. Tornillo*, 418 U.S. 241 (1974) (striking down a law requiring newspapers to provide space for replies to criticisms made in the newspapers).

Is there really a strong governmental information interest served by disclaimers? Consider the statement that candidates for federal office have been required to make on broadcast ads since 2003: "I'm ___, and I approve this message." Remembering that the ad must already state that it is authorized by the candidate, do voters wonder if a candidate approves an ad urging his election, or defeat of the opponent? The requirement has provided a significant amount of mockery—*see, e.g.*, https://www .youtube.com/watch?v=7M-cmNdiFuI. Has it really provided important information to the public?

In short, beyond the claims of a right to anonymity included in *McIntyre* and *Abell*, are disclaimer requirements vulnerable to challenge if they simply become too onerous? Where would a court draw the line?

D. Exemptions from Disclosure

In Part II-B of its opinion in *Buckley*, the Supreme Court held that the First Amendment required the government to grant an exemption from disclosure to minor parties and independents who were able to show a "reasonable probability" of "threats, harassment, or reprisals from either Government officials or private parties." The following case presents the question not only whether a particular minor party should be exempt from disclosing its contributors, but also whether it should be exempt from disclosing the recipients of its expenditures.

Brown v. Socialist Workers '74 Campaign Committee (Ohio)
Supreme Court of the United States
459 U.S. 87, 103 S. Ct. 416, 74 L. Ed. 2d 250 (1982)

JUSTICE MARSHALL delivered the opinion of the Court [in which CHIEF JUSTICE BURGER, JUSTICE BRENNAN, JUSTICE WHITE, and JUSTICE POWELL join, and in which JUSTICE BLACKMUN joins as to Parts I, III, and IV]. * * *

I

The Socialist Workers Party (SWP) is a small political party with approximately 60 members in the State of Ohio. The Party states in its constitution that its aim is "the abolition of capitalism and the establishment of a workers' government to achieve socialism." As the District Court found, the SWP does not advocate the use of violence. It seeks instead to achieve social change through the political process, and its members regularly run for public office. The SWP's candidates have had little success at the polls. In 1980, for example, the Ohio SWP's candidate for the United States Senate received fewer than 77,000 votes, less than 1.9% of the total vote. Campaign contributions and expenditures in Ohio have averaged about $15,000 annually since 1974.

In 1974 appellees instituted a class action * * * challenging the constitutionality of the disclosure provisions of the Ohio Campaign Expense Reporting Law. The Ohio statute requires every candidate for political office to file a statement identifying each contributor and each recipient of a disbursement of campaign funds. The "object or purpose" of each disbursement must also be disclosed. The lists of names and addresses of contributors and recipients are open to public inspection for at least six years. Violations of the disclosure requirements are punishable by fines of up to $1,000 for each day of violation.

* * * [T]he three-judge court concluded that under *Buckley* v. *Valeo*, 424 U.S. 1 (1976) [p. 933], the Ohio disclosure requirements are unconstitutional as applied to appellees. * * *

II

The Constitution protects against the compelled disclosure of political associations and beliefs. Such disclosures "can seriously infringe on privacy of association and belief guaranteed by the First Amendment." *Buckley* v. *Valeo, supra,* at 64. "Inviolability of privacy in group association may in many circumstances be indispensable to preservation of freedom of association, particularly where a group espouses dissident beliefs." *NAACP* v. *Alabama,* [357 U.S. 449], 462 [(1958)] [p. 919]. The right to privacy in one's political associations and beliefs will yield only to a "subordinating interest of the State [that is] compelling," *NAACP* v. *Alabama, supra,* at 463, and then only if there is a "substantial relation between the information sought and [an] overriding and compelling state interest."

In *Buckley* v. *Valeo* this Court upheld against a First Amendment challenge the reporting and disclosure requirements imposed on political parties by the Federal Election Campaign Act of 1971. The Court found three government interests sufficient in general to justify requiring disclosure of information concerning campaign contributions and expenditures: enhancement of voters' knowledge about a candidate's possible allegiances and interests, deterrence of corruption, and the enforcement of contribution limitations. The Court stressed, however, that in certain circumstances the balance of interests requires exempting minor political parties from compelled disclosures. The government's interests in compelling disclosures are "diminished" in the case of minor parties. Minor party candidates "usually represent definite and publicized viewpoints" well known to the public, and the improbability of their winning reduces the dangers of corruption and vote-buying. At the same time, the potential for impairing First Amendment interests is substantially greater:

> "We are not unmindful that the damage done by disclosure to the associational interests of the minor parties and their members and to supporters of independents could be significant. These movements are less likely to have a sound financial base and thus are more vulnerable to falloffs in contributions. In some instances, fears of reprisal may deter contributions to the point where the movement cannot survive. The public interest also suffers if that result comes to pass, for there is a consequent reduction in the free circulation of ideas both within and without the political arena." [424 U.S.], at 71.

We concluded that in some circumstances the diminished government interests furthered by compelling disclosures by minor parties does [*sic*] not justify the greater threat to First Amendment values.

Buckley v. *Valeo* set forth the following test for determining when the First Amendment requires exempting minor parties from compelled disclosures:

> "The evidence offered need show only a reasonable probability that the compelled disclosure of a party's contributors' names will subject them to threats, harassment, or reprisals from either Government officials or private parties." *Id.,* at 74.

The Court acknowledged that "unduly strict requirements of proof could impose a heavy burden" on minor parties. *Ibid.* Accordingly, the Court emphasized that "[minor] parties must be allowed sufficient flexibility in the proof of injury." *Ibid.*

> "The proof may include, for example, specific evidence of past or present harassment of members due to their associational ties, or of harassment directed against the organization itself. A pattern of threats or specific manifestations of public hostility may be sufficient. New parties that have no history upon which to draw may be able to offer evidence of reprisals and threats directed against individuals or organizations holding similar views." *Ibid.*

Appellants concede that the *Buckley* test for exempting minor parties governs the disclosure of the names of *contributors*, but they contend that the test has no application to the compelled disclosure of names of *recipients* of campaign disbursements. Appellants assert that the State has a substantial interest in preventing the misuse of campaign funds.[10] They also argue that the disclosure of the names of recipients of campaign funds will have no significant impact on First Amendment rights, because, unlike a contribution, the mere receipt of money for commercial services does not affirmatively express political support.

We reject appellants' unduly narrow view of the minor-party exemption recognized in *Buckley*. Appellants' attempt to limit the exemption to laws requiring disclosure of contributors is inconsistent with the rationale for the exemption stated in *Buckley*. The Court concluded that the government interests supporting disclosure are weaker in the case of minor parties, while the threat to First Amendment values is greater. Both of these considerations apply not only to the disclosure of campaign contributors but also to the disclosure of recipients of campaign disbursements. * * *[11]

---

10. This is one of three government interests identified in *Buckley*. Appellants do not contend that the other two interests, enhancing voters' ability to evaluate candidates and enforcing contribution limitations, support the disclosure of the names of recipients of campaign disbursements.

11. The partial dissent suggests that the government interest in the disclosure of recipients of expenditures is not significantly diminished in the case of minor political parties, since parties with little likelihood of electoral success might nevertheless finance improper campaign activities merely to gain recognition. * * * [But m]ost of the limited resources of minor parties will typically be needed to pay for the ordinary fixed costs of conducting campaigns, such as filing fees, travel expenses, and the expenses incurred in publishing and distributing campaign literature and maintaining offices. * * * We cannot agree, therefore, that minor parties are as likely as major parties to make significant expenditures in funding dirty tricks or other improper campaign activities. Moreover, the expenditure by minor parties of even a substantial portion of their limitod [*sic*] funds on illegal activities would be unlikely to have a substantial impact. Furthermore, the mere possibility that minor parties will resort to corrupt or unfair tactics cannot justify the substantial infringement on First Amendment interests that would result from compelling the disclosure of recipients of expenditures. * * * We * * * recognized [in *Buckley*] that the distorting influence of large contributors on elections may not be entirely absent in the context of minor parties. Nevertheless, because we concluded that the government interest in disclosing contributors is substantially reduced in the case of minor parties, we held that minor parties are entitled to an exemption

Moreover, appellants seriously understate the threat to First Amendment rights that would result from requiring minor parties to disclose the recipients of campaign disbursements. Expenditures by a political party often consist of reimbursements, advances, or wages paid to party members, campaign workers, and supporters, whose activities lie at the very core of the First Amendment. Disbursements may also go to persons who choose to express their support for an unpopular cause by providing services rendered scarce by public hostility and suspicion. Should their involvement be publicized, these persons would be as vulnerable to threats, harassment, and reprisals as are contributors whose connection with the party is solely financial.[14] Even individuals who receive disbursements for "merely" commercial transactions may be deterred by the public enmity attending publicity, and those seeking to harass may disrupt commercial activities on the basis of expenditure information. Because an individual who enters into a transaction with a minor party purely for commercial reasons lacks any ideological commitment to the party, such an individual may well be deterred from providing services by even a small risk of harassment.[16] Compelled disclosure of the names of such recipients of expenditures could therefore cripple a minor party's ability to operate effectively and thereby reduce "the free circulation of ideas both within and without the political arena." *Buckley*, 424 U.S., at 71.

We hold, therefore, that the test announced in *Buckley* for safeguarding the First Amendment interests of minor parties and their members and supporters applies not only to the compelled disclosure of campaign contributors but also to the compelled disclosure of recipients of campaign disbursements.

---

from requirements that contributors be disclosed where they can show a reasonable probability of harassment. 424 U.S., at 70. Because we similarly conclude that the government interest in requiring the disclosure of recipients of expenditures is substantially reduced in the case of minor parties, we hold that the minor-party exemption recognized in *Buckley* applies to compelled disclosure of expenditures as well.

14. The fact that some or even many recipients of campaign expenditures may not be exposed to the risk of public hostility does not detract from the serious threat to the exercise of First Amendment rights of those who are so exposed. We cannot agree with the partial dissent's assertion that disclosures of disbursements paid to campaign workers and supporters will not increase the probability that they will be subjected to harassment and hostility. Apart from the fact that individuals may work for a candidate in a variety of ways without publicizing their involvement, the application of a disclosure requirement results in a dramatic increase in public exposure. Under Ohio law a person's affiliation with the party will be recorded in a document that must be kept open to inspection by any one who wishes to examine it for a period of at least six years. The preservation of unorthodox political affiliations in public records substantially increases the potential for harassment above and beyond the risk that an individual faces simply as a result of having worked for an unpopular party at one time.

16. Moreover, it would be hard to think of many instances in which the state interest in preventing vote-buying and improper campaign activities would be furthered by the disclosure of payments for routine commercial services.

The header shows page number 966, "ANONYMOUS SPEECH", and "CH. 9".

III

The District Court properly applied the *Buckley* test to the facts of this case. The District Court found "substantial evidence of both governmental and private hostility toward and harassment of SWP members and supporters." Appellees introduced proof of specific incidents of private and government hostility toward the SWP and its members within the four years preceding the trial. These incidents, many of which occurred in Ohio and neighboring States, included threatening phone calls and hate mail, the burning of SWP literature, the destruction of SWP members' property, police harassment of a party candidate, and the firing of shots at an SWP office. There was also evidence that in the 12-month period before trial 22 SWP members, including 4 in Ohio, were fired because of their party membership. Although appellants contend that two of the Ohio firings were not politically motivated, the evidence amply supports the District Court's conclusion that "private hostility and harassment toward SWP members make it difficult for them to maintain employment."

The District Court also found a past history of Government harassment of the SWP. * * * Until at least 1976, the FBI employed various covert techniques to obtain information about the SWP, including information concerning the sources of its funds and the nature of its expenditures. The District Court specifically found that the FBI had conducted surveillance of the Ohio SWP and had interfered with its activities within the State. Government surveillance was not limited to the FBI. The United States Civil Service Commission also gathered information on the SWP, the YSA [Young Socialist Alliance], and their supporters, and the FBI routinely distributed its reports to Army, Navy and Air Force Intelligence, the United States Secret Service, and the Immigration and Naturalization Service.

The District Court properly concluded that the evidence of private and Government hostility toward the SWP and its members establishes a reasonable probability that disclosing the names of contributors and recipients will subject them to threats, harassment, and reprisals. There were numerous instances of recent harassment of the SWP both in Ohio and in other States.[20] There was also considerable evidence of

---

20. Some of the recent episodes of threats, harassment, and reprisals against the SWP and its members occurred outside of Ohio. Anti-SWP occurrences in places such as Chicago (SWP office vandalized) and Pittsburgh (shots fired at SWP building) are certainly relevant to the determination of the public's attitude toward the SWP in Ohio. * * * Appellants point to the lack of direct evidence linking the Ohio statute's disclosure requirements to the harassment of campaign contributors or recipients of disbursements. In *Buckley*, however, we rejected such "unduly strict requirements of proof" in favor of "flexibility in the proof of injury." [*Ibid.*] We thus rejected requiring a minor party to "come forward with witnesses who are too fearful to contribute but not too fearful to testify about their fear" or prove that "chill and harassment [are] directly attributable to the specific disclosure from which the exemption is sought." *Ibid.* We think that these considerations are equally applicable to the proof required to establish a reasonable probability that recipients will be subjected to threats and harassment if their names are disclosed. While the partial dissent appears to agree, its "separately focused inquiry" in reality requires evidence of chill and harassment directly attributable to the expenditure-disclosure requirement.

past Government harassment. Appellants challenge the relevance of this evidence of Government harassment in light of recent efforts to curb official misconduct. Notwithstanding these efforts, the evidence suggests that hostility toward the SWP is ingrained and likely to continue. All this evidence was properly relied on by the District Court.

IV

The First Amendment prohibits a State from compelling disclosures by a minor party that will subject those persons identified to the reasonable probability of threats, harassment, or reprisals. Such disclosures would infringe the First Amendment rights of the party and its members and supporters. In light of the substantial evidence of past and present hostility from private persons and Government officials against the SWP, Ohio's campaign disclosure requirements cannot be constitutionally applied to the Ohio SWP.

The judgment of the three-judge District Court for the Southern District of Ohio is affirmed.

It is so ordered.

[Justice Blackmun, concurring in part and concurring in the judgment, argued that the case did not properly present the question whether the anonymity of campaign disbursements should be subject to the same constitutional standard as the one applicable to contributions. Assuming, however, that the *Buckley* standard applied to both, he agreed that the Ohio law could not constitutionally be applied against the SWP, either as to contributions or expenditures.]

Justice O'Connor, with whom Justice Rehnquist and Justice Stevens join, concurring in part and dissenting in part.

I concur in the judgment that the Socialist Workers Party has sufficiently demonstrated a reasonable probability that disclosure of contributors will subject those persons to threats, harassment, or reprisals, and thus under *Buckley* v. *Valeo* the State of Ohio cannot constitutionally compel the disclosure. Further, I agree that the broad concerns of *Buckley* apply to the required disclosure of recipients of campaign expenditures. But, as I view the record presented here, the SWP has failed to carry its burden of showing that there is a reasonable probability that disclosure of recipients of expenditures will subject the recipients themselves or the SWP to threats, harassment, or reprisals. Moreover, the strong public interest in fair and honest elections outweighs any damage done to the associational rights of the party and its members by application of the State's expenditure disclosure law. * * *

[T]here are important differences between disclosure of contributors and disclosure of recipients of campaign expenditures — differences that * * * compel me to conclude that the balance should not necessarily be calibrated identically. First, unlike the government's interest in disclosure of contributions, its interest in disclosure of expenditures does not decrease significantly for small parties. The Court in *Buckley* recognized that knowing the identity of contributors would not significantly increase the voters' ability to determine the political ideology of the minor-party candidate, for the stance of the minor-party candidate is usually well known. Nor would identifying a minor party's contributors further the interest in preventing the "buying" of a candidate, because of the improbability of the minor-party candidate's winning the election. Thus, these two major government interests in disclosure of contributions are significantly reduced for minor parties.[3]

In sharp contrast, however, the governmental interest in disclosure of expenditures remains significant for minor parties. The purpose of requiring parties to disclose expenditures is to deter improper influencing of voters. Corruption of the electoral process can take many forms: the actual buying of votes; the use of "slush funds;" dirty tricks; and bribes of poll watchers and other election officials. Certainly, a "persuasive" campaign worker on election day can corral voters for his minor-party candidate with even a modest "slush fund." Even though such improper practices are unlikely to be so successful as to attract enough votes to elect the minor-party candidate, a minor party, whose short-term goal is merely recognition, may be as tempted to resort to impermissible methods as are major parties, and the resulting deflection of votes can determine the outcome of the election of other candidates. The requirement of a *full* and *verifiable* report of expenditures is important in deterring such practices, for otherwise the party could hide the improper transactions through an accounting sleight of hand.[6]

On the other side of the balance, disclosure of recipients of expenditures will have a lesser impact on a minority party's First Amendment interests than will disclosure of contributors. * * * Unlike silent contributors, whom disclosure would reveal to the public as supporters of the party's ideological positions, persons providing business services to a minor party are not generally perceived by the public as supporting the party's ideology, and thus are unlikely to be harassed if their names are disclosed. Consequently, the party's associational interests are unlikely to be affected by disclosure of recipients of such expenditures.

Other recipients of expenditures may have closer ideological ties to the party. The majority suggests that campaign workers receiving per diem, travel, or room expenses may fit in this category. It is certainly conceivable that such persons may be harassed or threatened for their conduct. Laws requiring disclosure of recipients

---

3. [T]he third governmental interest articulated in *Buckley* — using disclosures to police limitations on contributions and expenditures — has no application to either contributions or expenditures in Ohio, since the Ohio statute sets no limitations on them.

6. I therefore disagree with the majority's suggestion that the government interest in deterring corruption is not furthered by disclosure of all expenditures, including those for commercial services. Even if improprieties are unlikely to occur in expenditures for commercial services, full and verifiable disclosure is needed to ensure that other, improper expenditures are not hidden in commercial accounts.

of expenditures, however, are not likely to contribute to this harassment. Once an individual has openly shown his close ties to the organization by campaigning for it, disclosure of receipt of expenditures is unlikely to increase the degree of harassment so significantly as to deter the individual from campaigning for the party. Further, in striking the balance, the governmental concerns are greatest precisely for the actions of campaign workers that might improperly influence voters. Thus, whatever marginal deterrence that may arise from disclosure of expenditures is outweighed by the heightened governmental interest. * * *

Turning to the evidence in this case, it is important to remember that, even though proof requirements must be flexible, *Buckley, supra,* at 74, the minor party carries the burden of production and persuasion to show that its First Amendment interests outweigh the governmental interests. * * *

Here, there is no direct evidence of harassment of either contributors or recipients of expenditures. Rather, as the majority accurately represents it, the evidence concerns harassment and reprisals of visible party members, including violence at party headquarters and loss of jobs. I concur in the majority's conclusion that this evidence, viewed in its entirety, supports the conclusion that there will be a reasonable probability of harassment of contributors if their names are disclosed. This evidence is sufficiently linked to disclosure of contributors in large part because any person publicly known to support the SWP's unpopular ideological position may suffer the reprisals that this record shows active party members suffer, and the disclosure of contributors may lead the public to presume these people support the party's ideology.

In contrast, the record, read in its entirety, does not suggest that disclosure of recipients of expenditures would lead to harassment of recipients or reprisals to the party or its members. Appellees gave no breakdown of the types of expenditures they thought would lead to harassment if disclosed. The record does contain the expenditure statements of the SWP, which itemize each expenditure with its purpose while usually omitting the name and address of the recipient. The majority of expenditures, both in number and dollar amount, are for business transactions such as office supplies, food, printing, photographs, telephone service, and books. There is virtually no evidence that disclosure of the recipients of these expenditures will impair the SWP's ability to obtain needed services. Even if we assume that a portion of expenditures went to temporary campaign workers or others whom the public might identify as supporting the party's ideology, these persons have already publicly demonstrated their support by their campaign work. There is simply no basis for inferring that such persons would *thereafter* be harassed or threatened or otherwise deterred from working for the party by virtue of inclusion of their names in later expenditure reports, or that if any such remote danger existed, it would outweigh the concededly important governmental interests in disclosure of recipients of expenditures.

It is plain that appellees did not carry their burden of production and persuasion insofar as they challenge the expenditure disclosure provisions. I would therefore uphold the constitutionality of those portions of the Ohio statute that require the SWP to disclose the recipients of expenditures.

Notes and Questions

1. *Socialist Workers* was an as-applied challenge. How much evidence must a minor party produce to demonstrate a "reasonable probability of threats, harassment, or reprisals" so as to exempt it from reporting requirements?

At about the same time that it began pursuing the above litigation against the State of Ohio, the SWP also initiated litigation against the Federal Election Commission, seeking an exemption from the reporting requirements of the Federal Election Campaign Act, then 2 U.S.C. § 434(c), now 52 U.S.C. § 30104(c). *Socialist Workers 1974 National Campaign Committee v. Federal Election Commission*, Civil Action No. 74-1338 (D.D.C. 1979). In 1979, the parties entered into a consent decree that required the committees supporting the SWP candidates to maintain records in accordance with the Act and to file reports in a timely manner, but exempted the committees from the provisions requiring the disclosure of names, addresses, occupations, and principal places of business of contributors to SWP committees, as well as information related to political committees or candidates supported by SWP committees; lenders, endorsers, or guarantors of loans to the SWP committees; and persons to whom the SWP committees made expenditures. The decree applied through 1984, and it permitted the SWP to apply for extensions. Using the Advisory Opinion process of 2 U.S.C. § 437f (now 52 U.S.C. § 30108), the FEC has voted on five occasions to extend the SWP's exemption. Although earlier extensions were granted unanimously, later extensions became more controversial.

In 2003, the Commission extended the exemption by only a 4-2 vote. The evidence of ongoing harassment provided to the FEC by the SWP that year included statements from party officials and candidates that potential supporters feared public identification with the SWP, claims by party workers that they had difficulty selling subscriptions to the party newspaper because of fears their names would be placed on FBI watch lists, and statements from party fundraisers that long-time donors would refuse to contribute again if their names would be made public. What weight should the FEC, or perhaps a judge, place on such (self-serving?) statements? Might some potential donors say such things as excuses to avoid having to give an outright "no" to requests for support?

The SWP also supplied several examples of alleged harassment. Two typical examples: "SWP supporters were campaigning outside a factory in Newark when a man who identified himself as the factory's owner ripped a leaflet out of one of the supporter's hands, threatened to 'f*** up' the supporters, told them to 'get the f*** off his property' and repeatedly shoved them"; and "SWP supporters were staffing a table in the garment district of New York City [when] a man who said he owned the storefront business there told the SWP supporters they would have to move, and as they were moving he threatened to turn over the table." *See* Advisory Opinion

2003-02 (April 3, 2003). Are such incidents sufficient to demonstrate a need for an exemption? Are such episodes atypical of those faced by many demonstrators, pick-eters, leafletters, and volunteers for major-party campaigns?

The SWP's exemption was extended twice more, both times drawing at least one dissenting vote. In 2017, the FEC refused to extend the exemption. A few years earlier, the FEC refused to grant the Tea Party Leadership Fund an exemption from the same disclosure provisions.

If we wish to encourage more participation in politics, how much "harassment" and threats should people be expected to accept as normal? Does it matter that the government requires individuals to provide the information that may lead to their own harassment?

2. The Court in *Socialist Workers* focused not only on the level of theats and harassment necessary to entitle a party to a disclosure exemption, but also on the fact that the SWP was a minor party. Should minor-party status—as opposed to the level of threats and harassment—matter? At what point would a party cease to be a minor party? In 1996, the Reform Party nominee for President, Ross Perot, received 8.4% of the national popular vote. In 1998, Reform Party nominee Jessie Ventura was elected governor of Minnesota. However, no other Reform candidates have won federal or statewide office. Would the Reform Party have been considered a minor party heading into the 2000 election cycle?

3. After the 2004 presidential election, various contributors to major-party can-didates found their names and addresses listed as "targets" on a website maintained by an extremist animal-rights organization called Stop Huntingdon Animal Cruelty ("SHAC"), under the heading "Now You Know Where to Find Them." Members of SHAC had previously assaulted and vandalized property of various individuals working for Huntingdon Life Sciences, a London-based lab that used animals for drug testing. SHAC was listed as a domestic terrorist threat by the FBI. SHAC had compiled the list by searching the FEC's public database of donors who worked for companies that did business with Huntingdon Life Sciences. *See* Bradley A. Smith, *In Defense of Political Anonymity*, 20 City J. 74, 76–77 (2010).

In 2008, after California passed Proposition 8, a state constitutional amendment that prohibited state recognition of same-sex marriage, many financial support-ers of the Amendment found their businesses and employers boycotted or vandal-ized; others were fired or forced to resign from their jobs. These supporters were identified from information gleaned from mandatory disclosure reports. *Id.* at 77. Is it appropriate for government to force people to provide information that may subject them to harassment, vandalism, threats, and loss of employment? Alterna-tively, assuming lawful, non-violent means are used, is there any reason why people shouldn't be held "accountable" for their beliefs and votes? Is this merely part of the public's legitimate "right to know"? *Cf. Hollingsworth v. Perry*, 558 U.S. 183 (2010) (staying an order allowing cameras in the courtroom in a challenge to Proposition 8's validity).

4. In footnote 3 of her *Socialist Workers* opinion, Justice O'Connor noted that because Ohio at that time had no limits on contributions, reporting the names of contributors was not necessary to achieve the government's interest in policing limits on contributions. How much should the state's interest in enforcing contribution limits matter? Couldn't the state require reporting to the state, without making the information public (as with tax returns)? How much does it matter if the alleged threat of harassment comes from the government itself, in the form of official retaliation or surveillance?

Doe v. Reed

Supreme Court of the United States
561 U.S. 186, 130 S. Ct. 2811, 177 L. Ed. 2d 493 (2010)

CHIEF JUSTICE ROBERTS delivered the opinion of the Court [in which JUSTICE KENNEDY, JUSTICE GINSBURG, JUSTICE BREYER, JUSTICE ALITO, and JUSTICE SOTOMAYOR join].

The State of Washington allows its citizens to challenge state laws by referendum. * * * This case arises out of a state law extending certain benefits to same-sex couples, and a corresponding referendum petition to put that law to a popular vote. [The referendum, R-71, appeared on the November 2009 ballot. By a margin of 53% to 47%, the voters approved the law.] Respondent intervenors invoked the [Washington Public Records Act (PRA)] to obtain copies of the petition, with the names and addresses of the signers. Certain petition signers and the petition sponsor objected, arguing that such public disclosure would violate their rights under the First Amendment.

The course of this litigation, however, has framed the legal question before us more broadly. The issue at this stage of the case is not whether disclosure of this particular petition would violate the First Amendment, but whether disclosure of referendum petitions in general would do so. We conclude that such disclosure does not as a general matter violate the First Amendment, and we therefore affirm the judgment of the Court of Appeals. We leave it to the lower courts to consider in the first instance the signers' more focused claim concerning disclosure of the information on this particular petition, which is pending before the District Court. * * *

The compelled disclosure of signatory information on referendum petitions is subject to review under the First Amendment. An individual expresses a view on a political matter when he signs a petition under Washington's referendum procedure. In most cases, the individual's signature will express the view that the law subject to the petition should be overturned. Even if the signer is agnostic as to the merits of the underlying law, his signature still expresses the political view that the question should be considered "by the whole electorate." *Meyer* v. *Grant*, 486 U.S. 414, 421 (1988) [p. 647]. In either case, the expression of a political view implicates a First Amendment right. * * *

Respondents counter that signing a petition is a legally operative legislative act and therefore "does not involve any significant expressive element." It is true that signing a referendum petition may ultimately have the legal consequence of requiring the secretary of state to place the referendum on the ballot. But we do not see how adding such legal effect to an expressive activity somehow deprives that activity of its expressive component, taking it outside the scope of the First Amendment. * * *

We have a series of precedents considering First Amendment challenges to disclosure requirements in the electoral context. These precedents have reviewed such challenges under what has been termed "exacting scrutiny." See, *e.g., Buckley* v. *Valeo,* 424 U.S. 1, 64 (1976) [p. 933] (*per curiam*).

That standard "requires a 'substantial relation' between the disclosure requirement and a 'sufficiently important' governmental interest." To withstand this scrutiny, "the strength of the governmental interest must reflect the seriousness of the actual burden on First Amendment rights." *Davis* [v. *Federal Election Comm'n,* 554 U.S. 724, 744 (2008)].[1]

Respondents assert two interests to justify the burdens of compelled disclosure under the PRA on First Amendment rights: (1) preserving the integrity of the electoral process by combating fraud, detecting invalid signatures, and fostering government transparency and accountability; and (2) providing information to the electorate about who supports the petition. Because we determine that the State's interest in preserving the integrity of the electoral process suffices to defeat the argument that the PRA is unconstitutional with respect to referendum petitions in general, we need not, and do not, address the State's "informational" interest.

The State's interest in preserving the integrity of the electoral process is undoubtedly important. * * * The State's interest is particularly strong with respect to efforts to root out fraud, which not only may produce fraudulent outcomes, but has a systemic effect as well: It "drives honest citizens out of the democratic process and breeds distrust of our government." *Purcell* v. *Gonzalez,* 549 U.S. 1, 4 (2006) [p. 1158] (*per curiam*); see also *Crawford* v. *Marion County Election Bd.,* 553 U.S. 181, 196 (2008) [p. 999] (opinion of STEVENS, J.). The threat of fraud in this context is not merely hypothetical; respondents and their *amici* cite a number of cases of petition-related fraud across the country to support the point.

---

1. JUSTICE SCALIA doubts whether petition signing is entitled to any First Amendment protection at all. His skepticism is based on the view that petition signing has "legal effects" in the legislative process, while other aspects of political participation—with respect to which we have held there is a First Amendment interest—do not. That line is not as sharp as JUSTICE SCALIA would have it; he himself recognizes "the existence of a First Amendment interest in voting," which of course also can have legal effect. The distinction becomes even fuzzier given that only *some* petition signing has legal effect, and any such legal effect attaches only well after the expressive act of signing, if the secretary determines that the petition satisfies the requirements for inclusion on the ballot. Petitions that do not qualify for the ballot of course carry no legal effect.

But the State's interest in preserving electoral integrity is not limited to combating fraud. That interest extends to efforts to ferret out invalid signatures caused not by fraud but by simple mistake, such as duplicate signatures or signatures of individuals who are not registered to vote in the State. That interest also extends more generally to promoting transparency and accountability in the electoral process, which the State argues is "essential to the proper functioning of a democracy."

Plaintiffs contend that the disclosure requirements of the PRA are not "sufficiently related" to the interest of protecting the integrity of the electoral process. They argue that disclosure is not necessary because the secretary of state is already charged with verifying and canvassing the names on a petition, advocates and opponents of a measure can observe that process, and any citizen can challenge the secretary's actions in court. They also stress that existing criminal penalties reduce the danger of fraud in the petition process.

But the secretary's verification and canvassing will not catch all invalid signatures: The job is large and difficult (the secretary ordinarily checks "only 3 to 5% of signatures"), and the secretary can make mistakes, too. Public disclosure can help cure the inadequacies of the verification and canvassing process.

Disclosure also helps prevent certain types of petition fraud otherwise difficult to detect, such as outright forgery and "bait and switch" fraud, in which an individual signs the petition based on a misrepresentation of the underlying issue. The signer is in the best position to detect these types of fraud, and public disclosure can bring the issue to the signer's attention.

Public disclosure thus helps ensure that the only signatures counted are those that should be, and that the only referenda placed on the ballot are those that garner enough valid signatures. Public disclosure also promotes transparency and accountability in the electoral process to an extent other measures cannot. In light of the foregoing, we reject plaintiffs' argument and conclude that public disclosure of referendum petitions in general is substantially related to the important interest of preserving the integrity of the electoral process.

Plaintiffs' more significant objection is that "the strength of the governmental interest" does not "reflect the seriousness of the actual burden on First Amendment rights." According to plaintiffs, the objective of those seeking disclosure of the R-71 petition is not to prevent fraud, but to publicly identify those who had validly signed and to broadcast the signers' political views on the subject of the petition. Plaintiffs allege, for example, that several groups plan to post the petitions in searchable form on the Internet, and then encourage other citizens to seek out the R-71 signers.

Plaintiffs explain that once on the Internet, the petition signers' names and addresses "can be combined with publicly available phone numbers and maps," in what will effectively become a blueprint for harassment and intimidation. To support their claim that they will be subject to reprisals, plaintiffs cite examples from the history of a similar proposition in California and from the experience of one of the petition sponsors in this case.

In related contexts, we have explained that those resisting disclosure can prevail under the First Amendment if they can show "a reasonable probability that the compelled disclosure [of personal information] will subject them to threats, harassment, or reprisals from either Government officials or private parties." *Buckley*, *supra*, at 74; see also *Citizens United* [v. *Federal Election Comm'n*], 558 U.S. [310], 367 [(2010)] [p. 944]. The question before us, however, is not whether PRA disclosure violates the First Amendment with respect to those who signed the R-71 petition, or other particularly controversial petitions. The question instead is whether such disclosure in general violates the First Amendment rights of those who sign referendum petitions.

The problem for plaintiffs is that their argument rests almost entirely on the specific harm they say would attend disclosure of the information on the R-71 petition, or on similarly controversial ones. But typical referendum petitions "concern tax policy, revenue, budget, or other state law issues." Voters care about such issues, some quite deeply—but there is no reason to assume that any burdens imposed by disclosure of typical referendum petitions would be remotely like the burdens plaintiffs fear in this case.

Plaintiffs have offered little in response. * * * Indeed, what little plaintiffs do offer with respect to typical petitions in Washington hurts, not helps: Several other petitions in the State "have been subject to release in recent years," plaintiffs tell us, but apparently that release has come without incident.

Faced with the State's unrebutted arguments that only modest burdens attend the disclosure of a typical petition, we must reject plaintiffs' broad challenge to the PRA. In doing so, we note—as we have in other election law disclosure cases—that upholding the law against a broad-based challenge does not foreclose a litigant's success in a narrower one. See *Buckley*, *supra*, at 74 ("minor parties" may be exempt from disclosure requirements if they can show "a reasonable probability that the compelled disclosure of a party's contributors' names will subject them to threats, harassment, or reprisals from either Government officials or private parties"); *Citizens United*, *supra*, at 370 (disclosure "would be unconstitutional as applied to an organization if there were a reasonable probability that the group's members would face threats, harassment, or reprisals if their names were disclosed"). * * *

[*Affirmed.*]

JUSTICE BREYER, concurring.

In circumstances where, as here, "a law significantly implicates competing constitutionally protected interests in complex ways," the Court balances interests. *Nixon* v. *Shrink Missouri Government PAC*, 528 U.S. 377, 402 (2000) [p. 768] (BREYER, J., concurring). * * * As I read their opinions, this is what both the Court and JUSTICE

STEVENS do. And for the reasons stated in those opinions (as well as many of the reasons discussed by JUSTICE SOTOMAYOR), I would uphold the statute challenged in this case. With this understanding, I join the opinion of the Court and JUSTICE STEVENS' opinion.

JUSTICE ALITO, concurring.

The Court holds that the disclosure under the Washington Public Records Act (PRA) of the names and addresses of persons who sign referendum petitions does not as a general matter violate the First Amendment, and I agree with that conclusion. Many referendum petitions concern relatively uncontroversial matters, and plaintiffs have provided no reason to think that disclosure of signatory information in those contexts would significantly chill the willingness of voters to sign. Plaintiffs' facial challenge therefore must fail.

Nonetheless, facially valid disclosure requirements can impose heavy burdens on First Amendment rights in individual cases. * * * The possibility of prevailing in an as-applied challenge provides adequate protection for First Amendment rights only if (1) speakers can obtain the exemption sufficiently far in advance to avoid chilling protected speech and (2) the showing necessary to obtain the exemption is not overly burdensome. With respect to the first requirement, the as-applied exemption becomes practically worthless if speakers cannot obtain the exemption quickly and well in advance of speaking. To avoid the possibility that a disclosure requirement might chill the willingness of voters to sign a referendum petition (and thus burden a circulator's ability to collect the necessary number of signatures), voters must have some assurance *at the time when they are presented with the petition* that their names and identifying information will not be released to the public. The only way a circulator can provide such assurance, however, is if the circulator has sought and obtained an as-applied exemption from the disclosure requirement well before circulating the petition. Otherwise, the best the circulator could do would be to tell voters that an exemption might be obtained at some point in the future. Such speculation would often be insufficient to alleviate voters' concerns about the possibility of being subjected to threats, harassment, or reprisals.

Additionally, speakers must be able to obtain an as-applied exemption without clearing a high evidentiary hurdle. We acknowledged as much in *Buckley*, where we noted that "unduly strict requirements of proof could impose a heavy burden" on speech. 424 U.S., at 74. Recognizing that speakers "must be allowed sufficient flexibility in the proof of injury to assure a fair consideration of their claim," we emphasized that speakers "need show only a *reasonable probability*" that disclosure will lead to threats, harassment, or reprisals. *Ibid.* (emphasis added). * * *

In light of those principles, the plaintiffs in this case have a strong argument that the PRA violates the First Amendment as applied to the Referendum 71 petition. * * * The widespread harassment and intimidation suffered by supporters of California's Proposition 8 provides strong support for an as-applied exemption in the present case. * * * What is more, when plaintiffs return to the District Court, they will have the opportunity to develop evidence of intimidation and harassment of Referendum 71 supporters * * *. For example, plaintiffs allege that the campaign manager for one of the plaintiff groups received threatening e-mails and phone calls, and that the threats were so severe that the manager filed a complaint with the local sheriff and had his children sleep in an interior room of his home. * * *

As-applied challenges to disclosure requirements play a critical role in protecting First Amendment freedoms. To give speech the breathing room it needs to flourish, prompt judicial remedies must be available well before the relevant speech occurs and the burden of proof must be low. In this case—both through analogy and through their own experiences—plaintiffs have a strong case that they are entitled to as-applied relief, and they will be able to pursue such relief before the District Court.

JUSTICE SOTOMAYOR, with whom JUSTICE STEVENS and JUSTICE GINSBURG join, concurring. * * *

The Court today confirms that the State of Washington's decision to make referendum petition signatures available for public inspection falls squarely within the realm of permissible election-related regulations. Public disclosure of the identity of petition signers, which is the rule in the overwhelming majority of States that use initiatives and referenda, advances States' vital interests in "[p]reserving the integrity of the electoral process, preventing corruption, and sustaining the active, alert responsibility of the individual citizen in a democracy for the wise conduct of government." * * *

On the other side of the ledger, I view the burden of public disclosure on speech and associational rights as minimal in this context. As this Court has observed with respect to campaign-finance regulations, "disclosure requirements . . . 'do not prevent anyone from speaking.'" *Citizens United*, 558 U.S., at 366. When it comes to initiatives and referenda, the impact of public disclosure on expressive interests is even more attenuated. While campaign-finance disclosure injects the government into what would otherwise have been private political activity, the process of legislating by referendum is inherently public. To qualify a referendum for the ballot, citizens are required to sign a petition and supply identifying information to the State. The act of signing typically occurs in public, and the circulators who collect and submit signatures ordinarily owe signers no guarantee of confidentiality. For persons with the "civic courage" to participate in this process, the State's decision to make accessible what they voluntarily place in the public sphere should not deter them from engaging in the expressive act of petition signing. Disclosure of the identity of petition signers, moreover, in no way directly impairs the ability of anyone to speak and associate for political ends either publicly or privately.

Given the relative weight of the interests at stake and the traditionally public nature of initiative and referendum processes, the Court rightly rejects petitioners' constitutional challenge to the State of Washington's petition disclosure regulations. These same considerations also mean that any party attempting to challenge particular applications of the State's regulations will bear a heavy burden. Even when a referendum involves a particularly controversial subject and some petition signers fear harassment from nonstate actors, a State's important interests in "protect[ing] the integrity and reliability of the initiative process" remain undiminished, and the State retains significant discretion in advancing those interests. Likewise, because the expressive interests implicated by the act of petition signing are always modest, I find it difficult to see how any incremental disincentive to sign a petition would tip the constitutional balance. Case-specific relief may be available when a State selectively applies a facially neutral petition disclosure rule in a manner that discriminates based on the content of referenda or the viewpoint of petition signers, or in the rare circumstance in which disclosure poses a reasonable probability of serious and widespread harassment that the State is unwilling or unable to control. Cf. *NAACP* v. *Alabama ex rel. Patterson*, 357 U.S. 449 (1958) [p. 919]. Allowing case-specific invalidation under a more forgiving standard would unduly diminish the substantial breathing room States are afforded to adopt and implement reasonable, nondiscriminatory measures like the disclosure requirement now at issue. Accordingly, courts presented with an as-applied challenge to a regulation authorizing the disclosure of referendum petitions should be deeply skeptical of any assertion that the Constitution, which embraces political transparency, compels States to conceal the identity of persons who seek to participate in lawmaking through a state-created referendum process. With this understanding, I join the opinion of the Court.

JUSTICE STEVENS, with whom JUSTICE BREYER joins, concurring in part and concurring in the judgment.

This is not a hard case. It is not about a restriction on voting or on speech and does not involve a classic disclosure requirement. Rather, the case concerns a neutral, nondiscriminatory policy of disclosing information already in the State's possession that, it has been alleged, might one day indirectly burden petition signatories. The burden imposed by Washington's application of the PRA to referendum petitions in the vast majority, if not all, its applications is not substantial. And the State has given a more than adequate justification for its choice. * * *

[A]ny effect on speech that disclosure might have is minimal. The PRA does not necessarily make it more difficult to circulate or obtain signatures on a petition, or to communicate one's views generally. Regardless of whether someone signs a referendum petition, that person remains free to say anything to anyone at any time. If disclosure indirectly burdens a speaker, "the amount of speech covered" is small—only a single, narrow message conveying one fact in one place. And while the democratic act of casting a ballot or signing a petition does serve an expressive purpose, the act does not involve any "interactive communication" and is "not principally" a method of "individual expression of political sentiment."

Weighed against the possible burden on constitutional rights are the State's justifications for its rule. In this case, the State has posited a perfectly adequate justification: an interest in deterring and detecting petition fraud.[2] * * *

There remains the issue of petitioners' as-applied challenge. * * * Any burden on speech that petitioners posit is speculative as well as indirect. For an as-applied challenge to a law such as the PRA to succeed, there would have to be a significant threat of harassment directed at those who sign the petition that cannot be mitigated by law enforcement measures.[5] Moreover, the character of the law challenged in a referendum does not, in itself, affect the analysis. Debates about tax policy and regulation of private property can become just as heated as debates about domestic partnerships. And as a general matter, it is very difficult to show that by later disclosing the names of petition signatories, individuals will be less willing to sign petitions. Just as we have in the past, I would demand strong evidence before concluding that an indirect and speculative chain of events imposes a substantial burden on speech. * * *

Accordingly, I concur with the opinion of the Court to the extent that it is not inconsistent with my own, and I concur in the judgment.

JUSTICE SCALIA, concurring in the judgment. * * *

* * * Our Nation's longstanding traditions of legislating and voting in public refute the claim that the First Amendment accords a right to anonymity in the performance of an act with governmental effect. * * *

The filing of a [valid] referendum petition * * * has two legal effects: (1) It requires the secretary to place the measure referred to the people on the ballot at the next general election; and (2) it suspends operation of the measure, causing it only to have effect 30 days after it is approved during that election. A voter who signs a referendum petition is therefore exercising legislative power because his signature, somewhat like a vote for or against a bill in the legislature, seeks to affect the legal force of the measure at issue.[2]

---

2. Washington also points out that its disclosure policy informs voters about who supports the particular referendum. In certain election-law contexts, this informational rationale (among others) may provide a basis for regulation; in this case, there is no need to look beyond the State's quite obvious antifraud interest.

5. A rare case may also arise in which the level of threat to any individual is not quite so high but a State's disclosure would substantially limit a group's ability to "garner the number of signatures necessary to place [a] matter on the ballot," thereby "limiting [its] ability to make the matter the focus of statewide discussion." *Meyer* v. *Grant*, 486 U.S., [at] 423.

2. The Court notes that "only *some* petition signing has legal effect." That is true. Some petitions may never be submitted to the secretary; they are irrelevant here, since they will never be subject to the PRA. But some petitions that are submitted to the secretary may lack the requisite number of signatures. Even as to those, the petition signer has exercised *his portion* of the legislative power when he signs the petition, much like a legislator who casts a losing vote.

Plaintiffs point to no precedent from this Court holding that legislating is protected by the First Amendment. Nor do they identify historical evidence demonstrating that "the freedom of speech" the First Amendment codified encompassed a right to legislate without public disclosure. This should come as no surprise; the exercise of lawmaking power in the United States has traditionally been public. * * *

Moreover, even when the people *asked* Congress for legislative changes—by exercising their constitutional right to "to petition the Government for a redress of grievances"—they did so publicly. The petition was read aloud in Congress. The petitioner's name (when large groups were not involved), his request, and what action Congress had taken on the petition were consistently recorded in the House and Senate Journals. Even when the people exercised legislative power directly, they did so not anonymously, but openly in town hall meetings.

Petitioning the government and participating in the traditional town meeting were precursors of the modern initiative and referendum. * * * Plaintiffs' argument implies that the public nature of these practices, so longstanding and unquestioned, violated the freedom of speech. There is no historical support for such a claim.

Legislating was not the only governmental act that was public in America. Voting was public until 1888 when the States began to adopt the Australian secret ballot. * * * Initially, the Colonies mostly continued the English traditions of voting by a show of hands or by voice—*viva voce* voting. * * *

Although there was variation, the election official would ordinarily compile a poll with the name and residence of each voter, and the name of the candidate for whom he voted. To prevent fraud, the Colonies in Rhode Island, New York, and New Jersey adopted the English rule that "copies of the poll must be delivered on demand to persons who were willing to pay a reasonable charge for the labor of writing them." Some colonies allowed candidates to demand a copy of the poll and required the legislature to examine the poll in a contested election. Thus, as in this case, the government not only publicly collected identifying information about who voted and for which candidate, it also disclosed that information to the public.

Any suggestion that *viva voce* voting infringed the accepted understanding of the pre-existing freedom of speech to which the First Amendment's text refers is refuted by the fact that several state constitutions that required or authorized *viva voce* voting *also* explicitly guaranteed the freedom of speech. Surely one constitutional provision did not render the other invalid.

Of course the practice of *viva voce* voting was gradually replaced with the paper ballot, which was thought to reduce fraud and undue influence. There is no indication that the shift resulted from a sudden realization that public voting infringed voters' freedom of speech, and the manner in which it occurred suggests the contrary. States adopted the paper ballot at different times, and some States changed methods multiple times. * * *

The new paper ballots did not make voting anonymous. Initially, many States did not regulate the form of the paper ballot. Taking advantage of this, political parties began printing ballots with their candidates' names on them. They used brightly colored paper and other distinctive markings so that the ballots could be recognized from a distance, making the votes public. * * *

It was precisely discontent over the nonsecret nature of ballot voting, and the abuses that produced, which led to the States' adoption of the Australian secret ballot. * * * But I am aware of no contention that the Australian system was required by the First Amendment (or the state counterparts). That would have been utterly implausible, since the inhabitants of the Colonies, the States, and the United States had found public voting entirely compatible with "the freedom of speech" for several centuries. * * *

Plaintiffs raise concerns that the disclosure of petition signatures may lead to threats and intimidation. Of course nothing prevents the people of Washington from keeping petition signatures secret to avoid that—just as nothing prevented the States from moving to the secret ballot. But there is no constitutional basis for this Court to impose that course upon the States—or to insist (as today's opinion does) that it can only be avoided by the demonstration of a "sufficiently important governmental interest." And it may even be a bad idea to keep petition signatures secret. There are laws against threats and intimidation; and harsh criticism, short of unlawful action, is a price our people have traditionally been willing to pay for self-governance. Requiring people to stand up in public for their political acts fosters civic courage, without which democracy is doomed. * * *

JUSTICE THOMAS, dissenting. * * *

The expressive political activity of signing a referendum petition is a paradigmatic example of "the practice of persons sharing common views banding together to achieve a common end." *Citizens Against Rent Control/Coalition for Fair Housing* v. *Berkeley*, 454 U.S. 290, 294 (1981). A referendum supported by only one person's signature is a nullity; it will never be placed on the ballot. * * * For these reasons, signing a referendum petition amounts to "political association" protected by the First Amendment.

This Court has long recognized the "vital relationship between" political association "and privacy in one's associations," *NAACP* v. *Alabama ex rel. Patterson*, 357 U.S., [at] 462, and held that "[t]he Constitution protects against the compelled disclosure of political associations and beliefs," *Brown* v. *Socialist Workers '74 Campaign Comm. (Ohio)*, 459 U.S., [at] 91. This constitutional protection "yield[s] only to a subordinating interest of the State that is compelling, and then only if there is a substantial relation between the information sought and an overriding and compelling state interest." *Id.*, at 91–92. Thus, unlike the Court, I read our precedents to require application of strict scrutiny to laws that compel disclosure of protected First Amendment association. Under that standard, a disclosure requirement passes constitutional muster only if it is narrowly tailored—*i.e.*, the least restrictive means—to serve a compelling state interest.

Washington's application of the PRA to a referendum petition does not survive strict scrutiny.

Washington first contends that it has a compelling interest in "transparency and accountability," which it claims encompasses several subordinate interests: preserving the integrity of its election process, preventing corruption, deterring fraud, and correcting mistakes by the secretary of state or by petition signers.

It is true that a State has a substantial interest in regulating its referendum and initiative processes "to protect the[ir] integrity and reliability." But Washington points to no precedent from this Court recognizing "correcting errors" as a distinct compelling interest that could support disclosure regulations. And our cases strongly suggest that preventing corruption and deterring fraud bear less weight in this particular electoral context: the signature-gathering stage of a referendum or initiative drive. The Court has twice observed that "the risk of fraud or corruption, or the appearance thereof, is more remote at the petition stage of an initiative than at the time of balloting." [*Buckley* v. *American Constitutional Law Foundation*, 525 U.S. 182], 203 [(1999)] [p. 649] (quoting *Meyer* v. *Grant*, 486 U.S., [at] 427). * * *

We should not abandon those principles merely because Washington and its amici can point to a mere eight instances of initiative-related fraud. If anything, these meager figures reinforce the conclusion that the risks of fraud or corruption in the initiative and referendum process are remote and thereby undermine Washington's claim that those two interests should be considered compelling for purposes of strict scrutiny.

Thus, I am not persuaded that Washington's interest in protecting the integrity and reliability of its referendum process, as the State has defined that interest, is compelling. But I need not answer that question here. Even assuming the interest is compelling, on-demand disclosure of a referendum petition to any person under the PRA is "a blunderbuss approach" to furthering that interest, not the least restrictive means of doing so. The events that prompted petitioners' complaint in this case demonstrate as much.

As Washington explained during oral argument, after the secretary of state receives signed referendum petitions, his "first step . . . is to take them to his archiving section and to have them digitized. As soon as they're digitized, they're available on disks for anyone who requests them" under the PRA. In this case, two organizations announced their intention to obtain the digitized names and addresses of referendum signers and post them "online, in a searchable format."

There is no apparent reason why Washington must broadly disclose referendum signers' names and addresses in this manner to vindicate the interest that it invokes here. Washington * * * could put the names and addresses of referendum signers into a similar electronic database that state employees could search *without* subjecting the name and address of each signer to wholesale public disclosure. The secretary could electronically cross-reference the referendum database against the "statewide voter registration list" contained in Washington's "statewide voter registration database," to ensure that each referendum signer meets Washington's residency and voter registration requirements. Doing so presumably would drastically reduce or eliminate possible errors or mistakes that Washington argues the secretary *might* make, since it would allow the secretary to verify virtually all of the signatures instead of the mere "3 to 5%" he "ordinarily checks."

An electronic referendum database would also enable the secretary to determine whether multiple entries correspond to a single registered voter, thereby detecting whether a voter had signed the petition more than once. In addition, the database would protect victims of "forgery" or "'bait and switch' fraud." In Washington, "a unique identifier is assigned to each legally registered voter in the state." Washington could create a Web site, linked to the electronic referendum database, where a voter concerned that his name had been fraudulently signed could conduct a search using his unique identifier to ensure that his name was absent from the database — without requiring disclosure of the names and addresses of all the voluntary, legitimate signers. * * *

Washington nevertheless contends that its citizens must "have access to public records . . . to independently evaluate whether the Secretary properly determined to certify or not to certify a referendum to the ballot." * * * But Washington's Election Code already gives Washington voters access to referendum petition data. Under [Washington law], "[t]he verification and canvass of signatures on the [referendum] petition may be observed by persons representing the advocates and opponents of the proposed measure so long as they make no record of the names, addresses, or other information on the petitions or related records except upon" court order. Each side is entitled to at least two such observers[.] * * *

It is readily apparent that Washington can vindicate its stated interest in "transparency and accountability" through a number of more narrowly tailored means than wholesale public disclosure. Accordingly, this interest cannot justify applying the PRA to a referendum petition.

Washington also contends that it has a compelling interest in "providing relevant information to Washington voters," and that on-demand disclosure to the public is a narrowly tailored means of furthering that interest. This argument is easily dispatched, since this Court has already rejected it in [*McIntyre* v. *Ohio Elections Comm'n*, 514 U.S. 334 (1995)] [p. 922]. * * *

* * * People are intelligent enough to evaluate the merits of a referendum without knowing who supported it. Thus, just as this informational interest did not justify the Ohio law in *McIntyre*, it does not justify applying the PRA to referendum petitions. * * *

The difficulty in predicting which referendum measures will prove controversial — combined with Washington's default position that signed referendum petitions will be disclosed on-demand, thereby allowing anyone to place this information on the Internet for broad dissemination—raises the significant probability that today's decision will "inhibit the exercise of legitimate First Amendment activity" with respect to referendum and initiative petitions.

Notes and Questions

1. Justice Alito suggested that as-applied challenges, to be useful, must be handled on a timely basis and should not face a "high evidentiary" hurdle. Justice Sotomayor countered that courts should be "deeply skeptical" of any as-applied challenge, and Justice Stevens argued that proving an as-applied challenge would be "very difficult" and should require "strong evidence." Which approach makes the most sense? If the Sotomayor/Stevens approach is correct about the burdens facing an as-applied challenge, should the Court have been more willing to make a facial determination of unconstitutionality?

2. In May of 2010, a few weeks before *Doe* was decided, a multi-jurisdictional drug task force raided a "medical marijuana dispensary" near Tacoma, Washington, in the process seizing numerous completed petitions for a ballot initiative that would "remove state civil and criminal penalties for persons eighteen years or older who cultivate, possess, transport, sell, or use marijuana" in the state. Supporters of the initiative claimed that police intended to intimidate people out of signing petitions. Gavin Dahl, *Seized Marijuana Legalization Petitions Missing*, Raw Story, May 26, 2010, *at* http://rawstory.com/rs/2010/0526/case-marijuana-legalization-petitions-seized-drug-raid/. After *Doe*, police can simply obtain information on petition signatories through the Public Records Act. Would (should) a complaint based on such actions meet the Alito standard for obtaining as-applied relief? Would it meet the Sotomayor/Stevens standard?

3. Justice Scalia argued that disclosure statutes encourage "civic courage, without which democracy is doomed." Others, however, have expressed concern that there is little rational reason for voters to engage in political activity. *See* James Buchanan & Gordon Tullock, The Calculus of Consent: Logical Foundations of a Constitutional Democracy (1962). Buchanan and Tullock focused on the fact that any one person's vote was extremely unlikely to determine the outcome of an election, but it seems equally true that any one person's signature is unlikely to determine whether an initiative or referendum appears on the ballot. Likewise, any one person's financial contribution to a campaign is unlikely to determine the outcome. Given the often-tenuous incentives to participate in civic life, should we require the minority that does participate also to exhibit "civic courage" that goes beyond the norm?

In the wake of California's Proposition 8, which amended the state constitution to define marriage as being between a man and a woman, there were many reports of harassment and vandalism against supporters of the initiative. Relying on mandatory-disclosure laws, opponents of the measure publicized the names and addresses of supporters, organized boycotts, and in some cases published on the Internet maps to donors' homes. Said one leader opposed to Proposition 8, "Years ago we would never have been able to get a blacklist that fast and quickly." *See* Bradley A. Smith, *In Defense of Political Anonymity*, 20 CITY J. 74, 77 (2010). Assuming that private boycotts are a legitimate tool for attempting to create social change—indeed, a tool protected by the First Amendment, *see NAACP v. Claiborne Hardware Co.*, 458 U.S. 886 (1982)—should the state nonetheless be constitutionally prohibited from compelling the potential targets to disclose information that facilitates such boycotts and blacklists? Or is the proper balance between providing voters with information and protecting voters from harassment a classic matter for legislatures?

4. Justice Thomas argued that there were less-restrictive means available for the state to fulfill its anti-fraud goals. Yet some of these means, such as creating and maintaining a searchable website, would cost the state money. In an era of tight state budgets, to what extent should least-restrictive-means analysis take into account the financial costs to the state of providing a less restrictive alternative?

5. On remand, the district court held that the names of petition-signers could be made public. *Doe v. Reed*, 823 F. Supp. 2d 1195 (W.D. Wash. 2011). The court noted that by the time of the decision, some of the identities of the referendum's supporters were publicly known, and the court concluded that the plaintiffs had failed to show that those persons had been subject to harassment. Plaintiffs sought an injunction against disclosure of their identities, but the injunction was denied by the district court, the Ninth Circuit, and the Supreme Court, the last over the dissent of Justice Alito, with Justice Kagan taking no part in the decision. 565 U.S. 1048 (2011).

6. Is the act of signing a petition "speech"? Justice Scalia characterized it as a legislative act and analogized petition-signing to "a vote for or against a bill in the legislature," while the Court suggested that acts having governmental effect could also be speech when they constitute "the expression of a political view." Nevertheless, in *Nevada Commission on Ethics v. Carrigan*, 564 U.S. 117 (2011), an eight-Justice majority, in an opinion written by Justice Scalia, concluded that a vote in the legislature was not "speech" entitled to First Amendment protection:

> [A] legislator's vote is the commitment of his apportioned share of the legislature's power to the passage or defeat of a particular proposal. The legislative power thus committed is not personal to the legislator but belongs to the people; the legislator has no personal right to it. * * * In this respect, voting by a legislator is different from voting by a citizen. While "a voter's franchise is a personal right," "[t]he procedures for voting in legislative assemblies * * * pertain to legislators not as individuals but as political representatives executing the legislative process." *Coleman v. Miller*, 307 U.S. 433, 469–470 (1939) (opinion of Frankfurter, J.).
>
> * * * There are, to be sure, instances where action conveys a symbolic meaning—such as the burning of a flag to convey disagreement with a country's policies. But the act of voting symbolizes nothing. It *discloses*, to

be sure, that the legislator wishes (for whatever reason) that the proposition on the floor be adopted, just as a physical assault discloses that the attacker dislikes the victim. But neither the one nor the other is an act of communication. * * *

Even if it were true that the vote itself could "express deeply held and highly unpopular views," the argument would still miss the mark. This Court has rejected the notion that the First Amendment confers a right to use governmental mechanics to convey a message. * * * [A] legislator has no right to use official powers for expressive purposes.

564 U.S. at 125–27.

Is the analysis in *Carrigan* consistent with *Doe v. Reed*? Justice Alito, who concurred in the judgment on other grounds, thought not:

Voting has an expressive component in and of itself. * * * Just as the act of signing a petition is not deprived of its expressive character when the signature is given legal consequences, the act of voting is not drained of its expressive content when the vote has a legal effect. If an ordinary citizen casts a vote in a straw poll on an important proposal pending before a legislative body, that act indisputably constitutes a form of speech. If a member of the legislative body chooses to vote in the same straw poll, the legislator's act is no less expressive than that of an ordinary citizen. And if the legislator then votes on the measure in the legislative chamber, the expressive character of that vote is not eliminated simply because it may affect the outcome of the legislative process.

Id. at 134 (Alito, J., concurring in part and concurring in the judgment). The Court responded that "[i]t is one thing to say that an inherently expressive act [*e.g.*, signing a petition] remains so despite its having governmental effect, but is altogether another thing to say that a governmental act becomes expressive simply because the governmental actor wishes it to be so." *Id.* at 128 (opinion of the Court). Further, "[a] legislator voting on a bill is not fairly analogized to one simply discussing that bill or expressing an opinion for or against it. The former is performing a governmental act as a representative of his constituents; only the latter is exercising personal First Amendment rights." *Id.* at 128 n.5.

Should there be a constitutional right to anonymity in voting, *i.e.*, a right to the Australian ballot? Every state provides for secret balloting, but the Supreme Court has never been asked to decide on its constitutional status. For what it is worth, John Stuart Mill argued that except in rare circumstances, balloting should not be in secret. He believed that public voting would encourage responsibility and accountability for one's vote. *See* JOHN STUART MILL, ON REPRESENTATIVE GOVERNMENT 323–29 (Everyman ed. 1993).

Chapter 10

Election Day

A. Introduction

The constitutional protection of the right to vote is implicated throughout the electoral process. In Chapter 1, we began our discussion of the right by discussing attempts by states and municipalities to control *who* may exercise the right to vote. In subsequent Chapters we considered the impact on the right caused by, *inter alia*, the drawing of electoral districts and ballot-access limitations. The following cases concern challenges to state restrictions on *how* voters may exercise the right to vote. The cases struggle explicitly with the meaning and application of strict scrutiny in the electoral context, and provide an opportunity to consider the way the right to vote informs constitutional review of laws that affect all aspects of elections.

The right to vote is considered fundamental, but if strict scrutiny were applied to each law that limited the exercise of that right, it would be impossible to write rules for the orderly administration of elections. As a consequence, the Supreme Court has recognized that a lesser standard of scrutiny is appropriate when evaluating at least some election laws, lest elections descend into "chaos." *Storer v. Brown*, 415 U.S. 724, 730 (1974) [p. 513].The trick, of course, is in determining which regulations should be subject to more stringent scrutiny, and as to this issue the Court has not established a rule that is capable of consistent application.

The Court, instead, has used the balancing test from *Anderson v. Celebrezze*, 460 U.S. 780, 789 (1983) [p. 517], under which a reviewing court weighs the extent of the burden against the state's justifications for it. "Severe" burdens are constitutional only if they pass strict scrutiny, while lesser burdens are subject to less-stringent review. While it appeared to some after *Burdick v. Takushi*, 504 U.S. 428 (1992) [p. 990], that "reasonable, nondiscriminatory" regulations presenting less than "severe" burdens on the right to vote would be subject to the lenient rational-basis test, it now seems that such lesser burdens will be evaluated on a continuum, with the most deferential scrutiny applying only to the most minimal burdens on voting rights.

One particularly controversial voting regulation has been the requirement that voters present identification before being permitted to vote. Critics claim that such a law disproportionately harms the poor, the elderly, and minorities, each of whom might be thought to favor liberal candidates. Defenders of the requirement cite the need to guard against fraud. The Court, in *Crawford v. Marion County Election Board*, 553 U.S. 181 (2008) [p. 999], upheld a photo-identification requirement against a facial challenge, but did not foreclose the possibility that an as-applied challenge could succeed.

Sometimes government regulation, far from imposing burdens on casting ballots, seeks to alleviate them. Yet there, too, the regulations can cause constitutional problems. In *Burson v. Freeman*, 504 U.S. 191 (1992) [p. 1024], for example, the Court confronted a challenge to a state law that prohibited speech within one hundred feet of polling places. The law was aimed at preventing intimidation and harassment of voters. Because the law restricted speech in areas (streets and sidewalks) owned or controlled by the government but usually open to speech by private persons, the Court evaluated the law by applying the public-forum doctrine. Speech restrictions in traditional public fora (streets, parks, and sidewalks) are constitutional only if they pass strict scrutiny. In addition to the traditional public fora, "designated" public fora also provide government resources for private speech. The government need not set aside those areas for speech, but if it does, any content-based restrictions on speech within the designated fora will be reviewed under strict scrutiny. The government can also create a "limited" or "limited-purpose" public forum, where only certain speech by private persons is permitted—usually speech on a particular topic. For example, the government may hold a town-hall meeting at which members of the public are permitted to speak for up to five minutes on the question whether to build a park, without opening the discussion to other topics or permitting speakers to filibuster. Speech restrictions in "nonpublic fora"—government-controlled property that is open to the general public but for a purpose other than speech—are constitutional if they meet the much lower standard of being reasonable and viewpoint-neutral.

Burson upheld the campaign-free zone, reasoning that the state had compelling interests in protecting voters' access to the polls and ensuring against voter intimidation. Because strict scrutiny requires both a compelling interest and narrow tailoring, however, the Court had to assess whether a one-hundred-foot radius was narrow enough. The Court held that it was, but in so doing deferred substantially to the state's judgment and the judgment of history that such restrictions were necessary.

In *Minnesota Voters Alliance v. Mansky*, 585 U.S. __, 138 S. Ct. 1876 (2018), the Supreme Court considered the constitutionality of a speech restriction *within* polling places. The Court held that the area was a nonpublic forum, but the state's vague ban on wearing "political" apparel was not "reasonable." As you work through these cases and as you review the other cases we have encountered in this course, consider how deferential courts should be to the choices legislatures make in constructing election laws.

In our federalist system, both state and federal laws can affect voting procedures, and that is especially true when elections for federal office are administered by the states. We therefore consider, in § D of this Chapter, some federal rules—both constitutional and statutory—that affect the ways that states conduct federal elections. Presidential elections present their own complexities because of the operation of the electoral college. We will explore those complexities, including the extent of states' power to appoint electors and to control their votes once appointed.

Section E turns to the vote-counting itself and focuses on two primary issues: First, what rules determine whether a vote should count, *i.e.*, how is it determined whether a voter has cast a legal vote? Second, how should the votes be aggregated to determine a winner? Should we use the familiar system (known as the "first past the post" (FPTP) or "plurality" system) where the person who received the most votes wins, even if that turns out to be less than a majority? Or should we use an alternative designed to make it more likely that the winner is preferred by a majority of voters?

Throughout American history, the seemingly simple tasks of casting and counting votes have turned out to be anything but simple. Various techniques have been used in different parts of the country at different times—and the lack of uniformity persists to the present day. In some states at the beginning of the Republic, voting was a public, oral act. In other states, the voter wrote down his vote in a poll book underneath a picture of his preferred candidate. By the end of the nineteenth century, spurred by the increasing number of elective offices, most jurisdictions required votes to be indicated on preprinted ballots, although sometimes political parties would themselves print and help tabulate these ballots. All jurisdictions eventually came to use a written "Australian" ballot prepared by the government, administered to permit anonymous voting. In the twentieth century, many jurisdictions came to use a variety of machines to collate and count these ballots. Federal law now requires that votes be cast "by written or printed ballot, or voting machine the use of which has been duly authorized by the State law." 2 U.S.C. § 9. For a comprehensive overview of these developments, see ALEXANDER KEYSSAR, THE RIGHT TO VOTE: THE CONTESTED HISTORY OF DEMOCRACY IN THE UNITED STATES 23–24, 155, 261–62 (rev. ed. 2009).

As you read the cases and materials in this Chapter, consider the following themes. One is that the administration of elections in general, and the counting of votes in particular, are, or at least are perceived as, partisan. For example, in thirty-three states, the chief election officer, usually the Secretary of State, is elected as a partisan candidate. Critics have often accused such officers of making decisions for partisan reasons. Such accusations have led to calls for selecting election officials in nonpartisan ways.[a] Another theme focuses on efforts to centralize and nationalize the counting of votes. Such efforts include the Help America Vote Act (HAVA) of

---

a. For overviews of this controversy and calls for reform, see Jocelyn Friedrichs Benson, *Democracy and the Secretary: The Critical Role of Election Administrators in Promoting Accuracy and Access to Democracy*, 27 ST. LOUIS U. PUB. L. REV. 343 (2008); Richard L. Hasen, *Beyond the Margin of Litigation: Reforming U.S. Election Administration to Avoid Electoral Meltdown*, 62 WASH. & LEE L. REV. 937 (2005); David C. Kimball et al., *Helping America Vote? Election Administration, Partisanship, and Provisional Voting in the 2004 Election*, 5 ELECTION L.J. 447 (2006); and Daniel P. Tokaji, *The Future of Election Reform*, 28 YALE L. & POL'Y REV. 125 (2009). *See also* Michael J. Pitts, *Defining "Partisan" Law Enforcement*, 18 STAN. L. & POL'Y REV. 324 (2007) (arguing that charges of partisan

2002, 52 U.S.C. § 20901 *et seq.*, which was passed by Congress in the wake of controversies surrounding the 2000 presidential election. HAVA and similar statutes are discussed below.

A third theme is a separation-of-powers concern that has pervaded our study of election law: What should the role of the judiciary be in policing partisanship in elections? Do the frequent charges of partisan administration of election law suggest that courts should take an aggressive, or conversely a more passive, stand in enforcing election laws? Should courts defer to legislative judgments regarding the administration of elections? Can the judiciary ensure that elections are administered fairly, or will courts that enter the political thicket only draw the same criticism that is directed at other political actors?

B. Fraud Prevention and Burdens on Casting Ballots

Burdick v. Takushi

Supreme Court of the United States
504 U.S. 428, 112 S. Ct. 2059, 119 L. Ed. 2d 245 (1992)

JUSTICE WHITE delivered the opinion of the Court [in which CHIEF JUSTICE REHNQUIST, JUSTICE O'CONNOR, JUSTICE SCALIA, JUSTICE SOUTER, and JUSTICE THOMAS join].

The issue in this case is whether Hawaii's prohibition on write-in voting unreasonably infringes upon its citizens' rights under the First and Fourteenth Amendments. * * *

Petitioner is a registered voter in the city and county of Honolulu. In 1986, only one candidate filed nominating papers to run for the seat representing petitioner's district in the Hawaii House of Representatives. Petitioner wrote to state officials inquiring about Hawaii's write-in voting policy and [was informed] that the State's election law made no provision for write-in voting. Petitioner then filed this lawsuit, claiming that he wished to vote in the primary and general elections for a person who had not filed nominating papers and that he wished to vote in future elections for other persons whose names might not appear on the ballot. * * *

Petitioner proceeds from the erroneous assumption that a law that imposes any burden upon the right to vote must be subject to strict scrutiny. Our cases do not so hold.

It is beyond cavil that "voting is of the most fundamental significance under our constitutional structure." It does not follow, however, that the right to vote in any manner and the right to associate for political purposes through the ballot are

---

actions in this context are made too easily, and positing objective criteria to define true partisan actions).

absolute. The Constitution provides that States may prescribe "[t]he Times, Places and Manner of holding Elections for Senators and Representatives," Art. I, § 4, cl. 1, and the Court therefore has recognized that States retain the power to regulate their own elections. Common sense, as well as constitutional law, compels the conclusion that government must play an active role in structuring elections; "as a practical matter, there must be a substantial regulation of elections if they are to be fair and honest and if some sort of order, rather than chaos, is to accompany the democratic processes." *Storer* v. *Brown*, 415 U.S. 724, 730 (1974) [p. 513].

Election laws will invariably impose some burden upon individual voters. Each provision of a code, "whether it governs the registration and qualifications of voters, the selection and eligibility of candidates, or the voting process itself, inevitably affects — at least to some degree — the individual's right to vote and his right to associate with others for political ends." Consequently, to subject every voting regulation to strict scrutiny and to require that the regulation be narrowly tailored to advance a compelling state interest, as petitioner suggests, would tie the hands of States seeking to assure that elections are operated equitably and efficiently. Accordingly, the mere fact that a State's system "creates barriers . . . tending to limit the field of candidates from which voters might choose . . . does not of itself compel close scrutiny." *Bullock* v. *Carter*, 405 U.S. 134, 143 (1972) [p. 507].

Instead, * * * a more flexible standard applies. A court considering a challenge to a state election law must weigh "the character and magnitude of the asserted injury to the rights protected by the First and Fourteenth Amendments that the plaintiff seeks to vindicate" against "the precise interests put forward by the State as justifications for the burden imposed by its rule," taking into consideration "the extent to which those interests make it necessary to burden the plaintiff's rights." *Anderson* v. *Celebrezze*, 460 U.S. 780, 789 (1983) [p. 517]; *Tashjian* v. *Republican Party*, 479 U.S. 208, 213–214 (1986) [p. 443].

Under this standard, the rigorousness of our inquiry into the propriety of a state election law depends upon the extent to which a challenged regulation burdens First and Fourteenth Amendment rights. Thus, as we have recognized when those rights are subjected to "severe" restrictions, the regulation must be "narrowly drawn to advance a state interest of compelling importance." *Norman* v. *Reed*, 502 U.S. 279, 289 (1992). But when a state election law provision imposes only "reasonable, nondiscriminatory restrictions" upon the First and Fourteenth Amendment rights of voters, "the State's important regulatory interests are generally sufficient to justify" the restrictions. We apply this standard in considering petitioner's challenge to Hawaii's ban on write-in ballots.

There is no doubt that the Hawaii election laws, like all election regulations, have an impact on the right to vote, but it can hardly be said that the laws at issue here unconstitutionally limit access to the ballot by party or independent candidates or unreasonably interfere with the right of voters to associate and have candidates of their choice placed on the ballot. Indeed, petitioner understandably does not challenge the manner in which the State regulates candidate access to the ballot.

To obtain a position on the November general election ballot, a candidate must participate in Hawaii's open primary, "in which all registered voters may choose in which party primary to vote." The State provides three mechanisms through which a voter's candidate-of-choice may appear on the primary ballot.

First, a party petition may be filed 150 days before the primary by any group of persons who obtain the signatures of one percent of the State's registered voters. Then, 60 days before the primary, candidates must file nominating papers certifying, among other things, that they will qualify for the office sought and that they are members of the party that they seek to represent in the general election. The nominating papers must contain the signatures of a specified number of registered voters: 25 for candidates for statewide or federal office; 15 for state legislative and county races. The winner in each party advances to the general election. * * *

The second method through which candidates may appear on the Hawaii primary ballot is the established party route. Established parties that have qualified by petition for three consecutive elections and received a specified percentage of the vote in the preceding election may avoid filing party petitions for 10 years. The Democratic, Republican, and Libertarian Parties currently meet Hawaii's criteria for established parties. Like new party candidates, established party contenders are required to file nominating papers 60 days before the primary.

The third mechanism by which a candidate may appear on the ballot is through the designated nonpartisan ballot. Nonpartisans may be placed on the nonpartisan primary ballot simply by filing nominating papers containing 15 to 25 signatures, depending upon the office sought, 60 days before the primary. To advance to the general election, a nonpartisan must receive 10 percent of the primary vote or the number of votes that was sufficient to nominate a partisan candidate, whichever number is lower. During the 10 years preceding the filing of this action, 8 of 26 nonpartisans who entered the primary obtained slots on the November ballot.

Although Hawaii makes no provision for write-in voting in its primary or general elections, the system outlined above provides for easy access to the ballot until the cutoff date for the filing of nominating petitions, two months before the primary. Consequently, any burden on voters' freedom of choice and association is borne only by those who fail to identify their candidate of choice until days before the primary. But in *Storer* v. *Brown*, we gave little weight to "the interest the candidate and his supporters may have in making a late rather than an early decision to seek independent ballot status." 415 U.S., at 736. We think the same reasoning applies here and therefore conclude that any burden imposed by Hawaii's write-in vote prohibition is a very limited one. "To conclude otherwise might sacrifice the political stability of the system of the State, with profound consequences for the entire citizenry, merely in the interest of particular candidates and their supporters having instantaneous access to the ballot." *Ibid.*[7]

Because he has characterized this as a voting rights rather than ballot access case, petitioner submits that the write-in prohibition deprives him of the opportunity to cast a meaningful ballot, conditions his electoral participation upon the waiver of his First Amendment right to remain free from espousing positions that he does not support, and discriminates against him based on the content of the message he seeks to convey through his vote. At bottom, he claims that he is entitled to cast and Hawaii required to count a "protest vote" for Donald Duck, and that any impediment to this asserted "right" is unconstitutional.

Petitioner's argument is based on two flawed premises. First, in *Bullock* v. *Carter*, we minimized the extent to which voting rights cases are distinguishable from ballot access cases, stating that "the rights of voters and the rights of candidates do not lend themselves to neat separation." 405 U.S., at 143. Second, the function of the election process is "to winnow out and finally reject all but the chosen candidates," *Storer*, 415 U.S., at 735, not to provide a means of giving vent to "short-range political goals, pique, or personal quarrel[s]." Attributing to elections a more generalized expressive function would undermine the ability of States to operate elections fairly and efficiently.

Accordingly, we have repeatedly upheld reasonable, politically neutral regulations that have the effect of channeling expressive activity at the polls. Petitioner offers no persuasive reason to depart from these precedents. Reasonable regulation of elections *does not* require voters to espouse positions that they do not support; it *does* require them to act in a timely fashion if they wish to express their views in the voting booth. And there is nothing content based about a flat ban on all forms of write-in ballots.

* * * [W]e conclude that, in light of the adequate ballot access afforded under Hawaii's election code, the State's ban on write-in voting imposes only a limited burden on voters' rights to make free choices and to associate politically through the vote.

We turn next to the interests asserted by Hawaii to justify the burden imposed by its prohibition of write-in voting. Because we have already concluded that the burden is slight, the State need not establish a compelling interest to tip the

---

7. The dissent complains that, because primary voters are required to opt for a specific partisan or nonpartisan ballot, they are foreclosed from voting in those races in which no candidate appears on their chosen ballot and in those races in which they are dissatisfied with the available choices. But this is generally true of primaries; voters are required to select a ticket, rather than choose from the universe of candidates running on all party slates. * * *

If the dissent were correct in suggesting that requiring primary voters to select a specific ballot impermissibly burdened the right to vote, it is clear under our decisions that the availability of a write-in option would not provide an adequate remedy. *Anderson*, 460 U.S., at 799, n.26; *Lubin* v. *Panish*, 415 U.S. 709, 719, n.5 (1974).

constitutional scales in its direction. Here, the State's interests outweigh petitioner's limited interest in waiting until the eleventh hour to choose his preferred candidate.

* * * The prohibition on write-in voting is a legitimate means of averting divisive sore-loser candidacies. Hawaii further promotes the two-stage, primary-general election process of winnowing out candidates by permitting the unopposed victors in certain primaries to be designated office-holders. This focuses the attention of voters upon contested races in the general election. This would not be possible, absent the write-in voting ban.

Hawaii also asserts that its ban on write-in voting at the primary stage is necessary to guard against "party raiding." Party raiding is generally defined as "the organized switching of blocs of voters from one party to another in order to manipulate the outcome of the other party's primary election." Petitioner suggests that, because Hawaii conducts an open primary, this is not a cognizable interest. We disagree. While voters may vote on any ticket in Hawaii's primary, the State requires that party candidates be "member[s] of the party," and prohibits candidates from filing "nomination papers both as a party candidate and as a nonpartisan candidate." Hawaii's system could easily be circumvented in a party primary election by mounting a write-in campaign for a person who had not filed in time or who had never intended to run for election. It could also be frustrated at the general election by permitting write-in votes for a loser in a party primary or for an independent who had failed to get sufficient votes to make the general election ballot. The State has a legitimate interest in preventing these sorts of maneuvers, and the write-in voting ban is a reasonable way of accomplishing this goal.[9]

We think these legitimate interests asserted by the State are sufficient to outweigh the limited burden that the write-in voting ban imposes upon Hawaii's voters.[10]

Indeed, the foregoing leads us to conclude that when a State's ballot access laws pass constitutional muster as imposing only reasonable burdens on First and Fourteenth Amendment rights—as do Hawaii's election laws—a prohibition on write-in voting will be presumptively valid, since any burden on the right to vote for

---

9. The State also supports its ban on write-in voting as a means of enforcing nominating requirements, combating fraud, and "fostering informed and educated expressions of the popular will."

10. Although the dissent purports to agree with the standard we apply in determining whether the right to vote has been restricted, and implies that it is analyzing the write-in ban under some minimal level of scrutiny, the dissent actually employs strict scrutiny. This is evident from its invocation of quite rigid narrow tailoring requirements. For instance, the dissent argues that the State could adopt a less drastic means of preventing sore-loser candidacies, and that the State could screen out ineligible candidates through postelection disqualification rather than a write-in voting ban.

It seems to us that limiting the choice of candidates to those who have complied with state election law requirements is the prototypical example of a regulation that, while it affects the right to vote, is eminently reasonable. The dissent's suggestion that voters are entitled to cast their ballots for unqualified candidates appears to be driven by the assumption that an election system that imposes any restraint on voter choice is unconstitutional. This is simply wrong.

the candidate of one's choice will be light and normally will be counterbalanced by the very state interests supporting the ballot access scheme.

In such situations, the objection to the specific ban on write-in voting amounts to nothing more than the insistence that the State record, count, and publish individual protests against the election system or the choices presented on the ballot through the efforts of those who actively participate in the system. There are other means available, however, to voice such generalized dissension from the electoral process; and we discern no adequate basis for our requiring the State to provide and to finance a place on the ballot for recording protests against its constitutionally valid election laws.

[T]he right to vote is the right to participate in an electoral process that is necessarily structured to maintain the integrity of the democratic system. We think that Hawaii's prohibition on write-in voting, considered as part of an electoral scheme that provides constitutionally sufficient ballot access, does not impose an unconstitutional burden upon the First and Fourteenth Amendment rights of the State's voters. Accordingly, the judgment of the Court of Appeals is affirmed.

It is so ordered.

JUSTICE KENNEDY, with whom JUSTICE BLACKMUN and JUSTICE STEVENS join, dissenting. * * *

* * * In the election that triggered this lawsuit, petitioner did not wish to vote for the one candidate who ran for state representative in his district. Because he could not write in the name of a candidate he preferred, he had no way to cast a meaningful vote. Petitioner's dilemma is a recurring, frequent phenomenon in Hawaii because of the State's ballot access rules and the circumstance that one party, the Democratic Party, is predominant. * * *

Aside from constraints related to ballot access restrictions, the write-in ban limits voter choice in another way. Write-in voting can serve as an important safety mechanism in those instances where a late-developing issue arises or where new information is disclosed about a candidate late in the race. In these situations, voters may become disenchanted with the available candidates when it is too late for other candidates to come forward and qualify for the ballot. The prohibition on write-in voting imposes a significant burden on voters, forcing them either to vote for a candidate whom they no longer support or to cast a blank ballot. Write-in voting provides a way out of the quandary, allowing voters to switch their support to candidates who are not on the official ballot. * * *

* * * The right at stake here is the right to cast a meaningful vote for the candidate of one's choice. Petitioner's right to freedom of expression is not implicated. His argument that the First Amendment confers upon citizens the right to cast a protest vote and to have government officials count and report this vote is not persuasive.

As the majority points out, the purpose of casting, counting, and recording votes is to elect public officials, not to serve as a general forum for political expression.

I agree as well with the careful statement the Court gives of the test to be applied in this case to determine if the right to vote has been constricted. As the Court phrases it, we must "weigh 'the character and magnitude of the asserted injury to the rights protected by the First and Fourteenth Amendments that the plaintiff seeks to vindicate' against 'the precise interests put forward by the State as justifications for the burden imposed by its rule,' taking into consideration 'the extent to which those interests make it necessary to burden the plaintiff's rights.'" I submit the conclusion must be that the write-in ban deprives some voters of any substantial voice in selecting candidates for the entire range of offices at issue in a particular election. * * *

[S]ome voters cannot vote for the candidate of their choice without a write-in option. In effect, a write-in ban, in conjunction with other restrictions, can deprive the voter of the opportunity to cast a meaningful ballot. As a consequence, write-in prohibitions can impose a significant burden on voting rights. * * * The fact that write-in candidates are longshots more often than not makes no difference; the right to vote for one's preferred candidate exists regardless of the likelihood that the candidate will be successful.

Based on the foregoing reasoning, I cannot accept the majority's presumption that write-in bans are permissible if the State's ballot access laws are otherwise constitutional. The presumption is circular, for it fails to take into account that we must consider the availability of write-in voting, or the lack thereof, as a factor in determining whether a State's ballot access laws considered as a whole are constitutional. * * *

* * * The liberality of a State's ballot access laws is one determinant of the extent of the burden imposed by the write-in ban; it is not, though, an automatic excuse for forbidding all write-in voting. In my view, a State that bans write-in voting in some or all elections must justify the burden on individual voters by putting forth the precise interests that are served by the ban. A write-in prohibition should not be presumed valid in the absence of any proffered justification by the State. * * *

Because Hawaii's write-in ban, when considered in conjunction with the State's ballot access laws, imposes a significant burden on voters such as petitioner, it must put forward the state interests which justify the burden so that we can assess them. I do not think it necessary here to specify the level of scrutiny that should then be applied because, in my view, the State has failed to justify the write-in ban under any level of scrutiny. The interests proffered by the State, some of which are puzzling, are not advanced to any significant degree by the write-in prohibition. I consider each of the interests in turn.

The interest that has the best potential for acceptance, in my view, is that of pre-serving the integrity of party primaries by preventing sore loser candidacies during the general election. * * * A write-in ban does serve this interest to some degree by eliminating one mechanism which could be used by sore loser candidates. But I do not agree that this interest provides "adequate justification" for the ban. As an ini-tial matter, the interest can at best justify the write-in prohibition for general elec-tions; it cannot justify Hawaii's complete ban in both the primary and the general election. And with respect to general elections, a write-in ban is a very overinclusive means of addressing the problem; it bars legitimate candidacies as well as undesir-able sore loser candidacies. If the State desires to prevent sore loser candidacies, it can implement a narrow provision aimed at that particular problem.

The second interest advanced by the State is enforcing its policy of permitting the unopposed victors in certain primaries to be designated as officeholders without having to go through the general election. The majority states that "[t]his would not be possible, absent the write-in voting ban." This makes no sense. As petitioner's counsel acknowledged during oral argument, "[t]o the degree that Hawaii has abol-ished general elections in these circumstances, there is no occasion to cast a write-in ballot." If anything, the argument cuts the other way because this provision makes it all the more important to allow write-in voting in the primary elections because primaries are often dispositive.

Hawaii justifies its write-in ban in primary elections as a way to prevent party raiding. Petitioner argues that this alleged interest is suspect because the State created the party raiding problem in the first place by allowing open primaries. I agree. It is ironic for the State to raise this concern when the risk of party raiding is a feature of the open primary system the State has chosen. The majority suggests that write-in voting presents a particular risk of circumventing the primary sys-tem because state law requires candidates in party primaries to be members of the party. Again, the majority's argument is not persuasive. If write-in voters mount a campaign for a candidate who does not meet state-law requirements, the candidate would be disqualified from the election.

The State also cites its interest in promoting the informed selection of candidates, an interest it claims is advanced by "flushing candidates into the open a reasonable time before the election." I think the State has it backwards. The fact that write-in candidates often do not conduct visible campaigns seems to me to make it more likely that voters who go to the trouble of seeking out these candidates and writing in their names are well informed. The state interest may well cut the other way.

The State cites interests in combating fraud and enforcing nomination require-ments. But the State does not explain how write-in voting presents a risk of fraud in today's polling places. As to the State's interest in making sure that ineligible candidates are not elected, petitioner's counsel pointed out at argument that approximately 20 States require write-in candidates to file a declaration of candidacy and verify that they are eligible to hold office a few days before the election.

In sum, the State's proffered justifications for the write-in prohibition are not sufficient under any standard to justify the significant impairment of the constitutional rights of voters such as petitioner. I would grant him relief.

Notes and Questions

1. What are the implications of the Court's unanimous conclusion that, in Justice Kennedy's words, the "right to freedom of expression is not implicated" by Hawaii's ban on write-in voting? *See also Timmons v. Twin Cities Area New Party*, 520 U.S. 351, 363 (1997) [p. 526] ("Ballots serve primarily to elect candidates, not as forums for political expression."); *Rubin v. City of Santa Monica*, 308 F.3d 1008, 1016 (9th Cir. 2002) ("A ballot is a ballot, not a bumper sticker."). Is that concession consistent with Justice Kennedy's claim that "the right to vote for one's preferred candidate exists regardless of the likelihood that the candidate will be successful"? *See also United States v. Classic*, 313 U.S. 299, 318 (1941) ("The right to participate in the choice of representatives for Congress includes * * * the right to cast a ballot and to have it counted * * * *whether for the successful candidate or not*" (emphasis added)). Recall that the constitutional right to vote recognized in *Classic* is derived from Article I, § 2's implication that members of Congress must be chosen by elections (*see* p. 417, *supra*); what is the basis for a right to have a vote for a *losing* candidate counted?

If the sole purpose of voting is to serve as a mechanism for choosing between candidates (and for deciding ballot questions), then is voting a fundamental *individual* right at all? *See Reynolds v. Sims*, 377 U.S. 533, 561 (1964) [p. 122] (referring to the rights protected by the one-person, one-vote standard as "individual and personal in nature"); Pamela S. Karlan, *The Rights to Vote: Some Pessimism About Formalism*, 71 TEX. L. REV. 1705 (1993) (arguing that there are several "rights to vote," some of which are individual rights and some of which are group rights); Martin Shapiro, *Gerrymandering, Unfairness, and the Supreme Court*, 33 UCLA L. REV. 227, 232 (1985) (arguing that voting is an individual right, but the right to fair "representation" is a group right).[b]

---

b. As discussed in Chapter 4, much of the recent scholarly discussion on the group or individual character of the right to vote has concerned the nature of the right that members of minority groups have under § 2 of the Voting Rights Act to enjoy the same opportunity "to participate in the political process and to elect representatives of their choice" as held by "other members of the electorate," 52 U.S.C. § 10301(b). The individual/group nature of the right to vote is also at issue in *Shaw v. Reno*, 509 U.S. 630 (1993) [p. 362], and its progeny, which recognize voters' right to have districts drawn without the "predominant" consideration of race. *See, e.g., United States v. Hays*, 515 U.S. 737 (1995) (discussed at pp. 372–73, *supra*); *Shaw v. Hunt*, 517 U.S. 899, 917 (1996) (stating that the right to an undiluted vote belongs to the individual members of a minority group, rather than to the group as a whole).

2. Justice Kennedy would have held that Hawaii's write-in ban violated Burdick's "right to cast a meaningful vote for the candidate of [his] choice." What did Justice Kennedy mean by "meaningful"? In what respect would a vote for a candidate be meaningful if the candidate had no realistic chance of winning the election?

3. Under the Court's analysis in *Anderson v. Celebrezze*, 460 U.S. 780 (1983) [p. 517], and *Burdick*, "severe" restrictions on the right to vote are subject to strict scrutiny, while more modest restrictions are subject to a more permissive standard. The Court in *Burdick*, quoting *Anderson*, said that "reasonable, nondiscriminatory restrictions" will generally be justified by states' "important regulatory interests." What did the Court mean by "severe" and "reasonable"? Are they opposites in this context? Or can a "reasonable" restriction create a "severe" impairment on First and Fourteenth Amendment rights? Was Hawaii's write-in ban "reasonable"? Did it severely impair Burdick's (or anyone else's) right to vote?

4. Do you agree with one commentator that "the severe burden test is nebulous and unclear, resulting in vague decisions that fail to distinguish between constitutional and unconstitutional state election regulations"? Joshua A. Douglas, Note, *A Vote for Clarity: Updating the Supreme Court's Severe Burden Test for State Election Regulations that Adversely Impact an Individual's Right to Vote*, 75 Geo. Wash. L. Rev. 372, 373 (2007). Douglas suggested replacing the "nebulous" test with an empirical one drawn from the provisions of the Voting Rights Act that require certain jurisdictions to provide assistance for voters who do not understand English. Douglas would apply strict scrutiny if the challenged regulation affected more than 10,000, or five percent, of the voters in the jurisdiction. "If the regulation imposes a burden that exceeds either of these triggers, the regulation is per se severe and must survive strict scrutiny review." *Id.* at 386. Otherwise, rational-basis scrutiny would apply. *See id.* at 386–87. Is such a test an improvement over the existing one?

5. The next case considered the constitutionality of requirements that voters present state- or federal-government-issued photo identification. Should such requirements be considered "severe" burdens on the right to vote and therefore subject to strict scrutiny? If not, what test should apply?

Crawford v. Marion County Election Board

Supreme Court of the United States
553 U.S. 181, 128 S. Ct. 1610, 170 L. Ed. 2d 574 (2008)

Justice Stevens announced the judgment of the Court and delivered an opinion in which The Chief Justice [Roberts] and Justice Kennedy join.

At issue in these cases is the constitutionality of an Indiana statute requiring citizens voting in person on election day, or casting a ballot in person at the office of the circuit court clerk prior to election day, to present photo identification issued by the government.

Referred to as either the "Voter ID Law" or "SEA [Senate Enrolled Act] 483," the statute applies to in-person voting at both primary and general elections. The requirement does not apply to absentee ballots submitted by mail, and the statute contains an exception for persons living and voting in a state-licensed facility such as a nursing home. A voter who is indigent or has a religious objection to being photographed may cast a provisional ballot that will be counted only if she executes an appropriate affidavit before the circuit court clerk within 10 days following the election. A voter who has photo identification but is unable to present that identification on election day may file a provisional ballot that will be counted if she brings her photo identification to the circuit county clerk's office within 10 days. No photo identification is required in order to register to vote, and the State offers free photo identification to qualified voters able to establish their residence and identity. * * *

[Plaintiffs, including the Indiana Democratic Party and organizations representing elderly, disabled, poor, and minority voters,] allege that the new law substantially burdens the right to vote in violation of the Fourteenth Amendment; that it is neither a necessary nor appropriate method of avoiding election fraud; and that it will arbitrarily disfranchise qualified voters who do not possess the required identification and will place an unjustified burden on those who cannot readily obtain such identification.

[The district court granted] defendants' motion for summary judgment. * * * A divided panel of the Court of Appeals affirmed. * * *

In *Harper v. Virginia Bd. of Elections*, 383 U.S. 663 (1966) [p. 17], the Court held that Virginia could not condition the right to vote in a state election on the payment of a poll tax of $1.50. We rejected the dissenters' argument that the interest in promoting civic responsibility by weeding out those voters who did not care enough about public affairs to pay a small sum for the privilege of voting provided a rational basis for the tax. * * * Although the State's justification for the tax was rational, it was invidious because it was irrelevant to the voter's qualifications.

Thus, under the standard applied in *Harper*, even rational restrictions on the right to vote are invidious if they are unrelated to voter qualifications. In *Anderson v. Celebrezze*, 460 U.S. 780, 788 n.9 (1983) [p. 517], however, we confirmed the general rule that "evenhanded restrictions that protect the integrity and reliability of the electoral process itself" are not invidious and satisfy the standard set forth in *Harper*. Rather than applying any "litmus test" that would neatly separate valid from invalid restrictions, we concluded that a court must identify and evaluate the interests put forward by the State as justifications for the burden imposed by its rule, and then make the "hard judgment" that our adversary system demands.

In later election cases we have followed *Anderson*'s balancing approach. Thus, in *Norman v. Reed*, 502 U.S. 279, 288–289 (1992), after identifying the burden Illinois imposed on a political party's access to the ballot, we "called for the demonstration of a corresponding interest sufficiently weighty to justify the limitation," and concluded that the "severe restriction" was not justified by a narrowly drawn state interest of compelling importance. Later, in *Burdick* v. *Takushi*, 504 U.S. 428 (1992) [p. 990], we applied *Anderson*'s standard for "reasonable, nondiscriminatory restrictions," and upheld Hawaii's prohibition on write-in voting despite the fact that it prevented a significant number of "voters from participating in Hawaii elections in a meaningful manner." We reaffirmed *Anderson*'s requirement that a court evaluating a constitutional challenge to an election regulation weigh the asserted injury to the right to vote against the "precise interests put forward by the State as justifications for the burden imposed by its rule."[8]

In neither *Norman* nor *Burdick* did we identify any litmus test for measuring the severity of a burden that a state law imposes on a political party, an individual voter, or a discrete class of voters. However slight that burden may appear, as *Harper* demonstrates, it must be justified by relevant and legitimate state interests "sufficiently weighty to justify the limitation." We therefore begin our analysis of the constitutionality of Indiana's statute by focusing on those interests. * * *

[The State argues that the burdens imposed by the Voter ID Law are justified by the interests of deterring and detecting voter fraud, as well as safeguarding voter confidence.] The only kind of voter fraud that SEA 483 addresses is in-person voter impersonation at polling places. The record contains no evidence of any such fraud actually occurring in Indiana at any time in its history. Moreover, petitioners argue that provisions of the Indiana Criminal Code punishing such conduct as a felony provide adequate protection against the risk that such conduct will occur in the future. It remains true, however, that flagrant examples of such fraud in other parts of the country have been documented throughout this Nation's history by respected historians and journalists,[11] that occasional examples have surfaced in recent years,[12]

---

8. Contrary to JUSTICE SCALIA's suggestion, our approach remains faithful to *Anderson* and *Burdick*. The *Burdick* opinion was explicit in its endorsement and adherence to *Anderson*, and repeatedly cited *Anderson*. To be sure, *Burdick* rejected the argument that strict scrutiny applies to all laws imposing a burden on the right to vote; but in its place, the Court applied the "flexible standard" set forth in *Anderson*. *Burdick* surely did not create a novel "deferential 'important regulatory interests' standard."

11. One infamous example is the New York City elections of 1868. William (Boss) Tweed set about solidifying and consolidating his control of the city. One local tough who worked for Boss Tweed, "Big Tim" Sullivan, insisted that his "repeaters" (individuals paid to vote multiple times) have whiskers:

> "When you've voted 'em with their whiskers on, you take 'em to a barber and scrape off the chin fringe. Then you vote 'em again with the side lilacs and a mustache. Then to a barber again, off comes the sides and you vote; em a third time with the mustache. If that ain't enough and the box can stand a few more ballots, clean off the mustache and vote 'em plain face. That makes every one of 'em good for four votes."

12. [District] Judge Barker cited record evidence containing examples from California, Washington, Maryland, Wisconsin, Georgia, Illinois, Pennsylvania, Missouri, Miami, and St. Louis. * * * While * * * much of the fraud was actually absentee ballot fraud or voter registration fraud, there remain scattered instances of in-person voter fraud. For example, after a hotly contested gubernatorial election in 2004, Washington conducted an investigation of voter fraud and uncovered 19

and that Indiana's own experience with fraudulent voting in the 2003 Democratic primary for East Chicago Mayor—though perpetrated using absentee ballots and not in-person fraud—demonstrate that not only is the risk of voter fraud real but that it could affect the outcome of a close election.

There is no question about the legitimacy or importance of the State's interest in counting only the votes of eligible voters. Moreover, the interest in orderly administration and accurate recordkeeping provides a sufficient justification for carefully identifying all voters participating in the election process. While the most effective method of preventing election fraud may well be debatable, the propriety of doing so is perfectly clear.

In its brief, the State argues that the inflation of its voter rolls provides further support for its enactment of SEA 483. The record contains a November 5, 2000, newspaper article asserting that, as the result of [the National Voter Registration Act of 1993, which restricts the ability of states to remove names from lists of registered voters,] and "sloppy record keeping," Indiana's lists of registered voters included the names of thousands of persons who had either moved, died, or were not eligible to vote because they had been convicted of felonies. * * * Even though Indiana's own negligence may have contributed to the serious inflation of its registration lists when SEA 483 was enacted, the fact of inflated voter rolls does provide a neutral and nondiscriminatory reason supporting the State's decision to require photo identification.

Finally, the State contends that it has an interest in protecting public confidence "in the integrity and legitimacy of representative government." While that interest is closely related to the State's interest in preventing voter fraud, public confidence in the integrity of the electoral process has independent significance, because it encourages citizen participation in the democratic process. * * *

States employ different methods of identifying eligible voters at the polls. Some merely check off the names of registered voters who identify themselves; others require voters to present registration cards or other documentation before they can vote; some require voters to sign their names so their signatures can be compared with those on file; and in recent years an increasing number of States have relied primarily on photo identification. A photo identification requirement imposes some burdens on voters that other methods of identification do not share. For example, a voter may lose his photo identification, may have his wallet stolen on the way to the polls, or may not resemble the photo in the identification because he recently grew a beard. Burdens of that sort arising from life's vagaries, however, are neither so serious nor so frequent as to raise any question about the constitutionality of SEA 483; the availability of the right to cast a provisional ballot provides an adequate remedy for problems of that character.

"ghost voters." After a partial investigation of the ghost voting, one voter was confirmed to have committed in-person voting fraud.

The burdens that are relevant to the issue before us are those imposed on persons who are eligible to vote but do not possess a current photo identification that complies with the requirements of SEA 483. The fact that most voters already possess a valid driver's license, or some other form of acceptable identification, would not save the statute under our reasoning in *Harper*, if the State required voters to pay a tax or a fee to obtain a new photo identification. But just as other States provide free voter registration cards, the photo identification cards issued by Indiana's BMV are also free. For most voters who need them, the inconvenience of making a trip to the BMV, gathering the required documents, and posing for a photograph surely does not qualify as a substantial burden on the right to vote, or even represent a significant increase over the usual burdens of voting.[17]

Both evidence in the record and facts of which we may take judicial notice, however, indicate that a somewhat heavier burden may be placed on a limited number of persons. They include elderly persons born out-of-state, who may have difficulty obtaining a birth certificate; persons who because of economic or other personal limitations may find it difficult either to secure a copy of their birth certificate or to assemble the other required documentation to obtain a state-issued identification; homeless persons; and persons with a religious objection to being photographed. If we assume, as the evidence suggests, that some members of these classes were registered voters when SEA 483 was enacted, the new identification requirement may have imposed a special burden on their right to vote.

The severity of that burden is, of course, mitigated by the fact that, if eligible, voters without photo identification may cast provisional ballots that will ultimately be counted. To do so, however, they must travel to the circuit court clerk's office within 10 days to execute the required affidavit. It is unlikely that such a requirement would pose a constitutional problem unless it is wholly unjustified. And even assuming that the burden may not be justified as to a few voters,[19] that conclusion is by no means sufficient to establish petitioners' right to the relief they seek in this litigation. Given the fact that petitioners have advanced a broad attack on the constitutionality of SEA 483, seeking relief that would invalidate the statute in all its applications, they bear a heavy burden of persuasion. * * *

Petitioners ask this Court, in effect, to perform a unique balancing analysis that looks specifically at a small number of voters who may experience a special burden

---

17. To obtain a photo identification card a person must present at least one "primary" document, which can be a birth certificate, certificate of naturalization, U.S. veterans photo identification, U.S. military photo identification, or a U.S. passport. Indiana, like most States, charges a fee for obtaining a copy of one's birth certificate. This fee varies by county and is currently between $3 and $12. Some States charge substantially more.

19. Presumably most voters casting provisional ballots will be able to obtain photo identifications before the next election. It is, however, difficult to understand why the State should require voters with a faith-based objection to being photographed to cast provisional ballots subject to later verification in every election when the BMV is able to issue these citizens special licenses that enable them to drive without any photo identification.

under the statute and weighs their burdens against the State's broad interests in protecting election integrity. Petitioners urge us to ask whether the State's interests justify the burden imposed on voters who cannot afford or obtain a birth certificate and who must make a second trip to the circuit court clerk's office after voting. But on the basis of the evidence in the record it is not possible to quantify either the magnitude of the burden on this narrow class of voters or the portion of the burden imposed on them that is fully justified.

First, the evidence in the record does not provide us with the number of registered voters without photo identification * * *. Further, the deposition evidence presented in the District Court does not provide any concrete evidence of the burden imposed on voters who currently lack photo identification. * * * The record says virtually nothing about the difficulties faced by either indigent voters or voters with religious objections to being photographed. * * *

In sum, on the basis of the record that has been made in this litigation, we cannot conclude that the statute imposes "excessively burdensome requirements" on any class of voters. * * * When we consider only the statute's broad application to all Indiana voters we conclude that it "imposes only a limited burden on voters' rights." *Burdick*, 504 U.S., at 439. The "precise interests" advanced by the State are therefore sufficient to defeat petitioners' facial challenge to SEA 483. * * *

In their briefs, petitioners stress the fact that all of the Republicans in the General Assembly voted in favor of SEA 483 and the Democrats were unanimous in opposing it. * * * It is fair to infer that partisan considerations may have played a significant role in the decision to enact SEA 483. If such considerations had provided the only justification for a photo identification requirement, we may also assume that SEA 483 would suffer the same fate as the poll tax at issue in *Harper*.

But if a nondiscriminatory law is supported by valid neutral justifications, those justifications should not be disregarded simply because partisan interests may have provided one motivation for the votes of individual legislators. The state interests identified as justifications for SEA 483 are both neutral and sufficiently strong to require us to reject petitioners' facial attack on the statute. The application of the statute to the vast majority of Indiana voters is amply justified by the valid interest in protecting "the integrity and reliability of the electoral process."

The judgment of the Court of Appeals is affirmed.

It is so ordered.

JUSTICE SCALIA, with whom JUSTICE THOMAS and JUSTICE ALITO join, concurring in the judgment.

The lead opinion assumes petitioners' premise that the voter-identification law "may have imposed a special burden on" some voters, but holds that petitioners have not assembled evidence to show that the special burden is severe enough to warrant strict scrutiny. That is true enough, but for the sake of clarity and finality (as well as adherence to precedent), I prefer to decide these cases on the grounds that petitioners' premise is irrelevant and that the burden at issue is minimal and justified.

To evaluate a law respecting the right to vote—whether it governs voter qualifications, candidate selection, or the voting process—we use the approach set out in *Burdick* v. *Takushi*. This calls for application of a deferential "important regulatory interests" standard for nonsevere, nondiscriminatory restrictions, reserving strict scrutiny for laws that severely restrict the right to vote. The lead opinion resists the import of *Burdick* by characterizing it as simply adopting "the balancing approach" of *Anderson* v. *Celebrezze*. Although *Burdick* liberally quoted *Anderson*, *Burdick* forged *Anderson*'s amorphous "flexible standard" into something resembling an administrable rule. Since *Burdick*, we have repeatedly reaffirmed the primacy of its two-track approach. See *Timmons* v. *Twin Cities Area New Party*, 520 U.S. 351, 358 (1997) [p. 526]; *Clingman* v. *Beaver*, 544 U.S. 581, 586–587 (2005) [p. 460]. "[S]trict scrutiny is appropriate only if the burden is severe." *Id.*, at 592. Thus, the first step is to decide whether a challenged law severely burdens the right to vote. Ordinary and widespread burdens, such as those requiring "nominal effort" of everyone, are not severe. See *id.*, at 591, 593–597. Burdens are severe if they go beyond the merely inconvenient.

Of course, we have to identify a burden before we can weigh it. The Indiana law affects different voters differently, but what petitioners view as the law's several light and heavy burdens are no more than the different *impacts* of the single burden that the law uniformly imposes on all voters. To vote in person in Indiana, *everyone* must have and present a photo identification that can be obtained for free. The State draws no classifications, let alone discriminatory ones, except to establish *optional* absentee and provisional balloting for certain poor, elderly, and institutionalized voters and for religious objectors. Nor are voters who already have photo identifications exempted from the burden, since those voters must maintain the accuracy of the information displayed on the identifications, renew them before they expire, and replace them if they are lost.

The Indiana photo-identification law is a generally applicable, nondiscriminatory voting regulation, and our precedents refute the view that individual impacts are relevant to determining the severity of the burden it imposes. In the course of concluding that the Hawaii laws at issue in *Burdick* "impose[d] only a limited burden on voters' rights to make free choices and to associate politically through the vote," we considered the laws and their reasonably foreseeable effect on *voters generally*. We did not discuss whether the laws had a severe effect on Mr. Burdick's own right to vote, given his particular circumstances. That was essentially the approach of the *Burdick* dissenters, who would have applied strict scrutiny to the laws because of their effect on "some voters." Subsequent cases have followed *Burdick*'s generalized review of nondiscriminatory election laws. Indeed, *Clingman*'s holding that burdens are not severe if they are ordinary and widespread would be rendered meaningless if a single plaintiff could claim a severe burden. * * *

Insofar as our election-regulation cases rest upon the requirements of the Fourteenth Amendment, weighing the burden of a nondiscriminatory voting law upon each voter and concomitantly requiring exceptions for vulnerable voters would effectively turn back decades of equal-protection jurisprudence. A voter complaining about such a law's effect on him has no valid equal-protection claim because, without proof of discriminatory intent, a generally applicable law with disparate impact is not unconstitutional. The Fourteenth Amendment does not regard neutral laws as invidious ones, *even when their burdens purportedly fall disproportionately on a protected class. A fortiori* it does not do so when, as here, the classes complaining of disparate impact are not even protected.*

Even if I thought that *stare decisis* did not foreclose adopting an individual-focused approach, I would reject it as an original matter. This is an area where the dos and don'ts need to be known in advance of the election, and voter-by-voter examination of the burdens of voting regulations would prove especially disruptive. A case-by-case approach naturally encourages constant litigation. Very few new election regulations improve everyone's lot, so the potential allegations of severe burden are endless. A State reducing the number of polling places would be open to the complaint it has violated the rights of disabled voters who live near the closed stations. Indeed, it may even be the case that some laws already on the books are especially burdensome for some voters, and one can predict lawsuits demanding that a State adopt voting over the Internet or expand absentee balloting.

That sort of detailed judicial supervision of the election process would flout the Constitution's express commitment of the task to the States. See Art. I, § 4. It is for state legislatures to weigh the costs and benefits of possible changes to their election codes, and their judgment must prevail unless it imposes a severe and unjustified overall burden upon the right to vote, or is intended to disadvantage a particular class. Judicial review of their handiwork must apply an objective, uniform standard that will enable them to determine, *ex ante*, whether the burden they impose is too severe.

The lead opinion's record-based resolution of these cases, which neither rejects nor embraces the rule of our precedents, provides no certainty, and will embolden litigants who surmise that our precedents have been abandoned. There is no good reason to prefer that course.

---

* A number of our early right-to-vote decisions, purporting to rely upon the Equal Protection Clause, strictly scrutinized nondiscriminatory voting laws requiring the payment of fees. See, *e.g., Harper* v. *Virginia Bd. of Elections*, 383 U.S., [at] 670 (poll tax); *Bullock* v. *Carter*, 405 U.S. 134, 145 (1972) [p. 507] (ballot-access fee); *Lubin* v. *Panish*, 415 U.S. 709, 716–719 (1974) (ballot-access fee). To the extent those decisions continue to stand for a principle that *Burdick* does not already encompass, it suffices to note that we have never held that legislatures must calibrate *all* election laws, even those totally unrelated to money, for their impacts on poor voters or must otherwise accommodate wealth disparities.

The universally applicable requirements of Indiana's voter-identification law are eminently reasonable. The burden of acquiring, possessing, and showing a free photo identification is simply not severe, because it does not "even represent a significant increase over the usual burdens of voting." And the State's interests are sufficient to sustain that minimal burden. That should end the matter. That the State accommodates some voters by permitting (not requiring) the casting of absentee or provisional ballots, is an indulgence—not a constitutional imperative that falls short of what is required.

JUSTICE SOUTER, with whom JUSTICE GINSBURG joins, dissenting.

Indiana's "Voter ID Law" threatens to impose nontrivial burdens on the voting right of tens of thousands of the State's citizens, and a significant percentage of those individuals are likely to be deterred from voting. The statute is unconstitutional under the balancing standard of *Burdick* v. *Takushi*: a State may not burden the right to vote merely by invoking abstract interests, be they legitimate, or even compelling, but must make a particular, factual showing that threats to its interests outweigh the particular impediments it has imposed. The State has made no such justification here, and as to some aspects of its law, it has hardly even tried. I therefore respectfully dissent from the Court's judgment sustaining the statute.

Voting-rights cases raise two competing interests, the one side being the fundamental right to vote. As against the unfettered right, however, lies the "[c]ommon sense, as well as constitutional law . . . that government must play an active role in structuring elections; 'as a practical matter, there must be a substantial regulation of elections if they are to be fair and honest and if some sort of order, rather than chaos, is to accompany the democratic processes.'" [504 U.S.], at 433.

Given the legitimacy of interests on both sides, we have avoided pre-set levels of scrutiny in favor of a sliding-scale balancing analysis: the scrutiny varies with the effect of the regulation at issue. * * *

The first set of burdens shown in these cases is the travel costs and fees necessary to get one of the limited variety of federal or state photo identifications needed to cast a regular ballot under the Voter ID Law. The travel is required for the personal visit to a license branch of the Indiana Bureau of Motor Vehicles, which is demanded of anyone applying for a driver's license or nondriver photo identification. * * * Poor, old, and disabled voters who do not drive a car, however, may find the trip prohibitive[.][4] * * *

---

4. The State asserts that the elderly and disabled are adequately accommodated through their option to cast absentee ballots, and so any burdens on them are irrelevant. But * * * there are crucial differences between the absentee and regular ballot. Voting by absentee ballot leaves an individual without the possibility of receiving assistance from poll workers, and thus increases the likelihood of confusion and error. More seriously, * * * Indiana law "treats absentee voters differently from

Although making voters travel farther than what is convenient for most and possible for some does not amount to a "severe" burden under *Burdick*, that is no reason to ignore the burden altogether. It translates into an obvious economic cost (whether in work time lost, or getting and paying for transportation) that an Indiana voter must bear to obtain an ID.

For those voters who can afford the roundtrip, a second financial hurdle appears: in order to get photo identification for the first time, they need to present "a birth certificate, a certificate of naturalization, U.S. veterans photo identification, U.S. military photo identification, or a U.S. passport." As the lead opinion says, the two most common of these documents come at a price: Indiana counties charge anywhere from $3 to $12 for a birth certificate (and in some other States the fee is significantly higher), and that same price must usually be paid for a first-time passport, since a birth certificate is required to prove U.S. citizenship by birth. The total fees for a passport, moreover, are up to about $100. So most voters must pay at least one fee to get the ID necessary to cast a regular ballot. As with the travel costs, these fees are far from shocking on their face, but in the *Burdick* analysis it matters that both the travel costs and the fees are disproportionately heavy for, and thus disproportionately likely to deter, the poor, the old, and the immobile.

To be sure, Indiana has a provisional-ballot exception to the ID requirement for individuals the State considers "indigent" as well as those with religious objections to being photographed, and this sort of exception could in theory provide a way around the costs of procuring an ID. But Indiana's chosen exception does not amount to much relief.

The law allows these voters who lack the necessary ID to sign the poll book and cast a provisional ballot. As the lead opinion recognizes, though, that is only the first step; to have the provisional ballot counted, a voter must then appear in person before the circuit court clerk or county election board within 10 days of the election, to sign an affidavit attesting to indigency or religious objection to being photographed (or to present an ID at that point). Unlike the trip to the BMV (which, assuming things go smoothly, needs to be made only once every four years for renewal of nondriver photo identification), this one must be taken every time a poor person or religious objector wishes to vote, because the State does not allow an affidavit to count in successive elections. And unlike the trip to the BMV (which at least has a handful of license branches in the more populous counties), a county has only one county seat. Forcing these people to travel to the county seat every time

---

the way it treats Election Day voters," in the important sense that "an absentee ballot may not be recounted in situations where clerical error by an election officer rendered it invalid." The State itself notes that "election officials routinely reject absentee ballots on suspicion of forgery." * * * It is one thing (and a commendable thing) for the State to make absentee voting available to the elderly and disabled; but it is quite another to suggest that, because the more convenient but less reliable absentee ballot is available, the State may freely deprive the elderly and disabled of the option of voting in person.

they try to vote is particularly onerous [because] most counties in Indiana either lack public transportation or offer only limited coverage. * * *

All of this suggests that provisional ballots do not obviate the burdens of getting photo identification. And even if that were not so, the provisional-ballot option would be inadequate for a further reason: the indigency exception by definition offers no relief to those voters who do not consider themselves (or would not be considered) indigent but as a practical matter would find it hard, for nonfinancial reasons, to get the required ID (most obviously the disabled).

Indiana's Voter ID Law thus threatens to impose serious burdens on the voting right, even if not "severe" ones, and the next question under *Burdick* is whether the number of individuals likely to be affected is significant as well. Record evidence and facts open to judicial notice answer yes.

Although the District Court found that petitioners failed to offer any reliable empirical study of numbers of voters affected, we may accept that court's rough calculation that 43,000 voting-age residents lack the kind of identification card required by Indiana's law. * * * To be sure, the 43,000 figure has to be discounted to some extent, residents of certain nursing homes being exempted from the photo identification requirement. But the State does not suggest that this narrow exception could possibly reduce 43,000 to an insubstantial number.[24]

The upshot is this. Tens of thousands of voting-age residents lack the necessary photo identification. A large proportion of them are likely to be in bad shape economically. The Voter ID Law places hurdles in the way of either getting an ID or of voting provisionally, and they translate into nontrivial economic costs. There is accordingly no reason to doubt that a significant number of state residents will be discouraged or disabled from voting. * * *

Because the lead opinion finds only "limited" burdens on the right to vote, it avoids a hard look at the State's claimed interests. But having found the Voter ID Law burdens far from trivial, I have to make a rigorous assessment of "the precise interests put forward by the State as justifications for the burden imposed by its rule, [and] the extent to which those interests make it necessary to burden the plaintiff's rights." *Burdick*, 504 U.S., at 434. * * *

---

24. The State does imply that we should further discount the 43,000 estimate to exclude citizens who are not registered to vote, or who are registered but not planning to vote. But that argument is flatly contradicted by this Court's settled precedent. As our cases have recognized, disfranchisement is disfranchisement, whether or not the disfranchised voter would have voted if given the choice. That is why in *Dunn* v. *Blumstein*, 405 U.S. 330 (1972) [p. 74], the Court did not ask whether any significant number of individuals deprived of the right to vote by durational residence requirements would actually have chosen to vote. And in *Harper* v. *Virginia Bd. of Elections*, the Court did not pause to consider whether any of the qualified voters deterred by the $1.50 poll tax would have opted to vote if there had been no fee. Our cases make clear that the Constitution protects an individual's ability to vote, not merely his decision to do so.

[JUSTICE SOUTER argued that the state's justifications were insufficient, largely because of the lack of in-person voter-impersonation fraud.]

JUSTICE BREYER, dissenting.

Indiana's statute * * * imposes a burden upon some voters, but it does so in order to prevent fraud, to build confidence in the voting system, and thereby to maintain the integrity of the voting process. In determining whether this statute violates the Federal Constitution, I would balance the voting-related interests that the statute affects, asking "whether the statute burdens any one such interest in a manner out of proportion to the statute's salutary effects upon the others (perhaps, but not necessarily, because of the existence of a clearly superior, less restrictive alternative)." *Nixon* v. *Shrink Missouri Government PAC*, 528 U.S. 377, 402 (2000) [p. 768] (BREYER, J., concurring). Applying this standard, I believe the statute is unconstitutional because it imposes a disproportionate burden upon those eligible voters who lack a driver's license or other statutorily valid form of photo ID. * * *

Notes and Questions

1. Count the votes in *Crawford*. If a single opinion commands the agreement of a majority of the participating Justices, then the opinion is "of the Court." Where no opinion commands a majority, then one must look more closely at the opinions of the Justices who agree in the ultimate disposition of the case (affirmance, reversal, vacatur, etc.). The opinion representing the views of the most Justices who agree in the judgment is referred to as the "plurality" opinion. In *Crawford*, however, there was no plurality opinion because the six Justices who agreed to affirm the judgment of the Court of Appeals were split 3-3. Justice Stevens's opinion became the "lead opinion" because he had greater seniority than did Justice Scalia, who wrote for the other group of three Justices, but the Stevens opinion is not entitled to any greater precedential weight simply because it comes first in the U.S. Reports.

Rather, the precedential weight of the opinions is assessed by analyzing the Court's rule from *Marks v. United States*, 430 U.S. 188 (1977). Under the *Marks* rule, "[w]hen a fragmented Court decides a case and no single rationale explaining the result enjoys the assent of five Justices, 'the holding of the Court may be viewed as that position taken by those Members who concurred in the judgments on the narrowest grounds. . . .'" *Nichols v. United States*, 511 U.S. 738, 745 (1994). Thus, Justice Stevens's opinion will likely be given precedential weight because it was "narrowe[r]" than Justice Scalia's.

2. In *Crawford* there were six votes for reading *Burdick* as adopting an open-ended balancing test *à la Anderson*, rather than as dividing election regulations into those that present "severe" burdens on the right to vote and those that do not. Both the lead opinion and Justice Souter's dissent explicitly stated that courts should balance the need for election regulations against the burdens the regulations impose, even when such burdens are less than "severe," and Justice Breyer also applied a balancing analysis in evaluating the ID law. Review *Anderson* and consider whether

its standard is administrable or capable of being applied consistently. Is *Burdick's* two-tiered test any better from a perspective of administrability?

3. Justice Stevens's distaste for the two-tiered standard of review that Justice Scalia saw in *Burdick* was predictable. Justice Stevens authored the Court's opinion in *Anderson*, and had called for the abandonment of the tiers of scrutiny in equal-protection analysis. *See Craig v. Boren*, 429 U.S. 190, 211 (1976) (Stevens, J., concurring) ("There is only one Equal Protection Clause."). *See also Karcher v. Daggett*, 462 U.S. 725, 749 (1983) (Stevens, J., concurring) (same). According to Justice Stevens, the preferable approach would be to apply a single standard under which states would be required to "govern impartially." Under such an analysis, the justifications for disparate treatment would have to be progressively more convincing as the discrimination became more severe, but state classifications and justifications would be evaluated on a continuum rather than according to tiers. Such an approach has the advantage of allowing courts to make finer assessments as to whether states' classifications are justified, but places a large amount of discretion in the courts.

4. One lower court has characterized *Burdick* as creating a *three*-tiered standard of review: strict scrutiny for severe restrictions, rational basis for "reasonable, non-discriminatory restrictions," and the *Anderson* balancing test (weighing the burden on the right to vote against the "precise interests" offered by the state to justify the burden) for moderately burdensome restrictions. *See Obama for America v. Husted*, 697 F.3d 423, 429–34 (6th Cir. 2012). Is that the right way to read *Anderson* and *Burdick*? Is there any practical difference between the three-tiered standard of *Obama for America* and a standard that simply evaluates burdens along a continuum from least severe to most severe?

5. Recall Justice Breyer's argument that campaign-finance restrictions promote political equality, and therefore "constitutionally protected interests lie on both sides of the legal equation." *Nixon v. Shrink Missouri Government PAC*, 528 U.S. 377, 400 (2000) [p. 768] (Breyer, J., concurring). Do constitutionally protected interests lie on both sides of the debate about voter-ID laws? That is, does the Constitution protect not only the right to vote, but also the "right for each voter not to have his legitimate vote diluted or cancelled by an illegal vote"? J. Kenneth Blackwell & Kenneth A. Klukowski, *The Other Voting Right: Protecting Every Citizen's Vote by Safeguarding the Integrity of the Ballot Box*, 28 Yale L. & Pol'y Rev. 107, 109 (2009). For a defense of *Crawford* along that line, see *id.* at 116–17; *see also* Bradley A. Smith, *Broken Windows and Voting Rights*, 156 U. Penn L. Rev. Pennumbra 241 (2007).

6. A recurring question throughout election law is whether the government may limit individuals' ability to participate in politics because of a concern that the participation creates an appearance of impropriety. For example, limits on campaign fund-raising and judicial candidates' speech have been justified by such a concern, and appearances are significant in the law of electoral districting as well, as we saw in Chapter 4 when considering *Shaw v. Reno*, 509 U.S. 630 (1993) [p. 362], and its progeny.

In *Crawford*, Indiana relied in part on its belief that the voter-ID law served not only the interest in preventing *actual* fraud, but in strengthening the public's *faith* that the elections were not tainted by fraud. Justice Stevens agreed, and argued that "public confidence in the integrity of the electoral process" was important because it "encourages citizen participation in the democratic process." What significance should be given to the state's interest in preventing the *appearance* of voter fraud, even if Indiana could point to no instances of actual voter-impersonation fraud in the state's history? *See* Andrew N. DeLaney, Note, *Appearance Matters: Why the State Has an Interest in Preventing the Appearance of Voting Fraud*, 83 N.Y.U. L. Rev. 847 (2008); Joel A. Heller, Note, *Fearing Fear Itself: Photo Identification Laws, Fear of Fraud, and the Fundamental Right to Vote*, 62 Vand. L. Rev. 1871 (2009).

7. Should one assess the severity of election regulations from the perspective of voters generally, or from the perspective of the voters most inconvenienced by them? What do the Court's prior cases say about that question?

8. Consider the footnote in Justice Scalia's opinion. Was he in effect arguing that *Harper* was wrongly decided? Are you convinced by his attempt to distinguish that case? In answering these questions, does it matter whether the challenge to the poll tax in *Harper* is characterized as presenting a facial or an as-applied attack?

9. Justice Souter argued in his footnote 24 that the number of persons burdened by the photo-ID requirement should include persons who would choose not to vote even if there were no such requirement, because "the Constitution protects an individual's ability to vote, not merely his decision to do so." In what respect, however, does any limitation on voting burden someone who would not exercise the franchise even if there were no such limitation? Do the cases Justice Souter cited require counting those citizens who not only do not plan to vote, but who are unregistered? Note that the lead opinion pointed to the record as "not provid[ing] us with the number of *registered voters* without photo identification" (emphasis added).

10. Since the start of 2011, several states have enacted voter-ID laws or amended existing laws to increase ID requirements to register or to vote. A total of thirty-six states have laws requesting or requiring voters to show some form of ID, with thirty-five of those states' laws currently in effect. These laws differ in important details, such as the acceptable forms of identification, whether a photo-ID is required or whether a non-photo-ID will suffice, and whether a voter without ID can cast a ballot after signing an affidavit at the polling place. A useful catalogue of states' laws by the National Conference of State Legislatures is available at http://www.ncsl.org /default.aspx?tabid=16602.

Lower-court challenges to many of the new laws—some based on state law and others based on federal law—have reached disparate results. Georgia's and Oklahoma's laws were upheld in state court. *Democratic Party of Georgia v. Perdue*, 707 S.E.2d 67 (Ga. 2011); *Gentges v. Oklahoma State Election Board* (Okla. St. Dist. Ct. 2016) (upholding Oklahoma's voter-ID law), *reported at* Trevor Brown, *Judge Dismisses Challenge to State's Voter ID Law*, Oklahoma Watch, Aug. 16, 2016, at http://oklahomawatch.org/2016/08/16/judge-dismisses-challenge-to-states-voter -id-law/?platform=hootsuite. Pennsylvania's was struck down in state court. *Applewhite v. Commonwealth*, 2014 Pa. Commw. LEXIS 62 (Pa. Commw. Ct. 2014). Arkansas' law was struck down by a lower court, but the Arkansas Supreme Court vacated that judgment on procedural grounds. *Arkansas State Board of Election Commissioners v. Pulaski County Election Commission*, 437 S.W.3d 80 (Ark. 2014). Missouri's law was struck down in part because the law required voters without photo ID to execute an affidavit that was "misleading and contradictory." *Priorities USA v. Missouri*, 591 S.W.3d 448, 461 (Mo. 2020).

Wisconsin's law has been the subject of a legal saga, including several decisions by the Seventh Circuit in 2016 alone. In 2014, the Seventh Circuit upheld Wisconsin's law (overturning a district-court judgment striking it down). *Frank v. Walker*, 768 F.3d 744 (7th Cir. 2014). In 2016, however, the court held that any eligible voter who could not obtain ID with reasonable effort was entitled to an accommodation. *Frank v. Walker*, 819 F.3d 384 (7th Cir. 2016). The district court then issued an injunction requiring the state to waive the ID requirement for any voter who merely asserted that he could not obtain an ID through reasonable effort—"even if the voter has never tried to secure one, and even if by objective standards the effort needed would be reasonable (and would succeed)." The court of appeals promptly stayed the injunction pending appeal, allowing the ID law to be enforced. *Frank v. Walker*, 2016 WL 4224616, *1, 2016 U.S. App. LEXIS 14917, *3 (7th Cir. 2016). The court of appeals subsequently confirmed that the district court's injunction was inconsistent with *Crawford*, which permitted states to require that voters expend *some* effort to comply with ID laws. *See Luft v. Evers*, 963 F.3d 665, 678–79 (7th Cir. 2020). In yet another case, a district court held that any person requesting an ID would be entitled to receive a credential allowing him to vote, unless readily available information indicated that the person was not eligible to vote. *See One Wisconsin Institute, Inc. v. Thomsen*, 198 F. Supp. 3d 896 (W.D. Wisc. 2016). The state agreed to comply with that standard. *See Frank v. Walker*, 835 F.3d 649, 651–52 (7th Cir. 2016) (*en banc*) (*per curiam*) (denying petition for initial hearing *en banc*).

The Fourth Circuit struck down North Carolina's voter-ID law under the Federal Constitution and § 2 of the Voting Rights Act because, in the view of the court, the voter-ID law was passed with a racially discriminatory purpose. *North Carolina State Conference of the NAACP v. McCreary*, 831 F.3d 204 (4th Cir. 2016).

And Texas's law (like South Carolina's, discussed below), was the subject of a consent decree reached after the Fifth Circuit held that Texas was required by the Voting Rights Act to accommodate voters who lacked the necessary IDs. *Veasey v. Abbott*, 830 F.3d 216 (5th Cir. 2016) (*en banc*). Under the Texas consent decree, voters will be permitted to vote if they present any government document with their name on it and if they sign an affidavit saying that they could not easily obtain one of the IDs that the law purports to require. *See* Michael Wines, *Texas Agrees to Loosen Rules on IDs for November Election*, N.Y. TIMES, Aug. 4, 2016, at A9.

Additionally, the new voter-ID legislation has led to controversy surrounding the Voting Rights Act's preclearance requirement. The Department of Justice granted preclearance to some states' laws, including those in New Hampshire and Virginia. DOJ initially denied South Carolina's application, but the D.C. District Court granted preclearance after South Carolina offered an interpretation that gutted the law of most of its significance. *South Carolina v. United States*, 898 F. Supp. 2d 30 (D.D.C. 2012). Under this interpretation, voters could continue to use non-photo voter registration cards, as long as they provide a reason for not having a photo ID. The D.C. District Court denied Texas's request for preclearance of its photo-ID law. *See Texas v. Holder*, 888 F. Supp. 2d 113 (D.D.C. 2012), *vacated and remanded*, 133 S. Ct. 2886 (2013).

With the Supreme Court's invalidation, in *Shelby County, Alabama v. Holder*, 570 U.S. 529 (2013), of the VRA preclearance coverage formula, it appears that preclearance will no longer be an obstacle for the formerly covered jurisdictions. North Carolina, portions of which had been covered under the formula struck down in *Shelby County*, has attempted to take advantage of that decision to enact a new voter-ID law, but the Fourth Circuit struck down the law. *North Carolina State Conference of the NAACP v. McCreary*, 831 F.3d 204 (4th Cir. 2016). In addition to establishing an ID requirement, the law reduced the days available for early voting and also eliminated same-day registration. The court of appeals held that the law was passed with a racially discriminatory purpose, rejecting the district court's contrary factual finding as clearly erroneous, and therefore held that the law violated both the Constitution and § 2 of the Voting Rights Act. The Fourth Circuit relied on the fact that black voters disproportionately used the procedures that were restricted by the North Carolina law, and that blacks disproportionately lacked a satisfactory ID. The court also noted North Carolina's history of racial discrimination (although much of the post-1980 history did not involve proven *purposeful* discrimination), as well as information from the law's legislative history, including the unusually expeditious manner in which the law was enacted.

There is a move to use VRA § 3 to bail-in some of the formerly covered jurisdictions, and DOJ's suit against North Carolina asked for bail-in as well as for the invalidation of the photo-ID law. *See id.* To the extent such efforts are successful, preclearance will again be required for the areas bailed-in.

11. In *Arizona v. Inter Tribal Council of Arizona, Inc.*, 570 U.S. 1 (2013), the Supreme Court considered an Arizona law that required voters to present proof of citizenship upon registration. The Court held that the law was pre-empted by the National Voter Registration Act, 52 U.S.C. § 20505(a)(1), because the Arizona law imposed an additional registration requirement beyond completion of the federal form that, according to the NVRA, states must "accept and use."

While thus an apparent victory for challengers of such laws, the full story is much more favorable to states. The Court opined that Congress's power to regulate the times, places, and manner of federal elections did not include the power to decide "*who* may vote in" those elections. 570 U.S. at 16. And the government conceded that the federal form should require sufficient information to permit state officials to determine if applicants satisfied state-law qualifications for registration. Accordingly, Arizona could not require proof of citizenship in addition to the requirements listed on the federal form, but Arizona could likely demand that the federal form add a proof-of-citizenship requirement to its list of materials that prospective Arizona registrants must provide.

12. For one to classify a voting requirement as a "burden" on the right to vote, there must be an implicit assumption about the meaning of an "unburdened" right to vote. But voting always requires at least some effort—effort that may be greater for some people (notably the poor) than for others. For example, registration, especially pre-election-day registration, and even the obligation to go to a polling place impose burdens that may not be trivial for voters who lack easy access to transportation or who have jobs that make it difficult to leave during the appropriate hours. Are those requirements vulnerable after *Crawford* if one can show that they have a "disenfranchising" effect on some number of voters relative to alternatives such as Internet voting, registration or voting by mail, or an extended period of early (*i.e.*, pre-election-day) voting?[c]

Most people believe that a state may constitutionally limit voting to election day, and the Supreme Court has upheld requirements that voters register in advance of election day. *See Marston v. Lewis*, 410 U.S. 679, 680 (1973) (*per curiam*) (upholding a requirement that voters register fifty days in advance of an election, and noting that "States have valid and sufficient interests in providing *some* period of time—prior to an election—in order to prepare adequate voter records and protect its [*sic*] electoral processes from possible fraud."); *Dunn v. Blumstein*, 405 U.S. 330, 348 (1972) [p. 74] ("Fixing a constitutionally acceptable period [for registration prior to an election] is surely a matter of degree. It is sufficient to note here that 30 days appears to be an ample period of time for the State to complete whatever administrative tasks are necessary to prevent fraud. . . ."). Although many states allow early voting, nearly a third of states do not, and few people think that the Constitution requires states to amend their laws to provide for early voting. Is the constitutional issue any different if a state *does* have early voting and then eliminates or reduces it? Suppose that a state grants a period of early voting and same-day voter registration. If the state later amends the law to restrict the period of early voting and to eliminate same-day registration, is such a law unconstitutional because of its restriction on the right to vote? *See Ohio Democratic Party v. Husted*, 834 F.3d 620 (6th Cir. 2016). *Cf. Luft v. Evers*, 963 F.3d 665, 670 (7th Cir. 2020) ("If one party can make changes that it believes help its candidates, the other can restore the original rules or revise the new ones. The process does not include a constitutional ratchet.").

---

c. The Early Voting Information Center maintains a website discussing these and similar matters. *See* Early Voting Information Center, *EVIC*, http://earlyvoting.net.

13. If voting is a fundamental right, why should only "severe" restrictions on that right be subject to strict scrutiny? How can *Anderson* and *Burdick* be squared with cases such as *Kramer v. Union Free School District No. 15*, 395 U.S. 621 (1969) [p. 46], which held that strict scrutiny applies to laws restricting the franchise? Specifically, should *Anderson* and *Burdick* be limited to First Amendment challenges, or should they be applied to equal-protection challenges as well? Should they be limited to cases involving the administration of elections, or should they apply as well in any case involving regulation of the democratic process?

The Sixth Circuit has taken a particularly aggressive stance in applying *Anderson* and *Burdick* to a wide range of election laws. In *Obama for America v. Husted*, 697 F.3d 423, 430 (6th Cir. 2012), mentioned in Note 4, *supra*, the court applied *Anderson* and *Burdick* to evaluate an equal-protection challenge to a law that gave military personnel more time than others for early in-person voting. Was it correct to do so? A later Sixth Circuit opinion followed *Obama for America*, but expressed skepticism:

> It's unclear whether the Supreme Court ever intended *Anderson-Burdick* to apply to Equal Protection claims. That Court has only applied the framework in the context of generally applicable laws. [Here, the court cited *Crawford* (voter ID), *Burdick* (write-in voting), *Norman v. Reed* (ballot access), and *Anderson v. Celebrezze* (candidate filing deadlines).] * * *

> *Anderson-Burdick* first asks us to weigh the magnitude of the burden placed by the State's action on the plaintiff's right to vote. But State action making it easier for some voters to vote—such as providing them an extended deadline to register for absentee ballots—doesn't make it *harder* to vote for electors that don't get the same benefit. Rather, it's the generally applicable absentee ballot deadline that places the burden, if any, on Plaintiffs' right to vote. * * *

> The traditional Equal Protection tiers of scrutiny instead focus on how the State chooses to classify its citizens when drawing lines and then imposes differing requirements on the State's justifications for those classifications accordingly. They are thus better suited for analyzing disparate-treatment claims—even in the voting context. Nonetheless, we are bound by *Obama for America*, so we apply *Anderson-Burdick*.

Mays v. LaRose, 951 F.3d 775, 783 n.4 (6th Cir. 2020). *Mays* concerned a law that permitted no-excuse absentee voting, but required voters to request an absentee ballot by noon, three days before election day. Only voters who were unexpectedly hospitalized were permitted to request an absentee ballot after the deadline. The deadline and its hospital exemption were challenged by a voter who was jailed after the deadline and therefore could neither get to the polls nor request an absentee ballot. The court concluded that the deadline imposed only a "moderate" burden on the plaintiff's right to vote, because the plaintiff faced no greater burden on his right to vote than would be faced by any voter who was called away from home unexpectedly during the last three days before an election. *Id*. at 786. Is that a persuasive rationale for treating a burden as less than severe, when the effect of the law was to deprive him totally of the ability to vote? If you think the burden was severe and strict scrutiny should have applied, should the state be forced to accommodate every voter who finds himself unable to get to the polls because of illness, car trouble, work obligations, or the like? Is it better to answer those questions with *Anderson* and *Burdick* or with the equal-protection tiers of scrutiny?

Shortly after *Mays*, the Sixth Circuit again confronted the question of *Anderson-Burdick*'s scope. *Daunt v. Benson*, 956 F.3d 396 (6th Cir. 2020), involved a challenge to a Michigan constitutional provision establishing an independent redistricting commission. The constitutional provision required that five of the thirteen commissioners be unaffiliated with a political party, and that requirement was challenged by the Michigan Republican Party and individuals who objected to being excluded from those seats because of their partisan affiliation. In the course of upholding the structure of the redistricting commission, the majority of the court concluded that *Anderson-Burdick* applied:

> Although most — if not all — of the cases considered by the Supreme Court and this court under the *Anderson-Burdick* test have involved laws that regulate the actual administration of elections, the rationales for applying the *Anderson-Burdick* test — ensuring that "the democratic processes" are "fair and honest," *Storer v. Brown*, 415 U.S. 724, 730 (1974) [p. 513], and "maintain[ing] the integrity of the democratic system," *Burdick*, 504 U.S. at 441 — resonate here, too. At bottom, the *Anderson-Burdick* framework is used for evaluating "state election law[s]," *Burdick*, 504 U.S. at 434, and a law restricting membership of the body that draws electoral lines could conceivably be classified as an "election law." The [Michigan constitutional a]mendment is designed to further the exact goals described above: It requires commissioners to "perform their duties in a manner that is impartial and reinforces public confidence in the integrity of the redistricting process." For these reasons, we proceed to apply the *Anderson-Burdick* balancing test.

Id. at 406–07. Judge Readler, concurring in the judgment, disagreed. He argued that *Anderson-Burdick* was poorly suited to evaluate a challenge to a state's "means of self-governance" rather than "its election mechanics." *Id*. at 423 (Readler, J., concurring in the judgment). In his view, laws dealing with governmental structure "ha[ve] no actual impact (let alone burden) on voting" — and so it would be inappropriate to apply a balancing test that focuses on a law's burden on the right to vote. *Id*. at 424. *Compare Bates v. Jones*, 131 F.3d 843, 846–47 (9th Cir. 1997) (*en banc*) (applying *Burdick* to a challenge to California's term limits for state office), *with id*. at 859 (Rymer, J., concurring in the result) ("I would not start by analyzing Proposition 140 under the *Anderson/Burdick* test, because terms limits are a qualification for office — not for access to the ballot."). *Cf. Initiative & Referendum*

Institute v. Walker, 450 F.3d 1082, 1099–1100 (10th Cir. 2006) (*en banc*) (distinguishing between laws infringing on political speech, which trigger strict scrutiny, and those limiting citizens' use of initiatives and referenda, which do not); *Marijuana Policy Project v. United States*, 304 F.3d 82, 85 (D.C. Cir. 2002) (same). Should *Anderson-Burdick* apply to all challenges to laws affecting the "fair[ness]" or "integrity" of "the democratic system," *i.e.*, all laws that "conceivably" could be considered "election laws"? If not, is there a principled reason to apply it in ballot-access or election-administration cases but not others?

14. President Trump has alleged that millions of votes were fraudulently cast for his opponent in the 2016 election, although there appears to be no evidence to support such a claim. In May 2017, in an effort to combat such supposed voter fraud, the President issued an executive order establishing the Presidential Advisory Commission on Election Integrity. The bipartisan commission, which was chaired by Vice President Pence, was charged with submitting a report identifying "those vulnerabilities in voting systems and practices used for Federal elections that could lead to improper voter registrations and improper voting, including fraudulent voter registrations and fraudulent voting," as well as those laws and practices that either enhance or undermine public confidence in the integrity of elections. The full executive order is available at https://www.whitehouse.gov/the-press-office /2017/05/11/presidential-executive-order-establishment-presidential-advisory.

The commission requested states to provide publicly available voter data (such as names, addresses, birth dates, political-party registration, a list of elections in which each voter had voted, and the last four digits of voters' Social Security numbers), and that request created considerable controversy. Twenty-one states and the District of Columbia refused to provide any data, while others provided only some of the requested information. Some voters who objected to the disclosure of the information canceled their registrations in response to the request. Public-interest groups sued to block the commission from obtaining the data, although one such challenge was dismissed for want of standing. *Electronic Privacy Information Center v. Presidential Advisory Commission on Election Integrity*, 266 F. Supp. 3d 297 (D.D.C.), *aff'd*, 878 F.3d 371 (D.C. Cir. 2017). The commission was disbanded in January 2018.

15. Some states permit voters to cast "straight-ticket" votes, in which the selection of a party automatically casts a vote for each of that party's nominees in all of that year's elections. Most states, however, require voters to vote for each candidate individually.

Should the Constitution require states to provide an option for straight-ticket voting? Should it be constitutional to eliminate straight-ticket voting once it has been permitted? In a recent case, Michigan voted to eliminate straight-ticket voting, but its law was enjoined on the basis that it would increase waiting times for voting, thus burdening the right to vote, and would also cause voter confusion. Challengers also provided evidence that black voters were more likely than whites to use straight-ticket voting, so the elimination of that voting method would impose a disproportionate burden on blacks. *See Michigan State A. Philip Randolph Institute v. Johnson*, 833 F.3d 656 (6th Cir. 2016).

16. *Problem*. Indiana prohibits convicted sex offenders from coming within one thousand feet of schools, playgrounds, and similar areas. John Doe is a sex offender, having been convicted of child molestation, whose polling place is an elementary school. He may not request an absentee ballot because he will be within the county on election day, and does not satisfy any of the other conditions permitting use of an absentee ballot, such as hospitalization or status as an invalid. To comply with the prohibition and vote, he must appear in person before an absentee board in downtown Indianapolis. Is such a requirement constitutional? *See Does v. City of Indianapolis*, 2006 U.S. Dist. LEXIS 72865, 2006 WL 2927598, *9–*10 (S.D. Ind. 2006). Would the result change if Doe were able to request and cast an absentee ballot by mail? As Justice Souter pointed out in footnote 4 of his dissenting opinion in *Crawford*, there are certain advantages to casting a ballot in-person, including the assistance of poll workers if necessary and the reduced chance that a ballot will be rejected upon suspicion of fraud.

17. Commentators have continued to debate whether voter-ID laws, individually or collectively, disproportionately and negatively affect minority voter turnout. For different perspectives on the evidence, compare the majority opinion in U.S. Commission on Civil Rights: An Assessment of Minority Voting Rights Access in the United States (2018), with the dissent authored by Commissioner Gail Heriot; see also Ben Pryor et al., *Voter ID Laws: The Disenfranchisement of Minority Voters?*, 134 Pol. Sci. Q. 63 (Spring 2019) (discussing difficulties in drawing definitive conclusions from the large social-science literature analyzing the effect of voter-ID laws, in part due to studies based on self-reporting by non-voters).

18. The COVID-19 epidemic, which hit the United States in early 2020, brought to the fore questions about how best to protect both democracy and public health when an emergency occurs during a campaign or an election. As of May 2020, several states had made changes to their electoral rules. All three branches of government have been active, with governors and public-health officials issuing orders; legislatures amending election laws; and courts entertaining claims that states' action (or inaction) abridged the right to vote. The law is changing so rapidly that any attempt to catalogue all of the developments is bound to be overtaken by events nearly as quickly as it is written. Nevertheless, the following discussion should provide a sense of some of the responses that states have made to the crisis—and a sense of some of the contro¬versy that those responses have engendered.

The Democratic National Convention was pushed back a month—from July 13–16 to August 17–20—and conducted virtually because of concerns about the virus. The Republican National Convention was scheduled to be held in Charlotte, North Carolina, but when the Democratic governor and mayor refused to permit such a large in-person gathering, the RNC revised its plans and prepared to hold most of the convention events in Jacksonville, Florida. When it became clear that holding the convention in Jacksonville also presented an excessive public-health risk, the Republicans moved their convention online, except for a small amount of in-person business in Charlotte.

Many states considered postponing their primary elections or holding them exclusively by mail. In Pennsylvania, for example, a law was passed at the end of March moving the state's primary from April 28 to June 2 and also delaying the deadlines for voters to register and to request mail-in ballots, which are available to all voters. In all, fifteen states delayed their primaries, some more contentiously than others.

Ohio's Director of Public Health ordered the polls closed as a public-health measure less than twenty-four hours before voting in the state's March 17 primary was due to begin. The Ohio legislature shortly thereafter passed legislation creating an entirely vote-by-mail primary that required voters to submit their ballots by April 28. The vote-by-mail procedures were controversial, however. For example, even though there was no option of in-person voting, the state sent absentee ballots to only those voters who requested them. Charging that the procedures would cause thousands of Ohioans to lose their ability to vote, plaintiffs brought suit challenging the new procedures, but a federal district court refused to issue an injunction. Michigan's secretary of state, on the other hand, decided—without any explicit legislative authorization—to send mail-in ballots to all voters, even those voters who did not request them.

New York canceled its presidential primary, but the cancellation was overturned in court. *Yang v. Kellner*, __ F. Supp. 3d __, 2020 WL 2129597 (S.D.N.Y. 2020). Although New York's primary could not possibly determine the presidential nominee (Joe Biden had, practically speaking, secured the Democratic nomination), the court noted that the choice of convention delegates could have implications for the party beyond choosing the nominee, and, therefore, the cancellation abridged the right to vote.

Texas law permitted voters to vote by mail if they would be absent from the jurisdiction on election day and during the entire early-voting period, if they were at least age sixty-five, or if they had a "disability" that prevented them from voting in person. A federal district court ordered the state to permit every voter to vote by mail. In addition to finding that the right to vote was impaired by an in-person voting requirement during a pandemic, the court stated that permitting no-excuse mail-in voting for voters age sixty-five and over violated the Twenty-Sixth Amendment, which prohibits abridging the right to vote on account of age for anyone at least age eighteen. *See Texas Democratic Party v. Abbott*, __ F. Supp. 3d __, 2020 WL 2541971 (W.D. Tex. 2020). Saying that the district court's order "will be remembered more for audacity than legal reasoning," the Fifth Circuit promptly issued a stay. *Texas Democratic Party v. Abbott*, 961 F.3d 389, 394 (5th Cir.), *motion to vacate stay denied*, 140 S. Ct. 2015 (2020). The Court of Appeals held that the state was likely to succeed on the merits because the state's limitations on mail-in voting did not "absolutely prohibit[]" anyone from voting, *id.* at 404 (quoting *McDonald v. Board of Election Commissioners*, 394 U.S. 802, 808 n.7 (1969)), and the age classification was supported by a rational basis in easing the burdens on voting disproportionately felt by the aged, see *id.* at 406–08.

In Wisconsin, as elsewhere, the COVID-19 outbreak caused a substantial increase in the number of requests for absentee ballots. The resulting backlog meant that some voters in that state did not receive their ballots until after the April 7 election day — the day that state law not only designated for in-person voting, but the day by which absentee ballots were supposed to be received by election officials. A federal district court issued an injunction extending the deadline for absentee voting until April 13 and permitting voters to mail ballots after April 7, so long as they would be received by April 13. *Democratic National Committee v. Bostelmann*, __ F. Supp. 3d __, 2020 WL 1638374 (W.D. Wis. 2020). The Supreme Court, by a 5-4 vote, stayed part of the injunction, requiring voters to postmark their ballots by election day, but permitting a properly postmarked ballot to be counted even if it was not received until after election day. *Republican National Committee v. Democratic National Committee*, 589 U.S. __, 140 S. Ct. 1205 (2020) (*per curiam*). The Court relied on *Purcell v. Gonzalez*, 549 U.S. 1 (2006) [p. 1158], in holding that the district court's alteration of the electoral rules was particularly problematic because it occurred so close to the election. The "*Purcell* principle" is considered in more depth in Chapter 11. *See also Merrill v. People First of Alabama*, __ U.S. __, 2020 WL 3604049 (2020) (5-4) (staying a lower-court order that had eased requirements for voting by mail). *But see Republican National Committee v. Common Cause Rhode Island*, __ U.S. __, 2020 WL 4680151 (2020) (6-3) (denying a stay of an order that had eased similar requirements, when the order was entered pursuant to a consent decree).

While litigation over Wisconsin's absentee ballots was pending, there was uncertainty over whether the primary would be held on April 7 at all. The day before the election, Wisconsin's governor issued a decree delaying that state's primary election. The decree was immediately challenged, and on the same day, the Wisconsin Supreme Court overturned the governor's order by a 4-2 vote, holding that it exceeded the governor's authority under state law to respond to emergencies.

Stay-at-home orders not only made it difficult to cast ballots; they also hindered the ability to collect signatures on petitions. This hinderance took two forms. First, without exemptions for petition-circulation, stay-at-home orders prevented people from leaving their homes to collect signatures. Second, even if the circulators could leave their homes, it was much more difficult to collect signatures if stay-at-home orders prevented potential signatories from milling about in public areas. In addition, the virus itself made it potentially dangerous to collect signatures in person. Is it constitutional to require in-person signature-gathering during a pandemic?

In challenges to petition requirements during the pandemic, some courts reduced the number of required signatures, although decisions in this area were not consistent. *See Goldstein v. Secretary of Commonwealth*, 142 N.E.3d 560 (Mass. 2020) (reducing the number of required signatures and extending the deadline for collecting them); *Garbett v. Herbert*, __ F. Supp. 3d __, 2020 WL 2064101 (D. Utah 2020) (reducing the number of required signatures). *But see Murray v. Cuomo*, __ F. Supp. 3d __, 2020 WL 2521449 (S.D.N.Y. 2020) (denying a request for a further reduction in the number of required signatures after the governor issued an executive order reducing the requirement and shortening the time available for collecting signatures, so that they would be due three days after the order).

Some decisions have been relatively aggressive in insisting that governments accommodate signature-gatherers whose activity was hindered by stay-at-home orders. In *Esshaki v. Whitmer*, 813 Fed. Appx. 170 (6th Cir. 2020), the Court of Appeals affirmed a district-court decision enjoining Michigan from enforcing its petition requirements against a candidate who could not satisfy them because the stay-at-home order prevented people from leaving their homes to collect signatures. The Court of Appeals reversed the district court, however, as to the portion of its injunction requiring the state to reduce the number of required signatures by 50%, extending the deadline for collection of signatures, and requiring the state to accept petition signatures by mail. Thus, although the district court was within its authority in determining that Michigan's stay-at-home order made it unconstitutional to enforce the petition requirement, the district court exceeded its authority by rewriting the petition requirement to comply with constitutional requirements. In the Sixth Circuit's words, "federal courts have no authority to dictate to the States precisely how they should conduct their elections." *Id.* at 172; *see also SawariMedia, LLC v. Whitmer*, 963 F.3d 595 (6th Cir. 2020) (following *Esshaki* and holding unconstitutional Michigan's enforcement of its signature requirement despite the stay-at home order).

Similarly, a district court in Idaho required that state "either to certify an initiative for inclusion on the ballot without the requisite number of signatures, or to allow the initiative sponsor additional time to gather digital signatures through an online process of solicitation and submission never before used by the State. When the State chose neither option, the District Court authorized the sponsor to join with a third-party vendor to develop and implement a new online system over the course of nine days." *Little v. Reclaim Idaho*, 591 U.S. __, 2020 WL 4360897 at *1 (Roberts, C.J., concurring). The Supreme Court stayed the district court's order, with Justices Sotomayor and Ginsburg dissenting.

In *Thompson v. DeWine*, 959 F.3d 804 (6th Cir. 2020) (*per curiam*), the Sixth Circuit showed more reluctance to interfere in the state administration of elections. *Thompson* stayed a district-court order that had extended Ohio's signature-gathering deadline and had enjoined the state from enforcing its requirement that petition signatures be witnessed and that they be signed in ink. The Court of Appeals concluded that the state was likely to succeed on the merits of the challenge, because the restrictions put in place to control the virus did not impose a severe burden on the right to vote. The Sixth Circuit noted that, unlike the Michigan order at issue in *Esshaki*, the Ohio order exempted First-Amendment-protected activity—and specifically petition circulation—from the stay-at-home requirement. Further, the stay-at-home order ended five weeks before the petition deadline, giving petition circulators adequate time to collect signatures. The Michigan order in *Esshaki* was in effect through the deadline for circulating petitions, and it therefore presented a much more severe burden than the Ohio order did. Once again, the Sixth Circuit warned against using federal courts' injunctive powers to "'usurp[] a State's legislative authority by re-writing its statutes' to create new law." *Id.* at 812 (quoting Esshaki at 172) (alteration in original). *See also Hawkins v. DeWine*, 968 F.3d 603 (6th Cir. 2020) (following *Thompson*).

Other circuits have been less insistent that states "adapt the initiative process to account for new obstacles to collecting signatures." *Reclaim Idaho, supra*, at *1 (Roberts, C.J., concurring). In *Miller v. Thurston*, 967 F.3d 727 (8th Cir. 2020), the court upheld an Arkansas requirement that petitions be signed in the presence of a canvasser. The in-person-signature requirement, the court held, did not impose a severe burden on First Amendment rights and was a reasonable means of furthering the important interest in preventing fraud or mistakes in the petition-gathering process. Similarly, in *Morgan v. White*, 964 F.3d 649 (7th Cir. 2020) (*per curiam*), the court brushed aside the plaintiffs' claim that Illinois's petition requirements for initiatives and referenda were unconstitutionally onerous in light of the limitations put in place to deal with the pandemic. The court held that there was sufficient time to circulate petitions before the start of the pandemic, so there was no cause to grant emergency relief from the petition requirements. *Id.* at 651–52. The court also noted that there is no federal right to initiatives or referenda, and suggested that even if Illinois had simply decided "to skip all referenda for the 2020 election cycle, there is no federal problem. Illinois may decide for itself whether a pandemic is a good time to be soliciting signatures on the streets in order to add referenda to a ballot." *Id.* at 652.

Many jurisdictions revised their election policies after looking ahead to the November 2020 elections and anticipating the possibility of disruptions in the normal election procedure. New York's June 23 primary, which did not yield final results until well over a month following the election and in which more than 100,000 votes were invalidated, caused many observers to worry about similar delays in counting the votes in the general election, as many jurisdictions would be struggling to implement new voting rules and struggling to count millions of mail-in ballots during a highly contentious presidential election. Many states implemented reforms to make it easier for people to vote from home. In August 2020, for example, New York passed laws permitting voters to request absentee ballots because of the risk of illness, and allowing absentee ballots to be counted if postmarked by election day, even if not received until a week later.

Such reforms improved access to the ballot for voters who would have found it difficult to vote in person, but critics alleged that the increased use of absentee ballots would lead to higher printing and vote-tabulating expenses and delays, as well as risks of fraud. Republicans, and President Trump in particular, were critical of states that decided to mail ballots to all registered voters, even without a request from the individual voters. These critics feared that ballots could be stolen and cast illegally, especially in jurisdictions that allowed people to collect ("harvest") and submit others' ballots. Democrats, for their part, have called for additional funds for the U.S. Postal Service to enable it to deliver the large number of mail-in ballots that were anticipated. In late-March 2020, Congress passed a spending package to ease the economic effects of the coronavirus, and part of that package included $400 million in election funding to aid states in expanding voting by mail, as well as in ensuring safe in-person voting. As of this writing, there has been no agreement on additional funding for the Postal Service. For more discussion on election-related responses to the COVID-19 pandemic, see Richard L. Hasen, *Three Pathologies of American Voting Rights Illuminated by the COVID-19 Pandemic, and How to Treat and Cure Them*, SSRN, *available at* https://ssrn .com /abstract =3604668 (2020) (working paper).

C. Speech Restrictions in or near Polling Places

In Chapter 7, we discovered that the First Amendment's protection of "the freedom of speech" is most powerful when applied to speech concerning political campaigns. Nevertheless, the interest in free expression occasionally confronts other powerful societal interests, and even other constitutional rights. The following cases examine such a conflict, as they consider whether the need to protect voters from intimidation can justify restrictions on political speech inside or immediately outside polling places.

Burson v. Freeman

Supreme Court of the United States
504 U.S. 191, 112 S. Ct. 1846, 119 L. Ed. 2d 5 (1992)

Justice Blackmun announced the judgment of the Court and delivered an opinion, in which The Chief Justice [Rehnquist], Justice White, and Justice Kennedy join. * * *

The State of Tennessee has carved out an election-day "campaign-free zone" through § 2-7-111(b) of its election code. That section reads in pertinent part:

> "Within * * * [100 feet from the entrances], and the building in which the polling place is located, the display of campaign posters, signs or other campaign materials, distribution of campaign materials, and solicitation of votes for or against any person or political party or position on a question are prohibited."

Violation of § 2-7-111(b) is a Class C misdemeanor punishable by a term of imprisonment not greater than 30 days or a fine not to exceed $50, or both. * * *

[Section] 2-7-111(b) * * * [is a content-based restriction on political] speech in quintessential public forums. These forums include those places "which by long tradition or by government fiat have been devoted to assembly and debate," such as parks, streets, and sidewalks.[2] * * * Whether individuals may exercise their free speech rights near polling places depends entirely on whether their speech is related to a political campaign. The statute does not reach other categories of speech, such as commercial solicitation, distribution, and display. This Court has held that the First Amendment's hostility to content-based regulation extends not only to a restriction on a particular viewpoint, but also to a prohibition of public discussion of an entire topic.

As a facially content-based restriction on political speech in a public forum, § 2-7-111(b) must be subjected to exacting scrutiny: The State must show that the "regulation is necessary to serve a compelling state interest and that it is narrowly drawn to achieve that end." * * *

Tennessee asserts that its campaign-free zone serves two compelling interests. First, the State argues that its regulation serves its compelling interest in protecting the right of its citizens to vote freely for the candidates of their choice. Second, Tennessee argues that its restriction protects the right to vote in an election conducted with integrity and reliability. The interests advanced by Tennessee obviously are compelling ones. * * *

To survive strict scrutiny, however, a State must do more than assert a compelling state interest—it must demonstrate that its law is necessary to serve the asserted interest. While we readily acknowledge that a law rarely survives such scrutiny, an examination of the evolution of election reform, both in this country and abroad, demonstrates the necessity of restricted areas in or around polling places. * * *

[T]he history of election regulation in this country reveals a persistent battle against two evils: voter intimidation and election fraud. After an unsuccessful experiment with an unofficial ballot system, all 50 States, together with numerous other Western democracies, settled on the same solution: a secret ballot secured in part by a restricted zone around the voting compartments. We find that this widespread and time-tested consensus demonstrates that some restricted zone is necessary in order to serve the States' compelling interests in preventing voter intimidation and election fraud.

Respondent and the dissent advance three principal challenges to this conclusion. First, respondent argues that restricted zones are overinclusive because States

---

2. Testimony at trial established that at some Tennessee polling locations the campaign-free zone included sidewalks and streets adjacent to the polling places.

could secure these same compelling interests with statutes that make it a misdemeanor to interfere with an election or to use violence or intimidation to prevent voting. We are not persuaded. Intimidation and interference laws fall short of serving a State's compelling interests because they "deal with only the most blatant and specific attempts" to impede elections. Moreover, because law enforcement officers generally are barred from the vicinity of the polls to avoid any appearance of coercion in the electoral process, many acts of interference would go undetected. These undetected or less than blatant acts may nonetheless drive the voter away before remedial action can be taken.

Second, respondent and the dissent argue that Tennessee's statute is underinclusive because it does not restrict other types of speech, such as charitable and commercial solicitation or exit polling, within the 100-foot zone. We agree that distinguishing among types of speech requires that the statute be subjected to strict scrutiny. We do not, however, agree that the failure to regulate all speech renders the statute fatally underinclusive. * * * [T]here is, as summarized above, ample evidence that political candidates have used campaign workers to commit voter intimidation or electoral fraud. In contrast, there is simply no evidence that political candidates have used other forms of solicitation or exit polling to commit such electoral abuses. States adopt laws to address the problems that confront them. The First Amendment does not require States to regulate for problems that do not exist.

Finally, the dissent argues that we confuse history with necessity. Yet the dissent concedes that a secret ballot was necessary to cure electoral abuses. Contrary to the dissent's contention, the link between ballot secrecy and some restricted zone surrounding the voting area is not merely timing—it is common sense. The only way to preserve the secrecy of the ballot is to limit access to the area around the voter.[10] Accordingly, we hold that *some* restricted zone around the voting area is necessary to secure the State's compelling interest.

The real question then is *how large* a restricted zone is permissible or sufficiently tailored. Respondent and the dissent argue that Tennessee's 100-foot boundary is not narrowly drawn to achieve the State's compelling interest in protecting the right to vote. We disagree.

As a preliminary matter, the long, uninterrupted and prevalent use of these statutes makes it difficult for States to come forward with the sort of proof the dissent wishes to require. The majority of these laws were adopted originally in the 1890s, long before States engaged in extensive legislative hearings on election regulations. The prevalence of these laws, both here and abroad, then encouraged their

---

10. The logical connection between ballot secrecy and restricted zones distinguishes this case from those cited by the dissent in which the Court struck down longstanding election regulations. In those cases, there was no rational connection between the asserted interest and the regulation. See, *e.g.*, *Harper* v. *Virginia Bd. of Elections*, 383 U.S. 663, 666 (1966) [p. 17] ("Voter qualifications have no relation to wealth nor to paying or not paying this or any other tax").

reenactment without much comment. The fact that these laws have been in effect for a long period of time also makes it difficult for the States to put on witnesses who can testify as to what would happen without them. Finally, it is difficult to isolate the exact effect of these laws on voter intimidation and election fraud. Voter intimidation and election fraud are successful precisely because they are difficult to detect.

Furthermore, because a government has such a compelling interest in securing the right to vote freely and effectively, this Court never has held a State "to the burden of demonstrating empirically the objective effects on political stability that [are] produced" by the voting regulation in question. *Munro* v. *Socialist Workers Party*, 479 U.S. 189, 195 (1986).[11] Elections vary from year to year, and place to place. It is therefore difficult to make specific findings about the effects of a voting regulation. Moreover, the remedy for a tainted election is an imperfect one. Rerunning an election would have a negative impact on voter turnout. Thus, requiring proof that a 100-foot boundary is perfectly tailored to deal with voter intimidation and election fraud

> "would necessitate that a State's political system sustain some level of damage before the legislature could take corrective action. Legislatures, we think, should be permitted to respond to potential deficiencies in the electoral process with foresight rather than reactively, provided that the response is reasonable and does not *significantly impinge* on constitutionally protected rights." *Id.*, at 195–196 (emphasis added).

We do not think that the minor geographic limitation prescribed by § 2-7-111(b) constitutes such a significant impingement. Thus, we simply do not view the question whether the 100-foot boundary line could be somewhat tighter as a question of "constitutional dimension." Reducing the boundary to 25 feet, as suggested by the Tennessee Supreme Court, is a difference only in degree, not a less restrictive alternative in kind. As was pointed out in the dissenting opinion in the Tennessee Supreme Court, it "takes approximately 15 seconds to walk 75 feet." The State of Tennessee has decided that these last 15 seconds before its citizens enter the polling place should be their own, as free from interference as possible. We do not find that this is an unconstitutional choice.

---

11. This modified "burden of proof" does not apply to all cases in which there is a conflict between First Amendment rights and a State's election process—instead, it applies only when the First Amendment right threatens to interfere with the act of voting itself, *i.e.*, cases involving voter confusion from overcrowded ballots, like *Munro*, or cases such as this one, in which the challenged activity physically interferes with electors attempting to cast their ballots. Thus, for example, States must come forward with more specific findings to support regulations directed at intangible "influence," such as the ban on election-day editorials struck down in *Mills* v. *Alabama*, 384 U.S. 214 (1966) [p. 591].

At some measurable distance from the polls, of course, governmental regulation of vote solicitation could effectively become an impermissible burden akin to the statute struck down in *Mills* v. *Alabama*. In reviewing challenges to specific provisions of a State's election laws, however, this Court has not employed any "'litmus-paper test' that will separate valid from invalid restrictions." *Anderson* v. *Celebrezze*, 460 U.S. [780], 789 [(1983)] [p. 517]. Accordingly, it is sufficient to say that in establishing a 100-foot boundary, Tennessee is on the constitutional side of the line.

In conclusion, we reaffirm that it is the rare case in which we have held that a law survives strict scrutiny. This, however, is such a rare case. Here, the State, as recognized administrator of elections, has asserted that the exercise of free speech rights conflicts with another fundamental right, the right to cast a ballot in an election free from the taint of intimidation and fraud. A long history, a substantial consensus, and simple common sense show that some restricted zone around polling places is necessary to protect that fundamental right. Given the conflict between these two rights, we hold that requiring solicitors to stand 100 feet from the entrances to polling places does not constitute an unconstitutional compromise.

The judgment of the Tennessee Supreme Court is reversed, and the case is remanded for further proceedings not inconsistent with this opinion.

It is so ordered.

Justice Thomas took no part in the consideration or decision of this case.

Justice Kennedy, concurring.

* * * Under what I deem the proper approach, neither a general content-based proscription of speech nor a content-based proscription of speech in a public forum can be justified unless the speech falls within one of a limited set of well-defined categories. [But the regulation at issue here is not content-based.] * * * "[G]overnment regulation of expressive activity is content neutral so long as it is '*justified* without reference to the content of the regulated speech.'" *Ward* v. *Rock Against Racism*, 491 U.S. 781, 791 (1989).

[T]here is a narrow area in which the First Amendment permits freedom of expression to yield to the extent necessary for the accommodation of another constitutional right. That principle can apply here * * *; for under the statute the State acts to protect the integrity of the polling place where citizens exercise the right to vote. * * * The State is not using this justification to suppress legitimate expression. * * *

Justice Scalia, concurring in the judgment.

If the category of "traditional public forum" is to be a tool of analysis rather than a conclusory label, it must remain faithful to its name and derive its content from *tradition.* Because restrictions on speech around polling places on election day are as venerable a part of the American tradition as the secret ballot, § 2-7-111 does not restrict speech in a traditional public forum, and the "exacting scrutiny" that the plurality purports to apply is inappropriate. Instead, I believe that § 2-7-111, though content-based, is constitutional because it is a reasonable, viewpoint-neutral regulation of a nonpublic forum. I therefore concur in the judgment of the Court.

* * * Ever since the widespread adoption of the secret ballot in the late 19th century, viewpoint-neutral restrictions on election-day speech within a specified distance of the polling place — or on physical presence there — have been commonplace, indeed prevalent. By 1900, at least 34 of the 45 States (including Tennessee) had enacted such restrictions. It is noteworthy that most of the statutes banning election-day speech near the polling place specified the same distance set forth in § 2-7-111 (100 feet), and it is clear that the restricted zones often encompassed streets and sidewalks. Thus, the streets and sidewalks around polling places have traditionally *not* been devoted to assembly and debate. * * *

For the reasons that the plurality believes § 2-7-111 survives exacting scrutiny, I believe it is at least reasonable; and respondent does not contend that it is viewpoint discriminatory. I therefore agree with the judgment of the Court that § 2-7-111 is constitutional.

JUSTICE STEVENS, with whom JUSTICE O'CONNOR and JUSTICE SOUTER join, dissenting. * * *

Tennessee's statutory "campaign-free zone" raises constitutional concerns of the first magnitude. The statute directly regulates political expression and thus implicates a core concern of the First Amendment. Moreover, it targets only a specific subject matter (campaign speech) and a defined class of speakers (campaign workers) and thus regulates expression based on its content. In doing so, the Tennessee statute somewhat perversely disfavors speech that normally is accorded greater protection than the kinds of speech that the statute does not regulate. For these reasons, Tennessee unquestionably bears the heavy burden of demonstrating that its silencing of political expression is necessary and narrowly tailored to serve a compelling state interest.

Statutes creating campaign-free zones outside polling places serve two quite different functions — they protect orderly access to the polls and they prevent last-minute campaigning. There can be no question that the former constitutes a compelling state interest and that * * * the latter does not. Accordingly, a State must demonstrate that the particular means it has fashioned to ensure orderly access to the polls do not unnecessarily hinder last-minute campaigning.

Campaign-free zones are noteworthy for their broad, antiseptic sweep. The Tennessee zone encompasses at least 30,000 square feet around each polling place; in some States, such as Kentucky and Wisconsin, the radius of the restricted zone is

500 feet — silencing an area of over 750,000 square feet. Even under the most san-guine scenario of participatory democracy, it is difficult to imagine voter turnout so complete as to require the clearing of hundreds of thousands of square feet simply to ensure that the path to the polling-place door remains open and that the curtain that protects the secrecy of the ballot box remains closed.

The fact that campaign-free zones cover such a large area in some States unmis-takably identifies censorship of election-day campaigning as an animating force behind these restrictions. That some States have no problem maintaining order with zones of 50 feet or less strongly suggests that the more expansive prohibitions are not necessary to maintain access and order. * * *

Moreover, the Tennessee statute does not merely regulate conduct that might inhibit voting; it bars the simple "display of campaign posters, signs, or other cam-paign materials." Bumper stickers on parked cars and lapel buttons on pedestrians are taboo. The notion that such sweeping restrictions on speech are necessary to maintain the freedom to vote and the integrity of the ballot box borders on the absurd. * * * The abuses that [once] affected the electoral system could have been cured by the institution of the secret ballot and by the heightened regulation of the polling place alone, without silencing the political speech *outside* the polling place.[4] In my opinion, more than mere timing is required to infer necessity from tradition.

We have never regarded tradition as a proxy for necessity where necessity must be demonstrated. To the contrary, our election-law jurisprudence is rich with exam-ples of traditions [such as poll taxes, as in *Harper v. Virginia Bd. of Elections*] that, though longstanding, were later held to be unnecessary. Similarly, substantial bar-riers to candidacy, such as stringent petition requirements, see *Williams v. Rhodes*, 393 U.S. 23 (1968) [p. 495], property-ownership requirements, see *Turner v. Fouche*, 396 U.S. 346 (1970), and onerous filing fees, see *Lubin v. Panish*, 415 U.S. 709 (1974), were all longstanding features of the electoral labyrinth. * * *

Even if we assume that campaign-free zones were once somehow "necessary," it would not follow that, 100 years later, those practices remain necessary. Much in our political culture, institutions, and practices has changed since the turn of the century: Our elections are far less corrupt, far more civil, and far more democratic today than 100 years ago. These salutary developments have substantially elimi-nated the need for what is, in my opinion, a sweeping suppression of core political speech. * * *

---

4. The plurality's suggestion that "[t]he only way to preserve the secrecy of the ballot is to limit access to the area around the voter" is specious. First, there are obvious and simple means of pre-serving voter secrecy (*e.g.,* opaque doors or curtains on the voting booth) that do not involve the suppression of political speech. Second, there is no disagreement that the restrictions on cam-paigning *within the polling place* are constitutional; the issue is not whether the State may limit access to the "area *around the voter*" but whether the State may limit speech in the area *around the polling place.*

In addition to sweeping too broadly in its reach, Tennessee's campaign-free zone selectively prohibits speech based on content. * * * Within the zone, §2-7-111 silences all campaign-related expression, but allows expression on any other subject: religious, artistic, commercial speech, even political debate and solicitation concerning issues or candidates not on the day's ballot. Indeed, as I read it, §2-7-111 does not prohibit exit polling, which surely presents at least as great a potential interference with orderly access to the polls as does the distribution of campaign leaflets, the display of campaign posters, or the wearing of campaign buttons. This discriminatory feature of the statute severely undercuts the credibility of its purported law-and-order justification.

Tennessee's content-based discrimination is particularly problematic because such a regulation will inevitably favor certain groups of candidates. As the testimony in this case illustrates, several groups of candidates rely heavily on last-minute campaigning. Candidates with fewer resources, candidates for lower visibility offices, and "grassroots" candidates benefit disproportionately from last-minute campaigning near the polling place. * * *

* * * The plurality has effectively shifted the burden of proving the necessity of content discrimination from the State to the plaintiff. * * * Tennessee must shoulder the burden of demonstrating that its restrictions on political speech are no broader than necessary to protect orderly access to the polls. It has not done so.

I therefore respectfully dissent.

Notes and Questions

1. What justification is there for setting the limit of the "campaign-free zone" at one hundred feet from the entrances to polling places? Why did the plurality conclude that a one-hundred-foot limit (as opposed to, for example, a twenty-five-foot limit) was narrowly tailored to prevent the risks of election fraud and voter intimidation? Does your answer suggest that the plurality is not, in fact, applying strict scrutiny? Consider, in this regard, the plurality's footnote 11 and the accompanying text.

2. How far beyond one hundred feet can states extend "campaign-free zones" without violating the First Amendment? Justice Stevens noted that Kentucky and Wisconsin established five-hundred-foot zones; are they constitutional?

3. Do you agree with Justice Stevens that there is essentially no justification for "campaign-free zones" outside polling places at all?

4. Take another look at the statute. Within the designated area, the statute banned (1) "the display of campaign posters, signs or other campaign materials," (2) "distribution of campaign materials," and (3) "solicitation of votes." Are *all* of these prohibitions narrowly tailored ways of achieving compelling interests?

5. *Problem.* The Town of Snyder is holding an election for its fire commissioners. On election day, the fire hall is used as a polling place, as it is for all municipal elections in Snyder. The Town's "campaign-free zone" law is identical to the one in

Freeman. Voting booths are set up in the truck bay, adjacent to which each of the firemen keeps a locker containing fire-fighting equipment, civilian dress, toiletries, photos of loved ones, etc. The "lockers" have shelves and hooks for hanging clothing, but there are no doors that can be closed to secure each individual's belongings. In one of the lockers, visible to voters as they approach the booths, is a bumper sticker supporting one candidate. On what bases may the situation be challenged? If the statute is enforced against the fireman displaying the bumper sticker, would he succeed on a challenge to such enforcement? Does it matter if he is a volunteer or employed by the Town?

6. *Problem.* Consider this variation on the previous Problem. Jim Sullivan is running for Fire Commissioner in Snyder. Sullivan owns the house adjacent to the fire hall, and as a result, his yard falls within the campaign-free zone. In the month leading up to the election, Sullivan displayed a sign on his yard promoting his candidacy. Must he remove the sign on the day of the election? Would it make any difference if the campaign-free zone encompassed a substantial part, but not the entirety, of Sullivan's yard?

7. *Problem.* At a school bond election where the same "campaign-free zone" restriction is in effect, voters casting ballots at the school must walk by a bulletin board on which is posted, with notices about the honor roll, assemblies, try-outs, and such, a notice saying, "Encourage Your Parents to Vote for the School Bonds on November 5." Has the Constitution been violated? If the proceeds are to fund a new roof for the school, can the school enforce the restriction on campaign speech while holding the election in a room that requires several garbage cans to catch leaking rainwater? *Cf.* Jeremy A. Blumenthal & Terry L. Turnipseed, *The Polling Place Priming (PPP) Effect: Is Voting in Churches (or Anywhere Else) Unconstitutional?*, 91 B.U. L. REV. 561 (2011) (suggesting that polling places may affect voting behavior, and offering absentee and convenience voting as solutions). *See also* Jonah Berger *et al., Contextual Priming: Where People Vote Affects How They Vote,* 105 PROCEEDINGS OF THE NAT'L ACADEMY OF SCIENCES 8846 (2008) (finding, after controlling for other factors, that people voting at schools were more likely to support a school-funding initiative). Berger et al. suggest that governments might be able to minimize the biasing effect of polling locations by, "[f]or example, having people vote in a generic multipurpose room rather than a school hallway filled with children or a church room containing religious images." *Id.* at 8848.

8. Justice Scalia would have treated areas outside polling places as nonpublic fora. Such a designation, however, would not enable the state to regulate speech any way it pleased. As Justice Scalia recognized, regulations of speech in nonpublic fora must be "reasonable" and "viewpoint-neutral." *See Perry Education Association v. Perry Local Educators' Association,* 460 U.S. 37, 46 (1983) ("In addition to time, place, and manner regulations, the state may reserve the forum for its intended purposes, communicative or otherwise, as long as the regulation on speech is reasonable and not an effort to suppress expression merely because public officials oppose the speaker's view.").

9. What restrictions on political speech would be permissible in a nonpublic forum? In *Burson v. Freeman*, the speech restriction covered an area outside of the polling place, and only Justice Scalia would have treated that area as a nonpublic forum. In the next case, however, the challenged speech restriction operated *within* the polling place—an area that the Court agreed was a nonpublic forum. It may, then, be unsurprising that the Court was willing to accept speech restrictions in such a place. But at what point does a speech restriction—even one in a nonpublic forum—go too far? May a state ban voters from wearing clothing with political messages?

Minnesota Voters Alliance v. Mansky

Supreme Court of the United States
585 U.S. __, 138 S. Ct. 1876, 201 L. Ed. 2d 201 (2018)

CHIEF JUSTICE ROBERTS delivered the opinion of the Court [in which JUSTICE KENNEDY, JUSTICE THOMAS, JUSTICE GINSBURG, JUSTICE ALITO, JUSTICE KAGAN, and JUSTICE GORSUCH join].

Under Minnesota['s "political apparel ban," Minn. Stat. § 211B.11(1)], voters may not wear a political badge, political button, or anything bearing political insignia inside a polling place on Election Day. The question presented is whether this ban violates the Free Speech Clause of the First Amendment.

I * * *

There is no dispute that the political apparel ban applies only *within* the polling place, and covers articles of clothing and accessories with "political insignia" upon them. Minnesota election judges—temporary government employees working the polls on Election Day—have the authority to decide whether a particular item falls within the ban. If a voter shows up wearing a prohibited item, the election judge is to ask the individual to conceal or remove it. If the individual refuses, the election judge must allow him to vote, while making clear that the incident "will be recorded and referred to appropriate authorities." Violators are subject to an administrative process before the Minnesota Office of Administrative Hearings, which, upon finding a violation, may issue a reprimand or impose a civil penalty. That administrative body may also refer the complaint to the county attorney for prosecution as a petty misdemeanor; the maximum penalty is a $300 fine.

* * * Five days before the November 2010 election, [petitioner Minnesota Voters Alliance (MVA)] and other likeminded groups and individuals filed a lawsuit in Federal District Court challenging the political apparel ban on First Amendment grounds. * * * In response to the lawsuit, officials for Hennepin and Ramsey Counties distributed to election judges an "Election Day Policy," providing guidance on the enforcement of the political apparel ban. The Minnesota Secretary of State also distributed the Policy to election officials throughout the State. The Policy specified that examples of apparel falling within the ban "include, but are not limited to":

- "Any item including the name of a political party in Minnesota, such as the Republican, [Democratic-Farmer-Labor], Independence, Green or Libertarian parties.

- Any item including the name of a candidate at any election.

- Any item in support of or opposition to a ballot question at any election.

- Issue oriented material designed to influence or impact voting (including specifically the 'Please I.D. Me' buttons [worn by MVA members]).

- Material promoting a group with recognizable political views (such as the Tea Party, MoveOn.org, and so on)." * * *

* * * The District Court * * * granted summary judgment for the State * * *, and * * * the Court of Appeals affirmed. * * *

II

The First Amendment prohibits laws "abridging the freedom of speech." Minnesota's ban on wearing any "political badge, political button, or other political insignia" plainly restricts a form of expression within the protection of the First Amendment.

But the ban applies only in a specific location: the interior of a polling place. It therefore implicates our "'forum based' approach for assessing restrictions that the government seeks to place on the use of its property." Generally speaking, our cases recognize three types of government-controlled spaces: traditional public forums, designated public forums, and nonpublic forums. In a traditional public forum—parks, streets, sidewalks, and the like—the government may impose reasonable time, place, and manner restrictions on private speech, but restrictions based on content must satisfy strict scrutiny, and those based on viewpoint are prohibited. The same standards apply in designated public forums—spaces that have "not traditionally been regarded as a public forum" but which the government has "intentionally opened up for that purpose." In a nonpublic forum, on the other hand—a space that "is not by tradition or designation a forum for public communication"—the government has much more flexibility to craft rules limiting speech. *Perry Ed. Assn. v. Perry Local Educators' Assn.*, 460 U.S. 37, 46 (1983). The government may reserve such a forum "for its intended purposes, communicative or otherwise, as long as the regulation on speech is reasonable and not an effort to suppress expression merely because public officials oppose the speaker's view." *Ibid.* * * *

A polling place in Minnesota qualifies as a nonpublic forum. It is, at least on Election Day, government-controlled property set aside for the sole purpose of voting. * * * Rules strictly govern who may be present, for what purpose, and for how long. And while the four-Justice plurality in *Burson* [v. *Freeman*, 504 U.S. 191 (1992)] [p. 1024] and Justice Scalia's concurrence in the judgment parted ways over whether the public sidewalks and streets *surrounding* a polling place qualify as a nonpublic forum, neither opinion suggested that the interior of the building was anything but. See 504 U.S., at 196–197, and n.2 (plurality opinion); *id.*, at 214–216 (opinion of Scalia, J.).

We therefore evaluate MVA's First Amendment challenge under the nonpublic forum standard. The text of the apparel ban makes no distinction based on the speaker's political persuasion, so MVA does not claim that the ban discriminates on the basis of viewpoint on its face. The question accordingly is whether Minnesota's ban on political apparel is "reasonable in light of the purpose served by the forum": voting.

III

A

We first consider whether Minnesota is pursuing a permissible objective in prohibiting voters from wearing particular kinds of expressive apparel or accessories while inside the polling place. The natural starting point for evaluating a First Amendment challenge to such a restriction is this Court's decision in *Burson*, which upheld a Tennessee law imposing a 100-foot campaign-free zone around polling place entrances. * * *

[The *Burson* plurality] emphasized the problems of fraud, voter intimidation, confusion, and general disorder that had plagued polling places in the past. See *id.*, at 200–204 (plurality opinion). Against that historical backdrop, the plurality and Justice Scalia upheld Tennessee's determination, supported by overwhelming consensus among the States and "common sense," that a campaign-free zone outside the polls was "necessary" to secure the advantages of the secret ballot and protect the right to vote. *Id.*, at 200, 206–208, 211. As the plurality explained, "[t]he State of Tennessee has decided that [the] last 15 seconds before its citizens enter the polling place should be their own, as free from interference as possible." *Id.*, at 210. That was not "an unconstitutional choice." *Ibid.*

MVA disputes the relevance of *Burson* to Minnesota's apparel ban. On MVA's reading, *Burson* considered only "active campaigning" outside the polling place by campaign workers and others trying to engage voters approaching the polls. Minnesota's law, by contrast, prohibits what MVA characterizes as "passive, silent" self-expression by voters themselves when voting. MVA also points out that the plurality focused on the extent to which the restricted zone combated "voter intimidation and election fraud," 504 U.S., at 208—concerns that, in MVA's view, have little to do with a prohibition on certain types of voter apparel.

Campaign buttons and apparel did come up in the *Burson* briefing and argument, but neither the plurality nor Justice Scalia expressly addressed such applications of the law. Nor did either opinion specifically consider the interior of the polling place as opposed to its environs, and it is true that the plurality's reasoning focused on campaign activities of a sort not likely to occur in an area where, for the most part, only voters are permitted while voting. At the same time, Tennessee's law swept broadly to ban even the plain "display" of a campaign-related message, and the Court upheld the law in full. The plurality's conclusion that the State was war-ranted in designating an area for the voters as "their own" as they *enter* the polling place suggests an interest more significant, not less, *within* that place. *Id.*, at 210.

In any event, we see no basis for rejecting Minnesota's determination that some forms of advocacy should be excluded from the polling place, to set it aside as "an island of calm in which voters can peacefully contemplate their choices." Casting a vote is a weighty civic act, akin to a jury's return of a verdict, or a representa-tive's vote on a piece of legislation. It is a time for choosing, not campaigning. The State may reasonably decide that the interior of the polling place should reflect that distinction.

To be sure, our decisions have noted the "nondisruptive" nature of expressive apparel in more mundane settings. *Board of Airport Comm'rs of Los Angeles* v. *Jews for Jesus, Inc.*, 482 U.S. 569, 576 (1987) (so characterizing "the wearing of a T-shirt or button that contains a political message" in an airport); *Tinker* v. *Des Moines Inde-pendent Community School Dist.*, 393 U.S. 503, 508 (1969) (students wearing black armbands to protest the Vietnam War engaged in "silent, passive expression of opinion, unaccompanied by any disorder or disturbance"). But those observations do not speak to the unique context of a polling place on Election Day. Members of the public are brought together at that place, at the end of what may have been a divisive election season, to reach considered decisions about their government and laws. The State may reasonably take steps to ensure that partisan discord not follow the voter up to the voting booth, and distract from a sense of shared civic obligation at the moment it counts the most. That interest may be thwarted by displays that do not raise significant concerns in other situations.

Other States can see the matter differently, and some do. The majority, however, agree with Minnesota that at least some kinds of campaign-related clothing and accessories should stay outside. That broadly shared judgment is entitled to respect.

Thus, in light of the special purpose of the polling place itself, Minnesota may choose to prohibit certain apparel there because of the message it conveys, so that voters may focus on the important decisions immediately at hand.

B

But the State must draw a reasonable line. Although there is no requirement of narrow tailoring in a nonpublic forum, the State must be able to articulate some sensible basis for distinguishing what may come in from what must stay out. Here, the unmoored use of the term "political" in the Minnesota law, combined with hap-hazard interpretations the State has provided in official guidance and representa-tions to this Court, cause Minnesota's restriction to fail even this forgiving test.

Again, the statute prohibits wearing a "political badge, political button, or other political insignia." It does not define the term "political." And the word can be expansive. It can encompass anything "of or relating to government, a govern-ment, or the conduct of governmental affairs," Webster's Third New International

Dictionary 1755 (2002), or anything "[o]f, relating to, or dealing with the structure or affairs of government, politics, or the state," American Heritage Dictionary 1401 (3d ed. 1996). Under a literal reading of those definitions, a button or T-shirt merely imploring others to "Vote!" could qualify.

The State argues that the apparel ban should not be read so broadly. According to the State, the statute does not prohibit "any conceivably 'political' message" or cover "all 'political' speech, broadly construed." Instead, the State interprets the ban to proscribe "only words and symbols that an objectively reasonable observer would perceive as conveying a message about the electoral choices at issue in [the] polling place." * * * But far from clarifying the indeterminate scope of the political apparel provision, the State's "electoral choices" construction introduces confusing line-drawing problems.

For specific examples of what is banned under its standard, the State points to the 2010 Election Day Policy—which it continues to hold out as authoritative guidance regarding implementation of the statute. The first three examples in the Policy are clear enough: items displaying the name of a political party, items displaying the name of a candidate, and items demonstrating "support of or opposition to a ballot question."

But the next example—"[i]ssue oriented material designed to influence or impact voting"—raises more questions than it answers. What qualifies as an "issue"? The answer, as far as we can tell from the State's briefing and argument, is any subject on which a political candidate or party has taken a stance. For instance, the Election Day Policy specifically notes that the "Please I.D. Me" buttons are prohibited. But a voter identification requirement was not on the ballot in 2010, so a Minnesotan would have had no explicit "electoral choice" to make in that respect. The buttons were nonetheless covered, the State tells us, because the Republican candidates for Governor and Secretary of State had staked out positions on whether photo identification should be required.[4]

A rule whose fair enforcement requires an election judge to maintain a mental index of the platforms and positions of every candidate and party on the ballot is not reasonable. Candidates for statewide and federal office and major political parties can be expected to take positions on a wide array of subjects of local and national import. See, *e.g.,* Democratic Platform Committee, 2016 Democratic Party Platform (approved July 2016) (stating positions on over 90 issues); Republican Platform Committee, Republican Platform 2016 (approved July 2016) (similar). Would a "Support Our Troops" shirt be banned, if one of the candidates or parties had

---

4. The State also maintains that the "Please I.D. Me" buttons were properly banned because the buttons were designed to confuse other voters about whether they needed photo identification to vote. We do not doubt that the State may prohibit messages intended to mislead voters about voting requirements and procedures. But that interest does not align with the State's construction of "political" to refer to messages "about the electoral choices at issue in [the] polling place."

expressed a view on military funding or aid for veterans? What about a "#MeToo" shirt, referencing the movement to increase awareness of sexual harassment and assault? At oral argument, the State indicated that the ban would cover such an item if a candidate had "brought up" the topic.

The next broad category in the Election Day Policy—any item "promoting a group with recognizable political views"—makes matters worse. The State construes the category as limited to groups with "views" about "the issues confronting voters in a given election." The State does not, however, confine that category to groups that have endorsed a candidate or taken a position on a ballot question.

Any number of associations, educational institutions, businesses, and religious organizations could have an opinion on an "issue[] confronting voters in a given election." For instance, the American Civil Liberties Union, the AARP, the World Wildlife Fund, and Ben & Jerry's all have stated positions on matters of public concern. If the views of those groups align or conflict with the position of a candidate or party on the ballot, does that mean that their insignia are banned? See [State's Br.] (representing that "AFL-CIO or Chamber of Commerce apparel" would be banned if those organizations "had objectively recognizable views on an issue in the election at hand"). Take another example: In the run-up to the 2012 election, Presidential candidates of both major parties issued public statements regarding the then-existing policy of the Boy Scouts of America to exclude members on the basis of sexual orientation. Should a Scout leader in 2012 stopping to vote on his way to a troop meeting have been asked to cover up his uniform?

The State emphasizes that the ban covers only apparel promoting groups whose political positions are sufficiently "well-known." But that requirement, if anything, only increases the potential for erratic application. Well known by whom? The State tells us the lodestar is the "typical observer" of the item. But that measure may turn in significant part on the background knowledge and media consumption of the particular election judge applying it.

The State's "electoral choices" standard, considered together with the nonexclusive examples in the Election Day Policy, poses riddles that even the State's top lawyers struggle to solve. A shirt declaring "All Lives Matter," we are told, could be "perceived" as political. How about a shirt bearing the name of the National Rifle Association? Definitely out. That said, a shirt displaying a rainbow flag could be worn "*unless* there was an issue on the ballot" that "related somehow . . . to gay rights." A shirt simply displaying the text of the Second Amendment? Prohibited. But a shirt with the text of the *First* Amendment? "It would be allowed."

"[P]erfect clarity and precise guidance have never been required even of regulations that restrict expressive activity." *Ward* v. *Rock Against Racism,* 491 U.S. 781, 794 (1989). But the State's difficulties with its restriction go beyond close calls on borderline or fanciful cases. And that is a serious matter when the whole point of the exercise is to prohibit the expression of political views.

It is "self-evident" that an indeterminate prohibition carries with it "[t]he opportunity for abuse, especially where [it] has received a virtually open-ended interpretation." * * * We do not doubt that the vast majority of election judges strive to enforce the statute in an evenhanded manner, nor that some degree of discretion in this setting is necessary. But that discretion must be guided by objective, workable standards. Without them, an election judge's own politics may shape his views on what counts as "political." And if voters experience or witness episodes of unfair or inconsistent enforcement of the ban, the State's interest in maintaining a polling place free of distraction and disruption would be undermined by the very measure intended to further it.

That is not to say that Minnesota has set upon an impossible task. Other States have laws proscribing displays (including apparel) in more lucid terms. See, *e.g.,* Cal. Elec. Code Ann. § 319.5 (prohibiting "the visible display . . . of information that advocates for or against any candidate or measure," including the "display of a candidate's name, likeness, or logo," the "display of a ballot measure's number, title, subject, or logo," and "[b]uttons, hats," or "shirts" containing such information); Tex. Elec. Code Ann. § 61.010(a) (prohibiting the wearing of "a badge, insignia, emblem, or other similar communicative device relating to a candidate, measure, or political party appearing on the ballot, or to the conduct of the election"). We do not suggest that such provisions set the outer limit of what a State may proscribe, and do not pass on the constitutionality of laws that are not before us. But we do hold that if a State wishes to set its polling places apart as areas free of partisan discord, it must employ a more discernible approach than the one Minnesota has offered here.

Cases like this "present[] us with a particularly difficult reconciliation: the accommodation of the right to engage in political discourse with the right to vote." *Burson,* 504 U.S., at 198 (plurality opinion). Minnesota, like other States, has sought to strike the balance in a way that affords the voter the opportunity to exercise his civic duty in a setting removed from the clamor and din of electioneering. While that choice is generally worthy of our respect, Minnesota has not supported its good intentions with a law capable of reasoned application.

The judgment of the Court of Appeals is reversed, and the case is remanded for further proceedings consistent with this opinion.

It is so ordered.

Justice Sotomayor, with whom Justice Breyer joins, dissenting.

* * * I would certify this case to the Minnesota Supreme Court for a definitive interpretation of the political apparel ban under Minn. Stat. § 211B.11(1), which likely would obviate the hypothetical line-drawing problems that form the basis of the Court's decision today. * * *

Notes and Questions

1. Because the Court held that polling places were nonpublic fora, Minnesota had to demonstrate that its political-apparel ban was reasonable and viewpoint-neutral. The ban was clearly viewpoint-neutral, but the Court held that it was unreasonable because of the vagueness of the term "political" and the "haphazard interpretations" that the state had given to the term. Do you think the ban was reasonable? In considering that question, keep in mind that before one can determine whether a law is a reasonable way of accomplishing some goal, that goal must be identified. What was the government's goal here?

2. Would a more clearly stated prohibition on political apparel, such as the California and Texas statutes referenced in the Court's opinion, be a reasonable way of achieving the government's objective? How reasonable is it to prohibit, for example, the wearing of a T-shirt with a candidate's slogan or symbol? Consider Michael R. Dimino, Minnesota Voters Alliance v. Mansky *Strikes Down a Vague Ban on Speech in Polling Places, But Future Bans May Be Upheld*, 19 FED. SOC. REV. 134, 139 (2018) ("Wearing a 'Make America Great Again' hat or a 'Yes We Can' shirt * * * does nothing to undermine the purpose of a polling place because it does not intimidate voters or interfere with voters' ability to contemplate the questions on the ballot.").

3. As the Court noted, *Tinker v. Des Moines Independent Community School District*, 393 U.S. 503 (1969), held that a school could not prohibit its students from wearing black arm bands to protest the Vietnam War. *Minnesota Voters Alliance* distinguished *Tinker* on the ground that a polling place was a "unique context" that the state was entitled to keep free of "partisan discord" and "distract[ion]." Is a polling place much different from a school in that regard?

4. In footnote 4 of *Minnesota Voters Alliance*, the Court conceded that a state could "prohibit messages intended to mislead voters about voting requirements and procedures." Could a state ban "Please I.D. Me" buttons on the ground that they are intended to mislead voters about the identification requirements for voting? What if they are not *intended* to mislead, but the state fears they might have that effect?

5. As the Court noted, the government is prohibited from engaging in viewpoint discrimination even in a nonpublic forum. The Internet age has raised some questions about whether and how the First Amendment applies to certain online sites. For example, President Trump has used his Twitter account to communicate messages about his policies and to interact with the public. He established the account before he ran for President, however, and when he leaves office, he will retain control of the account. Is the President obligated to give the public access to the account on a viewpoint-neutral basis, or may he block Twitter users who post messages critical of him? *See Knight First Amendment Institute v. Trump*, 928 F.3d 226 (2d Cir. 2019) (holding that President Trump's personal Twitter account was a public forum). *See also Davison v. Randall*, 912 F.3d 666 (4th Cir. 2019) (holding similarly with respect

to a Facebook page used by a member of a county board of supervisors to distribute official government information).

6. Many states, in an attempt to limit vote-buying and voter coercion, have laws prohibiting voters from showing their votes to others. The rationale is that such a ban prevents voters from being able to prove how they voted; and attempts to buy a vote or to intimidate a voter into voting a certain way would be futile without a way of proving that the voter has voted the "right" way. Voters could still claim to have voted for one candidate or another, but there would be no way to be sure that the voter was telling the truth.

Those restrictions have come under increasing scrutiny in recent years with the rise of cell-phone cameras and social media. Some voters have taken and posted "ballot selfies" featuring their marked ballots, raising a conflict between the voters' free-speech rights and the government's interest in combating undue influence in elections.

Rideout v. Gardner

United States Court of Appeals for the First Circuit
838 F.3d 65 (1st Cir. 2016), *cert. denied*, 137 S. Ct. 1435 (2017)

LYNCH, Circuit Judge [with whom LIPEZ and THOMPSON, Circuit Judges, join].

In 2014, New Hampshire amended a statute meant to avoid vote buying and voter intimidation by newly forbidding citizens from photographing their marked ballots and publicizing such photographs. While the photographs need not show the voter, they often do and are commonly referred to as "ballot selfies." * * *

[In 1911, to prevent attempts to coerce voters into voting a certain way, the State] passed a statute[,] * * * codified in relevant part at [N.H. Rev. Stat.] section 659:35, I, which, until 2014, read: "No voter shall allow his ballot to be seen by any person with the intention of letting it be known how he is about to vote[.]" * * * In 2014, the New Hampshire legislature revised section 659:35, I as follows:

> No voter shall allow his <u>or her</u> ballot to be seen by any person with the intention of letting it be known how he <u>or she</u> is about to vote <u>or how he or she has voted</u> * * *. <u>This prohibition shall include taking a digital image or photograph of his or her marked ballot and distributing or sharing the image via social media or by any other means.</u>

Id. § 659:35, I (revisions underlined). The penalty for a violation of the statute is a fine of up to $1,000. * * *

[Although the legislative history suggested that the purpose of the bill was to prevent vote buying and voter coercion, t]he district court correctly held that "[t]he summary judgment record does not include any evidence that either vote buying or voter coercion has occurred in New Hampshire since the late 1800s." * * *

[The court first considered whether the ballot-selfie ban was a content-based or content-neutral restriction on speech. If the ban were content-based, strict scrutiny would apply, whereas if the ban were content-neutral, it would be evaluated under intermediate scrutiny. Ultimately the court held that it was unnecessary to resolve the question, because the law failed even under intermediate scrutiny.]

In order to survive intermediate scrutiny, section 659:35, I must be "narrowly tailored to serve a significant governmental interest." *McCullen* [v. *Coakley*], 134 S. Ct. [2518], 2534 [(2014)] (quoting *Ward* [v. *Rock Against Racism*], 491 U.S. [781], 796 [(1989)]). Though content-neutral laws "'need not be the least restrictive or least intrusive means of' serving the government's interests," *id.* at 2535 (quoting *Ward*, 491 U.S. at 798), "the government still 'may not regulate expression in such a manner that a substantial portion of the burden on speech does not serve to advance its goals,'" *id.* (quoting *Ward*, 491 U.S. at 799). The statute fails this standard.

Secretary Gardner essentially concedes that section 659:35, I does not respond to a present "'actual problem' in need of solving." Instead, he argues that the statute serves prophylactically to "preserve the secrecy of the ballot" from potential future vote buying and voter coercion, because ballot selfies make it easier for voters to prove how they voted. He characterizes the amendment in section 659:35, I as a natural update of the older version of the statute, done in response to the development of "modern technology, such as digital photography and social media," which may facilitate a future rise in vote buying and voter intimidation schemes.

As the district court noted, the prevention of vote buying and voter coercion is unquestionably "compelling in the abstract." But intermediate scrutiny is not satisfied by the assertion of abstract interests. Broad prophylactic prohibitions that fail to "respond[] precisely to the substantive problem which legitimately concerns" the State cannot withstand intermediate scrutiny. *Members of City Council of City of L.A. v. Taxpayers for Vincent*, 466 U.S. 789, 810 (1984).

Digital photography, the internet, and social media are not unknown quantities—they have been ubiquitous for several election cycles, without being shown to have the effect of furthering vote buying or voter intimidation. As the plaintiffs note, "small cameras" and digital photography "have been in use for at least 15 years," and New Hampshire cannot identify a single complaint of vote buying or intimidation related to a voter's publishing a photograph of a marked ballot during that period. Indeed, Secretary Gardner has admitted that New Hampshire has not received any complaints of vote buying or voter intimidation since at least 1976, nor has he pointed to any such incidents since the nineteenth century. "[T]he government's burden is not met when a 'State offer[s] *no* evidence or anecdotes in support of its restriction.'"[6]

---

6. Secretary Gardner does point to history abroad. He references the plebiscite held upon the German annexation of Austria in 1938, in which "Adolf Hitler instituted election rules that allowed voters to voluntarily show their ballot as they were voting." He also notes that Saddam Hussein employed ballots "contain[ing] a code number which he believed could be traced back to the

Secretary Gardner also highlights scattered examples of cases involving vote buying from other American jurisdictions. But Secretary Gardner admits that "there is no evidence that digital photography [of a ballot shared with others by a voter] played a[ny] role in any of the examples" he cites. A few recent instances of vote buying in other states do not substantiate New Hampshire's asserted interest in targeting vote buying through banning the publication of ballot selfies. * * *

New Hampshire has "too readily forgone options that could serve its interests just as well, without substantially burdening" legitimate political speech. At least two different reasons show that New Hampshire has not attempted to tailor its solution to the potential problem it perceives. First, the prohibition on ballot selfies reaches and curtails the speech rights of all voters, not just those motivated to cast a particular vote for illegal reasons. New Hampshire does so in the name of trying to prevent a much smaller hypothetical pool of voters who, New Hampshire fears, may try to sell their votes. New Hampshire admits that no such vote-selling market has in fact emerged. And to the extent that the State hypothesizes this will make intimidation of some voters more likely, that is no reason to infringe on the rights of all voters.

Second, the State has not demonstrated that other state and federal laws prohibiting vote corruption are not already adequate to the justifications it has identified. *See* 18 U.S.C. § 597 (prohibiting buying or selling votes); 52 U.S.C. § 10307(b) (prohibiting voter coercion or intimidation); *id.* § 10307(c) (prohibiting "pay[ing] or offer[ing] to pay or accept[ing] payment either for registration to vote or for voting" in some federal elections); N.H. Rev. Stat. Ann. § 659:40, I (prohibiting vote-related bribery); *id.* § 659:40, II (prohibiting voter coercion or intimidation); *id.* § 659:37 (prohibiting interfering with voters). * * *

As the district court observed, there are less restrictive alternatives available:

> [T]he state has an obviously less restrictive way to address any concern that images of completed ballots will be used to facilitate vote buying and voter coercion: it can simply make it unlawful to use an image of a completed ballot in connection with vote buying and voter coercion schemes.

Indeed, as to narrow tailoring, the plaintiffs [suggest that the state ban only those ballot selfies that are used "for the purpose of receiving pecuniary benefit . . . or avoiding harm"]. The ballot-selfie prohibition is like "burn[ing down] the house to roast the pig."

There are strong First Amendment interests held by the voters in the speech that this amendment prohibits. As the Supreme Court has said, "[t]he use of illustrations or pictures . . . serves important communicative functions: it attracts the attention

---

voter." There is no evidence that these historical examples from dictatorships have any material relationship to the present political situation in the State of New Hampshire, a democracy. Indeed, the restrictions on speech imposed by this amendment are antithetical to democratic values and particularly impose on political speech.

of the audience to the [speaker's] message, and it may also serve to impart information directly." *Zauderer* v. *Office of Disciplinary Counsel*, 471 U.S. 626, 647 (1985).

The restriction affects voters who are engaged in core political speech, an area highly protected by the First Amendment. As amici point out, there is an increased use of social media and ballot selfies in particular in service of political speech by voters. A ban on ballot selfies would suppress a large swath of political speech, which "occupies the core of the protection afforded by the First Amendment." Ballot selfies have taken on a special communicative value: they both express support for a candidate and communicate that the voter has in fact given his or her vote to that candidate.

Section 659:35, I reaches and prohibits innocent political speech by voters unconnected to the State's interest in avoiding vote buying or voter intimidation. The plaintiffs' examples show plainly that section 659:35, I "burden[s] substantially more speech than is necessary to further the government's legitimate interests." Indeed, several states have now expressly authorized ballot selfies, and those states have not reported an uptick in vote buying or voter intimidation.[10]

New Hampshire may not impose such a broad restriction on speech by banning ballot selfies in order to combat an unsubstantiated and hypothetical danger. We repeat the old adage: "a picture is worth a thousand words."

The judgment of the district court is *affirmed*.

Notes and Questions

1. The First Circuit in *Rideout* struck down New Hampshire's ban on "ballot selfies," but the Sixth Circuit, in *Crookston v. Johnson*, 841 F.3d 396 (6th Cir. 2016), reached a different conclusion as to Michigan's ban. The district court in *Crookston* struck down the law, but the court of appeals stayed, and later reversed, the district court's order. Most of the Sixth Circuit's opinion focused on the timing of the case — the court was unwilling to enjoin the state's law less than two weeks before the election — but the court also expressed "skeptici[sm]" about the merits of the First Amendment claim:

> The State's policy advances several serious governmental interests: preserving the privacy of other voters, avoiding delays and distractions at the polls, preventing vote buying, and preventing voter intimidation. Crookston tries to minimize the risk of vote buying as a relic of a bygone electoral era. But plenty of cases — in this circuit alone — show otherwise [citing three cases from 2013 to 2016 affirming vote-buying convictions].

---

10. See A.B. 1494, 2015–16 Reg. Sess. (Cal. 2016); S.B. 1287, 52d Leg., 1st Reg. Sess. (Ariz. 2015); H.B. 72, Gen. Sess. (Utah 2015); S.B. 1504, 77th Or. Leg. Assemb., 2d Reg. Sess. (Or. 2014) (effective Jan. 1, 2015); H.P. 1122, 125th Leg., 1st. Reg. Sess. (Me. 2011); R.I. State Bd. of Elections, ERLID No. 8372, Rules and Regulations for Polling Place Conduct (2016).

The links between these problems and the prohibition on ballot exposure are not some historical accident; they are "common sense." At the same time, it is far from clear that Crookston's proposal creates no risk of delay, as ballot-selfie takers try to capture the marked ballot and face in one frame—all while trying to catch the perfect smile.

Nor do we think much of Crookston's argument that the State has offered no evidence of ballot photography being used in vote-buying schemes or to intimidate voters. The Supreme Court made quick work of a similar argument in *Burson* [v. *Freeman*, 504 U.S. 191 (1992)] [p. 1024]. "The fact that these laws have been in effect for a long period of time," it reasoned, "makes it difficult for the States to put on witnesses who can testify as to what would happen without them." *Id.* at 208; see also *id.* at 214–16 (Scalia, J., concurring). Just so here.

It also is not clear whether a ban on ballot selfies "significantly impinges" Crookston's First Amendment rights. A picture may be worth a thousand words, but social media users can (and do) post thousands of words about whom they vote for and why. Although the loss of any potential First Amendment freedom deserves serious consideration, the government's interests in a stay outweigh any imposition on the expressive rights of Crookston and other would-be selfie-takers—particularly given the privacy interests of other voters [who might be captured in the background of a ballot selfie] in not having their votes made public.

841 F.3d at 400. *See also Crookston v. Johnson*, 854 F.3d 852 (6th Cir. 2016) (*per curiam*) (reversing the district court's preliminary-injunction order after the 2016 election, without additional analysis). Are you more persuaded by *Rideout* or *Crookston*? For a sample of commentary about whether ballot selfies should be permitted, see Richard L. Hasen, *Why the Selfie Is a Threat to Democracy*, REUTERS, Aug. 18, 2015, at http://blogs.reuters.com/great-debate/2015/08/17/why-the-selfie -is-a-threat-to-democracy/; Mark Joseph Stern, *Bring on the Ballot Selfies!*, SLATE, Oct. 1, 2012, *at* http://www.slate.com/articles/technology/future_tense/2016/09 /voting_booth_ballot_selfie_bans_violate_the_first_amendment.html; and Room for Debate, *Are Voting Booth Selfies Fun or Dangerous?*, N.Y. TIMES, Nov. 4, 2016, at *http://www.nytimes.com/roomfordebate/2016/11/04/are-voting-booth-selfies-fun-or -dangerous* (online debate between Professor Hasen and Elie Mystal).

2. The *Rideout* court did not decide whether ballot-selfie bans were content-based (resulting in the application of strict scrutiny) or content-neutral (resulting in the application of intermediate scrutiny). The issue is a difficult one given the Supreme Court's shifting jurisprudence on the subject.

The Supreme Court has held that a content-neutral law is one that is "justified without reference to the content of the regulated speech." *McCullen v. Coakley*, 573 U.S. 464, 477 (2014) (quoting *Ward v. Rock Against Racism*, 491 U.S. 781,

791 (1989)). Sometimes the Court applies this test by focusing on the government's purpose: If the government's interest is suppressing speech with particular content, then the law is content-based. If, however, the government's interest is something else—if it is suppressing speech with certain content in order to achieve some other result—then the law is content neutral. For example, in *Hill v. Colorado*, 530 U.S. 703 (2000), the Court held that a restriction on abortion "protest, education, or counseling" was content-neutral, because the government's interest was in protecting the patients at abortion clinics, rather than in suppressing speech with which the government disagreed. *See also McCullen*, *supra*, 573 U.S. at 479–82 (noting the content-neutral character of government interests in preserving public safety and preventing obstruction to healthcare); *City of Renton v. Playtime Theatres, Inc.*, 475 U.S. 41, 49–50 (1986) (holding that a zoning law applicable to adult theatres was content-neutral because it was aimed at combating the "secondary effects" of the speech rather than the speech itself).

Usually, however, the Court appears to apply a different test: whether the law's application to speech depends on the content of the speech. For example, in *Reed v. Town of Gilbert*, 576 U.S. 155 (2015), the Court held that a restriction on yard signs was content-based because it applied differently to signs depending on whether the content was "political," "ideological," or "directional." *See also McCullen*, *supra*, at 479–80 (noting that whether there was a violation of the content-neutral abortion-protest law at issue in that case did not depend on the content of what was said).

Ballot-selfie bans appear content-neutral if one focuses on the government's purposes, *e.g.*, deterring vote-buying or voter intimidation. On the other hand, ballot-selfie bans seem content-based if one focuses on whether the bans apply depending on the speech's content. The laws, after all, ban photos only if they contain particular content—a marked ballot.

3. In light of *Minnesota Voters Alliance v. Mansky*, 585 U.S ___, 138 S. Ct. 1876 (2018) [p. 1033], however, the question whether ballot-selfie bans are content-neutral may be irrelevant. That case, you will recall, held that the interiors of polling places are nonpublic fora. 138 S. Ct. at 1885–86. *See also Silberberg v. Board of Elections*, 272 F. Supp. 3d 454 (S.D.N.Y. 2017) (holding likewise in evaluating a ballot-selfie ban). As a result, speech restrictions inside polling places are constitutional so long as they are "reasonable" and "viewpoint neutral"—an easier test for the government to meet than either strict scrutiny or intermediate scrutiny. *See International Society for Krishna Consciousness v. Lee*, 505 U.S. 672, 678–79 (1992); *Perry Education Association v. Perry Educators' Association*, 460 U.S. 37, 46 (1983).

But what if ballot-selfie bans restrict conduct both within polling places and elsewhere? Ballot selfies must be *taken* inside the voting booth (unless they involve absentee or mail-in ballots), but may be *uploaded* later from a different location. According to *Silberberg*, "it suffices that the statute reasonably addresses conduct that could occur inside the polling booth, and in all cases begins in the voting booth." *Rideout*, however, implicitly held differently.

Perhaps the answer depends on the specific statute at issue. Laws that prohibit *taking* photographs in polling places might be thought to be a regulation of speech in a nonpublic forum (thereby triggering review only for reasonableness and viewpoint-neutrality), whereas laws that prohibit *distributing* photos might be evaluated under strict or intermediate scrutiny, depending on whether one considers those laws to be content-based or content-neutral. In *Hill v. Williams*, 2016 WL 8667798 (D. Colo. 2016), the court enjoined the government from enforcing a law prohibiting voters from "show[ing]" their ballots to other persons, but it explicitly stated that it was not enjoining the government from enforcing policies against taking photographs or videos. *See id.* at *8 & n.5.

If voters have a constitutional right to take ballot selfies, is there also a constitutional right to take selfies during a session of the Supreme Court? Cameras are prohibited in the courtroom during sessions, and there are only two known photographs of the Court in session. *See* Sonja West, *Smile for the Camera: The Long Lost Photos of the Supreme Court at Work—and What They Reveal*, SLATE, Oct. 1, 2012, *at* http://www.slate.com/articles/news_and_politics/jurisprudence/2012 /10/the_supreme_court_forbids_cameras_in_the_courtroom_but_twice_rogue _photographers_have_snapped_a_picture_of_the_justices_at_work_.html.

4. How severely does a ballot-selfie ban interfere with free speech? Does it matter that voters are free to announce their votes, even as they are prohibited from displaying photographic proof of them?

5. Should the constitutionality of a ballot-selfie ban depend on the prevalence of vote-buying or voter intimidation? If so, how is a state supposed to demonstrate that vote-buying is a significant potential problem if the ban itself has ensured that vote-buying could not take place?

6. The *Rideout* court indicated that a less-restrictive law—one that banned ballot selfies only when used in connection with vote-buying or voter intimidation—would have been a more narrowly tailored way of addressing the state's interests in avoiding those harms. Under intermediate scrutiny, however, the state need not adopt the least-restrictive alternative available. Do you believe the state's law was sufficiently tailored to survive intermediate scrutiny?

7. Would a ballot-selfie ban be sufficiently tailored to the government's separate interest in avoiding delays at the polls, or should the government simply be forced to use more polling stations to handle any increase in the time it takes to vote caused by people posing for selfies?

8. Similarly, assuming that the government has an interest in protecting the privacy of voters besides the self-portrait artists, is a ban on ballot selfies sufficiently tailored to protect the privacy of those other voters, or should states be forced to construct voting booths that would protect the occupant from being captured in someone else's ballot selfie? The *Crookston* court noted that "many Michigan voting stalls . . . are simply tall desks, placed next to each other, with three short dividers shielding the writing surface from view. In this setting, posing for a ballot selfie

could compromise the secrecy of another's ballot, distract other voters, and force a poll worker to intervene." *Crookston*, 841 F.3d at 399.

9. Or is your answer to all these questions "idk"? j/k lol. ☺

10. Although there is disagreement about whether bans on ballot selfies are appropriate ways of deterring vote-buying and voter-intimidation, there is widespread agreement that vote-buying and voter-intimidation are harmful and should be prohibited. In fact, every state and the federal government (*see* 18 U.S.C. §§ 597, 598) prohibit vote-buying. Professor Richard Hasen has identified three main rationales for vote-buying prohibitions: equality (the poor will sell their votes more readily than will the wealthy), efficiency (votes will be purchased so that government will be employed for the benefit of the purchasers, rather than for the general public), and inalienability (votes should not be transferable). *See* Richard L. Hasen, *Vote Buying*, 88 CALIF. L. REV. 1323 (2000). Do any of these rationales persuade you that vote-buying should be prohibited?

11. Is there a constitutional difference between vote-buying and vote-trading? In *Porter v. Bowen*, 496 F.3d 1009 (9th Cir. 2007), the Ninth Circuit held that there was. *Porter* involved two websites that facilitated vote-trading agreements during the 2000 presidential election, which was between Republican George W. Bush, Democrat Al Gore, and Green Party candidate Ralph Nader. The websites matched Gore supporters in non-competitive states with Nader supporters in swing states. After being matched, the voters were expected to agree to trade their votes, so that the original Nader supporter would vote for Gore, increasing the likelihood that Gore would receive the state's electoral votes and the presidency, while the original Gore supporter would vote for Nader, increasing the likelihood that Nader would receive five percent of the nationwide vote total, qualifying the Green Party for federal funding in future elections.

The California Attorney General argued that the websites were engaged in illegal activity, but the Ninth Circuit held that the websites and their vote-matching was protected by the First Amendment. The court explained that "unlike vote buying, vote swapping is not an 'illegal exchange for *private* profit' since the only benefit a vote swapper can receive is a marginally higher probability that his preferred electoral outcome will come to pass." 496 F.3d at 1020 (quoting *Brown v. Hartlage*, 456 U.S. 45, 55 (1982) [p. 568] (emphasis added in *Porter*)). Dissenting from the denial of rehearing *en banc*, Judge Kleinfeld argued that vote-trading *was* vote buying: The only difference was that votes were being bought not with "cash, or beer and cigars," but with reciprocal promises. *Porter v. Bowen*, 518 F.3d 1181, 1181 (9th Cir. 2008) (Kleinfeld, J., dissenting from denial of reh'g *en banc*). Reciprocal promises (as any law student who has studied bilateral contracts knows) satisfy the consideration requirement for contracts, and Judge Kleinfeld argued that it made no difference that the vote-trading was accomplished without an exchange of money. *See id.* at 1183.

Is vote-trading entitled to constitutional protection? If so, is it speech, expressive conduct, or neither? *Cf. Timmons v. Twin Cities Area New Party*, 520 U.S. 351, 363 (1997) [p. 526] ("Ballots serve primarily to elect candidates, not as forums for political expression.").

If, on the other hand, vote-trading is equivalent to vote-buying, could a state constitutionally punish an agreement to trade votes if it were made without a website or another enabling mechanism? For example, could a state prohibit two relatives living in different states from agreeing on their own to trade votes?

D. Federal Regulation of State-Run Elections

In Chapters 3 and 4, we extensively considered the Voting Rights Act of 1965, in which Congress limited states' control over elections to ensure that minorities' voting rights would be protected. The VRA is by no means the only federal law governing state-run elections. Federal law not only protects voting rights by ensuring that the franchise is open to certain people; federal law also is extensively involved in setting procedures for election administration. Congressional authority for such regulations comes from several different provisions in the Constitution. As we discussed in Chapter 3, the Enforcement Clauses of various Amendments permit Congress to "enforce, by appropriate legislation, the provisions of" the Amendments. Congress's powers under the Commerce Clause (U.S. Const. art. I, § 8, cl. 3), the Spending Clause (U.S. Const. art. I, § 8, cl. 1), and the Necessary and Proper Clause (U.S. Const. art. I, § 8, cl. 18) also permit Congress to enact measures that affect elections. Some constitutional provisions, however, are directly focused on Congress's power concerning election regulation.

The Constitution provides that "[t]he Times, Places and Manner of holding Elections for Senators and Representatives, shall be prescribed in each State by the Legislature thereof; but the Congress may at any time by Law make or alter such Regulations * * *." U.S. Const. art. I, § 4, cl. 1. Title 2 U.S.C. § 7, passed pursuant to that authority, is the law that establishes our election day as "[t]he Tuesday next after the 1st Monday in November, in every even numbered year * * *."[d] Federal law

---

d. States are permitted to have run-off elections *after* election day, at a time prescribed by state law, if the vote on election day failed to elect a candidate. 2 U.S.C. § 8(a). For example, states are free to require that winning candidates receive a majority, not just a plurality, of votes. In a multi-candidate race, the candidate with the most votes may have received less than a majority. A run-off election would then be held between the two candidates with the most votes. States may not, however, hold an election *before* the first Tuesday after the first Monday in November, with the run-off election (if necessary) being held on the federally chosen election day. *See Foster v. Love*, 522 U.S. 67 (1997).

In recent years, many states have experimented in various ways with modifying election "day," which previously had been a single day for all voters to cast their ballots in person. Over thirty states have adopted mail-in or absentee voting, which in effect can extend the voting period from also directs that members of Congress be chosen from single-member districts. 2 U.S.C. § 2c. *See generally Branch v. Smith*, 538 U.S. 254, 266–72 (2003). Furthermore, in any disputed congressional election, each house of Congress has the final word: "Each House shall be the Judge of the Elections, Returns and Qualifications of its own Members * * *." U.S. Const. art. I, § 5, cl. 1.

In presidential elections, the Constitution provides for the electoral college and specifies that the electors shall be appointed by "[e]ach State * * *, in such Manner as the Legislature thereof may direct," U.S. Const. art. II, § 1, cl. 2, but again the Constitution leaves a significant regulatory role for Congress: "The Congress may determine the Time of chusing the Electors, and the Day on which they shall give their Votes; which Day shall be the same throughout the United States." U.S. Const. art. II, § 1, cl. 4.[e]

Congress has exercised that authority. Title 3 U.S.C. § 1 directs that "[t]he electors of President and Vice President shall be appointed, in each State, on the Tuesday next after the first Monday in November, in every fourth year succeeding every election of a President and Vice President." Further, Congress has specified the day for the electors to cast their ballots: "The electors of President and Vice President of each State shall meet and give their votes on the first Monday after the second Wednesday in December next following their appointment at such place in each State as the legislature of such State shall direct." 3 U.S.C. § 7. Congress has also provided for the date (January 6), time (1:00 p.m.), and procedures of counting the electoral votes. *See* 3 U.S.C. §§ 15–18.

---

one day to several weeks. Courts have held that such systems do not violate *Foster*, in part because federal law also permits absentee voting in federal elections under some circumstances. *See Voting Integrity Project v. Keisling*, 259 F.3d 1169, 1175–76 (9th Cir. 2001) (Oregon's mail-in system); *Voter Integrity Project v. Bomer*, 199 F.3d 773, 777 (5th Cir. 2000) (Texas's early-voting system). One state court, drawing on *Foster*, has held that early-voting laws violate the state constitution's designation of one particular day for holding an election. *Lamone v. Capozzi*, 912 A.2d 674 (Md. 2006). Over thirty state constitutions have similar language, although *Lamone* appears to be the only successful challenge to early-voting systems on state-constitutional grounds. Ward Williams, Comment, 39 Rutgers L.J. 1117, 1125–27 (2008). Some studies of early voting show that it has little, if any, effect on increasing turnout, in part because it simply makes voting easier for those who would vote anyway. *See, e.g.*, Barry C. Burden et al., *Election Laws, Mobilization, and Turnout: The Unanticipated Consequences of Election Reform*, 58 Am. J. Pol. Sci. 95 (2014); Joseph D. Giammo & Brian J. Brox, *Reducing the Costs of Participation: Are States Getting a Return on Early Voting?*, 63 Pol. Res. Q. 295 (2010); Symposium, *Time Shifting the Vote: The Quiet Revolution in American Elections*, 10 Election L.J. 73 (2011).

e. As noted above, the Constitution vests both the initial power to make rules for congressional elections and the power to choose the manner of selecting presidential electors not simply in the states, but in the state *legislatures*. Despite this language, the Supreme Court has held that it is permissible for states to use independent redistricting commissions to draw congressional districts. Some states use the commissions as a way of lessening the self-interest and partisanship that inheres in districting by legislatures. The Court held that "Legislature" in Article I, § 4, cl. 1 includes any group—including the people of the state as a whole—that exercises the state's legislative power. *Arizona State Legislature v. Arizona Independent Redistricting Commission*, 576 U.S. 787 (2015) [p. 200].

1. The Help America Vote Act

The 2000 presidential-election debacle, with the outcome in doubt for more than a month until the Supreme Court's decision in *Bush v. Gore*, 531 U.S. 98 (2000), produced widespread agreement that America's voting processes needed to be improved. One of the responses from Congress was the passage of the Help America Vote Act of 2002 (HAVA), 52 U.S.C. § 20901 *et seq.*, which was designed to encourage and to assist states in improving and upgrading their administration of elections. The law reflected Democratic desires to improve access to the ballot and Republican concerns over the integrity of the voting process. HAVA, in its Title I, authorized the distribution of federal funds to states, and, in Title II, set up a new agency, the Election Assistance Commission (EAC). Title III imposed certain requirements on states with regard to voting-equipment standards, registration databases, identification requirements for first-time voters, and provisional voting. For discussion of the enactment of HAVA, see Leonard M. Shambon, *Implementing the Help America Vote Act*, 3 ELECTION L.J. 424 (2004). The following case involved a dispute concerning HAVA's language concerning the casting of provisional ballots.

Sandusky County Democratic Party v. Blackwell

United States Court of Appeals for the Sixth Circuit
387 F.3d 565 (6th Cir. 2004)

PER CURIAM. [CHIEF JUDGE BOGGS, CIRCUIT JUDGE GILMAN, and DISTRICT JUDGE WEBER (sitting by designation) join in this opinion.]

At bottom, this is a case of statutory interpretation. Does the Help America Vote Act require that all states count votes (at least for most federal elections) cast by provisional ballot as legal votes, even if cast in a precinct in which the voter does not reside, so long as they are cast within a "jurisdiction" that may be as large as a city or county of millions of citizens? We hold that neither the statutory text or structure, the legislative history, nor the understanding, until now, of those concerned with voting procedures compels or even permits that conclusion. Thus, * * * we hold that ballots cast in a precinct where the voter does not reside and which would be invalid under state law for that reason are not required by HAVA to be considered legal votes.

To hold otherwise would interpret Congress's reasonably clear procedural language to mean that political parties would now be authorized to marshal their supporters at the last minute from shopping centers, office buildings, or factories, and urge them to vote at whatever polling place happened to be handy, all in an effort to turn out every last vote regardless of state law and historical practice. We do not believe that Congress quietly worked such a revolution in America's voting procedures, and we will not order it.

The States long have been primarily responsible for regulating federal, state, and local elections. These regulations have covered a range of issues, from registration requirements to eligibility requirements to ballot requirements to vote-counting requirements. One aspect common to elections in almost every state is that voters are required to vote in a particular precinct. Indeed, in at least 27 of the states using a precinct voting system, including Ohio, a voter's ballot will only be counted as a valid ballot if it is cast in the correct precinct.

The advantages of the precinct system are significant and numerous: it caps the number of voters attempting to vote in the same place on election day; it allows each precinct ballot to list all of the votes a citizen may cast for all pertinent federal, state, and local elections, referenda, initiatives, and levies; it allows each precinct ballot to list only those votes a citizen may cast, making ballots less confusing; it makes it easier for election officials to monitor votes and prevent election fraud; and it generally puts polling places in closer proximity to voter residences. * * *

[The Help America Vote Act, 42 U.S.C. § 15301 *et seq.*, (HAVA)] was passed in order to alleviate "a significant problem voters experience[, which] is to arrive at the polling place believing that they are eligible to vote, and then to be turned away because the election workers cannot find their names on the list of qualified voters." H.R. Rep. 107–329 at 38 (2001). HAVA dealt with this problem by creating a system for provisional balloting, that is, a system under which a ballot would be submitted on election day but counted if and only if the person was later determined to have been entitled to vote.

Section 302 of HAVA, the section most pertinent to this appeal, requires States to provide voters with the opportunity to cast provisional ballots and to post certain information about provisional ballots at polling places on election day. The section's requirements relating to the casting of provisional ballots are as follows:

(a) Provisional voting requirements. If an individual declares that such individual is a registered voter in the jurisdiction in which the individual desires to vote and that the individual is eligible to vote in an election for Federal office, but the name of the individual does not appear on the official list of eligible voters for the polling place or an election official asserts that the individual is not eligible to vote, such individual shall be permitted to cast a provisional ballot as follows:

(1) An election official at the polling place shall notify the individual that the individual may cast a provisional ballot in that election.

(2) The individual shall be permitted to cast a provisional ballot at that polling place upon the execution of a written affirmation by the individual before an election official at the polling place stating that the individual is—

(A) a registered voter in the jurisdiction in which the individual desires to vote; and

(B) eligible to vote in that election.

(3) An election official at the polling place shall transmit the ballot cast by the individual or the voter information contained in the written

affirmation executed by the individual under paragraph (2) to an appropriate State or local election official for prompt verification under paragraph (4).

(4) If the appropriate State or local election official to whom the ballot
or voter information is transmitted under paragraph (3) determines that
the individual is eligible under State law to vote, the individual's provisional ballot shall be counted as a vote in that election in accordance
with State law. * * *

42 U.S.C. § 15482. * * *

On September 27, 2004, the Sandusky County Democratic Party, the Ohio
Democratic Party, and three labor unions ("Appellees") filed an action in the
United States District Court for the Northern District of Ohio against J. Kenneth
Blackwell, Ohio Secretary of State. Appellees' Complaint alleged that the Secretary's
promulgation to Ohio County Boards of Elections of Ohio Secretary of State Directive 2004-33 conflicts with the requirements of HAVA. Directive 2004-33 states, in
pertinent part, that:

> State law further provides that an eligible elector who moves from one
> Ohio precinct to another before an election may * * * update his or her exist-
> ing voter registration to the new voting residence address and vote a provi-
> sional ballot for the precinct in which the person's new voting residence is
> located. The provisional ballot will be counted in the official canvass if the
> county board of elections confirms that the person was timely registered to
> vote in another Ohio precinct, and that the person did not vote or attempt
> to vote in that election using the person's former voting residence address.

> Because R.C. 3599.12 specifically prohibits anyone from voting or
> attempting to vote in any election in a precinct in which that person is not a
> legally qualified elector, pollworkers in a precinct must confirm before issu-
> ing a provisional ballot that the person to whom the provisional ballot will
> be issued is a resident of the precinct, or portion of the precinct, in which
> the person desires to vote. . . . .

> Only after the precinct pollworkers have confirmed that the person is
> eligible to vote in that precinct shall the pollworkers issue a provisional bal-
> lot to that person. Under no circumstances shall precinct pollworkers issue
> a provisional ballot to a person whose address is not located in the precinct,
> or portion of the precinct, in which the person desires to vote.

Appellees alleged that Directive 2004-33 violates HAVA because, *inter alia*, it limits a voter's right to cast a provisional ballot to those situations where a voter has
moved from one Ohio precinct to another; allows poll workers to withhold a provisional ballot from anyone who is not—according to the poll worker's on-the-spot
determination at the polling place—a resident of the precinct in which the would-
be voter desires to cast a provisional ballot; does not require that potential voters

be notified of their right to cast a provisional ballot; and unduly limits the circumstances in which a provisional ballot will be counted as a valid ballot.

On October 14, 2004, the district court issued an Order granting preliminary injunctive relief to Appellees. * * * The district court's injunction required that the Secretary issue a revised directive that (1) permits any voter to cast a provisional ballot upon affirming that he or she is eligible to vote and is registered to vote in the county in which he or she wishes to vote; (2) requires poll workers to notify any voter making this affirmation of his or her right to cast a provisional ballot, even if the poll worker determines that the voter does not reside in the precinct in which he or she is attempting to vote; and (3) that provisional ballots cast by a voter in the county in which he or she is registered to vote must be counted as a valid ballot even if it was not cast in the precinct in which the voter resides. * * *

[The court first determined that plaintiffs may file a private lawsuit under 42 U.S.C. § 1983 to enforce their HAVA-created right to cast a provisional ballot. The court then turned to the merits.]

HAVA requires that any individual affirming that he or she "is a registered voter in the jurisdiction in which the individual desires to vote and that the individual is eligible to vote in an election for Federal office . . . shall be permitted to cast a provisional ballot." *See* 42 U.S.C. § 15482(a).

Directive 2004-33 contravenes this requirement because it requires that a voter's residence in a precinct be determined on the spot by a poll worker, and empowers poll workers to deny a voter a provisional ballot if the voter's residence in the correct precinct cannot be confirmed. *See* Directive 2004-33 ("Before issuing a provisional ballot as provided for under state or federal law, the pollworkers must confirm that the voting residence address claimed by the voter is located within the area shown on the precinct map and listed on the street listing."). As we explained above, the primary purpose of HAVA was to prevent on-the-spot denials of provisional ballots to voters deemed ineligible to vote by poll workers. Under HAVA, the only permissible requirement that may be imposed upon a would-be voter before permitting that voter to cast a provisional ballot is the affirmation contained in § 15482(a): that the voter is a registered voter in the jurisdiction in which he or she desires to vote, and that the voter is eligible to vote in an election for federal office.

Unfortunately, HAVA does not define what "jurisdiction" means in this context, which leaves unclear whether a voter must affirm that he or she is registered to vote in the *precinct* in which he or she desires to vote, the *county* in which he or she desires to vote, or even simply the *state* in which he or she desires to vote. The district court concluded that the term should be given the same meaning as the term "registrar's jurisdiction" is given in the NVRA; namely the geographic reach of the unit of government that maintains the voter registration rolls, *see* 42 U.S.C. § 1973gg-6(j), which in Ohio is each county board of election. The district court offered two bases for its conclusion: first, the statement by Senator Dodd on the Senate floor that "[i]t is our intent that the word 'jurisdiction' . . . has the same meaning as the term 'registrar's jurisdiction' in section 8(j) of the National Voter Registration Act," 148 Cong. Rec. S2535 (daily ed. Apr. 11, 2002); and second, the court's belief that permitting provisional ballots to be cast by voters outside their home precincts would further HAVA's purpose of preserving the federal franchise.

We disagree with the district court's interpretation of the term "jurisdiction." Senator Dodd's statement must be weighed against other statements in HAVA's legislative history that suggest quite the contrary—that jurisdiction means the particular state subdivision within which a particular State's laws require votes to be cast. Senator Bond, one of HAVA's floor managers, stated:

> Congress has said only that voters in Federal elections should be given a provisional ballot if they claim to be registered in a particular jurisdiction and that jurisdiction does not have the voter's name on the list of registered voters. . . . *This provision is in no way intended to require any State or locality to allow voters to vote from any place other than the polling site where the voter is registered.*

148 Cong. Rec. S10488, S10493 (daily ed. Oct. 16, 2002) (emphasis added). Senator Bond also noted:

> Additionally, it is inevitable that voters will mistakenly arrive at the wrong polling place. If it is determined by the poll worker that the voter is registered but has been assigned to a different polling place, it is the intent of the authors of this bill that the poll worker can direct the voter to the correct polling place. *In most states, the law is specific on the polling place where the voter is to cast his ballot. Again, this bill upholds state law on that subject.*

148 Cong. Rec. at S10491 (emphasis added).

Nor can the use of the NVRA's definition of "registrar's jurisdiction" be justified on the ground that doing so will further HAVA's purpose of preserving the franchise. For one thing, permitting voters to cast ballots in any precinct within their county of residence may cause logistical problems at certain favored polling places that outweigh some or all of the benefits expected by the district court. For another, even if importing language from the NVRA will in this case have the effect of expanding the opportunities of Ohioans to vote on election day, so too would ordering that provisional ballots may be cast by any Ohio voter anywhere in the state. Absent an independent reason for turning to the NVRA's definition, the mere fact that equating "jurisdiction" with "county" may have a salutary effect on the franchise cannot suffice to justify reading the language of HAVA in this way.

* * * In the absence of a compelling reason for defining HAVA's use of this term to mean the geographic reach of the unit of government that maintains the voter registration rolls, we look to the overall scheme of the statute to determine its meaning. * * * Nowhere in the language or structure of HAVA as a whole is there any indication that the Congress intended to strip from the States their traditional responsibility to administer elections; still less that Congress intended that a voter's eligibility to cast a provisional ballot should exceed her eligibility to cast a regular ballot. After all, the whole point of provisional ballots is to allow a ballot to be cast by a voter who claims to be eligible to cast a regular ballot, pending determination of that eligibility.

In Ohio, like many other states, a voter may cast a ballot only in his or her precinct of residence. *See* Ohio Rev. Code Ann. § 3503.01 (providing that an eligible voter "may vote at all elections in the precinct in which the citizen resides"); Ohio Rev. Code Ann. § 3599.12(A)(1) (making it a crime under Ohio law for a voter to knowingly vote anywhere except in the precinct in which he or she resides). As such, in Ohio, HAVA requires that a provisional ballot be issued only to voters affirming that they are eligible to vote and are registered to vote in the precinct in which they seek to cast a ballot. * * *

HAVA is quintessentially about being able to *cast* a provisional ballot. No one should be "turned away" from the polls, but the ultimate legality of the vote cast provisionally is generally a matter of state law. Any error by the state authorities may be sorted out later, when the provisional ballot is examined, in accordance with subsection (a)(4) of section 15482. But the voter casts a provisional ballot at the peril of not being eligible to vote under state law; if the voter is not eligible, the vote will then not be counted. * * *

In addition to finding that HAVA requires that voters be permitted to cast provisional ballots upon affirming their registration to vote in the county within which they desire to vote, the district court also held that provisional ballots must be counted as valid ballots when cast in the correct county. We disagree.

The only subsection of HAVA that addresses the issue of whether a provisional ballot will be counted as a valid ballot conspicuously leaves that determination to the States. That subsection provides:

> "If the appropriate State or local election official to whom the ballot or voter information is transmitted under paragraph (3) determines that the individual is eligible under State law to vote, the individual's provisional ballot shall be counted as a vote in that election in accordance with State law."

42 U.S.C. § 15482(a)(4). The district court interpreted this subsection to require the following procedure after a provisional ballot has been cast: First, an election official determines whether the individual who cast the ballot was eligible to vote in the broadest possible sense of that term. In essence, the district court would have state officials ask only whether a voter was eligible to vote *in some polling place* within the county at the start of election day. Even someone who has "voted 'improperly'" remains eligible in this sense of eligibility. Second, if the voter is deemed eligible to vote, the provisional ballot is deemed valid, and may then be tallied along with all the other valid ballots in accordance with State rules for tallying votes accurately and promptly. The district court, in other words, interpreted HAVA as leaving to state law only "*how* the ballots are counted" while federal law determines "*whether* they are to be counted." Because the district court found that voters are eligible to

vote under Ohio law anywhere in their county of residence, the court held that a provisional ballot cast anywhere in a voter's county of residence must be counted as valid.

The district court's interpretation of this subsection of HAVA is incorrect. To read "eligible under state law to vote" so broadly as to mean not only that a voter must simply be eligible to vote *in some polling place* within the county, but remains eligible even after casting an improper ballot would lead to the untenable conclusion that Ohio must count as valid a provisional ballot cast in the correct county even it is determined that the voter in question had previously voted elsewhere in that county; an impropriety that would not render that voter ineligible based upon the district court's interpretation of HAVA. State law concerning eligibility to vote is not limited to facts about voters as they arise from slumber on election day; they also stipulate, for example, that a voter is eligible to vote only once in each election, and, in Ohio, where a voter is eligible to cast a ballot. In other words, being eligible under State law to vote means eligible to vote *in this specific election in this specific polling place.*

Under Ohio law, a voter is eligible to vote in a particular polling place only if he or she resides in the precinct in which that polling place is located:

> Every citizen of the United States who is of the age of eighteen years or over and who has been a resident of the state thirty days immediately preceding the election at which the citizen offers to vote, is a *resident of the county and precinct* in which the citizen offers to vote, and has been registered to vote for thirty days, has the qualifications of an elector and *may vote at all elections in the precinct in which the citizen resides.*

Ohio Rev. Code Ann. § 3503.01 (emphasis added). * * * Indeed, it is a crime under Ohio law for a voter knowingly to vote anywhere except in the precinct in which he or she resides. Ohio Rev. Code Ann. § 3599.12(A)(1). Under Ohio law, then, only ballots cast in the correct precinct may be counted as valid.

There is no reason to think that HAVA, which explicitly defers determination of whether ballots are to be counted to the States, should be interpreted as imposing upon the States a federal requirement that out-of-precinct ballots be counted, thereby overturning the longstanding precinct-counting system in place in more than half the States. The phrase "eligible under State law to vote" certainly provides no reason to believe this was Congress's intent. Even if one concludes from our disagreement with the district court's interpretation of this phrase that it is somewhat ambiguous, that fact alone is an insufficient basis for inferring a congressional intent to impose federal requirements upon the States in this way. * * *

Nor does the legislative history of the statute provide any reason to believe that HAVA requires that ballots cast in the wrong precinct be counted. Senator Bond, for example, stated that "ballots will be counted according to state law. . . . It is not the intent of the authors to overturn State laws regarding registration or state laws regarding the jurisdiction in which a ballot must be cast to be counted." 148 Cong.

Rec. at S10491. Senator Dodd also noted: "Whether a provisional ballot is counted or not depends solely on State law, and the conferees clarified this by adding language in section 302(a)(4) stating that a voter's eligibility to vote is determined under State law." 148 Cong. Rec. at S10510. * * *

We therefore hold that HAVA does not require that any particular ballot, whether provisional or "regular," must be counted as valid. States remain free, of course, to count such votes as valid, but remain equally free to mandate, as Ohio does, that only ballots cast in the correct precinct will be counted.

It should be noted that this holding in no way rests upon our discussion above about the meaning of the term "jurisdiction." Even if the district court was correct to find that provisional ballots must be *offered* to any voter affirming residence in the county in which he or she desires to vote, it remains true that HAVA's single provision relating to the counting of ballots refers only to eligibility under State law to vote, and makes no reference either explicitly or implicitly to the jurisdiction in which a provisional ballot was cast.[5] In any event, there is no contradiction between requiring all voters in a county to be given a provisional ballot in case they are subsequently found to reside in the precinct in which they seek to vote, and then allowing the state to continue its practice of not counting votes cast outside of precinct. Although Congress certainly intended that some provisional ballots would be counted as valid after it was determined that voters should in fact have appeared on the list of qualified voters, there is no suggestion in either the legislative history of the statute or the statutory text that Congress intended all provisional ballots to be deemed valid. * * *

Notes and Questions

1. HAVA has been controversial since its inception. Under the statute, the EAC consists of two members from each major party, with a majority required for action. That and the limited powers granted by Congress have rendered the EAC largely toothless. It is authorized to distribute HAVA funds for election improvements and to engage in research, but it cannot issue regulations and otherwise is given relatively little power. Moreover, it has been plagued by disputes over commissioner appointments, limited funding, and failure to exercise what limited powers it does have. For an overview, see *Symposium, HAVA@10*, 12 ELECTION L.J. 111 (2013).

2. *Sandusky* held that voters had a private right of action through 42 U.S.C. § 1983 to enforce certain of the provisions found in § 302 of HAVA. In particular, the court determined that § 302 conveyed an enforceable individual right by providing that a voter "shall be permitted to cast a provisional ballot" upon affirming that he or she is registered and eligible to vote. In contrast, other decisions have refused to

---

5. Indeed, the requirement that ballots be issued county-wide is, even on the district court's reading, a federal requirement, which cannot be read into the statement that votes must be counted if a voter is determined to be eligible under State law.

infer private rights of action under other HAVA provisions. *E.g., Brunner v. Ohio Republican Party*, 555 U.S. 5 (2008) (*per curiam*) (saying, without elaboration, that the Party was "not sufficiently likely to prevail on the question whether Congress has authorized the District Court to enforce [HAVA] § 303 in an action brought by a private litigant to justify the issuance of a TRO [temporary restraining order]"); *Crowley v. Nevada*, 678 F.3d 730 (9th Cir. 2012) (HAVA § 301).

Does the result in *Brunner* call into question the result in *Sandusky*? The Sixth Circuit decision reversed in *Brunner* drew on *Sandusky* in suggesting that there was a cause of action under § 303, 544 F.3d 711, at 719–20 (6th Cir. 2008) (*en banc*), while the dissent argued that § 302 differed from § 303 in this regard. *Id.* at 726–30 (Moore, J., dissenting). For an argument that the cases do conflict, see J. Kenneth Blackwell & Kenneth A. Klukowski, *The Other Voting Right: Protecting Every Citizen's Vote by Safeguarding the Integrity of the Ballot Box*, 28 Yale L. & Pol'y Rev. 107, 119 n.51 (2009).

Is the result in *Brunner* desirable as a matter of policy? After that case, apparently the only way to enforce § 303 of HAVA is for the United States to sue the offending state. Should that be the preferred method of implementation? For further discussion of administrative versus private enforcement of federal election laws, see Daniel P. Tokaji, *Public Rights and Private Rights of Action: The Enforcement of Federal Election Laws*, 44 Ind. L. Rev. 113 (2010).

3. HAVA has been credited with encouraging states to abandon the traditional paper punchcard ballots, and to adopt newer technologies, such as optically scanned ballots or electronic voting machines. Refinements in voting technology have continued at the state level, even without the mandate of HAVA or other federal laws. For example, HAVA did not require states to implement a voter-verifiable paper record, but twenty-nine states have adopted some version of that requirement. Daniel Palazzolo et al., *Election Reform After HAVA: Voter Verification in Congress and the States*, 38 Publius: The Journal of Federalism 515 (2008). For further discussion of HAVA and related statutes and their impact, see Presidential Commission on Election Administration: The American Voting Experience: Report and Recommendations (2014); Election Administration in the United States: The State of Reform After *Bush v. Gore* (R. Michael Alvarez & Bernard Grofman eds., 2014); Martha Kropf & David C. Kimball, Helping America Vote: The Limits of Election Reform (2011); Kathleen Hale & Ramona McNeal, *Election Administration Reform and State Choice: Voter Identification Laws and HAVA*, 38 Pol'y Stud. J. 281 (2010); Daron Shaw et al., *A Brief Yet Practical Guide to Reforming U.S. Voter Registration Systems*, 14 Election L.J. 26 (2015).

It appears that fewer votes have been lost or not counted due to these various developments adopted in the wake of the passage of HAVA, as compared to earlier elections. Richard L. Hasen, *The Untimely Death of* Bush v. Gore, 60 Stan. L. Rev. 1, 16 (2007). *Compare* Robert M. Stein et al., *Voting Technology, Election Administration, and Voter Performance*, 7 Election L.J. 123 (2008) (comparing optically scanned paper ballots and electronic voting machines with regard to voter satisfaction and the time it takes to vote). In some places there is nostalgia for the punch-card system. Some election officials and voters argue that the punchcards were easier and quicker to use, while the optical-scan system takes more time, producing long lines at the polls, and requires voters to engage in a cumbersome and difficult process of filling in boxes with a pen. Barry M. Horstman, *No Easy Fix Proposed for Ballot Delays*, CINCINNATI ENQUIRER, Dec. 31, 2009, at B5.

In *Husted v. A. Philip Randolph Institute*, 584 U.S. __, 138 S. Ct. 1833 (2018), the Supreme Court, in a 5-4 decision, rejected a challenge to Ohio's policy of purging registered voters from the voting rolls. If a registered voter failed to vote for two years, Ohio sent a postage-prepaid card to the voter to determine if he had moved. If the registered voter did not return the card and failed to vote in a subsequent election for four more years, he was presumed to have moved and was removed from the rolls. Plaintiffs argued that this process violated the National Voter Registration Act's Failure-to-Vote Clause, as amended by HAVA, which generally prohibits states from removing people for failure to vote. 52 U.S.C. § 20507(b)(2). A different portion of the statute, however, permits the removal of a registrant who "(i) has failed to respond to a notice" and "(ii) has not voted or appeared to vote . . . during the period beginning on the date of the notice and ending on the day after the date of the second general election for Federal office that occurs after the date of the notice." 52 U.S.C. § 20507(d)(1)(B).

The Court held that the provisions only "forbid[] the use of nonvoting *as the sole criterion*" to remove a voter. 138 S. Ct. at 1842. Ohio, in contrast, used nonvoting *and* failure to respond to the notice, and therefore complied with the NVRA. The dissent, suggesting that few people respond to the notice cards, argued that Ohio's procedure violated the Failure-to-Vote Clause, as well as other statutory provisions that required states to make a "reasonable effort" to identify ineligible voters before removing names from the voter rolls. The majority responded that statutory provisions expressly contemplated that states would use the failure to respond to notices as such a way of identifying ineligible voters, and the record did not support the claim that few people used the notice cards.

At the outset of its opinion, the majority observed that it had been estimated that twenty-four million voter registrations, about one in eight, were either invalid or significantly inaccurate, and that about 2.75 million people are registered to vote in more than one state, citing a Pew Center report. Would greater use of same-day voter registration (or not requiring registration at all) obviate the need to purge voter rolls periodically? The majority also observed that states took a variety of approaches in culling their voting roles, and only five states besides Ohio sent notices in response to nonvoting. How much leeway do states have after *Husted* to comply with the relevant NVRA provisions? *Cf. American Civil Rights Union v. Philadelphia City Commissioners*, 872 F.3d 175 (3d Cir. 2017) (holding that the NVRA permitted, but did not require, the city to purge voter rolls of registered voters who were incarcerated due to a felony conviction, and were prohibited from voting under state law). For an extensive and critical discussion of *Husted*, see Lisa Marshall Manheim & Elizabeth G. Porter, *The Elephant in the Room: Intentional Voter Suppression*, 2018 SUP. CT. REV. 213.

4. Other federal laws, passed both before and after HAVA, regulate the manner in which states manage their voting systems with regard to participation in federal elections. Most states have long required voters to register in some way before they vote. Daniel P. Tokaji, *Voter Registration and Election Reform*, 17 WM. & MARY BILL RTS. J. 453 (2008). In 1993, Congress passed the aforementioned National Voter Registration Act (NVRA), 52 U.S.C. § 20501 *et seq.*, which requires states to link voter registration with applications for new or renewed driver's licenses. The NVRA has not led to robust increases in voting registration, one of its intended goals. Robert D. Brown & Justin Wedeking, *People Who Have Their Tickets But Do Not Use Them: "Motor Voter," Registration, and Turnout Revisited*, 34 AM. POL. RES. 479 (2006). NVRA contains a private right of action permitting a "person who is aggrieved by a violation" of NVRA to enforce the law in federal court. 52 U.S.C. § 20510. For examples of litigation under NVRA, see, *e.g.*, *ACORN v. Fowler*, 178 F.3d 350 (5th Cir. 1999) (holding that ACORN members lacked standing to bring an action absent evidence they had received a driver's-license-renewal form or had been purged from state voting rolls); *Harkless v. Brunner*, 545 F.3d 445 (6th Cir. 2008) (holding that the secretary of state was a proper defendant, and remanding for further consideration of ACORN's standing); *Arcia v. Florida Secretary of State*, 746 F.3d 1273 (11th Cir. 2014) (holding that the state violated NVRA when it conducted a program to remove suspected noncitizens from voter rolls within ninety days of a federal election). Other federal laws that regulate state voting practices are (1) the Voting Accessibility for the Elderly and Handicapped Act (VAEHA), 52 U.S.C. § 20101, passed in 1984, which requires states to facilitate voting in federal elections by voters who are handicapped or 65 years or older; (2) the Uniformed and Overseas Citizens Absentee Voting Act (UOCAVA), 52 U.S.C. § 20301 *et seq.*, passed in 1986, which requires states to facilitate absentee voting for federal elections by voters, including those in the military, who are overseas; and (3) the Military and Overseas Voter Empowerment Act, passed in 2009, amending UOCAVA and further requiring states to facilitate mail and electronic absentee voting in federal elections by members of the armed forces stationed outside the United States. For an overview and critique of NVRA, HAVA, and other federal laws, see Justin Weinstein-Tull, *Election Law Federalism*, 114 MICH. L. REV. 747 (2016).

5. In *Arizona v. Inter Tribal Council of Arizona Inc.*, 570 U.S. 1 (2013), the Court considered the preemptive effect of NVRA's mandate that states "accept and use" the federal voter registration form for elections to federal office. The form did not require evidence of citizenship; rather, it required only that the applicant aver that he was a citizen. Arizona required applicants using the form to present documentary evidence of citizenship. A majority of the Court held that Arizona's citizenship-documentation requirement was preempted by NVRA. The Court held that while the "accept and use" language might be subject to different interpretations, the "fairest reading of the statute is that a state-imposed requirement of evidence of

citizenship not required by the Federal form" was inconsistent with the federal statutory mandate.

The Court observed that the Elections Clause, art. I, § 4, cl. 1, imposes upon states the duty to prescribe the times, places, and manner of elections to the House and Senate, while conferring power upon Congress to alter or to supplant those regulations, including regulations dealing with voter registration. The Clause thus "empowers Congress to regulate *how* federal elections are held, but not *who* may vote in them." 570 U.S. at 16. Because the Clause "*necessarily* displaces some element of a pre-existing legal regime erected by" a state, the Court held that the traditional presumption against interpreting a federal statute to preempt state laws did not apply. *Id.* at 14. The Court suggested that Arizona could request the Election Assistance Commission to alter the federal form to include additional information. *See id.* at 19–20. For litigation filed as a result of the latter observation, see *Kobach v. United States Election Assistance Comm'n*, 772 F.3d 1183 (10th Cir. 2014) (affirming the EAC's refusal to change the federal form), *cert. denied*, 135 S. Ct. 2891 (2015). For a critique of whether and to what extent states should be able to set different standards for voter eligibility in state and federal elections, see Michael T. Morley, *Dismantling the Unitary Electoral System?: Uncooperative Federalism in State and Local Elections*, 111 Nw. U. L. Rev. 103 (2017).

6. Is federal regulation of the voting process at the state level, even limited to federal elections, always a good idea? Is that regulation inappropriately skewed in one direction? Commentators from various political persuasions have noted problems with an expanding federal presence in this regard. *See, e.g.*, Blackwell & Klukowski, *supra*, at 114 (noting that the NVRA and HAVA have facilitated voter registration and the casting of ballots, but arguing that one "looks in vain for [federal laws] strengthening the integrity of the ballot box"); Daniel J. Tokaji, *The Future of Election Reform: From Rules to Institutions*, 28 Yale L. & Pol'y Rev. 125, 146 (2009) (arguing that federal mandates on states should not be imposed without providing for significant federal administrative oversight). An alternative to significant federal oversight would be to encourage states to compete in a race to the top to improve voting systems. To a degree, HAVA and other provisions of federal law already attempt to do that. Another way is to measure and publicize comparative information about state election systems, as proposed in Heather K. Gerken, The Democracy Index: Why Our Election System Is Failing and How to Fix It (2009).

2. The Electoral College

As discussed above, federal law places constraints on states when state-run elections decide who shall serve in federal offices. The system for choosing the President is particularly esoteric. Presidential elections are governed by Article II, § 1 of the Constitution, which establishes the electoral college in this language: "Each State shall appoint, in such Manner as the Legislature thereof may direct, a Number of

Electors, equal to the whole Number of Senators and Representatives to which the State may be entitled in the Congress: but no Senator or Representative, or Person holding an Office of Trust or Profit under the United States, shall be appointed an Elector." Article II, §3, as modified by the Twelfth Amendment, specifies rules for the operation of the electoral college. Section 4 further provides, "The Congress may determine the Time of chusing the Electors, and the Day on which they shall give their Votes; which day shall be the same throughout the United States." Accordingly, the choice of President is made not by the American people directly, but by the electors chosen in each state. Five times in the nation's history (1824 (John Quincy Adams), 1876 (Rutherford B. Hayes), 1888 (Benjamin Harrison), 2000 (George W. Bush), and 2016 (Donald J. Trump))—and twice in the last generation—the candidate who received the most votes in the electoral college, and thus won the presidency, failed to win a plurality of the nation's popular votes.

The electoral college appears to be the product of the Framers' distrust of popular majorities. The Framers thought it unwise to leave the choice of President to the people directly because they would be ill-informed about issues and candidates (particularly those from outside their states). Instead, the state legislatures were to choose (or to choose a method for choosing) electors who would exercise their own independent judgment in electing a president. *See* THE FEDERALIST No. 68 (Alexander Hamilton). That system fell apart nearly as soon as it was instituted, and electors came to be chosen not because their independent judgment was trusted, but because they were known to favor particular presidential candidates. The Supreme Court held in 1952 that it was constitutional for a party to require its electors to commit to supporting the party and its nominees. *See Ray v. Blair*, 343 U.S. 214 (1952). That decision left unresolved the constitutionality of laws constraining the behavior of electors once they were appointed. Many states have laws requiring electors to vote in accordance with the popular vote in those states; electors who vote otherwise—the so-called "faithless electors"—can be removed or, in some instances, punished. Those laws are controversial because they appear to conflict with the reason that the Framers created an electoral college rather than permitting the people to elect the President directly.

Compared to a system giving equal weight to every popular vote, the electoral college is weighted in favor of small states. Each state, no matter how small, receives two senators and at least one representative, and each state has the same number of electors as its senators plus its representatives. And so Wyoming has three electoral votes compared to California's fifty-five, meaning that California has 18.3 times the number of electors that Wyoming has—even though California has 68 times the number of voters that Wyoming has.

Although early practice in the Republic was more diverse (with, for example, some state legislatures choosing electors directly), today every state selects its electors on the basis of the popular vote in that state. Every state except two (Maine and Nebraska) allocates its electors on a winner-take-all basis, meaning that the candidate who receives the most votes in the state receives all the state's electors. (Maine and Nebraska award two electors to the candidate who receives the most votes in the state, and one elector to the candidate who receives the most votes in each of the state's congressional districts.) Thus, in forty-eight states, if it is a foregone conclusion which candidate will receive the most votes in the state, it doesn't matter whether the other candidate receives 0% or 49%—the winner will take all the electors. Strategically, therefore, candidates concentrate on "swing states," where voters are closely divided and an effective campaign could make the difference between defeat and victory. Candidates will not spend much time campaigning in states such as New York, California, Utah, and Idaho, because neither Republicans nor Democrats want to spend time or money in a state where no amount of campaigning would alter the result. Likewise, voters in those states—whether Republican or Democratic—have little incentive to participate, because the election outcome is not in doubt.

The proposed the National Popular Vote Interstate Compact (NPVIC) is an effort to counter these perceived flaws of the electoral college (as well as its generally undemocratic nature), and to replace it with a system that would guarantee the presidency to the winner of the national popular vote. *See generally* National Popular Vote!, *Agreement Among the States to Elect the President by National Popular Vote, at* http://nationalpopularvote.com/written-explanation. The Compact is a proposed agreement among states to award their electors not on the basis of the popular vote in the respective states, but on the basis of the popular vote in the nation as a whole. Thus, if a majority of the national popular vote went to Candidate A, but Candidate B had more votes in State X, under the NPVIC all of State X's electoral votes would go to Candidate A. Because the Compact, by its terms, would go into effect only if enough states joined to yield a majority in the electoral college, the NPVIC would result in the winner of the national popular vote automatically receiving enough electoral votes to become President.

The Compact is controversial for both political and legal reasons. Politically, the NPVIC would take influence away from the swing states and increase the influence of large population centers, regardless of the states in which those centers were located. Indeed, candidates would not be competing to win states at all; rather, they would compete for the most total votes, and an extra vote in California or New York would matter as much as an extra vote in Ohio or Wisconsin. Many (but not all) observers believe that the NPVIC would inure to the advantage of Democrats, and so (of course) there is a partisan dimension to support for, and opposition to, the Compact.

Legally, the NPVIC may be vulnerable to a challenge under Article I, § 10, cl. 3 of the Constitution, which says that "[n]o State shall, without the Consent of Congress, * * * enter into any Agreement or Compact with another State * * *." Because congressional consent is unlikely, the NPVIC would be unconstitutional unless it is not the kind of "Agreement or Compact" covered by the Interstate Compacts Clause. Supporters of the NPVIC argue that the Clause covers only those interstate agreements that would threaten the supremacy of the national government, *see Virginia v. Tennessee*, 148 U.S. 503, 519 (1893), while opponents argue that the NPVIC should require congressional approval because it would disrupt relations between states and undermine the electoral college. For differing opinions on the constitutionality of the NPVIC, compare Akhil Reed Amar, *Some Thoughts on the Electoral College: Past, Present, and Future*, 33 Ohio N.U. L. Rev. 467 (2007); Robert W. Bennett, *Popular Election of the President Without a Constitutional Amendment*, 4 Green Bag 2d 241 (2001); Robert W. Bennett, *State Coordination in Popular Election of the President Without a Constitutional Amendment*, 5 Green Bag 2d 141 (2002); and Jennifer S. Hendricks, *Popular Election of the President: Using or Abusing the Electoral College?*, 7 Election L.J. 218 (2008), with Derek Muller, *The Compact Clause and the National Popular Vote Interstate Compact*, 6 Election L.J. 372 (2007); and Derek Muller, *More Thoughts on the Compact Clause and the National Popular Vote: A Response*, 7 Election L.J. 227 (2008).

McPherson v. Blacker

Supreme Court of the United States.
146 U.S. 1, 13 S. Ct. 3, 36 L. Ed. 869 (1892)

Mr. Chief Justice Fuller * * * delivered the opinion of the court [in which Mr. Justice Field, Mr. Justice Harlan, Mr. Justice Gray, Mr. Justice Blatchford, Mr. Justice Lamar, Mr. Justice Brewer, Mr. Justice Brown, and Mr. Justice Shiras join]. * * *

[Prior to 1892, Michigan allocated its presidential electors on a statewide, winner-take-all basis. In that year, the Michigan legislature passed a law that allocated the electors by congressional district, based on the winner of the popular vote for President in each district. Maine and Nebraska still use versions of this approach. Persons nominated to be presidential electors challenged the scheme in state court on various federal and state-law grounds, which were rejected by the Michigan Supreme Court.]

On behalf of plaintiffs in error it is contended that the act is void because in conflict with (1) clause two of section one of Article II of the Constitution of the United States; (2) the Fourteenth and Fifteenth Amendments to the Constitution; and (3) the act of Congress, of February 3, 1887.

The second clause of section 1 of Article II of the constitution is in these words: "Each State shall appoint, in such Manner as the Legislature thereof may direct, a Number of Electors, equal to the whole Number of Senators and Representatives to which the State may be entitled in the Congress; but no Senator or Representative, or Person holding an Office of Trust or Profit under the United States, shall be appointed an Elector."

The manner of the appointment of electors directed by the act of Michigan is the election of an elector and an alternate elector in each of the twelve Congressional districts into which the State of Michigan is divided, and of an elector and an alternate elector at large in each of two districts defined by the act. It is insisted that it was not competent for the legislature to direct this manner of appointment, because the State is to appoint as a body politic and corporate, and so must act as a unit, and cannot delegate the authority to subdivisions created for the purpose; and it is argued that the appointment of electors by districts is not an appointment by the state, because all its citizens otherwise qualified are not permitted to vote for all the presidential electors.

* * * [A State can act only] through such political agencies as are duly constituted and established. The legislative power is the supreme authority, except as limited by the constitution of the State, and the sovereignty of the people is exercised through their representatives in the legislature, unless by the fundamental law power is else-where reposed. * * * What is forbidden or required to be done by a State is forbidden or required of the legislative power under state constitutions as they exist. The clause under consideration does not read that the people or the citizens shall appoint, but that "each State shall"; and if the words, "in such manner as the legislature thereof may direct," had been omitted, it would seem that the legislative power of appoint-ment could not have been successfully questioned in the absence of any provision in the state constitution in that regard. Hence the insertion of those words, while operating as a limitation upon the State in respect of any attempt to circumscribe the legislative power, cannot be held to operate as a limitation on that power itself.

If the legislature possesses plenary authority to direct the manner of appoint-ment, and might itself exercise the appointing power by joint ballot or concur-rence of the two houses, or according to such mode as designated, it is difficult to perceive why, if the legislature prescribes as a method of appointment choice by vote, it must necessarily be by general ticket, and not by districts. In other words, the act of appointment is none the less the act of the State in its entirety because arrived at by districts, for the act is the act of political agencies duly authorized to speak for the state, and the combined result is the expression of the voice of the state, a result reached by direction of the legislature, to whom the whole subject is committed. * * *

Although it is * * * declared [in Article I, § 2 of the Constitution] that the people of the several States shall choose the members of Congress, (language which induced the State of New York to insert a salvo as to the power to divide into districts, in its resolutions of ratification,) the state legislatures, prior to 1842, in prescribing the times, places, and manner of holding elections for representatives, had usually apportioned the State into districts, and assigned to each a representative; and by act of Congress of June 25, 1842, * * * it was provided that, where a State was entitled to more than one representative, the election should be by districts. It has never been doubted that representatives in Congress thus chosen represented the entire people of the state acting in their sovereign capacity. * * *

The Constitution does not provide that the appointment of electors shall be by popular vote, nor that the electors shall be voted for upon a general ticket, nor that the majority of those who exercise the elective franchise can alone choose the electors. It recognizes that the people act through their representatives in the legislature, and leaves it to the legislature exclusively to define the method of effecting the object.

The framers of the Constitution employed words in their natural sense; and where they are plain and clear, resort to collateral aids to interpretation is unnecessary and cannot be indulged in to narrow or enlarge the text; but where there is ambiguity or doubt, or where two views may well be entertained, contemporaneous and subsequent practical construction are entitled to the greatest weight. Certainly, plaintiffs in error cannot reasonably assert that the clause of the Constitution under consideration so plainly sustains their position as to entitle them to object that contemporaneous history and practical construction are not to be allowed their legitimate force, and, conceding that their argument inspires a doubt sufficient to justify resort to the aids of interpretation thus afforded, we are of opinion that such doubt is thereby resolved against them, the contemporaneous practical exposition of the constitution being too strong and obstinate to be shaken or controlled. *Stuart* v. *Laird*, [5 U.S.] 1 Cranch, 299, 309 [(1803)].

It has been said that the word "appoint" is not the most appropriate word to describe the result of a popular election. Perhaps not; but it is sufficiently comprehensive to cover that mode, and was manifestly used as conveying the broadest power of determination. It was used in Article 5 of the Articles of Confederation, which provided that "delegates shall be annually appointed in such manner as the legislature of each State shall direct;" and in the resolution of Congress of February 21, 1787, which declared it expedient that "a convention of delegates who shall have been appointed by the several States," should be held. The appointment of delegates was, in fact, made by the legislatures directly, but that involved no denial of authority to direct some other mode. The Constitutional Convention, by resolution of September 17, 1787, expressed the opinion that the Congress should fix a day "on which electors should be appointed by the states which shall have ratified the same," etc., and that, "after such publication, the electors should be appointed, and the senators and representatives elected."

The Journal of the Convention discloses that propositions that the President should be elected by "the citizens of the United States," or by the "people," or "by electors to be chosen by the people of the several States," instead of by the Congress, were voted down, as was the proposition that the President should be "chosen by electors appointed for that purpose by the legislatures of the States," though at one time adopted. And a motion to postpone the consideration of the choice "by the national legislature," in order to take up a resolution providing for electors to be elected by the qualified voters in districts, was negatived in Committee of the Whole. Gerry proposed that the choice should be made by the State executives; Hamilton, that the election be by electors chosen by electors chosen by the people; James Wilson and Gouverneur Morris were strongly in favor of popular vote; Ellsworth and Luther Martin preferred the choice by electors elected by the legislatures;

and Roger Sherman, appointment by Congress. The final result seems to have reconciled contrariety of views by leaving it to the state legislatures to appoint directly by joint ballot or concurrent separate action, or through popular election by districts or by general ticket, or as otherwise might be directed.

Therefore, on reference to contemporaneous and subsequent action under the clause, we should expect to find, as we do, that various modes of choosing the electors were pursued, as, by the legislature itself on joint ballot; by the legislature through a concurrent vote of the two houses; by vote of the people for a general ticket; by vote of the people in districts; by choice partly by the people voting in districts and partly by the legislature; by choice by the legislature from candidates voted for by the people in districts; and in other ways, as, notably, by North Carolina in 1792, and Tennessee in 1796 and 1800. No question was raised as to the power of the State to appoint in any mode its legislature saw fit to adopt, and none that a single method, applicable without exception, must be pursued in the absence of an amendment to the Constitution. The district system was largely considered the most equitable, and Madison wrote that it was that system which was contemplated by the framers of the Constitution, although it was soon seen that its adoption by some States might place them at a disadvantage by a division of their strength, and that a uniform rule was preferable.

From [a] review [of the various ways States chose presidential electors between 1788 and 1892], * * * it is seen that from the formation of the government until now the practical construction of the clause has conceded plenary power to the state legislatures in the matter of the appointment of electors.

Even in the heated controversy of 1876–1877 the electoral vote of Colorado cast by electors chosen by the legislature passed unchallenged, and our attention has not been drawn to any previous attempt to submit to the courts the determination of the constitutionality of state action.

In short, the appointment and mode of appointment of electors belong exclusively to the States under the Constitution of the United States. They are, as remarked by Mr. Justice Gray in *In re Green*, 134 U.S. 377, 379 [(1890)], "no more officers or agents of the United States than are the members of the state legislatures when acting as electors of Federal senators, or the people of the States when acting as the electors of representatives in Congress." Congress is empowered to determine the time of choosing the electors and the day on which they are to give their votes, which is required to be the same day throughout the United States; but otherwise the power and jurisdiction of the state is exclusive, with the exception of the provisions as to the number of electors and the ineligibility of certain persons, so framed that Congressional and Federal influence might be excluded.

The question before us is not one of policy, but of power; and, while public opinion had gradually brought all the States as matter of fact to the pursuit of a uniform system of popular election by general ticket, that fact does not tend to weaken the force of contemporaneous and long continued previous practice when and as different views of expediency prevailed. The prescription of the written law cannot be overthrown because the States have latterly exercised in a particular way a power which they might have exercised in some other way. The construction to which we have referred has prevailed too long and been too uniform to justify us in interpreting the language of the Constitution as conveying any other meaning than that heretofore ascribed, and it must be treated as decisive.

It is argued that the district mode of choosing electors, while not obnoxious to constitutional objection, if the operation of the electoral system had conformed to its original object and purpose, had become so in view of the practical working of that system. Doubtless it was supposed that the electors would exercise a reasonable independence and fair judgment in the selection of the Chief Executive, but experience soon demonstrated that, whether chosen by the legislatures or by popular suffrage on general ticket or in districts, they were so chosen simply to register the will of the appointing power in respect of a particular candidate. In relation, then, to the independence of the electors the original expectation may be said to have been frustrated. But we can perceive no reason for holding that the power confided to the States by the Constitution has ceased to exist because the operation of the system has not fully realized the hopes of those by whom it was created. Still less can we recognize the doctrine, that because the Constitution has been found in the march of time sufficiently comprehensive to be applicable to conditions not within the minds of its framers, and not arising in their time, it may, therefore, be wrenched from the subjects expressly embraced within it, and amended by judicial decision without action by the designated organs in the mode by which alone amendments can be made.

Nor are we able to discover any conflict between this act and the Fourteenth and Fifteenth Amendments to the Constitution. * * * If presidential electors are appointed by the legislatures, no discrimination is made; if they are elected in districts where each citizen has an equal right to vote, the same as any other citizen has, no discrimination is made. Unless the authority vested in the legislatures by the second clause of section 1 of Article II has been divested and the State has lost its power of appointment, except in one manner, the position taken on behalf of relators is untenable, and it is apparent that neither of these amendments can be given such effect.

The third clause of section 1 of Article II of the Constitution is: "The Congress may determine the time of choosing the Electors, and the day on which they shall give their votes; which day shall be the same throughout the United States." * * *

By the act of Congress of February 3, 1887, entitled "An act to fix the day for the meeting of the electors of President and Vice President," etc., it was provided that the electors of each State should meet and give their votes on the second Monday in January next following their appointment. The state law in question here fixes the first Wednesday of December as the day for the meeting of the electors, as originally designated by Congress. In this respect it is in conflict with the act of Congress, and must necessarily give way. But this part of the act is not so inseparably connected in substance with the other parts as to work the destruction of the whole act. Striking out the day for the meeting, which had already been otherwise determined by the act of Congress, the act remains complete in itself, and capable of being carried out in accordance with the legislative intent. The state law yields only to the extent of the collision. The construction to this effect by the state court is of persuasive force, if not of controlling weight. * * *

We repeat that the main question arising for consideration is one of power and not of policy, and we are unable to arrive at any other conclusion than that the act of the legislature of Michigan of May 1, 1891, is not void as in contravention of the Constitution of the United States, for want of power in its enactment.

The judgment of the Supreme Court of Michigan must be

Affirmed.

Notes and Questions

1. What limits apply to the power of state legislatures to determine the manner of selecting electors? Could a state legislature limit or prohibit women or African Americans from voting in presidential elections or from serving as electors? Most people, we assume, would say no, and would point to the Fourteenth, Fifteenth, and Nineteenth Amendments, not to mention the Voting Rights Act and other laws. But can *McPherson* be interpreted to permit such restraints on the discretion of the state legislatures?[f] What if a state legislature directly appointed electors and, in doing so, refused to consider women or African Americans? Note that *McPherson* did consider the effect of the Fourteenth and Fifteenth Amendments, concluding that direct appointment of electors by state legislatures could not violate either Amendment, and that popular elections would likewise be constitutional so long as "each citizen has an equal right to vote."

If those Amendments prohibit state legislatures from discriminating on the basis of race, sex, and perhaps other characteristics, does the First Amendment prohibit state legislatures from discriminating on the basis of political ideology or partisan affiliation? Would the answer depend on whether electors were chosen by appointment or by popular election?

2. May state constitutions constrain state legislatures in selecting presidential electors? As you will see when you read *Bush v. Gore*, 531 U.S. 98 (2000) [p. 1085],

---

f. An analogous question is whether there are limits to Congress's power to make exceptions to the appellate jurisdiction of the Supreme Court. *See* U.S. Const. art. III, § 2, cl. 2. While the constitutional text provides no limitations, it is generally understood that there are, at a minimum, "external" limitations (*i.e.*, outside of Article III) that prevent Congress from stripping the Court of jurisdiction in a way that would, for example, violate equal protection. *See United States v. Klein*, 80 U.S. 128 (1872) (holding unconstitutional a "jurisdictional" limitation that would have undermined the President's pardon power).

one of the issues in the case was the claim that the Florida Supreme Court had usurped the Florida Legislature's role in choosing presidential electors by adopting an implausible interpretation of state election law. Does the U.S. Constitution forbid other branches of states' governments from interfering too much with the choices of the state legislatures?

Likewise, consider proposals to choose presidential electors based on the proportion of the statewide popular vote cast for each candidate, rather than through a winner-take-all system. Could a state, consistent with Article II, adopt such a system by citizen initiative, rather than by action by the state legislature? See Nicholas P. Stabile, Comment, *An End Run Around a Representative Democracy? The Unconstitutionality of a Ballot Initiative to Alter the Method of Distributing Electors*, 103 Nw. U. L. Rev. 1495 (2009).

3. Does the opinion in *McPherson* support or undermine the National Popular Vote Interstate Compact? If state legislatures have the plenary power to appoint electors, may they appoint electors on the basis of the national popular vote, even if it is contrary to the popular vote in their states and even if the NPVIC undermines the way the electoral college functioned in the past?

4. Do state legislatures have any power to control the behavior of electors once appointed? Electors are usually chosen because of their political commitments and loyalty, so it is rare for an elector to vote contrary to expectations. Occasionally, however, a "faithless elector" casts a ballot for a candidate other than the one who received the most votes in the state. May a state constitutionally remove a faithless elector and replace him or her with someone who will vote in the desired way? May a state simply refuse to accept a vote for the "wrong" candidate? May a state impose civil or criminal penalties on a faithless elector?

Chiafalo v. Washington

Supreme Court of the United States

591 U.S. __, 140 S. Ct. 2316, __ L. Ed. 2d. __ (2020)

Justice Kagan delivered the opinion of the Court [in which Chief Justice Roberts, Justice Ginsburg, Justice Breyer, Justice Alito, Justice Sotomayor, Justice Gorsuch, and Justice Kavanaugh join].

Every four years, millions of Americans cast a ballot for a presidential candidate. Their votes, though, actually go toward selecting members of the Electoral College, whom each State appoints based on the popular returns. Those few "electors" then choose the President.

The States have devised mechanisms to ensure that the electors they appoint vote for the presidential candidate their citizens have preferred. With two partial exceptions, every State appoints a slate of electors selected by the political party whose candidate has won the State's popular vote. Most States also compel electors to pledge in advance to support the nominee of that party. This Court upheld such a pledge requirement decades ago, rejecting the argument that the Constitution "demands absolute freedom for the elector to vote his own choice." *Ray v. Blair*, 343 U.S. 214, 228 (1952).

Today, we consider whether a State may also penalize an elector for breaking his pledge and voting for someone other than the presidential candidate who won his State's popular vote. We hold that a State may do so.

I * * *

* * * Article II, § 1, cl. 2 says:

> "Each State shall appoint, in such Manner as the Legislature thereof may direct, a Number of Electors, equal to the whole Number of Senators and Representatives to which the State may be entitled in the Congress: but no Senator or Representative, or Person holding an Office of Trust or Profit under the United States, shall be appointed an Elector."

* * * In the Nation's earliest elections, state legislatures mostly picked the electors, with the majority party sending a delegation of its choice to the Electoral College. By 1832, though, all States but one had introduced popular presidential elections. At first, citizens voted for a slate of electors put forward by a political party, expecting that the winning slate would vote for its party's presidential (and vice presidential) nominee in the Electoral College. By the early 20th century, citizens in most States voted for the presidential candidate himself; ballots increasingly did not even list the electors. After the popular vote was counted, States appointed the electors chosen by the party whose presidential nominee had won statewide, again expecting that they would vote for that candidate in the Electoral College.[1]

In the 20th century, many States enacted statutes meant to guarantee that outcome—that is, to prohibit so-called faithless voting. Rather than just assume that party-picked electors would vote for their party's winning nominee, those States insist that they do so. As of now, 32 States and the District of Columbia have such statutes on their books. They are typically called pledge laws because most demand that electors take a formal oath or pledge to cast their ballot for their party's presidential (and vice presidential) candidate. Others merely impose that duty by law. Either way, the statutes work to ensure that the electors vote for the candidate who got the most statewide votes in the presidential election.

---

1. Maine and Nebraska (which, for simplicity's sake, we will ignore after this footnote) developed a more complicated system in which two electors go to the winner of the statewide vote and one goes to the winner of each congressional district. See Me. Rev. Stat. Ann., Tit. 21–A, § 802; Neb. Rev. Stat. § 32–710. So, for example, if the Republican candidate wins the popular vote in Nebraska as a whole but loses to the Democratic candidate in one of the State's three congressional districts, the Republican will get four electors and the Democrat will get one. Here too, though, the States use party slates to pick the electors, in order to reflect the relevant popular preferences (whether in the State or in an individual district).

Most relevant here, States began about 60 years ago to back up their pledge laws with some kind of sanction. By now, 15 States have such a system.[2] Almost all of them immediately remove a faithless elector from his position, substituting an alternate whose vote the State reports instead. A few States impose a monetary fine on any elector who flouts his pledge.

Washington is one of the 15 States with a sanctions backed pledge law designed to keep the State's electors in line with its voting citizens. As all States now do, Washington requires political parties fielding presidential candidates to nominate a slate of electors. On Election Day, the State gives voters a ballot listing only the candidates themselves. When the vote comes in, Washington moves toward appointing the electors chosen by the party whose candidate won the statewide count. But before the appointment can go into effect, each elector must "execute [a] pledge" agreeing to "mark [her] ballots" for the presidential (and vice presidential) candidate of the party nominating her. [Wash. Rev. Code] § 29A.56.084. And the elector must comply with that pledge, or else face a sanction. At the time relevant here, the punishment was a civil fine of up to $1,000. See § 29A.56.340.[3]

This case involves three Washington electors who violated their pledges in the 2016 presidential election. That year, Washington's voters chose Hillary Clinton over Donald Trump for President. The State thus appointed as its electors the nominees of the Washington State Democratic Party. Among those Democratic electors were petitioners Peter Chiafalo, Levi Guerra, and Esther John (the Electors). All three pledged to support Hillary Clinton in the Electoral College. But as that vote approached, they decided to cast their ballots for someone else. The three hoped they could encourage other electors—particularly those from States Donald Trump had carried—to follow their example. The idea was to deprive him of a majority of electoral votes and throw the election into the House of Representatives. So the three Electors voted for Colin Powell for President. But their effort failed. Only seven electors across the Nation cast faithless votes—the most in a century, but well short of the goal. Candidate Trump became President Trump. And, more to the point here, the State fined the Electors $1,000 apiece for breaking their pledges to support the same candidate its voters had.

The Electors challenged their fines in state court, arguing that the Constitution gives members of the Electoral College the right to vote however they please. The

2. Ariz. Rev. Stat. Ann. § 16–212; Cal. Elec. Code Ann. §§ 6906, 18002; Colo. Rev. Stat. § 1–4–304; Ind. Code § 3–10–4–9; Mich. Comp. Laws § 168.47; Minn. Stat. §§ 208.43, 208.46; Mont. Code Ann. §§ 13–25–304, 13–25–307; Neb. Rev. Stat. §§ 32–713, 32–714; Nev. Rev. Stat. §§ 298.045, 298.075; N.M. Stat. Ann. § 1–15–9; N.C. Gen. Stat. Ann. § 163–212; Okla. Stat., Tit. 26, §§ 10–102, 10–109; S.C. Code Ann. § 7–19–80; Utah Code § 20A–13–304; Wash. Rev. Code §§ 29A.56.084, 29A.56.090.

3. Since the events in this case, Washington has repealed the fine. It now enforces pledges only by removing and replacing faithless electors. See Wash. Rev. Code § 29A.56.090(3).

Washington Superior Court rejected the Electors' claim in an oral decision, and the State's Supreme Court affirmed that judgment. * * *

II

[T]his Court has considered elector pledge requirements before. Some seventy years ago Edmund Blair tried to become a presidential elector in Alabama. Like all States, Alabama lodged the authority to pick electors in the political parties fielding presidential candidates. And the Alabama Democratic Party required a pledge phrased much like Washington's today. No one could get on the party's slate of electors without agreeing to vote in the Electoral College for the Democratic presidential candidate. Blair challenged the pledge mandate. He argued that the "intention of the Founders was that [presidential] electors should exercise their judgment in voting." *Ray*, 343 U.S., at 225. The pledge requirement, he claimed, "interfere[d] with the performance of this constitutional duty to select [a president] according to the best judgment of the elector." *Ibid.*

Our decision in *Ray* rejected that challenge. "Neither the language of Art. II, § 1, nor that of the Twelfth Amendment," we explained, prohibits a State from appointing only electors committed to vote for a party's presidential candidate. *Ibid.* Nor did the Nation's history suggest such a bar. To the contrary, "[h]istory teaches that the electors were expected to support the party nominees" as far back as the earliest contested presidential elections. *Id.*, at 228. "[L]ongstanding practice" thus "weigh[ed] heavily" against Blair's claim. *Id.*, at 228–230. And current voting procedures did too. The Court noted that by then many States did not even put electors' names on a presidential ballot. *See id.*, at 229. The whole system presupposed that the electors, because of either an "implied" or an "oral pledge," would vote for the candidate who had won the State's popular election. *Ibid.*

Ray, however, reserved a question not implicated in the case: Could a State enforce those pledges through legal sanctions? *See id.*, at 230. Or would doing so violate an elector's "constitutional freedom" to "vote as he may choose" in the Electoral College? *Ibid.* Today, we take up that question. We uphold Washington's penalty-backed pledge law for reasons much like those given in *Ray*. The Constitution's text and the Nation's history both support allowing a State to enforce an elector's pledge to support his party's nominee—and the state voters' choice—for President.

Article II, § 1's appointments power gives the States far-reaching authority over presidential electors, absent some other constitutional constraint. As noted earlier, each State may appoint electors "in such Manner as the Legislature thereof may direct." Art. II, § 1, cl. 2. This Court has described that clause as "conveying the broadest power of determination" over who becomes an elector. *McPherson v. Blacker*, 146 U.S. 1, 27 (1892) [p. 1065]. And the power to appoint an elector (in any manner) includes power to condition his appointment—that is, to say what the elector must do for the appointment to take effect. A State can require, for example, that an elector live in the State or qualify as a regular voter during the relevant time period. Or more substantively, a State can insist (as *Ray* allowed) that the elector pledge to cast his Electoral College ballot for his party's presidential nominee, thus tracking the State's popular vote. See *Ray*, 343 U.S., at 227 (a pledge requirement "is an exercise of the state's right to appoint electors in such manner" as it chooses). Or—so long as nothing else in the Constitution poses an obstacle—a State can add, as Washington did, an associated condition of appointment: It can demand that the elector actually live up to his pledge, on pain of penalty. Which is to say that the State's appointment power, barring some outside constraint, enables the enforcement of a pledge like Washington's.[6]

And nothing in the Constitution expressly prohibits States from taking away presidential electors' voting discretion as Washington does. * * * The Framers could have done it differently; other constitutional drafters of their time did. In the founding era, two States—Maryland and Kentucky—used electoral bodies selected by voters to choose state senators (and in Kentucky's case, the Governor too). The Constitutions of both States, Maryland's drafted just before and Kentucky's just after the U.S. Constitution, incorporated language that would have made this case look quite different. Both state Constitutions required all electors to take an oath "to elect without favour, affection, partiality, or prejudice, such persons for Senators, as they, in their judgment and conscience, believe best qualified for the office." The emphasis on independent "judgment and conscience" called for the exercise of elector discretion. But although the Framers knew of Maryland's Constitution, no language of that kind made it into the document they drafted.

The Electors argue that three simple words stand in for more explicit language about discretion. Article II, § 1 first names the members of the Electoral College: "electors." The Twelfth Amendment then says that electors shall "vote" and that they shall do so by "ballot." The "plain meaning" of those terms, the Electors say, requires electors to have "freedom of choice." If the States could control their votes, "the electors would not be 'Electors,' and their 'vote by Ballot' would not be a 'vote.'"

But those words need not always connote independent choice. Suppose a person always votes in the way his spouse, or pastor, or union tells him to. We might question his judgment, but we would have no problem saying that he "votes" or fills in a "ballot." In those cases, the choice is in someone else's hands, but the words still apply because they can signify a mechanical act. Or similarly, suppose in a system allowing proxy voting (a common practice in the founding era), the proxy acts on clear instructions from the principal, with no freedom of choice. Still, we might

---

6. The concurring opinion would have us make fine distinctions among state laws punishing faithless voting — treating some as conditions of appointment and others not, depending on small semantic differences. The Electors themselves raised no such argument, and they were right not to do so. No matter the precise phrasing, a law penalizing faithless voting (like a law merely barring that practice) is an exercise of the State's power to impose conditions on the appointment of electors. See *Ray v. Blair*, 343 U.S. [at] 227.

well say that he cast a "ballot" or "voted," though the preference registered was not his own. For that matter, some elections give the voter no real choice because there is only one name on a ballot (consider an old Soviet election, or even a down-ballot race in this country). Yet if the person in the voting booth goes through the motions, we consider him to have voted. The point of all these examples is to show that although voting and discretion are usually combined, voting is still voting when discretion departs. Maybe most telling, switch from hypotheticals to the members of the Electoral College. For centuries now, as we'll later show, almost all have considered themselves bound to vote for their party's (and the state voters') preference. Yet there is no better description for what they do in the Electoral College than "vote" by "ballot." And all these years later, everyone still calls them "electors"—and not wrongly, because even though they vote without discretion, they do indeed elect a President.

The Electors and their *amici* object that the Framers using those words expected the Electors' votes to reflect their own judgments. Hamilton praised the Constitution for entrusting the Presidency to "men most capable of analyzing the qualities" needed for the office, who would make their choices "under circumstances favorable to deliberation." The Federalist No. 68, p. 410 (C. Rossiter ed. 1961). So too, John Jay predicted that the Electoral College would "be composed of the most enlightened and respectable citizens," whose choices would reflect "discretion and discernment." *Id.*, No. 64, at 389.

But even assuming other Framers shared that outlook, it would not be enough. Whether by choice or accident, the Framers did not reduce their thoughts about electors' discretion to the printed page. All that they put down about the electors was what we have said: that the States would appoint them, and that they would meet and cast ballots to send to the Capitol. Those sparse instructions took no position on how independent from—or how faithful to—party and popular preferences the electors' votes should be. On that score, the Constitution left much to the future. And the future did not take long in coming. Almost immediately, presidential electors became trusty transmitters of other people's decisions. * * *

Begin at the beginning—with the Nation's first contested election in 1796. Would-be electors declared themselves for one or the other party's presidential candidate. * * * In some States, legislatures chose the electors; in others, ordinary voters did. But in either case, the elector's declaration of support for a candidate—essentially a pledge—was what mattered. Or said differently, the selectors of an elector knew just what they were getting—not someone who would deliberate in good Hamiltonian fashion, but someone who would vote for their party's candidate. * * * And when the time came to vote in the Electoral College, all but one elector did what everyone expected, faithfully representing their selectors' choice of presidential candidate.[7]

---

7. The reaction to even that single elector goes to prove the point that the system was non-discretionary. In the 1796 election, Pennsylvania held a statewide vote for electors under a winner-take-all rule (as all but two States have today). The people voted narrowly for the slate of electors

The Twelfth Amendment embraced this new reality—both acknowledging and facilitating the Electoral College's emergence as a mechanism not for deliberation but for party-line voting. [T]he Amendment grew out of a pair of fiascos—the election of [John Adams and Thomas Jefferson,] two then-bitter rivals as President and Vice President [in 1796], and the tie vote [in 1800 between Jefferson and Aaron Burr] that threw the next election into the House. Both had occurred because the Constitution's original voting procedures gave electors two votes for President, rather than one apiece for President and Vice President. Without the capacity to vote a party ticket for the two offices, the electors had foundered, and could do so again. If the predominant party's electors used both their votes on their party's two candidates, they would create a tie (see 1800). If they intentionally cast fewer votes for the intended vice president, they risked the opposite party's presidential candidate sneaking into the second position (see 1796). By allowing the electors to vote separately for the two offices, the Twelfth Amendment made party-line voting safe. The Amendment thus advanced, rather than resisted, the practice that had arisen in the Nation's first elections. An elector would promise to legislators or citizens to vote for their party's presidential and vice presidential candidates—and then follow through on that commitment. Or as the Court wrote in *Ray*, the new procedure allowed an elector to "vote the regular party ticket" and thereby "carry out the desires of the people" who had sent him to the Electoral College. *Ray*, 343 U.S., at 224, n.11. No independent electors need apply. * * *

State election laws evolved to reinforce that development, ensuring that a State's electors would vote the same way as its citizens. As noted earlier, state legislatures early dropped out of the picture; by the mid-1800s, ordinary voters chose electors. Except that increasingly, they did not do so directly. States listed only presidential candidates on the ballot, on the understanding that electors would do no more than vote for the winner. Usually, the State could ensure that result by appointing electors chosen by the winner's party. But to remove any doubt, States began in the early 1900s to enact statutes requiring electors to pledge that they would squelch any urge to break ranks with voters. Washington's law, penalizing a pledge's breach, is only another in the same vein. It reflects a tradition more than two centuries old. In that practice, electors are not free agents; they are to vote for the candidate whom the State's voters have chosen.

The history going the opposite way is one of anomalies only. The Electors stress that since the founding, electors have cast some 180 faithless votes for either

---

supporting Jefferson. But Federalist chicanery led to the Governor's inclusion of two Federalist electors in the State's delegation to the Electoral College. One of them, Samuel Miles, agreed to cast his vote for Jefferson, in line with the winner-take-all expectation on which the race had been run. If he thought other Federalists would forgive him for acting with honor, he was wrong. An irate voter reacted: "[W]hen I voted for the [Federalist] ticket, I voted for John Adams. . . . What! do I chuse Samuel Miles to determine for me whether John Adams or Thomas Jefferson is the fittest man for President of the United States? No—I chuse him to *act*, not to *think*." See Gazette of the United States, Dec. 15, 1796, p. 3, col. 1 (emphasis in original).

President or Vice President. But that is 180 out of over 23,000. And more than a third of the faithless votes come from 1872, when the Democratic Party's nominee (Horace Greeley) died just after Election Day.[8] Putting those aside, faithless votes represent just one-half of one percent of the total. Still, the Electors counter, Congress has counted all those votes. But because faithless votes have never come close to affecting an outcome, only one has ever been challenged. True enough, that one was counted. But the Electors cannot rest a claim of historical tradition on one counted vote in over 200 years. And anyway, the State appointing that elector had no law requiring a pledge or otherwise barring his use of discretion. Congress's deference to a state decision to tolerate a faithless vote is no ground for rejecting a state decision to penalize one. * * *

The judgment of the Supreme Court of Washington is

Affirmed.

JUSTICE THOMAS, with whom JUSTICE GORSUCH joins as to Part II, concurring in the judgment.

The Court correctly determines that States have the power to require Presidential electors to vote for the candidate chosen by the people of the State. I disagree, however, with its attempt to base that power on Article II. In my view, the Constitution is silent on States' authority to bind electors in voting. I would resolve this case by simply recognizing that "[a]ll powers that the Constitution neither delegates to the Federal Government nor prohibits to the States are controlled by the people of each State." *U.S. Term Limits, Inc. v. Thornton,* 514 U.S. 779, 848 (1995) [p. 538] (THOMAS, J., dissenting).

I * * *

In a somewhat cursory analysis, the Court concludes that the States' duty to appoint electors "in such Manner as the Legislature thereof may direct," Art. II, § 1, cl. 2, provides an express grant of "power to appoint an elector." [T]his interpretation erroneously conflates the imposition of a duty with the granting of a power. But even setting that issue aside, I cannot agree with the Court's analysis. The Court appears to misinterpret Article II, § 1, by overreading its language as authorizing the broad power to impose and enforce substantive conditions on appointment. The

---

8. The Electors contend that elector discretion is needed to deal with the possibility that a future presidential candidate will die between Election Day and the Electoral College vote. We do not dismiss how much turmoil such an event could cause. In recognition of that fact, some States have drafted their pledge laws to give electors voting discretion when their candidate has died. See, *e.g.,* Cal. Elec. Code Ann. § 6906; Ind. Code § 3–10–4–1.7. And we suspect that in such a case, States without a specific provision would also release electors from their pledge. Still, we note that because the situation is not before us, nothing in this opinion should be taken to permit the States to bind electors to a deceased candidate.

Court then misconstrues the State of Washington's law as enforcing a condition of appointment.

The Court's conclusion that the text of Article II, § 1, expressly grants States the power to impose substantive conditions or qualifications on electors is highly questionable. Its interpretation appears to strain the plain meaning of the text, ignore historical evidence, and give the term "Manner" different meanings in parallel provisions of Article I and Article II.

First, the Court's attempt to root its analysis in Article II, § 1, seems to stretch the plain meaning of the Constitution's text. Article II, § 1, provides that States shall appoint electors "in such Manner as the Legislature thereof may direct." * * * [This language] suggest[s] that Article II requires state legislatures merely to set the approach for selecting Presidential electors, not to impose substantive limitations on whom [*sic*] may become an elector. And determining the "Manner" of appointment certainly does not include the power to impose requirements as to how the electors vote *after they are appointed*, which is what the Washington law addresses. * * *

Historical evidence from the founding also suggests that the "Manner" of appointment refers to the method for selecting electors, rather than the substantive limitations placed on the position. * * *

Finally, the Court's interpretation gives the same term—"Manner"—different meanings in two parallel provisions of the Constitution. Article I, § 4, states that "[t]he Times, Places and Manner of holding Elections for Senators and Representatives, shall be prescribed in each State by the Legislature thereof." In *U.S. Term Limits*, the Court concluded that the term "Manner" in Article I includes only "a grant of authority to issue procedural regulations," not "the broad power to set qualifications." 514 U.S., at 832–833. Yet, today, the Court appears to take the exact opposite view. The Court interprets the term "Manner" in Article II, § 1, to include the power to impose conditions or qualifications on the appointment of electors.

With respect, I demur. "When seeking to discern the meaning of a word in the Constitution, there is no better dictionary than the rest of the Constitution itself." *Arizona State Legislature v. Arizona Independent Redistricting Comm'n*, 576 U.S. 787, 829 (2015) [p. 200] (Roberts, C.J., dissenting). While terms may not always have the exact same meaning throughout the Constitution, here we are interpreting the same word ("Manner") in two provisions that the Court has already stated impose "paralle[l]" duties—setting the "Manner of holding Elections" and setting the "Manner" of "appoint[ing] a Number of Electors." *U.S. Term Limits*, 514 U.S., at 804–805. Nothing in the Constitution's text or history indicates that the Court should take the strongly disfavored step of concluding that the term "Manner" has two different meanings in these closely aligned provisions.

All the Court can point to in support of its position is a single sentence in *Ray v. Blair*, 343 U.S. 214 (1952), which suggested that a State's power to impose a requirement that electors pledge to vote for their party's nominee comes from Article II,

§ 1, *id.*, at 227. But this statement is simply made in passing in response to one of the parties' arguments. It is curiously bereft of reasoning or analysis of Article II. We generally look to the text to govern our analysis rather than insouciantly follow stray, "incomplete" statements in our prior opinions. In my view, we should be guided by the text here.

Even accepting the Court's broad interpretation of Clause 2 of Article II, § 1, I cannot agree with its determination that this Clause expressly authorizes the Washington law at issue here. In an attempt to tie Washington's law to the State's "power to appoint an elector," the Court construes Wash. Rev. Code § 29A.56.340 as "enforc[ing] a pledge." But § 29A.56.340 did not involve the enforcement of a pledge or relate to the appointment process at all. It simply regulated electors' votes, unconnected to the appointment process.

To understand the Court's error, a brief summary of its theory is necessary. According to the Court, Article II, § 1, grants States "the power to appoint" Presidential electors "in such Manner as the Legislature thereof may direct." That "power to appoint an elector," the Court states, "includes power to condition his appointment." The power to condition appointment in turn allows the State to insist that an "elector pledge to cast his Electoral College ballot for his party's presidential nominee." And finally, "the State's appointment power . . . enables the enforcement of a pledge." The Court's theory is entirely premised on the State exercising a power to *appoint*.

Assuming the Court has correctly interpreted Article II, § 1, there are certain circumstances in which this theory could stand. Some States expressly require electors to pledge to vote for a party nominee as a condition of appointment and then impose a penalty if electors violate that pledge. * * * But not all States attempt to bind electors' votes through the appointment process. Some States simply impose a legal duty that has no connection to elector appointment. For example, New Mexico imposes a legal duty on its electors: "All presidential electors shall cast their ballots in the electoral college for the candidates of the political party which nominated them as presidential electors." N.M. Stat. Ann. § 1–15–9(A). And "[a]ny presidential elector who casts his ballot in violation of [this duty] is guilty of a fourth degree felony." § 1–15–9(B). California has a similar system. It first imposes a legal duty on electors to vote for the nominated candidates of the political party they represent if those candidates are alive. Cal. Elec. Code Ann. § 6906. It then imposes a punishment on "[e]very person charged with the performance of any duty under any law of this state relating to elections, who willfully neglects or refuses to perform it." § 18002. These laws penalize electors for their faithless votes. But they do not attempt to regulate the votes of electors through the appointment process. In fact, these laws have nothing to do with elector appointment.

The Court recognizes the distinction between these two types of laws, *i.e.*, laws enforcing appointment conditions and laws that regulate electors outside of the appointment process. But it claims this is merely a "small semantic differenc[e]."

Far from being semantic, the difference between the power to impose a "condition of appointment" and the power to impose restrictions on electors *that have nothing to do with appointment* is fundamental to the Court's textual argument. The Court's entire analysis is premised on States' purported Article II "power to appoint an elector" and "to condition his appointment." The Court does not, and cannot, claim that the text of Article II provides States power over anything other than the *appointment* of electors.

Here, the challenged Washington law did not enforce any appointment condition. It provided that "[a]ny elector who votes for a person or persons not nominated by the party of which he or she is an elector is subject to a civil penalty of up to one thousand dollars." [A] violation of § 29A.56.340 was not predicated on violating a pledge or any other condition of appointment. In fact, it did not even mention a pledge, which was set forth in a separate, unreferenced provision. See § 29A.56.320. Thus, § 29A.56.340 had no connection to the appointment process and could be enforced independent of the existence of any pledge requirement. While the Court's description of § 29A.56.340 as a law enforcing a condition of appointment may be helpful for the Court's claim that Washington's law was rooted in Article II, § 1's "power to appoint," it is simply not accurate. Thus, even accepting the Court's strained reading of Article II, § 1's text, I cannot agree with the Court's effort to reconcile Washington's law with its desired theory.

In short, the Constitution does not speak to States' power to require Presidential electors to vote for the candidates chosen by the people. The Court's attempt to ground such a power in Article II's text falls short. Rather than contort the language of both Article II and the state statute, I would acknowledge that the Constitution simply says nothing about the States' power in this regard.

II

When the Constitution is silent, authority resides with the States or the people. This allocation of power is both embodied in the structure of our Constitution and expressly required by the Tenth Amendment. The application of this fundamental principle should guide our decision here. * * *

As the Court recognizes, nothing in the Constitution prevents States from requiring Presidential electors to vote for the candidate chosen by the people. Petitioners ask us to infer a constitutional right to elector independence by interpreting the terms "appoint," "Electors," "vote," and "by Ballot" to align with the Framers' expectations of discretion in elector voting. But the Framers' *expectations* aid our interpretive inquiry only to the extent that they provide evidence of the original public meaning of the Constitution. They cannot be used to change that meaning. As the Court explains, the plain meaning of the terms relied on by petitioners do not appear to "connote independent choice." Thus, "the original expectation[s]" of the Framers as to elector discretion provide "no reason for holding that the power confided to the States by the Constitution has ceased to exist." *McPherson*, 146 U.S., at 36. * * *

Notes and Questions

1. Was the Court faithful to the original understanding of the constitutional provisions establishing the electoral college? The Court noted that the Constitution did not "expressly" or "explicit[ly]" prohibit states from binding electors to the states' respective popular votes, and the language that the Constitution did contain "took no position on how independent from—or how faithful to—party and popular preferences the electors' votes should be." Justice Thomas similarly argued that "the plain meaning of the [Constitution's] terms" did not impose limits on the states' ability to restrict electors' voting choices, and without such a textual indication, the contrary "expectations" of the Framers should be disregarded.

But is it proper to view the Constitution as silent on the question whether electors are entitled to vote independently? Is it plausible that the Framers would have forced state legislatures to choose electors (rather than allowing the state legislatures to cast votes for President directly) if the states could require the electors to vote a certain way? Why couldn't "original public meaning" be discerned from the constitutional structure, rather than from explicit language? *Cf., e.g., U.S. Term Limits, Inc. v. Thornton*, 514 U.S. 779, 806 (1995) [p. 538] ("[T]he text and structure of the Constitution, the relevant historical materials, and, most importantly, the 'basic principles of our democratic system' all demonstrate that the Qualifications Clauses were intended to preclude the States from exercising any such power and to fix as exclusive the qualifications in the Constitution.") (quoting *Powell v. McCormack*, 395 U.S. 486, 548 (1969)); *Morrison v. Olson*, 487 U.S. 654, 703–04 (1988) (Scalia, J., dissenting) ("The Court devotes most of its attention to such relatively technical details as the Appointments Clause and the removal power, addressing briefly and only at the end of its opinion the separation of powers. * * * I think that has it backwards."); *United States v. Nixon*, 418 U.S. 683, 711 (1974) ("Nowhere in the Constitution * * * is there any explicit reference to a privilege of confidentiality [for presidential communications], yet to the extent this interest relates to the effective discharge of a President's powers, it is constitutionally based."); *McCulloch v. Maryland*, 17 U.S. (4 Wheat.) 316, 406 (1819) ("Among the enumerated powers, we do not find that of establishing a bank or creating a corporation. But there is no phrase in the [Constitution] which, like the Articles of Confederation, excludes incidental or implied powers and which requires that everything granted shall be expressly and minutely described.").

2. If a state joined the National Popular Vote Interstate Compact, which is discussed in the notes before *McPherson*, could it require its electors to vote in accordance with the national popular vote, even if a different candidate received more votes in the state?

3. The Court said that "the power to appoint an elector (in any manner) includes power to condition his appointment. * * * [S]o long as nothing else in the Constitution poses an obstacle[,] a State can add, as Washington did, an associated condition of appointment: It can demand that the elector actually live up to his

pledge, on pain of penalty." The Court cited no authority for its conclusion that Washington could not only impose a condition on appointment but could also control the elector's conduct after the appointment. Does it follow from states' appointing authority that they also have the power to direct the performance of the elector while in office? Does such an authority extend to other appointed officials in the government? *Cf. Morrison v. Olson, supra* (upholding the independence of the independent counsel); *Humphrey's Executor v. United States*, 295 U.S. 602 (1935) (protecting the independence of members of the Federal Trade Commission from the control of the President). Surely the Court did not mean to suggest that the President's power to appoint federal judges gave him the authority to control judges' behavior in office. In the days before the Seventeenth Amendment, could a state legislature recall its U.S. Senator in the middle of his six-year term if it were unhappy with his performance in office? No Senator was ever recalled, and recall authority would appear quite inconsistent with the rationale of *U.S. Term Limits*. Can *Chiafalo* be squared with *Term Limits*? *See* Mike Rappaport, *The Originalist Disaster in* Chiafalo, Law & Liberty (Aug. 7, 2020), http://lawliberty.org/the-originalist-disaster-in-chiafalo/.

4. Should the number of faithless electors in the country's history have been relevant to the question of whether the Constitution protected electors' independence? If so, does the fact that there have been 180 faithless electors out of 23,000 indicate that there is historical support for electors' independence, or can those 180 electors be dismissed as "anomalies"?

5. Is there a difference between, on the one hand, a law that requires electors to pledge to vote for a candidate and then punishes electors who break that pledge, and, on the other, a law that does not require a pledge but directly requires electors to vote for the winner of the state's popular vote and punishes electors who fail to do so? Is that a merely "semantic difference[]," as the Court charged, or is it "fundamental to the Court's textual argument," as Justice Thomas argued?

E. Counting the Votes

We have discussed voter registration, districting, campaigns, and voting itself. Now it is time to discuss vote-counting. This section addresses two aspects of that fundamentally important topic: the standards to determine whether to count a vote and the rules for determining the results.

1. Constitutional Constraints on Vote-Counting

While most choices about the methods of casting and tabulating votes are made at the state and local levels, federal law—including the Constitution—imposes limits on those choices. For example, the Fifteenth and Nineteenth Amendments forbid race and sex discrimination, respectively, in voting, and the Equal Protection

Clause prohibits states from discriminating against other groups without sufficient justification. *See, e.g., Kramer v. Union Free School District No. 15*, 395 U.S. 621 (1969) [p. 46]; *Harper v. Virginia State Board of Elections*, 383 U.S. 663 (1966) [p. 17]; *Carrington v. Rash*, 380 U.S. 89 (1965) [p. 71].

The next case—the Supreme Court's decision striking down Florida's recount procedures in the 2000 presidential election between Republican George W. Bush and Democrat Al Gore—is undoubtedly the most famous instance of federal-court oversight of states' vote-counting processes. The case held that the Equal Protection Clause prevented states from making arbitrary distinctions in the tabulation of identically marked ballots.

Some background is necessary. While Gore had a substantial lead in the nation-wide popular vote, the electoral college was much closer. As election night came to an end, it became clear that the winner of Florida's electoral votes would win the Presidency. Initial counts there showed that Bush had prevailed by 1784 votes out of approximately six million cast. But that was just the beginning.

The closeness of the election triggered a recount under state law. A machine recount was held, with Governor Bush determined still to be the winner. Vice President Gore then asked for a manual recount, prompting controversy over the procedures governing such a recount. In particular, authorities in Florida were obligated to divine the intent of voters by interpreting marks on ballots, and different vote-counters used different standards to assess whether the marks sufficiently indicated an intent to cast a vote. Whether the differences in vote-counting were consistent with the constitutional guarantee of "the equal protection of the laws" was the principal question ultimately faced by the Supreme Court in the opinion that follows.

But *Bush v. Gore* was not the Supreme Court's first entry into the 2000 election controversy. In *Bush v. Palm Beach County Canvassing Board*, 531 U.S. 70 (2000) (*per curiam*) (*Bush I*), the Court was presented with a challenge to the recount deadline established by the Florida Supreme Court. The Florida court, after noting the Florida Constitution's protection of the right to vote and the importance of counting every vote, had imposed a deadline of November 26, despite the relevant statutes' apparent selection of November 14. The secretary of state objected that the court's reliance on the state constitution undermined the legislature's choice in violation of Article II, § 1, cl. 2 of the United States Constitution, which vests authority for determining the method of selecting presidential electors in state legislatures.

The Supreme Court did not decide the Article II issue, though. Instead, it vacated the Florida judgment and remanded to permit the Florida court more clearly to identify the source of its holding. On remand, the Florida Supreme Court maintained that its decision was merely an interpretation of the Florida statutes, and it therefore professed to be following, rather than contravening, the desires of the Florida Legislature. *See Palm Beach County Canvassing Board v. Harris*, 772 So. 2d 1273 (Fla. 2000).

Simultaneously with the recount-deadline litigation, Gore pressed separate election contests seeking manual recounts in two counties, and eventually the Florida

Supreme Court permitted the recounts to go forward. *Gore v. Harris*, 772 So. 2d 1243 (Fla. 2000). Republicans again appealed to the Supreme Court, which by a 5-4 vote stayed the lower court decision while the appeal was briefed and argued. *Bush v. Gore*, 531 U.S. 1046 (2000). As described in the opinion, the controversy in *Bush II* swirled around Florida's voting technology, the use of different ballot forms in different counties, and the process of conducting the recount that was mandated by Florida law, but *Bush I*'s concerns about the respective roles of courts and legislatures were not far in the background.

Bush v. Gore

Supreme Court of the United States
531 U.S. 98, 121 S. Ct. 525, 148 L. Ed. 2d 388 (2000).

PER CURIAM. [CHIEF JUSTICE REHNQUIST, JUSTICE O'CONNOR, JUSTICE SCALIA, JUSTICE KENNEDY, and JUSTICE THOMAS join in this opinion.] * * *

* * * On November 8, 2000, the day following the Presidential election, the Florida Division of Elections reported that petitioner Bush had received 2,909,135 votes, and respondent Gore had received 2,907,351 votes, a margin of 1,784 for Governor Bush. Because Governor Bush's margin of victory was less than "one-half of a percent . . . of the votes cast," an automatic machine recount was conducted under § 102.141(4) of the election code, the results of which showed Governor Bush still winning the race but by a diminished margin. Vice President Gore then sought manual recounts in Volusia, Palm Beach, Broward, and Miami-Dade Counties, pursuant to Florida's election protest provisions. * * *

On November 26, the Florida Elections Canvassing Commission certified the results of the election and declared Governor Bush the winner of Florida's 25 electoral votes. On November 27, Vice President Gore, pursuant to Florida's contest provisions, filed a complaint in Leon County Circuit Court contesting the certification. He sought relief pursuant to [Fla. Stat. Ann.] § 102.168(3)(c), which provides that "[r]eceipt of a number of illegal votes or rejection of a number of legal votes sufficient to change or place in doubt the result of the election" shall be grounds for a contest. The Circuit Court denied relief, stating that Vice President Gore failed to meet his burden of proof. He appealed to the First District Court of Appeal, which certified the matter to the Florida Supreme Court.

Accepting jurisdiction, the Florida Supreme Court affirmed in part and reversed in part. The court held that the Circuit Court had been correct to reject Vice President Gore's challenge to the results certified in Nassau County and his challenge to the Palm Beach County Canvassing Board's determination that 3,300 ballots cast in that county were not, in the statutory phrase, "legal votes."

The Supreme Court held that Vice President Gore had satisfied his burden of proof under § 102.168(3)(c) with respect to his challenge to Miami-Dade County's failure to tabulate, by manual count, 9,000 ballots on which the machines had failed to detect a vote for President ("undervotes"). Noting the closeness of the election, the court explained that "[o]n this record, there can be no question that there are legal votes within the 9,000 uncounted votes sufficient to place the results of this election in doubt." A "legal vote," as determined by the Supreme Court, is "one in which there is a 'clear indication of the intent of the voter.'" The court therefore ordered a hand recount of the 9,000 ballots in Miami-Dade County. * * *

The petition presents the following questions: whether the Florida Supreme Court established new standards for resolving Presidential election contests, thereby violating Art. II, § 1, cl. 2, of the United States Constitution and failing to comply with 3 U.S.C. § 5, and whether the use of standardless manual recounts violates the Equal Protection and Due Process Clauses. With respect to the equal protection question, we find a violation of the Equal Protection Clause. * * *

The individual citizen has no federal constitutional right to vote for electors for the President of the United States unless and until the state legislature chooses a statewide election as the means to implement its power to appoint members of the electoral college. U.S. Const., Art. II, § 1. This is the source for the statement in *McPherson* v. *Blacker*, 146 U.S. 1, 35 (1892) [p. 1065], that the state legislature's power to select the manner for appointing electors is plenary; it may, if it so chooses, select the electors itself, which indeed was the manner used by state legislatures in several States for many years after the framing of our Constitution. History has now favored the voter, and in each of the several States the citizens themselves vote for Presidential electors. When the state legislature vests the right to vote for President in its people, the right to vote as the legislature has prescribed is fundamental; and one source of its fundamental nature lies in the equal weight accorded to each vote and the equal dignity owed to each voter. The State, of course, after granting the franchise in the special context of Article II, can take back the power to appoint electors. See *id.*, at 35 ("[T]here is no doubt of the right of the legislature to resume the power at any time, for it can neither be taken away nor abdicated").

The right to vote is protected in more than the initial allocation of the franchise. Equal protection applies as well to the manner of its exercise. Having once granted the right to vote on equal terms, the State may not, by later arbitrary and disparate treatment, value one person's vote over that of another. See, *e.g.*, *Harper v. Virginia Bd. of Elections*, 383 U.S. 663, 665 (1966) [p. 17] ("[O]nce the franchise is granted to the electorate, lines may not be drawn which are inconsistent with the Equal Protection Clause of the Fourteenth Amendment"). It must be remembered that "the right of suffrage can be denied by a debasement or dilution of the weight of a citizen's vote just as effectively as by wholly prohibiting the free exercise of the franchise." *Reynolds* v. *Sims*, 377 U.S. 533, 555 (1964) [p. 122].

There is no difference between the two sides of the present controversy on these basic propositions. Respondents say that the very purpose of vindicating the right to vote justifies the recount procedures now at issue. The question before us, however, is whether the recount procedures the Florida Supreme Court has adopted are consistent with its obligation to avoid arbitrary and disparate treatment of the members of its electorate.

Much of the controversy seems to revolve around ballot cards designed to be perforated by a stylus but which, either through error or deliberate omission, have not been perforated with sufficient precision for a machine to register the perforations. In some cases a piece of the card—a chad—is hanging, say, by two corners. In other cases there is no separation at all, just an indentation.

* * * The recount mechanisms implemented in response to the decisions of the Florida Supreme Court do not satisfy the minimum requirement for nonarbitrary treatment of voters necessary to secure the fundamental right. Florida's basic command for the count of legally cast votes is to consider the "intent of the voter." This is unobjectionable as an abstract proposition and a starting principle. The problem inheres in the absence of specific standards to ensure its equal application. The formulation of uniform rules to determine intent based on these recurring circumstances is practicable and, we conclude, necessary.

The law does not refrain from searching for the intent of the actor in a multitude of circumstances; and in some cases the general command to ascertain intent is not susceptible to much further refinement. In this instance, however, the question is not whether to believe a witness but how to interpret the marks or holes or scratches on an inanimate object, a piece of cardboard or paper which, it is said, might not have registered as a vote during the machine count. The factfinder confronts a thing, not a person. The search for intent can be confined by specific rules designed to ensure uniform treatment.

The want of those rules here has led to unequal evaluation of ballots in various respects. See [*Gore* v. *Harris*, 772 So. 2d 1243,] 1267 [(Fla. 2000)] (Wells, C.J., dissenting) ("Should a county canvassing board count or not count a 'dimpled chad' where the voter is able to successfully dislodge the chad in every other contest on that ballot? Here, the county canvassing boards disagree"). As seems to have been acknowledged at oral argument, the standards for accepting or rejecting contested ballots might vary not only from county to county but indeed within a single county from one recount team to another.

The record provides some examples. A monitor in Miami-Dade County testified at trial that he observed that three members of the county canvassing board applied different standards in defining a legal vote. And testimony at trial also revealed that at least one county changed its evaluative standards during the counting process. Palm Beach County, for example, began the process with a 1990 guideline which precluded counting completely attached chads, switched to a rule that considered a vote to be legal if any light could be seen through a chad, changed back to the 1990 rule, and then abandoned any pretense of a *per se* rule, only to have a court order that the county consider dimpled chads legal. This is not a process with sufficient guarantees of equal treatment. * * *

The State Supreme Court * * * mandated that the recount totals from two counties, Miami-Dade and Palm Beach, be included in the certified total. The court also appeared to hold *sub silentio* that the recount totals from Broward County, which were not completed until after the original November 14 certification by the Secretary, were to be considered part of the new certified vote totals even though the county certification was not contested by Vice President Gore. Yet each of the counties used varying standards to determine what was a legal vote. Broward County used a more forgiving standard than Palm Beach County, and uncovered almost three times as many new votes, a result markedly disproportionate to the difference in population between the counties.

In addition, the recounts in these three counties were not limited to so-called undervotes but extended to all of the ballots. The distinction has real consequences. A manual recount of all ballots identifies not only those ballots which show no vote but also those which contain more than one, the so-called overvotes. Neither category will be counted by the machine. This is not a trivial concern. At oral argument, respondents estimated there are as many as 110,000 overvotes statewide. As a result, the citizen whose ballot was not read by a machine because he failed to vote for a candidate in a way readable by a machine may still have his vote counted in a manual recount; on the other hand, the citizen who marks two candidates in a way discernible by the machine will not have the same opportunity to have his vote count, even if a manual examination of the ballot would reveal the requisite indicia of intent. Furthermore, the citizen who marks two candidates, only one of which is discernible by the machine, will have his vote counted even though it should have been read as an invalid ballot. The State Supreme Court's inclusion of vote counts based on these variant standards exemplifies concerns with the remedial processes that were under way.

That brings the analysis to yet a further equal protection problem. The votes certified by the court included a partial total from one county, Miami-Dade. The Florida Supreme Court's decision thus gives no assurance that the recounts included in a final certification must be complete. Indeed, it is respondents' submission that it would be consistent with the rules of the recount procedures to include whatever partial counts are done by the time of final certification, and we interpret the Florida Supreme Court's decision to permit this. * * * This accommodation no doubt results from the truncated contest period established by the Florida Supreme Court in *Palm Beach County Canvassing Bd.* v. *Harris*, at respondents' own urging. The press of time does not diminish the constitutional concern. A desire for speed is not a general excuse for ignoring equal protection guarantees.

In addition to these difficulties the actual process by which the votes were to be counted under the Florida Supreme Court's decision raises further concerns. That order did not specify who would recount the ballots. The county canvassing boards were forced to pull together ad hoc teams of judges from various Circuits who had no previous training in handling and interpreting ballots. Furthermore, while others were permitted to observe, they were prohibited from objecting during the recount.

The recount process, in its features here described, is inconsistent with the minimum procedures necessary to protect the fundamental right of each voter in the special instance of a statewide recount under the authority of a single state judicial officer. Our consideration is limited to the present circumstances, for the problem of equal protection in election processes generally presents many complexities.

The question before the Court is not whether local entities, in the exercise of their expertise, may develop different systems for implementing elections. Instead, we are presented with a situation where a state court with the power to assure uniformity has ordered a statewide recount with minimal procedural safeguards. When a court orders a statewide remedy, there must be at least some assurance that the rudimentary requirements of equal treatment and fundamental fairness are satisfied. * * *

Upon due consideration of the difficulties identified to this point, it is obvious that the recount cannot be conducted in compliance with the requirements of equal protection and due process without substantial additional work. It would require not only the adoption (after opportunity for argument) of adequate statewide standards for determining what is a legal vote, and practicable procedures to implement them, but also orderly judicial review of any disputed matters that might arise. In addition, the Secretary has advised that the recount of only a portion of the ballots requires that the vote tabulation equipment be used to screen out undervotes, a function for which the machines were not designed. If a recount of overvotes were also required, perhaps even a second screening would be necessary. Use of the equipment for this purpose, and any new software developed for it, would have to be evaluated for accuracy by the Secretary, as required by Fla. Stat. Ann. § 101.015.

The Supreme Court of Florida has said that the legislature intended the State's electors to "participat[e] fully in the federal electoral process," as provided in 3 U.S.C. § 5. [*Palm Beach County Canvassing Bd. v. Harris,*] 772 So. 2d [1273,] 1289 [(Fla. 2000) *(Harris II)*]; see also *Palm Beach County Canvassing Bd. v. Harris*, 772 So. 2d 1220, 1237 (Fla. 2000) [*(Harris I)*]. That statute, in turn, requires that any controversy or contest that is designed to lead to a conclusive selection of electors be completed by December 12. That date is upon us, and there is no recount procedure in place under the State Supreme Court's order that comports with minimal constitutional standards. Because it is evident that any recount seeking to meet the December 12 date will be unconstitutional for the reasons we have discussed, we reverse the judgment of the Supreme Court of Florida ordering a recount to proceed.

Seven Justices of the Court agree that there are constitutional problems with the recount ordered by the Florida Supreme Court that demand a remedy. See *post* (SOUTER, J., dissenting); *post* (BREYER, J., dissenting). The only disagreement is as to the remedy. Because the Florida Supreme Court has said that the Florida Legislature intended to obtain the safe-harbor benefits of 3 U.S.C. § 5, JUSTICE BREYER's proposed remedy—remanding to the Florida Supreme Court for its ordering of a constitutionally proper contest until December 18—contemplates action in violation of the Florida Election Code, and hence could not be part of an "appropriate" order authorized by Fla. Stat. Ann. § 102.168(8). * * *

None are more conscious of the vital limits on judicial authority than are the Members of this Court, and none stand more in admiration of the Constitution's design to leave the selection of the President to the people, through their legislatures, and to the political sphere. When contending parties invoke the process of the courts, however, it becomes our unsought responsibility to resolve the federal and constitutional issues the judicial system has been forced to confront.

The judgment of the Supreme Court of Florida is reversed, and the case is remanded for further proceedings not inconsistent with this opinion.

It is so ordered.

CHIEF JUSTICE REHNQUIST, with whom JUSTICE SCALIA and JUSTICE THOMAS join, concurring. * * *

We deal here not with an ordinary election, but with an election for the President of the United States. * * *

In most cases, comity and respect for federalism compel us to defer to the decisions of state courts on issues of state law. That practice reflects our understanding that the decisions of state courts are definitive pronouncements of the will of the States as sovereigns. Of course, in ordinary cases, the distribution of powers among the branches of a State's government raises no questions of federal constitutional law, subject to the requirement that the government be republican in character. See U.S. Const., Art. IV, § 4. But there are a few exceptional cases in which the Constitution imposes a duty or confers a power on a particular branch of a State's government. This is one of them. Article II, § 1, cl. 2, provides that "[e]ach State shall appoint, in such Manner as the *Legislature* thereof may direct," electors for President and Vice President. (Emphasis added.) Thus, the text of the election law itself, and not just its interpretation by the courts of the States, takes on independent significance. * * *

In order to determine whether a state court has infringed upon the legislature's authority, we necessarily must examine the law of the State as it existed prior to the action of the court. Though we generally defer to state courts on the interpretation of state law, there are of course areas in which the Constitution requires this Court to undertake an independent, if still deferential, analysis of state law. * * *

This inquiry does not imply a disrespect for state *courts* but rather a respect for the constitutionally prescribed role of state *legislatures.* To attach definitive weight to the pronouncement of a state court, when the very question at issue is whether the court has actually departed from the statutory meaning, would be to abdicate our responsibility to enforce the explicit requirements of Article II.

Acting pursuant to its constitutional grant of authority, the Florida Legislature has created a detailed, if not perfectly crafted, statutory scheme that provides for appointment of Presidential electors by direct election. * * *

The state legislature has also provided mechanisms both for protesting election returns and for contesting certified election results. Section 102.166 governs protests. Any protest must be filed prior to the certification of election results by the county canvassing board. § 102.166(4)(b). Once a protest has been filed, "[t]he county canvassing board may authorize a manual recount." § 102.166(4)(c). If a sample recount conducted pursuant to § 102.166(5) "indicates an error in the vote tabulation which could affect the outcome of the election," the county canvassing board is instructed to: "(a) Correct the error and recount the remaining precincts with the vote tabulation system; (b) Request the Department of State to verify the tabulation software; or (c) Manually recount all ballots," § 102.166(5). In the event a canvassing board chooses to conduct a manual recount of all ballots, § 102.166(7) prescribes procedures for such a recount.

Contests to the certification of an election, on the other hand, are controlled by § 102.168. The grounds for contesting an election include "[r]eceipt of a number of illegal votes or rejection of a number of legal votes sufficient to change or place in doubt the result of the election." § 102.168(3)(c). * * * In Presidential elections, the contest period necessarily terminates on the date set by 3 U.S.C. § 5 for concluding the State's "final determination" of election controversies.

In its first decision, *Harris I*, the Florida Supreme Court extended the 7-day statutory certification deadline established by the legislature. This modification of the code, by lengthening the protest period, necessarily shortened the contest period for Presidential elections. Underlying the extension of the certification deadline and the shortchanging of the contest period was, presumably, the clear implication that certification was a matter of significance: The certified winner would enjoy presumptive validity, making a contest proceeding by the losing candidate an uphill battle. In its latest opinion, however, the court empties certification of virtually all legal consequence during the contest, and in doing so departs from the provisions enacted by the Florida Legislature.

The court determined that canvassing boards' decisions regarding whether to recount ballots past the certification deadline (even the certification deadline established by *Harris I*) are to be reviewed *de novo*, although the Election Code clearly vests discretion whether to recount in the boards, and sets strict deadlines subject to the Secretary's rejection of late tallies and monetary fines for tardiness. See Fla. Stat. Ann. § 102.112. Moreover, the Florida court held that all late vote tallies arriving during the contest period should be automatically included in the certification regardless of the certification deadline (even the certification deadline established by *Harris I*), thus virtually eliminating both the deadline and the Secretary's discretion to disregard recounts that violate it.

Moreover, the court's interpretation of "legal vote," and hence its decision to order a contest-period recount, plainly departed from the legislative scheme. Florida statutory law cannot reasonably be thought to *require* the counting of improperly marked ballots. Each Florida precinct before election day provides instructions on how properly to cast a vote, Fla. Stat. Ann. § 101.46; each polling place on election day contains a working model of the voting machine it uses, Fla. Stat. Ann. § 101.5611; and each voting booth contains a sample ballot, § 101.46. In precincts using punchcard ballots, voters are instructed to punch out the ballot cleanly:

> "AFTER VOTING, CHECK YOUR BALLOT CARD TO BE SURE YOUR VOTING SELECTIONS ARE CLEARLY AND CLEANLY PUNCHED AND THERE ARE NO CHIPS LEFT HANGING ON THE BACK OF THE CARD."

No reasonable person would call it "an error in the vote tabulation," Fla. Stat. Ann. § 102.166(5), or a "rejection of . . . legal votes," § 102.168(3)(c), when electronic or electromechanical equipment performs precisely in the manner designed, and fails to count those ballots that are not marked in the manner that these voting instructions explicitly and prominently specify. The scheme that the Florida Supreme Court's opinion attributes to the legislature is one in which machines are *required* to be "capable of correctly counting votes," § 101.5606(4), but which nonetheless regularly produces elections in which legal votes are predictably *not* tabulated, so that in close elections manual recounts are regularly required. This is of course absurd. The Secretary, who is authorized by law to issue binding interpretations of the Election Code, §§ 97.012, 106.23, rejected this peculiar reading of the statutes. The Florida Supreme Court, although it must defer to the Secretary's interpretations, rejected her reasonable interpretation and embraced the peculiar one.

But as we indicated in our remand of the earlier case, in a Presidential election the clearly expressed intent of the legislature must prevail. And there is no basis for reading the Florida statutes as requiring the counting of improperly marked ballots, as an examination of the Florida Supreme Court's textual analysis shows. We will not parse that analysis here, except to note that the principal provision of the Election Code on which it relied, § 101.5614(5), was * * * entirely irrelevant. The State's Attorney General (who was supporting the Gore challenge) confirmed in oral argument here that never before the present election had a manual recount been conducted on the basis of the contention that "undervotes" should have been examined to determine voter intent. For the court to step away from this established practice, prescribed by the Secretary, the state official charged by the legislature with "responsibility to . . . [o]btain and maintain uniformity in the application, operation, and interpretation of the election laws," § 97.012(1), was to depart from the legislative scheme. * * *

Given all these factors, and in light of the legislative intent identified by the Florida Supreme Court to bring Florida within the "safe harbor" provision of 3 U.S.C. § 5, the remedy prescribed by the Supreme Court of Florida cannot be deemed an "appropriate" one as of December 8. It significantly departed from the statutory framework in place on November 7, and authorized open-ended further proceedings which could not be completed by December 12, thereby preventing a final determination by that date.

For these reasons, in addition to those given in the *per curiam* opinion, we would reverse.

JUSTICE STEVENS, with whom JUSTICE GINSBURG and JUSTICE BREYER join, dissenting. * * *

The federal questions that ultimately emerged in this case are not substantial. Article II provides that "[e]ach *State* shall appoint, in such Manner as the Legislature *thereof* may direct, a Number of Electors." *Ibid.* (emphasis added). It does not create state legislatures out of whole cloth, but rather takes them as they come — as creatures born of, and constrained by, their state constitutions. Lest there be any doubt, we stated over 100 years ago in *McPherson v. Blacker*, 146 U.S., [at] 25, that "[w]hat is forbidden or required to be done by a State" in the Article II context "is forbidden or required of the legislative power under state constitutions as they exist." * * * The legislative power in Florida is subject to judicial review pursuant to Article V of the Florida Constitution, and nothing in Article II of the Federal Constitution frees the state legislature from the constraints in the State Constitution that created it. Moreover, the Florida Legislature's own decision to employ a unitary code for all elections indicates that it intended the Florida Supreme Court to play the same role in Presidential elections that it has historically played in resolving electoral disputes. The Florida Supreme Court's exercise of appellate jurisdiction therefore was wholly consistent with, and indeed contemplated by, the grant of authority in Article II.

It hardly needs stating that Congress, pursuant to 3 U.S.C. § 5, did not impose any affirmative duties upon the States that their governmental branches could "violate." Rather, § 5 provides a safe harbor for States to select electors in contested elections "by judicial or other methods" established by laws prior to the election day. Section 5, like Article II, assumes the involvement of the state judiciary in interpreting state election laws and resolving election disputes under those laws. Neither § 5 nor Article II grants federal judges any special authority to substitute their views for those of the state judiciary on matters of state law.

Nor are petitioners correct in asserting that the failure of the Florida Supreme Court to specify in detail the precise manner in which the "intent of the voter," Fla. Stat. Ann. § 101.5614(5), is to be determined rises to the level of a constitutional violation.[2] We found such a violation when individual votes within the same State were

---

2. The Florida statutory standard is consistent with the practice of the majority of States, which apply either an "intent of the voter" standard or an "impossible to determine the elector's choice" standard in ballot recounts. * * *

weighted unequally, see, *e.g.*, *Reynolds v. Sims*, 377 U.S., [at] 568, but we have never before called into question the substantive standard by which a State determines that a vote has been legally cast. And there is no reason to think that the guidance provided to the factfinders, specifically the various canvassing boards, by the "intent of the voter" standard is any less sufficient—or will lead to results any less uniform—than, for example, the "beyond a reasonable doubt" standard employed every day by ordinary citizens in courtrooms across this country.

Admittedly, the use of differing substandards for determining voter intent in different counties employing similar voting systems may raise serious concerns. Those concerns are alleviated—if not eliminated—by the fact that a single impartial magistrate will ultimately adjudicate all objections arising from the recount process. Of course, as a general matter, "[t]he interpretation of constitutional principles must not be too literal. We must remember that the machinery of government would not work if it were not allowed a little play in its joints." *Bain Peanut Co. of Tex.* v. *Pinson*, 282 U.S. 499, 501 (1931) (Holmes, J.). If it were otherwise, Florida's decision to leave to each county the determination of what balloting system to employ—despite enormous differences in accuracy[4]—might run afoul of equal protection. So, too, might the similar decisions of the vast majority of state legislatures to delegate to local authorities certain decisions with respect to voting systems and ballot design.

Even assuming that aspects of the remedial scheme might ultimately be found to violate the Equal Protection Clause, I could not subscribe to the majority's disposition of the case. As the majority explicitly holds, once a state legislature determines to select electors through a popular vote, the right to have one's vote counted is of constitutional stature. As the majority further acknowledges, Florida law holds that all ballots that reveal the intent of the voter constitute valid votes. Recognizing these principles, the majority nonetheless orders the termination of the contest proceeding before all such votes have been tabulated. Under their own reasoning, the appropriate course of action would be to remand to allow more specific procedures for implementing the legislature's uniform general standard to be established.

In the interest of finality, however, the majority effectively orders the disenfranchisement of an unknown number of voters whose ballots reveal their intent—and are therefore legal votes under state law—but were for some reason rejected by ballot-counting machines. It does so on the basis of the deadlines set forth in Title 3 of the United States Code. But, as I have already noted, those provisions merely provide rules of decision for Congress to follow when selecting among conflicting slates of electors. They do not prohibit a State from counting what the majority concedes

---

4. The percentage of nonvotes in this election in counties using a punchcard system was 3.92%; in contrast, the rate of error under the more modern optical-scan systems was only 1.43%. Put in other terms, for every 10,000 votes cast, punchcard systems result in 250 more nonvotes than optical-scan systems. A total of 3,718,305 votes were cast under punchcard systems, and 2,353,811 votes were cast under optical-scan systems.

to be legal votes until a bona fide winner is determined. Indeed, in 1960, Hawaii appointed two slates of electors and Congress chose to count the one appointed on January 4, 1961, well after the Title 3 deadlines. Thus, nothing prevents the majority, even if it properly found an equal protection violation, from ordering relief appropriate to remedy that violation without depriving Florida voters of their right to have their votes counted. As the majority notes, "[a] desire for speed is not a general excuse for ignoring equal protection guarantees."

Finally, neither in this case, nor in its earlier opinion in [*Harris I*] did the Florida Supreme Court make any substantive change in Florida electoral law. Its decisions were rooted in long-established precedent and were consistent with the relevant statutory provisions, taken as a whole. It did what courts do — it decided the case before it in light of the legislature's intent to leave no legally cast vote uncounted. In so doing, it relied on the sufficiency of the general "intent of the voter" standard articulated by the state legislature, coupled with a procedure for ultimate review by an impartial judge, to resolve the concern about disparate evaluations of contested ballots. If we assume — as I do — that the members of that court and the judges who would have carried out its mandate are impartial, its decision does not even raise a colorable federal question.

What must underlie petitioners' entire federal assault on the Florida election procedures is an unstated lack of confidence in the impartiality and capacity of the state judges who would make the critical decisions if the vote count were to proceed. Otherwise, their position is wholly without merit. The endorsement of that position by the majority of this Court can only lend credence to the most cynical appraisal of the work of judges throughout the land. It is confidence in the men and women who administer the judicial system that is the true backbone of the rule of law. Time will one day heal the wound to that confidence that will be inflicted by today's decision. One thing, however, is certain. Although we may never know with complete certainty the identity of the winner of this year's Presidential election, the identity of the loser is perfectly clear. It is the Nation's confidence in the judge as an impartial guardian of the rule of law.

I respectfully dissent.

JUSTICE SOUTER, with whom JUSTICE BREYER joins, * * * dissenting. * * *

Petitioners have raised an equal protection claim (or, alternatively, a due process claim), in the charge that unjustifiably disparate standards are applied in different electoral jurisdictions to otherwise identical facts. It is true that the Equal Protection Clause does not forbid the use of a variety of voting mechanisms within a jurisdiction, even though different mechanisms will have different levels of effectiveness in recording voters' intentions; local variety can be justified by concerns about cost, the potential value of innovation, and so on. But evidence in the record here suggests that a different order of disparity obtains under rules for determining a voter's intent that have been applied (and could continue to be applied) to identical types of ballots used in identical brands of machines and exhibiting identical physical characteristics (such as "hanging" or "dimpled" chads). I can conceive of no legitimate state interest served by these differing treatments of the expressions of voters' fundamental rights. The differences appear wholly arbitrary.

In deciding what to do about this, we should take account of the fact that electoral votes are due to be cast in six days. I would therefore remand the case to the courts of Florida with instructions to establish uniform standards for evaluating the several types of ballots that have prompted differing treatments, to be applied within and among counties when passing on such identical ballots in any further recounting (or successive recounting) that the courts might order.

Unlike the majority, I see no warrant for this Court to assume that Florida could not possibly comply with this requirement before the date set for the meeting of electors, December 18. * * *

I respectfully dissent.

Justice Ginsburg, with whom Justice Stevens joins, and with whom Justice Souter and Justice Breyer join as to Part I, dissenting.

I

The Chief Justice acknowledges that provisions of Florida's Election Code "may well admit of more than one interpretation." But instead of respecting the state high court's province to say what the State's Election Code means, The Chief Justice maintains that Florida's Supreme Court has veered so far from the ordinary practice of judicial review that what it did cannot properly be called judging. My colleagues have offered a reasonable construction of Florida's law. Their construction coincides with the view of one of Florida's seven Supreme Court justices. I might join The Chief Justice were it my commission to interpret Florida law. But disagreement with the Florida court's interpretation of its own State's law does not warrant the conclusion that the justices of that court have legislated. There is no cause here to believe that the members of Florida's high court have done less than "their mortal best to discharge their oath of office," and no cause to upset their reasoned interpretation of Florida law. * * *

No doubt there are cases in which the proper application of federal law may hinge on interpretations of state law. Unavoidably, this Court must sometimes examine state law in order to protect federal rights. But we have dealt with such cases ever mindful of the full measure of respect we owe to interpretations of state law by a State's highest court. * * *

II

I agree with Justice Stevens that petitioners have not presented a substantial equal protection claim. Ideally, perfection would be the appropriate standard for judging the recount. But we live in an imperfect world, one in which thousands of votes have not been counted. I cannot agree that the recount adopted by the Florida court, flawed as it may be, would yield a result any less fair or precise than the certification that preceded that recount.

Even if there were an equal protection violation, I would agree with JUSTICE STEVENS, JUSTICE SOUTER, and JUSTICE BREYER that the Court's concern about "the December 12 deadline" is misplaced. * * * Were that date to pass, Florida would still be entitled to deliver electoral votes Congress *must* count unless both Houses find that the votes "ha[d] not been . . . regularly given." * * *

I dissent.

JUSTICE BREYER, with whom JUSTICE STEVENS and JUSTICE GINSBURG join except as to Part I-A-1, and with whom JUSTICE SOUTER joins as to Part I, dissenting.

The Court was wrong to take this case. It was wrong to grant a stay. It should now vacate that stay and permit the Florida Supreme Court to decide whether the recount should resume.

I

The political implications of this case for the country are momentous. But the federal legal questions presented, with one exception, are insubstantial.

A

1

The majority raises three equal protection problems with the Florida Supreme Court's recount order: first, the failure to include overvotes in the manual recount; second, the fact that *all* ballots, rather than simply the undervotes, were recounted in some, but not all, counties; and third, the absence of a uniform, specific standard to guide the recounts. As far as the first issue is concerned, petitioners presented no evidence, to this Court or to any Florida court, that a manual recount of overvotes would identify additional legal votes. The same is true of the second, and, in addition, the majority's reasoning would seem to invalidate any state provision for a manual recount of individual counties in a statewide election.

The majority's third concern does implicate principles of fundamental fairness. The majority concludes that the Equal Protection Clause requires that a manual recount be governed not only by the uniform general standard of the "clear intent of the voter," but also by uniform subsidiary standards (for example, a uniform determination whether indented, but not perforated, "undervotes" should count). The opinion points out that the Florida Supreme Court ordered the inclusion of Broward County's undercounted "legal votes" even though those votes included ballots that were not perforated but simply "dimpled," while newly recounted ballots from other counties will likely include only votes determined to be "legal" on the basis of a stricter standard. In light of our previous remand, the Florida Supreme Court may have been reluctant to adopt a more specific standard than that provided for by the legislature for fear of exceeding its authority under Article II. However, since the use of different standards could favor one or the other of the candidates, since time was, and is, too short to permit the lower courts to iron out significant differences through ordinary judicial review, and since the relevant distinction was embodied in the order of the State's highest court, I agree that, in these very special circumstances, basic principles of fairness may well have counseled the adoption of a uniform standard to address the problem. In light of the majority's disposition, I need not decide whether, or the extent to which, as a remedial matter, the Constitution would place limits upon the content of the uniform standard.

2

Nonetheless, there is no justification for the majority's remedy, which is simply to reverse the lower court and halt the recount entirely. An appropriate remedy would be, instead, to remand this case with instructions that, even at this late date, would permit the Florida Supreme Court to require recounting *all* undercounted votes in Florida, including those from Broward, Volusia, Palm Beach, and Miami-Dade Counties, whether or not previously recounted prior to the end of the protest period, and to do so in accordance with a single uniform standard.

The majority justifies stopping the recount entirely on the ground that there is no more time. In particular, the majority relies on the lack of time for the Secretary of State to review and approve equipment needed to separate undervotes. But the majority reaches this conclusion in the absence of *any* record evidence that the recount could not have been completed in the time allowed by the Florida Supreme Court. * * * Whether there is time to conduct a recount prior to December 18, when the electors are scheduled to meet, is a matter for the state courts to determine. And whether, under Florida law, Florida could or could not take further action is obviously a matter for Florida courts, not this Court, to decide.

By halting the manual recount, and thus ensuring that the uncounted legal votes will not be counted under any standard, this Court crafts a remedy out of proportion to the asserted harm. And that remedy harms the very fairness interests the Court is attempting to protect. The manual recount would itself redress a problem of unequal treatment of ballots. As JUSTICE STEVENS points out, the ballots of voters in counties that use punchcard systems are more likely to be disqualified than those in counties using optical-scanning systems. According to recent news reports, variations in the undervote rate are even more pronounced. Thus, in a system that allows counties to use different types of voting systems, voters already arrive at the polls with an unequal chance that their votes will be counted. I do not see how the fact that this results from counties' selection of different voting machines rather than a court order makes the outcome any more fair. Nor do I understand why the Florida Supreme Court's recount order, which helps to redress this inequity, must be entirely prohibited based on a deficiency that could easily be remedied.

B

The remainder of petitioners' claims, which are the focus of THE CHIEF JUSTICE's concurrence, raise no significant federal questions. * * *

II * * *

Of course, the selection of the President is of fundamental national importance. But that importance is political, not legal. And this Court should resist the temptation unnecessarily to resolve tangential legal disputes, where doing so threatens to determine the outcome of the election.

The Constitution and federal statutes themselves make clear that restraint is appropriate. They set forth a road-map of how to resolve disputes about electors, even after an election as close as this one. That road-map foresees resolution of electoral disputes by *state* courts. See 3 U.S.C. §5 (providing that, where a "State shall have provided, by laws enacted prior to [election day], for its final determination of any controversy or contest concerning the appointment of . . . electors . . . by *judicial* or other methods," the subsequently chosen electors enter a safe harbor free from congressional challenge). But it nowhere provides for involvement by the United States Supreme Court.

To the contrary, the Twelfth Amendment commits to Congress the authority and responsibility to count electoral votes. A federal statute, the Electoral Count Act, enacted after the close 1876 Hayes-Tilden Presidential election, specifies that, after States have tried to resolve disputes (through "judicial" or other means), Congress is the body primarily authorized to resolve remaining disputes. See Electoral Count Act of 1887, 3 U.S.C. §§5, 6, and 15. * * * Given this detailed, comprehensive scheme for counting electoral votes, there is no reason to believe that federal law either foresees or requires resolution of such a political issue by this Court. * * *

The decision by both the Constitution's Framers and the 1886 Congress to minimize this Court's role in resolving close federal Presidential elections is as wise as it is clear. However awkward or difficult it may be for Congress to resolve difficult electoral disputes, Congress, being a political body, expresses the people's will far more accurately than does an unelected Court. And the people's will is what elections are about.

Moreover, Congress was fully aware of the danger that would arise should it ask judges, unarmed with appropriate legal standards, to resolve a hotly contested Presidential election contest. Just after the 1876 Presidential election, Florida, South Carolina, and Louisiana each sent two slates of electors to Washington. Without these States, Tilden, the Democrat, had 184 electoral votes, one short of the number required to win the Presidency. With those States, Hayes, his Republican opponent, would have had 185. In order to choose between the two slates of electors, Congress decided to appoint an electoral commission composed of five Senators, five Representatives, and five Supreme Court Justices. * * *

The Commission divided along partisan lines, and the responsibility to cast the deciding vote fell to Justice Bradley. He decided to accept the votes by the Republican electors, and thereby awarded the Presidency to Hayes.

Justice Bradley immediately became the subject of vociferous attacks. Bradley was accused of accepting bribes, of being captured by railroad interests, and of an eleventh-hour change in position after a night in which his house "was surrounded by the carriages" of Republican partisans and railroad officials. * * *

For present purposes, the relevance of this history lies in the fact that the participation in the work of the electoral commission by five Justices, including Justice Bradley, did not lend that process legitimacy. Nor did it assure the public that the process had worked fairly, guided by the law. Rather, it simply embroiled Members of the Court in partisan conflict, thereby undermining respect for the judicial process. And the Congress that later enacted the Electoral Count Act knew it.

This history may help to explain why I think it not only legally wrong, but also most unfortunate, for the Court simply to have terminated the Florida recount. Those who caution judicial restraint in resolving political disputes have described the quintessential case for that restraint as a case marked, among other things, by the "strangeness of the issue," its "intractability to principled resolution," its "sheer momentousness, . . . which tends to unbalance judicial judgment," and "the inner vulnerability, the self-doubt of an institution which is electorally irresponsible and has no earth to draw strength from." Those characteristics mark this case.

At the same time, * * * the Court is not acting to vindicate a fundamental constitutional principle, such as the need to protect a basic human liberty. No other strong reason to act is present. Congressional statutes tend to obviate the need. And, above all, in this highly politicized matter, the appearance of a split decision runs the risk of undermining the public's confidence in the Court itself. That confidence is a public treasure. It has been built slowly over many years, some of which were marked by a Civil War and the tragedy of segregation. It is a vitally necessary ingredient of any successful effort to protect basic liberty and, indeed, the rule of law itself. We run no risk of returning to the days when a President (responding to this Court's efforts to protect the Cherokee Indians) might have said, "John Marshall has made his decision; now let him enforce it!" But we do risk a self-inflicted wound—a wound that may harm not just the Court, but the Nation. * * *

I respectfully dissent.

Notes and Questions

1. It is difficult to overstate the attention and controversy that accompanied the *Bush v. Gore* litigation and its aftermath. The complex litigation that ensued played out over but a few weeks and was predicated on one of the closest presidential elections in American history. For useful overviews, see HOWARD GILLMAN, THE VOTES THAT COUNTED: HOW THE SUPREME COURT DECIDED THE 2000 PRESIDENTIAL ELECTION (2001); ABNER GREENE, UNDERSTANDING THE 2000 ELECTION: A GUIDE TO THE LEGAL BATTLES THAT DECIDED THE PRESIDENCY (2001).

2. It is also difficult to overstate the controversy in the legal academy's response to *Bush v. Gore*. One branch of scholarly response took seriously the doctrinal and

statutory analysis of the various opinions, and subjected them to traditional academic scrutiny. The focal point of much of this literature was whether the equal-protection analysis of the *per curiam* opinion properly followed from *Reynolds v. Sims* and other one-person, one-vote decisions. A second branch of scholarship took the analysis of the opinions (particularly those of the Justices constituting the majority) less seriously, and to varying degrees charged that the decision was a result-oriented attempt by Republican-appointed Justices to install a Republican President. It likewise bears mentioning that the Florida Supreme Court at this time was dominated by Democratic appointees.[g] For an overview and critique of both branches of scholarship, see Richard L. Hasen, *A Critical Guide to* Bush v. Gore *Scholarship*, 7 ANN. REV. POL. SCI. 297 (2004). Most scholars were very critical of the decision, though the decision has not gone unsupported by academics.[h]

3. The Article II rationale applied by the concurring opinion of Chief Justice Rehnquist in *Bush v. Gore* also attracted its share of scholarly attention. *Compare* Hayward H. Smith, *History of the Article II Independent State Legislature Doctrine*, 29 FLA. ST. U. L. REV. 731 (2001) (arguing that the provision was not intended to favor state legislatures to the exclusion of state courts), *and* Harold J. Krent, *Judging Judging: The Problem of Second-Guessing State Judges' Interpretation of State Law in* Bush v. Gore, 29 FLA. ST. U. L. REV. 493 (2001) (arguing that the Florida Supreme Court's construction of state election statutes was plausible), *with* Richard A. Posner, *Florida 2000: A Legal and Statistical Analysis of the Election Deadlock and Ensuing Litigation*, 2000 SUP. CT. REV. 1, 26 (charging that the Florida Supreme Court engaged in a "patent misreading of the election statute"). The Article II issue can come up in other settings, such as when state courts interpret state statutes that regulate other federal elections, and its resolution can implicate related constitutional issues (*e.g.*, Article I, § 4, of the U.S. Constitution, which vests in state legislatures the power to set rules for choosing members of Congress, absent congressional action, *see Arizona State Legislature v. Arizona Independent Redistricting Commission*, 576 U.S. 787 (2015) [p. 200]), and Article V, which gives state legislatures the power to ratify constitutional amendments, *see Coleman v. Miller*, 307 U.S. 433, 446–47 (1939) (dividing equally on the question whether there was jurisdiction to decide if Article V permitted a lieutenant governor to break a tie in favor of ratification)). For discussion of these possibilities, see Richard L. Hasen, *The Democracy Canon*, 62 STAN. L. REV. 69, 113–22 (2009).

---

g. For a small sampling of the enormous scholarly literature, see the numerous essays collected in BUSH V. GORE: THE QUESTION OF LEGITIMACY (Bruce Ackerman ed., 2002); THE VOTE: BUSH, GORE, AND THE SUPREME COURT (Cass R. Sunstein & Richard A. Epstein eds., 2001); and *Symposium, The Law of Presidential Elections: Issues in the Wake of Florida 2000*, 29 FLA. ST. U. L. REV. 325 (2001).

h. *Compare, e.g.*, Jack M. Balkin, Bush v. Gore *and the Boundary Between Law and Politics*, 110 YALE L.J. 1407 (2001), which itself is criticized as being partisan in Robert J. Pushaw, Jr., *Politics, Ideology, and the Academic Assault on* Bush v. Gore, 2 ELECTION L.J. 97 (2003), *with, e.g.*, Einer Elhauge, *The Lessons of Florida 2000*, 110 POL'Y REV. 15 (Dec. 2001 & Jan. 2002); *and* Nelson Lund, Bush v. Gore *at the Dawning of the Age of Obama*, 61 FLA. L. REV. 1101 (2009).

4. Chief Justice Rehnquist and Justices Scalia and Thomas would have held that the Florida Supreme Court's interpretation of that state's election statutes was so unreasonable as to go beyond the judicial role and invade the prerogative of the Florida Legislature to select the manner of appointing presidential electors. Did Chief Justice Rehnquist provide a judicially manageable standard for distinguishing between a judicial interpretation that is "absurd" and one that is merely wrong? Is it possible to develop such a standard?

5. *Problem.* As Justice Stevens pointed out in his dissent, different parts of an individual state often use different methods of tabulating votes, despite the fact that those different methods have different rates of rejecting votes. Is that discrepancy unconstitutional under the majority's reasoning? Suppose Voter A lives in a county that uses optical-scan technology, while Voter B's county uses punchcards. If Justice Stevens's statistics are accurate, it is more than twice as likely that Voter B's vote will be rejected than that Voter A's will. If Voter B brings an equal-protection challenge, should he succeed?

Consider *Stewart v. Blackwell*, 444 F.3d 843 (6th Cir. 2006), in which a divided court struck down Ohio's then-in-use punchcard system for counting votes. *Bush v. Gore* and related cases, the majority held, called for strict scrutiny to be applied to state practices that impaired the right to vote. The dissent argued that *Bush v. Gore* called for the application of rational-basis scrutiny, and in any event was a limited precedent not "designed to fundamentally transform federal election law." *Id.* at 887 (Gilman, J., dissenting). The Sixth Circuit granted the Ohio Secretary of State's motion to rehear the case *en banc*, and then dismissed the case as moot, 473 F.3d 692 (6th Cir. 2007), because Ohio had replaced the punch-card technology. For an extensive analysis of the challenge to Ohio procedures in the case, see Richard B. Saphire & Paul Moke, *Litigating* Bush v. Gore *in the States: Dual Voting Systems and the Fourteenth Amendment*, 51 VILL. L. REV. 229 (2006).

6. *Stewart v. Blackwell* notwithstanding, most challenges to state election procedures under *Bush v. Gore* have failed. *See, e.g., Wexler v. Anderson*, 452 F.3d 1226 (11th Cir. 2006) (holding that Florida's recount procedures for counties employing paperless touch-screen voting machines did not violate equal protection or due process, because strict scrutiny was not appropriate and the state had rational regulatory reasons to employ different recount procedures in counties with different voting machines); *Southwest Voter Registration Project v. Shelley*, 344 F.3d 914 (9th Cir. 2003) (*en banc*) (refusing to enjoin California's gubernatorial recall election despite continued use of punchcard technology); *Sheehan v. Franken*, 767 N.W.2d 453 (Minn. 2009) [p. 1103]; *Miller v. Treadwell*, 245 P.3d 867 (Alaska 2010) (holding write-in votes were properly counted since statutes did not require exact spellings); *SEIU v. Husted*, 698 F.3d 341 (6th Cir. 2012) (*per curiam*) (holding that the state need not count provisional ballots cast in the wrong polling place, even if due to poll-worker error).

7. A few challenges to state election procedures have successfully employed *Bush v. Gore.* Curiously, most have come from Ohio and the Sixth Circuit. *See, e.g.,*

League of Women Voters of Ohio v. Brunner, 548 F.3d 463 (6th Cir. 2008) (holding that problems regarding election administration, voter registration, the training of poll workers, the organization of polling places, the allocation of voting equipment, and other matters violated equal protection and substantive due process); *Northeast Ohio Coalition for the Homeless v. Husted*, 696 F.3d 580 (6th Cir. 2012) (*per curiam*) (addressing disparate treatment of deficient provisional ballots, including those cast in the wrong precinct due to poll-worker error); *Obama for America v. Husted*, 697 F.3d 423 (6th Cir. 2012) (holding that the state could not give only military and overseas voters preferential treatment regarding early absentee voting). *See generally* Richard L. Hasen, *The 2012 Voting Wars, Judicial Backstops, and the Resurrection of Bush v. Gore*, 81 Geo. Wash. L. Rev. 1865 (2013).

Sheehan v. Franken

Supreme Court of Minnesota
767 N.W.2d 453 (Minn. 2009)

Per Curiam. [Justices Page, P.H. Anderson, Meyer, Gildea, and Dietzen join in this opinion, Chief Justice Magnuson and Justice G.B. Anderson taking no part.]

Appellants, incumbent Republican United States Senator Norm Coleman and Cullen Sheehan, filed a notice of election contest under Minn. Stat. § 209.021 (2008), challenging the State Canvassing Board's certification that Democratic-Farmer-Labor challenger Al Franken was entitled to receive a certificate of election as United States Senator following the November 4, 2008 general election. After a trial, the three-judge trial court we appointed to hear the election contest issued its findings of fact, conclusions of law, and order for judgment, concluding that Franken received 312 more legally cast votes than Coleman and that Franken was entitled to a certificate of election for the office of United States Senator. The question presented on appeal is whether the trial court erred in concluding that Al Franken received the most legally cast votes in the election for United States Senator. Because we conclude that appellants have not shown that the trial court's findings of fact are clearly erroneous or that the court committed an error of law or abused its discretion, we affirm.

More than 2.9 million Minnesotans cast ballots in the November general election, including approximately 300,000 who voted or attempted to vote by absentee ballot. On November 18, 2008, the State Canvassing Board accepted the consolidated statewide canvassing report as showing that Coleman received 1,211,565 votes and that Franken received 1,211,359 votes for the office of United States Senator, a margin of 206 votes in Coleman's favor. Because the margin separating the two candidates was less than one-half of one percent of the total number of votes counted for that office, the State Canvassing Board directed the Minnesota Secretary of State's Office to oversee a manual recount, as required by [Minnesota law].

* * * During the recount, local election officials and the candidates reviewed the absentee ballot return envelopes that had been rejected on or before election day

and agreed that some of them had been improperly rejected. On January 3, 2009, the Secretary of State's Office opened and counted the 933 ballots identified during this process. On January 5, 2009, the State Canvassing Board certified the results of the election as 1,212,431 votes for Franken and 1,212,206 votes for Coleman, a margin of 225 votes in Franken's favor.

On January 6, 2009, appellants Coleman and Sheehan (hereinafter "Coleman") * * * contest[ed] the election results certified by the State Canvassing Board and [sought] a declaration that Coleman was entitled to the certificate of election as United States Senator. * * * No claim of fraud in the election or during the recount was made by either party. At the conclusion of the trial, the court determined that 351 additional absentee ballot return envelopes satisfied the statutory requirements and ordered that these envelopes be opened and the ballots inside counted.

On April 13, 2009, the trial court issued its findings of fact, conclusions of law, and order for judgment, finding that Franken received 1,212,629 votes and Coleman received 1,212,317 votes in the November 4, 2008 general election, a margin of 312 votes in Franken's favor. The court found that Franken received the highest number of votes legally cast in the election for United States Senator for the State of Minnesota and concluded that Franken was entitled to receive the certificate of election.

The State Canvassing Board's certification is prima facie evidence that Franken, the contestee, has been elected to the office. Coleman, the contestant, bears the burden of proof in the trial to show that the Board's certification was in error. * * *

Appellants raise essentially five issues: (1) whether the trial court violated Coleman's right to substantive due process by requiring strict, rather than only substantial, compliance with the statutory requirements for absentee voting; (2) whether Coleman's right to equal protection of the laws was violated, either by differences among jurisdictions in their application of the statutory requirements for absentee voting or by the court's rulings on the statutory requirements for absentee voting; (3) whether the court erred in excluding certain evidence; (4) whether the court erred in declining to order inspections of ballots and other election materials for precincts in which Coleman alleges that ballots may have been double-counted during the manual recount; and (5) whether the court erred by including in the final vote tally the election day returns from one Minneapolis precinct in which some ballots were lost before the manual recount.

I. * * *

During trial, the court identified, in an order issued February 13, 2009, ten categories of rejected absentee ballots that would not be considered legally cast as a matter of law because the ballots failed to comply with one or more of the statutory requirements for voting by absentee ballot. Coleman argues that this February 13 order imposed a standard of "strict" compliance with state law governing absentee ballots. Coleman asserts that the court's strict compliance standard departed from what had been a "substantial" compliance standard for acceptance of absentee ballots and application of a strict compliance standard resulted in a violation of substantive due process. * * *

* * * To prevail on a claim that a change in election standards violated substantive due process, the contestant must show a change that is patently and fundamentally unfair. In other words, the contestant must show likely reliance by the voters on an existing election procedure and a change in that procedure that results in significant disenfranchisement of the voters. Under this standard, in order to sustain a substantive due process violation, Coleman must prove as a threshold matter that the post-election change about which he complains—the trial court's adherence to a strict compliance standard—changed the procedures on which the voters relied on election day.

Coleman asserts that the trial court's February 13 order established a new standard of strict compliance with absentee ballot requirements, whereas precedent of this court and the practices of election officials, on election day and during the manual recount, required only substantial compliance.[9] If, in fact, strict adherence was not what the law required, so that voters could be said to have relied on something less, Coleman's argument might warrant further examination. But the law, both as provided by statute and in our precedent, requires strict adherence.

The Minnesota Legislature has established the process for voting by absentee ballot. Generally, a prospective voter first submits a written application for an absentee ballot. If the application complies with statutory requirements, the county auditor or municipal clerk sends the voter an absentee ballot, an absentee ballot return envelope, a ballot envelope (sometimes called a secrecy or security envelope), and a copy of the directions for casting an absentee ballot. If the applicant is not registered, the county auditor or municipal clerk includes a voter registration application.

The voter marks the ballot before a witness and puts the ballot in the secrecy envelope. The voter then puts the secrecy envelope (and the registration application, if any) in the ballot return envelope. The voter and the witness each sign the ballot return envelope. The completed ballot return envelope is returned to the county auditor or municipal clerk. The next step in the absentee voting process is acceptance or rejection of the ballot return envelope by local election officials. The decision to accept or reject the ballot return envelope is made at the precinct by local election judges on election day, or, if the local jurisdiction has an absentee ballot board, by the board in the 30 days before the election. The ballot return envelope is marked "Accepted" if officials are "satisfied" that:

---

9. The trial court concluded that it must enforce all requirements imposed by law upon voting by absentee ballot because our cases make those requirements mandatory for voters. The court found support for this conclusion in the facts that: (1) "the Minnesota Legislature has made voting in person relatively straightforward by permitting same-day voter registration," reflecting a policy decision to encourage voting in person on Election Day; and (2) "requiring compliance with the voting laws ultimately minimizes the risks of fraud and illegal voting that act as a detriment to a fair electoral process."

(1) the voter's name and address on the return envelope are the same as the information provided on the absentee ballot application;

(2) the voter's signature on the return envelope is the genuine signature of the individual who made the application for ballots and the certificate has been completed as prescribed in the directions for casting an absentee ballot, except that if a person other than the voter applied for the absentee ballot under applicable Minnesota Rules, the signature is not required to match;

(3) the voter is registered and eligible to vote in the precinct or has included a properly completed voter registration application in the return envelope; and

(4) the voter has not already voted at that election, either in person or by absentee ballot.

Minn. Stat. § 203B.12, subd. 2. Section 203B.12, subd. 2, makes clear that "[t]here is no other reason for rejecting an absentee ballot."

On election day, the absentee ballot return envelopes are delivered to the absentee voters' respective polling places. Before opening the accepted ballot return envelopes, election judges check each envelope against the precinct roster to be sure the voter has not voted in person or by another absentee ballot. If not, the election judges record those voters who voted by absentee ballot by marking the precinct roster with the notation "A.B." for each accepted absentee ballot return envelope. Once the roster has been so marked, the voter cannot vote again in that election. After the last mail delivery on election day, election judges open the accepted ballot return envelopes, remove the enclosed ballots from their secrecy envelopes, and then deposit the ballots in the ballot box.

The trial court's February 13 order closely tracks the requirements of these statutes. But Coleman contends that our precedent allows for something less than strict compliance with the statutory mandates. We disagree.

Although we have used a substantial compliance standard to judge errors by election officials, we have held voters strictly to statutory requirements. * * *

The distinction between errors by voters and errors by election officials is an important one. We have drawn "a clear distinction between the provisions and prohibitions in the election laws which are personal to the elector and those which apply to election officials over whose conduct he has no control." *Fitzgerald v. Morlock*, 120 N.W.2d 339, 345 (Minn. 1963). We have said that "any reasonable regulations of the statute as to the conduct of the voter himself" are mandatory, and a vote is properly rejected if the voter fails to comply with the law. *Id*. at 345. But if a voter complies with the law, his vote should not be rejected because of "irregularities, ignorance, inadvertence, or mistake, or even intentional wrong on the part of the election officers." *Id*.

In *Bell v. Gannaway*, we again explained that voting by absentee ballot is a privilege, not a right, and affirmed the mandatory nature of absentee voting requirements.

227 N.W.2d 797, 802–03 (Minn. 1975). We reiterated that because "the privilege of absentee voting is granted by the legislature, the legislature may mandate the conditions and procedures for such voting." *Id.* at 802.[11] We said there that strict compliance with the requirements for voting by absentee ballot is mandatory: "[V]oters who seek to vote under these provisions must be held to a strict compliance therewith." *Id.* at 803.

We conclude that our existing case law requires strict compliance by voters with the requirements for absentee voting. Thus, we reject Coleman's argument that only substantial compliance by voters is required. Having rejected this argument, we also conclude that the trial court's February 13 order requiring strict compliance with the statutory requirements for absentee voting was not a deviation from our well-established precedent.

Because strict compliance with the statutory requirements for absentee voting is, and has always been, required, there is no basis on which voters could have reasonably believed that anything less than strict compliance would suffice. Furthermore, Coleman does not cite, and after review of the record we have not found, any evidence in the record that election officials required only substantial compliance in any past election or any official pronouncements that only substantial compliance would be required in the November 4, 2008 election. Nor does Coleman point us to the testimony of any voter who neglected to comply with the statutory requirements for absentee voting in reliance on either past practice or official assurances that strict compliance was not required. Indeed, Coleman's counsel acknowledged during oral argument that Coleman cannot claim that any voters changed their behavior based on the alleged substantial compliance standard.

For all of these reasons, we hold that Coleman has not proven that the trial court's February 13 order violated substantive due process.

II.

We next examine Coleman's argument that the constitutional guarantee of equal protection was violated in this case. Coleman's equal protection argument is two-fold. First, he argues that the differing application and implementation by election officials of the statutory requirements for absentee voting violated equal protection. Essentially, Coleman contends that similarly situated absentee ballots were treated differently depending on the jurisdiction in which they were cast and that this disparate treatment violated equal protection. Second, Coleman contends that equal protection was violated when the trial court adhered to the statutory requirements for acceptance of absentee ballots, in contrast to the practices of local jurisdictions during the election.

---

11. At oral argument, Coleman posited that because of the increased use of the absentee voting method, it should now be treated as a right, not a privilege. But that is a policy determination for the legislature, not this court, to make.

Both parts of Coleman's equal protection argument depend on his assertion that differential application, either by election officials or by the trial court, of the statutory requirements for absentee voting violates equal protection. But equal protection is not violated every time public officials apply facially neutral state laws differently. The United States Supreme Court has held that "an erroneous or mistaken performance of [a] statutory duty, although a violation of the statute, is not without more a denial of the equal protection of the laws." *Snowden v. Hughes*, 321 U.S. 1, 8 (1944). The Court then explained that the "more" that is required for a violation of equal protection is intentional or purposeful discrimination. *Id.* The Court said:

> The unlawful administration by state officers of a state statute fair on its face, resulting in its unequal application to those who are entitled to be treated alike, is not a denial of equal protection unless there is shown to be present in it an element of intentional or purposeful discrimination.

Id.; *see also Vill. of Arlington Heights v. Metro. Hous. Dev. Corp.*, 429 U.S. 252, 265 (1977) (holding that proof of discriminatory intent or purpose is required to show a violation of the Equal Protection Clause); *Washington v. Davis*, 426 U.S. 229, 240–42 (1976) (same). * * *

Accordingly, in order to prevail on his equal protection claim of disparate application of a facially neutral statute, Coleman was required to prove either that local jurisdictions' differences in application or the trial court's application of the requirements for absentee voting was the product of intentional discrimination. Coleman neither claims nor produced any evidence that the differing treatment of absentee ballots among jurisdictions during the election was the result of intentional or purposeful discrimination against individuals or classes. Nor does Coleman claim that the trial court's February 13 order, establishing certain categories of ballots as not legally cast, was the product of an intent to discriminate against any individual or class.

On appeal, Coleman contends that he proved an equal protection violation by showing that local election officials made deliberate and intentional decisions to adopt particular interpretations of the statutory requirements for absentee voting. Under *Snowden*, however, the fact that the official's decision to act in a particular way was deliberate does not constitute discriminatory intent. *See* 321 U.S. at 10 (explaining that the requirement of intentional discrimination is not satisfied by allegations of willful, malicious conduct). Instead, *Snowden* requires a showing that the statutory standards were applied differently with the intent to discriminate in favor of one individual or class over another. *Id.* at 8.[13]

---

13. The Supreme Court observed in *Snowden* that intent to discriminate could also be demonstrated by evidence of systematic discrimination "so that the practical effect of the official breach of law is the same as though the discrimination were incorporated in and proclaimed by the statute." 321 U.S. at 9. Coleman neither claims nor introduced evidence of any systematic discrimination.

The trial court found that election judges applied the election laws in a consistent and uniform manner. The court found that election jurisdictions adopted policies they deemed necessary to ensure that absentee voting procedures would be available to their residents, in accordance with statutory requirements, given the resources available to them. The court also found that differences in available resources, personnel, procedures, and technology necessarily affected the procedures used by local election officials reviewing absentee ballots. But the court found that Coleman did not prove that these differences were calculated to discriminate among absentee voters. Our review of the record convinces us that the trial court's findings are supported by the evidence and are not clearly erroneous. As a result, we conclude that Coleman did not prove his equal protection claim.

Coleman makes the additional argument that the non-uniform application of the statutory standards for absentee voting nevertheless brings this case within the ambit of the United States Supreme Court's decision in *Bush v. Gore*, 531 U.S. 98 (2000) (per curiam) [p. 1085]. In *Bush*, the Court held that the statewide recount of the 2000 presidential election that had been ordered by the Florida Supreme Court violated equal protection. *Id.* at 103. Coleman argues that, in Minnesota's 2008 United States Senate election, different local election jurisdictions treated similarly situated absentee ballots differently and that the trial court imposed a stricter standard for compliance with absentee voting requirements than did election officials, and that those differences violate equal protection under *Bush*.

The trial court concluded that *Bush* is distinguishable in several important respects and, as a result, does not support Coleman's equal protection claim. We agree. In *Bush*, the Supreme Court specifically noted that it was not addressing the question of "whether local entities, in the exercise of their expertise, may develop different systems for implementing elections." 531 U.S. at 109. Variations in local practices for implementing absentee voting procedures are, at least in part, the question at issue here. As previously noted, the trial court here found that the disparities in application of the statutory standards on which Coleman relies are the product of local jurisdictions' use of different methods to ensure compliance with the same statutory standards; that jurisdictions adopted policies they deemed necessary to ensure that absentee voting procedures would be available to their residents, in accordance with statutory requirements, given the resources available to them; and that differences in available resources, personnel, procedures, and technology necessarily affected the procedures used by local election officials in reviewing absentee ballots. As we noted previously, Coleman has not demonstrated that these findings are clearly erroneous.

Additionally, the essence of the equal protection problem addressed in *Bush* was that there were no established standards under Florida statutes or provided by the state supreme court for determining voter intent; as a result, in the recount process each county (indeed, each recount location within a county) was left to set its own standards for discerning voter intent. *See id.* at 106. Here, there were clear statutory standards for acceptance or rejection of absentee ballots, about which all election officials received common training.

Finally, the decision to be made by Florida election officials with which the Supreme Court was concerned in *Bush* was voter intent—that is, for whom the ballot was cast—as reflected on ballots already cast in the election. In *Bush*, officials conducting the recount were reviewing the face of the ballot itself, creating opportunities for manipulation of the decision for political purposes. Here, the decision at issue was whether to accept or reject absentee ballot return envelopes before they were opened, meaning that the actual votes on the ballot contained in the return envelope were not known to the election officials applying the standards. In summary, we conclude that *Bush v. Gore* is not applicable and does not support Coleman's equal protection claim.

For all of these reasons, we conclude that Coleman has not proven that either election officials or the trial court violated his right to equal protection.

III. * * *

Coleman argued at trial that as a result of the trial court's February 13 order finding that certain ballots were not legally cast, there are absentee ballots included in the State Canvassing Board's certification of election results that would have been rejected if the strict compliance standard of the trial court had been applied to them. Coleman therefore argued that if the court did not adopt the substantial compliance standard that Coleman claims was used on election day, the court was required to apply a strict compliance standard to ballots already accepted and counted on election day and reduce the parties' vote totals for any ballots that did not meet that standard.

The trial court rejected Coleman's argument and the evidence Coleman offered to support it. Coleman made an offer of proof identifying absentee ballot return envelopes that had been opened and the enclosed ballots removed and counted on election day or during the manual recount. Coleman did not seek to present evidence identifying the ballots removed from those envelopes and could not have done so, because once the ballots were removed from the envelopes and deposited in the ballot box, they were commingled with other counted ballots and could not be identified. We conclude that the court did not abuse its discretion in excluding this evidence because the legislature has foreclosed any challenge to the legality of an absentee ballot based on the return envelope once the ballot has been deposited in the ballot box. * * *

Accordingly, we conclude that the court did not abuse its discretion in excluding the evidence. * * *

V.

Finally, Coleman contends that the trial court erred when it ruled that missing ballots from Minneapolis Ward 3, Precinct 1, were properly included in the State

Canvassing Board's January 5, 2009 certification of legally cast votes. During the manual recount, election officials could locate only four of the five envelopes of ballots from Minneapolis Ward 3, Precinct 1. Voting machine tapes showed a total of 2,028 ballots cast and counted in the precinct on election day, but only 1,896 ballots from the precinct were available for the recount, a difference of 132 ballots. The State Canvassing Board determined that an envelope of ballots had been lost and, rather than certify only 1,896 votes in the recount, accepted the election day returns for that precinct.

The trial court found no allegations or evidence of fraud or foul play and no evidence to suggest that the election day totals from the precinct are unreliable. The court therefore found "that 132 ballots from Minneapolis Precinct 3-1 were cast and properly counted on Election Day and were lost at some point after they were counted on Election Day but before the administrative recount." * * *

The ballots are missing, but Coleman introduced no evidence of foul play or misconduct, and the election day precinct returns are available to give effect to those votes. We hold that the trial court did not err in ruling that the election day precinct returns for Minneapolis Ward 3, Precinct 1, were properly included in the tally of legally cast votes.

VI.

For all of the foregoing reasons, we affirm the decision of the trial court that Al Franken received the highest number of votes legally cast and is entitled * * * to receive the certificate of election as United States Senator from the State of Minnesota.

Affirmed.

Notes and Questions

1. *Sheehan* found that the Minnesota recount procedures did not violate *Bush v. Gore*. The court argued that (1) variations in local practice "are the product of local jurisdictions' use of different methods to ensure compliance with the same statutory standards"; (2) unlike in Florida, the Minnesota statutes did have "clear statutory standards"; and (3) also unlike in Florida, the issue was not voter intent as such, but rather "whether to accept or reject absentee ballot return envelopes before they were opened." How persuasive are these arguments, alone or in combination? Does the continuing disagreement on how to interpret the equal-protection principles of *Bush v. Gore* make a coherent evaluation of *Sheehan* in this regard difficult? *See* Richard L. Hasen, *Bush v. Gore and the Lawlessness Principle: A Comment on Professor Amar*, 61 FLA. L. REV. 979, 985 (2009).

2. *Sheehan* held that the right to cast an absentee ballot was a privilege, not a right, and that as a result voters should be held to a standard of strict compliance with statutory requirements. In contrast, the court would use a "substantial compliance" standard when considering the effect of errors by election officials. Did the court

convincingly justify this distinction? Was the court right to suggest that changes in this legal regime should be made by the state legislature, not state courts? It appears that many state courts do not make this distinction, and instead permit absentee or other votes to be counted as long as there is substantial compliance with statutory requirements. *E.g., Miller v. Treadwell*, 245 P.3d 867 (Alaska 2010) (holding that it was proper to count misspelled write-in votes because statutes should be construed in favor of voter enfranchisement). *See generally* Richard L. Hasen, *The Democracy Canon*, 62 Stan. L. Rev. 69, 86–87 (2009). Is one view necessarily preferable? Should the answer depend, at least in part, on the precise statutory language in a particular state, and the history of absentee voting and related election issues in a particular state?

3. Another demonstration of the importance of state law for regulating federal elections comes from *Roudebush v. Hartke*, 405 U.S. 15 (1972). There, incumbent Senator C. Vance Hartke, Democrat from Indiana, defeated Republican challenger Richard Roudebush in an extremely close vote. Roudebush filed a petition in state court to order a recount, and Hartke responded by filing suit in U.S. District Court, requesting that it enjoin the state-court litigation. The federal court eventually did that, on the basis that the state's recount procedures would interfere with the Senate's power to judge the qualifications of its own members. On appeal, the Supreme Court reversed. The 5-2 majority held that the states possessed broad authority to regulate federal elections, and a manual recount was "within the ambit" of those powers. Such a recount would not prevent the Senate from later independently evaluating the election, or from conducting its own recount. There was no evidence to support the district court's holding that a recount "would increase the probability of election fraud and accidental destruction of ballots." The dissent argued that the Senate had a long tradition of independently resolving disputed elections by convening a special committee. There was a federal interest, the dissent contended, "in preserving the integrity of the evidence" of the disputed ballots, and for that reason it agreed with the district court.

The *Roudebush* decision gave a good deal of power to states, and state courts in particular, to resolve disputed congressional elections. But it apparently left intact the ability of the houses of Congress to take action concurrently to resolve such disputes. Since *Roudebush*, some disappointed candidates have simultaneously pursued remedies in state courts and in Congress. *See* Kristen R. Lisk, Note, *The Resolution of Contested Elections in the U.S. House of Representatives: Why State Courts Should Not Help with the House Work*, 83 N.Y.U. L. Rev. 1213 (2008) (discussing examples). Does such forum-shopping make sense in this context? At what point, in the words of *Roudebush*, do state actions "frustrate" the ability of Congress to judge the elections of its own members, should it care to do that? Conversely, as a general matter, should Congress presumptively defer to state action in this regard, absent specific congressional regulation on point? In the words of then-Circuit Judge Stevens, who sat on the lower court in *Roudebush*, would the work of the Senate "be facilitated, rather than impaired, by the availability of a fairly conducted recount * * * before undertaking its work"? *Hartke v. Roudenbush*, 321 F. Supp. 1370, 1378–79 (S.D. Ind. 1970) (*per curiam*) (three-judge court) (Stevens, J., dissenting), *rev'd*, 405 U.S. 15 (1972). *See generally* Lisa Marshall Manheim, *Judging Congressional Elections*, 51 GA. L. REV. 359 (2017); Paul E. Salamanca & James E. Keller, *The Legislative Privilege to Judge the Qualifications, Elections, and Returns of Members*, 95 KY. L.J. 241 (2007).

4. Some argue that the state political process, including litigation in state courts, is not an appropriate venue to settle election disputes for federal offices. The fear is that state officials, judges included, would act in parochial and partisan ways in resolving the disputes. While it is hard to argue that the members of the houses of Congress would be any less partisan than state officials would be in resolving election disputes, some might contend that federal judges with life tenure would be less partisan than their state counterparts. How compelling are these arguments? Anecdotal evidence cuts in different ways. Consider, for example, *Sheehan*, where a state supreme court consisting primarily, though not exclusively, of Democrats ruled unanimously in favor of the Democratic candidate. On the federal-court side, consider the lower, three-judge district-court decision in *Roudebush*. There, the Republican appointee (Stevens) ruled in favor of the Republican candidate, while the other two judges, both Democratic appointees, ruled in favor of the Democratic candidate.

The extant empirical evidence on partisan decision-making by judges in election-related cases is mixed. On the state-court side, compare Scott Graves, *Competing Interests in State Supreme Courts: Justices' Votes and Voting Rights*, 24 AM. REV. POL. 267 (2003) (finding state supreme courts acted in partisan ways in some circumstances in ballot-access cases), with Kyle C. Kopko, *Partisanship Suppressed: Judicial Decision-Making in Ralph Nader's 2004 Ballot Access Litigation*, 7 ELECTION L.J. 301 (2008) (finding state judges' partisan affiliations relatively insignificant in cases where Ralph Nader sought placement on the presidential ballot). On the federal-court side, compare Michael E. Solimine, *Institutional Process, Agenda Setting, and the Development of Election Law on the Supreme Court*, 68 OHIO ST. L.J. 767, 790–92 (2007) (arguing that the evidence did not show that lower-court federal judges systematically voted in a partisan fashion in election-law cases), with Adam C. Cox & Thomas J. Miles, *Judicial Ideology and the Transformation of Voting Rights Act Jurisprudence*, 75 U. CHI. L. REV. 1493 (2008) (arguing that federal judges often voted in partisan fashion in Voting Rights Act cases). For further discussion, see Richard L. Hasen, *Judges as Political Regulators: Evidence and Options for Institutional Change*, in RACE, REFORM, AND REGULATION OF THE ELECTORAL PROCESS 101 (Guy-Uriel E. Charles et al., eds., 2011); James B. Cottrill & Terri J. Perritti, *Gerrymandering from the Bench: The Electoral Consequences of Judicial Redistricting*, 12 ELECTION L.J. 261 (2013). *See generally* Michael S. Kang & Joanna M. Sheppard, *Judging Law in Election Cases*, 70 VAND. L. REV. 1755 (2017); Michael S. Kang & Joanna M. Shepherd, *The Long Shadow of* Bush v. Gore: *Judicial Partisanship in Election Cases*, 68 STAN. L. REV. 1411 (2016).

2. Determining a Winner

Our discussion thus far concerning the mechanics of vote-counting has elided a more fundamental question: What are the rules by which we determine who wins? In other words, what is the object of the electoral game?

In most American elections, the winner is the candidate who receives more votes than any other. Because there may be more than two candidates running, the winner may receive only a plurality, and not a majority, of votes. Both because plurality winners are opposed by majorities of the electorate and because losers receive no representation at all, plurality-winner systems can lead to results that are unrepresentative of the electorate's political opinions.

In multi-candidate contests, plurality-winner systems suffer from a spoiler effect. In such elections, a third-party candidate tends to take votes from the major-party candidate who is ideologically closer to the third-party candidate, thereby increasing the electoral chances of the candidate likely to be least palatable to supporters of the third-party candidate. *See generally* William H. Riker, *The Two-Party System and Duverger's Law: An Essay on the History of Political Science*, 76 AM. POL. SCI. REV. 753 (1982); Maurice Duverger, *Factors in a Two-Party and Multiparty System, in* PARTY POLITICS AND PRESSURE GROUPS 23 (1972). For this reason, plurality-winner systems tend to produce two (and only two) relatively centrist political parties, and may frustrate voters by giving them little choice if they want to avoid "wasting" their votes.

An example may help to illustrate the spoiler effect. In 2000, Green Party candidate Ralph Nader was ideologically more liberal than both of the two major-party candidates, Democrat Albert Gore, Jr., and Republican George W. Bush. Most of Nader's supporters, if forced to choose, would have preferred Gore to Bush. Their support of Nader rather than Gore, however, meant that Gore's vote total did not reflect their preferences, and Bush narrowly won the election. Similarly, in 1912, Democrat Woodrow Wilson prevailed when Bull Moose Theodore Roosevelt captured votes that would otherwise have given Republican William Howard Taft a victory.

Alternative methods of vote-counting give minor parties a much better chance of gaining representation in elected bodies, and result in legislatures that more closely reflect the electorate's range of political views. Proportional representation, for example, seeks to divide seats in a legislature proportionately according to the votes received by various parties. Thus, a minor party that receives 20% of the vote might receive no seats in a plurality system, but might receive 20% of the seats in a proportional system. Such a result might seem more fair, but note that proportional representation can lead to its own set of problems. Most significantly, it makes governing difficult, as the legislature must assemble coalitions of different parties to pass laws and even to select legislative leadership.

Single-transferable-vote (STV), or instant-runoff, systems provide a different means to enable voters to express a preference for minor parties. Under those systems, voters do not simply select their first-choice candidates. Rather, voters rank the candidates. First-choice votes are tabulated, and if one candidate receives a majority, that candidate is the winner. If no candidate receives a majority, however, the candidate with the least first-place votes is eliminated from contention. Voters who chose the eliminated candidate will have their second-choice votes counted in the next round, with the process repeating until one candidate receives a majority. For elections to fill multiple seats, STV systems also attempt to solve the problem of "wasted" extra votes cast for winning candidates. Once a candidate reaches a majority, a STV system applies all future votes cast for that candidate to the voters' second choices. That way, each voter has an increased opportunity to affect the outcome.

Ranked-choice voting (RCV), which includes STV and instant-runoff systems, is enjoying a resurgence of popularity in some quarters. It is used in about ten cities, including San Francisco and Cambridge, Massachusetts. It was not used for any state-wide elections until Maine adopted it by referendum in 2016, leading to the decision below. Katherine Q. Seelye, *Maine Adopts Ranked-Choice Voting. What Is It, and How Will It Work?*, N.Y. TIMES, Dec. 4, 2016, at A27. In November 2020, voters in Alaska and Massachusetts will consider whether to adopt RCV for their elections as well.

Other voting systems involve giving voters multiple votes to allocate to the candidates. One such system allocates zero votes to the voter's least preferred candidate, one to the candidate the voter prefers next, two to the next-preferred candidate, and so on. A second such system (known as "bullet-voting") gives each voter a certain number of votes and permits the voter to allocate votes as he or she sees fit. For example, a voter might have five votes to allocate between ten candidates running for five seats in a legislature, and might decide to give three votes to Candidate A and two to Candidate B. Because voters can allocate multiple votes to a single candidate, such a system permits voters who strongly support minor-party or minority-race candidates to overcome some of the disadvantage they face because of their smaller numbers.

It will not surprise you that the use of alternative vote-counting methods has led to legal challenges.

Opinion of the Justices

Supreme Judicial Court of Maine

162 A.3d 188, 2017 ME 100 (Me. 2017)

[Per Curiam. Chief Justice Saufley, Justice Alexander, Justice Mead, Justice Gorman, Justice Jabar, Justice Hjelm, and Justice Humphrey join in this opinion.]

The Senate seeks our opinions regarding the constitutionality of a statute recently enacted through citizen initiative, L.D. 1557, §§ 1–6, which established ranked-choice voting for elections of United States Senators, United States Representatives, Governor, State Senators, State Representatives, and federal and state primaries in Maine occurring on or after January 1, 2018.

The term "ranked-choice voting" is defined by the newly enacted Act as "the method of casting and tabulating votes in which voters rank candidates in order of preference, tabulation proceeds in sequential rounds in which last-place candidates are defeated and the candidate with the most votes in the final round is elected." As defined, ranked-choice voting contrasts with the statutory description of Maine's previous system of single-choice voting, by which voters voted for a single candidate for each seat. The crux of the Senate's inquiry is whether this statutorily enacted system of ranked-choice voting violates the provisions of the Maine Constitution by which successful candidates for office are identified "by a plurality" of all votes returned, namely, Me. Const. art. IV, pt. 1, § 5 (regarding the election of State Representatives); Me. Const. art. IV, pt. 2, § 4 (regarding the election of State Senators); and Me. Const. art. V, pt. 1, § 3 (regarding the election of the Governor). * * *

In arguing that the Act is unconstitutional, the Senate and others rely heavily on the constitutional history of the plurality requirement. As originally established when Maine became a State in 1820, the Maine Constitution provided for the election of Senators, Representatives, and the Governor by a majority vote.

Between 1830 and 1880, a number of elections yielded no candidate who achieved a majority vote. In those circumstances, the alternative means for election provided by the 1820 Constitution had to be utilized. For Representatives, that meant holding a series of new elections until a candidate won a majority. For Senators, that meant that the Representatives and the members of the Senate who had been elected by a majority would elect the winners by joint ballot. For Governor, it meant the House would select two of the candidates from those four candidates who received the highest number of votes and the Senate would elect the winner of those two.

The result was widespread discontent — and, in 1879, threats of violence * * * — caused by the expense and delay of holding repeat elections, by the election of candidates through legislative action rather than based on the will of the people, and by the claims of manipulation and allegations of self-dealing levied by opponents of the eventually-declared winners. In response to these challenges, by 1880, all three provisions had been amended to replace "majority" with "plurality" as is now found in the Constitution. The plurality requirements in these constitutional provisions have not changed since 1880.

As last amended to address the public's lack of confidence in the elective process in 1880, the language of the Maine Constitution today is clear. For Maine Senators, Maine Representatives, and the Governor alike, an election is won by the candidate that first obtains "a plurality of" all votes returned.

The Act, in contrast, provides for the tabulation of votes in rounds. Thus, the Act prevents the recognition of the winning candidate when the first plurality is identified. According to the terms of the Constitution, a candidate who receives a plurality of the votes would be declared the winner in that election. The Act, in contrast, would not declare the plurality candidate the winner of the election, but would require continued tabulation until a majority is achieved or all votes are exhausted. Accordingly, the Act is not simply another method of carrying out the Constitution's requirement of a plurality. In essence, the Act is inapplicable if there are only two candidates, and it is in direct conflict with the Constitution if there are more than two candidates.

The discrepancy between the Act and the Constitution is easily illustrated by the simplest of scenarios. If, after one round of counting, a candidate obtained a plurality of the votes but not a majority, that candidate would be declared the winner according to the Maine Constitution as it currently exists. According to the Act, however, that same candidate would not then be declared the winner.

Instead, the candidate, though already having obtained a plurality of the votes, would be subject to additional rounds of counting in which second, third, and fourth choices are accounted for and the lowest vote-garnering candidates are successively eliminated. Once those additional rounds are completed, a different candidate may be declared the winner — not because that second candidate obtained a plurality of the votes (which the first candidate had already obtained), but because that candidate obtained a *majority* of the votes after eliminating other candidates by taking into account the second, third, and fourth place preferences, or because the ballots have been exhausted. In this way, the Act prevents the candidate obtaining a "plurality" from being named the winner unless and until multiple rounds of vote-counting have occurred. * * *

[T]he Ranked-Choice Voting Act conflicts with the Maine Constitution.

Notes and Questions

1. In *Opinion of the Justices*, the Maine Supreme Judicial Court held that ranked-choice voting could not be used in the general elections to select state senators, representatives, or the governor. It was, however, used for the first time in the *primary* elections in June 2018. The Republican Party had objected to the use of ranked-choice voting in its primary elections, but a federal court rejected the Party's challenge. The court held that RCV did not improperly burden the party's associational rights or interfere with the party's internal governance, and it advanced

state interests in requiring candidates to show substantial support to appear on the general-election ballot. *Maine Republican Party v. Dunlap*, 324 F. Supp. 3d 802 (D. Maine 2018).

2. Was the constitutionality of ranked-choice voting as simple a question as the Maine Supreme Judicial Court seemed to think? Two scholars have argued that RCV is consistent with statutes and constitutional provisions, such as Maine's, that provide that an election shall be won by the candidate that receives "a plurality," the "highest," the "greatest," or "largest number of votes." *See* Richard H. Pildes & G. Michael Parsons, *The Legality of Ranked-Choice Voting* (Mar. 27, 2020), SSRN, *available at* https://ssrn.com/abstract=3563257 or http://dx.doi.org/10.2139/ssrn .3563257. The issue is important throughout the country—not just in Maine— because nearly forty states have constitutional provisions specifying that the winner of an election shall be the candidate receiving more votes than any other. *See id.* at 63–71 (listing state-constitutional provisions).

Chapter 11

Election Remedies

A. Introduction

Much election-law litigation, particularly litigation regarding elections that have already occurred, is undertaken to remedy perceived errors in the electoral process. To take but one example, in Chapter 10 we considered the Supreme Court's decision in *Bush v. Gore*, 531 U.S. 98 (2000) (*per curiam*) [p. 1085], which had its genesis in state-court litigation to recount certain ballots that were not properly cast. In this Chapter, we consider more systematically the ways legislators and courts deal with perceived and actual electoral errors.

Most states have fairly detailed statutory schemes that set out procedures for state and local officials to follow when confronting problems in an election. These statutes typically provide for an administrative process, followed if necessary by review in the state courts. Among the issues that state officials encounter are fraudulent votes, mistaken votes, and recounts when elections are extremely close. If and when a dispute reaches the judicial branch, a court must consider, often with little substantive guidance from the relevant statutes, whether an error has taken place and, if so, what the remedy should be.[a]

In § B of this Chapter, we consider two potentially controversial and complicated remedies for electoral errors that courts may order: conducting an entirely new election and adjusting existing vote totals. We find that courts are reluctant to order

---

a. For helpful discussion of these issues, see Edward B. Foley, Ballot Battles: The History of Disputed Elections in the United States (2016); Richard L. Hasen, Election Meltdown: Dirty Tricks, Distrust, and the Threat to American Democracy (2020); Richard L. Hasen, The Voting Wars: From Florida to the Next Election Meltdown (2012); Edward B. Foley, *Due Process, Fair Play, and Excessive Partisanship: A New Principle for Judicial Review of Election Laws*, 84 U. Chi. L. Rev. 655 (2017); Joshua A. Douglas, *Procedural Fairness in Election Contests*, 88 Ind. L.J. 1 (2013); Steven F. Huefner, *Remedying Election Wrongs*, 44 Harv. J. on Legis. 265 (2007); Steven F. Huefner, *Just How Settled Are the Legal Principles that Control Election Disputes?*, 8 Election L.J. 233 (2009) (book review); *Developments in the Law—Voting and Democracy*, 119 Harv. L. Rev. 1127, 1155–65 (2006). In 2010, the American Law Institute undertook a project to develop procedures for recounts and resolution of disputes over the casting and counting of ballots. *See* Steven F. Huefner & Edward B. Foley, *The Judicialization of Politics: The Challenge of the ALI Principles of Election Law Project*, 79 Brook. L. Rev. 1915 (2014). The result was Principles of the Law, Election Administration: Non-Precinct Voting and Resolution of Ballot-Counting Disputes (2019).

either remedy, particularly when a federal court is asked to overturn the results of a state election, but in extreme circumstances such remedies may be ordered.

Then, in § C, we turn to the question of how to remedy individual injuries. We first address violations of the right to vote, and consider a range of means of enforcement, from injunctions to criminal prosecutions to private damages actions. We also address whether remedies should be available to unsuccessful candidates who may have lost their elections because of others' violations of law.

As you read these materials, consider the inevitable trade-offs that seem to be required when a legislature, or a court, ponders whether and how to remedy election errors. Among the potentially conflicting values at stake are the perceived fairness, accuracy, and legitimacy of the remedial process itself; the desire of voters to be anonymous; the desire to resolve an election dispute with promptness and finality; and the efficiency (or lack thereof) and costs associated with any remedy. *See* Steven F. Huefner, *Remedying Election Wrongs*, 44 HARV. J. ON LEGIS. 265, 288–96 (2007). To what extent, if at all, are courts better situated than legislatures or state executive-branch officials to balance these values? Are these prototypical political questions, from which courts should abstain? At the very least, should courts give considerable deference to the efforts of the other branches of government to resolve any errors? Or does the inevitably politically freighted nature of many such errors suggest that courts should not hesitate to take action, since state officials may be inclined to take remedial actions that favor their own political parties or their own electoral fortunes? Do courts (particularly elected state courts) risk becoming politicized by remedying errors in elections for the other branches? And will recent statutory changes (*e.g.,* the Help America Vote Act, discussed in Chapter 10) that make registering and voting easier also have the unintended consequence of generating more remedial litigation concerning alleged errors in the registration and voting processes?

B. Correcting Faulty Elections

In this section, we consider two straightforward but drastic remedies for elections that may have been affected by violations of law: ordering a new election and adjusting the vote totals. State courts have taken several approaches in deciding whether a ballot was validly cast, whether to adjust vote totals, and when an irregularity should lead to a new election. For example, some states will order a new election, more-or-less automatically, simply if the number of invalid votes exceeds the margin of victory. Other states, in contrast, will order a new election only if there is a significant chance that the invalid votes would have affected the outcome. Some states will not deduct votes from a candidate unless there is direct evidence that invalid votes were cast for that candidate. Finally, some states undertake proportionate reduction, where the court will remedy invalid votes by estimating the number of such votes cast for each candidate, and reducing the vote totals accordingly.

As you read the cases below, consider what approach each court seemed to follow and ask how we should balance the desire for accuracy and fairness against other values, such as the need for legitimacy and finality.[b]

1. Re-Votes

Bell v. Southwell

United States Court of Appeals for the Fifth Circuit.
376 F.2d 659 (5th Cir. 1967)

Brown, Circuit Judge [with whom Goldberg and Ainsworth, Circuit Judges, join]:

A Georgia election was conducted under procedures involving racial discrimination which was gross, state-imposed, and forcibly state-compelled. Nevertheless the District Court by summary judgment held it could not set aside such election or order a new one even though in parallel cases the unconstitutional discriminatory practices were enjoined and all persons arrested were ordered discharged immediately. We reverse.

The underlying facts out of which the controversy grew may be quickly stated. The Justice of the Peace for the 789th Militia District in Americus, Sumter County, Georgia, died in June 23, 1965. The Ordinary on June 26, 1965, called a special election to fill the vacancy, which was held on July 20, 1965. Mrs. Mary F. Bell, one of the plaintiffs, a Negro, was a candidate as was the winner, J.W. Southwell, a defendant, and four other white men. Following Georgia procedure, the results of the election were canvassed and the defendant J.W. Southwell declared the winner. Of the 2,781 votes cast, Negroes actually voting numbered 403 out of a total of 1,223 registered and qualified Negro voters in the District. On July 29, 1965, and after the expiration of the time for election contest under Georgia laws, this suit was filed. The District Judge by opinion denied relief for three reasons, two Georgia and one Federal. First, even assuming the admitted racial discrimination intimidated Negroes from voting, if all of the qualified Negroes not voting were added to the confined [sic] vote of Southwell's opponents, the result could not have been changed. Second, if the election were voided, the Ordinary would be required to appoint the successor and the appointee would surely be Southwell. Third, Federal Courts simply do not have power to void a state election.

* * * The main charge [in the complaint] was that the election officials including the Ordinary had conducted the election in violation of the rights established

---

b. For further discussion of these issues, see *Developments in the Law—Voting and Democracy*, 119 Harv. L. Rev. 1127, 1157–61 (2006); Kevin J. Hickey, Note, *Accuracy Counts: Illegal Votes in Contested Elections and the Case for Complete Proportionate Deduction*, 83 N.Y.U. L. Rev. 167 (2008); Sarah E. LeCloux, Comment, *Too Close to Call? Remedying Reasonably Uncertain Ballot Results with New Elections*, 2001 Wis. L. Rev. 1541.

under the Constitution and laws of the United States. The specific allegations fell in two categories, one relating to the election system and the second to specific acts of intimidation. In the first it was alleged that voting lists for the election were segregated on the basis of race. Likewise, voting booths were segregated according to race, with one booth for "white males", another for "white women", and a third for Negroes. During the course of the election, a number of qualified Negro women voters were denied the right to cast their ballots in the "white women's" booth. In the second group were charges that the officials barred representatives of candidate Bell from viewing the voting, another was physically struck by an election official and police allowed a large crowd of white males to gather near the polls thus intimidating Negroes from voting. In addition, the plaintiffs were commanded by a deputy sheriff, acting under directions of the Ordinary, to leave the white women's polling booth and after their respectful refusal to do so on the ground that they had the constitutional right to vote without being subjected to racial discrimination, they were arrested. [T]he plaintiffs requested that the Court declare the defendant Southwell was not the legally elected Justice of the Peace, that he be enjoined from taking office, and that the Ordinary be ordered to call a new election. * * *

* * * Since it is clear that constitutional rights of the plaintiffs, the Negro voters as a class, indeed all voters, Negro and white, of the District were infringed, the sole question remaining is the sort of relief to be granted.

[T]he trial Court in unmistakable terms and action characterized the practices as flagrant violations of the Constitution. * * * Despite his determination that for the future these glaring racial discriminations could not go on, the trial Judge concluded that a Federal Court was either powerless—or at least ought not to exercise power—to set aside a State election. The Judge was apparently influenced by two factors. The first is one going to the existence of power or the propriety of its exercise. On the basis of *Reynolds v. Sims*, 1964, 377 U.S. 533 [p. 122], and other reapportionment cases, the trial Court recognizing that a prohibitory decree could took [*sic*] to the future, nevertheless held that it could not rectify the past since, as the Judge put it, "only a few minutes' reflection is needed to realize that the implications of such a decision would be staggering." The second [is] * * * that, granting the existence of this crude discrimination, there is no way to tell whether the result would have been different in its absence. Hence, no harm or injury is shown by these complainants. Neither of these factors warrant [*sic*], in our view, the complete denial of relief.

Drastic, if not staggering, as is the Federal voiding of a State election, and therefore a form of relief to be guardedly exercised, this Court in *Hamer v. Campbell*, 5 Cir., 1966, 358 F.2d 215, expressly recognized the existence of this power. Of course as that opinion emphasizes, not every unconstitutional racial discrimination necessarily permits or requires a retrospective voiding of the election. But the power is present * * *.

As to the second we do not think the Court could justify denial of effective, present relief because of any assumed inability to demonstrate that the outcome would have been different. The appellants seem to suggest that the existence of such flagrant racial discrimination would raise a presumption that the vote of every actual and potential voter was affected. On that approach, it is not Negroes alone who suffer, it is the body politic as a whole, both Negro and white. And this is certainly true at least to the extent that the trial Court legally could not assume — as it evidently did — that all white voters would vote for white candidates, all Negroes for Negroes, or that no whites would vote for Negroes in a free, untainted election.

[W]e think it is a mistake to cast this in terms of presumption. The fact is that there are certain discriminatory practices which, apart from demonstrated injury or the inability to do so, so infect the processes of the law as to be stricken down as invalid. Thus in jury-race exclusion cases, once the evidence, either direct or by inference from statistical percentages, establishes the existence of racial discrimination, the law requires that the indictment (or the petit jury verdict of guilty) be set side [sic] even though the accused is unable to demonstrate injury in fact. And at times demonstrated actual discrimination is not even required if the racially conscious system affords a ready opportunity for it in practice. * * * [I]n areas of such vital importance, state-imposed racial discrimination cannot be tolerated and to eliminate the practice or the temptation toward it, the law must extinguish the judgment wrought by such a procedure.

Even more directly, in connection with the elective process, the Supreme Court gave full play to this approach in striking down the Louisiana law requiring the designation of the race of each candidate on the ballot. *Anderson v. Martin*, 1964, 375 U.S. 399 [p. 536]. It takes little transposition to substitute for the ballot's written racial candidate label the state supplied racial marker for places and manner of voting. In each situation it is "placing a racial label * * * at the most crucial stage in the electoral process — the instant before the vote is cast." By each mechanism "the State furnishes a vehicle by which racial prejudice may be so aroused as to operate against one group because of race and for another." And in both situations this "is true because by directing the citizen's attention to the single consideration of race or color, the State indicates that * * * race or color is an important — perhaps paramount — consideration in the citizen's choice, which may decisively influence the citizen to cast his ballot along racial lines." And as much for one as for the other, the "vice lies not in the resulting injury but in the placing of the power of the State behind a racial classification that induces racial prejudice at the polls." * * *

* * * [T]he Georgia authorities * * * insist here that the relief sought was properly denied since the injunction was requested after the election was over. But * * * [t]here was really no effective relief available before the election. The moment the election process began, there was a protest by these Negro voters and others seeking an eradication of the discrimination and an opportunity for all members of that race, indeed for all voters, to vote without regard to race or color. That this self-help was not successful, indeed resulted in the unwarranted arrest and detention of those who protested, does not fault them for want of diligence. And within but a few days after the result of the election was published, this suit was filed as a part of an attack on many fronts.

Considering the gross, spectacular, completely indefensible nature of this state-imposed, state-enforced racial discrimination and the absence of an effective judicial remedy prior to the holding of the election, this is far removed from a belated effort to set aside retrospectively an election held long before on the ground that re-examination of the circumstances indicates a denial of constitutional rights on the part of candidates or voters, or both. The parties here moved with unusual diligence and * * * relief "if it is to be had, must perforce come from the Court or the voters must simply be told to wait four more years."

In the face of gross, unsophisticated, significant, and obvious racial discriminations in the conduct of the election and the now established power of a Federal Court to extinguish its effects even to the point of setting aside the election, the Georgia reasons relied on by the District Judge warrant but a brief comment. The Court's fundamental mistake was in assuming that this was an election contest as such in which the winner is challenged because of ineligibility, fraud or irregularities in the conduct of the election, the receipt or counting of illegal ballots which would change the result and the like, and which, as a separate special statutory proceeding, must be timely filed by specified persons following statutory procedures and in particular tribunals. Mrs. Bell and her co-plaintiffs alone or as members of the class did not challenge the eligibility of Mr. Southwell or the fact that he received an overwhelming majority. Indeed, Mrs. Bell as a former candidate did not seek to be selected over Southwell or any other opponent. What, and all, she and others sought was an election conducted free of such indefensible, racial distinctions. That being so, it was not the usual simple case of counting votes and denying relief for want of affirmative proof of a different result.

Equally lacking in merit is the Court's conclusion that setting aside the election would be ineffectual since * * * the Georgia statute prescribes that when an election is held and is determined not to have been valid, no re-election is held, but rather the Ordinary appoints a Justice of the Peace for the required term. The Court assumed, with unquestioned basis probably, that the Ordinary would have appointed Southwell. Clearly, the Federal Constitution and the Federal Courts are not so helpless or unresourceful as to condemn in words only to let go by default in fact such an open breach of constitutional demands.

This leaves only a tag end. There is a suggestion that the District Court enjoining Southwell from taking office pursuant to the election would be powerless to grant affirmative relief requiring that the Ordinary call a special election. In this vital area of vindication of precious constitutional rights, we are unfettered by the negative or affirmative character of the words used or the negative or affirmative form in which the coercive order is cast. If affirmative relief is essential, the Court has the power and should employ it.

The cause must therefore be reversed and remanded for the entry of an appropriate order setting aside the election and requiring the calling of a special election.

Ippolito v. Power

Court of Appeals of New York
22 N.Y.2d 594, 241 N.E.2d 232, 294 N.Y.S.2d 209 (1968)

Breitel, J. [with whom Fuld, C.J., and Keating and Jasen, JJ., join:]

The successful candidate for District Leader (Male) Part B of the 22nd Assembly District, Democratic party, in the County of Queens, appeals from an order directing a new primary election in a proceeding brought by the unsuccessful candidate under section 330 of the Election Law. Special Term, after a hearing, granted such order, and the Appellate Division affirmed by a divided vote.

The statute provides that the court may direct a new election where it "has been characterized by such frauds or irregularities as to render impossible a determination as to who rightfully was . . . elected." This is the statutory standard and it is stated in the alternative, namely, that frauds or irregularities may ground a court's discretion in directing a new election.

In the instant primary a total vote of 2,827 was cast, 1,422 for the winner and 1,405 for the loser. Thus the winning margin was a mere 17 votes. Concededly 101 possible votes in the aggregate number were suspect or invalid for some kind of irregularity without any evidence of fraud or intentional misconduct. According to the public counter on the machine, there were 68 more votes cast than there were qualified persons who signed the voter registration (buff) cards. To be sure, it may be that the public counter did not register actual votes but only openings and closings of the automatic voting machines. In any event, such excessive operations were as unlawful as if actual excess votes were cast, and are significant because of the impossibility of knowing, in the absence of positive evidence, whether that is all that happened when the machines were opened and closed. There were 19 suspect or invalid votes because of blank, void, or missing party enrollments, 7 voter registration cards that were not signed, one irregular card, and 6 signings-in by members of the Conservative party although there was no contested Conservative primary. These make up the total of 101 suspect or invalid votes.

It is evident that even a small portion of the suspect votes could undo the slight margin of the victor and change defeat into victory for the loser. Hence, the statutory standard is met precisely, justifying the lower court's exercise of discretion in directing a new primary election. On almost identical facts, this court affirmed a similar direction (*Matter of Nodar v. Power*, 18 N.Y.2d 697 [220 N.E.2d 267 (1966)]). In the *Nodar* case, 1,417 votes were cast for the contested position, 722 for the victor and 695 for the loser. There were 109 invalid or suspect votes, consisting of votes by 80 persons who were not enrolled and who signed in, and 29 excess operations of the machine according to the public counter. There, a victory margin of 27, when weighed against 109 irregular votes, was sufficient to require a new election without evidence of fraud or other intentional misconduct. *Matter of Acevedo v. Power* (18 N.Y.2d 700

[220 N.E.2d 269 (1966)]) and *Matter of O'Connor v. Power* (18 N.Y.2d 705 [220 N.E.2d 271 (1966)]), decided the same day as the *Nodar* case, reached an opposite conclusion. These were affirmances of exercises of discretion by the lower courts in declining to direct new elections, and were supported by entirely different probabilities. In the *Acevedo* case, there were 103 suspect votes against a victory margin of 95, and, in the other, some 262 suspect votes, of which Special Term refused to invalidate 102, leaving 160 against a victory margin of 165 votes. Obviously, a change in the result would require that the bulk of the questioned votes be shifted to the loser, a gross improbability, or even impossibility, before it could be inferred that the irregularities were influential (see *Matter of Badillo v. Santangelo*, 15 A.D.2d 341 [1962]).

There evolves from these cases a rational standard: if irregularities are sufficiently large in number to establish the probability that the result would be changed by a shift in, or invalidation of, the questioned votes, there should be a new election. As stated in the *Badillo* case, "An election will not be overturned upon a mere mathematical possibility that the results could have been changed, when the probabilities all combine to repel any such conclusion"; but in cases like the one now before the court, as in the *Nodar* case, it does not strain the probabilities to assume a likelihood that the questioned votes produced or could produce a change in the result.

While it is troubling to require new election for irregularities without evidence of fraud or other intentional misconduct, ignoring such irregularities would undoubtedly create the likelihood that skillfully manipulated "irregularities" would be used to mask corrupt practices. It is better to keep the standards high, even at the cost of penalizing some voters and candidates for the failures of election inspectors, than to increase the opportunities for fraud without possibility or likelihood of discovery. And the statute is explicit in directing that irregularities, as well as fraud, may justify the direction of a new election. * * *

Accordingly, the order directing a new election should be affirmed.

[BURKE, SCILEPPI, and BERGAN, JJ., dissenting.] * * *

Before considering the "specifics" relied upon by the majority, we would first comment on the setting in which the initial election was held. This year, for the first time, primaries were conducted State-wide. Accordingly, more voting machines were required. To meet this demand, a plan was initiated whereby the primary could be conducted without providing each political party a separate voting machine in each polling place. Instead, it was decided that the space on the individual machines could be split by the different political parties. To do this, it was first necessary that the machines be divided according to the parties, and that levers be installed which would limit a particular voter's choice to those persons on the machine who were aspirants for office in his own political party. Finally, to insure that each person was properly limited to voting for his party's candidates, each voter, after registering, was given a card of a distinctive color corresponding to the color ascribed to his party. Those persons operating the machines were thus informed of the voter's registration and would set the machine accordingly. The uniqueness of this procedure is apparent. It is equally obvious that such a plan, when used for the first time and because it encompassed more steps than the standard primary procedure, would produce more mechanical and human errors than are usually associated with elections. Discrepancies alone, therefore, between various cross references of figures are more likely to occur and, in light of all the claims asserted both in this court and the lower courts of this State pertaining to this primary election, it would indeed be suspicious for any district or area to report a totally unimpeachable result.

We do not agree with the majority that, to the extent the "irregularities" were attributed to the excess in the machine count over the number of signed cards, there is a basis for invalidating the difference. Even where there is an excess machine count in a case where machines were used for more than one party, it is pure speculation to assume *without any testimony* that there were repeaters. It is well settled that the results of an election are entitled to a presumption of regularity and that a party attempting to impeach these results carries the burden of proof. In *Matter of Nodar v. Power* there were 1,417 votes cast as against 2,827 in this case. Hence the percentage of irregularities here is 50% less than in *Matter of Nodar* which is, therefore, inapplicable.

An inexplicable inference, advanced by petitioner and accepted by the majority, arises from the Conservative vote in the district. The record before us indicates that there was no contested Conservative primary. From this evidence alone, the majority has concluded that Conservatives voted in the Democratic party. Proof of such a contention should lie, if at all, in the figures for registration and poll count amongst Democrats in the same district. Thus, if petitioner established that more Democratic votes were cast than could have been cast because of the Conservative registrants, there would indeed be a basis for this contention. Such evidence, however, does not exist. In fact, no testimonial evidence has been presented to support any allegation. * * *

It is evident that all these "irregularities" were in fact attributable to mechanical and human error. As the burden of establishing the adverse effect on him of the "irregularities" rests on the petitioner, it is inconsistent with the prevailing conditions at this primary as compared with the primary held in *Matter of Nodar* to refuse to dismiss the petition in this case as we did in *Matter of Acevedo v. Power* where the vote cast was equivalent to the vote cast here.

The order of the Appellate Division should be reversed and the petition dismissed.

Akizaki v. Fong

Supreme Court of Hawai'i.
51 Haw. 354, 461 P.2d 221 (Haw. 1969)

RICHARDSON, CHIEF JUSTICE [with whom JUSTICE LEVINSON, CIRCUIT JUDGE HAWKINS, and CIRCUIT JUDGE KING (the latter two sitting by designation) join].

In the November 1968 election to select six representatives in the [Hawaii] House of Representatives from the Fifteenth Representative District, five candidates were clearly elected without contest. The present case involves a controversy over the sixth seat.

In the final tabulation of the votes, the Republican candidate, Fong, received two more votes than did the Democratic candidate, Akizaki. Akizaki contested the election in the court below, and proved that of the ballots counted, at least nineteen were clearly invalid. These were absentee ballots which, because of late postmarks, failed to meet the requirements of HRS § 14-8. HRS § 14-8 provides that an absentee ballot received not later than noon on the sixth day following a general election may be counted, but only if it is postmarked not later than the day before the election. Due to a mistake on the part of the election officials, nineteen ballots postmarked too late to be opened and counted were nevertheless opened and counted. In the process they were commingled with valid absentee ballots so that it could not later be determined for whom the invalid ballots had been cast. Since the number of invalid ballots greatly exceeds the margin of victory, it is obvious that their presence could have affected the result. The court below resolved this problem by discarding 174 absentee ballots, among which were the nineteen invalid ones. On the basis of a tabulation without these 174 ballots, the court declared Akizaki to have been the winner of the election. From this determination Fong appeals to this Court. * * *

The fundamental interest to be protected here is that of the people of the Fifteenth Representative District in choosing whomever they please to represent them in the House of Representatives. The right to vote is perhaps the most basic and fundamental of all the rights guaranteed by our democratic form of government. Implicit in that right is the right to have one's vote count and the right to have as nearly perfect an election proceeding as can be provided. The result we reach must be consistent with these principles. * * *

We hold that * * * a new election should have been ordered. Because of the commingling of the valid and invalid absentee ballots, there is simply no way to determine what the actual result of the election was, and who should therefore be declared the winner. * * *

The trial court's approach was plausible; but to excise the entire absentee vote contained in the 174 ballots excluded by the court, in order to eliminate the nineteen ballots known to be invalid, inflicts too harsh a result on those absentee voters whose votes were validly cast. * * *

Reversed.

ABE, JUSTICE (dissenting). * * *

The House of Representatives in the proper exercise of this constitutional power by a majority vote of its members declared plaintiff Akizaki one of the six duly elected members from the Fifteenth Representative District and seated him. * * * I believe it is improper, to say the least, for this court, by its decision in this case, to attempt to undo what the House of Representatives has done. I disagree with the majority court and I believe its decision definitely shows not only utter disrespect but lack of confidence in a coordinate branch of our government. * * *

Fladell v. Palm Beach County Canvassing Board

Supreme Court of Florida
772 So. 2d 1240 (Fla. 2000)

PER CURIAM. [CHIEF JUSTICE WELLS, JUSTICE SHAW, JUSTICE HARDING, JUSTICE ANSTEAD, JUSTICE PARIENTE, JUSTICE LEWIS, and JUSTICE QUINCE join in this opinion.] * * *

The issue in this case concerns the legality of the form of the ballot used in Palm Beach County, Florida, in the November 7, 2000, general election for the President and Vice President of the United States. The remedy sought by the appellants is a re-vote, a new election, or a statistical reallocation of the election totals in Palm Beach County.

* * * In their briefs, the appellants [voters in Palm Beach County] * * * claim that the ballot is patently defective on its face in that the form and design of the ballot violated the statutory requirements of Florida election law. The appellants contend that the ballot was confusing and, as a result, they fear that they may have cast their vote for a candidate other than the one they intended.[c] * * *

As a general rule, a court should not void an election for ballot form defects unless such defects cause the ballot to be in substantial noncompliance with the statutory election requirements. *See Nelson v. Robinson*, 301 So. 2d 508, 510 (Fla.

---

c. This case involved the so-called "butterfly ballot." The standard form of the ballot listed all the candidates on the left side of the ballot. Voters would punch a hole to the right of their preferred candidate's name. The butterfly ballot listed candidates on both the right and left of the ballot, with a single line of perforated circles down the center. Apparently the rationale for the design was that having two columns of candidates' names would allow for the use of a larger font, which was thought to be beneficial for the elderly voters in Palm Beach County. Voters using the butterfly ballot would select the candidate listed in the top-left position by punching the top hole. Voters would select the candidate immediately below that candidate (*i.e.*, the one second-from-the-top, in the left column) by punching the *third* hole. Punching out the second hole would result in a vote being counted for the candidate listed on the top-right of the ballot. In the 2000 presidential election, George W. Bush was in the top-left spot; Pat Buchanan was in the top-right spot; and Al Gore was in the spot below Bush. It appears that several voters intending to vote for Gore—perhaps a large enough number to change the result in Florida, and thus the entire presidential election—cast a vote for Buchanan by mistake. The press nicknamed Theresa LePore, the supervisor of elections and designer of the ballot, "Madame Butterfly." —Eds.

2d DCA 1974) (rejecting a post-election challenge based upon an alleged defect in the alignment of the candidates' names on the ballot). When considering a petition alleging a violation in the form of the ballot, "a vital consideration guiding the courts in determining whether an election should be voided is the reluctance to reach a decision which would result in the disfranchisement of the voters. Indeed, as regards defects in ballots, the courts have generally declined to void an election unless such defects clearly operate to prevent that free, fair and open choice." *Id.*

In the present case, even accepting appellants' allegations, we conclude as a matter of law that the Palm Beach County ballot does not constitute substantial noncompliance with the statutory requirements mandating the voiding of the election. * * * Accordingly, we affirm the trial court's dismissal with prejudice of the complaints. * * *

It is so ordered.

Notes and Questions

1. As the *Bell* court acknowledged, it is extraordinary for a court (particularly a federal court) to take the "drastic" step of ordering a new election for a state office. According to the court, the remedy was necessary given the pervasiveness of the voting-rights violations. How often would you expect such circumstances to be found? It appears that federal courts have rarely found such circumstances, and so the holding in *Bell* is rarely replicated, even in cases from the same circuit. *See, e.g., Hamer v. Ely,* 410 F.2d 152, 156 (5th Cir. 1969) (Wisdom, J.) (refusing to order a new election, even when state officials did not appoint anyone to aid illiterate African-American voters, because the "serious violations of voting rights" found in *Bell* were not present); *Hutchinson v. Miller,* 797 F.2d 1279, 1287 (4th Cir. 1986) [p. 1168] (discussing how federal courts have rarely found the circumstances of *Bell* to be present). *See also Developments in the Law — Elections,* 88 Harv. L. Rev. 1111, 1335 (1975) (observing that courts rarely void elections, as in *Bell,* when there is no evidence that the violations would have changed the outcome). We will consider the impact of federalism on federal courts' ability to order election remedies later in this Chapter, in § C.

2. One scholar has contrasted *Bell* and *Bush v. Gore,* 531 U.S. 98 (2000) [p. 1085], arguing that the federal judges in the former case "courageously" and correctly voided the election, although "court intervention should be used sparingly." In contrast, he continued, *Bush v. Gore* is a "dangerous precedent to the extent that it eases the way for federal court intervention in state and local elections over nuts-and-bolts disputes better left to local authorities." Richard L. Hasen, Bush v. Gore *and the Future of Equal Protection Law,* 29 Fla. St. U. L. Rev. 377, 400 (2001). Do you agree? Would many critics of *Bush v. Gore* tend to herald *Bell,* and vice-versa? Are the cases in tension, or can they be harmonized in principled ways?

3. While the ordering of a new election, as in *Bell,* is unusual for federal judges, "the remedy is not uncommon in local elections" being reviewed by state judges,

often primarily or exclusively on state-law grounds. Steven F. Huefner, *Remedying Election Wrongs*, 44 Harv. J. on Legis. 265, 283 (2007). An example is the decision of Hawaii's Supreme Court in *Akizaki*. The court was unable to determine who had been rightfully elected, and found that ordering a new election did not violate separation of powers concerns. In other words, it was not a nonjusticiable political question (*see* Chapter 2). In contrast, the dissent found the result to be in "direct conflict" with the separation of powers. Whomever you may think had the better of the argument, note how *Akizaki* (in contrast to *Bell*) raised no federalism concerns because the litigation was in state court. Does that difference make it more justifiable for a state court than a federal court to order a new election?

4. *Fladell* was a less-noticed decision issued by the Florida Supreme Court during the *Bush v. Gore* controversy, albeit growing out of the same dispute. To order a new election, the court held, there must be "substantial noncompliance" with statutory requirements for the ballot. Courts should be wary of ordering a new election, the court held, since doing so would be tantamount to disenfranchising voters. Is that a fair characterization of the remedy? Why was the reticence displayed by *Fladell* absent in *Bell* and *Akizaki*? For an argument that the *Fladell* court should have ordered a new election, see Stephen J. Mulroy, *Right Without a Remedy? The "Butterfly Ballot" Case and Court Ordered Federal Election "Revotes,"* 10 Geo. Mason L. Rev. 215 (2001).

5. For a general discussion of the power of federal courts to set aside state elections, see Kenneth W. Starr, *Federal Judicial Intervention as a Remedy for Irregularities in State Elections*, 49 N.Y.U. L. Rev. 1092 (1974). Starr addressed the pros and cons of retroactively remedying an irregular election by ordering a new one, as opposed to issuing an order prospectively forbidding the challenged practice. The former, he noted, provides a more complete remedy, and seemingly returns voters to the status quo. The latter remedy, he observed, is less intrusive, and avoids the difficulty of truly restoring the status quo, since not all of the same voters may vote, time has passed, and it is almost impossible to rerun the same election. He saw the result of *Bell* as being justified due to the egregious, intentionally unlawful conduct of state officials. *Id.* at 1116–17. On the other hand, he argued, the "outrageous" criterion of *Bell* is a "highly subjective standard" and, therefore, difficult for courts to apply. *Id.* at 1117. In most instances, Starr concluded, a new election should be ordered only when the improprieties were outcome-determinative, that is, when they might have affected the outcome of the election. *Id.* at 1124–27.

6. Michael O. Finkelstein & Herbert E. Robbins, *Mathematical Probability in Election Challenges*, 73 Colum. L. Rev. 241 (1973), set out a formula to help determine whether invalid votes altered the outcome of an election. The formula considers the winner's plurality, the total number of votes cast, and the number of invalid votes cast. The formula assumes that the invalid votes were not systematically biased toward one candidate or another, *i.e.*, that the invalid votes were randomly distributed. In *Ippolito*, the court ordered a new election because "it does not strain the probabilities to assume a likelihood that the questioned votes produced or could

produce a change in the results." Finkelstein and Robbins criticized this analysis because under their formula, there was only a five percent chance that the outcome of the election at issue in that case would have been different. *Id.* at 243.

Does this analysis call into question the reasoning or result in *Ippolito*? Is the "intuitive" analysis of cases like *Ippolito* more, or less, persuasive than the formula? Finkelstein and Robbins acknowledged that their formula should not be used if there is "evidence of fraud or patterns of irregular voting." What type of evidence should be presented, or should a court demand, before invoking that exception? What do you make of the fact that no court has apparently ever applied the formula? Kevin J. Hickey, Note, *Accuracy Counts: Illegal Votes in Contested Elections and the Case for Complete Proportionate Deduction*, 83 N.Y.U. L. Rev. 167, 174 (2008).

2. Adjusting the Vote Totals

Marks v. Stinson

United States Court of Appeals for the Third Circuit
19 F.3d 873 (3d Cir. 1994)

Stapleton, Circuit Judge [with whom Greenberg, Circuit Judge, and Cowen, Circuit Judge, join]: * * *

Republican Bruce Marks and Democrat William Stinson ran in an election conducted on November 2, 1993, to represent Pennsylvania's second senatorial district. This election was held to fill the remaining portion of a term expiring in December 1994, and was of particular significance to both Republicans and Democrats because control of the Pennsylvania Senate was at stake. According to the certified results of the Philadelphia County Commissioners, sitting as the County Board of Elections ("the Board"), of the 38,818 votes cast on the voting machines on election day, 19,691 were cast for Marks, while 19,127 were cast for Stinson. However, of the 1,767 absentee ballots cast, Marks received only 371 votes, while Stinson received 1,396 votes. When all votes were added together, Stinson won by a final count of 20,523 to 20,062. The Board, therefore, certified Stinson as the winner of the election and he was subsequently sworn in as a Pennsylvania state senator. * * *

Under Pennsylvania law, a qualified elector may vote by absentee ballot if he or she is, *inter alia*, absent from the Commonwealth or county of residence "because his duties, occupation or business require him to be elsewhere during the entire period the polls are open" or is physically unable to go to the polls.[d] An elector who wishes to vote by absentee ballot must submit to the appropriate board of election an absentee ballot application, including a statement that the elector expects to be

---

d. Pennsylvania law now provides for no-excuse voting by mail. —Eds.

out of the county on election day or that the elector is physically unable to go to the polls[.] * * *

The Stinson campaign sent its workers into divisions of the district where a majority of the residents were white to solicit voter registration applications and absentee ballot applications. The goal was to obtain twenty absentee ballot applications from each division. Those who expressed a hesitancy to register because they did not wish to go to a polling place were told by campaign workers that they could fill out an absentee ballot application and obtain an absentee ballot as a matter of convenience. Many improper applications were received based on this misrepresentation. These absentee ballot applications stated that the basis for voting absentee was that the applicant would be out of the county at the time of the election, despite the fact that the applicant had no reason to believe that this would be the case. To conceal the fact that many of these improper absentee ballot applications were solicited several months before election day, Stinson campaign workers told canvassers not to fill in the true date on the application. The absentee ballots that the Stinson campaign obtained in this way were then submitted directly to [County] Commissioner Tartaglione's office and the corresponding absentee ballot packages were provided directly to the Stinson campaign. According to the testimony of one campaign worker, Stinson was aware of the improper conduct regarding the absentee ballots, yet he permitted the conduct to continue and even admonished campaign workers who questioned its legality.

About three weeks before the election, the Stinson campaign learned that a Democratic State Committee poll showed Marks running ahead of Stinson by four percentage points. The campaign responded by saturating the Hispanic and African-American areas of the district with absentee ballot applications using tactics similar to those earlier employed. This time, however, campaign workers solicited absentee ballot applications in person and by telephone by telling the Latino and African-American voters that there was a "new way to vote" from the convenience of one's own home. Campaign workers were paid $1.00 for each application or ballot that they were able to obtain in this way, and the campaign dispensed at least $500 to $700 dollars in this effort.

The Stinson campaign obtained approximately 1,000 absentee ballots applications from the minority sections of the district. The applications were then delivered by Stinson campaign workers directly to Commissioner Talmadge, and he provided the absentee ballot packages directly to the Stinson campaign. Stinson campaign workers then took the absentee ballots directly to applicants' homes. In numerous instances, Stinson workers executed applications, ballots, and declarations without the voter understanding the nature of the document. In other instances, Stinson workers instructed the voter to check certain places on the ballot, or filled out and forged the ballot. Voters were also assisted in completing applications and declaration packages after the statutory deadline for receipt by the Board had passed, and such ballots were counted by the Board. Many voters who cast absentee ballots testified that they were unaware that they had signed absentee ballot applications.

Almost 400 of the absentee ballot applications submitted by the Stinson campaign were rejected by the Board because they came from unregistered voters. These rejected applications were returned directly to Commissioner Talmadge, who then returned them to a Stinson campaign worker. Contrary to state law, no record was kept of the rejected applications.

Commissioners Tartaglione and Talmadge [both of whom were Democrats] and Board employees working with them were aware of the absentee ballot campaign of Stinson and his workers and assisted that campaign by delivering hundreds of absentee ballot packages directly to Stinson workers rather than mailing or delivering them to the electors whose names and addresses appeared on the applications. This assistance was designed to aid the Stinson campaign in obtaining more votes through personal contact between the electors and the Stinson campaign workers. No such assistance was provided to Marks or the Marks campaign. * * * The Board's assistance to the Stinson campaign was covert and was not disclosed to Republican Commissioner Kane at the time.

{On election day, November 2, * * * the Marks campaign attempted to challenge 551 absentee ballots at polling places * * *, but 351 absentee ballots were opened in apparent violation of [state law]. on November 18, the Board convened to consider Marks' challenge to the absentee ballots[.] * * * Marks attempted to present evidence of electoral fraud, but the Board heard from only one witness before determining that it could only consider testimony from authorized pollwatchers. None being present, the Board rejected all 551 challenges to the absentee ballots and certified Stinson as the winner.

{The federal district court made the following finding of fact with respect to the Board's November 18th certification of Stinson:

> * * * The decision to certify Stinson was made on November 18, 1993 when all other candidates for Election in the County of Philadelphia were certified on November 22, 1993.
>
> The Board certified Stinson during the hearing even though Commissioner Talmadge knew that the Election Code provided two days to appeal a decision of the Board with respect to challenges and even though he knew Marks was going to appeal. Marks did appeal. [State law] requires the County Board to suspend any action in canvassing, computing, and certifying the winner pending the 48 hour period during which Marks had a right to appeal the City Commissioners' decision and * * * requires the Board to suspend certification pending such appeal.
>
> The actions of the Board were designed to, and did in fact, prevent any realistic opportunity to appeal the certification in the State court system. The Board applied the Election Code in a discriminatory manner designed to favor one candidate. Certifying Stinson in this manner would end inquiries into the election abuse in which Commissioners Tartaglione and

Talmadge participated. The Board conducted nothing more than mock hearings and intentionally reached decisions that would not reveal their involvement in the ongoing absentee ballot voting scheme. * * * In short, the Board participated in an improper scheme and were then called upon to sit in judgment of that very conduct.

{On November 19, Marks and the Republican State Committee appealed the Board's dismissal of the absentee ballot challenge to Common Pleas Court. In addition, Marks filed an emergency petition with the Pennsylvania Supreme Court to request a stay to prevent Stinson from voting when the Pennsylvania Senate reconvened. The Pennsylvania Supreme Court refused to entertain a hearing or grant a stay.

{On November 22, the Pennsylvania Senate reconvened. The President of the Senate, Lt. Gov. Mark S. Singel, a Democrat, ruled that Stinson was properly seated. Sen. Robert C. Jubelirer, a Republican, objected, claiming that the Board's certification of Stinson was invalid. The Senate voted 25–24 that Stinson was "eligible to vote on his own seating in the Senate," with Stinson casting the decisive vote. The Senate then voted 25–24 that Stinson was "properly seated as a member of the Pennsylvania Senate," with Stinson again casting the decisive vote.

{The appeal from the Board's dismissal of the absentee ballot challenge was heard on December 14 before Judge Mark I. Bernstein of the Philadelphia Court of Common Pleas. Marks and the Republican State Committee * * * attempted to present evidence of electoral fraud, but Judge Bernstein found that he could consider only what had been presented to the Board[.] * * * Judge Bernstein accordingly affirmed the Board's certification of Stinson.

{Judge Bernstein also was assigned the election contest * * *. He ruled that the voters were required to post a $50,000 bond * * *. The bond was not raised and, on January 10, Judge Bernstein dismissed the contest without providing a hearing on the merits. * * *

{Marks and the Republican State Committee have appealed Judge Bernstein's dismissal of the absentee ballot challenge to the Pennsylvania Supreme Court. That appeal is currently pending. Marks has appealed the dismissal of the election contest to the Pennsylvania Senate which has scheduled no proceedings thereon.}

After setting forth its factual findings, the district court concluded that the plaintiffs had established a likelihood of success on their claims. Specifically, the court found a likelihood of success on the claims that the defendants' conduct violated: "i. the First Amendment rights of Plaintiffs by illegally discriminating in favor of Democrat Stinson over Republican Marks. . . . ii. the equal protection rights of Plaintiffs by illegally discriminating in favor of Democrat Stinson over Republican Marks with no rational reason or purpose[, and] the substantive due process right of Plaintiffs to a free and fair election." The district court also found that a likelihood of success had been shown with respect to the plaintiffs' Voting Rights Act claims. Finally, the district court concluded that plaintiffs, "and even the entire state," suffer irreparable injury when an "improperly seated . . . representative" of the people exercises the powers of his office and when "constitutional freedoms" are lost.

Having determined that a preliminary injunction should be issued, the district court turned to the form of the interim relief to be granted. The court stated in part:

> In light of the massive scheme of Candidate Stinson and the Stinson Campaign, and in light of the failure of the Board to fairly conduct its duties, it would be grossly inequitable to allow Stinson to remain in office and for the Board to continue to conduct business as it did during the 1993 Election. . . .

> The votes cast at the voting machines were not affected by the improper conduct of the Stinson Campaign or the Board, and no evidence indicates that the machine returns do not reflect the will of the electorate. The District should not be denied representation in the State Senate based on the efforts taken by the Stinson Campaign and the Board to conceal certain conduct relating to the absentee balloting procedures. . . .

> The will of the electorate is reflected in the votes cast on the voting machines. The public interest will be served by having Marks, the candidate who prevailed on the undisputed legal votes, serve the remaining months of the term, which expires in December, 1994, rather than declaring the seat vacant and scheduling a new election at the May primary.

The evidence and the factual findings of the district court clearly support its conclusion regarding the existence of irreparable injury and the likelihood of success on plaintiffs' Civil Rights Act claims, i.e., that the defendants operating under color of state law violated plaintiffs' rights under the First and Fourteenth Amendments. * * *

[W]e now turn to the remedy issue. The state elections process recognized Stinson as the winner of the election. While the district court found for purposes of plaintiffs' preliminary injunction motion that wrongdoing affected the election, it did not find, even for that limited purpose, that Stinson's election was attributable to wrongdoing. The district court did not find that Stinson failed to receive a plurality of the legally cast votes.

* * * Nor did the district court address the problem created by the fact that some electors who cast tainted absentee ballots undoubtedly would have cast valid votes at the polls had they not been misled (by a conspiracy knowingly supported by state actors) into believing there was a "new way to vote." Thus, while the district court concluded that "no evidence indicates that the machine returns do not reflect the will of the electorate," it did not affirmatively conclude that the winner of the machine vote would have won a plurality of the legal votes cast if the wrongdoing had not occurred.

The district court did conclude, with ample record support, that the wrongdoing was substantial, that it *could* have affected the outcome of the election, and that it

rendered the certified vote count an unreliable indicator of the will of the electorate. Having so concluded for the purposes of the preliminary injunction motion, we
cannot say that the district court abused its discretion in restraining Stinson from
exercising the powers of the office *pendente lite*.

The integrity of the election process lies at the heart of any republic. The people,
the ultimate source of governmental power, delegate to their elected representatives
the authority to take measures which affect their welfare in a multitude of important ways. When a representative exercises that authority under circumstances
where the electors have no assurance that he or she was the choice of the plurality
of the electors, the legitimacy of the governmental actions taken is suspect. Accordingly, where there is substantial wrongdoing in an election, the effects of which are
not capable of quantification but which render the apparent result an unreliable
indicium of the will of the electorate, courts have frequently declined to allow the
apparent winner to exercise the delegated power. *See, e.g., Bell v. Southwell*, 376 F.2d
659 (5th Cir. 1967) [p. 1121]. Having tentatively found the facts that it did, we cannot fault the district court for restraining Stinson from exercising the powers that
are delegated to a senator by the people, even though the court was not able to find
that he received less than a plurality of the legally cast votes.

However, the district court's tentative findings that there was "massive absentee
ballot fraud, deception, intimidation, harassment and forgery," and that "many"
of the absentee votes were tainted, do not, we conclude, justify its decision to order
the certification of Marks. Marks' only claim of authority to exercise the people's
delegated power rests upon his receiving a majority of the votes cast on the voting
machines. Equating the machine vote with the will of the electorate disenfranchises
the voters who cast legal absentee ballots. Moreover, it fails to take into account the
will of electors who would have voted at the polling places but who unknowingly
cast illegal absentee ballots relying on the assurances that were an integral part of
the scheme which "the Board participated in and later tried to conceal."

In the circumstances which confronted the district court, we believe the same
principle that justified the unseating of Stinson dictates that Marks not be certified
on the basis of the machine vote only. For the actions of a democratically elected
body of representatives to be legitimate, the electorate must be assured that each of
the representatives was the choice of the electorate. It follows, we believe, that Marks
should not be certified unless and until the district court is satisfied that Marks
would have won the election but for the wrongdoing. * * *

Plaintiffs argue that to require certainty of results here would be unfair to Marks.
They note that the district court tentatively found that the wrongdoing of Stinson
and the other defendants may have made it impossible to determine who would
have won a fair election. Assuming that it is in fact impossible to determine a certain winner, Marks will be forced to endure the hardship of running again if he still
wishes to fill the senate seat. Therefore, plaintiffs argue that Marks will, in effect,
be punished for the wrongdoing of the defendants. Plaintiffs suggest that the way

to deal with election results that are uncertain as a result of fraud is to have the "punishment" fall on the party who perpetrated the fraud. Plaintiffs' arguments, however, miss the mark. Our primary concern here is not to punish any individual candidate or party, but to promote the public's interest in having legislative power exercised only by those to whom it has been legally delegated. This interest is not served by arbitrarily ignoring the absentee vote, a substantial but undetermined portion of which was either legally cast or came from voters who would have gone to the polls but for the fraud. Just punishment for any wrongdoing that has been perpetrated may be pursued in other proceedings; it is not the objective here. * * *

We are mindful of the fact that our decision to sustain the preliminary injunction insofar as it relates to Stinson and to vacate it insofar as it relates to Marks will likely result in the voters of the second senatorial district being without representation in the Pennsylvania Senate during the pendency of this litigation. * * * [W]e do not think that concern justified the certification of a candidate who had not established his credentials.

Interim periods during which the voters of an area are without representation are inevitable. Vacancies periodically occur for a variety of reasons, and the process necessary to select someone to fill those vacancies necessarily takes time. Among the numerous factors that can make that period substantial are irregularities in the voting process and ensuing litigation. While substantial periods without representation are regrettable, the consequences of placing political power in unauthorized hands are of far graver concern.

We urge the district court to reach a final resolution of this case as soon as possible. The character and timing of further proceedings are, of course, left to its discretion. Those proceedings and the court's final judgment, however, should be consistent with this opinion. In particular, the district court should not direct the certification of a candidate unless it finds, on the basis of record evidence, that the designated candidate would have won the election but for wrongdoing.[14] *See, e.g.,* *Curry v. Baker*, 802 F.2d 1302 (11th Cir. 1986).

If the district court finds a constitutional violation, it will have authority to order a special election, whether or not it is able to determine what the results would have been in the absence of that violation. The district court need not exercise this authority, however. Depending on the circumstances existing at the time these proceedings are concluded, a special election to fill the vacancy for the remainder of the year may not be justifiable in terms of the expense to the state and the burden on the candidates, voters, and election officials. The district court may exercise its own discretion in light of the circumstances then existing or it may simply invalidate the

---

14. We do not suggest that such a finding would have to be made with mathematical precision. Courts, with the aid of expert testimony, have been able to demonstrate that a particular result is worthy of the public's confidence even though not established solely by applying mathematics to the record evidence. *See, e.g., Curry,* 802 F.2d at 1317–19. What is required is evidence and an analysis that demonstrate that the district court's remedy is worthy of the confidence of the electorate.

election, declare that there is a vacancy, and leave the decisions concerning a special election and the timing thereof to the appropriate state authorities.

We will vacate that portion of the district court's preliminary injunction that required the Board of Elections to certify Marks. The remainder of the preliminary injunction will remain in effect until further order of the district court.

Bradley v. Perrodin

California Court of Appeal, Second District, Division 1
106 Cal. App. 4th 1153, 131 Cal. Rptr. 2d 402 (2003)

ORTEGA, J. [with whom SPENCER, P.J., and MALLANO, J., join]. * * *

Appellant Irving and respondent Andrews were the top candidates in one of two city council races in the April 2001 primary election. * * * In the June 5, 2001, runoff election, Irving defeated Andrews by a vote of 5,414 to 4,863.

Andrews then filed the present election contest against Irving, contending that [city clerk Charles] Davis had erred by placing Irving's name above Andrews's on the runoff ballot. * * * Davis conceded below that Andrews's name should have been listed first [pursuant to the randomized alphabet compiled for such purposes] * * *. Davis stated, and the trial court agreed, that Irving's name was mistakenly placed before Andrews's due to Davis's unintentional error. The finding that Davis's error was unintentional is not disputed in this appeal. * * *

The trial court, after rejecting Irving's argument that the ballot name-order error should have been addressed in a preelection writ proceeding, found the error sufficient to overturn Irving's election. The court shifted 295 votes from Irving to Andrews based, as in the mayoral election contest, on the primacy effect theory,[5] and declared Andrews the winner.

In addition, the trial court found Irving had committed offenses against the elective franchise, either personally or through her agents, by: (1) knowingly soliciting nine noncitizens to register for absentee ballots * * *; (2) being present in the nine absentee voters' homes while they were voting and telling them how to vote * * *; (3) fraudulently registering the nine noncitizens and assisting them to vote or completing their absentee ballots for them * * *; and (4) soliciting illegal votes from the nine nonqualified voters[.] * * *

Irving appealed from the adverse judgment and petitioned for a writ of supersedeas. We denied the petition on March 7, 2002. Accordingly, Andrews has been serving on the city council while this appeal was pending. * * *

---

5. [T]he trial court based its primacy effect finding solely on [political scientist Jon] Krosnick's expert testimony that on average, those listed first on a ballot receive 3.32 percent more votes. There was no direct evidence from any voter regarding the effect of the name-order error on the voter's selection of a candidate.

When an otherwise successful candidate such as Irving is subsequently found to have committed an offense or offenses against the elective franchise, her election may be annulled even if the number of unqualified voters she fraudulently regis-tered or the number of votes she unlawfully solicited were too few to have changed the outcome of the election. As the California Supreme Court explained: "Each . . . 'offense against the elective franchise * * *' can furnish independent statutory grounds for contesting and annulling the election, separate and apart from the effects of any illegal votes actually counted." * * * We conclude [that] Irving's elec-tion was properly annulled [and Irving was disqualified from serving in the office] based on the finding, which was supported by substantial evidence, that she had committed offenses against the franchise[,] * * * despite the lack of evidence that Irving's offenses changed the outcome of the election. * * *

Given that this election contest involves questions broader than Irving's personal interest as a candidate for the contested office, we conclude the electorate's inter-est in this important legal issue requires that the primacy effect issue be addressed. Election contests are not typical adversary proceedings "between individuals assert-ing personal rights or interests, but involve the right of the people to have the fact as to who has been duly elected by them judicially determined. An election contest involves a question of broader import than the mere individual claim of a person to enjoy the honors and emoluments of a particular office brought directly into contest. The inquiry must be as to whether in a given instance the popular will has been, or is about to be, thwarted by mistake or fraud. The public interest imperatively requires that the ultimate determination of the contest shall reach the right result."

Turning to the merits of Irving's contentions, we find that by shifting votes from Irving to Andrews based solely on the primacy effect theory, the trial court exceeded its authority. Under sections 16203, 16402, and 16703 [of the California Elections Code], only *illegal* votes may be discarded in an election contest. If the court finds, after discarding the illegal votes given for the winning candidate, that another candidate "has the highest number of legal votes, the court shall declare that person elected." (§ 16703.) Otherwise, if discarding the illegal votes given for the winning candidate would not change the result of the election, and the win-ning candidate is disqualified from taking office due to having committed offenses against the elective franchise, the court shall enter judgment "annulling and setting aside the election." (§ 16603.)

In this case, the trial court found a total of 144 illegal votes had been cast in the runoff election, but found it impossible to determine in whose favor (other than the nine illegal votes for Irving) the illegal votes had been cast. Even if we were to assume that all 144 illegal votes had been cast for Irving, subtracting 144 illegal votes from Irving's total would still have left her the victor with 5,270 legal votes to Andrews's 4,863 legal votes. Therefore, the illegal votes cast for Irving did not change the result of the election, and there was no other candidate with more legal votes than Irving. Given Irving's disqualification from taking office due to her offenses against the elective franchise, the trial court should have entered a judgment "annulling *and setting aside* the election." (§ 16603, italics added.)

Instead, in a ruling unprecedented, to our knowledge, in this country, the trial court shifted 295 legal votes from Irving to Andrews based solely on the 3.32 percent primacy effect assumed to be enjoyed, on average, by those listed first on the ballot. While many courts and legislatures have recognized the advantage afforded to candidates whose names are listed first on the ballot, no judicial or statutory authority exists to reverse the results of an election where, due to *unintentional* clerical error, the ballot listed the candidates in the wrong alphabetical order.

Election results may only be challenged on one of the grounds specified in section 16100. Name-order error occurring in the absence of fraud and resulting purely from unintentional clerical error, as in this case, is not a valid ground for an election contest under section 16100. The fact that 295 legal votes may have been cast for Irving solely because her name was erroneously listed first on the ballot does not, in itself, impeach the integrity of those 295 votes. Legal votes randomly cast by the least informed or least interested voters are entitled to the same weight as legal votes cast by the most highly educated and informed voters in our society. The legality or illegality of a vote cast by a qualified voter in a lawful manner does not depend upon the voter's motive or purpose in voting a certain way. To shift 295 legal votes to "correct" the votes "randomly" cast for Irving solely as a result of her erroneous advantageous ballot position (and to award those same "random" votes to Andrews based solely on the primacy effect theory) would be, without any lawful justification, to disenfranchise those 295 voters.

We conclude the trial court erred in entering judgment for Andrews and declaring her elected when she had failed to win the highest number of legal votes in the June 5, 2001, election. Accordingly, * * * [t]he certificate of election for Andrews is annulled, and Andrews's city council seat shall be vacant upon the finality of this opinion. * * *

Notes and Questions

1. In *Marks*, the Third Circuit held that the district court should not have certified Marks as the winner unless the court found that Marks would have won the election absent any wrongdoing. How could Marks meet that standard, short of calling each absentee voter to testify about the way he or she voted? Do you agree with the court that "the same principle that justified the unseating of Stinson dictates that Marks not be certified on the basis of the machine vote only"?

2. The court in *Bradley* heavily relied on the expert evidence of political scientists in finding that there was a "ballot-order" or "primacy" effect (also called "position bias" or the "candidate-name-order" effect), *i.e.*, that candidates listed first on a ballot had an improper and unfair electoral advantage. For a sampling of the research on the ballot-order effect, see Nuri Kim et al., *Moderators of Candidate Name-Order Effects in Elections: An Experiment*, 36 Pol. Psych. 525 (2015);

Josh Pasek et al., *Prevalence and Moderators of the Candidate Name-Order Effect*, 78 PUB. OPINION Q. 416 (2014); Eric Chen et al., *The Impact of Candidate Name Order on Election Outcomes in North Dakota*, 35 ELECTORAL STUD. 115 (2014); Joanne M. Miller & Jon A. Krosnick, *The Impact of Candidate Name Order on Election Outcomes*, 62 PUB. OPINION Q. 291 (1998). For an argument that the social-science evidence for the effect is "muddled," and hence courts should be cautious before reallocating votes, or ordering a new election, based on the improper placement of names on a ballot, see R. Michael Alvarez et al., *How Much Is Enough? The "Ballot Order Effect" and the Use of Social Science Research in Election Law Disputes*, 5 ELECTION L.J. 40, 41 (2006). Given these complications, how confident should a court be when intervening to rectify errors regarding ballot order? *Cf.* Mary Beth Beazley, *Ballot Design as Fail-Safe: An Ounce of Rotation Is Worth a Pound of Litigation*, 12 ELECTION L.J. 18 (2013).

3. A particularly controversial recount and adjustment of votes took place after the 2004 gubernatorial election for the State of Washington. Initially, Republican Dino Rossi led Democrat Christine Gregoire by 261 votes out of more than 2.8 million cast. It was apparently the closest race for governor in American history. Two sets of recounts led to a lead by Gregoire of 129 votes. Rossi filed suit in state court, requesting a new election. Discovery in the case revealed that over 1600 voters had voted illegally, many of them disenfranchised felons. The challengers did not undertake the heavy burden of providing direct evidence of how the invalid voters voted. The trial judge refused to order a new election, because there was insufficient evidence of fraud. The court further found that proportionate deduction, the alternative remedy posited by the challengers, was not appropriate, in part because it could not assume that the mostly male felons were voting like non-felons. The challengers did not appeal the trial-court decision. Do decisions like this call into serious question the heretofore respectable theory of proportionate deduction? For discussion of the Washington election and its implications for this theory, see RICHARD L. HASEN, THE VOTING WARS: FROM FLORIDA TO THE NEXT ELECTION MELTDOWN 149–52 (2012); *Developments in the Law—Voting and Democracy*, 119 HARV. L. REV. 1127, 1155–65 (2006); Kevin J. Hickey, Note, *Accuracy Counts: Illegal Votes in Contested Elections and the Case for Complete Proportionate Deduction*, 83 N.Y.U. L. REV. 167 (2008).

4. For a discussion and a case study of statewide recounts, comparisons to initial, election-night vote tallies, and post-election audits in general, see Stephen Ansolabehere et al., *Learning from Recounts*, 17 ELECTION L.J. 100 (2018).

C. Federal-Court Remedies for State Elections

Roe v. Alabama

United States Court of Appeals for the Eleventh Circuit
43 F.3d 574 (11th Cir. 1995)

PER CURIAM [CHIEF JUDGE TJOFLAT and CIRCUIT JUDGE BIRCH join in this opinion]:

In Alabama, a person voting by absentee ballot must execute an "affidavit" in the presence of a "notary public or other officer authorized to acknowledge oaths or two witnesses 18 years of age or older." Ala. Code § 17-10-7. * * *

On November 8, 1994, Alabama held a general election for several statewide offices, including the offices of Chief Justice of the Supreme Court of Alabama and Treasurer of the State of Alabama. Between 1000 and 2000 absentee voters failed to properly complete their affidavits, either by failing to have their signatures notarized or by failing to have them witnessed by two people. Pursuant to the statutory mandate of [Ala. Code §] 17-10-10, and the statewide practice prior to the general election, these ballots were not counted: they were not removed from their affidavit envelopes and, therefore, were not placed in the ballot box.

The elections for Chief Justice and Treasurer, especially the former office, were quite close. Informal estimates place the two candidates for Chief Justice a mere 200 to 300 votes apart without counting the contested absentee ballots. Following the general election, two individuals who voted absentee, on behalf of themselves and similarly situated absentee voters, filed a complaint in the Circuit Court for Montgomery County, Alabama, seeking an order that the contested absentee ballots be counted. On November 17, 1994, the circuit court entered a "Temporary Restraining Order" requiring that "those persons counting the absentee ballots for each county shall count each ballot which contains: (1) the place of residence of the person casting the ballot; (2) the reason for . . . voting by absentee ballot; and (3) the signature of the voter. *Absentee ballots may not be excluded from being counted because of a lack of notarization or a lack of witnesses.*" (Emphasis added). The circuit court also ordered the Secretary of State to refrain from certifying the election until the vote totals, including the contested absentee votes, are forwarded to him; after receiving these revised totals, the Secretary must certify the election. Following the entry of this temporary restraining order, the election officials began counting the contested absentee ballots.

On December 5, 1994, the United States District Court for the Southern District of Alabama * * * entered a preliminary injunction against the Secretary and the election officials of Alabama's sixty-seven counties precluding them from complying with the circuit court's order. The district court, in its memorandum order granting the preliminary injunction, found from the evidence the parties presented that "the past practice of the Alabama election officials prior to [the] general election has been to refrain from counting any absentee ballot that did not include notarization or the signatures of two qualified witnesses," that "the past practice of the Secretary of State of Alabama has been to certify Alabama election results on the basis of vote counts that included absentee votes cast only by those voters who included affidavits with either notarization or the signatures of two qualified witnesses," and that the Montgomery County Circuit Court's order changed this past practice. The district court then concluded that, in obeying the circuit court's order, the defendant election officials were violating the Fourteenth Amendment. The district court, therefore, ordered that the contested ballots and other election materials be preserved and protected; that the Secretary refrain from certifying any election results based on a vote count that included the contested absentee ballots; that Alabama's sixty-seven county election officials forward vote totals to the Secretary without counting the contested absentee ballots; and that the Secretary, upon receipt of those vote totals from the county election officials, certify the election results. * * *

Appellants contend that the plaintiffs failed to allege, or to demonstrate, the violation of a right "secured by the Constitution" as required under section 1983. We disagree. In this case, [the plaintiffs] allege that "[t]he actions of the Defendants and the Defendant Class . . . would constitute a retroactive validation of a potentially controlling number of votes in the elections for Chief Justice and Treasurer" that "would result in fundamental unfairness and would violate plaintiffs' right to due process of law" in violation of the Fourteenth Amendment, and that this violation of "the plaintiffs' rights to vote and . . . have their votes properly and honestly counted" constitutes a violation of the First and Fourteenth Amendments.

* * * Generally, federal courts do not involve themselves in "'garden variety' election disputes." *Curry* [*v. Baker*, 802 F.2d 1302, 1315 (11th Cir. 1986)]. If, however, "the election process itself reaches the point of patent and fundamental unfairness, a violation of the due process clause may be indicated * * *. Such a situation must go well beyond the ordinary dispute over the counting and marking of ballots." *Id.* We address, then, whether the plaintiffs have demonstrated fundamental unfairness in the November 8 election. We conclude that they have.

The plaintiffs acknowledge that the State of Alabama is free to place reasonable time, place, and manner restrictions on voting, and that Alabama can require that voters be qualified electors. They argue, however, that section 17-10-7 of the Alabama Election Code clearly requires that affidavits accompanying absentee ballots be either notarized or signed by two witnesses; that the statewide practice in Alabama prior to the November 8 general election was to exclude absentee ballots that did not comply with this rule; and that the circuit court's order requiring the state's election officials to perform the ministerial act of counting the contested absentee ballots, if permitted to stand, will constitute a retroactive change in the election laws that will effectively "stuff the ballot box,"[13] implicating fundamental fairness issues. *Cf. United States v. Saylor*, 322 U.S. 385, 389 (1944).

We agree that failing to exclude the contested absentee ballots will constitute a post-election departure from previous practice in Alabama. This departure would have two effects that implicate fundamental fairness and the propriety of the two elections at issue. First, counting ballots that were not previously counted would dilute the votes of those voters who met the requirements of section 17-10-7 as well as those voters who actually went to the polls on election day. Second, the change in the rules after the election would have the effect of disenfranchising those who would have voted but for the inconvenience imposed by the notarization/witness requirement. * * *

Appellants point out that "[a] judicial construction of a statute is an authoritative statement of what the statute meant before as well as after the decision of the case giving rise to that construction." *Rivers v. Roadway Express, Inc.*, 511 U.S. 298, 312–13 (1994). Thus, appellants urge, the Montgomery County Circuit Court's ruling merely articulated in a clearer way what the law has always been in Alabama. This argument, however, ignores the fact that section 17-10-7, on its face, requires notarization or witnessing, that the Secretary and the Attorney General have acknowledged the requirement and that, as the district court found, the practice of the election officials throughout the state has been to exclude absentee ballots that did not meet this requirement. We consider it unreasonable to expect average voters and candidates to question the Secretary's, the Attorney General's, and the election officials' interpretation and application of the statute, especially in light of its plain language.

Appellants also argue that this case presents a case of enfranchisement of those who cast the contested absentee ballots, rather than a disenfranchisement of qualified voters, and thus does not rise to the level of a constitutional violation. They rely heavily on *Partido Nuevo Progresista v. Barreto Perez*, 639 F.2d 825 (1st Cir. 1980). In that case, the plaintiffs challenged the tallying of ballots in a local election in Puerto Rico. A section of the Electoral Law of Puerto Rico provided that, if a handwritten ballot was used in an election, the Electoral Commission had to guarantee that the elector was qualified to vote by making a mark in a specific place on the ballot. The section stated that if the mark was not made in the correct space, the ballot would be null and void. After the election, the Administrator of the Election Commission and the Commonwealth's Electoral Review Board held that several ballots were invalid because they were not marked correctly. The Supreme Court of Puerto

---

13. According to the record before the district court, in one Alabama county, Greene County, nearly 33% of the votes cast were from absentee voters. Secretary Bennett testified that he has "had concerns about absentee voter fraud for years" and that, if absentee ballots exceed 6% to 7% of the total votes cast, "bells and sirens ought to go off. There cannot be that many sick, infirm or out-of-county voters on one day."

Rico reversed, holding that, despite the section's clear language, the ballots should be counted. The *Barreto Perez* plaintiffs * * * alleged that the Puerto Rico Supreme Court's ruling constituted a change in the method of counting ballots after the election and, therefore, violated the Constitution.

The First Circuit did not agree for two reasons. First, the court found it significant that "this case does not involve a state court order that *dis*enfranchises voters; rather it involves a . . . decision that *en*franchises them—plaintiffs claim that votes were 'diluted' by the votes of others, not that they themselves were prevented from voting." *Id*. at 828 (emphasis in original). Second, the court found that "no party or person is likely to have acted to their detriment by relying upon the invalidity of [the contested] ballots." *Id*. Accordingly, the First Circuit found no constitutional injury. We need not address the court's apparent holding that dilution is not a constitutional injury because the facts of this case differ markedly from those of *Barreto Perez*. We believe that, had the candidates and citizens of Alabama known that something less than the signature of two witnesses or a notary attesting to the signature of absentee voters would suffice, campaign strategies would have taken this into account and supporters of [the losing candidates] who did not vote would have voted absentee.

The appellants contend that, since this case involves "a sensitive area of state policy," the district court should have stayed its hand and required the plaintiffs to invoke their state remedies—either an election contest in the legislature or a judicial declaration from the Supreme Court of Alabama. *See Railroad Comm'n v. Pullman*, 312 U.S. 496, 501–02 (1941). We agree that federal courts should refrain from holding a state election law unconstitutional when a reasonable alternative course of action exists. We are, therefore, reluctant to reach a final decision in this case while the proper application of the Alabama Election Code remains muddled.

There are two ways to show deference to the state decisionmakers in this matter: we can leave the plaintiffs to their state remedies; or we can certify a question to the Supreme Court of Alabama [regarding the requirements of a proper absentee ballot under Alabama law], retain jurisdiction, and await that court's answer. We choose the latter form of abstention; leaving the plaintiffs to their state remedies is neither workable nor appropriate in this case.

EDMONDSON, CIRCUIT JUDGE, dissenting:

I know of no other case involving disputed ballots in which a federal court has intervened in a state election where the plaintiff failed to show, in fact, either:

> 1. that plaintiff had "lost" the election but would have won the election if lawful votes only had been counted (that is, the alleged constitutional error changed the election result); or

2. that it was impossible ever to know that his opponent (the apparent winner) had truly won the election because of the nature of the voting irregularities (that is, the alleged constitutional error placed in everlasting doubt what was the true result of the election).

Nothing is known in this case about whether the alleged illegalities have affected or will affect the outcome of the pertinent elections. Yet today we plow into Alabama's election process and uphold a preliminary injunction that, in effect, overrules a pre-existing state court order which had directed that the contested votes be counted. And, instead, the federal courts (basically, stopping short the state election processes) order that the contested votes be *not* counted at all. This high level of federal activity seems unnecessary and, therefore, improper. So, I conclude that the district court abused its discretion.

For all we or anyone else knows, if the contested absentee votes in this case were counted, plaintiffs' candidates would win the elections, even taking those contested votes into account. In such event, none of the plaintiffs would be aggrieved by the decision to count absentee ballots not strictly complying with the state's statute. I believe everyone involved in this election dispute would understand that a court's allowing the simple adding up of which of the contested absentee votes went to which candidate would *not* be the same thing as saying that the contested votes will have value ultimately, as a matter of law, for deciding the final, official outcome of the elections. But instead of letting the votes be counted as an Alabama court has directed and then seeing *if* there is even a controversy about the election's outcome, the federal courts have jumped into the process and blocked the very step that might show there is no big problem to be dealt with by federal judges. * * *

This difference with my colleagues is more than just academic bickering about technicalities. Federal courts are not the bosses in state election disputes unless extraordinary circumstances affecting the integrity of the state's election process are clearly present in a high degree. This well-settled principle—that federal courts interfere in state elections as a last resort—is basic to federalism, and we should take it to heart. * * *

As I understand the law, "[o]nly in extraordinary circumstances will a challenge to a state election rise to the level of a constitutional deprivation." *Curry*, 802 F.2d [at] 1314. To my way of thinking, the federal courts have acted too aggressively too soon and have, as a result, become entangled in Alabama's state election too much. At a time when we do not know whether the contested votes, in fact, will make any difference at all in the outcome of the elections, it is hard for me to say that I am now facing the kind of extraordinary circumstances—patent and fundamental unfairness *tied to concrete harm*—that will amount to a constitutional deprivation and that will justify immediate significant federal interference in the election processes of a state. * * *

Scheer v. City of Miami

United States District Court for the Southern District of Florida
15 F. Supp. 2d 1338 (S.D. Fla. 1998)

EDWARD B. DAVIS, CHIEF JUDGE. * * *

* * * On November 4, 1997, the City of Miami held a general election for the position of Executive Mayor, with Joe Carollo and Xavier Suarez as the primary contenders. Neither Carollo nor Suarez received a majority of the overall votes; therefore, the City held a run-off election on November 13, 1997. In that election, Suarez defected [*sic*] Carollo in both precinct votes and absentee votes. On November 14, 1997, those results were certified and Suarez assumed the position of Mayor of the City of Miami.

Three Miami voters brought an *in rem* state lawsuit challenging the vote count in the first election pursuant to Section 102.166, Fla. Stat. Carollo and Suarez intervened in that action. The Plaintiffs in this case [absentee voters] did not.

Judge Thomas Wilson, Jr., for the Circuit Court of the Eleventh Judicial Circuit of Florida, found that massive absentee voter fraud tainted the electoral process.

> "Witness after witness testified, without contradiction, that they either 1) did not vote, 2) did not sign the ballots in question, 3) did not live in the district in which their ballot was cast, 4) did not live in the City of Miami, 5) did not know the person who 'witnessed' their signature or said someone other than the names [*sic*] witness actually 'witnessed' their vote, 6) did not live at the address that was given on the request for the absentee ballot, 7) did not request an absentee ballot and/or 8) did not qualify as 'unable to vote.'"

Judge Wilson found that this fraud scheme, "literally and figuratively, stole the ballot from the hands of every honest voter in the City of Miami." As a result, "the integrity of the election was adversely affected." Judge Wilson held that the appropriate remedy was to void the first Mayoral election and hold a new election.

The Third District Court of Appeal of Florida agreed that massive fraud occurred in the electoral process, but held that the appropriate remedy was to invalidate only the absentee ballots from the November 4, 1997, election. The court citing to almost sixty years of Florida precedent stated that it "refuse[d] to disenfranchise the more than 40,000 voters who, on November 4, 1997, exercised their constitutionally guaranteed right to vote in the polling places of Miami." Because Carollo received a majority (51.41%) of the machine vote in the initial election, the court declared him the Mayor of Miami.

In this case, Plaintiffs represent the class of absentee voters who lawfully cast their absentee votes but whose votes were not counted pursuant to the Third DCA's ruling. Plaintiffs, in their two count complaint for declaratory judgment and for injunctive relief, seek a new election. Plaintiffs basically contend that by voiding their votes, their constitutional rights under the First and Fourteenth Amendments were violated. * * *

This case presents the difficult question of when a federal court should involve itself with a state election dispute. There is no doubt that the right to vote is one of the most basic and fundamental of rights. However, federal courts can only intervene in a state election dispute in the most extreme circumstances. This case does not present one of those circumstances. Moreover, public policy dictates that this Court not meddle with the state process. Accordingly, the Court will grant summary judgment for the Defendants. * * *

* * * Only when election irregularities are fundamentally unfair and transcend "garden variety" problems do federal courts have a duty to step in to ensure that citizens' rights are protected. The Court, therefore, must determine whether this case is just another garden variety election dispute or whether Plaintiffs have been subjected to fundamental unfairness.[4]

More often than not, federal courts find that the problem is garden variety and do not intervene in state election disputes. *See, e.g., Gold v. Feinberg*, 101 F.3d 796, 801 (2d Cir. 1996) (refusing to intervene where human error resulted in miscounting of votes, presence of ineligible candidates on ballot, and delay in arrival of voting machines); *Bodine v. Elkhart County Election Bd.*, 788 F.2d 1270, 1272 (7th Cir. 1986) (mechanical and human error in counting votes); *Hendon v. North Carolina State Bd. of Elections*, 710 F.2d 177, 182 (4th Cir. 1983) (technical deficiencies in printing ballots); *Gamza v. Aguirre*, 619 F.2d 449, 454 (5th Cir. 1980) (negligent vote counting); *Hennings v. Grafton*, 523 F.2d 861 (7th Cir. 1975) (malfunction of voting machines); *Pettengill v. Putnam County R-1 School Dist.*, 472 F.2d 121, 122 (8th Cir. 1973) (counting votes that were illegally cast); *Powell v. Power*, 436 F.2d 84 (2d Cir. 1970) (non-party members mistakenly allowed to vote in congressional primary); *Johnson v. Hood*, 430 F.2d 610, 613 (5th Cir. 1970) (arbitrary rejection of 10 ballots).

In a case with strikingly similar facts, the Eleventh Circuit cautioned district courts not to meddle with a state election dispute. *Curry [v. Baker]*, 802 F.2d 1302 [(11th Cir. 1986)]. There, the plaintiffs argued that the state of Alabama incorrectly dealt with massive illegal voting. The Eleventh Circuit declined to answer that question for "reasons grounded in both law and public policy."

Curry involved a primary runoff election for the Democratic candidate for Governor of Alabama. Initially, it looked like Charles Graddick had won, but like this

---

4. Defendants argue that the Court need not reach this issue because absentee voting is a privilege and not a right. Defendants are correct that there is no right to vote by absentee ballot, but their characterization is misleading. Florida, of course, can restrict or perhaps even eliminate absentee voting under the appropriate circumstances *before* these votes are cast. The question then is whether Florida can restrict these votes after they are cast when there is evidence of massive fraud. As explained later, federalism and equity prevent this Court from telling Florida that it cannot in this case.

case, there was massive illegal voting. Therefore, the State Democratic Committee certified William Baxley, who received the majority of the legal votes, as the winner. Graddick and his supporters brought suit arguing that the election committee did not use the correct methods for counting and determining the lawfully cast votes. The district court agreed and ordered the Democratic Party to conduct a new primary and enjoined the disqualification of Graddick.

The Eleventh Circuit reversed, reasoning that it was not its role to "oversee the administrative details of a local election." *Id.* at 1315. As *Curry* clearly demonstrates, it is not the job of a federal court to involve itself with settling disputes as to how the state deals with counting votes after illegal votes are cast. Instead, a federal court should only intervene into state election disputes where the entire process is fundamentally unfair. "Episodic events" don't count. *Curry*, 802 F.2d at 1314. [There is] a distinction between state laws and patterns of state action that systematically deny equality in voting, and episodic events that, despite non-discriminatory laws, may result in the dilution of an individual's vote. Unlike systematically discriminatory laws, isolated events that adversely affect individuals are not presumed to be a [constitutional violation].

This instant action represents an isolated or "episodic event" that does not demonstrate that the entire process is fundamentally unfair.

Plaintiffs argue, however, that another Eleventh Circuit case is more similar to the instant action. *See Roe* [*v. Alabama*], 43 F.3d 574 [(11th Cir. 1995)] [p. 1143]. The Court disagrees.

In that case, the prior Alabama practice had been not to count absentee ballots unless they were notarized or witnessed; but after the 1994 election, an Alabama court ordered the improperly submitted absentee ballots to be counted. The *Roe* court determined that the election was fundamentally unfair for two reasons: 1) that Alabama was diluting the votes of those who had lawfully voted, and 2) that Alabama had disenfranchised those people who would have voted but for the inconvenience imposed by the notarization and witness requirements. *Id.* at 581. The difference between *Roe* and this case (as well as *Curry*) is that in *Roe*, the state changed its policy after an election. The Eleventh Circuit in *Roe* did not involve itself with settling an isolated dispute about fraud. Instead, it intervened because the state's policy changed after an election. Here, Florida did not change its policy at all. It stayed true to course—if there is massive fraud with absentee votes, they can be invalidated. In fact, there is a "complete absence of any Florida Appellate Court decision upholding the ordering of a new election in the face of such fraudulent conduct relating to absentee ballots."

Plaintiffs also rely on cases from the Third and First Circuits. These cases are persuasive, but in the end, do not control this Court's decision. * * * In *Marks* [*v. Stinson*], 19 F.3d [873,] 873 [(3d Cir. 1994)] [p. 1132], in Pennsylvania's second senatorial district election, the Republican candidate, Bruce Marks, received the majority of the machine votes over Democrat William Stinson. Stinson, however, won the bulk of the absentee votes. Because of the huge number of absentee ballots cast for Stinson, he won the election 20,523 to 20,062. Marks brought state and federal proceedings against Stinson alleging that his opponent engaged in absentee voter fraud. The district court, deciding not to abstain, voided all absentee votes finding that there was massive fraud and enjoined Stinson from assuming office and declared Marks the winner based solely on the machine vote. The Third Circuit remanded the case back to the district court to determine whether the results would have been the same absent the wrongdoing, with instructions that the district court "will have authority to order a special election, whether or not it is able to determine what the results would have been in the absence of that violation." *Id.* at 889.

Marks, however, did not present a situation where a federal court had to step in and invalidate sixty years of state law. Instead, the Third Circuit simply overruled the district court's decision to invalidate absentee votes. This case is fundamentally different because here, a federal district court would have to meddle with the state's determination of what an appropriate remedy is, and would also have to examine whether sixty years of precedent should be overturned. The Court declines to do so.

Plaintiffs also cite to a First Circuit case in which the court intervened, *Griffin v. Burns*, 570 F.2d 1065 (1st Cir. 1978). This case arose out of a Rhode Island local primary in which the state had encouraged citizens to vote by absentee ballot. After citizens took the bait, the Rhode Island Supreme Court found that absentee voting was not authorized for primary elections and invalidated those votes. The court then ordered the decertification of the winner and the board of canvassers certified a new winner based solely on the machine cast votes. *Id.*

The absentee voters then filed a class action in federal court alleging that the Rhode Island Supreme Court, by invalidating their votes violated the Due Process Clause of the Fourteenth Amendment. The district court agreed and the First Circuit affirmed, finding that plaintiffs had relied on the government's assurances that absentee ballots would be counted. Based on these unique circumstances, the First Circuit found "broad-gauged unfairness" which implicated the state's integrity and the integrity of the election results. The court recognized, however, that the Constitution confers the "power to control the disposition of contests over elections to . . . state and local offices." *Id.* at 1077.

Like Alabama in *Roe*, Rhode Island changed the rules half way through the game. The state told voters one thing before the election and changed its policy thereafter. This was unacceptable and of course, the First Circuit had to intervene. Florida, on the other hand, maintains its policy of remedying fraud. It has not changed the rules of the game and neither will this Court.

The Ninth Circuit, in refusing to meddle with a state election, summarized the law in all of these election cases:

> A general pattern emerges from all of these cases taken together. ***Mere fraud or mistake will not render an election invalid.*** However, a court will strike down an election . . . if two elements are present: (1) likely reliance by voters on an established election procedure and/or official pronouncements about what the procedure will be in the coming election; and (2) significant disenfranchisement that results from a change in the election procedures.

Bennett [*v. Yoshina*], 140 F.3d [1218,] 1226 [(9th Cir. 1998)] (emphasis added). This case is about mere fraud — nothing more. It has nothing to do with reliance on an established procedure or a change in the election procedures. If anything, the voters must be presumed to have known of Florida's procedure of voiding all absentee votes if there was evidence of fraud. * * *

Florida courts have established and followed this policy for good reason. The absentee voting scheme as it now exists in Florida lends itself to fraud, manipulation, and deceit. The state legislature continues to attempt improvements, but to date criminals have found ways to abuse the system. Accordingly, Florida courts for the past sixty years have constructed a means of dealing with absentee voter fraud. It is not this Court's province to upset this remedy as it has been well thought out by the state courts. For example, as the state appellate court in this case noted, "were we to approve a new election as the proper remedy following extensive absentee voting fraud, we would be sending out the message that the worst that would happen in the face of voter fraud would be another election." For these reasons, the Eleventh Circuit in *Curry* held that state election disputes were better dealt with by "the court system of the affected state." 802 F.2d at 1302.

Even if Plaintiffs were able to set forth a constitutional violation, the Court must take into account equitable considerations in fashioning the appropriate remedy in each case. "A federal court reaching into the state political process to invalidate an election necessarily implicates important concerns of federalism and state sovereignty. It should not resort to this intrusive remedy until it has carefully weighed all equitable considerations."

* * * Indeed, the old Fifth Circuit, whose decisions are of course binding on this Court, stated that even in cases of racial discrimination, the voiding of a state election is a "drastic if not staggering" remedy. *Bell v. Southwell*, 376 F.2d 659, 662 (5th Cir. 1967) [p. 1121]. The almost circus atmosphere surrounding this case makes the remedy Plaintiffs seek even more drastic and staggering. Plaintiffs could have intervened in the state case, as did Xavier Suarez. They did not. Instead, they waited until the trial was completed, the appeal and cross-appeal were filed, the appellate opinion was issued, rehearing and certification were petitioned for and denied, and discretionary review in the Florida Supreme Court was invoked before coming to this Court to request relief. The City of Miami has been scarred by the events that took place during and after the 1997 Mayoral election. The City and its citizens are finally starting to heal. Equity necessitates that the Court not re-open these wounds.

Federal courts rarely meddle with state election disputes. This case is no exception. The massive absentee fraud during the November, 1997, Mayoral election was an episodic event that was addressed by the state. The Eleventh Circuit as well as the majority of courts explain that it is not the job of the federal court to intrude into these brief episodes. Furthermore, equity demands that the Court stay on the sideline of this state dispute. * * *

Notes and Questions

1. The litigation in *Roe* continued throughout 1995. In response to the majority opinion, the Alabama Supreme Court answered the certified question by holding that the ballots in question were legal votes under Alabama law. *Roe v. Mobile County Appointment Board*, 676 So. 2d 1206 (Ala. 1995). The Eleventh Circuit then remanded the case to the district court to make findings of fact on whether the state courts had changed pre-election state law when they permitted the absentee ballots to be counted. *Roe v. Alabama*, 52 F.3d 300 (11th Cir. 1995) (*per curiam*). The district court found that the uniform practice in Alabama prior to the election had been to exclude absentee ballots like those at issue (although the Alabama Supreme Court seemed willing to overturn that practice), and the district court therefore ordered state authorities to certify the election of the chief justice and the treasurer without including the contested absentee ballots in the final count. *Roe v. Mobile County Appointing Board*, 904 F. Supp. 1315 (S.D. Ala. 1995). This decision was affirmed in *Roe v. Alabama*, 68 F.3d 404 (11th Cir. 1995) (*per curiam*). The entire federal-court litigation took almost one year to complete. Is it acceptable to allow election results to remain uncertain for so long? Should the courts have done anything differently to effect a quicker resolution? Were the fears of the dissent in the initial Eleventh Circuit decision realized?

2. The political affiliations of the state and federal judges in the protracted *Roe* litigation did not go unnoticed. For example, the state trial judge who originally ordered that the absentee ballots be counted was a Democrat, and the Alabama Supreme Court consisted of a majority of Democrats, while the Eleventh Circuit panel was comprised of Republican appointees. In grudgingly answering the certified question, the majority opinion of the Alabama Supreme Court complained about the intrusion of the federal courts into the state election dispute. 676 So. 2d at 1217. What should we make of this "tortured history"? One scholar argued that while the entire episode raised fears of politicized judging, federal-court intervention was warranted, since it appeared that voters' and candidates' settled expectations had been upset by the effort to count the absentee ballots. Richard L. Hasen, *The Democracy Canon*, 62 STAN. L. REV. 62, 119–22 (2009).

3. To invoke federal-court relief in a situation analogous to *Roe*, should voters and candidates need to show a change in state law *and* detrimental reliance on the pre-change practice? Or should the former be enough? See Richard H. Pildes, *Judging "New Law" in Election Disputes*, 28 FLA. ST. U. L. REV. 691 (2001).

4. Much as courts have been reluctant to order new elections under *Bell v. Southwell*, courts have often (though not always) been reluctant to order injunctive relief under *Roe. Compare Warf v. Board of Elections of Green County*, 619 F.3d 553 (6th Cir. 2010) (noting the principles of *Roe*, but refusing to intervene after a state court declared all absentee votes invalid, since state precedent was followed and there was no fundamental unfairness), *with Hunter v. Hamilton County Board of Elections*, 635 F.3d 219 (6th Cir. 2011) (noting deference to state authorities in cases like *Warf*, but holding that allegations of unequal treatment of different batches of miscast provisional ballots permitted a federal court to order a recount), *and Northeast Coalition for the Homeless v. Husted*, 696 F.3d 580 (6th Cir. 2012) (*per curiam*) (holding that the state improperly disqualified provisional ballots cast in the wrong precinct due to poll-worker error). For a recent example of the reluctance of federal courts to intervene in "garden-variety election irregularities" based on alleged failures to follow state law, see *Lecky v. Virginia State Board of Elections*, 285 F. Supp. 3d 908 (E.D. Va. 2018) (holding that the plaintiffs failed to show "that the assignment of voters to the incorrect house districts and the distribution of ballots associated with those incorrect house districts amount to the kind of broad gauged unfairness necessary to state a due process claim"). For a contrasting argument in favor of a more active federal-court role in such cases, see Ben Klein, Note, *A Vote for Clarity: Establishing a Federal Test for Intervention in Election-Related Disputes*, 86 Fordham L. Rev. 1361 (2017).

5. The decision in *Scheer* was preceded by state-court litigation. Carollo, the loser of the mayoral run-off election, filed an election protest. Finding demonstrable evidence of fraudulent absentee voting, the state appellate court nonetheless refused to order a new election. Among other things, the court reasoned that (1) the ability to vote absentee was a privilege, not a right; (2) Suarez, the run-off winner, had no knowledge of, and did not participate in, the fraud; and (3) a new election would disenfranchise those many voters who properly voted at the polls. The more appropriate remedy, the court held, was to void the absentee ballots only. *In re Protest of Election Returns*, 707 So. 2d 1170 (Fla. App. 1998) (*per curiam*). That decision was in effect subject to collateral review in *Scheer*. While the federal court did not agree with all aspects of the state-court decision, it left the result intact. To what extent, if at all, does it inform the analysis to label the right to cast an *absentee* vote as a privilege, not a right? Were these courts correct to disregard *all* absentee ballots, presumably including those that were correctly cast? Unlike Florida and other states that insist on "strict compliance" with election procedures, an apparent "majority of states . . . have [*sic*] concluded that absentee voting laws should be liberally construed in aid of the right to vote." *Adkins v. Huckabay*, 755 So. 2d 206, 216 (La. 2000). But there are other states that follow the right/privilege distinction for absentee ballots. *E.g., Sheehan v. Franken*, 767 N.W.2d 462 (Minn. 2009) [p. 1103]. For further discussion, see Hasen, *The Democracy Canon, supra*, at 86–87; Rebecca Guthrie, Note, *State Courts, the Right to Vote, and the Democracy Canon*, 88 Fordham L. Rev. 1957 (2020).

6. Did either *Roe* or *Scheer* display the appropriate balance between protecting federal rights and respecting state prerogatives? Were the cases distinguishable, as *Scheer* argued, or was there an inconsistency between *Roe*'s willingness to involve itself with Alabama's election processes and *Scheer*'s hesitancy to involve itself in Florida's?

D. Remedying Individual Electoral Injuries

1. Civil and Criminal Enforcement by the Federal Government

Federal statutes create a wide range of potential remedies that public entities or private parties can use to correct defective elections. Many of those statutes, and their remedial provisions, have been discussed in prior portions of this Casebook. For example, the Voting Rights Act is addressed in Chapters 3 and 4; the Federal Election Campaign Act and its predecessor statutes are addressed in Chapters 8 and 9; and the Help America Vote Act (HAVA) and the National Voter Registration Act (NVRA) are discussed in Chapter 10.

These statutes can be enforced, in various ways, by the federal government. Thus, the Federal Election Commission (FEC) can undertake to enforce the campaign-finance laws. The FEC can seek a variety of penalties against violators of those laws, but must request that courts enforce its orders. 2 U.S.C. §§ 437c–437h. The Civil Rights Division of the U.S. Department of Justice is charged with enforcing provisions of the Voting Rights Act, HAVA, and other laws. Both civil and criminal remedies are available.[e]

Not surprisingly, court decisions have played a major role in shaping the power of the branches of the federal government in enforcing these laws. For example, various statutes, such as 18 U.S.C. §§ 241–242, make it a crime for persons acting under color of state law to deprive persons of their constitutional right to vote. In the leading case of *United States v. Classic*, 313 U.S. 299 (1941), the Supreme Court upheld criminal prosecutions under those statutes of state election officials who had committed various frauds in a Democratic primary election for the U.S. House of Representatives. The officials argued that, while the ability to vote in a general congressional election was protected by Article I, § 2 ("The House of Representatives shall be chosen every second Year by the People of the several States * * *."),

---

e. For helpful overviews of the scope and enforcement of federal election law by federal authorities, see Joshua A. Douglas, *The Procedure of Election Law in Federal Courts*, 2011 Utah L. Rev. 433; David C. Rothschild & Benjamin J. Wolinsky, *Election Law Violations*, 46 Am. Crim. L. Rev. 391 (2009); United States Department of Justice, Federal Prosecution of Election Offenses (Richard C. Pilger ed., 8th ed. 2017), *available at* http://www.justice.gov/criminal/file/1029066/download.

a primary election was an internal matter for the party. Hence (they argued), depriving the voters of the ability to vote in a primary did not deprive them of a constitutional right. The Court rejected the argument, holding that primaries (especially in a state politically dominated by one party) were "an integral part of the procedure for the popular choice of Congressman." *Id.* at 314. *Classic* gave greater power to federal authorities to regulate elections for federal offices in the states, and emboldened private parties to use federal law to challenge such practices as the white primaries, as discussed in Chapter 5.

Thus, the remedial enforcement of federal election law is, as a practical matter, often a mix of administrative and court actions by public and private entities. As you read the materials below, consider the advantages and disadvantages of vesting enforcement authority in federal prosecutors or other federal officials, as opposed to private parties. The U.S. Department of Justice and other federal offices typically have limited resources, and can pursue only a limited number of investigations and court actions. Private enforcement would seem to be a necessary supplement to public prosecutions if one wished to ensure that violations would not go unaddressed, but private plaintiffs (often, interest groups) have their own agendas and may not pursue or serve the public interest. Courts have been faced with these issues when considering whether to infer a private right of action from a federal statute whose text provides for only administrative enforcement. *See, e.g., Allen v. State Bd. of Elections*, 393 U.S. 544, 556–57 (1969) [p. 252] (holding that an implied private right of action under § 5 of the Voting Rights Act was a necessary supplement to public enforcement); *Morse v. Republican Party of Virginia*, 517 U.S. 186, 230–34 (1996) (same with respect to § 10 of the Voting Rights Act);[f] *Sandusky County Democratic Party v. Blackwell*, 387 F.3d 565 (6th Cir. 2004) [p. 1051] (inferring a private right of action under § 302 of HAVA). *Cf. Alabama State Conference of the NAACP v. Alabama*, 949 F.3d 647 (11th Cir. 2020) (holding, over a strong dissent, that Congress impliedly abrogated states' sovereign immunity against private suits to enforce § 2 of the VRA). *See generally* Daniel P. Tokaji, *Public Rights and Private Rights of Action: The Enforcement of Federal Election Law*, 44 IND. L. REV. 113 (2010). The Supreme Court's jurisprudence has shifted over the years; its current approach strongly disfavors implied rights of action. *See Alexander v. Sandoval*, 532 U.S. 275 (2001).[g]

---

f. What weight, if any, should a court give in construing statutes in this context to an amicus brief from the Attorney General supporting the inference of a private right of action? *See Allen*, 393 U.S. at 557 n.23 (giving weight to such a brief); *Morse*, 517 U.S. at 231–32 (same).

g. For differing perspectives on what persons or entities should be entitled to sue to enforce election law and voting rights, see *Northeast Ohio Coalition for the Homeless v. Husted*, 837 F.3d 612 (6th Cir. 2016) (assuming the existence of a private right of action to enforce § 4 of the Voting Rights Act, which states that "no citizen shall be denied" the right to vote "because of his failure to comply with any test or device," but holding against the plaintiffs on the merits), *cert. denied*, 137 S. Ct. 2265 (2017); *In re: 2016 Primary Election*, 836 F.3d 584 (6th Cir. 2016) (holding that a federal court could not order extension of voting hours based on a "plaintiff-less complaint"—an anonymous phone call to the district clerk's office); Perry Grossman, *The Case for State Attorney*

As a matter of policy, whether one prefers public or private enforcement depends both on how much enforcement is desired and on who should decide whether enforcement is appropriate in a particular case. Exclusively public enforcement leaves enforcement discretion with the executive branch (which might be good or bad), while private enforcement is apt to lead to more enforcement, stripping the executive branch of the ability to assign enforcement priorities and to exercise prosecutorial discretion. Congress, in election-law and other contexts, frequently provides for both types of enforcement. Sean Farhang, *Public Regulation and Private Lawsuits in the American Separation of Powers System*, 52 Am. J. Pol. Sci. 821 (2008). What is the optimal mix of those options?

The materials below focus on private enforcement and describe the remedial options open to—and barriers faced by—private parties. We first consider suits by individuals who were allegedly denied the right to vote, and then we consider suits by candidates who claimed to have lost because the election was administered in a manner that violated the law. Would, or should, the holdings discussed below come out differently if public officials were bringing the cases?

2. Remedies for the Wrongful Denial of the Right to Vote

Most often, suits to vindicate the rights of would-be voters seek injunctions. And because of "the fundamental nature of the right to vote," courts have been willing—as we have seen in this Chapter and elsewhere—to grant equitable relief requiring election officials to register voters and to permit them to cast ballots. *See, e.g., Dillard v. Crenshaw County*, 640 F. Supp. 1347, 1363 (M.D. Ala. 1986).[h] Nevertheless, an award of damages is possible as well, *see Murphy v. Ramsey*, 114 U.S. 15, 37 (1885), and the propriety of awarding damages for the wrongful denial of the right to vote was recognized as early as *Ashby v. White*, 92 Eng. Rep. 126, *rev'd*, 1 Eng. Rep. 417—HL (1703).[i] *See generally* J.E. Macy, Annotation, *Personal Liability of Public Officer for Breach of Duty in Respect of Election or Primary Election Laws*, 153 A.L.R. 109 (1944).

a. The Timing of Injunctive Relief

The Supreme Court has signaled that courts should be wary of becoming involved in last-minute challenges to election procedures. That wariness now has a name—the "*Purcell* principle"—taken from the following case.

General Enforcement of the Voting Rights Act Against Local Governments, 50 U. Mich. J.L. Ref. 565 (2017).

h. The Supreme Court was not always so willing, though. As discussed earlier (*see* p. 16 n.f), *Giles v. Harris*, 189 U.S. 475 (1903), refused to order injunctive relief to correct an unconstitutional system of voter registration because the Court lacked the capacity to ensure that its injunction would be followed.

i. The Queen's Bench, 3-1, held for the defendant and against the would-be voter, over Chief Justice Holt's dissent. The judgment was reversed, however, in the House of Lords.

Purcell v. Gonzalez

Supreme Court of the United States
549 U.S. 1, 127 S. Ct. 5, 166 L. Ed. 2d 1 (2006)

PER CURIAM. [CHIEF JUSTICE ROBERTS, JUSTICE STEVENS, JUSTICE SCALIA, JUSTICE KENNEDY, JUSTICE SOUTER, JUSTICE THOMAS, JUSTICE GINSBURG, JUSTICE BREYER, and JUSTICE ALITO join in this opinion.] * * *

In 2004, Arizona voters approved Proposition 200. The measure sought to combat voter fraud by requiring voters to present proof of citizenship when they register to vote and to present identification when they vote on election day. * * *

In the District Court the plaintiffs in this action are residents of Arizona, Indian tribes, and various community organizations. In May 2006, these plaintiffs brought suit challenging Proposition 200's identification requirements. On September 11, 2006, the District Court denied their request for a preliminary injunction, but it did not at that time issue findings of fact or conclusions of law. These findings were important because resolution of legal questions in the Court of Appeals required evaluation of underlying factual issues.

The plaintiffs appealed the denial, and the Clerk of the Court of Appeals set a briefing schedule that concluded on November 21, two weeks after the upcoming November 7 election. The plaintiffs then requested an injunction pending appeal from the Court of Appeals. Pursuant to the Court of Appeals' rules, the request for an injunction was assigned to a two-judge motions/screening panel. On October 5, after receiving lengthy written responses from the State and the county officials but without oral argument, the panel issued a four-sentence order enjoining Arizona from enforcing Proposition 200's provisions pending disposition, after full briefing, of the appeals of the denial of a preliminary injunction. The Court of Appeals offered no explanation or justification for its order. * * *

Despite the time-sensitive nature of the proceedings and the pendency of a request for emergency relief in the Court of Appeals, the District Court did not issue its findings of fact and conclusions of law until October 12. It then concluded that "plaintiffs have shown a possibility of success on the merits of some of their arguments but the Court cannot say that at this stage they have shown a strong likelihood." The District Court then found the balance of the harms and the public interest counseled in favor of denying the injunction. * * *

Faced with an application to enjoin operation of voter identification procedures just weeks before an election, the Court of Appeals was required to weigh, in addition to the harms attendant upon issuance or nonissuance of an injunction, considerations specific to election cases and its own institutional procedures. Court orders affecting elections, especially conflicting orders, can themselves result in voter confusion and consequent incentive to remain away from the polls. As an election draws closer, that risk will increase. So the Court of Appeals may have deemed this consideration to be grounds for prompt action. Furthermore, it might have given some weight to the possibility that the nonprevailing parties would want to seek en banc review. * * * These considerations, however, cannot be controlling here. It was still necessary, as a procedural matter, for the Court of Appeals to give deference to the discretion of the District Court. We find no indication that it did so, and we conclude this was error.

Although at the time the Court of Appeals issued its order the District Court had not yet made factual findings to which the Court of Appeals owed deference, by failing to provide any factual findings or indeed any reasoning of its own the Court of Appeals left this Court in the position of evaluating the Court of Appeals' bare order in light of the District Court's ultimate findings. There has been no explanation given by the Court of Appeals showing the ruling and findings of the District Court to be incorrect. In view of the impending election, the necessity for clear guidance to the State of Arizona, and our conclusion regarding the Court of Appeals' issuance of the order we vacate the order of the Court of Appeals. * * *

JUSTICE STEVENS, concurring.

Allowing the election to proceed without enjoining the statutory provisions at issue will provide the courts with a better record on which to judge their constitutionality. At least two important factual issues remain largely unresolved: the scope of the disenfranchisement that the novel identification requirements will produce, and the prevalence and character of the fraudulent practices that allegedly justify those requirements. Given the importance of the constitutional issues, the Court wisely takes action that will enhance the likelihood that they will be resolved correctly on the basis of historical facts rather than speculation.

Republican National Committee v. Democratic National Committee

Supreme Court of the United States
589 U.S. __, 140 S. Ct. 1205, 206 L. Ed. 2d 452 (2020)

PER CURIAM. [CHIEF JUSTICE ROBERTS, JUSTICE THOMAS, JUSTICE ALITO, JUSTICE GORSUCH, and JUSTICE KAVANAUGH join in this opinion.]

The application for stay presented to JUSTICE KAVANAUGH and by him referred to the Court is granted. The District Court's order granting a preliminary injunction is stayed to the extent it requires the State to count absentee ballots postmarked after April 7, 2020.

Wisconsin has decided to proceed with the elections scheduled for Tuesday, April 7 [despite the COVID-19 epidemic]. The wisdom of that decision is not the question before the Court. The question before the Court is a narrow, technical question about the absentee ballot process. In this Court, all agree that the deadline for the municipal clerks to receive absentee ballots has been extended from Tuesday, April 7, to Monday, April 13. That extension, which is not challenged in this Court, has afforded Wisconsin voters several extra days in which to mail their absentee ballots. The sole question before the Court is whether absentee ballots now must be mailed and postmarked by election day, Tuesday, April 7, as state law would necessarily require, or instead may be mailed and postmarked after election day, so long as they are received by Monday, April 13. Importantly, in their preliminary injunction motions, the plaintiffs did not ask that the District Court allow ballots mailed and postmarked after election day, April 7, to be counted. That is a critical point in the case. Nonetheless, five days before the scheduled election, the District Court unilaterally ordered that absentee ballots mailed and postmarked after election day, April 7, still be counted so long as they are received by April 13. Extending the date by which ballots may be cast by voters—not just received by the municipal clerks but cast by voters—for an additional six days after the scheduled election day fundamentally alters the nature of the election. And again, the plaintiffs themselves did not even ask for that relief in their preliminary injunction motions. Our point is not that the argument is necessarily forfeited, but is that the plaintiffs themselves did not see the need to ask for such relief. By changing the election rules so close to the election date and by affording relief that the plaintiffs themselves did not ask for in their preliminary injunction motions, the District Court contravened this Court's precedents and erred by ordering such relief. This Court has repeatedly emphasized that lower federal courts should ordinarily not alter the election rules on the eve of an election. See *Purcell* v. *Gonzalez*, 549 U.S. 1 (2006) (*per curiam*) [p. 1158]; *Frank* v. *Walker*, 574 U.S. 929 (2014); *Veasey* v. *Perry*, 574 U.S. __, 135 S. Ct. 9 (2014).

The unusual nature of the District Court's order allowing ballots to be mailed and postmarked after election day is perhaps best demonstrated by the fact that the District Court had to issue a subsequent order enjoining the public release of any election results for six days after election day. In doing so, the District Court in essence enjoined nonparties to this lawsuit. It is highly questionable, moreover, that this attempt to suppress disclosure of the election results for six days after election day would work. And if any information were released during that time, that would gravely affect the integrity of the election process. The District Court's order suppressing disclosure of election results showcases the unusual nature of the District Court's order allowing absentee ballots mailed and postmarked after election day to be counted. And all of that further underscores the wisdom of the *Purcell* principle, which seeks to avoid this kind of judicially created confusion.

The dissent is quite wrong on several points. First, the dissent entirely disregards the critical point that the plaintiffs themselves did not ask for this additional relief in their preliminary injunction motions. Second, the dissent contends that this Court should not intervene at this late date. The Court would prefer not to do so, but when a lower court intervenes and alters the election rules so close to the election date, our precedents indicate that this Court, as appropriate, should correct that error. Third, the dissent refers to voters who have not yet received their absentee ballots. But even in an ordinary election, voters who request an absentee ballot at the deadline for requesting ballots (which was this past Friday in this case) will usually receive their ballots on the day before or day of the election, which in this case would be today or tomorrow. The plaintiffs put forward no probative evidence in the District Court that these voters here would be in a substantially different position from late-requesting voters in other Wisconsin elections with respect to the timing of their receipt of absentee ballots. In that regard, it bears mention that absentee voting has been underway for many weeks, and 1.2 million Wisconsin voters have requested and have been sent their absentee ballots, which is about five times the number of absentee ballots requested in the 2016 spring election. Fourth, the dissent's rhetoric is entirely misplaced and completely overlooks the fact that the deadline for receiving ballots was already extended to accommodate Wisconsin voters, from April 7 to April 13. Again, that extension has the effect of extending the date for a voter to mail the ballot from, in effect, Saturday, April 4, to Tuesday, April 7. That extension was designed to ensure that the voters of Wisconsin can cast their ballots and have their votes count. That is the relief that the plaintiffs actually requested in their preliminary injunction motions. The District Court on its own ordered yet an additional extension, which would allow voters to mail their ballots after election day, which is extraordinary relief and would fundamentally alter the nature of the election by allowing voting for six additional days after the election.

Therefore, subject to any further alterations that the State may make to state law, in order to be counted in this election a voter's absentee ballot must be either (i) postmarked by election day, April 7, 2020, and received by April 13, 2020, at 4:00 p.m., or (ii) hand-delivered as provided under state law by April 7, 2020, at 8:00 p.m. * * *

Justice Ginsburg, with whom Justice Breyer, Justice Sotomayor, and Justice Kagan join, dissenting. * * *

Wisconsin's spring election is scheduled for tomorrow, Tuesday, April 7, 2020. At issue are the presidential primaries, a seat on the Wisconsin Supreme Court, three seats on the Wisconsin Court of Appeals, over 100 other judgeships, over 500 school board seats, and several thousand other positions. * * *

While I do not doubt the good faith of my colleagues, the Court's order, I fear, will result in massive disenfranchisement. A voter cannot deliver for postmarking a ballot she has not received. Yet tens of thousands of voters who timely requested ballots are unlikely to receive them by April 7, the Court's postmark deadline. Rising concern about the COVID–19 pandemic has caused a late surge in absentee-ballot requests. The Court's suggestion that the current situation is not "substantially different" from "an ordinary election" boggles the mind. Some 150,000 requests for absentee ballots have been processed since Thursday, state records indicate. The surge in absentee-ballot requests has overwhelmed election officials, who face a huge backlog in sending ballots. As of Sunday morning, 12,000 ballots reportedly had not yet been mailed out. It takes days for a mailed ballot to reach its recipient—the postal service recommends budgeting a week—even without accounting for pandemic-induced mail delays. It is therefore likely that ballots mailed in recent days will not reach voters by tomorrow; for ballots not yet mailed, late arrival is all but certain. Under the District Court's order, an absentee voter who receives a ballot after tomorrow could still have voted, as long as she delivered it to election officials by April 13. Now, under this Court's order, tens of thousands of absentee voters, unlikely to receive their ballots in time to cast them, will be left quite literally without a vote.

This Court's intervention is thus ill advised, especially so at this late hour. See *Purcell* v. *Gonzalez*, 549 U.S. [at] 4–5. Election officials have spent the past few days establishing procedures and informing voters in accordance with the District Court's deadline. For this Court to upend the process—a day before the April 7 postmark deadline—is sure to confound election officials and voters.

What concerns could justify consequences so grave? The Court's order first suggests a problem of forfeiture, noting that the plaintiffs' written preliminary-injunction motions did not ask that ballots postmarked after April 7 be counted. But unheeded by the Court, although initially silent, the plaintiffs specifically requested that remedy at the preliminary-injunction hearing in view of the ever-increasing demand for absentee ballots.

Second, the Court's order cites *Purcell*, apparently skeptical of the District Court's intervention shortly before an election. Nevermind that the District Court was reacting to a grave, rapidly developing public health crisis. If proximity to the election counseled hesitation when the District Court acted several days ago, this Court's intervention today—even closer to the election—is all the more inappropriate.

Third, the Court notes that the District Court's order allowed absentee voters to cast ballots after election day. If a voter already in line by the poll's closing time can still vote, why should Wisconsin's absentee voters, already in line to receive ballots, be denied the franchise? According to the stay applicants, election-distorting gamesmanship might occur if ballots could be cast after initial results are published. But obviating that harm, the District Court enjoined the publication of election results before April 13, the deadline for returning absentee ballots, and the Wisconsin Elections Commission directed election officials not to publish results before that date.

The concerns advanced by the Court and the applicants pale in comparison to the risk that tens of thousands of voters will be disenfranchised. Ensuring an opportunity for the people of Wisconsin to exercise their votes should be our paramount concern.

* * *

The majority of this Court declares that this case presents a "narrow, technical question." That is wrong. The question here is whether tens of thousands of Wisconsin citizens can vote safely in the midst of a pandemic. Under the District Court's order, they would be able to do so. Even if they receive their absentee ballot in the days immediately following election day, they could return it. With the majority's stay in place, that will not be possible. Either they will have to brave the polls, endangering their own and others' safety. Or they will lose their right to vote, through no fault of their own. That is a matter of utmost importance—to the constitutional rights of Wisconsin's citizens, the integrity of the State's election process, and in this most extraordinary time, the health of the Nation.

Notes and Questions

1. Should the *Purcell* principle apply only when the litigation could have been brought well in advance of an election but instead was brought at a time when an election was imminent? In other words, is *Purcell* based on a latches principle or does it suggest that courts should refuse injunctive relief close to an election even when the plaintiffs are not at fault? In *Purcell*, plaintiffs waited a year and a half to file suit challenging the ID requirement. In *R.N.C. v. D.N.C.*, by contrast, plaintiffs brought suit in response to a rapidly changing public-health crisis. Should *Purcell* have applied in that case?

2. If *Purcell* did have relevance to the resolution of *R.N.C. v. D.N.C.*, which way did it cut? In *R.N.C. v. D.N.C.*, both the Court and the dissent invoked *Purcell*. The majority thought that the district court was wrong to change the rules of the election so close to election day, while the dissent thought that the Supreme Court's intervention itself violated the *Purcell* principle. Which was right? *See also Texas Democratic Party v. Abbott*, 961 F.3d 389, 412 (5th Cir. 2020) (rebuking the plaintiffs for their "chutzpah" in arguing, "[j]ust days after themselves obtaining an injunction intervening in forthcoming elections, * * * that *we* should now refrain from intervening ourselves, given 'the proximity of a forthcoming election and the mechanics and complexities of state election laws.'") (footnote omitted) (emphasis in original).

3. The Court in *R.N.C. v. D.N.C.* found it exceptional that the district court would extend the time voters had to cast absentee ballots. Is that a fundamentally different kind of relief from the portion of the district court's order that was unchallenged before the Supreme Court—extending the deadline for the government to *receive* ballots? Even if your answer is "yes," did the district court adequately address potential objections by prohibiting the government from releasing election results before the new deadline for receiving ballots?

b. The Availability of Damages

Wiley v. Sinkler

Supreme Court of the United States
179 U.S. 58, 21 S. Ct. 17, 45 L. Ed. 84 (1900)

Statement by MR. JUSTICE GRAY:

This was an action brought March 11, 1895, in the circuit court of the United States for the district of South Carolina, by a resident of the city of Charleston in that state, against the board of managers of a general election at a ward and precinct in that city, to recover damages in the sum of $2,500 for wrongfully and wilfully rejecting his vote for a member of the House of Representatives of the United States for the state of South Carolina on November 6, 1894. * * *

The court * * * sustained the demurrer and dismissed the complaint because it did not state facts sufficient to constitute a cause of action, in that it failed to state that the plaintiff was a duly registered voter of the state of South Carolina. The plaintiff sued out a writ of error from this court. * * *

MR. JUSTICE GRAY, after stating the case as above, delivered the opinion of the court [in which MR. CHIEF JUSTICE FULLER, MR. JUSTICE HARLAN, MR. JUSTICE BREWER, MR. JUSTICE BROWN, MR. JUSTICE SHIRAS, MR. JUSTICE WHITE, MR. JUSTICE PECKHAM, and MR. JUSTICE MCKENNA join]: * * *

The Circuit Court of the United States has jurisdiction, concurrent with the courts of the State, of any action under the Constitution, laws, or treaties of the United States, in which the matter in dispute exceeds the sum or value of $2,000.

This action is brought against election officers to recover damages for their rejection of the plaintiff's vote for a member of the House of Representatives of the United States. The complaint, by alleging that the plaintiff was at the time, under the constitution and laws of the State of South Carolina and the Constitution and laws of the United States, a duly qualified elector of the state, shows that the action is brought under the Constitution and laws of the United States.

The damages are laid at the sum of $2,500. What amount of damages the plaintiff shall recover in such an action is peculiarly appropriate for the determination of a jury, and no opinion of the court upon that subject can justify it in holding that the amount in controversy was insufficient to support the jurisdiction of the circuit court.

The Circuit Court therefore clearly had jurisdiction of this action, and we are brought to the consideration of the other objections presented by the demurrer to the complaint. * * *

The constitution and the laws of [South Carolina] require that, in order to entitle any one to have his vote received at any election, he must not only have the requisite qualifications of an elector, but he must have been registered. By elementary rules of pleading, both these essential requisites must be distinctly alleged by the plaintiff in any action against the managers of an election for refusing his vote.

The complaint in this case alleges that the plaintiff was a duly qualified elector; but it contains no allegation that he was ever registered as such. Because of this omission the complaint does not state facts sufficient to constitute a cause of action. * * *

Judgment affirmed.

Notes and Questions

1. Although the Court ultimately ruled against the plaintiff voter, to reach the merits the Court first had to conclude both that there was a federal question involved in the case and that the amount-in-controversy requirement was satisfied. Today there is no amount-in-controversy requirement in federal-question suits, *see* 28 U.S.C. § 1331, but from 1875, when Congress first provided for general federal-question jurisdiction, until 1980, federal-question suits not meeting a certain amount-in-controversy had to be brought, if at all, in state courts. *See* Richard H. Fallon, Jr., et al., Hart and Wechsler's The Federal Courts and the Federal System 783 (7th ed. 2015).

Wiley held, following *Ex Parte Yarbrough*, 110 U.S. 651 (1884), that the right to vote for representatives arose under the Constitution, for the Constitution created the office and provided that anyone entitled to vote for "the most numerous Branch of the State Legislature" would also be entitled to vote in congressional elections. U.S. Const. art. I, § 2, cl. 1. Thus, the Constitution adopted the voting qualifications used by the states, but did not give the states any power to set the qualifications of voters in congressional races as such. The Court thus found unconvincing the defendant's argument that the right to vote for Congress depended on whether one had been granted the right, under state law, to vote for the state legislature. *See also Swafford v. Templeton*, 185 U.S. 487 (1902).

2. As for the amount-in-controversy requirement, the Court held that the appropriate damages for the wrongful denial of the right to vote were "peculiarly appropriate for the determination of a jury," and therefore the plaintiff's demand for $2500 satisfied the requirement. *See also Wayne v. Venable*, 260 F. 64, 66 (8th Cir. 1919) ("In the eyes of the law this right [to vote] is so valuable that damages are presumed from the wrongful deprivation of it without evidence of actual loss of money, property, or any other valuable thing, and the amount of the damages is a question peculiarly appropriate for the determination of the jury, because each member of the jury has personal knowledge of the value of the right."). Ordinarily the amount claimed by the plaintiff controls, so long as it is made in good faith, unless it "appear[s] to a legal certainty that the claim is really for less than the jurisdictional amount." *St. Paul Mercury Indemnity Co. v. Red Cab Co.*, 303 U.S. 283, 289 (1938). Two thousand five hundred dollars in 1900 would be worth about $75,000 today. Would such an award be — as a matter of law — excessive? How much is one's vote worth?

Assigning a dollar value to the right to vote is difficult for several reasons. First, there is no market against which to measure a damages award. Every state and the federal government have laws prohibiting the buying or selling of votes, *see, e.g.,* 18 U.S.C. §§ 597, 598; Richard L. Hasen, *Vote Buying*, 88 CAL. L. REV. 1323 (2000), and as a result we cannot be certain how much a vote is "worth" in that sense. Second, if we were to approximate the value of a vote based on the behavior of eligible voters (many of whom choose not to vote), that value would be very low. *Cf. Crawford v. Marion County Election Board*, 472 F.3d 949, 951 (7th Cir. 2007) (Posner, J.) ("[S]ome people who have not bothered to obtain a photo ID will not bother to do so just to be allowed to vote, and a few who have a photo ID but forget to bring it to the polling place will say what the hell and not vote, rather than go home and get the ID and return to the polling place"), *aff'd*, 553 U.S. 181 (2008) [p. 999]). *See generally, e.g.,* ANTHONY DOWNS, AN ECONOMIC THEORY OF DEMOCRACY 260–76 (1957). Third, if we view the right in narrow instrumental terms—the chances any particular vote will make the difference in an election—the value is infinitesimally small, at least in national and state elections. Fourth, taking a broader view, the value of voting—of subjecting government to popular accountability—is incalculably high. Indeed, the behavior of generations of Americans who have fought and died to protect democracy might indicate that the right has an extremely large value.

The Supreme Court has indicated that the narrower vision of the right is appropriate. "The 'value of the right' [to vote] is the money value of the particular loss that the plaintiff suffered—a loss of which 'each member of the jury has personal knowledge.' It is *not* the value of the right to vote as a general, abstract matter, based on its role in our history or system of government." *Memphis Community School District v. Stachura*, 477 U.S. 299, 312 n.14 (1986). If damages are to be based on "the money value of the particular loss that the plaintiff suffered," was *Wiley* correct to sustain jurisdiction?

3. Cases deciding claims of voting-rights violations are fact-intensive and require detailed analyses not only of facts but context. Appellate decisions must also consider the appropriate amount of deference to give to trial courts' determinations of these factual and contextual matters. For one such painstaking analysis by a well respected circuit judge, see *Taylor v. Howe*, 225 F.3d 993 (8th Cir. 2000) (R. Arnold, J.). In *Taylor*, several voters and candidates (all black) sued poll workers for racial discrimination. The plaintiffs asked for damages, along with other remedies, under 42 U.S.C. § 1983, which provides a private right of action for violations of constitutional rights. Some of the plaintiffs were turned away at the polls, and others suffered a variety of indignities and harassment. Still others were permitted to vote, but only after enduring a more difficult and complicated process than should have occurred. Because the constitutional claims required the plaintiffs to prove that the defendants discriminated against the plaintiffs because of their race, the key question was the defendants' intent. That intent, of course, had to be inferred from the defendants' behavior and the context.

The trial court ruled in favor of the defendants, but the Eighth Circuit reversed in part, rejecting some of the district court's conclusions as clearly erroneous. The court of appeals heavily relied on the facts that the problems arose in a very small community in Arkansas that was *de facto* segregated by race. The court noted that, in many cases, blacks were denied the ability to vote ostensibly because of concerns about whether they lived in the district, even though they were personally known to the poll workers. Further, the poll workers sometimes acted contrary to the law and their training, for example, by forbidding voters from receiving assistance from others. The poll workers' over-zealous and illegal behavior towards black voters contrasted with their much more generous behavior towards at least some white voters.

Still, other challenged behavior by the poll workers was not so clearly racially motivated as to require the court of appeals to reject the district court's conclusions that there had not been racial discrimination. For example, a voter was denied the ability to cast a ballot when the precinct register indicated that he was sent an absentee ballot. There was no indication that he had voted his absentee ballot, and the poll workers should have checked to see whether he was eligible to vote in person, rather than simply turning him away. Similarly, the poll workers excluded black candidates from the polling place, over-enforcing the state law against "electioneering" within 100 feet of a polling place. *See generally Burson v. Freeman*, 504 U.S. 191 (1992) [p. 1024]. The court concluded, however, that the poll workers' behavior, while a misapplication of law, may not have been the product of racial bias. One is reminded of the caution reflected in Hanlon's Razor: "Never attribute to malice that which can be adequately explained by stupidity."

On remand in *Taylor v. Howe*, the district court awarded seven plaintiffs between $500 and $2000 each in compensatory damages, and did not award any punitive damages. Six of those seven plaintiffs appealed, arguing that the award was grossly inadequate, but the court of appeals, applying the clearly-erroneous standard, affirmed. *Taylor v. Howe*, 280 F.3d 1210 (8th Cir. 2002).

4. Most jurisdictions, but not all, require a showing of malice or other improper motive before recovery may be had for wrongfully denying the right to vote. *Compare, e.g., Lincoln v. Hapgood*, 11 Mass. 350 (1814) (applying strict liability), *with, e.g., Jenkins v. Waldron*, 11 Johns 114 (N.Y. 1814) (requiring malice).

5. Ordinarily, municipalities are not liable under § 1983 for constitutional violations unless "the action that is alleged to be unconstitutional implements or executes a policy statement, ordinance, regulation or decision officially adopted and promulgated by that body's officers," or is the result of a governmental "custom." *Monell v. Department of Social Services*, 436 U.S. 658, 690–91 (1978); RICHARD H. FALLON, JR., ET AL., HART AND WECHSLER'S THE FEDERAL COURTS AND THE FEDERAL SYSTEM 998–1003 (7th ed. 2015). The "policy or custom" limitation on liability prevents local governments from being liable for constitutional violations simply on a *respondeat superior* theory, which would force taxpayers to pay for the behavior

of rogue employees. It is on this ground that *Taylor* refused to impose liability on some of the poll workers in their *official* capacities, which would, in effect, amount to imposing liability on the county.

Municipalities can also be liable for behavior that can be attributed to the municipalities themselves—most notably, failure to train employees. There too, however, not all constitutional violations are compensable. Liability may be imposed on the municipality "only where the failure to train amounts to deliberate indifference to the rights of persons with whom the [trainees] come into contact." *City of Canton v. Harris*, 489 U.S. 378, 388 (1989).

3. Remedies for Unsuccessful Candidates

Hutchinson v. Miller

United States Court of Appeals for the Fourth Circuit
797 F.2d 1279 (4th Cir. 1986)

WILKINSON, CIRCUIT JUDGE [with whom PHILLIPS, CIRCUIT JUDGE, and GORDON, SENIOR DISTRICT JUDGE (sitting by designation) join]:

Plaintiffs are three unsuccessful candidates for public office who seek to recover approximately $9 million in damages under 42 U.S.C. § 1983, 18 U.S.C. § 1964 (Racketeer Influenced and Corrupt Organizations Act—RICO), and the common law of West Virginia, for alleged irregularities in the 1980 general election. The district court granted motions to dismiss, summary judgment, or directed verdicts in favor of all defendants, various election officials and those alleged to have conspired with them to fix the election. The court found plaintiffs had failed to prove the existence of a conspiracy, on which their case depended, or to show a fundamentally unfair election amounting to a constitutional deprivation.

We conclude that federal courts are not available for awards of damages to defeated candidates. * * *

Our constitution does not contemplate that the federal judiciary routinely will pass judgment on particular elections for federal, state or local office. The conduct of elections is instead a matter committed primarily to the control of states, and legislative bodies are traditionally the final judges of their own membership. The legitimacy of democratic politics would be compromised if the results of elections were regularly to be rehashed in federal court. Federal courts, of course, have actively guarded the electoral process from class-based discrimination and restrictive state election laws. This suit, however, asks us to consider the award of damages for election irregularities that neither disenfranchised a class of voters nor impugned state and federal procedures for the proper conduct of elections. In this essentially factual dispute, we defer to those primarily responsible for elections and we refuse to authorize yet another avenue for those disgruntled with the political process to keep the contest alive in the courtroom.

I.

Plaintiffs were Democratic candidates in the 1980 general election in West Virginia. John Hutchinson sought re-election to the United States House of Representatives in the Third Congressional District of West Virginia. This district included Kanawha and Boone Counties—where the disputed elections occurred—as well as twelve other counties. Plaintiff Leonard Underwood was the incumbent delegate to the state house from Kanawha County, and plaintiff William Reese sought election as a County Commissioner for Kanawha County. Hutchinson and Reese were defeated by wide margins, while Underwood's loss was a narrow one.

Underwood requested a recount of all computer punchcard ballots cast in the election. When the Kanawha County Commission denied this request, Underwood sought a writ of mandamus in the Circuit Court of Kanawha County to compel a hand count of ballots. That action was dismissed, and a similar attempt before the state Supreme Court was found to be time barred. Hutchinson filed a formal election complaint with the United States Attorney in January, 1981. The resolution of that complaint is not revealed in the record, but apparently was not satisfactory to Hutchinson. Plaintiffs filed their original complaint in this suit in February, 1983.

As amended, the complaint in essence charges that the election night totals were pre-determined by defendants, who then conspired to cover up their activities. Named as defendants in the suit were both local officials and private citizens alleged to have acted in concert with those officials. * * *

[V]oters indicated their choices on computer punch cards. After polls were closed, these cards were transported to countywide tabulation centers in locked and sealed ballot boxes. The ballots were removed by teams of workers, who arranged them for feeding into the computer and noted in log books the time when ballot boxes were opened. Plaintiffs cite as evidence of election fraud the fact that the log shows one box was opened after the computer tabulation was printed out.

Plaintiffs' main allegations focus on events at the central tabulation center for Kanawha County. They rely largely on the testimony of Walter Price, incumbent candidate for the House of Delegates who was at the center on election night. Price testified that he observed [defendant and county clerk] Margaret Miller manipulating computer toggle switches during the election count, purportedly in an attempt to alter vote counts. He saw an "unknown gentleman"—whom plaintiffs identify as Carl Clough—placing a phone receiver into his briefcase. Plaintiffs suggest that this activity is consistent with the use of a portable modem, perhaps in an effort to change vote totals. Price also testified that Stephen Miller [the husband of Margaret Miller] took computer cards from his coat pocket and gave them to his wife, who allegedly fed the cards into the computer.

Finally, plaintiffs assert that numerous irregularities occurred after the election, including improper handling of the ballots and release of exact returns prior to the canvass, and destruction of ballots that violated the terms of [state law]. Plaintiffs make similar, though less detailed, allegations with respect to the election process in Boone County. * * *

The [district] court considered motions for directed verdicts at the close of plaintiffs' case. It found that plaintiffs' claims failed for several reasons. The court held that plaintiffs had failed to prove a conspiracy, noting that the only evidence the election was rigged was "purely speculative . . . mere suspicion." It also found that plaintiffs Reese and Hutchinson had not shown that they were harmed by the alleged actions; there was no evidence that their large losses would have been victories in the absence of the alleged conspiracy. Further, finding only "mere election irregularities" and no evidence to suggest that the election was fundamentally unfair, the court held that plaintiffs had failed to prove a deprivation of a constitutional right essential to a § 1983 action. Finally, the court dismissed plaintiffs' claims under RICO, finding "absolutely no proof" that would allow it to consider the claim.

II. * * *

As in any suit under § 1983 the first inquiry is "whether the plaintiff has been deprived of a right 'secured by the Constitution and laws.'" *Baker v. McCollan*, 443 U.S. 137, 140 (1979).[3] In their complaint, plaintiffs alleged that defendants deprived them of "their constitutionally protected right to participate fully and fairly in the electoral process," and "their constitutional right to vote or receive votes," and their Fifth Amendment right to hold property, in this case public office. The district court found that plaintiffs proceeded at trial as "defeated or disenfranchised candidate[s] rather than as . . . disenfranchised voter[s]." Thus, plaintiffs essentially assert that they have been deprived of their "right to candidacy."

Courts have recognized that some restrictions on political candidates violate the Constitution because of their derivative effect on the right to vote. * * * We assume, without deciding, that plaintiffs have sufficiently alleged a deprivation of constitutional rights to meet the basic requirements of a § 1983 cause of action. That assumption, however, cannot end the matter. As Judge Rubin has noted for the Fifth Circuit: "constitutional decision must not be confined merely to the logical development of the philosophy of prior decisions unfettered by other considerations. The functional structure embodied in the Constitution, the nature of the federal court system, and the limitations inherent in the concepts both of limited federal jurisdiction and of the remedy afforded by section 1983 must all be fully attended." *Gamza v. Aguirre*, 619 F.2d 449, 452 (5th Cir. 1980). The functional allocations and structural mandates of our Constitution lead us to conclude, like the court in *Gamza*, that this complaint must be dismissed. * * *

---

3. Though we speak here in terms of § 1983, our discussion applies as well to the RICO and common law counts. Our review of the limited role of federal courts does not depend on the specific theory under which a particular suit is brought, but rather upon the institutional structure established by the constitution and administered through other state and federal remedies.

III. * * *

Where state procedures produce contested results, the Constitution dictates that, for congressional elections, "Each House shall be the Judge of the Elections, Returns and Qualifications of its own Members." Art. I, Sec. 5, cl. 1. The House accordingly has the authority "to determine the facts and apply the appropriate rules of law, and, finally, to render a judgment which is beyond the authority of any other tribunal to review." This plenary power is paralleled at the state level by the power of the West Virginia legislature to review the elections of its own members. Contests for county offices, such as that of plaintiff Reese, are resolved by county courts.

We thus proceed with awareness that the resolution of particular electoral disputes has been primarily committed to others in our system. The express delegation to Congress and the states of shared responsibility for the legitimation of electoral outcomes and the omission of any constitutional mandate for federal judicial intervention suggests the inadvisability of permitting a § 1983 or civil RICO action to confer upon federal judges and juries "a piece of the political action," no matter what relief is sought. Consideration of the various ways in which these other bodies have regulated and monitored the integrity of elections only confirms our hesitation to consider the disputed details of political contests.

Those with primary responsibility have not abandoned their duty to ensure the reliability and fairness of democratic elections. The House of Representatives, for example, has developed a body of guiding precedent regarding election contests, *see* 2 *Deschler's Precedents of the United States House of Representatives*, 323–888 (1977), and has enacted detailed procedures designed to ensure due process and just consideration of disputes. *See* Federal Contested Elections Act, 2 U.S.C. §§ 381–396. * * * Had the framers wished the federal judiciary to umpire election contests, they could have so provided. Instead, they reposed primary trust in popular representatives and in political correctives.

Dissatisfied candidates for office in West Virginia are also presented with numerous avenues by which to challenge election results, some of which parallel the federal model. The legislature is directed by Art. 4, § 11 of the West Virginia Constitution "to prescribe the manner of conducting and making returns of elections, and of determining contested elections," and has accordingly enacted procedures for ballot control and recounts, and election contests. * * *

State and federal legislatures, moreover, are not concerned solely with election results, but have subjected the entire electoral process to increasing regulation. * * * Thus it seems fair to conclude that the demonstration of judicial restraint under 42 U.S.C. § 1983 will not leave American elections unsupervised or unregulated.

Finally, both state and federal authorities have employed criminal penalties to halt direct intrusions on the election itself. Federal conspiracy laws such as 18 U.S.C. § 241 have been applied to those engaged in corruption of election procedures. *See also*, 18 U.S.C. § 594 (prohibiting intimidation of voters); 18 U.S.C. § 600 (prohibiting promise of employment or other benefit for political activity). Criminal sanctions are also available under West Virginia law for those found to have filed false returns, tampered with ballots, bought or sold votes, and the like. A state grand jury investigated the very allegations at issue here, and issued one indictment, which did not result in a conviction.

IV.

Though the presence of even exhaustive alternative remedies does not usually bar an action literally within § 1983 or other statutes, we are persuaded in this context that we must refrain from considering the particulars of a disputed election, especially in a suit for damages. To do otherwise would be to intrude on the role of the states and the Congress, to raise the possibility of inconsistent judgments concerning elections, to erode the finality of results, to give candidates incentives to bypass the procedures already established, to involve federal courts in the details of state-run elections, and to constitute the jury as well as the electorate as an arbiter of political outcomes. These costs, we believe, would come with very little benefit to the rights fundamentally at issue here—the rights of voters to fair exercise of their franchise. Instead, plaintiffs, who voluntarily entered the political fray, would stand to reap a post-election recovery that might salve feelings of rejection at the polls or help retire debts from the campaign but would bear very little relationship to the larger public interest in partisan debate and competition undeterred by prospects of a post-election suit for damages.

Plaintiffs' theories in this case illustrate the ways in which a lawsuit such as this could intrude on the role of states and Congress to conduct elections and adjudge results. In their complaint, plaintiffs allege damages including, *inter alia*, loss of income (salary from holding public office), earning capacity, time expended for election purposes and various election expenses, as well as injury to reputation. These losses, of course, would have resulted from election defeat absent any conspiracy by defendants. * * *

Thus, plaintiffs in order to recover damages must perforce rely on the theory that defendants' alleged conspiracy cost them an election they otherwise would have won. In presenting their case plaintiffs would essentially ask a jury to review the outcome of the election. As explained above, however, the task is reserved for states and legislatures, and though the jury's review would not directly impair their primary responsibility to adjudge elections, its re-examination of election results would be inconsistent with proper respect for the role of others whose job it is to canvass the returns and declare a prevailing party. This intrusion, moreover, would not be limited to that of a jury, for the judiciary itself would doubtless be asked to review the jury's judgment of the election in post-trial motions. Principles of separation of powers and federalism, therefore, dictate that both jury and court avoid this inquiry.

Just as the review of electoral results by judge or jury is inconsistent with proper respect for the role of states and Congress, so too the outcomes of these deliberations are potentially inconsistent with the results of the electoral process. Were plaintiffs successful in convincing the jury that they should have won the election or should receive an award of damages, the courts would enter a judgment at odds with the judgment of Congress and of West Virginia, which have seated the apparent victors in these elections. The difficulties inherent in such continuing assaults on political legitimacy would be obvious and might impair the respect to which the enactments of those duly elected are entitled.

Closely related to the problem of inconsistent judgments is the need for finality in elections. Inconsistent judgments, of course, call into question the results of an election in a way that detracts from finality. Even without inconsistent judgments, suits asking federal courts to replay elections cast into limbo contests that should have been long since decided. This case is illustrative. The election at issue occurred in 1980. Plaintiffs did not even bring their suit until 1983, after plaintiff Hutchinson's term would have expired. Now, nearly six years after the election, the parties remain in court essentially to contest the integrity of the election. So long as such avenues are available to defeated candidates, the apparent finality of election outcomes will be illusory.

Maintenance of this action might also provide incentives to losing candidates to ignore the principal routes established to challenge an election and to proceed instead to have the election reviewed in federal courts in hopes of gaining monetary compensation. * * *

We further believe that federal courts are ill-equipped to monitor the details of elections and resolve factual disputes born of the political process. As one court has noted, "[w]ere we to embrace plaintiffs' theory, this court would henceforth be thrust into the details of virtually every election, tinkering with the state's election machinery, reviewing petitions, election cards, vote tallies, and certificates of election for all manner of error and insufficiency under state and federal law." *Powell v. Power*, 436 F.2d 84, 86 (2d Cir. 1970). Elections are, regrettably, not always free from error. Voting machines malfunction, registrars fail to follow instructions, absentee ballots are improperly administered, poll workers become over-zealous, and defeated candidates are, perhaps understandably, inclined to view these multifarious opportunities for human error in a less than charitable light. Quite apart from the serious problems of federalism and separation of powers problems raised by these tasks, we find sifting the minutae [*sic*] of post-election accusations better suited to the factual review at the administrative and legislative level, where an awareness of the vagaries of politics informs the judgment of those called upon to review the irregularities that are inevitable in elections staffed largely by volunteers.

To ask a jury to undertake such tasks, moreover, is to risk the intrusion of political partisanship into the courtroom, where it has no place. From the exercise of jury strikes to the final rendering of verdict, the spectre of partisanship would intrude and color court proceedings. Such disputes belong, and have been placed, in the political arena, and we cannot accept the substitution of the civil jury for the larger, more diverse, and more representative political electorate that goes to the polls on the day of the election.

These concerns suggest that the federal judiciary should proceed with great caution when asked to consider disputed elections, and have caused many courts to decline the requests to intervene except in extraordinary circumstances. The unique nature of this case convinces us that the requested intervention is inappropriate under any circumstances, for plaintiffs' suit for damages strikes us as an inapt means of overseeing the political process. It would provide not so much a correction of electoral ills as a potential windfall to plaintiffs and political advantage through publicity. Those who enter the political fray know the potential risks of their enterprise. If they are defeated by trickery or fraud, they can and should expect the established mechanisms of review—both civil and criminal—to address their grievances, and to take action to insure legitimate electoral results. In this way, they advance the fundamental goal of the electoral process—to determine the will of the people—while also protecting their own interest in the electoral result. A suit for damages, by contrast, may result principally in financial gain for the candidate. We can imagine no scenario in which this gain is the appropriate result of the decision to pursue elected office, and we can find no other case in which a defeated candidate has won such compensation. Nor do we believe, in light of the multitude of alternative remedies, that such a remedy is necessary either to deter misconduct or to provide incentives for enforcement of election laws.

V.

We accordingly hold that federal courts do not sit to award post-election damages to defeated candidates. Equitable relief, though theoretically available, has properly been called a "[d]rastic, if not staggering" intrusion of the federal courts, and "therefore a form of relief guardedly exercised." *Bell v. Southwell*, 376 F.2d [659,] 662 [(5th Cir. 1967)] [p. 1121]. Courts have therefore repeatedly refused to intervene in routine election disputes, acting instead only in instances of "patent and fundamental unfairness" that "erode[] the democratic process." * * *

In short, the general attitude of courts asked to consider election disputes, whatever the relief sought, has been one of great caution. Intervention has come only in rare and extraordinary circumstances, for courts have recognized and respected the delegation of such disputes to other authorities. Such intervention, moreover, has never included the grant to defeated candidates of monetary compensation. Because such compensation is fundamentally inappropriate, we hold that it is unavailable as a form of post-election relief. The parties here have asked for nothing more, and we need not consider under what circumstances equitable remedies might be appropriate. Accordingly, the judgment of the district court dismissing this lawsuit is hereby

Affirmed.

Notes and Questions

1. What was the holding of *Hutchinson*? Was it that the statutes on which the plaintiffs relied did not provide a damages remedy for losing candidates, or was it that federal courts lack the constitutional authority to grant a damages remedy even if a congressional statute purports to make one available? If *Hutchinson*'s holding was based on an interpretation of the statutes, should the court have relied more on statutory language and precedents about the meaning of the statutes? If the holding was constitutional, on the other hand, can it really be that federal courts lack the authority to order a damages remedy for the violation of constitutional rights just because that victim was a candidate? Did the court appropriately exercise restraint or did it abdicate a responsibility that Congress gave to federal courts when it passed the statutes on which the plaintiffs relied?

2. Are damages in some sense a *less* intrusive remedy for a federal court to order in this context than prospective, injunctive relief? Or are both types of remedies on an equal footing when it comes to interpreting and applying congressional statutes (*e.g.*, 42 U.S.C. § 1983)? That is, has the remedial choice already been made by the statutory language? In light of these issues, how persuasive was *Hutchinson* in favoring injunctive relief over damages in suits by disappointed candidates?

3. Another distinction made by *Hutchinson* was between suits by voters (damages permitted) and those by disappointed candidates (damages not permitted). How persuasive was this distinction? What if a plaintiff asserts that she is suing both as a voter and as a disappointed candidate? *Cf. White-Battle v. Democratic Party of Virginia*, 323 F. Supp. 2d 696, 703 (E.D. Va. 2004) (finding that the plaintiff asserted claims only as a disappointed candidate, although she claimed to be both a voter and a candidate).

4. The bar against suit by disappointed candidates in *Hutchinson* has been followed by both federal (*e.g.*, *White-Battle, supra*, 323 F. Supp. 2d at 705–06) and state (*e.g.*, *Hill v. Stowers*, 680 S.E.2d 66, 77 (W. Va. 2009)) courts, which have emphasized that other remedies were available to contest an allegedly improper election. Should these decisions turn on the robustness of these remedies, or should their simple existence be enough? Almost all states have some form of election-contest statute, but the scope and efficacy of those statutes vary from state to state. Steven F. Huefner, *Just How Settled Are the Legal Principles that Control Election Disputes?*, 8 ELECTION L.J. 233, 236 (2008) (book review).

5. Courts have also held that disappointed candidates cannot bring suit for alleged violations of the Voting Rights Act. Section 2 of the Act provides that "an aggrieved person" has a private right of action to sue for certain violations of the Act. 52 U.S.C. § 10302. In *Roberts v. Wamser*, 883 F.2d 617 (8th Cir. 1989), the court held that this language did not include losing candidates. While the language might have been read to cover such persons, the court was not "convinced that

Congress intended it to be stretched that far," because (1) the primary purpose of the Act was to protect minority voters; (2) the interests of a candidate might diverge from those attempting to enforce their right to vote, and (3) "state and local election contests are quintessentially state and local matters"; to permit suit in federal court by disappointed candidates "would violate principles of federalism in a highly radical way." *Id.* at 621. *But see id.* at 624–28 (Heaney, J., dissenting) (arguing that the legislative history indicated that Congress wanted the statute to be applied in a broader way).

Index